Management and Organisational Behaviour

SECOND EDITION

Dear Student,

Thank you for buying a copy of the second edition of *Management and Organisational Behaviour*. We hope you find this book useful for your course and we hope it helps you pass your exams! Wendy Bloisi has made significant changes to this edition to ensure that it contains the latest coverage you need to pass your course and that it is loaded with examples that you'll find interesting and relevant.

As well as being written to help you pass your first introductory management and OB course, *Management and Organisational Behaviour*, second edition is also a great reference for your future management and OB courses. We hope you'll continue to find the book useful throughout your degree and well into your future career in management.

We understand that you may not be completing a degree in management and OB so, if you choose not to keep this book as an essential reference, let us know. We can buy back your copy of *Management and Organisational Behaviour*, second edition and help make your future book buying easier! After completing your introductory management and OB course, return your copy of *Management and Organisational Behaviour*, second edition to us and **receive 50% off your next McGraw-Hill textbook purchase!** Simply register your details using the link below and we will email you details of how to take advantage of this special offer.

Wishing you every success in your studies,
McGraw-Hill Education

WIN A NEW ipod nano!!!

Every student who logs onto www.mcgraw-hill.co.uk/student and registers will be entered into a prize draw for a new ipod nano. further details are available on the website.

Management and Organisational Behaviour

SECOND EDITION

Wendy Bloisi
Curtis W. Cook
Phillip L. Hunsaker

The **McGraw·Hill** Companies

London Boston Burr Ridge, IL Dubuque, IA Madison, WI New York San Francisco
St. Louis Bangkok Bogotá Caracas Kuala Lumpur Lisbon Madrid Mexico City
Milan Montreal New Delhi Santiago Seoul Singapore Sydney Taipei Toronto

Management and Organisational Behaviour , European Edition
Wendy Bloisi, Curtis W. Cook and Phillip L. Hunsaker
ISBN-13 978-0-07-711107-6
ISBN-10 0-07-711107-9

Published by McGraw-Hill Education
Shoppenhangers Road
Maidenhead
Berkshire
SL6 2QL
Telephone: 44 (0) 1628 502 500
Fax: 44 (0) 1628 770 224
Website: www.mcgraw-hill.co.uk

British Library Cataloguing in Publication Data
A catalogue record for this book is available from the British Library

Library of Congress Cataloging in Publication Data
The Library of Congress data for this book have been applied for from the Library of Congress

Acquisitions Editor: Kirsty Reade
Development Editor: Hannah Cooper
Senior Marketing Manager: Alice Duijser
Senior Production Editor: Beverley Shields

Text design by Hard Lines
Cover design by Ego Creative
Typeset by Wearset Ltd, Boldon, Tyne and Wear
Printed and bound in Italy by Rotolito Lombarda

First Edition published in 2003 by McGraw-Hill Education

Dedication

To my son Alexander, older and wiser.

Brief Table of Contents

Detailed Table of Contents

The second European edition of *Management and Organisational Behaviour* reflects the differences in working practices, culture and language between Europe and the USA, which is intended to make it more appropriate for a European audience. At the outset of writing this edition I thought the process would be quite straightforward – after all, at least in the UK, we share a similar language. However, after a few chapters it became apparent that it was more than a matter of simply changing words. The way we do business in Europe differs from the way it is done in the USA, as does how we communicate and relate to one another. Many of the examples in this book are UK based since, apart from brief experiences of working in Germany and Thailand, that is where my working life has been spent. However, I have included several case examples from Europe, which I hope European students will be able to relate to. I have also included examples of cases from the voluntary sector, education, local authorities and the police, since management and organisational behaviour is not the prerogative of big business. Neither has America or the rest of the world been ignored as to do so would be to disregard a wide body of knowledge that forms the basis of many of our theories of organisations. New to this edition are integrated cases, which pull together some of the topics discussed in the different chapters. Applied questions also mean that students have the chance of relating theory to practice, which helps add meaning.

A textbook should hold the interest of the reader and draw them into learning the subject field. It should also provide the lecturer with an inviting and useful text, and offer rich pedagogical features and ancillary support.

Enjoy the journey.

Wendy Bloisi
London, 2006

Why integrate management and organisational behaviour?

Students readily learn the applied skills and perspectives of organisational behaviour (OB) when concepts and techniques are integrated into a management context; conversely, essential management subjects come alive when infused with lessons and techniques from the behavioural sciences.

This European edition provides even more integration of the two fields, starting with modest rearrangement of content and the infusion of new material and extensive contemporary examples in response to comments from many users. This edition of the text deepens our commitment of responsiveness to three changing educational forces: business practices, student needs and student-centred learning.

Business practices

The world of organisations generally, and business firms in particular, is fast changing, driven in part by quickly evolving technology and shifts in environmental forces. Since the previous edition, the Internet has significantly altered practices, both in terms of opening up market opportunities for new products and services (e.g. new dotcom start-ups) and in introducing efficiencies into business processes. Electronic commerce has quickly become a way of life within the wired (and increasingly wireless) new economy. As described in many of the examples and boxed inserts, these business transformations impact management and organisational behaviour practices.

Student needs

At present the student reader is likely to be taking an OB module as part of an undergraduate degree course. Our vision is that most students who use this text will not be in managerial roles for, say, another five years. Therefore they need to know how to be effective performers both individually and in teams within organisations. They also need to know how to work with managers and to begin preparing for the time when they are likely to assume managerial and leadership responsibilities. Part of their success requires them to understand the macro aspects of organisational behaviour, which of necessity involves managerial skills and ways of strategic thinking.

Student-centred learning

With cutbacks in class contact, certainly in the area of higher education, students are expected to spend more time on independent study. The teacher is seen as a facilitator guiding the students, rather than as an instructor. This edition with its wealth of cases allows the student to gain an insight into what is happening in organisations. The 'Your turn' exercises, discussion questions and case questions allow students to contribute to their own learning.

Given these forces, the merger of OB and management topics is a natural one. Because dealing with OB issues will be students' dominant need as they enter organisational life, about two-thirds of the book's content is anchored in time-tested and emergent OB subjects. About one-third focuses on issues and practices that every manager, or everyone who reports to a manager, needs to know.

A note to organisational behaviour faculties

Management and Organisational Behaviour provides a comfortable and contemporary feel for those who teach from an OB perspective. Of particular note are the behavioural exercises at the end of each chapter (one personal and one team) and other pedagogical elements, such as the 'Your turn' instrument for personal evaluation found within every chapter. From the behavioural perspective, the text includes chapters on skill-building topics such as:

- personality and perception from a learning perspective (Chapter 4)
- motivation fundamentals, theories combined with research findings and examples (Chapter 5)
- a practice-based survey of motivational applications (Chapter 6)
- self-management of careers and the stresses that complicate work performance (Chapter 7)
- communication from the perspective of sharing and influencing results (Chapter 8)
- interpersonal relationships, which promote experiential explorations of OB (Chapter 9)
- how groups and teams function, and how to influence them (Chapter 10)
- the reality that power and organisational politics are critical to success (Chapter 13)

- organisational culture, with a heavy infusion of values and expectations (Chapter 16)
- a venture into organisational change and learning from a behavioural perspective (Chapter 18).

A note to management faculties

While this book may have more the look and feel of an organisational behaviour text, it clearly provides coverage of topics essential to understanding management functions. For those who prefer a management perspective, every business student should know the practical skills associated with managerial success (e.g. how to engage in group-based planning, rather than just to know how managers are supposed to plan). In addition to management applications through skill-building lessons, examples, cases and exercises (including web-based applications), the text emphasises management through chapters that focus on:

- an introduction to human resource management as a consideration of organisational behaviour (Chapter 1)
- organisational strategy, planning and behavioural approaches to continuous improvement (Chapter 3)
- job design, reinforcement and other applied motivation practices (Chapter 6)
- building teams as a way to get work done using group techniques (Chapter 10)
- conflict management and negotiation, which overcome the illusion of rationality (Chapter 11)
- ethical problem-solving and decision-making, to advance socially responsible goals (Chapter 12)
- leaders, and what they do to develop people and transform organisations (Chapter 14)
- structure, as a way of organising communities in which people work (Chapter 15)
- the role of human resource management in organisations (Chapter 17)
- how managers promote organisational change, development and innovation (Chapter 18)

What makes the text a multidimensional learning resource?

Thanks to the constructive feedback received from academics in the UK, Europe and North America at different stages of this project, *Management and Organisational Behaviour* is a text designed to achieve several goals. The text and instructional ancillaries are a learning package with a balance of concepts, examples and practical applications. Included are pedagogical alternatives that help students develop personal skills and organisational insights. It also promotes an understanding of how organisations function, and why they do the things they do, within applied contexts that are highly visual and interesting to read.

Each chapter incorporates a repertoire of features and pedagogical aids aimed at holding reader interest and encouraging the student to bridge an understanding of concepts and theories with skill-building capabilities and applications. This multidimensional resource approach provides the teacher with several options to use the text features most compatible with his or her personal approach to stimulating learning. Chapters include the features described below.

Learning outcomes

As an introductory overview, learning outcomes help students quickly grasp the essentials they are expected to learn from each chapter. Outcomes are reinforced by directly linking them to the study and discussion questions at the end of the chapter. At the end of each chapter there is a learning checklist, which again links back to the learning outcomes and allows students to check that they have understood the relevant chapter before moving on.

Opening vignettes

To provoke preliminary thought about the practical lessons of the chapter, an opening real-world scenario or issue introduces students to the value of learning the chapter material. For example, Chapter 2 opens with insights into how entrepreneur Richard Branson develops strategies for his business, the Virgin Group. The vignette demonstrates how a business evolved from a small mail-order business to a multinational company. It looks at how Branson exploited opportunities and fought back when external threats were about to destroy his business.

Your turn

Students encounter self-reflective exercises designed to apply the lessons of the chapter to themselves. The objective is to encourage the student to reflect upon personal preferences and behaviours, or other factors that reveal something about how he or she functions on one or more dimensions explained in the chapter. In Chapter 17, for example, students are asked to answer 16 questions that profile a personal tolerance for ambiguity (propensity to cope with change) based on responses to issues of novelty, complexity and insoluble problem-solving situations.

Boxed features

To enable students to grapple with real-world key issues facing managers and organisations, five types of boxes appear throughout the text. Four kinds of boxed materials link chapter content to the four emphasised themes: diversity, ethics, technology, and global perspectives. Each of these boxes is new for this edition, with several reflecting the dynamics of organisations functioning in the 'new economy' and the recent upsurge in dotcom firms. Students are also given an opportunity to evaluate their own thoughts and ideas through 'Your turn' exercises within each chapter. Here's an up-close review of each type of box.

Dynamics of Diversity

Details a situation in which factors of gender, race, ethnicity or disability call for managerial sensitivity and/or change. The 'Dynamics of Diversity' box in Chapter 1, for example, demonstrates what happened when Lego in Denmark did not think about the consequences of its advertising in other countries.

Eye on Ethics

Spotlights the ethical dilemmas or action situations facing managers who confront the ideological issues involved in choosing between right and wrong. The 'Eye on Ethics' box in Chapter 12, for example, presents the idea of lecturers' performance-related pay being awarded by their students. What could be the impact of such action? What might lecturers do to ensure they receive the extra pay?

Technology Transformation

Illustrates 18 organisations caught up in the dynamics of introducing or incorporating new technology into their customer offerings or internal operations. The 'Technology Transformation' box in Chapter 12, for example, looks at the introduction of Compstat to allow the police to identify crime hotspots; however, politics starts to impact on the success of the scheme.

World Watch

Brings world events, people and organisations into focus for the purpose of learning about life in other cultures and to reduce the tendency to judge others through the filters of one's own culture. The 'World Watch' box in Chapter 2, for example, probes the three distinct strategies used by Japanese businesses to increase their power on the global stage, and raises questions about whether their capabilities and commitments to manufacturing have put them at a disadvantage in increasingly service-orientated markets.

Research focus

Although theories of management and organisational behaviour are incorporated throughout the text, many students are keen to have an overview of how the theories were formulated. Research focus boxes highlight some of the major research in the various topic areas and demonstrate how theories have developed, as well as their impact on current organisational and management thinking. Chapter 1 evaluates the Hawthorne experiment and shows that, although its findings were not as expected and the method was flawed, it has still had a major impact on management thinking.

'A second look'

Because the chapter opener confronts readers with an example or situation before they have learned the chapter concepts and techniques, at the end of each chapter we revisit the lead-off situation for a 'second look'. This closure typically extends the company experience to more complex levels and applies some of the tools of analysis to increase learning from the example.

Exhibits

Tables, charts and diagrams remain time-tested ways of summarising comparative data, the relationships among variables or the actions that lead to a desired outcome. Typically each chapter includes a half-dozen or so colour-enhanced exhibits to provide the visual learner with a break from text reading and an easy summary of ideas conveyed in a graphical form.

Margin definitions

The technical language of management and OB is summarised in key terms. These appear with definitions in the page margins beside the point in the text where they are introduced and discussed.

Summary

Some students find it helpful to turn from the chapter objectives immediately to review the summary. They then begin reading the text and features. Those who do will find that the summaries provide highlights that relate back to chapter objectives and key topics.

Further reading

New to this edition, these direct students to current research published in peer-reviewed journals. This enables students to keep abreast of developments in the different fields of management and organisational behaviour.

Areas for personal development

Each chapter provides six to eight instruction sets on how to bridge concepts with development of personal skills appropriate to effective organisational performance. These development areas provide guidance on how to initiate actions that enable students to practise several principles of managing organisational behaviour. For example, the 'Areas for personal development' section for Chapter 11 advises readers about behaviours essential for managing conflict productively in both interpersonal and intergroup situations, including how to assess the nature of the conflict, identify the sources of conflict, use the most appropriate style orientation for managing a specific conflict, empathise with the other conflict parties, apply a plan and concrete strategy, address problems – not personalities, maintain a rational goal-orientated frame of mind, emphasise win-win solutions, create a climate of trust, and adapt to culture differences.

Questions for study and discussion

Whenever appropriate, main headings within the chapters are presented as questions to be answered by reading the text, exhibits, boxes and photo essays. End-of-chapter questions provide ways to help students ensure that chapter outcomes are learned.

List of key concepts

At the end of each chapter is a list of key terms and the page on which each is introduced and defined.

Experiential exercises

Many OB faculties like to use selected in-class exercises as a way of encouraging students to learn from direct experiences. Two types of exercise at the end of each chapter provide variety in how different types of activity can be used to stimulate experiential learning behaviours.

Personal skills exercise

The individual learner is given an opportunity to work through an issue, process or technique that stimulates experiential learning. (Some personal skills exercises extend individual learning by incorporating a dyad or small group follow-on to either demonstrate individual differences or add complexity to the assignment.) Chapter 17's exercise applies force-field analysis as a way of working through a personal problem or challenge.

Team exercise

Because so much of what happens in organisations occurs with people interacting, the team exercises stimulate learning by first having a group of students work through the content issues of an activity, then debriefing the behavioural dynamics and processes that facilitated or interfered with task accomplishment and learning. In Chapter 14 the team exercise is a role play that gives all class members an opportunity to exert leadership influence in one of six groups. Through the two-phase dynamics of the exercise, students form impressions about their own leadership tendencies and learn through social observation which leadership behaviours do and do not work in different situations.

Cases

Business education has a long history of engaging students in discussion of cases as a way of learning from experience. End-of-chapter cases provide vivid descriptions of an organisation's experience, followed by a few questions to encourage students to think critically about the case situation in relation to concepts explained in the text. The case in Chapter 7, for example, invites students to make inferences about why communication has caused problems with the implementation of a company magazine.

WWW exercise – manager's Internet tools

These end-of-chapter exercises link use of the Internet to organisations described in the chapters. Students are guided to certain websites, directed to selected pages and asked to search for answers to a set of questions that connect with concepts in the chapter. Chapter 17's WWW exercise explores how Solar Turbines prepared for and used the Baldrige National Quality Award process to improve performance by continuously improving quality while cutting costs (and, along the way, they won the Baldrige Award).

References

For the research minded, full details of all texts cited are collected at the end of each chapter. These conform to the Harvard system of referencing, which is the preferred method in many universities. They also help direct further reading.

Integrated cases

These are new for this edition and have been requested by lecturers who want longer cases that pull together the different aspects of management and organisational behaviour. These appear at the end of each part of the book and there are five in total, ranging from well-known organisations such as eBay to lesser-known organisations such as Vanderlande.

Online supplements
Online Learning Centre

This European edition offers an accompanying Online Learning Centre (www.mcgraw-hill. co.uk/textbooks/bloisi). This is an added resource for lecturers and students alike. Included here are: an overview of information about the text, professional resources, downloadable supplements (for teachers), learning outcomes, chapter self-quizzes, key terms, Internet exercises, a career corner, message board and much more. Visit the OLC to make use of these valuable resources for your course.

Supplements for lecturers
Lecturer's manual

No lecturer's manual (LM) is intended to supplant the creativity and perspectives on learning that each lecturer brings to his or her class. However, lecturers often find the LM a helpful guide in planning class sessions. The *Lecturer's Manual* for this edition of the text was written by the authors themselves, based on their combined 60-plus years of teaching this material in diverse learning environments. For preparing the course syllabus, the *Lecturer's Manual* provides alternative suggestions for management- and/or OB-focused courses. The *LM* also suggests shortcuts to making decisions – for example, about which cases or exercises to assign, and how to sequence chapter assignments. To offer teaching suggestions, the *LM* provides the following elements for each chapter:

- chapter overview
- key terms from the text, with definitions
- learning outcomes
- answers to study and discussion questions
- synopsis of the experiential exercises and debriefing questions/answers
- synopsis of the case and perspective answers to questions
- a summary of each boxed item
- a teaching note for each line-drawing exhibit
- supplemental handouts – an exercise, case, example or self-assessment instrument.

PowerPoint slides

Supplemental exhibits and teaching points (as well as visuals for the exhibit drawings that appear in the text) are available as a Microsoft PowerPoint presentation. Some review each chapter's key points. Some include a self-quiz or chapter quiz to use as a review. Some summarise key points likely to be taught as a mini-lecture. Overall, the combination gives instructors considerable choice in drawing upon resources beyond those they have personally created for the classroom.

Supplements for students

A range of resources for students accompany this book on the Online Learning Centre (www.mcgraw-hill.co.uk/textbooks/bloisi). Tailored specifically to the book, they are organised by chapter to make learning and revising easier. Chapter-by-chapter resources include:

- learning objectives
- Internet exercises
- multiple-choice quiz
- true or false
- web links.

There is also a general Glossary, and a Business Skills area offering a practical context for students to apply their management and organisational behaviour skills.

Guidelines for study

Time management

As a student, whether full or part time, you are likely to have a lot of constraints on your time. You may be fitting your study around work or vice versa, you may have family responsibilities. Whatever the constraints, you need to decide how much time you can devote to study.

Here are some tips, identified by students, on managing time.[1]

- Be consistent. How much time can you realistically devote to study? Timetable it in your diary.
- Be realistic. Set aside time, divide time equally for everything – socialising, study, part-time work, family, hobby and community.
- Allocate activities. If you know you have assignment deadlines or seminar activities, write them in your diary.
- Rest is important. If you work instead of sleep occasionally, make provision to catch up – have a 'power nap'. Do not stay up too late before exams as this is likely to affect your performance. If you have planned properly you shouldn't have to.
- Who will benefit? Are you studying for yourself? If so, ask people to respect your time-management goals, and provide encouragement and support. It will not last for ever.
- Ask for help. If you get stuck, don't leave work until the last minute, ask your tutor, peers or friends for help. You will be glad that you did. Go for it, don't be lazy, you can do it!
- Stay flexible. Take account of changing circumstances and adjust accordingly.
- Don't get stressed. Stay calm, make a priority list, be self-disciplined and *enjoy!*

Academic writing

As part of your study you will be expected to engage in a variety of academic writing tasks including essays, reports, projects, case studies and examinations.

Before you start make sure you know what is required. Are you writing an academic paper, essay or report? Look for key words in the question. Highlight them to make sure you understand what is required. Plan your outline with an introduction, which should include an outline of what you are doing and how you are going to do it. The main body should include your arguments, ideas and evidence, and a conclusion to summarise your main points. Make sure you refer back to the main question to ensure that you have answered it. You will also need to include references and a bibliography (see below).

When writing, students should take care not to mix fact and opinion. You need to think about what is a fact and what is an opinion – especially in this day and age, when more and more information is obtained from the Internet. You need to think about who put it there and what their background is, in other words do they have an axe to grind? Are they trying to sell something? The 'Research focus' boxes offer some examples of how, sometimes, opinions can be stated as fact, even when they have been based on research. Academic journals are often peer reviewed, which means that other academics will have looked at published research and either tried to replicate it or offered alternative research arguments that either prove or disprove the research. When referring to journals check if they have been peer reviewed.

Take care when writing as it is often difficult to express absolute certainty and you should be careful to monitor your use of language.[2]

Sources/referencing

Whenever you are required to write a piece of coursework – either as an essay or academic paper – you will be expected to make references (also known as citations or a bibliography) to the books and articles that you have drawn on to produce your coursework.

Referencing is important as it helps to trace the history of an idea and identifies where the work came from. It provides evidence that you have knowledge of the subject you are discussing; it identifies the perspectives and research of different writers; it provides evidence to support your argument and it will show that you are able to produce work of acceptable academic practice.

When you start your background reading and researching in order to produce an assignment, write down the bibliographic details of the books, articles and other sources that you consult or take notes from. 'Bibliographic details' are those details about a book or article that enable the reader to identify and, if necessary, get hold of or access, the book or article that you are referring to. Many people use index cards to record bibliographic details.[3]

Proper referencing also protects you against charges of plagiarism. Essentially, plagiarism is about using the expressions of an author you have read as if they were your own personal voice, or failing to give credit to the ideas, theories and opinions of other writers by presenting them as if they were (written) reflections of your own thinking. Plagiarism is cheating and most academic institutions take it very seriously and may fail students.[4]

Referencing systems

There are a number of referencing systems used in academic writing.

The *Harvard system* uses the name of the author and date of publication in the body text. The Bibliography or References at the end of the book will then list the authors' names in alphabetical order with the date of publication, followed by the title and publisher. You will find that we have used this system throughout the main part of this book, with the full details given at the end of each chapter.

The *numeric system* (as used in this section) gives a number at the end of each quote. A correspondingly numbered list is then provided at the end of the book or chapter, giving full publishing details. This helps the reader to identify the source of information provided in the text.

The difference between a reference list and a bibliography

A reference provides the full bibliographic details of the citation of an author's work that you have actually consulted and specifically referred to in your coursework. This may be by quoting an author in the body of your coursework, or by referring to the theories, ideas or opinions of an author in the body of your coursework. At the end of your coursework there should be a list of references in alphabetical order, if you are using the Harvard system, or in numerical order, of all the citations you have made in the body of your coursework.[5]

Strictly speaking, a bibliography is a list of all the texts you have consulted as part of your background reading or researching that have *influenced* your writing, but that have not been cited *directly*. So some of the references in your bibliography may not be to work that you have *specifically* cited in your coursework. If, in practice, your reference list and bibliography amount to the same thing there is no need to produce an additional bibliography. This is why the Harvard system is so popular, as often only one list is needed.[6]

Do not forget to ask your tutors about their expectations regarding the referencing practices they require for the particular coursework they have set for you to do.

Make a record of who and what you are reading – get into the habit of making a note of the bibliographic details of what you are reading at the time of your reading, and you will begin to find that writing up coursework is not a punishment – it is a personal and rewarding challenge.

Using case studies

Case studies are a description of a situation in an organisational context over a particular period of time. They are used in education as a means of acquiring knowledge and developing various skills. It is for this reason that we have included a case study in each of the chapters of this book. Many students find case studies difficult as they are not being taught but instead are having to use their problem-solving skills alone. You may be using case studies in class as a means of clarifying your understanding of a topic area, or in an exam as a summative assessment of your learning. Analysing case studies can often strike fear in the hearts of students, especially if they are used to right or wrong answers. There is also no set method of analysing the case – it is very much up to the individual to find the method they prefer. However, the more you deal with case studies the better you will become.

Geoff Easton recommends the following in his seven-step approach.[7]

1 Understanding the situation: What is happening in the case? Is it relevant? Is it all there? What is missing? Can I make decisions based on the information?

2 Diagnosing the problem areas: What is the situation now? What should it be? The difference between the two is the problem. You will need to identify the factors involved and the different relationships to find out if you have the right cause, as not all the symptoms may lead to the problem.

3 Generating alternative solutions: Be creative. You may want to produce a mind map or decision tree to identify various solutions. There is information on organisational decision-making in Chapter 11, could you use one of these methods for your case study? You are unlikely to implement all your solutions, but it will enable you to examine them and make decisions.

4 Predicting outcomes: What would happen if you implemented a particular solution? You need to try to predict all possible outcomes and think about what happens to other problems if you solve one problem and not another. You need to weigh up the risks with the benefits.

5 Evaluating alternatives: You will need to choose your alternative solutions. They need to be qualified and quantified before you justify your choice.

6 Rounding out the analysis: How much detail do you need to include? You may need to go back to the case and go through the stages again. This will add breadth and depth to your analysis.

7 Communicating the results: How are you going to report the results? Is it a written or an oral presentation? You need to spend time on this – especially if you are going to be marked for it. Think about professionalism – especially if you are looking for a future in management.

Exam techniques

You will notice in each chapter that there are questions for study and discussion; some of these questions may be similar to those you may encounter in an exam. The better prepared you are for exams the less stress you are likely to feel. When you start an exam, read the instructions carefully. Do you have to answer every question? How many marks are allocated to each question? Divide up your time to make sure that you will be able to answer the required questions, also allowing some time to check through the paper at the end.

Check the wording of the exam. Are you being asked to – describe, discuss, evaluate, analyse, etc. Before you start your answer draw up a brief plan, this often helps the thought processes and can be crossed out afterwards.[8]

Make sure your writing is legible. Perfectly able students have been known to fail exams because their handwriting couldn't be read.

When the exam is over forget about it. Don't dwell on what you may or may not have done; and it is often better not to discuss it with others, as this can often cause anxiety. You can't do anything until the results are published so you may as well relax and chill out.

Notes

[1] Thanks to BX 101 undergraduates at London Metropolitan University who provided the study tips (2002).

[2] Unpublished paper on academic writing by Linda Johnson at London Metropolitan University (1998).

[3] Egan, S. (1978) 'Citation Indexes: Background, Description and Evaluation with Special Reference to SSCI', MA thesis, University of Sheffield.

[4] Ibid.

[5] Kaplan, N. (1965) 'The Norms of Citation Behavior: Prolegomena to the Footnote', *American Documentation*, 16(3), pp. 179–184.

[6] Martyn, J. (1966) 'Citation Indexing' *The Indexer* 5(1), pp. 5–15.

[7] Easton, G. (1982) *Learning from Case Studies*. Prentice Hall, Chapter 2.

[8] Study Skills and Learning Materials Booklet (unpublished). London Metropolitan University, 2002.

Further reading

Buzan, T. with Buzan, B. (1985) *The Mind Map Book*. London, BBC Books.

Cameron, S. (2002) *The Business Students Handbook* (2nd edn). Financial Times, Prentice Hall.

Guided tour

Learning Outcomes

As an introductory overview, learning outcomes help students quickly grasp the essentials they are expected to learn from each chapter.

Opening Vignettes

An opening real-world scenario or issue introduces students to the value of learning chapter material. At the end of each chapter we revisit the lead-off situation for a 'second look.'

Your Turn

These self-reflective exercises are designed to enable students to apply lessons of the chapter to themselves.

Boxed Features

To enable students to grapple with real-world key issues facing managers and organisations, four key theme boxes appear throughout the text: dynamics of diversity, eye on ethics, technology transformation and world watch.

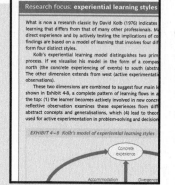

Research Focus

The research focus boxes highlight some of the major research in the various topic areas, demonstrate how theories have developed, and explore their impact on current organisational and management thinking.

Margin Definitions

The technical language of management and OB is summarised in key terms in the margins. At the end of each chapter is a list of the key concepts and page numbers.

Summary

The summary provides highlights that relate back to chapter objectives and key topics.

Areas for Personal Development

Each chapter provides six to eight instruction sets on how to bridge concepts with development of personal skills appropriate to effective organisational performance.

Questions for Study and Discussion

End-of-chapter questions provide ways to help students ensure that chapter outcomes are learned.

Team exercise
Problem-solving within Lightning Rod S

Purpose This is a team-based exercise designed to:

1 analyse the motivational implications of data gene
   for Lightning Rod Steel (LRS)
2 develop and present to the class a theory-supporte
   of the engineers
3 use the same criteria developed by the engineers to
   in a work situation.

Time about 35 minutes

Procedures Perform the following five tasks.

1 Divide into groups of five to seven people.
2 As a team, read the background material, including
3 Each group should analyse the Lightning Rod situa
   motivation among engineers. Then, use one establi
   for developing an action plan of recommendatio
   company's engineers. What specific actions shoul
   plan is feasible and reasonable for the managers to
4 Each individual group member should score the 19
   neers in Exhibit 5-6. Determine how much each fa
   an ideal work situation. Assign points from 0 to 5,
   0 indicates 'unimportant'. Record your points in
   exhibit. Then think of any factors important to you

Experiential Exercises

Two exercises, 'personal skills exercise' and 'team exercise', at the end of each chapter provide variety in how different types of activity can be used to stimulate experiential learning behaviours.

Case study: Volvo's Uddevalla plant, Sweden

Volvo's production plant at Uddevalla used 40 small parallel te
production pace, individual cycle times ranged from 1.5 to 3.5 h
and a materials shop. The usual number of teams was eight
precise number of teams changed as a consequence of const
Uddevalla's whole-car assembly was reminiscent of craft work.
kits in a largely automated process using sophisticated new tech
nical aids were developed to make the small-scale assembly effic
cally vastly superior to line assembly. Furthermore, the holist
intellectual quality supported an extended collaboration am
designers and product engineers, which made for a potentially
to the static character of traditional craft work.

Management believed that the plant's combination of high
short feedback loops would automatically result in excellent qua
sation structure was flat, but for a long time the advanced asse
management hierarchy, underscored by the detached and seclu
their offices.

During the early years the plant developed despite this an
clear signs of stagnation. The plant could not advance only o
needed a congenial plant organisation and managerial structur
of soul-searching, management put in place a different and
headed by a new plant manager who had been extremely succe
Volvo's development and product engineering departments. In
only two hierarchical levels: shop-floor and plant management.
shops had on average 70 workers organised in teams with rotati
nicated directly with the shop managers, who in turn made up

Cases

End-of-chapter cases provide vivid descriptions of an organisation's experience, followed by a few questions to encourage students to think critically about the case situation in relation to concepts explained in the text.

WWW exercise
Manager's Internet tools

Web tips: examining motivation on the Internet
The world of work is changing, with the use of teleworki
that are here today and gone tomorrow. Also, in times of
skilled staff, employers need to be able to maintain a conte
to foster an environment where people enjoy coming to wo
tion. When Joanna Read of Morpheus (in the opening vign
staff retention, she sought help and realised that it was he
change. She also recognised that the different life cycles of a
depending on whether it was in the initial start-up phase o
that if these types of firm are really different to work for, wh
start-up versus a more mature organisation?

World Wide Web search
Examine some dotcom websites, particularly the areas dedi
job openings. Examine some of the job postings and
employees. What are some of the motivating factors listed?
Because the Internet industry is changing rapidly, there
up websites to examine.

1 Are there actual or perceived differences between the
  different companies? If so, what are the different motiva
2 Would stock option plans motivate you to join a parti
  would motivate you to join an Internet start-up? A matt

WWW Exercise

These end-of-chapter exercises link use of the Internet to organisations described in the chapters.

Further reading

Bradberry, T. and Greaves, J. (2005) 'Heartless Bosses?', *Harvar*
   p. 24.
Gabel, R.S., Dolan, S.L. and Cerdin, J.L. (2005) 'Emotional
   Adjustment for Success in Global Assignments', *Caree*
   pp. 375–397.
Liptak, J.J. (2005) 'Using Emotional Intelligence to Help Coll
   place', *Journal of Employment Counseling* 42(4), December, p

References

Bennis, W.G., Berlew, D.E., Schein, E.H. and Steele, F.I. (1973
   Chicago, IL: Dorsey Press, pp. 495–518.
Berman, L. (1995) 'The Gospel According to Mary', *Working W*
Bernstein, P.W. (1980) 'Things the B-school Never Taught', *Fo*
Castro, J. (1992) 'Sexual Harassment: A Guide', *Time*, 20 Januar
Coffey, R.E., Athos, A.G. and Raynolds, P.A. (1975) *Behaviour*
   View (2nd edn). Englewood Cliffs, NJ: Prentice Hall, pp. 150
Cohen, A.R., Fink, S.L., Gadon, H., Willits, R.D. and Josefow
   Organisations (5th edn). Homewood, IL: Irwin, p. 256.
Costley, D.L. and Todd, R. (1987) *Human Relations in Organi*
   lishing Company, pp. 232–235.
Covey, S.R. (1989) *The 7 Habits of Highly Effective People*. New
   pp. 188–189.

References

For the research minded, references are collected at the end of each chapter. This also helps to direct further reading.

Technology to enhance learning and teaching

Online Learning Centre (OLC)

After completing each chapter, log on to the supporting Online Learning Centre website. Take advantage of the study tools offered to reinforce the material you have read in the text, and to develop your knowledge of management and organisational behaviour in a fun and effective way.

Resources for students include:

- *Business skills area*
- *Self-test multiple choice questions*
- *Weblinks*

Also available for lecturers:

- *PowerPoint slides*
- *Lecturer's manual*
- *Interactive CD-Rom test bank*

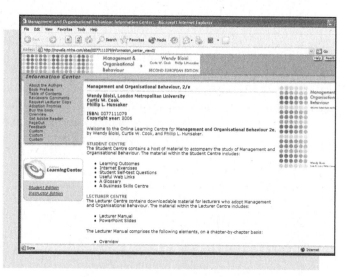

EZ Test

EZTest, a new computerised testbank format from McGraw-Hill, is available with this title. EZTest enables you to upload testbanks, modify questions and add your own questions, thus creating a testbank that's totally unique to your course! Find out more at: *http://mcgraw-hill.co.uk/he/eztest/*

Visit **www.mcgraw-hill.co.uk/textbooks/bloisi** today

Lecturers: customise content for your courses using the McGraw-Hill Primis Content Centre

Now it's incredibly easy to create a flexible, customised solution for your course, using content from both US and European McGraw-Hill Education textbooks, content from our Professional list including Harvard Business Press titles, as well as a selection of over 9000 cases from Harvard, Insead and Darden. In addition, we can incorporate your own material and course notes.

For more information, please contact your local rep, who will discuss the right delivery options for your custom publication – including printed readers, e-Books and CD-Roms. To see what McGraw-Hill content you can choose from, visit *www.primisonline.com*.

Study skills

Open University Press publishes guides to study, research and exam skills to help undergraduate and postgraduate students through their university studies.

Visit *www.openup.co.uk/sg/* to see the full selection of study skills titles, and get a **£2 discount** by entering the promotional code **study** when buying online!

Computing skills

If you'd like to brush up on your computing skills, we have a range of titles covering MS Office applications such as Word, Excel, PowerPoint, Access and more.

Get a £2 discount on these titles by entering the promotional code **app** when ordering online at *www.mcgraw-hill.co.uk/app*.

Acknowledgements

Our thanks go to the following reviewers for their comments at various stages in the development of the text:

Jimmy Donaghey, Queen's University, Belfast
Annet de Lang, Vrije University, Netherlands
Sam Lynch, University of Kent, UK
Alma McCarthy, National University of Ireland, Galway
Michaela Schippers, Erasmus University, Netherlands
Paul Stokes, Sheffield Hallam University, UK
Billie Taylor, Nottingham Trent University, UK
Yoke Eng Tan, Canterbury Christ Church University College, UK

Authors' acknowledgements

Thanks also go to the first-year undergraduates at London Metropolitan University who tried some of the activities.

Every effort has been made to trace and acknowledge ownership of copyright and to clear permission for material reproduced in this book. The publishers will be pleased to make suitable arrangements to clear permission with any copyright holders whom it has not been possible to contact.

PART 1

What managers and organisations do

Part contents

Introduction to management and organisational behaviour

LEARNING OUTCOMES ☑

After studying this chapter you should be able to:

- ☑ **understand** the historical foundations of management

- ☑ **identify** the different schools of management theory

- ☑ **compare** and contrast the different schools of management theory

- ☑ **understand** the need for management and organisational research and the methodologies used

- ☑ **recognise** that international competition, quality, diversity and ethical behaviour are major management issues.

The opening vignette introduces a leading manager and entrepreneur from a well-known hairdressing chain. We look at what makes him successful and how he sees himself as a manager.

Toni & Guy: hair affair

Toni Mascolo is the man behind the most recognisable hairdressing brand on the UK high street. Thirty years on from opening his first salon, the business is still growing and he says he won't stop until he is in a wooden box.

▶ Toni Mascolo has built his Toni & Guy hairdressing business up from a single south London salon to an empire spanning two global salon chains and the Tigi hair products range. Here he tells us what it takes to be a successful businessman, how he has learnt from his mistakes, about his management style, and why he thinks entrepreneurs should follow their hearts and not their accountants.

Toni, whose real name is Guiseppe, admits that he had thought of hairdressing as a hobby and had different ambitions, such as becoming an accountant or lawyer. After opening his first salon with his brother in Clapham, London in the early 1960s he soon had a growing clientele. By the 1970s business was going well and they had published four books and a video. They were now being asked for by name.

One of the greatest challenges in building the business was the failure of the first franchise in 1989. The manager wanted to work under his own name rather than the Toni & Guy logo and in the end the franchise went bankrupt. To avoid financial disaster Toni had to pay the rent and take over the running of the shop. This was also the year Toni & Guy came close to bankruptcy because of huge rent increases caused by a recession. By refinancing at a high interest rate, he set about improving service and raising standards. The business survived because it had expanded to America, which was not in recession at that time. During the difficult economic times in the UK financial support was sustained by the US operation.

In order to build a successful business, management skills are required. Toni had come to England from Italy at the age of 14; he left school early, admitting he had learned nothing. As a manager, Toni tries to teach people to help themselves. He believes managers' decisions have to come from the heart and when a decision has been made people should stick with it.

Over the years Toni admits that his management style has changed. He acknowledges that at one time he was viewed as being quite cocky and confident; now when he looks back he realises he has made some blunt decisions. One example is when he invested with the wrong person in Barcelona. The chosen person had the best record ever, was a marvellous manager and had £280 000 in cash to invest. But the trouble was he wanted to open a franchise and just relax. Another example of following his heart was when Toni invested in Toni & Guy in Verona, not because Toni believed in it, but through following his instincts. The Verona manager was artistic, but no one had a good word for him. The prospective manager had decided he wanted to be the best franchisee. Toni didn't believe him and thought he would leave in a year's time, since the manager was creative rather than a businessman. However, he now looks as if he could be their best franchisee ever.

Toni admits that he thinks for himself and does not always listen to others. When he was advised by his accountant, lawyer and architect not to buy a building in West Drayton, Toni ignored them. 'Deep in my heart I felt it would be a great opportunity but they gave me all the reasons it would be a bad buy. Then I remembered my father telling me: "Do whatever you want. If you make a bad decision you'll learn by it." That passed through my mind and I banged my fist on the table and said: "I've decided I want to buy it!" and they said "Yes sir!"'

When people say that being a manager is a lonely job, Toni does not agree. He says he talks to everybody. If someone comes into one of his salons and asks if he works there, he says yes. When he goes to the warehouse he talks football and has tea with the workers. If he goes to a salon he spends time with the apprentices.

Toni identifies his main personal quality as being down to earth. He says he gets his inspiration from Julius Caesar, who won battles without lifting his sword. Toni also loves watching football and, as a supporter of Chelsea Football Club, he finds inspiration from the balance between consistent strong defenders and superstars. Toni believes that balance is the most important thing in any company.

Toni acknowledges that management also involves some tough decisions. 'Making people redundant is a big dilemma. When Tigi was de-merged, quite a few people were made redundant. I try and offer those who started their careers with me anything I can to get them going again.'

Toni says he gets his entrepreneurial spirit from a love of helping people and, the more he can achieve, the more people he can help – it is this that keeps him interested in the business. His greatest satisfaction is from giving people the opportunity to help themselves. He thinks that the ability to achieve is infinite.

Toni predicts that the company will open another 10 000 Essensuals salons globally in five to ten years and another 100 Toni & Guy salons.

Source: adapted from *Growing Business*, October 2002.

Discussion questions

1 What does this case tell us about the functions of a manager?

2 Does an entrepreneur make a good manager?

To be an effective manager requires knowledge and experience. A study of management and organisational behaviour will not necessarily mean you will become a good manager, this knowledge would need to be combined with experience, but it will help you to understand how people have used their management skills and how research into organisations can guide your management of people. The opening vignette identifies a successful businessman and how he has built his empire. However, Toni has had no formal management training and seems to have run his business by instinct, rather than sound business sense. Many new businesses do not last beyond the first year and yet Toni Mascolo, with very little education, emigrates from Italy to England, opens his first shop and then 10 years later expands abroad. He follows this with hair-care products and then develops a second chain called Essensuals. How can we explain Toni's business success?

Is it to do with his personality? He obviously has strong motives and drives. Or, has he been successful because of his management style and his ability to develop people? Many may argue that he is not a successful manager as the case has illustrated that he does not listen to advice. Therefore could it be just an element of luck?

How can we find this out? And how can we identify why his strategies are successful so that we can use them to make our organisations successful? Also, what about the structure and design of the organisation? How does it respond to the environment? This is what the study of organisational behaviour and management is about. By working your way through this book you will meet other entrepreneurs and managers of both large multinational companies and small family-owned businesses and we will look at their strategies, which may or may not have been successful.

Another method of helping us to understand management and organisational behaviour is to look at the research that has been done before. To prepare for the future it is useful to know what has gone before and what has and has not been successful. Theories can help us do this.

This chapter introduces you to the development of management and organisational behaviour theories and later explains why the study of the different theories and methodologies is important. But it is also important not to study the theories in isolation; we need to think about how they can be applied to the workplace and how we can use them to make us better managers. As you progress through this book you will see plenty of practical examples of how theories are applied to the management of organisations and how managers deal with the everyday tasks of planning, leading, organising and controlling.

First, we will take a look at the historical foundations of management and OB theories. This will help us to identify how theories were developed, and their relevance and application in today's business environment.

Historical foundations of management and OB theories

Henry Towne proposed to a meeting of the American Society of Mechanical Engineers in 1886 that management should have its own body of theory (Duncan, 1990). In the audience was Frederick Taylor, whose subsequent research, writing and principles created the 'scientific management' movement and the first serious study of managing behaviour in organisations. From these engineering origins the study of management has branched out and become more formalised over the last century. This chapter provides a foundational perspective on the history of management and organisational behaviour theories and how they have shaped what we know and appreciate about organisations. It concludes with a brief note on the methods of conducting behavioural research.

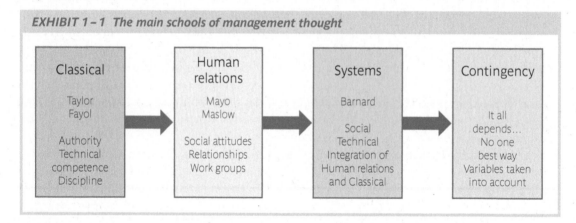

EXHIBIT 1–1 The main schools of management thought

The classical perspectives

In the first 20 years of the twentieth century, several streams of thought emerged independently that focused on the revolutionary idea that management could be learned and codified systematically. This was an era when mass production and economies of scale first became the accepted path to business success. Henry Ford introduced his moving assembly line in 1914, enabling production of a Model T Ford in two hours. The price of a Model T dropped from £600 in 1908 to about £250 (Duncan, 1990).

Among the notables to leave a permanent mark on the study of behaviour in organisations and the practice of management during this emerging industrial era were the Americans Frederick Taylor and Lillian Gilbreth, the Frenchman Henri Fayol and the German Max Weber.

Scientific management

From Frederick Taylor's assumption that the interests of management and employees could be integrated through the principle of economically motivated self-interest emerged scientific management. He clearly distinguished between managerial and non-managerial work, and was one of the first to do so. Taylor believed scientific observation of people at work (through time and motion studies) would reveal the one best way to do any non-managerial task. Once the best way had been determined and the requisite skills identified, managers could hire appropriate people and train them to perform the specialised job. With performance requirements and tools specified, Taylor also established a 'differential piece rate' pay system that rewarded work output in excess of established standards.

scientific management
An early 1900s movement that elevated the status of managers and held that scientific observation of people at work would reveal the one best way to do any task.

Taylor placed his emphasis on the 'task' or the tangible elements of a job, which he saw as the 'most prominent single element in modern scientific management' (Taylor, 1914). He replaced haphazard rules of thumb with systematic, measured, empirically derived *principles*. Taylor was the first to emphasise the prediction of behaviour, followed by goals, training and other management techniques to influence work outcomes. However, Taylor (1914) espoused a rather mechanistic view of workers. He wrote that successful pig iron handlers were so 'stupid and so phlegmatic' that they appeared to resemble more in 'mental makeup the ox than any other type of animal'. Nevertheless, Taylor's contributions to the emergence of management are legendary and several of his original concepts still provide the foundation for current management practices.

Research focus: **Frederick Taylor**

Taylor believed managers had the responsibility to plan, organise and determine the best methods for performing a job. His work stemmed from his job as a foreman in the Midvale Steel Company. One of the best illustrations of Taylor's work is at Bethlehem Steel Company in the 1890s.

Bethlehem Steel Company had been dumping pig iron in an open field as a result of its smelting processes. However, during the Spanish-American War the price of pig iron increased enough for there to be a viable market for it. The mountains of dumped pig iron needed to be loaded on to railway trucks. When Taylor (1914) first analysed the task he found a group of 75 men working at the rate of 12.5 tons per man per day. By calculating the ideal walking speed and the percentage of time a worker needed to be free of a load to avoid excessive fatigue, Taylor found a method of increasing productivity by almost four times. By following Taylor's instructions of when to lift, when to carry and when to rest, the workers succeeded in loading 47.25 tons per day, and found that the new method was no more exhausting than the old one.

Development of the theory of scientific management into practice

The Taylor Society proposes the following aims of scientific management.

1 To gauge industrial tendencies and the market in order to thereby regularise operations in a manner which will serve the investment, sustain the enterprise as an employing agency, and assure continuous operation and employment.

2 To assure the employee not only of continuous operation and employment by correct gauging of the market, but also to assure by planned and balanced operations a continuous earning opportunity.

3 To earn, through waste-saving management and processing techniques, a larger income from a given expenditure of human and material energies, which shall be shared through increased wages and profits by workers and management.

4 To make possible a higher standard of living as a result of increased income to workers.

5 To assure a happier home and social life to workers through the removal, by increase of income, of many of the disagreeable and worrying factors in the total situation.

6 To assure healthful as well as individually and socially agreeable conditions of work.

7 To assure the highest opportunity for individual capacity through scientific methods of work analysis and of selection, training, assignment, transfer and promotion of workers.

8 To assure by training and instructional foremanship the opportunity for workers to develop new and higher capacities, and eligibility for promotion to higher positions.

9 To develop self-confidence and self-respect among workers through opportunity afforded for the understanding of one's work specifically, and of plans and methods of work generally.

10 To develop self-expression and self-realisation among workers through the stimulative influence of an atmosphere of research and valuation, through understanding of plans and methods, and through the freedom of horizontal as well as vertical contacts afforded by functional organisation.

11 To build character through the proper conduct of work.

12 To promote justice through the elimination of discrimination in wage rates and elsewhere.

13 To eliminate factors of the environment which are irritating and the causes of friction, and to promote common understandings, tolerances, and the spirit of teamwork.

Source: Person, H.S. (ed.) (1929) *Scientific Management in American Industry*. Copyright Taylor Society and H.S. Person, Harper Row, Publishers, Inc.

Evaluation of scientific management

Scientific management has been regarded as being too preoccupied with productivity. It may be true that many factory owners have employed Taylor's methods without providing rewards, but this is not what Taylor had in mind. Taylor's writings do not ignore the worker. He believed in careful selection and training and that they should be suitable for the work. In some respects he had an idealistic view that workers, managers and owners could work together in harmony and profit from it.

Lillian Gilbreth, one of the first women to earn a PhD in the field of psychology, took the 'task' concept of scientific management and embellished it as a goal-setting process. She viewed task determination as a means–ends process of *analysis* (separating complex things into their constituent elements) and *synthesis* (putting the elements back together into a logical system). This interaction between analysis and synthesis became the basis for empirically based goal-setting. To Gilbreth (1973), a goal was not an idealised aspiration, but the result of an objectively determined study of work tasks based on what 'has actually been done and what can be expected to be repeated'. Her pioneering 1914 work on analysis and synthesis as the basis of goal-setting provided the foundation for later management practices such as *management by objectives (MBO)* and the use of rewards to reinforce behaviour. This is another reason why the study of the history of management is important, as past research impacts on future research. More can be found about management by objectives in Chapter 6.

Your turn

How efficient are you?

Many of you may have worked, or are working now, to support your studies. Apply the following fundamental principles of Taylor's scientific approach to your job.

1 Replace rules of thumb with science.
2 Obtain harmony in group action, rather than discord.
3 Achieve the co-operation of human beings, rather than chaotic individualism.
4 Work for maximum output, rather than restricted output.
5 Develop workers to the fullest extent for their own and their company's highest prosperity.

If your organisation applied the above scientific principles would you still want to work for it?

Administrative principles

The French industrialist Henri Fayol developed the first management principles that focused on the administrative aspects of the manager's job. He published *General and Industrial Management* in bulletin form in 1916, although it was not available in an English translation until 1949. Fayol (1949) elevated the study of management from the shop floor (Taylor's emphasis) to the total organisation. He viewed business as a composite of six subsystems: purchasing, production, sales, finance, accounting and administration. To handle the subsystems, he described the five *management functions* of planning, organising, co-ordinating, directing and controlling (see Exhibit 1-2).

These management functions remain the basic platform for the principles of management texts in use today. In this text our approach is to blend management and organisational behaviour. The first part of Fayol's book emphasised that *management principles* (a theory of management) needed to be developed so that they could be taught to managers. Fayol complemented his five functions with 14 principles of administrative management, which included such teachings as *division of labour* to achieve specialisation for maximum efficiency and *unity of command* so that workers receive directives from only one superior in order to eliminate confusion.

EXHIBIT 1–2 Henri Fayol's functions of management

To build 'unity through management', Fayol (1949) described how managers administer operations through five functional activities.

1 **Planning** – studying the future and arranging the means for dealing with it, which encompasses forecasting, setting goals and determining actions.

2 **Organising** – designing a structure to assist in goal accomplishment that effectively relates human and non-human resources to the tasks of the enterprise.

3 **Co-ordinating** – uniting activities that take place within the organisation so that elements are given proper resources and the means to accomplish goals.

4 **Commanding (directing)** – engaging in those activities that ensure effective operation, including leadership and motivation of employee action towards goals.

5 **Controlling** – ensuring that everything is carried out according to the plan.

Sources: Henri Fayol's *General and Industrial Management* (1949), as summarised in W. Jack Duncan, *Great Ideas in Management* (San Francisco: Jossey-Bass, 1990), pp. 91–97.

Research focus: **Henri Fayol**

Fayol's principles are based on his observations as a businessman. He based his writings on his experience from a long managerial career. He made no attempt to develop a logical theory or to develop a philosophy of management. However, his observations fit closely with current developments in management theory.

Fayol observed that the qualities required by a manager were to be fit, both physically and mentally, have a moral code, be interested in the acquisition of knowledge and have technical expertise and experience. It is on this basis that Fayol recognised the need for principles of management and for management to be taught. He then set about developing his theory.

Fayol's 14 principles of management (1949)

1 Division of Work – specialisation is to create efficiency, not just for technical work but also for managerial work.

2 Authority and Responsibility – if you have responsibility you must have authority. This would be not only from position but also from personality.

3 Discipline – this is required at all levels and ensures the outward marks of respect.

4 Unity of Command – employees should receive orders from only one boss.

5 Unity of Direction – for each group of activities there should be one boss and one plan.

6 Subordination of Individual Interest to the General Interest – if there are differences managers must reconcile them.

7 Remuneration – should be fair and equitable for both the employee and the employer.

8 Centralisation – the extent to which authority is concentrated in one place or dispersed. Who holds the power?

9 Scaler Chain – there should be a line of authority from highest to lowest.

10 Order – a place for everyone and everything and everyone and everything in its place.

11 Equity – through kindliness and justice which will create loyalty and devotion.

12 Stability of Tenure – unnecessary labour turnover can be both the cause and the effect of bad management.

13 Initiative – managers should encourage initiative from their employees and nurture it.

14 Esprit de Corps – (unity is strength) this emphasises the need for teamwork.

Source: Henri Fayol (1949) *General and Industrial Management*. London: Pitman.

Fayol's teachings are still valid today. Fayol argues that, since all organisations require managing, the formulation of a theory of management is necessary for its effective teaching.

Bureaucracy theory

Although conventional wisdom associates the word bureaucracy with inefficiency and indifference to clients, it was originally put forward by Max Weber to be an ideal design for efficiency. A sociologist concerned about society in Germany, Weber introduced several underlying structural principles for organisational effectiveness under the umbrella of the concept of bureaucracy. To Weber (1947), **bureaucracy** meant:

bureaucracy
Max Weber's rational–legal authority structure for organising specialised functions and standardising procedures to achieve efficiency.

- a hierarchy of command based on a rational–legal authority structure established by a person's rank in the hierarchy
- specialisation and division of labour by organisational function, such as engineering, production and sales
- an explicit system of rules and policies that standardises how things are to be done, to ensure equitable treatment of everyone
- promotion and tenure based on competence, developed through training and experience, and measured by objective standards
- impersonal treatment of people through consistent application of rules and decisions to prevent favouritism.

Weber assumed work was not necessarily meant to be pleasant but rather to be efficient, with minimum conflicts of interest. Managers were expected to be unemotional and treat people as though they were interchangeable.

Although he wrote as a sociologist concerned about preserving social order, one of Weber's most significant contributions to management was his *focus on authority* (Weber, 1947). He believed organisations require order to regulate human behaviour, and employees accept directives and guidelines from management to improve harmony and productivity. The most significant source of authority is from the legal system, which gives the manager legitimate authority; the weakest is charismatic authority based on the esteemed personal qualities of the leader or manager. In Weber's view, people comply with authority because it is in their best interest to do so, which suggests a passive human nature. This impersonal treatment of people was seen as a limitation of Weber's theory once groups were recognised as social systems made complex because of non-mechanistic human behaviour.

The behavioural approaches

Regardless of whether practised in the United Kingdom, United States, France or Germany, the previously described classical theories of management held a limited view of people as employees. They all viewed the rank-and-file worker as rather passive, lacking in self-direction and motivated mainly by economic self-interest. Three forces combined to hasten the decline of the mechanistic point of view in favour of a more human-centred orientation: the hardship of the Great Depression; enactment of progressive legislation on social security, pay and working hours; and an intellectual climate that raised social consciousness. The original shift in focus away from a rational-economic picture of employees to a more social-behavioural perspective came from an attempt to refine and extend scientific management.

Hawthorne studies spawn human relations movement

The theoretical turning point in management philosophy and practice was the work of Elton Mayo in his famous Hawthorne studies. Mayo's (1933) research project to determine the relationship between physical working conditions and worker productivity at Western Electric's Hawthorne Works near Chicago yielded puzzling results. The productivity of the initial work groups selected for observation seemed to increase constantly regardless of changes in a variety of physical variables such as temperature, lighting or duration of work. What seemed to be important were social elements such as involvement in decision-making, work relationships, and group attitudes and values.

The Hawthorne Works research methodology has been widely criticised. Some allege that simply because the experimental subjects (the employees) were being paid attention, their behaviour changed – a research-confounding effect called the Hawthorne effect. Yet more than any other single body of research, the decade of Western Electric experiments (involving more than 20 000 workers) shifted the management paradigm from largely mechanistic principles to a human relations orientation built around the behavioural complexities of people with diverse needs functioning in a complex, informal social system. Organisational behaviour became important as a field of study and a concern of management.

Hawthorne effect
The unintentional biasing of research outcomes due to the possibility that simply paying attention to the experimental subjects causes their behaviour to change.

Research focus: **The illumination studies**

The illumination studies were set up to identify what the proper level of lighting, identified as a requirement of scientific management, should be.

The illumination studies looked at the effect of light intensity on worker productivity. Three formal experiments were set up with different groups of workers. These experiments increased or decreased the amount of lighting while productivity levels were measured. The results were not as expected. It was found that productivity levels often increased whether the room was lighter or darker. The test was repeated on a control group and the result was the same. The experiment was then carried out on two groups using 10 candles for light. The control group's light remained constant, while the other group had one candle at a time removed. Both groups' efficiency increased slowly, until production had to cease as the experimental group could no longer see.

An informal experiment was then carried out where two workers were locked in a room and the light was reduced to that of moonlight. Again both workers maintained their efficiency.

The investigators were beginning to think that the workers were responding to something other than the physical environment and the experiment was developed further. This time the workers were asked what they felt about the increases and decreases in lighting. The response was that they felt they worked better under bright lights. When the investigators increased the lighting the workers said they preferred it, but they also said the same when the investigators only pretended to increase the lighting. When the investigators announced that they had decreased the lighting the workers complained. When the investigators pretended to decrease the lighting again the workers complained. However, throughout the experiment the production output did not change.

From this research the investigators concluded that light was only a minor factor affecting employee performance. The attempts to measure the effects of lighting had failed as other factors had not been controlled. The experiment was therefore flawed as it was decided that the measuring process rather than the level of lighting influenced production more. It was the fact that the workers knew their performance was being measured that increased production. This became known as the Hawthorne effect (Roethlisberger and Dickson, 1967).

Impact of research

The illumination studies and other similar studies leading on from them have had a greater impact on the history of management than any other study. As the 'Research focus' shows, there were serious flaws in the method and logic of these studies. Mayo claimed that changes in productivity were caused by the attitudes of the employees and that management practices influenced this. Therefore, friendly supervision was considered far more important than the physical environment.

From this viewpoint managers were taught that people were more important than productivity and that concern for people did not mean lower outputs.

Evaluation of the Hawthorne studies

■ The research stimulated many new ideas but they did not have a solid scientific foundation.

■ As we have identified above, the studies showed many flaws in their method and logic.

Some critics claimed that the research that followed on from these studies was the opposite to what the researchers claimed. Financial incentives through piece rates were thought to be a powerful motivator and yet the Hawthorne researchers could not find a substantial link (Roethlisberger and Dickson, 1967).

Towards a humanistic psychology

During the era of the late 1940s and the 1950s a popular (but widely misunderstood) theory of motivation was expressed by Abraham Maslow (1943) and his followers, such as Douglas McGregor (1960). They pushed the humanistic frontier even further in focusing on the complexities of human behaviour as a critical variable in organisational effectiveness. Maslow defined human motivation as 'the study of ultimate human goals' in his 1954 book *Motivation and Personality* (Maslow, 1954). He emphasised the uniqueness of human needs and at the same time called attention to the different ways cultures impact on the satisfaction of those needs.

As explained in Chapter 6, Maslow recognised that some needs deal with overcoming basic human deficiencies, whereas others pull us in the direction of individualistic, growth-motivated goals. This concept shifted management attention away from simply providing basic needs and towards an awareness that people's growth needs could be achieved at work, benefiting both the individual and the organisation. Many present-day practices such as empowerment, team-building, and building high-commitment organisations are based on the humanistic realities originally advocated by Maslow and refined by many others.

The systems approach

One of the most influential writers in the field of management was Chester Barnard. He had an extensive career in management and was also a respected academic who lectured at Harvard. Barnard's analysis of the manager was a social systems approach as he felt that to be able to comprehend and analyse the functions of management, it was necessary to examine the major tasks in the system where they operate (Roethlisberger and Dickson, 1967).

In determining that the task of managers was one of maintaining a system of co-operation in a formal organisation, Barnard addressed himself first to the reasons for, and the nature of, co-operative systems.

Research focus: **Chester Barnard**

Barnard's (1938) research resulted in the publication of *The Functions of the Executive*. An analysis of his research can be seen in the following steps.

1 Physical and biological limitations of the individuals lead them to co-operate. Because of these limitations once people co-operate, psychological and social limitations will also add to that co-operation. This results in group work and team effort.

2 The act of co-operation leads to the establishment of co-operative systems. Barnard would see a group as a co-operative system made up of the physical environment as well as the people. The continuation of effectiveness depends on the ability to achieve set goals with the minimum of dissatisfaction to members.

3 Any co-operative system may be divided into two parts: 'organisation', which includes only the behaviour of people; and 'other elements'.

4 Organisations can be divided into 'formal', where there are set conscious interactions, and 'informal', which refers to the social interactions that are unconscious.

5 The formal organisation cannot exist unless there are persons who are (a) able to communicate with one another, (b) are willing to contribute to group action, (c) have a conscious common purpose.

6 Every formal organisation must include the following elements: (a) a system of functioning so that people can specialise, (b) a system of effective and efficient incentives that will induce people to group action, (c) a system of authority and power to direct group members, (d) a system of logical decision-making.

7 The functions of the manager in this organisation are therefore: (a) the maintenance of communication systems, (b) to gain the commitment of individuals in the organisation, (c) the formulation and definition of purpose, the mission and plan.

8 The management functions are integrated by the manager as a means of finding the best balance between conflicting forces and events.

To make the manager effective requires responsible leadership. Barnard (1938) comments, 'Co-operation, not leadership, is the creative process; but leadership is the indispensable fulminator of its forces.'

   This is a social systems approach, concentrating on major elements of the manager's job. The research has had a major influence on management thought.

Systems theories with contingency adjustments

The last half of the twentieth century saw a proliferation of theoretical refinements largely consistent with the systems concept of organisations. Several contributors helped create the concept of contingent-based administrative behaviour within an open system.

Systems theory

systems theory
Emphasises that the whole is greater than the sum of the parts, and that the parts or subsystems are related to each other and to the whole.

Systems theory holds that the whole is greater than the sum of the parts, and that the parts, or subsystems, are related to one another and to the whole. Two works were especially notable for examining organisations as social systems. The first was George Homans' (1950) *The Human Group*, which presented a social systems model of group behaviour. The other milestone was

The Social Psychology of Organisations by Katz and Kahn (1966), which built on the work of Parsons (1951) to emphasise the close relationship between the organisation and its supporting environment. The systems approach allows the level of analysis to run up and down the hierarchy and from the outside environment to individual behaviour, depending on the behaviour that is the focus of attention. More than any other model, the systems perspective examines growth and decline in terms of predicted patterns of effectiveness. How organisations behave as systems can be seen in Chapter 2.

Administrative behaviour

Mary Parker Follett wrote across a number of management topics. Lyndall Urwick edited the essence of Follett's most important ideas in *Freedom and Coordination* (1949). In seeking to develop a more enlightened theory of administration 'Follett maintained that there are two basic qualifications for a profession: it must be founded on science, and its knowledge must be used in the service of others' (Duncan, 1990). One of Follett's major contributions was to articulate the reciprocal nature of power. Unlike Weber, who had a hierarchical view of authority, Follett believed that power came from the nature of the task performed. Power is thus function based, or embedded in the plan of the organisation, not in the individual.

To Follett, the exercise of power simply makes things happen, and managers use power as an agent of change. She did not accept the prevailing belief that managers have power 'over' other people. Rather, she introduced the concept of power 'with' others as a process for jointly developing solutions and coactive behaviours as opposed to power as a lever of coercion (Graham, 1995). By both influencing others and accepting the influence of others, a genuine environment of participation is possible.

Follett favoured replacement of authority with careful education of people in the best practices for carrying out work. She emphasised the 'law of the situation', cautioning managers to think through the total situation before issuing commands – to think holistically before acting impulsively. When possible, commands should not be directed towards individuals. Directives can provide guidance in a non-finger-pointing way if people understand why they must do certain things that are in their best interest.

Herbert Simon (1946) broke new ground with the publication of his *Administrative Behaviour*. In this and other works, Simon introduced the concept that managers are decision-makers who are not always rational because they do not have 'the wits to maximise'. Instead, the administrator works within a realm of subjective rationality to maximise outcomes subject to what is known about the decision situation. Thus, the decision-maker is limited by *bounded rationality* rather than perfect knowledge and ends up making *satisficing* (acceptable) instead of maximising decisions.

Cyert and March (1992) extended Simon's lead in their book, *A Behavioural Theory of the Firm*, to observe that managers engage in sequential searches of alternative solutions, often with ill-defined outcome preferences. Collectively, this body of research shifted attention away from the people being managed to the imperfections and limitations of those who manage and who are responsible for decisions to better the organisation.

The contingency perspective

For the first 50-plus years of management research, scholars and practitioners alike tried to uncover universal principles that would hold up regardless of circumstances. These proved to be elusive. More recently, researchers and managers have recognised that organisational behaviour cannot be engineered by consistently applying one theory to solve a particular problem. In most situations, multiple sources influence outcomes, so the contingency approach within a systems model is viewed as more workable. The contingency approach builds an 'it all depends' perspective into the applications of management theory.

But contingency does not mean simply that anything goes. Rather, useful **contingency theories** identify the circumstances in which a particular practice is more likely to obtain desired results. For example, if employees are new and unsure of themselves, the manager hypothesises on how to get better results by being considerate yet firmly task directed; if employees know how to handle their job, being more relationship focused and less intense about task directives is more likely to promote effective performance (Vecchio, 1987). The lesson from contingency approaches is that the manager must examine the situation to discover its relevant variables, diagnose the problem and then adapt some independent variable (often the manager's own behaviour) to fit the need. This discussion invites a brief overview of research methods.

contingency theories
Theories that identify the circumstances in which a particular practice is more likely to obtain desired results.

Research and methodological foundations

The study of management and organisational behaviour has evolved from industrial engineering and the various behavioural and social sciences to serve practical purposes. It provides knowledge that can be applied in organisational settings to improve performance and to increase efficiency and effectiveness at three levels of analysis: that of the individual, the small group and the entire organisation.

Beyond *industrial engineering* (which gave birth to scientific management), five social science disciplines have been major contributors to management and organisational behaviour knowledge. *Psychology* focuses directly on understanding and predicting individual behaviour. *Sociology* studies how individuals interact with one another in social systems. *Social psychology* is a behavioural science hybrid that integrates psychology and sociology to study why individuals behave as they do when part of a group. *Anthropology* studies the relationship between individuals and their environments and how a person or a group adapts to its environment. *Political science* studies individuals and groups in governmental and public policy-making environments and has relevant OB applications through its focus on power, conflict and rivalry.

The scientific method

Although the behavioural sciences may appear to lack the universal precision of the physical sciences, they all embrace the fundamentals of the scientific method. The **scientific method** uses a theory to guide systematic, empirical research from which generalisations can be made to influence applications. Rather than rely on intuition or a few ad hoc observations, the scientific method draws on facts through theory-guided investigations of behaviour in organisations. It works only because behaviour is caused or enacted rather than random. Research based on the scientific method progresses through four stages: from description, to understanding, to prediction and, finally, to control to bring about predicted outcomes. These stages parallel what those managers go through as they learn to become more skilled and ultimately to influence behavioural outcomes.

scientific method
The use of theory to guide systematic, empirical research from which generalisations can be made to influence applications.

Exhibit 1-3 portrays the flow of the scientific method as applied to the study of organisational behaviour. Some researchers begin with observing and gathering facts from the real-world behaviour of individuals, groups and organisations. From their specific preliminary

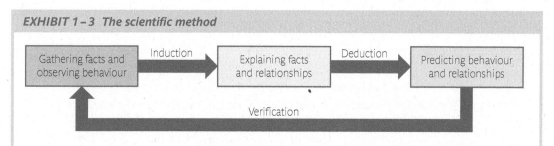

EXHIBIT 1–3 The scientific method

Research that employs the scientific method results in a cycle of ever-expanding knowledge based on the empirical verification of predicted hypotheses and models.

Source: based on Eugene F. Stone (1978), *Research Methods in Organisational Behaviour*. Glenview, IL: Scott Foresman.

observations, they inductively reason possible general explanations or theories of the cause of behaviour and/or its effects. Or researchers can apply deductive logic by building on their logical-rational thoughts about phenomena to state testable hypotheses or models of predicted behaviour in general organisational situations.

In reality, there is no separation of inductive and deductive approaches to theory development, but rather an essential continuity (Parkhe, 1993). The interplay between conceptualising general explanations of phenomena (deductive reasoning) and empirically studying the relationships among specific phenomena (inductive reasoning) is 'the essence of modern scientific method' (Sax, 1968).

Managers can also apply the scientific method. For example, in making appraisals of employees a manager can study multiple performance events over a period of time instead of drawing inferences from a single event. An inference based on a single snapshot can lead to an erroneous conclusion if the employee is having an off day (or a superior day). Similarly, if only one dimension of behaviour was observed (such as friendliness) the conclusion might be equally misleading. Instead, the more reliable approach is to use multiple criteria with episodes documented at different intervals of time. Documentation at the time of the event is important, for lapsed time between events and evaluations tends to blur the details of what actually happened.

Hypothesised relationships among variables

Once a model or hypothesis has been specified, the researchers verify (or disconfirm) hypothesised relationships by means of systematic data collection and analysis using experimentation, survey methods or field investigations of an appropriate sample. (See Exhibit 1-4 for notes on research methods.) Most research is conducted to establish relationships between two or more variables.

A **hypothesis** is a statement about the proposed relationship between the variables. An **independent variable** (also called the treatment, experimental or antecedent variable, represented by the symbol X) is thought to cause an effect on one or more **dependent variables** (often called the criterion or predicted variable, symbolised by Y). It might be hypothesised, for example, that leaders who are more considerate and team centred will realise higher group output and higher employee

hypothesis
A statement about the proposed relationship between independent and dependent variables.

independent variable
The variable thought to affect one or more dependent variables.

dependent variable
The outcome studied through research and believed to be caused or influenced by an independent variable.

EXHIBIT 1 – 4 Research designs for studying behaviour

The empirical investigation of behaviour in organisations draws on four primary alternatives for collecting data: interviews, questionnaires, observation of a sample of respondents, and secondary sources (such as company records). Researchers have a number of design options to choose from to provide answers to the questions (hypotheses) being investigated. Here are the basics of four common research designs.

1 **Case study:** The researcher focuses on a single organisation and does an in-depth study using a variety of data-collection methods, including interviews, observation and reviews of existing records. Case studies are useful in uncovering new insights into behavioural phenomena or making a limited exploration of a deductive model. Generalisation of results is limited.

2 **Field survey:** This method gathers data about perceptions, feelings and opinions through interviews and questionnaires administered to people in their actual work setting. Large numbers of people should be surveyed to obtain valid conclusions from the sample that will apply to the general population. Data tend to be correlational in nature (indicating that relationships exist); surveys lack cause → effect conclusions.

3 **Field experiment:** Field experiments allow the researcher to manipulate independent variables in actual organisations in an attempt to control variables and explain causality. At times, the subjects know they are being observed under experimental conditions (as in the Hawthorne studies). In other situations the experimental treatment is part of an actual management pilot programme and less influenced by the Hawthorne effect.

4 **Laboratory experiment:** Control of independent variable manipulation without intervening environmental effects is at its maximum in lab experiments conducted in artificial settings. Conclusions of causality can be highly reliable, but generalisation is often difficult because the artificial conditions are devoid of organisational complexities.

---

satisfaction than leaders who are directive and task centred. The research design to test such a hypothesis would treat variation in leadership style as the independent variable, and group output and employee satisfaction as the dependent variables.

moderating variable

A variable believed to influence the effects of the independent variable on the dependent variable.

In some research designs, a moderating variable might be specified – one that is believed to influence the effects of the independent variable on the dependent variable. For example, working conditions may moderate the effect of leadership on output. (In the Hawthorne research, working conditions such as lighting were hypothesised as independent variables thought to directly cause a change in output – a hypothesised relationship that was difficult to prove.)

reliability

The consistency of the data obtained from a particular research method.

Reliability is the consistency of the data obtained from a particular research method. A performance evaluation is reliable, for example, if it gives the same score to people who perform at the same level, or to the same person who performs consistently over several evaluation periods. Different performance scores for truly equivalent performers mean that the research method or data-gathering instrument is not reliable.

Before basing research conclusions on the data collected by a particular instrument, the data need to be proven reliable. If your bathroom scale displays a different weight reading each of the five times you step on it during a one-minute reliability trial, you will certainly dismiss the data as unreliable. The same reliability expectations should hold for research instruments or methods of measuring organisational performance.

validity

The degree to which a research method actually measures what it is supposed to measure.

Validity is the degree to which the research actually measures what it is supposed to measure. A research design or instrument has *internal validity* if the independent variable really did produce a change in the dependent variable. The research has *external validity* if the findings can be generalised to populations beyond the sample. A researcher might find, for example, that differences in leadership style (as measured by a particular instrument) among a sample of university undergraduates did produce predictable outcomes in groups participating in an experiment (that is, internal validity might be high). However, generalising the results to managers in actual work settings might be questionable. The external validity would be low because the experimental findings are not generalisable beyond a population of university students.

Research implications for managers

Managers can obviously learn from the results of published research. But, like scientists, managers need to control for extraneous events that distort conclusions about particular circumstances or people. For example, managers need to consider the factors beyond the control of an employee when evaluating his or her performance. Without being aware of moderating forces the manager risks a distorted perception of the extent to which an individual's or group's behaviour contributed to observed or measured performance outcomes.

In a different application, when managers act as change agents they can think like scientists by conceptualising a model, or hypothesising relationships among critical variables. By thinking through mutual dependencies or cause–effect relationships, the manager should also be able to identify appropriate measures of key outcomes before and after the change. The practice of measuring organisational variables has become more common in the last few years as firms adopt benchmarking and continuous improvement techniques. Measurements, statistical process controls and model building all indicate that the scientific method is useful to managers as well as researchers.

Current issues in the organisational context and the challenges for managers

Every generation of managers faces a set of forces and issues that seems to dominate the context if not the content of many decisions. Most informed managers are aware that their organisations have to contend with external forces such as:

- the acceleration of technology that affects work processes as well as the development and positioning of products in the marketplace
- the tenacity of competing interests, not just as rivals jockey to gain customers, but as constituent interest groups vie for resources or elevate conflict to dramatise their views
- the swings in social behaviours that usually begin externally with shifts in expectations and values by one or more segments of society, whose members then affect organisations as employees, customers, suppliers and regulators
- the uncertainties of geopolitical and economic forces that in some situations flare up into aggressive hostilities and in others pull nations together in treaties and business relationships.

These current issues take on greater specificity, as they are perceived by managers to present immediate threats or opportunities to their organisations. As socio-techno-economic changes take on greater specificity, four thematic issues emerge to affect most managerial practices regardless of industry. The challenge of *managing technology* has become a driving force affecting practically all organisational processes in response to pressures to improve productivity and to keep up with or lead competitors. Enabled by technology transformations, firms turn to *global business*, where they are caught up in competition for customers and suppliers on a worldwide stage. With the increased flow of people across national borders and pressures to safeguard the civil rights of all people, managers are expected to promote and benefit from *human diversity* and equity. Finally, in spite of the complex pressures facing people in today's organisations, the expectation of *ethical behaviour* is stronger today than in previous generations.

These four themes are woven throughout the fabric of this book and reflect some of the current issues facing managers today; other issues, such as knowledge management, e-commerce and flexible workforces, are also dealt with in this and the following chapters. Detailed examples are provided in boxes under the headings of Technology Transformation, World Watch, Eye on Ethics and Dynamics of Diversity. While each theme is a valid issue in its own right, there are threads of interdependency among them. Let's examine some of the forces within each.

Technology transformation

For centuries, technology has had a transforming effect on how we work, live, communicate and travel. Anthropologists have documented the effect primitive technologies such as harnessing fire or making tools out of stone had on nomadic tribes as our early ancestors sought to increase control of their environments. Surely the invention of the steam engine, mass production and interchangeable parts in the nineteenth century brought about major transformations in the world of work and standards of living as large numbers of people became employees and wage earners. It seems that each successive wave of technology increases the pace and complexity of societal and organisational transformation. The new technologies of the last quarter of the twentieth century – from computing and information networks to biotechnology and genetic engineering – set the stage for organisational and lifestyle changes in the twenty-first century.

Two types of organisation are especially buffeted by technology change. One is the high-tech firm, the organisation whose mission is to create products/services and markets for the latest whiz-bang technology. This is the world of the *dotcoms* (such as Amazon.com or Lastminute.com) and of in-the-news firms that produce technology-based products and profits, such as Cisco, Dell, Intel and Microsoft.

The other type of organisation is more pervasive, for it includes all that employ technology to streamline and enhance business processes and services. The Internet revolution in particular is rapidly transforming the ways organisations make decisions, fulfil customer needs and cluster work activities. Says Alan McCarthy, of PinkRoccade UK, 'The delivery rate of innovations in technology over the last five years has been overwhelming. Businesses have been pushed along, trying to keep up with their competitors. This has mainly been driven by the Internet and anything prefixed by E' (McCarthy, 2002).

Beyond the Technology Transformation boxes, we weave throughout this book examples and lessons involving the organisation–technology–manager interface.

Knowledge management

According to Liebowitz (2004) knowledge management is: 'the process of creating value from an organisation's intangible assets. The ability to share and leverage knowledge internally and externally to create knowledge innovation is the cornerstone of knowledge management' (2004, p. 1).

Knowledge management is important as managers are facing the need to work smarter; not only that but people tend to move from job to job more quickly, some people may be at the end of their working life, and economic demands may also mean a shrinking workforce. Electronic business and advances in technology also mean that knowledge is spread.

Whatever the reason, it is important that managers capture the knowledge available in the workplace. The four key areas of the knowledge management process can be seen in Exhibit 1-5.

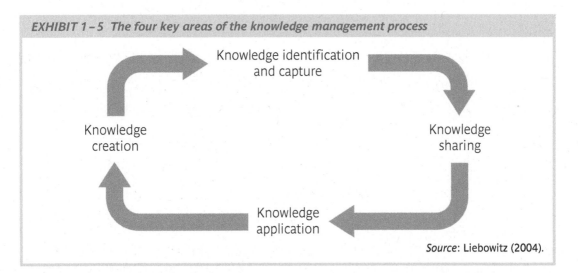

EXHIBIT 1 – 5 The four key areas of the knowledge management process

Knowledge identification and capture

Knowledge sharing

Knowledge application

Knowledge creation

Source: Liebowitz (2004).

Knowledge identification and capture should identify where the knowledge is in the organisation and the necessary expertise to enable it to be captured. Often expertise is held by outside contractors. A knowledge audit can help identify the knowledge needed for an organisation, who has it, what knowledge is available and what knowledge is missing.

According to Liebowitz (2004), asking the following questions can be helpful:

■ What knowledge competency is at risk of being lost if an expert leaves?

■ Who is the expert in this area?

■ On a scale of 1–10, how would you rate this area in relation to the mission and goals of the organisation?

However, there is also the problem of why someone should want to give up their knowledge. One method could be to include knowledge sharing as part of the appraisal process. A more effective method would be to embed knowledge management activities into everyone's working life. Online communities can be helpful here.

Knowledge sharing needs to be recognised and rewarded formally to make it a reality. People are often reluctant to share their expertise, especially if knowledge is seen as power. Managers trained in knowledge capture often have the expertise to enable this to happen. In many organisations there are functional silos and it is important that these are broken down to allow for knowledge sharing. People not only like to hoard their knowledge, but they also tend to stick to their work culture – for example, accountants, engineers or lawyers may be reluctant to share their knowledge with people who they perceive to be outsiders.

Knowledge application refers to the taking of shared knowledge and applying it to the workplace. Often this can be in the form of lessons learnt from past problems, possibly in other parts of the organisation.

Knowledge creation is the result of the sharing and application of knowledge, which should ultimately end in the creation of new knowledge. This new knowledge should enable an innovative and dynamic organisation to develop.

The process of knowledge identification and capture, knowledge sharing, knowledge application and knowledge creation tends to be continuous. Not only that, but the proper resources need to be put in place to allow it to happen. The use of new technology can be a tool to enable this to happen.

technology transformation

Microsoft enjoys monopoly power

Chance at times plays a role in organisational success. Bill Gates was still twentysomething when he dropped out of college and, with Paul Allen, co-founded the Microsoft organisation. Microsoft's early success was boosted by a decision IBM made in 1981 when its management was sceptical of the viability of what was then an emerging technology called the personal computer. Rather than develop its own technology in personal computers (PCs), IBM decided to purchase the MS-DOS operating system from fledgling Microsoft (and microprocessor chips from Intel). IBM's contracts did not prevent Microsoft (or Intel) from selling products to other customers. Thus, hundreds of firms produced PC clones controlled originally by the DOS, and then by the Windows, operating systems and software. Today Microsoft is one of the world's most valuable companies, thanks in large part to the 90 per cent market share enjoyed by its Windows PC operating system.

Says Gates, 'I think the success of Microsoft has come from knowing [that technology and business] have a relationship with each other. The two sides drive each other. I think business is very simple. Profit. Loss. Take the sales, subtract the costs, you get this big positive number. The maths is quite straightforward.' This simple approach to maths has enabled thousands of Microsoft employees to become multimillionaires.

But such visible business success as a technology giant comes at a cost to Microsoft and its competitors. Judge Thomas Penfield Jackson, presiding in a Department of Justice suit against Microsoft, wrote in his findings of fact that 'Microsoft enjoys monopoly power' and the result 'is that some innovations that would truly benefit consumers never occur for the sole reason that they do not coincide with Microsoft's self-interest.' Judge Jackson subsequently ordered that Microsoft be broken into two separate competing companies. His ruling focuses the tense debate on the role of regulation versus free markets in stimulating technology innovation and serving the interests of the public.

Technology requires entrepreneurs with big visions and the motivation to take risks.

Sources: adapted from Richard Conniff (2000) 'The Natural History of the Rich', *Worth*, December/January, pp. 136–143, 160; Adam Cohen (1999) 'Microsoft Enjoys Monopoly Power', *Time*, 15 November, pp. 60–69; William J. Cook with David Bowermaster (1993) 'The New Rockefeller', *US News & World Report*, 15 February, pp. 64–69; 'Microsoft May Lose Grip on Windows', *New York Times*, 25 February 1993; and Joel Brinkley (2000) 'Federal Judge Orders Breakup of Microsoft', *New York Times* News Service, 8 June.

Discussion questions

1 At what point do one entrepreneur's actions begin to stifle market opportunities for potential competitors who would bring new technology to customers?

2 How does technology innovation impact on law, ethics and business practice?

Globalisation of business

From a historical perspective the United States was (and still is) the dominant economic power in the world throughout the twentieth century. During most of that century few American businesses acted as if the world was their stage: it was really during the last third of the century that businesses began to focus globally. One way to mark the beginning of this period was the publication of the French historian Servan-Schreiber's (1967) best-selling book *The American*

Challenge. The book was a warning to Europeans that the United States would dominate the world economy because of its management expertise. However, it seemed during the 1970s and 1980s that Japanese firms were seizing centre stage with phenomenal growth into world markets. Japanese management first began to export, and then followed up with manufacturing and distribution in key markets within Europe and the United States. Japanese firms such as Toyota and Sony challenged management practices with an emphasis on work teams and total quality management (TQM). Through the process of continuous quality improvement and just-in-time (JIT) manufacturing, Japanese products became the world-class standards of quality and innovation in consumer products. But the Japanese economic engine overheated, managers began to believe their decisions were infallible, firms and properties were acquired worldwide at inflated prices – and the bubble burst (see the World Watch box).

Japan entered the 1990s in a recession that turned to prolonged stagnation. The once assumed sacred practice of lifetime employment within the families of large firms crumbled as managers began to lay-off employees to cut costs and scale back on excess production capacity. At about the same time the former military powerhouse, the USSR, began to crumble in November 1989 with the symbolic destruction of the Berlin Wall that for two generations had divided East Germany and West Germany. The break-up of the Soviet Empire in the early 1990s into independent republics shifted the world political-economic order. A decades-old cold war stand-off between NATO forces in the West and Russia quickly thawed, and Moscow's importance as a centre of world power plummeted. Europe began a new era of technology and economic growth, with historically protected industries such as telecommunications and banking transformed through open competition and mergers and acquisitions on a global scale as the European Union became reality (Rossant, 1999). Then, in 1998, overheated economies in Asia, Indonesia and Thailand in particular, devalued their currencies and the ripple effect of economic destabilisation extended to Latin America and other emerging regions. Servan-Schreiber's (1967) prediction became true as the millennium ended with the United States once again the clear global leader in political and military influence, and in business practice and success. Since the collapse of Enron and financial malpractices in other multinational organisations, repercussions have been felt around the world, with the uncertainty reflected in the stock markets. This short-term history of world events over the past 30 years emphasises the wild swings of instability that herald an era of global business, both competition and co-operation. A global view becomes critical to managing in the twenty-first century.

In today's market organisations are often concerned with increased competition, often from the emerging economies such as China, as well as those mentioned above. To survive, large organisations need to adopt a global perspective.

Organisations that focus only on one market, one supplier or one customer base are ultimately going to run into problems. This has been one of the problems that has faced Marks & Spencer, a UK department store, which in the past insisted on sourcing goods from only British suppliers. The result was that it was unable to compete against other retailers that imported their goods from developing countries. Once it changed its strategy it became more competitive; however, it now faces other problems, such as competition from Primark's policy of 'pile 'em high, sell 'em cheap'. The globalisation of world trade affects both the domestic economy and can also change market characteristics in that country. Starbucks' infiltration into China has helped to develop a coffee culture, turning the Chinese away from their traditional drink of tea; there are concerns that this may have a negative impact on local tea producers. Many countries in Africa also complain that European and American subsidies provided for their home producers mean that developing countries are unable to compete on a level playing field, which pushes them further into debt.

Why trade globally?

According to the UK Government the basic economic argument for international trade remains that of 'comparative advantage': more trade leads to a better use of the world's resources, as countries produce more of those things that, in relative terms, they are better at producing.

Many of the gains from imports also flow from inward investment, which can raise the overall level of investment and productivity in an economy and play a major role in transferring technology and know-how. Foreign investors often work in partnership with local business, which can stimulate ripple-through effects, improving knowledge transfer and working practices in the domestic market.

Although removing trade barriers can help trade to flow, other factors also need to be taken into account. In general terms, countries with open markets seem to grow faster, but the extent to which this growth is driven by trade liberalisation varies from country to country. Some countries that have opened their economies to trade and investment have, for other reasons, not seen an increase in trade, growth and prosperity. Many developing countries often have to deal with the following concerns before they can develop free trade:

- the skills and health of their citizens need strengthening – not just for international trade, but to improve productivity across the economy
- they need improved trade-related capacity, such as efficient customs, trade infrastructure, including roads and ports, to enable them to bring goods to market competitively
- they need the capacity to cope with economic change, such as opportunities to re-skill, and a flexible dynamic economy that continually creates new jobs
- institutions need to be put in place to safeguard people through change.

Many benefits can be seen from the liberalisation of trade. In 1973, 35 per cent of UK trade was with EU countries; in 2003 this had risen to 53 per cent, with 3 million UK jobs linked to EU trade (Ardy *et al.*, 2004).

The removal of tariffs and the creation of a level playing field for EU countries has given EU firms access to the largest market in the world.

It is the developed countries that hold the largest share of world trade, although recent developments in Brazil and China are likely to start to make an impact. It is the countries of sub-Saharan Africa that are having the most difficulty in response to freer trade and the reasons for this are as follows.

- Poor levels of education mean it is hard to compete globally with knowledge economies.
- HIV and AIDS mean that many workers are either absent from work as they need to care for their sick families, or are themselves dying and in need of medical care.
- Political conflict, weak governments and corruption undermine economic development.
- Low levels of investment make it difficult for organisations to develop and expand.
- Poor infrastructure means that there are difficulties with transport and communication networks.
- Entrepreneurs are not given access to financial services, market information and technical expertise.
- There is an over-reliance on primary commodities, such as tea and cocoa, which are subject to volatile prices.

- Tariffs have been imposed by developed nations on the importation of products from developing nations.
- Subsidies are provided to producers in developed nations (as is the case with EU farmers).

The international integration of production

In the past products such as cars were made and exported from the country of origin. For example, Nissan cars were made in Japan and exported from Japan to Europe. That is no longer the case, and Japanese cars can easily be made in Europe, although their parts may be sourced from countries such as China or South Korea. Often this is thought of as a one-way process, with production shifting from the richer countries to poorer countries, but this is not necessarily the case. Companies that want to dominate the global market cannot just consider the cost of production, they also need to consider research and development, the skills of the workforce, transportation of goods and services, and innovation. What is becoming clear is that many companies will focus on the most important parts of the business in the home country and outsource other parts of their work.

Offshoring

The offshoring of business is when an organisation decides to move some of its operation to another country to save on operating costs. The best-known examples of offshoring are call centres. Many financial services organisations have relocated their call centres to other English-speaking countries such as India, South Africa or the Philippines, where employment costs are lower and there is a ready supply of educated labour. However, it is not only the cost of labour that has made this possible. There has also been a significant drop in the cost of telecommunications and significant advances in technology that have made phone calls reliable and cheap.

Organisations that decide to offshore should not just consider the cost. They also need to decide whether they can keep sufficient control over their operations and maintain a good relationship with their customers. This is dependent on the complexity of the tasks the call centres are expected to deal with. Often, routine enquiries can be dealt with overseas, while more complex tasks are dealt with in the home country.

The future developments in technology mean that it may not only be call centres operating in India. Tele-medicine could follow, where X-rays, scans and other medical analyses are carried out in other countries by qualified doctors and fed back to the patient through their doctor in their home country.

For organisations, offshoring requires serious consideration and cannot be rushed into in a bid to save costs.

Organisations need to:

- consider their long-term interests and gain a better understanding of the risks
- consult their workers properly in decisions on offshoring
- address the concern that offshored work may be carried out in conditions that do not satisfy core labour standards
- think about how this will improve their competitiveness and productivity
- help home country employees to improve their skill levels
- help people to find new employment as quickly as possible if they lose their jobs as a result of offshoring.

Offshoring is often seen as having a negative impact on home employment but it can also have a positive impact, in that it can give an organisation the prospect of growing and prospering in the long term.

world watch

Groomed so not to marry: Porsche claims exemption from merger mania

In the early 1990s, the production floor of Porsche's factory was not a pretty sight. Workers would storm off in a huff. Managers would fume. Voices would rise above the hum and bang of the line. Porsche's assembly line looked like a dark warehouse. On either side were shelves eight feet high with huge parts bins filled with 28 days of inventory. To get a part workers often had to climb ladders, wasting enormous amounts of time. Half-built engines sat on the side of the assembly line, while workers left their work spaces to dig for parts and others stood around waiting until they returned.

Porsche could afford this type of inefficiency in the early 1980s when the economic boom fuelled sales to more than 50 000 vehicles a year. But then the recession of the early 1990s hit, and Porsche sales plummeted to 14 000 units in 1993. From the dizzy heights of the mid-1980s when yuppies, not to mention staid German executives, had to have one, Porsche went to the brink of bankruptcy in 1992. Recession had crippled sales, and costs were out of control. That was when the company's family owners called in 43-year-old Mr Wendelin Wiedeking to be Porsche's chief executive and solve its problems.

From the beginning, Wiedeking's idea was to bring in the Japanese style of management. First, he eliminated one-third of his managers and gave those remaining new assignments, so they would be struggling to learn new jobs – 'rather than waiting for me to make a mistake'. Next, he took his management team on extensive tours of Japanese auto plants. They benchmarked by timing precisely how long it took Porsche to assemble body parts and engines and instal carpeting and dashboards, and then studied comparable times in Japan. On most tasks, Porsche was taking almost twice as long. These comparisons gave Porsche management a traumatic understanding of what had to be done.

In late 1992 Wiedeking brought the Shin-Gijutsu group, a cadre of former Toyota engineers, to the Porsche plant and gave them carte blanche to revitalise the system. It was a painful process. The Japanese engineers unleashed demanding explanations – scolding, lecturing and browbeating some of Germany's finest automobile craftsmen – about how poorly they were doing their jobs. The result was the salvation of Porsche AG, Germany's ultimate symbol of racing car performance and autobahn freedom.

With help from the Japanese engineers, assembly time for a car was reduced from 120 hours to 72. The number of errors per car fell 50 per cent, to an average of three. The workforce shrank 19 per cent, to about 6800 employees from more than 8400 in 1992. Parts bins have been entirely eliminated, and assemblers now take only the parts needed for each stage of assembly. The line itself has been shortened and inventories have been cut back so much that factory space has been reduced by 30 per cent. All this means Porsche was making more cars at lower cost. And, in 1996, the company reported its first profit in four years, after £200 million in losses.

Since 1996, peace has prevailed on the Porsche line. The production changes imposed by the Shin-Gijutsu group produce more cars faster, with fewer people, without losing technical sophistication and road performance. Putting the losses behind it, the company now concentrates on developing new models and new markets. In 1997 Porsche sold over 10 000 of its new Boxster roadsters, its least expensive model, produced to go along with its re-engineered, top-of-the-line 911s. In 2002 the company introduced a sport-utility vehicle with typical Porsche high-performance characteristics.

The team of Japanese consultants now returns only about four times a year because the German engineers are continuing the innovations they initiated. Workers on the line submit 2500 suggestions a month. Porsche still hopes to strip another 10 hours off car assembly time, making the company comparable to the best Japanese car makers. Porsche is also working with its suppliers to cut costs and improve quality and deliveries. While it works away at this goal, Porsche has formed Porsche Consulting to spread to other German manufacturers the Japanese manufacturing concepts it has learned.

As other car makers have scurried to merge and acquire, foreseeing a future controlled by fewer than 10 mega motor conglomerates, tiny Porsche has rescued itself, by itself, from near bankruptcy. Dismissing what seem impossible odds, Porsche declares it will never marry. Finances are in order, sales are strong and very profitable, and new products are coming. Porsche has restored its reputation as a clear-headed, focused, unique car company.

Sources: J.R. Healey (1999) 'Groomed So Not to Marry: Porsche Claims Exemption From Merger Mania', *USA Today* (6 August), pp. B-1–B-2; J. Kandell (1998) 'Ferdinand Porsche, Creator of the Sports Car That Bore His Name, Is Dead at 88', *New York Times* (28 March), p. A12; N.C. Nash (1996) 'Putting Porsche in the Pink: German Craftsmanship Gets Japanese Fine-Tuning', *New York Times* (20 January), pp. 17–18; J. Mateja (2000) 'Image-conscious Porsche to Offer an All-wheel SUV', *San Diego Union-Tribune* (13 May), p. WHEELS-8.

Discussion questions

1 How does this compare with your understanding of scientific principles?
2 What impact do you think management initiatives have had on the workforce?

Managing diversity

People tend to feel more comfortable with people they see as similar to themselves. But people are different, and differences are at the root of diversity. Differences in gender, race, language, size, physical impairments and age are clearly visible. Less visible are differences in education, religion, nationality, economic status, sexual orientation and learning disabilities.

The United Kingdom and North America have long been recognised as a melting pot for their ability to assimilate people from other cultures into their own. Today the melting pot has melted and much of northern Europe and North America has become multicultural. New immigrants are the fastest-growing segment of the population. Whether in London or Birmingham, companies increasingly find their employees were born in countries other than the one in which they are employed.

At the organisational level, managers are learning to build on the strengths of differences among employees and customers.

Affirmative action or positive discrimination and managing diversity are not the same. The goal of affirmative action is to ensure that people are given fair opportunities to be hired or admitted to organisations regardless of gender, race, nationality, religion or age. Progress has been made in minority entry into organisations. However, it is believed by many that affirmative action will one day no longer be necessary because women and minorities will no longer need a helping hand to break through the barriers of discrimination. The challenge today is less one of guaranteeing entry than of granting people of all kinds equal opportunities to reach their potential in all functions and at all levels of management and leadership. This means reducing barriers to equal opportunity and introducing progressive practices for taking advantage of diversity as a stimulus to innovation and market segment understanding.

My biggest mistake: Martin Lindstrom
All I had for Christmas was a couple of very embarrassing misjudgements

Martin Lindstrom, 31, was chief operating officer of Digitas Europe, a multinational marketing agency turning over £220 million. He explains here how his misjudgements not only cost a company money but could also have had a serious impact on its reputation.

In 1996 I was working for BBDO, the advertising agency, and one of my clients was Lego. I had been a Lego fan since I was a child. When I was 14, I built my own Legoland in my back garden and charged people a fee to come and see it. So working with Lego was a thrill.

Lego was one of the first companies to use the Internet to promote its toys, and in 1996 it wanted to find new ways to use interactivity to activate kids.

I came up with what I thought was a brilliant idea, which was to produce an online advent calendar. You have 24 small doors to open leading to Christmas, and on 24 December you get a big surprise. I'm from Denmark, where advent calendars are popular. I assumed the concept was known and loved across the world.

So I suggested this to Lego, and they thought it was a great idea. They saw it as a risk-free activity and a cheap way to create a contact between the brand and the end-user. The first problem was that kids in New Zealand were furious because they couldn't open the door on the right day since they were 24 hours ahead of some parts of the world.

We managed to get over that by hiring one of the world's best Java programmers, who managed to write a script looking for the user's nationality then deciding the time of opening. Today this technique is very widely used but it was one of a kind back then.

But the real problem was that advent calendars are related to Christianity, and Lego was suddenly seen by many people as promoting that religion. On 1 December, I went to work and when I opened my inbox there were hundreds, if not thousands, of emails from angry people all over the world, particularly Jews, who said, 'We've always been a major fan of Lego, we love the product but suddenly you are promoting Christianity. What's it all about?' Some of them sent pictures of their family playing with Lego years ago, showing how devoted their family had always been to the product. I went into a serious panic.

Here were all these complaints about a product that is so well known and respected around the world. People were in danger of changing their perception of the brand, and I was responsible.

The people at Lego were furious, but they were also furious at themselves because they had accepted this concept and had then made the same mistake as I had.

How on earth was I going to answer all these emails? We had to get several people in to help out. It wasn't just a matter of answering the emails but of taking every one of them extremely seriously. Unfortunately, I started to get a bit lazy and I arranged a standard signature line. It said, 'We really apologise for the inconvenience this has caused. We hope you continue playing with Lego and enjoying it. Merry Christmas and a Happy New Year.'

I had made the same mistake a second time.

I can laugh about it now, but it took me about two years to get my sense of humour back about it.

Luckily, this was still the beginning of the popularity of the Internet so relatively few people were involved. If this happened now – when there are tens of millions of members of the Lego Club – it would have been even more serious.

But I learned a lot from the experience, especially to respect different cultures around the world, and to think about that now that, with the Internet, everything is global.

We were lucky. Lego learned a lot from it and became one of the most successful companies in the toy industry on the Internet. We made some major mistakes in the beginning, and I was responsible. But I think that's why today Lego are a little bit more advanced than others around the world, because they learned from it

Source: © Alice Woolley (2001) *The Independent*, 20 June.

Discussion questions

1 What advice would you give Lindstrom to prevent him making the same mistake again?

2 What does this tell us about operating in a global market?

Promoting ethical behaviour

The fourth management theme woven throughout this text is that of striving to inculcate norms of ethical behaviour as a healthy and profitable way of conducting business. Pressures arising from international competition and accelerating diversity increase the complexities of organisational behaviour. Too many self-centred people are not prepared to cope in ways that ensure fair and moral treatment of others. Many fail to anticipate how often people are injured by one person's or one firm's decisions.

The examples of probable wrongdoing are legion. Corporate and industry images have been tarnished by unethical (and illegal) practices in savings and loan debacles, fraudulent practices in selling junk bonds, the mislabelling of products, the cover-up of tobacco's addictive power, the recent collapse of Enron, the wrongful discharge of employees, or sweatshop practices condoned by western firms with operations in developing-world countries.

Unethical and even illegal actions can occur at all levels in organisations. In subsequent chapters we introduce ways of thinking systematically about making moral decisions and behaving with ethical integrity. Acting ethically promotes long-term benefits. Bowing to immediate pressures by dropping the ethical filter may seemingly solve one problem, but inevitably one bad decision creates many more serious ones. Acting ethically is synonymous with practising effective organisational behaviour.

Human resource management and organisational behaviour

The study of organisational behaviour involves the study of people as individuals or as groups. Most organisations would claim that successful people management is vital for their success. Human resource management is about choosing and developing people to ensure that strategies are implemented and organisations can grow. As you work your way through this book you will come to realise that organisations cannot exist without people and these people need to

eye on ethics

End of Andersen

At lunch on one of those bright but chilly early February London days, a stone's throw from the smart headquarters of Andersen on the Strand, a senior executive of one of Britain's rival Big Five accountancy firms could talk of little else. 'What the hell were they doing?' he yelled. 'Yes, Andersen needed to front up. But to go on *Newsnight*? Bloody hell. What control do you have over your message? You just don't do *Newsnight*.' He was talking of the excruciating 10 and a half minutes spent a week earlier by John Ormerod, managing partner of Andersen in the UK, getting grilled by Jeremy Vine on BBC TV's nightly inquisition.

The greatest business scandal ever – Enron – was engulfing its auditors. Andersen had been accused of avoiding the press. Yet according to his peers, the decision by Ormerod, at 53 a highly experienced and intelligent chartered accountant but something of a media novice in the *Newsnight* bear pit, was more foolhardy than brave.

Ormerod left the BBC studios savaged and having failed miserably to rescue his company's reputation. Within 10 weeks, he had given up making excuses and was instead signing away the independence of Andersen's UK arm to arch-rival Deloitte & Touche. By the end of the summer the once proud name of Andersen had been expunged from commercial daily life.

It was all over, almost in a trice. And this was not just any old firm of dusty bookkeepers going to the wall. Andersen may have been the smallest of the Big Five, but it was also the proudest.

This was all to change.

News had started to filter across the Atlantic of a company called Enron. Andersen staff read reports on Enron with increasing dismay and incredulity: the creation of off-balance sheet financing vehicles and the collusion of colleagues to cover up the true financial state of the global energy trader.

Enron filed for bankruptcy and there was talk of legal action against its auditor, Andersen.

Andersen's worldwide boss gave a frank testimony: 'Andersen will have to change ... the accounting profession will have to reform itself. Our system of regulation and discipline will have to improve.'

His further admission, that accounting systems had 'turned out wrong', was a statement that no accountant had ever made, inside or outside a law court.

The full implications of the impact of Enron did not come out until later, with the first tangible evidence of the extent of the cover-up: Andersen staff had shredded Enron documentation.

Clients wanted explanations. Andersen offices around the world – the firm was made up of different national partnerships – went into huddles. Should they merge with another Big Five player to save themselves from financial disaster? Should they split off audit and non-audit functions?

More worryingly, some of Andersen's top clients refused to back the company publicly. One, London-listed fund management group Amvescap, said it was conducting 'due diligence' on its auditor.

In addition, investigators' files were open on Andersen's role at two major audit clients, Wickes and SSL, both hit by fraud accusations. Another client, Allied Carpets, had been battered by a five-year accounting scam.

It was against this background that Ormerod's public relations advisers decided to right perceived media wrongs with his ill-fated appearance on *Newsnight*.

With fraud investigations in the USA the death knell had been sounded and the various parts of Andersen were sold off. The ship has sunk for good but the ripples continue to spread. For a generation or more to come, the name Andersen will be synonymous with collusion, complicity and fraud. Not only has it tainted the people who worked for the firm, but it is even worse for tens of thousands more chartered accountants in the wider profession.

Source: adapted from an article by Robert Lea (2002) 'End of Andersen',
Management Today, October, pp. 46–53.

Discussion questions

1 How can unethical behaviour affect business?

2 Do you think that senior management at Andersen should have talked to the media?

be managed effectively. A human resource department should not just be involved with working conditions and wages – it needs to engage and co-operate at all levels within the organisation to ensure that staff can be motivated and developed to reach their full potential, not only for their own satisfaction but also for the growth and development of the organisation.

Many people who work in human resource departments would be expected to have a basic understanding of organisational behaviour, after all how can you develop staff if you do not know about motivation? How can you interview prospective employees fairly if you do not have an understanding of personality and perception and how it can influence your view of the world? How can organisations expand globally if managers lack an understanding of the impact of culture on the workplace? Organisations change and to keep up with developments the human resource manager needs to understand how they change and how people cope with change. They will need to understand that change needs to be managed to ensure minimum disruption to the organisation's growth and development.

Managing the human resource is vital for the success of organisations, regardless of size or industry sector. Whether you are going to specialise in human resources, a specialist department such as finance, or general management you will be responsible for leading and managing people. It is the responsibility of everyone in the organisation to manage people effectively, and the study of management and organisational behaviour will help managers make informed decisions that, in turn, will help organisations grow and develop.

Overview of the book

There are no easy answers to the effective management of organisational behaviour. Nevertheless, this text exposes you to numerous issues, situations, research conclusions and techniques that, if learned well, will improve your chances of being an effective organisational performer. Your behaviour should also be more efficient because you will have less need to learn by trial and error, having gained insights from your study of management and organisational behaviour. Exhibit 1-6 shows how the pieces of this book fit together, stretching from Part 1, which sets the stage with a macro all-encompassing perspective of organisations, to the final linking together of managing organisational and personal change strategies in Part 5.

Part 1 continues looking at why we study organisational behaviour, identifies why people need to be managed, examines the purpose of organisations and how they implement strategy,

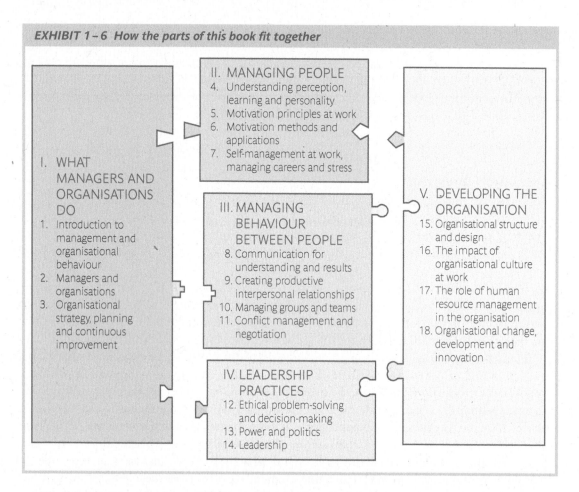

EXHIBIT 1 – 6 *How the parts of this book fit together*

I. WHAT MANAGERS AND ORGANISATIONS DO
1. Introduction to management and organisational behaviour
2. Managers and organisations
3. Organisational strategy, planning and continuous improvement

II. MANAGING PEOPLE
4. Understanding perception, learning and personality
5. Motivation principles at work
6. Motivation methods and applications
7. Self-management at work, managing careers and stress

III. MANAGING BEHAVIOUR BETWEEN PEOPLE
8. Communication for understanding and results
9. Creating productive interpersonal relationships
10. Managing groups and teams
11. Conflict management and negotiation

IV. LEADERSHIP PRACTICES
12. Ethical problem-solving and decision-making
13. Power and politics
14. Leadership

V. DEVELOPING THE ORGANISATION
15. Organisational structure and design
16. The impact of organisational culture at work
17. The role of human resource management in the organisation
18. Organisational change, development and innovation

and builds on from the historical perspective with a look at what managers actually do. We revisit the systems approach and take a look at what it means to be a successful manager.

The focus shifts in Part 2 to the smallest unit of analysis – the individual – and the tasks involved in managing people. Since people are the reason why life in organisations is interesting and challenging, you will study such fundamentals of individual behaviour as personality, perception, learning and motivation, and will learn how to engage motivational practices through empowering people, setting goals and objectives, designing jobs and administering rewards.

In Part 3 you will learn about critical behaviours in managing relationships with others. Here you will begin to see how and why managers go about the process of influencing the thoughts and actions of others through communications, interpersonal relationships, and functioning in groups and teams. Because not everyone will agree with the direction of the workplace or how it should function, managing conflict becomes critical to managerial success.

Part 4 focuses squarely on the manager's exertion of influence and leadership. You will learn about problem-solving and decision-making within an ethical context. You will also get the opportunity to push back the veil of power and politics, a natural part of every organisation. This part concludes with a review of what leaders do and the ways in which leadership helps groups achieve their performance expectations and transform entire organisations.

Finally, in Part 5 you will learn how managers develop the organisation and manage change. Part of change management is to lead the process of change and organisational learning. This ranges from modest changes in a work unit's internal processes to transforming large parts of an organisation through substantial organisational development efforts and innovation. At a personal level of performance, everyone needs to manage their career and learn skills to cope with stress.

Regardless of your intended career path, this book can help make your life in organisations more knowledgeable, controllable, meaningful and satisfying.

Toni & Guy: a second look

Toni says the best advice he can give is 'Think big and you get big. Make a decision and don't stray from it. Make sure the decision comes from your heart and you'll achieve it.'

One of the methods used to expand the Toni & Guy empire was through franchising. Toni Mascolo first came across franchising during a business trip to the USA in the 1980s. He recalls coming back to the UK with a bump. 'I went to my bank manager for an appointment because I was so excited about franchising and I thought he might feel proud of me.' This guy, a terrifying man with glasses and a smart suit, said, 'What's franchising? Be serious man!' The bank manager was obviously too conservative to try anything different.

Undeterred, Toni opened his first franchised salon in south-west London. Five years on, the salon manager had parted company with Toni & Guy and gone bankrupt, leaving Mascolo paying the rent on the property.

Despite this early setback, he is convinced of the benefits of franchising. Today almost all Toni & Guy and Essensuals salons are franchises, with the parent company owning a minority stake and acting as the head lessee on the property.

Prospective franchisees are let loose in their own salon only once they have worked for the company for five years and passed hairdressing and management exams at a Toni & Guy academy. Standards are monitored regularly and no franchisee is allowed to manage more than one salon. This way, Toni says, the brand is not diluted.

Source: adapted from *Growing Business*, October 2002.

Summary

- An extensive body of literature that we have not been able to do justice to in this chapter aids the study of management and organisational behaviour.

- The main schools of managerial thought are classical, human relations, systems and contingency. You will be meeting many of them again on your journey through this book.

- Scientific management, developed by Frederick W. Taylor in the early 1900s, is based on the principles of task specialisation, division of labour and piece-rate incentive pay.

- Some of the most important insights into management have come from Max Weber, with his descriptions of bureaucracy, and Henri Fayol, with his description of management principles. Both of these writers were European and had a major impact in a world where the majority of management writers were North American.

- The human relations movement developed as a reaction against scientific management and resulted from the Hawthorne studies. These studies concluded that human relations were an important part of productivity.

- Systems theory, which will be dealt with in more detail in the next chapter, builds on the foundations laid by Chester Barnard, whose work contained extraordinary insights on decision-making and leadership.

- The contingency approach arose from the assumption that no management principle was universally appropriate in every situation. The outcome of this thinking was that management principles were contingent on the situation. In other words, it all depends...

- Through research we are able to develop theories explaining the world around us. Good theories help us direct and interpret our observations, predict future behaviour and direct our research efforts. The understanding of these theories is important as it can help us predict behaviour and build on past experiences to avoid mistakes and improve our management of organisations. The end result will be an innovative and flexible organisation that meets the needs of its stakeholders.

- The changing workforce means that it is important that organisations develop strategies for managing knowledge.

- Globalisation is having a major impact on how we do business, not only in our home country but also in developing countries.

- Throughout the rest of this book you will be able to see how research has influenced current practice.

Areas for personal development

Managers can learn from past events and published research. As a manager you will need to think through problems, maybe conceptualise a model or develop a hypothesis of what is happening. Looking at past research can help us focus on current problems and enable us to try solutions in a new situation.

Know the different schools of management thought. Where did they come from? How did they develop over time? We can use this to give us a foundational perspective on the history of management and organisational behaviour theories and how they have shaped what we know and appreciate about organisations.

Identify the behavioural approaches. The classical approach viewed the worker as someone rather passive and lacking in self-direction. What caused the move away from this approach? Can you identify how the Hawthorne studies influenced the future study of organisational behaviour? How does this help your study of organisational behaviour?

Define systems theories. Can you analyse an organisation using the systems approach? Look at an organisation with which you are familiar. The systems approach allows the level of analysis to run up and down the hierarchy and from the outside environment to individual behaviour, depending on the behaviour that is the focus of attention. Why do people in organisations want different outputs? How do managers manage this?

Define contingency theory. What influences your behaviour at work? Are they the same influences as your colleagues'? You will find as an employee or manager there will be many influences on your behaviour from both the external and internal environment. By now you should have an awareness of the origins of some of the different theories of management. When applied to an organisation, will the theory work all the time or does it 'all depend'? If the latter is so, you will be using the contingency approach.

Examine the use of theories in management research. As a student you are likely to be asked to carry out small-scale research either as an academic paper or as a dissertation. Can you identify the different research designs for studying behaviour? How can you be sure that the research you are reading is valid and that the research method actually measures what it is supposed to measure? You may be able to read final-year dissertations, or you could find some published research on the web. What methods have been used? Do the methods measure what they are supposed to measure? Is the hypothesis either proved or disproved?

❓ Questions for study and discussion

1 Identify the five principles of scientific management. How do these differ from the fundamental beliefs of the modern manager?

2 Is the process of management a science or an art? Can the same style of management be applied to an office and a factory?

3 Critically examine the systems approach to management. What are the elements of the systems approach and how do managers operate in an open system?

4 Management theorists such as Taylor and Fayol have been accused of recommending the 'one best way' of managing. How accurate is this accusation?

5 Why has Henri Fayol been called 'the father of modern operational management'?

6 The contingency approach to organisational behaviour leads some people to believe that the correct answer to any question about organisational behaviour is 'It depends...'. What implications does this have for the study of management and organisational behaviour?

7 To understand history is to understand ourselves. Critically discuss what are some of the most important things we learn from the history of management and organisational behaviour that can help us as managers today.

8 The human relations movement was a reaction against scientific management. Using relevant theories, why is the human relations movement important for the impact of management today?

9 The classical school of management views human beings as inert objects that are to be used as management requires. What are the origins of this theory and how does it impact on management and organisational behaviour today?

10 Using relevant theories critically evaluate the impact of the classical and human relations approach to organisational behaviour and management.

🔑 Key Concepts

scientific management, *p. 7*

bureaucracy, *p. 10*

Hawthorne effect, *p. 12*

systems theory, *p. 14*

contingency theories, *p. 16*

scientific method, *p. 16*

hypothesis, *p. 17*

independent variable, *p. 17*

dependent variable, *p. 17*

moderating variable, *p. 18*

reliability, *p. 18*

validity, *p. 18*

Personal skills exercise

Purpose To understand that systems are either 'open' or 'closed'. A system is considered open if it reacts with the environment through the exchange of information or materials.

Time 30 minutes

Materials Flip chart for class discussion.

Procedure View your university or college as an open system.
- What are the inputs?
- What are the transformation processes?
- What are the outputs, both intended and unintended?
- How does the external environment affect the transformation processes?
- How does management ensure that the intended outputs are achieved? (You may have to spend time researching this.)

Group discussion

Does the group view all transformation processes in the same way? The group may want to look at this from different perspectives, such as: students; lecturers; administrators; finance; admissions, etc.

Team exercise

Purpose This exercise involves using principles of scientific management and applying them to a production problem.

Time 60 minutes

Materials Sheets of plain paper, scissors.

Procedure Divide the class into groups of four. Each group will be assigned one of the following goal-setting conditions.
- No minimum: the group sets its own standard.
- Low minimum: the group is told to produce 15 paper chatterboxes per 15-minute production run.
- High minimum: the group is told that it is expected to produce 30 chatterboxes per 15-minute production run.

Making chatterboxes
- Cut a piece of paper into an even square.
- Fold the four corners to the centre. You will now have another smaller square.
- Repeat to make another smaller square.
- Turn the paper over and again fold all corners to the centre.
- Place a finger and thumb under each flap on the underneath and push the points together to form a pyramid.
- You should now be able to open and close the mouth of the chatterbox.

Scoring All paper must be obtained before the beginning of the production period. Each sheet is worth £1. Each chatterbox can be sold for £5. However, they must meet quality standards.

Production standards
- The paper must not be torn.
- All points must meet exactly.
- The folds must not overlap each other.
- If the chatterboxes are torn, they are worthless.
- If the points do not meet or the folds overlap they can be sold as seconds for £3.
- At the end of the 15-minute production period deduct the cost of materials from the sales price of the chatterboxes and calculate the total profit.

Questions for discussion

1 Did any of the groups use scientific principles such as task specialisation and division of labour?

2 What were the effects of the different goal-setting conditions on the performance of the task?

Case study: **Fontel Ltd transforms its systems**

Fontel Ltd is an expanding distributor of components for mobile phones and is likely to become one of the major players in Europe. Like most organisations, Fontel experienced difficulties through a period of growth, with a misalignment of systems, processes, equipment and people.

Rather than attempt to fit new challenges into the ways of the old methods and structures, Fontel actively reorganised the way it functioned. It began with a new mission statement that emphasised the firm's commitment to adding value to customers through innovation and continuous improvement. As management at Fontel examined the needs and opportunities for turning around performance, it adopted a systems approach. The systems model examines all elements of an organisation as an interacting whole, sensitive to external pressures. Fontel managers learned that, as they changed one element, such as ways of transacting with suppliers, they would also have to change internal processes and even their relationships with customers.

What they realised was that they had to shift from focusing only on results, to looking at the processes within the system that were producing those results. They also knew that a redesign of organisational systems needed to provide flexibility so that people could adapt their behaviour to changing circumstances in daily activities. As a starting point for systematically learning about management and behaviour within organisations, Fontel identified two key mental models: one emphasising the dynamic nature of managerial roles, and the other identifying the macro options managers have available for changing organisational performance.

Discussion questions

1 How can Fontel's managers measure outputs to ensure that they achieve their mission?

2 Why is it helpful for managers to understand that they must be prepared to engage in a constantly changing set of roles throughout the day?

3 Why can the transformation process affect outputs?

4 How can managers ensure that their intended outputs are achieved?

Applied questions

5 If Fontel had decided to adopt a scientific management approach, do you think systems and people could be aligned?

6 Using systems theory as a predictor of organisational effectiveness, how can management ensure that the subsystems at Fontel can integrate to form an effective whole system?

WWW exercise

Using the web for research

Throughout this book you will be referred to the web as a source of information, either for a specific exercise or for more general research.

Go to a search engine. You may find your university has access to electronic journals that you could search. Type in one of the key concepts that you have studied in this chapter. Examples could be: classical management, scientific management, systems approach to management, etc.

1 How many examples can you find for one key word?

2 How relevant are they?

3 Who wrote it?

4 How do you know if the research is valid?

Specific exercise

Most companies have websites where they advertise their products, but they can also be used for corporate information. This is where investors can find out about the company.

Look at the corporate information for the following companies:

- www.airtours.co.uk
- www.marconi.co.uk
- www.tesco.co.uk
- www.virgin.co.uk

1 Can you identify which companies are having financial difficulties?

2 Is the information biased? Could you rely on the validity of the information for management research?

LEARNING CHECKLIST

Before you move on you may want to reflect on what you have learnt in this chapter. You should now be able to:

- ☑ understand the historical foundations of management

- ☑ identify the different schools of management theory (the scientific management movement, Henri Fayol's 14 principles of management, bureaucracy theory, the Hawthorne experiments, systems theory, the contingency approach)

- ☑ compare and contrast the different schools of management theory

- ☑ understand the need for management and organisational research and the methodologies used

- ☑ identify the different types of research

- ☑ understand the term validity

- ☑ understand what a hypothesis is

- ☑ recognise that international competition, quality, diversity and ethical behaviour are major management issues.

Further reading

Parker, L. and Ritson, P. (2005) 'Fads, Stereotypes and Management Gurus: Fayol and Follett Today', *Management Decision* 43(10), pp. 1335–1357.

Smith, I. and Boyns, T. (2005) 'British Management Theory and Practice: The Impact of Fayol', *Management Decision* 43(10), p. 1317.

Smith, I. and Boyns, T. (2005) 'Scientific Management and the Pursuit of Control in Britain to c.1960', *Accounting, Business & Financial History* 15(2), July, p. 187.

References

Ardy, B., Begg, I. and Hodson, D. (2004) 'UK Jobs Dependent on the EU', European Institute, South Bank University, April.

Barnard, C.I. (1938) *The Functions of the Executive.* Cambridge, MA: Harvard University Press.

Cyert, R.M. and March, J.G. (1992) *A Behavioral Theory of the Firm.* Englewood Cliffs, NJ: Prentice Hall; 2nd edn, Cambridge, MA: Blackwell.

Duncan, W.J. (1990) *Great Ideas in Management.* San Francisco: Jossey-Bass, p. 3.

Fayol, H. (1949) *General and Industrial Management.* C. Storrs, trans. London: Pitman.

Gilbreth, L.M. (1973) *The Psychology of Management.* Easton, PA: Hive Publishing, p. 130.

Graham, P. (ed.) (1995) *Mary Parker Follett: Prophet of Management.* Boston, MA: Harvard Business School Press.

Homans, G.C. (1950) *The Human Group.* New York, NY: Harcourt Brace & World.

Katz, D. and Kahn, R.L. (1966) *The Social Psychology of Organizations.* New York, NY: John Wiley & Sons.

Liebowitz, J. (2004) 'Will Knowledge Management Work in the Government?' *Electronic Government* 1(1).

Maslow, A. (1943) 'A Theory of Human Motivation', *Psychological Review*, July, pp. 370–396.

Maslow, A. (1954) *Motivation and Personality.* New York, NY: Harper & Row.

Mayo, G.E. (1933) *The Human Problems of an Industrial Society* (2nd edn). New York, NY: Macmillan.

McCarthy, A. (2002) of PinkRoccade UK, in IBIS (Best Practice Business Improvement), Institute of Ideas and Solutions, p. 7.

McGregor, D. (1960) *The Human Side of Enterprise.* New York, NY: McGraw-Hill.

Parkhe, A. (1993) '"Messy" Research, Methodological Predispositions, and Theory Development in International Joint Ventures', *Academy of Management Review* 18, April, p. 237.

Parsons, T. (1951) *The Social System.* New York, NY: Free Press.

Roethlisberger, F.J. and Dickson, W.J. (1967) *Management and the Worker.* Cambridge, MA: Harvard University Press.

Rossant, J. (1999) 'Europe Ten Years Later', *Business Week*, 8 November, pp. 56–61.

Sax, G. (1968) *Empirical Foundations of Educational Research.* Englewood Cliffs, NJ: Prentice Hall, p. 31.

Servan-Schreiber, J.J. (1967) *The American Challenge.* New York, NY: Athenaeum.

Simon, H.A. (1946) *Administrative Behavior.* New York, NY: Free Press.

Taylor, F.W. (1914) *The Principles of Scientific Management.* New York, NY: Harper & Row, p. 39.

Vecchio, R.P. (1987) 'Situational Leadership Theory: An Examination of a Prescriptive Theory', *Journal of Applied Psychology* 72, August, pp. 444–451.

Weber, M. (1947) *The Theory of Social and Economic Organization* (A.M. Henderson and T. Parsons, eds and trans.). New York, NY: Free Press.

Managers and organisations

The opening vignette will introduce you to a well-known entrepreneur and illustrate how he turned his vision into a multinational company.

The Virgin Group: Richard Branson's vision

Richard Branson, founder of the Virgin Group, grew up in a middle-class family where initiative and independence were encouraged. Sent away to a boarding school, he was seen as a troublemaker. Dyslexia and poor eyesight rendered him unable to read and write at the age of eight. He succeeded in the English public school system only due to his ability in sport, but even that was thwarted by injury. His entrepreneurial streak emerged while at school, when he decided to make money by growing Christmas trees; the venture was not successful. His next venture, breeding budgerigars, failed when they escaped.

Branson had been brought up to believe he could change the world and one of the places he decided to start was at school, with the production of a school magazine, which later became a student magazine. With his poor academic record, Branson's headmaster predicted that he would either go to prison or become a millionaire, fortunately for him he chose the latter.

Branson's philosophy of business is to create something that is original, useful and stands out from the crowd. Branson feels that business has to be involving and fun and to exercise your creative instincts.

Branson and his colleagues continued with the magazine when they left school and from this came the idea of selling records by mail order. By undercutting the high-street stores they were able to capture the student record market. This venture nearly collapsed with the postal strike of 1971, but by opening a shop that reflected the student culture of the time they were able to continue trading. From selling records Virgin moved into recording studios and from here evolved the ideas of its own record label and Virgin book publishing.

Branson's philosophy was, when Virgin had money, to look for new opportunities. Some resulted in failure such as the attempt to buy *Time Out* magazine where he was outbid, the expansion of Virgin Books into an already saturated market, or the film venture Virgin Vision where the competition was too high. Other ideas were successful, such as the airline Virgin Atlantic, where the Virgin Group met a gap in the market.

Virgin floated on the Stock Exchange in 1986 only to be re-privatised after the stock market crash of 1988.

Branson sees the survival of the Virgin Group as being down to keeping on top of costs, protecting the downward risk as much as possible and keeping a tight control of cash. Sometimes he would break these rules when he felt there were opportunities not to be missed – such as the signing of Janet Jackson to the Virgin record label.

Branson puts Virgin's success down to his need for business to be fun and creative. He and his team continually look for new opportunities and he is not frightened to take on the opposition when he feels threatened, as he did with British Airways. He sees business as a fluid, changing substance and if you have a good team around you and a fair share of luck then you might make something happen.

Source: Richard Branson (1998) *Losing My Virginity, the Autobiography*. Virgin Publishing Ltd.

Discussion questions

1 What qualities does Richard Branson possess as a manager?

2 How did Richard Branson turn his vision into a multinational business?

Managers are responsible for working with and through others to achieve objectives by influencing people and systems in a changing environment. Some managers are also leaders and visionaries, the qualities that become necessary as managers take on central decision-making roles within organisations.

Richard Branson has a vision and does not shy away from influencing people and systems within the Virgin Group. His influence has developed the Virgin Group's organisational culture, beliefs, values and assumptions about how to succeed in business from one idea of selling records to a student market, to a diverse business that ranges from travel to drinks and from finance to holidays. His drive and determination have made the Virgin Group an organisation that cannot be ignored in a very competitive marketplace.

Management and Organisational Behaviour provides theories, insights, examples and practices that will help you achieve a productive and satisfying life within organisations, whether or not you aspire to be a manager. The emphasis is on helping you first to understand the range of human behaviour and managerial practices in a variety of organisational contexts. Second, you will learn to develop the judgement and skills you need to succeed as an organisational performer in managing your own behaviour and, at times, in managing the behaviour of others.

Why study management and organisational behaviour?

Chances are better than nine to one that over the next 30-plus years you will spend half your daylight hours (or evenings if you prefer) working for organisations. Whether or not you look forward to that prospect, the reality is that organisations of people working collectively for a common purpose long ago displaced individual workers as the providers of goods and services. Organisations are the dominant generators of employment and economic wealth (in the case of business firms) or the reallocators of income and wealth (in the case of governments). As an educated adult the quality of your life will be dependent on the quality of the organisations with which you regularly interact, be they firms, government agencies, schools, hospitals or other non-profit organisations.

The business environment

In understanding the business environment, a manager can become skilled in how to manage an organisation so that it can survive and grow in a complex and changing world. This means that managers need to understand not only the internal environment but also the external environment, as will be discussed below. Managers need to understand both the micro and macro environment. They need to understand how the subsystems of an organisation fit together and how the whole organisation can be influenced by what is happening in the wider economic, political and social environment. Organisational behaviour can help provide a road map, and managers who have an understanding of organisational behaviour can help an organisation adapt to the opportunities and threats provided by both the internal and external business environment.

Organisational behaviour (OB) provides a road map

Because organisations large and small dominate society, you increase the odds of achieving a meaningful involvement with organisations if you formally study how they function. In effect, the study of organisational behaviour provides a road map to the many twists, turns and detours that make life in organisations both complex and exciting. **Organisational behaviour** (often referred to as OB) refers to the behaviour of individuals and groups within organisations and the interaction between organisational members and their external environments. Organisational behaviour is a behavioural science field of study that

organisational behaviour
OB for short. Refers to the behaviours of individuals and groups within an organisation, and the interactions between the organisation and environmental forces.

borrows its core concepts from disciplines such as psychology, sociology, social psychology and anthropology. As you have seen from Chapter 1, these behavioural science disciplines have extensive research foundations that explain human behaviour using the scientific method as an investigative tool.

People bring to their work in organisations their hopes and dreams as well as their fears and frustrations. For much of the time, people around you in organisations may appear to be acting quite rationally, doing their fair share of work and going about their tasks in a civil manner. But often, without warning, one or more of your colleagues may appear distracted, their work slips, and they become snappy or withdrawn. Worse, you may find that someone has taken advantage of you to further his or her own personal aims. Another example may be that your manager may not seem to be treating everyone fairly, and may appear to single out someone for preferential treatment.

Occasionally you are likely to get caught up in anxiety-provoking organisational changes that involve reassignments or even redundancies. Such a range of human behaviours makes life in organisations perplexing. But those who know what to look for and have some advance ideas about how to cope with pressures are more likely to respond in ways that are functional, less stressful and even career advancing.

Students of organisational behaviour seek to improve the effectiveness of organisations (and their lives in organisations) through the application of behavioural science concepts and research. The assumption that study and analysis can improve organisational behaviour is based on the premise that behaviour is not completely random. Rather, it represents mutual dependencies or cause-and-effect links that can be anticipated, sometimes predicted, and often influenced to varying degrees. A comprehensive knowledge of organisational behaviour helps prepare managers or aspiring managers for the tasks of influencing and transforming organisational systems. For non-managers, understanding organisational behaviour makes organisational life more predictable and allows for greater self-control over organisational outcomes.

Management provides direction and organisation

As we have already discussed in Chapter 1 the practice of management is thousands of years old, but the formal study of management and organisational behaviour is a product of the twentieth century. Management is the practice of directing, organising and developing people, technology and financial resources in task-orientated systems that provide services and products to others. Managers are the ones who practise management, with job titles ranging from supervisor to chief executive.

management
The practice of organising, directing and developing people, technology and financial resources to provide products and services through organisational systems.

For the foreseeable future, two forces of change complicate the actions managers choose in their efforts to guide organisations and keep them viable. First, the speed of change on practically all fronts is accelerating, from technological developments to competitive strategies. Second, the forces that affect organisational performance, such as governmental actions and the expectations and behaviour of employees, are becoming more complex and apparently less controllable.

The speed and complexity of change are what make life in organisations challenging and uncertain. Corresponding to these forces of change, knowledge of behaviour in organisations has increased exponentially over the last 50 years. Such knowledge enables managers and non-managerial professionals alike to be better informed and more prepared to cope with the challenges they will encounter in twenty-first-century careers. Research provides clues as to why people behave as they do in organisational settings and indicators of the factors that affect performance. Practical applications of behavioural research help managers improve the probability that their influence will be effective. This knowledge also helps in preparing for twenty-first-century careers.

The purpose of organisations

Organisations are the product of human ingenuity, created to serve one or more specific needs of a community, be it a town, a county or multiple nations. An **organisation** is a group of

organisation

A group of people working in a network of relationships and systems towards a common objective.

people working in a network of relationships and systems towards a common objective of providing value to the people served. Although serving different purposes, the state school is an organisation, as are banks, hospitals, professional football teams and fire stations. Churches, the local social club, charitable groups such as Friends of the Earth, and local social groups such as mother and toddler clubs are organisations that serve the spiritual or social needs of members, and in the process often provide public services that create benefits for non-members.

Organisations of even modest size create systems to use financial and technical resources to provide products, services and/or experiences valued by one or more segment(s) of society, including customers, employees and, in the special case of businesses, owners. Thus, the local McDonald's restaurant is an organisation created to provide fast access to prepared food of consistent quality, at reasonable prices, in a clean and cheerful eating environment. McDonald's also provides employment for hundreds of thousands of people and rewards for its franchise owners and corporate investors.

Organisations work to benefit multiple stakeholders

stakeholders

Definable clusters of people who have an economic and/or social interest in the behaviour and output of an organisation.

Formulating a purpose and goals in an organisation is complicated by the need to balance the interests of various groups who have a stake in its actions and outcomes. **Stakeholders** are definable clusters of people who have an economic and/or social interest in the behaviour and output of an organisation. Exhibit 2-1

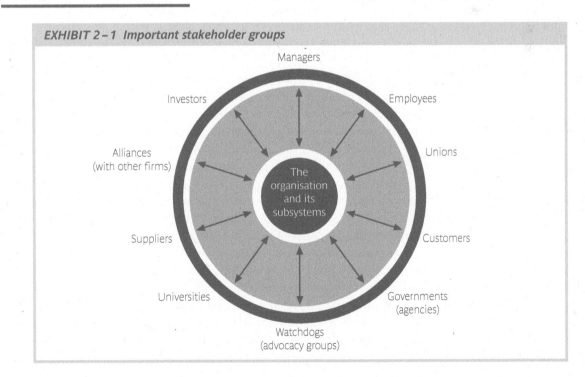

EXHIBIT 2–1 Important stakeholder groups

Managers

Investors

Employees

Alliances (with other firms)

Unions

The organisation and its subsystems

Suppliers

Customers

Universities

Governments (agencies)

Watchdogs (advocacy groups)

identifies 10 stakeholder constituencies common to business firms. The stakeholders of a college or university would include students, faculty, alumni, recruiters and the board of governors, among others.

All organisations interact with various stakeholder groups. Some of these stakeholders or constituency groups, such as employees and managers, function as insiders. Others are clearly external and seek to constrain the organisations' behaviours, as do watchdog advocacy groups and certain government regulatory agencies. Still others are both internal and external, such as alliances and joint ventures with other firms that may serve as suppliers or customers or true partners in producing a joint product.

A conceptual model by Pierce et al. (1991) infers that stakeholders can be either external or internal. External stakeholders include suppliers, customers, competitors, regulators, special interest groups, government and society. Managers and employees are internal stakeholders. Shareholders might be either, depending on their degree of influence over organisational actions and their investment goals. Shareholders in large firms are usually outside investors. Smaller firms tend to have more inside investors, so that owners' and managers' goals coincide. To link the role of employee/investor, many firms with rapid growth prospects use stock options as financial incentives for employees, where the employee profits from rising prices per share of stock.

An important challenge for managers is to identify the relevant stakeholders and to operate the organisation in ways that optimise the returns to each group. Zammuto (1984) argues that such decisions are often made in the context of considerable pressure and conflict created by each stakeholder group pursuing its own interests. Traditionally, owners/investors have wanted to maximise profits and minimise costs, but employees want to maximise personal income and security, which is a cost paid as salaries, wages, bonuses and fringe benefits. Sometimes the interests of these stakeholders are in conflict. External investors are concerned about financial performance, while managers may be more interested in surviving in a high-status, highly paid position. One way to balance these apparent conflicts is to work aggressively for continuous improvement, being ever mindful of adding value to clients.

Purpose is focused by mission and goals

mission
An organisation's fundamental purpose, articulated to define the nature of the business and unify human and other resources.

An organisation's **mission** articulates its fundamental purpose in such a way that it both defines the business of the enterprise and articulates values about the use of human, technical and financial resources. A well-framed mission statement provides a sense of purpose and establishes parameters that focus effort and resources. For example, easyJet, the low-cost airline, states its mission as 'To provide our customers with safe, good value, point-to-point air services. To effect and to offer a consistent and reliable product and fares appealing to leisure and business markets on a range of European routes. To achieve this we will develop our people and establish lasting relationships with our suppliers.' One of the missions of the cosmetic company, the Body Shop, is 'To passionately campaign for the protection of the environment, human and civil rights and against animal testing within the cosmetics and toiletries industry.'

Choosing a mission is not a one-time decision. Any organisation's mission statement is open to change as needs shift and new technologies displace old products and services. Hewlett-Packard (H-P) began business in a garage in 1938 with a focus on making more accurate measuring instruments. Sixty-one years later it spun off its original business so that management could concentrate on computing and imaging, for H-P had become the world leader in computer printers, a product that was non-existent when H-P framed its first mission. In 1999 it became the most visible of the Dow 30 (American stock exchange) firms to appoint a woman as CEO. In 2002 CEO Carly Fiorina revealed the importance of keeping the mission on track. After the recent merger with Compaq, she proclaimed, 'We've kept our eye on the ball. We're hitting all our integration milestones and are on track to meet our second-half targets' (Hopkins, 2002). As recently as the mid-1990s, it was a rare futurist who would have envisioned the sudden success of dotcom companies fuelled by newly emergent entrepreneurs who devised missions to capitalise on the rising popularity of the Internet.

Beyond defining its mission, founders and top managers are responsible for articulating the organisation's fundamental values, goals and guiding concepts. Such statements provide a sense of direction, conveying how the game of business is to be played by organisation members. **Superordinate goals** are the highest goals of the organisation, its fundamental desired outcomes stated in ways that enable managers to measure and assess specific performance targets relative to overall mission aspirations.

superordinate goals
The highest goals of an organisation; fundamental desired outcomes that enable managers to assess performance relative to its mission.

The Body Shop states that it is an ethical business and its founder Anita Roddick believed that business was about human relationships. The Body Shop believes that, by listening to stakeholders, the better the business will be run. The superordinate goals can be seen as 'To creatively balance the financial and human needs of our stakeholders: employees, customers, franchisees, suppliers and shareholders.' This demonstrates to the stakeholders in the organisation where the business is and where it is going.

Organisations serve themselves by serving customers/clients

Throughout this book we focus on organisations that are goal-striving and that hire employees to serve the needs of customers or clients. By focusing on serving customers or clients, organisations indirectly help society when they accomplish the purpose for which they were created. Although we more often use examples of business firms because they have been more fully researched and frequently described than other types of organisation, managers in all types of organisation (from museum to military) face common tasks even though purposes differ. When it comes to business, management philosopher Peter Drucker identifies in simple terms the common purpose of private enterprise:

> To know what a business is we have to start with its purpose. Its purpose must lie outside itself. In fact, it must lie in society since business enterprise is an organ of society. There is only one valid definition of business purpose: to create a customer.
> (Drucker, 1974)

When an organisation is in its start-up phase, the founder or founders are usually fixated on two goals: one a narrowly defined customer-focused goal, the other a goal of financial viability and possible personal rewards. For Netscape, the customer-orientated goal is to be the browser of choice for navigating the Internet. For Dell, it is to be the premier maker of computers custom-outfitted to customer specifications through direct Internet, telephone or mail order. For technology companies such as Netscape and Dell, founders dream of personal financial wealth when shares are sold through the initial public flotation and they profit from future share options.

Lumpkin and Dess (1995) suggest that simplistic goals and strategies that contribute to performance early in the life of an organisation may become detrimental as the firm grows. What happens is that the organisation becomes preoccupied with a single goal and factor such as marketing, to the neglect of other factors, such as procurement and manufacturing.

During every organisation's early years, energies and resources are focused on making viable the concept around which the organisation was created. In the case of business firms this means designing the technology or processes that create products and services of value to customers, finding financing and working to secure a position in the market differentiated from competitors. Profits are the reward and reinforcement for taking the risk in which enterprise managers bet they will be able to better serve customers than can competitors.

While we expect rewards to flow to organisations that provide a superior product or better service, there are times that luck and timing also contribute to success. As can be seen in the previous chapter, even software giant Microsoft had a lucky helping hand when getting started. However, now its leaders must divert attention to the legal challenges that raise issues with its actions to achieve technical and market success. Sciona Ltd demonstrates how a new development can attract investment and help build a profitable company (see Technology Transformation box).

Once success for the emerging firm takes hold and growth takes off, managers often branch out to offer products or services beyond those that established the original business. The firm then runs the risk of becoming unfocused, of trying to be too many things to too many people. To survive the complexity brought on by growth, the firm's managers turn to focusing more on strategies for positioning products within the competitive marketplace. They design a rational organisation structure, establish policies and procedures for consistent handling of recurring events, and give attention to nurturing an organisational culture that embodies the beliefs and values on which they plan to build success.

Mitroff *et al.* (1994) state: 'In the past, organisations have been structured around largely autonomous, self-contained, traditional functions such as accounting, finance, human resources, law, marketing, strategic planning, and so on. While important, they are no longer the building blocks of today's organisations.' Today, success depends more on integrating processes that co-ordinate horizontal flows across functional areas. Such forces tug at an organisation periodically to refocus its mission and goals.

Knowledge promotes socially responsible behaviour

Because organisations are a collection of human decisions and behaviours, none is perfect and 100 per cent predictable. Unlike a finely tuned machine, the inputs to performance as well as performance itself vary over time. One source of variation that frustrates some is the clash between personal values such as integrity and honesty and the questionable things that people are pressured to do on behalf of the organisation. Many employees are more motivated to work diligently for organisations that fulfil socially desirable purposes than for firms whose managers define their principal objective as profit-taking or engaging in practices that question ethical norms. Ethical issues and the need for consistent ethical behaviour are not limited to the business community, as suggested by the trade sanctions implemented by various governments around the world described in the Eye on Ethics box, when the consequences of government action can have far-reaching effects on people's lives.

Within the business community, two contrasting examples underscore managerial values and the benefits of being socially responsible. The Body Shop is an excellent example of a company dedicated to serving not only its customers but also the environment from which it

Self-testing bio firm nets £3 million

Hampshire-based biotechnology company Sciona Ltd has raised £3 million to develop new screening products aimed at healthcare professionals.

Founded by Chris Martin, Rosalyn Gill-Garrison and Manuel Sanchez-Felix in September 2000, Sciona focuses on turning technology-derived genetic research into tangible products.

Despite the relative youth of the company, the first of these products is already on the market. Available through nutritionists, dieticians and also the Body Shop, it is a self-testing kit that uses genetic samples swabbed from the mouth to provide information on an individual's nutritional requirements.

Chief executive Chris Martin said the company was now developing tools aimed at helping healthcare professionals to create personalised treatment regimes for their patients using genetic information.

To raise the cash required to fund its research and development operation, the company turned to Prelude Trust as lead investor.

According to Martin there was a natural fit: 'Prelude specialises in early stage technology companies – we saw them as a value-added proposition. I think they saw us as a company that had managed to turn a promising technology into a set of products.'

As lead investor, Prelude put up £1.25 million of the total £3 million required, with the rest coming from private investors.

Martin sees a promising market for Sciona's screening products, particularly in the realm of disease management. The company claims that Britain's healthcare service currently wastes tens of millions of pounds every year on inappropriate prescription drugs. Martin argues that by using genetic information doctors will be better able to understand how debilitating disease can best be treated on a case-by-case basis.

With just 14 employees, Sciona is a small firm playing in an international arena and the company is seeking partnerships with larger firms to help gain inroads into the key markets of mainland Europe, Japan and North America. Martin says the company has the expertise to do business beyond the UK. 'I have experience setting up companies in Europe, North America and the Far East,' he says.

Sciona will be seeking additional funding from strategic investors and venture capitalists in 18 months' time – probably in North America – and will eventually make a public offering.

Source: *Growing Business*, May 2002 p. 53.

Discussion questions

1 What do you think Sciona's vision is?

2 Do you think their mission will change if they globalise?

takes its products. In contrast, Railtrack, whose core business is maintaining and renewing Britain's railways, was placed in administration after a series of rail disasters allegedly due to lack of investment and poor management. Organisational behaviour is usually not random. Thorndike (1965) argues that the law of effect is the behavioural tendency for people to work persistently to attain the goals for which they are rewarded. But not all managerially imposed goals and rewards promote socially responsible behaviours. For the Body Shop, the goal of balancing financial and human needs has

law of effect

People tend to behave in ways that enable them to attain the goals for which they are rewarded.

eye on ethics

The gospel of free trade

Free trade may have been invented in Britain two centuries ago, but it has taken as long as that to persuade the rest of the world that it is a good idea.

When George Bush increased tariffs on steel imported into America, the Russian Government banned US chicken drumsticks for failing domestic health and safety standards.

George Bush's decision has been seen as purely political in an attempt to win votes in swing states before the mid-term elections, but the results are now spiralling out of control. This move is even viewed with cynicism in America, where a protected workforce is likely to push up manufacturing costs and be less competitive.

According to the European Commission the two-way trade between the EU and the USA generates around £1 trillion. This latest trade war could derail growth, start costly litigation and paralyse innocent business sectors. International trade experts fear that a full-blown trade war will break out, when the EU decides the level of sanctions it can impose on the USA. If the EU gets its way the sanctions could be as high as £3.5 million.

If Europe were to proceed with sanctions, it would follow the tactics employed by the USA in the recent banana trade war, when America accused the EU of using import quotas to favour Caribbean producers over the Latin American ones with US-based distributors. This would mean that small but politically sensitive industries would suffer, as happened when the USA refused to allow in Scottish cashmere and Austrian chandeliers.

While Europe seems to be morally right, America is likely to hit back when a change in the Common Agricultural Policy comes into force. It is likely that America will try to stop Europe's refusal to import genetically modified crops or hormone-injected beef on the grounds of discrimination.

Many observers see the US handling of trade as hypocrisy: it berates developing countries for not liberalising their institutions and industries and yet it imposes tariffs if they try to export to them. This may have worked well for the USA in the past, but the looming trade war looks set to harm many of them, with US chicken farmers being only the first victims.

Source: adapted from the *Observer*, 10 March 2002.

Discussion questions

1 Is it right that the short-term view should have such an effect on so many people?
2 Does the power to decide what is ethical behaviour reside with those who have the power?
3 What could be the overall consequences of trade sanctions?

enabled it to become a global business and increase value to all stakeholders. Railtrack's alleged record of poor maintenance and lack of investment has led to loss of life and loss of money to shareholders. Managerial teams in Internet companies (so-called dotcoms) are rewarded by revenue growth through stock value appreciation. The stock market seems to temporarily reward these companies and managers by running up stock prices based more on market share than future profitability. Without some capacity for generating profits, in time market values plunge as shareholders sell off the stock and shift to firms with balanced growth in revenue and profits.

The systems behaviour of organisations

The basic model we use to help understand how organisations behave is that of an integrated system. A **system** is a set of interrelated elements and interacting subsystems that together form an integrated whole. Consider a house as an integrated system for shelter and comfort made up of elements such as concrete, wood, metal and glass. The raw materials in stock at a DIY store are not a system until assembled following the architect's plan. The framing provides a structure, into which are built key subsystems such as plumbing, electrics and heating. Each element or subsystem contributes to the whole; without each functioning effectively, the overall comfort or safety level diminishes. The failure of the heating subsystem on a winter's night or a blocked drain in the plumbing subsystem causes distress to occupants, for the system is not responding as expected. To see how this theory developed we can look at research by the Tavistock Institute.

system
An integrated whole formed by a set of interrelated elements and interacting subsystems.

Research focus: **Systems theory**

When organisations are viewed as systems an integrated and complex web of relationships forms between structures, technology and employees, as well as technical and social processes.

Research by Trist and Bamforth (1951) at the Tavistock Institute in London developed the socio-technical systems approach.

The Tavistock Institute developed a distinctive approach in its classic studies in the British coal-mining industry and later in the Indian textiles industry, where it looked at the effects of technology on the social system of work. Trist had been investigating reasons for the failure of mechanisation in the coal industry to increase productivity. Before mechanisation small teams worked on different sections of the coal face, the miners shared the tasks and pay was distributed by group consensus. This resulted in highly cohesive work groups.

New technology changed the old methods, machinery was now used to cut the coal and conveyor belts carried it to the surface. This resulted in a change in social relationships. Each shift now consisted of a large group of miners under a supervisor. The team was divided into specialists with an elaborate pay structure. The result meant a hierarchy developed and with it an industrial relations problem. The impact of technological change included difficulties in co-ordination, difficulties in workload and problems of control as the miners resented supervision.

The researchers recognised the central problem was the impact of technological advances on traditional group working practices. Trist argued that any solution would have to involve 'the general character of the method so the social as well as a technological whole can come into existence'.

This research led to the concept of the organisation as a *socio-technical system*. It implied that the workplace has to be seen in terms of two interrelated systems: a social and a technical system, each with its own independent characteristics. Trist and his colleagues argued that when improvements were made in the technological system, this should not be to the detriment of the social system.

From this research, the Tavistock Institute observed how some groups of miners adapted to the new working methods. Some groups managed to adapt to the new technology under modified working conditions. From these observations, the researchers developed a 'composite' method where miners were divided into shift teams. Practices were adopted where the miners

▶ could learn new skills, choose which task they wanted and which shift they worked. According to Trist and Bamforth (1951) these changes reduced the co-ordination and supervision problems, as well as satisfying the miners' socio-psychological needs.

The results of this research led to its application by Rice (1951) to an Indian textile mill with a similar conclusion.

Socio-technical principles (Rice, 1951)

- A system cannot operate in a vacuum. It is the total sum of its parts and must be viewed as a whole.

- Redesign must be interactive. Employees should actively participate in changes.

- Redesign must be holistic. Employees' participation and socio-technical principles have to take place in every part of the redesign process – especially at the beginning.

- Social partnership is possible. There can be a balance between the social needs of work and the economic and production needs.

Systems depend on input-transformation-output processes

organisations

Complex forms of social systems comprising people, other resources and subsystems integrated for the purpose of transforming inputs into mission-relevant outputs.

As we have seen from the previous research, **organisations** are a form of *social system* made up of people and a variety of resources and subsystems integrated to transform inputs into mission-appropriate outputs. For example, employee selection, training, evaluation and rewards are a few of the processes performed by the human resource subsystem. The human resource subsystem in turn interacts with and provides services to other subsystems, such as production, marketing and finance.

Any business organisation is an *input-transformation-output system* that takes in resources, converts them into goods and services, and passes along these outputs to customers and others. In the simplified model shown in Exhibit 2-2, each of the three functional subsystems in the shaded box represents several departments or work units that contribute to the transformation or resource conversion process. A Burger King restaurant orders inputs of minced beef, buns, lettuce and other ingredients. Cooks transform these into outputs of hamburgers, and servers fill customer orders and collect money. However, as systems are not perfectly efficient, some outputs are disposed of as rubbish or waste by-products.

Assume the organisation consists of the subsystems within the shaded box in Exhibit 2-2. Various inputs are imported from the environment, which are then transformed by the firm's subsystems into products and services. These are subsequently exported to different sectors of the environment in the form of outputs.

Organisation systems are open and dynamic

Early writers of social science such as Bertalanffy (1968) and Boulding (1956) identified that

closed systems

Systems that operate without environmental or outside disturbances.

systems can be either closed or open. This later led to the open view of systems being applied to organisations by Katz and Kahn (1968). **Closed systems** operate without interference from outside their boundaries. For example, within a building we know that each time we flip a specific switch the light on that circuit will turn

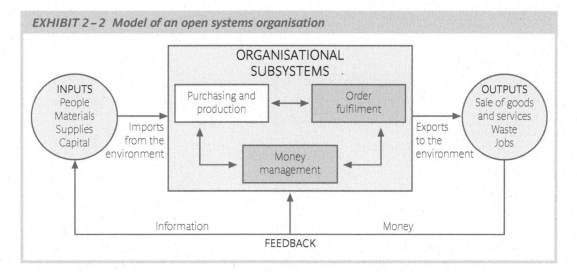

EXHIBIT 2–2 Model of an open systems organisation

on, unless the bulb is burned out. **Open systems** are subject to pressures and inputs from outside their boundaries and are thus more complex and more difficult to control than closed systems A **dynamic system** changes over time. Its essential elements, functions and structures shift and adapt to external disturbances and conditions. All business organisations are thus open dynamic systems. As an open system, firms are subject to outside forces by competitors, customers, suppliers and regulators. As a dynamic system, a business can change its product mix, enter new markets, restructure its sources of financing, hire new managers or redesign its compensation policy in anticipation of, or in response to, outside forces.

Microsoft can be thought of as an open dynamic system continuously working to improve its line of software and information services in an effort to stay ahead of competitors. Yet each Microsoft manager defines his or her own subsystem differently by selecting a boundary that makes sense in terms of his or her desired sphere of influence. A purchasing manager attends to a different set of external constituents than does a sales manager or engineering manager. But senior managers within Microsoft had to shift attention from growing the business to defending its superior market position in PC software when the US Law Courts claimed it used monopoly power to crush competition. US District Judge Thomas P. Jackson ruled in his fact-finding that, yes, Microsoft was acting like a monopoly, a ruling that left Microsoft managers coping with the uncertainty of penalties, ranging from closer supervision to break-up. Judge Jackson subsequently ruled a few months later that Microsoft should be divided into two firms, which increased uncertainty even more (Martinson, 2000).

Systems interact with environmental forces

Organisations are linked with environmental forces through exchanges or transactions. Exhibit 2-3 identifies the key environmental forces that directly impact any business system's suppliers, regulators, competitors and customers.

Business firms conduct exchanges directly with persons and entities in their immediate transacting environment. In the more distant macroenvironment are forces that indirectly influence the behaviour of the firm by altering the behaviour of the transacting forces.

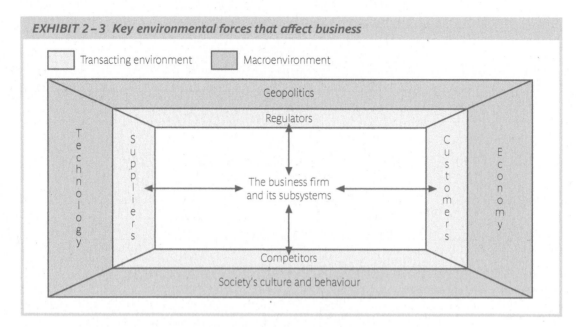

EXHIBIT 2–3 Key environmental forces that affect business

□ Transacting environment   ▨ Macroenvironment

Geopolitics

Regulators

Technology

Suppliers

The business firm
and its subsystems

Customers

Economy

Competitors

Society's culture and behaviour

The exhibit also identifies the more distant macroenvironmental forces that indirectly influence behaviour in any one organisation, such as technology, the economy, geopolitical behaviour and social behaviour.

Most links to the transacting forces occur through specialised subsystems and the people who hold jobs within them. Purchasing transacts with suppliers; salespeople with customers; corporate lawyers with regulators, customers and vendors; and financial officers with bankers and investors. The management of open dynamic systems requires careful attention to these important **boundary-spanning transactions** that link the organisation to specific external sectors. As circumstances change, the relative importance of specific boundary-spanning links will shift. In one time phase, the need might be to maintain the supply of a critical component from vendors. With the shifting of priorities over time, in phase two, obtaining additional financing might be most critical. Look at the World Watch box to see how external forces created change for Japanese businesses.

boundary-spanning transactions
Those actions that link an organisation to specific external sectors; exchanges that make the system dynamic and open.

An organisational system is interdependent with environmental forces because each influences both the organisation and its environment. To illustrate, imagine that Bio-Instruments, a manufacturer of medical diagnostic instruments, depends on a select few suppliers for the parts and components that go into its final assembled instruments. If even one supplier who is the sole source of a component interrupts the supply flow, then Bio-Instruments' production schedules are disrupted. Shipments of products ordered by hospitals and clinics will be delayed, which may lead to cancelled orders or even redundancies if the delay stretches too long. In one study, by Goodman *et al.* (1995), of customer transactions with supplier organisations, researchers found an interesting result: customers who were more involved with their suppliers were more dissatisfied if the product performance did not meet expectations than were peripherally involved customers.

In a different scenario, a competitor begins to market an improved model of a diagnostic tool at a lower price. Sales of the Bio-Instruments model drop precipitously, and unsold

world watch

Japanese business: up, down, sideways

Japan is a highly nationalistic society caught up in cultural contradictions and chaos. Because its island landmass is poor in natural resources, Japan pursued three different strategies during the twentieth century to shore up its economy and presence on the world stage.

Strategy one: take and fight

In part its aggressive actions in the 1930s and early 1940s (culminating in the Second World War) were attempts to seize natural resources in China and Indonesia. As a consequence of the Second World War, Japan's industrial capacity was 55 per cent destroyed and the surviving population faced widespread food shortages immediately following the war.

Strategy two: make and export

To help Japan rebuild its shattered economy, the United States allowed Japanese firms unrestricted access to US markets. Japanese firms quickly used their manufacturing efficiency to become an exporting powerhouse, selling everything from televisions to automobiles through their network of trading companies. By the 1970s, Japanese firms became recognised as world-class leaders in flexible, just-in-time (JIT) manufacturing systems organised around teams within strong organisational cultures. The banking system became an agent of state planning to provide low-cost loans to strategically important industries.

Strategy three: invest and build abroad

Faced with lower-wage competition from other Asian nations and increasing protectionism in major western markets during the 1980s, Japan reinvented itself as a multinational player. Japanese firms bought property in North America and Europe, and built production plants within major markets. They also constructed supplier hubs for manufacturing lower-cost components in Asian nations such as China, Thailand and Indonesia.

Largely because Japanese business is highly efficient in manufacturing consumer products, Japan's economy is the second largest in the world. Japan entered the decade of the 1980s the envy of the business world, and seemed destined for sustained growth and prosperity. But by 1989 its economy was in shambles – equity stocks and land prices lost two-thirds of their value. In the 1990s Japanese business reacted to its bloated bureaucracies by laying off mid-level managers and abandoning unprofitable product lines, practices very foreign to its cultural values.

Ironically, today Japan seems to be held hostage by the very thing that made it successful – manufacturing expertise. The twenty-first century begins with an emphasis on technology and services as industries of the future. How quickly will Japanese industry adopt a fourth strategic thrust that leaps beyond manufacturing as the source of global competitive advantage? History will let us know.

Source: adapted from Walter Russell Mead (2000) 'The Great Japanese Stock Market Recovery', *Worth* (December/January), pp. 124–134.

Discussion questions

1 How has the external environment affected Japanese businesses?
2 Where does the concept of change fit into the functions of management?

inventories begin to stockpile. This ties up working capital, adding to costs. Unless sales of alternative products take up the slack, the firm will begin to lay-off employees to bring costs into line with reduced revenues. Employee morale will probably decline, and employee stress over future uncertainty will increase.

This latter scenario is common in plants designed to produce only one product, such as one type of car. Such pressures make the manager's job challenging, forcing him or her to change roles throughout the day. Let us examine what managers do to carry out their task of analysing and influencing the system.

What successful managers do

Managers are people responsible for working with and through others to achieve objectives by influencing people and systems in a changing environment. This implies that the manager must understand the totality of his or her organisation and then influence system components such as tasks, technology, structure, people, and perhaps even organisational culture, to achieve desired outputs.

managers
People responsible for working with and through others to achieve objectives by influencing people and systems in a changing environment.

Additionally, managers must be aware of the environments in which their systems operate and how external forces alter the performance of internal subsystems and processes. A manager then seeks to align the organisation and its output with its changing environment by shifting resources and what people do to fit that alignment (Miles and Snow, 1991). The merger of H-P and Compaq left former Compaq staff under no illusion about the changes they would have to make (Clark, 1999). The Compaq logo disappeared under the new 'HP Invent' logo. To enable the company to remain competitive ruthless cost-cutting also had to take place.

A manager diagnoses and influences systems and organisational practices by working with people and allocating resources to carry out tasks and achieve goals. Nevertheless, we recognise that managers do not have total control over that part of the organisation for which they are responsible. Many factors other than a manager's actions, which often are attempts to influence other people, ultimately determine why organisational outcomes unfold as they do. No manager can absolutely predict and control environmental forces, as evidenced by Railtrack being placed in administration. Even internal forces that involve human behaviour are often unpredictable and people will thwart attempts by managers to influence them. Now to help you ponder some personal issues about managerial realities, spend a couple of minutes completing the 'your turn' exercise.

The rational view: managers plan, organise, direct and control

'If you ask a manager what he does, he will most likely tell you that he plans, organises, co-ordinates, and controls. Then watch what he does. Don't be surprised if you can't relate what you see to these four words.' This contradiction, observed by Mintzberg (1990), suggests two contrasting views of managers: the rational heroic view and the chaotic realistic view. We can see how he developed his view on page 58.

The rational heroic view is a legacy of early descriptions and prescriptions of the nature of the manager's job. Writers such as Henri Fayol, Fredrick Taylor and Lillian Gilbreth began chronicling the role of management in the early twentieth century. They, and many researchers to follow, characterised the manager as one who engages in reflective planning, takes time to carefully organise structures and systems, directs and co-ordinates an orchestrated flow of activities, and then exercises timely control to keep critical elements in harmony (Fayol, 1949).

Your turn

Do you have the right stuff to be a manager?

Envision yourself in a professional work environment. Which of the following would you like to experience at work? Tick Yes or No for each statement.

		Yes	No
1	To perform a great quantity of work at a hectic pace, driven to keep on top of changing demands.	☐	☐
2	A workday with a great variety of unrelated tasks, fragmented into brief encounters with a number of people.	☐	☐
3	To react to issues and problems that are largely unplanned and initiated by others.	☐	☐
4	To receive more information than you generate, and to spend as much time with people in other departments as you do with people in your department.	☐	☐
5	Verbal communication (whether face to face, in meetings or on the phone) more than written reports, mail and correspondence.	☐	☐
6	To feel that you are a puppet with others pulling on the strings, yet somehow you still manage to move in the direction you want to go.	☐	☐

Scoring These six statements describe how typical managers actually work. If you ticked Yes five or six times, you have the personal characteristics that will enable you to feel comfortable with a manager's responsibilities. If you ticked No five or six times, you are likely to feel uncomfortable with the demands of being a manager. With three or four Yes answers, it's a mixed call. As you read the forthcoming section on the chaotic view of management, you will discover why a manager is more likely to answer Yes to all the above.

According to this rational heroic view, the manager is expected to have an overall feel for where the unit is going, know what is going on, and accept responsibility for problem-solving and the department's success or failure.

Such a rational heroic view of management may have been valid in slower and simpler times, but today's organisations are subjected to fast rates of change and ever increasing complexity. For example, managers in fast-changing, high-technology environments have learned to focus on concept development of new products and keep specifications as flexible as possible until late in a project so as to maintain flexibility and responsiveness to changing market and technological forces (Iansite, 1995).

All managers do some work that is not purely managerial – for example, building relations with clients. All forces considered, the rational heroic model places too much emphasis and responsibility on the manager and not enough on teams and followers within the organisation. When managers act as if they should be the only ones 'in control' they deprive followers of job challenges and create delays in decisions. Heroism sets up a self-defeating cycle: the more the manager commands responsibility for departmental success, the more likely subordinates will be to yield it. This leaves the manager with more to do, with less creative and problem-solving input from those who carry out the work (Bradford and Cohen, 1984).

Research focus: **The managerial roles approach**

This approach was developed by Mintzberg (1990). By systematically studying the activity of five chief executives in a variety of organisations, Mintzberg came to the conclusion that managers do not carry out the classical managerial functions identified by Fayol. He concluded that managers actually fill a series of 10 roles. These can be seen in Exhibit 2-4.

EXHIBIT 2 – 4 Mintzberg's 10 managerial roles

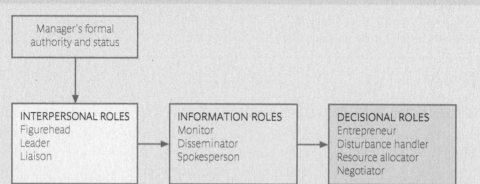

The manager's job is far from routine. Mintzberg suggests that the job of manager can be broken into 10 identifiable roles, each within one of three clusters. As the manager goes about performing his or her job, there is a general flow from interacting with people to handling information to making decisions.

Source: reprinted by permission of *Harvard Business Review*. An exhibit from 'The Manager's Job: Folklore and Fact' by Henry Mintzberg (March–April 1990).

Evaluation of Mintzberg's approach

- Mintzberg has been accused of removing the first-level classification of the managerial function of planning, leading, organising and controlling. He later denied this.

- The research sample was too small and the conclusion was sweeping.

- Many of the activities that Mintzberg found include planning, leading, organising and controlling. For example the interpersonal roles are evidence of leading.

- The roles also appear to be incomplete – where is developing strategies or selection of staff?

However, looking at what managers do is important. In analysing activities, an effective manager might wish to find out how activities and techniques fall into various fields of knowledge reflected in the basic functions of a manager.

The chaotic view: managerial life is intense, fragmented and complex

Chaos well describes the circumstances under which today's managers flourish. Tom Peters devoted an entire book to the premise that managers and organisations 'thrive on chaos' (Peters, 1987). In the 1990s business researchers developed entire projects to explain to increasingly troubled managers how to manage amid chaos (Wheeler, 1997). Amid this environment of chaos, Henry Mintzberg found that instead of being the reflective and systematic planners described in traditional books on management, most managers are actually caught up in a variety of intense, brief, disconnected activities. Few managers work for very long without interruption by phone calls, people dropping into their office, impromptu meetings, other fragmented events, and the frequent 'beep' to announce incoming email. In observations of chief executives, half their activities lasted less than nine minutes. Over 90 per cent of their verbal contacts were ad hoc, short, unplanned episodes that shifted quickly from one topic to another.

Managers prefer action to reflection, according to both Mintzberg (1990) and Kotter (1982). The 'plans' of managers often exist largely in their heads. Managers have several informational media at their disposal (documents, telephone calls, email, scheduled meetings, unscheduled meetings, and observational tours). Of these options, they prefer oral mediums over written information. Mail, email, and reports are usually dispensed with by a quick scan. Verbal contacts with others are the manager's principal source of information, gossip, ideas, opinions and facts. From such contacts emerge a sense of direction and, ultimately, actions.

Managers work in multiple roles

Whether chief executive, managing director, supervisor, coach, bishop, dean, superintendent or brigade chief, all managers share common work characteristics. Mintzberg (1990) writes:

> All these managers are vested with formal authority over an organisational unit. From formal authority comes status, which leads to various interpersonal relations, and from these comes access to information. Information, in turn, enables the manager to make decisions and strategies for his unit.

Having formal authority and status simply sets the stage for managerial activity, which is classified into 10 unique roles. Managerial roles are those distinct patterns of behaviour that managers engage in while working at different tasks. As events and needs shift throughout the manager's working day, the roles keep changing as well.

The interpersonal roles

Managers interact in different ways with people. Interpersonal roles involve three key functions served by managers when representing the organisation and communicating with people: figurehead, leader and liaison. Women are often said to have good interpersonal skills; however, they are not well represented at senior management level. Read the Dynamics of Diversity box for an insight into why this could be.

Figurehead

All managers at times play a figurehead role by participating in ceremonial duties. Some of these duties are routine and have little if any apparent impact on work unit performance, such as when the vice chancellor puts in an appearance at a university party honouring the retirement of the dean of science. When the sales director has lunch with a sales manager and key customer, the figurehead role is important to goal achievement and work unit performance.

Leader

When acting as a leader, the manager focuses on exerting influence over people. As leaders, managers strive to motivate and encourage team members to follow their agenda and to develop their people. Often leader effort overlaps the activities of other roles. (Chapter 14 provides a thorough discussion of leadership.)

dynamics of diversity

Old girls network takes on male bastion

Women make up 44 per cent of the British workforce and their spending power is crucial to the success of companies from Marks & Spencer through Prudential to Unilever. Yet almost half of our top companies have no women on the board. Only eight of them employ female executive directors – and the number is falling not rising. Perhaps the most surprising thing about these statistics, which have been published in a study by Cranfield School of Management, is that the survey's co-author, Val Singh, finds them 'encouraging' and 'evidence for some cautious optimism. Women are showing they can do it.' But does the lack of female representation matter? Certainly there is growing recognition that women can bring a different perspective to board discussions.

Kate Avery, who is the Legal & General director responsible for relationships with its partners such as Barclays and Alliance & Leicester, says: 'As boards recognise they need a different skill mix, not just financial and actuarial, they realise that some of these are more appropriate to a female. Women bring a different direction.'

Beverley Hodson, managing director of WHSmith Retail, believes that this different way of thinking is attractive not just to women but to younger men. 'What we have been working on for the past four years is to get a balanced agenda between what you could call the emotional contribution and the need to drive shareholder value through business efficiency.'

This means performance appraisals for senior executives are based not just on the achievement of financial targets but also on their behaviour, including criteria such as their skills as team leader.

Since Smith started using this approach, the number of women in senior positions has risen from 22 per cent to 40 per cent – and sales growth has averaged 10 per cent a year while profits have jumped by 70 per cent.

There are also signs that chairmen and chief executives are keen to recruit women. Hilary Sears, vice president of executive search at AT Kearney, says that some boards do say they would like to find a woman – but not at any cost. 'One chief executive made the point that, although they ideally wanted a woman, and there were two on the long list of 12, neither made it to the shortlist.'

That could be down to two things: either there are not enough suitable women to get the top jobs – or bosses are using selection criteria biased in favour of men. Singh finds it hard to believe that talented women are in short supply. 'Women started having career ambitions in the 1970s, so we are 30 years downstream ... There must be some talented women about – and if not? Why are they not being given the opportunities?'

There do seem to be plenty of women just below board level. Singh's own survey found that, of the FTSE companies that list their full senior management teams – about half the total – 15 per cent are female. That is still way above the proportion of women in very senior positions.

Less elevated women still complain that it is difficult to make the first leap into a senior position. 'You have to make it into the club. Once you get in it is easier to get others', says Norman Broadbent's Marx.

That is borne out by the survey: 44 per cent of the total, and 73 per cent of the non-executives, also have other corporate directorships.

The old girl network appears to be taking shape.

Source: adapted from *Observer*, Business, 25 November 2001.

Discussion questions

1 What is meant by the term 'You have to make it into the club'? Is it more important to network than develop top-class management skills?

2 How could the selection criteria be changed to reduce inequality? Would any change be good for business?

Liaison

The liaison role encompasses the manager's interactions with others outside his or her vertical chain of reporting relationships. Liaison activities typically involve lateral contacts, or attempts to influence peers in other parts of the organisation. Observational studies typically find about half a manager's time is filled by discussions with peers in other parts of the organisation.

The informational roles

All organisations depend on information as the basis for making decisions and taking action. Toffler (1981) identified that information may well be the most critical resource in post-industrial societies like Britain, the United States, France and other technology-mediated countries. The informational roles of a manager involve obtaining or exchanging relevant information as monitor, disseminator or spokesperson.

Monitor

The monitor role means scanning the environment, asking questions, maintaining a network of contacts, and in general finding out what is going on. It places the manager in the role of information collector and assimilator.

Disseminator

When managers share information with unit members – especially proprietary or goal-affecting information – they are fulfilling the disseminator role. Selective dissemination also helps the manager build a power base, which can be good or bad depending on how that influence is exercised. (Power is the subject of Chapter 13.)

Spokesperson

Managers are at work in the spokesperson role when they share information with influential people outside the unit. The spokesperson role is at work when the chief financial officer makes a speech before a group of visiting security analysts, and independently the director of information systems keeps division managers informed of progress on a technology system changeover.

The decisional roles

Making decisions is the natural consequence of working with the output of informational roles. Decisional roles are exercised when the manager acts on information to commit the organisation to new courses of action, whether as entrepreneur, disturbance handler, resource allocator or negotiator. (Chapter 12 examines ethical decision-making and problem-solving techniques.)

Entrepreneur

The entrepreneurial role involves attempting to adjust the organisation to its environment. Entrepreneurial behaviour includes modifying the product line or repositioning products for a new customer segment, converting operations to a new technology or altering the compensation scheme for salaried professionals. Entrepreneurial behaviour exists at all levels and in all functions, in the public as well as the private sector.

Disturbance handler

While the entrepreneurial role causes managers to act as an agent of change, the disturbance handler role typically draws them in involuntarily. A major breakdown in a critical machine, a union work stoppage or the bankruptcy of an important vendor may all be relatively unanticipated events that call on the manager to restore functionality and performance.

Resource allocator

Whether initiated through entrepreneurial foresight or the compelling need to handle a threatening disturbance, the resource allocator role is one all managers perform. Resource allocations can be as far reaching as restructuring the organisation or authorising capital expenditure for a new plant, or as mundane (yet politically charged) as assigning one member of the work unit to a vacant office with a window.

Negotiator

None of the other roles by itself prevents conflict. Thus the manager inevitably shifts into the negotiator role when bargaining with a union steward over an employee grievance or working out a solution to a new product design dispute between engineering and manufacturing. Negotiations and the management of conflict are a way of life for managers. (Chapters 9, 10 and 11 discuss conflict in interpersonal and group relationships.)

The 10 roles just discussed span the work activities of the manager. They provide clues to the abilities that managerial aspirants must learn if they are to succeed. Yet, there is a danger in decomposing the manager's job into a series of discrete roles. Katz (1955) argues that real managerial success comes from integrating the roles so that behaviour flows naturally across roles. In practice, the relative emphasis given to different roles depends on where the manager is within the organisational hierarchy and the pressures felt at the time. A first-line supervisor is dependent primarily on liaison, monitor, disturbance handler and negotiator roles. At the top of the organisation, the figurehead, leader, spokesperson and entrepreneur roles consume a manager more.

How managers influence organisation systems

An important function of managing is to adapt or transform system elements to achieve goals within a dynamic environment. In dynamic open systems, especially those feeling the effects of weak performance, system variables become misaligned with environmental forces over time and need to be realigned or changed (Boeker and Goodstein, 1991). Managers need to understand and diagnose their systems and then influence select variables to transform system capabilities.

Select options for changing an organisation

The key resource variables or capabilities that managers seek to influence and transform include tasks, technology, organisation, people and organisational culture. Exhibit 2-5 shows a model of these change options within an open systems framework. The model is intended to simplify the complexity of a real organisation and serves as a conceptual framework to help managers decide where and how to make changes. Managers evaluate these key internal system elements in

EXHIBIT 2–5 Resources elements for transforming organisational systems

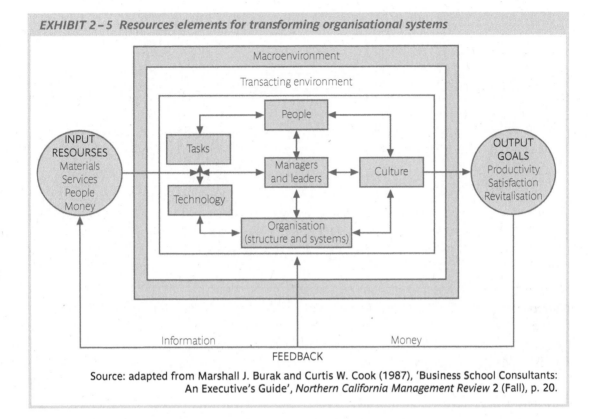

Source: adapted from Marshall J. Burak and Curtis W. Cook (1987), 'Business School Consultants: An Executive's Guide', *Northern California Management Review* 2 (Fall), p. 20.

planning how they will bring about organisational innovation and continuous improvement. The model also reminds managers that key system variables are interactive: a change in one potentially impacts and changes other variables.

Every organisation uses a few basic internal resources to convert and transform external inputs into value-added outputs. The five resource elements (people, tasks, technology, organisation and culture) are dynamically interactive – a change in one potentially affects the others. Managers not only work to keep these resource elements in balance, but they also use them to trigger changes that transform the entire system. The leaders in many firms are now trying to bring about a transformation to total quality, using these resource elements as their instruments of change.

Tasks

Tasks are the jobs or work that people do in pursuit of enterprise purpose. Tasks begin with goals and can be designed to be simple or complex, easy or difficult, physical or mental, and so on. The job of carpenters who specialise in cutting and nailing wall partitions is simpler and less mentally challenging than the jobs of carpenters responsible for framing the walls and roof. How managers design tasks is crucial to motivating and helping people achieve desired outputs.

Technology

Technology includes the knowledge, equipment, subsystems, software and methods for accomplishing work tasks. In manufacturing, technology choices are matched to the expected quantity of outputs and methods for producing products. Production ranges from custom made (one of a kind) to batch produced (in small quantities or lots) to systems for mass or continuous

production. While computers, robots and lasers are obvious technology tools, we also include the knowledge needed to use that hardware and software in our definition of *technology*. Today, electronic commerce is rapidly streamlining the business processes for speeding the flow of goods from producers to customers by using instantaneous web-based information exchanges.

People

People energise and give life to systems. People make the fundamental decisions that influence system outputs for better or worse. To begin with, managers have to decide how many people to employ in a certain task and what knowledge and skills they require. Managers are then responsible for selecting and training people who have or can develop the skills needed to achieve the organisation's goals.

Organisation

Organisation, as used here, refers to a structural network and the processes that define and link key subsystems within the enterprise. Organisation encompasses the communication and decision-making network among work units that guides and limits people's behaviour within an organisation's structure. A chart, drawing or map that depicts the decision authority and communication relationships among people and the ways in which tasks are grouped into departments or subunits simplistically symbolises organisation structure. In a realistic sense, managers view structure in a broader way to include all those elements that help govern people's behaviour at work. These include goals, plans, policies and rules, as well as the authority and communication networks.

Organisational culture

The entire foregoing elements combine to form a network of social systems, and from these evolve an organisational culture. By culture we mean the beliefs, values and assumptions people have about their particular organisation and the expected behaviour within it. Culture includes the norms that influence the member's behaviour and how they present themselves to the outside world. Hewlett-Packard is guided by a formal code of conduct, the 'H-P way', that espouses consensus-orientated management; Asda uses technology and management to energise its in-store merchandising and the behaviour of its associates (employees) around the cultural norm that 'the customer is number one'. (Work through the WWW exercise assignment at the end of this chapter to personally draw out comparisons between H-P and Asda supermarkets.)

Management: the integrating responsibility

In the centre of this transformation network, we show *managers* and *leaders*. Traditionally, they are the ones responsible for planning, co-ordinating, organising, controlling and directing the other elements in the rational view of management. They are responsible for ensuring that appropriate inputs are received and processed through the transformation system in timely ways. Managers are assessed in part on the extent to which their part of the system (typically a subsystem such as manufacturing or supply) produces appropriate outputs that satisfy customers or users. At times, managers make significant breakthroughs in the way they go about analysing systems and making changes in the more chaotic view of management.

Anticipate dependency among system elements

The planned changes managers make in a system to achieve intended results commonly lead to unintended second-order consequences. When Ford came under pressure from the media and a union campaign to keep the Halewood plant open by maintaining some sort of vehicle production, former CEO at Ford, Jack Nasser, agreed in principle, and the senior management team were given the task to lead the transition from restrictive production practices to a flexible and productive mobile workforce. The senior management team produced a vision statement and negotiated the Halewood Gateway agreement which, although after a series of strikes, was eventually implemented when Ford threatened to pull out completely (Oxtoby, 2002). Today a change in the plant's culture and processes has made it one of the most successful in the UK. In the Ford example, a planned change in one variable 'organisation' caused subsequent changes in tasks and technology. In this case although there was resistance the impact was positive. When one system variable is changed, it is likely that some or all of the mutually dependent variables will also change. For more detail of what exactly happened at Halewood, see the opening case in Chapter 6.

Achieve balance among essential output goals

In diagnosing how and where to influence an organisational system, managers typically start with outputs because they are important to all organisations. For a business, outputs are goods and services that provide value to customers. All organisations try to produce outputs that meet the quality, quantity, timeliness and price expectations of customers. To do so, they need to set specific goals that address three output criteria: productivity, satisfaction and revitalisation.

Productivity

To put the concept of productivity into a managerial perspective, think of the output (product or service) that is the purpose for being in business. The output of IBM is principally computers, software and information-related services. For Barclays Bank, output refers to the services of protecting deposits, providing loans and charge card accounts, and administering trusts. For Gap, output is merchandising and selling casual clothing to young people. As a starting point, productivity compares the level of output from one reporting period to another. For manufacturing, it is the number of units produced; for accounting, the information collected, organised and disseminated; for research and development, the number of innovations patented and commercialised.

In producing outputs, costs are incurred as inputs are consumed. Costs include both capital investments (in physical facilities and infrastructure) and operational expenses (including payroll and supplies or services consumed). Operational costs are often sensitive to volume of activity, which has an impact on profits (Clancy and Madison, 1997). Thus, a more meaningful concept of productivity refers to how outputs are achieved.

Productivity is the ratio of outputs of acceptable quality to inputs consumed and is a measure of how well an organisation attains its goals. A five-person production team that produced 100 units of a product in quarter one and then produced 110 units in quarter two improved productivity by 10 per cent. Over time, productivity depends on both efficiency and effectiveness.

Efficiency means doing things right, or getting the most output for the least input. Typical measures of efficiency are sales per employee, inventory turns per year, student–faculty ratios, and number of acceptable units produced per person-hour or per shift.

Effectiveness means producing the right outputs – those that are sufficiently valued by stakeholders to sustain the organisation. For easyJet, direct selling on the Internet and operating ticketless travel has enabled them to cut costs and be effective and efficient.

productivity
Ratio of acceptable quality outputs to inputs consumed; a measure of how well the organisation achieves its goals.

efficiency
Doing something right or getting the most output for the least input.

effectiveness
Producing the right output or doing things right to create value for stakeholders.

It is possible to have efficiency without effectiveness and vice versa. An accounting department might collect certain data very efficiently (at low cost), but it might not provide the data needed for managerial decision-making. The ideal is to achieve a balance of effectiveness and efficiency, although effectiveness is usually more critical. Porsche nearly went out of business, for although it was producing a high-quality product, its work practices were inefficient (Healey, 1999).

Satisfaction

Satisfaction Another key goal of organisations is to keep stakeholders satisfied. Satisfaction refers to the overall positive feelings people have about an organisation, whether as an employee, customer, supplier or regulator.

Satisfaction can be measured informally by listening to people talk or by asking them how they feel about the organisation. Satisfaction can also be measured through focus groups or by administering attitude surveys to employees, customers and/or vendors. Alternatively, it can be inferred by studying employee data such as absenteeism, turnover and number of grievances. Firms also measure customer satisfaction by examining trends in sales volume, number of product returns/complaints, or number of repeat purchases per customer. The example of Internet service providers suggests yet another indicator of customer satisfaction: the number of defectors (cancellations) per month.

satisfaction
Positive feelings people have about an organisation, whether as an employee, customer, supplier or regulator.

One of the pervasive problems facing managers is to manage the relationship between productivity and satisfaction. Managers commonly think that happy people are productive people. However, research suggests otherwise, for the causality between satisfaction and productivity is low. Instead, high productivity more often leads to satisfaction. Here is clearly a case in which research overturns conventional beliefs.

Workers who are dissatisfied with their work, and maybe even negative towards their employer, can still be very productive. Assembly-line workers often typify this positive–negative combination. On the other hand, sometimes even satisfied workers are not productive. You may know some university lecturers in this category! As you will see later on, research into empowerment and self-governing teams suggests that productivity and satisfaction often improve when management relaxes. Less management can produce more results (Lawler, 1992).

Revitalisation and organisational renewal

A third major output criterion is the capacity of the organisation to develop and renew itself.

revitalisation
Ability to take care of tomorrow's problems as well as today's by renewing strategies, resources, technology and skills.

Revitalisation refers to the ability to take care of tomorrow's problems as well as today's by renewing the strategies, resources, technology and skills required for future success. Rather than deplete the resource base to get immediate results, companies must periodically or continually reinvest, renew and reinvent.

Revitalisation naturally occurs when a firm replaces worn-out or technically obsolete equipment. Revitalisation also involves people, for without training and professional development of human resources an organisation slips in its capacity to compete. Reinvention occurs when firms invest in the research and development of new products and the improvement of internal processes (such as streamlining the number of steps required to pay accounts receivable). Marks & Spencer has recently changed direction in an attempt to revitalise a business that has been losing its market share.

Each of these output criteria – productivity, satisfaction and revitalisation – can be applied to individuals, groups, organisations and even societies. Sims and Lorenzi (1992) suggest that the overall job of any manager is:

- to identify clearly the output requirements of his or her system
- to devise measures of efficiency and effectiveness
- to develop core skills and capabilities within the organisation to do the job well
- to promote improvement and innovation
- to make changes when results fail to measure up.

Both researchers and managers realise that the critical issues that affect organisational practices change with time. As issues emerge in the search for ways to improve organisational performance, some become the constant subject of discussions, conferences, workshops and research agendas, and are eventually put into practice. Four such central themes, of globalisation, ethics, diversity and technology, concern managers who expect to achieve balance among output goals in the early years of the twenty-first century.

Richard Branson of Virgin: a second look

Richard Branson has created a diverse organisation. Today it is the third most recognised brand in the UK – it is now becoming the first global brand name of the twenty-first century.

Virgin is involved in planes, trains, finance, soft drinks, music, mobile phones, holidays, cars, wines, publishing, bridal wear and more. What ties these brands together are the values of the brand and the attitudes of the people.

Virgin has created over 200 companies worldwide, employing over 25000 people. The total revenues in 1999 exceeded £3 billion.

Virgin states:

> We believe in making a difference. In our customers' eyes, Virgin stands for value for money, quality, innovation, fun, sense of competitive challenge. We deliver a quality service by empowering our employees and we facilitate and monitor customer feedback to continually improve the customers' experience through innovation.

When Virgin starts a new venture it bases it on hard research and analysis:

> Typically, we review the industry and put ourselves in our customers' shoes to see what could make it better. We ask fundamental questions: is this an opportunity for restructuring a market and creating competitive advantage? What are the competitors doing? Is the customer confused or badly served? Is this an opportunity for building the Virgin brand? Can we add value? Will we interact with our other businesses? Is there an appropriate trade-off between risk and reward?

Virgin puts forward the idea that:

> Once a Virgin company is up and running, several factors contribute to making it a success. The power of the Virgin name; Richard Branson's personal reputation; our unrivalled network of friends, contacts and partners; the Virgin management style; the way talent is empowered to flourish within the Group. To some traditionalists, these may not seem hardheaded enough. To them, the fact that Virgin has minimal management layers, no bureaucracy, a tiny board and no massive global HQ is an anathema.

Virgin sees itself as part of a family rather than a hierarchy. Empowered to run their own affairs and yet helping each other out when there are problems. It operates on the idea of being a community, with shared ideas, values, interests and goals. Virgin sees success as having a strong business promise, and keeping it.

Source: www.virgin.com.

Summary

- Organisations are open, dynamic systems for transforming resource inputs into outputs of useful products and services that satisfy the needs of customers and provide value to stakeholders.
- The interests of various stakeholders (whether employees, clients, suppliers, shareholders or regulators) are not always aligned. This places conflicting pressures and demands on managers.
- At the highest organisational level, managers seek to navigate competitive environmental forces by developing a mission to define the firm's unique business purpose and crafting superordinate goals to challenge and guide employees.
- At all levels, managers diagnose and influence systems by working with people and allocating resources to carry out tasks and achieve goals within an environment of change.
- In performing their jobs managers behave differently in various roles, frequently shifting emphasis among interpersonal, information and decision-making roles.
- To maintain organisational viability managers work to achieve goals in the areas of productivity, satisfaction and revitalisation.
- One of the realities of life in organisations is that today's effective practices are not likely to suffice tomorrow.
- Whether pulled by the success of growth or jolted by crisis and downturn, managers must periodically transform the system to adapt to environmental realities.
- In the process of transformation managers can target changes in the key internal resources such as tasks, technology, organisation, people and culture.
- Maintaining a dynamic balance among these resources is what organisational behaviour is all about.
- The study of organisational behaviour is important because of the growing complexity and turbulence of the business environment and the related growth in research knowledge about behaviour within and between organisations.

Areas for personal development

More than 90 per cent of the readers of this book will devote most of their income-earning life to working within or with organisations. Be they business enterprises, not-for-profits or governmental departments, organisations are the dominant system for combining human talent and other resources to carry out collective purposes. To improve your personal effectiveness as an organisational member and stakeholder, begin to develop or hone your skills by applying the following suggestions to your daily life.

1 **Know your organisations.** Knowledge is power when used to understand the circumstances in which one makes decisions and influences others to bring about desired goals. Begin now to learn as much as you can about the organisations that impact your life. As a student, ask questions of faculty, staff and administrators to learn more about how your university functions: how it is organised, how decisions and changes are made, why various systems are used, and how people are chosen for various jobs. Do the same at work, at church and even in organisations you frequent as a customer.

2 **Create a satisfied customer.** Just as every organisation, even a non-profit one, wants to build and serve a base of customers, every individual needs to create and serve a base of customers for his or her talents. Who are your customers? Who do you need to please and satisfy by use of your talent and energy? What are their needs, their preferences both in the output you might deliver and in the way you conduct yourself in providing your 'product'? Learn not just to do what you want to do in life, but to collect sufficient data to know that there is a market for your product or service and that you are providing customer satisfaction.

3 **Develop a personal mission.** To serve customers effectively, it helps to know not only the nature of your 'business' but also where you are going. Write out a personal mission statement that defines what you have to offer that is attractive to others and that articulates your primary values. Start by writing possible themes as short phrases, and then link them together through several drafts until you have a single statement of about 20 words or fewer that gives meaning to what you do and what you seek to become.

4 **Define the transactions among subsystems within a network.** To refine your learning about organisations, begin to map the work and informational flows among subsystems. Sketch out the relationships among departments or activity centres in organisations where you work or learn. Pay particular attention to boundary-spanning transactions, where the organisation receives inputs or provides outputs. What kind of work product is exchanged, what kind of information? Where could bottlenecks or problems occur? Become a system analyser and, as opportunities or needs arise, you will be better prepared to influence the system, either by changing the behaviour of people performing within it or changing the tasks and processes.

5 **Broaden your managerial roles.** While you may not now be a manager, begin to develop the skills and roles that a manager uses in diagnosing and influencing how systems are organised and function. Review your responses to the 'Your turn' exercise. As you find yourself in different situations throughout the day, ask yourself, 'What kind of role am I playing now? What kind of role is needed as I move back and forth between interpersonal, informational and decisional activities?'

6 **Target an option for organisational change.** You have undoubtedly experienced situations as a customer or member of an organisation where you thought, 'This isn't working, this isn't right.' Rather than simply complain or keep your frustration within you, practise diagnosing and working through the change options that might permanently improve the situation. Use Exhibit 2-5 as a simple organising scheme where you think through (and write down) what is the task to be performed, what kind of technology or equipment is involved, how is it organised, who are the people (and their skills, attitudes) and what do I infer about the organisational culture (the beliefs, values and assumptions of organisational members). Work through the exercise: 'What ultimately do I want to change? How do I get there: by focusing on the element apparently causing the problem or by starting with another source?'

7 **Balance efficiency and effectiveness.** In your task assignments, define what will make your output or result effective. This involves doing the right thing so that you and your customer are satisfied. Also organise your activities so that you are efficient and getting the most output for the least input.

❓ Questions for study and discussion

1 Critically challenge or defend the statement, 'The mission of a business firm is to produce profits.'

2 Identify the three primary clusters of managerial roles and, for each, give examples of at least two specific roles.

3 What key elements and relationships define a business as a dynamic open system? Provide an example of why a systems understanding of organisations and their environments is useful to managers.

4 What are the fundamental internal system elements managers commonly target in their change or transformation of organisations? Describe an example that demonstrates the potential interdependency among at least three change variables.

5 Think about the themes we characterise in this book as Technology Transformation, World Watch, Dynamics of Diversity and Eye on Ethics. Provide at least one reason why each is an important managerial issue for organisations entering the twenty-first century.

🔑 Key Concepts

organisational behaviour, *p. 43*

management, *p. 44*

organisation, *p. 45*

stakeholders, *p. 45*

mission, *p. 46*

superordinate goals, *p. 47*

law of effect, *p. 49*

system, *p. 51*

organisations, *p. 52*

closed systems, *p. 52*

open systems, *p. 53*

dynamic system, *p. 53*

boundary-spanning transactions, *p. 54*

managers, *p. 56*

productivity, *p. 66*

efficiency, *p. 66*

effectiveness, *p. 66*

satisfaction, *p. 66*

revitalisation, *p. 67*

Personal skills exercise

Analysing Joyce Johnson's system

Purpose This exercise involves step-by-step analysis, prediction and planning. Your task is to advise Joyce Johnson, CEO of Johnson Aerospace Ltd, and to experience working as an impromptu team.

Time about 20 to 30 minutes

Procedure Perform, step by step, the tasks called for in each part of the exercise. Do not read ahead until you have answered the questions.

Part 1 Joyce Johnson is CEO and general manager of a small aerospace parts manufacturing company that has been operating for nine years. Johnson Aerospace Ltd was profitable in its second year, and in each of the succeeding five years sales and profits increased moderately. Two years ago, sales and profits peaked, but they have since been declining. During the decline, customers have complained that deliveries of Johnson parts are often delayed and the parts are sometimes of unacceptable quality and are no longer price competitive with two other competitors.

Johnson knows that two-thirds of her sales are to three key customers who value product quality, timely delivery and price, in that order. Johnson is also aware that morale and commitment among her 125 employees are not strong and seem to be slipping with declining sales. Turnover of employees has risen from 2 per cent to 15 per cent over the past two years. Her key managers have been driving people to get more work out, but with little progress.

Joyce Johnson's goals have been to try to differentiate Johnson Aerospace Ltd from its competitors. The company has done this by identifying what the customer wants and then quickly agreeing to supply the desired parts at specified quality levels, by a specific delivery date, at a quoted price. Being relatively small, Johnson Aerospace has historically been able to respond to customer needs. Johnson thinks her strategy is appropriate but knows something has to change since competitiveness has slipped.

Before you go on to Part 2, decide on answers to the following three questions, and agree on a rationale for each answer:

1 Johnson needs more quality-control inspectors.

☐ Agree ☐ Disagree

Why? _____

2 Johnson needs to immediately get employee attention by doing something dramatic like promising bonuses for sales and profits improvements.

☐ Agree ☐ Disagree

Why? _____

3 Johnson should concentrate on reducing the production cycle time in order to make on-time deliveries.

☐ Agree ☐ Disagree

Why? _____

Part 2 Before doing anything, Johnson thought she ought to diagnose her situation using a systems model framework. She began to list a series of questions to help guide her analysis. Johnson started with: 'Do we have the right kinds of resources?' Write out at least five other questions that would be most helpful to Johnson in analysing her business system.

1 _____

2 _____

3 _____

4 _____

5 _____

As you reflect on your questions, does it appear that:

1 most of Johnson's problems are people problems?

☐ Agree   ☐ Disagree

Why? _____

2 most likely, Johnson has a number of interdependent systems problems that require transformation or change?

☐ Agree   ☐ Disagree

Why? _____

Part 3 Once Johnson has her list of system-guiding questions and begins seeking information to answer them, she discovers several areas that could be improved. In trying to understand why morale and commitment are declining, she finds many of the workers feel they benefit little from increasing output performance. Their pay stays the same, their opportunities for advancement in the small company are slight, and they expect continuing pressure to produce more regardless of the level of their output. Some find their jobs boring, and most think supervisors spend more time pressuring employees to produce more than showing appreciation for what has been produced.

Johnson also discovers that three essential machines are old and frequently require repair. Machine operators feel frustrated using them and production is held up when the machines are down for repairs. In addition, Johnson finds that friction between production and quality-control people results in considerable loss of time and energy, and causes considerable rework. Finally, it appears that the layout of the manufacturing process is not as efficient as employees believe it could be.

Although you do not have enough information to solve all Johnson's problems, conclude this exercise by helping Johnson provide a big-picture sense of direction to employees within the firm.

1 Write a one-sentence mission statement to guide Johnson Aerospace Ltd appropriately in its future behaviour.

2 Write two or three superordinate goals that will help employees focus on and support this mission.

(a) _____

(b) _____

(c) _____

Part 4 *As an option*, your tutor may ask you to form groups in class and share individual output to each of the three parts to the exercise, and come up with a team response. If so, discuss similarities and differences among your responses. How does your work compare with the responses of others? What insights did others have that provide you with a more comprehensive understanding of Johnson Aerospace? Did you use disagreements and conflict to push for deeper insight into understanding the situation at Johnson Aerospace? Alternatively, did your group agree to the first idea anyone expressed? How can a group benefit from having disagreements and differences of opinion among members?

Team exercise

The vision of McDonald's: from burgers to system

Purpose Everyone knows McDonald's, the hamburger chain that spans the globe. In Britain there is one in nearly every high street. This exercise gives groups of students the opportunity to analyse a familiar business from a systems perspective.

Time about 25 minutes total

Materials Flip chart and coloured markers preferred.

Procedure Divide the class into teams of four to six members.

1   Each team meets to share reflections about what members know about McDonald's. Express these observations and conjectures in one or more diagrams that represent the system elements and interdependencies within a McDonald's restaurant (about 15 minutes). Use the various system diagrams within this chapter as clues for how you might go about presenting your analysis, but be specific to McDonald's. The following questions suggest elements you may want to include, but you are not bound to these – be creative:

   ■ What are the major output goals?
   ■ How might McDonald's evaluate performance?
   ■ Who are the customers? How might customers be segmented into distinct product markets (based on demographics)? What adds value to customers' needs?
   ■ What are the major resource inputs? What types of vendors might McDonald's need?
   ■ Who are the stakeholders, and what do they want from their relationship with McDonald's?
   ■ What are the principal work subsystems within the restaurant? How are the inputs transformed into saleable outputs?
   ■ How do the internal resource elements (tasks, technology, organisation, people, culture and managers) come together in an alignment that aids in accomplishing the mission?
   ■ What changes or adjustments in the system would have to be made to accommodate a new cooked menu item?

2   Each group displays its systems design(s) or drawing(s) and discusses why it chose both the features and the mode of representation in its drawing(s).

3   Discuss and debrief by calling attention to similar and different elements across groups. Discuss the group process using the following questions for guidance.

   ■ What helped and what hindered the process of performing this task?
   ■ How did you handle disagreements among members about how to format your presentation and what to include?
   ■ In what ways did your group function as a mission-guided system? On the other hand, did it dissolve into a variety of disconnected opinions?

Case study: Who's in charge of purchasing at Logistix?

John Smith, the Logistix Company's chief executive, decided to move his organisation towards centralising support functions and began with the purchasing department. He took this action to save time, cut inventory costs, streamline processes linking sales to final customers, and out of fear that the economy was entering a phase of possible shortages and higher prices in some key supply sectors. Logistix had a tradition of promoting local autonomy among its divisions (they now number 14 in Britain, three in Ireland and four in mainland Europe). With its decentralisation emphasis, purchasing practices had never been co-ordinated. Each division was left to buy whatever it needed from any source of supply. Each division provided monthly consolidated reports to head office.

As part of his move towards centralisation, Smith decided to create a new position: vice president of purchasing. Michelle Jones had been a divisional purchasing manager before becoming a strategic planner for the chief financial officer. Well known throughout the company, she made known her aspirations for the new position. Jones was disappointed when she read a company-wide email that, with the approval of the board of directors, Smith was appointing David Evans into the newly created position. Evans had worked for 18 years with other firms, and to help his transition into Logistix, Smith appointed Jones to be his assistant.

Although Logistix was diversified into several lines of business, most of the purchasing managers were entering their busiest season of the year, which would peak in about a month. The new vice president was aware of this and thought he would initiate his new appointment by announcing a policy calling for head office review of pending purchasing contracts. After some contemplation Evans thought he would ask divisional purchasing managers to transmit to him copies of all pending contracts over £15 000. He planned to email each of the 21 purchasing managers a copy of his new policy directive (which had been approved by Smith) but thought he would first test the communiqué on Jones. Evans called Jones into his office, handed her the draft and asked, 'What do you think of this as a way of getting started?' The message read:

> TO: Divisional Purchasing Managers
>
> FROM: David Evans, Vice President, Purchasing
>
> SUBJECT: Implementation of a policy of review on pending contracts
> I am sure you are all concerned about maintaining a steady flow of quality
> supplies and components at the best possible prices. As you know from the
> recent announcement, Mr Smith has appointed me to co-ordinate purchasing
> among our 21 divisions. Therefore, to get started at this task I am initiating a
> change in policy with the approval of Mr Smith and the board. As you negotiate
> contracts with values of £15 000 or more, please fax or email to head office for
> my review a copy of each pending contract before it is signed.
>   With the forecast shortages in some supplier markets, I know you will
> appreciate the value of what we in head office can do to assure the best prices
> and delivery terms. Realising this is a busy time, I assure you that we will give a
> prompt response on all contracts. As we move into a new era of vendor relations,
> I count on your continued professionalism to help us get the most from our
> relations with suppliers.

Jones read the draft message twice and then told Evans, 'The policy change seems appropriate enough, but I'm not sure about sending an email memo as the method of implementing it. Wouldn't you rather personally inform the purchasing managers of the necessity for this policy and how it will work?

Evans abruptly responded, 'Haven't got time. There is too much to do in networking our key suppliers and reviewing our processes. If any questions arise, why don't you act as the point person and convince the purchasing managers this is in their best interest?'

Jones decided to let it pass. Evans spun around in his chair, hit the 'send' button on his email and transmitted it immediately to the 21 plants. Within the next week, he received several replies from the purchasing managers. Each said, in so many words 'I understand your policy and you can count on our co-operation.'

Four weeks later, Evans had yet to receive a pending contract. During executive meetings in head office, the other vice presidents reported that, during their visits to the plants, they found business to be booming and plants were producing at near-capacity levels.

Questions for managerial action

1 What concepts of management and organisational behaviour do you see in this situation or infer from the case?

2 What thoughts could have possibly gone through Evans' mind as he contemplated sending out his new policy on contract reviews? Were there any system factors he should have analysed but, based on his actions, probably did not?

3 What would you do if you were in Jones' position once Evans sent his memo? What are the motivational implications of this situation for Jones?

4 What would you do if you were one of the 21 divisional purchasing managers? In what ways might they have some advantage or power over Evans? What external and internal forces influence them as they consider what to do about the new policy?

5 What is your evaluation of Evans as a manager? As a leader? Why do you believe he took the action he did? What should he do at this point?

Applied questions

6 Using Mintzberg's managerial roles can you identify which management activities are Smith, Jones and Evans involved in? Which are effective and which roles are less effective?

7 Exhibit 2-2 illustrates a model of an open systems organisation. How would a centralised purchasing system impact on the whole organisation? You may want to illustrate your answer with a diagram.

Source: based on Lawrence and Seiler (1965).

WWW exercise

Manager's Internet tools

Web tips: corporate management messages on the web

The Internet is a fast-growing tool for companies to broadcast some of their management ideas. A company's website can be the first point of contact between an individual and that company, or individuals can frequent a company's website on a recurring or sporadic basis. Therefore, the Internet can be used as an effective tool for management communication.

A favourite organisation

Besides just products and services, a company's website can be used to communicate much about the values, goals, visions, innovations and operations of the organisation. For example, go to one of your favourite organisations via its http://www.___.___ address and see what you can learn in answer to the following.

- What is the organisation about and where is it heading?
- What are some of the core management values and beliefs?
- How does the organisation view its employees and customers?
- What does the organisation expect of its employees?

Specific exercise

A comparison exercise

The above themes are just some of the messages companies can communicate over the Internet. Look at two specific websites:

- *http://www.hp.com*
- *http://www.asda.co.uk*

Hewlett-Packard (H-P) and Asda, a subsidiary of the American supermarket giant Wal-Mart, are two well-known companies that have distinguished themselves not only for their financial successes, but also by their innovative management techniques. Browse their websites, looking for messages on their management beliefs about their employees and their customers. On the Asda site there is a link to the Wal-Mart site, read some of the examples provided about the company's culture. Do you think this culture will be acceptable to British workers. On the H-P website pay particular attention to the 'H-P Way'.

1 What do the cultural stories imply about Asda management philosophy? How does Asda view its customers? Its employees? Does the Wal-Mart philosophy match the Asda one? What about cultural differences?

2 How does H-P view 'profit'? What themes are consistent between H-P's thoughts about its customers and its employees? What does H-P expect of its employees in terms of performance? How do these messages relate to the view of 'profit'?

3 What similarities exist between Asda and H-P in their management themes?

LEARNING CHECKLIST ☑

Before you move on you may want to reflect on what you have learnt in this chapter. You should now be able to:

☑ explain how business firms attempt to balance the profit motive with serving customer needs

☑ understand how an organisation's mission and superordinate goals guide employee behaviour towards desired quality outcomes

☑ identify the following key elements and relationships that characterise organisations as dynamic open systems
- – inputs
- – outputs
- – transformation processes

☑ use Mintzberg to explain a manager's interpersonal, informational and decisional roles

☑ explain how managers can influence the five basic resources to transform their organisations

☑ defend the premise that international competition, quality, diversity and ethical behaviour are the major management issues of the early twenty-first century.

Further reading

Iaffaldano, M.T. and Muchinsky, P.M. (1985) 'Job Satisfaction and Job Performance: A Meta-analysis', *Psychological Bulletin*, March, pp. 251–273.

McCracken, M. and Winterton, J. (2006) 'What About the Managers? Contradictions Between Life-long Learning and Management Development', *International Journal of Training & Development* 10(1), March, p. 55.

Minkes, A.L. (2002) 'Business and a Behavioural Tradition Revisited: A Personal View', *International Journal of Management & Decision Making* 3(2), p. 107.

Murray, K. and White, J. (2005) 'CEOs' Views on Reputation Management', *Journal of Communication Management* 9(4), pp. 348–358.

Petty, M.M., McGee, G.W. and Cavender, J.W. (1984) 'A Meta-analysis of the Relationship Between Individual Job Satisfaction and Individual Performance', *Academy of Management Review* 9, October, pp. 712–721.

References

Bertalanffy, L.V. (1968) *General Systems Theory: Foundations, Development, Applications.* New York, NY: George Braziller.

Boeker, W. and Goodstein, J. (1991) 'Organizational Performance and Adaptation: Effects of Environment and Performance on Changes in Board Composition', *Academy of Management Journal* 34, December, pp. 805–826.

Boulding, K.E. (1956) 'General Systems Theory – The Skeleton of Science', *Management Science* 2, April, pp. 200–201.

Bradford, D.L. and Cohen, A.R. (1984) *Managing for Excellence.* New York, NY: John Wiley & Sons, p. 17.

Clancy, D.K. and Madison, T.F. (1997) 'Cost-Volume-Profit Analysis and Changing Costs: Reconciling Theory and Practice', *Journal of Cost Analysis*, Fall, pp. 89–108.

Clark, D. (1999) 'H-P and Oracle to Announce Marketing Pact', *Wall Street Journal*, 21 September, p. B4.

Drucker, P.F. (1974) *Management Tasks, Responsibilities, Practices.* New York, NY: Harper & Row, p. 61.

Fayol, H. (1949) *General and Industrial Management.* London: Pitman [orig. 1916], trans. C. Storrs.

Goodman, P.S., Fichman, M., Lerch, F.J. and Snyder, P.R. (1995) 'Customer–Firm Relationships, Involvement, and Customer Satisfaction', *Academy of Management Journal* 38, October, pp. 1310–1324.

Healey, J.R. (1999) 'Groomed so as not to Marry: Porsche Claims Exemption from Merger Mania', *USA Today*, 6 August, pp. B1–B2.

Hopkins, N. (2002) 'Fiorina Under Fire as Dell knocks HP off the Top', *The Times*, 16 November, p. 57.

Iansite, M. (1995) 'Shooting the Rapids: Managing Product Development in Turbulent Environments', *California Management Review* 38, pp. 37–58.

Katz, D. and Kahn, R.L. (1968) *The Social Psychology of Organizations.* New York, NY: John Wiley & Sons, and C. West Churchman, *The Systems Approach.* New York, NY: Dell.

Katz, R.L. (1955) 'Skills of an Effective Administrator', *Harvard Business Review* 33, January–February, pp. 33–42.

Kotter, J.P. (1982) *The General Managers.* New York, NY: Free Press.

Lawler III, E.E. (1992) *The Ultimate Advantage: Creating the High-involvement Organization.* San Francisco, CA: Jossey-Bass.

Lawrence, P.R. and Seiler, J.A. (1965) 'Inspired by a Classic, "The Dashman Company"', *Organizational Behaviour and Administration: Cases, Concepts, and Research Findings.* Homewood, IL: Irwin, pp. 16–17.

Lumpkin, G.T and Dess, G.G. (1995) 'Simplicity as a Strategy-making Process: The Effects of Stage of Organizational Development and Environment on Performance', *Academy of Management Journal* 38, October, pp. 1386–1407.

Martinson, J. (2000) 'Judge Orders Microsoft Breakup', *Guardian*, 8 June, p. 2.

Miles, R.E. and Snow, C.C. (1991) 'Fit, Failure, and the Hall of Fame', in Barry M. Staw (ed.) *Psychological Dimensions of Organizational Behaviour.* New York, NY: Macmillan, pp. 632–646.

Mintzberg, H. (1990) 'The Manager's Job: Folklore and Fact', *Harvard Business Review* 90, March–April.

Mitroff, I.I., Mason, R.O. and Pearson, C.M. (1994) 'Radical Surgery: What Will Tomorrow's Organizations Look Like?', *Academy of Management Executive* 8, May, pp. 11–21.

Oxtoby, B. (2002) 'Driving High Performance Working', *People Management*, 18 April, pp. 37–42 (CIPD).

Peters, T. (1987) *Thriving on Chaos: Handbook for a Management Revolution.* New York, NY: Harper & Row.

Pierce, J.L., Rubenfeld, S.A. and Morgan, S. (1991) 'Employee Ownership: A Conceptual Model of Process and Effects', *Academy of Management Review* 16, January, pp. 121–144.

Rice, A.K. (1951) *Productivity and Social Organization.* London: Tavistock Institute.

Sims, H.P. Jr and Lorenzi, P. (1992) *The New Leadership Paradigm.* Newbury Park, CA: Sage, Chapter 13.

Thorndike, E.L. (1965) *Animal Intelligence: Experimental Studies.* New York, NY: Hafner [orig. 1911], p. 244.

Toffler, A. (1981) *The Third Wave.* New York, NY: Bantam Books.

Trist, E.L. and Bamforth, K.W. (1951), 'Some Social and Psychological Consequences of Coal Getting', *Human Relations* 1, Tavistock Institute.

Wheeler, D. (1997) 'Why it's all Over for Them and Us', *Independent on Sunday*, 20 April.

Zammuto, R.F. (1984) 'A Comparison of Multiple Constituency Models of Organizational Effectiveness', *Academy of Management Review* 9, October, pp. 606–616.

Organisational strategy, planning and continuous improvement

The opening vignette demonstrates how a successful business can bring about social change and be profitable.

Anita Roddick: the Body Shop

Anita Roddick opened the first Body Shop in Brighton, England, in 1976. This one small shop, selling around 25 hand-mixed products, developed into a multi-million-pound business with a worldwide network of shops. Anita Roddick, a once unemployed mother, went on to become Businesswoman of the Year, Communicator of the Year, Retailer of the Year, and the recipient of the United Nations Environmentalist Award to the Amazon, where she started cottage industries to help save the rainforest.

Anita Roddick's philosophy is that you can run a successful business and make money, but you can also use that money for social change. She has become an ambassador for free enterprise, social consciousness and success.

Roddick started her business retailing home-made, naturally inspired products with minimal packaging. The franchising of her ideas in the late 1970s and early 1980s saw new shops opening at the rate of two a month. In 1985 it became a public company. In spite of now being accountable to shareholders, it sponsored Greenpeace and later set up its own in-house environmental department. In 1989 it set up its first franchise in the USA. By 1990, the Body Shop was trading in 39 countries. In 1994 the direct selling arm of Body Shop was launched; by 2001, in the UK alone, there were over 3000 consultants selling its products.

The Body Shop has continued its environmental practices, its head office uses renewable sources of energy and its aim is to convert all its shops to green electricity. It campaigns against animal testing and has linked up with Amnesty International to highlight the plight of human rights defenders around the world.

In 1995, the Body Shop put its beliefs to the test when it committed its first social audit. The results of its audits were independently verified and published in the Body Shop's Values Report. These reports were recognised by the United Nations Environment Programme as 'trailblazing', and ranked highest in its reviews of international corporate environmental reports.

In 2001, the Body Shop celebrated 25 years of 'business as unusual': 'Celebrating 25 years of a great experiment – an experiment which proved it is possible to build a huge global enterprise and still challenge, campaign, trade honourably, give back to the community and have a good time while doing it.'

The Body Shop has a vision – even today it still retains its trademark emphasis on naturally inspired products using traditional recipes. Its community trade programme creates sustainable trading relationships with disadvantaged communities around the world. The goal is to help build livelihoods and to explore trade-based approaches to supporting sustainable development by sourcing ingredients and accessories from socially and economically marginalised producer communities.

The Body Shop is a stakeholder-led company. It believes its success is dependent upon its relationships with all its stakeholders, including its employees, franchisees, customers, communities, suppliers, Body Shop at Home consultants, shareholders and campaigning partners.

The Body Shop has evolved from one small shop to a public company listed on the London stock exchange. The company has 5000 employees worldwide. It trades through over 1900 stores in 50 markets around the world. It has done all this while maintaining its mission statement of 'A Company with a Difference'.

In early 2006 the Body Shop agreed a deal with cosmetics giant L'Oréal. Critics have suggested that Body Shop is getting into bed with 'the enemy' because L'Oréal has not abandoned animal testing; something rejected by Dame Anita, who said the £652 million deal was a chance to strike a fairer deal for the world's poor.

However, Anita Roddick stated that the Body Shop was about values and not just animal testing, saying, 'The most exciting thing about this is that L'Oréal is asking us to teach it about community trade, which is the best poverty eradicator in the world.' Roddick will remain in her current role as a consultant and insists that Body Shop's ethics will not change. 'I don't see it as selling out,' she says. 'For both Gordon [her husband] and I, this is without doubt the best 30th anniversary gift the Body Shop could have received. L'Oréal has displayed visionary leadership in wanting to be an authentic advocate and supporter of our values.'

L'Oréal agrees that, 'The acquisition reinforces the portfolio of L'Oréal brands with a brand that is very complementary and with a strong identity and strong values. L'Oréal undertakes to respect these values. A partnership between our companies makes perfect sense. Combining L'Oréal's expertise and knowledge of international markets with the Body Shop's distinct culture and values will benefit both companies.'

Supporters of Roddick's campaigns for fairer trade and on green issues were dismayed by the deal and *Ethical Consumer* magazine, which ranks firms according to their ethical credentials, urged consumers to boycott Body Shop if the deal goes through.

Source: www.bodyshop.co.uk.

Discussion questions

1 Do you think the Body Shop would be as successful if it had decided that ethics were not important?

2 Who are the stakeholders of the Body Shop?

3 Do you think the Body Shop will be able to sustain its ethical credibility now that it is part of the L'Oréal group?

Strategic thinking, planning and continuous improvement are fundamental to every organisation, even those that are not as global in perspective as the Body Shop. Whether pulling people together to publish a newspaper, film a movie, fight a war or manufacture television sets, crafting strategies and planning results-orientated actions are a part of all organised human activity. Having a vision and a mission and bringing people together to plan the actions necessary to carry out strategies are essential to achieving goals and bolstering organisational success. But a vision and plan need careful implementation and evaluation with a focus on adjustments and continuous improvement.

Nadler *et al.* (1995) point out that it is not just the tangible 'plans' that are important. Also important is the process by which plans are developed, for increasingly managers are drawing in people at lower levels in the organisation to participate in the planning process. Everyone expects senior managers to be strategic thinkers. But if first-line managers and technically experienced professionals are to be engaged in business planning, they too need to develop the skills to think strategically.

How a manager begins to think strategically

All organisational professionals improve their skills by learning to think strategically. **Strategic thinking** involves envisioning and planning a workable fit between organisational competencies and limitations on the one hand and external opportunities and threats on the other, with the aim of continuously improving the relationship between the organisation and its environment. Thinking strategically means anticipating what actions and behaviours are most likely to help the organisation prosper in a changing environment. Mintzberg (1987) argues that managing strategy involves the craft of balancing stability and consistency over time with changes when needed. For established, mature organisations, much of the time strategic decisions involve refining a basic way of doing business rather than abruptly charting a new course.

strategic thinking
A process of envisioning and planning to create a workable match between organisational competencies (and limitations) and external opportunities (and threats) with the goal of better serving customers.

Exhibit 3-1 shows the cycle of strategy-related processes common to all types of organisations. It suggests a sequential flow of decisions throughout the organisation, although in practice there may be a dynamic interplay among these activities. The exhibit serves as a reminder of important strategic elements in planning ways to add value to the organisation and keep it viable over time. But Exhibit 3-1 is just one way to model planning, with numerous variations on the theme. Because planning is more art than science, the critical need for any specific organisation is to tailor its planning processes and strategy cycle to its unique strengths and competencies (Campbell, 1999).

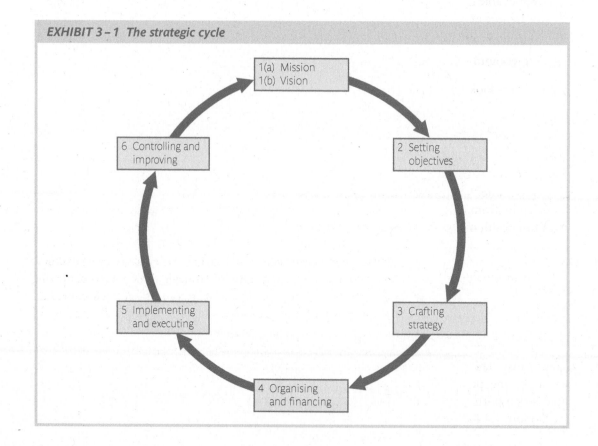

EXHIBIT 3 – 1 The strategic cycle

1(a) Mission
1(b) Vision

2 Setting objectives

3 Crafting strategy

4 Organising and financing

5 Implementing and executing

6 Controlling and improving

Managing strategically involves striking a balance among environmental forces and the available human, technical and financial resources. The strategic cycle can be symbolised by a circular flow among these six key processes.

As introduced in Chapter 2, the *vision* and *mission* that are articulated by managers and reiterated at every opportunity should serve as guides for organisational behaviour. This is especially true in *setting key objectives*, articulated as mission-consistent measurable results to be achieved by specific times in the future. Objectives help frame the choices for *crafting strategy* that charts a course for the future make-up of products and services and targeted customer bases. Any strategy, whether revised or new, requires commitments to *organising* who and which units will carry out the plan, as well as budgeting and *financing* the resources to achieve the objectives. The saying 'the devil is in the detail' certainly applies to the processes of *implementing the strategy*, for it is here that products and systems are changed or created, incentives and rewards established, information networks linked, and leadership provided to mobilise human energy and shape interactions within and across units throughout the organisation. Finally, it is critical to *control and improve on* the intended strategy with the aim of achieving continuous improvement. All these tasks draw on the manager's perception, learning and problem-solving skills. Goals and objectives are not worthwhile unless they are capable of being measured and achieved. Another way of saying this is that objectives need to be *SMART*.

SMART objectives are:

- **Specific** – they need to be focused and relevant to the vision of the organisation
- **Measurable** – there must be some quantifiable method to measure the objectives
- **Achievable** – an objective must be seen as being within reach; no one will make the effort to achieve an unattainable objective
- **Realistic** – all objectives should deal with a manageable feature of the organisation
- **Timebound** – there should be a deadline.

We will now look in more detail at the six key processes depicted in Exhibit 3-1.

1(a) Craft a mission to define a common purpose

Whether a business firm, a non-profit organisation or a government agency, every organisation has a mission, or cause, intended to unite and provide direction to its members. Some organisations are created out of community need. A police force is created to protect people within the community from careless or criminal acts. A hospital cares for the health needs of the community, from health maintenance to active treatment.

mission

The fundamental purpose of an enterprise that defines the nature of its business and provides strategic direction to unify the use of human and other resources.

Chapter 2 introduced the mission of an enterprise as its fundamental purpose, articulated to define the nature of its business and provide a unifying sense of strategic direction in deploying human, technical and financial resources. A well-conceived mission answers the questions: Why do we exist and what do we do? Who are we and where are we headed? A mission should serve as a rallying cry to induce organisational members to take up its cause. This is epitomised by VSO's (Voluntary Service Overseas) mission, which wants to attract young people to volunteer during their gap year, or Fairtrade, an organisation that actively supports producers in countries in the developing world to give them a better deal.

Exhibit 3-2 lists five essential characteristics of a well-framed mission statement. Once the

---

EXHIBIT 3 – 2 *Purpose served by a well-articulated mission statement*

To be useful, a statement of mission should:

1 articulate the vision that defines the business, what it is, what it is not, and what it should be in the future

2 communicate to internal members and external constituencies a clear sense of meaning and direction that is motivating and energising

3 convey which customer wants or needs it will seek to satisfy, and the target markets it will serve

4 identify the value-adding functions it will perform, realising its specific enabling actions will change over time while the purpose endures

5 be of bumper-sticker length – brief enough to be incorporated into corporate communications and easily remembered.

---

mission statement is cast, it is expected to provide guidance for specific goals and strategies for years to come. But with the passage of time, mission statements have to be reassessed and even reformulated.

When Marks & Spencer started as a market stall in 1884 it was very different from what it is today as one of the UK's leading retailers of clothing, foods, homeware and financial services, serving 10 million customers a week in over 300 UK stores. Yet its survival has been down to its ability to reinvent itself and respond to changes in the market to keep it competitive.

Missions become complicated when an organisation branches beyond its original line of business. This was highlighted in the example of the Virgin Group in Chapter 2. A company that started out selling records has a very different mission from a company that includes an airline, holidays and financial services.

1(b) Use a vision to set the direction for a desired future

The concepts of mission and vision are sometimes used interchangeably by managers. The two are interrelated, but to distinguish between the two: a mission is normally expected to provide direction that stretches beyond the foreseeable future; visions change more frequently, are often more detailed, and can be specific to a product, programme or project. A **vision** incorporates current realities and expected future conditions to create a desired organisational scenario and outcome within a relevant time frame: 'A vision belongs to what we may term a process of direction setting. Direction setting connotes the identification of something in the future (a vision scenario), often the distant future, and a strategy for getting there' (El-Namaki, 1992). Three elements are fundamental to a comprehensive, meaningful vision: a purpose, a goal and an image of results (Collins and Porras, 1991).

vision

A desired future image of the organisation, and its processes and products, that integrates current realities and expected future conditions within a specific time frame.

A statement of purpose

First, ideology and core values are combined in an explicit *statement of purpose*. The purpose need not be meaningful to outsiders but should inspire and motivate insiders. The executives of Kodak Film, realising that in the future digital imaging will experience a more robust market than photos, expanded its purpose with the aim: 'to be the world's best in chemical and electronic imaging'.

A tangible goal

The second element of a vision, *creation of a tangible goal*, begins with a vision statement that frames a clear, specific and compelling goal that focuses people's efforts. A well-framed goal has a target and a time frame for its attainment. To achieve one of Asda parent company Wal-Mart's visions of maintaining consistent growth, founder Sam Walton gave employees their goal for the 1990s at the 1990 annual shareholders' meeting. The target was to double the number of stores and increase income volume per square foot by 60 per cent, and the time frame was to accomplish this by the year 2000. This was a very tangible and meaningful goal that was attained ahead of schedule before the end of the decade. This goal helped focus effort and signal what was meaningful, furthermore, although Walton's goal focused on the US market, Wal-Mart had already become the largest retailer in Mexico and was well on its way to achieving the same status in Germany and other countries by the end of the decade (Feldman, 1999). However, with limited experience in cross-cultural adaptability, its progress towards achieving growth goals outside the United States was far from smooth, as noted in the World Watch box.

Wal-Mart takes on the French in Argentina

One of the guiding principles for multinational firms is to 'think globally, act locally'. But for organisations whose success has been proven in one country before extending their reach beyond domestic borders, adapting to foreign local realities is often a lesson learned by trial and error – a lot of error. Such was the case with Wal-Mart's entry into Argentina during the late 1990s.

Carrefour, the French general merchandise chain (second largest in the world), arrived in Argentina in 1982, and by 2000 was well established as the dominant retailer in that country with 23 big stores. Argentine shoppers have become accustomed to all things French, from fashion to late-night dining. Yet with globalisation, a greater acceptance of American influences began to creep into the Argentine culture in the 1990s – more casual dress, consumption of more beer and less wine, and even jazz and the blues. Thus, when Wal-Mart entered the Argentine market, it did so with a team of American managers and store models that worked in big- and small-town America.

Wal-Mart's merchandising and facilities were not an immediate hit with Argentine shoppers: jewellery including emeralds, sapphires and diamonds was not of great interest to women who prefer the simplicity of gold and silver. Tools and appliances wired for 110-volt electrical power were useless with Argentina's 220-volt standard. Carpeted aisles were too narrow and difficult to keep clean given the Argentine habit of shopping daily, which meant more traffic and, thus, crowded, dirty aisles.

Given its early difficulty in learning to get it right with the Argentines, Wal-Mart overhauled its top management team four times in four years for its 13-store operation. Concedes Donald C. Bland, president and CEO of Wal-Mart Argentina, as it entered the 2000s, 'Following our blueprint too closely wasn't a good idea.'

Argentine economist Martin Redrado observed, 'Carrefour better understood from the beginning the local idiosyncrasies and managed its strategy around local conditions.' And, adds retail analyst David Shriver, 'They [Wal-Mart] have adapted pretty well, and they have stolen a lot of ideas from Carrefour.'

Source: adapted from Clifford Krauss (2000) 'French Give Wal-Mart a Sales Lesson', *New York Times* News Service, 16 January.

world watch

Discussion questions

1 How important is it to know the culture before expanding into other countries?
2 How did Wal-Mart's lack of flexibility affect the business in Argentina?

An image of results

The final element in crafting a vision is creating a *vivid image of the results*. The image should paint a compelling picture using crisp language. Henry Ford projected this in his original vision for Ford: 'I will build a motor car for the great multitude – it will be so low in price that no man making a good salary will be unable to own one. When I'm through everybody will be able to afford one, and everyone will have one. The horse will have disappeared from our highways, the automobile will be taken for granted.' Ford's vision conveyed a clear picture of the future, and it was realised within two generations.

Although, ideally, a vision should contain these three elements – a statement of purpose, a tangible goal and an image of results – research by Kriger (1990), Hunt (1991), Nanus (1992) and Greenwood and Hinings (1993) suggests that one finding can be generalised: the faster an industry changes, the more the articulation of a vision needs to be communicated to insiders. A vision enables the people who design, build, sell and service products to internalise a greater sense of purpose and meaning in the projects and activities they undertake (Kouzes and Posner, 1995; Larwood *et al.*, 1995).

2 Set objectives to define measurable results

If visions are to become tangible, the broad-based visionary goal of building a better mousetrap needs to be broken apart into operational objectives. Objectives convert visionary intentions into specific performance targets that can be measured at designated points in time. A well-framed objective requires effort and teamwork to achieve. It should be bold and aggressive, and exhibit a sense of urgency. By using quantitative measures organisations can also compare their unit's performance over time and to outcomes achieved in other organisations, a process called benchmarking. However, Campbell (1999) suggests that an organisation should not end up simply chasing the best practices of others, for to do so runs the risk of moving away from the core competencies that already add value to the venture.

objectives
Specific performance targets that can be measured at designated points in time.

benchmarking
Comparing a unit's performance to outcomes achieved in other outstanding organisations.

Management by objectives (MBO) is a widely applied method of managing, but it is not always clear what is meant by MBO. The 'Research focus' box discusses the work of Peter Drucker, a writer on management and organisations. We will also be meeting MBO again when we discuss methods and applications of employee performance in Chapter 7.

Research focus: Management by objectives (Peter Drucker)

Many organisations have tried to place the emphasis of accountability on the results expected of employees rather than their activities. This has become known as management by objectives (MBO).

Drucker (1989b) noted the advantages of managing managers by 'objectives' rather than 'drives'. Each manager, from the highest to the lowest, has clear objectives that reflect and support the objectives of the organisation. All managers take part in the goal-setting process and then exercise 'self-control' over their own performance; this means they monitor and evaluate their performance against their objectives and correct it where necessary.

The focus of MBO

MBO is a general management philosophy, applied both to performance and evaluation. There is no one best way to manage by objectives. MBO must be adapted to the needs of the organisation. It reflects the positive and proactive, rather than reactive method of managing.

MBO focuses on:

- predicting and shaping the future of the organisation by developing long-range organisational objectives and strategic plans
- accomplishing results rather than performing activities
- improving individual competence and organisational effectiveness
- increasing participation and involvement of employees in all aspects of the organisation.

MBO also consists of a series of integrated management functions:

- the development of clear, precise organisational objectives
- the formulation of co-ordinated individual objectives to help achieve the overall organisational objectives
- the systematic measurement and evaluation of performance
- the use of corrective actions to achieve the planned objectives.

Phases of MBO

Phase one

Evaluating the performance of managers. The emphasis is on developing measurable objectives for each manager and evaluating them at the end of a set time period.

Phase two

The MBO programmes are integrated into the organisation's planning and control and budgetary processes. Management support is obtained. The emphasis is placed on the training and development of employees.

Phase three

This is the fully implemented MBO system. All the major organisational functions are integrated in a logical manner. These functions include performance evaluations, financial planning, development of strategic plans and goals, employee and management development. The emphasis for integration is on teamwork and flexibility during the goal-setting process and by emphasising individual development and performance.

Benefits of MBO

- Improved management: MBO forces managers to think about planning for results, how the results are to be accomplished and the resources required.
- Clarity of the organisation: it forces managers to clarify organisation roles and structures, and makes sure they have the key people where they are needed.
- Personal commitment: it encourages people to commit themselves to goals. Employees have a part in setting their objectives and have support from managers to enable them to achieve their goals. This helps to create commitment.

- Effective control: MBO involves the measuring of results, evaluating and taking action. A clear set of goals makes measurement and control easier.

Evaluation of MBO

- MBO is widely practised in management, but sometimes it is not as effective as it could be. This is due in part to faulty implementation.
- MBO is often applied as a mechanistic technique that focuses on selected aspects of the management process without integration as a whole.
- MBO has been compared with scientific management, as it concentrates too much on the individual performance and requires vast amounts of data and analysis (Crainer, 1998).
- Excessive concern with economic results can lead to unethical behaviour.
- It is not always easy to set targets for senior management or jobs where a high degree of interpersonal skills are required.
- Many goals are short term. Managers may concentrate on these at the expense of long-term goals.
- It can be inflexible. If goals cease to be meaningful managers may not want to change employees' objectives as it may affect the plan.

Any type of organisation needs to specify objectives focusing on two types of performance outcome: financial and strategic. Even in non-profit or government organisations, *financial objectives* are critical to guiding the long-term viability of the enterprise. A variety of financial measures can be used, including expenditure variances against budget, unit costs per activity, revenue per employee, contribution margins (profits as a percentage of revenues) or earnings per share. Notwithstanding the new economy's willingness to bid up the share price of dotcom firms without a record of profitability, the attainment of financial objectives is a fact of life for business managers, regardless of industry (Vickers and Coy, 2000).

Strategic objectives are used to assess performance against the specific design of a strategy. Here a variety of measures are used, some more or less common across strategies, others more programme-specific. Common measures are competitive product performance features, time to market (in designing and delivering new products), market share and customer satisfaction. Strategic objectives in particular need to be time-specific in order to be able to assess short-term performance against longer-term criteria.

The 3M Company illustrates how objectives can be set in both financial and strategic terms:

> To achieve annual growth in earnings per share of 10 per cent or better, on average; a return on stockholders' equity of 20–25 per cent; a return on capital employed of 27 per cent or better; and have at least 30 per cent of sales come from products introduced in the past four years.

So stated, these objectives are tangible and measurable, and thus effective guides for human behaviour.

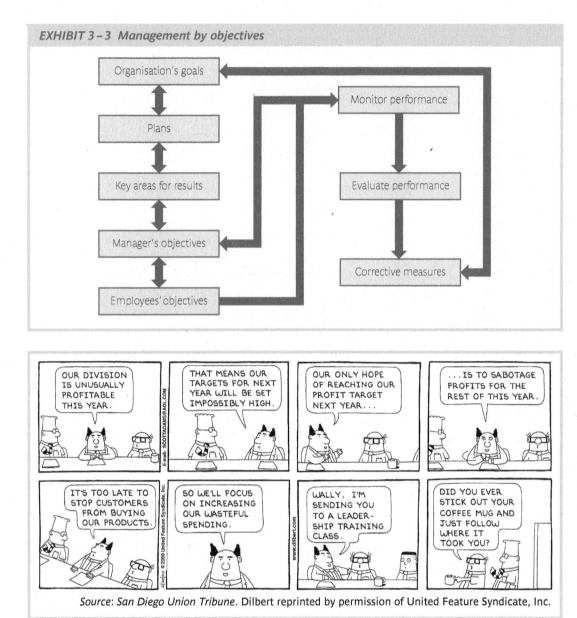

EXHIBIT 3–3 Management by objectives

Source: *San Diego Union Tribune*. Dilbert reprinted by permission of United Feature Syndicate, Inc.

3 Craft strategy to fulfil the mission and vision

strategy

A plan of actions to achieve a favourable position within the competitive marketplace by strengthening the relationship between an organisation's capabilities and its changing environment.

To achieve the objectives that flow from the mission and vision, every organisation – be it governmental, non-profit or a business – needs to craft multiple strategies. A **strategy** is a plan of major actions crafted to achieve a favourable position within the competitive marketplace by strengthening the relationship between an organisation's capabilities and its changing environment. Strategies pertain to those destiny-shaping decisions concerning:

- the choice of technologies on which products and services are based
- the development and release of new products and services

- the processes for producing products and services
- the way products and services are marketed, distributed and priced
- the ways in which the organisation responds to rivals.

Businesses as well as non-business entities depend on strategies to help employees or members plan new programmes or revitalise services so that constituencies are better served. Consider the essential decisions Federal Express (FedEx) had to make in crafting its initial strategy.

Federal Express was created by Frederick Smith on the premise that organisations would pay for guaranteed next-day delivery of parcels, something the postal service could not guarantee at the time. Fundamental to this vision was the strategy of routing all aircraft through a single airport hub in the country of operation. It meant that a package shipped from Paris on Tuesday afternoon destined for Rome would be sorted at Geneva during the night and then shipped aboard another plane to Rome for delivery by Wednesday morning. To make the hub-and-spoke concept work in shipping packages, FedEx had to create an international network of airports, aeroplanes, trucks and computers. It also had to find financing, organise people into a network structure, and create systems to provide consistency and reliability.

4 Organising and financing to support strategy

Two planning processes are close companions to crafting strategy, and they must be resolved before (or at least concurrently with) implementation. The **organising** function plans the supportive structures and systems needed to align people to the strategy. **Financing** requires budget preparation and finding or determining sources of funding to meet both capital requirements (for facilities, equipment and technology) and for operating expenses (such as payroll and purchasing of supplies and materials).

In organising, **structure** provides a way of grouping people and tasks into departments or subunits, and defining the linkages among departments so that work flows and decision authority are co-ordinated and communicated. At FedEx, a geographical structure had to be organised to connect managers and operations at terminals in each major airport and to grant terminal managers the authority to organise employees into work groups to perform tasks in each location. Structures also had to be created for managing the logistics of scheduling aircraft and pilots, and for purchasing airplanes and trucks.

Systems provide guidelines or processes for handling recurring transactions and events in a standardised or consistent way. FedEx systems had to be developed and maintained, beginning with the computers and information system for routing and tracking parcels, accounts receivable, aircraft and delivery vans. The systems extended from accounting for employee time to purchasing barcode labels and billing corporate accounts. The combination of structures and systems enabled FedEx to organise to carry out the hub-and-spoke strategy.

organising
The management function that plans supportive structures and systems that align people to the strategy.

financing
The management function involving budget preparation and finding or determining sources of funding to meet requirements for capital investments and operating expenses.

structure
Organisational groupings of people and tasks into departments or work units to promote co-ordination of communication, decisions and action.

systems
Guidelines or structured processes for handling recurring transactions and events in a standardised or consistent way.

5 Implementing and executing strategy

The greatest concentration of management and non-management effort occurs with implementation (or execution) of strategy. This is the stage where most managers and certainly most non-managers are involved and where investments are made and costs incurred. Implementation involves everything from acquiring facilities and developing products/services (sometimes by acquisition or merger), to developing channels of distribution, and marketing tactics. It also often involves recruiting new employees or contract personnel (including temporaries) and providing incentives and rewards.

Above all, implementation requires leadership, the formation of teams and the nurturing of a supportive organisational culture. Implementation is a very action-orientated activity that converts all the planning that came before into make-it-happen results. Typically this is where the efforts of several different activity centres are supposed to flow together, where conflicts occur, and where integration and co-ordination are put to the test. Most of the chapters of this book provide insights and techniques for guiding the implementation process.

6 Controlling results to sustain continuous improvement

If objectives have been clearly established, control of strategy implementation typically requires measurement of results and comparisons with target expectations. Control involves the detailed assessment of performance outcomes and contributors to the outcome – something more than simply achieving a satisfactory 'bottom line'. If you have studied micro economics or finance, you might have been taught that the unique purpose of business firms is to create profits, or to maximise shareholder wealth. True, the owners and managers of businesses expect that, if they are successful, they will be profitable. Bottom-line profits generate resources for reinvestment and affect a firm's attractiveness to capital markets. But profits are the result, or the derivative, of doing several things well. While a certain level of profitability may be one objective, other objectives and measures are needed to ensure that people are focusing effort and resources on the things they have to do to bring about favourable results, to create customer satisfaction, and the like (Drucker, 1974).

A manufacturer of tennis racquets aims to create certain performance and design characteristics that appeal to a particular segment of tennis players. A software firm defines objectives and crafts a strategy to get ahead of the competition by introducing an application package that will enable potential users to do certain things more easily, quickly or accurately than they ever imagined. For the tennis player, the newly designed product may have satisfied a current need. The new software may have brought a latent need to the surface by suggesting that a product that will take the drudgery out of performing certain tasks is finally available. For either organisation evaluation needs to include measures of customer satisfaction with the new product in addition to quality checks on design and performance features of the product itself. Other measures track costs of design and development, as well as production, marketing and distribution costs, inventory levels, and other indicators of the success of the strategy.

Periodic reviews are useful if the control system and assessment process are used for defining the causes of problems and initiating corrective action. Successful organisations practise **continuous improvement**, where assessment data feed back to the teams responsible for results for the purpose of finding better ways to design, produce, package, price and deliver the product or service. Improvements may be incremental and uneven, but the processes for bringing them about are systematic rather than haphazard.

continuous improvement
Ongoing assessment and problem-solving aimed at improving designs, processes and outcomes.

Assessment therefore completes the strategic cycle, and in the process generates new visions, just as it promotes organisational learning of new skills and knowledge bases. Tools and techniques for improvement practices are explained throughout the book, based on the belief that individuals and organisations want to learn best practices and produce consistently high quality.

IKEA: trying to assemble a perfect reputation

eye on ethics

IKEA's global reach is rivalled only by McDonald's. It employs workers in some of the world's most impoverished countries, and has aggressive expansion plans for its huge retail complexes – the bane of planning authorities and traffic controllers everywhere. So how come its name is not writ large alongside those of Nike, Wal-Mart and McDonald's among the anti-globalisation protesters from Seattle to Doha.

Chief executive Anders Dahlvig is uncomfortable with the question and takes pains to highlight IKEA's past PR disasters – most notably over child labour in Asia. He knows IKEA will doubtless come a cropper again. 'There will be things we don't see. You can't protect yourself from problems altogether', he said.

Since the early 1990s, when a Swedish documentary showing children chained to the weaving looms of a supplier in Pakistan triggered protests, IKEA has made strenuous efforts to protect its 58-year-old brand.

Beyond tightening up its monitoring of suppliers, it has conducted a root-and-branch examination of its business to see where it can lessen its environmental and social impact – and has disarmed critics by enlisting their support. IKEA has given money to UNICEF to set up schools in Indian villages, and to Greenpeace, which Dahlvig describes as its 'roving conscience'.

IKEA has increased its purchasing from developing countries from 23 to 48 per cent over the past five years in its relentless drive to keep prices low. The further it goes into such countries, the more important the issue becomes. Dahlvig has only been CEO since 1999, but his first big project was to complete a code of conduct for IKEA's suppliers – a three-page document called *The IKEA way on the environment*, a tortuous process that took a year to complete.

I-way defines a single set of standards for its 1400 suppliers – the same rules apply in Sweden (still its main source of supply) as in China – and three levels of check include independent auditing. *I-way* sits on the shelf beside IKEA's other bible, *Kamprad's Furniture Dealer's Testament*, which permits only economy-class flights and budget hotels, even for himself and Dahlvig.

'We're lucky because our business idea, values and vision all actually help us and point towards taking social and environmental responsibility,' Dahlvig says. 'It's in IKEA's DNA, so to speak.'

But this is not altruism. What makes the environment such a critical issue is that there is no room for compromise on the biggest part of IKEA's DNA by far: its massive warehouse retail outlets. The company operates in 22 countries but has only 143 stores, each averaging the size of three football pitches, allowing it to keep its overheads low. It vies with MFI for the top UK furniture retailer spot despite having just 11 stores. And IKEA has ambitious plans for more: it will open another 10 stores worldwide in 2001–2002 and 20 the year after; and in the UK it wants to open another 20 in the next 10 years, tripling its presence.

To maintain its position as a top furniture retailer it helps to be ethical and have a conscience.

Source: © Terry Slavin, *Observer*, 25 November 2001.

Strategic questions every manager should explore

There are no hard-and-fast rules for learning to think and manage strategically. Rather, the process is a way of analysing, planning and thinking that evaluates and anticipates the relationship between the organisation and its environment to add value in ways unique to the unit. Leaders who effectively guide strategy formulation and implementation, whether for a total organisation or a subunit, draw others into the process – a form of teaching and learning.

The teachable point of view

Executives have found that people at all levels of the organisation become strategically focused if involved in learning through teaching personal lessons about how to succeed (Wetlaufer, 1999). As researched and described by Tichy (1999), the *teachable point of view* puts the leader in front of his or her people by writing about and interactively teaching his or her personal beliefs, assumptions and models of change. Leaders teach consumer value, how to knock out competition, and how to drive strategic change down to the people who are producing value for customers and capital markets. They do this in part by sharing philosophy, and then asking, debating and finding answers to the questions on which the viability of the organisation depends.

Hinterhuber and Popp (1992) suggest that individually and collectively, managers and salaried employees learn to shape and share responses to questions such as the six that follow, to understand what they mean for the organisation. These are the types of question a manager ponders in discussions with colleagues in the hallway, over lunch, in conference rooms and in formal workshops. Eisenhardt and Galunic (2000) suggest that often the collective answers emerge over time as individual ideas are shared and actions co-evolve. Other questions raised by Ghosal *et al.* (1992) may be equally effective in provoking strategic thinking, but these are representative of the reasoning that leads to strategic organisational learning and action.

1 What business are we in?

The most basic question any organisation must answer is: 'What product or service should we market?' A related question is: 'Who is our customer and how can we provide value to that customer?' Research by Porter (1998) substantiates that organisations do best if they remain focused on a core business that takes advantage of the unique capabilities that give them competitive advantage over rivals. Even a non-profit organisation can excel if focused on a very selective set of services that match its capabilities with its mission.

Sony excels at producing and marketing consumer electronics products, but has not done so well with the acquisition of a movie studio. The difference between being a 'consumer electronics business' and an 'entertainment business' is profound, for the talent needed to make great innovative products (boxes for entertainment) is vastly different than the talent needed to produce entertainment content (movies and TV programmes).

Some businesses have only one or a few customers, such as the local smallholding that supplies the nearby hotel. Others, such as Boeing, sell a limited number of aircraft models (with airline customisation) to a hundred or so customers throughout the world. Still others, such as Procter & Gamble, sell hundreds of consumer products to thousands of retailers, which in turn sell them to millions of individual consumers.

This 'What business are we in?' question should be asked by every manager. *Every unit must serve a customer*, regardless of the department's or unit's level, function or size. For most units, the customer is one or more other departments or divisions within the organisation that receive(s) its output. Even then, however, the same dedication to increasing value for the customer should apply. For example, an information systems manager should work with other departments to find solutions to their information-processing needs. In effect, all managers of work units should think of themselves as entrepreneurs serving customer markets – and if they do not serve them well, other customers (whether external or internal) should be free to buy where they find the best deal. When Alcoa, an aluminium firm, declared that all line and staff units were free to conduct business with outside companies, productivity and sales among line units doubled.

2 What are our internal strengths and weaknesses?

A firm (or a line of business within it) should be aware of its core capabilities and sources of competitive advantage. A sustainable competitive advantage is created if a firm's core capabilities cannot readily be copied by competitors. Core capabilities are the critical skills and processes that an organisation executes so well that its reputation builds around them. Core capabilities develop if people consistently carry out the actions necessary to achieve the intended strategy.

core capabilities
The critical skills and processes that an organisation executes so well in carrying out its intended strategy that its reputation builds around them.

For example, there is nothing unique about the strategy of Marriott Corporation: simply attract travellers and diners by providing them with consistently excellent service. Marriott realises it must ignite within each employee a deep commitment to outstanding customer service. Employees are empowered to use their initiative in meeting customers' needs, backed by training and guidelines to make sure details are not overlooked. Housekeeping staff, for example, follow a 66-point guide in making up rooms; nothing is left to chance.

In addition to knowing its strengths, an organisation must recognise its limitations. Whether limited by a poorly equipped production facility or a salesforce that merely quotes prices and delivery dates, a business that acknowledges its weaknesses forces managers to assess their processes and systems. Many will conclude that they should concentrate on the functions at which they excel and outsource functions that can best be performed by vendors.

3 What external opportunities and threats do we face?

External and internal environments present both driving and restraining forces. Opportunities may occur suddenly: a key supplier agrees to form a joint venture, a regulation is relaxed, or a competitor encounters a major problem (such as a product recall). Conversely, managers need to be aware of looming threats and plan for them. Legal action, competitor product breakthroughs, and even industry-wide price cuts (common at times in the airline industry) all threaten a firm's current strategies. Undoubtedly the announced acquisition by AOL (the Internet service provider) of Time Warner (the diversified media and cable TV company) was seen as threatening to smaller Internet service providers, phone companies and video rental stores.

Furthermore, in unstable or hostile environments, managers need to plan for contingencies, adopting a 'What will we do if?' preparedness to respond to likely threats.

With the fast pace of globalisation and technology changes, what may initially present itself as an opportunity may become a threat if organisational responsiveness is too slow or not well planned. The rapid rise of the Internet with video streaming capabilities provides universities with the opportunity to use technology creatively to mediate or modify how instruction is delivered to students. Schools either lacking in resources or slow to develop competence in managing the technology–learning interface may find new competitors drawing away their students without regard to geography.

The combination of questions that assess internal *strengths* and *weaknesses* and external *opportunities* and *threats* are the keys to a process called SWOT analysis. Managers perform a **SWOT analysis** (or situational audit) whenever they assess conditions in their relevant environment in relation to internal resources and competence; that is, when they assess the relationships among strengths, weaknesses, opportunities and threats. Few experienced managers would think of planning strategies without making SWOT analysis part of the process. Exhibit 3-4 shows the SWOT elements radiating out to impact on the key strategy processes.

SWOT analysis

An assessment of internal resources and competence (Strengths and Weaknesses) in relation to conditions in an organisation's external environment (Opportunities and Threats).

Few managers will attempt to manage the strategic cycle processes without keeping in mind conclusions drawn from a SWOT analysis. To do so, they synthesise what they know about relevant external and internal forces into the four components of internal strengths and weaknesses, and external opportunities and threats.

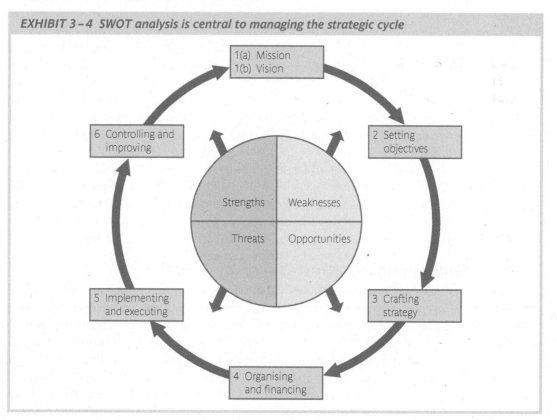

EXHIBIT 3–4 SWOT analysis is central to managing the strategic cycle

4 What business(es) should we be in?

With this question, managers seek to control their organisation's destiny. This critical question encourages managers to infuse their own values, ideology, creativity and desires into the strategic planning process, creating a vision of what the organisation is capable of becoming. Even managers of functional departments (such as marketing or design engineering) are capable of drastically altering the types of services they provide. There are really two ways to respond to this question.

First, the traditional interpretation focuses on lines of business – product and market combinations. In some firms the vision of the future organisational unit may be one of expanding output and sales by finding new markets for a basic product line, such as the Body Shop has done in moving into diverse trade channels and global markets. In other organisations, the vision is one of diversification by branching out, of moving into a broader offering of lines of business involving new combinations of products and markets. Richard Branson of Virgin expanded into other operations when he realised Virgin was being blocked by the large record companies. Virgin's first shop was the result of a postal strike and, from there, every time it has found a gap in the market it has diversified into it. In rare cases a firm may abandon its original business and redirect its resources elsewhere. Vauxhall cars, owned by General Motors, has pulled out of car manufacturing at its Luton plant to concentrate on its van business. Its cars are to be built elsewhere in the UK and Europe.

Second, management might probe the internal business processes used to bring products and services to the market. Hagel and Singer (1999) argue that three basic process networks or businesses are found in most organisations: a product innovation business, a customer relationship business, and an infrastructure business that builds and manages facilities for high-volume repetitive tasks. As transactions from any of these business processes move onto electronic networks, managers who question 'What business should we really be in?' will realise that not all of these are best performed inside the organisation. By outsourcing non-core capabilities, the organisation concentrates on what it can do better than others.

5 How do we get there?

Responses to the preceding questions cascade down into planning how to strategically position or reposition resources and actions to achieve the desired business objectives. This strategy design and implementation process involves setting direction for obtaining and allocating resources, establishing systems and policies, and, when necessary, restructuring the organisation (as indicated earlier in the strategy process cycle). Often the key is to recognise emerging possibilities and help them take shape. Mintzberg (1987) claims, 'The job of the manager is not just to preconceive specific strategies but also to recognise their emergence elsewhere in the organisation and intervene when appropriate.'

For example, managers might extend a particular product line, drive down costs by simplifying product design (to reduce labour costs and improve quality), streamline production, strengthen customer service, develop new channels of distribution, restructure the pricing policy and perhaps simplify the organisation. To successfully carry out operational strategies the firm needs a planning process that identifies critical resources, events and timetables for converting intentions into actions.

Strategies can also be enacted to phase out products that no longer contribute to the core business. Many banks have both cut back on full-service branches and extended access to ATMs and supermarket 'branches', and expanded into new lines of financial services business.

Caution pays off when launching speech-operated services

I wanted to go to Tobago but the voice on the other end of the line seemed determined to send me to Tokyo. There was no arguing with her since I was talking to a computer at the new British Airways flight information system.

Such mix-ups have become a fundamental barrier to adoption of voice-activated technology – few businesses are willing to trust a computer with their mission-critical applications while glitches remain.

However, the BA computer system quickly showed why confidence in the technology is growing. Within seconds of its mistake, the computer redeemed itself by asking whether the details were correct and on being told they were not accepted the right information. I could fly to Tobago – and the entire information had taken a few minutes, against a much longer time I might normally have had to wait to talk to a human operator in a call centre.

Furthermore, BA estimates that the cost to the company per call falls from about £2 using a call centre operator to 8 pence with the computer system. Three months since its launch, with 12 000 calls a day being made to the new service, the company expects to quickly recoup its – undeclared – investment. Cost is essential to wider adoption.

'We are now seeing a wide array of products where economic benefits of speech technology are being validated,' says Stuart Patterson, president and CEO of Speechworks, a voice technology group. 'This is helping to drive the market because we are in an environment where companies are looking to cut costs without compromising service.'

The success of high-profile projects such as the BA initiative is crucial says Ron Croen, head of rival company Nuance. 'It spreads confidence that here is a technology that is robust and reliable.' The growing awareness of such cost and service benefits is driving a diverse range of initiatives.

The UK Government recently introduced a voice-enabled tagging scheme whereby young offenders under curfew can call a police computer that recognises their voices and verifies the time and location of their calls.

Betting company Ladbrokes introduced its first voice-activated computer for the Grand National horse race in April 2002, which proved so popular that it is being extended to other events.

Lastminute.com was more cautious and has introduced voice technology gradually. It uses voice-activated systems for only parts of its organisation, although it expects their use to expand as consumer acceptance grows. One area it has targeted is technology to allow its suppliers, such as hotels and airlines, to update their inventory lists. Thus, where a hotel would have called or faxed through changes in its room availability, it can now transfer the information more speedily and cheaply with Lastminute.com's voice system.

While caution is the watchword among big corporate users, Serafino Abate, senior technologist at Ovum, the technology research group, sees more rapid growth in voice service provision. In the same way that Internet service providers currently offer web hosting services, he says, they may also provide voice-activated services.

ISPs are more likely to offer voice portals – computerised voice-activated services ranging from calendars to email to entertainment, he says.

'This could be a big opportunity for the ISPs to test new services before the advent of the next-generation 3G services.'

Source: adapted from Christopher Price (2002) 'Investment: a Voice You can Trust', *Financial Times*, 14 June, p. 13.

> ### Discussion questions
> 1 What are the problems of new technology in business?
> 2 How could poor implementation of new technology affect business?

6 How do we know we are still on the right course?

Plans need to have milestones and controls to ensure that actions correspond to plans, or to evaluate whether intended actions and goals are still feasible. **Milestones** are future dates by which certain events are scheduled to occur. Milestones are useful when a plan has several distinct components, each of which must be completed at a specified time for the entire event to occur. Managers also use controls to evaluate efficiency by comparing actual with planned performance. Actual costs can be compared with budgeted costs, or the number of service calls handled within a targeted response time can be compared with set standards or historical results.

milestones
Future dates by which certain events are planned to occur.

A control system works if it prevents deviations from a well-conceived plan. If a deviation does occur, the control process should trigger actions to bring out-of-control elements back into line with the plan's goals and milestones. For example, a local pizza delivery company guarantees to deliver within the hour or the pizza is free. Managers monitor this to ensure the pizza chefs and delivery drivers keep to target.

Results are the pay-off

results
An external acceptance or rejection of what an organisation does – satisfied customers are the hallmark of positive results.

All the plans, actions, milestones, goals and controls managers use to shape business strategy culminate in performance results. Management philosopher Drucker (1989a) emphasises that **results** are an external acceptance or rejection of what the enterprise does:

> The single most important thing to remember about any enterprise is that results exist only on the outside. The result of a business is a satisfied customer. The result of a hospital is a healed patient. The result of a school is a student who has learned something and puts it to work ten years later. Inside an enterprise, there are only costs.

The previous six questions, or variations of them, should not be asked only when an organisation is in trouble. Rather, they should be asked periodically to help managers look ahead to opportunities as well as threats. Such questions serve as the focus for management retreats, meetings and conversations with peers. Together, they create an integrated way of thinking and acting strategically within an organisation. You can practise thinking strategically by asking yourself similar questions about your 'business' and where you are going. Take a moment now to complete the 'Your turn' exercise.

Developing competitive advantage

In a practical sense, strategy begins by making decisions about which markets to compete in and what products and services to provide so that customers' needs are met and expectations exceeded. According to Welch and Nayak (1992), strategy then includes decisions about:

- how much of the product the firm should make, and how much it should buy from other firms
- whether to be technology or labour intensive
- whether to distribute through independent dealers, wholesale trade channels, a business-owned dealer network, or the Internet
- whether to aim for high-volume economies of scale, or flexibility with short product life cycles and greater customised production
- whether to price products to gain market share or to improve gross margins.

Exhibit 3-5 summarises the key concepts that come into play when an enterprise seeks to sustain a competitive advantage.

Competitive advantage occurs whenever an organisation is able to sustain an edge over its rivals in attracting customers and defending itself against competitive forces. Behind every organisation that enjoys a superior competitive advantage is a unique set of core capabilities that develop with experience and focused use of resources. For diversified firms, these capabilities should limit the lines of business that make up the portfolio of corporate strategy. Within each business unit, managers craft competitive strategies that affect actions involving technology, production, product development, marketing, pricing and other means of building a favourable position within the marketplace.

Your turn
Strategically planning your career

To give you insights into strategically focusing your career, write down your answers to the following questions. Periodically thinking through such questions can keep your career from drifting.

1 What business are you in? What is your product (the service or value you create for others)? Who is your market (what type of employer or client is willing to buy your service)?

2 What are your strengths and weaknesses as an employee or self-employed provider of services? What are your core skills and competencies?

3 What external opportunities and threats do you anticipate? Where could you best use your competencies following graduation? What can go wrong in controlling your career?

4 What business should you be in? Where would you like your career to be, say, three, five or ten years from now? What vision do you value?

5 How do you get there? What actions do you need to undertake now to reach your career vision?
   (a) What added education/training do you need?
   (b) What organisational experience do you need?

6 How do you know you are still on the right course? What milestones do you have for periodically checking up on your career progress?
                    Note: For additional help in planning your career, see Chapter 16.

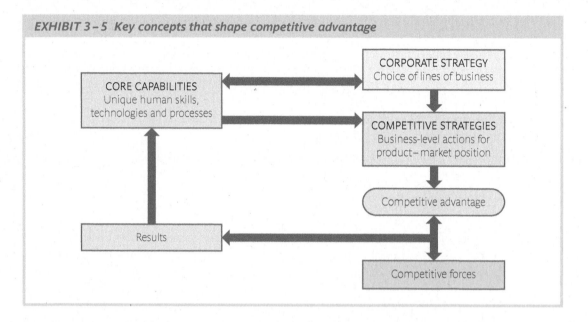

EXHIBIT 3 – 5 Key concepts that shape competitive advantage

Craft strategic actions to win competitive advantage

competitive advantage
Occurs whenever a business is able to sustain an edge over its rivals by attracting customers and defending itself against competitive forces.

A business enjoys a competitive advantage whenever it is able to sustain an edge over its rivals by attracting customers and defending itself against competitive forces (Porter, 1995). For decades the Kodak Company was the undisputed market leader in chemical-based photographic film. But, externally, the combination of world competition in film (especially by Fuji) and the emergence of digital imaging stalled Kodak's growth and profitability. Internally, a dysfunctional organisational culture and a dispirited workforce hindered Kodak. Kodak was losing its competitive advantage.

George Fisher gave up his post as CEO of Motorola, Inc. to take the helm of Kodak. He reorganised and changed strategy to reposition the rapidly fading Kodak. Fisher sold off its unrelated Sterling Drug division so that management could refocus on imaging. He also slashed debt by £8 billion to save on interest costs, reignited photography growth in global markets (especially Asia), invested heavily in digital technology, and began shaking up the sluggish management system by stressing accountability, quality and cycle time (Maremont, 1995). In short, he worked to restore and sustain Kodak's competitive advantage based in part on building capabilities in new digital technologies.

Assets and skills build organisational capabilities

To achieve a strategic competitive advantage all enterprises build their strategies around a core of physical assets, business processes, and the skills and talents of their people. The critical question is how well assets and skills combine to endow the organisation with unique capabilities. Hayes and Pisano (1994) argue that core capabilities provide the keys to long-term success by enabling the firm to combine assets and skills to do certain things better than competitors. Firms need to be cautious, however, that extreme success in combining technology with other capabilities may be viewed as restraint of trade with monopoly power – an issue that continues to confront Microsoft (Boscheck, 1994).

Hayes and Pisano (1994) conclude that the key to competitive success within manufacturing organisations is not in having equipment resources, but in 'the ability to produce [a product] efficiently, sell it efficiently, or advance it over time. Such superior organisational capabilities provide a competitive advantage that is much more sustainable than one based on something you can build or buy.' Similarly, close relationships with customers are being recognised as a source of competence since they often provide the laboratories for testing products, solving problems and even helping in the design of new product requirements for technology firms such as Cisco Systems (Prahalad and Ramaswamy, 2000).

Skills and knowledge are also critical: Hayes and Pisano (1994) argue that 'A company's capabilities are more than its physical assets. In fact, they are largely embodied in the collective skills and knowledge of its people and the organisational procedures that shape the way employees interact.' For Sun Microsystems, skill-based capabilities include rapid high-technology product development and rollout, and production flexibility. Tesco has shown the capability to consistently spot market trends, it introduced loyalty cards, recognised the need for a value range at one end of the market and a gourmet range at the other, and constantly changes its products in response to market demands (Saunders, 2002). Both companies pursued their unique strategy for managing knowledge as a critical resource – a core capability.

Corporate strategy for managing a diversified enterprise

corporate strategy

For multibusiness firms, the highest-level decisions and actions about what lines of business to be in and how to manage them.

diversification

In complex organisations, a corporate strategy of branching out beyond the core business by offering different combinations of products and markets that establish new lines of business.

For the firm as a whole, corporate strategy involves senior executive decisions about what lines of business to be in and how to manage them. Diversification is the corporate strategy of branching beyond the core capabilities that define the product technologies and markets of the current core businesses. The enterprise George Fisher took over at Kodak had been diversified into several business lines – from film, photographic paper and chemicals to cameras, digital imaging and pharmaceuticals. Porter's (1982) research on diversified firms found that competition occurs only at the business-unit level, which in a diversified firm involves a plant or division targeting a focused product line at a specific market. Consistent with this finding, one of Fisher's early corporate strategies was to refocus on photography and imaging, and to get out of the pharmaceuticals business where Kodak had no distinctive capabilities and thus no strong basis for competitive advantage.

Today many diversified (multibusiness) firms are using a couple of basic strategies to plan robust futures. One is to narrow their focus by downsizing and exercising control over fewer industries but ones they know well – their core businesses (Pound, 1992). Firms are unloading

outsourcing

The strategy of purchasing services or components from suppliers to prevent over-extending the firm beyond its core capabilities.

relative quality degradation

Occurs when the rate of improvement of an enterprise falls behind that of competitors and relegates it to second-class performance.

support services and activities that are not critical to core businesses; they are even outsourcing information technology services, facilities management and human resources (Kenny, 2002). Outsourcing is the strategy of purchasing services or components from suppliers to prevent over-extending the firm beyond its core capabilities.

Managers realise that they must not lose strength in their core businesses, otherwise their relative quality will be degraded. Relative quality degradation occurs when an enterprise's rate of continuous improvement falls behind that of competitors.

Even if product quality improves in an absolute sense, the rate of improvement relative to competitors determines growth or decline. It is better for an enterprise to be a world-class competitor in a few select lines of business than a second-class one in many.

A second basic strategy is to transform a hierarchical, bureaucratic organisation into a series of flexible internal enterprise units. The objective is to create internal markets and businesses among relatively small, semi-autonomous enterprise units. Hewlett-Packard is an example of how internal enterprise units balance freedom with control:

> Units are converted into enterprises by accepting controls on performance in return for freedom of operations. Hewlett-Packard (H-P) is famous for its entrepreneurial system that holds units accountable for results but gives them wide operating latitude. As one H-P executive described it, 'The financial controls are very tight, what is loose is how [people] meet those goals.' (Halal, 1994)

The Swedish-Swiss firm ABB has excelled at stimulating innovation by granting local autonomy among its 4500 semi-autonomous profit centres, each a separate legal entity with its own financial statements. Especially for global enterprises like ABB, competitive advantage is created more by setting up businesses in locations that offer unique capabilities than by shifting production facilities globally in pursuit of low-cost labour (Bartmess and Cerny, 1993).

Competitive strategies at the business-unit level

competitive strategy
Actions at the level of a specific line of business intended to create a competitive advantage by planned actions about where to compete and how to compete.

Many firms compete across multiple lines of business – they have pursued diversification. Competitive strategy is possible only within specific lines of business, where competitive advantage can be created through making choices about *where to compete* (the markets and segments, the type of rivals one goes up against) and *how to compete* (on the basis of product features, manufacturing, pricing, distribution, and so on) (Aaker, 1989).

Designing an integrated set of competitive strategies requires creativity and innovation in one or more spheres of business activity. In researching how companies succeed in international markets, Porter (1990) states:

> Companies achieve competitive advantage through acts of innovation. They approach innovation in its broadest sense, including both new technologies and new ways of doing things. They perceive a new basis for competing or find better means for competing in old ways.

National competitiveness through innovation

On a global level, if one nation's firms in a once-dominant industry begin to lag behind competitors in another region of the world, that nation loses global market share. Once the decline begins, it often accelerates, as has occurred in the UK clothes manufacturing industry. When Asian countries were able to produce goods of equal quality but at a lower cost, UK manufacturers lost out. After completing a four-year study in 10 countries, Porter (1990) concluded, 'A nation's competitiveness depends on the capacity of its industry to innovate and upgrade.' Furthermore, 'Once a country achieves competitive advantage through an innovation, it can sustain it only through relentless improvement.' Porter also found that a primary driver of such innova-

clusters
Geographic concentrations of interconnected organisations in a particular field.

tion is the dominance of regional industry clusters: 'Clusters are geographic concentrations of interconnected companies and institutions in a particular field [that] encompass an array of linked industries and other entities important to competition.' Clusters provide local knowledge, relationships, motivation, sources of capital, and infrastructure that stimulates dynamic co-operation as well as competition. Well-known examples are Hollywood for movies, Dagenham, Essex, for Ford cars.

Craft strategy before action

Strategy is the glue that holds the organisation together by unifying plans throughout. Competitive strategy is the pattern of actions that focus an organisation's resources and core competencies on achieving a sustained competitive advantage in chosen environments. Managing strategically is a process of 'making choices that best align the organisation with environmental demands' (Thakur and Calingo, 1992). Every manager, regardless of position within the organisation, needs to think strategically before initiating major actions, for every organisational unit is responsible for strategy. Exhibit 3-6 provides an example of how a successful entrepreneur develops strategy before starting new ventures.

Why planning is an exercise in organisational learning

The preceding discussion suggests that planning should be a rational, analytical process based on the facts of a situation. In reality, planning is more about organisational learning than about programming a series of activities to attain an objective (De Geus, 1988). As the former head of planning at Shell noted, 'The real purpose of effective planning is not to make plans but to change the ... mental models that ... decision-makers carry in their heads.' A generation ago, senior executives got caught up in strategic planning as 'the thing to do' but in this earlier

---

EXHIBIT 3 – 6 Four steps for success in business start-up planning

Norm Brodsky has started six new businesses, three of which have been included in the Inc. 500. After observing the business of entrepreneurs and checking out their performance numbers, he offers the following advice (applicable primarily to non-dotcom businesses). Although your text focuses on understanding human behaviour, numbers remain important and cannot be ignored. For entrepreneur Brodsky, the numbers are fundamental to disciplining the mind of the manager. He recommends the following:

1 'Get a grip on your emotions and decide on your goals.' He emphasises goals that centre on preserving capital and maintaining gross profit margins in early years.

2 'Make sure you understand what cash flow is and where it's going to come from.' The centrepiece of a business plan is cash flow, and cash flow is about making the right kind of sales. Realise that capital is limited and make sure it lasts long enough to make the business viable with sufficient cash to cover expenses.

3 'Recognise the sales mentality before it's too late.' Successful entrepreneurs fixate on making sales go up every day, every week, every month. Sales, rather than earnings, should be the early goal. But entrepreneurs should also protect capital, and go after the highest gross margin the business can sustain while keeping sales increasing.

4 'Learn to anticipate and recognise the changes in your business.' The biggest change occurs once critical mass is attained. Critical mass is a threshold necessary for the business to take off, such as the size of the customer base. Critical mass is the point at which internally generated cash flow allows the business to grow without needing outside investment.

Source: Bo Burlingham (1995), 'How to Succeed in Business in 4 Easy Steps', *Inc.* 17 (July), pp. 30–42. Reprinted by permission of *Inc.*

approach to planning, planning was divorced from doing; it was something to assign to staff analysts. Thus, strategic planning became detailed analyses to support strategies managers had already envisioned.

Today, planning is the responsibility of all managers and typically of work teams, and it involves participation, empowerment and commitment more than it does making calculations. When managers plan, the emphasis is on strategic thinking, not on strategic planning. As Mintzberg (1994) emphasised:

> Strategic planning is not strategic thinking. Indeed, strategic planning often spoils strategic thinking, causing managers to confuse real vision with the manipulation of numbers ... Strategic thinking ... is about *synthesis*. It involves intuition and creativity. The outcome of strategic thinking is an integrated perspective of the enterprise, a not-too-precisely-articulated vision of direction.

Mintzberg's words are not an indictment of planning, but an encouragement not to treat it as a mechanistic, highly analytical and formalised process to be delegated to staff. Organisations do need to plan, but planning begins when managers lead, rather than delegate, the process.

Planning helps reorientate vision and direction

All firms that expect to grow or reposition themselves need to plan their strategic moves. After a few years of successful growth, most leaders latch on to a formula that seems to work; they develop core capabilities and learn how to be competitive. But most organisations encounter periods of crisis in which the winning formula that created success under one set of conditions no longer propels growth. Drucker (1980) refers to this as the need to 'slough off yesterday' and reposition for the future.

In part because of their size and past success, industry giants encounter difficulty when yesterday's collective decisions no longer fit new realities. Peters (1992) declares bluntly, 'Success breeds failure. The challenge of reinvention is absolutely required.' Nevertheless, the need to reinvent the future and slough off yesterday applies even to the smallest organisational unit. Any department or subunit needs to plan how it will continually revitalise its contribution. Otherwise, it may be absorbed into another unit or axed altogether.

British Airways, Marks & Spencer, General Motors, IBM and Kodak have all experienced struggles to reorientate their organisations to futures that differ from the success factors of an earlier era. In some firms management beliefs are too anchored to the past and the senior executive too entrenched. In others, management is blind to internal weaknesses (such as too many layers of managers) or key environmental changes (such as shifting customer demands or rapid advancements in technology). In still others, plans are poorly conceived and executed, whether they focus on product development, acquisition or defences against anti-trust litigation. Competent managers typically think of planning and implementation as a continuous process, a responsive flow of values, information, goals, decisions and resources throughout the organisation. General Electric (GE) has made significant progress in repositioning its 20 lines of business through such processes (Colvin, 2000). Exhibit 3-7 identifies the key issues GE managers work through in their planning process.

planning
The process of establishing objectives and specifying how they are to be accomplished in a future that is uncertain.

Planning and controlling events, behaviours and resources are critical parts of every manager's job. **Planning** is the process of establishing objectives and specifying how and when they are

---

EXHIBIT 3–7 GE's simple formula for global competitiveness

To reduce the bureaucratic hierarchy and speed up the flow of strategic decisions at General Electric, the top 100 or so managers meet together as the corporate executive council (CEC) for two days every quarter. CEO Jack Welch at times asks leaders of GE's business units to reduce their analyses to one-page answers to each of five questions.

1 What are your global market dynamics today; where are they going over the next few years?

2 What actions have competitors taken in the last three years to upset those global dynamics?

3 What have you done in the last three years to upset those global dynamics?

4 What are the most dangerous things your competitor could do in the next three years to upset those dynamics?

5 What are the most effective things you could do to bring your desired impact on those global dynamics?

Sharing responses to these questions allows everyone to know the basic game plan and plays across the 14 or so major lines of business.

Sources: adapted from Noel Tichy and Ram Charan (1989), 'Speed, Simplicity, Self-confidence: An Interview with Jack Welch', *Harvard Business Review* 67 (September–October), p. 115; and Terence P. Paré (1994), 'Jack Welch's Nightmare on Wall Street', *Fortune* 130 (5 September), pp. 40–48.

---

to be accomplished in an uncertain future. When it works well, planning helps individuals and groups visualise desired outcomes and anticipate the behaviours and resources necessary to make them a reality. Controlling is the process of evaluating whether outcomes match objectives and, if not, analysing why and taking corrective action. Control involves measuring and assessing performance to increase the probability that behaviours and resources support plans or that plans are re-evaluated as circumstances change.

controlling
The process of evaluating the degree to which outcomes match objectives; and, when they do not, analysing why and taking corrective action.

The dynamics of planning and managing strategically cannot be distilled into a predetermined set of steps. Nevertheless, managers draw on common elements to give direction and meaning to their plans. Effective managers combine ideology with environmental scanning perceptions to articulate a strategic vision. A manager's ideology is his or her values and beliefs about how to succeed in business, which runs the gamut from economic assumptions to ethical ideals. Although these factors vary among firms and managers, a manager's ideology weaves its way into his or her approach towards planning, as well as into the outcomes of planning.

ideology
Beliefs and values held by a manager about how to succeed in business; encompasses economic assumptions and ethical ideals.

The paradox of managing by ideology in the information age

management by information
A structured system of information management based on developing clear, specific goals and plans for all managers to use in analysing problems by studying cause–effect relationships.

Two systems of management have been identified by Cummings (1983), one based on information and the other on ideology. Organisations that encourage management by information believe in developing clear, specific goals and plans, where managers analyse problems by studying cause-and-effect relationships. Thought processes are expected to be logical and directed towards well-defined systems and structures. Upper managers manipulate the symbols of success: promotions and bonuses, larger offices on higher floors, prestigious job titles, and so on. Lower managers are rewarded for passing relevant information upwards and carrying out operational plans that emanate from higher up. Information is believed to be truth.

Does this sound like your ideal approach to management? If so, take comfort in the fact that for generations it was *the* way to get things done in organisations. But its emphasis on predictability makes information-driven planning limited in effectiveness. It is most applicable when environmental conditions are reasonably stable, which is increasingly atypical for any type of organisation.

management by ideology

A system of information management based on trust in individual managers to be sensitive to the attitudes and perceptions of all participants in a decision situation and to do what is best for all by applying appropriate values and beliefs.

An alternative approach encourages self-expression and individuality among managers and professionals. **Management by ideology** means being sensitive to the attitudes and perceptions of participants; managers are expected to 'do what is right' in a situation rather than base decisions on information that may be inadequate, distorted or outdated. Cummings sees value in basing plans on ideology: 'Trust and credibility begin to centre more on ideology, values, and basic beliefs, as opposed to ... the accuracy and completeness of information. If one cannot trust others' information because of environmental change and turbulence, then one must trust others' values' (Cummings, 1983).

The recent rush to create Internet companies that emphasise digital distribution – the so-called dotcom firms – dramatises this reality. Even though the business model relies on instant information, the entrepreneurial decisions that bring the firm into being are based largely on innovative ideas, assumptions and beliefs about what might succeed in the marketplace. These are commitments made with a high degree of risk, driven by ideology. 'Dozens of Microsoft's best and brightest have traded in their cushy corporate perches for the folding-chair atmosphere of web startups' (Moeller, 1999).

Ideology guides environmental scanning

The combination of increased environmental turbulence and better-educated managers has made management by ideology more common. If ideology is the driver, information can be used creatively to reinvent the future. In part, this shift has occurred to help organisations respond to faster, more complex external changes:

> In management by ideology, innovation is sought and positions are advocated that, in fact, reward innovative policies and structures. Contrary to the usual assumption, on the other hand, in management by information real innovation is to be avoided ... Technological and information systems are designed to ensure the status quo or, at most, the gradual and incremental modification of organisational policies and designs. (Cummings, 1983)

Organisations led by people with a coherent ideology are able to use what they have learned in the past to make sense of all the conflicting information that surrounds them. Managers engage in **environmental scanning** to monitor current events in the business environment and forecast future trends, a process that combines quantitative data with qualitative perceptions (Wilson, 1980). Ideology filters the manager's environmental scanning perceptions of everything from external forces (especially opportunities) to internal dynamics.

environmental scanning

The monitoring of current and anticipated trends and events in the external environment through quantitative data and qualitative perceptions.

Active environmental scanning opens managers to a broader array of possibilities, especially if they evaluate data guided by ideology. Research by Thomas *et al.* (1993) found that hospital administrators who paid attention to environmental cues had a more reliable frame of reference for making decisions. Therefore, they initiated more product and service improvements and performed better than those who paid less attention to their environments. Even, according to Stepanek (1999), large organisations such as Shell, Procter & Gamble and DaimlerChrysler are using cyberspace teams to round up ideas from employees and outsiders to innovate new products without the usual constraint of big bureaucracies. A quick environmental scan subjects information to the judgement of team members, who act on the most promising possibilities. At times, quasi-structured group processes are used to speed up the pooling of individual perceptions and ideological evaluation of data leading to new visions and plans.

How group techniques promote innovative visions

Regardless of the size or age of an enterprise, managers have at times to take innovative actions to promote the organisation's prosperity. Such actions require periodically examining the organisation from different perspectives to help it better adapt to turbulent environments. To do so, managers can draw upon quasi-structured group techniques to share perceptions, promote innovative visions and stimulate organisational learning. In this section we walk through the details of a sample of techniques suggested by Cowley and Domb (1997) to illustrate how they are administered for creative planning.

Each of these four activities can be completed within an hour or two; or, when combined, they provide a comprehensive workshop for the better part of a day (as they are illustrated here). Since innovation planning usually links organisational activities to outside stakeholders, stakeholder representation should be included in the process. To make the process manageable, these techniques are well suited for groups of 10 to 12 people. If larger numbers of people are to be invited, subgroups of 8 to 10 people each can be formed, with each group either tackling a slightly different assignment or using the same agenda to compare results. It helps if the facilitator is an outsider – someone not ultimately responsible for carrying out the plan. (Supplies needed for carrying out these four techniques include: a flip chart on an easel and coloured felt-tip markers, several pads of 3- and 5-inch Post-it Notes and, for each participant, a felt-tip pen and a dozen or more half-inch-diameter adhesive dots.)

Activity 1: identify stakeholder needs and requirements

By way of welcome and introduction, the lead manager informs participants about the general purpose of the session, usually to create innovative visions for strengthening a programme or developing a new product and/or market. For small organisations, the purpose might be to reinvent the entire enterprise if its future appears threatened, off-course or on the threshold of a new opportunity that would radically alter its mission.

As a warm-up activity the group brainstorms a list of possible stakeholders affected by the project, with responses recorded on a flip chart. Next, participants brainstorm lists of the specific needs or requirements of any stakeholders with whom they have experience. From these overall impressions participants are collectively asked to categorise (a)· the strength of these needs and (b) the degree to which they are satisfied by the organisation's current offerings (or, in the case of potential new products, the extent to which they are satisfied by whatever is currently available). Two columns (representing a and b) are marked off on the flip chart. Each stakeholder is evaluated using the two criteria, with the group's consensus represented by symbols such as □ (strong), △ (medium) and ○ (weak). A comparison of needs and their fulfilment usually reveals unfulfilled needs. (See photo A in the six-picture photo essay.) Strong needs that are weakly satisfied at present are candidates for visioning new offerings or initiating corrective actions.

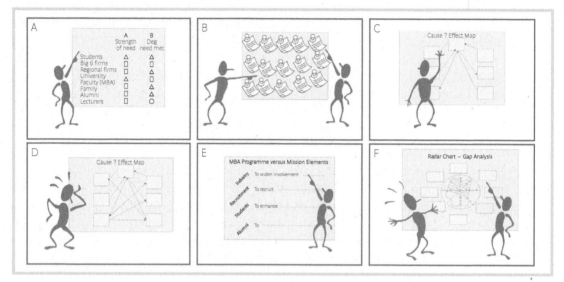

Activity 2: initiate visioning through an affinity diagram

As defined earlier a vision is a statement of elements that captures what planners want a business or programme to look like in the future. The first step in crafting a vision via a group process is to identify the elements essential to make it happen. The second step is to define what the group wants the business or product/service offering to look like at some time in the future – say, three years. In effect, a plan becomes a bridge between the present state and the desired future state. Participants then proceed by (1) viewing the stakeholder analysis as a picture of the present state, (2) creating a vision of the future, and (3) working out details of the plan as the bridge between the present and future.

Participants are asked individually to write a series of statements, one item per Post-it, in response to the second task, creating a vision of the future. For example, participants planning a business school curriculum intended to emphasise electronic commerce might be guided by the question, 'What will be the characteristics of a successful business school programme with a strong electronic commerce emphasis three years from today?' As a prompt, the facilitator suggests that participants think about internal capabilities, customer needs, competition, the economic environment, obstacles to overcome, technology trends and opportunities to exploit.

affinity diagram
An output from a quasi-structured group process created by arranging individual responses to a focusing question into groupings in which individual statements appear to have an affinity relationship to each other.

Participants individually write their responses, and then post their statements randomly on a wall until everyone has exhausted his or her possibilities. Next comes the creative part. The group is asked to silently create an **affinity diagram** by individually and collectively arranging groupings in which individual statements appear to have a relationship to each other. They do this by moving all statements around on the wall to create thematic clusters (see photo B).

This affinity mapping often results in 6 to 10 clusters for most visioning tasks. The group then decides on a thematic title for each affinity set, writes it on a Post-it, and then draws a border around it to distinguish integrating themes from individual items.

Activity 3: convert cause-and-effect diagram to a vision statement

A duplicate set of thematic labels is written and posted in a circle on a flip chart sheet. The next group task is to evaluate the relationships (if any) between items in the circle, looking for cause and effect linkages. Connecting arrows are drawn to show cause and effect relationships. The group discusses each possible pairing; some relationships are easy to agree on, others generate controversy and a deeper probing of the interplay between forces (see photo C).

Once the network of cause and effect arrows has been completed, the group counts the number of incoming and outgoing arrows for each theme and tabulates scores beside the label (using $C = x$, where x is the number of causal elements; and $E = y$, where y is the number of effects). The group then labels the two or three thematic elements that have the largest number of outgoing arrows as *PC* for *primary cause*. The same is done for the *PE*, or *primary effect*, themes (see photo D).

For planning purposes the PC elements are the ones that focus attention. If primary cause elements are acted on and strengthened, the primary effects will be likely to occur. From this cause-and-effect diagram, the group then collectively articulates a written *vision statement* of what the future should look like. Each stakeholder should be able to see their role in this vision (see photo E).

Activity 4: use a radar chart to show vision–reality gaps

One further refinement allows individual participants to evaluate each thematic element in a creative, graphic way. The facilitator draws a large circle on a blank flip chart page, and then places a 'hub' dot in the centre. Thematic labels are then placed around the outer circumference of the circle and a series of 'spokes' are drawn, one for each theme.

Participants are told to let the hub represent a score of zero (0) on a theme – the complete absence of performance or lack of any value added. The point at which the spoke connects the outer circumference of the wheel represents a perfect score of 10 (10) – the future state desired three years from now (or whatever the time horizon is). Each person then pastes an adhesive-backed dot on each spoke at the point where he or she judges the organisation to be currently performing on that thematic element. Participants may differ in their evaluations so a spoke may have dots pasted at several points along it, although typically a few spokes will have a tight clustering.

To tie results together the facilitator asks the group to visually estimate the central tendency of dots on each thematic spoke. A hash mark is drawn to represent the estimated midpoint, or average score, and a number approximating its value (ranging from 0 to 10) is written beside the mark. Once midpoints are determined connecting lines are drawn between midpoints of pairs of spokes. The results look like a web or radar display within the circle. The facilitator then shades in the inner portion of the web to represent distance already travelled in crossing the bridge to the future. This completes the 'radar chart' (see photo F).

The non-shaded area represents the *gap*, where future progress must be accomplished. Radar charts can also be constructed for principal competitors as a way to compare or benchmark performance.

Map alternative paths to bridge the future

With this visual, graphic, intuitive-analytic work accomplished, participants have a shared sense of where they must concentrate planning efforts. They can now use their collective creativity to map out alternative routes for crossing the bridge between present and future (and closing the gap). Since few organisations can be all things to all people, some elements with an overall low impact are usually discarded as not providing enough benefits for the resources expended. Subgroups can be formed to use the original affinity statements and other visualisation outputs as a way to consider planning options. Most important, this interactive process usually energises participants and gives them a broader shared vision of the project, which is difficult to accomplish when just one or two people sit down to plan.

Such a group approach to planning emphasises four Ps: *participation* of people in a series of *processes* that collectively produce a variety of visualisation *products* that guide action to achieve *performance* results.

Vision planning works best under fast-changing conditions

Visual planning approaches (rather than the more traditional linear and quantitative forecasting methods of planning) are preferred by managers whose industries require fast, imaginative outlooks and decisions. Statistical interpretations (using factor analysis) of a survey of top executives confirms that the rate of industry change affects corporate visioning (Larwood *et al.*, 1995). Twenty-two executives in one cluster who saw their industries as being slow to change also saw their visions as involving far-reaching but conservative strategic planning. These executives expressed little need for acceptance of their vision by others. In contrast, 97 executives in a second cluster characterised their firms as involved in rapid change. These executives embraced the belief that visions, in addition to providing strategic direction, should empower others and to be widely accepted throughout the organisation.

An executive who believes in vision planning to stimulate innovation is Ed McCracken, CEO of Silicon Graphics, the computer company that pioneered three-dimensional visual computing and simulation. McCracken (1995) anticipates a thousandfold improvement in information technology per decade, which transforms industries that enable people to learn, to be entertained, to improve productivity and to communicate.

Accordingly, firms participating in the transformation of technology require long-term visioning but cannot tolerate long-range planning. He says, 'If a product takes one year to design, the operational planning can be for no more than one year out.' Silicon Graphics relies more on 'dynamic step-wise planning in which we do it [plan] at the last minute'. McCracken's (1995) ideology has no illusions about 'controlling' talented employees. He prefers to 'trust intuitive wisdom' in people throughout the organisation. When technology changes so rapidly, people have 'to make decisions quick, at the right level, and without concern over making mistakes'. In making such statements, McCracken personifies the leader who uses controls to help bring about continuous improvement, the concept that concludes this chapter.

How control systems impact continuous improvement

Control is one of the most widely misunderstood organisational concepts because many people think of it in narrow terms, as management through coercion and punishment (Kouzes and Posner, 1995). Although negative connotations persist, evaluation and control systems are a must in organisations. A **control** is 'any process that helps align the actions of individuals with the interests of their employing firm' (Snell, 1992). As dynamic, open social systems, established organisa-

control
Any process to help align the actions of people and systems with the goals and interests of the organisation.

control system
Evaluative and feedback processes to let people know their managers are paying attention to what they do and can tell when undesired deviations occur.

tions are efficient and effective when control systems are in place and working (Wilkins and Ouchi, 1983). A **control system** is 'the knowledge that someone who knows and cares is paying close attention to what we do and can tell us when deviations are occurring' (O'Reilly, 1989).

Control systems help narrow the gap

Control systems can be formalised and structured, such as those based on assembly-line fault tolerances, accounting comparisons of expenses with budgets, or performance appraisals. However, as defined above, control systems also include behavioural sources of control, such as organisational culture and leadership. Whether structured or social, control systems are used to narrow the gap between objectives or expectations and actual outcomes.

For social system controls to work, people need to know that someone in authority knows what they are doing and is willing to call attention to gaps between performance and objectives. When Jan Carlzon took over as CEO of the airline SAS, one of his main concerns was the decline in on-time departures. To give ground and flight crews the message that on-time departures were important and had to increase, Carlzon (1987) made it known that he was personally monitoring the departure times of all flights. Within two years the record had improved from 83 to 97 per cent on-time departures. Crews knew that Carlzon knew which flights were late, and they did not want to be on his list.

Behaviours and outcomes are assessed/measured

Control systems evaluate and, wherever possible, measure outcomes and/or behaviours. Measurement is preferred when outcomes can be quantified, which is the purpose of formalised control systems such as accounting or six sigma. In sales, for example, outcomes are compared to each person's quota or target and to productivity measures such as sales per week, sales per customer or orders per 10 calls. In manufacturing, controls may measure defects per million, output per shift or on-time shipments.

To be effective any evaluation or measurement needs to assess outcomes or behaviours that are affected by actions of the unit or individual. O'Reilly (1989) observes that it makes little sense to evaluate a nursing staff based on, for example, whether patients get well. Restoring health to wellness is really the responsibility of a physician. Assessment of nurses' behaviours makes more sense – determining whether medical procedures are followed and whether medications are given or patient monitoring carried out at appropriate times. In other environments, evaluation focuses on both behaviours and outcomes. In some retail establishments, behaviours such as courteous treatment of customers and promptness of completion of sales transactions are as important as sales volume per employee or gross margins.

Social expectations can control behaviour

One paradox of management is that social expectations conveyed within an organisation's culture provide better controls over people than do formal measurement systems. O'Reilly (1989) states, 'With formal systems people often have a sense of external constraint that is binding and unsatisfying. With social controls, we often feel as though we have great autonomy, even though paradoxically we are conforming much more.'

The purpose of social controls is to get people to commit themselves to the organisation.

Commitments require actions, not just attitudes, even though the more a person likes a job the more willing he or she is to stay with the organisation. Maguire and Ouchi (1975) found that supervisors who focus on output increase employee satisfaction, but those who focus on close behaviour monitoring do not. The research by Maguire and Ouchi on retail department stores focused on the control of organisations and included the selection, training, socialisation process, formalisation and measure of outputs. They found two independent forms of control serving different functions: **behavioural control**, which refers to supervision and is responsive to the needs of the task and the ability of the manager, and **output control**, which is based on the measurements of outputs and results and serves the needs of the organisation.

behavioural control
Refers to supervision and is responsive to the needs of the task and ability of the manager.

output control
Based on measurements of output and results. It serves organisational needs.

A summary of the effects of supervisory controls on employee commitment is captured in the following statement by Salancik (1991): 'We would expect that high output monitoring coupled with low behavioural control would lead to the greatest felt responsibility on the part of the worker.' Whether this condition leads to greater satisfaction depends on the extent to which the employee can handle the task. Overall, an important positive contribution of controls is that at least people know what is expected of them. If no one is willing to tell an employee what is expected, that employee is likely to receive little or no performance feedback and will not be particularly attentive to performance.

Two methods for achieving quality through continuous improvement

To undertake systematic evaluation for the purpose of continuous improvement, leaders can draw upon some rather well-known quality enhancement methods such as the framework for the Malcolm Baldrige National Quality Award, six sigma or total quality management (TQM). Let us take a look at the Baldrige framework, a very process-driven model, and then a brief excursion into six sigma, a measurement technique.

The Malcolm Baldrige National Quality Award framework

Baldrige
The Malcolm Baldrige National Quality Award framework for evaluating the qualities and processes of organisations dedicated to quality performance as measured by seven dimensions of organisational life, ranging from leadership practices to performance results.

The Baldrige has widespread appeal because it has become the recognised standard for evaluating the qualities and processes of organisations dedicated to quality performance. Winning the Baldrige award is a coveted achievement since only a handful of organisations are so recognised each year. Nevertheless, many leaders engage their people in a Baldrige-type evaluation process because it is broad-based and provides an eye-opening experience for participants that typically dramatises the gaps between current performance and desired results.

The Baldrige framework probes into seven dimensions of organisational life, ranging from leadership practices to data that measure performance results. It is not a mechanistic formula-driven model. Rather, it is a flexible process for identifying factors critical to performance, coupled with a problem-identification and problem-solving process focused on bringing about improvement. Exhibit 3-8 identifies the seven basic elements in the Baldrige framework and how they flow together. Explanations of these seven key elements are given below (Ruben and Lehr, 1997).

1 **Leadership.** Senior leaders are involved in creating and sustaining consensus regarding the organisation's mission, values, plans and goals, and focus on the stakeholder groups being served.

2 **Planning.** The processes for short-, intermediate- and long-range plans are communicated and aligned throughout the organisation.

3 **Service orientation.** Processes are provided for learning about the needs and expectations of the groups for which services are provided, and satisfaction for these groups is monitored and improved (especially relative to peer and benchmark institutions).

4 **Information and analysis.** Information is assessed and managed to track and improve overall organisational effectiveness and service excellence.

5 **Employees and workplace climate.** Employees at all levels are encouraged to develop their full potential relative to the organisational mission and goals, supported by an environment conducive to excellence, participation, appreciation of diversity and personal/organisational growth.

6 **Process management.** Key processes are developed, managed and improved to achieve superior organisational performance and a service orientation.

7 **Excellence levels and trends.** Achievements and improvements are documented in key excellence areas, relative to past performance and to peer and benchmark organisations.

The Baldrige assessment model focuses on seven areas. The numbers in parentheses in Exhibit 3-8 represent the maximum point values for Baldrige Award scoring (total score = 1000 maximum).

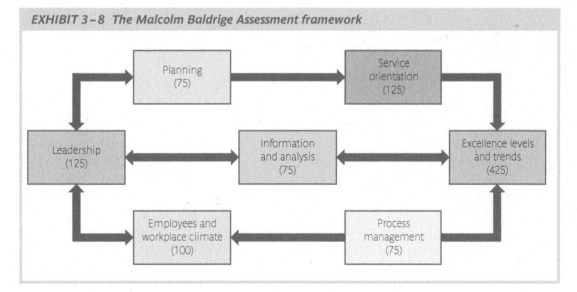

EXHIBIT 3 – 8 The Malcolm Baldrige Assessment framework

dynamics of diversity

Short skirts and daggers at work

Employees' dress codes have long troubled Britain's tribunals and courts. Until the recent arrival of the Human Rights Act, disgruntled workers seeking to change the law had to rely on sex or race discrimination laws.

It has not been easy to reconcile the tension between the rights of men and women to be treated equally and the different dress conventions for the sexes. The courts have generally adopted a pragmatic approach. In a celebrated 1996 case, the Court of Appeal upheld Safeway's ban on long hair for male delicatessen staff even though it was allowed for women. The court said that employers could lay down different rules for male and female staff as long as similar standards were imposed overall.

Unsurprisingly the courts have been less sympathetic to bans on women wearing trousers. In January 2000 Judy Owen, a training manager, won a sexual discrimination case against the Professional Golfers' Association, which would not let her wear a smart trouser suit to work.

Less enlightened was the approach of the Spanish Supreme Court in a case in 2001. Renfe, the Spanish national train company, required hostesses on high-speed trains to wear skirts 'at least' 2 cm above the knee. The court said the rule was neither sexist nor discriminatory but appropriate for a company seeking to project a 'high-quality brand'.

Race discrimination claims have often been made against employers that have objected to Rastafarian hairstyles or to the beards, bracelets, daggers and turbans of Sikhs. Such cases do not have predictable outcomes. In one case, Rowntree Mackintosh, the confectionery group, successfully argued that it was justified in rejecting a Sikh man for a post in its factory on the basis that his beard could jeopardise food hygiene. In another, a tribunal rejected attempts to justify forbidding a Sikh to wear a hidden dagger.

Two big legal developments may increase the scope for employees to challenge dress restrictions. One is the Human Rights Act 2000, which provides for freedom of expression. While employees cannot bring claims in an unemployment tribunal for breach of the Act, its provisions are relevant to many employment tribunal claims, such as a complaint of unfair dismissal. Even then the right to freedom of expression has its limits. Paul Kara, a training administrator, received short shrift from the European Commission on Human Rights in 1999 when he argued that Hackney Council's refusal to allow him to wear women's clothes to work breached his human rights.

The second important legal development will be the outlawing of religious discrimination in the workplace by the end of 2003. In a recent case in France Habiba Charni, a Muslim, worked as a sales assistant in a food store. For seven years she had worn her headscarf tied away from her face. However, on returning from a pilgrimage to Mecca, she insisted on wearing a veil. Last year the French Court of Appeal upheld the consequent dismissal, having taken account of Mrs Charni's client contact, the employer's attitude in allowing her to wear a headscarf tied up and to having taken additional leave to make her pilgrimage, and the employer's additional argument that some customers would be uncomfortable with the veil across her face.

It will be interesting to see the approach UK employment tribunals take to similar cases. Perceived client preferences or prejudices will not generally justify sex, race or disability discrimination in the UK, so it may be difficult for employers to use client contact to justify dress codes that restrict religious expression.

Employers are increasingly prepared to adopt a relaxed attitude to dress and appearance at work and, where appropriate, to allow their staff more scope for self-expression. The key is to establish clear policies so staff know where they stand. Such policies should not differentiate between the sexes unnecessarily and should accommodate ethnic differences or religious beliefs wherever possible. Above all, employers need to approach the issue objectively and avoid restrictive rules unless there is a sound business justification for them.

Source: adapted from James Davies writing in the *Financial Times*, 29 April 2002.

Discussion questions

1 Do you think employers should be able to dictate their employees' dress?
2 How could the above be reflected in the mission statement?

Six sigma statistical method

Imagine customers doing business with an airline that always had a customer service representative to answer telephone calls within five seconds, always billed the correct lowest fare, produced on-time arrivals, and never lost or misrouted a checked bag. Organisations that employ the six sigma methodology strive, through vigorous use of performance data and statistical interpretations, to achieve such error-free results (Harry. 1994). As a statistic, six sigma represents the value of six standard deviations from the arithmetic mean. When applied to quality measures it represents the probability that a defect or unwanted variance from the standard will occur no more than 3.4 times out of one million transactions – perfection, or at least coming within a whisker of it.

six sigma
A high-performance, data-driven approach to analysing the root causes of business problems and solving them after first aligning the outputs of a business directly with marketplace requirements.

Motorola popularised six sigma as a 'do it right' philosophy and technique to promote continuous improvement of essential operational processes. Six sigma is, according to Blakeslee (1999), 'a high-performance, data-driven approach to analysing the root causes of business problems and solving them' after first linking 'the outputs of a business directly to marketplace requirements'. Organisations that embrace six sigma analyse their customers' requirements, and then build their internal processes in a highly disciplined manner to fulfil those requirements by driving out variances from the standard. They do this by measuring and tracking performance, sharing data with those involved in the process, analysing why deviations occur and then working to eliminate causes of unacceptable performance. Critical to all this working is close attention to employee training in statistical methods and the techniques for process improvements. In this regard it is more an intervention to affect organisational behaviour than it is a statistical tool.

When work teams in organisations begin to measure their performance outputs, they often find they are in the two to four sigma range (three sigma performance means roughly 67 000 defects per million operations). Mechanised manufacturing operations tend to be on the higher side; service operations dependent on human judgement are usually lower or more variable in results. As a control system, organisations committed to six sigma results create a climate of alignment that is guided by top management to provide the resources and create a culture supportive of measurement and change. Employees have access to timely data, are trained to understand statistics and use problem-solving techniques, and provided with incentives to work towards error-free results.

Managerial values influence patterns of control systems

Control systems differ across organisations depending on managerial values and commitments. One study of financial executives by Jablonsky *et al.* (1992) identified three different types of managerial control orientations: competitive team, command and control, and conformance.

1 A *competitive team orientation* focuses on adding value to the market, with controls used to enhance the organisation's core competence and strategic competitiveness. Information flows laterally and informally throughout the organisation to help people make timely decisions.

2 The classic *command and control orientation* is used most often in firms that rely on a chain-of-command structure to emphasise operating efficiency and conservation of corporate resources. Controls focus on internal events, with vertical flows of information up the hierarchy for top management review and oversight.

3 The *conformance orientation* of control is found most often in organisations doing business with the government. Work is organised around a bureaucracy, with fixed control routines for processing information and externally reporting it in compliance with government regulations. The Inland Revenue Service is the archetype of an organisation focused on conformance control.

Such variations in control orientations underscore the reality that organisations differ significantly in how managers seek to bring about satisfactory performance. As elaborated throughout this text, some managers learn to emphasise team performance by building on the core values of service and involvement, knowledge of the business and customer service. Team-orientated leadership is typical of organisations operating in dynamic, fast-changing, high-tech environments (Keating and Jablonsky, 1990). In contrast, the more stereotypical view of control is seen in the core values of managers who view their roles more to police activities and people. They emphasise oversight and surveillance, and administration of rules and procedures.

While managers voice an intent to shift towards advocating customer service and building competitive teams, being consistent with these values is not easy since it requires risk-taking and innovation (Jablonsky *et al.*, 1992). The team-centred manager is more likely to use social expectations combined with quality-orientated methods to foster commitment and self-accepted responsibility than the manager who polices the behaviour of others.

The Body Shop: a second look

The Body Shop International plc is a values-driven, high-quality skin and body care retailer operating in 50 countries with over 1900 outlets spanning 25 languages and 12 time zones.

It is estimated that the Body Shop sells a product every 0.4 seconds, with over 77 million customer transactions through stores worldwide, with customers sampling its current range of over 600 products and more than 400 accessories.

The Body Shop has always believed that business is primarily about human relationships: 'We believe that the more we listen to our stakeholders and involve them in decision-making, the better our business will be run.'

In 1999, the Body Shop was voted the second most trusted brand in the UK by the Consumers Association. According to 1997 Interbrand survey criteria, the company was named

28th top brand in the world, second in the retail sector. In a 1998 report, a survey of international chief executives in the *Financial Times* ranked the Body Shop the 27th most respected company in the world.

The Body Shop mission statement gives the following statements as to its reason for being.

- To dedicate our business to the pursuit of social and environmental change.
- To creatively balance the financial and human needs of our stakeholders: employees, customers, franchisees, suppliers and shareholders.
- To courageously ensure that our business is ecologically sustainable: meeting the needs of the present without compromising the future.
- To meaningfully contribute to local, national and international communities in which we trade, by adopting a code of conduct that ensures care, honesty, fairness and respect.
- To passionately campaign for the protection of the environment, human and civil rights, and against animal testing within the cosmetics and toiletries industry.
- To tirelessly work to narrow the gap between principle and practice, while making fun, passion and care part of our daily lives.

These goals are very idealistic and in some respects are in opposition to the commonly held belief that to be in business is to make a 'fast buck', regardless of the cost to others. Anita Roddick and the Body Shop have shown that this need not be the case, and that a company can gain more respect by giving as well as taking.

Source: www.bodyshop.co.uk

Summary

- You do not have to be an executive to benefit from learning to think like a strategist. Strategic thinking involves having a vision of a desired future that leads to a workable fit between the organisation and its environment.

- Visions are crafted to be consistent with the organisation's mission, a crisp statement of fundamental purpose that focuses on adding value to customers.

- From mission and vision, leaders craft a circular flow encompassing objectives, strategies, financing, organising, implementing and controlling.

- No matter what your position in the organisation, you can use a series of all-encompassing questions to investigate, evaluate and plan strategic actions.

- Two of these questions enable managers to develop a SWOT analysis of internal strengths and weaknesses and external opportunities and threats.

- Because every work unit can be thought of as a business that creates value for others, thinking through these questions strategically can help any performance-minded person think and plan more effectively.

- One purpose of strategy is to provide products and services that give the organisation a competitive advantage. Doing so builds on organisational capabilities, the combination of assets and skills that enables one firm to do certain things better than competitors, usually by combining unique resources and employee talents into programmes and services that rivals cannot duplicate.

- Competitive strategies are possible only within lines of business where specific products jockey for position within a competitive market. For diversified businesses in multiple lines of business, corporate strategies are the choices senior executives make about what businesses to be in and how to compete.

- Planning is not a mechanistic exercise of programming actions to attain objectives; rather it is a process for organisational learning. Guiding the process is the manager's ideology, which shapes his or her environmental scanning perceptions as well as mission and goals.

- In fast-changing environments, representative stakeholders using group techniques to move from defining a vision to detailing specific actions can quickly craft planning.

- Affinity diagrams are one planning tool to help pull ideas into clusters of related elements that frame a desired future state. These key themes can then be evaluated using the tools of a cause-and-effect diagram and a radar chart to identify gaps between current performance and future expectations.

- Control systems help narrow the gap between current performance and forward-looking goals. To help guide and develop an emphasis on quality and continuous improvement, leaders of organisations can turn to using the Baldrige Quality Award framework and/or six sigma method.

- Managers committed to continuous improvement realise that success combines controlling social expectations and measuring process outputs.

Areas for personal development

Learning to think strategically requires practice. To begin the process of developing strategic thinking skills, apply these practices at every opportunity. They are part of learning to 'manage oneself'.

1 **Craft a personal mission to define your purpose.** Every organisation and professional needs a mission statement. Write out a personal mission statement that summarises what you are committed to achieve and who you plan to serve – in effect answering the question 'What is my purpose?' (See Exhibit 3-2 for guidelines.) Then, at least weekly, recite your mission from memory and ask, 'How am I focusing my decisions and actions so that I'm fulfilling my mission?'

2 **Emphasise adding value to customers.** When crafting a mission, do not focus on your personal gratification, but on how your actions help others (whether people or organisations). Ask, 'What have I done to benefit or add value to my "customers" this week?'

3 **Know your business and what it should become.** Every person is a strategist and every person can think of himself or herself as a business. Think, 'Who are my customers and what do they value?' Then, what will it take to have a stronger, more robust business two to five years from now?

4 **Visualise goals as scenarios come true.** While a mission is a global guide to choice of actions, visions are more focused and specific. Visions are best framed as graphic or descriptive scenarios of what success would look like at some specific time in the future. Practise developing visions as written scenarios that describe some future outcome. Your vision may be stated as what you have learned by the time of graduation, what you will be doing at work two years after graduation, or what your personal relationships will look and feel like five years out.

5 **Focus on your sources of competitive advantage.** People are not created equal (although they should have equal opportunity). Appraise your true sources of competitive advantage over others and how you best learn. It is easier to build on known strengths than it is to try to shore up weaknesses. Strengthen your sources of competitive advantage through practising introspection and self-appraisal.

6 **Scan your environment.** Neither individuals nor organisations function as islands. Scan your environment by looking for clues as to how well you are performing (do not rely on a boss for feedback) and for signs of significant changes in the world external to you that will impact you.

7 **Practise gap analysis between present and future states.** After visualising a scenario (outcome) you desire at a specific time in the future develop an inventory of the contributing factors that will cause it to happen. Periodically assess 'Where am I now on each causal

factor relative to the goal?' Use a radar chart to picture the distance yet to be travelled – the gap – to dramatise where emphasis should be placed (see photo F in the photo essay on page 110).

8 **Evaluate behaviours and outcomes for self-control.** Self-control in work tasks means aligning your actions with the interests of the task group or organisation. Focus on targeted results or outcomes and evaluate, 'How are my behaviours (and the behaviours of others) affecting results?' A retired navy captain states it most simply by asking, 'What is victory? How do we achieve victory?' Personal plans and controls improve the likelihood of victory being achieved.

❓ Questions for study and discussion

1 Why does an organisation need to develop strategy, and what are some of the elements or processes involved in planning strategy as a circular flow of decisions and actions?

2 Apply the six questions that form a basis for strategic thinking to the organisation with which you are most experienced. What new insights into the organisation do you gain by this process?

3 What is a SWOT analysis? How can a SWOT analysis be used to plan within one department of a larger organisation? Give an example.

4 In what ways does management ideology influence the planning process? Why is managing by ideology more useful than managing by information within many organisations?

5 Describe the group processes managers and stakeholders would use to create an affinity map, a cause-and-effect diagram and a radar chart. Explain how each device contributes to planning.

6 How do quality methods such as the Baldrige framework and six sigma exemplify control systems used to promote continuous improvement?

🔑 Key Concepts

strategic thinking, *p. 84*

mission, *p. 85*

vision, *p. 86*

objectives, *p. 88*

benchmarking, *p. 88*

strategy, *p. 91*

organising, *p. 92*

financing, *p. 92*

structure, *p. 92*

systems, *p. 92*

continuous improvement, *p. 93*

core capabilities, *p. 96*

SWOT analysis, *p. 97*

milestones, *p. 100*

results, *p. 100*

competitive advantage, *p. 102*

corporate strategy, *p. 103*

diversification, *p. 103*

outsourcing, *p. 103*

relative quality degradation, *p. 103*

competitive strategy, *p. 104*

clusters, *p. 105*

planning, *p. 106*

controlling, *p. 107*

ideology, *p. 107*

management by information, *p. 107*

management by ideology, *p. 108*

environmental scanning, *p. 108*

affinity diagram, *p. 110*

control, *p. 112*

control system, *p. 113*

behavioural control, *p. 114*

output control, *p. 114*

Baldrige, *p. 114*

six sigma, *p. 117*

Personal skills exercise
What's your SWOT analysis?

Purpose This is a quickly administered combination individual and group exercise that gives students an opportunity to apply the essentials of SWOT analysis. It provides a lively, practical application of one of the most widely used tools for strategic thinking.

Time 15 to 20 minutes

Materials Several blank flip-chart sheets (or transparencies) and markers. Masking tape if flip-chart sheets are used.

Procedure The instructor lists on the board or screen several organisations that are likely to be familiar to students (such as McDonald's, Littlewoods, Pizza Hut, Homebase, AOL, Microsoft). We suggest listing one organisation for every six to seven students. Prominent local firms can be included.

Step 1: Individual SWOT Each student selects one organisation from the list. Working individually, on a sheet of paper the student identifies the firm at the top and then draws a 2 × 2 matrix and writes in the labels 'strengths, weaknesses, opportunities, threats' as shown in Exhibit 3-9. Next, the student fills in each cell by writing short phrases that assess the firm as he or she perceives it on each of the four SWOT analysis criteria. (Time required: 4 to 5 minutes.)

Step 2: Pooled SWOT profiles Divide into groups, one for each organisation. Students join the group representing the firm they individually analysed. Group size will naturally vary, so if any one firm was chosen by, say, about half the class, split it into two or three groups for greater efficiency. Now, on the flip chart record a pooling of the individual SWOT analysis themes.

EXHIBIT 3–9 Example of SWOT analysis applied to Philip Morris companies

Strengths
- High profits from tobacco
- World's largest advertiser
- Operational efficiencies
- Etc....

Weaknesses
- Dependence on tobacco
- Some acquisition mismatch
- Management blunders
- Etc....

Opportunities
- Global tobacco markets
- Many food companies for sale
- Price power over ad media
- Etc....

Threats
- Tobacco regulation as a drug
- Customer product boycotts
- Competitor retaliation
- Etc....

SWOT analysis provides a structured framework for assessing relevant internal and external factors affecting an organisation's strategies. This PM example is highly abbreviated – your group may want to provide greater detail for each key element.

1 Brainstorming a list of stakeholders and evaluating how well their needs and requirements are being met.

2 Creating an affinity map to cluster planning elements into key affinity themes.

3 Starting to identify cause → effect relationships among key planning themes.

4 One group's completed cause → effect diagram shows a network of arrows used to identify primary causes and effects.

5 Results of the previous planning output are articulated into a comprehensive written vision statement.

6 Construction of a radar chart dramatises gaps in planning elements between the present and desired future.

Do this in a round-robin fashion where each student in turn offers one analytical thought (rather than one person giving his or her entire list). Start with 'strengths'; then when everyone has exhausted their 'strength' offerings, move on to 'weaknesses, opportunities and threats' in rotation. (Time required: about 10 minutes.)

Step 3: Class sharing Each group shares its results with the class. Tape the flip-chart sheets to a wall and have one member briefly summarise the completed SWOT as represented by pooling the individual assessments for that organisation. (Time required: about 5 minutes.)

Step 4: Debriefing Discuss issues such as the following.

1 What did you learn about the thoroughness of analysis comparing personal SWOTs with pooled group SWOTs? What does this suggest about whether strategic planning should be performed by one person (the most senior leader) or by a team?

2 In what ways did the four-factor SWOT analysis cause you to see critical elements about the organisation that you probably would have overlooked if you were not using a structured framework?

3 To what extent does the profile of elements suggest any strategies that ought to be changed or initiated? To what extent does it reinforce the efficacy of current strategies?

4 What did you observe about the group process during the pooling stage that made this a productive (or unproductive) exercise? What behaviours facilitated task accomplishment; what behaviours got in the way? Did the same behaviours that promoted efficiency also promote effectiveness? Why?

Team exercise

Group techniques for planning a vision (Drucker 1999)

Purpose This exercise enables in-class teams to develop skills for group-based vision planning by focusing on an organisation that everyone knows. Specifically, the team task is to plan actions that would strengthen the academic programme in which you are enrolled. The process engages teams in the hands-on experience of creating affinity maps, cause-and-effect diagrams and radar charts.

Time about 60 minutes if students have read the chapter section on group processes for visioning.

Materials One or two pads of Post-it Notes per team (minimum size 3×3 inches, preferably larger), two or three sheets of blank newsprint per team, a roll of masking tape (for taping newsprint to wall), about a dozen adhesive-backed dots for each person.

Procedure Form teams of 7 to 10 persons each and hand out materials. Then work through tasks 1 to 4.

Task 1: Individual visioning Once teams have been assembled, each person should write brief responses to the question below. Write each response on a single Post-it, boldly enough to be read from a distance of six to eight feet. Write as many statements as you believe are relevant, but use only one theme or idea per Post-it. For planning purposes, focus on a time horizon of three years in the future. The following question is suggested as a way of focusing on a tangible task, although your instructor may present a different question:

As a student, you are concerned about the quality of the academic programme in which you are enrolled. What practices or qualities should be part of this educational programme three years from now to help students receive the greatest benefit from the experience? In effect, what features would enable this programme to be truly excellent?

Task 2: Creation of a team affinity diagram

(a) After three or four minutes of writing, members randomly post their responses on a wall, with each team's responses in one area.

(b) Members arrange responses into clusters. This is a silent activity, with everyone working individually. Simply link themes based on any kind of affinity relationship that comes to mind. Feel free to break up groupings others have made.

(c) As a group, decide on a brief title for each affinity cluster. Then write that title on a separate Post-it, draw a border or box around it, and post it at the top of the cluster.

Task 3: Creation of a cause-and-effect diagram Tape a sheet of newsprint to the wall near your affinity map (one for each team). Make a duplicate set of title labels and stick them to the newsprint in a large circle (similar to an analogue clock face). Now draw arrows to show cause-and-effect relationships between each pair of themes (that is, the arrow pointing away from the cause towards the effect). Refer back to the photo essay on p. 110 and text for guidance if needed.

Task 4: Creation of a radar chart for gap analysis On another flip-chart sheet, draw a large circle and post another set of labels around the outer circumference. Place a hub and spokes using the text and photo essay as guides. With the circumference (outer rim) representing an ideal score of 10 and the hub 0, each person places an adhesive-backed dot on each spoke to spatially represent your institution's current performance. When completed, collectively determine the midpoint for each line of dots, draw a connecting line between the midpoints of each adjacent pair of spokes and shade in the inner area. The white space represents the gap between performance now and the ideal future for the themes.

Debriefing Reflect on the process and learning implications of this exercise by discussing the following questions.

1 What obstacles did you encounter, if any? What behaviours or processes seemed to help get the task done in both an efficient and an effective manner?

2 In what ways are your affinity diagrams, cause-and-effect diagrams and radar charts more complex because they were developed by a group rather than by you alone? Does the collective effort more accurately represent reality? What do your answers say about whether planning should be done by individuals or teams?

3 If your university was to use this process for actual programme planning, what other stakeholders or constituents would you want to include?

4 Now that you have identified cause-and-effect relationships and performed a gap analysis, what specific actions would you plan to bring about the vision created by your group?

Case study: **Marconi – a big name on the brink**

Marconi, one of the big names in British industry, is on the brink of financial collapse as the banks tighten the screws on companies that borrowed millions of pounds to gamble on expansion during the economic boom.

Marconi was once a company that had a name synonymous with technological know-how and financial prudence. Now the company is fighting for its survival after lenders have refused to grant fresh funds. With its share price falling the city consensus is that it will be wound up soon.

Boom has not yet turned to bust for the UK economy as a whole, but many telecommunications and media businesses are staring into the abyss after going on an unprecedented spending spree in the late 1990s. Marconi is not the only company in trouble, ITV Digital is having problems as are cable TV companies Telewest and ntl.

The common thread running through these companies is that they over-extended in the heady days of 1999 – 2000, but did not have the critical mass or profitability to withstand a sudden lessening of economic pace. Internet and telecommunications-related companies have become commodity businesses, selling services and products in a market that is heaving with over-capacity.

The Marconi story illustrates most clearly how management can get things wrong. The company was built up by Lord Weinstock in the 1970s and 1980s, and was renowned for its conservative approach to expansion and risk-taking.

When a new team arrived in the mid-1990s under Lord Simpson, the former Rover boss, and John Mayo, a City banker with experience in the pharmaceuticals industry, investors looked forward to a lucrative unwinding of the Weinstock empire.

At first all went well as Simpson and Mayo negotiated the £6 billion sale of Marconi's defence systems division to BAE, the former British Aerospace. Afterwards they calculated that a rapid expansion into telecommunications and the Internet would be the best way to invest the proceeds.

In fairness, many City brokers and bankers egged them on as these sectors were seen as offering the most attractive growth prospects.

Shares in technology firms were reaching new heights, although many of them did not expect to be profitable for several years. Investors were blinded by market hype and backed the strategy of the new Marconi management. Simpson acquired several large American competitors with cash, rather than by issuing new equity.

This was to prove a fatal mistake when the economy turned down. Interest payments and start-up costs running into billions wiped out money generated from relatively new businesses. Marconi had gambled and lost.

Marconi has realised that its financial structure is no longer appropriate for its trading position. This became clear when its trading figures had deteriorated to such an extent that recovery had been pushed even further into the future.

An executive at one of the lending banks said, 'You could say that this could have been sorted out four to six months ago if the company had been willing to listen and less eager to pursue its own agenda . . . It is not that we are getting tougher, it is that the company's circumstances have changed. It does not have much of a balance sheet now.'

Marconi thought it could trade its way out of its position, but it is having to use its money to pay interest to bondholders so as to prevent then from demanding instant repayment. Marconi is now embracing the idea of a debt for equity swap, but will its lenders agree? If they do it could end up with the banks and bondholders owning 75 per cent and equity investors taking the remaining 25 per cent. The question is, will this give them a better return than pulling the plug now.?

Source: *Observer*, 24 March 2002.

Questions for managerial action

1 What are the strengths and weaknesses of Marconi at present? You may have to search its website for more information about the company.

2 What is currently going on in the competitive marketplace of telecommunications? What external opportunities and threats are there?

3 From your SWOT analysis (responses to questions 1 and 2), what would you recommend if Marconi were to be kept afloat?

4 What has happened to the concept of managing by strategic vision?

5 If Marconi were restructured what type of controls could be put in place to ensure it never end up in this position again?

Applied questions

6 Using the Malcolm Baldrige National Quality Award framework can you identify how the seven key elements could have been applied to Marconi to turn it around?

7 GE has a simple formula for global competitiveness, as illustrated in Exhibit 3-7. How could Marconi have used its five questions in an attempt to improve its own competitive advantage?

WWW exercise

Manager's Internet tools

Web tips: Communicating company missions on the World Wide Web
In the last chapter we discussed the Virgin Group. When people mention the name Virgin what image comes to your mind? Is it that of a record company, an airline, or is it Richard Branson the entrepreneur and action man?

World Wide Web: Virgin
Go to http://www.virgin.com. What is your first impression of the website? Was it what you expected? What do the first couple of sentences imply about the company's mission? Look through the various pages on the website and note all the different products. Examine Virgin Trains, Virgin Wines, Virgin Atlantic and Virgin Music.

1 Why do you think Virgin has developed such a diverse set of companies? Why has it given them all the Virgin name?

2 How do you think the company's mission and strategies have changed since the 1970s? What are the primary variables that influenced these changes?

LEARNING CHECKLIST ☑

Before you move on you may want to reflect on what you have learnt in this chapter. You should now be able to:

☑ describe the essential processes that help a manager begin to think strategically, starting with vision and mission and cycling through to controlling and improving

☑ understand the questions that help you think strategically about planning actions, whether for an entire business or an organisational subunit

☑ understand the concept of management by objectives (MBO)

☑ conduct a SWOT analysis to evaluate an organisation's limitations and potential when you read a complex case or study the options for responding to environmental conditions

☑ explain how organisational capabilities translate into competitive advantage when linked to strategies for where and how to compete

☑ discuss why planning is more about organisational learning than about programming actions, and why a manager's ideology may be more useful than managing by information

☑ describe how group processes help create a shared vision through the use of planning tools such as an affinity map, a cause-and-effect diagram and a radar chart

☑ explain how assessment controls can lead to continuous improvement

☑ explain the Malcolm Baldrige Assessment framework

☑ explain the six sigma statistical method.

Further reading

Collins, J.C. and Porras, J.I. (1991) 'Organisational Vision and Visionary Organisations', *California Management Review* 34, Fall, pp. 30–52.

Estrella Tolentino, P. (2002) 'Hierarchical Pyramids and Heterarchical Networks: Organisational Strategies and Structures of Multinational Corporations and its Impact on World Development', *Contributions to Political Economy* 21(1), p. 69.

Hansen, M.T., Nohria, N. and Tierney, T. (1999) 'What's Your Strategy for Managing Knowledge?', *Harvard Business Review*, March–April, pp. 106–116.

McPhee, N. (2002) 'Gaining Insight on Business and Organisational Behaviour: The Qualitative Dimension', *International Journal of Market Research* 44(1), pp. 53–70.

Ritti, R.R. (1998) *The Ropes to Skip and the Ropes to Know – Studies in Organisational Behaviour* (5th edn). John Wiley & Sons.

Thompson Jr, A.A. and Strickland III, A.J. (1999) *Strategic Management Concepts and Cases.* Boston, MA: Irwin McGraw-Hill, Chapter 1

Wheelen, T.L. and Hunger, J.D. (2000) *Strategic Management and Business Policy.* Upper Saddle River, NJ: Prentice Hall, Chapter 1.

References

Aaker, D.A. (1989) 'Managing Assets and Skills: The Key to a Sustainable Competitive Advantage', *California Management Review* 31, Winter, pp. 91–106.

Bartmess, A. and Cerny, K. (1993) 'Building Competitive Advantage Through a Global Network of Capabilities', *California Management Review* 35, Winter, pp. 78–103.

Blakeslee, J.A. Jr (1999) 'Implementing the Six Sigma Solution', *Quality Progress*, July, p. 78.

Boscheck, R. (1994) 'Competitive Advantage: Superior Offer or Unfair Dominance?' *California Management Review* 37, Fall, pp. 132–151

Campbell, A. (1999) 'Tailored, Not Benchmarked: A Fresh Look at Corporate Planning', *Harvard Business Review*, March–April, pp. 41–50.

Carlzon, J. (1987) *Moments of Truth*. Cambridge, MA: Ballinger.

Cohen, A. (1999) 'Microsoft Enjoys Monopoly Power', *Time*, 15 November, pp. 60–69.

Collins, J.C. and Porras, J.I. (1991) 'Organizational Vision and Visionary Organizations', *California Management Review* 34, Fall, pp. 30–52.

Colvin, G. (2000) 'America's Most Admired Companies', *Fortune*, February, pp. 108–111 (GE ranked number one for three consecutive years).

Cowley, M. and Domb, E. (1997) *Beyond Strategic Vision: Effective Corporate Action with Hoshin Planning*. Boston, MA: Butterworth-Heinemann, especially Chapter 13.

Crainer, S. (1998) *Key Management Ideas: Thinkers that Changed the Management World* (3rd edn). Financial Times, Prentice Hall, p. 75.

Cummings, L.L. (1983) 'The Logics of Management', *Academy of Management Review* 8, October, pp. 532–538.

De Geus, A. (1988) 'Planning as Learning', *Harvard Business Review* 66, March–April.

Drucker, P.F. (1974) *Management: Tasks Responsibilities, Practices*. New York, NY: Harper & Row, p. 61.

Drucker, P.F. (1980) *Managing in Turbulent Times*. New York, NY: Harper & Row, pp. 43–45.

Drucker, P.F. (1989a) *The New Realities*. New York, NY: Harper & Row, p. 230.

Drucker, P.F. (1989b) *The Practice of Management*. Heinemann, p. 59.

Drucker, P.F. (1999) 'Managing Oneself', *Harvard Business Review*, March–April, pp. 64–74.

Eisenhardt, K.M. and Galunic, D.C. (2000) 'Coevolving: At Last, a Way to Make Synergies Work', *Harvard Business Review*, January–February, pp. 91–101.

El-Namaki, M.S.S. (1992) 'Creating a Corporate Vision', *Long Range Planning* 25(6), p. 25.

Feldman, A. (1999) 'How Big Can It Get?' *Money*, December, pp. 158–164.

Ghoshal, S., Arnzen, B. and Brownfield, S. (1992) 'A Learning Alliance between Business and Business Schools: Executive Education as a Platform for Partnership', *California Management Review* 35, Fall, pp. 50–67.

Greenwood, R. and Hinings, C.R. (1993) 'Understanding Strategic Change: The Contribution of Archetypes', *Academy of Management Journal* 36, October, pp. 1052–1081.

Hagel III, J. and Singer, M. (1999) 'Unbundling the Corporation', *Harvard Business Review*, March–April, pp. 133–141.

Halal, W.E. (1994) 'From Hierarchy to Enterprise: Internal Markets Are the New Foundation of Management', *Academy of Management Executive* 8, November, p. 72.

Harry, M.J. (1994) *The Vision of Six Sigma: A Roadmap for Breakthrough*. Phoenix, AZ: Sigma Publishing.

Hayes, R.H. and Pisano, G.P. (1994) 'Beyond World-class: The New Manufacturing Strategy', *Harvard Business Review* 72, January–February, pp. 77–86.

Hinterhuber, H.H. and Popp, W. (1992) 'Are You a Strategist or Just a Manager?' *Harvard Business Review* 70, January–February, pp. 105–113.

Hunt, J.G. (1991) *Leadership: A New Synthesis*. Newbury Park, CA: Sage.

Jablonsky, S.F., Keating, P.J. and Heian, J.B. (1992) *The Management Communication and Control Systems Diagnostic Questionnaire: Core Values and Organizational Learning*. New York, NY: Financial Executives Research Foundation.

Keating, P.J. and Jablonsky, S.F. (1990) *Changing Roles of Financial Management: Getting Close to the Business*. New York, NY: Financial Executives Research Foundation.

Kenny, D. (2002) 'It's Time to Test the True Value of Facilities Management Outsourcing', Institute of Business Ideas and Solutions, December, pp. 2–3.

Kouzes, J.M. and Posner, B.Z. (1995) *The Leadership Challenge*. San Francisco, CA: Jossey-Bass.

Kriger, M.P. (1990) 'Towards a Theory of Organizational Vision: The Shaping of Organizational Futures', paper presented at the Academy of Management annual meeting, San Francisco, CA.

Larwood, L., Falbe, C.M., Kriger, M.P. and Miesing, P. (1995) 'Structure and Meaning of Organizational Vision', *Academy of Management Journal* 38, June, pp. 740–769.

Maguire, M.A. and Ouchi, W.G. (1975) 'Organizational Control and Work Satisfaction', research paper no. 278, Graduate School of Business, Stanford University.

Maremont, M. (1995) 'Kodak's New Focus', *Business Week*, January, pp. 62–68.

McCracken, E. (1995) 'The Information Super Highway: How Entertainment Will Drive its Technological Development into the 21st Century', Business Alumni Association Executive Breakfast Briefings, San Jose State University, 22 June.

Mintzberg, H. (1987) 'Crafting Strategy', *Harvard Business Review* 65, July–August, pp. 66–75.

Mintzberg, H. (1994) 'The Fall and Rise of Strategic Planning', *Harvard Business Review* 72, January–February, pp. 107–114.

Moeller, M. (1999) 'Outta Here at Microsoft', *Business Week*, November, pp. 156–160.

Nadler, D.A., Shaw, R.B. and Walton, A.W. (1995) and associates, *Discontinuous Change: Leading Organizational Transformation*, San Francisco, CA: Jossey-Bass.

Nanus, B, (1992) *Visionary Leadership: Creating a Compelling Sense of Direction for Your Organization*. San Francisco, CA: Jossey-Bass.

O'Reilly, C. (1989) 'Corporations, Culture, and Commitment: Motivation and Social Control in Organizations', *California Management Review* 31, Summer, p. 11.

Peters, T. (1992) High Tech Summit Visioning Conference, sponsored by Joint Venture: Silicon Valley, presented at Santa Clara, CA, 14 October.

Porter, M.E. (1982) 'From Competitive Advantage to Corporate Strategy', *Harvard Business Review* 64, May–June, pp. 43–59.

Porter, M.E. (1990) 'The Competitive Advantage of Nations', *Harvard Business Review* 68, March–April, p. 74.

Porter, M.E. (1995) 'The Competitive Advantage of the Inner City', *Harvard Business Review* 73, May–June, pp. 55–71.

Porter, M.E. (1998) 'Clusters and the New Economics of Competition', *Harvard Business Review*, November–December, pp. 77–90.

Pound, J. (1992) 'Beyond Takeovers: Politics Comes to Corporate Control', *Harvard Business Review* 70, March–April, pp. 83–93.

Prahalad, C.K. and Ramaswamy, V. (2000) 'Co-opting Customer Competence', *Harvard Business Review*, January–February, pp. 79–87.

Ruben, B.D. and Lehr, J.K. (1997) *Excellence in Higher Education: A Guide to Organizational Self-assessment, Strategic Planning and Improvement*. Dubuque, IA: Kendall/Hunt.

Salancik, G.R. (1991) 'Commitment and the Control of Organizational Behaviour and Belief', in Barry M. Staw (ed.) *Psychological Dimensions of Organizational Behaviour*. New York, NY: Macmillan, p. 310.

Saunders, A. (2002) 'Double First', *Management Today*, December, pp. 45–53.

Snell, S.A. (1992) 'Control Theory in Strategic Human Resource Management: The Mediating Effect of Administrative Information', *Academy of Management Journal* 35, June, p. 293.

Stepanek, M. (1999) 'Using the Net for Brainstorming', *Business Week*, December, pp. EB55–EB57.

Thakur, M. and Calingo, L. (1992) 'Strategic Thinking is Hip, but Does it Make a Difference', *Business Horizons* 35, September–October, p. 48.

Thomas, J.B., Clark, S.M. and Gioia, D.A. (1993) 'Strategic Sensemaking and Organizational Performance: Linkages among Scanning, Interpretation, Action, and Outcomes', *Academy of Management Journal* 36, April, pp. 239–270.

Tichy, N. (1999) 'The Teachable Point of View: A Primer', *Harvard Business Review*, March–April, pp. 82–83.

Vickers, M. and Coy, P. (2000) 'A New Net Equation', *Business Week*, 31 January, pp. 38–40.

Welch, J.A. and Nayak, P.R. (1992) 'Strategic Sourcing: A Progressive Approach to the Make-or-buy Decision', *Academy of Management Executive* 6, February, pp. 23–31.

Wetlaufer, S. (1999) 'Driving Change: An Interview with Ford Motor Company's Jacques Nasser', *Harvard Business Review*, March–April, pp. 77–88.

Wilkins, A.L. and Ouchi, W.G. (1983) 'Efficient Cultures: Exploring the Relationship between Culture and Organizational Performance', *Administrative Science Quarterly* 28, September, pp. 468–481.

Wilson, I.H. (1980) 'Environmental Scanning and Strategic Planning', Business Environment/Public Policy Conference Papers, St Louis, American Assembly of Collegiate Schools of Business, pp. 159–163.

Part 1: Integrated case study

Vanderlande Industries: a global marketplace

As you rush off the aircraft and through passport control on your way to baggage reclaim, have you ever wondered how your bag has managed to get to the carousel? The chances are the technology and operating system were provided by Vanderlande Industries.

Anybody who's ever flown will be familiar with the conveyor belts that carry away your baggage once you've checked in. Whether or not you ever see your suitcases again depends on the effectiveness of the airport's baggage-handling system. Your baggage has to go through a security check and then find its way onto the right plane in good time for take-off. That may sound simple, but given that your suitcase is just one of thousands – at some airports, hundreds of thousands – of other pieces of baggage, it's a very precise process and this is where Vanderlande Industries has built its expertise.

The company produces a whole range of different kinds of baggage-handling systems, big and small, ranging from simple conventional solutions to complex high-tech systems. Vanderlande has supplied more than 300 airports throughout the world, from London's Heathrow to Kiev's Borispyl and from Rio de Janeiro in Brazil to Chengdu in China.

Background

Vanderlande Industries is an international company, originating in the Netherlands, dedicated to the design, implementation and service of automated material-handling systems, not only in airports but also for mail-order companies.

The company has a broad expertise in many branches of industry and is particularly recognised for its capabilities to implement integrated material-handling solutions in distribution centres, express parcel-sorting facilities and the manufacturing industry. In addition, it is one of the leading suppliers of baggage-handling systems at airports worldwide.

Vanderlande is a global player and was recently recognised as such when it was awarded the Ontario Global Traders Award by the Ontario Government in Canada, recognising its alliance with Brock Solutions.

Brock's strategic alliance with Vanderlande was established in response to the tragedy of 9/11 and the subsequent mandate of heightened security requirements at US airports, and is specifically aimed at supplying turnkey baggage-handling systems to large airports in the United States. The partnership has resulted in the implementation of numerous explosives detection systems (EDS) into existing baggage-handling systems (BHS), as well as complete systems implementations involving the design and deployment of BHS and EDS systems at new terminals in airports throughout the United States.

The result of such collaboration has meant that, in 2005, sales rose by 26 per cent. The most important contributions to this increase were provided by the activities in the USA and London's Heathrow Terminal 5 contract.

Based on the expected market growth, the continuous investments in research and development, and the record order book position, the company expects to achieve a further increase in net sales and an improved operating profit in the next financial year. At present the company has 1201 employees; these future developments will also lead to further growth in the number of employees. For example, the company currently has more than 60 vacancies, particularly for technicians and IT specialists at HBO (higher vocational training) and WO (graduate) level.

Building a successful organisation

Vanderlande Industries has gained global recognition by becoming a knowledge-intensive international company that specialises in the design, implementation and maintenance of automated material-handling systems and related services.

The company is among the top five in the world in its field. For the supply of material-handling solutions, the company possesses core competences in all the relevant disciplines, from system design and engineering through supply chain management and production to IT, project management and continuing service and customer support.

Vanderlande operates globally with a presence in all key regions of the world. The company operates locally through customer centres in the Netherlands, Belgium, Germany, France, the UK, Spain, China, South Africa and the USA, which handle all key business functions and maintain direct contact with the customer.

It has achieved this success because it is dedicated to improving its customers' business processes and strengthening their competitive position by enabling them to optimise their performance.

It does this by providing effective automated material-handling systems. These systems provide fast, efficient, reliable and labour-saving goods-handling solutions in distribution centres, express parcel-sorting facilities and the manufacturing industry, and for baggage handling at airports. The company implements material-handling systems of all sizes, ranging from the world's largest facilities to many local sorting depots, airports and distribution centres.

In every case the emphasis is on a close partnership with the customer, extending from initial analysis of the underlying business processes through to total life cycle support, including upgrades and refurbishment. To enable it to do this, the company possesses core competencies in all the relevant disciplines, ranging from system design and engineering, through supply chain management and manufacturing, to information and communication technology, system integration, project management and continuing customer service and support.

Core capabilities

Core capabilities of the company are system concepting, design, engineering, information technology, integration, project management and services. The company is dedicated to the application of state-of-the-art technology and is continuously developing new products and software solutions that improve its customers' competitiveness. Vanderlande company has subsidiaries in the Netherlands, Belgium, France, Germany, Great Britain, Spain, Asia (Hong Kong SAR), South Africa and the USA.

The changing face of baggage handling

It wasn't all that long ago that individual airports decided how baggage was dealt with and what the system should be like. But that situation has now changed. Nowadays, baggage handling is considered to be such a complex process that it's too expensive for an airport to have the necessary expertise in-house. As a result, stringent specifications have been replaced by a programme of requirements based on performance indicators. In line with this approach, maintenance and operation are increasingly being contracted out.

That trend has greatly benefited Vanderlande Industries because the company is an expert in all aspects of baggage handling. Vanderlande designs and constructs the systems itself and, if the client wishes, can also look after maintenance and operation. According to Rob Houben, vice president baggage handling systems at Vanderlande, 'That's why we can give guarantees, more than any other player. After all, nobody knows a product better than the people who designed and produced it.' Houben makes clear that capacity at Vanderlande Industries links up with a trend that he notes in customer demand. 'Airports first let us know what they need. They then want to know what the life cycle costs will be, in other words what the system is going to cost them over the next 10 years. Because we design and construct so much in-house, we can give a precise answer to that question and that makes us extremely competitive.' That's not just true where the price is concerned because Vanderlande also thinks along with the client. A combination of customised work and the most complete product package – from simple baggage conveyors to high-tech systems – means that Vanderlande can always come up with the right solution. Recently, for example, an airport asked Vanderlande to provide a 'rush baggage' facility for last-minute passengers. The system will take the baggage concerned directly from the check-in desk to the aircraft. The patented BAGTRAX system transports the baggage to the plane at up to 40 kilometres an hour. 'This is an example of a client asking us for total process control,' says Houben, 'We look after the passenger's case from the moment he or she lets go of it.'

BAGTRAX and other 'destination coded vehicle' systems developed by Vanderlande operate at airports such as Amsterdam Schiphol Airport, Charles de Gaulle (Paris), Oslo and Zurich. BAGTRAX consists of an extensive system of aluminium rails on which run four-wheeled carts, each carrying a single piece of baggage. On the straight sections of the system, the carts may reach a speed of up to 40 kilometres an hour. In many cases, BAGTRAX follows a circular route around all the piers, the baggage hall, and the loading and unloading stations. The system also includes lines for transporting empty carts, a security inspection zone and a maintenance area. The whole system is controlled by a computer, which also controls functions such as the loading and unloading of the carts, merging the carts into and diverting them from the main line, transport on inclined sections, sorting sections, and scanning and monitoring stations. The strength of the system is in its simplicity. It has few moving parts, meaning that little maintenance is necessary, and it is highly reliable. It can handle 99.99 per cent of all bags smoothly, regardless of their shape or size. The running costs are also low. For example, each motor runs only when it has a cart directly above it, thus saving energy and increasing the life of the system. 'Robustness has always been one of our guiding principles,' says Houben. 'Whether a complex system or a single conveyor is concerned, we always work on the basis that a baggage-handling system needs to work effectively and punctually.'

For airports, that principle is one of the main factors determining how successful they are in the competition to attract passengers. It's therefore not surprising that Vanderlande takes on contracts all over the world. More than half the world's 500 large and medium-sized airports use systems produced by the company, transporting a total of 1.1 million pieces of baggage a day. 'In fact, we're everywhere,' says Houben. 'We've recently been carrying out assignments in Boston, Chengdu and Leipzig. The projects are always different. Sometimes they're really challenging because we need to integrate new systems with existing facilities and we therefore need to get our software to talk to the programs that are already installed. And sometimes all we need to do is instal some perfectly ordinary conveyors. Whatever the situation, we always strive for top quality, and we give operational guarantees.' Vanderlande remains highly innovative. It is currently working on prototypes of a do-it-yourself check-in system for some European airports. Passengers will be able to check in at unmanned desks all over the airport. A machine will dispense their boarding pass and receive their baggage, which will then be forwarded underground. 'The passenger will be able to get rid of his baggage right away. He won't need to stand in a queue but will be able to go shopping or fill in time in some other way. The gain for the passenger is convenience and for the airport it's extra income. We are a factor that promotes that effect.'

Discussion questions

1 What strategies have enabled Vanderlande Industries to be one of the main players in the baggage-handling industry?
2 What part does innovation play in helping Vanderlande achieve success?
3 Vanderlande is a global business, what factors have contributed to its global success?
4 What is meant by global partnership?

Applied questions

5 Using a model of an open system, how do Vanderlande's subsystems come together to form a cohesive whole?

6 The six sigma and Malcolm Baldrige National Quality Award framework are two methods of examining an organisation to ensure continuous improvement. How can these methods be applied to Vanderlande?

PART 2

The individual: managing people

Part contents

4

Understanding perception, learning and personality

LEARNING OUTCOMES

After studying this chapter you should be able to:

- ☑ **explain** what is meant by person–job fit and the psychological contract

- ☑ **illustrate** the impact of perceptions and attributions on people's behaviour in organisations

- ☑ **describe** three theories of learning and how they apply to organisational settings

- ☑ **contrast** four basic individual styles of learning and know in which roles each is effective

- ☑ **illustrate** the impact that values and attitudes have on perceptions and behaviour

- ☑ **describe** and illustrate different personality types and traits, and their significance for behaviour.

The opening vignette looks at how important it is for the performance of people in an organisation to be not just physically fit but also mentally fit.

Liechtenstein Global Trust: learning to learn

Prince Philipp of Liechtenstein, chairman of the multinational bank the Liechtenstein Global Trust (LGT), once received a letter from the wife of a senior executive member of staff. 'Thank you for giving me my husband back,' she wrote. Her husband had decided to work smarter, not harder, after attending a six-week course at the LGT Academy to learn about the ideas of Tony Buzan, the creator of 'mind mapping'.

Internationally renowned for his work on using the brain and body together for maximum performance, Buzan was called in to LGT in 1995 to design a programme for the bank's 700 staff.

Every employee went through the multi-million-pound initiative, learning mental and physical skills. These included creative innovation, learning and memory, mind mapping, reading and studying, physical stamina training such as martial arts, self-management, change management, leadership, art, music, philosophy, psychology, poetry and communication.

The training, which still goes on today, has transformed the organisation according to Prince Philipp. 'Not only has it made people more efficient and better communicators, the physical and mental health of the organisation is demonstrably superior,' he told Buzan.

The creative thinking expert has long advocated the benefits of using brain and body together effectively. 'The way we think affects our bodies. If you're thinking clearly, creatively and positively, then you will be strengthening yourself and actually using the complexity and sophistication of your brain effectively,' he says.

Buzan believes the reverse is also true: a healthy body leads to a more effective mind. 'But if you know the entire relationship and you train them both, you get an even greater return,' he adds. Now we are living in the knowledge economy, Buzan's message could be more relevant than ever. What he believes in translates easily into the corporate world. Unilever, IBM and LGT are among a handful of companies that have already used the mind and body principle of healthy body, healthy mind – healthy mind, healthy body – to deliver improved performance.

'Within the next 10 years, before anyone in the company does any training, they will be required to have accomplished skills in learning how to learn,' Buzan predicts.

According to Buzan two drivers in particular will lead to the mind and body principle taking hold in the corporate world. First, in an economy where employees are the competitive advantage, companies are increasingly demanding learning skills. 'In the global marketplace, employers are looking for thinkers. They are looking for people who can, above anything else, learn.' Second, there is the stress factor. 'Stress is one of the main damaging effects to any company and its bottom line,' Buzan says. 'When people are stressed, a business disintegrates by definition.'

Organisations are spending millions shoring themselves up against the pressure of stress, paying for medical bills and bringing in cover for absent employees. According to the Health & Safety Executive, 6.5 million working days are lost each year through stress-related illnesses, costing employers £370 million.

Buzan claims that if a person is mentally fit – through being accomplished in the arts, mind sports such as chess, reading, studying, and so on – they can, by definition, handle stress better. And if they are physically fit, they can get a pint more blood circulating around the body, giving them 20–50 per cent more energy.

Source: originally published in *People Management*, 7 February 2002: Buzan, T. 'Head Strong', Thorsons, reproduced with permission.

Discussion questions

1 How does this case demonstrate the importance of being mentally fit for work?

2 What effect can stress have on an organisation?

Perception, learning and personality are important facets of human behaviour. This chapter explores some of the important elements that managers should consider in understanding and managing people. Topics include the importance of person–job fit and the impact of perceptions, attributions learning, values, attitudes and personality in an organisational setting. Personality is the window through which others view your predictable behaviour patterns. While development of your personality has essentially been moulded by the time you are a young adult, the ways in which you perceive the world around you and the opportunities for learning develop and become more complex over a lifetime. We saw this illustrated in the opening vignette, where LGT found it could shape how its employees learn. This chapter begins with the ways in which you make sense of the world around you and concludes by opening windows to personality differences as part of the process of adapting to and successfully fitting in to your environment.

How the psychological contract bonds person–job fit

Organisations need to attract people who are able and willing to do the work necessary for achieving company and unit objectives. People, in turn, hope to work for organisations that help them satisfy their needs and wants. Both organisations and normal individuals hope to achieve a good fit between them.

person–job fit
The degree of fit between a person's abilities and motives and a job's demands and rewards.

Person–job fit is the term used to describe how well the abilities and motives of an individual fit the job demands and rewards offered by the organisation. Exhibit 4-1 illustrates this concept. A manager's job includes making the best fit possible between employees and their jobs.

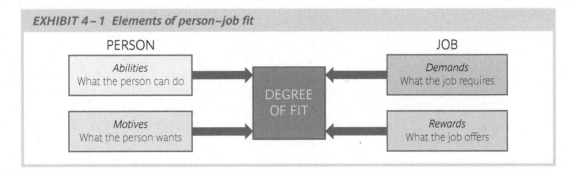

EXHIBIT 4–1 Elements of person–job fit

PERSON		JOB
Abilities — What the person can do	DEGREE OF FIT	*Demands* — What the job requires
Motives — What the person wants		*Rewards* — What the job offers

The psychological contract

When people enter organisations and jobs they bring their own expectations about what they will have to contribute and what they will receive in response, a set of expectations called the psychological contract. Individuals may not be fully conscious of this 'contract', for usually it is implicit and unwritten. People feel satisfied as long as the contract is fulfilled, but if it is not they are likely to feel tension and behave in ways that either even up the contract or change it.

psychological contract
Workers' implicit expectations about what they are expected to contribute to an organisation and what they will receive in return.

Individuals contribute such qualities as their skills, effort, time, loyalty and commitment to an organisation. In return, the organisation offers such things as pay, benefits, security and opportunities to satisfy such motives as the need for achievement, power, status and affiliation.

Both the individual and the organisation feel satisfied if they perceive the psychological contract as fair. If not, either party can initiate a change. For example, people can withhold effort or quit if they do not get an expected raise, promotion and/or reassignment. The organisation can require employees to exert more effort or to learn a new skill. The psychological contract is dynamic because the expectations and contributions of both the individual and organisation change over time. An awareness of psychological contracts should remind managers of the reciprocal relationship between individuals and the organisation, and the need to keep those contracts fair, equitable and up to date.

Economic cycles and business trends affect the terms of the psychological contract. During the mid-1990s it became apparent that all was not right with many employee–employer contracts. Most companies proclaimed the importance of teamwork, empowerment, participation and employee loyalty. Yet many of these same companies were downsizing and laying off large numbers of people, many of whom were long-term employees. Mergers and acquisitions also led to many people losing their jobs. These actions were taken to reduce costs and stay competitive. Many companies also began to replace long-term employees with temporary and part-time workers.

The chasm between company pronouncements and company actions was obvious. Kuttner (1993) and Csoka (1995) highlighted the opinion that employees wondered why they should give their loyalty and commitment to companies that did not reciprocate with commitments to long-term relationships. And yet, as they entered the twenty-first century, most organisations had put consolidation and downsizing behind them. A wave of entrepreneurism was creating new businesses and jobs, and economic conditions of full employment caused many organisations to scramble to improve the terms of the psychological contract if they were to retain or recruit employees.

Movement towards a new social contract

social contract
Term used to describe collective psychological contracts within a national culture.

The term social contract is sometimes used to describe collective psychological contracts that prevail within a national culture. Although there have always been important variations, for many years the general social contract in the United Kingdom and the United States included two common elements identified by Weidenbaum (1995). One was that employees would give regular attendance and effort, along with loyalty, to the organisation. In return, employers would provide 'fair' pay and benefits, advancement based on seniority and merit, and job security within reasonable limits. This social contract was never followed universally, but it was strongly implied and accepted by large numbers of companies and employees. During recent years that has changed.

Weidenbaum (1995) suggests that a new social contract needs to be developed. Many paradoxes will have to be faced and reconciled. For example, when productivity must be enhanced, why is the workforce often reduced? Companies encourage workers to give their commitment and loyalty without promising the same in return.

According to Csoka (1995) a revised social contract will probably include the following in defining new relationships. Employees will be expected to provide a high level of performance, a commitment to the company's objectives, and a willingness to innovate or make suggestions and train to improve behaviour. Employers, in turn, will provide interesting and challenging work, learning, flexibility, performance-based compensation, and opportunities for participation and involvement. This means that many workers will have to change from their psychological dependence on their employers to a commitment to their craft or profession. Workers will have to develop knowledge and skills that are transferable to other companies and jobs.

In spite of a more ambiguous social contract, one of the manager's major challenges remains making the best possible fit between individuals and jobs. To meet this challenge, managers must understand employees' abilities as they pertain to their daily job tasks.

People's performance depends on their abilities and motives. Ability is about 'can do' and motives are about 'will do'. Both are important to performance, and managers need to know the difference. Some people are able to perform specific tasks but are unwilling to do so; others compensate for their lack of ability by being motivated to learn and work hard. This section focuses on ability; motives will be discussed in Chapter 5.

Ability versus aptitude

ability
The capacity to perform physical and intellectual tasks.

aptitude
The capacity to learn an ability.

Ability is the capacity to perform physical and intellectual tasks. **Aptitude** is the capacity to learn an ability. People differ both in their abilities and aptitudes. Few, if any, can play football as well as David Beckham or sing as well as Luciano Pavarotti. Most of us do not have the aptitude required to match their abilities. Managers should know what abilities are required to perform various jobs and should try to match the jobs with people who have appropriate abilities, or at least the aptitude to learn. Physical ability can be distinguished from intellectual ability.

Physical ability includes such factors as strength, dexterity, co-ordination, stamina and quickness. Intellectual ability is the capacity to learn, reason, manipulate data and apply knowledge to new situations. According to Gardner (1983), intelligence is sometimes thought of as a single factor, but evidence suggests there are multiple intelligences, including linguistic, musical, logical, mathematical, spatial, bodily-kinaesthetic and personal intelligence. Tests have been designed to measure both physical and intellectual skills.

It is useful for managers to understand the difference between ability and aptitude. People who lack either the ability or aptitude to perform a job will likely fail and feel dissatisfied. Those who have the aptitude but not the ability to perform a certain job can learn to do so. Too much ability, however, can also be a problem. Those who are overqualified for certain jobs can become bored and unmotivated. The key is to find the best person–job fit possible.

Managing the person–job fit involves more than simply matching a person's abilities and motives with job requirements and rewards. How an individual performs is also impacted by such variables as perceptions, learning, attitudes and personality. Consider now how perceptions impact on how people behave in an organisation.

dynamics of diversity

Hidden talents

Reed Executive, a top recruitment company, hears constantly that recruiting top talent is still the number one priority.

Winning the recruitment war continues to be crucial, and had apparently got harder rather than easier for more than one-third of those surveyed by the company. As one respondent put it, 'even in a recession, top talent is scarce'.

Its concerns are reflected in the statistics. Despite the current economic slowdown, UK unemployment remains at its lowest level since the mid-1970s. Half of all companies in the UK still report skill shortages when they recruit, although this has improved on the 70 per cent who cited such difficulties at the peak of the recent economic boom.

One problem is that the UK has too many unskilled people. We have seen plummeting demand for unskilled workers over the past decades. Many of them are unemployed and some are economically inactive for other reasons.

Overall the UK has a bigger proportion of very low-skilled workers than other rich European countries, making this an issue that affects this country more than similar European states and one we cannot ignore.

At the same time, where people have skills they may not have the right ones. The effects of this appear to be greater than employment figures suggest. Even for workers with 'new skills', recruitment patterns have changed unexpectedly, making it hard for employers to read the market.

While no one pretends it is easy to ride the waves of this rather unpredictable job market, employers do unfairly ignore the talents of certain groups. Unemployment among minority ethnic groups has dropped over the past decade, but it remains consistently more than double the rate for white unemployment – 12 per cent compared with 5 per cent.

One of the obstacles identified by Reed was the wrong fit between an organisation's profile and what the best candidates actually wanted. Moreover, this is backed up by the views of the candidates themselves. Reed analysed responses from over 3500 questionnaires that were filled in on its website. An interesting trend emerged.

It became clear just how important it was to get the psychological fit right for each role, as well as the skills, to ensure the person is, to coin a phrase, 'fit for work'. This means more than creating the right personality spec. Different job-seekers look for different types of working style – some, for instance, love teamwork while others want only to be rewarded for individual effort – and each person brings their own preferences to work with them.

Moreover, nearly three-quarters of workers questioned have suffered 'job shock' in their working lives, where they found a huge difference between what they had expected the working style to be and the reality. Finding the right workplace was a major issue, according to Reed's research; 85 per cent said it affected their motivation at work, 66 per cent felt it affected their productivity, 61 per cent felt getting this fit right affected their initial attraction to the job, and almost half said that it affected their retention in the job.

One of the most striking findings of the survey was just how diverse people's psychological preferences were when it came to job style. While 41 per cent liked a flat structure, for instance, 38 per cent actually preferred to work in a hierarchical organisation. Half wanted a co-operative environment, but nearly a third would rather have a competitive one.

Among all this divergence, there was a fascinating area of agreement: an astonishingly high 92 per cent of workers chose a challenging work style in preference to a predictable one, emphasising just how important this is within a job profile.

Clearly different jobs require different working styles, yet 26 per cent of job-seekers felt that employers failed to do enough to communicate these when they were recruiting. Addressing the dynamics of diversity can help in the vital task of getting the best, most productive new staff member.

Source: adapted from *People Management*, 16 May 2002, 'Hidden Talents' by John Reed, CEO Reed Executive, pp. 32–34.

Discussion questions

1 Would testing candidates help to ensure the correct fit between the person and the job?
2 What can employers do to ensure that employees are satisfied with their work?

Perceptions and attributions

Each of us has experienced perceiving someone or something differently than others do. For example, two subordinates may evaluate their supervisor quite differently. One might perceive the boss as an effective leader because he or she provides structure and direction, while the other may perceive him or her as a rigid and controlling manager. Understanding the perceptual process helps explain why such differences occur.

Perception defines one's reality

perception
The selection, organisation and interpretation of sensory data.

Perception is the selection, organisation and interpretation of sensory data. This critically important process helps people define their world and provides clues for guiding their behaviour. Exhibit 4-2 illustrates the general perceptual process.

People do not see objective reality, but they believe what they perceive is real. Our perceptions are our personal reality whether they are objective or not, and they influence our behaviour. Imagine a manager named Joe walking into his subordinate's office unexpectedly.

His subordinate, Daniel, is leaning back in his chair, feet on the desk and eyes closed. How will Joe react? That will depend on how Joe perceives the situation.

He might respond with anger because he thinks Daniel is sleeping on the job, or he might quietly withdraw because he assumes Daniel is thinking through a problem. Joe's past experience with Daniel will temper his perceptions. For example, he may know Daniel likes to party and stay out late at night, and he may assess him as a below-average employee. Alternatively, he may know that Daniel has been working hard on a difficult project and that in the past he has been productive. Joe knows he himself sometimes leans back and shuts the world out while thinking about a difficult problem.

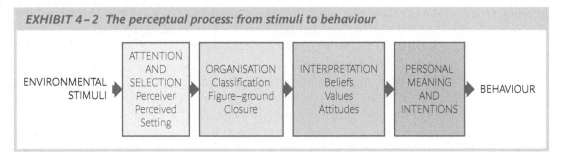

EXHIBIT 4–2 *The perceptual process: from stimuli to behaviour*

ENVIRONMENTAL STIMULI → ATTENTION AND SELECTION (Perceiver, Perceived, Setting) → ORGANISATION (Classification, Figure–ground, Closure) → INTERPRETATION (Beliefs, Values, Attitudes) → PERSONAL MEANING AND INTENTIONS → BEHAVIOUR

In either case, Joe is noticing certain things and relating them to what he already believes. He then adds meaning and interprets what he sees. The result is his personal perception, which in turn influences his behaviour towards Daniel. Joe may behave inappropriately if he misperceives the situation.

Understanding the perceptual process helps managers know better why people perceive things as they do and why they often perceive things differently. This understanding enables them to deal better with such differences and minimise some of the distortions that occur.

Attention and selection

Each of us is bombarded with multiple sensory stimuli, and it is impossible to attend to them all. We selectively respond to meaningful stimuli and minimise or ignore others. The perceiver, the perceived and the setting influence this part of the process.

The perceiver

People tend to notice what is important to them. A hungry person is more likely to be aware of food than someone whose stomach is full. An unemployed person is more likely to read a job advertisement than someone gainfully employed. Individuals are more likely to notice positive or negative characteristics of others depending on whether they like them or not. People tend to perceive what they need, want and expect to see.

The physical, mental and emotional condition of the perceiver affects attentiveness. A person who is tired, ill, stressed or emotionally upset may not perceive as accurately as someone who is alert, well, at ease or calm. In addition, the perceiver's beliefs, attitudes, values, motives and expectations influence what he or she perceives as relevant. For example, a student who values grades more than learning may not pay attention to parts of a classroom lecture but may perk up when the instructor mentions a possible test question.

The perceived

Certain general attributes of the perceived object or person influence what is noticed and what is not. These include size, novelty, motion, proximity and intensity of the stimulus. Loud noises, sudden quietness, unusual motions and bright colours tend to attract attention. Objects that are novel or unusual stand out. These characteristics also apply to people. Those who are very large or small often attract attention. So do those who are loud, dress in bright colours or unusual styles, and behave in unusual ways. People who are unusually attractive or unattractive are noticed when others are not. The status of a person may also influence attention.

The setting

Time and physical conditions such as temperatures, lighting, noise, smell and clutter are examples of contextual factors that may influence what is noticed and what is not. If an individual is tired and it is late in the day, he or she might be less sensitive to external stimuli than when feeling bright and alert. People generally see more in the light than in the dark, although they might hear more in the dark than in the light.

The nature of the setting can also be relevant. Boisterous laughter might be appropriate in a social setting and not noticed as much as it would be in a work setting. A manager might go unnoticed in jeans and a T-shirt at the company picnic but would attract considerable attention dressed that way in the office. The nature of the setting influences what is perceived as appropriate or normal.

Organisation

The next step after sensory stimuli have been selected and received is to organise the various stimuli into more meaningful patterns. Three concepts relate to this process: classification, figure–ground differentiation and closure.

Classification

We classify people in a variety of categories such as age, gender, race, nationality, physical categories, education, occupation and status. We also attach the assumptions, beliefs and attitudes we hold about those groupings. Classifying sensory inputs helps us sort and recall sensory data faster than if we did not have an organisational system. However, classification can also lead to stereotypes and inaccurate perceptions.

For example, assume a job applicant is directed to visit Chris Taylor, the human resources manager. The applicant approaches two people, a young man and a middle-aged woman, looks at the man, and says, 'Mr Taylor?' The man smiles and replies, 'No, I'm Ed Smith. This is Chris Taylor.' This embarrassing perceptual error is probably based on the mistaken assumption that men are more likely to be managers and women secretaries. A person who is aware of the perceptual process would recognise the ambiguity in this situation and avoid the mistake.

Figure–ground differentiation

figure
The dominant feature being perceived.

ground
The surrounding, competing stimuli being perceived.

A major element in perceptual accuracy is the ability to distinguish **figure** (dominant features) from **ground** (surrounding, competing stimuli). Why, in a crowded and noisy restaurant, are you are able to hold a meaningful conversation with a colleague? Because you are capable of distinguishing the sight and sound of your colleague (figure) from the sight and sound of the other people and objects present (ground). Although you perceive the entire scene, you respond selectively to the most relevant stimuli. If you were to respond to all the stimuli non-selectively, nothing meaningful would result.

It is the same for managers in organisations. People pay more attention to some stimuli than others and run the danger of overlooking relevant clues. For example, the job applicant looking for Chris Taylor might have focused on the ages of Taylor and Smith as well as on their gender. He or she may have assumed (correctly in this case) that the older of the two was more likely to be the manager. If Joe (in our earlier example) notices only Daniel's closed eyes and relaxed position, he may overlook the piles of work on his desk and his rumpled clothing, which might indicate Daniel had worked all night on a project.

Look quickly at Exhibit 4-3 and then look away. How do you interpret the figure? Most people focus on the individual figures enclosed with lines, and few see any meaning. However, if you focus on the space between the figures, the word WEST appears. If you put a piece of paper along the bottom of the figure, the word becomes even more apparent.

EXHIBIT 4–3 A figure–ground experiment

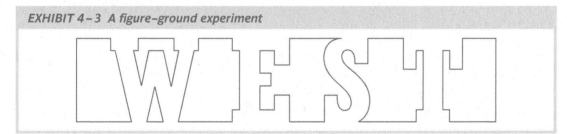

What we see depends on what we see as figure and what we see as ground. We attend selectively to stimuli by focusing on features that capture our attention. A major purpose of studying organisational behaviour is to alert you to possible important stimuli. Key theories and concepts (such as power, motivation and leadership) call attention to variables that affect organisational performance. The trained manager knows what to look for as the dominant figure against a complex background of organisational forces.

Closure

If normal channels of sensory awareness receive incomplete information, the mind often fills in the gaps. **Perceptual closure** occurs when we receive some data that we judge important but incomplete and allow our minds to fill in the missing data, especially if the situation or topic is familiar. Instances of perceptual closure often arise at work when someone in authority delivers a command or instruction but fails to explain it adequately. Typically, the conscientious receiver will think, 'What did she mean by that?' or 'Why is he making me do this?' Our answers fill the gaps to give us a sense of closure. Sometimes our answers are incorrect!

perceptual closure
The mind's tendency to fill in missing data when it receives incomplete information.

Given insufficient information, people often make assumptions about the missing data. However, if the stimulus is insufficient to effect closure and thus to cope with an ambiguous situation, then frustration, anxiety and stress may result. Some managers deliberately assign tasks in an ambiguous manner, believing this will encourage subordinates to develop their own problem-solving skills and become more self-reliant. However, if the level of ambiguity is excessive for the individual's job maturity level, this tactic is likely to prove dysfunctional. Lacking closure on the task, and left without clues as to how to proceed, the subordinate may become disorientated, fearful, defensive and withdrawn. Alert managers watch for these symptoms and help employees work through their feelings by listening and offering suggestions.

Exhibit 4-4 illustrates the perceptual closure concept. Conjecture is easy in the bottom row, but most people would have difficulty completing the top row based on the information given. Closure would not occur.

It would be difficult to complete the symbols in the top row because of insufficient information. The symbols in the bottom row could be considered complete because sufficient information is provided.

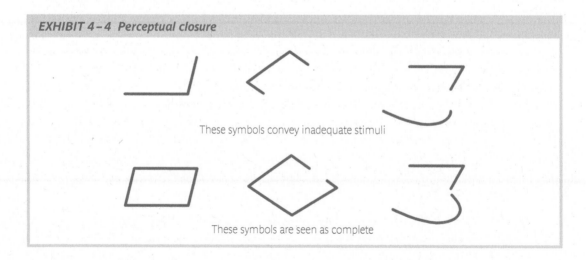

EXHIBIT 4–4 Perceptual closure

These symbols convey inadequate stimuli

These symbols are seen as complete

Interpretation

Keep in mind that the perceptual process happens instantly. It happens much faster than the time it takes you to read about it! Sensory inputs are selected, filtered through our past and present experience and then interpreted. We add meaning to data we take in. Our past learning and experience as well as our current beliefs, assumptions, attitudes and values, all influence the meaning we add to what we take in. Combined, they form our individual **frame of reference**, which is a mental filter through which perceptions are interpreted and evaluated.

frame of reference
Mental filter through which perceptions are interpreted and evaluated.

For example, in our earlier example Joe actually interpreted what he saw as Daniel needing a well-deserved break. Although startled at seeing him stretched out with his eyes closed, he knew that Daniel was a conscientious, productive person. He noticed the rumpled clothes and piles of work, and he correctly assumed he had spent the night at his desk. Based on his perception, he quietly withdrew and decided to contact Daniel later.

Fortunately, in this case Joe perceived correctly. However, the perceptual process is difficult and subject to various errors and distortions. Research by Henriques and Sadorsky (1999) shows that if managers do not perceive a stakeholder (such as those in the 'environmental protection' classification) as important to the organisation's mission, they will take a more reactive or defensive posture. This distorts their interpretation of the potential relevance of the stakeholder's agenda. We will identify some of the more common errors.

Perceptual distortions

People's perceptions become distorted in several ways. These involve selective perception, stereotypes, halo effects and projection. An understanding and awareness of these distortions can help people avoid them. Each of these distortions tends to obscure individual differences and has the potential to make us oversimplify or misread other people and situations.

People tend to focus on those attributes of people and situations that fit their frame of reference. This is called **selective perception**. Two examples are failing to see the faults of a loved one or the good points about someone we dislike. The potential danger of selective perception is that we miss important data and the omission causes a distorted view of a person or situation.

selective perception
The tendency to focus on those attributes of people and situations that fit our frame of reference.

stereotype
A rigid, biased perception of a person, group, object or situation.

Alternatively, we might misperceive because of stereotypes. A **stereotype** is a rigid, biased perception of a person, group, object or situation. We tend to categorise people by their obvious, and sometimes less obvious, differences. Based on past experiences and learning, those who stereotype think and behave as though all people in that category are the same. Stereotypes can be either positive or negative. People stereotype others on criteria ranging from age, gender, race, religion and nationality, to education level, occupation and political affiliation. Unwarranted negative stereotypes can lead to bias, which in turn leads to destructive attitudes such as sexism, racism and nationalism. Managers should be aware of their own inappropriate stereotypes and the need to confront those of their employees when they lead to destructive relations within a group.

halo effect
The tendency to overrate a person based on a single trait.

In sharp contrast to stereotyping, at times we attribute a **halo effect** to others. A halo effect is the tendency to overrate a person based on a single trait. An example would be assuming that an attractive person is intelligent without having an objective basis for that judgement. Halo effects can lead to incomplete and inaccurate judgements and, like stereotypes, may prompt someone to miss individual differences.

projection
Attributing to others one's own thoughts, feelings, attitudes and traits.

Another common perceptual distortion is projection, which is attributing to others one's own thoughts, feelings, attitudes and traits. People sometimes read their own motives or feelings into another. Someone who is very tired or stressed may see those same feelings in another person, who in fact may not be feeling that way. A person who tends to be suspicious of others may perceive others as being suspicious, just as someone who is trusting perceives others to be the same way.

Accurately perceiving other people is difficult because of the various kinds of errors we can make. It is even more difficult because we see only behaviours. Much of what causes these behaviours is not observable. We do not see others' thoughts, motives, intentions, attitudes, values or feelings. We satisfy our need for perceptual closure by making inferences about why others behave as they do, a process called attribution.

Attribution

attribution
An assumed explanation of why people behave as they do, based on our observations and inferences.

Attribution is an assumed explanation of why people behave as they do, based on our observations and inferences. In other words, the process of giving reasons for why things happen. Heider (1958) argued that people act like 'naive scientists', gathering factual information and using it to form theories about the possible causes of that information.

The way we identify these causes is known as the process of attribution. We also make attributions about our own behaviour. Past studies by Kelley and Michela (1980), Staw (1975), Kelley (1971) and Bettman and Weitz (1983) have identified how people assign causes to

Research focus: theories of attribution

Theory suggests that when people observe another's behaviour they use certain criteria to determine whether it fits that person's general personality or is affected by other factors. This attribution process is often subconscious.

Heider suggests that when we observe behaviour we decide whether it was internally or externally caused. We believe internally caused behaviours are under the control of the individual, whereas externally caused behaviours occur through outside forces beyond the person's control.

According to Kelley (1971), three types of information determine the attribution we make:

1 distinctiveness – whether the individual displays different behaviours in different situations, or the behaviour is common

2 consensus – whether the behaviour applies to everyone in the same situation

3 consistency – whether the behaviour is usual for the person.

Exhibit 4-5 illustrates, when consistency, distinctiveness and consensus are all high, we are likely to make a situational attribution. The practical example below shows how this theory works in practice.

distinctiveness
An attribution process used to explain whether a person's behaviour fits with other behaviours.

consistency
An attribution process used to explain the degree of variance in behaviour over time.

consensus
An attribution process used to determine how others behave in similar situations.

and explain behaviour. This has led to the development of attribution theory.

Assume Fernando Garcia submits a financial analysis needed for a proposal a day late. His supervisor, Kris White, instinctively assesses the meaning of this behaviour. Kris is likely to consider Fernando's past performance, including such things as quality and quantity of work, attendance, promptness and attitude. She will also be aware of situational factors, including workloads, time pressures, available resources, support and performance standards. Attribution theory suggests that she will then use three criteria in understanding why Fernando submitted the report late: **distinctiveness**, **consistency** and **consensus**.

Distinctiveness

If Fernando's analyses are sharp, his writing clear, his presentations professional, and if he has performed effectively and reliably over a range of different assignments, his late submission would be distinctive – a deviation from normal expectations.

According to Kelley (1971), consistency, distinctiveness and consensus information help us determine whether to make personal or situational attributions for someone else's behaviour.

Consistency

Has Fernando missed other deadlines, or is this an exception? Does he come to work and appointments on time? Is he usually reliable? If Kris decides Fernando's late submission fits a pattern of frequent tardiness, his behaviour would be judged consistent.

Consensus

Do Fernando's peers submit reports late? How frequently? If they are often late, there is consensus.

Attributions of internal–external causality

After assessing her observations using the above criteria, Kris is likely to attribute the cause of Fernando's behaviour to either internal or external factors. Internal causes are those over which

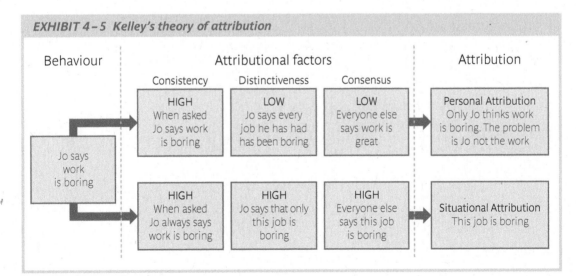

EXHIBIT 4–5 Kelley's theory of attribution

Behaviour	Attributional factors			Attribution
	Consistency	Distinctiveness	Consensus	
Jo says work is boring	HIGH When asked Jo says work is boring	LOW Jo says every job he has had has been boring	LOW Everyone else says work is great	Personal Attribution Only Jo thinks work is boring. The problem is Jo not the work
	HIGH When asked Jo always says work is boring	HIGH Jo says that only this job is boring	HIGH Everyone else says this job is boring	Situational Attribution This job is boring

the individual, Fernando in this case, is perceived to have control, such as effort, competence or attitude. External causes are those over which the individual is perceived to have little control; examples include poor or inadequate training, unrealistic workloads and deadlines, an equipment failure, insufficient resources and inadequate supervision.

If Kris decides that Fernando was late because he is lazy, is incompetent or has a poor attitude, she is attributing his behaviour to internal causes. If instead she thinks Fernando was late because the deadline was unrealistic or the computer file was destroyed, she will attribute Fernando's tardiness to external causes. Of course, a mix of internal and external attributions might be made. Kris's behaviour towards how she handles Fernando's late report will be influenced by the attributions she makes. Exhibit 4-6 illustrates the attribution process.

Fernando will make self-attributions about being late. He may be more aware than Kris of perceived external factors. Most people tend to give themselves credit for successes but to rationalise failures as based on perceived external factors. This tendency is modified by the degree of the individual's internal or external orientation. Both Kris or Fernando can each make inappropriate attributions, and we turn now to two errors people commonly make.

Attributional error and self-serving bias

attributional error
The tendency to overestimate internal factors and underestimate external factors when making attributions about others.

self-serving bias
The tendency of individuals to attribute their own positive performance to internal factors and their negative performance to external factors.

Miller and Lawson (1989) argue that when people make attributions about others there is evidence that they overestimate internal factors and underestimate external factors, a phenomenon called **attributional error**. One study by Schermerhorn (1986) showed that managers are more likely to attribute the poor performance of their subordinates to internal factors, such as ability and effort, than to negative factors inherent in the situation. However, the managers attributed their own poor performance to lack of support, an external factor. This **self-serving bias** is the tendency of individuals to attribute their own positive performance to internal factors and their negative performance to external factors.

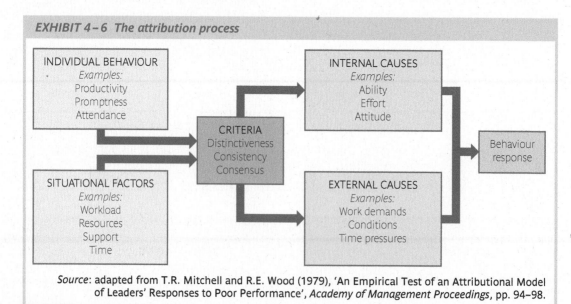

EXHIBIT 4–6 The attribution process

INDIVIDUAL BEHAVIOUR
Examples:
Productivity
Promptness
Attendance

SITUATIONAL FACTORS
Examples:
Workload
Resources
Support
Time

CRITERIA
Distinctiveness
Consistency
Consensus

INTERNAL CAUSES
Examples:
Ability
Effort
Attitude

EXTERNAL CAUSES
Examples:
Work demands
Conditions
Time pressures

Behaviour response

Source: adapted from T.R. Mitchell and R.E. Wood (1979), 'An Empirical Test of an Attributional Model of Leaders' Responses to Poor Performance', *Academy of Management Proceedings*, pp. 94–98.

Applications of perception and attribution

The behaviour of people in organisations is continuously influenced by perceptions and attributions. The interviewer who sizes up an applicant and the manager who evaluates employee performance are basing their judgements on perceptions and attributions. So are people who perceive others, deciding if they like them or not and want to co-operate or compete with them. We should be aware that others perceive us differently from how we may want to be seen, and vice versa. The need for self-awareness and empathic understanding is clear, as is the need to work continuously to avoid the common errors of perception and attribution.

Perception enables people to learn about and make sense of their worlds. The ability to learn is an important distinguishing characteristic of human beings and is vital to both individuals and organisations. In the next section, we will look at some of the basic theories of how individuals learn.

How people learn

Change pervades businesses and organisations. Individuals must be able to learn new knowledge and skills in order to survive. In the opening vignette at the beginning of this chapter, you were introduced to new ways of learning that have improved performance in the multinational bank LGT. In today's fast-changing world, everyone who works is periodically required to learn new knowledge and skills. This is dramatically apparent from the mushrooming uses of the Internet, as it changes the ways people perform routine functions and discover new ways of obtaining and acting on information.

We saw this illustrated in the vignette where LGT found it could shape its employees for the better using the ideas of Tony Buzan. His technique is simple, but nevertheless a useful learning tool and one you may like to use – especially if you have to write an assignment or revise for an exam, as you can see from the 'Research focus'.

learning
The acquisition of knowledge, skill or values through study, practice or experience.

An important distinguishing characteristic of human beings is their ability to store information and to learn. **Learning** is the acquisition of knowledge, skill or values through study, practice or experience. Learning is usually considered to lead to relatively permanent changes in behaviour as the learner develops capabilities for functioning in his or her environment.

The learning process takes place primarily in the brain. One useful metaphor for the brain is a computer. It has the capacity to receive inputs, organise and store them, and respond to some calls for retrieval. New data can be entered and existing data can be reorganised or deleted. Memory is similar to computer files, and perception and learning are the processes through which new data are added and old data revised.

Computers differ in their capacity to receive, store, process and retrieve information quickly and to manipulate the data in order to solve problems. These differing capacities are somewhat analogous to different individuals' intelligence and ability to think. Intelligence is a fuzzy

intelligence
The ability to adapt to novel situations quickly and effectively, use abstract concepts effectively, and grasp relationships and learn quickly.

concept. According to Chaplin (1985) generally, **intelligence** includes three different aspects: (1) the ability to adapt to novel situations quickly and effectively; (2) the ability to use abstract concepts effectively; and (3) the ability to grasp relationships and to learn quickly. Goleman (1994) has recently identified another aspect of intelligence, which he labels 'emotional intelligence'.

Research focus: using the mind map

The opening vignette introduced you to a manager who changed his life by using a technique described by Tony Buzan.

The mind map is a diagramming technique that helps you think. In the case of Liechtenstein Global Trust (LGT) it helped a manager to change his work strategies and become more productive and less stressed.

There are several variants of the mind map – you may know it as a spidergram, spray diagram or relevance tree.

To construct a mind map, start in the centre of the page with the main word or phrase that illustrates your idea. Then branch out into themes and subthemes. These branches can then be subdivided again. You could also use colour to represent a theme or pictures (see Exhibit 4-7).

Buzan illustrates the following advantages of using a mind map over conventional notes.

- The central idea is more clearly defined.
- The position indicates its importance – main headings near the centre are seen as more important than those on the outside.
- The lines create links and show connections between concepts.
- Recall and review is more effective as links can be seen.
- It is easy to add ideas to the structure.
- Patterns will differ from each other, making them easier to remember.

Buzan (1989) suggests that when using patterns creatively, the brain can easily make new connections.

EXHIBIT 4–7 Mind map showing stress and possible causes

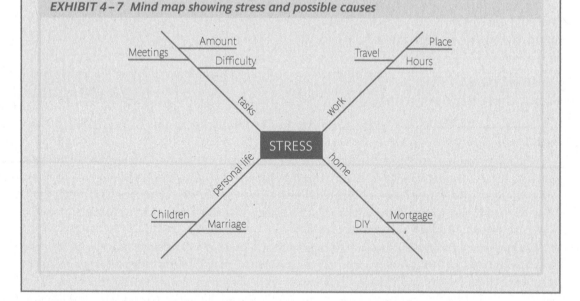

It reflects the functioning of a person's emotional brain, which generates and regulates feelings. Goleman suggests emotional intelligence relates to a person's ability to get along with others, exert control over one's life, and think and decide clearly.

Individuals differ in memory, intelligence and ability to learn. Now you have the opportunity to learn some of the basic theories of how individuals learn. The main theories we will consider are: (1) behavioural conditioning, (2) social learning and (3) cognitive discovery. We will also look at different individual styles of learning, because people tend to differ from one another in how they learn.

Behavioural conditioning

The development of learning theory began in the early twentieth century when the Russian physiologist Ivan Pavlov found he could condition dogs to salivate in response to the sound of a tuning fork, a previously neutral stimulus. Pavlov's work led to the development of classical conditioning, which is an experimental approach that associates a conditioned stimulus with an unconditioned stimulus to achieve a conditioned response.

classical conditioning
An experimental approach that associates a conditioned stimulus with an unconditioned stimulus to achieve a conditional response.

Dogs and other animals naturally salivate (*unconditional response-R*) when they are hungry and food (*unconditional stimulus-S*) is present. Pavlov experimented by preceding the presentation of food with the sound of a tuning fork (*conditional stimulus-S'*) and over time taught the dogs to salivate (*conditional response-R'*) at the sound alone. Pavlov's (1927) experiments provided the intellectual basis for an empirical approach to the study of learning.

People experience classical conditioning in their everyday lives without realising it. For example, assume you frequently walk by a bakery early in the morning and smell (*S*) the freshly baked bread. If you have not had breakfast you are likely to salivate and feel hunger pangs (*R*). The odour is an unconditioned stimulus, and your physical reaction is an unconditional response. Assume this happens frequently. Then one day you drive by the bakery and cannot smell the bread, but you salivate and feel hungry anyway. The sight of the shop (*S'*) has become a conditioned stimulus and your physical response, which now occurs without the actual odour, is also conditioned (*R'*).

Conditioning through management of reinforcement

operant conditioning
Learning in which reinforcement depends on the person's behaviour.

The psychologist B.F. Skinner extended the work of Pavlov and others to develop operant conditioning, which is learning in which reinforcement depends on the person's behaviour. In operant conditioning the critical learning element is the direct linkage of significant contingent consequences to an operant behaviour.

A *contingent consequence* is a reinforcer; it may be positive, negative or neutral. The term *operant* simply means that the individual 'operates' in his or her environment to obtain some desired consequences and avoid adverse or negative consequences. Individuals learn to anticipate or expect a certain consequence following specific behaviours. They learn to behave in ways that achieve positive consequences. The more frequently we get the desired consequences or avoid undesirable ones, the firmer the learning.

For example, assume Donna works extra hard on a special project to meet a tight deadline. Her boss is appreciative of Donna's efforts, gives her special praise and celebrates by treating her to lunch at an upmarket restaurant. Donna enjoys the recognition and is likely to work hard again to receive the desired compliments. If she gets no response at all, she will probably feel less inclined to work hard. If Donna is late with her report and is reprimanded, she is likely to work harder the next time to avoid the negative consequence.

According to Thorndike (1913) the basic assumption underlying conditioning theory is simple: people tend to repeat those behaviours that lead to desirable consequences and avoid

technology transformation

Whistles and bells

Ken Sung's job selling menswear is only part-time. But his familiarity with computers has landed him a new role helping Birmingham's House of Fraser store, Rackham's, to implement online learning.

Sung first sat in front of a computer at the age of four. This is a good deal earlier than many of his older colleagues. His supervisor, for instance, has only had a computer at home for two weeks, while many others have never been near one.

So Sung, in his final year at Birmingham University, found himself accompanying two or three staff at a time to the training room (where the company had installed three PCs) and showing them how to download and work through customer service modules.

Now, with the backing of his manager, he has devised a questionnaire to explore employees' computer awareness. The aim is to work out how much support they need so that training sessions are better planned.

The exercise is one store's response to the group-wide introduction of e-learning last year. And it is an example of how organisations launching such systems can support learners with traditional training methods. While information through cash tills has been available for two years, Rackham's has found computers are much more of a challenge to staff.

'When I've shown people what to do, they have been very positive, and all asked for user names so they can come back,' says Sung.

The computer is not replacing the way we have always learnt but is certainly aiding it. Only experience can teach you, but computers give you a theoretical underpinning.

House of Fraser piloted online learning last year in five stores and for selected office managers, using off-the-shelf modules from software firm Xebec McGraw-Hill. After successful evaluation it is now available in all stores and offices. Up to three dedicated terminals are provided in each store. There is also a booking system, which ensures that everyone is able to have a go.

Colin Robinson, the company's management development manager, says that in the past the company has relied on in-house advisers to train its managers. It now mixes this with online learning and on-the-job training.

Denise Harvie had been a first-line manager in the fashion industry for 15 years before taking a job in House of Fraser's buying department just over a year ago. Having never received any management training, she grabbed the chance to work through some basic computer modules on leadership, time management, dealing with stress and motivating a team. She enjoyed working at her own pace and at convenient times.

But she admits, 'Once I'd accomplished a particular section of a module, I felt I didn't have to think about it again. I wasn't the only one like that.'

So when she and her colleagues heard they were going on a three-day workshop, they did some swotting up. Once there, they discovered that the workshop neither duplicated the online learning nor taught an entirely new set of skills, but reinforced what had already been learnt: 'The skills covered on the computer are cleverly incorporated into the course,' says Harvie.

The epitome of blended learning at House of Fraser is the 12-month management training programme launched in May 2001 to produce more internally promoted managers. It combines workshops, workbooks, seminars and online learning, with every type of on-the-job development from 'sitting by Nellie', to assignments, coaching, job rotation and shadowing. Participants also have a mentor.

The recognition of a need to blend e-learning and offline development clearly emerged from last year's pilot, which showed it was helpful for managers who were working through the modules to get together afterwards and discuss what they had learnt.

'Online learning does not have to be lonely learning. There still needs to be follow-up when somebody has been on a management skills module. People will absorb the knowledge. We have to make sure they apply it. It's about consolidated learning,' says Robinson.

Source: adapted from *People Management*, 7 February 2002, 'Whistles and Bells' by Neil Merrick and Jane Pickard, pp. 44–45.

Discussion questions

1 Do you think it is important for all employees to be technologically aware?

2 How would you persuade 'technophobes' to develop new skills?

---

those that lead to negative results. Conditioning theory underlies many of the behaviours managers and teachers use in an attempt to motivate people and teach them to behave in certain ways. Today, Skinner's (1964) principles of operant conditioning are commonly applied in organisational settings to help change many types of human behaviours: drug addicts, students with learning disabilities, smokers, sex offenders and phobics, as well as employees. The use of reinforcement for purposes of behaviour modification is extended in Chapter 6.

Self-management of contingencies

It is possible for a person to manage his or her own contingencies. For example, one principle of time management has evolved from the premise that a person will complete 'have-to' tasks quite expediently if the reward (positive reinforcement) is engaging in tasks that are more creative, enjoyable or satisfying. Premack (1959) formalised this self-management strategy of pairing tasks or events.

Premack principle
The pairing of disagreeable tasks with enjoyable tasks or events to hasten their completion.

The **Premack principle** is based on the finding that when tasks are paired, the more probable (more pleasurable) behaviour will tend to reinforce or bring about the less probable behaviour. For example, complete the report, then play football or tennis. Well-organised students and workers may find they have adopted the Premack principle without even knowing that it had a name. If you have not used it for self-management, try it.

Social learning theory

Behaviourist psychologists believe that operant conditioning or reinforcement theory is the most valid explanation for how people learn. However, many researchers disagree with Skinner's (1971) contentions that humankind is simply an instrument of society and that people are passively subject to shaping by environmental events and by those in control.

Unwilling to accept the fact that reinforcement alone is the answer, Bandura (1974) has

social learning theory
The belief that we learn many behaviours by observing and imitating others.

researched the social learning aspects of human development. **Social learning theory** is based on the process of observational learning through modelling and imitation. It holds that rather than learning exclusively through reinforcement and the shaping of successive approximations towards a desired behaviour, we acquire much behaviour simply through imitation. Imitation is especially strong when the learner identifies with and desires to be like the role model or mentor. Imitators are in conscious control of whether or not to act like the model. Weaver *et al.*'s (1999), research found that the success of corporate ethics programmes is most strongly linked to top management's commitment to ethical behaviour – employees will model what they see in leaders.

Bandura (1974) suggests that people are capable of anticipatory control – of choosing how they will respond in various situations. Because people are capable of observing the effects of their behaviours, they can anticipate consequences across a variety of circumstances. For example, Carlo's boss may say something in a meeting that angers him. Carlo can choose whether or not to express his anger

anticipatory control
Bandura suggests that people are capable of choosing how they will respond in various situations.

publicly. He is capable of anticipating his boss's response, based on his experiences with the boss and others in authority positions. He may let it pass based on anticipatory self-control.

Even though the organisational world acts on them, adults at work still choose what situations to get involved in and how to act in them to produce a desired outcome. Bandura and Walters (1963) found that we learn through social observation to expect that certain socially desirable behaviours will be reinforced, and we learn the value of the reinforcer. While social learning theory acknowledges and builds on many principles of reinforcement, it moves closer to the concept of learning cognitively through insight and self-discovery.

The cognitive view: new patterns of thought

The perceptual-cognitive view of learning focuses on what happens within the individual: motives, feelings, attitudes, memory and cognition (thought). Sensory mechanisms are of primary importance in the key cognitive activity, which is observation based. Through speech and knowledge of language, humans form abstract concepts for organising perceptions and manipulating ideas. Thus, cognitive learning involves selective interpretation of perceptual data organised into new patterns of thoughts and relationships. A manager who asks a subordinate if he has a few minutes to talk illustrates this kind of learning. The latter says, 'Well … OK [voice dropping].' Although the words

cognitive learning
Selective interpretation of perceptual data organised into new patterns of thoughts and relationships.

indicate consent, the boss notices a look of frustration and reads into the pause and tone of voice a strong unwillingness. The boss's ability to observe multiple stimuli and to interpret the non-verbal along with the verbal communication can be learned through training and experience.

Human beings are capable of rearranging thought patterns into new configurations, or gestalts. Gestalt is a German word meaning 'shape, configuration or the arrangement of relationships in a total situation'. Patterns of concepts and relationships may occur suddenly, through insight, or they may evolve gradually as elements are linked together with new data.

gestalt
A German word meaning 'shape, configuration or the arrangement of relationships in a total situation'.

Insight

Often known as the Eureka! ('I've found it!') or a-ha! experience, insight is best described as the sudden discovery of the answer to a problem. We achieve insight into a situation, relationship or problem when we suddenly grasp an idea or see a relationship

insight
The sudden discovery of the answer to a problem.

that helps us to understand the situation better or solve the problem. Insight often comes while doing something and observing what happens (Bigge, 1964).

Kohler (1925) presented the first experimental evidence on insight in the 1920s, when he demonstrated the results of his work with a chimpanzee named Sultan. The turning point in Kohler's research occurred when he enclosed Sultan and a short stick inside a barred cage, outside of which he placed a longer stick and a banana – both too far away for Sultan to reach. Sultan first picked up the short stick and attempted to rake in the banana. However, the elusive banana remained beyond the chimp's extended reach. Unable to obtain results, Sultan sat cowering in the cage, gazing at the objects around him. Suddenly he jumped up and reached for the short stick. With it, he raked in the long stick; then he used the long stick to rake in the banana. Eureka! The chimp had discovered a solution! Today we know that two of the learning processes involved in the phenomenon of insight are discrimination and generalisation.

Discrimination

discrimination
The process by which universal or previously unstructured elements are placed into more specific structures.

Sometimes called differentiation, discrimination is the process by which universal or previously unstructured elements are placed into more specific structures (Blaker, 1976). People learn to read by discriminating among symbols – first individual letters, then groupings of letters (words), and finally meaningful groupings of letters separated by spaces and punctuation. Discrimination also occurs when three cars are seen as a Mercedes, a Volkswagen and a Porsche, or considered in terms of their components: tyres, engines, doors, seats. Managers discriminate a general concept such as 'organisation' into people, positions, structures, policies, power, leadership, and so on.

James Holden: will he fit the driver's seat at DaimlerChrysler?

Every organisation needs one or more persons (such as James P. Holden) who think independently, who test reality unencumbered by the party line, and who revitalise people and groups when needed. Holden grew up in Canada, moved up a fast-track career at Ford in Detroit, and then jumped to troubled Chrysler in 1981, as a truck division sales manager, because he wanted 'the challenge of being part of something that could be wonderful, but was screwed up'.

Holden developed a reputation as a problem-solver. One of his earlier mentors, Patrick Keegan, says, 'If it's broken, he can fix it.' Part of his problem-solving abilities comes from his penchant for sizing people up. According to a dealer, 'Jimmy is smart, he can read people good.' Such talents have enabled Holden to be a star behind-the-scenes reformer at Chrysler and have now landed him his biggest challenge. Let us review three missions assigned to Holden.

In 1992, Robert J. Eaton joined Chrysler as CEO, replacing the flamboyant Lee Iacocca. Eaton quickly selected Holden and a few other rising executives to help put in motion the strategic and cultural changes necessary to restore financial health. In a designated leaderless group, Holden quickly emerged as the de facto leader. After benchmarking the world's best practices, the team came up with a proposal to rebuild such 'soft' areas of practice as customer service and human resources. Holden confronted Eaton and said emphatically that unless Chrysler's top 25 managers embraced the new approach, it was futile to proceed. With Eaton's support against some resistance within the top 25, Holden extracted commitments of four hours a week from each of these senior managers to learn the new philosophy – and then to teach it to their subordinates.

Then in 1995 Eaton entered Holden's office, closed the door, and gave a mysterious assignment by saying, 'I need you to go do a project. You're probably going to disappear for a while.'

world watch

The mission was to explore the feasibility of doing a massive joint venture with Daimler-Benz (the German producer of Mercedes) to sell cars and trucks in Asia, eastern Europe and Latin America. After completing his analysis, Holden concluded that such a venture would fail in developing countries where neither company had a strong market presence because, 'We're trying to combine our weaknesses not our strengths. Either we don't do it, or we go all the way' and combine operations in markets where both were powerful.

Following Holden's advice, Chrysler walked away from a joint venture then, but in May 1998 stunned the industry by announcing a $36 billion merger, in effect going 'all the way'. Now Holden's earlier assignments come full circle as in the autumn of 1999 he was named president of DaimlerChrysler's US operations. His mission this time: deliver the merger synergies expected when the deal was announced and restore morale and the entrepreneurial spirit back into the Chrysler organisation. The job will not be easy, for there are frictions between the Chrysler and Daimler cultures and a number of Chrysler's key people have already jumped ship. But James Holden's easy-going interpersonal style combined with his tough-minded problem-solving abilities will certainly produce changes, the impact of which remains to be seen. Holden will also be well served by his work philosophy, 'Do you stand at the beginning of the next decade and say: 'Those were the glory days?' No. The answer has to be who do you want to be in 2010?'

Source: Joann Muller (1999) 'Your Turn to Drive, Mr Holden', *Business Week*, 29 November, pp. 194–198.

Discussion questions

1 How important is it to have independent thinkers in an organisation?

2 How could a manager's personality cause problems in an organisation?

Generalisation

When concepts, functions, objects and events are grouped into categories, generalisation is at work. **Generalisation** is the means through which we transfer learning from one situation to another as well as categorise information. Whereas discrimination breaks down the general into the specific, generalisation unites previously separate elements into meaningful universal themes or clusters. Generalisation helps people map out and programme their memories so that not every event has to be experienced as something totally new.

generalisation
The means through which we transfer learning from one situation to another as well as categorise information.

Managers generalise when they categorise an organisational behaviour problem as one of communication, for example, or of conflict, motivation, job design or leadership. Then they differentiate its possible causes and probable solutions. They remember the consequences of attempted actions and apply that learning when diagnosing current problems and deciding how they will act. The ability to discriminate, generalise and develop insight is vital to conceptual skill, which is critically important for successful managers, accountants, analysts, scientists and other knowledge workers.

Because insight is a human resource, a manager may draw others into a group problem-solving process. An idea offered by Simon may trigger a thought by Sheila, which prompts a creative suggestion from Susan. One insight tends to generate another in the search for an effective group solution.

How people differ in how they learn

One of the most important abilities an individual can possess is the ability to learn. A manager's long-term success depends more on the ability to learn than on the mastery of specific skills or technical knowledge. However, people learn in different ways. We now discuss two ways of differentiating how people learn, one based on behavioural styles the other on brain dominance.

Research focus: experiential learning styles

What is now a research classic by David Kolb (1976) indicates that managers favour a style of learning that differs from that of many other professionals. Managers learn most readily from direct experience and by actively testing the implications of concepts to new situations. Kolb's findings are based on a model of learning that involves four different abilities; they combine to form four distinct styles.

Kolb's experiential learning model distinguishes two primary dimensions of the learning process. If we visualise his model in the form of a compass, one dimension ranges from north (the concrete experiencing of events) to south (abstract conceptualisation of ideas). The other dimension extends from west (active experimentation or testing) to east (reflective observations).

These two dimensions are combined to suggest four main learning abilities or processes. As shown in Exhibit 4-8, a complete pattern of learning flows in a circular direction. Beginning at the top: (1) the learner becomes actively involved in new concrete experiences, and (2) through reflective observation examines these experiences from different perspectives (3) to form abstract concepts and generalisations, which (4) lead to theories or assumptions that can be used for active experimentation in problem-solving and decision-making.

EXHIBIT 4–8 Kolb's model of experiential learning styles

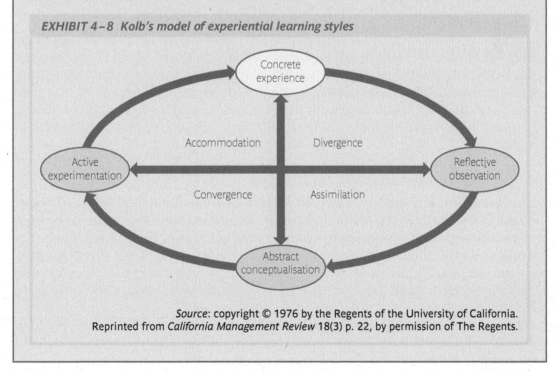

Source: copyright © 1976 by the Regents of the University of California. Reprinted from *California Management Review* 18(3) p. 22, by permission of The Regents.

Kolb's personal learning styles

Most people become highly skilled at one or two processes rather than all four. When two adjacent processes are emphasised, a dominant learning style emerges. The four characteristics identified in Exhibit 4-8 – divergence, assimilation, convergence and accommodation – represent distinct personal learning styles.

The Diverger

Divergers learn best by reflecting on specific experiences and drawing new inferences. The Diverger tends to be highly imaginative, excels at brainstorming and likes involvement in the generation of creative ideas. Divergers have an uncanny ability to view concrete situations from many perspectives. Academically, such learners are often interested in the liberal arts, humanities and fine arts. Human resource managers are often Divergers.

The Assimilator

With their capability to combine reflective observation and abstract conceptualisation, Assimilators are good at creating theoretical models. Inductive reasoning is the forte that permits integrating diverse observations into a coherent explanation. Dealing with abstract ideas is the Assimilator's domain, more so than seeking practical applications or working with people. Individuals who adopt this learning style are attracted to basic research; in business, you may find them staffing corporate research and planning departments.

The Converger

Convergers use abstract concepts as a basis for active experimentation. They focus on specific problems, looking for answers and solutions. Like the Assimilator, the Converger prefers working with ideas and specific tasks to working with people. Convergers tend to do well in the physical sciences and engineering.

The Accommodator

This style focuses on doing. The Accommodator's domain is active experimentation and the carrying out of plans that lead to real experiences. Such people are risk takers, able to adapt quickly to new situations. If a theory does not fit the situation, the Accommodator discards the concept and works from the facts. Although at ease with people, Accommodators tend to be impatient and assertive. Accommodation is often the dominant style of individuals trained for the business world, especially those who gravitate towards action-orientated management or sales jobs.

The need to combine skills and styles

Kolb's research finds that managers tend to be orientated towards learning by active experimentation and concrete experience. Many managers are Accommodators. By contrast, many business school faculties tend to be strong on reflective observation and abstract conceptualisation. This makes them Assimilators. Because Accommodator managers tend to make fewer inferences from data and are less consistent in their actions than Assimilators, both learning styles are necessary within organisations. To blend styles within an organisation, Kolb (1976) offers two recommendations.

First, managers and organisations should value and consciously seek learning from experience by budgeting time for the learning process. Second, managers and organisations should value and include those with different learning styles and perspectives. Action-orientated people should be combined with those who are reflective, and those involved in concrete experience should be joined with those who are analytical. Learning can be enhanced when style differences are valued, just as it can by integrating people from different cultures and ethnic backgrounds. (To increase your own awareness of learning style preferences and the need to develop complementary abilities, complete the Personal Skills Exercise at the end of this chapter.)

Two hemispheres of learning

Another explanation of differences in learning is based on brain-hemisphere dominance. Neurologists and psychologists have long known that the left hemisphere of the brain controls movements on the right-hand side of the body, and vice versa. Ornstein (1973) has carried this further by suggesting that our dominant brain hemisphere may play a significant role in how we learn.

The linear/systematic left

The brain's left hemisphere assimilates information in ordered, systematic ways. The process of analysis and planning (usually a central theme of the business school curriculum) is linear in structure. Accounting systems and management science quantitative models are based on rational logic. Their underlying assumption is that, if data are channelled into a formula or model, a working solution can be found.

The left hemisphere of the brain handles quantification and written language. Many organisational activities are well served by predictability and logic. In stable environments structured, planned behaviour is likely to be effective. However, organisations do not survive and grow without creativity and change.

The holistic/relational right

Mintzberg (1976) suggests that when it comes to running organisations, planning occurs on the left side of the brain, managing on the right. He writes, 'it may be that management researchers have been looking for the key to management in the lightness of logical analysis whereas perhaps it has always been lost in the darkness of intuition'. In drawing insights from observing managers' behaviours, Mintzberg adds, 'effective managers seem to revel in ambiguity; in complex, mysterious systems with relatively little order'.

The world of the right-hemisphere-dominant manager involves holistic, simultaneous, creative learning. In addition, it emphasises learning from face-to-face verbal exchanges rather than from written reports. Through verbal communication, managers can interpret non-verbal cues and act simultaneously on real-time data. Synthesis of soft data-impressions – feelings, intuition – provides the basis for acting more than hard-data analysis does.

Hunches and judgement are mental processes from which insights and new possibilities spring forth. With brief time sequences for processing information, action – not reflection – is more the executive norm, as you may recall from Chapter 2. Orderly agendas are atypical in a world beset with interruptions and unplanned activities.

In an article on why and how to develop right-hemisphere intuitive powers, another researcher cited the experiences of a number of executives who relied heavily on intuitive decisions. One of them, Paul Cook, founder and former president of Raychem Corporation, 'replied that nearly all of his decisions were based on intuition, and that the only major decisions he regrets were ones not based on it' (Agor, 1984). Be cautioned, however, that the intuition of which Cook speaks builds on years of experience and learning. It is not impulsive.

Lifelong learning

Both the Kolb model of learning styles and the notion of brain-hemisphere specialisation emphasise the ongoing nature of individual learning. Life is a series of learning episodes and processes. Those who are managers will find their jobs involve knowing both how to learn themselves and how to influence the learning of others.

Now that you are familiar with the different ways of learning, you can probably see for yourself why no one theory works all the time across all situations. Applied behaviour modification principles, for example, are best used in situations in which reinforcing environmental consequences can be structured. Those who learn best through direct experience are not likely to become reflective/conceptual learners. Each approach and style has its essential place in organisations.

E-learning

e-learning
The instruction and delivery of training through electronic means, such as computer packages and the Internet.

According to Rosenberg (2001) **e-learning** refers to instruction and delivery of training by computers through electronic means such as the Internet or computer packages. E-learning includes web-based learning, distance learning, virtual classrooms and the use of CD-Roms.

The three basic characteristics of e-learning are as follows.

1 It involves electronic networks that allow information and instruction to be delivered, shared and updated instantly.

2 E-learning is delivered to the trainee via computers with Internet technology.

3 It focuses on learning solutions that go beyond traditional training to include information and tools to improve performance.

The features of e-learning can be seen in Exhibit 4-9.

As can be seen from Exhibit 4-9, the features of e-learning include collaboration and sharing of information, links to further resources, often via a web link. The learner is also in control, she or he is able to dictate their pace of learning and can receive instant feedback through a variety of assessment techniques. In organisations, e-learning can be developed to contribute to the organisational objectives. According to Galagan (2000) this gives it advantages over other training methods. It enables participants to engage with learning from their difference locations and therefore can cut down on time needed away from the workplace. The learning materials provided can range from video clips and graphics, to sound and text, and can therefore appeal to different learning styles. One multinational finance house, Meryll Lynch, uses e-learning to provide employees with training in basic financial planning techniques as well as more advanced concepts such as investment techniques. In the past these trainees would have had to attend a training centre, which would have meant not only the cost of replacing them at work, but also the costs of instructors and training facilities. The learner is also in control, he or she can become involved in the learning through self-pacing exercises. Learners can also expand on their learning by following links to other experts, as well as having group interaction through message boards and online discussions. As can also be seen from the example of House of Fraser in the Technology Transformation box on page 156, training can be customised both to meet the needs of the learner and the organisation.

Another special area of learning relates to values and attitudes. We will discuss the importance of an organisation's value system as part of its culture in a later chapter. Here we will focus on individual values and attitudes, which are important because they influence percep-

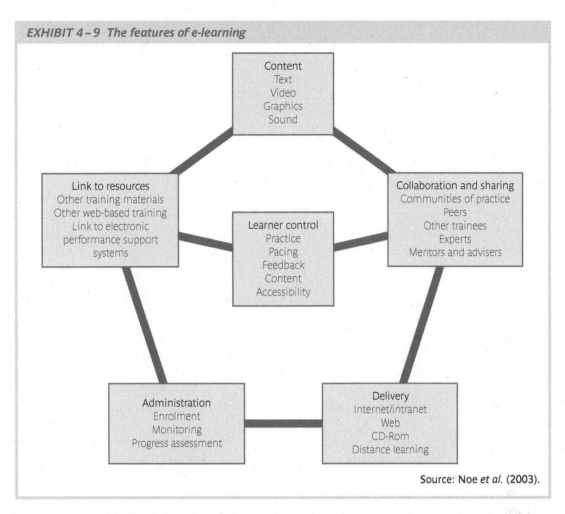

EXHIBIT 4–9 The features of e-learning

Content
Text
Video
Graphics
Sound

Link to resources
Other training materials
Other web-based training
Link to electronic
performance support
systems

Learner control
Practice
Pacing
Feedback
Content
Accessibility

Collaboration and sharing
Communities of practice
Peers
Other trainees
Experts
Mentors and advisers

Administration
Enrolment
Monitoring
Progress assessment

Delivery
Internet/intranet
Web
CD-Rom
Distance learning

Source: Noe *et al.* (2003).

tions and impact behaviour and performance at work. We turn now to an examination of these two important manifestations of learning.

How personal values differ from attitudes

Naomi Fujioka was faced with a dilemma. She was about to receive her MBA from a prestigious business school and had two job offers. One offer was to be an investment banker at a high salary, the other was at a modest salary in a non-profit organisation that helps poor children in developing countries. Naomi's choice was heavily influenced by her values. Both jobs were attractive. Naomi valued earning a good income from a challenging position, but she valued even more using her talents to help people in need. She joined the non-profit organisation.

The function of values

values
Permanent beliefs or ideals held to be important, which influence thought and behaviour.

Values are stable, enduring beliefs about what is worthwhile, which influence thought and behaviour. Values are learned, beginning soon after birth, as parents and others indicate that certain behaviours are good and others bad. Children in many cultures learn quickly that it is good to be obedient and bad to disobey. They may learn that honesty, cleanliness, politeness, and similar traits and behaviours are good – and therefore valued.

Values are relatively stable and deep-seated and they influence an individual's perceptions of what is good and bad, important and unimportant. For example, if an individual values being on time, he or she will be motivated to behave so as to be on time. The thought of being late may stimulate feelings of stress and a subsequent adrenaline rush to hurry to the appointment. Conversely, if punctuality is not valued, there is no need to be stressed about being late.

The values of the larger culture and society greatly influence what individuals learn. Parents, teachers, peers, heroes and heroines, the media, art, music and personal experience also play a role. The country and culture in which one is born, the nature of its economy and political system, and the level of its technology are some of the important variables that influence values, as you will discover in later chapters. For example, young people in the United Kingdom are taught the value of independence, whereas in Japan young people learn the value of dependence and interdependence. In the United Kingdom people learn to value individualism, and in Japan they learn to value groups. People in both countries learn to value ambition.

Different cultural values often create dissonance for those entering a new culture, especially for expatriates who are expected to work and live in another country. One model by Osland and Bird (2000) of cross-cultural sensemaking (for interpreting cultural clues) looks at the interplay between specific situational context and cultural values. The natural tendency for an expatriate manager is to cross-reference his or her own cultural values with his or her stereotypes of the new culture. However, general stereotypes (such as the Japanese and Costa Ricans being more collectivist than individualist), which do not hold true in specific business contexts (such as decision-making at meetings or in evaluating a subordinate), can cause a manager to behave inappropriately.

Two simple recommendations may prevent cross-cultural mistakes. One: when assigned to another culture, seek out a cultural mentor, such as someone from the culture who is familiar with the social environment. Two: approach learning another culture much like a scientist who treats cultural stereotypes like hypotheses to be reality-tested against a specific work situational context.

The Eye on Ethics box illustrates one of the complexities of values and how they can differ among different employees in organisations.

Types of values

An early classification of values was developed by Allport *et al.* (1951). Their categories included the following.

- **Theoretical:** values the discovery of truth, and emphasises critical and rational approaches to problems.
- **Economic:** values utility and practicality, and emphasises standard of living.
- **Aesthetic:** values form, grace and harmony, and emphasises the artistic aspects of life.
- **Social:** values love of people and altruism, and emphasises concern for others.
- **Political:** values power, position and influence, and emphasises competition and winning.
- **Religious:** values unity and people's relationship to the universe, and emphasises high ideals and the reasons for being on earth.

Researchers have found that the values people emphasise vary with their occupations. For example, scientists of all kinds are often theoretically inclined; business people – particularly the

Respect employees' values: low morale in many workplaces caused by employers' lack of human care

Companies that fail to respect employees' personal values are risking their long-term business performance as well as the health of their staff, experts have claimed.

Pauline Crawford, founder and managing director of consultancy Corporate Heart, said its research into high-performance work cultures had revealed low morale in many workplaces caused by employers' lack of human care.

'How can leaders expect their staff to follow them when mistrust and dishonesty threaten the core of their work existence?' she asked.

Adrian Gilpin, chairman of the Institute of Human Development, said, 'If companies ask employees to compromise their values or corporate responsibility, all the human energy is chipped away and the impact can be devastating, such as in the case of Enron.'

But Robert Mecrate-Butcher, a partner in the employment department at law firm Pinsent Masons, said the core bargain involved in an employment contract meant staff must accept a degree of compromise when carrying out their work.

Even so, he said that employers would benefit by trying to reduce the degree of conflict: 'One way to do this may be to talk with staff to identify core values.'

Neil Crofts, managing director of consultancy Authentic Business, said this approach had worked for ANZ bank in Australia: 'It transformed itself by asking staff what their values were and how they could be manifested in the business. Three years on, ANZ has gone from the least popular bank in Australia to work for to the most popular and its share value has tripled,' he said.

Recent research from the Institute of Business Ethics among 759 staff found one in four UK employees had felt pressure to compromise their organisation's ethics; and one in five had noticed behaviour by colleagues that violated the law or did not accord with their organisation's standards.

Source: originally published in *People Management*, 29 September 2005, and reproduced with permission.

Discussion questions

1 Why is it important to respect employees' values at work?

2 What could be the consequences of ignoring personal values?

British and Americans – are high in economic value. Artists have a high aesthetic value; psychologists, social workers and many teachers are inclined towards social values. Executives in all fields often have a high political value; and philosophers and the clergy often hold high religious values.

A second way of classifying values was developed by Rokeach (1973) and Rokeach and Ball-Rokeach (1989). He distinguishes between two sets of values. *Instrumental values* describe desirable beliefs about what behaviours are appropriate in reaching desired goals and ends. Examples include being loving, honest and ambitious. *Terminal values* describe desirable ends that are worth striving to reach. Examples include a comfortable, prosperous life, world peace, wisdom and salvation. The 'Your turn' exercise will help you rank your own values. Following Rokeach, rank your ultimate values (similar to what Rokeach calls terminal values). Then rank how you value those traits that help you achieve your ultimate values. Compare your rankings with those of someone who knows you well.

Merging personal and organisational values

People enter the workforce with a personal value system in place. A **personal value system** is a relatively permanent perceptual framework – an enduring organisation of beliefs – that shapes and influences the general nature of an individual's behaviour. However, because organisations incorporate selected values into their cultures, there can at times be a tug of war between personal and organisational values.

personal value system
A relatively permanent perceptual framework (an enduring organisation of beliefs) that shapes and influences an individual's behaviour.

What researchers have found is that managers (as one type of much studied worker) carry with them a set of *intended values* that are socially or culturally induced. These ideals may be personally important. However, to be successful in an organisation managers may learn *adopted values*, a set of values that are part of the organisation's culture. When personal values (intended) and organisational values (adopted) are congruent, these become highly pragmatic *operative values*. That is, they provide a frame of reference for consistency in making decisions and in relationships with others. Research by Oliver (1999) has shown that the fundamental values within these three systems have remained remarkably stable over 30 years – with the exception of 'money', which has moved up in strength to become an operative value.

Where the organisation reinforces personal values, the consistency makes it highly probable that those core values will guide behaviour – values such as productivity, organisational efficiency, industrial leadership, ambition, achievement, success, ability and skill. In the adopted values category – associated with organisational success but not personally important – are power and aggressiveness. Intended values that are personally important but not related to success within organisations include employee welfare, trust, loyalty and honour.

Moral dilemmas, internal conflicts and ethical compromises occur when personally intended and organisationally induced values clash. Ironically, this calls into question the overarching value of integrity. **Integrity** defines a loyalty in demonstrated action to rational principles and one's values. According to Becker (1998), 'That is, integrity is the principle of being principled, practicing what one preaches regardless of emotional or social pressure, and not allowing any irrational consideration to overwhelm one's rational convictions.' This does imply acting in accordance with a morally justifiable value

integrity
Defines a consistency in demonstrated action to rational principles and one's values, or the principle of being principled, practising what one preaches regardless of emotional or social pressure.

system, although it does not mean that a person cannot change his or her mind as knowledge increases. People can change their values or goals, but only for good reasons.

Changes in values with time

Although values are relatively enduring – with the possible exception of those adopted as a result of organisational membership – they can and do shift over time (Cooper, 1979). Important local, national and world events lead to changing attitudes, needs and values. Young people in Britain during the prosperous 1960s valued their right to rebel against authority and seek individual happiness. Economic conditions grew tighter during the early 1970s, jobs were scarcer, and young people became more conservative and conformed more closely to traditional organisational values. Prosperity returned for many during the 1980s, and people tended to value money and the acquisition of material goods.

According to research by Yankelovich (1981), 'The shift from the eighties to the nineties has turned out to be about as abrupt as you can imagine.' He says: 'People are tired of one group of people making points off another. And their intuition tells them that the trouble we're in is moral, that there really is such a thing as decadence.' Whether this apparent shift in values will be sustained and how it will manifest itself remain to be seen.

An awareness of values can help managers understand and predict the behaviour of others. For example, they would know that workers in their thirties, fifties and sixties are more likely to be accepting of authority than are workers in their forties. They might reasonably predict that older workers are more likely to be loyal to the organisation than those who are younger, although this may be changing as our earlier discussion of a changing social contract indicated.

Your turn

Your values

Instructions Rank the first column, *Ultimate values*, from 1 (most important) to 16 (least important). Rank the second column, *Means values*, from 1 (most important) to 23 (least important). Suggestion: think about what your own past behaviour tells you about your values. Think about the difference, if any, between what you say you value (ultimate values) and what you do value (means values). Pay particular attention to your top five values in each column.

Rank	Ultimate values	Rank	Means values
_____	Achievement	_____	Action-orientated
_____	Aesthetics	_____	Ambitious
_____	Contentment	_____	Athletic/physical
_____	Equality	_____	Brave
_____	Excitement	_____	Compassionate
_____	Health	_____	Competent
_____	Liberty	_____	Considerate
_____	Love	_____	Creative
_____	Peace	_____	Decisive
_____	Pleasure	_____	Dependable
_____	Prosperity	_____	Disciplined
_____	Security	_____	Energetic
_____	Self-esteem	_____	Friendly
_____	Social status	_____	Good-natured
_____	Spirituality	_____	Honest
_____	Wisdom	_____	Intelligent
		_____	Open
		_____	Orderly
		_____	Outgoing
		_____	Rational
		_____	Reserved
		_____	Spontaneous
		_____	Tough-minded

The function of attitudes

attitude
Readiness to respond in a certain way to a person, object, idea or situation.

When people say 'I like my job' or 'I'm proud to be a part of this company' or 'I'm against unions', they are expressing their attitudes. An **attitude** is a predisposition or readiness to respond in a certain way to a person, object, idea or situation. Attitudes differ from values in that they are more specific and can be less stable and enduring. Although some attitudes may remain relatively stable over time, others are subject to change with the accumulation of new information and experience.

Breckler (1984) suggests that attitudes have three components: cognition, affect and behaviour. The cognitive component is beliefs and perceived knowledge about the subject of the attitude. The affective component includes the feelings associated with the subject, often conveying likes and dislikes. The behavioural component stems from the perceptions and feelings as an intention to behave in a certain way.

These three components can be illustrated by John Wainwright's attitude towards his boss. John believes his boss is unfair and authoritarian, whereas he (John) values honesty and independence. John's beliefs when evaluated against his values create feelings of dislike for his boss, and he intends to seek a transfer. John's attitude thus influences his behaviour.

Although attitudes influence behaviour, predictions about actual behaviour cannot be made with certainty. For example, although John intends to change jobs, he may choose to suppress his feelings and stay on the job because he does not have a good alternative. In such a case, John would probably feel frustrated and would experience what is known as cognitive dissonance.

Cognitive dissonance is a term popularised by psychologist Festinger (1957) to describe a state of inconsistency between an individual's attitudes and their behaviour. The discomfort experienced by people feeling cognitive dissonance leads to efforts to reduce the tension by (1) changing the attitude; (2) changing behaviour; or (3) rationalising the inconsistency.

cognitive dissonance
A state of inconsistency between an individual's attitudes and behaviour.

For example, John might change his perceptions to emphasise his boss's positive traits and minimise his negative traits, making his overall attitude more positive. On the other hand, he might go ahead with the transfer to another job. Alternatively, he might reason that part of working is putting up with difficult superiors. Any one of these three alternatives would lessen the tension caused by John's conflicting attitudes and behaviour.

Attitudes affect productivity

It was noted earlier that attitudes influence behaviour, but our discussion of cognitive dissonance illustrates that behaviour can also influence attitudes. For example, if John behaves in a certain way to please his boss, the response might be positive and John might find his attitude of disliking changing to liking. In this case, his own behaviour would have contributed to his change in attitude.

Employee attitudes towards their job and company are important because they can influence productivity and satisfaction. An employee's general attitude towards his or her job is called job satisfaction. Research by Mowday *et al.* (1982) has shown a negative relationship between job satisfaction and absenteeism and turnover. Employee attitudes are important enough for companies to periodically measure them by means of attitude surveys.

Job satisfaction surveys ask employees to rate their attitudes towards their work, pay and benefits, supervisor, upper management, peer groups, opportunities for advancement, and

Research focus: theory of cognitive dissonance

Festinger's (1957) theory of cognitive dissonance has been one of the most influential theories in social psychology and has led to many studies in an attempt to gain a better understanding of what determines an individual's beliefs, how decisions are made based on such beliefs and what happens when such beliefs are questioned.

Festinger's (1957) work is largely based on Heider's (1958) ideas. Festinger proposed that cognitive dissonance is a major source of attitude change. Cognitive dissonance occurs when we find our attitudes and beliefs contradict one another, either because they are not balanced views, as argued by Heider (1958), or because they are in direct conflict with one another.

The resulting conflict can be dealt with in one of two ways:

1 we can change one of the attitudes, or
2 we can add additional attitudes that allow us to interpret the situation differently.

Festinger *et al.* (1956) carried out a famous study through participant observation of a religious cult. The sect believed that a US city was about to be destroyed by flood. The members of the cult would survive since they would be rescued by a flying saucer. Cult members sold all their possessions and went on a hill near the city to wait for the event to happen. Festinger *et al.* found that when the event didn't happen, the cult coped with the cognitive dissonance by adding an additional belief: that the city had been saved as a result of the prayers of the cult.

In another study, by Festinger and Carlsmith (1959), subjects were asked to perform the very boring tasks of putting pegs in a hole and giving them a quarter-turn for an hour. At the end of the hour they were asked how they found it and all described the task as boring. Next they were asked to introduce the task to another group of subjects, telling them the task was fun and interesting. First, they were divided into two groups: one group was paid $1 while the other group received $20 for explaining the task. After the task was completed they were asked how they felt. Festinger and Carlsmith found that those who had been paid $20 still found the task boring and repetitive. But those who had only been paid $1 rated the task as much more enjoyable than previously and enjoyed it more than the other group.

Festinger argues that this was a result of cognitive dissonance. The highly paid group could justify lying to the new subjects as they had done it for money. But the low-paid group hadn't earned enough to make lying worthwhile, so they had changed their attitudes to reduce the dissonance between how they felt and what they told the new subjects.

Festinger argues that cognitive dissonance is a major factor in inducing attitude change. But people with strong feelings on an issue are often highly resistant to information that contradicts their beliefs and they will tend to defend against it. They may simply ignore the information; or they may distort it so that it becomes consistent with their beliefs. They can do this by doing one of the following:

■ discrediting the source of information
■ re-analysing the information so it is seen as having different implications
■ being highly selective about which bits of information they will notice or recall.

According to Festinger, the presence of dissonance gives rise to an uncomfortable feeling that motivates the person to lessen or eliminate the dissonance.

Although there has been much research over the years to test the theory, most researchers agree that some form of psychological discomfort will motivate change. The example below shows how this can happen in the workplace.

other items. Effective managers augment such formal surveys with informal observations and indirect indicators such as absenteeism and turnover. The value of survey and related forms of data depend largely on how skilfully and effectively managers use these results to improve identified problem areas.

So far in this chapter we have seen that people vary in their abilities, perceive and learn differently from one another, and vary in their values and attitudes. It is not surprising that they also behave differently. We turn now to the concept of personality, which is another factor that managers must consider in managing a diverse workforce.

How personalities differ

Personality is the set of traits and behaviours that characterises an individual. The longer and better we know someone, the more likely we are to recognise the pattern of how that individual responds to various people and situations. The clearer and more enduring the pattern of responses, the more we attribute it to the individual's personality. Managers and others use personality to understand and predict an individual's behaviour and to define the essence of an individual.

Heredity and learning determine personality

Personality emerges over time from the interaction of genetic and environmental factors. To a large extent, genes predetermine an individual's physical characteristics, and they contribute to other important personality characteristics such as intelligence and temperament. Gender, race, size, appearance, and even health and energy are influenced significantly by genes (Couchard, 1990).

personality
The set of traits and behaviours that characterises an individual.

Although heredity plays a role in the development of personality, it is clear that learning is also vitally important. One of the major characteristics that distinguishes humans from other species is that people have a significantly greater capacity to learn, remember and think about what has happened in the past, is happening in the present and might happen in the future. We have already seen how people learn, including how they acquire knowledge, abilities, values and attitudes. Individuals learn their own motives. Over time, their patterns of behaviour become identified as their personalities.

People's personalities become clearer and more stable as they grow older. Personality can change and may do so slowly over the years. The more set an individual's personality becomes, the greater the need for conscious effort to modify it. For example, someone who is used to arguing strongly for their point of view would probably find it difficult to listen passively to those who differed.

The 'big five' personality factors

Because personality comprises many elements, psychologists work to identify critical factors that help people observe and understand an individual's style and differences. One such set of factors is referred to by some psychologists as the 'big five' (Harary and Donahue, 1992). Each factor represents one aspect of an individual's personality and style. The five factors include the following.

1 **Expressive style:** how individuals express themselves verbally and behaviourally. For example, people's behaviour may range from quiet and reserved to talkative and outgoing.

2 **Interpersonal style:** how individuals behave while interacting with others. For example, people's behaviour may range from being cool and distant to warm and close.

3 **Work style:** how people work and meet responsibilities. For example, individuals' styles may range from performing work in a detailed and structured manner to a general and spontaneous way.

4 **Emotional style:** how people express their emotions. For example, individuals' behaviours may range from unemotional and stable to highly emotional and volatile.

5 **Intellectual style:** how individuals learn, think and decide. For example, individuals' styles may range from learning, thinking and deciding in simple and traditional ways, to complex and novel ways.

Each factor helps us to know what behaviour patterns to observe in understanding someone's personality. For example, the expressive style factor leads us to observe whether a person is generally quiet and reserved, or talkative and outgoing, or somewhere in between. Each of the other factors helps in a similar fashion. Key elements of each factor combine to provide an overall understanding of an individual's personality. This ability to understand different personalities is helpful to managers in being better able to predict an individual's behaviour in different situations.

For example, assume a manager, Karen, is deciding which of two people she will appoint as a task force leader. The task will be to develop a new approach to marketing an established product. She has observed one person, Wayne, who is quiet and reserved and interacts relatively little with his work peers. He is very bright, a hard worker and very reliable in doing detailed, structured work. He has never been observed to express either positive or negative emotion.

The other person, Ursula, is talkative and outgoing. She interacts easily with others and has a warm, outgoing style. She is sometimes careless about details and is easily bored with repetitive, routine work. However, she enjoys solving new problems and makes good decisions in ambiguous situations. Her peers can tell what Ursula is feeling because she is quite expressive, but she has not let her emotions get out of control at work even when under stress. The more difficult the problem, the more she enjoys it.

You are correct if you predict that Karen decided to appoint Ursula. She fits the team leader role better than Wayne. Karen used the 'big five' personality factors to observe and organise relevant aspects of Wayne's and Ursula's behaviour.

Different psychological types and cognitive styles

One of the earliest theories of personality was developed by Jung (1933). Briggs and Myers (1987) further developed a personality test called the Myers–Briggs Type Indicator (MBTI) to measure the traits posited by Jung. Today it is the most widely used personality test in the world and is used by many major corporations primarily to develop awareness of and sensitivity to the differences among people (Moore, 1987).

The Jungian framework

Basic to Jung's framework is the differentiation between introversion and extroversion. Those who are *introverts* are more orientated towards their inner thoughts and feelings, they like to work quietly and without interruption. *Extroverts* are orientated towards the outer world of people and things. They enjoy communicating verbally with people and prefer to experience life rather than reflect on it.

Jung also differentiates between perceivers and judgers. Those who are *judgers* like to live in an orderly, planned way. They prefer control, structure and closure. *Perceivers*, on the other hand, prefer flexibility and spontaneity. They enjoy gathering information and adapting to life as it unfolds.

cognitive style
The way an individual perceives and processes information.

Cognitive style describes how individuals perceive and process information. Cognitive style is complex and can be defined and measured in several ways. We will concentrate on one way that is based on Carl Jung's theory of psychological types. According to Jung, individuals develop, mostly unconsciously, preferred ways of gathering information and evaluating it to make decisions. The two opposite ways of *gathering information* are through a sensing method and by intuition, and the two opposite ways of *evaluating information* are thinking and feeling. Exhibit 4-10 illustrates these alternative processes. Alternatives for gathering information are on the vertical axis; ways for evaluating information appear on the horizontal axis.

Obtaining information by sensation/intuition

Managers who collect information by sensing seek details, hard facts and quantitative reports. *Sensers* like to apply structures for organising data logically, step by step. They are especially comfortable working within a structure of organisational policies and rules that provide clear guidelines for action. Senser managers learn best from concrete experience; they can be thought of as left-brain-hemisphere processors.

Intuitive managers may ignore routine, structured reports and rely more on hunches and non-verbal perceptions of problems. Data collection by this type of manager often appears to be unsystematic, with considerable jumping back and forth. *Intuitives* excel at synthesis – that is, taking a large amount of data from a number of sources and drawing seemingly spontaneous conclusions. These managers are imaginative, futuristic and often good at drawing creative ideas out of others. They are more dependent on the right-brain hemisphere.

Evaluating information by thinking/feeling

Two opposite ways of processing and evaluating information are *thinking* and *feeling*. Evaluation is the process of integrating information to solve a problem or to make a decision. Managers who depend on thinking use analysis and rational logic as the basis for problem-solving.

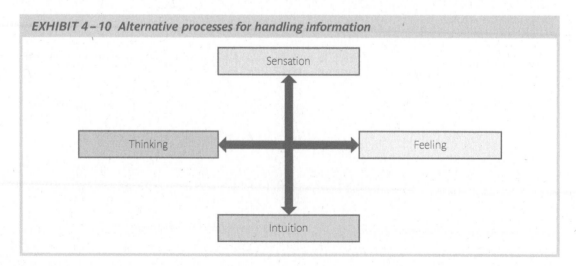

EXHIBIT 4–10 Alternative processes for handling information

They tend to be unemotional in applying data to models or problem-solving techniques. The forte of these managers is the use of the scientific method (systematic evaluation of empirical data), devoid of personal considerations.

Managers who arrive at decisions through feeling rely heavily on person-centred values. They personalise their evaluations and are sensitive to the concerns, ideas and feelings of those around them. Placing a major emphasis on the human aspects of problems, these managers dislike creating conflict. They value harmony and tend to conform to the wishes of others rather than consider alternatives based on logic or analysis.

Four types of problem-solving behaviour

These different ways of gathering and evaluating information combine to form a matrix of four problem-solving behaviours. Exhibit 4-11 illustrates how these four personality types emerge. Each type has its virtues and shortcomings, but in a complex organisation all are necessary. The following descriptions are based on research into the problem-solving behaviours of managers by Slocum and Hellriegel (1983).

Sensation thinkers (ST)

Steve Tinker is the archetypal bureaucrat, concerned with formulating and enforcing rules. Because sensation and thinking dominate his functions, Steve is persistent, yet decisive. He weighs costs and benefits, plans a logical schedule, and has an infinite capacity to absorb and remember details.

Steve is a hard worker, a good co-ordinator and a dependable leader. His penchant for analysis and logic makes him quite predictable. However, as a sensation thinker, Steve tends to become impatient with those who are not equally detailed, organised and rational. He avoids abstractions and seldom provides feedback to others unless it is based on measured performance. Steve is so concerned with preserving accepted practices and tradition that he overlooks possibilities for creative improvement.

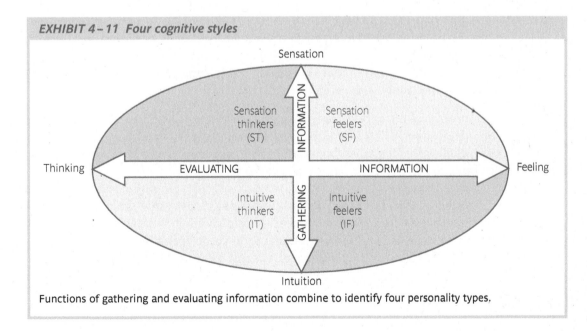

EXHIBIT 4–11 Four cognitive styles

Functions of gathering and evaluating information combine to identify four personality types.

Intuitive thinkers (IT)

Ida Tucker exemplifies the intuitive thinker. She is a manager who looks ahead, always searching for innovative possibilities. Although she tends to be impersonal, Ida is quick to analyse the power dynamics within an organisation. She is noted for her intellectual capabilities and pioneering ideas. Ida is a great designer of new methods and projects. She then depends on her staff to flesh out the details of her proposals.

Once a project has been initiated, Ida relinquishes its administration to someone better suited to establishing organisational routines. Gifted in abstract creativity, Ida is sometimes insensitive to the personal needs and wishes of others. Nevertheless, as an intuitive thinker she responds to the ideas and problems of others when they are logical and reasonable. She finds it difficult to accept anything other than competent, professional performance. Ida frequently expects more than others are prepared to deliver.

Sensation feelers (SF)

Sensation feelers are exemplified by Sally Field, who is a methodical manager. She is great at analysis based on detailed observation. Sally deals efficiently with here-and-now problems. Her decisions and actions result from quick interpretation of the facts. She loves to find the causes of problems in standardised operations and excels at extracting higher efficiency from programmed procedures.

Yet Sally does not like to see changes sweep too far in new directions. She would rather fix an old system than conceptualise a new approach. Sally generally gets along well with coworkers. She reinforces good performance by giving praise, writing memos of thanks and publicly acknowledging others' accomplishments.

Intuitive feelers (IF)

Ian Fuller is the quintessential intuitive feeler. He is a charismatic leader who communicates fluently and is quick to visualise possibilities for improvement. He draws out ideas from others and always consults co-workers before moving ahead on significant actions. Given the freedom to manage, Ian creates a high level of *esprit de corps* within his team. Ian believes in psychological rewards and makes sure they come in timely response to his workers' emotional needs.

Yet Ian himself needs recognition from others. He tends to back away from his personal ideas when they appear to conflict with views held by esteemed others. He is very popular among his co-workers, but because he wishes to retain this popularity Ian is at times hesitant to act. Sometimes the opportunity of the moment is lost because of his indecision.

The behaviour patterns of these four managers indicate extreme personalities. While managers may tend towards sensation or intuition, thinking or feeling, usually their dominant combinations do not preclude use of the other functions. In fact, most managers rely to some extent on all four functions.

Still, the message for organisations is clear: to be effective across the entire range of problems – those that demand change and those that require stability, those that call for quantitative analysis and those that require creative thought – an organisation needs all four types of manager. In the ideal management team, individual styles complement one another. A built-in system of checks and balances is possible when team members are of different personality types.

Personality traits

Pervin (1985) has identified other personality attributes that are relevant for behaviour in organisations. In this section we discuss several of these.

locus of control
The degree to which people believe that they, rather than external forces, determine their own lives.

Locus of control is a dimension of personality that explains the degree to which people believe that they, rather than external forces, determine their own lives (Rotter, 1966). People who believe that what happens to them depends on themselves are *internals*. Those who believe that what happens is caused by fate, luck or other external forces are *externals*. For example, assume that two employees, one an internal and one an external, both fail to get an increase in salary. The internal is likely to attribute this to his or her own performance, while the external will probably blame an unfair boss or some other outside force. Internals are likely to perform better on jobs that require initiative and offer autonomy. Externals are more likely to seek structured jobs with clear direction.

authoritarianism
The degree to which a person believes that status and power differences are appropriate in an organisation.

Authoritarianism is the degree to which a person believes that status and power differences are appropriate in an organisation (Adorno, 1989). People high in authoritarianism tend to be autocratic and demanding with subordinates but are likely to accept orders and directions from superiors without question. High-authoritarian types would not fit well in organisations that require flexibility and quick change or sensitivity to people and co-operative behaviour. They would fit better in a highly structured organisation that values conformity.

dogmatism
The degree of flexibility or rigidity of a person's views.

Machiavellianism
A personality attribute that describes the extent to which a person manipulates others for personal gain.

Dogmatism refers to the degree of flexibility or rigidity of a person's views. Those high in dogmatism tend to be rigid and closed. They often view the world as threatening and cling to their beliefs. People low in dogmatism are more open-minded and receptive to considering views that differ from their own.

Machiavellianism is a personality attribute that describes the extent to which a person manipulates others for personal gain. Named after Niccolo Machiavelli, who wrote *The Prince* in the sixteenth century, the concept refers to a rational, pragmatic approach to situations and emotional distance from subordinates (Christie and Gies, 1970). Machiavelli believed that the end justifies the means. Psychologists have developed instruments designed to compare a person's orientation with that of Machiavelli. High 'Machs' perform better in loosely structured situations and when they can interact face to face with others.

risk propensity
A person's willingness to take risks.

Risk propensity refers to a person's willingness to take risks. People with a high propensity for risk make decisions faster and are willing to take chances. Risk-aversive people are more cautious, make decisions more carefully and try to minimise risk. High-risk managers may make costly decisions, although they may also enable their organisation to respond quickly to fast-changing environments. Low-risk managers may also make costly decisions if they respond too slowly to changing competitive conditions. The appropriateness of each depends on the organisational situation.

self-esteem
The judgement one makes about one's own worth.

Self-esteem is the judgement one makes about one's own worth. People with high self-esteem tend to like themselves, have high expectations for success, and feel confident they can achieve their goals. Those with low self-esteem lack confidence and look to others for praise and reinforcement. In so doing they tend to avoid conflict and conform to expected norms (Meeker, 1990).

self-monitoring
The degree to which people are sensitive to others and adapt their own behaviour to meet external expectations and situational needs.

Self-monitoring refers to the degree to which people are sensitive to others and adapt their behaviour to meet external expectations and situational needs (Snyder, 1987). High self-monitors are similar to actors in that they can assume a personality to satisfy an audience. They are adept at separating their private from their public selves. People who are low self-monitors reveal themselves much more clearly and tend to be themselves regardless of the situation or others' expectations. The high self-monitor may be more flexible in interacting with different types of people. One researcher (Ibarra, 2000) even advocates that young professionals observe a broad range of executive personalities and pick out specific behaviours that might fit into one's own repertoire of styles. The intention is to develop flexibility and effectiveness in interacting with a range of people and situations.

Assessing individual differences

Before offering someone a job employers want to know as much about the person as possible to make sure they have the characteristics they require for the job. The most widely used method in the selection process of potential employees is the interview, but, as we have said earlier in this chapter, how can we ensure that our perceptions are accurate? One method used to try to overcome this is to make the interview more standardised and structured – in other words, more like a test.

psychometric assessments
Structured assessments to identify a candidate's behaviour type.

Psychometric assessments involve all the candidates being given the same questions in the same order. The questions are worded in such a way that the responses will demonstrate a behaviour type (Jackson, 1996).

Tests commonly used are:

- dexterity tests – used for manual skills
- general ability tests – used to test the general intelligence of an individual
- aptitude tests – test multiple abilities such as verbal, spatial, numerical and mechanical
- critical thinking tests – more often used in management and simulate problem-solving situations
- personality tests – try to provide clues as to how people will cope in different situations; some of these are not too different from the personality questionnaires often found in magazines
- personal qualities – used to try to test honesty and integrity.

The tests are interpreted using norm referencing, criterion referencing or content referencing (Jackson, 1996).

- Norm referencing refers to where an individual's behaviour is in relation to others.
- Criterion referencing tries to find out if the person would be successful in the job.
- Content referencing adds information value to the score by interpreting the pattern of performance. In other words, it identifies where the strengths are of candidates who may have the same score. One candidate may be more technically competent while the other may be better at reasoning. A decision can then be made as to whom to employ.

Care needs to be taken in the application of these tests to ensure their reliability and validity. Before testing candidates it is also necessary to have carried out a systematic job analysis otherwise how do you know you have the right candidate for the job? This is often the fundamental element that employers neglect and why there is so much criticism of the testing process (Woodruffe, 1993).

Learning how to learn: a second look

Kim Lafferty, chief knowledge architect at integrated learning specialists Academee, has been working closely with Tony Buzan to disseminate his ideas.

Lafferty believes it is acceptable to talk about 'healthy minds and healthy bodies' in organisations because there is a growing awareness that personal fitness, health and lifestyle have an impact on performance.

'My frustration is that it plays at the level of the individual, not the level of the corporation,' she says. 'I still see resistance from corporations, not because they don't believe it but if you have a budget, you are more likely to spend it on, say, presentation skills because – to a large extent – you can't control your employees' diet.'

Controversially, Buzan believes the hurdle to effective mind and body in the workplace lies in a 'complete misinterpretation' of HR development. Businesses never consider what a human resource is. 'If you're going to develop it you need to know what that resource is, how it's made and how to care for it.'

One example is to categorise personal skills as 'soft' skills.

'The profit-making skills are thinking, learning, innovation, self-management, mental and physical fitness, communication and leadership, and those have to be taught if a company is going to survive,' Buzan warns.

With most training, a company is lucky if 5 per cent of what is taught is applied. But when you teach people about how they function, the application rate is between 50 per cent and 100 per cent, he claims.

'Any company that implements a "learning how to learn" model will be more efficient and more effective and therefore will dominate in the marketplace. This is an inevitability; it is not optional.'

Buzan concludes, 'I am extremely hopeful that this will mean the marketplace and the workplace are going to be much more enjoyable, creative, productive, much less stress-ridden, more communicative and fun.'

Source: People Management, 7 February 2002, Buzan, T. 'Head Strong', Thorsons.

Summary

- People enter organisations with different abilities and motives. A manager's role is to achieve the best person–job fit possible, which means matching the individual's abilities and motives with the job requirements and rewards.

- Each individual develops a psychological contract with the organisation, which includes expectations about what each party will give and receive.

- The perceptual process includes the selection, organisation and interpretation of sensory stimuli.

- Individuals often perceive differently from one another, and this makes communication in organisations more difficult.

- Selective perception, stereotyping, halo effects and projection are perceptual errors that make managing behaviour in organisations more difficult.

- Attributions are individuals' efforts to explain the reasons for behaviour. Externals look for causes outside themselves; internals look within.

- A common attributional biasing error is for people to blame their own failures on external factors and credit internal factors for their successes.

- Individuals learn by responding to positive and negative reinforcers in their environment, by observing others and imitating certain behaviours, and by using their cognitive skills to observe, reason and choose an appropriate course of action.

- People develop different styles of learning. Some learn by experiencing and others learn by observing and reflecting.

- Individuals also favour one side of their brains in learning: either the left (linear/systematic) side or the right (holistic/relational) side. Learning is a lifelong activity, made even more important by today's fast-changing world.

- Values and attitudes shape people's perceptions and behaviour. Values are relatively stable and enduring, affirming what is important. They guide people in deciding how to behave and what to seek, and employees may adopt value systems espoused by the organisation.

- Attitudes are more specific and subject to change. They include cognitive, affective and intentional components, and represent how people feel about others, objects and situations. Attitudes about jobs and organisations influence attendance, turnover and, sometimes, commitment and productivity. For this reason managers should monitor employee attitudes about important organisational variables.

- Each individual develops a unique personality, which is the set of traits and behaviours that characterises a person. Managers who are sensitive to these differences are better able to understand and predict their employees' behaviours. However, because people are so complex, complete understanding is an elusive goal.

Areas for personal development

Although your personality is well established at this point in your life, you can still improve on perceptual accuracy and how you learn – you may even develop greater flexibility in your behavioural styles. These affect managerial performance.

1 **Write out a psychological contract from your point of view.** Every time you join an organisation you develop a psychological contract of your expectations of what each party gives and receives. If you belong to a club, a church, a volunteer organisation or hold a job, select one membership and write out a psychological contract. Now do the same for the organisation where you expect to be working for the two years following graduation.

2 **Match abilities to aptitudes.** Develop a list of your abilities and a list of your aptitudes (where you have the capacity to learn). Where you have aptitudes that are not yet fulfilled with abilities, write a plan of what you need to do to develop abilities. Distinguish between what you can do while still a student and what you can better learn while working over the next five years or so.

3 **Hone perceptual organisation and interpretation.** Reflect back over the past 24 hours and identify four or five ambiguous situations that potentially hold significance for you. It could have been something said (but not understood) in class, an unusual expression on the face of a friend, an observation you offered at a meeting but to which no one responded, or something else. Write a brief phrase as a frame of reference for each, and then write two or more action alternatives for each. These are actions you could have initiated to improve the accuracy of your perception in the situation. Become proactive in reality testing your perceptions so you respond more to facts than inferences.

4 **Differentiate between internal and external attribution.** Do you find yourself at times defending something you have done that was associated with a less than desirable outcome? If so, you may be resorting to rationalisation to justify that your actions were not contributing to the disappointment. Step back and answer honestly to yourself 'Do I have some responsibility for this problem or setback?' Own up to internal attributions when justified, and external attributions when it is obvious the event or outcome was caused by others, by chance or by external forces.

5 **Apply the Premack principle of reinforcement.** When deciding on the sequence of your 'to do' list, pair tasks and do the less satisfying one first. Do something that is more enjoyable or fulfilling as reinforcement for having done the one that is more of a chore.

6 **Follow the flow of experiential learning styles.** Refer back to Exhibit 4-8 and, using the descriptors for Kolb's four styles of learning, identify the one that is most characteristic of you. As each style represents the combination of two learning abilities, observe the two alternative abilities you seem to use less frequently. Practise following the flow of the model when you are learning something complex. That way you will include the less-developed abilities and complete the learning loop.

7 **Clarify your personal values.** If you have not done so, complete the 'Your turn' activity on page 169. For each column, circle the five values you ranked from 1 to 5. Do the five in the 'Ultimate values' column really represent what is important to you to find fulfilment in life? Do the five 'Means values' most appropriately describe your current behaviours? If not, rethink your list(s).

8   **Become aware of your personality characteristics.** Jung's cognitive styles (of gathering and evaluating information) represent opposites (similar to Kolb's learning abilities). Using the model in Exhibit 4-10, what combination is most characteristic of you in terms of your self-perception? Share the model with a friend and ask 'How would you describe me using these terms?' Then reciprocate by offering your perceptions of your friend, who also defines his or her self-perception. Are you the same or different? If different, in what ways do you complement one another? If you tend to attract kindred spirits, think through what you can do to move away from your comfort zone and begin to appreciate more diversity among personalities.

❓ Questions for study and discussion

1   Give one example of a good person–job fit, and give one example of a poor person–job fit. What alternatives can be considered in improving the poor person–job fit?

2   Joanne Kraus has just been hired as a management trainee with a large regional bank. She is a management graduate with a 2:1 classification from a well-known business school. She is 22 and plans to have a career in banking. What might be some of the elements of her psychological contract?

3   Explain what is meant by the statement 'Some of what you see in me is really in you, and some of what I see in you is in me.' Give some examples illustrating the statement.

4   What are some alternative ways of responding to someone who has perceptions that differ from yours? What is likely to be the impact of each on your interactions with that person?

5   Give one example of a self-attribution and one example of an attribution about another person.

6   Give an example of how the manager of an e-commerce unit might apply each of these three learning theories: (1) behavioural conditioning; (2) social learning theory; (3) cognitive theory.

7   Albert Einstein attributed his famous theory of relativity to sudden insight. Many executives say that when it comes to personnel and product-related problems, their intuition serves them better than objective, rational study. What is your view? Are insight and intuition unrelated to analytical reasoning? Provide illustrations of how differences in the nature of the problems invite either left-brain-hemisphere or right-brain-hemisphere approaches.

8   What are some alternative ways of finding out the values of another person? How about your own? How reliable is each approach?

9   Can attitudes be changed? If so, how? If not, why?

10 Develop a brief job description that would appeal to each of the following types of manager:
    (a) sensation thinker
    (b) sensation feeler
    (c) intuitive thinker
    (d) intuitive feeler.

🔑 Key Concepts

person–job fit, *p. 141*

psychological contract, *p. 142*

social contract, *p. 142*

ability, *p. 143*

aptitude, *p. 143*

perception, *p. 145*

figure, *p. 147*

ground, *p. 147*

perceptual closure, *p. 148*

frame of reference, *p. 149*

selective perception, *p. 149*

stereotype, *p. 149*

halo effect, *p. 149*

projection, *p. 150*

attribution, *p. 150*

distinctiveness, *p. 151*

consistency, *p. 151*

consensus, *p. 151*

attributional error, *p. 152*

self-serving bias, *p. 152*

learning, *p. 153*

intelligence, *p. 153*

classical conditioning, *p. 155*

operant conditioning, *p. 155*

Premack principle, *p. 157*

social learning theory, *p. 157*

anticipatory control, *p. 158*

cognitive learning, *p. 158*

gestalt, *p. 158*

insight, *p. 158*

discrimination, *p. 159*

generalisation, *p. 160*

e-learning, *p. 164*

values, *p. 165*

personal value system, *p. 168*

integrity, *p. 168*

attitude, *p. 170*

cognitive dissonance, *p. 170*

personality, *p. 172*

cognitive style, *p. 174*

locus of control, *p. 177*

authoritarianism, *p. 177*

dogmatism, *p. 177*

Machiavellianism, *p. 177*

risk propensity, *p. 177*

self-esteem, *p. 177*

self-monitoring, *p. 178*

psychometric assessments, *p. 178*

Personal skills exercise
Reflections on learning styles

Continual learning is fundamental to functioning successfully within organisations. Therefore, those who aspire to careers in organisations should be aware of how they prefer to learn, and work to develop complementary learning skills where those abilities are low. To think more personally about learning processes, begin by answering the following questions. Circle the number that best describes you for the eight questions below. (This entire activity can be completed in about 5 to 7 minutes.)

1 I enjoy venturing into new experiences and relationships to see what I can learn.
This describes me   *This does not describe me*
1   2   3   4   5

2 I actively participate in here-and-now experiences that enable me to become aware of how I affect my environment and others.
This describes me   *This does not describe me*
1   2   3   4   5

3 I am a careful observer of events and people, and find myself reflecting on what I see and hear from what goes on about me.
This describes me   *This does not describe me*
1   2   3   4   5

4 I find myself talking with others about our recent experiences so that I can make sense of what people say and do and of why events turn out as they do.
This describes me   *This does not describe me*
1   2   3   4   5

5 I like to manipulate abstract ideas and symbols to visualise how concepts and things are related.
This describes me   *This does not describe me*
1   2   3   4   5

6 I find myself engaging in 'what if' forms of reasoning and synthesising ideas into hypotheses for future testing.
This describes me   *This does not describe me*
1   2   3   4   5

7 I enjoy taking risks by testing my ideas on others or in actions to see if they work.
This describes me   *This does not describe me*
1   2   3   4   5

8 I am decisive, a practical problem-solver who enjoys putting plans into action.
This describes me   *This does not describe me*
1   2   3   4   5

There are no right or wrong answers to the above questions. It is not intended to be a scientifically valid instrument, but simply to serve as a stimulus to your thinking and learning. To interpret your answers, add your 'scores' for each pair of questions (1 + 2, 3 + 4, etc.) in the table below:

Scores from questions			Learning processes (abilities)
1 _____	+ 2 _____	= _____	Concrete experience
3 _____	+ 4 _____	= _____	Reflective observation
5 _____	+ 6 _____	= _____	Abstract conceptualisation
7 _____	+ 8 _____	= _____	Active experimentation

Your lowest score(s) suggest the learning processes that you tend to favour. The higher the score, the less inclined you are to use that process or ability.

Now turn back to Exhibit 4-8 and write your total scores on each of the four processes next to the appropriate label in the diagram. Are your two lowest scores adjacent to one another in the flow process (for example, 'concrete experience' and 'reflective observation')? If so, circle the learning style indicated by the combination of the two (such as 'divergence' in the above example). This is suggestive of your dominant style of learning. Read again the description of this style and reflect on whether you believe that it appropriately describes you.

If you do have a dominant style, is the total of your other two processes at least twice as high as your two lowest scores? If so, you might want to strengthen them as this suggests they are seldom used. Write three action steps you could take to activate learning using these process alternatives. Then seek to practise them.

1 _____

2 _____

3 _____

You may want to compare your results with those of a classmate. If the two of you differ in learning styles, you can learn from one another how to strengthen your less-used abilities.

Team exercise

Diversity dilemma: a role play

Procedure Form groups of four to six people. Read the 'situation' described below, and then decide who will role play Jeff and who Daneisha as the two meet to discuss her request.

Time 20 to 30 minutes

Situation Jeff Birnbaum faces a dilemma. Daneisha Tinson has just asked him to recommend her for the bank's development programme for upper-management secretaries. Being accepted in that programme would give Daneisha both experience and visibility that could help her gain a promotion to an executive secretary position.

Jeff is 42, white and the compensation manager for Midshires Bank, which employs 9500 people. He values employee development and is a strong advocate of affirmative action and equal employment opportunity.

Daneisha is 26 and has worked for five years at Midshires. She started as an administrative assistant, was promoted in six months to the word-processing department, and two years later was promoted to secretary. Jeff rates her performance as outstanding. She is highly skilled, works hard, and can be trusted to produce top-quality work.

Proud of her African heritage, Daneisha enjoys wearing colourful African-style prints, head wraps and jewellery to work. Jeff knows the senior bank executives, who are all men, are ultra-conservative. They wear dark suits, white shirts and club ties, and care about presenting the right image to clients and employees. Their executive secretaries all wear tailored dresses and suits. Jeff wonders if Daneisha would be accepted on the executive floor. He has no doubts about her ability and potential but wonders if her expression of ethnic identification might lead to rejection. If all others must conform, why not Daneisha? Jeff knows the clash between corporate and ethnic cultures could lead to trouble. He wonders what he should say to Daneisha.

Role play Two people enact the conversation Jeff has with Daneisha (within your small group). The following questions may provide ideas for the meeting.

1 Should Jeff recommend Daneisha for the development programme? Why or why not?

2 What, if anything, should Jeff tell Daneisha in communicating his opinion?

3 Is this an individual issue or a corporate issue?

Case study: **Tesbury's Supermarket plc**

James Fox, a senior director of Tesbury's Supermarket, felt anxious and tense. He and Martin Miller, the CEO, frequently seemed to clash. They disagreed so much that James wondered if he should resign.

Martin Miller was 51. He started with one small store in a small English town and had gradually expanded to become one of Britain's largest supermarket chains. Tesbury's performed well as a public limited company and had been the market leader in its sector, although in the last year it had dropped to third place. Martin also had considerable personal wealth, the majority of which came from when the company went public. In addition to being CEO he was the largest shareholder. Martin was seen by most people as focused, determined and intelligent. He was considered by most to be a 'straight talker'.

The promotion and clash of views

James Fox, 38, has a BA in Retail Management and an MBA. He was 27 when he started with Tesbury's. He quickly moved ahead and, until nine months ago, was senior manager of retail operations. At that time he was promoted two levels to a senior director's position because his predecessor had unexpectedly resigned. James had not interacted much with Martin Miller because Martin had delegated most operational matters to the former senior director, and James himself had reported to a another director. James's perceptions of Martin had changed during the past months, and he suspected Martin's views of him had also changed.

A major issue between the two concerned pricing and competition. Martin believed strongly that some of his competitors were becoming too big as they were buying up smaller supermarkets. He was lobbying to refer one particular company to the Monopolies and Mergers Commission. He was also not happy with the 'value brands', which were often sold at a loss, or the 'gourmet brands', which were expensive to develop. James, on the other hand, felt that Tesbury's had no problem competing, but needed to concentrate on creating customer loyalty with incentive schemes and creating new ranges such as 'The restaurant at home' gourmet range. Martin was startled and disappointed with James's response to his views.

Martin said James was naive and inexperienced in strategic matters, and that his ideas were impractical. He indicated clearly that he, as CEO, was the one to be concerned with such decisions. Martin even said that if James wanted to question his (Martin's) competence, he should do so directly instead of insinuating indirectly.

James works quietly behind the scenes

Because Martin was so vehement, James decided to back away and to avoid discussions in which he differed with Martin. James disliked arguments, so he decided to execute his duties by conforming closely to Tesbury's policies and ways of operating. However, because Martin was frequently away, James interpreted policies rather broadly. He began to quietly take small steps to reshape the organisation along the lines he thought appropriate. For example, he began to develop a new customer loyalty card. He also influenced the product development department to focus less on value products and more on a gourmet range in an attempt to increase appeal to higher socio-economic groups.

When Martin questioned James on some of these changes, James would back away from the discussion to avoid bombastic arguments. He would focus for a while on areas of less interest to Martin but that would still help move Tesbury's towards improved performance.

However, James became increasingly aware of how much his own philosophy differed from Martin's. He felt disturbed that he could not talk openly with Martin, and he observed that the two interacted less and less. James wondered what the limits of his own authority were. Although he feared a repeat of previously uncomfortable discussions, he suggested to Martin that they meet to discuss their respective areas of authority and responsibility. Martin agreed and said they would meet as soon as possible. Three weeks passed and James had heard nothing.

Martin begins to rethink James's appointment

Conversely, Martin was bothered by James's behaviour since he became a senior director. One of Martin's first concerns followed James's recommendation to spend large sums of money on marketing the new customer loyalty scheme. Martin questioned the amount and whether this would provide the expected returns in increased sales. He also thought James exhibited poor judgement in his willingness to abandon Tesbury's traditional market, and the customer loyalty scheme James was recommending did not seem to provide the incentives that their competitors offered. Martin decided James was not willing to support his own case because he quickly backed down when Martin challenged him.

Martin was also irritated at some of the product development changes that had been made. He would like to have discussed some of these with James to help his own thinking on the moves, but he could never pin James down to a clear position. Martin was wondering just how much authority he could give James. Martin felt particularly annoyed at what he perceived to be James's building support for his own ideas behind Martin's back. Changes were made that would be difficult to undo. Martin did not understand why James was not as direct with him as he (Martin) was with James. Martin enjoyed an energetic go-at-'em exchange in which viewpoints could be tested. However, James just did not seem willing to stand up for his views. Martin pondered how to work with a man like James and wondered if he should continue in the executive vice president role.

Discussion questions

1 What is happening in this case?

2 How do you think Martin and James perceive each other? How do they perceive themselves?

3 What do you think each should do? Why?

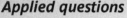

Applied questions

4 The perceiver, the perceived and the setting all influence how we respond to stimuli. How and why are Martin and James reacting differently to the situation?

5 Attribution is an assumed explanation of why people behave as they do based on our behaviour and inferences. Using Kelley's theory of attribution, how are Martin and James judging each other?

WWW exercise

Manager's Internet tools

Web tips: cross-cultural values and expatriate managers on the web

In a globally competitive world, companies routinely send managers overseas. For many companies, this is part of the 'grooming process' for career advancement. The effective manager and executive will be the one that is not only functionally and technically competent, but one who can manage people with diverse backgrounds, cultures, languages and values. However, the risks to the firm are great: if the expatriate does not work well in a foreign environment, it can affect the current and future performance of the firm in its foreign dealings.

It is imperative, therefore, that expatriate managers learn and prepare for the assignment. Beyond all the logistical aspects, it is important that expatriates prepare for the cultures in which they are going to be immersed. Cultures of the world have different values and norms, as you are aware. While values are very personal in nature, they do take on a cultural aspect. For the expatriate, the more one knows about a culture, the fewer 'cultural mistakes' he or she will make and the easier it will be to integrate. Success in a foreign assignment has a lot to do with one's ability to learn quickly: to integrate, understand, sympathise and relate to the local people.

World Wide Web search

Pick a country in which you would be interested in living. Using a search engine, find some information about the culture(s) in that country, particularly the cultural values. Search with keywords like 'cultural values in X', or 'living in X'. Are the cultural values you found what you expected? Are they different from your personal value set?

Specific website: Integrated Resources Group

The Integrated Resources Group (IRG) works with multinational corporations in preparing for expatriate assignments and developing solutions for cross-cultural problems. Look at the IRG website (www.expatrepat.com/home.html) and pay particular attention to these areas:

- the challenge of working in a foreign culture
- the importance of cross-cultural preparation
- assessing who would be good candidates for overseas assignments
- preparing for the international move
- maintaining ties to home.

1 Do you think you would be a good candidate for an international assignment? Why?

2 What personal values might you have to adjust when working in a foreign culture?

3 What learning style do you have? Would you need to develop a different learning style for working in a foreign culture? Which learning style would be most effective? Why?

LEARNING CHECKLIST ☑

Before you move on you may want to reflect on what you have learnt in this chapter. You should now be able to:

☑ explain what is meant by person–job fit and the psychological contract

☑ illustrate the impact of perceptions and attributions on people's behaviour in organisations

☑ describe three theories of learning and how they apply to organisational settings

☑ contrast four basic individual styles of learning and know in which roles each is effective

☑ illustrate the impact that values and attitudes have on perceptions and behaviour

☑ describe and illustrate different personality types and traits and their significance for behaviour

☑ identify various methods of testing potential employees.

Further reading

Haslam, N., Bastian, B., Bain, P. and Kashima, Y. (2006) 'Psychological Essentialism: Implicit Theories and Intergroup Relations', *Group Processes & Intergroup Relations* 9(1), January, p. 63.

Huey, J. (1993) 'Finding New Heroes for a New Era', *Fortune*, 25 January, pp. 52–69.

Machiavelli, N. (1961) *The Prince*, George Bull (trans.) Middlesex: Penguin.

Magnet, M. (1987) 'The Money Society', *Fortune*, 6 July, pp. 26–31.

Noe, R., Hollenbeck, J., Gerhart, B. and Wright, P. (2003) *Human Resource Management – Gaining Competitive Advantage.* McGraw-Hill Irwin.

Sinclair, S., Huntsinger, J., Skorinko, J. and Hardin, C.D. (2005) 'Social Tuning of the Self: Consequences for the Self-evaluations of Stereotype Targets', *Journal of Personality and Social Psychology* 89(2), August, p. 160.

Wegener, D.T., Petty, R.E. and Clark, J.K. (2006) 'Not all Stereotyping is Created Equal: Differential Consequences of Thoughtful Versus Non Thoughtful Stereotyping', *Journal of Personality and Social Psychology* 90(1), January, p. 42.

References

Adorno, T.W. (1989) 'Who Becomes an Authoritarian?' *Psychology Today*, 1989, pp. 66–70.

Agor, W.H. (1984) 'Using Intuition to Manage Organisations in the Future', *Business Horizons* 27, July–August, p. 51.

Allport, G.W., Vernon, P.E. and Lindzey, G. (1951) *Study of Values*. Boston, MA: Houghton Mifflin.

Bandura, A. (1974) 'Behaviour Theory and the Models of Man', *American Psychologist* 29(12), pp. 859–869.

Bandura, A. and Walters, R.H. (1963) *Social Learning and Personality Development*. New York, NY: Holt, Rinehart & Winston, p. 2.

Becker, T.E. (1998) 'Integrity in Organizations: Beyond Honesty and Conscientiousness', *Academy of Management Review* 23, January, pp. 154–161 (quote on p. 157).

Bettman, J.R. and Weitz, B.A. (1983) 'Attributions in the Board Room: Causal Reasoning in Corporate Annual Reports', *Administrative Science Quarterly*, June, pp. 165–183.

Bigge, M.L. (1964) *Learning Theory for Teachers*. New York, NY: Harper & Row, p. 214.

Blaker, K.E. (1976) *Behaviour Modification*. Morristown, NJ: General Learning Press, pp. 19–20.

Breckler, S.J. (1984) 'Empirical Validation of Affect, Behaviour, and Cognition as Distinct Components of Attitude', *Journal of Personality and Social Psychology*, May, pp. 1191–1205.

Briggs, K. and Myers-Briggs, I. (1987) *Myers–Briggs Type Indicator*. Palo Alto, CA: Consulting Psychologists Press, Inc.

Buzan, T. (1989) *Use your Head*. BBC Publications.

Chaplin, J.P. (1985) *Dictionary of Psychology* (rev. 2nd edn). New York, NY: Bantam Doubleday Dell, pp. 233–234.

Christie, R. and Gies, F.L. (1970) *Studies in Machiavellianism*. New York, NY: Academic Press.

Cooper, M.R. (1979) 'Changing Employee Values: Deepening Discontent?', *Harvard Business Review*, January–February, pp. 117–125.

Couchard, T.J. Jr (1990) 'Sources of Human Psychological Differences: The Minnesota Study of Twins Reared Apart', *Science* 250, 12 October, pp. 223–228.

Csoka, L.S. (1995) 'A New Employer–Employee Contract?', *Employee Relations Today*, 22 June, pp. 21ff.

Festinger, L. (1957) *A Theory of Cognitive Dissonance*. Palo Alto, CA: Stanford University Press.

Festinger, L. and Carlsmith, L.M. (1959) 'Cognitive Consequences of Forced Compliance', *Journal of Abnormal and Social Psychology* 58, pp. 203–210.

Festinger, L., Rieken, H.W. and Schachter, S. (1956) *When Prophecy Fails*. Minneapolis: University of Minneapolis Press.

Galagan, P. (2000) 'The E-learning Revolution', *Training and Development*, December.

Gardner, H. (1983) *Frames of Mind: The Theory of Multiple Intelligences*. New York, NY: Basic Books.

Goleman, D. (1994) *Emotional Intelligence*. New York, NY: Bantam Books.

Harary, K. and Donahue, E. (1992) 'Who Are You?', *Psychology Today*, May–June, p. 69.

Heider, F. (1958) *The Psychology of Interpersonal Relations*. New York, NY: Wiley.

Henriques, I. and Sadorsky, P. (1999) 'The Relationship between Environmental Commitment and Managerial Perceptions of Stakeholder Importance', *Academy of Management Journal* 42, February, pp. 87–99.

Ibarra, H. (2000) 'Making Partner: A Mentor's Guide to the Psychological Journey', *Harvard Business Review*, March–April, pp. 146–155.

Jackson, C. (1996) *Understanding Psychological Testing*. Leicester: BPS Books.

Jung, C.G. (1933) *Psychological Types*. New York, NY: Harcourt.

Kelley, H.H. (1971) *Attribution in Social Interaction.* Morristown, NJ: General Learning Press.

Kelley, H.H. and Michela, J.L. (1980) 'Attribution Theory and Research', *Annual Review of Psychology*, pp. 457–501.

Kohler, W. (1925) *The Mentality of Apes.* New York, NY: Harcourt Brace and World.

Kolb, D.A. (1976) 'Management and the Learning Process', *California Management Review* 18, Spring, pp. 21–31.

Kuttner, R. (1993) 'Talking Marriage and Thinking One-night Stand', *Business Week*, 18 October, p. 16.

Meeker, B.F. (1990) 'Cooperation, Competition, and Self-Esteem: Aspects of Winning and Losing', *Human Relations*, March, pp. 205–220.

Miller, A.G. and Lawson, T. (1989) 'The Effect of an Informational Option on the Fundamental Attribution Error', *Personality and Social Psychology Bulletin*, June, pp. 194–204.

Mintzberg, H. (1976) 'Planning on the Left Side and Managing on the Right', *Harvard Business Review* 54, July–August, p. 53.

Moore, T. (1987) 'Personality Tests Are Back', *Fortune*, 30 March, pp. 74–82.

Mowday, R.T., Porter, L.W. and Steers, R.M. (1982) *Employee Organization Linkages: The Psychology of Commitment, Absenteeism, and Turnover.* New York, NY: Academic Press.

Oliver, B.L. (1999) 'Comparing Corporate Managers' Personal Values Over Three Decades, 1967–1995', *Journal of Business Ethics* 20, June, pp. 147–161.

Ornstein, R.E. (1973) 'Right and Left Thinking', *Psychology Today*, May, pp. 87–92.

Osland, J.S. and Bird, A. (2000) 'Beyond Sophisticated Stereotyping: Cultural Sensemaking in Context', *Academy of Management Executive* 14, February, pp. 65–77.

Pavlov, I.P. (1927) *Conditional Reflexes*, GV Anrep (trans.). London: Oxford University Press.

Pervin, L. (1985) 'Personality', in Mark Rosenzweig and Lyman Porter (eds) *Annual Review of Psychology* 36, Palo Alto, CA: Annual Reviews.

Premack, D. (1959) 'Toward Empirical Behaviour Laws: 1. Positive Reinforcement', *Psychological Review* 66.

Rokeach, M. (1973) *The Nature of Human Values.* New York, NY: Free Press.

Rokeach, M. and Ball-Rokeach, S.J. (1989) 'Stability and Change in American Value Priorities, 1968–1981', *American Psychologist*, May, pp. 775–784.

Rosenberg, M. (2001) *E-learning Revolution: Strategies for Delivering Knowledge in the Digital Age.* New York, NY: McGraw-Hill.

Rotter, J.B. (1966) 'Generalized Expectancies for Internal versus External Control of Reinforcement', *Psychological Monographs* 80(609).

Schermerhorn, J.R. Jr (1986) 'Team Development for High Performance Management', *Training and Development Journal* 40, November, pp. 38–41.

Skinner, B.F. (1964) *The Shaping of a Behaviourist.* New York, NY: Harper & Row, Chapter 8.

Skinner, B.F. (1971) *Beyond Freedom and Dignity.* New York, NY: Bantam-Vintage Books.

Slocum, J.W. Jr and Hellriegel, D. (1983) 'A Look at How Managers' Minds Work', *Business Horizons* 26, July–August, pp. 58–68.

Snyder, M. (1987) *Public Appearance/Private Realities: The Psychology of Self-monitoring.* New York, NY: W.H. Freeman.

Staw, B.M. (1975) 'Attribution of the Causes of Performance: A General Alternative Interpretation of Cross-sectional Research on Organisations', *Organisational Behaviour and Human Performance*, pp. 414–432.

Thorndike, E.L. (1913) *Educational Psychology: The Psychology of Learning.* New York, NY: Columbia University Press, II, 4.

Weaver, G.R., Treviño, L.K. and Cochran, P.L. (1999) 'Corporate Ethics Programs as Control Systems: Influences of Executive Commitment and Environmental Factors', *Academy of Management Journal* 42, February, pp. 41–57.

Weidenbaum, M. (1995) 'A New Social Contract for the American Workplace', *Challenge*, January, pp. 51ff.

Woodruffe, C. (1993) *Assessment Centres: Identifying and Developing Competence* (2nd edn). London: IPM.

Yankelovich, D. (1981) 'New Rules in American Life: Searching for Self-fulfillment in a World Turned Upside Down', *Psychology Today*, April, pp. 35–86.

Motivation principles at work

LEARNING OUTCOMES ☑

After studying this chapter you should be able to:

☑ **identify** two need-based theories of motivation and describe how each influences approach–avoidance behaviours in a work setting

☑ **explain** why removing sources of job dissatisfaction will not necessarily rekindle the motivation to work

☑ **distinguish** among the motives of achievement, power and affiliation, and tell how each affects success as an entrepreneur or manager

☑ **relate** the three basic factors of expectancy theory to typical work conditions that increase or diminish motivation

☑ **distinguish** between satisfaction and motivation, and indicate how the two are related

☑ **explain** why equity evaluations (and perceptions of work justice) can alleviate motivational problems

☑ **tell** why motivation theories based on individual behaviour are increasingly inadequate for explaining behaviour in multicultural organisations.

Despite the decline in manufacturing in the United Kingdom there is still hope for the British car industry. The opening vignette demonstrates how, given the right conditions, workers can have influence in the workplace.

Top gear
People often used to blame the British car industry's poor performance on workers. But employees at Halewood in Merseyside have shown they can rival the best in the world, given the right conditions.

Jimmy Rooney has worked at Ford's Halewood plant on Merseyside for 28 years. However, he has to think back only two years to remember it as a dark and dirty old factory with grime on the floor and boxes of car parts cluttering the aisles between production lines. Operators used to eat their sandwiches perched on benches by the line. Many even sat in the cars: once the seats had been installed, they were more comfortable.

It was hardly surprising that the plant, which then produced Ford Escorts, had one of the lowest productivity and quality records in the company.

It also has a history of poor labour relations, as many who recall the frequent walkouts of the 1970s and 1980s will know. The press often blamed the 'bolshie Scouse' workforce, whose parents and grandparents worked in the docks and brought a militant tradition with them to the new factories, such as Halewood, which were built on the outskirts of Liverpool in 1962. So it may seem strange that the company, after a certain amount of soul-searching, chose the site in 1998 to produce its new 'baby' Jaguar, the X-type. This would replace Escort production, which was being wound up.

In fact the media headlines had always been somewhat misleading. Senior management knew, even then, that the productivity record of the plant could not be entirely blamed on the workforce. The company was also under pressure from a union campaign to keep Halewood open by maintaining some sort of production there.

Ford's president, Jack Nasser, agreed to this in principle and was then faced with the need to bring forward plans for the X-type. Perhaps he also had enough faith in humanity and the transforming effects of good management to believe that Halewood, widely seen as a stain on the face of automotive manufacturing, could be a star.

Visiting the factory today it is hard to believe the descriptions of its former incarnation. The shell of the main building remains but is covered on the outside at the front with a silver metallic cladding befitting a luxury car. Inside, the assembly area has been gutted, cleaned, given a new (white) floor and refitted with the paraphernalia of a modern car plant. Wide aisles, clearly marked with pedestrian and forklift lanes for safety, divide assembly lines to which parts are delivered just-in-time. Screens display management announcements and statistics, and every so often there is a large square rest area, designed like a cafe with tables and refreshments, or a management area where hundreds of record sheets on production times, errors or quality improvement proposals cover notice boards. These are made up by production workers and team leaders themselves and use words, charts and pictures. One, for instance, had a picture of a car boot, the work 'leak' and two arrows pointing graphically to either side.

An orange cord runs at head height all the way along the line. Any operator can pull this to stop the line if they feel it necessary. In other words, this is a factory designed to be as pleasant as possible to work in and to be micro-managed by the workers. Moreover, the workers quite like it. Many, such as Rooney, are enthusiastic.

'In the old days, if we could see a quality issue that needed tackling, we just ignored it. Now we are asked to give our input. Management listens to what we have to say. Years ago, arguments didn't even get to the table. We would just have to walk. Now you can get around a table and have a chat.'

So how was the transformation managed? It was a little wobbly at first. Initially, an agreement had to be drawn up with the unions to enable the plant to operate the kind of flexible Japanese practices now common elsewhere, including Jaguar's other plants. In addition,

500 jobs were to go, which strengthened resistance from a workforce that had already seen numbers drop from 13 000 at Halewood's peak to fewer than 4000 by 1998.

The senior management team, formed that year to lead the transition, produced a vision statement and negotiated the Halewood Gateway Agreement in which unions agreed flexibility, mobility and new working practices – including not eating in the cars. But when it was implemented there was a series of protest strikes.

In response Ford threatened to withdraw the project from Halewood, effectively closing it down unless workers signed up to the 'Halewood Charter' consenting to operate the agreement. Early retirement and redundancy were on offer to those who did not want to make the change, but there was a commitment to no compulsory redundancy. More than 90 per cent signed.

With the union leaders and at least the majority of members behind them, the management team running Halewood knew that the key to success was to change the plant's culture at the same time as its processes; they needed genuine buy-in from people, not half-hearted compliance driven by carrot and stick.

David Crisp, corporate affairs manager and part of the change team, explains: 'The priority was to change from a volume-driven culture to a quality-driven culture. Halewood never really talked about the customer. Quality management had been introduced and the plant would achieve its targets for a short period but they were not sustained. There were rapid management changes and not enough investment. But before we started trying to make all these changes across the board, we fell flat on our faces because it was too big and too great.'

So the new team, then headed by David Hudson, a Jaguar veteran and now manufacturing director, opted for a three-pronged strategy: cranking up quality, changing the Halewood culture and, crucially, delivering these changes gradually through centres of excellence – bite-sized elements of the business.

In the centres of excellence, new processes and a more open management style were introduced and the boxes of components cleared away. Engineers, managers, supervisors and shop-floor operatives in the section were all involved in talking through the changes.

Shop-floor workers wrote their own job descriptions and operating processes and timed each other using video cameras. Work groups were reduced in size from 20–30 down to six or eight, giving each group leader more control. A series of assessment centres was set up to choose new managers for the centres of excellence who were comfortable with leading culture change and operating lean production methods.

Source: originally published in *People Management*, 18 April 2002, Barrie Oxtoby, 'Driving High Performance Working' from the CIPD's HRD 2002 conference. Reprinted with permission.

Discussion questions

1 Why is it important for managers to listen to the workforce?
2 Why has performance improved at Halewood?

Motivation is at the heart of how innovative and productive things get done within work organisations. As demonstrated by Halewood in the opening vignette, management has to get it right to enable others in the organisation to produce effectively. Those who lead need to be aware of how they use language and behaviour to arouse in followers a desire to direct effort into activities that benefit the organisation and themselves. This chapter focuses on the basic motivational factors that can energise a person's work, on the distractions that compete for attention, and on how motives are learned through experience. Several theories have evolved to help explain different facets of motivation.

We begin with the concept that people have different needs that direct their behaviour. Some of these needs depend on personal circumstances and outside events. Needs can cause people to seek out experiences that enrich their lives. Alternatively, needs can trigger behaviour to avoid threatening conditions and feelings of deprivation. Other needs are learned from rewarding experiences. These learned needs become relatively persistent motives that influence a person to seek out experiences that satisfy a particular motive, such as the need for achievement or power.

Beyond human needs and the acquired taste for specific motives, a different explanation of motivation focuses on expectancies, or people's expectations about whether they can affect performance outcomes and how closely desired rewards are linked to performance. People also consider the equity of how they are treated, and those evaluations help determine whether they will appear motivated or not. As you develop in the workplace and possibly find yourself challenged with managerial responsibilities, you will be more productive if you understand the needs, expectations and conditions that enable individuals and groups to learn and exhibit qualities of effective motivation.

How human needs differ in content

Throughout most of the last century managers tried to find the key that unlocks people's motivation to work. With the help of research we have come to realise that motivation involves several distinct elements. It is not simply a case of some people having it and others not.

Motivation involves a conscious decision to perform one or more activities with greater effort than one performs other activities competing for attention. This definition of motivation contains three elements: (1) some need, motive or goal that triggers action; (2) a selection process that directs the choice of action; and (3) a level of effort intensity that is applied to the chosen action. In essence, motivation governs behaviour selection, direction and level of effort.

motivation
A conscious decision to perform one or more activities with greater effort than other competing activities.

One explanation of human motivation focuses on the content of people's needs. The content theories of motivation identify specific human needs and describe the circumstances under which these needs activate behaviour. Some theories arrange needs in hierarchical levels, with each level activating a different behaviour aimed at satisfying that need. Another theory suggests that individuals learn to be strongly attached to certain kinds of needs, typically called motives, because they produce satisfaction whenever they are acted on. Learned motives cause people to be predictable in the choice of tasks and behaviours they undertake.

content theories of motivation
Theories based on identifying specific human needs and describing the circumstances under which these needs activate behaviour.

Before we venture too far into detailed explanations of needs and other sources of motivation, take a couple of minutes to complete the 'Your turn' exercise. It will get you thinking about personal applications of the motivational theories you learn in this chapter.

Your turn

Motivational forces that affect you

For each of the following statements, check the option that best describes you in work or organisational situations.

	Usually	Sometimes	Never
1 I am bothered by lack of creature comforts and security.	☐	☐	☐
2 I need the frequent companionship of others.	☐	☐	☐
3 I seek out novel experiences and learning opportunities.	☐	☐	☐
4 I really get turned on by achievement-related tasks.	☐	☐	☐
5 I delight in building friendships and helping people.	☐	☐	☐
6 I am at my best when in charge and influencing others.	☐	☐	☐
7 My effort and abilities affect my task performance.	☐	☐	☐
8 I am rewarded when I perform well, punished when I fail.	☐	☐	☐
9 I value the rewards and punishments I encounter.	☐	☐	☐
10 I am treated fairly compared to others.	☐	☐	☐
11 I appreciate others rewarding me for my good work.	☐	☐	☐
12 No one needs to acknowledge when I do good things.	☐	☐	☐

Interpretation This exercise gives you a chance to reflect on what motivates you. Those statements for which you checked 'Usually' are motivating factors that affect you; those checked 'Never' probably do not affect you. Here is a summary of the 12 factors described in this exercise and in this chapter: (1) existence needs; (2) relatedness needs; (3) growth needs; (4) achievement motive; (5) affiliation motive; (6) power motive; (7), (8) and (9) combine for an expectancy outlook; (10) equity; (11) extrinsic rewards; and (12) intrinsic rewards. As you read about each factor in the chapter, turn back to this exercise to understand your answer within the context of the relevant theory. Which motivational forces do you want to change? Why?

Needs trigger approach–avoidance behaviours

A basic observation about human behaviour is that people will make an effort to do or have some things, but they will actively try to avoid or reduce the impact of others. Psychologists refer to this basic human condition as a struggle between *approach* and *avoidance behaviours*. On the one hand, people willingly seek out or approach desirable conditions – relationships, tasks, events, and so on. Alternatively, they try to minimise or avoid troubling or debilitating conditions. According to Maslow (1998), the opposing behaviours are energised by two very different types of needs. One has to do with reducing threatening deficiencies, the other with seeking personal growth experiences.

---

deficiency reduction needs
Rather universally experienced needs that trigger avoidance behaviours where the aim is to find relief from deficiencies, deprivations or unpleasant tensions.

Deficiency reduction needs

Nobody wants to be hungry, injured, rejected by others or taken advantage of. **Deficiency reduction needs** trigger behaviours of avoidance – the aim is to find relief from deficiencies, deprivations or unpleasant tensions, and return to a more neutral state of existence free from discomfort. A person who feels hunger pangs will act to relieve that discomfort. The worker troubled over accumulating bills may take a second job to earn extra money and pay off personal debts. Once the normal state has been reattained the need diminishes and behaviour can be directed to satisfying other needs.

Growth aspiration needs

growth aspiration needs
Somewhat unique personal needs influencing choices to seek out goals and experiences that will be meaningful and satisfying.

Whereas humans generally want to avoid threatening or unpleasant deprivations, growth goals are more personal, even unique. **Growth aspiration needs** motivate people to approach or seek out goals and experiences that they find personally meaningful. Growth needs involve the active pursuit of learning, meaningful personal relationships, and new challenges and experiences. Once a particular growth need or goal has been achieved, people typically direct their behaviour towards another challenge or pleasurable experience.

Shifts between growth and deficiency reduction needs

Thinking about these two different types of needs as sets of opposing forces helps explain why a person's behaviour will change many times during a day. We understand the working parent who abruptly leaves work to tend to an injured child or who stays home in bed with the flu. We may also expect the survivors of a mass lay-off, who have been reassigned to other departments during the subsequent reorganisation, to be disorientated, bewildered and anxious during the first few days. Under such circumstances, a manager who uses only growth 'challenges' to motivate is not likely to receive an enthusiastic response from people trying to protect themselves from the threat of job loss. Conversely, people whose essential needs have been met tend to be striving for growth most of the time. Managers should allow such people to channel their energies into solving problems, enhancing their knowledge and abilities, and engaging in new experiences.

Imagine that Theresa, a technical writer and single parent, has been earning a good salary and benefits that enable her to provide for her family's physical well-being – ample food, comfortable housing and clothing, good medical care. Then her company announces it is downsizing and will be reducing its workforce by 10 per cent, and she fears being laid off (which triggers a safety need). She is unlikely to be overly concerned about the higher-order need of belonging to a group or her own self-esteem need to perform creative and technically accurate work. Rather, she is likely to be motivated to do whatever she believes will enable her to keep her job and/or to begin looking discreetly for other employment. Once the lay-offs have been announced and Theresa realises she is not on the list, she breathes a sigh of relief and then re-engages work with a higher-order need energising her behaviour. Interestingly, one research study by Brockner *et al.* (1992) suggests that a moderate threat of lay-off leads to a greater increase in work effort than does either high or low job insecurity.

Limitations of the hierarchy of needs

Although popular among managers because of its intuitive appeal, Maslow's theory has been controversial among researchers. When the theory has been applied to industrial environments, results have been mixed at best. Generally, they fail to confirm the lockstep sequence of the five hierarchical levels and the principle that lower needs must be gratified before higher needs (Wahba and Bridwell, 1976).

Research focus: **Maslow's hierarchy of needs**

When managers talk about theories of motivation, almost inevitably they name Abraham Maslow and his hierarchy of needs theory. Maslow (1998) originally proposed a five-level hierarchy of needs as the basis of his original explanation of needs-based motivation. The hierarchy of needs begins with physical well-being as the most basic, and then progresses successively through safety, belonging, esteem and self-actualisation needs (see Exhibit 5-1). According to Maslow's hierarchical theory, once a lower-level need has been largely satisfied, its impact on behaviour diminishes. The individual is then free to progress to the next higher-level need, which becomes a major determinant of behaviour.

hierarchy of needs
A five-level needs theory proposed by Maslow in which lower-level basic needs must be satisfied before advancing to a higher-level need.

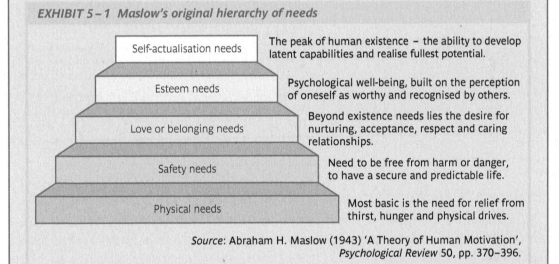

EXHIBIT 5–1 *Maslow's original hierarchy of needs*

Self-actualisation needs — The peak of human existence – the ability to develop latent capabilities and realise fullest potential.

Esteem needs — Psychological well-being, built on the perception of oneself as worthy and recognised by others.

Love or belonging needs — Beyond existence needs lies the desire for nurturing, acceptance, respect and caring relationships.

Safety needs — Need to be free from harm or danger, to have a secure and predictable life.

Physical needs — Most basic is the need for relief from thirst, hunger and physical drives.

Source: Abraham H. Maslow (1943) 'A Theory of Human Motivation', *Psychological Review* 50, pp. 370–396.

Abraham Maslow identified five levels of needs as the sources of different motivating behaviours. According to his theory, once a lower-level need has been satisfied, a person can activate the next higher-level need.

There have been several research studies in organisations using Maslow's theory. One such study, by Porter (1961), found that managers higher up the organisation placed a greater emphasis on self-actualisation needs and were generally more able to satisfy their growth needs than lower-level managers. Several other studies also show some support for Maslow's theory.

However, a review of research findings by Wahba and Bridwell (1976) on the hierarchy of needs concept found an interesting paradox. The review examined three propositions of Maslow's model:

1 the existence of the hierarchy

2 the proposition that an unfulfilled need leads individuals to focus exclusively on that need

3 the proposition that satisfaction of one need activates the next higher need.

> The examination revealed that there was no clear evidence showing that human needs are classified into five distinct categories, or that the categories are structured into a hierarchy. Most of the studies found two categories – those of deficiency and growth needs. The second proposition found mixed results. Some studies supported the need for individuals to focus on their unfulfilled needs, others did not. The third proposition of moving from lower to higher needs was also not supported. It was found by Maddi (1972) that higher-level needs can influence behaviour even when some of the lower-level needs are unfulfilled.
>
> Despite the lack of empirical support Maslow's theory is still popular and can provide a useful model for personal development, as we will see below.

Maslow (1965) even questioned its applicability to organisational behaviour, realising he based it on a study of neurosis. He wrote, 'But I of all people should know just how shaky this foundation is as a final foundation [of motivation in industry]. My work on motivation came from the clinic, from a study of neurotic people.' Few managers, let alone authors, are aware of the unusual origins of this popular theory.

The theory is perhaps most useful as a reminder of the full range of motivational forces in people. It may, for example, have relevance in building a workforce in developing countries. A firm from the United Kingdom planning to set up a factory in China, where per capita income is less than £300 per year, is likely to find the theory useful as a developmental guide over time. At first the firm will satisfy basic physical and safety needs; then, as individual workers learn and become more competent, an increasing array of opportunities for fulfilling higher-order needs can be built into job tasks and organisational practices.

Existence, relatedness and growth needs

Alderfer (1969) developed a needs-specific model of motivation that relaxes some of Maslow's original assumptions and combines levels of needs. Alderfer calls his model the ERG theory, based on the initials of three categories of motivating needs: existence, relatedness and growth. *Existence* needs refer to basic survival needs (similar to Maslow's physiological and safety needs) that everyone must satisfy to maintain life. *Relatedness* needs draw people into interpersonal contact for social-emotional acceptance, caring and status. *Growth* needs involve personal development and a sense of self-worth.

ERG theory
Alderfer's simplified content theory that identifies existence, relatedness and growth as need categories, and acknowledges that multiple needs may be operating at one time without being hierarchically determined.

Alderfer rejects Maslow's premise that lower-level needs must be satisfied before higher-level needs are activated. He believes a person can seek growth experiences when relatedness and maybe even existence needs have not been adequately met. Artists are often so consumed with their work that creature comforts are unimportant to them; the Dutch post-impressionist painter Vincent Van Gogh being a good example. Alderfer does suggest, however, that the longer lower-level needs (existence, and to some degree relatedness) go unfulfilled, the more they will be desired. But when growth needs are thwarted, a person will regress towards seeking relatedness or existence needs, which are generally more attainable.

Alderfer also believes that humankind is complex, and more than one need may be operating at a time. During the course of a business day, for example, one person eats lunch (existence needs) with two colleagues in part for social interaction (relatedness needs) and in part to obtain support in solving a problem (growth needs). Research by Wanous and Zwany (1977) and Schneider and Alderfer (1973) appears to provide better support for ERG theory than for Maslow's original five-level needs hierarchy. Unlike Maslow's clinical study of neurosis, Alderfer focused on understanding adult behaviour in task-orientated organisations.

The needs-based theories discussed so far illustrate the complexity of human behaviour. Needs vary within an individual over time, they vary across people within an organisation or culture, and they vary across national cultures. Approach–avoidance struggles can create cross-cultural ethical dilemmas, as illustrated by the problem South Korea has with the practice of businesses paying bribes to politicians (see World Watch box). Nevertheless, some persons are consistently driven by higher-order needs. This is because people are capable of learning to be guided by specific motives.

What will motivate Koreans to do business without bribes and corruption?

The motives that underlie commonly accepted business practices differ around the world because of local values and learned traditions. In South Korea firms who do not pay bribes do not do business. For more than a decade, a US electronics firm did business in South Korea through a local distributor who made up to £3 million per year. Thinking it could improve margins, the electronics firm dropped its Korean distributor to handle distribution itself. A bad decision. In the following five years the US firm lost £12 million trying to do business in South Korea. According to the former Korean distributor, the answer is simple: 'The Americans refuse to pay bribes to customers to win contracts.'

The CEO of a medium-sized Korean business says: 'Any businessman in Korea who has survived the last 30 years is to some degree corrupt, including myself. The whole country was this way. The president was corrupt, the ministers were corrupt, the banks were corrupt. How else could you survive?'

South Korea is no longer an underdeveloped country. Today it is the world's 12th largest economy. But for three decades its spectacular growth came through a highly centralised alliance between government and big, diversified businesses (called *chaebols*). Four firms – Hyundai, Samsung, Daewoo and LG – account for a third of South Korea's total sales. Korea's political leaders demanded 'donations' from companies to gain access to capital and licences, and businesses in turn expected payments to secure contracts. The locals are motivated to learn quickly the rules of business survival.

But in late 1991, Hyundai's founder, Chung Ju Yung, announced that rather than pay off politicians he would form his own political party. Chung's efforts to challenge the tradition of bribery resulted in the then president, Roh Tae Woo, pulling strings to starve Hyundai's access to capital. Bank loans were cancelled, attempts to sell more shares were blocked by securities officials, and tax inspectors stormed the company. The isolation strategy continued until Kim Young Sam was elected president in December 1992. Kim worked to control widespread corruption and bribery by changing tax laws and making laws to force more disclosure by politicians.

Another Kim in office during the turn of the century, president Kim Dae Jung, pushed for further economic stability and reform. His intended plans included privatisation of 10 state-run companies and corruption reforms to have the *chaebols* (beyond Hyundai) stop the practice of paying bribes to political parties and politicians. Kim also sought to break up the *chaebols* so that their business units would function independently. But Kim is finding progress slow and faces opposition referenda on his reforms.

Sources: Moon Ihlwan (2000) 'South Korea: Can Reform Survive the Next Election?' *Business Week*, 13 March, p. 60; Kevin Sullivan (1995) 'Bribes Part of Business in S. Korea', *Washington Post*, 26 November; Laxmi Nakarmi (1995) 'Seoul Yanks the *Chaebol's* Leash', *Business Week*, 30 October, p. 58; and Jeffrey A. Fadiman (1995) 'Bribery and American Business Ethics: A Resolvable Dilemma', *Northern California Executive Review* 9, Fall/Winter, pp. 15–22.

Discussion questions

1 If South Korea really wants to do business on a global scale, what will motivate politicians and businesses alike to do business without bribery?

2 How important is culture in the application of the principles of motivation?

The effect of needs on work-related motivation

Two lines of motivational research focus specifically on work-related needs. One, by Frederick Herzberg, postulates that for workers to be motivated, the content of the job itself must be motivating – simply improving working conditions will not necessarily energise employees' behaviour. The other, by Douglas McGregor, distinguished a 'Theory X' from a 'Theory Y' approach to managing employees, based on assumptions about employees' willingness to take responsibility for work.

Research focus: Herzberg's dual-factor theory

A needs-based model intended to provide direct managerial applications evolved from Frederick Herzberg's research into the sources of job-related satisfaction and dissatisfaction. Herzberg (1966) carried out 203 interviews with accountants and engineers using the critical incident method. They were asked two questions: What made them feel good about their job and what made them feel bad. The interviewees were asked to relate the sequence of events leading up to the feelings. The responses revealed that there were two different factors affecting motivation and work. From the research Herzberg concluded that:

1 job satisfaction and job dissatisfaction derive from different sources

2 simply removing the sources of dissatisfaction will not cause a person to be motivated to produce better results.

Herzberg blended these two premises into a dual-factor explanation of motivation. Dual-factor theory refers to two different types of needs:

dual-factor theory
Herzberg's motivation content theory based on two independent needs: hygiene and motivator factors.

1 hygiene factors, which involve working conditions and can trigger dissatisfaction if inadequate

2 motivator factors, which originate from the nature of the job itself and can create job satisfaction.

Dissatisfiers as hygiene factors

hygiene factors
Job context factors such as working conditions and benefits that cause dissatisfaction if inadequate.

Herzberg drew the term hygiene factors from his public health experience. **Hygiene factors** are those basic factors surrounding the job – job security, working conditions, quality of supervision, interpersonal relationships, and adequacy of pay and fringe benefits – which, if lacking, can cause dissatisfaction. Such factors are largely *extrinsic*, or external to the nature of the job itself, and can therefore be thought of as job context features.

Hygiene factors do not produce job satisfaction. If adequate, they simply produce neutral feelings with the realisation that basic maintenance needs are taken care of. Like a city's water and sanitation systems, these factors do not cause people to be healthy and robust. They simply prevent disease and unhealthy conditions – they provide good hygiene.

Satisfiers as motivator factors

motivator factors
Job content factors such as responsibility and achievement that provide feelings of satisfaction when experienced.

According to Herzberg (1993), only when a person feels the potential for satisfaction is he or she able to muster significant work motivation. **Motivator factors** such as job challenge, responsibility, opportunity for achievement or advancement, and recognition, provide feelings of satisfaction. These are associated with job content and are *intrinsic*, or unique to each individual in his or her own way.

Herzberg's dual-factor theory suggests that if motivators are not present in a job a person will not necessarily be dissatisfied. However, that person will simply not be in a position to experience satisfaction, since nothing about the work itself is a motivational turn-on. When motivator factors are inherent in the job, satisfaction is perceived as possible and work-directed energy is aroused or sustained. Only then can a person be consistently motivated, according to Herzberg. Exhibit 5-2

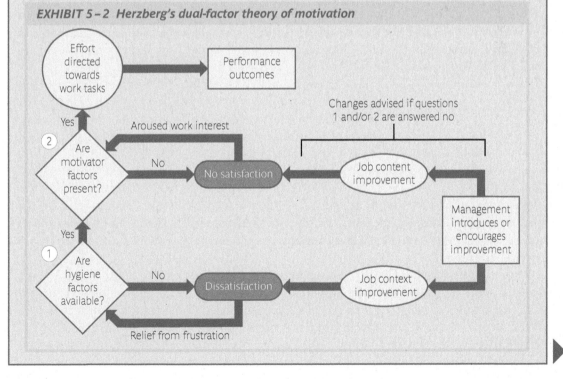

EXHIBIT 5 – 2 Herzberg's dual-factor theory of motivation

▶ presents the four alternative combinations of hygiene and motivator factors derived from the theory.

To improve motivation to work, managers are first advised to provide an adequate job context of working conditions and benefits for their people. This will satisfy lower-level hygiene needs, which, if not met, cause dissatisfaction. But to arouse work interest and promote self-directed task motivation, managers also need to ensure that the content of the job itself is reasonably satisfying – that jobs contain responsibility, challenge, and the opportunity to learn and advance.

Evaluation of Herzberg's theory

According to House and Wigdor (1967):

- although the initial study has been replicated by Herzberg (1993) and others using the same methodology and supporting evidence was found, studies using different methodology fail to support the theory

- the theory is 'method bound' – in other words, it supports the results only when one method is used

- it oversimplifies the complex sources of satisfaction and dissatisfaction and the relationship between satisfaction and motivation; satisfiers and dissatisfiers are not the same for everyone.

Nevertheless, Herzberg's theory is an excellent illustration of how theory need not be perfect to provide a valuable contribution. The concern should be that it is helpful rather than right or wrong.

Applications and limitations of the dual-factor theory

According to this theory the most effective way to stimulate motivation is to improve the nature of work itself. At the time the theory was developed, most jobs were relatively structured and routine (and many still are). Therefore, Herzberg (1987) argued, the most appropriate technique for building in motivation factors was to enrich jobs.

job enrichment
A means to encourage motivation by building greater responsibility and variety into a job.

Job enrichment involves giving a job greater scope (variety) and depth (responsibility for planning and control of the work). Job enrichment means expanding the critical functions and challenges of individual jobs. These design features are emphasised in the next chapter.

Research into the appropriateness of dual-factor theory has been criticised for its original reliance on engineers and accountants as subjects, since these two types of professional are not as subject to lower-level needs as are people working in low-skilled jobs. The theory has been difficult to replicate without asking for self-reports of past events, in which respondents tend to take credit for positive events (internal attribution) and blame externalities for negative ones (external attribution).

Some variables, such as quality of supervision or pay, seem to be more unstable than Herzberg specified. Other research by Lawler (1981), House and Wigdor (1967) and Fein (1973) has uncovered a link between pay and increasing levels of motivation. Researchers such as Whitsett and Winslow (1967) have found that a specific variable can be a source of either satisfaction or dissatisfaction, depending on the person. Furthermore, the theory does not include the impact of external factors (such as health and family tensions) on work behaviour.

Creativity has also been linked with intrinsic motivation where the work itself is challenging. One academic, Amabile (1998), has articulated the 'Intrinsic Motivation Principle of Creativity: people will be most creative when they feel motivated primarily by the interest, satisfaction, and challenge of the work itself – and not by external pressures.' Amabile (1998) finds that managers can influence three components of creativity: expertise, creative thinking skills and motivation. She adds, 'But the fact is that the first two are more difficult and time consuming to influence than motivation.' Managers can activate up to five motivating levers to spur creativity: the amount of challenge given to employees; the degree of freedom granted about processes; the way work groups are designed; the level of encouragement provided; and the nature of organisational support.

McGregor's Theory X and Theory Y

Maslow's ideas about motivation influenced the thinking of Douglas McGregor, who constructed a philosophy based on differing managerial practices. McGregor (1960) presented a sharp contrast between two different sets of managerial assumptions about people (Theory X and Theory Y), reasoning that a manager's ideas about people influence how he or she attempts to manage (see Exhibit 5-3).

Theory X

A managerial assumption that people act only to realise their basic needs and therefore do not voluntarily contribute to organisational aims.

Theory Y

A managerial assumption that people are motivated by higher-order growth needs and will therefore act responsibly to accomplish organisational objectives.

A Theory X set of assumptions about human behaviour postulates that people act to realise basic needs, and therefore do not voluntarily contribute to organisational aims. When these are the expected employee characteristics, managers believe that their task is to direct and modify human behaviour to fit the needs of the organisation. Managers must persuade, reward, punish and control those who do not naturally strive to learn and grow.

By contrast, a Theory Y view of human behaviour sees people as motivated by higher-order growth needs. According to Theory Y, management's task is to enable people to act on these needs and to grow in their jobs. Management's essential task is to

---

EXHIBIT 5–3 The contrast between Theory X and Theory Y

Managers who subscribe to *Theory X* basically believe that:

1 people dislike responsibility and lack ambition; therefore, they prefer to be led, and management must direct their efforts

2 the average person is passive, indolent and works as little as possible; thus, people need to be coerced and controlled

3 people are self-centred and indifferent to organised needs; therefore, they are by nature resistant to change.

Theory Y assumes that:

1 people seek responsibility and have the capacity to direct and control organisational tasks if they are committed to the objectives

2 people by nature are not passive or indifferent to organisational needs, for work is as natural as rest or play

3 employees at all levels have the ability to be creative and use ingenuity in solving organisational problems.

Source: Douglas McGregor, *Leadership and Motivation*. ©1966 The MIT Press.
Used with permission of The MIT Press.

structure the work environment so that people can best achieve their higher-order personal goals by accomplishing organisational objectives.

McGregor's concept was meant to be provocative and was not the product of empirical research. It has therefore not been empirically validated, but rather has served to make managers reflect on how their own assumptions about people affect their behaviour towards employees. McGregor intended Theory X and Theory Y to represent extreme ends of a continuum of beliefs.

McGregor stopped short of advocating that all managers become Theory Y managers. His intention was to make managers aware of how stereotyped views of human nature can lead to self-fulfilling prophecies. McGregor saw Theory Y as a way to align the goals of employees with those of the organisation. If people could satisfy their personal goals by accomplishing organisational objectives, their greater productive energy would benefit everyone. The manager who delegates authority and provides people with the resources to do a job often finds that they behave responsibly. According to McGregor, management based primarily on satisfying lower-level needs (Theory X) fails over time to obtain desired results other than maintenance of the status quo.

Limitations of classic need theories

Today's generation of senior managers has had ample exposure to these pioneering attempts to understand motivational forces, and some have tried to relate them directly to their organisations. Exhibit 5-4 shows the pattern of similarities among the theories of Maslow, Alderfer, Herzberg and McGregor. A knowledge of an employee's level of needs provides clues about the likely direction that person's behaviour will take. If Katrina is experiencing difficulties with her manager or with a co-worker, she will probably act to minimise contact with the person. If John perceives that his growth aspirations can be met by challenging work assignments, he is likely to direct his energy towards job tasks that enable him to learn and to contribute to group goals.

There are many parallels among the popular theories of Maslow (original hierarchical theory and revised dual-level theory), Alderfer, Herzberg and McGregor. The needs at the top of the model shown in Exhibit 5-4 all lead towards approach behaviours, while those at the

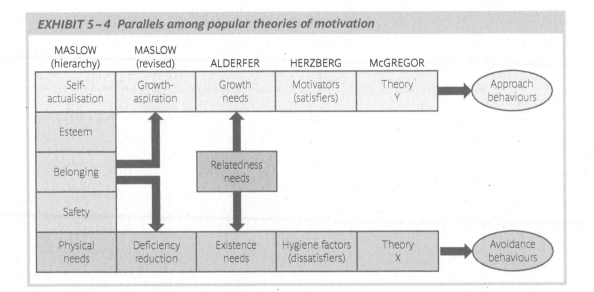

EXHIBIT 5–4 Parallels among popular theories of motivation

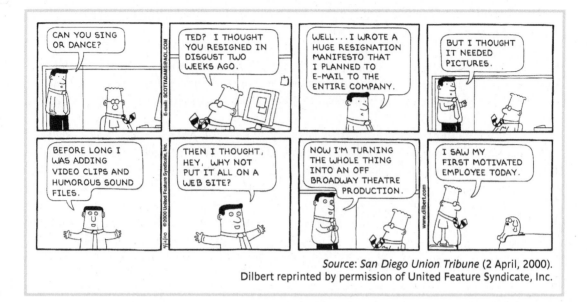

Source: *San Diego Union Tribune* (2 April, 2000).
Dilbert reprinted by permission of United Feature Syndicate, Inc.

bottom propel people towards avoidance behaviours if not adequately obtained. Those in the middle (Maslow's belonging and Alderfer's relatedness) are potentially unstable and can direct behaviour, in either direction, depending on the circumstances.

It is more difficult, however, to predict how a person will act when motivated by a lower-level or hygiene need. If Rosa, George and Kim perceive their pay as inadequate, how will each behave in response? Rosa might assume the situation will not improve and avoid doing any more work than is absolutely necessary to hold her job (to restore a sense of equity – a concept we will explore shortly). George may become active in union affairs to press for better pay. Kim may work harder to gain the boss's favour, expecting that her efforts will be recognised. So while need theories may provide clues to unsatisfied desires, they do not always tell us how an individual is likely to behave to satisfy them. Moreover, for organisations, the way behaviour is directed (combined with its intensity) is the key to performance.

How learned motives influence work behaviour

The discussion so far assumes that a person's current circumstances determine which level of need will be acted on. However, a different category of needs is learned, or socially acquired, and more stable over time. Depending on your personal experience, you may have one or two strong socially learned needs. Learned through repeated experiences, these needs motivate your behaviour whenever you perceive an opportunity to satisfy them.

Motives are learned from experience

Some people learn to be consistently energised when they encounter circumstances that offer the opportunity of experiencing feelings of satisfaction. Examples of learned motives include the need for achievement, power, affiliation, competence, status and autonomy. This learning can be either conscious or unconscious. These learned motives have profound relevance for organisational behaviour because they activate employee behaviour selection, direction and level of effort.

Individuals differ in the importance they assign to specific motives (Stahl, 1986; McClelland and Burnham, 1995). Some people have a clearly dominant motive, such as Trevor's need for *achievement*, Cynthia's for *power*, or Kim's for *affiliation*. Regardless of the situation, these individuals are likely to behave consistently with the motive that is dominant in their lives. Alternatively, Coreen might have several motives that are activated by different situations. At work her dominant motive might be power or achievement; at home, affiliation; and in social events, status.

Managers can motivate others if they are sensitive to the learned motives of individual employees. For this reason we will examine the motives that have been researched most extensively: achievement, power and affiliation.

The achievement motive

**need to achieve
(or achievement motive)**
A learned motive that satisfaction can be found in seeking tasks that will provide a sense of accomplishment.

People who have a high **need to achieve** are usually self-motivated; they seek tasks that will provide them with a sense of accomplishment. They will choose an opportunity to confront a challenging but doable task rather than attend the company's Friday-afternoon pizza social (unless they plan to seek ideas from others that promote task accomplishment). Many people of Anglo descent like to think of themselves as being achievement-orientated, undoubtedly because achievement is highly valued in most western societies.

Research focus: achievement motivation theory

McClelland (1961, 1965) and Atkinson (1964) conducted the pioneering research on work-related motives, particularly the achievement motive. They assumed the achievement motive could be measured by what people say, do or write. Several behavioural characteristics distinguish the achievement-motivated person.

1 Achievers prefer a moderate level of difficulty or challenge. Just as they avoid tasks that are too easy, they also shy away from those that are extremely difficult. Being realistic, they know their limitations. The most desired task is one that requires a high level of exertion but carries a reasonable probability of success.

2 High achievers also like to feel that they are in reasonable control of an outcome. If the element of chance or luck is a primary factor in success, or if others over whom they have little influence are involved, there is reduced incentive to try.

3 Achievement-motivated people also like to receive frequent and specific feedback about how well they are doing. This does not mean they need constant praise from their supervisors. Ideally, the task itself should provide enough feedback so they can evaluate themselves; self-approval is good feedback for an achiever.

A high need for achievement has long been associated with entrepreneurial success. It has not been especially predictive of managerial success, except in smaller or more decentralised organisations. McClelland (1995) found in a study of PepsiCo, which consists of thousands of reasonably independent decentralised business units, that managers with a high need for achievement are more successful than those with a high power motive concerned more with influencing others.

The power motive

need for power (or power motive)
A learned motive that finds satisfaction from being in charge and controlling and influencing others.

Power is the ability to influence others to behave as we want. People who have a high **need for power**, or power motive, find satisfaction from being in charge and influencing others. While it is important to have some high achievers in management, an organisation will not function effectively without its share of take-charge types for whom power is the dominant motive. These people are willing to specify organisational goals and influence others to achieve them. It is difficult to be a successful manager without a need for power, especially in large organisations.

McClelland (1975) differentiates managers with strong power needs into two kinds: either personal power managers or institutional power managers. Managers with high *personal power needs* exemplify the stereotypical self-serving, exploitative, dominating boss. Such a need for power reflects the aim of personal gain through manipulation and control of others without exhibiting self-control and inhibition. A personal-power boss may coerce and even threaten subordinates in a forceful attempt to get them to carry out commands (and may take credit for their successes). Contrary to what is presented in soap operas, these managers usually don't make it to the top of an organisation because people they have stepped on earlier find ways to sabotage their careers (Kelly, 1987).

Managers with high *institutional power needs* temper their influence over others with inhibition and self-control. They are altruistic and believe power should be used more for the good of the organisation than for personal advantage. Satisfaction is obtained more from the process of influencing others to carry out their work in pursuit of organisational goals than from their own personal success. Research indicates that higher-level managers in large organisations are more likely to be successful if they possess a high need for power that is institutionalised (with high inhibition and self-control) combined with low affiliation needs.

The affiliation motive

need for affiliation (or affiliation motive)
A learned motive to seek satisfaction from the quality of social and interpersonal relationships.

Persons with a high **need for affiliation** find satisfaction in the quality of their social and interpersonal relationships. Affiliators avoid isolation (whereas achievers may welcome it), since interaction with others is so important for them. Such people easily develop wide circles of friends, both in and out of the workplace. They are prone to show concern for the feelings of others and to be sympathetic to opposing views. Given the opportunity, they often try to help others work through problems.

People who are high affiliators often make weak bosses. McClelland (1975) found that only 20 per cent of the 'above-average' sales departments in a research sample were supervised by managers whose affiliation needs were more dominant than their power needs. Of the 'below-average' departments in their sample, 90 per cent were run by affiliation-motivated managers. By contrast, power-motivated managers ran 80 per cent of the best and only 10 per cent of the worst departments. The researchers concluded that because of their need to be liked, affiliation-motivated managers made 'wishy-washy decisions'. They bent company rules to make particular individuals happy, and in the process they were seen as unfair.

One of the interesting findings of this research is that the achievement drive can be taught. Teaching programmes that concentrated on the thinking and language patterns of high achievers, emotional support, prestige and the practicality of effecting change could increase the achievement motive (McClelland and Winter, 1969).

Attributions and learning affect motive development

personal attribution
The process of rationalising causality (either to external or internal (personal) factors) as to why personally involving events turn out as they do.

A person engages in **personal attribution** when rationalising causality as to why events turn out as they do. To develop strong motives a person learns to see him or herself as personally responsible for positive outcomes. Achievers, in particular, establish a pattern of *internal attribution* of success (Weiner, 1974). Through repeated opportunities to succeed or fail, high achievers learn to attribute success to their own efforts or abilities. They take on responsibilities because accomplishment of a task provides self-satisfaction and pride. Achievement-motivated employees often strive for higher goals and standards of performance than those assigned by supervisors.

When high achievers fail, however, they are reluctant to place all the blame on themselves. Achievers often attribute some of the blame for failure to one or more external circumstances – bad luck, unforeseen events, impossible tasks, or interference by powerful others (Cook, 1983). This helps them retain self-confidence. When they accept responsibility for an unsuccessful outcome they engage in problem-solving to learn from the experience.

Individuals with low achievement needs perceive success or failure in a different light. To them life is capricious. They tend to attribute their successful outcomes to external factors (good luck, easy tasks, powerful others) and thus feel little or no personal pride in accomplishment. Conversely, they often accept blame for failures. Given their inability to enjoy success, people with low achievement needs seek out situations where individual achievement is not a factor.

Being successful at work is more complex than simply being motivated to achieve (McClelland and Winter, 1969). In fact, some highly achievement-motivated people are so concerned with their own achievement that they are not very adept at helping others achieve. While they may make good entrepreneurs in start-up companies, high achievers do not necessarily make good managers in large bureaucratic organisations. On balance, the competent manager displays motivational behaviours that include 'self-control, self-confidence, an ability to get a consensus from people, and strong motivations for achievement, power, or both' (McClelland, 1995).

Motives help predict behaviour

Differences in the strength of specific motives help explain why some people are more predictable than others. People tend to develop motivation patterns that represent the needs they consistently seek to satisfy. However, motivation patterns are sometimes difficult to infer simply by observing behaviour. For example, Mark might have a dominant need for power. He finds that one way to get power is to achieve, so that he will be sought after as an expert. People observing him might assume he has a high achievement motive. Nevertheless, in his case achievement is merely a means of satisfying a power need. By contrast, Jennifer has a high need for achievement. In achieving success she attains considerable power and influence. People might incorrectly assume that she has a high power need because she is promoted to positions of leadership in which she can influence group performance. These contrasting examples suggest that people use different behavioural strategies to satisfy motive needs.

Be cautious in making attributions about another's motives. However, correctly recognising another's motive patterns helps a manager select assignments that energise that person. For example, the achiever is excited by his assignment to a challenging project. The power-motivated person enjoys representing her group in a negotiating session. Both feed a dominant motive.

Personal ideology promotes motivational consistency

Because motives are learned they promote consistency in motivated behaviour. A related learned source of motivational consistency is one's self-ideology. A person's values, moral obligations and sense of self provide a mental image of his or her personal ideology. **Personal ideology** is an individualised conception of one's place in the world, a conception that includes human obligations in relation to meaningful activities that promote a sense of self-worth.

personal ideology
A source of personal consistency based on one's values and conception of one's place in the world in relation to meaningful activities that promote a sense of self-worth.

One's concept of personal ideology influences motivation. Unlike needs or motives that vary in strength according to situational forces at the time, ideology is a stabilising force behind behaviour. According to Shamir (1991) this is because it draws on a 'concept of values as "conceptions of the desirable" as distinct from the desired'. A person with a strong personal ideology desires to enhance self-concept, self-esteem and sense of self-consistency. To be true to one's self-image, a person does not always work for direct personal gain; sometimes the emphasis at work is to behave in ways consistent with that image.

Ideological factors that support work motivation

Ideological concerns that promote self-consistency may include being respected by colleagues, meeting a manager's expectations, contributing to the production of something of value, sustaining respect by family, feeling pride in being helpful, and carrying one's own weight at work. One study in Britain, by Carlisle and Manning (1994), found that even when jobs were threatened by new technology, motivation to do good work did not wane. This outcome was attributed to ideological values that linked self-respect with work performance. Even in a factory where employees lacked loyalty to the firm because termination was imminent, they were no less work motivated than employees who were not threatened with job loss.

Ideological beliefs related to work and personal economic values have even been shown to relate to differences in growth rates and income levels across countries – two implicit indices of national motivation. In a study of about 12 000 people in 41 countries, investigators found that individual competitiveness, the desire for money, and a willingness to save are predictors of the growth rate of a region. However, according to Furnham *et al.* (1994), these same three ideological components are negatively associated with per capita income. Competitiveness – the drive to be better than others at what one does – is especially important as a stimulant of growth in less developed nations such as Bangladesh, China and India. It may be, however, that after a country has become affluent, 'co-operativeness' becomes more valued than competitiveness. Such national cultural values feed into the evolution of personal ideologies.

Emotional intelligence feeds passion for work

Goleman (1998) arrives at interesting conclusions about the concept of 'emotional intelligence' in leaders, a concept that feeds into one's ideology. Goleman found that when predicting outstanding leaders, emotional intelligence was twice as important as either technical skills or IQ (intelligence) as a driver of outstanding performance.

The five key components of emotional intelligence are self-awareness, self-regulation, motivation, empathy and social skill. (These are extensively discussed and include a 'Your turn' exercise in Chapter 9.) Of the five components, Goleman (1998) singles out motivation as all-critical:

> If there is one trait that virtually all effective leaders have, it is motivation. They are driven to achieve beyond expectations – their own and everyone else's. The key word here is achieve. . . . The first sign is a passion for the work itself – such people seek out creative challenges, love to learn, and take great pride in a job well done.

The effect of expectations on work motivation

In contrast to identifying the content of need-based theories of motivation, another approach, by Steers *et al.* (1996), focuses on the mental processes used to evaluate cause-and-effect relationships. **Process theories of motivation** explain how and why workers select behaviours and how they determine whether their choices were successful. Since people are creatures of perception, thought and a certain degree of rationality, they are capable of making informed choices about where and how to channel energy. In making choices, the human tendency is to embrace the most advantageous option or at least avoid functioning at a disadvantage. This premise underlies the process theories based on expectancy and equity.

process theories of motivation
Theories that focus on the ways people think through motivation issues and how they determine whether their actions were successful.

dynamics of diversity

As the business grows an organisational framework will develop in which each role has its own set of competencies. Appropriate packages of pay and benefits can be set at each level.

It is important to ensure that nothing done at the outset will cause problems later. In the early stages of business, people are recruited on an ad hoc basis and you may have agreed certain deals for people who do not fit in well with the framework of a more mature business.

Typically, the structure would involve a broad-based salary band in which individuals are paid according to their qualities, skills and performance. The classic approach is the performance-based plan in which senior directors' bonuses and pay rises are linked either to personal targets or to the overall corporate performance, or both.

With staff below board level, performance can be graded into bands such as poor, average, good and outstanding, and bonuses triggered accordingly.

To be successful the appraisal policy should encourage people to think about the performance they need to deliver in terms of the way they behave, as well as meeting targets. It should also deal effectively with poor performance, identifying shortcomings and taking appropriate action.

Most individuals care as much about their career as how much they are being paid. Providing on-the-job coaching or other means of training and development ensures not only that employees have the skills and knowledge to deliver the business objectives, but the satisfaction of improving their own prospects as well.

Kellett concludes: 'What you are aiming to do is to develop a performance culture that helps people achieve their own aspirations and goals, as well as those of their team and the business.'

Source: Robert McLuhan (2002) 'Dynamic Growing Businesses', in association with Andersen Consulting, pp. 11–12, May.

Discussion questions

1 According to McClelland, what are the motives that drive entrepreneurs?

2 How does the above case take into account people's different motivations?

Expectancy theory raises three questions

Motivation based on expectancy theory focuses on a person's beliefs about the relationships among effort, performance and rewards for doing a job, as discussed in the 'Research focus'.

Research focus: expectancy theory

Vroom (1994), while attacking Herzberg's two-factor theory as being too dependent on the content and context of the work roles of the interviewees, offered an expectancy approach to the study of motivation.

expectancy theory
A theory of motivation based on a person's beliefs about effort performance–outcome relationships.

This theory proposes that people will be motivated to achieve a desired goal as long as they expect that their actions will achieve the goal. Expectancy theory was originally expressed as a probability relationship among three variables labelled expectancy, instrumentality and valence – terms defined in Exhibit 5-5. While these psychological terms mean more to researchers than managers, the concepts and their interrelationship provide the foundation for another useful way of thinking about work motivations.

Research by Wanous *et al.* (1983) supports the validity of expectancy relationships in work settings but acknowledges that the jargon used by psychologists is difficult to apply (see Exhibit 5-5). Using this theory Vroom came up with the expectancy equation of:

$$\text{Force (F)} = \text{Valence (V)} \times \text{Expectancy (E)}$$

The basics of expectancy theory for organisational practitioners can be converted into a series of three questions that people often ask themselves about their work situation (Cook, 1980).

1 Does how hard I try really affect my performance? To be motivated you must have a positive answer to this *expectancy question*. You must believe that your personal efforts have the potential to make a positive performance difference. You must also have the capacity for internal attribution, or a willingness to take personal credit or blame for your performance. Positive task motivation begins when you see a link between personal effort and task performance.

2 Are personal consequences linked to my performance? In some jobs or roles there is little association between effort and rewards or punishments. To answer this *instrumentality question* you must believe that task performance results (a first-order outcome) serve to obtain second-order personal consequences or pay-offs. Increased motivation is possible when you perceive a positive personal consequence arising from satisfactory task performance.

3 Do I value the consequences available to me? Answers to this *valence question* depend on how much you value a particular expected personal outcome or pay-off. If you really do not care about the potential pay-off, it provides little, if any, incentive value. Suppose you want recognition but your boss simply gives you another assignment and sends you off on another trip to out into the sticks. As a result you therefore discount the value of possible pay-offs, and your expectation of being rewarded in a meaningful way diminishes. A person must value the pay-off if the expectancy loop is to be positive and motivational.

Vroom's theory recognises the importance of individual needs and motivations and is therefore less simplistic than those of Maslow or Herzberg. Expectancy theory recognises that individuals have personal goals that may differ from the organisation's. However, these can be harmonised. The theory is also consistent with management by objectives, which we met in earlier chapters. The difficulty with the approach is with its application. How can it be researched and applied in practice when motivation is so complex?

EXHIBIT 5–5 Three variables frame expectancy theory

The original expectancy theory consists of the interrelationships among three variables.

1 *Expectancy*. The probability (from 0 to 1) that an individual believes his or her work effort directly affects the performance outcome of a task.

2 *Instrumentality*. The probability (from 0 to 1) that an individual anticipates that an attained level of task performance will have personal consequences.

3 *Valence*. The value (from positive to negative) that a person assigns to the personal consequences that follow work performance.

For example, Todd expects he will have a significant influence over the audits he performs as an accountant. He believes that performing high-quality audits will result in substantial pay increases and his promotion to manager. His number one goal is to make manager within five years and to be paid more than his peers.

Source: H.J. Arnold (1981) 'A Test of the Multiplicative Hypothesis of Expectancy-Valence Theories of Work Motivation', *Academy of Management Journal* 24, March, pp. 128–141. Republished with permission of *Academy of Management Journal*.

Think of your own experiences for a moment. Do you often mull over in your mind questions similar to those listed in the 'Research focus'? If so, you find yourself in agreement with academics such as Porter and Lawler (1968) and Lawler (1994). They find that motivation is enhanced when a person answers yes to all three expectancy-related questions: (1) when effort is believed to be performance related; (2) when performance is linked to personal consequences; and (3) when the consequences or pay-offs available are highly valued. Conversely, when one or more answers is negative, motivation potential diminishes.

It is important for managers to realise that not all people value the available outcomes or rewards in the same way. Managers who want to motivate by expectancies must weigh whether employees place a greater value on extrinsic or intrinsic rewards. However, for some people there is a dynamic interplay between extrinsic and intrinsic rewards, especially as highly energetic and talented individuals rush into Internet start-ups that provide creative challenges and the lure of monetary incentives. AT&T has experienced a brain-drain of key executives who have abandoned the bureaucracy for life in the fast but uncertain lane. After nearly 20 years, Daniel Schulman left as head of AT&T's Consumer Services Division to pursue the adrenaline rush of being CEO of the start-up Priceline.com (which gave him an extrinsic £60 million multi-year compensation package) (Rosenbush, 2000).

Motivational implications of intrinsic and extrinsic rewards

There are two basic sources of rewards or pay-offs. Many people depend on and highly value **extrinsic rewards** – rewards that are externally bestowed, such as praise from a supervisor, a promotion or pay rise, or the grade received for coursework. Others place a high value on **intrinsic rewards** – their own personal feelings about how well they performed the task or simply the satisfaction they derived from doing it. Managers need to realise the distinction between the two and how their employees view them. For example, in work conditions where employees seek extrinsic rewards but believe their degree of effort is not clearly visible to supervisors, 'social loafing' or reduced effort is likely to occur. However, where there is a high intrinsic involvement in the task, social loafing will be low even when effort is not visible to the manager (George, 1992).

extrinsic rewards
Rewards externally bestowed, as by a supervisor, teacher or organisation.

intrinsic rewards
Postulate that motivation is moderated by perceived fairness or discrepancies between contributions and rewards.

According to Steers and Porter (1987) although most people look for some mix of intrinsic and extrinsic rewards, people clearly differ as to which is the more compelling motivational force. If a manager always praises an achievement-motivated professional who excels largely for the feelings of intrinsic satisfaction, this person will probably begin to look on his manager as shallow or fake. He may think to himself, 'I know I did a superb job on this project. Why does she keep stating the obvious? I wish she'd stop being so condescending.'

Even within the extrinsic rewards arena, people look for different types of reward. Praise may be perfectly acceptable to the person motivated by relatedness needs or affiliation, but may do nothing for the person expecting a more tangible pay-off – something that can be banked. Typical extrinsic rewards are favourable assignments, trips to desirable destinations, tuition reimbursement for courses in which a good grade is earned, pay rises, bonuses and promotions.

Research initiated by Deci (1971) offers evidence that when too many extrinsic rewards are provided, work effort may decline. He found that the introduction of extrinsic rewards for work previously performed for intrinsic pleasure tends to reduce motivation. Over-abundant

technology transformation

Net's queen bee still buzzes

'Dotcom queen bee' was just one of Julie Meyer's soubriquets as she buzzed around Europe with her First Tuesday technology forums. Her popular networking organisations became symbols of the late-1990s Internet frenzy.

Two years on the buzzing has not stopped. The queen bee has a swarm of workers out pollinating the brightest flowers of the European technology industry.

Meyer co-founded First Tuesday, which matched entrepreneurs with investors, in 1998. She turned the group into an international media phenomenon almost singlehanded, but the success turned sour in 2000 and she left following acrimony among the founders over a £33 million sale to the Israeli company Yazam.

Out of the experience of First Tuesday, Meyer has created Ariadne Capital – part venture capital, part adviser, part sales team and part headhunters.

The company helped TenUK buy its two main rivals – Liberate and Entrust – in the concierge market, taking TenUK's market share to almost 80 per cent. Ariadne also brokered a deal between Casino's By The Dealer betting game with Lycos Europe. It also helped New.net, a domain name registry offering its services to customers of telecoms firm Tiscali.

By connecting complementary businesses across Europe, she is helping build 'Europe.net'. In techie terms Ariadne is acting as a 'network router'.

But the lessons of the dotcom frenzy have also led to a more sober business. 'We're focused less on exit and more on executions,' she says.

In addition, there is none of the 'funky business' approach. 'We're not a high fixed cost business,' she explains and neither are there any 'spacehoppers' in their offices in a converted City of London townhouse.

In a sense her business model is formalising and updating a more familiar form of gentlemanly capitalism. The stereotype of Home Counties gentlemen farmers that pile en masse into the latest tech 'play' is not sustainable Europe-wide.

Meyer's hectic schedule makes it difficult to escape Ariadne.

'I like and respect the people I work with so much that they are difficult to separate. It does begin to take over your life.'

Moreover, being a woman in the male-dominated world of technology has only contributed to her success. 'It's a strategic asset to be a woman. You're more likely to get noticed as a 5 ft 10 in blonde American woman that as a native UK man.'

Meyer is one of 100 global leaders for tomorrow identified by the World Economic Forum. However, she is happy with her current business role.

'It's far more enjoyable to get in at the beginning, at the ground floor, rather than being a cog in the wheel of the machine. We want a big impact, more that just investing in the companies. I want Ariadne to have a macro impact in shaping Europe.net.'

She says 12 people working out of a converted townhouse in the heart of the City are not going to change the world alone. 'But using the extended network of angel investors and contacts, we can.'

Buzzing is no longer enough for this queen bee. She wants the honey and it is that which keeps her motivated.

Source: © Guardian Newspapers Ltd, 2002, Faisal Islam.

Discussion questions

1 What do you think are Julie Meyer's drives?
2 Do you think Julie Meyer would be effective in motivating her workforce?

extrinsic rewards are likely to lessen the need to seek intrinsic satisfaction. People may perceive extrinsic rewards as diminishing their control of the work situation. However, if rewards serve primarily as feedback, this negative effect is minimal.

Managing motivational expectancies

A manager does not need to be a psychologist to benefit from applying expectancy theory. First, the theory is most applicable to those jobs in which an individual has discretion as to how and when work is performed. For example, it would have somewhat greater applicability for airline reservation agents (who can either be thorough and helpful or abrupt and indifferent) than for operators on a machine-paced assembly line. However, it probably has even greater relevance for professionals such as accountants, market researchers, stockbrokers, design engineers and systems analysts.

To get the best from their people, managers should emphasise anticipated reward value, whether extrinsic or intrinsic (Bradt, 1991). The manager's job is to strengthen effort–performance–reward expectancies. For employees who have difficulty attributing outcomes to their performance, managers must make sure they realise performance–reward connections and then provide performance feedback.

Clarify performance–reward linkages

Not all employees know about or understand extrinsic organisational rewards. Survey data also suggest levels of satisfaction with extrinsic rewards are diminishing, although that may be changing with new economy start-ups and electronic business. The managerial challenge is to clarify rewards available to employees and relate them to personal and team performance (Quick, 1990). While many organisations provide little performance-based pay differentiation among people of the same salary grade, there are other extrinsic rewards a manager can bestow. For example, a manager can allocate more favourable job assignments to those who meet or surpass performance expectations. The key is to make obvious in advance the pay-off people can expect for certain levels of performance, and then follow up on satisfactory performance with feedback and appropriate rewards (Knippen and Green, 1990).

Provide performance feedback

Managers need to provide feedback both to demonstrate that they know what others are doing and to acknowledge improved performance or a job well done. Especially for employees who seem unsure of themselves or tend to externally attribute success, a manager should point out ways in which the employee is improving (Villere and Hartman, 1990). Praising specific accomplishments or improvements helps bolster employee esteem and promote internal attribution. It helps forge the link between focused effort, performance improvement, and the personal outcome of recognition from powerful others and personal feelings of pride.

How perceptions of equity affect motivation

Along the path to expectancy motivation things can go wrong. One of the most disruptive situations is when the pay-offs or personal outcomes are perceived to be inequitable or unfair. Managers need to be aware of equity perceptions and reduce gaps in rewards or conditions of employment where possible. From one perspective this is a matter of sustaining motivation; from another point of view it can be a matter of justice and ethics.

Perceptions of equity moderate motivation

Expectancy motivation works best if people perceive an underlying fairness among effort–performance–reward relationships. Research by Stacy Adams originally popularised this idea in what is called equity theory. **Equity theory** suggests that motivation is moderated by the perceived fairness or discrepancy between personal contributions and rewards, relative to what others receive. There are two basic dimensions to the equity process.

equity theory
The idea that motivation is moderated by perceived fairness or discrepancies between contributions and rewards.

Ratio of personal outcomes to inputs

People often think in terms of the ratio of their personal outcomes to work inputs. That is, their perceptions of equity depend on how they answer the question, 'What is the pay-off to me (in terms of status, benefits, recognition, money, promotion and job assignments) relative to my inputs of effort exerted, skills, job knowledge and actual task performance?'

External comparisons

People also compare their own outcomes/input ratio to those they perceive for other people doing comparable work. These comparisons may be made on three levels.

1 **Comparisons to specific other individuals.** For example, Ben might conclude, 'I think Karen really has been outperforming me.' Ben would expect Karen to be getting more in the way of rewards and recognition.

2 **Comparisons to another reference group.** Workers might think, 'Our department is getting much better treatment than the shipping department.' This comparison recognises that there are differences in pay-offs and 'our group' is getting a better deal. However, it does not indicate that better treatment is the result of better performance, and therefore deserved. We will return to this situation in a moment.

3 **Comparisons to general occupational classifications.** At times people compare themselves to people in similar positions in other organisations. A physical therapist at a private hospital might observe, 'According to national salary survey data, my pay is at only the 20th percentile – way below what someone with my experience should be earning.' Another common comparison is across gender within the same occupation, where women often experience discrepancies of earning 20 to 40 per cent less pay than men.

Adjusting for equity gaps

You might think that equity concerns would be activated only when a person believed he or she was being taken advantage of, or was under-compensated relative to others. This is not always the case. While this may be the more common experience, people sometimes conclude that they are over-compensated. This might have been the case in the second comparison listed above if the conclusion had been 'Our group is receiving better treatment but performing no better than the group in shipping.'

Mowday (1987) suggests that the equity concept affects motivation whenever a person perceives a meaningful difference in personal or group outcomes and then adjusts behaviour or perceptions to reduce the gap. In a research experiment by Brockner *et al.* (1986), those who survived a job lay-off and thought their co-workers' dismissals were random worked harder than when they believed those caught in the lay-off had produced less. Similarly, if Bernice believes she is inequitably over-compensated, she might intensify her efforts to produce more to be worthy of the superior benefits she receives. Alternatively, she may simply change her frame of reference to reduce the perceived equity gap by, for example, comparing her pay with national rather than company data. Conversely, when people perceive that they are under-compensated relative to the frame of reference (which is more common), they will probably reduce or redirect their efforts in an attempt to beat the system so they end up with a fair deal. These adverse consequences are more pronounced with extrinsic inequities (especially monetary rewards) than intrinsic inequities (Tyagi, 1990).

Slim pickings

William Wordsworth reckoned he once saw 10 000 daffodils at a glance. 'I gazed and gazed but little thought', the awe-struck bard recalled, 'What wealth to show me had brought'. Ask a Cornish flower grower what the sight of 10 000 blooming daffodils brings to mind and you can be pretty sure it will not be 'wealth'. Financial ruin more likely.

About a third of all daffodils grown in Cornwall never make it to market. Along with an unusually mild winter, which caught growers unawares, the tight local labour market and tougher immigration policies are largely to blame.

Finding people willing to stand around in a rainy Cornish field all day, plucking flowers from the ground for less than a penny per stem is never going to be easy. Seasonal flower picking in Britain has traditionally been the privilege of hard-up eastern European students. However, police crackdowns on illegal immigrants have made farmers wary of employing foreigners. Not wanting to fall foul of the law, they are turning away potential workers whom they might once have taken on.

Jim Hosking, a daffodil farmer, has found that as unemployment has dropped in Cornwall, the local labour pool has dried up. 'In particular, fewer women are doing that sort of work. Twenty years ago, more than 50 per cent of daffodil pickers would have been women,' he says. Picking daffodils is a taxing business for anyone. 'It's a lot of hard work, with your bum in the air all day', another old hand explains. As a waiter or bartender, a light pay packet can at least be supplemented by tips.

The problem has grown more acute as short-term labour has increased. So-called ornamental crops are a popular alternative to conventional food crops.

Booting out visa-less labourers and rumbling people-smugglers is good for the circulation of tabloid newspapers, but it ignores the important role such labour plays in the domestic economy. At present 15 200 youngsters are allowed into the country each year under the Seasonal Agricultural Worker's Scheme (SAWS). This will increase to 20 200 over the next two years, but Harvey Guntrip, who is investigating the short-term labour situation for the National Farmer's Union, thinks that is nowhere near enough to meet the demand. Anyway, SAWS operates only between May and November, which does not help all those outdoor daffodil growers whose season starts in January and ends in March.

Unless regulations are relaxed to allow short-term workers into Britain, full-time British jobs will be put at risk and the demand for illegal labour will continue to grow. High VAT, labour and utility costs, along with the strong pound (which makes imported flowers cheap), further handicap British farmers.

The government is mindful of all this. A government report on the future of food and farming, published in January, recommends raising the SAWS quota to 50 000, and a

White Paper on immigration and asylum gestures towards increased flexibility and plans to extend SAWS.

Overall, the horticultural industry is booming. The market in cut flowers is growing at a rate of 10 per cent a year. It is worth about £2 billion – roughly the same as the retail music industry. With a few tweaks to labour and farming policies, it could be worth a good deal more.

Source: © The Economist Newspapers Ltd, London, 13–19 April 2002.

Discussion questions

1 Why do you think people are no longer motivated to do traditional jobs?
2 What do the employers have to do to attract workers to their industry?

Fairness involves distributive and procedural justice

distributive justice
The perceived fairness of the amount and allocation of rewards among individuals.

procedural justice
The perceived fairness of the means used to determine the amount and distribution of rewards.

Research into the equity issue focuses on the fairness of both distributive and procedural justice. Distributive justice refers to the perceived fairness of the *amount* of compensation or rewards employees receive. Procedural justice describes the perceived fairness of the *process* used to determine the distribution of rewards among employees. Whereas equity theory has historically focused on the amount individuals receive relative to others (distributive justice), procedural justice shifts attention to the fairness of how managers arrive at those decisions. Although managers might not be as generous to all employees as they would like to be, they remain responsible for determining the process by which reward distributions are made.

Perception of what might have been

How do employees feel about reward distributions and the procedures used for making them? Research finds that distributive satisfaction influences primarily personal outcomes such as satisfaction and attitudes towards pay and promotion decisions. Procedural justice reflects more on organisational outcomes in terms of employee commitment and trust in supervisors (Folger and Konovsky, 1989).

referent cognitions theory
Postulates that people evaluate their work and rewards relative to 'what might have been' under different circumstances.

A related line of research, called referent cognitions theory, indicates that employees are capable of evaluating their work and reward experiences by reflecting on 'what might have been' under different circumstances and procedures (Folger, 1986). For example, would a different process have led to a more favourable personal outcome on a pay rise or expected promotion? Obviously, resentment peaks when the distribution of rewards is perceived as inequitable and the criteria used to arrive at that distribution are believed to be unfair. Furthermore, according to Fortado (1992), there is a cumulative effect when a person 'experiences mounting feelings of injustice at work'.

Equity begins with fair procedures

A study of union grievances by Fryxell and Gordon (1989) found that the administration of procedures was more important than the outcomes in influencing workers' satisfaction with their union. Satisfaction with management depended on the extent to which workers found the workplace to be just and moral. Another study, by McFarlin and Sweeney (1992), involving a sample of 675 bank employees, also found that procedural justice is the more important of the two.

Such research implies that if an organisation's procedures treat employees fairly, they will view the organisation as positive even if dissatisfied with personal outcomes such as pay. As long as the procedure is seen as fair, employees find it difficult to envision a more positive alternative for distributing rewards. They are therefore likely to remain committed to the organisation and to trust in the fairness of managers. This important bottom-line issue of equity suggests that groups and group perception are important in managing motivation.

Should motivation focus on individuals or groups?

Theories of motivation in western countries focus on the individual. Alternatively, not all cultures emphasise the individual. In many cultures, the group (family, tribe, village or team) is the centre of attention, and individual behaviour gets attention only if it deviates from group norms. Even in North America and Europe, organisations are beginning to spotlight the team, not just the individual. The emphasis on self-managed teams is an example of this (you can read more about this in the opening vignette in Chapter 10, about Pocklington Coachworks).

Globally, many cultures disregard individual motivation

There are major limitations to western ideas of motivation. As you will find out in the later chapter on culture, Hofstede's (1983) investigation of dominant cultural values in 50 countries found that the United States ranks highest in individualism. Westerners mostly base their identity more on personal and professional achievements than on family roles or their role within a social group. It is natural for managers in the United States, Great Britain and some parts of Canada to emphasise individual initiative in evaluating and seeking to motivate employees. Yet, according to Sitkin and Pablo (1992), groups are known to be critical to risk-taking propensity in these countries. Thus Hofstede (1980) suggests that the Scandinavians, for whom social needs and the quality of life take precedence over self-actualisation and achievement or power needs, are perhaps better prepared motivationally to provide the collaboration and co-operation necessary for teamwork.

In other parts of the world family connections are the usual way of gaining employment – something that is vilified in the British tradition. The British expect people to maximise individual gain or personal utility. The British view of motivation overlooks the power of the family and social fabric that dominates collectivist countries, or the impact of the government in assigning people to jobs, as is common in state-owned enterprises in the People's Republic of China (Boyacigiller and Adler, 1991). Theories of motivation would be richer if they encompassed cultural forces most westerners find mystifying.

Even in France the quality of life – vacations, socialising and enjoying free time – is generally more highly valued than achievement and work-related accomplishments. Notwithstanding cultural differences that may shift the focus of motivational forces, interesting work is something desired in many cultures. One study by Harpaz (1990) of seven countries found 'interesting work' to rank number one among eleven possible work goals in Belgium, Britain, Israel and the United States; and in Japan, the Netherlands and Germany it ranked either number two or three.

Innovation goals shift motivation towards teams

Most of the research about motivation was undertaken in an era of big business, mass markets and relatively standardised products. The pace of major changes in the design and technology of products was relatively moderate and predictable. During this era (through the third quarter of the twentieth century) management and motivation theory focused on the individual. Researchers asked, 'What affects an individual's choice of behaviours and intensity of work effort?' Managers wondered, 'How can I get Dick or Jane to vigorously pursue my goals?' Such concerns are useful, but they may be less in tune with today's organisational needs than yesterday's.

In the late twentieth century and early twenty-first, the critical motivational task has been to energise and empower individuals and teams to improve quality and bring about innovation (Randolph and Posner, 1992). Individual behaviours remain important, however producing continuous improvements and innovations is principally a team task. For Honda Motors the motivation of teams to make continuous improvements flows from its goal to be number one in producing cars.

As managers seek to cope with motivational challenges in the twenty-first century, they are advised to rethink the motivational goals and expectations of their teams and to change their managerial procedures. Using the car industry as a case in point, Cole (1990) observes that 'management has come to recognise that management behaviour is the root cause of quality problems'. Pickard (2002) reports that management consistently underestimates the interest of hourly employees in improving quality; even the Transport and General Workers Union in the Jaguar plant discussed at the beginning of this chapter, supports quality improvements. According to Cohen (1993), better technology is not always the answer, for in the late 1980s GM's Buick division achieved dramatic improvements in quality at two plants by reducing automation and initiating in its place plant-level teamwork. Innovation and performance result when teams are motivated to improve. Chapter 10 extends this concept by examining the processes for developing groups into motivated teams.

Halewood: a second look

Barrie Oxtoby, a consultant and former senior HRD manager at Rover, who did an audit of Halewood for the Greater Merseyside Learning and Skills Council, says: 'The people in the first four or five centres of excellence were really proud of being selected and used to tell other people what they were doing. In the car industry, there is a "me-too" culture. Once people see something being done that works, their attitude is: if he's got one, I want one.'

Alan Walker, the plant's finance director, puts much of the success down to several key areas: the involvement of people in developing the values and behaviours; the culture change and team-building workshops; a certain stability in the management team; and a willingness to be actively involved.

But he stresses that 'we are not there yet. The danger is to think we are there. It's still fragile here. We can destroy it as quickly as that,' he says, clicking his fingers. 'The thing we must do is keep communicating and we must do what we say. If there is an issue, people must feel free to say what they think.'

This may be true. Nevertheless, Halewood has certainly scored some spectacular successes. Even before Escort production finished there, the plant had already halved defect rates since 1998, halved inventories and achieved quality certification, making it the top quality Escort line in Europe. Productivity was up 20 per cent. This was with largely the same workforce and equipment as before.

The Greater Merseyside Learning and Skills Council has identified Halewood as a model plant. After his audit for the LSC, Oxtoby created what he calls the Jaguar template, a model for culture change that the Council is now planning to replicate around the region.

Tony Woodley, the Transport and General Workers Union's chief negotiator for the car industry, who led the original campaign to save Halewood, says, 'The people are in the main the same people. It's not a miracle. It's just a case of putting in good, firm processes and giving high-quality training to an already competent workforce along with serious investment in the plant.'

The biggest prize for all those involved in the Halewood transition came in November after the week-long annual audit by Ford's own inspectors. The plant emerged with a score of 4.5 out of 7 – making it the best Ford assembly plant in the world. 'Four years ago we were on our knees. Now look at us,' says David Crisp, corporate affairs manager.

Source: *People Management*, 18 April 2002, Barrie Oxtoby, 'Driving High Performance Working' from the CIPD's HRD 2002 conference.

Summary

- One of life's basic conflicts is whether to approach (actively engage) or to avoid a person, task or event. The direction and intensity of movement towards or away from a situation reflect one's motivation at the time.

- Motivation is our conscious decision to direct our effort more towards one or more activities than other possibilities, and/or to vary the level of effort exerted.

- Several theories seek to identify individual needs or motives and suggest how each activates different behaviours.

- Maslow originally identified five hierarchical levels of needs but later simplified his theory to define needs as either deficiency reduction or growth aspiration forces.

- Alderfer distilled Maslow's theory into three non-hierarchical needs: existence, relatedness and growth. This simplification has produced generally favourable research support.

- Herzberg focused entirely on work motivation and claimed that simply providing for hygiene or maintenance needs does not motivate. Only motivators – the sources of satisfaction found in the nature of work itself – will motivate.

- Some needs become such compelling sources of satisfaction to an individual that they become socially learned motives.

- People will consistently engage in activities that satisfy their dominant motive, such as a need for power, achievement or affiliation. Managers do well to draw on socialised power needs, and entrepreneurs usually have high achievement needs.

- Expectancy theory provides the central explanation of motivation as a process. It explains how individuals evaluate effort–performance–outcome relationships in making behaviour choices. Moderating motivation (regardless of need, motive or expectancy) are people's perceptions of equity, which are separated into the fairness arenas of distributive justice and procedural justice.

- Theories of motivation popular in Britain focus on individual behaviour. Yet many organisations are shifting to group-based practices, and globally in many cultures the individual is already subordinate to the group. A new stream of motivation research is expected to focus on providing greater insights into group-based motivation.

Areas for personal development

Everyone experiences motivation – it is the causal energy within us that affects our choice of behaviours and the intensity with which they are done. As a personal force within the individual, motivation is thus a perfect candidate for personal development. To learn to use your motivation potential for productive pursuits, apply the following skills to your daily life.

1 **Get in touch with your needs.** Needs change many times within a day, often many times within an hour. For one waking day, make a record of your needs as they happen, and the way you feel as you act on each need. Then review your record several ways. Which of your needs seem to be orientated to avoiding some form of deficiency or discomfort; which pull you towards something that is more pleasurable, exciting or interesting? How do you feel when experiencing relief? How do you feel when engaged in something that you are actively wanting and pursuing? Look in particular for patterns of feelings across the needs you might classify as existence, relatedness or growth (to use Alderfer's theory).

2 **Know your sources of dissatisfaction and satisfaction.** As an extension of skill 1, develop an awareness of the factors that seem to be sources of dissatisfaction or negative tension in your life. Do the same with sources of satisfaction. Do the satisfiers (using Herzberg's terminology) seem to originate from situations where you feel more in control (more intrinsic in nature)? Are the dissatisfiers more extrinsic? If so, how could you organise your life so you can experience more of the internal satisfaction that comes from engaging in events or tasks where you can influence the outcome?

3 **Attribute success to yourself.** Actively work to develop the socially acquired motives that you believe will contribute to your life's success. If you believe you need to be more achievement orientated, develop the capacity to realise how your efforts and talents contribute to the successes you experience. If you believe the power motive needs to be elevated, seek out experiences in which you can work to influence others in seeking team or organisationally relevant behaviours. See yourself as causing positive outcomes – reject the tendency to attribute them to luck or others if you are so inclined.

4 **Clarify your expectations when engaged in jobs.** Use the three expectancy questions to help understand your motivational choices and energy in work-related situations. Ask yourself the following questions. Does my effort affect performance? Are personal consequences linked to my performance? Do I value the available consequences? Thinking through your answers to these questions provides clues as to where you will experience positive pay-offs when you have some range of task options. If you can answer 'yes' to all three questions for most of the tasks you face, consider yourself positively motivated.

5 **Know how you adjust to inequities.** Not everything in your life will be fair. Be alert to how you handle disappointments that seem inequitable. What do you use as comparisons? Other individuals? Another reference group? Occupational classifications? What actions do you take to try to end up with a fair deal? Try to find a way that results in a win–win outcome for all involved, rather than just complaining or brooding in silent frustration.

6 **Be a team contributor.** You have probably experienced dysfunctional teams, possibly in class assignments. Realise that much of your working life will probably involve working in

groups that, hopefully, function as teams. Look for ways you can influence the teams in your life to draw in the motivational commitment of all players. Use the combination of awareness of individual motives with the expectancy framework as ways to pull in the contributions of others.

7 **Assess group motives.** Especially when working in teams, probe with questions that get not only at ideas about what to do to bring about improvement, but at the underlying motives and attitudes that are blocking better performance. Seize opportunities to practise cause-and-effect assessment of team performance so that the team learns to remove motivational obstacles, rather than pointing blame to one or more individuals who appear to be unmotivated.

❓ Questions for study and discussion

1 Whitehead (1929) proposed that all human beings seek three purposes: first to be alive, next to live well and, finally, to live better. Compare this thought to the theory of motivation you believe most closely parallels it.

2 Under what circumstances do needs serve as reliable motivators at work? Which theory based on needs do you believe to be most useful to managers? Give two ways in which a manager could apply the theory to strengthen the motivation of team members so that they approach rather than avoid essential tasks.

3 Suppose an executive made the statement: 'Entrepreneurs are driven by achievement motivation, managers in big firms need to be power motivated, but affiliation-motivated people make lousy managers.' Explain the underlying validity of each of the three observations.

4 What are the three main variables of expectancy theory? Give one example of how a person's evaluation of each of the three could lead to a conclusion to increase motivation on a task. Give an example of an evaluation leading to the opposite conclusion.

5 Can a person who is 'satisfied' still be motivated? Explain the distinction and relationship between satisfaction and motivation.

6 In what ways might a person adjust her behaviour if she believed she was unjustly under-compensated? Over-compensated? In considering such equity issues, how does procedural justice differ from distributive justice?

7 Theories of motivation have focused primarily on explaining individual behaviour. What are some of the emerging forces that suggest that group-based motivation will become more important in the future?

8 What action would you recommend as a manager to motivate a work group to thrive on organisational learning?

🔑 Key Concepts

motivation, *p. 196*

content theories of motivation, *p. 196*

deficiency reduction needs, *p. 197*

growth aspiration needs, *p. 198*

hierarchy of needs, *p. 199*

ERG theory, *p. 200*

dual-factor theory, *p. 202*

hygiene factors, *p. 203*

motivator factors, *p. 203*

job enrichment, *p. 204*

Theory X, *p. 205*

Theory Y, *p. 205*

need to achieve (or achievement motive), *p. 208*

need for power (or power motive), *p. 209*

need for affiliation (or affiliation motive), *p. 209*

personal attribution, *p. 210*

personal ideology, *p. 211*

process theories of motivation, *p. 212*

expectancy theory, *p. 213*

extrinsic rewards, *p. 215*

intrinsic rewards, *p. 215*

equity theory, *p. 218*

distributive justice, *p. 220*

procedural justice, *p. 220*

referent cognitions theory, *p. 220*

Personal skills exercise
What is your motive?

Purpose Managers who are successful at motivating others often pick up clues about the motives of colleagues from their behaviour and spoken words. They then try to alter work tasks or elements that direct and energise others. Although brief, this personal + 1 (dyad) exercise provides practice in reading motive clues from a peer, and then responding with intended motivational-enhancing strategies.

Time about 15 to 20 minutes

Procedure Form groups of two. One person takes the position of A, the other B.

1   A begins by describing two recent events: one event in which he or she was really turned on, putting a lot of conscious effort into doing something that was personally meaningful; the other event in which A just could not put much into it, where the effort was, at most, half-hearted. (Time: about 2 minutes for each.)

2   B then analyses and describes whatever clues he or she can discern from these scenarios about A's motives or needs. B should draw on whatever theories of motivation may provide diagnostic insights into the other person's behaviour in response to the two different situations – maybe there is an explanation based on achievement, affiliation or power motives, or perhaps there were underlying unsatisfied needs, expectancies or equity factors. (Time: 2 to 3 minutes.)

3   Having attempted to interpret analytically the clues provided by A, B then describes a work situation in which B is a manager and A is a member of B's group. B now recommends actions he or she would take as a manager to bring out the motivational best in A. Then, A provides feedback about the likely impact of B's strategies or actions on A's behaviour. (Time: 2 to 3 minutes.)

4   Reverse roles and repeat steps 1 to 3 with the spotlight on B.

Debriefing Time permitting, the tutor may want to bring out some best practices by sharing them with the class. Think about the analysis and interpretation your partner offered about your personal situations.

1   Was your partner's interpretation especially insightful, one that accurately reflects one or more of your learned motives or other motivational tendencies? If so, have two or three dyads share those insights. The one making the interpretation should explain how he or she 'read' the clues.

2   Did your partner interpret your scenarios based on his or her own motives? In other words, did your partner seem to interpret your stories based on what is important to him or her, in effect reading his or her personal motives into your situation? If so, this is not uncommon for people with highly accentuated learned motives. Have one or two dyads discuss this situation.

3   Would your partner's managerial action recommendations be appropriately motivating for you? If so, have a couple of dyads explain, with the one being 'motivated' reflecting on why it would be personally motivating.

Team exercise
Problem-solving within Lightning Rod Steel

Purpose This is a team-based exercise designed to:

1 analyse the motivational implications of data generated by a group of engineers working for Lightning Rod Steel (LRS)

2 develop and present to the class a theory-supported action plan for improving motivation of the engineers

3 use the same criteria developed by the engineers to assess motivational factors affecting you in a work situation.

Time about 35 minutes

Procedures Perform the following five tasks.

1 Divide into groups of five to seven people.

2 As a team, read the background material, including Exhibit 5-6 (about 3 minutes).

3 Each group should analyse the Lightning Rod situation to determine the presumed lack of motivation among engineers. Then, use one established theory of motivation as the basis for developing an action plan of recommendations to 'improve the motivation' of the company's engineers. What specific actions should the managers take? Make sure your plan is feasible and reasonable for the managers to accept (10 to 15 minutes).

4 Each individual group member should score the 19 motivational factors listed by the engineers in Exhibit 5-6. Determine how much each factor contributes to *your* motivation in an ideal work situation. Assign points from 0 to 5, where 5 means 'extremely desirable' and 0 indicates 'unimportant'. Record your points in the 'Your ideal scores' section of the exhibit. Then think of any factors important to you that are missing from the list. Compare your responses to those of the engineers and your team members. Plan to comment to the class on why your team scores were similar to or different from those of the engineers (about 7 minutes).

5 Present your recommendations and observations to the class. Debrief the activity to look for insights into how motivational expectations and motives differ among your peers (about 10 minutes).

Background of Lightning Rod Steel (LRS) Lightning Rod produces a number of rolled, bar and tubular steel products from a single mill fuelled by two electric hearth furnaces that melt recycled scrap metal. Kent Olsen, the director of manufacturing services, and his two engineering managers are concerned that, given a soft market for steel and the constant need to cut costs by improving efficiencies, 'we aren't getting 100 per cent from our engineering staff'. Engineers number about three dozen and are of two types. Design engineers work on special projects for plant modernisation. Industrial engineers update work standards, work method improvements, compensation incentives and similar projects.

1 Olsen approaches your consulting group with a couple of questions: 'One of the issues we've been unable to resolve among ourselves is how to determine the productivity of engineering professionals, and then how to improve it. Second, why aren't more of our engineers being pirated away by our seven operating general managers for higher-paying managerial jobs?' He hands you a page (Exhibit 5-6) developed by the engineers during a recent training session. The data were developed in response to the question, 'Brainstorm

a list of what you would like to experience more often or have more of in your work situation, then evaluate ideal and actual conditions on a 0- to 5-point scale.' Olsen continues, 'Maybe this gives you some clues as to what we could do better to motivate engineers.'

EXHIBIT 5–6 What LRS engineers expect at work

Scores reflect the group mean, with 5 points maximum.

Work factors	Engineers' scores		Your ideal scores
	Ideal conditions	Actual experience	
1 Open and honest communication	4.8	2.2	_____
2 A sense of fairness and justice	4.3	2.0	_____
3 Seeing the results of my work	4.3	2.7	_____
4 The opportunity to get my job done	4.2	2.5	_____
5 Feedback about how I am doing	4.0	2.0	_____
6 Interesting work assignments	4.0	2.2	_____
7 Opportunity for advancement	4.0	0.5	_____
8 Being compensated for performance	4.0	1.5	_____
9 Upward and/or lateral job mobility	4.0	0.8	_____
10 Recognition for work accomplishments	3.8	1.8	_____
11 A say in things that affect me	3.8	1.8	_____
12 A sense of involvement in the company	3.7	2.0	_____
13 Being informed of policies/job openings	3.5	0.7	_____
14 Working for a winning/successful team	3.2	1.7	_____
15 Even work distribution (no peaks/troughs)	3.0	2.0	_____
16 Equitable access to benefits	3.0	2.8	_____
17 A variety of tasks (job rotation)	2.8	1.8	_____
18 Security of not working myself out of job	2.5	1.5	_____
19 Good physical working environment	2.0	1.3	_____

Case study: **Ralph Henry's motivational crisis, by Elaine Chiang**

Ralph Henry had worked as a production chemist at Systems Diagnostics Corporation (SDC) for seven years. The last four of those years were with the MED group, during which he received two promotions to become the group's senior chemist. Conscientious and thorough in his work, Ralph was a stickler for details in the lab yet always willing to help others. Co-workers liked Ralph's pleasant, friendly manner and his lively conversations about sports and running (his major avocations). However, beyond the immediate group Ralph was rather private. He interacted with few people outside the MED group and rarely attended social functions and company parties.

Ralph had always enjoyed his career as a chemist. He was particularly pleased with the laboratory environment which allowed him to work freely and independently, pursuing whatever challenge or idea that came along. It was no big surprise, then, when Ken Chang asked Ralph to become supervisor of the MED group and take over a role Chang had held for three years.

The reorganisation

Systems Diagnostics Corporation makes diagnostic reagent kits and pharmaceutical instrumentation for hospitals, clinical laboratories and some government agencies. The firm was having difficulties containing costs and had recently announced the third consecutive decline in quarterly profits. Although sales were steady, with the latest announcement of profit erosion, senior management also announced a reorganisation to consolidate product lines. Because of the reorganisation, Ken Chang was promoted to production manager of a newly created division, leaving vacant his former position as supervisor of the MED group. While a supervisor, Ken spent much of his time outside the group and, in doing so, granted considerable autonomy to his chemists.

When offered the supervisor's position, Ralph initially baulked. He explained to Ken his reluctance to leave the lab bench and his feelings of uneasiness about supervising a group of long-time peers. All his education was in pure science; he had no management training or experience. Ken promised that Ralph could participate in management training seminars and expressed his confidence that Ralph would quickly master the art of management.

The promotion

After a week of contemplation, Ralph accepted. When his appointment was announced, members of the MED group were delighted and hosted a congratulatory luncheon for him.

Six months into the supervisory job, Ralph's attitude was as conscientious and upbeat as ever. Much of his time was spent thoroughly checking each group member's work. Unlike Ken in the role of supervisor, Ralph required that all product tests be documented in detail and often requested that routine lab testings be repeated to confirm accuracy. Rather than delegate difficult problems to group members Ralph took on most of these complex lab tasks himself and often worked late into the evening.

The crisis

In mid-December a major crisis required Ralph's immediate attention. The deadline on a large Navy contract assigned to the MED group was moved from mid-February to mid-January. Management wanted very much to make good on this contract, as the Navy was a potential major customer. But because of technical difficulties, Ralph did not believe MED would meet the deadline since SDC had a tradition of shutting down during the holidays. To respond to the pressure, Ralph called a meeting of all group members, something he rarely did. He spelled out the situation: 'As you're all aware, we are having a big technical problem with the Navy contract. To compound our troubles, I just got word from management that the deadline has been moved up one month to mid-January. This really puts us in a jam because the plant is scheduled to be shut down for 10 days over the holidays.

'Personally, I know the project is more important than my holiday plans, so I'm cancelling them. What I'd like to know is who will be willing to work with me, say, a few of the 10 days? Of course, you will get time off in lieu or overtime pay if you prefer. How many of you will be willing to work with me?'

The group was silent. Not one of the 10 members raised a hand or spoke up.

Questions for managerial action

1 What motivates Ralph Henry? How do these forces affect his behaviour as a chemist? As a supervisor?

2 What probably motivates the other chemists in the MED group? How well does Ralph understand these motivational forces and adjust his supervisory behaviour to bring out their best? Compare the motivational impact on the chemists of Ken Chang's approach to supervision with that of Ralph Henry.

3 Why the 'no hands' response to Ralph's request for help? What does it indicate about Ralph's development as a supervisor? Given no volunteers, what does Ralph do now?

Applied questions

4 Using Victor Vroom's expectancy equation can you identify what Ralph's motivations are and which elements are hindering his ability to motivate his team?

5 McClelland and Atkinson suggest that the achievement motive could be measured by what people say, do or write. If this is the case can you identify Ken and Ralph's achievement motive? What evidence are you using to draw conclusions?

WWW exercise

Manager's Internet tools

Web tips: motivational factors on the web

The job market in the late 1990s and in early 2000 was very tight. Established companies have been challenged by new entrants: the dotcoms. Competition between 'new economy' and 'old economy' firms has redefined everything from products to technology, and how companies view, treat and motivate their employees. With these changes, the demand for skilled labour has risen to high levels, further forcing companies to attract talent and differentiate themselves by creating exciting and new environments. 'Perks' such as stock options, flexitime, casual dress, on-site childcare, an area for employee pets, gym membership, video games and football machines, and even time set aside for surfing are being used to attract and retain talent, *and* to motivate workers.

Specific websites

What type of work environment motivates you? Are you more attracted to the dotcom environment, or to a more traditional environment? Look at some of the websites of the dotcom start-up companies; search for information about their environment and the climate they nourish to motivate employees. Some recommended sites are:

http://www.yahoo.com/
http://www.lastminute.com/
http://www.scient.com/
http://www.amazon.com/

Then, look at some of the websites of companies from the 'old economy'. Some recommended sites are:

http://www.ibm.co.uk
http://www.hp.co.uk
http://www.britishairways.co.uk

1 What factors motivate you? Are they different at work versus outside of work?

2 What are some of the motivating messages on the dotcom sites? The 'old economy' sites? What differences are noticeable; what similarities do you see? Which corporate environment better suits you?

LEARNING CHECKLIST ☑

Before you move on you may want to reflect on what you have learnt in this chapter. You should now be able to:

☑ identify two need-based theories of motivation and describe how each influences approach–avoidance behaviours in a work setting

☑ explain why some theories can be useful even if they are unreliable

☑ explain why removing sources of job dissatisfaction will not necessarily rekindle the motivation to work

☑ distinguish among the motives of achievement, power and affiliation, and tell how each affects success as an entrepreneur or manager

☑ relate the three basic factors of expectancy theory to typical work conditions that increase or diminish motivation

☑ distinguish between satisfaction and motivation, and indicate how the two are related

☑ explain why equity evaluations (and perceptions of work justice) can alleviate motivational problems

☑ tell why motivation theories based on individual behaviour are increasingly inadequate for explaining behaviour in multicultural organisations.

Further reading

Alderfer, C.P. (1972) *Existence, Relatedness, and Growth*. New York, NY: Free Press.

Bassett-Jones, N. and Lloyd, G.C. (2005) 'Does Herzberg's Motivation Theory have Staying Power?', *Journal of Management Development* 24(10), pp. 929–943.

Bossé-Smith, L. (2005) 'More than Motivation, Training and Development', *Alexandria* 59(10), October, pp. 22–24.

Herzberg, F. (1993) *The Motivation to Work*. New Brunswick, NJ: Transaction Publications.

Martin, A.J. (2004/2005) 'The Role of Positive Psychology in Enhancing Satisfaction, Motivation and Productivity in the Workplace', *Journal of Organizational Behavior Management* 24(1, 2), p. 113.

Maslow, A.H. (1965) *Eupsychian Management: A Journal.* Homewood, IL: Richard D. Irwin, p. 55.

Maslow, A.H. (1987) *Motivation and Personality* (2nd edn). Reading, MA: Addison-Wesley.

Rauschenberger, J., Schmitt, N. and Hunter, J.E. (1980) 'A Test of the Need Hierarchy Concept by a Markov Model of Change in Need Strength', *Administrative Science Quarterly* 25, December, pp. 654–670.

References

Alderfer, C.P. (1969) 'An Empirical Test of a New Theory of Human Needs', *Organisational Behaviour and Human Performance* 4, May, pp. 142–175.

Amabile, T.M. (1998) 'How to Kill Creativity', *Harvard Business Review* 76, September–October, pp. 77–87.

Atkinson, J.W. (1964) *An Introduction to Motivation.* Princeton, NJ: Van Nostrand.

Boyacigiller, N.A. and Adler, N.J. (1991) 'The Parochial Dinosaur: Organizational Science in a Global Context', *Academy of Management Review* 16, April, pp. 274–276.

Bradt, J.A. (1991) 'Pay for Impact', *Personnel Journal* 70, May, pp. 76–79.

Brockner, J., Greenberg, J., Brockner, A., Bortz, J., Davy, J. and Carter, C. (1986) 'Layoffs, Equity Theory and Work Performance: Further Evidence of the Impact of Survivor Guilt', *Academy of Management Journal* 29, June, pp. 373–384.

Brockner, J., Grover, S., Reed, T.F. and Dewitt, R.L. (1992) 'Layoffs, Job Insecurity, and Survivors' Work Effort: Evidence of an Inverted-U Relationship', *Academy of Management Journal* 35, June, pp. 413–425.

Carlisle, Y.M. and Manning, D.J. (1994) 'The Concept of Ideology and Work Motivation', *Organisation Studies* 15, December, pp. 683–700.

Cohen, S.G. (1993) 'New Approaches to Teams and Teamwork', in Jay R. Galbraith, Edward E. Lawler III and associates, *Organizing for the Future.* San Francisco, CA: Jossey-Bass, pp. 194–226.

Cole, R. (1990) 'US Quality Improvement in the Auto Industry: Close but No Cigar', *California Management Review* 32, Summer, p. 72.

Cook, C.W. (1980) 'Guidelines for Managing Motivation', *Business Horizons* 23, April, pp. 61–69.

Cook, R.E. (1983) 'Why Jimmy Doesn't Try', *Academic Therapy* 19(2), pp. 153–163.

Deci, E.L. (1971) 'Effects of Externally Mediated Rewards on Intrinsic Motivation', *Journal of Personality and Social Psychology* 18.

Fein, M. (1973) 'Work Measurement and Wage Incentives', *Industrial Engineering*, September, pp. 49–51.

Folger, R. (1986) 'Rethinking Equity Theory: A Referent Cognitions Model', in H.W. Bierhoff, R.L. Cohen and J. Greenberg (eds) *Justice in Social Relations.* New York, NY: Plenum, pp. 145–162.

Folger, R. and Konovsky, M.A. (1989) 'Effects of Procedural and Distributive Justice on Reactions to Pay Raise Decisions', *Academy of Management Journal* 32, March, pp. 115–130.

Fortado, B. (1992) 'The Accumulation of Grievance Conflict', *Journal of Management Inquiry* 1, December, p. 288.

Fryxell, G.E. and Gordon, M.E. (1989) 'Workplace Justice and Job Satisfaction as Predictors of Satisfaction with Union and Management', *Academy of Management Journal* 32, December, pp. 851–866.

Furnham, A., Kirkcaldy, B.D. and Lynn, R. (1994) 'National Attitudes to Competitiveness, Money, and Work Among Young People: First, Second, and Third World Differences', *Human Relations* 47, January, pp. 119ff.

George, J.M. (1992) 'Extrinsic and Intrinsic Origins of Perceived Social Loafing in Organizations', *Academy of Management Journal* 35, March, pp. 191–202.

Goleman, D. (1998) 'What Makes a Leader?', *Harvard Business Review* 76, November–December, pp. 93–102 (quote on p. 99).

Harpaz, I. (1990) 'The Importance of Work Goals: An International Perspective', *Journal of International Business Studies*, First Quarter, pp. 75–93.

Herzberg, F. (1966) *Work and the Nature of Man*. Cleveland, OH: World.

Herzberg, F. (1987) 'One More Time: How Do You Motivate Employees?', *Harvard Business Review* 46, September–October, pp. 109–120.

Hofstede, G. (1980) 'Motivation, Leadership, and Organisation: Do American Theories Apply Abroad?', *Organisational Dynamics*, Summer, p. 55.

Hofstede, G. (1983) 'Dimensions of National Cultures in Fifty Countries and Three Regions', in J.B. Deregowski, S. Dziurawiec and R.C. Annis (eds) *Explanations in Cross-cultural Psychology*. Lisse, Netherlands: Swets and Zeitlinger, pp. 335–355.

House, R.J. and Wigdor, L.A. (1967) 'Herzberg's Dual Factor Theory of Job Satisfaction and Motivation: A Review of the Evidence and a Criticism', *Personnel Psychology* 20, pp. 369–389.

Kelly, C.M. (1987) 'The Interrelationship of Ethics and Power in Today's Organisations', *Organisational Dynamics* 5, Summer.

Knippen, J.T. and Green, T.B. (1990) 'Boost Performance Through Appraisals', *Business Credit* 92, November–December, p. 27.

Lawler III, E.E. (1981) *Pay and Organizational Development*. Reading, MA: Addison-Wesley.

Lawler III, E.E. (1994) *Motivation in Work Organizations*. San Francisco, CA: Jossey Bass.

Maddi, S. (1972) *Theories of Personality, A Comparative Analysis* (rev. edn). Homewood, IL: The Dorsey Press.

Maslow, A.H. (1955) 'Deficiency Motivation and Growth Motivation', in M.R. Jones (ed.) *Nebraska Symposium on Motivation*. Lincoln: University of Nebraska Press.

Maslow, A.H. (1998) *Toward a Psychology of Being*. New York, NY: Wiley & Sons.

McClelland, D.C. (1961) *The Achieving Society*. New York, NY: Van Nostrand Reinhold.

McClelland, D.C. (1965) 'Achievement Motivation Can Be Developed', *Harvard Business Review* 43, November–December, pp. 6–8.

McClelland, D.C. (1975) *Power: The Inner Experience*. New York, NY: Irvington.

McClelland, D.C. (1995) 'Retrospective Commentary to McClelland and Burnham', *Harvard Business Review* 73, January–February, pp. 138–139.

McClelland, D.C. and Burnham, D.H. (1995) 'Power Is the Great Motivator', *Harvard Business Review* 73, January–February, pp. 126–139.

McClelland, D.C. and Winter, D.G. (1969) *Motivating Economic Achievement*. New York, NY: Free Press.

McFarlin, D.B. and Sweeney, P.D. (1992) 'Distributive and Procedural Justice as Predictors of Satisfaction with Personal and Organizational Outcomes', *Academy of Management Journal* 35, August, pp. 626–637.

McGregor, D. (1960) *The Human Side of Enterprise*. New York, NY: McGraw-Hill.

Mowday, R.T. (1987) 'Equity Theory Predictions of Behaviour in Organizations', in R.M. Steers and L.W. Porter (eds) *Motivation and Work Behaviour* (4th edn). New York, NY: McGraw-Hill, pp. 91–113.

Pickard, J. (2002) 'Top Gear', *People Management*, 18 April, pp. 37–42.

Porter, L.W. (1961) 'A Study of Perceived Need Satisfactions in Bottom and Middle Management Jobs', *Journal of Applied Psychology* 45, pp. 1–10.

Porter, L.W. and Lawler III, E.E. (1968) *Managerial Attitudes and Performance.* Homewood, IL: Richard D. Irwin.

Quick, T.L. (1990) 'Simple is Hard, Complex is Easy, Simplistic is Impossible', *Training and Development Journal* 44, May, pp. 94–99.

Randolph, W.L. and Posner, B.Z. (1992) *Getting the Job Done! Managing Project Teams and Task Forces for Success.* Englewood Cliffs, NJ: Prentice Hall.

Rosenbush, S. (2000) 'The Talent Drain at AT&T', *Business Week,* 13 March, pp. 94–100.

Schneider, C.P. and Alderfer, C.P. (1973) 'Three Studies of Measures of Need Satisfaction in Organisations', *Administrative Science Quarterly,* December, pp. 489–505.

Shamir, B. (1991) 'Meaning, Self and Motivation in Organisations', *Organisation Studies* 12, pp. 405–424.

Sitkin, S.B. and Pablo, A.L. (1992) 'Reconceptualizing the Determinants of Risk Behaviour', *Academy of Management Review* 17, January, pp. 9–38.

Stahl, M.J. (1986) *Managerial and Technical Motivation: Assessing Needs for Achievement, Power, and Affiliation.* New York, NY: Praeger.

Steers, R.M. and Porter, L.W. (1987) *Motivation and Work Behaviour* (4th edn). New York, NY: McGraw-Hill.

Steers, R.M., Bigley, G.A. and Porter, L. (eds) (1966) *Motivation and Leadership at Work* (6th edn). New York, NY: McGraw-Hill.

Tyagi, P.K. (1990) 'Inequities in Organisations, Salesperson Motivation and Job Satisfaction', *International Journal of Research in Marketing* 7, December, pp. 135–148.

Villere, M.F. and Hartman, S.J. (1990) 'The Key to Motivation is in the Process: An Examination of Practical Implications of Expectancy Theory', *Leadership and Organizational Development Journal* 11(4), pp. i–iii.

Vroom, V.H. (1994) *Work and Motivation.* San Francisco, CA: Jossey-Bass.

Wahba, M.A. and Bridwell, L.G. (1976) 'Maslow Reconsidered: A Review of Research on the Need Hierarchy Theory', *Organizational Behaviour and Human Performance* 15, pp. 212–240.

Wanous, J.P. and Zwany, A. (1977) 'A Cross-sectional Test of Need Hierarchy Theory', *Organisational Behaviour and Human Performance* 18, May, pp. 78–97.

Wanous, J.P., Keon, T.L. and Latack, J.C. (1983) 'Expectancy Theory and Occupational/ Organizational Choices: A Review and Test', *Organizational and Human Performance,* August, pp. 66–86.

Weiner, B. (1974) *Achievement Motivation and Attribution Theory.* Morristown, NY: General Learning Press.

Whitehead, A.N. (1929) *The Function of Reason.* Boston, MA: Beacon Press.

Whitsett, D.A. and Winslow, E.K. (1967) 'An Analysis of Studies Critical of the Motivation-hygiene Theory', *Personnel Psychology,* pp. 391–416.

Motivation methods and applications

The opening vignette shows what can happen when faced with staff retention problems. Morpheus, a corporate website developer, decided to look for outside help and turned to the local Business Link.

Joanna Read at Morpheus: turning point

Running a small business can leave you feeling rather isolated. You become tied up in day-to-day problems and consequently develop an introverted management style. It often seems difficult to get impartial, outside advice. With hindsight, these were certainly the symptoms of our own management style. Our philosophy tended to be 'Do it yourself or it won't be done properly.'

Our communication process was ad hoc to say the least. Staff reviews were carried out only when there was a problem or a pay rise was requested and our stance was, with hindsight, quite aggressive and combative. We were ill-equipped to deal with staff issues and our attempts to improve the office environment often had an adverse effect.

As such, we had a problem with demoralised workers, recruitment and retention. We could not keep people and much of this was down to our initial selection of unsuitable candidates.

It all sounds very bleak, so why did we bother? Well, because we always held on to the belief that we had something to offer. We were determined to make it work and enjoy it. After all, even with these problems we had survived three years and made a profit each year without borrowing a penny. We had built some fantastic solutions and had a strong client base – we would not give up.

However, we were tired of dealing with staff problems and also of trying to control every aspect of the business. We knew it could not stay like this.

The major turning point came a year ago. We lost virtually our entire staff and were in effect back at the start, but wiser and with a bigger office. We knew we needed external guidance, but were not sure where to get it.

I made a call to our local Business Link and a meeting was arranged with one of their advisers. The first session was uncomfortable but necessary. We were told that our management style was providing the major barrier to our growth. Coming from an experienced outsider, this was just the jolt we needed to reassess our approach to the business and to become more analytical in solving problems.

Source: Joanna Read in *Growing Business*, May 2002.

Discussion questions

1 Why is it important to have proper selection procedures for staff?
2 Why do you think management style can affect motivation?

Motivating the behaviour of employees is a managerial challenge with many options. Managers can set goals, apply selective rewards such as stock options, redesign jobs, develop conditions of empowerment to unleash motivation, and even reinforce routine behaviours using organisational behaviour modification. Chapter 5 surveyed several influential theories of motivation and their implications for understanding human behaviour in organisations. This chapter extends the principles of motivation by surveying several techniques designed to direct, focus and energise human behaviour at work, ranging from goal-setting to organisational learning.

Joanna Read at Morpheus realised she had a problem with staff retention, which usually means that there is a problem with motivation. She also realised that if the company was to grow the problem needed to be solved.

By seeking external help it was made obvious that Morpheus needed to look at its management style and how it viewed workers. Think back to McGregor in the previous chapter. It was also time to concentrate on team-building as a means of making staff feel valued.

One of the problems with motivational practices in many organisations, especially mature ones, is that techniques are based on gimmicks, which range from paying celebrities thousands of pounds for a brief inspirational speech to handing out prizes that cost a few pounds. Human resource managers are always looking for the ideal solution that will solve the challenge of how to motivate workers. Yates (1995) commented that at one 'motivation show', more than 40 000 corporate people looked over the offerings of 3200 sales displays. For sale was everything from products to ideas proclaimed to get people to work more productively.

Rather than relying on fads and gimmicks, this chapter reviews motivational practices that are widely used and that have been researched to reveal strengths as well as limitations. Buhler (1994) suggests that flexibility and some variety of approaches are advocated, for people are motivated by different needs and goals, as can be seen in the case of the Beardmore Hotel in the Dynamics of Diversity box.

The Beardmore Conference Hotel, Clydebank: pick and mix benefits

The four-star Beardmore Conference Hotel in Clydebank, Glasgow, is part of the Best Western consortium and boasts 168 bedrooms, 12 conference rooms and a 170-seater tiered auditorium; 82 full-time employees and 15 casual staff look after guests, most of whom are either business-based conferences, tourists or wedding parties.

Like the rest of the hospitality industry, the hotel faces a problem recruiting and retaining staff, with stiff competition from several call centres, a business park and major supermarkets in the Clydebank Shopping Centre. But flexible working patterns, including time off for dependants and career breaks, are a crucial tool in its approach to staffing. Managers work as and when required, but the rest of the staff all work annualised hours, with the same size pay cheque each month, as HR assistant Carol Hampson explains.

'They work 1950 hours, which is the equivalent of 37.5 hours a week. If we're busy one week and need extra food and beverage staff or housekeepers – perhaps there are extra rooms to clean – staff are prepared to stay longer until the work is done. In return, they'll leave earlier the following week if we're not so busy. Or it may be a question of them working very hard for a four-month stretch during the summer, with a quieter time and therefore shorter hours during the winter. If they leave the company before they've been able to recoup their hours, the extra is paid back to them in cash. It's important, though, to monitor individual working patterns to make sure that the demands on them are not too great in terms of hours per week.'

Sixteen-year-old Danielle Henderson is a room attendant at the hotel and she finds the flexible approach suits her down to the ground: 'I'm a singer and although I've only worked here for a few months the company is really helpful, giving me time off to go for auditions and recordings. They're happy to let me get away early or change the schedule to fit in with my timings.'

Other flexible benefits on offer include childcare vouchers, pension, life assurance, health insurance, educational funding and driving lessons.

dynamics of diversity

The driving lessons proved very popular with young people who felt they did not want a pension or insurance.

Other benefits include a taxi home after 11 p.m., counselling, staff meals, staff discounts and incentives.

Carol sees considerable benefits for the company in the way it treats it's staff. 'I have a meeting with each member of staff who has joined the benefits scheme and the feedback I receive is that the benefits are valued by staff and certainly at the recruitment stage it appears to be a valued attraction. Local employers may sometimes offer higher rates of pay but they don't offer a flexible benefit package like we do. Add our benefits to an employee's salary and in the long run they know they will be better off with us.'

Source: 'Worklife Balance – A Good Practice Guide for the Hospitality Industry' in conjunction with the HCIMA and DTI.

Discussion questions

1 Why is it important to recognise different people's motivations?

2 How can flexible benefits improve business performance?

Enhancing motivation by goal-setting

Work performance is affected by company policies and practices, manager–employee relationships and organisational goals. According to Locke (1978), there is an abundant stream of research that suggests goal striving is a common element in most motivational theories. A **goal** is the desired outcome of an action; it becomes motivational when an individual wants it and strives to achieve it. The goal of a football team is to win the next game, then the league championship. A goal of a marketing department might be to increase global market share three points in the next 12 months.

goal
The desired outcome of an action, which becomes motivational when a person wants it and strives to achieve it.

Difficult goals stimulate effort and commitment

Yearta *et al.* (1995) suggest that the use of goals to motivate performance draws on two primary attributes: the content of the goal and the level of intensity in working towards it. *Content* emphasises the features of the goal, how it is to be measured or assessed, and its level of specificity – which implies a level of difficulty in attaining it. *Intensity* considers the process by which a goal is set – the extent of participation – and the degree of commitment and intention to bring it about.

Content-level of difficulty

Apart from the specificity or tangibility of a goal, most content-related research has concentrated on the relationship between goal difficulty and performance. Using meta-analysis (an analysis of many other studies), Wood *et al.* (1987) investigated the following hypothesis: 'Given adequate ability and commitment, more difficult goals stimulate greater effort and performance than easier goals.' They concluded that 175 of 192 laboratory and field research studies produced partial or full support for the hypothesis. Thus, managers and professionals should heed this lesson when setting goals – if a task is worthy of a goal it should be challenging and require considerable effort to achieve. Occasionally, an unexpected crisis provokes a sudden goal that needs to be achieved quickly.

Research focus: **goal-setting theory**

According to Locke (1968), performance can be affected by the setting of goals and therefore goal-setting can be used as a means of motivation. Locke suggests goals are used to direct effort and also provide guidelines for deciding how much effort should be put into each activity when there are multiple goals. Involving individuals in setting realistic and achievable goals increases self-belief, which in turn can increase motivation.

Locke's theory assumes that:

- the goal is the most important part of motivation and performance
- the harder the goal the greater the level of performance
- task performance depends on goal commitment.

Goal-setting theory assumes that behaviour is a result of conscious goals and intentions. Therefore, a manager should be able to influence an employee's behaviour by setting goals. Locke's (1968) original goal-setting theory looked at two specific goal characteristics: goal difficulty and goal specifity.

Goal difficulty is the extent to which the goal is challenging and requires effort. This is based on the idea that if people work hard to achieve goals, then they will worker harder to achieve more complex goals. However, the goal should not be so difficult that it is unattainable.

Goal specifity is the clarity and precision of the goal. If a goal can be quantifiable then it can be made specific. In other words, cutting costs by 10 per cent is far more specific that telling employees that they need to cut costs. Further research by Latham and Baldes (1975), on truck drivers hauling timbers, found that setting specific loads and increasing the difficulty of the task significantly increased productivity.

It is easy to be specific when goals can be quantifiable; it is much harder when setting gaols for improving customer satisfaction or employee well-being. Here, thought needs to be given as to how it can be measured.

Locke (1979) later improved his model by expanding his theory to include two further characteristics: goal acceptance and goal commitment.

Goal acceptance is the extent to which a person accepts a goal as his or her own.

Goal commitment is the extent to which he or she is personally interested in reaching the goal.

Exhibit 6-1 shows the expanded model and the complexities of goal-setting theory.

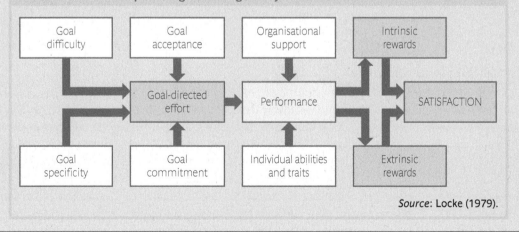

EXHIBIT 6–1 *The expanded goal-setting theory of motivation*

Source: Locke (1979).

▶
> To be effective, goal-setting needs to involve participants in the process. Goals should not be imposed but should be negotiated, agreed and accepted. The amount of organisational support can do much to help or hinder the process. Positive support may mean ensuring that adequate resources are available, whereas negative support may mean that appropriate training has not been given or equipment needed to do the tasks is not available. Rewards for achieving goals, both intrinsic and extrinsic, also need to be considered.

Intensity – degree of participation

Researchers Latham and Locke (1969) have examined goal-setting in three types of environment: (1) when goals are assigned by management; (2) when members participate in goal-setting; and (3) when members are told 'do your best'. Results indicate that either having a goal assigned or participating in goal-setting are associated with higher performance than the simple instruction to 'do your best'. Any manager giving an admonition to 'do your best' is really abandoning the goal-setting process. Without a goal there is nothing to measure, no way to compare results with targets. One action is as good as the next.

Ironically, according to Erez *et al.* (1985), while participation often produces greater commitment to goals and perceptions of self-control and fairness, participation does not necessarily lead to higher performance than manager-assigned goals. One workable hybrid is for managers to assign goals, hold people responsible for results, grant them the autonomy to plan their actions and exercise control over how they do their work, and then measure results. People who have the capability to do the task and are committed to achieving it will generally perform well regardless of their degree of participation in setting the goal (Latham and Marshal, 1982). Goals that are met will motivate higher performance only when they lead to the setting of higher goals.

According to Quick (1990), participative goal-setting can focus on four kinds of goal: (1) routine goals, an extension of what people are already doing; (2) problem-solving to overcome shortcomings; (3) innovation; and (4) personal development to spur greater achievement. Berlew (1986) suggests that, by focusing on goals rather than controls, a manager can align people behind organisational purposes and then allow individual initiative without sacrificing co-ordination. The relaxation of external controls helps people develop a greater capacity for internalising their commitment to relevant and meaningful tasks. Managers at Birkenstock Footprint Sandals, a company of a few hundred employees, encourage people to form task forces to solve complex problems (such as how to use recycling to save energy) (Rothman, 1993).

Intentions combine goals and action plans

Understanding personal intentions is central to fully understanding any cognitive approach to motivation practices, such as goal-setting. Intentions encompass more than goal-setting alone. A goal represents the desired outcome of action. An **intention** is a 'cognitive representation of both the objective [or goal] one is striving for and the action plan one intends to use to reach that objective' (Tubbs and Ekeberg, 1991). Even more explicitly, an intention contains a target combined with some specific action that is focused on bringing about an event within a specified time (Ajzen, 1995).

intention

Mental awareness of having both a goal and an action plan to obtain the goal.

actions

Deliberate choices about where to direct behaviours combined with intense, persistent efforts to achieve a goal over some time period.

Actions involve choices about the direction of effort, combined with intensity and persistence over some time period. Toby's goal is to simplify the steps involved in purchasing transactions within his organisation to generate 20 per cent cost savings over the next 12 months. He plans to achieve this outcome by converting paper forms to an Internet protocol through engaging several employees and vendors in a task force involving problem-solving and innovation. In effect, Toby's goal-setting process incorporates an action-taking component, energised with the intention to reduce the gap between the current situation and his targeted future outcome. He knows he must provide leadership and guidance to enable the task team to finish its plans within the next four months so the new Internet process can be implemented in time to produce the 20 per cent savings goal.

The more a manager specifies goals, the easier it is for others to frame their intentions for achieving them. However, Latham and Locke (1969) suggest that if an assigned goal is either too difficult or too easy, personalised intentions are likely to vary from those envisioned by the manager. It also helps if the employee engages in internal attribution and is hopeful of achieving the goal. 'Having *hope* means believing you have both the will and the way to accomplish your goals, whatever they may be. . . . Hope has proven a powerful predictor of outcome in every study we've done so far,' reports a research psychologist. In a study of 3920 students researchers found that the amount of hope among entering undergraduates was more predictive of academic success than either school-leaving qualifications or SAT scores, the two conventional predictors (Snyder, 1999). Data suggest people with high hope tend to be reality centred, set higher goals for themselves and actively work to attain their expectations. In short, they are motivated.

Management by objectives (MBO) sets priorities

You will remember that we discussed management by objectives (MBO) in Chapter 3, but it is important to look at it again in the context of motivation.

Dave Matthews, former director of training for the Water Council of Scotland, opens his general management training programmes with the statement: 'Management by objectives. Ladies and gentlemen, I ask you, is there any other way to manage?' Matthews is speaking of identifying the main objectives to be achieved within a specific time period. Many within the last two generations of managers have made objective-setting a systematic part of their business planning.

management by objectives (MBO)

The practice of manager and subordinate jointly determining time-specific objectives.

The formal process of **management by objectives**, popularly known as **MBO**, is based on the philosophy that the manager and the managed ought to negotiate or collaborate on defining the objectives the subordinate is to pursue over the next time period. The concept originated with management writer Drucker (1954) and was popularised by Odiorne (1965, 1979). Numerous organisations adopt MBO as a formal management practice and link it to performance appraisals and compensation. As a practice, MBO is supposed to provide a cross-reference of the purposes pursued by managers at different organisational levels and to co-ordinate objectives from top to bottom.

The intent of MBO is threefold: (1) to strengthen planning; (2) to encourage participative decision-making; and (3) to motivate performance of tasks that have a high pay-off for the organisation. In a formal MBO process, four steps are typically employed by the manager and subordinate (Kondrasuk, 1981):

1 agreement on key goals or objectives
2 action planning to work on the objectives
3 self-control and corrective actions to keep on target
4 periodic measurements, formal reviews and performance appraisals.

The give and take of setting objectives

The MBO process is intended to give participants a clearer idea of organisational priorities and of where intentions and effort should be concentrated. Ideally, people reporting to a manager who uses MBO are responsible for drafting individual job objectives. The manager then reviews each person's objectives in a face-to-face, give-and-take planning session until they generally agree on the priorities and expected levels of accomplishment. Although some organisations make MBO a formal management practice, today it is common to have some form of MBO practised in only some parts of the organisation or by only some managers.

During their objective-setting review, Arlene, a senior manager, might tell Jay, one of her subordinate managers, 'I agree fully with your objectives one to four and number six. These are critical to your department's success. From my point of view, objective five is not necessary, but if you have time and want to pursue it, OK. However, number seven needs to be more challenging and performed sooner. Let us come back to it and see if a higher level of performance isn't possible. However, don't waste time on eight, for the company is about to restructure that function so you'd just be spinning your wheels. Now, about that seventh objective...'.

In theory, this process of agreeing to objectives is one of collaboration. In practice, the manager may veto, change or impose objectives. Regardless of the degree of participation in objective-setting, the important factor is for both people to have a shared expectation of what needs to be done during the next planning cycle. Roslund (1989) suggests that then it is necessary for both to periodically review progress towards the objectives, and where necessary to make adjustments in their priority or scope or in the actions taken in pursuit of them. At the Ritz-Carlton Hotel, every day each department that directly serves customers receives and discusses Service Quality Scores from the previous day and how they compare with set targets. The objective is to reduce sources of guest dissatisfaction and increase employee pride in their work.

Limitations versus benefits

MBO works well if there is respect and trust between the subordinate and manager, and if the subordinate keeps the manager informed of progress and setbacks. If the relationship is strained or adversarial, or if MBO is required by the organisation but not accepted by a manager, then the process is risky. Authoritarian managers seldom change their style and can use objectives as a club. Formula-driven MBO may also reduce flexibility, increase conflict, diminish innovation and consume time. Moreover, according to Kelly (1983), in a worst-case scenario some jobs just do not have sufficient flexibility for a person's motivation and ability to affect performance.

Although the concept of MBO is widely known to managers and has been used by about half the large corporations, research suggests the success rate is lower than anticipated (Schuster and Kindall, 1974). As also found in the total quality management (TQM) movement, substance can give way to form when a practice is forced on managers without really becoming part of their working philosophy. However, for managers who believe that a shared understanding of priorities is an important precursor of action, MBO can focus and guide behaviours. Seyna (1986) suggests that, from an equity viewpoint, it also means that performance reviews and reward processes can be based on results rather than personal characteristics or extraneous variables.

Goals should be clear, specific, challenging

Dangot-Simkin (1991) proposes that to activate energetic, task-focused behaviour, a person needs clear, specific and challenging goals. Especially when delegating tasks, managers should describe clearly what is wanted and provide specific feedback as to the appropriateness of work being done. Suggestions on how to write goals that satisfy clear, specific, challenging criteria are offered in Exhibit 6-2.

Here are two brief examples of complete operational objectives.

1 To decrease time lost by equipment failure to no more than 10 minutes per day during the next quarter.

2 To develop marketing forecasts on the gamma product line acceptable to the CEO by December 1.

Source: demonstrated by Edward J. Harrick at a USAID-sponsored organisation development workshop in Bombay, India.

For example, Rose Banks, assistant director of human resources for a large insurance company, was concerned that Ed Tran, her manager of training and development, had been using too many contract training programmes from outside consultants and trainers, programmes that were not central to company needs. During a performance review with Tran 18 months ago, Banks stated, 'Next year your staff needs to develop and deliver more in-company training for sales agents and cut back on off-the-shelf contract programmes.'

During the review a year later, Banks expressed disappointment that courses originated by the training staff accounted for only 30 per cent of the total, although she acknowledged this was up almost 5 per cent. She decided to be more explicit: 'Ed, for this next year I want you to target 60 per cent of your training days for staff-delivered programmes and only 40 per cent for outside vendors. You develop a plan for achieving it, and let's review it and then meet monthly to review progress towards that plan and the milestones you set.' Six months later, Tran was ahead of plan and close to a 50–50 milestone. Participant satisfaction ratings were up nearly 25 per cent, a major improvement in the quality of sales training. Banks celebrated the progress by taking Tran and his group to a celebration luncheon.

EXHIBIT 6–2 *Four steps to writing clear goals*

Goals need to be clear, specific and challenging, and one way to achieve this is to write operational objectives. A four-step approach is suggested, as follows.

1 Begin with an *action verb* preceded by the word 'to'. Examples: To build, To complete, To present, To learn, To improve, To decrease, To prevent, To sell.

2 Identify a relevant *key result area* that is the performance target. Examples: customer service, reports, orders, inventory, accidents, attendance, accounts receivable.

3 State a *performance indicator* or *measurement standard* that specifies the targeted degree of quality and quantity to be achieved. Indicators can be stated in monetary units, resource units consumed, average time per task, percentages or changes.

4 Provide a *time frame* by or during which the key result will be produced. Examples: by Friday noon, by the 15th of each month, each week, one week before the IRS deadline.

The incident between Banks and Tran demonstrates the complex impact of participation in goal-setting. When initially given freedom to set his own goals, Tran failed to make the shift Banks was apparently looking for. Tran was then assigned an ambitious goal by his boss, but he was responsible for planning how to achieve the target, and did so.

Modifying behaviour with reinforcement

A goal requires cognitive or mental involvement by those who pursue it. Let's now consider reinforcement, a less cognitive-dependent technique to modify or shape desired behaviours. **Reinforcement** is the process of managing behaviour by having a contingent consequence follow a behaviour with the intent of promoting a consistent pattern of behavioural responses (Kazdin, 1975). Reinforcement is the product of a *behaviourism* philosophy, meaning that behaviour is believed to be shaped by environmental consequences.

reinforcement
The use of contingent consequences following a behaviour to shape a consistent behaviour pattern.

There are different types of reinforcement, each designed to promote a specific behavioural response. The buzzing of an alarm clock may send you promptly hopping out of bed to catch a plane or to meet a friend if you anticipate positive consequences. The identical sound may be greeted with less enthusiasm, but may still produce the same on-time behaviour if you aim to avoid a negative consequence, such as a late start on an exam or a reprimand for turning up late at work. The first incident is an example of positive reinforcement – pleasant consequences to promote a desired behaviour. The second reflects negative reinforcement – potentially adverse consequences where the desire to avoid something unpleasant promotes the desired behaviour. It is possible for the same behaviour to be motivated by very different consequences.

Behaviour modification follows an ABC sequence

Management applications of reinforcement theory rest on the assumption that people in positions of authority can be taught to use environmental consequences to stimulate and shape the behaviours of others. While a somewhat questionable assumption, authorities such as teachers and managers who use reinforcement to shape the behaviours of others apply an $A① \to B① \to C$ *model* structured around *antecedent, behaviour* and *consequence.*

Antecedent

A represents the antecedent condition or cue that precedes a set of behaviour alternatives – the stimulus or circumstance that invites a desired behaviour. The traffic light turning amber, the alarm clock ringing, the manager asking for a report, a calendar note reminder of a noon luncheon meeting – these are all antecedent conditions.

Behaviour

B is the behaviour in response to the antecedent circumstance. Applying the car brakes rather than speeding up, getting out of bed rather than going back to sleep, submitting a comprehensive report on time rather than saying 'I was too busy', or showing up for the noon meeting on time – these behaviours represent the desired responses to the antecedent cues.

Consequence

C represents an environmental consequence that is contingent on an appropriate behaviour. As noted in Exhibit 6-3, the most common consequence is *positive reinforcement* of a desired

Royal Bank of Scotland Business Banking: using technology to increase business and develop staff

With several hundred years of history behind it, Royal Bank of Scotland (RBS) has few problems in persuading businesses that it is a reputable and secure provider of their banking needs. The greater challenge is to demonstrate to customers that it is flexible and responsive enough to serve their twenty-first century needs.

The way RBS Business Banking has met this challenge persuaded judges that it should be Highly Commended in the Unisys Management Today Service Excellence Awards.

Based in Edinburgh, RBS provides banking services to businesses throughout the UK via its branch network. Most customer contact is conducted through relationship managers based in individual branches, who receive the backing of central support staff at the Scottish HQ.

In this competitive and politically sensitive market, RBS has devised a number of approaches that are quite unique. For example, its mentor consulting service provides business customers with advice on employment law, health and safety issues and taxation, helping smaller enterprises in particular to cope with the ever-growing burden of red tape.

A priority for RBS has been to make it easy for business customers to do business with the bank. To this end they can contact their relationship manager by direct line, mobile phone and email; if a relationship manager is on holiday, the nearest colleague becomes his or her 'buddy' and deals with a customer during the manager's absence. The bank's research suggested that business customers like continuity, so RBS introduced a four-year tenure for managers.

RBS was also first to the market with Internet banking for business; and there is a further alternative for those who want access to their bank at any time of the day or night: a 24-hour phone-based service called Direct Banking for Business. The focus on customers has been a driving force in the way RBS recruits and develops its own people. The bank's policy here is to 'hire the smile, train the skill', believing that all employees should be developed beyond mere competency to a higher level. Newly inducted staff now go through a 'customer service review' to find out what it is like to be on the other side of the desk, asking to borrow money.

A further innovation is a diploma in customer relationship management (CRM), which the bank has instituted for relationship managers – believed to be the first in the industry.

RBS Business Banking impressed the judges with its use of technology and internal communications, including a dedicated Business TV channel, and its willingness to learn from elsewhere, through its Service Masterclass benchmarking visits and talks from other organisations.

Moira Clark, director CRM Research Forum at the Cranfield School of Management and one of the judges, commented: 'Few banks manage to develop and maintain mutually trusting and profitable relationships with their business customers, and what impressed me at RBS was the sincerity in what they do. The way they individually counselled farmers during the foot and mouth crisis, and have put managers in place for four years to establish continuity are both excellent examples of building lasting relationships.' By doing this RBS also demonstrates that it is able to retain and develop staff.

Source: adapted from *Management Today*, September 2001, Unisys Service Excellence Awards.

Discussion questions

1 Why is training important when motivating staff?

2 How can improved communication help with staff development?

> ### EXHIBIT 6-3 Four common reinforcers
>
> The objective of reinforcement is to apply consequences (reinforcers) following a behaviour that will shape a patterned response to a given antecedent condition.
>
> 1 **Positive reinforcers** – pleasant, rewarding or otherwise satisfying contingent consequences, that are used to initiate or increase a desired behaviour. They should increase in frequency as the desired behaviour increases. Praise and tangible rewards or gifts are positive reinforcers widely used at work. So are more attractive office space, a more prestigious job title, extra time off and off-site meetings at resorts.
>
> 2 **Negative reinforcers** – the removal or reduction of an aversive condition following a desired behaviour to initiate or increase the desired behaviour. The contingent consequence of the desired behaviour is relief or escape from something unpleasant, threatening or dissatisfying. Negative reinforcement is at work when one person acts to avoid another's wrath or ridicule or to prevent personal harm. It keeps us paying our bills on time and obeying the speed limit.
>
> 3 **Punishment** – an aversive event or the removal of a positive event following a behaviour, designed to reduce the frequency of the behaviour or to eliminate it altogether. Punishment in the workplace is less severe than in the criminal justice system and may involve warnings, withdrawal of privileges or assignment to unpleasant tasks. The most severe punishment is probably dismissal.
>
> 4 **Omission** – a completely neutral response to a negative behaviour to encourage its diminishment. It is often the ideal response to chronic complainers and others with annoying habits, such as telling offensive jokes.
>
> *Source*: Lee W. Frederikson (ed.) (1982), *Handbook of Organizational Behavior Management*. New York, NY: John Wiley & Sons. Reprinted by permission of John Wiley & Sons, Inc.

behaviour, such as public praise from the manager for submitting an analytically sound and persuasive report. At times the consequence is *negative reinforcement* of a desired behaviour, which reduces or avoids a potential negative outcome. Negative reinforcement occurs when a person shows up on time for work to avoid having his or her pay docked. *Punishment* is used to decrease an undesired behaviour (for example, when a police officer gives a speeding ticket to a motorist). *Omission* – a neutral response to either a desired *or* undesired behaviour – also tends

law of effect

The principle that the consequences of behaviour should be immediate to reinforce the link between the two.

to diminish offending behaviour, such as ignoring someone who tries to be a comedian at a meeting.

The **law of effect** advocates that consequences should immediately follow behaviour in order to reinforce the link between the two. With repeated reinforcement over time the desired behaviour becomes systematic.

Managing environments with organisational behaviour modification (OB mod)

Luthans and Kreitner (1985) suggest that when managers deliberately apply the $A① \rightarrow B② \rightarrow C$

organisational behaviour modification (OB mod)

Deliberate management application of the antecedent → behaviour → consequence sequence to shape desired employee behaviours.

sequence to shape the behaviour of others, they are applying what is popularly called **organisational behaviour modification**, or **OB mod** for short. OB mod is potentially useful in improving tangible, observable, measurable, repeatable behaviours (behaviours that are typically different from the goals included in MBO). It has been found to help reduce absenteeism, reduce substandard output, increase total output, decrease costs and

improve safety (by increasing the number of accident-free days).

Komake (1982) recognises that, although simple in principle, OB mod is difficult to apply consistently in most organisational settings if it is left to the manager to apply the contingent reinforcer. Managers often lack systematic control over the workplace environment. Also, it is no easy task to apply timely consequences that are reasonably free from distortion by extraneous feedback. For this reason, some of the most significant behaviour modification programmes rely on automatic, computer-generated feedback.

In fact, feedback alone has been found by O'Hara *et al.* (1985) to be a very useful reinforcer, eliminating the need for any tangible rewards (or punishments). Computer networks are useful in providing employees with up-to-date reports of current output compared to past statistics. These reports serve to reinforce acceptable results. Research into FTSE 500 companies, by Howat (2002), has shown that IT service management has had a 70 per cent increase in improved performance to customers by highlighting specific problem areas.

Research focus: **principles of behaviour modification**

To apply the principles of behaviour modification using other than automatic feedback requires planning a multi-step process that typically begins with data collection to establish a baseline. This process is best demonstrated with an example. Examine in Exhibit 6-4 the steps of a programme described by Luthans and Martinko (1976) to modify a common organisational problem – absenteeism. (According to Steers and Rhodes (1991), it is estimated that each year millions of work days are lost because of employee absenteeism – about five days per employee.) On a more descriptive level, here are the four key processes that are typically employed when implementing an OB mod programme to reinforce behaviour change.

1 **Establish baseline data.** To provide a point of reference, measure or chart the frequency with which the undesirable behaviour occurs in the normal, unmodified environment. In many problem situations (absenteeism is only one), existing records will provide an historic database. Frequencies of absence should be charted according to the day of the week, department and other relevant benchmarks. The objective is to document the problem behaviour in a way that reveals the circumstances under which it most frequently occurs.

2 **Analyse current behavioural contingencies.** Examine the current environment to identify any antecedent cues that encourage or discourage the desired behaviour. Interviews, group discussions or a survey, are likely to reveal the circumstances that affect attendance. Absenteeism cues might include group norms that encourage or discourage attendance, patterns of family illness, substance abuse, marital problems, lack of daycare for children, availability of transportation, lack of an alarm clock, or even the day of the week (Mondays are notorious). Further investigation may show that punitive measures already taken have not worked. If absenteeism increases following a reprimand, the warning may actually have reinforced the undesirable behaviour (which may be seen as a way of gaining attention or getting even).

3 **Develop a reinforcement strategy.** Those responsible for correcting the problem evaluate possible reinforcers and select the one(s) thought to be most conducive to improving behaviour. According to Frayne and Latham (1987), three factors should be considered in structuring a reinforcement programme.

- The reinforcer selected should be meaningful enough to increase the desired behaviour and offset the competing reinforcers (of absenteeism).

- The reinforcers should follow timely evidence of improved behaviour to cement the cause-and-effect relationship.

- Criteria for achieving the reinforcer should be realistic, directly related (to attendance), attainable by most employees and less expensive than the cost (of absences).

If groups are generally cohesive (meaning people stick together and respect one another), some form of group reward might be appropriate. Some companies allow groups to finish early on Fridays or to build points towards a monthly beer and pizza celebration for perfect group attendance. To reward individuals the company might pick up more of the cost of health benefits currently borne by the employee. Alternatively, individuals could accumulate points towards a lottery of prizes. Interestingly, a one-in-four chance at a £16 prize has as much reinforcement effect as the certainty of receiving £4. The lottery idea is an example of intermittent, or variable, ratio reinforcement.

4 **Implement the reinforcement and chart results.** A management team might start with posting attendance records and giving praise as a modest first step. If results are not as strong as desired, the managers could move to one of the more substantive reinforcement plans noted above. As attendance improves the schedule of reinforcement may be shifted to an interval or ratio basis until behaviours become self-reinforcing.

OB mod requires a systematic planning and strategy process based on data, analysis and contingent reinforcement. The goal is to establish a desired $A \textcircled{1} \rightarrow B \textcircled{1} \rightarrow C$ sequence.

EXHIBIT 6 – 4 Steps in organisational behaviour modification

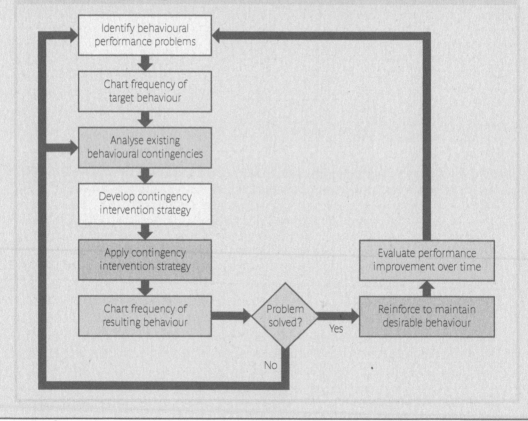

An example of a shift from a continuous (daily) to an intermittent reinforcement ratio is shown in Exhibit 6-5, which examines how muffins and bagels were used to reward and reinforce punctuality.

It is also possible for a person to manage his or her own contingencies. As explained in the previous chapter, one common principle of time management is to quickly complete 'have to' tasks and then reward yourself by doing something more enjoyable or satisfying.

Remember – this is known as the *Premack principle*, which means that pleasurable tasks or events are paired with less pleasurable tasks to encourage completion of the latter (Premack, 1959). You may find yourself adopting this principle of self-management without even being aware that it has a name and research support, when you complete a task assignment before engaging in, say, an athletic activity.

Beware the danger of rewarding *A* while hoping for *B*

Kohn (1993) argues that reinforcement practices in industry are controversial; for some industry observers, any form of reward manipulates at best a temporary change in behaviour (more about this in the next section). More generally, what management wants, what it rewards, and what it gets from employees are not always the same: 'If innovation is espoused, but doing things by the book is what is rewarded, it doesn't take a psychologist to figure out what the firm actually values' (O'Reilly, 1992). This all too common practice was originally documented by Kerr (1975) in examples ranging from battlefields to orphanages.

Universities typically say they emphasise teaching, but most of the rewards they grant are linked to research, and faculties quickly learn where to channel their energy for maximum payoff. Businesses often say they want to take care of their customers, and then reward managers for cutting costs in ways that negatively impact customers. The lesson is that often, without thinking, managers reinforce the wrong behaviour. Such errors in judgement suggest that the selective use of rewards should be well thought out if the intent is to motivate employees to behave congruently with managerial expectations.

EXHIBIT 6 – 5 OB mod example: the early birds get the goods

Carol King, director of a public health clinic associated with a US midwestern state university, was concerned about the tardiness of her part-time staff. Early morning was a busy time, since the clinic opened at 7.30 am and many students sought to obtain services before their 9.00 am classes. Seven graduate students worked as counsellors, staffing the reception and intake desks. These part-time employees had the annoying habit of drifting in any time between 7.30 and 8.30. King tried pleas and then warnings; she even docked pay cheques to discourage tardiness, but none of these methods worked.

Then King decided to experiment with positive reinforcement. At 7.00 one Monday morning, she arrived with two dozen assorted muffins and bagels and placed them next to the coffee pot in the staffroom. She set up a small, hand-lettered sign:

GOOD MORNING, EARLY BIRDS!
HELP YOURSELF TO THE GOODIES.
– CAROL KING

Promptly at 7.30 am, King removed all unclaimed baked goods but left the sign. Staff members who arrived early or on time that day were rewarded unexpectedly; those who were late saw only the sign. On Tuesday there were more muffins and bagels. Again, any not claimed were promptly removed at 7.30. By Wednesday, six of the morning staff arrived on time, partly out of curiosity to see if the goodies would be there. King said nothing about punctuality all week.

A muffin or bagel on one's desk soon became a status symbol – 'here works an early bird'. During the second week, King began to skip a day or two between muffin or bagel deliveries. This, too, was an effective procedure. The uncertainty of intermittent reinforcement kept tardiness at a low level during the remainder of the year.

Source: thanks to a communication from one of the early birds.

The link between rewards and behaviour

Bob Clark began working for Wal-Mart, Asda's American owner, as a truck driver in 1972, when the firm had only 15 drivers. He remembers attending a safety meeting during his first month, during which founder Sam Walton proclaimed, 'If you'll just stay with me for 20 years, I guarantee you'll have £75,000 in profit sharing.' Clark thought to himself at the time, 'Big deal. Bob Clark never will see that kind of money in his life.'

Twenty years later, he told Sam Walton (now deceased): 'Well, last time I checked, I had £500 000 in profit sharing, and I see no reason why it won't go up again ... When folks ask me how I like working for Wal-Mart ... I tell them about my profit sharing and ask them, "How do you think I feel about Wal-Mart?"' (Walton, 1992).

The realisation of a consistent build-up of monetary rewards increased Bob Clark's commitment to Wal-Mart. However, generalised rewards (such as profit sharing) only indirectly related to one's personal actions do not necessarily equitably reinforce individual (or team) task-appropriate behaviours. This may seem illogical, but remember: reinforcement occurs only when some form of consequence increases a desired behaviour or decreases an undesired one. If there is no observable change in behaviour following a reward, reinforcement has not occurred.

Economic and symbolic 'rewards' intended to act as reinforcers frequently fall short of the mark. Sometimes they have no impact, as though employees are saying to themselves, as Bob Clark originally did, 'Big deal.' At other times they may have the opposite impact from that desired (managers follow the folly of rewarding A while hoping for B). As expectancy and equity theories of motivation suggested in Chapter 5, symbolic rewards such as certificates and recognition luncheons may lead the recipient to question, 'Is this all I get for all that I've done?' Feelings of being under-appreciated can then lead to a slacking off, where the consequences produce a behaviour that is contrary to that intended (McFarlin and Sweeney, 1992).

Performance means behaviour has been evaluated

Whenever systematic performance objectives, appraisals and rewards are lacking in an organisation, members usually experience three emotions:

1 ambiguity – Exactly what is expected of me as an employee?

2 Uncertainty – How well am I performing or measuring up to my boss's expectations?

3 suspicion – Are promotions and rewards (or lay-offs and discharges) being administered equitably around here?

Many kinds of behaviours occur throughout an organisation. However, a collection of behaviours does not necessarily produce performance results. Campbell *et al.* (1973) emphasise: 'Behaviour is simply what people do in the course of work (e.g. dictating letters, giving directions, sweeping the floor). **Performance** is behaviour that has been evaluated (e.g. measured) in terms of its contribution to the goals of the organisation.'

performance
Behaviour that has been evaluated or measured as to its contribution to organisational goals.

The overarching goal is to make as many behaviours as possible be performance contributors to specific goals. Previously we said that performance can be evaluated on the basis of productivity (including quality), growth and satisfaction. Ivancevich (1979) argues that research has yet to confirm clearly causality in the performance–satisfaction relationship. That is, we do not yet know with a high level of confidence if performance causes satisfaction or vice versa, or if the two occur simultaneously.

Although individuals differ in their sources of motivation, the manager who systematically sets performance objectives, monitors outcomes and administers reinforcement or rewards, is more likely to stimulate task-directed performance than the manager who does not.

The concept of pay-for-performance rewards

As firms moved into mass production and mass distribution during the industrial era, compensation systems followed suit. They became more impersonal, moving towards standardisation just like the products being produced. Most employees over the last half-century have been paid on the basis of non-performance factors, such as their job classification, pay grade, hours worked and/or seniority. Uniform systems of pay may seem equitable but from a motivational perspective such non-performance payments do not necessarily encourage stellar performance. One could even claim they are not equitable because the best performer gets compensated the same as the worst performer.

By the mid-1990s, nearly 60 per cent of firms participating in a national compensation survey were offering 'results-sharing' programmes. The Walt Disney Company began offering an annual bonus programme for animators, directors and producers who work on its profitable animated movies. A majority of its employees receives bonuses based on division profitability. Moreover, in the executive suite, after years of defending shareholder charges of 'fat cat' salaries, corporations are aggressively linking executive pay to performance. Although the recent bonus paid to the CEO of Vodafone, which recently made a massive loss, does little to reassure investors.

A major performance benchmark for CEOs is the firm's stock performance, and boards of directors do cut back on bonus payments when per-share earnings or stock price decline. When Quaker Oats stock fell by 13 per cent, CEO William D. Smithburg received an 11 per cent cut in salary and bonus to £1 million. Such a scenario, with fluctuating rewards, is becoming more commonplace. Nevertheless, every year there are hundreds of annual shareholder meetings where shareholders protest against increases in executive compensation that race ahead of profit performance.

As competitiveness across industries became global, the norm for systems of rewards incorporated more pay-for-performance factors. Performance-based compensation schemes are consistent with the expectancy theory of motivation. Employees compare rewards received for performance with what they expect to receive (just as investors compare a firm's quarterly profit performance with financial analysts' projections – and immediately reward or punish the stock price depending on whether expectations were satisfied). They also compare what they receive with what others receive (the equity factor). Overall, satisfaction is likely to be a composite of how the employee perceives both the extrinsic and intrinsic rewards from the job (Lawler, 1981).

Piecework or standard-hour systems

piecework
The practice of rewarding performance by paying for the amount produced consistent with quality standards.

The classic performance-based reward system is based on **piecework**, or payment for the amount produced consistent with specified quality standards. Piecework systems work when a person can directly affect his or her rate of output, and the output (quality and quantity) can easily be measured or verified. Some programmers' pay depends on how many lines of code they write; magazine writers are often paid by the number of words in their articles; shirtmakers in developing countries are paid a few cents for each shirt they sew.

A pay-for-performance variation is to use a *standard-hour plan*. Such plans specify the normal time required to complete a task, coupled with a standard rate of pay. For example, the standard for a dental hygienist to clean a patient's teeth may be 45 minutes at a rate of £25. The more skilful technician may be able to serve more patients per day, receiving pay for each at the standard rate.

The difficult issues in any piece- or standard-rate plan are twofold. One is evaluating work methods to arrive at an equitable standard and rate; since managers like to adjust periodically one or both compensation factors, the issue of equity can be controversial. The second concern is the quality–quantity trade-off. Without appropriate controls, quality may be sacrificed to reach quantity targets. As previously noted, behaviour tends to focus on what is measured (Hammer, 1975).

Merit pay ties performance to add-on rewards

Rather than tie pay only to output, an alternative is to provide a base salary or hourly wage and then an incentive or bonus based on output. Where the base plus merit incentive system is used, the performance-based portion depends on some measurable level of output over which the employee has control. Output could be measured by volume, defect rate (or quality) or cost savings. Sales representatives often earn a base salary plus commission based on the level of sales above a set base figure. Intranet-based performance tracking systems now allow firms to provide real-time rewards for salespeople who serve clients better rather than just close deals.

Bonus and profit-sharing plans

Many compensation plans are based on the overall performance of the enterprise rather than the individual's contribution. Profit sharing has become common in many firms, including the John Lewis Partnership, where everyone owns stock and profits are distributed back to members. In merit-based pay plans a pool of money is divided among eligible employees based on some performance evaluation or rating system. The objective of merit plans such as profit sharing, bonuses and stock options is to link everyone's fate to overall performance, reinforcing corporate cultures that emphasise group results over individual performance.

For the John Lewis Partnership, profit sharing is a major part of employee compensation. Every employee who has worked for at least a year is eligible for profit sharing. The firm contributes a percentage of every eligible employee's wages or salary. This makes the organisation one of the leading retail employers in the country and this reflected in the quality of service received in any of the Partnership's stores.

In recent years, directors' compensation packages have been loaded with bonuses and stock option add-ons often totalling several times base salary. However, shareholders are revolting against greedy CEOs. There is a realisation that people who work for money are not always effective and that the best CEOs are those who have developed a good reputation by doing the right things. They are likely to have a checklist in their back pocket that represents their set of personal ethics: Is it right? Is it good for customers and employees?

Beyond line managers, companies have also sought to link the compensation of directors to company performance, believing that money motivates. Graef Crystal, a compensation specialist, reports that firms as diverse as the Body Shop and Johnson & Johnson have devised plans to compensate outside board members in company stock. The assumption is that significant equity ownership assures high motivation to safeguard corporate interests. However, will outside directors really change their behaviour? Based on stock price changes, Crystal (1995) selected 15 high-performing companies and 15 low performers. His question and answer:

> Is there any evidence to suggest that companies in which outside directors own lots of stock outperform companies in which outside directors own little stock? The answer is an unequivocal 'no'.... No matter what the time period chosen ... there was simply no significant statistical association between outside director shareholdings and subsequent company performance.

Gainsharing plans

Gainsharing is an umbrella term for approaches to encourage employees at all levels to be responsible for improving organisational efficiency. According to Welbourne and Gomez-Mejia (1995), **gainsharing** plans link financial rewards for all employees to improvements in performance of the entire business unit. One survey by Markam *et al.* (1992) of 10 000 members of the Society for Human Resource Management found that gainsharing is used in all industries, including the public sector. Another, by Alexander (1992), concluded that for the 1990s, except for healthcare, gainsharing was the most important human resource topic, more important than work design, managing diversity and other issues. Exhibit 6-6 lists several reasons why gainsharing is increasing in popularity as a motivational incentive, to be made available to all employees in an organisational unit.

gainsharing
A pay-for-performance system that shares financial rewards among all employees based on performance improvements for the entire business unit.

Panhandle Eastern Corporation introduced gainsharing following deregulation of the natural gas industry in an effort to make employees more cost and profit conscious. In its plan, if the company achieves earnings per share of £1.50, all Panhandle employees receive a bonus of 2 per cent of their salary at year-end. For earnings of £1.60 or more per share, the bonus climbs to 3 per cent. Panhandle's gainsharing expectancies reach all organisational levels.

EXHIBIT 6–6 Why gainsharing plans are growing in use

Survey research reveals seven fundamental reasons why gainsharing continues to grow in popularity as a pay-for-performance strategy.

1 The basic design of jobs is undergoing fundamental change from individuals to teams.

2 Other pay-for-performance systems often lead to disappointing results, especially those that reward individuals (because of the difficulty of untangling individual performance from the contributions of other employees).

3 Gainsharing is easy to sell to top management because financial payouts are generally modest and employees share proportionately with the organisation the gains of targeted performance improvements.

4 Gainsharing has a long history, which makes it easy to imitate successful plans.

5 There are many consulting firms that specialise in helping organisations implement gainsharing (and several governmental commissions in the United States and Canada have advocated its widespread implementation).

6 Gainsharing provides flexibility in choosing pay-off criteria from such diverse factors as profitability, labour costs, material savings, safety records, reject rates, meeting deadlines and customer satisfaction.

7 Gainsharing complements the move towards participative management and employee involvement, as many plans incorporate committee structures to evaluate and act on employee recommendations.

Source: Theresa M. Welbourne and Luis R. Gomez-Mejia (1995) 'Gainsharing: A Critical Review and a Future Research Agenda', *Journal of Management* 21, September, pp. 559 ff. Copyright 1999, with permission from Elsevier Science.

Randy Watson, a mailroom employee, has cut mailing costs 43 per cent simply by changing 'rush' delivery times to arrive at 10.30 a.m. the next day instead of 10.00 a.m.

Rewards as a cafeteria of benefits

One method for skirting around the complexities of equitable performance evaluations and merit compensation while maintaining sensitivity to expectancy motivation is to offer cafeteria-style benefits. Historically compensation was based on the belief that one size fits all, that people could be uniformly rewarded. Today's increasingly popular practice is to let people select from among a portfolio, or menu, of benefits.

With his non-working wife and three children, Arthur may be quite concerned that he has comprehensive family medical coverage with minimum deductions. Fellicia, single and in her early twenties, might opt for increased holiday allowances and paid study fees in exchange for an increased payment to her pension plan. Such flexibility in selecting benefits, while not necessarily related to employee output, helps promote a positive answer to the expectancy question, 'Do I value the rewards available to me?'

Individuals want and need different things from their employment. Discover your own preferences by completing the 'Your turn' exercise. Then compare your profile to the profile of a cross-section of employees shown in Exhibit 6-7.

Your turn

What do you want from your job?

Rank the following 16 work-related rewards and outcomes from 1 (most important) to 16 (least important) to you.

Good health insurance and other benefits	_____
Interesting work	_____
Job security	_____
Opportunity to learn new skills	_____
Having a week or more of vacation	_____
Being able to work independently	_____
Recognition from co-workers	_____
Regular hours (no weekends, no nights)	_____
Having a job in which you can help others	_____
Limiting job stress	_____
High income	_____
Working close to home	_____
Work that is important to society	_____
Chances for promotion	_____
Contact with a lot of people	_____
Flexible hours	_____

Interpretation Compare your rankings with the scores reported in Exhibit 6-7. What factors can you control to increase the probability of satisfaction?

EXHIBIT 6–7   What employees want from their work

The most important things workers look for in their employment do not necessarily cost the firm money. Providing 'interesting work' (rated no. 2) is inherently less costly for many firms than paying a 'high income' (rated no. 11). These data were collected by the Gallup Poll of Princeton, NJ, from a cross-section of employees in differing industries and jobs. The figures reflect responses to the questions: How important is each of the following characteristics to you? How satisfied are you with it in your current job?

	Percentage of workers who said they:	
	ranked it as very important	were satisfied
Good health insurance and other benefits	81%	27%
Interesting work	78	41
Job security	78	35
Opportunity to learn new skills	68	31
Having a week or more of vacation	66	35
Being able to work independently	64	42
Recognition from co-workers	62	24
Regular hours (no weekends, no nights)	58	40
Having a job in which you can help others	58	34
Limiting job stress	58	17
High income	56	13
Working close to home	55	46
Work that is important to society	53	35
Chances for promotion	53	20
Contact with a lot of people	52	45
Flexible hours	49	39

The average 'importance' of each characteristic is 61.8%, whereas the average 'satisfaction' is only 32.8%. Employers have a long way to go in closing this expectation–satisfaction gap. (Be aware, though, that this poll aggregates the answers of people in many types of jobs, so its averages should not parallel your own, except by chance.)

Source: reprinted with permission, *Inc.* magazine, November 1992. Copyright 1992 by Goldhirsh Group, Inc., 38 Commercial Wharf, Boston, MA 02110.

Controversial consequences of incentives and rewards

Beyond making differential pay adjustments among employees, managers can adjust rewards by varying the assignments they hand out, the praise (or reprimands) they give, the equipment or offices they provide, and the special privileges they grant. Nevertheless, rewards that bear no relationship to personal or team performance invite people to redirect and/or reduce their effort. One typical response by people who experience inequities is to engage more in activities they enjoy than in those that need to be done. Little wonder that managers believe performance should be the most important determinant of compensation, whether the reward is a salary increase or bonus (Lawler, 1966). However, controversy typically surrounds pay plans that rely heavily on performance-based compensation.

Except in cases where performance can easily be measured, employees often believe that the person evaluating them relies too much on subjective judgement. With subjective assessments, they question the fairness of merit pay (as do many trades unions). Even though team-based reward plans that provide for gainsharing when groups accomplish strategic goals are on the increase, issues of fairness and equity make them troublesome to administer (Ost, 1990). Therefore, some managers try to alter a group's perception that it is treated inequitably. For example, managers might present results of a wage and salary survey of comparable jobs that shows the company pays in the top 10 per cent of all firms surveyed. Although employees may still desire more money, their opinion of their employer will be more favourable.

On a more general level, some view the use of rewards as unethical and dysfunctional. Research by Kohn (1993) found that, 'Most managers too often believe in the redemptive power of rewards' even though some research finds that 'rewards typically undermine the very processes they are intended to enhance'. He further claims, 'Incentives do not alter the attitudes that underlie our behaviours. . . . Rewards do not create a lasting commitment. They merely, and temporarily, change what we do.' In effect, Kohn views rewards as 'bribes' and concludes, 'Do rewards motivate people? Absolutely. They motivate people to get rewards.' Cumming (1994), however, claims that Kohn's somewhat valid criticism of behaviourist theory (behaviour modification) when generalised to all forms of rewards and incentives is unsubstantiated.

Certainly when placed within a cross-cultural perspective, employees in some countries find the concept of rewards for performance confusing. In Australia such policies tend to be reserved only for top executives, where the rank and file prefer to do their work and expect to be paid on an hourly or salary basis – they accept responsibility to work, so why pay them more for doing their job? In one policy initiative to provide financial rewards to highly paid government managers, the concept was strongly resisted by the armed forces (who were originally to have been included). To them, pay for performance simply made no sense to an officer performing his or her duty.

While goals, incentives and rewards can energise and focus behaviour in some countries, there are potential pitfalls in using them as motivational systems: quality may be traded off for quantity and vice versa, dysfunctional inertia may occur if employees cling to ineffectual methods rather than innovate, and behaviours may be focused on the goal only to the detriment of other activities. People may also believe the end justifies the means and engage in illegal or unethical behaviours – as occurred when Kwik-Fit employees overcharged customers for unnecessary repairs when the retailer instituted product-specific quotas, commissions and standard job pay rates (Wright, 1994). Because such potential drawbacks are associated more with individualised reward plans, many organisations are abandoning individual and departmental pay-for-performance plans in favour of more simplified plans focused on total business performance (Nulty, 1995).

In addition to or instead of the difficulty in achieving equity balance among complex compensation plans, some organisations have begun to open their books to employees. **Open book management** is the practice of sharing with all employees the essential financial information of the organisation, often including details on salaries and compensation packages. Ken Anderson of Anderson & Associates, a 170-employee firm that designs roads and government infrastructure projects, learned that a big advantage in opening the books to all within the organisation was trust-building:

open book management
The practice of sharing key financial information, often including salaries and compensation, with all employees.

There was widespread fear and consternation in our company when we decided to put all our financial information, including salaries, on our wide area network (WAN) in 1987 and then on our intranet in the early 90s. People feared our competitors would get the numbers and use them against us – scare our clients, steal our employees.... But that just hasn't happened. And I don't believe it will.... I can't say we're more profitable because of OBM ... but we do have a great deal of trust here, and our employees stick with us. (Anderson, 1999)

The key factors in job design

Beyond practices that emphasise goals and rewards, behavioural scientists have for decades concluded that the design of a person's job has significant motivational impact on behaviour.

job design
The process of incorporating tasks and responsibilities into meaningful, productive, satisfying job responsibilities.

Job design is the process of incorporating tasks and responsibilities into jobs to make them meaningful, productive and satisfying. During much of the past century job design was the responsibility of managers and industrial engineers, who emphasised productivity over meaningfulness or satisfaction. One could even make the claim that managerial work did not begin to be respected as a profession, until bosses recognised that factory jobs could be designed and structured into specific tasks to make it easier for managers to supervise the work of others.

As described in Chapter 1, one of the breakthrough practices of the early twentieth century was scientific management. Scientific management, advocated by Frederick W. Taylor, provided a methodology to structure highly specialised jobs, which simplified hiring, training and supervising people with the requisite capabilities. Once trained, the manager's job was to see to it that all those reporting to him were performing according to defined job standards. Scientific management provided an orderliness to the work of organisations (Wrenge and Perroni, 1974). It helped fuel the rise of large businesses producing high volumes of standardised goods – everything from textiles to breakfast cereal to cars and radios.

scientific management
An early twentieth-century methodology advocated by Frederick W. Taylor in which work tasks were structured into highly simplified, standardised jobs to simplify hiring, training and supervision.

In keeping with the principles of scientific management, job design has historically involved analysing a complex task, then breaking it down into specific subtasks. One or more of these specific subtasks or jobs are then combined into departmental work units, where managers oversee the work of employees (Hammer, 1990). Managers are responsible for staffing jobs with competent people, then holding their people accountable for carrying out the assigned tasks. In the hotel industry, for example, specific jobs are clustered into specific responsibility units such as front desk, housekeeping, food and beverage.

This manager-in-charge, 'command and control' approach worked reasonably well during the first three-quarters of the twentieth century, when most jobs were readily defined. Today, however, industrial growth comes more from flexible, smaller firms (or divisions of diversified large firms) than from large producers of mass commodities. Giants such as IBM, GM and others have become painfully aware of this trend (Miller, 1992). In Chapter 15 you will learn that, increasingly, responsibility for the design of work is shifting to the workers themselves and to self-managed teams, rather than residing with managers or industrial engineers. Nevertheless, there are some fundamental concepts involved in designing jobs, whether for individuals or teams, guided by the objective of improving work motivation and performance.

Task scope and task depth

Two typical dimensions used for defining or describing all types of job, from general manager to routine production operator, are task scope and depth. **Task scope** describes the horizontal characteristics of a job, or the degree of variety in the activities a person is expected to perform. A job narrow in scope has few activities. A court reporter, for example, transcribes verbatim what is said during a trial; a lab technician draws blood samples eight hours a day. A cleaner who only empties waste bins has a narrower task scope than one who also mops, vacuums, dusts, and washes windows.

task scope
The degree of task variety built into a job, typically called horizontal job loading, when jobs are formally designed.

Task depth addresses how much vertical responsibility or individual accountability is expected in a job. Depth increases when the employee is given responsibility to schedule the sequence of work, to initiate self-control if activities or output begin to get out of balance, to identify and solve problems as they occur, or to originate innovative ways of improving the process or the output. Task depth is shallow when managers determine what job-holders are to do, when they are to do it, in what quantities, and then monitor results to determine if work output matches the standards handed down.

task depth
The degree of responsibility and autonomous decision authority expected in a job, often thought of as vertical job loading when formally designed.

Combining scope and depth into four job profiles

Task scope and depth can be considered ways of 'loading' work into jobs. When combined into a 2×2 matrix, high or low loadings on each of the two variables identify four types of broad job classifications. Exhibit 6-8 illustrates how these job features produce different work experiences.

Four distinct types of jobs are identified by the ways in which task scope (variety) and task depth (responsibility) combine. To the employee, jobs are more meaningful as they become less routine and more enriched, since competent, motivated people like to believe that their jobs provide variety and give them responsibility and the resources to carry out tasks.

Ultimately, managers should ask themselves the following questions. Do our job structures and technology fit the capabilities of the people we employ? Do these jobs promote high-quality

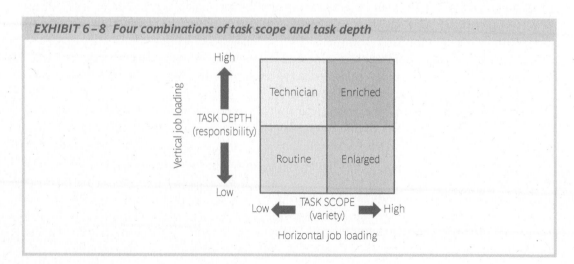

EXHIBIT 6–8 Four combinations of task scope and task depth

work, satisfying to those who produce it? Too often, the answer to both questions will be no. All the media attention showered on high technology and dotcom start-ups notwithstanding, many jobs still incorporate narrowly defined requirements that were common 20 or more years ago. Routine jobs low in scope and depth are prone to under-utilise the mental competencies of employees, and thus reduce the quality level attained by the organisation.

Routine jobs

Routine jobs are programmed to be repetitive and narrow in scope and are often restricted by technology. People in these simplistic and repetitive jobs are expected not to do much independent thinking, just pay attention to detail. Examples of routine jobs include data entry, assembly, clerical and cashier jobs. Skills are mastered in a matter of hours or days; there is no expectation of career growth unless one becomes a supervisor over those performing these routine jobs.

Technician jobs

Technician jobs offer greater opportunities for independent thinking and deciding what to do and when, but provide employees with little variety in their daily tasks. The technician may have a university education or need professional training to learn how to perform the job of, say, a pharmacist or stockbroker. The work may be valued by the client, but research suggests that people such as medical technicians find their jobs become meaningless over time because their job tasks are repetitive and there is little growth opportunity (Lengel, 1976).

Enlarged jobs

Enlarged jobs provide an expanded variety or diversity of tasks. At times jobs are deliberately expanded, either by adding on sequential tasks or by allowing employees to rotate among different jobs. Decreasing the number of separate job classifications or titles in a traditional industry typically affords employees enlarged variety or a change of pace.

Enriched jobs

Enriched jobs enable an individual to feel responsible for whole tasks. Most professional jobs that require analysis and manipulation of symbolic data (managers, scientists and teachers, for example) are enriched to give the individual responsibility for doing whatever is necessary to get the job done. The work presents challenges and novelty, with the incumbent empowered to solve problems and find innovative solutions to shifting performance demands.

Changing task scope and depth

The car mechanic who is allowed to troubleshoot and correct problems whenever they occur experiences job enrichment. The mechanic who only fixes braking system problems is more rigid in character, and the person who simply changes oil probably views the job as routine.

horizontal job loading
The process of enlarging jobs by combining separate work activities into a whole job that provides for greater task variety.

Jobs can be changed if they are found to be overly confining and thus fail to use the full capabilities of the people employed. Variety in a position can be increased by combining all the separate steps or tasks required to complete a whole job. This process is called horizontal job loading because the enlarged job can be viewed as a horizontal chain of multiple work activities performed in a sequence. The 'horizontal' concept builds from the logic that, in most organisations, work can be analysed as a series of tasks that are sequential in their structure. Thus, the processes of procurement or accounts payable can each be defined as a chain of end-to-end tasks. To enlarge (and ultimately enrich) jobs, one person is given responsibility for more links of the chain.

vertical job loading
The process of structuring a greater range of responsibility for planning, control and decision-making authority into a job.

Task depth is increased by **vertical job loading**, or the structuring of a job to allow a greater range of responsibility and authority. When management reserves exclusive responsibility for planning and control, employees have little task depth. Lawler (1994) suggests that companies that subscribe to the principles of quality management and employee involvement actively expand vertical loading for what have typically been routine production or narrowly defined service jobs. They move away from the top-down approach to let employees decide what needs to be done for quality improvement.

Many of today's jobs are more complex, subject to change, and require analytic or symbol-manipulation skills. Thus, managers may not be the best people to tell other professionals what to do – they must delegate responsibility to others. This lesson is illustrated by the way in which Sweden's Atlas Copco moves managers laterally across the globe and vertically gives them a change of responsibility so they become leaders allowing their people to solve problems (see the World Watch box).

Sweden's Atlas Copco AB rotates managers

'The only thing that differentiates people is their responsibility.' Such a statement by Giulio Mazzalupi, the Italian CEO and president of Swedish-based Atlas Copco, reflects one of the qualities that differentiates this £6 billion manufacturer from many of its competitors. The second quality is the firm's commitment to moving managers across countries to new international assignments.

Atlas Copco manufactures compressors, electric and pneumatic tools, and construction and mining gear in plants around the globe, many of them acquired. With more than 125 years of business experience, this firm grows by developing talent through dramatically changing the experiences of its human resources, especially managers. In a recent six-year period more than 80 per cent of Atlas Copco's top managers changed jobs, with more than half moving to responsibilities in another country.

To illustrate, the head of Atlas Copco Compressors in Mount Holyoke, Illinois, is British and previously worked for Atlas in South Korea. The CEO of its Chicago Pneumatic Tool Company plant in South Carolina is Turkish and previously led the company's operations in Japan.

When Giulio Mazzalupi moved from executive vice president of the firm's largest business unit to the CEO position, he gave a rather simple explanation of what most British people would consider a significant promotion: 'The difference is the responsibility, not the authority. When you move up in a Swedish organisation, it doesn't make you a better or more important person – you just grow in your responsibilities. . . . I am not Swedish, but I am CEO. This is a strong message to the organisation that there are no prejudices and that if you do well, you can go anywhere.'

Organisational learning is important to Mazzalupi as it reinforces his belief in getting 'employees to understand where they are in the work flow [because each employee is] the centre

world watch

of the organisation. We must get people to work together, because it is people who solve problems, not managers. Managers have to create an environment so that people are in the best position to solve problems.'

Source: adapted from Michael A. Verespej (1998) 'Widespread Responsibility', *Industry Week*, 19 January, pp. 31–36.

Discussion questions

1 Why are people so important to an organisation?

2 Why do people have different motives at different levels in the organisation?

The effect of job design on work outcomes

Scope and depth are the most basic descriptors of any job. But other dimensions of a job affect the attitudes of workers, their willingness to perform successfully, the productivity and reliability of their work output, and corresponding side effects such as accidents, absenteeism and job stress.

Research focus: job enrichment

An integrating motivational theory of job design

Hackman *et al.* (1976) have developed an integrating theory of job design. The objective is to help managers understand and build into work the conditions that will inspire people to turn in high-quality performances. They used the following three-sequence model to provide recommendations for enriching jobs:

Core job dimensions ① → *Psychological states* ① → *Personal/work outcomes*

core job dimensions
The underlying characteristics of a job and how they relate to a person's job involvement, motivation, performance and satisfaction.

Core job dimensions

In the design of jobs, core job dimensions are the underlying characteristics of a job and how they relate to a person's job involvement, motivation, performance and satisfaction (Hackman and Lawler, 1971). The six original dimensions are described in detail in Exhibit 6-9. These researchers found that the first four of the original core job dimensions (*autonomy, task variety, task identity* and *feedback*) had greater impact on the outcome measures of job involvement, motivation, performance, and satisfaction than did numbers five and six (*friendship opportunities* and *dealing with others*). As a result of independent research by Kiggundu (1981), two other core job dimensions have been added: *task significance* and *task interdependence*.

In considering person–job matches, Hackman and Lawler (1971) found these core dimensions had a better fit and greater meaning for self-motivating individuals who desire opportunity, personal growth, challenge, autonomy and feedback. Such individuals have high growth needs and tend to be intrinsically motivated, as explained in Chapter 5.

psychological states
Three possible job qualities – experienced meaningfulness, experienced responsibility, knowledge of results – that shape individual job motivation and satisfaction of growth needs.

Psychological states

To assess the impact of core job dimensions on three psychological states that shape individual job motivation and satisfaction, researchers or human resource

> **EXHIBIT 6 – 9** *Six core job dimensions for evaluating jobs*
>
> These core job dimensions are introduced in order of their pervasiveness in affecting the outcome measures of job involvement, motivation, performance and satisfaction.
>
> 1 **Autonomy** – the degree of control a person has over his or her own job actions, such as responsibility for self-governing behaviours to perform the job and the absence of a pro-grammed sequence of activities (essentially, task depth).
>
> 2 **Task variety** – the degree to which normal job activities require performing multiple tasks (breadth of task scope).
>
> 3 **Task identity** – the extent to which a person has a whole task to complete, with visible starting and ending points.
>
> 4 **Feedback** – the frequency and completeness with which the task provides information about work progress and results of personal efforts.
>
> 5 **Friendship opportunities** – the extent to which the work setting provides opportunities for close interpersonal contacts.
>
> 6 **Dealing with others** – the degree to which task flow or accomplishment requires interaction with others in contributory or collegial ways.
>
> *Source*: copyright 1975 by the Regents of the University of California. Reprinted from *California Management Review* 17(4). By permission of the Regents.

professionals can use a diagnostic instrument, the Job Diagnostic Survey. Generally, people whose jobs enable them to experience the following three psychological states will have a positive 'motivating potential' because these cognitions satisfy personal-professional growth needs.

1 **Experienced meaningfulness.** Occurs when an individual perceives his or her work as worthwhile or in tune with personal values (influenced by skill variety, task identity and task significance dimensions).

2 **Experienced responsibility.** Realised when a person feels personally accountable for the outcomes of his or her efforts (influenced by the autonomy dimension).

3 **Knowledge of results.** Experienced when an individual can determine on a fairly regular basis whether the performance outcomes of his or her work are satisfactory (influenced by the feedback dimension).

Personal/work outcomes

Favourable core job dimensions create a positive motivating potential which often yields high personal and work outcomes. *Job outcomes* are measured by job involvement, motivation and satisfaction at the personal level, and performance at the work level. For example, Lisa has strong growth needs and perceives her production-scheduling job as one of significant respons-ibility. She receives positive feedback about her results and believes her work to be meaningful both to co-workers and customers. These positive psychological states enable her to enjoy high self-esteem and job satisfaction. She is highly involved in her job and thus internally motivated to excel. Lisa's performance produces high-quality work of a timely and accurate nature, rarely disrupted by absences. We conclude that her job dimensions produce positive psychological states, which in turn lead to high personal and work outcomes. If any of the three psychological states were missing (meaningfulness, responsibility, knowledge of results) her motivating potential would probably be lower.

A manager thinking of enriching jobs to build in more of the positive core job dimensions will find those individuals with high growth needs stimulated by learning and challenges and therefore more receptive to these changes. Another person in Lisa's job who lacks strong growth needs or who has low self-esteem is less likely to accept such changes in the structuring of his or her work. Outcomes will therefore be diminished for both the individual and organisation. Jobs with high levels of responsibility and variety are not for everyone. Some want security and structure more than autonomy or challenge. However, not everyone wants money, as can be seen in the Eye on Ethics box.

Drug baron at Oxfam: former SmithKline high-flier moves to Oxfam. Who says it is money that motivates?

When David Earnshaw took up a highly paid job for SmithKline Beecham in 1986 he knew it was not a sinecure that would see him to a well-padded retirement.

That was just as well. Earlier this year, after being made redundant during a merger with Glaxo Wellcome, he took a well-publicised 50 per cent cut in his salary to join Oxfam, where he is now working on the other side of the barricades on issues such as HIV drugs for Africa.

Of course Oxfam has somewhat different objectives from the multinational drug companies when it lobbies the European Parliament. But Earnshaw says that he was never an apologist for the drugs industry – he was always outspoken in his criticisms.

Earnshaw was not surprised that his head was on the block in the merger. 'My views weren't an insignificant factor in me being made redundant,' he says, choosing his words carefully.

But working at Oxfam is more a return to form for the Rochdale-born Earnshaw. Before the SmithKline job his career had been mainly academic – he was a lecturer in European politics – and political – he worked for the European Parliament. But armed with an MBA he jumped at the chance to cross into the corporate sector and work with one of Europe's biggest multi-nationals.

He is just as happy to have jumped back – though the return trip, with its steep drop in salary, did require a sharp intake of breath.

'I'm 42. If I don't do something like work for Oxfam now, I'm not going to. I believe in humanity and global equity and I don't want to become so attached to an income that I divorce myself from those values.'

Earnshaw says it is refreshing to work for Oxfam rather than a large corporate bureaucracy.

His main concern was that his 16-year-old stepdaughter, whom he is raising, should not see any change in her standard of living. She was consulted before he took the Oxfam job. 'It was important that she liked the idea. If she hadn't that would imply I hadn't brought her up to see organisations such as Oxfam as important.'

Source: © Terry Slavin, *Observer*, 17 June 2001.

eye on ethics

Discussion questions

1 What do you think Earnshaw's motives were for moving to Oxfam?

2 Do you think money is a motivator?

Interdisciplinary approaches to job design

The approach to job design advocated by Hackman and colleagues clearly emphasises the motivating potential of work. While popular, there are other philosophies and approaches to job design that affect several other outcomes. Research by Campion (1988) and his colleagues distinguishes approaches to job redesign into four distinct fields, each with a rather predictable trade-off of costs and benefits. His four approaches, each based on a different premise or research discipline, are motivational, mechanistic, biological and perceptual/motor.

Motivational approach

Several theories (including Hackman's) aim to increase the outcomes of job satisfaction, job involvement and performance by enabling people to realise growth needs through experiencing challenging work. Added benefits of jobs rating high in motivational design are lower boredom and absenteeism. Campion (1987) notes, however, that in striving to produce jobs that are stimulating and mentally demanding, the motivational approach may have the unintended consequence of creating staffing difficulties, increasing training times, and having higher mental overload and stress.

Source: *San Jose Mercury News* (14 June 1995).
Reprinted with permission of United Feature Syndicate, Inc.

Mechanistic approach

The earliest techniques for designing jobs emerged from classical industrial engineering with extensions to scientific management. They were based on time and motion studies and work simplification. Mechanistic approaches are orientated towards efficiency in the use of human resources by simplifying staffing and training requirements through the design of standardised, simplified work tasks that require less experience.

Mechanistic jobs have lower mental overload and stress but more boredom and physical demands (along the lines of the routine or technician-type jobs described earlier).

Biological approach

ergonomics
A biomechanic approach to minimise physical strain and stress on a worker based on the healthy design of work methods and technology.

From the study of work physiology and biomechanics emerged a concern about job ergonomics. **Ergonomics** emphasises the minimisation of physical strain and stress on the worker, based on work methods and technology. Biological methods involve making jobs physically comfortable and matched to physical strength and endurance, combined with attention to noise, climate requirements and the design of equipment. Where jobs are well designed biologically, workers report less physical effort and fatigue, fewer aches and pains, and have fewer health complaints. The likelihood of accidents is reduced, employees have more favourable attitudes towards their workstation and sometimes experience slightly higher job satisfaction. On the cost side, equipment investments are higher and training requirements increase.

Perceptual/motor approach

From human factors engineering, experimental psychology and human information processing studies, lessons are focused on human processes and performance. Perceptual/motor approaches seek to match job characteristics to human mental capabilities (and limitations) with a primary emphasis on how people concentrate and what helps them pay attention to job requirements. Favourable outcomes from this approach are improved reliability by reducing errors and accidents, and positive worker reactions by reduced fatigue, mental overload and stress. Staffing and training requirements are reduced, but boredom increases.

Such research about how different disciplines contribute to job design emphasises that there is no one approach that is best for all types of people and jobs. Like so many other managerial challenges, job design involves seeking a balance among approaches to achieve results that best fit situational realities. Campion (1988) concludes:

> Jobs can be simultaneously high on the mechanistic and perceptual/motor approaches because they both generally recommend design features that minimise mental demands, but the motivational approach gives nearly opposite advice by encouraging design features that enhance mental demands. As such, jobs high on the motivational approach may be more difficult to staff, require more training, have greater likelihood of error, and more mental overload and stress. Jobs high on the mechanistic and perceptual/motor approaches may have less satisfied and motivated employees and higher absenteeism. This suggests a basic trade-off between organisational benefits, such as efficiency and reliability, and individual benefits, such as satisfaction.

Strategies to enhance jobs through redesign

Recent task and process design successes by firms who have won the Malcolm Baldrige National Quality Award (such as Ritz Carlton Hotels, Solar Turbines and Solectron) suggest actions that organisations can take to improve overall job effectiveness. Most of the strategies learned from best practices of such award-winning companies apply mainly to employees who seek growth challenges and enjoy learning. As summarised in Exhibit 6-10, the orientation of such job enhancement strategies is principally through the motivational approach. Five of many strategies suggested by Blackburn and Rosen (1993) are as follows:

1 **Combine tasks.** To improve skill variety, task identity and interdependence, job enlargement combines tasks that, over time, have become overly specialised and fragmented. Tasks may be combined by having one individual complete a larger module of work or by establishing teams in which members periodically switch tasks. Critical also is the elimination of tasks that no longer add value to necessary processes.

2 **Load jobs vertically.** To improve autonomy, empower employees by combining responsibilities for planning, executing and adjusting work activities. A manager authorises staff members to schedule their own work, decide on work methods, troubleshoot problems, train others and monitor quality. They are also provided with cost and performance reports.

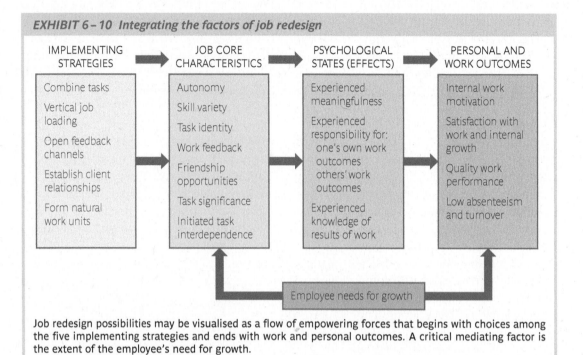

EXHIBIT 6–10 Integrating the factors of job redesign

IMPLEMENTING STRATEGIES	JOB CORE CHARACTERISTICS	PSYCHOLOGICAL STATES (EFFECTS)	PERSONAL AND WORK OUTCOMES
Combine tasks	Autonomy	Experienced meaningfulness	Internal work motivation
Vertical job loading	Skill variety	Experienced responsibility for: one's own work outcomes others' work outcomes	Satisfaction with work and internal growth
Open feedback channels	Task identity		Quality work performance
Establish client relationships	Work feedback		Low absenteeism and turnover
Form natural work units	Friendship opportunities Task significance Initiated task interdependence	Experienced knowledge of results of work	

Employee needs for growth

Job redesign possibilities may be visualised as a flow of empowering forces that begins with choices among the five implementing strategies and ends with work and personal outcomes. A critical mediating factor is the extent of the employee's need for growth.

3 **Open feedback channels.** To improve interaction with others and clarify task significance, managers should develop systems where employees directly receive all possible feedback about factors that affect their work. The best feedback sources are the job itself, peers and access to computerised databases, not the manager's perceptions and judgemental comments.

4 **Establish client relationships.** To improve skill variety, autonomy, interaction with others and feedback, employees whose actions impact on customers should periodically interact directly with customers. Three steps are suggested: (1) identify a relevant client or customer contact for employees; (2) structure the most direct contact possible, such as on-site visits for commercial customers; and (3) have the work group set up criteria by which the customer can evaluate work quality and channel any remarks directly to the employee or work team.

5 **Form natural work teams.** To improve skill variety, task significance, friendship and interdependence, link people together when the job performed by one person affects others. Regardless of work flow sequences, bringing people together as a team enhances identification with the whole task and creates a sense of shared responsibility. To provide a team project focus some Hewlett-Packard divisions have moved design engineers into the middle of the production area. They interact with assemblers and manufacturing operators and obtain clues to improving manufacturing processes. Such experiences are expanding the use of teams to engage non-managers in wide-ranging problem-solving and quality improvement.

Motivating by empowerment

A generation ago managers began to discover the motivational power of empowerment. True, some managers have always been empowering people by delegating considerable autonomy, providing ample information, and backing projects that showed creativity or initiative. Likewise, many individuals have learned over the years to be self-motivated and self-empowered – they seize opportunities to make their work more meaningful and are willing to make choices, to experiment and to have an impact on the organisation. However, until the term *empowerment* entered the manager's vocabulary, little was done to encourage the practice as a conscious way to promote self-motivation, innovation and system-wide continuous improvements.

Empowerment enhances self-perceptions and behaviours

empowerment
Describes conditions that enable people to feel competent and in control of their work, and energised to take initiative and persist at meaningful tasks.

self-concept
How we think about ourselves or see ourselves in a role.

self-esteem
How we generally feel about our own worthiness – our self-acceptance.

Empowerment describes conditions that enable people to feel competent and in control, and energised to take the initiative and persist at meaningful tasks (Conger and Kanungo, 1998). Empowerment is a multifaceted and highly personal motivational force. Empowerment can come from within the individual, from peers or from a manager. As suggested by its definition, empowerment aspires to bring about positive self-perceptions (self-concept, self-esteem and self-efficacy) and task-directed behaviours. Exhibit 6-11 graphically portrays these forces, and the following text describes some of the interplay among them.

Changed self-perceptions are an important manifestation of empowerment. Your **self-concept** is how you think about yourself or see yourself in a role. Self-concept changes as you shift roles – say from friend to student to employee. **Self-esteem**

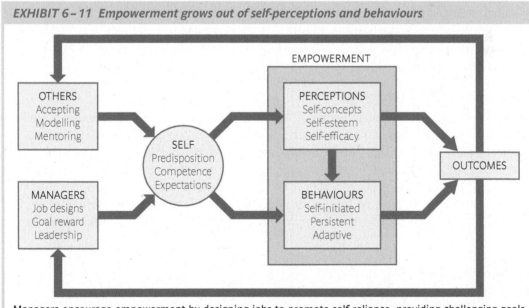

EXHIBIT 6–11 Empowerment grows out of self-perceptions and behaviours

Managers encourage empowerment by designing jobs to promote self-reliance, providing challenging goals and meaningful rewards, and exerting considerable leadership. Other people are empowering if they are accepting, provide a model for others to be self-motivated performers and exert the patience to be mentors.

is how you generally feel about your own worthiness – your self-acceptance that you are worthy of self-respect. A specific aspect of self-esteem is self-efficacy, a concept closely linked to empowerment. **Self-efficacy** is an individual's self-perceived ability to perform a certain type of task. Bandura (1988) suggests that your feelings of self-efficacy are important because they influence performance and a sense of personal well-being.

self-efficacy
Our self-perceptions about our ability to perform certain types of task.

Individuals develop a sense of self-efficacy based on past experience with actual or similar tasks, comparisons with others and feedback from others. A person's self-assessment of ability (knowledge and skills), general physical and emotional condition, and personality (including overall self-esteem) all influence his or her feelings of task-specific self-efficacy (Gist and Mitchell, 1992). How skilfully and with how much effort an individual approaches tasks also influences personal performance and the subsequent feeling of self-efficacy. Empowering conditions help strengthen self-efficacy.

Self-initiated empowerment

An individual can initiate personal actions to bring about self-empowerment and greater feelings of self-efficacy. People who are intrinsically motivated internal attributors usually initiate personal efforts to expand the nature of their jobs and their power. They are willing to take on additional responsibilities and/or creatively work on ways to improve organisational processes or products. Self-empowering people are in effect entrepreneurs who work actively to alter the organisation in ways that make them proud of their results.

Empowerment by others

Colleagues and co-workers have a significant impact on work-related self-perceptions. Peers who promote empowerment influence how individuals within a group feel about themselves and the group itself. Within groups, people feel empowered when they are respected and treated as professionals, and encourage co-workers to accept responsibility and have the sponsorship of a personal mentor. Individuals are empowered when peers seek their advice, confide in them, and include them in projects from which they can learn and make contact with others, and that might help their careers.

Empowerment by managers

The most talked-about source of empowerment is the behaviour of managers or leaders in interacting with staff. The empowering manager actively gives power to individuals and enables them to be self-motivated. This is done by changing employee expectations so they believe they are in control of their destiny and can shape their work and make it meaningful within their organisation. Empowering managers also share information so people can perform their jobs more accurately and confidently. Information technology and systems that allow employees to have on-demand access to whatever information they need is by itself a major empowering factor.

As a management practice, empowerment also means managers open communications, delegate power, share information and cut away at the debilitating tangles of corporate bureaucracy. The manager who deliberately works to empower his or her employees gives them a licence to pursue their visions, to champion projects, and to improve practices consistent with the organisational mission and goals. According to Cohen and Bradford (1984), the manager who shares responsibilities with subordinates and treats them as partners is likely to get the best from them. For these reasons, it is common to think of empowerment as a principal quality of leaders. At Sun Microsystems, CEO Scott G. McNealy has built an empowering corporate culture within his Internet-focused company around his playful motto 'Kick butt and have fun' (Hoff, 1996).

Empowerment results in personal changes

The empowered person undergoes two types of personal change. One is *motivational enhancement*, especially when the source of empowerment is positive change initiated by a manager (Kappelman and Prybutok, 1995). Empowered people usually intensify their task focus and are energised to become more committed to a cause or goal. They experience self-efficacy, which stimulates motivation by enabling people to see themselves as competent and capable of high performance. Empowerment is also manifested in active *problem-solving behaviours* that concentrate energy on a goal. Thomas and Velthouse (1990) suggest that the empowered person is more flexible in behaviour, tries alternative paths when one is blocked, and eagerly initiates new tasks or adds complexity to current ones. Behaviour becomes self-motivated when the individual seeks to carve out greater personal autonomy in undertaking tasks without the manager's help, or to draw support from team members.

W.L. Gore & Associates, a privately held firm of over 6000 associates most noted for its Gore-Tex and other products made from Teflon, has an unusual organisation and culture that supports empowerment. All activities are structured around teams, the firm has sponsors rather than managers, and hiring decisions are a team-based process. Once a team decides another person is needed, its members recruit, interview and select, and then assign that person a sponsor who acts as a mentor. 'Usually we choose the person [on the team] who has the most invested in making the new person successful,' says Sally Gore. 'If you sponsor someone, you want them to be successful. You will offer them appropriate opportunities to sit in on meetings and seminars, and do things so that they will be successful.' Then teams and individuals are rewarded with profit sharing based on the value they add to the company. 'Seniority and education are not the criteria. The criterion is contribution, pure and simple [to create] an atmosphere where associates are motivated to innovate' (Hasek, 2000).

Empowerment alters expectations

Although managers often set the stage for empowerment by promoting initiative and relaxing bureaucratic obstacles, ultimately the individual decides whether to act in an empowered way. Because empowerment depends in part on how people perceive reality, not everyone on a team responds in the same way to empowerment opportunities (Thomas and Velthouse, 1980).

Naomi, a market analyst, has self-confidence and self-esteem because she believes she can influence organisational outcomes. Bandura (1986) suggests that this occurs in part because her manager enthusiastically supports her reports and allows her to present them to top management. Such repeated experiences lead to a personal belief that she is truly competent, which positively influences her expectations about future events. Naomi believes her competence transfers across situations, and she looks forward to challenging assignments. By contrast, Scott, her accounts receivable colleague, generally sees himself as weak in analytical reasoning and persuasion skills. He has low self-efficacy associated with learned helplessness in these areas. His manager audits his work, points out deficiencies and hounds him for faster turnaround times. Scott avoids situations that he expects will require analytical or persuasion skills.

Expectancy motivation comes into play in empowerment whenever a person raises questions about himself or herself and the task at hand. Managers help bring about empowerment when they encourage their people to diminish such bureaucratic thoughts as 'It's not my responsibility' or 'It's beyond my control' or the classic, 'It wasn't invented here.' One way to overcome self-deluding excuses is to have people identify the customers served by their work, even if customers are other departments within the firm. This shifts the focus away from thinking of one's tasks as trivial 'busywork' and towards perceiving one's importance in the flow of interdependent tasks.

Morpheus: a second look

Business Link has helped us to set some targets for growth and reassess our vision so that it is easily understood by everyone in the company. We all know where we're heading.

The help was there at the right time, and the experience has made us realise you can seek external help to expand thinking and be a bit more objective to take the business forward. We have seen it as a starting point and are aiming to achieve Investors in People standard this year, which is a reflection on how far we have come.

I do think that focusing on staff retention and team-building has to come at the right time. It takes a lot of time and effort, which for many companies in the early stages would mean a happy team, but no customers. I also think you need to experience bleak periods which will inevitably occur in a growing business, to be able to handle future issues.

One of the hardest aspects of running your own business is to let others take some control, but you must if you are to let it grow and evolve beyond being a lifestyle environment, to an effective business system that can operate independently of its owners.

Source: Joanna Read in *Growing Business* May 2002.

Summary

- Managers have found many ways to apply and extend the fundamental theories of motivation.

- One of the common applications of motivation theory is goal-setting.

- Management by objectives (MBO) is a specific managerial application of goal-setting that has been widely used in organisations.

- Participation in goal-setting helps raise aspirations, but it does not necessarily lead to better performance than when goals are set by management.

- People are more likely to perform actions leading to the desired results if they have clear, specific and challenging goals. This can be done by writing goals that begin with an action verb, identify major result areas, provide a measurement standard and specify a time for completion. Once a person has a goal, intentions lead to an action plan to reach the objective.

- The most direct application of motivational theories is organisational behaviour modification (OB mod), which uses reinforcement to shape behaviour. Reinforcement involves managing the environment, usually by linking a positive consequence to a desired behaviour (to increase the likelihood of its being repeated).

- However, OB mod can also rely on negative reinforcement (removal of an aversive or negative condition following a desired behaviour), or even punishment or omission of any reinforcement to shape behaviour.

- Linked to goals are rewards and benefits. In pursuit of continuous improvements in quality, organisations are increasing their use of performance-based compensation systems such as gainsharing that focus on the total business unit rather than on departmental or individual pay-for-performance plans.

- In addition to bonuses and profit sharing, managers are also allowing employees greater choice in selecting benefits from a cafeteria-style menu. Such a movement recognises that people have different needs, and compensation systems should reflect those differences.

- Historically, jobs have been designed around task depth (autonomy and responsibility) and task scope (variety). As jobs become enriched (by building in greater depth and scope), employees potentially experience greater meaning in their work and satisfaction from the experience.

- The newest and most conceptually abstract of the applied motivational practices is empowerment. Empowerment enables people to feel competent and in control of their work by granting them authority, providing information and reducing bureaucratic restrictions.

- Empowerment leads to a combination of greater motivation and more energetic problem-solving behaviours.

Areas for personal development

Motivational applications are found in many organisational practices, including goal-setting, reinforcement, rewards, job design, empowerment and organisational learning. Practise some of the skill-building behaviours that will strengthen your motivation for high performance.

1 **Learn to set measurement-orientated goals.** Manage your own behaviour by objectives (personalised MBO) by writing operational objectives for your major tasks. Begin with an action verb 'to _____', then state a major result area, followed by a measurement standard or performance indicator, concluding with a time frame by which the key result will occur. Then follow up to evaluate if you did it on time and to the degree of performance you specified. Remember that objectives should be SMART – Specific, Measurable, Achievable, Relevant and Timebound.

2 **Provide self-reinforcement for those major tasks.** Once concluded, administer some form of appropriate self-reinforcement depending on the result produced. If you met your objective, apply some type of personally meaningful positive reinforcement to produce satisfaction, or apply negative reinforcement by removing some aversive or threatening condition so that you experience relief. If the results are disappointing, apply some form of punishment, perhaps by denying yourself something pleasant you were otherwise going to do.

3 **Performance is behaviour that has been evaluated.** If your behaviour is to be performance orientated, get used to evaluating what you have done at the end of the day. Learn to realise when you are behaving in ways that contribute to some goal-orientated performance activity, then reward yourself from whatever cafeteria of benefits is meaningful and available to you.

4 **Structure tasks that expand the core job dimensions.** During the course of a week, work to engage in a sufficient number of tasks that enable you to include all six of the core job dimensions of autonomy, task variety, task identity (a whole task with visible beginning and end), feedback, friendship opportunities and dealing with others. Being able to activate these six will help you experience positive cognitions on the three psychological states of experienced meaningfulness, experienced responsibility and knowledge of results. Realising these makes you a more motivated person.

5 **Empower yourself to enhance self-efficacy.** Self-efficacy is your perception that you have the abilities to perform various tasks. Enhance yours by realising the contributions you make to the positive things that happen in your life. Self-empowerment means taking charge of your life and feeling accountable for your behaviour. Being empowered enables you to feel competent and in control, energised to take on meaningful tasks.

6 **Learn from self-evaluation of outcomes.** Question your personal motives as you evaluate how you have performed on various tasks. Rather than simply acknowledging the quality or level of your performance, probe as to what caused the outcome. Accept personal accountability for outcomes by questioning your own assumptions and behaviour so that you can learn to improve when there is room for improvement.

❓ Questions for study and discussion

1 Write a comprehensive goal statement of a major task you need to undertake. Include the four elements of an action verb, a major result area, a measurement standard and a time frame.

2 Different forms of management by objectives (MBO) are widely practised, yet MBO remains controversial. Place yourself in a familiar work situation and describe what your manager would do to include you in an MBO process. What four objectives would you probably initiate?

3 What are the differences among the four basic types of reinforcement: positive, negative, punishment and omission? Why is positive reinforcement advocated more than punishment?

4 The management of a health-conscious firm wants to stamp out smoking among its employees. A senior vice president asks you to devise an OB mod programme that would use reinforcement to help people stop smoking. What steps would you recommend?

5 Describe each of these types of pay-for-performance system: piecework, bonuses on top of a base salary, profit sharing, gainsharing and cafeteria-style benefits. Give an example of each. Why should firms design their compensation systems to maintain equity while at the same time promoting individual expectancies?

6 Examine the 2×2 model that characterises types of jobs by depth and scope (Exhibit 6-8). For each of the four cells, identify a specific type of job that fits that particular cell and explain why. Then, for the cells identified as routine, technician and enlarged, explain what changes you would make in task scope and/or task depth to enrich each job you have identified.

7 Identify a career-orientated job you would like to hold following graduation. Describe the conditions under which that job would rate favourably on each of the six core job dimensions identified in Exhibit 6-9. Make sure your descriptions reflect job qualities that produce overall positive psychological states of experienced meaningfulness, experienced responsibility and knowledge of results.

8 'When the managers of an organisation actively work to empower their people, there is little need to be concerned about individual motivation.' Critically evaluate this statement. In what ways might empowerment shift concerns about motivation away from individuals to the team?

9 Henry argues, 'For every worker there is one best motivational application to drive performance.' Sarah responds, 'Nonsense – there is no single best way to motivate anyone.' Who is correct? Explain.

🔑 Key Concepts

goal, *p. 240*

intention, *p. 242*

actions, *p. 243*

management by objectives (MBO), *p. 243*

reinforcement, *p. 246*

law of effect, *p. 248*

organisational behaviour modification (OB mod), *p. 248*

performance, *p. 252*

piecework, *p. 253*

gainsharing, *p. 255*

open book management, *p. 258*

job design, *p. 259*

scientific management, *p. 259*

task scope, *p. 260*

task depth, *p. 260*

horizontal job loading, *p. 261*

vertical job loading, *p. 262*

core job dimensions, *p. 263*

psychological states, *p. 263*

ergonomics, *p. 266*

empowerment, *p. 269*

self-concept, *p. 269*

self-esteem, *p. 269*

self-efficacy, *p. 270*

Personal skills exercise
How does the design of jobs affect you?

Purpose To quickly bring out personal reactions to different job profiles, and to understand why any one job design profile may be appealing or repulsive.

Time can be completed within about 7 minutes (as an option, individuals can combine with three or so other students for the third phase, in which case the time is doubled)

Phase 1 (5 minutes) From the five job profiles given below, select the one you believe is your most preferred and the one that is your least preferred. Four of these profiles are based on the concepts of task scope and task depth (summarised in Exhibit 6-8). The fifth (team) was explained briefly in this chapter and in greater detail in Chapter 15. The profiles are:

- *routine jobs* (low scope, low depth)
- *technician jobs* (low scope, high depth)
- *enlarged jobs* (high scope, low depth)
- *enriched jobs* (high scope, high depth)
- *team-based jobs* (high interaction, high interdependence).

For each of the two profiles you have selected, place the name of your profiles at the top of separate pages, and then draw a large 'T' with the two subheadings 'What turns me on' and 'What turns me off'. For the next 4 minutes generate lists of the pros and cons (turn-ons, turn-offs) of the job profiles you are describing. Think of the profile as a set of job attributes or characteristics, some of which you may like, some of which you may not.

Phase 2 (2 minutes) Now evaluate how strongly each item on the two lists affects you personally. Do so by using a simple plus/minus scoring system, with your scores marked on the page beside each item. Use two plus signs (+ +) if it is a strong turn-on for you, one plus sign (+) if moderate; two minus signs (− −) if a strong turn-off, one minus sign (−) if a moderate turn-off. Now examine your job-related likes and dislikes and brainstorm five to eight job titles you believe will be most satisfying for you.

Phase 3 (Optional: 7 minutes) Form into teams with three to four other students and share your choices of profiles, your job attributes and the types of job title you believe are most satisfying. Were there any commonalties among the profiles that were most and least desired? What accounts for the similarities? The differences? Engage in a general team discussion of how different job profiles stimulate the reactions they do.

Team exercise
Class behaviour feedback and goal-setting

Purpose This exercise gives you and a colleague experience in the give and take of providing feedback and setting goals. Each pair will have the opportunity to establish a helping relationship for purposes of self-improvement.

Time 30 minutes

Materials Paper and pen or pencil for each person.

Instructions Pair up with a colleague with whom you have had some working experience, perhaps in a previous exercise or another class. Make a managerial decision as to who will be A and who will be B.

A's self-disclosure (2 minutes) At a signal from your tutor, A will have 2 minutes to answer the question 'Who am I?' while B listens. A will talk about himself/herself without interruption or questioning from B. A should talk about whatever A is comfortable sharing – family background, relationships with friends, jobs, hobbies or interests. Any subject is fair game as long as it reveals something about A.

B's self-disclosure (2 minutes) Reverse roles. B tells A about himself/herself.

B's positive feedback to A (1 minute) B now has 1 minute to provide A with feedback on what was heard. The only stipulation is that the feedback should reflect totally positive regard for A. B should not be critical but should emphasise the strengths or interesting qualities perceived about A in the spirit of unconditional positive regard for A.

A's positive feedback to B (1 minute) Now reverse roles and let A tell B the positive attributes heard or perceived.

B's class performance appraisal of A (2 minutes) Once the pair is comfortable in making self-disclosures and giving feedback, the focus shifts to observed classroom behaviour. B will assume the role of appraiser and provide candid feedback to A about A's behaviour and performance in class. B should try to identify critical incidents or specific events that reflect on A's behaviour as a student or team member. This segment opens two-way communication, for A may ask questions or seek clarification. The intent of the feedback is to improve A's future performance as a student. Since feedback is often perceived by the receiver as criticism, which increases defensiveness, the intent should be to engage in a problem-solving approach where feedback suggests room for self-improvement.

A's class performance appraisal of B (2 minutes) Now reverse roles while A gives feedback on B's behaviour.

A sets objectives with B's help (5 minutes) Now it's time to set personal performance objectives. A begins by discussing some aspect of his/her career aspirations that may benefit from better planning and behaviour focusing. With B's help, A writes at least two complete objective statements including, as explained in Exhibit 6-2, an appropriate action verb, a key result area, a performance indicator or measure, and a relevant time frame.

B sets objectives with A's help (5 minutes) Switch roles. The spotlight is now on B, who will develop at least two complete objective statements with A's help.

Conclusion The learning value of this exercise rests solely on personal introspection. To some the exercise – especially the objective-writing phase – may seem tedious, for few people like to write objectives in the presence of others. However, with the proper attitude, the outcome should be useful. Don't just close the book on your objectives and forget about them. Remember them next week, next month, next year.

Case study: **Volvo's Uddevalla plant, Sweden**

Volvo's production plant at Uddevalla used 40 small parallel teams to build complete cars. At regular production pace, individual cycle times ranged from 1.5 to 3.5 hours. The plant had six assembly shops and a materials shop. The usual number of teams was eight in each assembly shop, although the precise number of teams changed as a consequence of constant efforts to improve work patterns. Uddevalla's whole-car assembly was reminiscent of craft work. Materials were collected in individual kits in a largely automated process using sophisticated new technology. In addition, a number of technical aids were developed to make the small-scale assembly efficient and, at the same time, ergonomically vastly superior to line assembly. Furthermore, the holistic kind of assembly and its upgraded intellectual quality supported an extended collaboration among assemblers, industrial engineers, designers and product engineers, which made for a potentially dynamic work organisation, in contrast to the static character of traditional craft work.

Management believed that the plant's combination of highly motivated and skilled workers and short feedback loops would automatically result in excellent quality. In the assembly shops, the organisation structure was flat, but for a long time the advanced assembly teams coexisted with a traditional management hierarchy, underscored by the detached and secluded building where the managers had their offices.

During the early years the plant developed despite this anomaly, but, in early 1992, there were clear signs of stagnation. The plant could not advance only on the strength of its team systems; it needed a congenial plant organisation and managerial structure. In mid-1992, after a difficult period of soul-searching, management put in place a different and very process-orientated organisation headed by a new plant manager who had been extremely successful in reorganising the pilot plants in Volvo's development and product engineering departments. In Uddevalla's new structure there were only two hierarchical levels: shop-floor and plant management. As before, the assembly and materials shops had on average 70 workers organised in teams with rotating, hourly team leaders. They communicated directly with the shop managers, who in turn made up the bulk of the new management committee of the plant. This participation of first-line managers in Uddevalla's central governing body reflected the very strong emphasis on process and process development (including cross-team learning) in the new organisational design. For the new plant manager, the compressed hierarchy was only the first step.

The advanced team structure turned out to be ideally suited for sustaining continuous improvement activities. In March 1993, team members commented, 'Previously, we had only felt pressure from management to reach our targets. Now we really got support and did many things, often small improvements we had never bothered to do.'

Using the holistic and reflective principles, the whole team felt part of the organisation.

The holistic principle recognises the importance of understanding the whole (in this case the assembly of the whole car) and the interdependencies of all constituent parts. Accordingly, the learning process encompassed the work in its entirety.

The reflective principle recognises skill formation as an integration of mental maps and manual skills. For assembly workers at the Uddevalla plant, performing long and complex tasks was not enough; equally important was achieving an articulated and detailed intellectual understanding of the process. Job design and training were thus very different from conventional job enlargement, which is usually merely a quantitative inclusion of additional repetitive tasks. Another indication of the power of the holistic assembly principles was the emerging dialogue and interaction between assembly teams and product engineers during pilot runs of new annual models. According to Gothenburg product engineers, who had experienced all Volvo's assembly plants, discussions with skilled workers at Uddevalla, especially the whole-car assemblers, were often very productive. These problem-solving dialogues were not constrained by the rigid sequencing of the assembly line system; the workers could question proposed assembly methods and develop innovative solutions.

Swedish manufacturing firms in the 1980s encountered a very demanding labour market, probably the most exacting in the world. Four important Swedish contributions to the renewal of work organisation and job design were as follows.

1 Integration of fragmented mass production work to holistic tasks. The Swedish carmakers' 'assembly trajectory' demonstrates that alternatives to repetitive and confined work structures are possible. They are technically feasible, compatible with very varied market demands and socially desirable because they result in qualitative job enrichment and a reduction in physical workloads.

2 Comprehensive improvement in the ergonomics of manual work. At Uddevalla, this effort was explicitly related to the high proportion of female workers (40 per cent) and the need to adapt tools and methods to human differences, recognising that all workers are not the same size and strength.

3 Efforts to make work systems less rigidly coupled and more adaptable to diverse human needs. This too was a response to an advanced labour market with high labour force participation, a large number of female workers and virtually no unemployment. Car firms were not able to target a carefully selected, male workforce and had to accommodate employees who had important obligations outside work.

4 Dealing with a high degree of union involvement – in decision-making and planning processes – as independent partners with their own legitimate interests. The participation may cause controversy and complications, but it also creates a way to articulate complex social demands.

Uddevalla's autonomous teams and holistic job design were supported by a participative and hard-driving management; the result was accelerated and simultaneous advances in productivity, quality and market responsiveness.

However, in May 1993, the Uddevalla plant was shut down. Because of disastrous markets and low capacity utilisation, Volvo decided to consolidate all Swedish production at its main factory in Gothenburg and close the small final assembly plants in Uddevalla and Kalmar. Volvo management emphasised, however, that this was not because of competitive failures.

Source: adapted from *Sloan Management Review*, Winter 1994, 35(2), p. 37(9).

Questions for discussion

1 What are the lessons to be learned about motivation from the practices at Uddevalla?

2 To what extent could the best management practices at Uddevalla be transferred to a multiplant company such as General Motors, Ford or Chrysler? Under what conditions would such a transfer of practices be likely to be successful?

3 Do you think the Uddevalla plant would still be in operation if scientific principles had been used?

4 Historically, auto assembly jobs have been designed to be routine (narrow in both job scope and depth). How would you characterise the design of jobs in Uddevalla's manufacturing operation using the variables of variety (scope) and responsibility (depth)? Why?

Applied questions

5 Management by objectives (MBO) helps strengthen planning, encourage participative decision-making and motivate performance. Can you identify how and where MBO has been implemented at Uddevalla?

6 Exhibit 6-4 identifies the steps in organisational behaviour modification (OB mod). Using the diagram can you identify how management changed the behaviour of workers at Uddevalla?

WWW exercise

Manager's Internet tools

Web tips: examining motivation on the Internet

The world of work is changing, with the use of teleworking and Internet start-up companies that are here today and gone tomorrow. Also, in times of low unemployment and a lack of skilled staff, employers need to be able to maintain a contented workforce. Management needs to foster an environment where people enjoy coming to work and a culture that fosters motivation. When Joanna Read of Morpheus (in the opening vignette) realised she had problems with staff retention, she sought help and realised that it was her management style that needed to change. She also recognised that the different life cycles of a business needed different strategies, depending on whether it was in the initial start-up phase or the growth phase. The question is that if these types of firm are really different to work for, what would motivate you to work at a start-up versus a more mature organisation?

World Wide Web search

Examine some dotcom websites, particularly the areas dedicated to company information and job openings. Examine some of the job postings and note what benefits are offered to employees. What are some of the motivating factors listed?

Because the Internet industry is changing rapidly, there are likely to be recent Internet start-up websites to examine.

1 Are there actual or perceived differences between the inferred work environments at the different companies? If so, what are the different motivating factors mentioned or implied?

2 Would stock option plans motivate you to join a particular company? What other factors would motivate you to join an Internet start-up? A mature organisation?

3 Some of the websites began as start-up companies, but were acquired by larger firms. How do you think an acquisition would change the work environment of the original company? Would an acquisition change your motivation to work for that firm? If so, how and why?

LEARNING CHECKLIST ☑

Before you move on you may want to reflect on what you have learnt in this chapter. You should now be able to:

☑ write a simple, clear, challenging goal statement that includes an action verb, key result area, measurement standard and time frame

☑ write objectives that are SMART

☑ identify the desired processes in an effective management by objectives (MBO) programme

☑ differentiate among the four alternative forms of behaviour-shaping reinforcement (positive, negative, punishment, omission)

☑ describe how to implement an organisational behaviour modification programme to change a routine behaviour

☑ describe three types of incentive or reward plans, and explain their links to equity and expectancy motivation

☑ use the principles of task scope and task depth to differentiate among jobs that are classified as routine, technician, enlarged or enriched

☑ evaluate a job's psychological health (experienced meaningfulness, responsibility and knowledge of results) using the six core job dimensions that characterise work

☑ illustrate three practices managers can use to empower employees and thereby reduce the need for managerial control.

Further reading

Campion, M. (1987) 'Ability Requirement Implications of Job Design: An Interdisciplinary Perspective', paper presented at 95th conference of the American Psychological Association, New York (August).

Ehrlich, C. (2006) 'The EFQM-model and Work Motivation', *Total Quality Management & Business Excellence* 17(2), p. 131.

Eskildsen, J.K., Kristensen, K. and Westlund, A.H. (2004) 'Work Motivation and Job Satisfaction in Nordic Countries', *Employee Relations* 26(1/2), p. 122.

Hackman, J.R. (1987) 'The Design of Work Teams', in J.W. Lorsch (ed.) *Handbook of Organizational Behaviour*. Englewood Cliffs, NJ: Prentice Hall, pp. 315–342.

Snyder, C. (1991) in 'To Succeed, You Gotta Have Hope, Studies Show', *New York Times*, 26 December.

Woodruffe, C. (2005/2006) 'Employee Engagement – the Real Secret of Winning a Crucial Edge Over Your Rivals', *British Journal of Administrative Management*, Dec/Jan, pp. 28–30.

References

Ajzen, B.I. (1985) 'From Intentions to Actions: A Theory of Planned Behaviour', in J. Kuhl and J. Beckman (eds) *Action Control: From Cognition to Behaviour*, Springer-Verlag, pp. 11–39.

Alexander (1992) 'Health Care Costs, Quality Top List of Human Resources Concerns', *Employee Benefit Plan Review* 47(3), Alexander Consulting Group, pp. 38–39.

Anderson, K. (1999) 'By the (Open) Book', *Inc. Technology* 21(3), pp. 33–34.

Bandura, A. (1977) *Social Learning Theory*. Englewood Cliffs, NJ: Prentice Hall.

Bandura, A. (1986) *Social Foundations of Thought and Action: A Social-cognitive View*. Englewood Cliffs, NJ: Prentice Hall.

Bandura, A. (1988) 'Self-regulation of Motivation and Action Through Goal Systems', in V. Hamilton, G.H. Bower and N.H. Frijda (eds) *Competence Considered: Perceptions of Competence and Incompetence Across the Lifespan*. Dordrecht, Netherlands: Kluwer Academic Publishers, pp. 37–61.

Berlew, D.E. (1986) 'Managing Human Energy: Pushing Versus Pulling', in S. Srivastva (ed.) *Executive Power*. San Francisco, CA: Jossey-Bass, pp. 35–50.

Blackburn, R. and Rosen, B. (1993) 'Total Quality and Human Resources Management: Lessons Learned from Baldrige Award-Winning Companies', *Academy of Management Executive* 7, August, pp. 49–66.

Buhler, P. (1994) 'Motivating the Employee of the 90s: Managing in the 90s', *Supervision* 55, July, pp. 8–10.

Campbell, J.P., Dunnette, M.D., Arvey, R.D. and Hellervik, L.V. (1973) 'The Development and Evaluation of Behaviourally Based Rating Scales', *Journal of Applied Psychology*, February, p. 15.

Campion, M. (1987) 'Ability Requirement Implications of Job Design: An Interdisciplinary Perspective', paper presented at 95th conference of the American Psychological Association, New York (August).

Campion, M.A. (1988) 'Interdisciplinary Approaches to Job Design: A Constructive Replication with Extensions', *Journal of Applied Psychology* 73, pp. 467–481.

Cohen, A.R. and Bradford, D.L. (1984) *Managing for Excellence: The Guide to High Performance in Contemporary Organizations*. New York, NY: John Wiley & Sons.

Conger, J.A. and Kanungo, R.N. (1998) 'The Empowerment Process: Integrating Theory and Practice', *Academy of Management Review* 13, July, pp. 471–482.

Crystal, G. (1995) 'Growing the Pay Gap', *Los Angeles Times*, 23 July.

Cumming, C.M. (1994) 'Incentives That Really Do Motivate', *Compensation and Benefits Management* 26, May, pp. 38–40.

Dangot-Simpkin, G. (1991) 'Getting Your Staff to Do What You Want', *Supervisory Management* 36, January, pp. 4–5.

Drucker, P.F. (1954) *The Practice of Management*. New York, NY: Harper & Row.

Erez M., Earley, P.C. and Hulin, C.L. (1985) 'The Impact of Participation on Goal Acceptance and Performance: A Two-step Model', *Academy of Management Journal* 28, February, pp. 50–66.

Frayne, C.A. and Latham, G.P. (1987) 'Application of Social Learning Theory to Employee Self-management of Attendance', *Journal of Applied Psychology*, August, pp. 387–392.

Gist, M.E. and Mitchell, T.R. (1992) 'Self-efficacy: A Theoretical Analysis of its Determinants and Malleability', *Academy of Management Review* 17, April, pp. 183–211.

Hackman, J.R. and Lawler III, E.E. (1971) 'Employee Reactions to Job Characteristics', *Journal of Applied Psychology* 55, pp. 259–286 (defines the first six core job dimensions).

Hackman, J.R., Oldham, G.R., Janson, R. and Purdy, K. (1976) 'A New Strategy for Job Enrichment', *California Management Review* 17, Summer, pp. 57–71.

Hammer, M. (1990) 'Reengineering Work: Don't Automate, Obliterate', *Harvard Business Review* 68, July–August, p. 107.

Hamner, C.W. (1975) 'How to Ruin Motivation with Pay', *Compensation Review* 21, pp. 88–89.

Hasek, G. (2000) 'The Right Chemistry', *Industry Week*, 6 March, pp. 36–39.

Hof, R.D. (1996) 'Scott McNealy's Rising Sun', *Business Week*, 22 January, pp. 66–73.

Howat, I. (2002) 'Don't Let the IT Tail Wag the Business Dog', Institute of Ideas and Solutions, December, p. 9.

Ivancevich, J.M. (1979) 'High and Low Task Stimulation Jobs: A Causal Analysis of Performance–Satisfaction Relationships', *Academy of Management Journal* 22, June, p. 220.

Kappelman, L.A. and Prybutok, V.R. (1995) 'A Small Amount of Empowerment Pays Off Big in a Regional Bank', *National Productivity Review* 14, 22 September, pp. 39–42.

Kazdin, A.E. (1975) *Behaviour Modification in Applied Settings*. Homewood, IL: Dorsey Press, pp. 33–34.

Kelly, C.M. (1983) 'Remedial MBO', *Business Horizons*, September–October, pp. 64–65.

Kerr, S. (1975) 'On the Folly of Rewarding A, While Hoping for B', in B.M. Staw (ed.) *Psychological Dimensions of Organizational Behaviour*. New York, NY: Macmillan, 1991, pp. 65–75. Originally in *Academy of Management Journal* 18, pp. 769–783.

Kiggundu, M.N. (1981) 'Task Interdependence and the Theory of Job Design', *Academy of Management Review* 6, July, pp. 499–508.

Kohn, A. (1993) 'Why Incentive Plans Cannot Work', *Harvard Business Review* 71, September–October, pp. 54–63.

Komake, J. (1982) 'Why We Don't Reinforce: The Issues', *Journal of Organizational Behaviour Management*, Fall–Winter, pp. 97–100.

Kondrasuk, J.N. (1981) 'Studies in MBO Effectiveness', *Academy of Management Review* 6, July, pp. 419–430.

Latham, G.P. and Baldes, J.J. (1975) 'The Practical Significance of Locke's Theory of Goal-setting', *Journal of Applied Psychology* 60(30), pp. 122–124.

Latham, G.P. and Locke, E.A. (1969) 'Goal Setting – A Technique that Works', *Organisational Dynamics* 8, Autumn, pp. 68–80.

Latham, G.P. and Marshal, H.A. (1982) 'The Effects of Self-set, Participatively Set and Assigned Goals on the Performance of Government Employees', *Personnel Psychology* 35, pp. 399–404.

Lawler III, E.E. (1966) 'Managers' Attitudes Toward How Their Pay is and Should Be Determined', *Journal of Applied Psychology* 50, pp. 273–279.

Lawler III, E.E. (1981) *Pay and Organizational Development*. Reading, MA: Addison-Wesley.

Lawler III, E.W. (1994) 'Total Quality Management and Employee Involvement: Are They Compatible?' *Academy of Management Executive* 8, February, pp. 68–76.

Lengel, F. (1976) 'The Existence and Impact of Alienating Job Conditions in the Hospital Medical Laboratory', a master's degree report, Wayne State University, Detroit.

Locke, E.A. (1968) 'Toward a Theory of Task Performance and Incentives', *Organisational Behaviour and Human Performance* 3, pp. 157–189.

Locke, E.A. (1978) 'The Ubiquity of the Technique of Goal Setting in Theories and Approaches to Employee Motivation', *Academy of Management Review* 3, July, pp. 594–601; with more recent integration in E.A. Locke and G.P. Latham (1990) *A Theory of Goal Setting and Task Performance*. Englewood Cliffs, NJ: Prentice Hall.

Luthans, F. and Kreitner, R. (1985) *Organizational Behaviour Modification and Beyond: An Operant and Social Learning Approach*. Glenview, IL: Scott, Foresman, pp. 46–49.

Luthans, F. and Martinko, M. (1976) 'An Organizational Behaviour Modification Analysis of Absenteeism', *Human Resource Management* 15, Fall, pp. 11–18.

Markham, S.E., Scott, K.D. and Little, B.L. (1992) 'National Gainsharing Study: The Importance of Industry Differences', *Compensation and Benefits Review* 24(1), pp. 34–35.

McFarlin, D.B. and Sweeney, P.D. (1992) 'Distributing and Procedural Justice as Predictors of Satisfaction with Personal and Organization Outcomes', *Academy of Management Journal* 35, August, pp. 626–637.

Miller, M.W. (1992) 'IBM Shares Tumble by 7.6% on Pessimism Over Actions', *Wall Street Journal Europe*, 17 December, p. 4.

Nulty, P. (1995) 'Incentive Pay Can Be Crippling', *Fortune*, 13 November, p. 235.

Odiorne, G.S. (1965) *Management by Objectives.* New York, NY: Pitman.

Odiorne, G.S. (1979) *MBO II: A System of Managerial Leadership for the 80s.* Belmont, CA: Pitman.

O'Hara, K., Johnson, C.M. and Beehr, T.A. (1985) 'Organizational Behaviour Management in the Private Sector: A Review of Empirical Research and Recommendations for Further Investigation', *Academy of Management Review* 10, October, pp. 848–864.

O'Reilly, C. (1992) 'Corporations, Culture, and Commitment: Motivation and Social Control in Organizations', in A.A. Thompson Jr, W.E. Fulmer and A.J. Strickland III (eds) *Readings in Strategic Management* (4th edn). Homewood, IL: Irwin, p. 465.

Ost, E.J. (1990) 'Team-based Pay: New Wave Strategic Incentives', *Sloan Management Review*, Spring; and in A.A. Thompson Jr, W.E. Fulmer and A.J. Strickland III (1992) (eds) *Readings in Strategic Management* (4th edn). Homewood, IL: Irwin, pp. 485–499.

Premack, D. (1959) 'Toward Empirical Behaviour Laws: Positive Reinforcement', *Psychological Review* 66, pp. 123–180.

Quick, T.L. (1990) 'Using the "Three" to Achieve Your Goals', *Sales and Marketing Management* 142, September, pp. 170–171.

Roslund, J.L. (1989) 'Evaluating Management Objectives with the Quality Loss Function', *Quality Progress*, August, pp. 45–49.

Rothman, H. (1993) 'The Power of Empowerment', *Nations Business* 81, June, pp. 49–52.

Schuster, F.E. and Kindall, A.F. (1974) 'Management by Objectives, Where We Stand – A Survey of the Fortune 500', *Human Resource Management* 13, Spring, pp. 8–11.

Seyna, J. (1986) 'MOB: The Fad that Changed Management', *Long-Range Planning*, December, pp. 116–123.

Snyder, C.R. (1999) *Hope for the Journey.* Boulder, CO: Westview Press.

Steers, R.M. and Rhodes, S.R. (1991) 'Major Influences on Employee Attendance: A Process Model', in B.M. Staw (ed.) *Psychological Dimensions of Organizational Behaviour.* New York, NY: Macmillan, pp. 151–164.

Thomas, K.W. and Velthouse, B.A. (1990) 'Cognitive Elements of Empowerment: An "Interpretative" Model of Intrinsic Task Motivation', *Academy of Management Review* 15, October, p. 673.

Tubbs, M.E. and Ekeberg, S.E. (1991) 'The Role of Intentions in Work Motivation: Implications for Goal-setting Theory and Research', *Academy of Management Review* 16, January, pp. 180–199.

Walton, S. (1992) with John Huey, J., *Sam Walton: Made in America.* New York, NY: Doubleday, pp. 132–133.

Welbourne, T.M. and Gomez-Mejia, L.R. (1995) 'Gainsharing: A Critical Review and a Future Research Agenda', *Journal of Management* 21, September, p. 559.

Wood, R.E., Mento, A.J. and Locke, E.A. (1987) 'Task Complexity as a Moderator of Goal Effects: A Meta-analysis', *Journal of Applied Psychology* 72, pp. 416–425.

Wrenge, C.D. and Perroni, A.G. (1974) 'Taylor's Pig-tale: A Historical Analysis of Frederick W. Taylor's Pig-iron Experiments', *Academy of Management Journal* 17, pp. 6–27.

Wright, P.M. (1994) 'Goal Setting and Monetary Incentives: Motivational Tools That Can Work Too Well', *Compensation and Benefit Review* 26, May, pp. 41–50.

Yates, R.E. (1995) 'Can Motivational Techniques Release Corporations Within? Firms Take New Age Approach to Finding Success in Workplace', *Chicago Tribune*, 15 October, p. 1C.

Yearta, S.K., Maitlis, S. and Briner, R.B. (1995) 'An Exploratory Study of Goal Setting in Theory and Practice: A Motivational Technique that Works?', *Journal of Occupational and Organisational Psychology* 68, September, pp. 237ff.

Self-management at work: managing careers and stress

The opening vignette illustrates how local authorities are trying to encourage workers back into social work – a profession that is notorious for its high stress factors.

Social work: encouraging former social workers back into the profession makes better financial sense than training new recruits from scratch – and conditions have improved

So severe is the nationwide shortage of social workers that people who left the profession years ago are being targeted by local authorities. 'It is expensive to qualify a new social worker from scratch. So it makes sense to win back those who have already trained, and spend much less on

▶ brushing up their skills – particularly as there are thousands of qualified social workers currently not employed as such,' says Ian Johnston, director of the British Association of Social Workers.

Vic Citarella, adviser to the Local Government Association, has been involved in researching why so many people have left their careers in social work. 'Two of the main reasons are bringing up children and moving sideways into other areas of work. Many of these people would be interested in coming back into the profession for the same reasons that they joined initially, so it's important that we start communicating with them and find ways to meet their needs.'

The Training Organisation for Personal Social Services (TOPSS) has been funded by the Department of Health to do just that. 'We are at the very early stages of looking into developing a retraining package for returner social workers that would consist of a combination of training input and employer support,' explains Richard Banks, principal of the standards and qualifications framework at TOPSS. It's no mean feat, he admits, because the 150 local authorities – the main employers of social workers – all work completely independently. 'But we have created regional forums of employers in the past couple of years. Through these, we hope to get groups of employers to take part in pilot schemes and then roll out those that are successful.'

In the meantime a growing number of local authorities have already started creating their own local campaigns to recruit returner social workers and are working in partnership with local academic institutions to create tailor-made refresher courses. Michael Leadbetter, president of the Association of Directors of Social Services and director of social services in Essex, explains, 'What we have done in Essex is to determine the major gaps in skills and knowledge, which may be due to the passing of time or old qualifications. Then, we have agreed with an academic institution to put in place appropriate modules as well as providing additional practice placement opportunities.' Generally, training is accompanied by a mentoring service, as well as intense supervision and support in the workplace.

Both employer and employee gain, says Leadbetter. 'Retraining and support doesn't cost the new recruit a penny and the employer pays a lot less than they would to put a new recruit through the two-year Diploma in Social Work (DipSW), which is the recognised qualification in social work.'

Even for those who left the profession some years ago as unqualified social workers, there are increasing opportunities not only to return but also to be seconded by the local authority to qualify. Indeed, the Department of Health is increasingly supporting employers to take on such people and then put them through part- or full-time DipSW courses.

Among the greatest fears and anxieties of people who left social work years ago – whether qualified or unqualified – is that they are simply out of touch. 'But in fact, the skills involved in bringing up children or being in other employment tend to be highly transferable into the field of social work and are therefore not just valued but sought after by local authorities,' explains Leadbetter. 'We have a couple of social workers in Essex who took time out to do VSO [Voluntary Service Overseas] and they have a better perspective of social work because of their outside experiences than if they'd never left.'

The increased use of computers and changing standards and legislation are other concerns. However, says Leadbetter, these areas tend to be covered in-depth by employers at the retraining stage.

Then there is the issue of salaries. Can people really afford to go back into what is a notoriously low-paid profession? 'I am a qualified social worker who moved to work in an education department many years ago,' says Louise O'Shea. 'I'd love to return to social work but I am prevented from doing so because the poor pay makes it impossible with children to support and relatively high mortgage payments.'

The good news is that salaries are improving. 'They now start at around £17 000 – more in London – and you can fairly quickly progress to the £23 000 level,' says a spokeswoman for the General Social Care Council. 'As a team manager you can expect around £30 000, and directors of social services earn around £80–90 000.' Many local authorities are offering 'golden hellos' as well as annual retention payments, while others are focusing on offering benefits such as assistance with housing and childcare and flexible working arrangements.

Stress caused by heavy workloads, traumatic cases and the risk of being blamed or even scapegoated for errors is another source of concern for people thinking about coming back into social work. The media has placed heavy emphasis on such stories in recent years, rarely reporting all the good that social workers achieve and the job satisfaction they enjoy on a daily basis.

Owen Davies, national secretary for social services at UNISON, believes this is the biggest discouragement of all. 'However hard you work and however dedicated you are, social work is a largely thankless job,' he admits. 'And if something goes wrong, you risk huge blame. It's a powerful anxiety.'

Many social services departments, however, are introducing stress management, additional supervision and support, as well as decreasing workloads, in an attempt to overcome these concerns. 'Social work is inevitably a stressful job because of the nature of the people you're trying to help, but employers are waking up to the fact that stress can be reduced,' Davies says.

Others think they are too old to start again in a fast-changing profession. The new social work degree, which begins next year and will eventually replace the DipSW, will undoubtedly attract a younger crowd. In fact, however, the number of people starting social work in their thirties, forties and fifties remains on the increase with many people entering into it as a second or third career, as a result of wanting to do something more socially useful with their working lives.

Source: © Kate Hilpern, *Independent*, 23 July 2002.

Discussion questions

1 What are the costs of stress to the employer and the employee?

2 Who should take responsibility for stress at work?

More and more organisations are changing their approach to work in an attempt to create workplaces and policies that allow people to deal with the demands of their personal as well as work lives. Pay-offs for organisations include healthier employees, increased productivity, cost savings associated with fewer absences and medical expenses, and the caring corporate citizen image. On the other hand, employees who take advantage of the physical, emotional, social, financial and other professional services available in creating work–life balance, can experience benefits. The responsibility for achieving a satisfactory work–life balance is really the responsibility of each individual. To achieve a successful career, and a successful life, individuals need to be skilled in effective self-management.

The meaning of work

Work can mean different things to different people and people work for a variety of reasons, not just for financial reward. We often think of work as 'paid', and fail to acknowledge work done in the home or in the voluntary sector as meaningful. Work needs a broader definition – as parents who raise children are performing just as much of a useful service to society as any office worker.

People also respond differently to work and some sort of work do appear to be more meaningful than others. However, even when jobs are the same the individual's response can differ. I am sure you are now aware of this after studying the previous chapters on personality and motivation.

Four of the major functions of work are economic, social, social status and self-esteem.

1 **Economic.** People are paid for the work they do. For most people this is a necessity, as they need to support themselves and their families. But money is not the only motivator, other satisfactions are also important; think of nurses, paramedics or the social workers discussed in the opening vignette. However, if the pay is not adequate they may have to leave their job despite their commitment to it.

2 **Social function.** Work provides social interaction and gives individuals the chance to make new friends. The majority of people who work outside the home will spend more time with their colleagues than their family. Friendship with colleagues provides a social support function and is often one of the reasons mothers of young children return to work even though they may not be much better off financially.

3 **Social status function.** The type of work and the place in the organisation hierarchy often extend into a person's social life. They may have a higher status in the community; they may even be offered incentives such as tickets to cup finals. They are also often approached to serve on voluntary bodies, which all adds to their status.

4 **Self-esteem function.** Work provides a sense of identity. It tells us who we are. When people introduce themselves, they will quite often mention their profession on the assumption that it is important in defining who we are. This helps us identify our contribution to society and how we benefit others. It makes us feel good about ourselves (Terkel, 1972).

Unemployment

Often in times of organisational change one of the first things that springs to mind is 'Will I lose my job?' In the 1980s **downsizing** became common as organisations became sleeker and more streamlined. Changes driven by new technologies and the redesign of work practices have also meant some workers have found themselves obsolete. The impact this can have on a person can be devastating, not only during the period of uncertainty of whether they will survive the

downsizing
The process of deliberately becoming smaller by reducing the size of the workforce, or amalgamating or losing divisions.

change, but also what happens if they do have to suffer the pain of unemployment and financial insecurity.

We have discussed the meanings of work and why people do it; dealing with unemployment will mean not only financial loss but also loss of status, esteem and the social support network often found through work. Although we may not be able to avoid redundancy we can certainly take steps to ensure that we remain employable by keeping our skills up to date and ensuring we are able to manage ourselves and be flexible. You never know – finding ourselves unemployed could be the impetus for starting our own business or changing to a company that better meets our needs and goals.

Managing yourself

According to Bennis (1987), for most people the central issue and aspiration is a life worth living. Bennis found that the one characteristic that all successful leaders share is full deployment of themselves. They measure themselves accurately and use themselves fully. He further observed that anyone who measures him or herself accurately and uses him or herself fully could be said to be not only successful, but also happy. The test is how one feels each day in anticipation of the day's experience. The same test is the primary predictor of good health and longevity.

Unfortunately, most people have been brought up to live by rules that have nothing to do with making our lives worth living. Some of these rules, in fact, are guaranteed to make life not worth living. Bennis (1987) suggests that most of our institutions and traditions introduce cultural distortions into our vision, impose beliefs and definitions on us that do not work, distract us from the task of building lives that are worth living, and persuade us that other things are more important. Consequently, the jobs of measuring ourselves accurately and using ourselves fully so that we can not only be successful, but also happy in our careers and lives, are ours, and ours alone. In addition, the key to accomplishing these goals lies in successfully managing ourselves.

Drucker (1999) agrees with Bennis that success in the knowledge economy comes to those who know themselves – their strengths, their values and how they best perform. He notes that history's great achievers – a Napoleon, a da Vinci, a Mozart – have always managed themselves. That, in large measure, is what makes them great achievers. But they are rare exceptions, so unusual in both their talents and their accomplishments as to be considered outside the boundaries of ordinary human experience. However, Drucker believes that now most of us, even those of us with modest endowments, will have to learn to manage ourselves. We will have to learn to develop ourselves. We will have to place ourselves where we can make the greatest contribution. Moreover, we will have to stay mentally alert and engaged during a 50-year working life, which means knowing how and when to change the work we do. So what do we need to do to manage ourselves effectively?

Determine your strengths

We can only perform well from strength. We cannot really excel in areas where we are weak, let alone on something we cannot do at all. Therefore, we need to know our strengths in order to know what kind of organisation and careers we belong in.

feedback analysis
A written expectation that you expect will happen because of a key decision or action, and the comparison of the actual results 9 or 12 months later.

One way to discover your strengths is through **feedback analysis**. Whenever you make an important decision or take an important action, write down what you expect will happen. Nine or twelve months later compare the actual results with your expectations. Practised consistently, this simple method will show where your strengths are, what you are doing or failing to do that deprives you of the full benefits of your strengths, and where you are not particularly competent. Finally, it will show you where you have no strengths and cannot perform.

Several implications for action follow from feedback analysis. First, concentrate on your strengths. Put yourself where your strengths can produce results. Second, work on improving your strengths. Analysis will rapidly show where you need to improve skills or acquire new ones. It will also show gaps in your knowledge that need to be filled. Third, discover where you have disabling ignorance and overcome it. Many people – especially people with great expertise in one area – are contemptuous of knowledge in other areas. First-rate engineers, for instance, tend to take pride in not knowing anything about people. Human resource professionals, by contrast, often pride themselves on their ignorance of elementary accounting or quantitative methods. However, taking pride in such ignorance is self-defeating. Go to work on acquiring the skills and knowledge you need to fully realise your strengths. Finally, it is essential to remedy your bad habits – the things you do or fail to do that inhibit your effectiveness and performance.

Determine how you perform best

Different people work and perform differently. If you are working in ways that are not your best ways, you will not be able to perform at your optimum level. A person's way of performing can be slightly modified, but it is unlikely to be completely changed – and certainly not easily. Just as people achieve results by doing what they are good at, they also achieve results by working in ways they best perform. Ask questions and analyse your answers about how you prefer to work. How much pace, structure and stress do you prefer? How you prefer to learn – reading, listening or doing? Do you prefer to work alone or with others in teams? Do you prefer being a leader or a subordinate, a decision-maker or an adviser? Then act on your knowledge if you want to perform to your optimum.

Determine your values

Figure out what you stand for, what kind of person you want to be and what behaviours you believe are desirable. Ask yourself what kind of person you want to see in the mirror in the morning. Then determine your organisation's values. To be effective in an organisation, a person's values must be compatible with the organisation's values. They do not need to be the same, but they must be close.

Take responsibility for relationships

Very few people work by themselves and achieve results by themselves. Whether they are members of an organisation or independently employed, most people work with others and need to be effective with other people. Managing yourself requires taking responsibility for relationships in two ways.

The first is to accept the fact that other people are as much individuals as you yourself are. They too have their strengths; they too have their ways of getting things done; they too have their values. To be effective, therefore, you have to know the strengths, the performance modes and the values of your co-workers. The purpose is to understand the people you work with and depend on so that you can make use of their strengths, their ways of working and their values. Working relationships are as much based on the people as they are on the work.

The second part of relationship responsibility is taking responsibility for communication. Today the great majority of people work with others who have different tasks and responsibilities. The majority of 'personality' conflicts in organisations arise because people do not know what other people are doing and how they do their work, or what contribution the other people are concentrating on and what results they expect. The reason they do not know is that they have not asked and therefore have not been told.

To understand your co-workers and be able to work most productively with them you could do two things. One is to share with your associates what you are good at, how you prefer to work, what your values are, the contribution you plan to concentrate on, and the results you expect to deliver. Second, you should ask others what their strengths are, how they prefer to perform, their values and their proposed contributions. You should request this of everyone with whom you work, whether as subordinate, superior, colleague or team member.

For example, the marketing director may have come out of sales and know everything about sales, but know nothing about the things he or she has never done – pricing, advertising, packaging and the like. Therefore, the people who do these things must make sure that the marketing director understands what they are trying to do, why they are trying to do it how they are going to do it and what results to expect. Conversely, it is the marketing director's responsibility to make sure that all co-workers understand how he or she looks at marketing: what his or her goals are, how he or she works, and what he or she expects of him or herself and of each co-worker.

Determine your career match

Most people do not really know where they belong in terms of a career until they are well past their mid-twenties. By that time, however, they should know the answers to the three questions: What are my strengths? How do I perform? What are my values? At that point, they are better able to decide a good career match. At least, they should be able to decide where they *do not* belong. The person who has learned that he or she does not perform well in a big organisation should have learned to say no to a position in one. The person who has learned that he or she is not a decision-maker should have learned to say no to a decision-making assignment.

Equally important, knowing the answer to these questions enables a person to say to an opportunity, an offer or an assignment, 'Yes, I will do that. However, this is the way I should be doing it. This is the way it should be structured. This is the way the relationships should be. These are the kind of results you should expect from me, and in this time frame, because this is who I am.'

Successful careers are not planned. They develop when people are prepared for opportunities because they know their strengths, their method of work and their values. Knowing where one belongs can transform an ordinary person – hard-working and competent but otherwise mediocre – into an outstanding performer. Let us look a little more closely at some ideas for managing your career.

Career management

It used to be that most people went to work for large companies and expected to stay with them for most of their careers. People were loyal to companies and vice versa. Career ladders were clearly designed. Managers, specialists and those who had been with a company for many years could count on holding their jobs. People who obtained a good education, worked hard and were loyal were normally assured of a job and opportunity to build a career.

However, this is no longer the case. Rice (2001) suggests many people find that they have to change career path because of changes in the economy; jobs in advertising and marketing are often the first to go in times of difficulty. Many higher-level managers, technical specialists and employees with 20 or more years of service are being released from their jobs and companies.

Today most people expect to work at several different jobs in several different organisations; often, they may also expect to change careers several times. Others opt to start their own businesses. Success in today's culture is no longer measured by money, position and status alone, but also by family, lifestyle, geographic location and personal autonomy. No longer do people assume that the organisation has unilateral control over their careers. Rice (2002) also suggests that a service- and knowledge-based economy has fundamentally shifted our aspirations about how we work and live. The Dynamics of Diversity box illustrates how occupational psychology can identify who would do well in certain careers.

dynamics of diversity

Why your job is all in the mind: occupational psychology is increasingly used to spot which people will do best in particular careers

An occupational psychologist is not, as some might think, a soothsayer drafted in by the England football team manager to divine a winning technique. She or he is closer to the white-coated scientific community.

Occupational psychologists look at behavioural patterns in the workplace – anything from the design of interview centres to models of stress in world leaders. They also aim to identify what kinds of personalities do best in specific careers. Moreover, as companies are increasingly drafting them in to assess you, it pays to understand a little of what they do. Occupational psychologists have, for instance, devised an examination that will forecast whether someone will make a good keyhole surgeon. Traditionally, assessing which trainees can succeed in this highly specialised branch of surgery has been difficult, and often shortcomings are not discovered until after expensive training or, worse, when an operation has gone wrong.

Now a computer test, which measures hand–eye co-ordination, has been developed. The trainee has to trace around a shape on a computer screen while their speed and accuracy are measured. No previous experience is needed and the test has proved to be an accurate predictor.

The use of computers in the field of careers advice is not new but tests are increasingly being used in reverse – to find out whether the individual is suitable for the job. Two academics from Nottingham University, Dr Eamonn Ferguson and Professor David James, say that more frequent use of psychometric tests supports both the applicant and the employer. They say that up to 17 per cent of medical trainees drop out, but that this figure could be reduced if universities were to review their selection procedures.

More startlingly, a test has now been devised to spot people who may have a 'dark side'. Personality tests are usually concerned with benign characteristics such as sociability, prudence or thinking style. But the Hogan Development Survey, being used in the UK by psychologists from private consultancy PCL called, ironically, Geoff Trickey and Gillian Hyde, is designed to expose the 'counter-productive behaviour' that can surface when an individual is particularly stressed.

The test, which is based on research of managers who have 'gone off the rails', is primarily designed to be used in staff appointments – usually of senior managers – or staff development. If an existing employee is identified as displaying traits like arrogance or mistrustfulness then they can be trained in strategies to avert their crushing staff morale.

The test lasts for 20 minutes and executives are asked to give true or false answers to 168 simple questions such as 'Do you feel that you are ambitious?' and 'Do you feel that you are witty and entertaining?' The test is designed to make it difficult to cheat, as people are encouraged to highlight their strengths.

Mr Trickey says, 'This often relates to strong features of a personality which, in moderation, are positive, but which, when an individual is stressed, become negative.' Examples of people with a dark side are Charlie Chaplin, brilliantly creative but very difficult to work with, and Peter Sellers, whose exuberance could turn manic.

He adds that until the 1980s there was a huge divergence between personality tests, but psychologists now all use the Five Factor test to identify to what degree a person demonstrates desirable traits.

1 **Surgence:** this relates to how sociable, energetic and ambitious a person is.

2 **Agreeability:** a person's ability to get on with people and empathise.

3 **Openness to experience:** whether the person will keep up to date with new technology.

4 **Consciousness:** this relates to self-control and prudence.

5 **Adjustment:** this, says Trickey, is the most important factor – how emotionally stable a person is.

Alexander Lowen, an American psychologist, has identified five personality types, which he says will indicate precisely what sort of an employee a prospective candidate will make.

1 **Hold-together personality:** this is formed in response to damaging experiences encountered from birth onwards, such as staying in hospital longer due to premature birth. As a child, the person tries to hold on to themselves in hostile environments, which leads to an adult who is difficult to understand and a perfectionist. They are committed and hard working but in an insular way. In conflict situations they appear to withdraw.

2 **Hold-on personality:** this personality type is formed from being deprived of touch and attention in early life. Hold-ons, because of their desire for attention, present well and network effectively. They tend to prefer to think rather than do and can appear lazy. They also find it difficult to be truthful and forthcoming. They tend not to reach senior executive positions.

3 **Hold-up personality:** children who were not given the opportunity to develop their own identity often show this trait as adults, which means they tend to hold themselves up above the rest of the world in a heroic or grandiose stance. They are charming, successful and excellent strategists but can be scheming and ruthless. At best, they make soft, heroic-like leaders but, at worst, they are tyrannical. High-flyers tend to fall into this mould.

4 **Hold-in personality:** hold-in personalities are formed when children are over-disciplined. They hold in their feelings so as not to upset their parents and in later life are likely to display a lack of assertiveness and find receiving feedback a traumatic experience.

5 **Holdback personality:** children who are not given the chance to come to terms with their own sexuality emerge as adults who hold back their feelings. They compensate for this by striving for excellence, in a rational, goal-orientated way, rather than seeking inspiration or creativity. When encountering failure, they need a long time to bounce back.

There are dangers, however, with over-reliance on such tests. Although they provide analyses and often highlight faults, one obvious drawback is that their effectiveness depends on the person administering them and the person analysing the results.

It could be argued that many of the tests are biased towards white, middle-class males, designed as they are to select people for the boardroom, and the overwhelming majority of board members are ... white, middle-class and male. Another danger is that only bland people are employed. Mr Trickey denies, however, that using the dark-side test universally could result in a *Brave New World*-esque workplace, where all employees are clones of each other. He contends that companies will still employ these people but will design specific training or counselling for them to prevent their going off the rails.

However, according to research from Cranfield University School of Management, there are other factors that determine who will make the best employee. Age is a key indicator of a person's managerial ability – older senior managers will take a balanced view when reaching a decision and are better at fostering positive relationships with people in their office and in other companies

Source: © Liz Stuart, *Guardian*, 30 January 1999.

Discussion questions

1 How important are selection procedures in assessing someone's suitability for a job?

2 Do you think such tests are biased to white, middle-class males?

Factors that drive career trends

Many factors have contributed to these changes. Competition has intensified as the nations of the world move closer to a global economy. Technological advances continue to enhance productivity and spur new product development. Employees are better educated and more empowered to make decisions and act at work.

These and other factors have stimulated many companies to become leaner, flatter and more efficient, thus reducing the number of jobs. That trend, in turn, has eroded the feelings of loyalty among workers, managers and technical people at all levels. Many people are wary of trusting or identifying too closely with a company and it could be that working too long in the same company could count against you as it may be perceived that you lack a sense of adventure. For some, the impact on their self-esteem and aspirations is devastating.

The accelerating rate of change stimulated by technological advances means that in the future people will change companies and even careers more frequently than in the past. Rather than planning for a career in one field, industry or company, young people would do better to assume they will work in three or more companies and career areas and to focus on developing transferable skills. Not only are advancement paths unclear, so are career opportunities.

Sir Terry Leahy, chief executive of Tesco Stores plc, demonstrates how someone from a non-traditional background can rise to the top. Leahy's humble background, a Liverpool council house and UMIST management course, and his unflashy image could not disguise his ambition and world-class talent. In this cut-throat sector profits are up by 13 per cent and Tesco remains the supermarket others have to beat.

What is a career?

To most people a career is a series of separate but related experiences that occur in the process of moving upwards in their chosen occupation or profession. Traditionally this process involved increases in salary, responsibility, status, prestige and power. However, today an individual can remain in the same job, developing new skills, without necessarily moving upwards in an organisation. It is also becoming common for people to move laterally among various jobs in different fields and different organisations.

The concept of 'career' applies not only to working for pay, but also to a variety of other life pursuits, such as homemaking and volunteer work. Hall (1976) defines **career** as 'the individually perceived sequence of attitudes and behaviours associated with work-related experiences and activities over the span of the person's life'. Current research has indicated that today there may be at least four dominant career concepts replacing the traditional one of moving up an organisational ladder (see 'Research focus').

career
The individually perceived sequence of attitudes and behaviours associated with work-related experiences and activities over the span of the person's life.

Research focus: career concepts

In many, if not most, organisations a career has traditionally been defined as a steady progression towards positions of increasing authority and responsibility. Career success has been measured in terms of position in an organisational hierarchy. A pluralistic framework, on the other hand, specifies that there are markedly different ways of defining career success and, consequently, markedly different approaches to career management and development in organisations.

Brousseau *et al.* (1996) have developed a more contemporary, multiple career concept model that identifies four fundamentally different patterns of career experience. The four patterns – or career concepts – basically differ in terms of direction and frequency of movement within and across different kinds of work over time. The four concepts can be combined in various ways to form hybrid concepts that, in turn, can be used to describe many different patterns of career experience. Distinctly different sets of motives underlie each of the four concepts. Exhibit 7-1 presents a summary of the concepts and key associated motives.

EXHIBIT 7–1 Four career concepts

	Key features and motives			
	Linear	Expert	Spiral	Transitory
Direction of movement	Upward	Little movement	Lateral	Lateral
Duration of stay in one field	Variable	Life	7–10 years	3–5 years
Key motives	Power Achievement	Expertise Security	Personal growth Creativity	Variety Independence

The linear career concept

The ideal linear career consists of a progressive series of steps upwards in a hierarchy to positions of ever increasing authority and responsibility. People who see the ideal career in linear terms often find it difficult to imagine any other definition of success. In the West, in particular, the linear concept is deeply rooted in the cultural emphasis society places on upward mobility. Chief among the motives that people with strong linear concepts bring to their careers is power and achievement. They are motivated by opportunities to make important things happen.

The expert career concept

The expert career is one involving a lifelong commitment to some occupational field or speciality. Once the career choice has been made, the individual focuses on further developing and refining his or her knowledge and skills within that speciality. If there is upward movement, it is roughly from apprentice to journeyman to master, a reflection of the origins of the expert concept in the medieval guild structure. Old as it is, many people view the expert career concept as descriptive of their ideal career.

People with strong expert career concepts know clearly that what they desire most in their careers is expertise or technical competence, and security or stability. Getting ahead means becoming increasingly proficient in their specialities. The nature of the work they perform is an integral part of their self-identity. A quick linear trip up the corporate ladder could be an alienating experience for an individual with a strong expert career concept.

The spiral career concept

The spiral career is one in which a person makes periodic major moves across occupational areas, specialities or disciplines. Ideally, these moves come every seven to ten years, a span that seems to permit individuals sufficient time to develop in-depth competence, if not full mastery, in many fields before moving on to new ones. The ideal spiral move is from one area (e.g. engineering or research) into an allied area (e.g. product development). The new field draws on knowledge and skills developed in the old field, and at the same time throws open the door to the development of an entirely new set of knowledge and skills. Like their linear career counterparts, spirals bring numerous motives to their careers, but the primary ones are personal development and creativity.

The transitory career concept

The transitory career is the least traditional, and one of consistent inconsistency. The ideal transitory career is one in which a person moves every three to five years from one field or job to a very different or wholly unrelated field or job. People who intentionally pursue transitory careers often do not think of themselves as actually having careers. They are merely treating themselves to a fascinating mix of work experiences, seeking variety and independence.

Implications of career concepts

Individuals who differ in their career concepts and motives do not merely differ; they clearly complement each other as well. Organisations that support pluralistic concepts of careers stand to gain the advantage of developing and maintaining within their workforces diverse sets of complementary skills and capabilities. These skills provide distinct competitive and survival advantages in a fast-moving, unpredictable and largely unforgiving world.

Career stages

Many people begin to prepare for a career without even thinking about it. As children's personalities develop and they go through school, they begin to fantasise about what they will do when they get older. Their thoughts are usually influenced by their socio-economic status, family background and educational environment.

Many young people enter the world of work through part-time jobs, and they begin to learn more about what they like and do not like to do and what they hope to achieve. These young people are in the first of several career stages, shown in Exhibit 7-2. Most people progress through these stages, although the exact timing of each varies.

Planning your career

Planning your career requires a lot of self-management. In order to know what type of career you will be happy in, you need first to determine your life priorities, values and interests. We turn to these topics in this section.

Know yourself well

Not everyone aspires to be director of a company, nor does everyone want to be a manager. However, virtually all people want to be successful and happy. Definitions of success and happiness are elusive, largely because both are self-defined. What constitutes success to one person may not to another, and what brings happiness is highly personal. *Success is achieving your objectives.* Happiness is feeling satisfied with your situation. Thus, one of the first steps in career planning is to begin identifying your goals, values and aspirations. Career planning should be approached in the context of your whole life.

EXHIBIT 7 – 2 Career stages

Individuals may differ in the age at which they transition from one stage to the next, but for most people the role of work in their lives progresses through rather predictable career stages.

Age	Stage	Description
0–14	Early childhood	Parents, schools, peers and experiences influence attitudes, values and expectations about work
15–24	Exploration and initial jobs	Temporary jobs and first full-time job to earn money, develop independence, test self and learn own strengths and weaknesses, and investigate possibilities and limits of specific jobs
25–34	Trial work period	Move from testing self to clearer view of self and direction in work context; individuals can feel confident and successful or confused, uncertain, frustrated
35–44	Establishment	Find and accept role and career path that is satisfying, or resign self to not fully achieving aspirations and accepting what must be endured, or trying a different path
45–65	Stability and maintenance	For some, continuing advancement and growth; for many, plateauing and stabilising and making contributions in a satisfying way; for some, frustration; and for some, trying a different path
65+	Post-retirement	Letting go and finding new activities and outlets for satisfaction

Life planning

Life planning is deciding how you want to live your life. Although some people value career and work highly, most believe there is more to life than work. Other important factors include family, leisure-time activities, social life, spiritual development, education and personal development, and civic and philanthropic involvement. **Life planning** includes making choices about what mix of these various aspects of life most closely matches your values and aspirations. Some people emphasise career and work over the other factors. Others focus on family or spiritual development or social life. Some try to achieve a relatively even balance.

life planning
Making choices about what activities you want to spend your time on in your life.

The first 'Your turn' exercise shows selected aspects of life, based on work by Clawson *et al.* (1992). How important is each to you? This exercise can help you gain perspective on your values and so help you plan a more satisfying life. Making these choices can be difficult because each choice involves costs as well as benefits. Each person has the same amount of time each day, and it is impossible to do everything. Choosing one activity often means another cannot be pursued.

Your turn

Valuing selected aspects of life

Allocate a total of 100 points among these different aspects of life according to how much you value each. If one aspect is very important, you might give it 30 to 50 points. Some might receive zeros. Your total should be 100.

_____	Work/career/profession	_____	Intellectual growth
_____	Family	_____	Spiritual growth
_____	Wealth (money)	_____	Social life (friends)
_____	Material possessions	_____	Physical fitness/health
_____	Political/societal concerns	_____	Recreation

Where have I come from?

One way of getting to know yourself, including what motivates you, what you like and dislike doing, and what is important to you, is to answer the questions 'Where have I come from? What is my background and how does it relate to how I think and feel about myself?' One way to answer these questions is to write your autobiography (Clawson *et al.*, 1992).

Set aside some uninterrupted time during which you can give exclusive attention to writing freely about yourself. Just start writing what comes to mind without worrying about organisation or whether you are getting the 'right' things down. When finished, review your results to analyse what areas seem most and least important to you. A more structured alternative is to complete the second 'Your turn' exercise. You could also use the questions in the exercise to help diagnose your autobiography.

Your turn

This has been my life

Write down your answers to the following questions. This exercise helps you sort out your main values, motives and aspirations up to this stage of your life.

1 What have I liked to do most? Least?

2 What successes have I had? Failures?

3 What have been my most important relationships, and what impact have they had on me?

4 How important have relationships been to me?

5 What were the most important incidents in my life and what meaning do they have for me?

6 Have there been any turning points in my life so far?

7 When did I feel happiest and most fulfilled? Discontented and least fulfilled? What was the context of these feelings?

8 How does my past experience help me understand my present feelings about myself? My degree of self-esteem? My present personality and behaviour?

Know your values

The previous exercises have already required that you identify your values to some extent. You can expand your awareness by completing the third 'Your turn' exercise, which is designed to help you rank your values. After you have identified the relative importance of different aspects of your life and their associated values, it is helpful to identify your interests.

Determine your interests

Your autobiography and responses to the 'Your turn' exercises probably pointed towards some of your interests. According to Holland (1973), by the time people are in college or beginning to choose their occupations, they have developed a predisposition towards various clusters of jobs. What you liked and did not like doing reveals your interests.

One source of help is the Strong Interest Inventory (SII), which is a widely used vocational interest test. The SII relates your interests to major occupational groups and selected jobs. It is based on Holland's (1973) theory that most occupations can be grouped in one of six general occupational themes. Exhibit 7-3 provides examples of interests, activities, skills and values of people who fall into each of the SII themes. Exhibit 7-3 is only suggestive and is not a substitute for the SII, which gives information that is much more complete.

Know your skills

Knowing your values and interests helps in determining *what you want* from a job and career. Knowing your abilities and skills helps in determining *what you can give* to an organisation. Begin recording your personal inventory of skills. Avoid comparing yourself to others. One suggestion is to brainstorm on this subject, listing as many skills as you can. Then you can rank them according to those you feel best about and those you want to improve. Keep your list where you can add to it as you identify new skills or more fully develop existing skills. An excellent source of help in identifying your skills is Bolles' (2000) *What Color is Your Parachute?* (revised annually).

Your turn

What do I value?

Place a + (plus sign) in front of any item that you value and that is so important to you that you consistently try to experience it. For any item that you disdain or seek to avoid, put a − (minus sign). Skip any item that is neutral, or does not influence you. When you have finished, study your results to find patterns that suggest what you might want to experience in your career.

_____	Achieving	_____	Advancing
_____	Being logical	_____	Being relaxed
_____	Being creative	_____	Being challenged
_____	Being alone	_____	Being close
_____	Being higher than others	_____	Being praised
_____	Being independent	_____	Being secure
_____	Being safe	_____	Being expert
_____	Competing	_____	Controlling
_____	Co-operating	_____	Creating ideas or things
_____	Directing others	_____	Doing mental work
_____	Enjoying work	_____	Experiencing stability
_____	Feeling comfortable with ambiguity and uncertainty	_____	Feeling in control
_____	Focusing on one job at a time	_____	Finishing a job
_____	Having variety	_____	Having routine
_____	Having unstructured work	_____	Having work structured
_____	Having several balls in the air	_____	Having order
_____	Receiving clear direction	_____	Helping others
_____	Working with simple ideas	_____	Taking risks
_____	Working with people	_____	Working with things
_____	Working outdoors	_____	Working with hands
_____	Working alone	_____	Working in groups
_____	Working with details	_____	Working with general ideas
_____	Others?	_____	Working with complex ideas and problems
		_____	Others?

Skills can be developed through school, training and experience. A good career plan identifies current skills, those needed for the next job, and those likely to be required in the future. The plan can then provide for when and how the needed skills will be developed. The next step is to plan how to find the right position to move you along in your career.

EXHIBIT 7 – 3 *Six occupational themes*

Theme	Interests	Work activities	Potential skills	Values
Realistic (R)	Machines, tools, outdoors	Operating equipment, using tools, building, repairing	Mechanical ingenuity and dexterity, physical co-ordination	Tradition, practicality, common sense
Investigative (I)	Science, theories, ideas, data	Performing lab work, solving abstract problems, researching	Maths, writing, analysis	Independence, curiosity, learning
Artistic (A)	Self-expression, art appreciation	Composing music, writing, creating visual art	Creativity, musical talent, artistic expression	Beauty, originality, independence, imagination
Social (S)	People, teamwork, human welfare, community service	Teaching, explaining, helping	People skills, verbal ability, listening, showing understanding	Co-operation, generosity, service to others
Enterprising (E)	Business, politics, leadership, influence	Selling, managing, persuading	Verbal ability, ability to motivate and direct others	Risk-taking, status, competition
Conventional (C)	Organisation, data, finance	Setting up procedures, organising, operating computers	Maths, data analysis, record-keeping, attention to detail	Accuracy, stability, efficiency

Getting the career you want

Finding your ideal job can be difficult because some factors are out of your control. Economic conditions, the availability of jobs, and the number of people looking for similar jobs are a few of those factors. This leads some people to settle for taking any job they can get, at least temporarily, and sometimes that may be appropriate. However, a better approach is to get a clear picture in your mind of the kind of job and career you want, and then seek diligently to find and obtain that job.

Define what you want to do

You have already laid the groundwork for defining the kind of job and career you want through the preceding self-assessment process. Your results can help you answer questions, like those that follow, that will further define the job you want.

- What are your best skills and where do you want to use them?
- What kinds of people would you like to work with or help?
- In what kind of place would you like to work?
- What fields or industries feel compatible with your skills and interests?

- What salary level do you want?
- What developmental and advancement opportunities do you want?

In answering these and similar questions, you can begin to define the specific jobs or careers that will enable you to use your skills and fulfil your interests and aspirations.

Identify potential organisations

Begin to identify specific organisations that have the kinds of jobs you want. Do this by word of mouth, by reading business periodicals, and by using school or college career guidance services. Read the recruitment advertisements in the business section of your local paper and the *Financial Times*. List specific organisations that have potential for you. Then request information about these companies. You may even want to visit some. Such a visit is not to secure a position, but to obtain information that will help you assess the fit with your own skills and interests. If you have an informational interview, go with questions in mind and keep the meeting brief. Enquire about the company's employment needs and the goals it is trying to achieve.

Build a network of contacts

Start your career planning immediately, even if you have some years of study ahead of you.

network
Contacts who can help provide information, advice and help in your career.

Begin to build a **network** of contacts that can help you obtain information, give you advice and help you get introductions into the companies of your choice. Talk with the successful friends of your parents and the parents of your friends. Ask them for the names of others that might help. Become acquainted with the people in your school who can give you information and advice and can serve as referees. You will be surprised how wide a network you can develop if you work at it.

Placements

Summer and part-time work can be just a source of money or it can provide important skills and information. Look for work that fits your job and career interests. Such a job may be more valuable to you in the end than one that pays more, and above-average performance may be rewarded by valuable contacts and references.

Design your curriculum vitae

Carefully design a one- or two-page curriculum vitae (CV) that effectively describes your goals, qualifications and skills. You may want to have more than one CV for use in trying to achieve different types of job. The basics should stay the same, but the goals and emphasis on skills may vary. Refine your CV until you feel it represents you in the best manner possible. If you want some advice from professionals, a survey by Scripps (1999) of 1687 human resource managers and executive recruiters yielded the following key findings:

- a strong preference for two-page CVs (63 per cent)
- a strong preference for a chronological CV format (70 per cent)
- the importance of the CV's readability followed by overall appearance (more than 50 per cent)
- dislike for fancy papers with designs and shading (they do not copy well)
- use of a covering letter (84 per cent) with CV – 'The cover letter is what sells us on you. Tell us why we should hire you,' says one executive
- it is OK to fax or email CVs; a follow-up of a mailed hard copy is recommended, though.

At the end of the survey, respondents were asked: 'If you could give the CV writer one piece of advice, what would it be?' One respondent summarised much of the advice: 'Grammar/spelling 100 per cent correct. No typing errors. Personalised covering letter. No more than two pages. Emphasise accomplishments, factors that might distinguish you from other applicants. Concise/well written.'

Prepare and practise for interviews

Prepare and practise. Those are the keys to successful interviews. Your preparation is already far along if you have carefully assessed your values, goals, interests and skills, and determined the kind of job you want. List the questions you think an interviewer might ask, and write answers to them. Ask a few interviewers what questions they ask and what they look for in an applicant. Then practise interviewing. Professors, business people and career services personnel may be willing to conduct a mock interview with you. This kind of practice and accompanying feedback can improve your chances of receiving job offers.

Obtain interviews

Do some research and try to discover the decision process in the companies you have targeted. If you can, try to have your interview with the decision-maker. This is not always possible, and you should be careful not to antagonise people you might be trying to bypass. However, sometimes it is possible through contacts to get an interview directly with the person who makes the decision. Remember that the interview is a two-way process. The organisation is interviewing you, and you are interviewing the organisation. Your mutual goal is to decide if you have a good fit. Some people make the mistake of selling themselves into a job and company they later discover they dislike. Exhibit 7-4 suggests a few caveats for interviewing.

How do I manage my career?

Think of managing your life and career as a part-time task you will perform for the rest of your life. This section is designed to stimulate you to think about some important steps to take in managing your own career.

Make a mission statement

Think of yourself metaphorically as a small company. Covey (1989) suggests developing a mission statement that expresses your philosophy and central values. In your statement include

---

EXHIBIT 7 – 4 Suggestions for employment interviews

To increase your chances of success:
- research the company before your interview
- focus on the employer's needs and how you meet them
- listen carefully, respond succinctly and always be courteous
- be early, appropriately dressed, and be considerate of the interviewer's time
- ask about salary and developmental opportunities near the end of the interview if those subjects have not been addressed; avoid being the first to introduce these subjects
- be clear on what follow-up is appropriate
- send a thank you note
- follow up by phone or letter if appropriate
- sometimes it is appropriate to ask for feedback and advice after an unsuccessful interview.

who you want to be, what you want to do, and your most central values. Who you are describes your character; what you do describes the contributions you want to make.

Establish and visualise your goals

Covey (1989) urges people to 'begin with the end in mind'. He points out that all things are created twice. First, there is the mental creation, or visualisation, of what might be. Second, there is the actual creation. Covey argues that people who have a clear vision of their values and goals tend to direct their behaviour towards fulfilling their mission. Peak performers are frequently visualisers.

Be aware of career stages

Keep in mind the opportunities and pitfalls related to each of the career stages you will pass through. The first stage usually runs from your twenties into your thirties. In this stage your goal should be to gain a variety of experiences and to develop basic skills that will be transferable to other positions. Often a big company is a good place to go through this stage, but some small companies also have advantages. Avoid over-specialisation. One suggestion is that by your mid-thirties you have a 'T-shaped experience profile: a wide array of general managerial skills with at least one "deep groove" of expertise'.

Communicate a positive attitude

Enthusiasm and positive outlooks are contagious. For some people, expressing these traits comes easily. Others have to work at it. The benefits make it worth the effort.

Perform

This is as obvious as it is crucial. Yet, some people lope rather than run in their first jobs, and some focus so much on the jobs ahead they forget to perform in the present one. Excellent performance becomes a habit, just as does mediocre performance.

Capitalise on luck and build on setbacks

Luck often comes to those who have worked hard and prepared themselves for unexpected events. Do not count on luck to help implement your life and career plans, but if it should come, rejoice and be ready to capitalise on it. Setbacks come to everyone, but successful people respond positively to them. They find ways to learn from and build on the setbacks to help them get back on track towards reaching their goals.

Develop a network

Some people concentrate so much on the job at hand that they fail to develop relationships throughout the organisation. Usually some conscious effort has to be directed towards building such a network. Those who have established relationships enjoy the benefits of being hooked into informal communications. In addition, friends in strategic places can help you achieve results that might be difficult if you rely only on the formal organisation.

Find a mentor, be a mentor

mentor
An experienced person who helps a less experienced person achieve their career goals.

A mentor is someone, usually older and more experienced, who helps another person achieve his or her career goals. The mentor serves as a guide, coach, adviser and counsellor. Some companies, such as IBM, have formal mentoring programmes. Others rely on informal mentoring because they think it is more effective.

If there is no formal mentoring programme, find someone in your organisation you trust and like. However, remember that a mentor is no substitute for performance. Often a mentor is not a direct superior but someone who cares enough about you to share his or her accumulated wisdom and experience. As you develop experience, look for opportunities to serve as a mentor. Helping others achieve success is an important attribute of successful managers and professionals.

Special situations to be aware of

We now turn to three topics important in many people's careers. They are the 'mummy and daddy tracks', the 'glass ceiling' and plateauing.

Family career path

Schwartz (1989) has suggested that companies should recognise that not all women are alike and that different career paths should be open to them. She proposed that those who opted to devote time to having and caring for children should be given opportunities to work but with lower expectations of rewards. This career path became known as the **mummy track**, a career path for mothers that provides opportunities to work without the pressure of striving to advance as high as others.

mummy track
A career path for mothers with less advancement pressure and fewer rewards so that mothers can spend more time with their families.

To balance family and career demands, Schwartz suggested that people should stop trying to 'have it all'. The implication was that women choosing this track should be willing to give up getting to the top because they had chosen to spend some time and energy with their families. Some critics suggested that women should not have to make such choices and should have full access to the top without being penalised for devoting time to families.

There was little evidence that men had to make such choices, the implicit assumption being that women were charged with raising children even if they worked, while men were free to pursue their careers full-time. However, according to Mehren (1993), today there is some indication that some men are on the **daddy track**. They find they have to choose between family and career, a dilemma that has always faced working mothers. Some fathers are basing their career decisions on how their children will be affected more than on their own advancement.

daddy track
A career path for fathers with less advancement pressure and fewer rewards so that fathers can spend more time with their families.

This painful dilemma of choosing between family and career faces many people today. The increasing number of women in advanced positions and professions, and the number of couples with dual careers, pose a host of challenges not encountered by past generations. Pressure is growing for organisations to recognise these problems and help solve them. Flexible schedules, telecommuting, childcare, family leave and reduced pressure for mobility as a criterion for advancement, are things organisations can do to alleviate some of the new problems. The pay-off for the organisation is an expanded talent pool and image of caring about its employees.

The 'glass ceiling'

glass ceiling
An invisible barrier that limits the advancement of women and minorities.

Morrison *et al.* (1987) define the **glass ceiling** as an invisible barrier that limits the advancement of women and minorities. This ceiling is supported by inappropriate stereotypes about gender, race and age. For example, Schwartz (1989) suggests that some assume that women who behave as men do are unfeminine, that women who emphasise family are not committed to their careers, and that women will not move to new career opportunities. The lack of female and minority managers at higher levels indicates that organisations are still not taking positive steps to break the barriers holding back qualified women and minorities.

An 18-month study in the early 1990s by Garland (1991) found that the height of glass ceilings varied from company to company. In some organisations the ceiling was not much above the supervisory level, which may account for women holding only 6.6 per cent and minorities only 2.6 per cent of corporate executive positions. The study found that minorities hit the glass ceiling even earlier than women.

One common stereotype is that women will not stay with their companies. Yet a recent study showed that many women left their jobs out of frustration with career progress, not because of home or children. During the early 1990s, the number of women-owned start-ups grew at twice the rate of all other business start-ups, and one study showed that 73 per cent of women who left large companies moved to another organisation. Only 7 per cent left to stay at home (Moore, 1991).

A related problem is that women and men are paid differently for comparable work. One study, by Stroh *et al.* (1992), showed that women lagged behind men in salary progression and job transfers although the women were fully and comparably qualified.

Pressure is building to break this artificial ceiling. Forward-looking organisations are taking proactive steps to ensure that women and minorities have full and fair opportunities to advance. Today, although the glass ceiling definitely still exists, an increasing number of women are breaking through it. With the help of new government legislation in the UK concerning transparency of pay, with luck it should become easier.

Plateauing

Virtually everyone who works for a company eventually reaches a plateau beyond which he or she does not advance. For some, this is frustrating both because they want to continue advancing and are qualified to do so. But in pyramidal organisations the openings at the top become increasingly scarce. Some find **plateauing** a normal experience and continue to contribute and find satisfaction in their work. Expectations and attitude have

plateauing
The ending of career advancement.

much to do with how employees experience plateauing. Those who find a large gap between their expectations and reality are likely to feel dissatisfied and frustrated.

According to Nussbaum (1993), the trend towards downsizing with its attendant lay-offs of people at all levels has forced many to find alternatives to working for large companies and they often find the changes positive and satisfying. Some buy a franchise, do consulting, join a small business or start a new business. Many people, though not all, find the career changes energising and satisfying, and some even find their new careers more lucrative. Nevertheless, these unplanned career changes cause stress, which needs to be managed effectively if you are to have a successful career and satisfying life. Take the true case of Nancy Bauer, for example, illustrated by Schlossberg (1990).

Nancy Bauer walked away from a successful five-year career in marketing communications. Why leave a prestigious client list, a healthy income and a central office at age 38? In a single word, stress. The harder Bauer tried to be a corporate superwoman, the more her stress levels increased. 'I was handling 15 accounts, had 12 people working for me, and at a minimum was dealing with 30 people at a time.' On top of all the work stress, Bauer wanted to get pregnant. 'I was 38 years old and didn't have any children.' Bauer said she was a product of the 'male-held perceptions' that rule the corporate world – 'the value system of produce, produce, produce and work, work, work'.

As the grip of stress tightened, her weight fluctuated. She began to lose strands and then clumps of hair. She spent her weekends sleeping. 'I would come home and sleep all weekend as a way to replenish myself. I was that drained.' Her doctor told her she needed a break. However, in her company, 'people who take career breaks are looked at as if they are not cut out to be a superperson. Moreover, the City tends to glorify people who live on just four hours sleep a night … always doing, doing, doing. It's a sense of being invincible, rather than being vulnerable, yet strong,' Bauer says.

'I forgot my own definition of success,' she recalls, 'and started living according to one that fitted the circumstances, no matter how disagreeable.' Other people in the company had ulcers and cholesterol problems and they were still working at outrageous levels. Nevertheless, her doctor told her, 'You have to take a leave from your job, to save your life. Go away. Get out of the City. Reflect for a while.'

With her hair falling out, her physiology a wreck, her professional life in turmoil, and still childless, Bauer took her doctor's advice and flew to India for several weeks of meditation, where she successfully got back on track. She no longer works 90 hours a week. She resigned from her corporate position to start her own freelance business and again has time for her husband and even herself. Bauer feels that the stress-management technique of meditation was responsible for allowing her to find appropriate balance in her life. The next section takes a closer look at what causes work stress and what you can do to manage it productively.

Stress management

The real-life case of Nancy Bauer demonstrates that work stress can have a disastrous effect on quality of life. Work stress knows no boundaries. It affects men and women, executives and secretaries. According to Bales (1991), 46 per cent of workers and 70 per cent of managers believe that stress is a huge and growing problem in the workplace. Stress is created by a multitude of overlapping factors such as overwhelming workloads, ethical dilemmas, difficult relationships with bosses and colleagues, and international uncertainties. Although stress can sometimes stimulate and challenge us, too much stress for too long a time has negative effects on both our work quality and personal life. Work stress will not go away, but it can be managed productively. The Eye on Ethics box demonstrates the practical measures employers can take to alleviate workplace stress.

What is stress?

Taking a final exam, having a serious accident, giving a formal speech, ending a significant relationship and missing a deadline can all be stressful. However, different people have different

stress
The body's reaction to a demand that is perceived as threatening.

stressors
Environmental demands that are perceived as threatening.

feelings and reactions in response to the same event: some negative and some positive. Stress refers to the body's psychological, emotional and physiological responses to any demand that is perceived as threatening to a person's well-being. These are natural changes that prepare a person to cope with stressors, which are threatening environmental conditions, either by confronting them (fight) or by avoiding them (flight).

Think of how you would react to seeing a car speeding straight at you as you were crossing the road. Your emotional reaction would be fear, which would cause you psychologically to

NHS staff stress rife, bosses say

Most NHS employers think up to half of their staff may be suffering from workplace stress, a report says.

A survey for NHS Employers found that 62 per cent of health service organisations estimated that half their workforce might be under stress. But only a third of the 177 health chiefs quizzed said their trusts had carried out a stress risk assessment.

Work stress is responsible for 30 per cent of staff sickness in the NHS and costs the service £300m to £400m each year. But despite the toll of stress, less than a third of health service managers questioned said their organisation had a stress policy, while a further 6 per cent said they had plans for such a policy.

Julian Topping, NHS Employers' head of workplace health and employment, said: 'Our lives are becoming increasingly more hectic and stress levels are soaring. Stress has become one of the biggest causes of staff sickness and costs the NHS millions of pounds every year. Employers have a legal duty to manage stress among staff, and staff have a legal duty towards making sure they are safe and well. The main problem is that many people don't recognise when they, or their employees, are stressed until it is too late and, if they do, they very often don't know what to do about it.'

This has resulted in promoting a campaign to tackle workplace stress. Topping says that NHS Employers – the employers' organisation for the NHS in England – would be starting a campaign to help NHS organisations and staff recognise stress and deal with it effectively. Counselling, job restructuring and stress management were the most popular methods of alleviating stress. Physiotherapists said stress was being felt by workers in all professions.

Tessa Campbell of the Chartered Society of Physiotherapy says that around five million people in the UK feel very or extremely stressed by their work. 'Small amounts of stress can actually help stimulate, excite and boost performance. But when stress levels become too high and are experienced over time, they can seriously affect people's health, personal lives and work performance.'

Source: adapted from www.bbc.co.uk/business.

Discussion questions

1 What could be the consequences of workplace stress?
2 How can NHS managers implement work practices to alleviate stress?

experience increased tension, anxiety and alertness brought on by hormones released from the pituitary, thyroid and adrenal glands. These hormonal changes would then cause physiological increases in your metabolism, blood pressure, heart rate, breathing rate, muscle tension and pupil dilation to prepare you to cope with the threatening situation. These same reactions might occur when you are faced with a non-physical stressor like giving a speech, meeting a deadline or resolving a disagreement, when the threat is to your self-esteem or relationship with others.

The degree of stress experienced depends on many factors. Lazarus and Folkman (1984) suggest that, first, the demand must be *perceived* (people must be aware that it exists) as *threatening* (having the potential to hurt them if they do not react appropriately). Second, the threat must be to something that is *important* to people (has the potential to substantially affect their well-being). Finally, people experiencing the threatening demand must be *uncertain* about the

Research focus: **the physiology of stress**

In 1939 Hans Selye, an endocrinologist, described what he called the general adaptation system (GAS), which was a major discovery in understanding the stress response.

Selye (1976) made a distinction between a stress and a stressor. He defined stress as the non-specific response of the body to any demand. A stressor was the object or the event that caused the stress. Selye stated that when a stressor is present a sequence of biological events can be triggered by different situations, these can be both pleasant and unpleasant. It is the different situations that Selye called GAS. The GAS consisted of three stages: alarm, resistance and exhaustion.

Alarm stage
This reaction occurs when a stressor is recognised. A biochemical message is sent from the brain to the pituitary gland, which controls the endocrine system. This secretes a hormone which, in turn, causes the adrenal gland to secrete adrenaline. During this stage a general alarm is sent to all the systems in the body. The alarm reaction has also been referred to as the 'fight or flight' response, where the body is prepared for physical action.

Resistance stage
During this stage the body tries to return to a state of equilibrium once the immediate threat has passed. The exact opposite of the reactions that caused the alarm stage occur as the body tries to regain a state of balance even if the stressor is still present.

Exhaustion stage
This stage occurs if the stressor continues and the body exhausts its ability to adapt. The symptoms of the exhaustion stage are similar to the alarm reaction. If this happens for too often or too long the body may remain in a constant state of tension with high blood pressure, rapid heartbeat and digestive problems. The effects on health can be serious.

outcome (not sure if they can deal with it effectively). Nancy Bauer, in the earlier example, probably would not have experienced any stress if she were invited to lunch with an established client to put the final touches to an advertisement that was already approved. On the other hand, if her boss asked her to sign five new accounts in the next month, she might not have escaped from her job without a nervous breakdown.

Constructive versus destructive stress

In its everyday usage, the word *stress* connotes something unpleasant and undesirable. We often use the word to refer to the aggravation brought about by traffic jams, troubled relationships, dwindling finances or heavy workloads. This uncomfortable state of mind and disturbing physical symptoms are all forms of **distress** – that is, stress that has a negative impact. Later in this chapter we will elaborate on some of its destructive consequences, such as ulcers, heart attacks, depression, murders and suicide, to name a few.

distress
Stress that has a negative consequence on a person's well-being.

On the other hand, Schwartz and Levin (1990) suggest that stress can have positive effects, such as the feeling of excitement before an athletic contest or speech that arouses us to 'get up' for the event and perform in a superior way. Some degree of emotional and physiological arousal is necessary to motivate us for most of our daily activities. This positive stress gives us the energy we need to get up in the morning, to excel at work and to be creative.

Stress itself is neither good nor bad. It depends on existing conditions how we perceive and react to it. Stress can be conceptualised as akin to body temperature. It is always there, and maintaining the optimal degree is an essential component of health. A temperature that climbs too high or dips too low signals some physical malfunction that needs to be attended to.

Episodic versus chronic stress

Early in the morning, our stress level may be very low. If we encounter traffic problems on the way to work and expect to be late to an important meeting, our stress level will increase. If we find that the meeting has been postponed, our stress drops back to a more comfortable level. Throughout a normal day, week, month or year, we are likely to experience a whole range of stress levels, from crises to relaxation, as we react to deadlines, emergencies, weekends and vacations.

A pattern of high degrees of stress followed by intervals of relief is referred to as **episodic stress**. We endure the anxiety, cope with the challenge and then relax. This is the kind of stress that was functional for our ancestors, who at times needed to run to escape a sabre-toothed tiger or to fight off an enemy. Elevated stress was functional

episodic stress
A pattern of high stress followed by intervals of relief.

Research focus: the Michigan Organisational Stress model

The first basic model of job stress was developed by the Institute for Social Research (ISR) at the University of Michigan and has become known as the Michigan Organisational Stress model.

The basic model combines different conceptual categories rather than a particular theory of stress, whereas a more developed model by Kahn and Byosiere (1992) attempts to define factors more closely and determine the interrelationships into a more elaborate person–environment fit model.

As can be seen from Exhibit 7-5, the Michigan model consists of four groups of variables arranged in a causal sequence.

The sequence flows from problems with the organisational characteristics; these could include company size, hierarchical structure and job description. The resulting problems may then lead to psychological stress such as role conflict, role ambiguity and role overload. These stressors may then lead to stress reactions such as physiological symptoms or behavioural problems. If the organisational problems are not resolved then the employee may develop a stress-related illness. (Types of stress-related illness are discussed later in this chapter.)

The Michigan model is not based on theoretical research and although it offers an inclusive view of stress it does not offer any hypotheses that could be tested. A more detailed model can be seen in Exhibit 7-6.

EXHIBIT 7–5 The Michigan Organisational Stress model

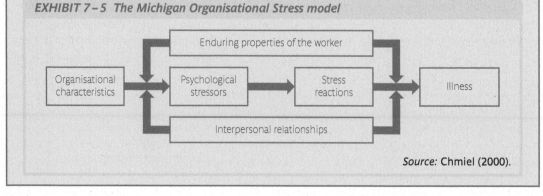

Source: Chmiel (2000).

because it created a state of readiness to fight or flee. After the stressor had been dealt with, relaxation and renewal followed.

Unfortunately, the stressors many people face now – job insecurity, the rising cost of living, constant deadlines, and poor interpersonal relationships with bosses or co-workers – are contin-

chronic stress
The stress caused by continual confrontation of stressors without relief.

ual. These types of stressors put a person in a state of readiness to deal with threats that can neither fight nor flee. They produce **chronic stress**, which is constant and additive. Each stressor contributes to increasing tension that cannot be released productively. Although some people may snap and punch their boss in the nose or even kill someone because of these conditions, most people just grin and bear the pressure because there is no way to relieve it productively. The cost of maintaining continuous high levels of chronic stress, however, is often a serious health breakdown (Archer, 1991).

The causes of stress

Kim Edwards is a 37-year-old company director who supervises bond trading and underwriting for a small bank. She has to sell twice as many bonds as she did five years ago to make the same profit. She is also concerned about her job. Her employer is the last bank in the area that has not been acquired by a bigger rival. She figures she would lose her job if the bank were bought out. Meanwhile, her schedule is so full that she has little free time for stress-alleviating activities, such as exercise (Noles, 1990).

Many factors contribute to the stress experienced by people such as Kim Edwards. The organisational environment may provide a host of potential stressors. Others are due to changes in our personal lives, and some are the result of personality characteristics. These multiple contributors to work stress are illustrated in Exhibit 7-6.

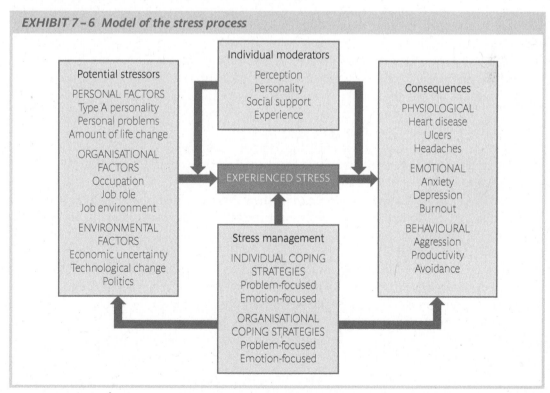

EXHIBIT 7–6 Model of the stress process

Personal factors

A particularly dangerous type of stress is generated internally by individuals who place constant demands on themselves. This is demonstrated by Barnett (1982), who gives the example of a senior manager who gets up at 4.15 a.m., is at the office at 5.35 a.m. at the latest, and grabs a sandwich in the office at lunch if possible. He keeps two meetings going on at once and just goes from one to the other, schedules a business appointment for dinner at 10.00 p.m., and goes home at 11.30 p.m. If he does not have a dinner meeting, he goes home between 10.00 and 11.00 p.m. He sleeps only three and a half to four hours a night. He starts to get tired if he cuts it below three. This is a prime example of the Type A personality.

Type A and Type B personalities

Friedman and Rosenman (1974) have identified two distinct personality patterns and labelled them Type A and Type B. They contend that Type A individuals, like the senior manager described above, are three times more likely to suffer from heart disease than are their opposites, Type B people. Typically, people with Type A personality are impatient, restless, competitive, aggressive, under intense perceived time pressure, and always attempting to accomplish several things at once. The Type B personality, on the other hand, does not feel under pressure; Type Bs take things much more slowly and enjoy a variety of non-work-orientated activities.

Type A personality
Personality characterised by impatience, restlessness, competitiveness, aggressiveness and a sense of intense time pressure.

Type B personality
A personality that does not feel under pressure, is easy-going and seldom impatient.

Because Type As thrive in an environment of tight deadlines and devote long hours to accomplishing volumes of work, they often achieve rapid promotion through the middle level of management. If they perceive a high degree of control over their job environment, Type As experience high job satisfaction and performance, although they do report high incidence of health complaints (Lee *et al.*, 1990). Unfortunately, they seldom manage to remain in good health and only a few obtain top-level management positions. Part of the problem is that Type As do not slow down enough to make thoughtful analyses of complex issues. In addition, their impatience and hostility produce stress and discomfort among those with whom they work. Consequently, most successful top executives are Type B individuals, who have the patience and more amiable interpersonal style required to maintain organisational harmony (Jackson, 1988).

According to Williams (1984), of all the Type A characteristics, hostility and anger are the most 'toxic' contributors to heart disease for both men and women. Brief *et al.* (1981) suggest that, since 61 to 76 per cent of managers in most organisations are Type As, they need to be open to feedback that they are hostile, and then do something about it. Suggestions from Williams (1989) include reducing cynical mistrust of the motives of others; reducing the frequency and intensity of their anger, frustration, and rage; and learning to treat others with kindness and consideration.

Most Type A individuals are unaware of, or refuse to acknowledge, their problem or their need to change. Williams (1989) suggests that many attribute their past successes to Type A behaviours, and others fear that seeking help to change their behaviour will be viewed as a sign of weakness. If it continues in this manner, Type A behaviour could become a major social problem. Check the World Watch box to see the damage it has caused in work-obsessed Japan.

Stressed to death in Japan

world watch

In Japan, *karoshi* is recognised as a fatal mix of apoplexy, high blood pressure and stress, which doctors relate directly to too many hours on the job. Its victims, which some estimates put in the tens of thousands, are often middle managers and supervisors in their forties and fifties who are known in the companies as *moretsu sha-in* (fanatical workers) and *yoi kigyo senshi* (good corporate soldiers).

Millions of Japan's 55 million workers routinely put in 13- and 14-hour workdays, mainly because it is expected. Despite a recent revision of the labour standards law that reduced the 48-hour working week to 46 hours, Japanese workers spend an average of 2250 hours annually on the job – about six weeks more than most westerners.

A recent Health Ministry report called *karoshi* the second leading cause of death (after cancer) among Japanese workers. 'Our research shows that there are conservatively at least 30 000 *karoshi* victims every year in Japan,' said Hiroshi Kawahito, an attorney with the Defense Council of Victims of Karoshi, a legal support group for victims, 'and the number is growing.' A survey conducted late in 1989 by the Fukoku Mutual Life Insurance Co. revealed that 46 per cent of all Japanese aged 30 to 60 consider it likely they will die from the effects of *karoshi*.

Some men respond to the pressure by dropping from sight. Japan's National Police Agency said 9964 men were reported missing last year. Authorities say investigations of each case showed the men apparently simply chose to disappear. 'These men appeared to have gone underground rather than face the grind of their jobs. They just couldn't take it any more,' a police official said.

Still others immerse themselves in their office life, said Toru Sekiya, director of a Tokyo neuropsychiatric clinic and author of the best-selling book *Daddy Cannot Come Home!*.

'The stress and the long hours spent on the job result in an irrational feeling of alienation from their families and a phobia about going home and staying home,' Sekiya said. 'Many remain in their offices or spend the night in hotels and 24-hour coffee shops.'

Source: Ronald E. Yates, *Chicago Tribune*. Used with permission.

Discussion questions

1 How does a country's culture impact on the work ethic and lead to stressful situations?

2 What impact can lack of work–life balance have on family life?

Personal problems

Family difficulties can create a lot of stress. One example is when a two-career family balances conflicting demands concerning childcare, career moves, time conflicts, priorities and expectations. Stress can also be created by financial problems or health problems. In addition, poor relationships with spouses or children can be a major source of job and life dissatisfaction. Katz and Kahn (1978) argue that when people feel they are surrounded by others that really care, stressors are perceived as being less severe and much anxiety is alleviated. Revicki and May (1985) propose that this is true whether the support is from a cohesive work group or an understanding family.

Amount of life change

Research by Holmes and Rahe (1967) suggests that positive and negative life changes combine to create stress as the individual strives to adjust to each new situation. Too much change in too short a period of time increases a person's chances of developing serious health problems.

Your turn

Life change unit scale

Fill in the mean values for the life events you have experienced in the past 12 months, then total your personal points.

Rank	Life event	Mean value	Personal points
1	Death of spouse or significant other	100	
2	Divorce	73	
3	Marital (or significant other) separation	65	
4	Jail term	63	
5	Death of close family member	63	
6	Personal injury or illness	53	
7	Marriage	50	
8	Fired from work	47	
9	Marital (significant other) reconciliation	45	
10	Retirement or quit job	45	
11	Change in health of family member	44	
12	Pregnancy (or of wife/significant other)	40	
13	Sex difficulties	39	
14	Gain of new family member (sibling, step-parent, etc.)	39	
15	Business readjustment (decrease in income)	39	
16	Change in financial state	38	
17	Death of a close friend	37	
18	Change to different line of work	36	
19	Change in number of arguments with significant other	35	
20	Loan over £10 000 (for car, studying, etc.)	31	
21	Foreclosure on loan	30	
22	Change in responsibilities at work	29	
23	Son or daughter leaving home (or leaving parents' home)	29	
24	Trouble with nuclear family members (e.g. in-laws)	29	
25	Outstanding personal achievement	28	
26	Wife/husband/roommate begins or stops work	26	
27	Begin or end school	26	
28	Change in living conditions	25	
29	Revision of personal habits	24	
30	Trouble with boss or teacher	23	
31	Change in work hours or conditions	20	
32	Change in residence	20	
33	Change in schools	20	
34	Change in recreation	19	

continued ▶

Rank	Life event	Mean value	Personal points
35	Change in church activities	19	
36	Change in social activities	18	
37	Loan less than £10 000	17	
38	Change in sleeping habits	16	
39	Change in number of family get-togethers	15	
40	Change in eating habits	15	
41	Holidays	13	
42	Christmas	12	
43	Minor law-breaking (e.g. speeding)	11	
Total points: _____			

Interpretation Holmes and Rahe (1967) found that people with a points total of less than 150 generally have good health the following year. Those with scores between 150 and 199 have a 37 per cent chance of developing health problems, while those with scores of between 200 and 300 have a 51 per cent chance. People scoring over 300 points have a 70 per cent chance of having a major illness.

Source: this scale was first published as 'The Social Readjustment Rating Scale' in an article by Thomas H. Holmes and Richard H. Rahe (1967) *Journal of Psychosomatic Research* 11, pp. 213–218.

The stress of changes adds up in a cumulative fashion and eventually overloads the endocrine system, thereby depleting stress-coping resources and suppressing the immune system, which makes the body more susceptible to certain types of disease. To determine if the amount of change in your life has the potential to contribute to stress-related illness, complete the life change unit scale in the 'Your turn' exercise.

Overwhelming amounts of change can be very stressful. But the research does not indicate that it will always lead to major health problems for everyone. According to Monroe (1983), some people experience high levels of change in their lives without any illness at all. If your score on the life change unit scale alarms you and you are experiencing difficulties, postpone any further changes that are under your control until your score settles down.

Organisational factors

Exhibit 7-7 compares the frequency with which 15 different stressors are experienced by managers in 10 different countries. Time pressures and deadlines, mentioned by over half the respondents, were the most frequently cited source of work stress, closely followed by work overload.

High-stress occupation

High-stress occupations allow incumbents little control over their jobs, impose relentless time pressures, have threatening or unpleasant physical conditions or carry weighty responsibilities. High-stress jobs, such as manager, supervisor and secretary, possess these high-stress characteristics, while low-stress jobs, such as stock handler, artisan and college professor, do not. Jobs in the top 10 per cent for stress have 4.8 times the heart attack risk of those in the bottom

EXHIBIT 7 – 7 Global comparison of work stressors

Source of stress	Percentage of respondents mentioning source	Most often mentioned by managers in	Least often mentioned by managers in
1 Time pressures and deadlines	55.3	Germany (65.4%)	Japan (41.8%)
2 Work overload	51.6	Egypt (76.7%)	Brazil (38.1%)
3 Inadequately trained subordinates	36.4	Egypt (65.0%)	Britain (13.1%)
4 Long working hours	29.0	Nigeria (40.5%)	Brazil (19.6%)
5 Attending meetings	23.6	South Africa (28.5%)	United States (16.3%)
6 Demands of work on my private and social life	22.1	Sweden (31.7%)	Singapore (12.9%)
7 Demands of work on my relationship with my family	21.4	Nigeria (29.7%)	Brazil (8.2%)
8 Keeping up with new technology	21.4	Japan (32.8%)	Egypt (10.0%)
9 My beliefs conflicting with those of the organisation	20.6	United States (30.2%)	Egypt (13.3%)
10 Taking my work home	19.7	Egypt (30.0%)	Japan (13.4%)
11 Lack of power and influence	19.5	United States (46.5%)	Sweden (11.0%)
12 Interpersonal relations	19.4	Japan (29.8%)	Singapore (12.9%)
13 The amount of travel required by my work	18.4	Nigeria (29.7%)	Brazil (9.3%)
14 Doing a job below the level of my competence	17.7	Brazil (23.7%)	Sweden (10.3%)
15 Incompetent boss	15.6	United States (30.2%)	Britain (9.1%)

Source: reprinted with permission. © *International Management*, 1993. Reed Business Publishing.

10 per cent. Even managers and professionals can only bob and weave for so long through the successive waves of downsizings, acquisitions, consolidations and recessionary lay-offs typical of the early 1990s (Zemke, 1991).

Job role

Whatever the occupation, certain negative characteristics of a person's role at work can increase the likelihood of his or her experiencing stress. Job role stressors include impossible workloads, idle periods of time, job ambiguity and conflicting performance expectations (Matteson and Ivancevich, 1987).

Overload

When people are expected to accomplish more than their ability or time permits, they feel pressured and under stress. This is role overload, which was shown in Exhibit 7-7 to be the number one source of work stress around the world. For both upper- and middle-level managers, unreasonable deadlines and constant pressure are the most frequent stressors in their jobs (Zemke, 1991). This *quantitative role overload* exists whenever people are required to produce more work than they can comfortably complete in a given period of time. *Qualitative role overload* exists when the requirements of the job are greater than the skills or knowledge of the employee.

An example of the dire consequences of overload was described in a lawsuit blaming it for the suicide of 27-year-old Charles McKenzie, who jumped off a building during his first year as a solicitor at a law firm. New solicitors at large law firms are routinely expected to work between 60 and 80 hours per week, with minimum time off for holidays and sick days, which many do not take because of the billable hours they would miss (Stevens, 1994).

Underutilisation

Most people prefer a job that has enough tasks to keep them busy and enough challenges to keep them involved. Underutilisation occurs when people have insufficient work to fill their time or are not allowed to use enough of their skills and abilities. White-collar workers fare best in having good job–ability fits, followed by skilled blue-collar workers. Unskilled workers experience the most boredom and apathy with their jobs because of underutilisation of skills and abilities, low levels of responsibility, lack of participation and uncertain futures. The resulting stress symptoms include weariness, frequent absence and proneness to injury. Machine-paced assembly lines are an example of such a work environment. Operating nuclear power plants involves periods of boredom that must be endured simultaneously with sufficient alertness to respond to potential emergencies. Cooper (1987) argues that an awareness of the costs of an ineffective response to an emergency makes these jobs all the more stressful.

Role ambiguity

Role ambiguity exists when people work without a clear understanding of their job definition, performance expectations, preferred methods of meeting those expectations, or consequences of their behaviours. The incidence of role ambiguity is greater among managers than among many other occupations because managerial tasks are often hard to define, and a high degree of freedom and autonomy goes with the job (Girdano et al., 2000).

Role conflict

Role conflict exists when a job's function contains duties or responsibilities that conflict with one another. It is most commonly found among middle managers, who find themselves caught between top-level management and lower-level managers (Girdano et al., 2000). A classic example of role conflict is that of the worker who is caught between a supervisor's demand for increased output and the pressure of peers for restricted output. Another type of role conflict occurs when an individual is told by superiors to ignore some legal or ethical practice.

Role conflict not only causes increased interpersonal tension and decreased job satisfaction, but also destroys trust and respect for those who exert the conflicting role pressures. The resulting social and psychological withdrawal can be costly for both the individual and the organisation (Girdano et al., 2000).

Responsibility for others

A job that carries responsibility for either the well-being or the task performance of others is likely to cause stress. People in supervisory positions are more susceptible to such disorders as ulcers and hypertension than are the people they supervise (Riley and Zaccaro, 1987).

Poor working conditions

Prolonged continuous exposure to extreme heat, cold, noise or crowding can be very stressful, as can high visibility and lack of privacy. Workers on rotating work shifts experience more stress than do those on regular shifts (Riley and Zaccaro, 1987).

Organisational politics

A survey by Kiev and Kohn (1979) of over 2500 managers found that the political climate of the organisation was the third most frequently cited stressor (following heavy workload and differences between what managers had to do and would like to accomplish). A by-product of power struggles within an organisation is heightened competition and increased stress for participants. Managers caught up in power games and political alliances also pass on pressure to subordinates (Matteson and Ivancevich, 1987).

Poor work relationships

Stress can be generated from poor relationships with co-workers, whether they be the boss, peers, subordinates or workers in other departments. In study after study across organisations, occupations, geographic locations and time periods, at least 60 per cent of workers report that the most stressful aspect of their job is their immediate supervisor (Hogan and Morrison, 1990). Difficult peers can also be unpleasant to work with for a variety of reasons. Gutek (1990) argues that this is especially true for women, who are often encumbered by major stresses on the job rarely encountered by men, such as sexual harassment, role overload, role conflict, pay inequality and discrimination based on sex.

Environmental factors

People cannot just ignore what is going on in the world around them. Most of us read newspapers, look at news broadcasts on the television and radio, talk to colleagues about what is going on, and notice what is happening in the physical, economic and political environments. These varying elements cause us stress because they are uncertain and may affect us in some important ways. The anxiety aroused by uncertain environmental factors carries over into the workplace and our personal lives.

Economic uncertainty

Downsizing, rightsizing, reductions in head count, and so on, are all in the name of efficiency and cost reduction to increase profitability. The problem is that we may be the ones made redundant and forced to find another means of sustenance. Even if it is only the stock market that is declining, that is where our pension funds are invested, and we have all heard of the Great Depression of the 1930s.

Technological change

Technology, computers and robots have contributed greatly to productivity, but have also displaced workers and forced them to relearn skills for different occupations. Even if a worker's skills are not made completely obsolete by technological advances, they usually necessitate learning new ones to be able to remain a viable contributor in the workplace. How many of your fellow students do not possess computer skills today? Probably not one. That was not the case 15 years ago, and older employees may find learning the necessary computer-age skills challenging and stressful.

Politics

Jobs, for many people, directly depend on which party is in political office. For others, indirect relationships exist because of employment in government-funded organisations like aerospace, defence and science. Even the unemployed can feel stressed by political uncertainties since these might affect their social security, pensions or student grants.

Individual factors
Individual stress moderators

The same stressor will not cause the same reaction in all people. The demands of something that will overwhelm one person will challenge another to produce a brilliant performance. Some of the factors that moderate the degrees of stress experienced by different individuals as a result of the same potential stressor are perception, personality, social support and experience.

Perception

For people to experience stress, they must first perceive an environment that has the potential to significantly hurt their well-being. Students receiving an oral report assignment for the following week, for example, will experience a wide range of reactions. Some will not experience much stress because they have many friends in the classroom, were on their school debating team and know the topic well. At the other end of the spectrum may be foreign students who have no friends yet, have never given a speech before in their second language, know little about the topic, and doubt their ability to gather the necessary information and present it in an articulate manner. While the first type of student may do little more than brush up on the subject matter and go about business as usual, the second type may agonise for days about little else but the dreaded presentation. Cooper and Payne (1988) concluded that these different students are faced with the same demand but have very different perceptions of its importance, impending rewards and costs because of their different perceptions of their own situation in the class, level of coping skills and self-confidence that they can prepare in time.

Personality

Differences in personality characteristics have been found to moderate the degree of stress experienced. We have already discussed how Type A personalities create and experience more stress than do Type B personalities. In the discussion of the 'big five' personality factors in Chapter 4, it was evident that people whose personality styles were not very expressive, were not open to new experiences and had negative emotions, experienced more stress than their opposites (Burke *et al.*, 1993). In fact, almost all the different personality types, styles and traits discussed in Chapter 4 are potential stress moderators. We will illustrate the predominant ones below: self-esteem, locus of control, extroversion and hardiness.

High *self-esteem* causes people to feel good about themselves and have high confidence in their abilities to cope effectively. Consequently, Girdano *et al.* (2000) argue that people with high self-esteem experience less stress when experiencing threatening situations than do those with low self-esteem.

Gemmill and Heisler (1972) suggest that people with an internal *locus of control* believe that they make a difference and that their destinies are primarily under their own control. Those with an external locus of control believe that whatever happens is either a matter of chance or determined by forces external to them. Internal attributors tend to perceive their jobs as less stressful and more satisfying than do external attributors, regardless of their education level, length of time on the job or managerial level. Externals are more likely to feel helpless to deal productively with stressors, so they experience more stress (Murphy, 1986).

Introverts are inner-directed, private, reserved people who spend time in their inner world of thoughts. *Extroverts* are more outer directed, friendly and expressive. Consequently, introverts experience more stress when attempting to cope with the interpersonal aspects of role conflict (Kahn *et al.*, 1964).

hardiness
A personality characteristic of people who are more immune than most to the negative consequences of experiencing stress.

Hardiness is a combined personality characteristic of people who believe that they are in control of their lives, have the ability to respond to and transform potentially negative situations, and actively seek out novelty and challenge. They welcome change and have a high tolerance for ambiguity. Consequently, 'hardy' managers experience far lower than average rates of illness in high-stress environments than do others (Matteson and Ivancevich, 1987).

Social support

Cummings (1990) and House (1981) argue that positive relationships with colleagues and supervisors can lessen the impact of stress. The same is true for supportive relationships outside of the job, with family members and friends. Anderson (1991) agrees that social support provides comfort and assistance, which buffers such people from the negative consequences of stress.

Experience

Experience teaches people how to deal with recurring situations that were originally threatening because of their novelty, uncertainty, and threats to self-esteem and well-being. Research by Motowidlo *et al.* (1987) has verified common sense and demonstrated that more experience on a specific job is negatively correlated with stress because those who remain in a stressful job are either more hardy or they have learned to cope with it productively.

French and Caplan (1973) suggest another reason for this effect is that people who do not enjoy a job probably resign. The fit between a person's abilities and needs, and the demands of the job assignment, is inversely related to the degree of stress experienced. The more a person's needs are satisfied and the greater his or her ability to perform effectively, the less stress is likely to be experienced on the job.

The consequences of stress

A variety of physiological, psychological and behavioural changes can affect a person who is experiencing unhealthy, chronic stress. These symptoms may not be obvious at first. Schwimer (1991) argues that people who adopt a fast-track lifestyle may forget how it feels to be free of stress and accept their harried state as a fact of life. Because the symptoms of stress are so varied, they may be overlooked or mistaken. Special attention should be given to prolonged headaches, elevated blood pressure, fatigue and depression.

Physiological consequences

Early physiological symptoms of stress include elevated blood pressure, increased heart rate, sweating, hot flushes, headaches and gastrointestinal disorders. Chronic stress is often accompanied by more severe disorders like increased cholesterol levels and hypertension, two conditions that precipitate a number of serious health impairments. Medical experts attribute between 50 and 75 per cent of all illness, including ulcers, arthritis and allergies, to stress-related sources. Perhaps the most significant stress-related illness is heart disease, which kills one in four males. In fact, significant correlations between job dissatisfaction and heart disease have been discovered among workers from more than 40 different occupations (Fletcher, 1988).

Gender studies show that on average women experience lower mortality rates from stress-related illness than do men, and exhibit a lower incidence of heart disease, cirrhosis and suicide.

Men are more likely to develop serious illnesses, but women are likely to experience higher rates of psychological distress (Jick and Mitz, 1985).

Psychological consequences

Watson and Tellegen (1985) found that chronic stress can cause boredom, dissatisfaction, anxiety, depression, tension and irritability. All these detract from feelings of well-being, and contribute to poor concentration, indecision and decreased attention spans. If they are unable to alter or escape from their stressors, people may resort to psychological substitutes such as negativism, anger, feelings of persecution, criticism, displacement, denial, apathy, fantasy, hopelessness, withdrawal, forgetfulness or procrastination (Fletcher, 1988).

When prolonged exposure to stress uses up available adaptive energy, exhaustion can take the form of depression, mental breakdown or what is termed

burnout
Exhaustion that develops from experiencing too much pressure and too few sources of satisfaction.

burnout. **Burnout**, according to Golembiewski and Munzenrider (1988), is a feeling of exhaustion that develops when an individual simultaneously experiences too much pressure and too few sources of satisfaction. Rogers (1984) found that over 18 per cent of business owners, managers, professionals and technical personnel suffer from burnout. When we confront continual role ambiguity, performance pressures, interpersonal conflicts or economic problems while simultaneously trying to fulfil our own and the organisation's expectations, the most likely effects are fatigue, frustration, helplessness and literal exhaustion. Exhibit 7-8 presents data on some additional factors that contribute to the high risk of burnout.

Behavioural consequences

Some of the first behavioural consequences for individuals experiencing chronic stress are sleep disorders, changes in eating habits, increased smoking, more alcohol consumption and nervous mannerisms such as rapid speech, fidgeting and rudeness towards others. When normally very agreeable people stop interacting politely with their peers and start yelling at subordinates and

EXHIBIT 7–8 Who burns out more?

Factor	Who burns out more?
Sex	Females more than males
Age	Younger more than older (especially beyond age 50)
Pay	Lower paid more than higher paid
Position	Lower status more than higher status
Ethnicity	Hispanics more than any other race
Customer contact	Those with direct customer contact more than those with no customer contact
Seniority	Longer-term employees more than those with less than 10 years of service
Job preference	Those in a non-preferred job more than those in a preferred job
Marital status	Singles more than married
Potential	Those with low promotion potential more than those with high potential

Source: R.T. Golembiewski and R.F. Munzenrider (1988) *Phases of Burnout: Developments in Concepts and Applications*. New York, NY: Praeger, pp. 132–138. Copyright 1988, Greenwood Publishing Group, Inc., Westport, CT. Reproduced with permission.

secretaries, it is often because of negative stress. DeAngelis (1993) noted that the most extreme cases of excessive stress result in workplace violence, where a person ends up physically attacking, or even killing, co-workers, or is attacked by irate customers, as has happened in some NHS hospitals, or they may attack their equipment, as highlighted in the Technology Transformation box (on page 327). Performance decline is perhaps the most studied behavioural consequence of stress. It is estimated that 75 per cent of all work loss is due to stress (Bell, 1990). Not all stress is bad for performance, however. For example, athletes 'get up' for critical performances, performers experience nervousness before going on stage, and the stress students feel during final exams energises them to work harder to achieve their goals.

Archer (1991) demonstrates that the relationship between stress and performance resembles an inverted U-shaped curve, as shown in Exhibit 7-9. Stress is like a violin string: the optimal degree of tension is essential to obtaining the proper performance. A string that is too tight or too loose will not produce the desired effect. Insufficient stress leads to boredom, apathy and decreased motivation.

Increasing stress from an insufficient level yields better performance through increased arousal and concentration – up to an optimal point. Jamal (1985) suggests that problem-solving groups, for example, become more receptive to new information provided by others when the group is under increased stress. After that, according to Bales (1991), if stress continues to increase and persists for long periods of time, the ability to perform effectively will decrease because of depleted energy, overload and anxiety. Examples of performances impaired by excessive stress are when students suffer from test anxiety and cannot remember material they know well for their answer, athletes who 'choke' during critical contests, and performers who make mistakes while on stage.

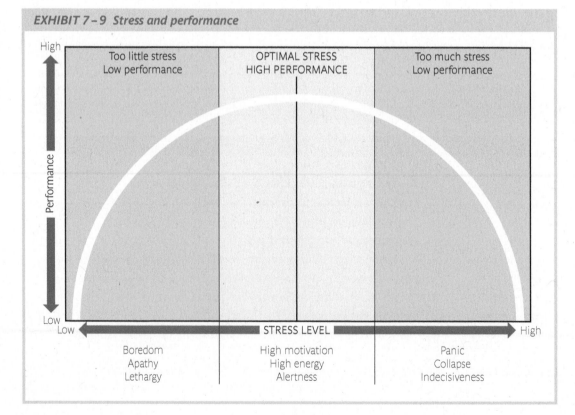

EXHIBIT 7–9 Stress and performance

Research focus: **the demand–control–support model of job stress**

The job demand–control (JD–C) model developed by Karasek (1979), and expanded by Karasek and Theorell is one of the major contributors to research into stress.

The model, shown in Exhibit 7-10, argues that the main sources of stress lie within two basic job characteristics: psychological job demands and job decision latitude.

According to the JD–C model, jobs that are most likely to cause extreme reactions to job-related stress such as exhaustion or cardiovascular diseases, are those that combine high demands with low decision latitude. The JD–C model labels this as high strain as opposed to low strain, which would predict lower than average stress reactions, as can be seen in Exhibit 7-10.

This model also assumes that motivation, learning and personal growth will occur where job demands and decision latitude are high. This has been referred to as good stress, as job stressors are translated into direct action such as effective problem-solving (Karasek *et al.*, 1998). In passive jobs, which may not utilise an employee's skills effectively, the opposite can occur with a situation of 'learned helplessness' (Lennerhöf, 1998). This results in poor performance due to a lack of motivation.

The JD–C model demonstrates that psychological demands and decision latitude affect two psychological mechanisms. One is adverse and affects the health of the employee while the other influences motivation and the learning behaviour of the employee.

This JD–C model was expanded to include a third characteristic of work, that of workplace social support. This is known as the DCS model and can be seen in Exhibit 7.11.

The DCS model includes the psychological job demands and job decision latitude, although for this model they are known as job demands and job control, and also includes the third dimension of workplace social support. The strain and activity characteristics of the workplace are split into isolated and collective conditions. This model argues that when there are high job

EXHIBIT 7–10 The job demand–control model

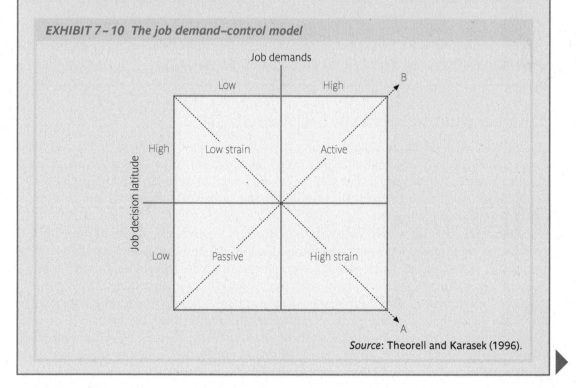

Source: Theorell and Karasek (1996).

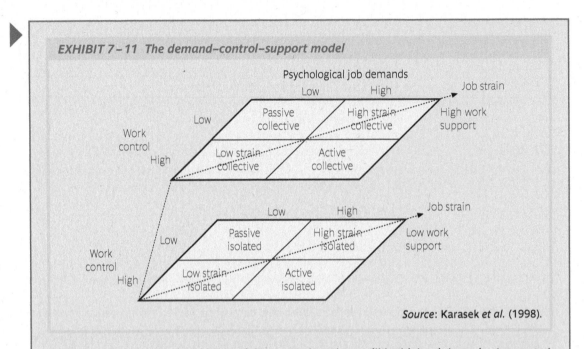

EXHIBIT 7–11 The demand–control–support model

Source: Karasek *et al.* (1998).

demands, low job control and low social support then there will be higher job strain. Jones *et al.* (1998) refer to this as *iso-strain*. The social support is seen as a buffer to reduce the amount of psychological stress.

De Jonge and Kompier (1997) have evaluated the JD–C and DCS models and suggest that evidence produced from research studies confirms that where there is a high job demand and low control stress is likely to be higher; yet they suggest that the social support is not confirmed by research studies, but the three elements of the DCS model each have different impacts on job stress, rather than a collective effect.

The usefulness of these models is that they focus on the characteristics of the work situation and highlight that, often, it is the job and not individual characteristics that create stress and it is important that employers respond appropriately.

The productive management of stress

Stress is an unavoidable condition of life. Although we cannot eliminate it, we can use our understanding of stress to control its effects and thereby enjoy more productive, satisfying lives both at work and elsewhere. In this section we will prescribe techniques that organisations and individuals can implement to reduce the likelihood of stressful situations and to cope with those that will inevitably arise.

Stress management at both individual and organisational levels consists of three steps. The first is *awareness* of negative stress symptoms such as the individual and organisational consequences just discussed – decreased performance, irritability, absenteeism, and so on. The second step is *determining the source* – what are the stressors contributing to the distress and its negative consequences? The third step is *doing something constructive to cope* more effectively with the stress. Folkman and Lazarus (1988) conclude that there are two types of coping: problem-focused coping, where the stressors are dealt with directly by either removing or changing them; and emotion-focused coping, where people learn how to modify or manage their stressful feelings and reactions in more constructive ways.

Millions are driven to attack their computers: 'desk rage' is the new office epidemic as stressed staff strike back at torrents of email

It is known as 'desk rage', and it is becoming an epidemic. One in four Britons admits to beating their computer – and the attacks are often sparked by a torrent of annoying emails.

A study of the computer habits of 4200 workers by computer firm Novatech showed that a quarter of Britons happily admit to attacking their computers.

Experts say people feel increasingly under the control of their computer, whether it is because of the machine breaking down or a deluge of 'you have mail' signs.

'This is a new phenomenon,' said Dr Frank Bond, an occupational psychologist at City University, London. 'But there are trends behind it. We live in an increasingly violent society and, in the workplace, we are put under large amounts of pressure. Britain works harder than the rest of Europe. This kind of stress will decrease your ability to keep under control and to react adequately. The natural checks that keep you from strangling your boss are just not there any more.'

The levels of violence revealed in the anonymous survey were equally alarming. One user admitted to breaking his finger as he lashed out at a monitor.

'One afternoon, after a day of glitches and errors,' said another confession, 'to the shock of my office I wrenched the screen free from my computer, stormed outside and chucked it down the fire escape stairs . . . [later] I gave it a decent burial in a skip.'

Experts fear the outbreak may be a result of 'inbox tyranny', described by the work think-tank, the Industrial Society, as 'the dread of feeling that your inbox is silently filling up'.

Gallup and the Institute For The Future estimate the average British working day consists not only of 171 messages, 46 telephone calls, 15 internal memos and 19 items of external post, but of 22 emails as well.

Diane Miller, employment relations adviser at the Chartered Institute for Personnel Development, said: 'We have all this new technology but have not thought through our working policies to make best use of it. People get 100 emails a day, and because it is so quick they feel that they must respond to them immediately. It is a distraction. A computer becomes a machine whose demands must be met.'

A recent survey by computer manufacturers Compaq and pollsters MORI questioned more than 1250 workers in Britain. Nearly half felt frustrated by the time taken to solve IT problems and two in five blamed computer jargon for exacerbating the issue. A quarter of under 25 year olds questioned said they had seen colleagues kick computers, and one in eight respondents had seen co-workers bully the IT department when things went wrong.

Research shows the problem is likely to increase. Internet analysts Jupiter project that marketing-related email messages will increase 40-fold by 2006. Ferraris Research estimates that by next year workers will spend four hours a day reading and answering on average 50 work-related messages. Today we deal with 30 a day, up 50 per cent from last year.

While the Health & Safety Executive recommends workers spend between 20 and 40 minutes a time at a computer on health grounds, there is, yet, little research on whether time spent at terminals should be limited on stress grounds. The International Stress Management Association ranks emails among the top 20 causes of stress. Twenty per cent of people said that new technology was a source of stress, whereas 19 per cent referred to domestic relationships as 'stressful'.

▶   The TUC considers stress the UK's top workplace hazard. Two-thirds of the 9000 organisations the TUC surveyed late last year considered stress a severe problem. This rise is accompanied by TUC figures showing one in five workers are subjected to violence at work. The last British Crime Survey reported 1.2 million incidents of work-related violence.

'We communicate a lot by computer,' adds Bond. 'We may get bad news from it. And these stresses may lead us to retaliate. We might shoot the messenger. Organisations are getting increasingly concerned about sabotage. People are getting increasingly angry and starting to take it out on the company, not in an overt way, but covertly – by leaving a computer virus on their disk, for example.'

Source: © Guardian Newspapers Ltd, 2001, Nick Paton Walsh.

Discussion questions

1 Do you think new technology is making work more or less stressful?

2 How can we improve communication to decrease stress?

Individual coping strategies

Because stress is such a multidimensional phenomenon, the ultimate responsibility for stress management rests with the individual. There are a number of things people can do by themselves to cope better with stress. Some of these proven strategies are discussed below.

Problem-focused strategies

Problem-focused strategies for coping with individual stress need to attack the specific stressor directly. If a student is worried about finding a job after graduating, stress will start to be reduced to the extent that he or she starts the job search process. Once several job possibilities have been located, interviews set up and information on the companies gathered, the stress level will start to decrease. The same is true for a worker who has just been given an assignment that is not clear and has an impossible deadline. Once the worker shares these concerns with management and gets help and an extended deadline, stress levels drop. There are several general strategies that can aid in dealing with most stressors that can be decreased by solving a problem: time management, seeking help and, if all else fails, changing jobs.

Time management

Not being in control of your time can generate serious anxiety, frustration and even panic. Time management consists of applying the principles of management to yourself – in other words, planning, organising and controlling the use of your time. It means using schedules and other control mechanisms to keep your performance flowing smoothly along some desired time line. In general, time management strategies entail deciding what goal is to be accomplished by what date or time, and then making a list of all the activities necessary to accomplish the goal, prioritising the tasks from most important to least important, estimating how long it will take to accomplish the tasks, and planning activities, starting with the most important task first, until the goal is accomplished (Lakein, 1973).

Seeking help

Getting help from a colleague, advice from your boss or training from the human resources department can provide a stressed person with the knowledge and skills to deal productively

mentoring
The process of a senior performer coaching a junior one.

with a stressor. Just knowing that such support is available from others is helpful in coping with stress. Longer-term support systems can be set up through **mentoring**, where a junior employee is personally coached by a more senior and proven performer. Mentoring has been found to relieve stress caused by high performance demands, pressures for change and low job challenge (Kram and Hall, 1989).

If the cause of stress is due to improper employee training, classes, coaching or another appropriate form of instruction should be undertaken. Not only will proper training eliminate qualitative job overload, but it also increases self-esteem and confidence as employees begin to perform more effectively on the job.

The organisation you work for probably has a number of things available to you that can help ease your stress. Take advantage of them. In addition to training and mentoring, your company may offer things like daycare facilities, employee assistance programmes, fitness promotion and personal time off.

Change jobs

If, after exhausting all available problem-solving techniques, job-related stress is still not reduced to a satisfactory level, changing the nature of your job or even leaving the organisation in favour of alternative employment may be the answer. Sometimes renegotiating your job role can eliminate the stress caused by role ambiguity, conflict, overload or underload (French and Bell, 1990). If this does not work, however, no job is worth sacrificing your physical and mental health, and it may be best to seek other job opportunities. According to Schlossberg (1990), hanging in there until burnout occurs only compounds the stress.

Emotion-focused strategies

If the stressor cannot be reduced or eliminated through problem-focused strategies, or if an individual decides to live with the stressor for some reason, emotion-focused strategies can be used to decrease the level of stress experienced to more healthy and comfortable levels. Certain emotion-focused strategies work better for some people than others. Anything that works to reduce stress for you in a healthy, productive manner should be used. Some common emotion-focused strategies include relaxation, exercise, psychological strategies, recreation and companionship.

Relaxation

Relaxation decreases muscle tension, which in turn decreases heart rate, breathing rate and blood pressure (Smith, 1990). Benson (1975) suggests that to elicit the relaxation response, you must find a quiet place, then assume a comfortable position, close your eyes, and concentrate on relaxing all your muscles while you listen intently to your own breathing for 20 minutes. A study of 126 employees at the Converse Rubber Company found that after just a month of two daily 15-minute relaxation breaks using Benson's relaxation response, employees demonstrated significant increases in work performance and sociability, and decreases in stress, blood pressure levels and sick days (Hart, 1987). A similar study of the relaxation response at two high-tech corporations found that participating employees demonstrated significant decreases in anxiety, depression and hostility, and showed better coping skills.

To practise meditation, sit comfortably with your eyes closed for about 20 minutes and engage in the repetition of a special sound, called a *mantra*. Those who practise meditation can vouch for the fact that following this procedure twice a day reduces your heart rate, oxygen consumption and blood pressure (Woolfold *et al.*, 1982).

An easy way to start meditation is to breathe in a full and relaxed manner. Every time you exhale, calmly let the word 'one' float through your mind. You may also want to imagine that you are in a safe place while you continue this process for 15 minutes (Smith, 1991).

To get high-tech help for relaxing there is the *biofeedback process*, which involves detecting small changes in body tension through galvanic skin responses picked up by electrodes attached to the body. When these responses are amplified and displayed to individuals connected to the biofeedback machine, the individuals can learn how to control their body responses in ways that reduce stress (Girdano *et al.*, 2000).

Exercise

Medical science has shown that the physiological and biochemical changes resulting from exercise reduce the effects of stress (Mobily, 1982). Matteson and Ivancevich (1987) have reported that exercisers experience lower degrees of anxiety, depression and hostility than do non-exercisers. Regardless of whether you choose jogging, cycling, tennis, walking, swimming or one of countless other activities, the evidence is unequivocal that proper exercise enhances physical health and mental well-being.

Psychological strategies

There are a number of psychological strategies that can control the amount of stress experienced and its impact on an individual. Two of these are increased self-awareness and perceptual adaptation.

Increased self-awareness about how you normally behave on the job and in social situations and an ability to recognise early signs of tension make up the first step in managing personal stress. Your self-awareness will signal you to withdraw from overload situations and seek help when necessary.

Through perceptual adaptation or reframing, individuals can learn to condition their minds to handle those stressors they are not able to control or eliminate (Shepherd, 1990). The 'thousand year test', for example, can help you reduce tension. Just ask yourself, 'A thousand years from now, will anyone really care if I miss this deadline?' Alternatively, 'What is the worst thing that can actually happen to me if things do go wrong, and can I cope with it?' Often, you can reduce stress just by realising that you will be able to survive even if the worst happens.

Recreation

If all you do is work, you are bound to experience stress, no matter how much you love your job. Everyone needs hobbies and recreational interests that have no purpose beyond the relaxation and pleasure they bring. It is especially important that Type A personalities take their minds off work and relax with some sport or hobby that forces them to forget their job-related troubles. It does not matter what they do, so long as it is enjoyable and not related to work.

Companionship

Stress tends to intensify when a person is alone. If you live by yourself, invite others to share in your leisure pursuits. People who develop close, supportive relationships have a powerful antidote to stress. One study of middle-aged men who lost their jobs found that those who had social support from wives, family or friends survived the resulting stress relatively unharmed. Those without such support, however, suffered physical as well as mental problems (Ganster *et al.*, 1986).

Time management

Time management is an important issue for both individuals and managers. Time is a basic resource yet it is also something that can pass quickly and is often difficult to capture.

Managing personal time

Balancing aspects of you life is important and the aim of time management is to spend time doing the things that help you achieve your goals as well as the things you personally prioritise and value. Often people have to balance home, work, study and a social life, and an unexpected problem in one area could lead to a build-up of problems in another. You may well remember being nagged when at school to do your homework when you get it and you may well remember ignoring such advice and having to spend a long Sunday night completing your tasks so as not to get in trouble the next day. As people get older they also have more responsibilities, and poor planning can lead to poor time management, a lack of control and also, possibly, to symptoms of stress.

Blair (2005) suggests that the three 'effs' can help in capturing the time resource with very little effort. These 'effs' are:

1 effective – having a definite or desired effect

2 efficient – productive with minimum waste or effort

3 effortless – seeming without effort, natural, easy.

To be effective you need to prioritise your goals. What is important to you? It may help to rank them in order from 1–10. Try to be realistic and definite. Identify what needs to be done, when and by whom. If the goals are major then they may need to be broken up into smaller steps.

To be efficient means having to plan. How will you allocate your time? Using a timetable can be quite helpful. If there are certain activities that you have to do each week then write them down and plan around them. Also think about the best time for you: can you work early in the morning, or are you a late-night person? If you are studying you may find it easier to complete tasks before going to college rather than at the end of the day. It is also important to review your plan regularly. If your schedule is not working, think about why. What can be changed, and how? It is also important to remember that 'all work and no play makes Jack or Jill a dull person', therefore allow for some 'me' time doing the things you like.

To be able to appear effortless is a sign of good planning: the supermum who always seems to be able to do everything probably not only has a coherent plan but also a contingency plan for when things go wrong.

To practise good time management:

■ look carefully at your priorities

■ identify your goals

■ look carefully at the way you work

■ look carefully at where you allocate your time.

Organise your time

To find enough time and use it effectively it is a good idea to find a system that works for you. A personal diary or organiser can be useful as it enables forward planning.

A review of the following issues can also help you identify how you spend your time.

- Look carefully at what you need to do each day. Prioritise those tasks that are urgent and recognise those that can be put off or that someone else could do.

- Do the tasks as soon as possible rather than delaying, as this can cause a build-up that then leads to anxiety.

- Make sure your work area is suitable for the tasks. This means ensuring you have adequate space and lighting.

- Create a routine. Your time plan should help you identify when you need to do tasks and how much time needs to be allocated.

- Break tasks into manageable portions as this gives a sense of achievement when they are accomplished.

- Learn how to say no. If a task is likely to take you away from your goals then be firm and don't do it.

- Reward yourself with something you enjoy when you achieve a task.

- Decide not only your starting times but also your finishing times, so you can plan for other activities.

A good manager needs to be able to manage not only their own time but also that of others, so it is important to apply these strategies to the workplace. Time management is really the application of common-sense strategies and although it may not solve your problems, it can reveal them and provide you with a structured plan to help you deal with them.

Social work: a second look

Chris Giles, 47, left his career in social work in the mid-1990s but he missed the challenges and job satisfaction, and returned to the profession in 2001.

'Having qualified as a social worker in 1981 and after working in childcare and mental health for a couple of years, I got a job helping to set up a juvenile justice team in Epping Forest, where I became project leader. After that, I managed a generic team of seven social workers.

'I began to miss working in an inner city and moved to Tower Hamlets, where I got a similar job. I was promoted to principal officer in charge of three social work teams and then to be in charge of all front-line services of a political ward.

'My career came to an end in 1996, following the local elections of 1994, which saw political control of the council switch from Liberal to Labour. Labour ordered a complete reorganisation of the borough and I was forced to reapply for alternative jobs, none of which I got. I believe it was Labour's way of getting people they wanted in jobs rather than those they had inherited. It was a devastating experience for me, having been in the job 23 years, and I swore I'd never work for local government again.

'For the next five years, I had many jobs – in the private sector, voluntary sector and even running my own business. As each one failed to become permanent, I started to realise that I am best off when using my people skills and that the best use of people skills is, in my opinion, in social work. So, last year, I put aside my old feelings and reapplied.

'Although I had been at the top of the tree, I knew I would have to come in again at the bottom. However, I did not mind, particularly when I saw a job ad for a reviewing officer for older people. It was part of a new team looking at care packages for older people. Working with older people involves a lot of positive feedback and, being a returner and feeling quite vulnerable, it proved to be perfect.

'My employers were brilliant at arranging relevant retraining courses and offering both practical and emotional support in the workplace. In five years you miss a lot in social work. Key legislation changes, for one thing. However, with help at hand, I had a good feel for the job within just six months.

'Another positive aspect of returning to the profession was that my skills from my previous careers as a social worker and in other jobs were both valued and utilised. In the private sector, people can be quick to use you but quick to drop you; that is never the case in social work. I'm a better manager than practitioner and may try to move in that direction again, but for now I'm really enjoying and valuing being put back in touch with people at the coalface of the profession. Most importantly, my sense of self-worth has been re-established.'

Source: © Kate Hilpern, *Independent*, 23 July 2002.

Summary

- Whether focusing on career development, personal wellness or daily productivity, self-management is the name of the game in today's rapidly changing world.

- Success in the knowledge economy comes to those who know their strengths, their values and how they best perform. Given this information, people are in good shape to manage their stress and careers.

- Some people leave their careers to chance. Wiser people plan, which is especially important now because careers are likely to be quite different in the future.

- Career paths are more variable and less predictable than they were in the past. Planning your career requires that you understand how future changes will influence it.

- Intense worldwide competition, fast-changing technology, and changing organisational forms and management will cause people to change jobs, organisations and even careers more frequently than in the past. You should expect change and uncertainty and be prepared to manage your own career.

- Career planning is part of life planning, which means prioritising the work, family, social, financial and spiritual aspects of life.

- Decide what kind of person you want to be and what you want to do. Identify your values, interests and skills so that you can decide how well they fit particular jobs and careers.

- To achieve your career goals and get the job you want, define what you want to do. Then initiate a process of identifying potential organisations, building a network of contacts, working part-time, designing your CV, and preparing for interviews. The final step is to conduct interviews until you find a job and organisation that fit you best.

- In today's rapidly changing workplace, you must assume responsibility for managing your own career. Develop your personal mission statement and clearly establish and visualise your goals. Be aware of which career stage you are in, as each has its own opportunities and pitfalls.

- Women and minorities face special problems. Women who value both careers and families often feel the pressure of juggling the conflicting demands of family and work. Both minorities and women encounter the 'glass ceiling', which is an invisible barrier that blocks advancement.

- All people reach a plateau in their career; the critical factor is how each individual reacts to and manages that stage. For some, the experience is frustrating and discouraging; others take it in their stride and continue to contribute and find satisfaction.

- Work-related stress is a major concern in the 2000s. Never before have people been so concerned about 'burning out' at work. Successive waves of downsizing, acquisitions and consolidations have added to the traditional stressors of overwork, time deadlines and ambiguity. Yet stress in the workplace has always been with us, and it often serves as the motivator for outstanding accomplishments.

- As our natural reaction to threatening situations, stress is our ally in survival. Too much or too little stress, however, can negatively affect our performance and well-being.

- Monitoring our stress symptoms can help us know how well we are coping and when to do something constructive about the challenge we are experiencing.

- Failure to monitor and react appropriately to chronic stress can lead to immense organisational costs, including significant health problems and even death.

- Although stress may originate from a variety of organisational sources, such as work overload and time pressures, it can also be caused by problems in a person's home life or personality make-up. A variety of factors, such as social support and personal ability, moderate the consequences of stress for various individuals.

- It may be impossible or even undesirable to eliminate stress, but it can be managed productively. Organisations can help by providing personal assistance and applying appropriate management principles. Of course, it is the individuals who are experiencing the stress who must personally manage it for themselves, using both organisational and personal resources.

Areas for personal development

Management guru Peter Drucker said years ago, 'If you can't manage yourself, you can't manage anyone else.' It is also often true that if you do not manage yourself, somebody else will do it for you. In addition to these very significant reasons, self-management is also imperative for successful stress and career management. You can be more effective managing yourself if you apply the following interpersonal skills.

1 **Test how you feel each day in anticipation of the day's experience.** This will tell you if you are managing yourself successfully. If your feelings are positive, you are on the right track. If they are negative, you need to find out why and change something.

2 **Practise feedback analysis.** Whenever you make a major decision or take a major action, write down what you expect will happen. Nine or 12 months later, compare the actual results with your expectations. Practised consistently this simple method will show where your strengths are, what you are doing or failing to do that deprives you of the full benefits of your strengths, and where you are not particularly competent. Finally, it will show you where you have no strengths and cannot perform.

3 **Take responsibility for relationships.** Share with your associates what you are good at, how you prefer to work, what your values are, the contribution you plan to concentrate on, and the results you expect to deliver. Second, ask others what their strengths are, how they prefer to perform, what their values are and what their proposed contributions are.

4 **Continually do life planning.** This includes making choices about what mix of the primary aspects of life – family, leisure-time activities, social life, spiritual development, education and personal development, civic and philanthropic involvement, and work – most closely match your values and aspirations. Then you need to check how you are spending your time in comparison to these priorities.

5 **Know your values.** Determine what is desirable to you in terms of both ends – the goals you want to achieve – and the means (the behaviours you think are acceptable). Rank what you value in both areas and monitor yourself to make certain that your time is spent consistently.

6 **Determine your interests.** What you like and do not like doing reveals your interests. You will perform better if you choose areas that you like to work in.

7 **Determine your strengths.** That is, define what you are good at doing, and what you are weak in. Concentrate your performance in areas where you are strong.

8 **Plan your career.** After you have determined your life priorities, values, interests and strengths, you are in good shape to define what you want to do. Answer the following questions to define the job you want. What are your best skills and where do you want to use them? What kinds of people would you like to work with or help? In what kind of place would you like to work? What fields or industries feel compatible with your skills and interests? What salary level do you want? What developmental and advancement opportunities do you want?

9 **Build a network of contacts.** Build a network of contacts who can help you obtain information, give you advice and help you get introductions into the companies of your choice. Talk with the successful friends of your parents and the parents of your friends. Ask them for the names of others that might help.

10 **Manage your stress productively.** Apply the three-step stress-management process of *awareness, determining the source* and *doing something constructive* to cope more effectively with stress. Use time management to keep yourself organised and in control of your life.

Seek help from friends or company resources when you need assistance. Get out of dysfunctional stress situations by changing jobs, relationships or locations. If you cannot eliminate the stressor directly, manage how you experience the stress by relaxation, exercise, psychological strategies, recreation and companionship.

❓ Questions for study and discussion

1 Warren Bennis said that, for most people, the central issue and aspiration is a life worth living. What does a 'life worth living' consist of for you?

2 Why is self-management important?

3 What is a successful career for you?

4 What are your strengths and preferred ways of performing? How can you apply this knowledge to develop a successful career?

5 What are your most common stress symptoms? How do these symptoms affect your performance, interpersonal relationships and happiness?

6 What are the major stressors contributing to the stress symptoms you are currently experiencing? If you are not currently experiencing stress symptoms, how do you account for this state of affairs?

7 How do you and other students you know cope with the stress of final examinations? What are the short-term and long-term consequences of these various methods?

8 How do you react to the stress of giving a speech? Check out how five of your friends feel about public speaking. Why is it considered stressful? Why do some people perceive it as more stressful than do others?

🔑 Key Concepts

downsizing, *p. 290*

feedback analysis, *p. 292*

career, *p. 297*

life planning, *p. 300*

network, *p. 304*

mentor, *p. 306*

mummy track, *p. 307*

daddy track, *p. 307*

glass ceiling, *p. 307*

plateauing, *p. 308*

stress, *p. 309*

stressors, *p. 309*

distress, *p. 311*

episodic stress, *p. 312*

chronic stress, *p. 313*

Type A personality, *p. 314*

Type B personality, *p. 314*

hardiness, *p. 322*

burnout, *p. 323*

mentoring, *p. 329*

Personal skills exercise

Tensing muscles relaxation technique

Purpose To experience a stress-reduction technique.

Time 10 minutes

Instructions It is recommended that the instructor or a class member be selected to read the following instructions to the class while class members are relaxing with their eyes closed. If preferred, students can read the exercise and do it on their own in class or elsewhere.

1 Select a comfortable sitting or reclining position.

2 Loosen any tight clothing.

3 Tense your toes and feet (curl the toes; turn your feet in and out). Hold and study the tension. Relax.

4 Now tense your lower legs, knees and thighs. Hold the tension and study the tension, then relax your legs.

5 Now tense your buttocks. Hold and study the tension. Relax your buttocks.

6 Tense the fingers and hands. Hold and study the tension, then relax.

7 Tense your lower arms, elbows and upper arms. Hold and study the tension, then relax.

8 Tense your abdomen. Hold and study the tension, then relax.

9 Now tense your chest. Hold and study the tension, then relax. Take a deep breath and exhale slowly.

10 Tense your back. Hold and study the tension, then relax.

11 Now tense your shoulders. Hold and study the tension, then relax.

12 Finally, tense your neck. Hold and study the tension, then relax.

13 Now relax every part of your body and be as quiet as possible for a couple of minutes.

14 How do you feel?

Debriefing After the exercise is finished, simply ask participants to share how they feel and what they experienced during the exercise. Participants can also share other relaxation techniques with one another that they have experienced, such as deep breathing, visual fantasies and meditation.

Team exercise
Diagnosing stress and its causes

Purpose To diagnose the stress symptoms, causes and coping strategies that you have experienced. Compare them with the experiences of others in similar situations to gain a broader perspective of the stress process and increase your repertoire of stress-management options.

Time The total time for all four steps is 50 to 75 minutes. If time is limited, step 4 can be omitted and smaller groups can be formed.

Step 1 Individually think about a stressful situation you have experienced. Then write down your answers to the following questions (5 minutes).

1 What caused the stress (what were the stressors)?

2 What symptoms of stress did you experience?

3 What were the consequences of the stress?

4 How did you try to cope with the stress?

Step 2 In groups of four to six, compare your answers to the questions in step 1 in round-robin fashion (10 to 15 minutes). When all have shared their experiences, compare them according to the following guidelines (20 minutes).

Step 3

1 Identify common elements in the stressful situations just described by your group members. Write them down for later class sharing.

2 List all the symptoms of stress that individuals in your group experienced in the stressful situations they shared. Note the common symptoms across situations.

3 Specify the causes of stress and their frequency of occurrence in group members' experiences.

4 Describe the different processes that group members used to reduce the stress in the situations they reported.

5 Suggest additional ways for reducing the stress in the original situations described and for managing stress in similar situations in the future.

Step 4 Choose a spokesperson from your group to share your group's answers with the entire class. Discuss, as a class, the groups' summaries just shared. Use the following questions as guidelines (30 minutes).

1 What are the most common symptoms of stress?

2 What are the most common causes of stress?

3 What means of stress reduction are effective?

4 What have you learned from this exercise that can help you cope with current or potential stressors?

Case study: a hectic day at Westland Bank

Tony Cruickshank awoke to the ring of the telephone next to his bed. It was after midnight. Tony thought instantly of his ageing mum and dad in Kent and reached for the receiver with a feeling of dread. But it was the desk sergeant at the local police station, making what was to him a routine call.

'Mr Cruickshank. The back door down here at Westland Bank is unlocked. You're going to have to come down and check the place with our officer and lock up the building.'

Tony was both relieved and agitated. 'So what else can go wrong at work?' he asked himself as he grappled in the dark for jeans and a sweatshirt.

Tony was assistant director of Westland Bank, a small financial institution that had come into its own in the 10 years since Tony had started work there. At that time, there were only two employees: the managing director, Mark Picton, and himself. Now there were 18.

As Tony drove towards town, he began to recall the events of the preceding day at work. It had been one of those days that were becoming increasingly common. Such days left him exhausted – so much so that at home he had begun to argue with his wife and to scold his three children for minor things that had once left him unruffled.

Yesterday the turmoil had started early in the morning when the chairman of the board burst into his office and created a disturbance because she had not yet received last month's statistical data. She had to review it before that afternoon's board of directors' meeting, she informed him. Tony had intended to get the statistical information together, but in what little spare time he could find between customers he had made out the monthly report for the Bank of England instead. That deadline could not be ignored.

After the chairman of the board departed, Tony went to tell Picton that he needed another administrator to help relieve his workload. Picton asserted that the bank was currently overstaffed and that more efficient use of the personnel on board would solve the problem. Tony agreed with him that the present number of personnel should be adequate, but their efficiency was poor. Picton took this as a direct criticism of the niece and two cousins he had employed, and a heated argument developed between the two men. Eventually their tempers cooled, and Tony returned to his office and resumed his work.

About two o'clock in the afternoon, Tony stepped out of his office and spotted two customers waiting at the counter. Not a single cashier was in evidence. His quick investigation disclosed three cashiers downstairs having coffee. Another had gone out for cigarettes, and the fifth was in the supply room stocking up on forms for his window. Tony called Picton out of his office and quickly pointed out the situation. Picton snapped, 'You take care of it!' Then he ducked back into his office and slammed the door. Tony herded the cashiers out of the canteen with a sharp reprimand and then went to see Anita Fall, who was supposed to supervise them.

Anita was in her mid-twenties and had worked for Westland Bank for nearly five years. At first she had shown marginal interest in her work, but after she got married and her husband entered law school, her interest picked up; now she was progressing quite rapidly.

Tony asked Anita for an explanation of the cashier situation. Anita advised him that she had no real control over the cashiers. She told Tony that she had asked Picton for help but got none, and that on occasions when she had attempted to discipline certain cashiers, Picton had reprimanded her for doing so. By this time Tony was sorely frustrated, but he managed to keep himself under control.

Just before five o'clock, Tony's secretary (a Picton cousin) brought him the typed letters that he had dictated earlier that day. As Tony prepared to sign them, he noted two contained so many errors that he decided to stay late and retype them himself.

Now, as the steeple clock in the centre of town struck a single chime, Tony Cruickshank drove into the car park pondering why the back door was unlocked. Hadn't Picton been the last person to leave? 'But Mark always checks both doors before he leaves the building ... could I myself have forgotten?'

Questions for managerial action

1 What symptoms of stress is Tony exhibiting in this case?

2 What are the sources of his stress? Is Tony himself responsible for any of these?

3 What could Tony do to improve his management of stress in this situation?

4 How could Tony apply time-management techniques to help him regain control and reduce stress?

5 What kind of role conflict exists here? From Tony's perspective, what would be the most effective method of dealing with it?

Applied questions

6 Selye identified three stages in the physiology of stress. What stage is Tony at?

7 Exhibit 7-6 illustrates a model of the stress process. How can Tony moderate either his own behaviour or the organisation's to ensure he doesn't suffer from the physiological, emotional or behavioural consequences of stress?

WWW exercise

Manager's Internet tools

Web tips: providing stress management training through the Internet

As the information age accelerates change and the speed with which business is done, companies around the world will need to pay special attention to the effects of work-related stress on their employees. Although there are many resources to which companies can turn to get information on dealing with stress, there may not be as many resources for companies with offices around the world. An important resource that companies should consider is the International Stress Management Association (ISMA), a non-profit organisation dedicated to creating a less stressful world.

ISMA seeks to advance the education of professionals and students and to facilitate methodically sound research in several professional interdisciplinary stress management fields: business and industry, counselling, dentistry, education, medicine, nursing, occupational therapy, physical therapy, psychiatry, psychology and speech pathology. The need for ISMA's efforts has become critical in recent years, as medical and psychological service providers are overwhelmed with patients who have been unable to cope effectively and are suffering from a wide variety of stress-related disorders. ISMA's intention is to establish minimum standards and criteria for a credential that does not duplicate clinical services but focuses on clearly defined educational principles and skill development.

World Wide Web search

ISMA is dedicated to promoting research, encouraging professional communication, and supporting publication of articles on stress management and health around the world. Started in the United States, ISMA has quickly expanded globally, with offices opening in the United Kingdom, Germany, the Netherlands, France, Spain, Russia, the Republic of Georgia, India, Japan, Hong Kong and Australia. Visit ISMA's comprehensive website, links and resources at http://www. isma.org.uk and find out how ISMA can help you learn how to manage stress better.

Specific website

Go to the website totaljobs.co.uk and get your career plan ready to look for the perfect job. Your new job may be just a click away. What other advice does it offer? Are you able to plan your career and find information on the right job for you?

1 What kind of education about work-related stress worldwide is available at ISMA? Does it offer workshops or certifications if you wanted to move towards a professional career in stress management?

2 What career and job search advice can you obtain from the totaljobs.co.uk job search guide?

3 What do you think are the advantages and disadvantages of being able to upload your actual CV right onto the website as a shotgun approach to job searching, as compared to actually meeting with company representatives?

LEARNING CHECKLIST ☑

Before you move on you may want to reflect on what you have learnt in this chapter. You should now be able to:

☑ understand the meanings of work

☑ apply principles of self-management

☑ self-manage your own career

☑ recognise stress symptoms

☑ identify the major causes of stress

☑ discuss the consequences of stress

☑ apply strategies for coping with stress.

Further reading

Gonzalez-Roma, V., Schaufeli, W.B., Bakker, A.B. and Lloret, S. (2006) 'Burnout and Work Engagement: Independent Factors of Opposite Poles?', *Journal of Vocational Behavior* 68(1), p. 165.

Kohler, J.M., Munz, D.C. and Grawitch, M.J. (2006) 'Test of a Dynamic Stress Model for Organisational Change: Do Males and Females Require Different Models?', *Applied Psychology* 55(2), p. 168.

Ter Doest, L., Maes, S., Gebhardt, W.A. and Koelewijn, H. (2006) 'Personal Goal Facilitation through Work: Implications for Employee Satisfaction and Well-being', *Applied Psychology* 55(2), p. 192.

References

Anderson, J.G. (1991) 'Stress and Burnout Among Nurses: A Social Network Approach', *Journal of Social Behavior and Personality* 6(7), pp. 251–272.

Archer Jr, J.A. (1991) *Managing Anxiety and Stress.* Muncie, IN: Accelerated Development, Inc., pp. 12–13.

Bales, J. (1991) 'Work Stress Grows, but Services Decline', *APA Monitor* 22(11), November, p. 32.

Barnett, C. (1982) 'Workaholics: They're Not All Work Enthusiasts', *Republic Scene*, January, p. 39.

Bell, J. (1990) 'Managing Stress', *Accountant's Magazine* 94, August, pp. 14–16.

Bennis, W. (1987) 'Bennis Offers Psychologists His "Secret of Success"', *USC School of Business Administration, The Quarterly*, Summer, p. 7.

Benson, H. (1975) *The Relaxation Response.* New York, NY: William Morrow.

Blair, G. (2005) Personal Time Management for Busy Managers, at www.see.ed.ac.uk.

Bolles, R.N. (2000) *What Color is Your Parachute 2000.* Berkeley, CA: Ten Speed Press, pp. 194–228.

Brief, A.P., Schuler, R.S. and Van Sell, M. (1981) *Managing Job Stress.* Boston, MA: Little Brown & Co., p. 138.

Brousseau, K.R., Driver, M.J., Eneroth, K. and Larsson, R. (1996) 'Career Pandemonium: Realigning Organizations and Individuals', *Academy of Management Executive* 10(4), pp. 52–66.

Burke, M.J., Brief, A.P. and George, J.M. (1993) 'The Role of Negative Affectivity in Understanding

Relations Between Self-reports of Stressors and Strains: A Comment on the Applied Psychology Literature', *Journal of Applied Psychology* 78, pp. 402–412.

Clawson, J.G., Kotler, J.P., Faux, V.A. and McArthur, C.C. (1992) *Self-assessment and Career Development* (3rd edn). Englewood Cliffs, NJ: Prentice Hall.

Chmiel, N. (2000) *Introduction to Work and Organisational Psychology*. Blackwell Publishers.

Cooper, C.L. (1987) 'The Experience and Management of Stress: Job and Organisational Determinants', in A.W. Riley and S.J. Zaccaro (eds) *Occupational Stress and Organizational Effectiveness*. New York, NY: Praeger, pp. 53–69.

Cooper, G.L. and Payne, R. (1988) *Causes, Coping and Consequences of Stress at Work*. New York, NY: Wiley, pp. 216–220.

Covey, S.R. (1989) *The 7 Habits of Highly Effective People*. New York, NY: Simon & Schuster, pp. 106–139.

Cummings, R.C. (1990) 'Job Stress and the Buffering Effect of Supervisory Support', *Group and Organization Studies*, March, pp. 92–104; and J.J. House (1981) *Work Stress and Social Support*. Reading, MA: Addison-Wesley.

DeAngelis, T. (1993) 'Psychologists Aid Victims of Violence in Post Office', *APA Monitor*, October, pp. 144–145.

De Jonge, J. and Kompier, M.A.J. (1997) 'A Critical Examination of the Demand–Control–Support Model from a Work Psychological Perspective', *International Journal of Stress Management* 4(4), pp. 235–258.

Drucker, P.F. (1999) 'Managing Oneself', *Harvard Business Review*, March–April, pp. 65–74.

Fletcher, B. (1988) 'The Epidemiology of Occupational Stress', in C.L. Cooper and R. Payne (eds) *Causes, Coping and Consequences of Stress at Work*. New York, NY: John Wiley & Sons, pp. 3–52.

Folkman, S. and Lazarus, R.S. (1988) 'Coping as a Mediator of Emotion', *Journal of Personality and Social Psychology* 54, pp. 466–475.

French, J.R.P. and Caplan, R.D. (1973) 'Organizational Stress and Individual Stress', in A.J. Marrow (ed.) *The Failure of Success*. New York, NY: AMACOM, pp. 30–36.

French, W.L. and Bell Jr, C.H. (1990) *Organizational Development: Behavioral Science Interventions for Organization Improvement*. Englewood Cliffs, NJ: Prentice Hall.

Friedman, M. and Rosenman, R. (1974) *Type A Behaviour and Your Heart*. New York, NY: Alfred A. Knopf.

Ganster, D.C., Fusilier, M.R. and Mayes, B.T. (1986) 'Role of Social Support in the Experiences of Stress at Work', *Journal of Applied Psychology* 71, pp. 102–110.

Garland, S.B. (1991) 'Throwing Stones at the "Glass Ceiling"', *BusinessWeek*, 19 August, p. 29.

Gemmill, G.R. and Heisler, W.J. (1972) 'Fatalism as a Factor in Managerial Job Satisfaction, Job Strain, and Mobility', *Personnel Psychology* 25, pp. 241–250.

Girdano, D.A., George, S. and Everly, D. (2000) *Controlling Stress and Tension* (6th edn). New York, NY: Benjamin/Cummings, pp. 140–141.

Golembiewski, R.T. and Munzenrider, R.F. (1988) *Phases of Burnout: Developments in Concepts and Applications*. New York, NY: Praeger, pp. 6–10.

Gutek, B. (1990) 'Women's Fight for Equality in the Workplace', paper presented at the American Psychological Association and National Institute for Occupational Safety and Health Conference, Washington, DC, November.

Hall, D.T. (1976) *Careers in Organization*. Pacific Palisades, CA: Goodyear.

Hart, K.E. (1987) 'Managing Stress in Occupational Settings: A Selective Review of Current Research and Theory', in C.L. Cooper (ed.) *Stress Management Interventions at Work*. Rochester, England: MCB University Press Limited, pp. 11–17.

Hogan, R. and Morrison, J. (1990) 'Work and Well-being: An Agenda for the '90s', paper presented at the American Psychological Association and National Institute for Occupational Safety and Health Conference, Washington, DC, November.

Holland, J. (1973) *Making Vocational Choices: A Theory of Careers*. Englewood Cliffs, NJ: Prentice Hall.

Holmes, T.H. and Rahe, R.H. (1967) 'The Social Readjustment Rating Scale', *Journal of Psychosomatic Research* 11, pp. 213–218.

House, J.J. (1981) *Work, Stress and Social Support*. Reading, MA: Addison-Wesley.

Jackson, H. (1988) 'Type-A Managers Stuck in the Middle', *Wall Street Journal*, 17 June, p. 17.

Jamal, M. (1985) 'Relationship of Job Stress to Job Performance: A Study of Managers and Blue-collar Workers', *Human Relations*, May, pp. 409–424.

Jick, T.D. and Mitz, L.F. (1985) 'Sex Differences in Work Stress', *Academy of Management Review* 10, pp. 408–420.

Jones, F., Bright, J.E.H., Searle, B. and Cooper, L. (1998) 'Modelling Occupational Stress and Health: The Impact of the Demand–Control Model on Academic Research and on Workplace Practice', *Stress Medicine* 14(4), pp. 231–236.

Kahn, R.L. and Byosiere, P. (1992) 'Stress in Organizations', in M.D. Dunette and L.M. Hough (eds) *Handbook of Industrial and Organisational Psychology, Vol. 3*. Palo Alto, CA: Consulting Psychologists Press, pp. 571–650.

Kahn, R.W., Wolfe, D.M., Quinn, R.P., Snoek, J.D. and Rosenthal, R.A. (1964) *Organizational Stress*. New York, NY: Wiley, pp. 72–95.

Karasek, R.A. (1979) 'Job Demands, Job Decision Latitude and Mental Strain: Implications for Job Redesign', *Administrative Science Quarterly* 24, pp. 285–308.

Karasek, R.A. and Theorell, T. (1990) *Healthy Work: Stress, Productivity and the Reconstruction of Working Life*. New York, NY: Basic Books.

Karasek, R.A., Brison, C., Kawakami, N., Houtman, I., Bongers, P. and Amick, B. (1998) 'The Job Content Questionnaire (JCQ): An Instrument for Internationally Comparative Assessments of Psychosocial Job Characteristics', *Journal of Occupational Health Psychology* 3(4), pp. 322–355.

Katz, D. and Kahn, R. (1978) *The Social Psychology of Organizations* (2nd edn). New York, NY: Wiley.

Kiev, A. and Kohn, V. (1979) *Executive Stress: An AMA Survey Report*. New York, NY: AMACOM.

Kram, K.E. and Hall, D.T. (1989) 'Mentoring as an Antidote to Stress during Corporate Trauma', *Human Resource Management*, Winter, pp. 493–511.

Lakein, A. (1973) *How to Get Control of Your Time and Your Life*. New York, NY: Peter H. Wyden.

Lazarus, R.S. and Folkman, S. (1984) *Stress, Appraisal, and Coping*. New York, NY: Springer.

Lee, C., Ashford, S.J. and Bobko, P. (1990) 'Interactive Effects of Type A Behavior and Perceived Control of Worker Performance, Job Satisfaction, and Somatic Complaints', *Academy of Management Journal* 33, December, pp. 870–882.

Lennerhöf, L. (1998) 'Learned Helplessness at Work', *International Journal of Health Services* 18(2), pp. 207–222.

Matteson, M.T. and Ivancevich, J.M (1987) *Controlling Work Stress*, San Francisco, CA: Jossey-Bass, pp. 41–52.

Mehren, E. (1993) 'On the Daddy Track', *Los Angeles Times*, 30 June, pp. E1ff.

Mobily, K. (1982) 'Using Physical Activity and Recreation to Cope with Stress and Anxiety: A Review', *American Corrective Therapy Journal*, May/June, pp. 62–68.

Monroe, S.M. (1983) 'Major and Minor Life Events as Predictors of Psychological Distress: Further Issues and Findings', *Journal of Behavioral Medicine*, June, pp. 189–205.

Moore, R. (1991) 'How to Keep Women Managers on the Corporate Ladder', *BusinessWeek*, 2 September, p. 64.

Morrison, A.M., White, R.P. and Van Velsor, E. (1987) *Breaking the Glass Ceiling*. Reading, MA: Addison-Wesley.

Motowidlo, S.J., Packard, J.S. and Manning, M.R. (1987) 'Occupational Stress: Its Causes and Consequences for Job Performance', *Journal of Applied Psychology*, November, pp. 619–620.

Murphy, L.R. (1986) 'A Review of Organizational Stress Management Research', *Journal of Organizational Behavior Management*, Fall–Winter, pp. 215–227.

Noles, B. (1990) 'Fear and Stress in the Office Take Toll', *Wall Street Journal*, 6 November, p. B1.

Nussbaum, B., Cuneo, A., Carlson, B. and McWilliams, G. (1993) 'Corporate Refugees', *Business-Week*, 12 April, pp. 58–65.

Quick, J.C. and Quick, J.D. (1984) *Organizational Stress and Preventive Management*. New York, NY: McGraw-Hill, p. 8.

Revicki, D.A. and May, H.J. (1985) 'Occupational Stress, Social Support and Depression', *Health Psychology* 4, pp. 61–77.

Rice, M. (2001) 'The Way Back', *Management Today*, September, pp. 80–85.

Rice, M. (2002) 'Balancing Acts', *Management Today*, September, pp. 52–59.

Riley, R.W. and Zaccaro, S.J. (eds) (1987) *Occupational Stress and Organizational Effectiveness*. New York, NY: Praeger, pp. 56–59.

Rogers, D.P. (1984) 'Helping Employees Cope with Burnout', *Business*, October–December, pp. 3–7.

Schlossberg, H. (1990) 'Meditation Uplifts Her Life on the Fast Track', *Marketing News*, 1 October, pp. 10–11.

Schwartz, A.E. and Levin, J. (1990) 'Combatting Feelings of Stress', *Supervisory Management* 35, February, pp. 4–5.

Schwartz, F.N. (1989) 'Management Women and the New Facts of Life', *Harvard Business Review*, January–February, pp. 65–76.

Schwimer, D. (1991) 'Managing Stress to Boost Productivity', *Employee Relations Today*, Spring, pp. 23–27.

Scripps, H. (1999) 'Advice for Resume Writers: Don't Make a Novel Out of It', *The San Diego Union-Tribune*, 29 November, p. C-2.

Selye, H. (1976) *The Stress of Life*. New York, NY: McGraw-Hill.

Shepherd, J.S. (1990) 'Manage the Five C's of Stress', *Personnel Journal* 69, July, pp. 64–68.

Smith, J.C. (1990) *Cognitive–Behavioral Relaxation Training*. New York, NY: Springer Publishing Company.

Smith, J.C. (1991) *Stress Scripting: A Guide to Stress Management*. New York, NY: Praeger, pp. 162–163.

Stevens, A. (1994) 'Suit Over Suicide Raises Issue: Do Associates Work Too Hard?', *Wall Street Journal*, 15 April, pp. B1, B7.

Stroh, L., Brett, J. and Reilly, A. (1992) 'All the Right Stuff: A Comparison of Female and Male Managers' Career Progression', *Journal of Applied Psychology* 77(3), pp. 251–260.

Terkel, S. (1972) *Working*. New York, NY: Avon Books.

Theorell, T. and Karasek, R.A. (1996) Current Issues Relating to Psychological Job Strain and Cardiovascular Disease Research', *Journal of Occupational Health Psychology* 1(1), pp. 9–26.

Watson, D. and Tellegen, A. (1985) 'Toward a Consensual Structure of Mood', *Psychological Bulletin* 98, pp. 219–235.

Williams, R. (1989) 'The Trusting Heart', *Psychology Today*, January/February, pp. 35–42.

Williams Jr, R.B. (1984) 'Type A Behavior and Coronary Heart Disease: Something Old, Something New', *Behavior Medicine Update* 6, pp. 29–33.

Woolfold, R.L., Lehrer, R., McCann, B. and Ronney, A. (1982) 'The Effects of Progressive Relaxation and Meditation on Cognitive and Somatic Manifestations of Daily Stress', *Behavioral Research and Therapy* 20, pp. 325–338.

Zemke, R. (1991) 'Workplace Stress Revisited', *Training*, November, p. 35.

Part 2: Integrated case study

SABMiller: a global company with a local strategy – gaining competitive advantage through the leadership of people

SABMiller is a large brewing company, 31 per cent of its workforce is based in Africa. The Eagle Lager project provides Ugandans with an affordable and healthy quality beer made from a locally produced primary raw material such as sorghum.

From its South African origins, SABMiller has become one of the world's largest brewing companies. With operations in over 40 countries, it has more beer brands in the world's top 50 than any other brewer and it ranks among the top three brewers in more than 30 countries. Every minute of every day, consumers the world over drink an average of over 46,000 pints of SABMiller beer.

SABMiller is passionate about brewing. From local beers steeped in tradition to brands that are recognised around the world, the company's ambition is always to offer an outstanding product. Its quality is backed by some of the most efficient brewing and distribution operations in the industry – not to mention its long and successful record of market research, brand development and superb marketing in all corners of the world. Its success also lies in the way it conducts its business – with respect for partners and employees and a desire to do the best for the local community.

SABMiller's history is one of exceptional growth and returns to shareholders. With its global footprint, strong portfolio of brands and spread of operations in both mature and developing markets, SABMiller is well placed to continue its growth.

Although a worldwide organisation, SABMiller takes a local view when it comes to leading and motivating its employees, as can be seen from its Africa operations.

The Africa division has major brewing or beverage interests in 28 countries, which includes the traditional African beer made from sorghum. These also involve 18 African countries through its strategic alliance with the Castle group, as well as Kenya and Zimbabwe, where it has minority shareholdings in brewing interests.

Key African brands include Castle Lager, Castle Milk Stout, Hansa Pilsener, Kilimanjaro, Chairman's ESB, Club Pilsener, Nile Special, Eagle (clear sorghum beer), Mosi, Rhino, N'gola, Chibuku (sorghum beer), Golden Pilsener, St Louis, Club, 2M and Laurentina. For SABMiller in 2004, Africa produced strong earnings growth. However, its two largest operations, Tanzania and Botswana, have contributed the bulk of its profits in Africa for some time and both again did well – exceptionally so in the case of Tanzania. Among SABMiller's smaller businesses, Mozambique excelled and Angola continued its strong growth in soft drinks.

The company thinks that, in general, prospects in Africa are hopeful, with increasing economic stability.

The chairman states that:

> As incomes rise, we're seeing the same trading up among beer drinkers that is evident in South Africa. The challenge is to make sure our products are readily available, particularly in rural areas. We're also working hard to improve productivity, recognising that there's some way to go to match the standards we've achieved in South Africa.

SABMiller's group strategy, in Africa, is looking forward to establishing its operation and developing opportunities for growth as countries open their markets.

The stakeholders

SABMiller, in both a regulatory and socio-economic sense, depends on the support of all its stakeholders, from governments and local communities to its employees, suppliers and investors. Maintaining an open and honest dialogue with these groups, including reporting their progress, it sees as critical to its success.

Developing strong, interactive relationships with its stakeholders not only provides SABMiller with a rich source of ideas to improve the performance of its business, it is also a social and commercial obligation. It states that it has to be accountable for its actions.

During 2004, SABMiller held productive discussions with a large number of stakeholders. At a global level, these included organisations such as the World Health Organization, the Commission for Africa and the European Commission for Health and Consumer Safety. Locally, its businesses maintained regular contact with its local stakeholders, including relevant government departments and civil society groups.

In terms of reporting its corporate social responsibility (CSR) progress, SABMIller documents its advances in publications, produces an annual corporate accountability report and provides progress reports on the web (www.sabmiller.com). Its corporate accountability report provides a fuller explanation of its CSR progress, as well as its CSR governance and management structure and principles, which can also be accessed via the website. Several of its businesses, including companies in Botswana, Hungary and Poland, have also produced their own local CSR/corporate accountability reports.

The relentless pursuit of excellence is a hallmark of SABMiller. Its continuous focus on quality and performance has helped it to become one of the world's most successful beer businesses, with operations in over 40 countries across four continents – from China to El Salvador, from Russia to South Africa – which suggests it is passionate about its brands and how it produces them.

As it strives for quality, SABMiller is determined to conduct its activities in an exemplary manner. It believes in being a responsible employer to its 40 000-plus employees, in supporting the communities in which it operates and being mindful of its impact on the environment.

It is equally proud of its record and the excellent returns it has been able to offer its shareholders. However, it recognises that, without developing and motivating its employees, this would not be possible.

Employees

SABMiller state that:

> Healthy, motivated and skilled staff are the key to higher productivity and profitability. To enable them to realise their full potential, we support a range of training and healthcare programmes, among other initiatives.

HIV/AIDS is a significant issue in many of SABMiller's markets, including Africa, Asia and eastern Europe. To limit its impact on staff, it runs a comprehensive HIV/AIDS programme, currently focused on Africa but due to be rolled out across the group. Supported by educational campaigns, this includes voluntary counselling and testing for staff and their dependants in Africa, as well as fully funded anti-retroviral treatment for employees and their dependants who test HIV positive. So far, about 60 per cent of staff in Africa have agreed to voluntary testing, rising to more than 80 per cent, in certain locations. Its new group-wide HIV/AIDS strategy is due to be unveiled shortly.

The continued motivation of employees and management towards overall productivity enhancement in the business, by increasing empowerment, is a fundamental feature of the group's operating philosophy and is key to the management of risk. It achieves this through training, development, information sharing and progressive co-operative contributions to operating methods and planning, supported by rewards at competitive levels, including short- and long-term incentives where appropriate.

It is the aim of the group to be the employer of choice in each country in which it operates. In order to achieve this, each company designs employment policies that are appropriate to its business and markets, and that attract, retain and motivate the quality of staff necessary to compete.

The group is committed to an active equal opportunities policy from recruitment and selection, through training and development, appraisal and promotion to retirement. In southern Africa, there is a special focus on achieving demographic balance across management grades.

Within the constraints of local law it is the company's policy to ensure that everyone is treated equally, regardless of gender, colour, national origin, disability, marital status, sexual orientation, religion or trades union affiliation.

SABMiller also recognises that communicating with its employees is important and, as a result, some operations have conducted an employee opinion survey. The information gained showed that employees were relating more strongly to their own departments and were not seeing enough of the bigger picture.

As a result, SABMiller reacted by creating internal communications initiatives aimed at improving communications at every level. Survey results are now shared with employees and a six-monthly board roadshow was launched to give every employee the opportunity to have direct access to senior management. Info-kiosks have been provided, so that all employees can access information on the company intranet, and the company internal magazine, *SWIAT PIWA*, is now published monthly rather than bi-monthly. The SABMiller performance management processes have been introduced, which include empowerment through joint goal-setting, regular one-on-one meetings and formal performance feedback.

The changes have had considerable impact; the latest employee opinion survey reveals two important developments. Employees are now much more likely to see problems as opportunities, and they are making use of the new communications channels to talk more openly and freely about the issues that concern them.

Like all responsible multinationals, SABMiller invests heavily in the professional and personal development of its staff through training programmes and other schemes. It places particular emphasis on developing local staff, exemplified by its business in Tanzania. Over the last three years the business has run workshops and training programmes, as well as rotated local staff through different positions, to create a sense of ownership and enable employees to take on more senior positions. In the last two years, several local staff have reached top managerial posts, replacing expatriate staff.

SABMiller has set out the following employment strategies.

- SABMiller seeks to be a preferred employer.

- SABMiller remunerates its employees fairly, according to skills and performance, by reference to competitive industry and country conditions and within a rewarding work environment.

- SABMiller recognises that productivity is directly related to the health, safety and welfare of its employees. SABMiller companies promote continual improvement in health and safety performance, through the involvement of employees and the auditing of compliance with health and safety legislation and industry safety standards.

- SABMiller seeks to create an environment in which all individuals and teams may develop their full potential for the benefit of themselves and the group.

- SABMiller companies understand and respect the wide range of human diversity in which they operate and encourage inclusiveness with regard to human resource practices, irrespective of (among others) nationality, race, gender and physical disabilities.

- SABMiller is committed to fair treatment of employees: timely, honest and respectful communication, and freedom of expression. SABMiller plc recognises the right to freedom of association of employees and further recognises that trades unions and collective bargaining form a normal part of labour/management relations. Appropriate employee participation in problem-solving and decision-making is encouraged.

- SABMiller promotes ethical behaviour and will not tolerate violation of human rights nor any illegal activity, including bribery and corruption. Group employees may not comment unfavourably on the products, management or operations of competitors

In the community

SABMiller also recognises that a good employer also contributes to improving the quality of life in the communities in which it operates. Therefore it has developed the following strategies:

- to have a positive impact on local economies, through profitable and sustainable commerce
- to acknowledge that alcohol products and gaming services can be issues of concern, and therefore promoting the responsible use of its products and services
- to seek to be actively involved in partnerships that bring measurable benefits to people in communities where it operates
- to seek to be a good neighbour in local communities – 'We will consult on social issues and the environmental impacts of our operations.'

The results of such aims meant that, in 2005, SABMiller won the Oracle International Award, Awards for Excellence 2005, through developing the Eagle Lager project.

The Eagle Lager project is a public–private sector partnership between SABMiller and the Ugandan Government. The project encourages responsible alcohol consumption, engagement with and investment in local communities and agricultural development.

The project was developed to respond to the very specific characteristics of the Ugandan alcohol market: 60 per cent of Ugandans live on less than €1 per day. They cannot afford alcohol from the formal market. Many communities therefore make their own crude unrefined alcohol, which is high in alcoholic content and unhealthy.

The objectives were to stimulate agricultural research and development into the use of sorghum for brewing, and create a permanent and stable market for local sorghum farmers who would be contracted to Nile Breweries, which would replace expensive imported brewing ingredients and enable the company to apply for lower excise tax rates.

A recent evaluation of the project with local government representatives in the Sorote District of Uganda has confirmed that it has contributed directly to the Ugandan Government's Poverty Eradication Action Plan (PEAP), which is aligned with the poverty alleviation objectives of the Millennium Development Goals.

The Eagle Lager project demonstrates the benefits of approaching development issues from a commercial perspective and clearly shows the central role the private sector can play in assisting African countries to reach the targets set out in the Millennium Development Goals.

Impact

- Four years later, the beer is now Nile Breweries' top brand, with a market share of around 20 per cent.
- The use of sorghum has created a permanent and stable market for 3500 local Ugandan farmers who have contracts to grow it. As demand increases it is expected that output will increase to 3000 tonnes per year, creating more jobs and wealth for Ugandan farmers.
- The business benefits of the Eagle Lager project for SABMiller have been significant. It has resulted in increased sales and improved profitability, with Eagle Lager becoming Nile Breweries' top-selling Ugandan brand with over 20 per cent of the country's market share.

SABMiller has shown that a global business can develop corporate social responsibility through strong leadership, managing and developing its people, and participation with its environment. The result is a growing company with a strong competitive advantage.

Discussion questions

1 Why is communication with employees so important for improved performance and motivation?

2 Africa is a developing continent, with high unemployment and many people living below the poverty line. How has the leadership of SABMiller worked with the communities rather than exploited them? Why does this make good business sense?

3 A healthy workforce is a happy workforce. Why should this be important to an employer?

4 How can global organisations help developing countries?

Applied questions

5 Maslow's hierarchy of needs, illustrated in Exhibit 5-1, identifies five levels of need as the sources of different motivating behaviour. How could the motivations of workers from developing countries differ from those of workers in the developed world?

6 A manager from Europe may have different perceptions of an African workforce than does a local African manager. How can a European manager ensure that his or her perceptions are fair?

PART 3

Groups and teams: managing behaviour between people

Part contents

Chapter 8

Communicating for understanding and results

LEARNING OUTCOMES ☑

After studying this chapter you should be able to:

☑ **describe** the functions, types and directions of communication channels in organisations

☑ **identify** the barriers to effective communication and know how to avoid them

☑ **actively listen** and obtain feedback to understand others and to build rapport

☑ **read** non-verbal communication signals

☑ **appreciate** the diversity of communication styles

☑ **improve** cross-cultural communication

☑ **increase** the credibility and clarity of the messages you send to others

☑ **understand** the impact of unethical communication

☑ **commit** to staying abreast of new communications technology.

The opening vignette is an example of how good communication can make good business sense.

Mr easyJet – colossus with the common touch: Stelios Haji-Ioannou

Stelios Haji-Ioannou head of easyGroup, is Britain's Business Communicator of the Year for 2002, beating fellow CEOs and chairmen, including Charles Dunstone of Carphone Warehouse, Sir Christopher Gent of Vodafone, Peter Kenyon of Manchester United and Martin Sorrell of WPP.

▶

The award, created by the Public Relations Consultants Association (PRCA) in association with *The Business* newspaper and independent research company Datops, went to the founder of the budget airline easyJet because of his willingness to address various business constituencies, the consistency and volume of his messages and his great ability to project himself as the public persona of his company.

The television programme *Airline*, which goes behind the scenes at easyJet, shows how much he loves to engage with the public.

Although Haji-Ioannou, the son of a Greek shipping tycoon, was born a multimillionaire, employees at his company confirm his ability to get on with people at all levels.

Speaking at the award ceremony, Haji-Ioannou remarked on his public image, 'It works positively for us, warts and all. How many other companies achieve this level of free coverage during prime-time television? As a direct sell operation, we have to rely on our customers coming to us, so making sure they know who we are and what we do is crucial. The *Airline* series has made a significant contribution to easyJet becoming a household name.'

The importance of good communications to a successful business was underlined by Tom Watson, chairman of the PRCA, who said, 'All the shortlisted candidates understood the whole value of business reputation, not just the bottom line necessities of the City.

They all used, or were advised on, a range of objectives-driven public relations techniques to reach all their audiences. Ten years ago, their focus would have been 95 per cent financial; now they are communicating about the whole of the business and the benefits were demonstrable. That's real progress.'

One of the main themes that emerged during the process of selecting an eventual winner was that communicating well when the business environment is bad is critical.

In what has been the worst of times for airlines since 11 September [2001], with several companies confronting bankruptcy, easyJet shrugged off adversity and executed a profitable business plan.

As Andrew Harvey, an ITN business broadcaster, puts it, 'Stelios Haji-Ioannou is an excellent example of how effective communications at the top can make a real difference to a business, particularly as a new entrant to a market.'

Source: *Financial Times*, 12/13 May 2002, p. 29.

Discussion questions

1 Why is good communication important to a successful business?

2 How does Stelios demonstrate his communication skills?

Communication is a crucial aspect of any situation where two or more people interact to accomplish an objective. As demonstrated in the opening vignette, Stelios not only communicates with his workforce but also with the external environment through a variety of media. Communication is important to keep employees informed about what, when and how to act. It is also vital for enabling managers to discover and solve problems, and build trust and rapport with employees.

Communication is an activity that can take up most of a manager's time. Managers rarely find themselves alone at their desks contemplating alternatives to problems. When they are not talking in person with supervisors, peers or subordinates, they are usually communicating by telephone or email, or reading or writing memos and letters. Reece and Brandt (1987) suggest that it is unusual for a manager to work without interruption for more than the occasional half-hour two or three times a week. Communication takes up a major portion of time for non-managerial professionals as well.

This chapter examines the all-important impact of communication in organisations. We begin by discussing the importance of communication and how information is processed. After describing the basic communication process, we explore the various channels of communication and their inherent barriers. Finally, we explain how barriers can be overcome and communication effectiveness and efficiency increased.

What is communication?

Communication begins when one person sends a message to another with the intent of evoking a response. Effective communication occurs when the receiver interprets the message exactly as the sender intended. Efficient communication uses less time and fewer resources. Communicating with each subordinate individually, for example, is less efficient than addressing all subordinates as a group. The most efficient communication is not necessarily the most effective, however. What a manager wants to achieve is effective communication in the most efficient way.

communication
The process of one person sending a message to another with the intent of evoking a response.

The importance of communication to organisational effectiveness

Effective communication is essential for the functioning of any organisation. Managers need to transmit orders and policies, build co-operation and team spirit, and identify problems and their solutions. Employees need to clarify directives, provide feedback and make their problems known. Team members need to share feelings and perceptions to solve problems and resolve conflicts.

Communication breakdowns contribute to a host of organisational problems, from failure to carry out simple directives properly to low productivity and quality. When addressing employees many managers engage in one-way communication, giving employees the impression that their feelings and input do not matter. To ensure that effective communication occurs, managers should encourage employees to express their feelings, acknowledge such expressions and be tactful when expressing their own feelings. According to Reece and Brandt (1987), poor communication in the workplace costs the economy more than £1 billion annually and contributes to a significant number of employee injuries and deaths, particularly in industries where workers operate heavy machinery or handle hazardous materials.

Baskin and Aronoff (1980) suggest that communication in organisations serves three major purposes. It allows members to co-ordinate actions, share information and satisfy social needs. Pincus (1986) argues that when employees are happy with how their supervisors communicate with them, their job satisfaction and work output increase and they are more committed to the organisation. According to Putti *et al.* (1990) listening to what employees have to say can also be a useful motivational tool.

When the senior management at the Halewood plant (which we looked at in the opening vignette in Chapter 5) began to listen to and trust employees by encouraging discussion between managers and employees, output increased 8 per cent and absenteeism decreased. Over a recent two-year period, the opening-up of communication also cut overall defects by 90 per cent and assembly hours by 41 per cent.

Communication processes within organisations are changing rapidly. In addition to still vital face-to-face, telephone and written communications, voicemail, electronic mail, videoconferencing, faxing and personal computers make a vast magnitude of complex information immediately available for problem-solving and decision-making. Knowing how to obtain, transmit and process information through the multitude of existing communication channels is essential for any manager and most organisation members. To do so effectively through any medium, however, requires that managers understand the basic communication process. The Technology Transformation box describes how the availability of technology can enable the smaller firm to communicate effectively.

Rest on your laurels – at your peril

Websites not updated at regular intervals are losing out to rival sites that realise the customer's need for up-to-the-minute information, coupled with the facility for interactive communication. There is little wonder content management solutions has become a hot IT topic.

Companies complacent about maintaining static design and content on their web pages are failing to deliver the service demanded by customers. 'If your site is not a valuable information resource, it is time to improve communication through a content management solution, thereby adding to the credibility and integrity of your organisation,' says Peter Prior of QED IT Group Limited.

Customers have no incentive to revisit a site if the content never changes – it takes on the appearance of an advertisement and consequently fails to be used to maximum effect in the marketplace. However, when content changes at frequent intervals and the very latest information is available on the site, customers want to make regular visits.

Good content management solutions give a wide cross-section of staff the ability to create and publish new content on the site, as well as editing current information and removing out-of-date material. All of this can be achieved online without affecting the design, functionality, brand and image of your site.

A prime example of poor content management is the site that purports to have the latest news on a topic that in all probability has not been updated during the last six months. Delays in updating information on a site reflects badly on a company, often leaving customers at best bewildered and at worst dissatisfied with the level of service on offer. The missed business opportunities that result from poor management of the site will more than likely go to rival companies.

In the past updating was left to IT specialists, which wasted the expertise of experienced specialised staff. A content management solution allows non-technical staff to create, publish and update an organisation's website. There are obvious advantages to businesses as it allows the transferring of responsibility for updates to those people who actually create the content. This improves efficiency and the use of technical resources. There is no longer an IT bottleneck by using specialists to improve and update information channels and it also provides an opportunity for more interactive communications, which produce a dynamic site that customers will enjoy visiting.

The wise use of content management solutions is now separating the men from the boys. Good management keeps customers informed and provides them with interactive communication. QED IT develops solutions to business needs to ensure companies get the maximum business returns from their websites. 'We have recognised this direction by signing an agreement with Emojo to deliver its Affino™ content management solution. Affino represents a breakthrough in the content management system market by delivering a solution at a much lower cost than has been possible in the past,' says Peter Prior.

Until recently, such content management solutions have been the main preserve of large conglomerates but now this system offers the service to medium-sized businesses. They too are now able to offer their customers current and lively sites, encouraging repeat, sustainable business.

QED's first public installation of the Affino content management solution was at Crosshall Infant School in Cambridgeshire. It is a perfect example of a medium-sized organisation using an affordable system to publish a variety of information. The school subsequently raised its profile to prospective pupils and parents alike.

There is no doubt that the real beauty of a website is in how it delivers its message to the website visitor, and how it adds value to the website owner. It is in these areas that content management is absolutely key.

In any business it is important to be able to communicate with the customer, to remain innovative and give customers what they want, thereby adding value to the business. Content management solutions is the new key in the IT world to achieving these aims.

Source: adapted from Peter J. Prior, QED IT Group Limited in IBIS, *Business News Extra*, June 2002.

Discussion questions

1 Why is it important for organisations to develop the use of new technology for communication?

2 Do you think everyone should have access to the implementation of new technology in the workplace, or should it just be senior management?

The communication process

Communication is a complex process and one of the best ways to try to understand it is from a theoretical standpoint, as detailed in the 'Research focus' box.

Encoding

sender
The person communicating a message.

receiver
The person receiving a message.

encoding
Translating information into a message appropriate for transmission.

message
The physical form into which the sender encodes information.

transmission
The act of conveying a communication.

Starting in the left-hand column of Exhibit 8-1, the **sender** desires to communicate to the **receiver** some idea, feeling or intention. Let us imagine that a manager wishes to communicate information about a new deadline. First, the manager must encode the message. **Encoding** is translating the information into a format that will get the idea across. The result is the **message**, which is now ready for **transmission** to one or more of the receiver's senses through speaking, writing, gesturing or touching.

Research focus: the communication process

An early model comes from the works of Berlo (1960), Schramm (1953) and Shannon and Weaver (1948), and an example of this, from Rogers and Agarwala-Rogers (1976), can be seen in Exhibit 8-1, which depicts the communication process. The main components of this model are the sender, the receiver, the message and the channel. The communication process includes the sequential steps of encoding, transmission and decoding.

The following points need to be noted before exploring the model.

■ It specifies the components that should be present in communication, and the functions they perform, which should make it useful as a diagnostic tool when there are communication problems. It is not an exact representation of communication in practice.

■ There are three elements that have a huge impact on the communication process yet they were not shown as part of the communication process. These are the structure of the organisation, the technology and culture.

■ It also needs to be mentioned that communication is two-way and often the receiver will become the sender of return communications, yet this is not always reflected in information-processing models.

A more detailed focus on the components of the model can be seen in the exhibit and is described in the text that follows.

EXHIBIT 8 – 1 A model of the interpersonal communication process

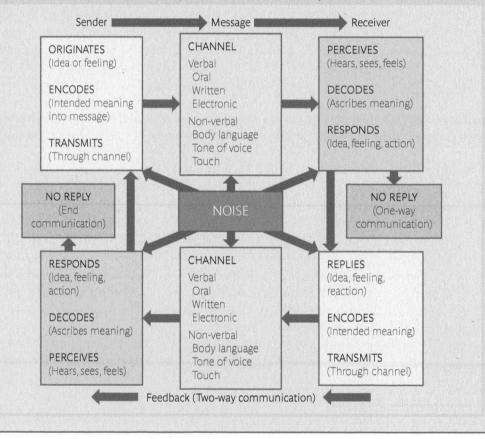

Transmission channels

channel
The medium through which a message is transmitted.

verbal
Words spoken and transmitted through sound waves.

The **channel** is the medium through which the message is transmitted. Oral communication via sound waves is the **verbal** channel utilised in speeches, meetings, telephone calls or informal discussions. Luthans and Larson (1986) suggest that face-to-face oral communication accounts for 81 per cent of a manager's communication each week, of which 45 per cent is with subordinates, 15 per cent with superiors, 18 per cent with peers and 24 per cent with people external to the organisation. As we can see from the opening vignette, Stelios Haji-Ioannou has built the easyGroup into a multimillion-pound industry, through using effective communication channels.

Non-verbal channels, according to Kiechel (1990), such as touch, facial expression and tone of voice, can convey nuances of meaning mere words are not capable of communicating. Although aware of non-verbal signals, many of us fail to recognise their importance in amplifying, changing or negating verbal communication.

non-verbal
All ways of communicating without words, such as tone of voice, facial expression and gestures.

Written communication channels include letters, memoranda, reports, manuals and forms. Written materials provide hard copies for storage and retrieval in case documented evidence is needed later.

Electronic channels include email, voicemail, portable telephones, facsimile (fax) machines, telecommuting, networked computers (integrated databases, online 'chat sessions', etc.) and videoconferencing. Electronic mail (email) enables people to exchange messages through computers. Interpersonal messages can just as easily be transmitted overseas as to an adjacent office. Computer-to-computer communications can also involve bill payments, invoices or purchase orders. Voicemail is a computer-based answering machine system accessed by telephone to receive or transmit messages. Cellular telephones can be utilised while travelling, during luncheon meetings or while walking between appointments. Portable fax machines can be hooked up in a car or other location when hard copies of communications are required. Telecommuting refers to one of the ultimate uses of electronic communications where employees actually work at home while linked to the office through computers, data networks, fax machines and telephones.

Online technology can improve communication efficiency and result in better productivity. Trevino *et al.* (1990), however, suggest that, on the other hand, minimising face-to-face contact and opportunities for soliciting feedback can lead to misunderstandings and lack of non-verbal support, which are often the keys to effective communication and motivation. Face-to-face discussions have the potential for being the most complete and effective channel, followed by telephone conversations, informal letters and memos, electronic mail, formal written documents, and formal quantitative documents such as computer printouts or financial statements. Sam Walton created a way to get the best of both technology and face-to-face communication. Every Saturday morning, Walton and 300 top managers met at Wal-Mart's headquarters where market information was shared and decisions made. Messages from the managers at these meetings were transmitted via satellite to all Wal-Mart stores, and frequently Sam would appear on television speaking to almost a quarter of a million employees just as if he were in the room talking to a handful of people he knew by name.

Decoding

Communication does not take place if the receiver's senses fail to perceive the sender's message. Decoding is the receiver function of perceiving communication stimuli and interpreting their meaning. It encompasses both comprehending the content of the message and determining the sender's intention in transmitting it. The closer the receiver's decoding is to the sender's intended message, the more effective the communication has been.

decoding
The receiver function of perceiving communication stimuli and interpreting their meaning.

After the message has been decoded into information meaningful to the receiver, how the receiver feels about and responds to the message will depend on the receiver's needs. No matter how clearly information has been encoded, misunderstanding is always possible in its decoding because the receiver's past experience, personal interpretations and expectations influence this process.

Noise

Noise is anything that interferes, at any stage, with the communication process. A sender may be inarticulate, have an irritating writing style or speak too softly to be heard. During transmission, extraneous noise from nearby conversations, music or machines can impede hearing, and irrelevant visual activities may be distracting. A less obvious type of noise occurs when the receiver simply fails to pay attention or is not receptive to the message because of hostile attitudes, past experiences, mental/emotional distractions or contrary frames of reference. According to Copeland and Griggs (1985), in the international arena, considerable noise and confusion can occur; for example, this occurs when Americans, who prefer to get right to the point of a business negotiation, interact with Arabs, who may prefer to talk about social topics for a while before addressing the business objective.

noise
Anything that interferes with the communication process.

The success of the communication process depends to a large degree on overcoming various sources of noise. Some enlightened organisations are providing training to increase communication skills. The British Government's recent initiative on life-long learning is involving more and more businesses in the provision of basic skills that include communication. Much of the remainder of this chapter addresses ways to overcome communication noise. A basic method to determine whether noise has occurred and to correct communication errors caused by noise is to use feedback.

Feedback

After the sender, or source, has encoded and transmitted the message and the receiver has received and decoded it, the feelings, ideas and intentions generated in the receiver are usually communicated back to the sender. In this reversal, the receiver now becomes the responder, the original sender becomes the receiver, and the process continues. An important component of the second stage of the communication process is feedback. Feedback is the message that tells the original sender how clearly his or her message was understood and what effect it has had on the receiver. Feedback is the manager's primary tool for determining whether or not instructions have been understood and accepted. It can be transmitted through a variety of formal and informal organisational communication channels. With advances in technology, feedback can be unobtrusively obtained by simply monitoring employees' behaviour and actions on their

feedback
A message that tells the original sender how clearly his or her message was understood and what effect it has had on the receiver.

computers. New technologies allow managers to monitor computer, email and Internet actions from a remote location. This can be an effective channel to gather feedback; however, it also raises ethical concerns. The Eye on Ethics box describes the delicate trade-off between employee monitoring and corporate concerns.

Electronic spying on employees: performance booster or invasion of privacy?

Big Brother is watching. And it is increasingly likely that the Omniscient One is your boss. Implemented correctly, monitoring of employee performance by computer or telephone can improve service, productivity and profits. Done incorrectly, it just bugs the staff – in both senses. Fortunately or unfortunately, advances in technology are permitting corporations to increase the amount and methods of monitoring employee performance (and, hence, employee actions).

With the advent of new technologies, corporations are employing new techniques for customer service improvements. At the Electric Insurance Company (EIC), managers utilise a computer-telephony integrated (CTI) recording system to not only digitally record conversations between customers and employees, but also to record 'screen captures' of employee–computer actions. This enables managers to evaluate the service agent's verbal and technical abilities together. Employees who verbally work well with customers must also be able to enter correctly customer information or requests in order to provide effective customer service.

Therefore, the ability of EIC to record and synchronise an employee's verbal and technical actions during a call permits the company to evaluate correctly the entire customer–agent experience. There are multiple benefits of using the CTI system for the Electric Insurance Company. First, the digital recording (and compression) of calls and screen captures reduces administrative costs (versus tape recording) and increases manager productivity. Unneeded calls or incomplete calls are quickly deleted from the system. Also, the storage of calls requires little space. Second, it improves agent quality because agents are less casual and more careful about transactions that are permanently recorded. The consistency of agent evaluation is improved with the elimination of paperwork and handwritten notes, and all employees are evaluated on a common set of criteria. Third, the CTI system facilitates improved employee training since EIC has easy database access to 'good' versus 'bad' calls. Finally, the company can further increase employee productivity by identifying and correcting cumbersome and complicated software procedures.

While the EIC employees know they are being monitored, what reactions might employees have if they were to discover their actions were being recorded and evaluated without their knowledge? A recent management study indicates that perhaps two-thirds of all companies record and monitor employees' phone calls and computer actions (e.g. email, Internet browsing, downloads). Advances in technology allow companies to digitally record and compress all employee calls and computer actions, cataloguing and storing them for later retrieval. Employee monitoring allows companies to protect themselves against espionage, unwanted lawsuits for illegal activities (e.g. accessing child pornography on the Internet, engaging in sexual harassment via email), and unproductive time (e.g. playing computer games at work). Therefore, many corporations feel monitoring is necessary and that since the phone and computer are company property, they should be used for company business only.

However, the increased frequency of monitoring is raising ethical concerns. Should companies be required to inform employees they are being monitored? Additionally, what actions should be monitored, and when? Is it permissible for an employee to play computer games in his or her lunch break? Additionally, the impact of monitoring on employee morale must also be considered. It can be argued that employee monitoring creates an untrusting environment, where employee productivity will be negatively impacted. However, there is no doubt that improvements in technology will continue to increase the methods, ease and frequency of monitoring.

Sources: Liz Stevens (1999) 'Careful! Your Boss May Be Eavesdropping', *San Diego Union Tribune*, 6 October, p. A1; Garry Shearer (1998) 'Voice/Screen Capture System Boosts Quality and Productivity', *Call Centre Solutions*, November, pp. 100–103; Greg Meckbach (1998) 'The Secret World of Monitoring Software', *Computing Canada*, 4 May, pp. 1, 4; Bill Hancock (1999) '45% of Big Firms Monitor Workers', *Computers & Security*, 18(4), pp. 284–285; and Joaquim Menezes (1999) 'More Employers Spying on Workers', *Computer Dealer News*, 9 July, p. 52.

Discussion questions

1 Should organisations be able to monitor their employees' communication and if so should the employees be informed?

2 How can a balance be struck between company interests and employee privacy?

Using communication channels in organisations

Communication between organisational members can be vertical or lateral, formal or informal. Managers are responsible for establishing and maintaining internal communication channels in downward, upward, and horizontal directions. Just as important in most organisations are informal networks, which convey feelings and reactions among employees.

Internal communication

The main objectives for internal communication are to:

- pass on or transmit instructions or requests along the lines of command – for example, from marketing director to sales manager to floor staff
- inform staff on new policies, arrangements, developments, processes, etc.
- request information from any employee in the company to assist in making decisions for the company or provide feedback after analysing situations
- encourage or reassure staff in certain circumstances, and to persuade and motivate them to work as individuals and as part of a team
- provide confirmations, responses and information upwards
- pass on suggestions, ideas and developments along the chain of command.

Formal communication channels

Formal communication channels are established within the organisation's chain of command in order to accomplish task objectives. Exhibit 8-2 illustrates the three directions of formal communication flow, the types of information conveyed and the functions they perform.

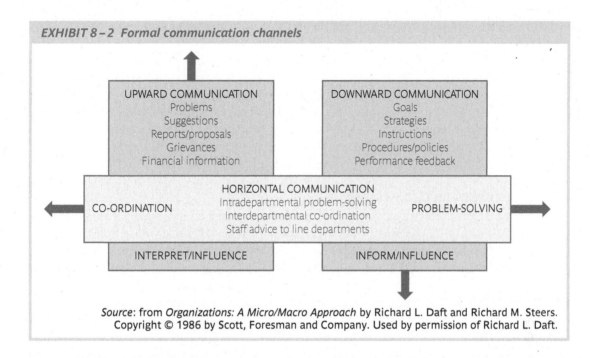

EXHIBIT 8–2 Formal communication channels

UPWARD COMMUNICATION
Problems
Suggestions
Reports/proposals
Grievances
Financial information

DOWNWARD COMMUNICATION
Goals
Strategies
Instructions
Procedures/policies
Performance feedback

CO-ORDINATION

HORIZONTAL COMMUNICATION
Intradepartmental problem-solving
Interdepartmental co-ordination
Staff advice to line departments

PROBLEM-SOLVING

INTERPRET/INFLUENCE

INFORM/INFLUENCE

Source: from *Organizations: A Micro/Macro Approach* by Richard L. Daft and Richard M. Steers. Copyright © 1986 by Scott, Foresman and Company. Used by permission of Richard L. Daft.

Downward communication

Downward communication is used by managers to assign goals, provide job instructions, inform about policies, procedures and practices, provide performance feedback, point out problems, and socialise with employees. The most costly communication breakdowns occur when instructions are given or received poorly. Howell (1991) suggests that even though nearly 90 per cent of all instructions are considered routine, it is necessary for managers to confirm them repeatedly. Downward communication can take many forms: speeches, memos, company newsletters, bulletin boards, and policy and procedure manuals. Surveys of employees by Maud (1991) show that they do not think the information in downward employee reports is relevant to them, and they have difficulty understanding it because it is communicated in head-office language. Employees rely on and trust their supervisors most for relevant downward information.

Upward communication

Upward communication provides managers with information about current problems, updates on employees' progress towards goals, suggestions for improvement, proposals for innovations, employee grievances and feedback about employee attitudes. Upward communication can take the form of employee surveys, suggestion boxes, face-to-face encounters, open-door policies or required reports. According to Hawken (1987), employees at Smith & Hawken, a gardening supply company, are encouraged to submit to their supervisor every Friday a '5–15 report', which requires no more than 15 minutes to write and 5 minutes to read. Brassil (1984) suggests that by improving upward communication from employees to management, some companies have experienced profit increases of as much as 30 to 40 per cent.

Horizontal communication

Horizontal communication takes place among peers and can cut across departments and work groups. These lateral communications benefit the organisation by providing support, co-ordination and information more efficiently than could vertical channels. Some organisations form task forces and committees to facilitate information exchange and co-ordination between departments.

Another form of lateral communication occurs outside the walls of any particular organisation – communication with customers and suppliers. Boeing Commercial Airplanes, for example, buys approximately 60 per cent of its aeroplane parts from outside suppliers. Since Boeing wants to get the highest-quality parts, it has recently begun programmes to increase lateral communication with suppliers about quality requirements and procedures. Boeing has also asked customers to identify their requirements more specifically and to provide specific feedback so that Boeing can satisfy those requirements (Certo, 1991).

Informal communication channels

Informal communication channels exist to serve the interests of those people who comprise them regardless of their position in the organisation. Modic (1989) suggests that they are not formally sanctioned by management and do not follow the organisation's hierarchy; however, informal communications are often perceived by employees as more believable than communications received through formal organisational channels. Some typical informal channels are the grapevine, social gatherings, informal one-to-one discussions and small-group networks.

The grapevine

The **grapevine** is the informal communication channel for gossip and rumours and is outside the control of management. According to Modic (1989), it is perceived by most employees as more believable and reliable than top management communication channels. The grapevine satisfies social needs, helps clarify orders and decisions, and serves as a way of getting information that cannot be expressed adequately through formal channels. Simmons (1985) argues that about 80 per cent of grapevine communications is work related, and over 80 per cent of the time the grapevine is accurate.

grapevine
The informal communication channel for gossip and rumours.

Studies by Davis (1953) have determined that only about 10 per cent of managers actually pass on rumours and gossip – regardless of their importance – to more than one other person. When a manager was contemplating resignation from one company, for example, 81 per cent of the other managers knew about it, but only 11 per cent shared this information with others. Although managers may not be part of the actual gossip chain, they can keep an ear to the grapevine through loyal subordinates or colleagues who will discreetly share information with them. Then they can pass on news that will improve relationships or act to eliminate gossip that might be harmful to organisational performance (Kiechel, 1985).

It is important that managers recognise that a grapevine will exist whether they want it to or not. Additionally, managers can do little to control the direction, speed and accuracy of grapevine rumours. What managers can do, however, is diminish the amount of grapevine rumours with effective communication. By clearly communicating in a timely, accurate manner, addressing all aspects of issues or a decision, managers can reduce the amount of anxiety employees have and, hence, reduce the need for grapevine communication.

Social gatherings

Each of Tandem Computers' 132 worldwide offices holds a Friday-afternoon beer-drinking session to create an informal communication channel for employees. 'Over beer and popcorn, employees are more willing to talk openly,' says CEO Jim Treybig. Similar social opportunities for informal information exchange can be created at office parties, company picnics and lunches (O'Boyle and Hymowitz, 1985).

Management by wandering around

Peter Anderson, when CEO of ZTEL, a maker of television switching systems, preferred not to personally communicate with employees. By maintaining distance between himself and his employees, however, some analysts think Anderson failed to provide an informal communication channel for employees, which contributed to ZTEL's eventual bankruptcy (Therrien, 1985). Anderson's preference is not unusual, but managers do not have to break into ongoing coffee groups or buy a round of beer to enter into informal communication with employees. Peters and Waterman (1982) suggest that managers can simply walk around their organisations and chat informally with all levels of employees to learn about their concerns, ideas and problems. Informally talking with employees is commonly called 'management by wandering around'.

Small-group networks

The pattern and direction of communication flows have important consequences for both task accomplishment and personal satisfaction. Exhibit 8-3 diagrams the types of small-group networks. The chain network typifies the organisation with a strong vertical hierarchy, where information travels only upwards and downwards. People communicate only with their immediate superior and subordinate. It also exists between people working on a production line. In the circle network, people can communicate only to others on either side. This pattern often occurs between people in departments at the same horizontal level in organisations. The star configuration distributes the flow of communication most evenly. It prevails in informal groups with no assigned leader or tasks to accomplish. The wheel represents the other extreme, where all communications are channelled through a central position. The wheel would rely on Kate, who could be the group leader or manager, to make sure that each member has the information

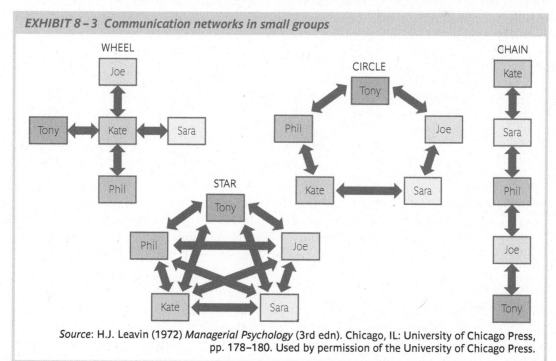

EXHIBIT 8–3 Communication networks in small groups

Source: H.J. Leavin (1972) *Managerial Psychology* (3rd edn). Chicago, IL: University of Chicago Press, pp. 178–180. Used by permission of the University of Chicago Press.

he or she needs. Air traffic controllers would be the hub of a circle of aeroplane pilots attempting to land at the same airport.

Leavitt (1972) suggests that the effectiveness of communication networks varies according to the task. The centralised wheel-type formation provides more efficient and accurate problem-solving of simple and routine tasks. For ambiguous and complex problems, however, the more egalitarian star network is much more effective. Overall group satisfaction is greater in star-type networks because group members participate more evenly. In centralised wheel networks, individuals holding the central position are much more active, satisfied and likely to become leaders than those in peripheral locations.

Research by Ibarra (1993) found that a frequent problem for women and minorities in organisations is limited access to or exclusion from informal interaction networks. This limited access produces disadvantages such as restricted knowledge of what is going on in the organisation and difficulty in forming the alliances vital to career advancement and social support.

Actually, a number of barriers exist for all organisational members in each of the communication channels just reviewed. Barriers to effective understanding also can be found within the sender or receiver of information.

The barriers to communication

The image and credibility of the sender, stereotyping, past experiences, overexposure to data, attitudes, mindsets, perceptual filters, trust and empathy all impact on what receivers of communication 'hear' and how they interpret its meaning. These communication barriers occur in everyday business communications.

Misinterpretation occurs when the receiver understands the message to his or her own satisfaction but not in the sense that the sender intended. Misinterpretation can be a consequence of sender or channel noise, poor listening habits, erroneous inferences on the part of the receiver, or differing frames of reference. An example of this occurs when unclear instructions lead employees to 'hear' the wrong procedures for doing their work.

Frames of reference

A combination of past experience and current expectations often leads two people to perceive the same communication differently. Although each hears the actual words accurately, he or she may catalogue those words according to his or her individual perceptions, or **frame of reference**. For example, many teenagers refer to things that are good as 'wicked' or 'cool'; to a person of another generation or nationality this may mean something evil or cold.

frame of reference
A person's mindset, based on past experience and current expectations, which determines what is perceived and how it is interpreted.

Within organisations, people with different functions often have different frames of reference. Marketing people may interpret things one way and production people another. An engineer's interpretation is likely to differ from that of an accountant.

Semantics

Just as individual frames of reference lend different meanings to identical words or expressions, so can variations in group semantics. *Semantics* pertains to the meaning and use of words. This is especially true when people from different cultures are trying to communicate. Consider, for example, a Japanese businessman who is trying to tell his Norwegian counterpart that he is uninterested in a product. The Japanese businessman politely says, 'That would be very diffi-cult.' The Norwegian businessman interprets that to mean that there are still problems, not that the deal is off. Since he does not understand that the Japanese have more than a dozen subtle ways to say no, the Norwegian businessman responds by asking how his company can help solve the problem. The Japanese businessman, who thinks that he has communicated that the sale is off, is totally confused (Adler, 1986).

Many professional and social groups adopt a specialised technical language called *jargon* that provides them with a sense of belonging and simplifies communication within the ingroup. But sophisticated technical or financial terms can intimidate and confuse outsiders, especially when members of a specialised group use them to project a professional mystique.

The same is true of words that cause emotional reactions in others. The same word does not cause the same reaction in all people. Often only the members of certain groups experience emotional reactions, such as when a grown woman is referred to as a girl.

Value judgements

Value judgements are a source of noise when a receiver evaluates the worth of a sender's message before the sender has finished transmitting it. Often such value judgements are based on the receiver's previous experience either with the sender or with similar types of communi-cation. A professor may tune out when a student begins to describe a workload problem because 'students are always complaining about something'. Unfortunately, many managers react similarly in work organisations. When listeners form value judgements, speakers are usually aware of this through verbal and non-verbal feedback. Subsequently, the senders become guarded and defensive, which often inhibits transmission of their real concerns.

Whereas the sender usually knows what he or she intends to communicate, the receiver must infer what is really meant. Because of different frames of reference, the frequent result is a highly distorted understanding of what the sender intended to communicate. A receiver's degree of trust and confidence in the sender directly affects his or her reaction to the words and gestures of the message. In businesses where union leaders are perceived as political exploiters, management will rarely hear their messages without making some inference as to the speaker's intent.

Selective listening

Value judgements, needs, and expectations cause us to hear what we want to hear. When a message conflicts with what a receiver believes or expects, selective listening may cause them to block out the information or distort it to match preconceived notions. Feedback to an employee about poor performance, for example, may not be 'heard' because it does not fit the employee's self-concept or expectations.

selective listening
Receiver behaviour of blocking out information or distorting it to match preconceived notions.

At times people become so absorbed in their tasks that when someone initiates conversation they are not able to disassociate and listen effectively. Not only is it difficult for a preoccupied person to receive the message the sender intends, but obvious body language may make it appear that the receiver does not care about the sender or the message. This can create negative feelings and make future communications even more difficult.

This problem occurs frequently in emotionally charged conversations or philosophical debates, when receivers listen only for an opening to speak, rather than pay attention to the content of the sender's message. Such receivers often miss the sender's entire meaning in their haste to get a personal point across.

Filtering

filtering
The sender conveys only certain parts of the relevant information to the receiver.

Filtering is selective listening in reverse; in fact, we might call it 'selective sending'. When senders convey only certain parts of the relevant information to receivers, they are said to be filtering their message. Filtering often occurs in upward communication when subordinates suppress negative information and relay only the data that will be perceived by superiors as positive. Filtering is very common when people are being evaluated for promotions, salary increases or performance appraisals.

A different kind of filtering occurs in times of information overload or intense time pressure. When managers are deluged with more information than they can process effectively, one response is to screen out and never decode a large number of messages. With time pressure, even the information that a manager has absorbed and processed may not be communicated to all employees concerned. Information overload and time pressures also compound the difficulty of making good decisions and solving complex problems.

Distrust

A lack of trust on the part of either communicator is likely to evoke one or more of the barriers we have just examined. Senders may filter out important information if they distrust receivers, and receivers may form value judgements, make inferences, and listen only selectively to distrusted senders. Such situations are complicated by the fact that the distrust itself may have arisen from earlier communications that were impeded by some of the same barriers. In other words, neither party is dishonest, but their poorly developed communication skills have led them to distrust one another.

Distrust is sometimes caused by status differences. Lower-status employees can be intimidated by higher-status job titles, plush offices, sophisticated modes of dress, and perhaps even a particular manager's reputation. Rather than take the risk of being judged incompetent or being ridiculed, subordinates may refrain from seeking help or requesting needed information from a high-status manager.

Many times these barriers to effective communication can be neutralised or avoided altogether if the sender and receiver practise certain communication techniques. The next section addresses how a sender can be more effective and the section after that explains how receivers can increase their effectiveness.

Sending messages more effectively

Consistently effective communication requires considerable skill in both sending and receiving information. In this section, we will examine how to achieve better transmission of messages by increasing the clarity of messages, developing credibility, communicating ethically and soliciting feedback. Later in the chapter, we will explore the receiver skills that enhance our understanding of the messages others send to us.

Increase the clarity of messages

A sender should take the initiative in eliminating communication barriers by making sure a message is clear and understandable to the receiver. Be specific, explain exactly what you want and how you expect it to be achieved.

Use multiple channels

The impact of a message can be increased by using more than one channel or mode of transmission to send it. Examples are matching facial and body gestures to a message or drawing it on a piece of paper. This kind of multiple-mode communication of the same message ensures that the receiver has the opportunity to receive the message through more than one sense. A consultant speaking about the need to increase quality of production, for example, may convey the urgency of the message through the multiple channels of words, voice tones, facial expressions, gestures, pictures, postures and audio-visual presentations.

Be complete and specific

When the subject matter of a message is new or unfamiliar to the receiver, the sender can make the message complete and specific by providing sufficient background information and details. Once the receiver understands the sender's frame of reference, he or she is more likely to interpret the message accurately. By referring to concrete deadlines and examples, a sender can decrease the probability of misinterpretation.

Claim your own message

To claim the message as their own, senders should use personal pronouns such as 'I' and 'mine'. This indicates to the receiver that the sender takes responsibility for the ideas and feelings expressed in the message. General statements like 'everyone feels this way' leave room for doubt (someone might *not* feel that way). However, an 'I' message, such as 'I feel strongly about this', is not ambiguous. The sender is stating a personal opinion. It is better, too, to be up-front rather than put the receiver on the defensive. Say, 'I think improvement is necessary' if that is what you mean, rather than asking 'Don't you think you can do better?'

Be congruent

Make sure your messages are congruent with your actions. Being incongruent by saying one thing and doing another confuses receivers. If, for example, managers tell subordinates that they are 'always available' to help them but then act in a condescending and preoccupied way when those people come to them with problems, they are communicating something quite different from the verbal message.

Simplify your language

Complex rhetoric and technical jargon can confuse individuals who do not use such language. In addition, most organisations develop a 'lingo', or language distinctly the company's own, made up of words and phrases for people, situations, events and things. At Walt Disney, for example, all employees are called 'cast members'. They are 'on stage' when they're working and 'off stage' when at lunch or taking a break. Any situation or event that is positive is a 'good mickey'. Anything less is a 'bad mickey'.

Jargon and lingo serve a purpose in an organisation. They make the organisation more distinctive and unique, which tends to build employees' identity with and commitment to the company. They are also efficient ways to communicate inside the organisation. However, used with associates outside the company who do not know the jargon, lingo can hinder communication (Miller, 1987). Effective communicators avoid jargon, slang, clichés, and colourful metaphors when communicating with people outside the industry or those who do not speak the language fluently. By being empathetic and envisioning themselves in the receiver's situation, managers can encode messages in terms that are meaningful to the specific receivers.

Develop credibility

credibility
The sender's degree of trustworthiness, as perceived by the receiver.

The **credibility** of a sender is probably the single most important element in effective interpersonal communications (Johnson, 1981). Sender credibility is reflected in the receiver's belief that the sender is trustworthy. According to Garside and Kleiner (1991), factors that increase the clarity of communication, like congruence of verbal and non-verbal messages, contribute to the sender's credibility, as do the additional dimensions discussed below.

Expertise

Receivers will be more attentive when they perceive that a sender has expertise in the area about which he or she is communicating, as when instructions are given by someone authorised to dispense that information.

Mutual trust

Receivers prefer to have a sender's motives clarified: are they selfish or altruistic? Owning up to motives at the very beginning of a conversation eliminates the receiver's anxiety about a sender's real intentions and does much to establish common trust.

Reliability

A sender's perceived dependability, predictability and consistency in providing all relevant information (being consistent in applying performance criteria when evaluating subordinates and treating subordinates fairly and equally, for example) reinforce the sender's perceived trust-worthiness.

Warmth and friendliness

A warm, friendly, supportive attitude is more conducive to managerial credibility than is a posture of hostility and arrogance, especially when subordinates need to tackle new or uncertain tasks.

Dynamic appearance

A sender who is dynamic, confident and positive is more credible than one who acts in a passive, withdrawn and unsure manner. Receivers tend to be more attentive to a message when the sender is confident.

Personal reputation

If other members of the organisation have told the receiver that a sender is credible, the receiver will usually tend to believe it. If, on the other hand, a sender's reputation has been tarnished by a history of untrustworthiness, a receiver is likely to believe the negative peer opinions.

Communicate ethically

Interpersonal communications are ethical when they facilitate a person's freedom of choice by presenting accurate, relevant information. They are unethical when they prevent another person from securing information relevant to a choice. According to DeVito (1992) unethical communications may cause a person to make a choice he or she would not normally make or to not make a choice he or she would normally make, or both.

Deception is the conscious alteration of information to significantly influence another's perceptions (Knapp and Comadena, 1979). Deception includes lying, which is concealing or distorting truthful information, and engaging in behaviours that do not reflect our true feelings or beliefs, like smiling at people we dislike or acting busy to avoid being given more work.

An overt lie is a false statement made with the deliberate intent to deceive. Covert lying occurs when one omits something relevant, leading others to draw incorrect inferences. Lying or hiding the truth is unethical because it prevents another person from getting complete and correct information to explore fully all possible alternatives.

McLellan (1993) suggests that interpersonal deception is very prevalent in the workplace. It is mainly used to avoid punishment, but also serves to present a better image, protect others' feelings, attain personal goals and avoid embarrassment. Since honesty and trust are so important for productive interpersonal relationships, however, deception can be a serious flaw.

Deception can be detected by noticing behavioural changes. When people are practising deception, they display more vagueness, uncertainty and reticence, their messages are less plausible, and their speech contains more errors and is less fluent (Cody *et al.*, 1978). Kraut (1978) suggests that liars avoid eye contact and have a tendency to squirm more than honest people. The Eye on Ethics box on page 361 discusses how some companies are obtaining information from employees, with or without their employees' knowledge. Are these companies acting ethically? In what circumstances would you consider the companies monitoring employee communications to be acting in an ethical manner?

Ethical behaviour has very important consequences for a sender's credibility. In every national poll, the most important thing people want in a leader, friend, partner or workmate is honesty. According to McLellan (1993), the biggest cost of lying is that you may lose the trust of other people who depend on you and on whom you depend. Mayer and Davis (1995) confirm this by arguing that working with others in organisations involves interdependence, so lying should be confronted and eliminated in order to maintain mutual trust.

Obtain feedback

Effective communication means both top-down and bottom-up communication. Lewis and Spiker (1991) suggest that, all too often, management concentrates on communicating its message to employees without providing the feedback mechanism for response and input from workers. The Dynamics of Diversity box shows how effective communication can help a company to grow and learn.

Recall that feedback is the receiver's response to the sender's message. Its purpose is to tell the sender what the receiver heard and what the receiver thinks the meaning of this message is. If the receiver's response indicates a lack of understanding, the sender can modify the original message to make sure his or her intentions are understood. If senders are unable to obtain feedback on how their messages are being received, inaccurate perceptions on the part of a receiver may never be corrected.

When a manager says 'Call me later and we'll discuss it' while walking out the door, does the manager mean 15 minutes from now, two hours from now, tomorrow or next week? Statements that carry a number of potential meanings are highly susceptible to misunderstanding on the part of their receivers. Hunsaker and Alessandra (1986) suggest that, unless they are clarified, such ambiguous directions are unlikely to be followed according to the sender's intentions, and the relationship between the parties will be strained. By listening to feedback, managers can transform such highly ambiguous statements into very specific, effective communications.

dynamics of diversity

Simon Jersey: learning organisation

Simon Jersey shows that communication is not just about talking, it is also about listening to customers and employees.

A year ago, corporate clothing specialist Simon Jersey's operations impressed all judges in the UNISYS Management Today Service Excellence awards, but it was felt that the company still had some way to go in other areas, particularly in gathering feedback from customers about its service. The actions the business has taken since then to improve on these points has made it the natural candidate for the 2001 Learning Organisation award, sponsored by Cranfield School of Management. The company beat wire manufacturer John Pring and Kraft Foods' Away from Home division with honours.

Simon Jersey provides uniforms worn by DHL delivery men, American Airlines ground staff, chefs, nurses, bank staff and other occupations around the UK and Europe, via both bespoke contracts and a catalogue of more than 1000 stock garments. The clothes are designed at the company's architecturally acclaimed HQ in Accrington, Lancashire, then manufactured in sites in Britain and around the world, from Romania to Morocco, Indonesia and Malaysia.

It is a complex operation in a competitive market, where logistics, design and price each play a vital part in achieving satisfied customers. The diverse range of clients that Simon Jersey serves, both in size and sector, makes the goal of customer satisfaction an even more daunting challenge. For service purposes, the company has divided into four principal groups: smaller catalogue buyers, major catalogue buyers accounts, bespoke customers and export.

Over the past 12 months Simon Jersey has introduced a Voice of the Customer programme dedicated to ensuring that the needs of each group are fully understood, and to establish how they could be better served. The programme involves sending 10 000 questionnaires a year to catalogue customers, surveying buyers on all major accounts (many for the first time), initiating surveys of direct customers in Europe, and introducing 'mystery shoppers' to compare Simon Jersey's service with that of rivals as well as non-competitors such as Next and Racing Green.

'We have been seeking to make improvements wherever we can,' says technical director Richard Mullen. 'Our job specs used to be quite woolly; now they all have measurable parameters. We visited a German company where performance data were displayed on every wall, so we are now increasing the visibility of our own data. We have tasked each of our managers to come up with one measurable improvement.'

Simon Jersey puts great emphasis on employee training and education. In 1988 the company created a Learning Centre, which has a dual purpose: it serves as a classroom for departments to train members on specific issues, but employees can also use it outside office hours for their own personal development. The company set up a 'signing' class at the request of one deaf employee, so that she would be able to communicate with her colleagues.

In a complex organisation it is vital that all departments work well together, so Simon Jersey introduced a Department of the Year trophy, voted on by all employees and awarded to the department judged to have delivered the best service to its own customers. Last year it was won by IT.

The readiness to learn, adapt and seek out constant improvement has been paying dividends. Sales have virtually quadrupled over five years from £7.3 million in 1995 to £28.6 million in 2000. But at Simon Jersey there is no time for complacency; improvement is a journey with no end in sight.

It also shows that listening to staff and customers improves communication and this in turn improves performance.

Source: UNISYS Management Today Service Excellence Awards, published in *Management Today*, September 2001.

Discussion questions

1 What does the above case tell us about the importance of good communication?

2 How can training help with communication in the workplace?

Verbal feedback allows parties to clarify facts, feelings and needs. It can also be used to show others that they are recognised and appreciated, as when a manager says, 'You did a really good job. I have confidence in you.' This kind of feedback prompts others to continue their positive performance. When someone's behaviour requires negative feedback, it can be given constructively. Ignoring an inadequate performance or poor work behaviour by remaining silent may be construed as tacit approval. Direct comments such as 'Sarah told me she's afraid to work with you because you are so aggressive' provide people with the type of verbal feedback they need to correct inadequate behaviour.

To ensure that each party understands what the other is trying to communicate, interpretations of received messages can be fed back for confirmation. Clarifying feedback typically begins with a statement such as 'Let me be sure I understand what you have said' or 'Let me see if I can summarise the key points we've discussed.' Often it ends with a question: 'Did I understand you properly?', 'Were those your major concerns?' Feedback can provide the needed information for quality and productivity enhancement.

Through the use of their bodies, eyes, faces, postures and senses, receivers communicate a variety of positive or negative attitudes, feelings and opinions that serve as feedback about how they react to a sender's message. All signals communicated back to the sender by the receiver, other than the actual words spoken or written, comprise non-verbal feedback. Examples are eye contact, gestures, facial expressions and vocal intonations. Although most people react subconsciously to non-verbal feedback, perceptive communicators use it to structure the content and direction of the conversation. By changing the pace of their words, tone of their voice or their physical position, for example, skilled speakers gain or regain attention and interest.

Feedback can be used to clarify needs and reduce misunderstanding, to improve relationships and keep both parties updated, to determine which issues need further discussion, and to confirm all uncertain verbal, vocal and visual cues. The proper and effective use of feedback skills can lead to mutual understanding, less interpersonal tension, increased trust and credibility, and higher productivity. Some rules for giving and receiving feedback effectively are summarised in Exhibit 8-4.

Receiving messages more accurately

We have just discussed how a sender can increase the effectiveness of a transmission. Now let us look at how the receiver can ensure understanding through the use of questions, listening and non-verbal communications.

EXHIBIT 8–4 *Guidelines for giving and receiving feedback*

Criteria for giving feedback

1 Make sure your comments are intended to help the recipient.
2 Speak directly and with feeling based on trust.
3 Describe what the person is doing and the effect the person is having.
4 Don't be threatening or judgemental.
5 Be specific, not general (use clear and recent examples).
6 Give feedback when the recipient is open to accepting it.
7 Check to ensure the validity of your statements.
8 Include only things the receiver can do something about.
9 Don't overwhelm; make sure your comments aren't more than the person can handle.

Criteria for receiving feedback

1 Don't be defensive.
2 Seek specific examples.
3 Be sure you understand (summarise).
4 Share your feelings about the comments.
5 Ask for definitions.
6 Check out underlying assumptions.
7 Be sensitive to sender's non-verbal messages.
8 Ask questions to clarify.

Source: summarised from Phillip L. Hunsaker and Anthony J. Alessandra (1986), *The Art of Managing People*. New York, NY: Simon & Schuster, pp. 209–213. Reprinted by authors' permission.

Ask questions

Do not be afraid to ask questions, even questions you might consider 'stupid'. Stupid questions are easier to handle than dumb mistakes. Only people who know all the answers can dispense with the use of questions. We need to ask questions to obtain the information we need from managers, peers, subordinates, computers and sometimes even ourselves. Davidson (1991) suggests that questions motivate communication and open channels of communication, providing an environment in which employees also feel free to state their feelings, which helps managers communicate more effectively with a diverse workforce.

Questions allow us to gain information about people and problems. They can help us uncover motives and gain insights into another person's frame of reference, goals and motives. Questions can convey information: 'Did you know we have an education reimbursement programme?' They can be used to check understanding or interest and to obtain subordinate participation. Finally, questions can bring attention back to the subject and start others thinking. According to Hunsaker and Alessandra (1986), there are three main types of question: closed-end, open-end and clarifying.

Closed-end questions require narrow answers to a specific inquiry. Typical answers will be 'yes', 'no', or something nearly as brief. Questions of this nature are useful for obtaining facts, gaining commitment or directing the conversation to a desired area. *Open-end questions* are often used to draw out a wide range of responses to increase understanding or solve a problem. These questions involve other people by asking for feelings or opinions about a topic. They usually cannot be answered by a simple 'yes' or 'no', begin with 'what' or 'how', and do not lead others in a specified direction. *Clarifying questions* are essentially restatements of another person's remarks to determine if you have understood exactly what the speaker meant. These questions are useful for clarifying ambiguities and inviting the speaker to expand on ideas and feelings.

Listen

Listening is an intellectual and emotional process in which the receiver integrates physical, emotional and intellectual inputs in search of meaning. Listening to others is our most important means of gaining the information we need to understand people and assess situations. Kharbanda and Stallworthy (1991a) suggest that many communication problems develop because listening skills are ignored, forgotten or just taken for granted. Check your own listening proficiency by completing the following 'Your turn' exercise.

---

listening

The intellectual and emotional process in which the receiver integrates physical, emotional and intellectual inputs in search of meaning.

Listening is not the same as hearing, and effective listening is not easy. People usually hear the entire message, but too often its meaning is lost or distorted. Research by Goldhaber (1980) suggests that when listening to messages of only 10 minutes in duration, most people are likely to understand and retain only about 50 per cent of what is said; 48 hours later, this relatively poor retention rate drops to a still less impressive 25 per cent. This means that most people's memory of a particular conversation that took place more than a couple of days ago will always be incomplete and will usually be inaccurate.

Poor listeners miss important messages and emerging problems. Consequently, the ideas they propose are often faulty and inappropriate; sometimes they even address the wrong problems. Failure to listen also creates tension and distrust and results in reciprocal non-listening by others. The first step to overcome listening barriers is being aware of them.

Barriers to effective listening

Hunsaker and Alessandra (1986) suggest that many people identify listening as a passive, compliant act and develop negative attitudes towards it. From early childhood onwards, we are encouraged to put our emphasis on speaking as opposed to listening. We are taught that talk is power. When two people are vying for attention and control, however, they not only fail to listen to each other, but also generate increased tension along with decreased trust and productivity.

To listen well you have to care about the speaker and the message. Lack of interest makes listening effectively very difficult. Differences in prior learning and experience between senders and receivers can also detract from listening ability. For example, people with poorly developed vocabularies find it difficult to listen attentively to those with extensive vocabularies. Similar difficulties occur when the parties to a conversation have disparities of language, dialect or colloquial usage.

Classifying or prejudging the speaker in either positive or negative ways can distort the message accordingly. When we like a speaker, we view their message in a favourable and sympathetic way. When we dislike a speaker, we do just the opposite.

Our beliefs and values also influence how well we listen. If the actual message is in line with what we believe, we tend to listen much more attentively and regard the words in a more favourable light. However, if the message contradicts our current values and beliefs, we tend to criticise the speaker and distort the message. How we communicate is also affected by how much information we have – as can be seen from the 'Research focus'.

Your turn

Listening inventory

Instructions

Go through the following questions, checking yes or no next to each one.
Mark it as you actually behave, not as you think you should behave.

		Yes	No
1	I frequently attempt to listen to several conversations at the same time.	☐	☐
2	I like people to give me only the facts and then let me make my own interpretation.	☐	☐
3	I sometimes pretend to pay attention to people.	☐	☐
4	I consider myself a good judge of non-verbal communications.	☐	☐
5	I usually know what another person is going to say before he or she says it.	☐	☐
6	I usually end conversations that don't interest me by diverting my attention from the speaker.	☐	☐
7	I frequently nod, frown or whatever to let the speaker know how I feel about what he or she is saying.	☐	☐
8	I usually respond immediately when someone has finished talking.	☐	☐
9	I evaluate what is being said while it is being said.	☐	☐
10	I usually formulate a response while the other person is still talking.	☐	☐
11	The speaker's 'delivery style' frequently keeps me from listening to content.	☐	☐
12	I usually ask people to clarify what they have said rather than guess at the meaning.	☐	☐
13	I make a concerted effort to understand other points of view.	☐	☐
14	I frequently hear what I expect to hear rather than what is said.	☐	☐
15	Most people feel that I have understood their point of view when we disagree.	☐	☐

Interpretation According to communication theory, the correct answers are as follows: *No* for questions 1, 2, 3, 5, 6, 7, 8, 9, 10, 11 and 14; *Yes* for questions 4, 12, 13 and 15. If you missed only one or two questions, you strongly approve of your own listening habits, and you are on the right track to becoming an effective listener in your role as manager. If you missed three or four questions, you have uncovered some doubts about your listening effectiveness, and your knowledge of how to listen has some gaps. If you missed five or more questions, you probably are not satisfied with the way you listen, and your friends and co-workers may not feel you are a good listener either. You can work on improving your active listening skills by applying the ideas in this chapter.

Source: Ethel C. Glenn and Elliott A. Pood (1989) 'Listening Self-inventory', *Supervisory Management*, January, pp. 12–15. Copyright 1989 American Management Association International. Reprinted by permission of the publisher. All rights reserved.

Lack of concentration and attention often results from the mistaken assumption that we can do two things at the same time. The best you can possibly hope for when doing two things at the same time is to divide your attention equally between them.

People can think nearly four times as fast as they can speak. This leaves the listener with approximately three times the mental capacity he or she actually needs to hear the message. This 'dead space' is used by skilled listeners to summarise and relate data, whereas poor listeners simply let their minds wander.

Skilled listeners attempt to be objective by consciously trying to understand the speaker without letting their personal opinions influence the decoding of the speaker's words. They try to understand what the speaker wants to communicate, not what they want to understand.

Research focus: the Johari Window

As we have said above, perceptual differences on the part of the sender and receiver can cloud our judgement. As we mentioned in Chapter 4, people interpret the world according to their own backgrounds and prior experiences and this will have a strong impact on how they behave when communicating.

Often when we communicate with another person we have a wariness, as we do not know everything about the other person and they do not know everything about us. So the communication situations can be classified according to the amount of information each person has at the outset of the communication. According to Luft (1961) the three categories for communication are:

1 the knowledge of the issue
2 the person's own view on the subject under discussion
3 the other person's view.

For two-person communication, this can be classified along two dimensions:

1 the amount of information possessed by oneself
2 the amount possessed by the other person.

This can be shown in a model developed by Luft (1961), which is known as the Johari Window (see Exhibit 8-5).

■ **Blind spot situation** – the sender is at a disadvantage as the receiver knows more about the issues being communicated, his or her reactions to it and the reactions of the sender.

■ **Unknown situation** – neither knows much about the situation and communication could be poor as any meaningful dialogue will happen only by chance.

■ **Façade situation** – the sender knows much more about the situation than the receiver. As a result the receiver may pretend to know more than they actually do or the sender may withhold information.

■ **Arena situation** – both the sender and receiver know all they need to know about the situation and each other's views. Therefore, interpersonal communication is likely to be effective.

EXHIBIT 8–5 The Johari Window (Luft, 1961)

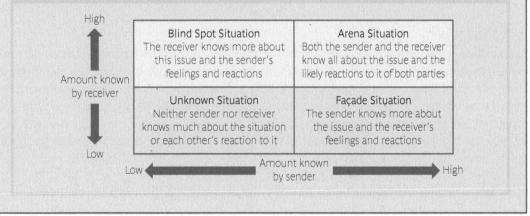

The problem with the Johari Window is that three of the situations may result in communication being only partially effective. Polsky (1971) argues that effectiveness comes from a willingness to engage in self-disclosure and a willingness to give and receive feedback. Because people differ greatly in these respects, the result is characteristic patterns of behaviour, as identified by Polsky (1971) (see Exhibit 8-6).

- **Self-exposing style** – the sender of the message encourages the receiver to focus on the sender by asking for feedback.
- **Self-bargaining style** – the sender is willing to open up to the receiver and give a measure of feedback. This may only be done if the receiver does the same.
- **Self-protective style** – the sender is unwilling to be open with the receiver about his or her own feelings and will tend to probe the other person's views and give feedback on these. This can often result in a façade situation.
- **Self-actualising** – they are willing to provide a great deal of information about themselves, and give and receive feedback, which results in an arena situation.

Polsky's analysis has its problems. It is useful in telling us that a person's style has an impact on communication, but it suggests that the self-actualising style is best and that something is wrong with communication if this is not used everywhere. Although the self-actualising style encourages communication because it encourages a person to adopt a self-disclosing approach and give feedback, it is also necessary to focus on the other aspects of behaviour.

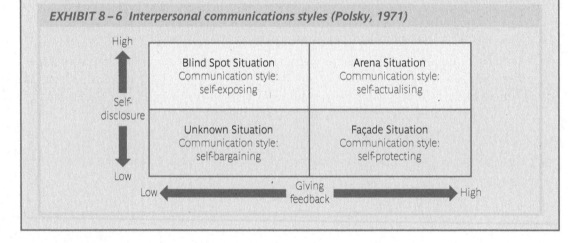

EXHIBIT 8–6 Interpersonal communications styles (Polsky, 1971)

Active listening

If you refrain from evaluating other people's words, try to see things from their point of view, and demonstrate openly that you are trying to truly understand, you are using the technique of active listening (Hunsaker and Alessandra, 1986). Active listeners are not only attentive to the words being spoken, but also 'put themselves in the other person's shoes'. They search for the intent and feeling of the message and indicate their understanding both verbally and non-verbally. Active listeners do not interrupt. They look for verbal and visual cues that the other person would like to say something more. Guidelines for effective listening are provided in Exhibit 8-7.

An active listener practises sensing, attending and responding. *Sensing* is the ability to recognise the silent messages that the speaker is sending through non-verbal clues such as vocal

EXHIBIT 8 – 7 Guidelines for effective listening

1 Stop talking. It is impossible to listen and talk at the same time.

2 Listen for main ideas.

3 Be sensitive to emotional deaf spots that make your mind wander.

4 Fight off distractions.

5 Take notes.

6 Be patient. Let others tell their stories first.

7 Empathise with other people's points of view.

8 Withhold judgement.

9 React to the message, not the person.

10 Appreciate the emotion behind the speaker's words.

11 Use feedback to check your understanding.

12 Relax and put the sender at ease.

13 Be attentive.

14 Create a positive listening environment.

15 Ask questions.

16 Be motivated to listen.

Source: summarised from Phillip L. Hunsaker and Anthony J. Alessandra (1986) *The Art of Managing People*. New York, NY: Simon & Schuster, pp. 137–141. Used with authors' permission.

intonation, body language and facial expression. *Attending* refers to the verbal, vocal and visual messages that an active listener sends to the speaker to indicate full attention. These include eye contact, open posture, affirmative head nods and appropriate facial and verbal expressions.

In *responding*, the active listener summarises and gives feedback on the content and feeling of the sender's message. He or she encourages the speaker to elaborate, makes the speaker feel understood, and attempts to improve the speaker's own understanding of the problems or concerns.

Sensory aspects of communication

When we communicate with the outside world we use our senses. We mentioned in Chapter 4 how we make assumptions about people from what we see and hear, either from the way they dress or the way they speak. If we were to lose one of our senses it would have a serious impact not only on how we communicate but also on how we can learn and understand. This can affect the decisions we make. There is an old saying that says 'I hear I forget, I see I remember, I do I understand'. Fifty-five per cent of non-verbal communication is visual. Think back to your lectures, the ones you are more likely to remember will probably have used a visual display, either diagrams or bullet points on a projector or maybe a video illustrating a point. Also, think about the lectures where someone has stood in front of the class either reading from notes or ad-libbing. How much of it can you remember? Probably not very much, unless they had an animated tone of voice. Tone of voice can account for 35 per cent of our understanding of communication. We know when someone is angry, sad, interested or uninterested not by what they say but by how they say it; we can pick this up by using our auditory senses as well as our visual senses by looking at face and body movements. This leaves only 10 per cent of what we understand of the communication to its actual content. Therefore, if we were to lose one of our senses we would have a serious problem in understanding the context to a communication.

Reading non-verbal communication cues

The amount of non-verbal feedback exchanged is not as important as how the parties interpret and react to it. Very often a person says one thing but communicates something totally different through vocal intonation and body language. These *mixed signals* force the receiver to choose between the verbal and non-verbal aspects of a message. Mehrabian (1972) suggests that, most often, the receiver chooses the non-verbal aspect. Mixed messages also create tension and distrust because the receiver senses that the communicator is hiding something or is being less than candid.

As much as 93 per cent of the meaning that is transmitted between two people in a face-to-face communication can come via non-verbal channels. This means that as little as 7 per cent of the meaning we derive from others may come through their words alone. Non-verbal communications are actually more reliable than verbal communications when they contradict each other. Consequently, they function as a 'lie detector' to aid a watchful listener in interpreting another's words. According to Ekman (1993), although many people can convincingly misrepresent their emotions in their speech, focused attention on facial and vocal expressions can often detect leakage of the concealed feelings. Williams (1989) suggests that non-verbal communication is made up of visual, tactile and vocal aspects, and the use of time, space and image.

Visual aspects of non-verbal communication

The visual component of non-verbal communication has been called *body language*, or *kinesics*. It includes facial expressions, eye movements, posture and gestures.

The face is the best communicator of non-verbal messages. By 'reading' a person's facial expressions we can often detect unexpressed feelings like happiness, sadness, surprise, fear, anger and disgust. Caution is advised, however, because different cultures impose emotional restraints to hold back true feelings, and the same facial expression can mean different things in different cultures. For example, agreement or approval is indicated by up-and-down head nods in British culture, but is expressed by side-to-side head movements in India (Gibson and Hodgetts, 1986).

We've all heard the phrases 'One glance is worth a thousand words' and 'The eyes are the windows to the soul.' How do you feel when you are talking to someone wearing mirrored sunglasses? Most of us are uncomfortable because we are cut off from the most significant body expression of that person's mood.

Eye contact allows us to read and communicate a number of things. Direct eye contact, for example, is generally perceived as a sign of honesty, interest, openness and confidence. If eye contact is avoided, we feel that the other is embarrassed, nervous or hiding something. As with all body language, eye contact varies by culture. According to Gibson and Hodgetts (1986), in some African cultures, for example, children are taught not to look directly in the face of an adult (superior) – behaviour that, in an adult, could be interpreted by a British manager as a sign of deceit.

Posture provides clues about the attitude of the bearer. How we carry ourselves signals such feelings as self-confidence, aggressiveness, fear, guilt or anxiety. An example of using posture to appear in charge is when a manager stands up and leans forward over an employee's desk to peer down and give a reprimand. Self-confidence could be portrayed by a relaxed posture, such as sitting back in a chair with legs stretched out and hands behind the head. Contrast the image to that of someone hunched down, looking away, and biting his or her fingernails. A shift in posture means that something is changing, but it is up to the receiver to figure out what (Mehrabian, 1972).

Gestures combine facial expressions and posture movements to indicate meaning, control conversation, or complement words. Some gestures have universal symbolism. Raising both hands above the head indicates surrender and submission. A salute, a tip of the hat, a handshake, a wave of farewell, a V for victory, an O for OK, and a wink of the eye, are just a few of the familiar symbols that transcend most language and cultural barriers.

According to Kharbanda and Stallworthy (1991b) most gestures are culturally bound and susceptible to misinterpretation, however. It is very easy for British people to misread Japanese body language, for example. Japanese people try to avoid personal confrontation; they usually exhibit a non-controversial demeanour and use excessive politeness and tact to smooth over any differences that arise. When negotiating among themselves, this presents no difficulties. However, for the British, serious misinterpretations can arise.

Each isolated gesture is like a word in a sentence and should be considered in light of the other simultaneous forms of communication. When individual gestures are put together in clusters, they paint a more precise picture of what the other person is feeling and thinking.

Nierenberg and Calero (1973) suggest that, to the sender of a message, a receiver's gestures serve as feedback; by observing the emotions and attitudes that are expressed non-verbally, he or she can tell how acceptable the message is. For example, disagreement will be evident when someone shakes her head or raises her eyebrows in amazement or doubt. A smile and a nod, on the other hand, will signal agreement.

Tactile aspects of non-verbal communication

Tactile communication is the use of touch to impart meaning, as in a handshake, a pat on the back, an arm around the shoulder, or a push or slap. Gentle touching like a hand on an arm, a kiss or a hug indicates support, liking or intimacy. Rough touching like squeezing someone's hand too hard, kicking people under the table and bumping into them in the hallway, is hostile behaviour indicating negative sentiment.

Vocal aspects of non-verbal communication

Vocal intonations are how things are said, as exemplified by the common phrase, 'It's not what you say but how you say it.' Simply changing the intonation of your voice can alter the meaning of words. Try changing your vocal qualities while you say the word 'no'. You can express mild doubt, amazement, terror and anger; you can give a command, decline an invitation, or answer a simple question. Each vocal intonation conveys a separate and unique feeling. Changes in loudness, pitch, rate, rhythm and clarity all produce different meanings.

According to Gibson and Hodgetts (1986), vocal meanings also vary across cultures. For example, if a British person raises his or her voice, we assume that the person is excited or angry and usually have a difficult time concentrating on what is being said once the volume has risen beyond what we consider a comfortable level, focusing instead on the projected emotions. In Italian cultures, however, noise level is generally higher than in Britain. The normal British vocal level would be considered too subdued to indicate genuine involvement and appropriate concern for what the Italian is communicating.

The most important aspect of vocal intonation is a change in vocal quality. Rosenthal *et al.* (1974) suggest that when people change their normal vocal qualities, it is a sign that they are communicating something extra. One example is statements tinged with sarcasm, where the vocally transmitted message has a meaning quite different from that of its actual verbal content.

Use of time as non-verbal communication

Time is a continuous and irreversible scarce resource. Consequently, whom we spend it with and how much we give, communicate our feelings about who and what are important to us. Most men probably try to arrive a little early for a first date with an important woman so that they do not insult her by being late. Yet, in order to hide their eagerness, they probably will not go up to her door until exactly the agreed-upon time. If either party had been very late, a suitable explanation would have been in order to ease the assumption of indifference. Similarly, it may be common for a manager to assume that a subordinate who is frequently late to department meetings does not care about them, whether this is accurate or not.

Use of time also communicates how we view our own status and power in relation to others. If the president of a company calls a junior manager to his or her office for a meeting, the manager will probably arrive well before the appointed time. Because of the difference in status, most managers would probably feel that any inconvenience in waiting ought to be theirs. The president's time is assumed to be worth more and therefore not to be wasted, as opposed to the perceived less valuable time of subordinates.

Special aspects of non-verbal communication

Proxemics is the way we use physical space to communicate things about us. How do you feel when you return from a class break and find someone sitting in your seat? Or when someone is standing so close to you that you wonder how long ago he had the tuna sandwich? Or when your boss looks down on you from his or her plush leather chair behind the expensive oak desk in their large office? Managers need to understand at least three aspects of proxemics for effective communication: territory, things and personal space zones (Hunsaker, 1984).

proxemics
The use of physical space and things to communicate meaning.

Virtual proxemics

How can we use physical space when we communicate more and more by email? We can create distance by how we communicate. If you send an email to your boss, how do you word it and do you check your spelling? Many people seem quite happy to send emails full of typos when they would never do the same with a letter. Do you begin 'Dear...' or launch straight in to the subject matter? Again, if you were communicating to a friend, what would be the difference? How we communicate can give an indication of how close we want to be to the person with whom we are communicating.

Territory

Although how space is used to communicate differs by culture, people seek to extend their territory in many ways to attain power and intimacy. We silently say things by manipulating space, as when we intrude on another person's space or guard our own. For example, your office or work area is a *fixed-feature territory* with permanent boundaries such as walls, partitions and doors. When you walk into a meeting or classroom, you establish a *semi-fixed feature territory* by fixing movable objects; for example, by laying out notebooks, folders and a coffee cup, or hanging a jacket on a chair. Being assigned fixed-feature territory is a sign of increased status compared to having only semi-fixed feature space, because a rare resource has been assigned for your exclusive use and you can communicate how important you or others are by shutting people out or holding private meetings. The larger your office, the more status and importance communicated.

People like to protect and control their territory; this is easier to do in fixed-feature areas because you can shut or even lock the door. In semi-fixed feature areas your best protection is your physical presence, backed up by other people's respect in honouring your territory. If you return from a break and find someone sitting in your seat or, even worse, enter your office and find someone looking for something in your filing cabinet, you will probably be angry with the violator.

How things communicate

The things within your space also communicate things to others. A clean desk communicates efficiency versus the disorganisation conveyed by a messy one. An attractive reception area communicates that the organisation cares about visitors. Expensive things communicate higher status than do cheap ones. Personal things in your space such as trophies, photographs, pictures, plants and other decorations, also convey messages about you to others.

Personal space zones

We all carry an invisible personal territory, much like a private air bubble. We feel a proprietary right to this space and resent others entering it unless they are invited. The exact dimensions of these private bubbles vary from culture to culture and person to person, but adult British people usually have four personal space zones.

1 The *intimate zone*, from actual physical contact to about 2 feet away, is reserved for closest family and friends. A husband and wife often touch and interact enjoyably in this zone, but British businessmen or businesswomen confined to the intimate zone in a crowded subway or elevator would not.

2 The *personal zone*, from approximately 2 feet to 4 feet, usually reserved for family and friends. How other people react if you enter their personal space can be a non-verbal signal about how comfortable they are with you.

3 The *social zone*, extending from nearly 4 feet to roughly 12 feet, is where most business transactions, such as sales calls or negotiations, occur. It is far enough away to allow some feeling of security, yet close enough to communicate acceptance and closeness if desired.

4 The *public zone*, stretching from 12 feet away to the limits of hearing and sight, is most often used for lectures or speeches. It is the most formal zone and represents the farthest limit at which we can effectively communicate face to face.

People can generally be classified into two major proxemic categories. Although space preferences are based on personal and experience factors, northern Europeans typify the non-contact group due to the small amount of touching and relatively large space between them during their transactions. Arabs and southern Europeans are in the contact group, who normally stand very close to each other and use a lot of touching when they communicate.

When people do not appreciate differences in personal zones, discomfort, distrust and mis-understanding can occur. Contact people can unknowingly get too close to or touch non-contact people, as happened when a Moroccan and an English person were discussing business at a cocktail party. For the Moroccan, the appropriate zone for interaction was the personal zone, and he used frequent touching to make a point. That was about half the distance (minus touch) that the English person needed to be in his comfortable social zone. The Moroccan would step closer and the English person would back away, in a strange proxemic dance, until both gave up the relationship as a lost cause because of the other's 'cold' or 'pushy' behaviour.

Image as communication

Hunsaker and Alessandra (1986) suggest that, as irrational as it may seem, people do judge a book by its cover. Through clothing and other dimensions of physical appearance, we communicate our values and expectations. It is an unusual person who can overcome a bad initial impression and reveal genuine assets hidden underneath. People react favourably to an expected image. Consequently, managers who look and act like executives tend to be more successful than those who do not. In *Business Buzzwords*, for example, 'suits' is defined as a 'blue-collar term for white-collar managers, as in: "look busy. Here come the suits."' (Johnson, 1990).

First impressions made by the initial impact of your clothing, voice, grooming, handshake, eye contact and body posture, are lasting images. Projecting both a depth and breadth of knowledge about your job or area of expertise builds your credibility, commands respect from others and helps develop rapport. Flexibility, enthusiasm and sincerity in your work relationships create a positive image that can enhance your communication effectiveness. In terms of dress, colours have meanings (e.g. brown for trusting, white for purity, dark colours for power) as do style (e.g. formal versus casual for more or less status respectively) and material (e.g. synthetic fibres like polyester convey lower class versus pure fibres like wool for higher class) (Raffaeli and Pratt, 1993).

Electronic communication

Miles and Snow (1986) argue that with more and more organisations using information and communication technologies (ICTs) new organisations are emerging. According to Davidow and Malone (1992), these may be known as 'virtual organisations' or 'networked organisations'. New methods in communication using email and the web have enabled these organisations to develop. They do not exist in the physical sense, but in cyberspace; they tend to be a loose network of knowledge workers and have fluid boundaries that can expand or contract as needed. More information on virtual organisations and their development can be found in Chapter 17. The one thing about e-commerce is that it can operate across boundaries: a hotel in the USA can be booked from England at any time, day or night, without having to think about time differences and, because the process is automated, there is often an immediate response, where a letter could have taken days or weeks to answer. However, there are also stresses associated with such communication as people find they have to respond faster to requests for information, as can be seen from the 'desk rage' case in Chapter 7. The World Watch box on page 388 illustrates how new methods of communication can help us to talk to people in different countries.

The problem with electronic communication is that it is everywhere; this means that people have access to vast amounts of data, which may lead to the extra pressures of sifting through and evaluating information. The other issue is the way work culture is changing: already there is the term 'telecommuting', which is used for people who work at home and link up online with other colleagues. This could mean a future of people staying at home but doing their business electronically.

There are both advantages and disadvantages of such as system, as can be seen below. The advantages are:

- a fast speed of transmission
- versatility in that text and graphics can be exchanged and video links allow face-to-face communication.

- accuracy – data can be recorded and does not need to rely on conversations
- feedback and exchange of information can be instant.

The disadvantages to this are:

- the large volume of transmitted data can make it hard to absorb within set time limits
- costs in providing hardware, software and networks need to be considered
- legal implications as paper signatures are dispensed with
- instant delivery could mean that email messages etc. can cause upsets if they are composed in anger and then unretrievable after being sent.

Dealing with electronic communication

The problem with email is that we tend to be bombarded with information; most junk mail can be filtered out using spam filters, but often we are still left with a large volume of mail that needs to be answered. The same strategies for dealing with paperwork can be adopted for use with electronic sources.

- Prioritise and try to deal with incoming letters, memos and notes immediately.
- Treat electronic communication as you would paperwork – deal with email messages right away, forward or copy as appropriate, then delete.
- Deal with each piece of paper only once. When you pick it up, do something towards getting rid of it – take the necessary action or copy it to the right place, then throw it away.
- Delete emails when you have finished with them.
- File only the material you will need; review your files periodically and clean out any you no longer refer to.
- At the end of your day, go through any remaining communication and either take any appropriate action, or send it to a relevant person, or file it or throw it away.
- Check any items off against your to-do list so you can start with a clean slate tomorrow.

Managing electronic communication

Electronic communication certainly has its advantages in that it speeds up the transfer of information, however it raises other issues with both the employer and employee on how it should be managed. Johns (2005) argues that employers are using monitoring and surveillance on a regular basis to ensure that staff are prevented from acting unethically or passing on information that could cause a scandal for the organisation.

Mancini and Kahn (2005), in a survey of 1000 organisations, found that many which used electronic communication were either poorly managed or not managed at all. This suggests that many employers do not have strategies in place for ensuring their information is secure or protecting their workers from viruses, spam etc. The research also found that the internal management of emails was poor: while 86 per cent of organisations had a policy on how to use email, only 39 per cent had policies about how it should be stored and retained. Email is now forming a central part of an organisation's workload and yet its management is often considered as an add-on rather than an integral part of the organisation.

With electronic communication becoming more common many managers need to think about how they manage communications between workers.

The TUC (2005) suggests the following criteria, which should be communicated to all members of the organisation.

■ Set out clearly the circumstances in which workers may or may not use the employer's phone systems (including mobile phones), email system and the Internet for private communications.

■ Make clear the extent and type of private use that is allowed – for example, any restrictions on overseas phone calls or limits on the size or type of email attachments

■ Specify clearly any restrictions on web material that can be viewed or copied. A simple ban on 'offensive material' is unlikely to be sufficiently clear for workers to know what is and is not allowed. Employers should at least give examples of the sort of material that is considered offensive (e.g. material containing racist terminology or images of nudity).

■ Advise workers what personal information they are allowed to include in particular types of communication, or the alternatives that should be used (e.g. communication with the company doctor should be sent by internal mail rather than email).

■ Lay down clear rules regarding personal use of communication equipment when used from home (e.g. facilities that enable external dialling into a company network).

■ Explain the purposes of any monitoring, its extent and the means used.

■ Outline how the policy is enforced and the penalties for breaching it.

Control and surveillance

According to Porter and Griffaton (2003), the number of email users increased from 8 million in 1991 to 108 million in 2000. In 2000, 40 million employees exchanged more than 60 billion messages daily.

With just a few clicks of a mouse, an employer may lose valuable trade secrets and confidential information, be liable for violating copyright laws, or be exposed to claims that it permitted a hostile work environment. The pervasive and ubiquitous nature and exponential growth of electronic mail and the Internet highlight the need to monitor the electronic workplace to curb that liability.

While most employees have been trained about improper office behaviour – for example, sexual harassment – many do not view email as an avenue for harassment and tend to treat their incoming and outgoing messages more casually than a letter or memo written on a company letterhead.

According to a 2001 survey by Elron Software, more than 40 per cent of respondents admitted to receiving company confidential information such as client lists, financial statements and product specifications from 'outside their organisations – a 356 per cent increase since 1999'.

Most electronic monitoring by employers, like the monitoring of employees' conduct in general, is conducted in the workplace, but some employers also monitor and even discipline employees' off-duty conduct.

The type of software available for monitoring generally falls into the following categories.

■ **Blocking software.** This type of software filters virtually anything on the Internet that the employer deems inappropriate for employees to access while at work. When employees type in questionable words or search inappropriate sites, which have been predetermined by the employer, not only are they prevented from entering, but they may be directed automatically to the company's electronic communications policy. The software can also alert employers when an off-limits site is visited.

- **Direct surveillance.** This software takes a picture of an employee's screen at periodic intervals, which enables the employer to see the sites employees are visiting or the messages they are emailing.
- **Flagging.** This software not only monitors employees' Internet use but also screens their email for potentially offensive or inappropriate messages. This software scans employee emails for questionable keywords predetermined by the employer. For example, an employer concerned with the theft of its trade secrets can list the names of its primary competitors as keywords. This software also can automatically email 'flagged' messages to a company representative.
- **Keystroke logging.** This software maintains a record of keystrokes and tracks computer idle time. This software can even recreate 'deleted' documents because the keystrokes are logged and stored even if deleted.

Many employers want to be able to monitor staff to ensure that they don't misuse company property, and most staff accept the need for this. However, it is important to be able to find a balance between respecting the rights of both employees and employers. Excessive surveillance can be viewed by employees as a lack of trust and this has been confirmed by research from the Chartered Institute of Personnel and Development, which has found that organisations that seek to monitor their employees excessively are unlikely to create a culture that fosters trust, loyalty and commitment. The research report reveals that employees who are closely monitored tend to have more negative attitudes towards work and are more likely to suffer from stress, (CIPD, 2005).

Protection for employees under data protection and human rights legislation means that employers need to be careful as there can be a fine line between acceptable and unacceptable practices. To ensure that employers do not fall foul of such legislation a risk assessment is a useful tool. The assessment should identify the purpose of monitoring, the benefits it's likely to deliver and any likely adverse effects. It should also consider alternatives to surveillance or less intrusive ways in which to do it.

Once employers have decided on the type of employee conduct they expect, they need to communicate it to the employees; this usually takes the form of policy documents. These set out what is acceptable and what is not, and the consequences of breaking the rules. For example, the use of pornographic websites would in most cases be seen as unacceptable and consequences could result in dismissal, while the private use of email may be seen as acceptable.

The monitoring code generally succeeds in helping employers walk the fine line between respecting employees' privacy and protecting their own interests. For example, the code allows an organisation to check employees' emails in their absence if they have been informed that this will happen. An employee's privacy must be respected if they clearly mark that an email is personal, unless the employer has a valid and defined reason to examine its content. The code also protects staff from covert monitoring except in exceptional circumstances, such as where there are grounds for suspecting criminal malpractice.

Employers need to be aware that employees have the right to privacy and dignity at work, but employees need to be aware that employers need to be protected from behaviour that could bring the organisation into disrepute.

Tongue-tied companies: online attempts to speak to customers in their own language are decidedly patchy

Almost half the UK's top 100 companies do not have any foreign content on their websites, according to a study by SDL, a language specialist, as part of the International Multilingual Content Survey of FTSE 100 companies. Should we be appalled? Not really.

For one thing translating a website is expensive. If a company has decided that the cost outweighs the benefit, that is a reasonable commercial judgement. For another, the commercial web is still in its infancy, and there is evidence that companies are trying, even if they have not got that far yet.

What is worrying is that few organisations have a consistent language policy on what is, after all, the World Wide Web. Too often the result is a mess.

The exceptions are some of the big technology providers, such as Microsoft and Xerox, which have created massive multilingual sites based on a common template. Vodafone has local sites in foreign languages as diverse as Albanian and Romanian. Electrolux shows that organisation rather than translation is the key. Most, though not all, subsidiaries use the same template but have modules of translated content dropped in as appropriate. This is localisation, not just translation at low cost.

Most airlines have a range of non-English sites with the exception of American and Delta. But the big hotel groups are rather hopeless, although Marriott managed to have a site in Japanese.

SDL says that 'Business users are three times as likely to buy when addressed in their own language.'

While Japan and the big European countries have fully translated sites, Latin Americans have to cope with English, while Scandinavians are offered an Anglo-local hybrid.

The lack of language policy is even more clear on corporate sites. While many offer plenty of non-English material, it is inconsistent and just as confusing – inconsistently presented.

One company that has got it right is Electrolux. It started work on localisation several years ago and developed its own processes to allow copy to be translated locally using a split screen. In other words, it has a mass production system, whereas other giants are still largely in the costly age of hand-building.

Where does the expense of business translation leave small organisations? Well, they should at least consider machine translation. Yes, it produces sometimes farcical results – but if you want to communicate with a prospective Portuguese customer, it may be better to offer bad Portuguese than good English.

That is what Queen Ethelburga's school in York does. It provides eight languages including Korean and Japanese to lure prospective parents. It uses a computer translation of the original web page, although it says it should not be regarded as complete or accurate. This may be so, but at least it attempts to communicate with non-English speakers.

Source: adapted from David Bowen in *Financial Times*, 28 June 2002.

Discussion questions

1 What are the implications of providing a foreign-language website for attracting overseas business?

2 What are the problems with machine translations of languages?

Improving cross-cultural communication

Achieving effective communication is a challenge to managers worldwide even when the workforce is culturally homogeneous, but when one company includes a variety of languages and cultural backgrounds, it becomes even more difficult. The greater the differences in backgrounds between senders and receivers, the greater the differences in meanings attached to particular words and behaviours. This is equally true for communicators from different countries, different sexes or different subcultures in the same country.

Global differences

While most European businesspeople speak several languages, the average British businessperson speaks only English. The same year that 20 million Japanese were studying English, only a few thousand Britons were studying Japanese (Harris and Moran, 1991). The vast majority of people in the world do not understand English, making foreign language training a necessity in today's international business environment.

Even if two communicators are speaking the same language, the same words and phrases may mean different things to people from different cultures. For example, the phrase 'That would be very hard to do' means to the British that some adjustments or extra contributions may be necessary, but the deal is still possible. To Japanese, the phrase clearly means, 'No, it won't be possible.' For a non-verbal example, the British think that maintaining eye contact is important and others who do not are dishonest or rude. Japanese, on the other hand, lower their eyes as a gesture of respect when speaking with a superior (Salacuse, 1991).

Working in a global environment requires employees and managers to acknowledge and understand how different cultures interpret, behave and interact. It is inappropriate (and generally impossible) to assume that a particular working style or mode of communication that works in Britain is transferable across cultures. A British manager might be shocked if not a single person shows up to a 2 p.m. meeting in Italy, when it is siesta time. Additionally, the manager might not understand why some Italians are still working at 8 p.m., as they do not realise that they have had a three-hour lunch break.

When working in a global environment, it is important that managers recognise the difficulties of cross-cultural communication. Cross-cultural misinterpretation is influenced by several factors managers need to be aware of. The use of categories and stereotypes, either consciously or subconsciously, allows people to make order or sense of different situations. However, Adler (1997) suggests that in a multicultural environment, the use of categories and stereotypes can cause significant misunderstanding. The British manager could stereotype the Italian colleagues who did not show up to the meeting as 'lazy', or 'not serious about the project'. However, the British manager is not recognising the fact that his Italian colleagues worked until 8 p.m. The rush to categorise or stereotype, rather than attempting to objectively understand, permitted the British manager to quickly, but incorrectly, explain to himself why the Italian colleagues did not show up to the meeting.

Gender differences

Gender can create subculture communication barriers within the same country. In Britain, for example, men frequently use talk to emphasise status differences because of their need for independence, while women more often use it to create interpersonal connections based on common ground because of their greater need for intimacy. Men frequently complain that women talk a lot about their problems, and women criticise men for not listening. Men tend to present information in attempts to establish power positions, however women tend to focus on relationships and gain a consensus to a larger extent than men (Daly and Ibarra, 1996). Tannen (1991) suggests that what men are doing is asserting their independence and desire for control by providing solutions that women do not necessarily want in their quest for support, understanding and connection.

Male managers' communication behaviours are often characterised by task orientation, dominance, challenges to others, and attempts to control the conversation. For example, males talk more and interrupt more often than do females. Females are usually more informative, receptive to ideas, focused on interpersonal relations and concerned for others. They are more reactive and show more emotional support (Bard and Bradley, 1979).

Hunsaker and Hunsaker (1991) suggest that women are more precise in their pronunciation than men who, for example, tend to shorten the ends of words (using 'in' instead of 'ing'). Males and females also differ in word choice. Females tend to select more intense adverbs, such as 'extremely friendly', whereas males use words that are more descriptive and defining.

Women more often use *qualifying terms*, which are phrases that soften or qualify the intent of communication. They make language less absolute and less powerful. Examples include 'maybe', 'you know what I mean', and 'it's only my opinion' (Eakins and Eakins, 1978).

Women also frequently use *tag questions*, which are qualifying words at the end of a sentence that ask the other for confirmation of the statement presented. When using these, they automatically defer to others: 'It's really time for a break now, right?', 'We did the job right, didn't we?' By adding the tag question, the speaker gives the impression of being unsure and surrenders decision-making power (Hunsaker and Hunsaker, 1991).

Guidelines for improving cross-cultural communication

Thousands of successful cross-cultural business communications take place every day. Familiarising yourself with cultural differences and being aware of your own cultural frame of reference can help you communicate more effectively when working with people from different cultures or subcultures. The following more specific guidelines, suggested by Adler (1997), can facilitate cross-cultural communications.

Assume differences until similarity is proven

Effective cross-cultural communicators know that they do not know how people with different backgrounds perceive a situation or interpret certain forms of communication. They do not assume that a person from another culture interprets a word or behaviour the same way that they do. Therefore, to avoid embarrassing misinterpretations, effective managers first assume that individuals from different cultures will interpret communication or behaviours differently until some similarities are proven.

Emphasise description rather than interpretation or evaluation

Effective cross-cultural communicators delay judgement until they have observed and interpreted the situation from the perspectives of all cultures involved. Description emphasises observation of what has occurred rather than interpretation or evaluation, which are based more on the observer's culture and background than on the facts.

Empathise

When trying to understand the words, motives and actions of a person from another culture, try to interpret them from the perspective of that culture rather than your own. When you view behaviours from your own perspective, you can completely misinterpret the other's actions if he or she has different values, experiences and objectives. Therefore, to reduce cross-cultural misinterpretations, it is important to reflect and view behaviours from another's culture.

Treat your interpretations as guesses until you can confirm them

If in doubt check with people from other cultures to make sure that your evaluation of a behaviour is accurate. Treat your first interpretations as working hypotheses rather than facts, and pay careful attention to feedback in order to avoid serious miscommunications and resulting problems.

Mr easyJet: a second look

The PRCA awards are essentially about good communication of issues, including business performance, and it was agreed by the panel of judges that Stelios had done a first-class job of convincing customers and shareholders that he had the right strategy. It was felt that his recent exit as chairman of easyJet had been handled well and he remained the popular face of the company, notwithstanding dissenters.

Like Sir Richard Branson and his Virgin empire, Stelios has often come under fire from city bankers and journalists for over-extending the 'easy' brand, but the wider public has warmed to his ideas of cheap car rental, Internet cafes and low-cost cinemas and hostels. One member of the panel likened his popularity to that of Sir Freddie Laker, the pioneering low-cost airline operator of the 1970s, but felt that Stelios had already achieved a good deal more.

Now, following his resignation as chairman in favour of Sir Colin Chandler, former chairman of aerospace firm Vickers, chief executive Ray Webster will increasingly become the face of the airline. Stelios is now simply an investor in the airline and will become, says his spokesman James Rothnie, 'a net seller of easyJet over the years'.

If he figures in 2003's PRCA Communicator of the Year, it will be as the figurehead of easyGroup, a leisure services company which, in Rothnie's phrase, 'is customer-pointing in what it seeks to do'.

Stelios has endeared himself to the press, the City and the public. But the British are notoriously a nation for suddenly withdrawing affection. It will be another challenge for him to sustain his appeal.

On his communication skills Lord Bell says, 'As a business communicator, Stelios stands out in the crowd. He always seems to get it right – he even resigned as chairman at the right time and in such a way as to minimise the impact to the core business. He demonstrated that he understood the impact of 11 September. While others went under, his business thrived. He is also a business leader of real quality and vision.'

Source: Financial Times, 12/13 May 2002, p. 29.

Summary

- Effective communication is essential for transmitting directives, building co-operation and team spirit, optimising performance and satisfaction, and avoiding and solving problems.

- Formal communication channels flow in downward, upward and horizontal directions. Informal networks are more useful when there is a need to tap into current feelings and reactions of employees.

- Messages need to be encoded carefully so that they clearly communicate intentions, feelings and expectations. They should be sent through the most appropriate channels, and feedback should be solicited from the receiver to be sure that the message was decoded as intended.

- Communication is complicated by such barriers as frames of reference, value judgements, selective listening, filtering and distrust. These are especially prevalent in multicultural environments.

- Barriers can be overcome by sending clear, complete and specific messages.

- Credibility can be enhanced by demonstrating expertise, clarifying intentions, being reliable and dynamic, exhibiting warmth and friendliness, and building a positive image. Soliciting and providing specific feedback can also enhance communication effectiveness.

- Questions can help a person gain information, uncover motives, give information, obtain participation, check understanding, start others thinking, induce agreement and refocus attention.

- Active listening skills build rapport with others and help obtain relevant information.

- Body language is useful both in reading the emotions and attitudes of others and in reinforcing your own verbal messages.

- Understanding vocal qualities can enhance your reading of other people's messages and help to project your own messages more effectively.

- Unethical interpersonal communication can damage relationships and prevent further communication between people. Deception and lying are two examples of unethical communication that prohibit effective communication.

- Managers should avoid unethical communication because it destroys their own credibility and rapport among people in the organisation.

Areas for personal development

Effective communication is vital to a successful organisation. Managers need to communicate directions and tasks, and provide employee performance feedback. Employees need to provide answers and opinions, and communicate issues back to management. Furthermore, effective teamwork requires clear communication between team-mates. Breakdowns in communication cause organisational problems, rumours to surface, low productivity and poor quality. Consequently, you should apply the following skills to ensure you are communicating effectively.

1 **Choose the most effective method to communicate.** It is important that the 'right message' is communicated using the 'right method'. Focus on the message being sent and choose the most appropriate method to send it. For example, it might be most appropriate to sit down with an employee to discuss a performance appraisal, giving the employee your full attention. Email might not be a very effective form of communication for situations requiring a lot of rapport and understanding. However, for routine communications where little room for misinterpretation exists, email might be the best communication form. Even a clear and meaningful message can be lost if an ineffective delivery method is utilised.

2 **Send clear, complete and specific messages.** Enhance your credibility by demonstrating expertise, clarifying intentions, being reliable and dynamic, and exhibiting warmth and friendliness.

3 **Actively listen.** Active listening is hard work, but worth it because it builds rapport with others and helps you obtain relevant information. You need to physically attend and mentally concentrate on what the speaker is conveying. You can also ask clear questions and paraphrase to ensure understanding.

4 **Ask appropriate questions.** Questions can help gain information, uncover motives, give information, obtain participation, check understanding, start others thinking, induce agreement and refocus attention.

5 **Read and apply non-verbal communication.** The best message, combined with the best delivery method, can be completely lost if non-verbal communication is incongruent. Focus on forms of non-verbal communication like body language, facial expressions and tone of voice. Even a strong message will lose its meaning if the communicator looks uneasy or unsure. It is important that you read non-verbal cues well. When giving directions, notice how employees receive the direction (hence, read non-verbal cues). Do employees' faces indicate they are confused, frustrated or happily receiving the directions? Does their body language indicate they are tired or uninterested? Adjust your verbal and non-verbal communication to respond to your receiver's non-verbal reactions.

6 **Utilise informal communication channels.** Informal communication channels include the 'grapevine', social gatherings, management by wandering around, and small-group networks. Informal communication channels can be used effectively, or they can lead to damaging situations. For example, management by wandering around gives managers an opportunity to observe and to understand employee morale. However, false rumours spread through the grapevine can unnecessarily damage employee morale.

7 **Clarify other communicators' frames of reference.** For effective communication it is important that each party understands the other's frame of reference. For example, marketing people may view certain issues and goals much differently than do production people. Use questions such as, 'Let me see if I understand your point of view' or 'Have I understood this correctly?' to better understand people's frame of reference.

8 **Be careful with your use of semantics.** Uses of different terms or language (semantics) can lead to confusion when others are not aware of their meaning. Semantics are especially important in international settings where different cultures may have a different meaning for the same word or expression. Try to use specific, generic terms in your communication and request the other party to reflect back your message if you see signals that it may be misinterpreted.

9 **Avoid value judgements.** Value judgements tend to put others on the defensive, or belittle their self-identity. For example, avoid using statement such as, 'That's not a good idea' or 'Only an idiot would think of that!' Try to understand versus evaluate.

10 **Be careful of tendencies to use selective listening.** Filtering out what you do not want to hear from others can cause them to think that you do not care or you never really hear what they are saying. If you appear preoccupied or not receptive to opinions being expressed, negative feelings will surface and damage the quality of communication that is taking place.

11 **Recognise gender differences and communicate appropriately.** The identical message might be most effectively communicated to men through a different channel and using a different technique than it would be communicated to women. A competitive challenge using a sports analogy might motivate a man, while it could alienate a woman, who may prefer less hype and a supportive atmosphere. Take the time to know which technique is most effective with each individual, male or female.

12 **Recognise cultural differences and communicate appropriately.** In cross-cultural situations, assume differences in meaning and understanding until similarity is proven. What you might view as a negative value judgement or a distrustful statement might merely be the result of a language barrier or semantics. Be patient and actively listen. Paraphrase and ask questions like, 'Can you summarise what I have just told you?' 'Did I hear you say ____, and does that mean ____?' Additionally, your usual associations of particular non-verbal cues (body language, facial expressions, etc.) to particular meanings should be discarded. Do not assume anything is the same when communicating with a person of a different culture until you build some experience with that culture. Treat impressions as guesses until the impressions are confirmed.

❓ Questions for study and discussion

1 Explain why you cannot be an effective manager unless you are an effective communicator. How well do you communicate with others now? How can you improve?

2 What are the components of the communication process? Explain how noise can occur within each.

3 What are the barriers to effective communication? How can they be overcome?

4 What is feedback, and why is it such an important factor in effective two-way communication? What can you do to ensure that you transmit productive feedback? How can you get the most out of the feedback you receive?

5 How can questions be used to enhance the communication process? What types of questions are commonly used?

6 What are the benefits of active listening? What poor listening habits do you currently possess? How can your listening skills be enhanced?

7 How can vocal tones reinforce verbal messages?

8 Why is body language such an important part of effective communications? What are the major ways that you can send messages via your body? What common gestures and gesture clusters are you aware of? What do they mean?

9 What are some of the ways in which men and women communicate differently? Why is it important to recognise the differences?

10 In a multicultural environment, what steps can a manager take to reduce cultural misinterpretations?

🔒 Key Concepts

communication, *p. 355*

sender, *p. 357*

receiver, *p. 357*

encoding, *p. 357*

message, *p. 357*

transmission, *p. 357*

channel, *p. 359*

verbal, *p. 359*

non-verbal, *p. 359*

decoding, *p. 360*

noise, *p. 360*

feedback, *p. 360*

grapevine, *p. 364*

frame of reference, *p. 366*

selective listening, *p. 367*

filtering, *p. 368*

credibility, *p. 370*

listening, *p. 375*

proxemics, *p. 382*

Personal skills exercise

Listening to understand problems

Purpose To practise the skills of active listening under difficult communication conditions.

Time 45–50 minutes

Procedure Form groups of three. Each person will take it in turns to play the role of listener, speaker and observer. Decide who will play each role for the first round, then work through the following steps.

1 The speaker chooses an unresolved interpersonal problem to explain to the listener.

2 The speaker explains the problem to the listener and shares his or her personal feelings concerning the problem. (Take no more than 10 minutes.)

3 During this exercise, the listener should attempt to use as many of the active listening skills (attending, paraphrasing, concentrating, and so on) as possible to understand (not solve) the speaker's problem.

4 The observer should remain totally silent during the exercise and take notes on the listener's effective and ineffective listening behaviours.

5 At the conclusion of the exercise, first the observer and then the speaker should give the listener feedback on points they felt indicated effective or ineffective listening skills. (Take no more than 5 minutes for this feedback.)

6 Steps 1 to 5 should be repeated twice more so that each person in the group has a chance to play each role once.

Team exercise

Multicultural communication

Introduction Communicating in a multicultural environment can be difficult. However, in a global business environment, effective managers need to possess the appropriate skills to communicate and manage.

Purpose To practise and experience communication in a multicultural environment.

Time 10 minutes

Procedure Choose a female and a male student to be the 'managers'. The rest of the class will be the 'culture'. Work through the following steps.

1 Inform the two managers that they are going on a foreign assignment into a new culture. They will leave the classroom and, upon re-entry, should attempt to understand the 'cultural rules' of the new environment (there will be three rules). They can utilise any channel of communication and engage with anyone to understand the rules. Have the two managers exit the room.

2 The class now needs to form a new culture with three 'cultural rules'. The rules can be anything, but everyone in the classroom must adhere to them during the exercise. For example, a rule can be 'men talk only to men, women only to women'. Alternatively, a rule could be a 'yes' answer to a question actually means 'no'. Be creative. However, make sure everyone can participate in using the rules. Remember, they are 'cultural'.

3   Once the rules are formed, the instructor should invite the two managers back into the new culture. Allow the two managers about 5 minutes to engage with the new culture to see if they can determine the three cultural rules.

4   Once the first exercise is over (either time has expired or they have figured out the rules), then choose two different managers and repeat the exercise.

5   When you have completed the exercise, hold a class discussion about it. Discuss the following aspects.

   ■ How did the first two managers attempt to figure out the culture? What techniques did they employ? How did they feel during the exercise?

   ■ How did the second two managers attempt to figure out the culture? Did they have more success than the first two? If so, why?

   ■ Incorporate the ideas presented in this chapter about techniques on how to improve cross-cultural communication.

Case study: the team-spirit tailspin

Richard Johnson, newly appointed CEO of Century Airlines, knew the company's survival depended on customer service, which in turn depended on motivated employees. So he created the Century Spirit programme, to build team spirit by encouraging employee participation, individual initiative and open communication. Among the programme's early successes was a newspaper started by a group of flight attendants. The *Plane Truth* published information about benefits and work conditions as well as feature stories and humorous articles. It quickly became popular not only with flight attendants but with pilots, ground crew and baggage handlers.

As time went on, though, the *Plane Truth* began to run articles critical of the company. When management cut back workers' hours, the newspaper questioned what sacrifices the executives were making. When the technical services department released figures showing long turnround times, the paper questioned the ground crew's work ethic.

Worried that customers might see the newspaper, Johnson wanted to cancel it. The president of the flight attendants' union also wanted to see it go because it was stirring up trouble with the ground crew.

Joan Raffin, Century's human resources director, was asked to stop the publication. But she hesitated. She knew that employee morale was on the brink, but she did not know whether the newspaper was venting workers' frustrations and reinforcing team spirit or stirring up old animosities and bringing the whole company down. Was it creating more tension than unity or vice versa?

Questions for managerial action

1   What communication issues are involved at Century Airlines?

2   What communication channels are being utilised?

3   What are the barriers to this communication vehicle?

4   How can this communication channel be used most effectively?

5   What should Joan Raffin do? Why?

Applied questions

6 Look again at the model of interpersonal communication illustrated in Exhibit 8-1. How could Century Airlines utilise such a model to improve communications?

7 The Johari Window can help to identify where there may be problems with communication. Using the Johari Window can you identify where Century Airlines is at present and how it can improve to become more effective at communicating?

WWW exercise

Manager's Internet tools

Web tips: communication on the World Wide Web

The Internet is the fastest-growing tool for communication. Information can be passed on, relayed or found in seconds, which enhances communication efficiency and volume tremendously. However, the Internet may be thought of by some as 'impersonal communication' because direct face-to-face contact is lost, unless communicators are using videoconferencing. Does this imply that one can forget all the effective communication techniques described in this chapter when using the Internet? Absolutely not! Consider why by answering the following questions.

1 What new or additional challenges does the Internet pose to effective communication, and what concepts in this chapter should be applied when using email, chat sessions, or even developing web pages?

2 What aspects of communication are 'lost' or difficult to control over the Internet? How should an effective manager tackle these challenges?

World Wide Web search

There are many sites on the Internet, including many specific companies, devoted to improving communication skills. Using a search engine, find some sites that are targeted to helping develop communication skills. What do these sites and/or companies have to offer, and what are the similarities to the concepts presented in this chapter?

Specific website exercise

Look at some of the following websites:

www.ibm.com
www.zerox.com
www.vodafone.com
www.unilever.com
www.hsbc.com
www.electrolux.co.uk

If you were a non-English speaker how easy would it be for you to use the above websites? You may also try the address with .de, .fr, .it, etc. instead of .com. Are you now able to access the sites in another language?

If your mother tongue is a non-English language, look at www.queenethelburgas.edu. This site has been computer translated. Would it attract you as an overseas student?

LEARNING CHECKLIST ☑

Before you move on you may want to reflect on what you have learnt in this chapter. You should now be able to:

☑ describe the functions, types and directions of communication channels in organisations

☑ identify the barriers to effective communication and know how to avoid them

☑ actively listen and obtain feedback to understand others and to build rapport

☑ read non-verbal communication signals

☑ identify the diversity of communication styles

☑ improve cross-cultural communication

☑ increase the credibility and clarity of the messages you send to others

☑ understand the impact of unethical communication

☑ understand the importance of staying abreast of new communications technology.

Further reading

Hunsaker, P.L. and Cook, C.W. (1986) *Managing Organisational Behaviour*, Reading, MA: Addison-Wesley, p. 216.

Hunsaker, P.L. and Frayne, C.A. (1983) 'More and Better Results through Concentration', *Supervisory Management*, February, pp. 14–19.

McKinnon, C. (2005) 'Challenges Facing the Public Sector', *KM World*, 14(6) pp. 3–4.

Mehrabian, A. (1968) 'Communication without Words', *Psychology Today*, September, pp. 53–55.

Scott, C.R. and Rains, S.A. (2005) 'Anonymous Communication in Organizations: Assessing Use and Appropriateness', *Management Communication Quarterly: McQ* 19(2), November, pp. 157–197.

Tourish, D. (2005) 'Critical Upward Communication: Ten Commandments for Improving Strategy and Decision Making', *Long Range Planning* 38(5), October, p. 485.

Tsai, W.-C., Chen, C.-C. and Chiu, S.-F. (2004) 'Exploring Boundaries of the Effects of Applicant Impression Management Tactics in Job Interviews', *Journal of Management* 31(1), p. 108.

References

Adler, N.J. (1986) *International Dimensions of Organizational Behaviour*, Boston, MA: Kent, p. 53.

Adler, N.J. (1997) *International Dimensions of Organizational Behaviour* (3rd edn). Cincinnati, OH: South-Western College Publishing, pp. 74–75.

Bard, J. and Bradley, P. (1979) 'Styles of Management and Communication: A Comparative Study of Men and Women', *Communication Monographs* 46, pp. 101–111.

Baskin, O.W. and Aronoff, G.E. (1980) *Interpersonal Communication in Organizations*, Santa Monica, CA: Goodyear, p. 2.

Berlo, D.K. (1960) *The Process of Communication*. New York, NY: Holt, Rinehart and Winston.

Brassil, J. (1984) 'Communication in Business: Encouraging Upward Communication', *Pace*, November/December, p. 39.

Certo, S.C. (1991) *Profiles in Quality: Blueprints for Action from 50 Leading Companies*. Boston, MA: Allyn and Bacon, pp. 45–48.

CIPD (2005) 'Pressure at Work and the Psychological Contract', Chartered Institute for Personnel Development.

Cody, M., Marston, P. and Foster, M. (1978) 'Deception: Paralinguistic and Verbal Leakage', in R. Bostrom (ed.) *Communication Yearbook*. Beverly Hills, CA: Sage Publications.

Copeland, L. and Griggs, L. (1985) *Going International*. New York, NY: Random House, p. 103.

Daly, K. and Ibarra, H. (1996) 'Gender Differences in Managerial Behaviour: The Ongoing Debate', in M.C. Gentile (ed.) *Managerial Excellence through Diversity*. Prospect Heights, IL: Waveland Press, p. 32.

Davidow, W. and Malone, T. (1992) *The Virtual Organisation*. New York, NY: Harper and Row.

Davidson, E. (1991) 'Communicating with a Diverse Work Force', *Supervisory Management* 36(12), December, pp. 1–2.

Davis, K. (1953) 'Management Communication and the Grapevine', *Harvard Business Review*, September–October, pp. 43–49.

DeVito, J.A. (1992) *The Interpersonal Communication Book* (6th edn). New York, NY: HarperCollins Publishers, p. 77.

Eakins, B. and Eakins, R. (1978) *Sex Differences in Human Communication*. Boston, MA: Houghton Mifflin Company, pp. 117–119.

Ekman, P. (1993) 'Facial Expression and Emotion', *American Psychologist*, April, pp. 384–392.

Garside, S.G. and Kleiner, B.H. (1991) 'Effective One-to-one Communication Skills', *Industrial & Commercial Training* 23(7), pp. 24–28.

Gibson, J.W. and Hodgetts, R.M. (1986) *Organizational Communication: A Managerial Perspective*. Orlando, FL: Academic Press, p. 95.

Goldhaber, G.M. (1980) *Organizational Communication* (4th edn). Dubuque, IA: William C. Brown, p. 189.

Harris, P. and Moran, R. (1991) *Managing Cultural Differences* (3rd edn). Houston, TX: Gulf Publishing, p. 13.

Hawken, P. (1987) *Growing a Business*. New York, NY: Simon & Schuster.

Howell, A. (1991) 'Communicating for Productivity', *Bobbin* 3(4), December, pp. 20–21.

Hunsaker, J. and Hunsaker, P. (1991) *Strategies and Skills for Managerial Women*. Cincinnati, OH: South-Western Publishing, pp. 252–253.

Hunsaker, P.L. (1984) 'The Space Case', *Registered Representative*, April, pp. 67–72.

Hunsaker, P.L. and Alessandra, A.J. (1986) *The Art of Managing People*. New York, NY: Simon & Schuster, pp. 202–213.

Ibarra, H. (1993) 'Personal Networks of Women and Minorities in Management: A Conceptual Framework', *Academy of Management Review* 18(1), pp. 56–87.

Johns, P. (2005) 'Shades of gray: what is "acceptable and tolerable" in electronic communication?', *RMA Journal* 88(2), October, p. 33.

Johnson, D.W. (1981) *Reaching Out* (2nd edn). Englewood Cliffs, NJ: Prentice Hall, pp. 65–66.

Johnson, M. (1990) *Business Buzzwords*. Cambridge, MA: Blackwell.

Kharbanda, O.P. and Stallworthy, E.A. (1991a) 'Listening: A Vital Negotiating Skill', *Journal of Managerial Psychology* 6(4), pp. 6–9, 49–52.

Kharbanda, O.P. and Stallworthy, E.A. (1991b) 'Verbal and Non-verbal Communication', *Journal of Managerial Psychology* 6(4), pp. 10–13, 49–52.

Kiechel III, W. (1985) 'In Praise of Office Gossip', *Fortune*, 19 August, pp. 253–256.

Kiechel III, W. (1990) 'Breaking the Bad News to the Boss', *Fortune*, 9 April, pp. 111–112.

Knapp, M. and Comadena, M. (1979) 'Telling it Like it Isn't: A Review of Theory and Research on Deceptive Communication', *Human Communication Research* 5, pp. 270–285.

Kraut, R. (1978) 'Verbal and Nonverbal Cues in the Perception of Lying', *Journal of Personality and Social Psychology* 36, pp. 380–391.

Leavitt, H.J. (1972) *Managerial Psychology* (3rd edn). Chicago, IL: University of Chicago Press, pp. 189–196.

Lewis, E. and Spiker, B.K. (1991) 'Tell Me What You Want Me to Do', *Manufacturing Systems* 9(12), December, pp. 46–49.

Luft, J. (1961) 'The Johari Window', *Human Relations and Training News*, January, pp. 6–7.

Luthans, F. and Larsen, J.K. (1986) 'How Managers Really Communicate', *Human Relations*, February, pp. 167–168.

Mancini, J.F. and Kahn, R. (2005) 'Electronic Communication: Policies and Procedures', *AIIM E – Doc Magazine* 19(3), Silver Spring, May/June, p. 8.

Maud, P. (1991) 'Dialogue with Employees: Why Most Well-intentioned Efforts Fail', *Practicing Manager* 11(3), October, pp. 33–36.

Mayer, R.C. and Davis, J.H. (1995) 'An Integrative Model of Organizational Trust', *Academy of Management Review*, July, pp. 709–734.

McLellan, D. (1993) 'That's a Lie', *Los Angeles Times*, 9 February, p. E3.

Mehrabian, A. (1972) *Nonverbal Communication*. Chicago, IL: Aldine/Atherton, pp. 25–30.

Miles, R.E. and Snow, C. (1986) 'Network Organizations: New Concepts and New Forms', *California Management Review* 28(1), pp. 62–73.

Miller, M.W. (1987) 'At Many Firms, Employees Speak a Language That's All Their Own', *Wall Street Journal*, 29 December, p. 15.

Modic, S.J. (1989) 'Grapevine Rated Most Believable', *Industry Week*, 15 May, p. 14.

Nierenberg, G.I. and Calero, H.H. (1973) *How to Read a Person Like a Book*. New York, NY: Pocket Books.

O'Boyle, T.F. and Hymowitz, C. (1985) 'More Corporate Chiefs Seek Direct Contact with Staff, Customers', *Wall Street Journal*, 27 February, pp. 1, 12.

Peters, T. and Waterman, R. (1982) *In Search of Excellence*. New York, NY: Harper & Row, pp. 173–174.

Pincus J.D. (1986) 'Communication Satisfaction, Job Satisfaction, and Job Performance', *Human Communication Research*, Spring, pp. 395–419.

Polsky, H.W. (1971) 'Notes on Personal Feedback in Sensitivity Training', *Sociological Enquiry* 41(2), pp. 175–182.

Porter, W.G. and Griffaton, M.C. (2003) 'Between the Devil and the Deep Blue Sea: Monitoring the Electronic Workplace', *Defense Council Journal* 70(1), January, pp. 65ff.

Putti, J.M., Aryee, S. and Phua, J. (1990) 'Communication Relationship, Satisfaction, and Organisational Commitment', *Group and Organisational Studies*, pp. 44–52.

Rafaeli, A. and Pratt, M.G. (1993) 'Tailored Meanings: On the Meaning and Impact of Organizational Dress', *Academy of Management Review* 18(1), pp. 32–55.

Reece, B.L. and Brandt, R. (1987) *Effective Human Relations in Business* (3rd edn). Boston, MA: Houghton Mifflin, p. 97.

Rogers, E.M. and Agarwala-Rogers, R. (1976) *Communication in Organizations*. New York, NY: Free Press, pp. 10–14.

Rosenthal, R., Archer, D., Koivumaki, J.H. and Rogers, P. (1974) 'Body Talk and Tone of Voice: The Language without Words', *Psychology Today*, September, pp. 64–68.

Salacuse, J. (1991) *Making Global Deals.* Boston, MA: Houghton Mifflin, pp. 14–15.

Schramm, W. (1953) 'How Communication Works', in W. Schramm (ed.) *The Process and Effects of Mass Communication.* Urbana, IL: University of Illinois Press.

Shannon, C. and Weaver, W. (1948) *The Mathematical Theory of Communication.* Urbana, IL: University of Illinois Press.

Simmons, D.B. (1985) 'The Nature of the Organisational Grapevine', *Supervisory Management,* November, pp. 39–42.

Tannen, D. (1991) *You Just Don't Understand: Women and Men in Conversation.* New York, NY: Ballantine Books, pp. 24–25.

Therrien, L. (1985) 'How ZTEL Went from Riches to Rags', *Business Week,* 17 June, pp. 97–100.

Trevino, L.K., Lengel, R.H., Bodensteiner, W., Gerloff, E.A. and Kanoff-Muir, N. (1990) 'The Richness Imperative and Cognitive Style: The Role of Individual Differences in Media Choice Behaviour', *Management Communication Quarterly* 4, pp. 176–197.

TUC (2005) Policy on electronic communication, at www.tuc.org.uk.

Williams, F. (1989) *The New Communications.* Belmont, CA: Wadsworth, p. 45.

Creating productive interpersonal relationships

After studying this chapter you should be able to:

- ☑ **appreciate** the importance of good interpersonal relations at work
- ☑ **understand** the importance of emotional intelligence
- ☑ **appreciate** the impact of personality differences on relationships
- ☑ **assess** interaction climates
- ☑ **recognise** differences in self-disclosure
- ☑ **deal** effectively with male/female differences in work behaviours
- ☑ **understand** the importance of ethics in interpersonal relations
- ☑ **get along better** with people with different interpersonal styles.

The opening vignette show how companies use 'away days' to expose and develop interpersonal skills in an effort to match the right person to the right job.

Fast track: a steep learning curve – want to teach your graduate trainees a lesson? Send them to Lapland

Awaiting my flight at Heathrow last week alongside nine strangers with whom I was expected to 'team-build' over the next four days, I felt scared. It's one thing learning about individual strengths, compensating for weaknesses and improving interpersonal skills in the safe

▶

environment of an office. However, it's quite another when it's beyond the Arctic Circle where snowmobiling is the chief means of transport and temperatures are as low as −20°C.

Nevertheless, an increasing number of graduate recruits are experiencing assessment, development and training in extreme climates. Team Dynamics International – a British company which runs such trips – claims the latter half of the 1990s has seen a huge growth in bookings abroad.

'Employers have one of three objectives,' explains Colin Wallace, director. 'First, they use the trips as a recruitment tool. After all, graduates do not have a record of accomplishment and many employers want something other than interviewing and psychometric testing to reveal for sure true characteristics. Second, the trips are a method of deciding what role would suit the graduates once they have been recruited. Third, they are a means of team-building.' Additionally, of course, it is a perk – a way for an employer to say 'We value you.' Finnish Lapland, for instance, is one of the world's most untouched and exotic regions. One participant asked me: 'Where else are you likely to go this year in which a single afternoon incorporates visiting a husky dog farm, playing snow golf, reindeer sleighing and eating in an ice restaurant?'

The bonus for the firms themselves is that it is not much more expensive a location than Scotland or the Lake District.

But are such trips more than a 'jolly'? Even our first morning (8 a.m. start after arriving at the hotel at 3 a.m. – a theme to be repeated throughout the weekend, although often through choice) suggested they must be.

A series of indoor projects based on tactics for survival – including one exercise involving decisions over how to stay alive in an avalanche – demonstrated that teams consistently made more sound decisions than individuals, even where experts were present.

With this in mind we were deemed ready for the harsher environment outside. Although one last indoor assignment – completing the Myers–Briggs Personality Type Indicator questionnaire – revealed the best and worst each of us would be likely to bring to any given team. For my team the results were particularly interesting since we all had the same profile of being extrovert rather than introvert, feeling rather than thinking, and perceiving rather than judging. The result? We threw ourselves into the afternoon's tasks (getting a team member on top of 14 crates balanced on ice without touching him, and hoisting a team member up a tree while the rest of us were blindfolded) with enthusiasm, taking mistakes in our stride, and ignoring time management.

'All good fun,' laughed our co-ordinator afterwards. 'But what if you worked on a company project in that way?'

Indeed, every group activity over the ensuing days included a review process so comprehensive that each of us was forced to analyse every participant's behaviour and relate it to the office. How could we make our enthusiasm more productive? What individual qualities could be worked on to balance the chaos of the way the group worked?

But cannot such lessons be learned in any location? Kumud, a course participant, believes not. Having attended other programmes back in England, she says: 'The surreal surroundings allow the imagination to think that anything is possible. Also, the clean air and feeling of altitude is uplifting.'

Source: © Kate Hilpern, *Independent*, 8 April 1999.

Discussion questions

1 How useful do you think such an event would be for your development?

2 Do you think it gives an accurate interpretation of a potential employee's future performance?

In the new information era, interpersonal communication is a valuable business tool. Understanding different mindsets, technical backgrounds and cultural perspectives is more crucial than ever for managers today and in the future. To deal effectively with diversity, managers have to be flexible in how they relate to people from different cultures and backgrounds. No one's personal set of behavioural rules will prevail intact in organisations designed to incorporate diversity and still provide a common integrating culture that promotes the organisation's goals.

To make organisations with diverse workforces viable and to be effective leaders, managers need to learn a new respect for differences. As with the opening vignette, employers often use different methods to find out about their employees' interpersonal skills. Pure technical knowledge will only get you so far; beyond that, interpersonal skills become critical and how well are managers equipped to deal with diverse workforces? Probably not nearly as well as required. Consequently, many managers are being sent to away days like those described in the opening vignette. This chapter discusses concepts and skills necessary for successfully managing interpersonal relations with different types of people in organisations.

What influences interpersonal relations?

A Gallup (1991) survey of executives investigated the biggest challenges management will face by the year 2000. The foremost finding was the importance they placed on interpersonal and communication skills. Possessing interpersonal skills was noted more often than any other response by senior and middle-level executives as a sign that a recent hire had the potential to develop into a senior-level executive. Robbins and Hunsaker (1996), in a corresponding finding of this and other studies, found that although interpersonal skills are determined to be essential for management development, they are named more often than any other management skill by recently recruited graduates as the attribute least emphasised in university and development programmes.

Most work either requires or encourages interaction among individuals. The more a job requires two people to work together, the more important becomes the nature of the relationship between them. 'There are lots of brilliant people who can't relate with others,' says Robert LoPresto, an executive recruiter. 'We replace that kind of person every day' (Sanholz, 1987). Even where interaction is only peripheral to the task, relationships can still be a source of satisfaction or frustration and affect the total work effort in many ways. According to Cohen *et al.* (1992), good interpersonal relations support the work effort; bad ones inhibit it. This can be especially true in international situations, as the World Watch box illustrates.

It can be very frustrating trying to figure out all the possible reasons people do or do not get along well together. You have already been introduced in previous chapters to some concepts that can help you understand what contributes to interpersonal differences in perception,

Rule number 1: Don't offend the locals

When deciding whom to assign to an important foreign client, many companies select employees who are aces at technical matters or have an outstanding record in management. A recent study by Prudential Relocation Intercultural Services, a subsidiary of Prudential Insurance, discovered a number of horror stories about such selection criteria. One company sent an evangelical Christian to Saudi Arabia, where he offended locals by setting up a Bible group and got booted out of the country. An American oil company transferred an executive to Peru where he told jokes deriding the natives' industriousness and excluded them from his parties. Indigenous employees complained to government officials, who cancelled the company's oil concession. American multinational companies admit that about 90 per cent of their overseas placements are mistakes primarily due to their employees' failures to adjust properly to a new culture.

Prudential's survey of 72 personnel managers working at multinationals found that 35 per cent agreed that the best trait for overseas success was cultural adaptability, which includes patience, flexibility and tolerance of others' beliefs. Only 22 per cent of the respondents listed technical or managerial skills.

Fortunately, there are a variety of training techniques available to better prepare people for intercultural work. They include: (1) reading programmes to expose people to the country's socio-political history, geography, economics and cultural institutions; (2) cultural assimilators who expose trainees to specific incidents critical to successful interaction with a target culture; (3) language preparation; (4) sensitivity training to increase people's self-awareness; and (5) exposing trainees to mini-cultures within their own country during short field exercises.

Sources: 'Rule Number 1: Don't Diss the Locals', *Business Week*, 15 May 1995, p. 8; and P. Christopher Earley (1987) 'Intercultural Training for Managers: A Comparison of Documentary and Interpersonal Methods', *Academy of Management Journal* 30, August, pp. 685–698.

Discussion questions

1 How important is it to understand the culture before working in another country?

2 How can training help overcome these problems?

---

motivation and communication. This chapter focuses on emotional intelligence, personal, behavioural and situational factors that can create difficulties in relationships. Strategies for effectively managing interpersonal relationships are also described.

Emotional intelligence

emotional intelligence
A person's ability to be aware of personal emotions and those of others in order to interact with others in productive ways.

Emotional intelligence (EQ) is very different from the common intelligence measure IQ. While IQ measures intellectual ability, EQ focuses on interpersonal and communication skills. Fisher (1998) suggests that emotional competence includes a large number of attributes such as self-awareness, impulse control, persistence, confidence, self-motivation, empathy, social deftness, trustworthiness, adaptability and the ability to work collaboratively.

In today's business world, the importance of EQ is overriding sheer intellectual ability for many managers and high-level personnel. The more people one must interact with, the more important interpersonal and communication skills become. Think of a manager who must lead a project team of diverse people. That manager may possess all the technical knowledge sufficient to complete tasks. However, it is of extreme importance for the team's success that the manager be able to lead, understand and 'connect with people', and know how to conduct himself or herself in both positive and negative situations. A recent study of what characteristics corporations are seeking in MBA candidates revealed that the three most desirable traits are communication skills, interpersonal skills and initiative. All three of these traits are part of one's emotional intelligence.

Although it is important to understand what emotional intelligence is, it is more important to understand how one can continually improve one's interpersonal skills. As one ascends into higher management positions, the degree of interaction with other people increases. Additionally, the ability to lead and obtain a consensus increases dramatically. While technical skills and fundamental business skills are important and serve as a decision basis, one's ability to articulate ideas and build rapport and trust will be of increasing importance. A manager's success will largely be dependent upon his or her interpersonal skills, hence emotional intelligence (see the Technology Transformation box on the importance of interpersonal skills in a technology environment). To get an estimate of your own EQ, complete the 'What's your emotional intelligence at work?' inventory, adapted from Weisinger (1998), in the 'Your turn' exercise.

Managers who are attuned to their own feelings and the feelings of others can use their understanding to enhance the performance of themselves and others in their organisation. Murray (1998), Fisher (1998) Goleman (1998) and Daft (1999) have identified the five basic components of emotional intelligence most important for managers, these are discussed below. Review the following discussion of the five components of emotional intelligence, and think about what you might do to develop those areas where your score was low.

Self-awareness

This is the basis for all the other components of emotional intelligence. Self-awareness means being aware of what you are feeling, being conscious of the emotions within yourself. People who are in touch with their emotions are better able to guide their own lives. Managers need to be in touch with their emotions in order to interact effectively and appreciate emotions in others. Managers with high levels of self-awareness learn to trust their 'gut feelings' and realise that these feelings can provide useful information about difficult decisions. Answers are not always clear about who is at fault when problems arise or when to let an employee go, reorganise a business or revise job responsibilities. In these situations managers have to rely on their own feelings and intuition.

Managing emotions

The second key component of emotional intelligence is managing emotions. Operationally this means the manager is able to balance his or her own moods so that worry, anxiety, fear or anger do not get in the way of what needs to be done. Managers who can manage their emotions perform better because they are able to think clearly. Weisinger (1998) suggests that managing emotions does not mean suppressing or denying them, but understanding them and using that understanding to deal with situations productively. Managers should first recognise a mood or feeling, think about what it means and how it affects them, and then choose how to act.

IT experts need mobility

In the 1980s computer-related careers seemed a fairly safe bet. The proliferation of computers in the workplace would create a continuing demand for specialists with up-to-date knowledge of equipment, able to design and implement systems for specific industries.

However, at the start of the 1990s the number of computing jobs advertised plummeted, seemingly as a result of the recession. As Chris Phillips, deputy director of Manchester University Careers Service, says: 'The majority of computing jobs in this country are service jobs and they rely on other organisations investing and re-investing in new technology. Organisations were not able to invest that money.' That has now been reversed and Phillips claims the industry has shown more growth in graduate opportunities than any other over the past 12 months. Expansion still lies within software and services but as the leisure market grows and technology enters all areas of industry, workers of all disciplines and skill levels are in demand.

Computer science courses are run by most universities although programming languages and specialisations vary. Technology-based BSc courses range from artificial intelligence at Birmingham to informatics at Anglia and software engineering at Edinburgh. Entrance criteria relate to course content but previous programming experience is not expected. All courses include some mathematics – algebra, numerical analysis or combinatorics.

Postgraduate MSc and research courses are available for graduates in technology and for those new to the discipline. Specialist courses may demand a strong scientific background but one-year conversion courses are available for graduates in the arts, humanities and social sciences who have little computing experience. Giving a basic grounding in IT application, rather than how it works, these courses are ideal for graduates who wish to combine technology with their previous area of study.

The growth in home and business computing enabled the Granville Technology Group to expand rapidly from a Burnley cornershop at the end of the 1980s to today's 120 000-square-foot warehouse. A microcosm of the industry itself, the workforce has tripled in the last two years to 320 staff who assemble, package, sell and support computers.

Made up of six different companies, each targeting services and products to discrete markets, practically everything is done in-house.

During its expansion, Granville identified a lack of skills among the local workforce. A partnership was established between Granville and the Burnley ITeC (one of 22 Information Technology Centres) allowing employees to attend college on day release. Newcomers take courses on software, hardware and components.

ITeC's Sue Goodbrand, whose job is to liaise with companies, says the relationship means classroom theory is put into practice on site. Training at Granville always had the feeling of an apprenticeship and now the pooling of resources between the ITeC and East Lancashire TEC means the company is the first to offer an official Modern Apprenticeship in computing, recognised by the government scheme aimed at the young jobless, taking staff to NVQ Level 3.

Ian Wilson, the company's human resources officer, says Granville's size means employees can be developed through many areas of the business. An appraisal system identifies strengths and weaknesses and possible career moves.

Knowledge of how a computer fits together, gained on the assembly line where recruits begin, provides a base on which to build other skills – reconditioning machines, handling customer enquiries or managing component stock. The company is able to encourage and nurture future management material from any part of the company.

While computer knowledge is necessary, interpersonal skills make a successful career. New products and techniques can be learned but if that knowledge is not applied in the right manner it is useless. 'Personality is essential when you're dealing with the public,' notes Wilson. 'You have to create the right impression so you can respond to their needs.'

Paul Honour discovered this while helping to recruit for Logica, an international software consultancy. 'I thought there was no such thing as a Logica person – it requires such a broad range of abilities – but when I started interviewing it became obvious who would fit in and who wouldn't.'

The key again was personality. Would they be happy at Logica and work within a team? Honour is perfectly placed to assess candidates but does not work in personnel. He joined Logica around five years ago and is now in transport. Giving recruitment responsibility to a relatively new employee may seem a radical move but the personnel department ultimately benefits from the opinions of someone who has recently experienced their first years in the company.

Throughout the recession Logica continued to take on graduates and now recruits 300 to 400 each year. Jim McKenna, group head of personnel, argues this high level of recruitment reflects the fact that graduates are its primary source of new employees. Had it also reduced its profile in universities, consequent recruitment may have been jeopardised.

Recruits are not taken exclusively from scientific and computing backgrounds, although there must be clear evidence of competency. Each recruit is assigned to one of nine divisions.

Recruits are given responsibility at an early stage. Laure De Herrypon, a mathematics graduate, joined the broadcasting division in 1994 and four months later found herself designing an automated TV system for a new station in Paris.

'I was involved in the design, the coding, testing the product and support work – every stage,' she says. 'It's so exciting you don't realise how much you're learning while you're doing it.' Having pioneered the system, the implementation and training programme, she has opened a further three stations across Europe and will continue globe-trotting as further clients are secured.

Immediate responsibility means interpersonal skills are an imperative. The company may employ 3700 people but, for her clients, De Herrypon is Logica. McKenna also stresses the importance of developing employees' marketing and financial skills at this early stage. De Herrypon went to Logica on a work placement during a postgraduate computer conversion course and was later offered a full-time contract. In the 18 months since she arrived, Logica has recognised her expertise in TV systems, even using her to advise on the in-house television information service.

Paul Honour, although now helping with recruitment, has, over the years, worked on larger and more long-term projects. His work destroys the image of the computer boffin shackled to his machine in an office. Leading Logica staff in implementing traffic control systems at the Channel Tunnel, he spent many days directing traffic around the Folkestone site in rain and snow, observing how the automated system of barriers and lights performed. Working conditions were difficult and the number of subcontractors and contractors made identifying personal responsibilities problematic. 'Everything was done by consensus,' explains Honour. 'If something wasn't working we just fixed it rather than sort out whose responsibility it was.'

▶ Honour clearly revels in the experience, knowledge and trust this kind of teamwork provides. The depth of involvement in a client's work is exemplified in the case of one project for Ford where Logica workers won internal quality awards.

But working in and out of short-term projects does not suit everyone. Some people need the security of a single employer and location. Honour says staff have to cope with a sense of loss when a project is completed: 'You feel a little bit desperate. It's like a divorce – you've been concentrating on one thing for so long and then it's not there any more.'

The project model of working may appear completely unstructured and a nightmare to navigate for employees and personnel managers alike. Employees have ultimate responsibility for what they will do but the structure can make this difficult and career development seem intangible. Logica provides every employee with a staff or resource manager to advise on the projects and experiences they should be accumulating.

Updates on future and current projects are circulated to project managers and opportunities are advertised on the in-house TV information service. Employees can apply for any project that interests them and if they need new skills in order to participate they can take the necessary course.

The company delivers an average of six training days per employee per year. There is another, informal way of joining a project team: 'Managers will say, "I'm going to bid for this project so I want these members of staff",' explains McKenna.

He is confident the company can offer new challenges rather than losing staff. This can mean changing roles from one division to another, from one part of a project to another, or even from one country to another. Perfect mobility benefits the client, the company and the employee.

Paul Honour found involvement in the initial research and bidding stages of a project particularly refreshing: 'It's really good fun. You have four or five people thinking up whacky technical solutions to problems and then phoning people up to see if their equipment will do what you want. The advantage we have is the ability to take that expertise wherever it is needed worldwide.' Retaining that asset also means creating an attractive and supporting culture for staff. The plethora of social and sporting activities within Logica are now administered by a dedicated full-time member of staff.

Both Granville and Logica's working culture reflect the business in which they work. Technological advances take place constantly and new skills, ideas and products must be swiftly assimilated.

'In an environment where 90 per cent of our staff are on projects being formed or dissolved, you don't want a rigid structure that could easily fall over,' explains Jim McKenna. 'Technology changes quickly and you need a structure which reflects that.'

Source: © Guardian Newspapers Ltd, 1996, Simon Kent.

Discussion questions

1 Is it important for technology workers to have good interpersonal skills?

2 How important is Logica's appraisal scheme in employee development?

Your turn

What's your emotional intelligence at work? (Weisinger, 1998)

For each item below, rate how well you are able to display the ability described. Before responding, try to think of actual situations in which you have had the opportunity to use the ability.

	Very low ability		Moderate ability		Very high ability
1 Associate different internal physiological cues with different emotions.	1	2	3	4	5
2 Relax when under pressure in situations.	1	2	3	4	5
3 'Gear up' at will for a task.	1	2	3	4	5
4 Know the impact that your behaviour has on others.	1	2	3	4	5
5 Initiate successful resolution of conflict with others.	1	2	3	4	5
6 Calm yourself quickly when angry.	1	2	3	4	5
7 Know when you are becoming angry.	1	2	3	4	5
8 Regroup quickly after a setback.	1	2	3	4	5
9 Recognise when others are distressed.	1	2	3	4	5
10 Build consensus with others.	1	2	3	4	5
11 Know what senses you are currently using.	1	2	3	4	5
12 Use internal 'talk' to change your emotional state.	1	2	3	4	5
13 Produce motivation when doing uninteresting work.	1	2	3	4	5
14 Help others manage their emotions.	1	2	3	4	5
15 Make others feel good.	1	2	3	4	5
16 Identify when you experience mood shifts.	1	2	3	4	5
17 Stay calm when you are the target of anger from others.	1	2	3	4	5
18 Stop or change an ineffective habit.	1	2	3	4	5
19 Show empathy to others.	1	2	3	4	5
20 Provide advice and emotional support to others as needed.	1	2	3	4	5
21 Know when you become defensive.	1	2	3	4	5
22 Know when you are thinking negatively and head it off.	1	2	3	4	5
23 Follow your words with actions.	1	2	3	4	5
24 Engage in intimate conversation with others.	1	2	3	4	5
25 Accurately reflect people's feelings back to them	1	2	3	4	5

Scoring Add your responses to the 25 questions to obtain your overall emotional intelligence score. Your score for *self-awareness* is the total of questions 1, 6, 11, 16 and 21. Your score for *managing emotions* is the total of questions 2, 7, 12, 17 and 22. Your score for *motivating oneself* is the sum of questions 3, 8, 13, 18 and 23. Your score for *empathy* is the sum of questions 4, 9, 14, 19 and 24. Your score for *social skill* is the sum of questions 5, 10, 15, 20 and 25.

Interpretation This questionnaire provides an indication of your emotional intelligence. If you received a total score of 100 or more, you have high emotional intelligence. A score from 50 to 100 means you have a good platform of emotional intelligence from which to develop your managerial capability. A score below 50 indicates that you realise you are probably below average in emotional intelligence. For each of the five components of emotional intelligence – self-awareness, managing emotions, motivating oneself, empathy, and social skill – a score above 20 is considered high, while a score below 10 would be considered low.

Motivating oneself

This is the ability to be hopeful and optimistic despite obstacles, setbacks or even outright failure. This ability is crucial for pursuing long-term goals in life or in business. A classic example of this occurred when the Metlife insurance company hired a special group of job applicants who tested high on optimism but failed the normal sales aptitude test. Compared to salespeople who passed the regular aptitude test but scored high on pessimism, the 'optimistic' group made 21 per cent more sales in their first year and 57 per cent more in the second (Gibbs, 1995).

Empathy

The fourth component is empathy, which means being able to put yourself in someone else's shoes, to recognise what others are feeling without them needing to tell you. Most of the time people do not tell us what they feel in words but rather in tone of voice, body language and facial expression. Empathy is built from self-awareness; being attuned to one's own emotions makes it easier to read and understand the feelings of others.

Social skill

The ability to connect with others, build positive relationships, respond to the emotions of others and influence others is the final component of emotional intelligence. Managers need social skills to understand interpersonal relationships, handle disagreements, resolve conflicts and pull people together for a common purpose.

Personality factors

When trying to understand your feelings and behaviours, it helps to be aware that how you think and feel about yourself and others may be very unlike how they think and feel about themselves and you. These different evaluations and reactions depend on each individual's self-concept, frame of reference, defences, interpersonal relationship needs and feelings.

Self-concept

Starting with messages from parents, which are later reinforced by significant others, you learn to view and evaluate yourself in a certain way. The identity and evaluation of yourself that you come to accept is your **self-concept**, which may be anything from essentially positive ('I am worthwhile') to negative ('I am worthless'). You protect yourself from any attempts to change your self-concept, even if your view of yourself is a painful one.

self-concept
Our perception and evaluation of ourselves.

Even if not ideal, your self-concept allows you to cope, and it is safer to hold on to something known than to let go and take the risk of something new. Yet feedback occurs and learning takes place, causing you to choose between the need to know and the fear of knowing about yourself, especially if the knowledge may force you to change your self-concept.

Through observation and interaction, you learn what significant others think is important. The messages about how you 'ought' to feel and behave become your guiding values for later interactions. You also learn what you 'ought' to want to achieve, such as graduation from college or freedom from responsibility. Finally, you learn certain techniques that are acceptable to your significant others to gain their approval. These beliefs about what behaviours, feelings, goals and techniques are desirable become internalised into your **value system**.

value system
Internalised beliefs about what behaviour, feelings, goals and techniques are desirable.

Research focus: the A-B model

The A-B model developed by Turner and Lombard (1969) and shown in Exhibit 9-1 illustrates the chain of rapid events that occur between two interacting people.

Both parties have *needs* they want to satisfy and sets of *values* indicating the most desirable ways of doing so. Sometimes needs are satisfied through defence mechanisms that protect established self-concepts and frames of reference regardless of their current appropriateness. Based on past experiences, both people also make *assumptions* about the nature of the other and of the particular kind of situation they are in (e.g. competitive or co-operative). Each person develops positive or negative *feelings* that contribute to enhanced or diminished *perceptions* of self, the other, and the current situation. These perceptions contribute to *evaluations* of the other person in this situation and lead to the formulation of *intentions* to interact in specific ways to accomplish personal objectives. The *consequences* of that behaviour and subsequent *interactions* generate new input for another loop of reactions.

Relationships tend to be *reciprocal* in nature, meaning that one person will most often treat another the same way he or she is, or expects to be, treated by that person. In enduring productive relationships, people expect positive reciprocity – an exchange of benefits in their interpersonal transactions. For example, physical and mental efforts may be 'traded' for money or recognition. Help and kindness may be exchanged for affection and respect. The exchange need not be equal, but unless it is perceived as fair by both parties, tension will probably rise.

reciprocity
The exchange of benefits in interpersonal transactions.

On the other hand, if A assumes that B perceives him or her negatively, A may feel diminished, causing him or her to perceive B negatively and interact with B accordingly. Even if A's first assumption was incorrect, his or her subsequent behaviour may make this incorrect assumption come true and a negatively reciprocal relationship may emerge. Many times the stage is set for a particular type of reciprocity by various personality factors or pre-existing interaction climates.

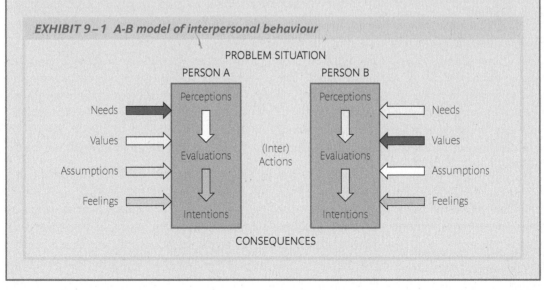

EXHIBIT 9–1 A-B model of interpersonal behaviour

Personal frame of reference

personal frame of reference
How we see the world based upon our past experiences and self-concept.

As discussed in Chapter 4, your self-concept and perceptions of other people and things develop into a **personal frame of reference** for perceiving and interpreting experiences. Two people with different frames of reference may do very different things in the same situation to try to satisfy the same needs. For example, two students in a highly interactive seminar may perceive the emphasis on participation very differently. One who has been praised for contributing in classes in the past may feel comfortable and view the situation as potentially rewarding. The other, who has had past class contributions rejected and ridiculed, however, may see the class as very threatening. Consequently, to protect and enhance their self-concepts, these two students are likely to behave in opposite ways in the seminar.

Frames of reference are abstractions of reality, and everyone sees reality differently because of different needs and past experiences. Furthermore, new experiences and changing needs keep the reality changing somewhat. It is very difficult to understand how others perceive their world, especially since we tend to filter their behaviour through our own unique frame of reference. Our actions are logical to us given our frame of reference, but so are other people's different behaviours to them, although they may not make sense to us because of their alternative perception of the situation.

Cultural backgrounds are a frequent source of different frames of reference. Paul Nolan is director of corporate training for the Lincoln Savings Bank, which has a diverse employee mix including young and old men and women who are Mediterranean, Chinese, Asian, African-Caribbean and Arabic. After going through a number of multicultural training sessions, he believes that he is a better manager. 'I've always seen life through white, male eyes,' he says. 'Even now, when I speak to white males, I'm very structured, very aggressive, succinct. But if I were talking to a Chinese person, I'd ask open-ended questions, such as "Tell me what you think about this" instead of "This is what I think"; I've learned that others can perceive me as "this white man telling me what to do".' Nolan's new, more flexible approach has dramatically increased the participation rate of minorities on the staff (Edwards, 1991). The Dynamics of Diversity box illustrates how managing emotions is a global issue.

To understand others, you need to understand their frames of reference without judging them in terms of your own values. This does not mean that you must accept for yourself the means they are using to satisfy their needs. Nor should you expect others to always accept your own behaviour as the most satisfying for them. But you can benefit from continuously exploring with others your own perception of reality compared to theirs. Failure to be accepting and understanding can cause defensiveness, inhibit personal growth and cause conflicts.

Defensiveness

defence
A cognitive distortion that protects the self-concept against being diminished.

One response to an interpersonal encounter that threatens your self-concept or frame of reference is to apply one or more psychological defences. A **defence** is a cognitive distortion that protects the self-concept from being diminished. Defensiveness occurs when you protect yourself by denying, excusing or rationalising your actions to protect your self-concept against the threat of being damaged by failure, guilt, shame or fear.

All defence mechanisms involve a degree of distortion of the true relationships between the individual and external reality. Although defence mechanisms provide some relief from tension and anxiety, they do not satisfy underlying needs. Individuals learn defence mechanisms at an early age and continue to use those that have worked for them in the past. According to Costley

Why workers need to have feelings

If you want to get ahead in business nowadays, you will need more than a head. Research shows you will need a heart as well.

That's the theory behind the growing focus on 'emotional intelligence' as a key tool for workplace success. Fans of the classic British 1970s television comedy *Fawlty Towers* know all about a manager who lived life on a short fuse. It portrayed stressed-out hotel owner, Basil Fawlty, forever infuriated by the apparent stupidity of his staff and guests.

This raises the issue of the need to understand the role of emotions in the workplace. Mr Fawlty might have been well educated, but he never quite managed to understand or control his own emotions.

Personal development trainer Cheryl Buggy says that process is surprisingly important.

'While we like to think we're thinking, rational human beings, we're actually primarily motivated by our feelings, our emotions,' she says. 'The success of any organisation will often be down to the relationships people are having within that organisation with each other, and then with clients.'

So a growing number of employers are selecting and training staff by looking not just at skills and qualifications, but 'emotional intelligence'. The phrase covers a basket of personality traits including self-control, trustworthiness, conscientiousness, adaptability and innovation – and it seems to have a real cash value.

Many organisations are now noticing that emotional intelligence is good for business.

One company that has turned to emotional intelligence to test candidates is cosmetics giant L'Oréal. It found that sales staff chosen on emotional intelligence sold goods worth almost $100 000 (£62 000) a year more than their colleagues, and far fewer left their jobs early. This is because people with emotional intelligence 'are more likely to be proactive than reactive,' says Ms Buggy.

For this reason, it could be worth companies learning not just how to spot emotional intelligence but how to foster it. Lack of motivation 'really does hold you back and therefore could hold an organisation back,' she says.

It is not only in the UK that emotional intelligence is an issue. In Hong Kong, a series of workshops has been looking for ways to develop new skills in its workforce of the future.

Ms Buggy says the authorities there are 'rather concerned' that academically well-qualified graduates might still lack vital skills for commercial success – such as innovation, flexibility, creativity, and the ability to anticipate and solve problems.

'I certainly got the feeling that there was concern that the education system in China and in Hong Kong wasn't producing those sorts of graduates,' she says.

One Hong Kong parent who agrees with this diagnosis is Florence Leung, who works for tobacco company Philip Morris. She is determined that her seven-year-old daughter Joyce will emerge from school with more than academic qualifications.

'I think those people who can communicate well . . . who have good integrational skills and show respect for other people, those are people who can really accomplish more in the workplace,' she says.

dynamics of diversity

▶ She is concerned that children 'don't actually learn a lot of these skills from school'.

Add emotional intelligence skills to your qualifications, get in touch with your feelings and those of your colleagues, and get ahead.

Source: adapted from Chris Carnegy, BBC World Service business reporter,
www.bbc.co.uk/business.

Discussion questions

1 What is the solution for the workforce of the twenty-first century?
2 Can emotional intelligence be taught?

and Todd (1987), defence mechanisms affect the way individuals relate to each other and the way they understand and adapt to their relationships. Some of the more common defences are summarised in Exhibit 9-2.

Defences alleviate painful feelings, but they fail to deal with the causes of the problem. If overused, defences can be dysfunctional because they inhibit individual growth and interactions with others. Defensiveness may distort ideas, obscure solutions or hinder interpersonal communication. Individuals can respond non-defensively by acknowledging and accepting the threatening event and then attempting to cope with it by eliminating or moderating their behaviour. One way to avoid your own defensive behaviour is to acknowledge what is being said as at least partially true. If you are frequently late, for example, and someone criticises you for it, you could simply acknowledge, 'Yes, I often am late' as opposed to trying to convince the other person that you are really not always late or that there are always good reasons why you are late.

One way to reduce another person's defensiveness is to use active listening, as described in Chapter 8. This means using verbal and non-verbal responses to show that you are listening non-judgementally to truly understand the other person. By reflecting back your perception of the other's concerns in a non-judgemental way, he or she may feel safe and understood enough to reduce defences.

Interpersonal relationship needs

Schutz (1958) contends that people have three dominant interpersonal needs. The first is *inclusion* – the need to establish and maintain relationships with other people. Inclusion concerns balancing the desire to be part of a group against the desire for solitude. The second is *control* – the need to maintain a satisfactory balance of power and influence in relationships. Control concerns trade-offs between the desires for structure and authority versus the desire for freedom. Finally, there is the need for *affection* – the need to form close and personal relationships with others. Affection concerns balancing desires for warmth and commitment against those for maintaining distance and independence.

Each of these three needs has two subdimensions – the *expressed* desire to give, or impose the need on others, and the *wanted* desire to receive the need from others; for example, the need to invite or include others in our activities, and the need to be invited and included in others' activities. These three interpersonal needs and their two subdimensions are illustrated in Exhibit 9-3. Complete the 'Your turn' exercise to determine the relative strengths of your interpersonal needs.

If you have strong interpersonal needs, you desire to interact with others and are probably outgoing and gregarious. If you have low interpersonal needs, you may not mind being alone and are more reserved around others. Hill (1974) found that typically, marketing and human

EXHIBIT 9–2 Common defence mechanisms

Defence	Psychological process	Illustration
Rationalisation 'Everybody does it.'	Justifying behaviours and feelings that are undesirable by providing explanations that make them acceptable.	You pad your expense account because 'everybody does it'.
Repression 'Motivated forgetting'	'Forgetting' painful and frustrating events by unconsciously putting them out of your memory.	You 'forget' to tell the boss about an embarrassing error you made because you feel guilty.
Reaction-formation 'Methinks the lady doth protest too much.'	Repressing unacceptable urges and exhibiting the opposite attitudes and behaviours.	The manager who represses the desire to have an affair with his secretary crusades against such activities.
Projection 'It's all your fault.'	Protecting yourself from awareness of your own undesirable traits or feelings by attributing them to others.	In a crisis, the manager tells employees not to panic, to hide his own undesirable feelings of panic.
Regression 'Disneyland, here I come.'	Responding to frustration by reverting to earlier and less mature forms of behaviour; attempting to go back to a more comfortable time.	A manager who cannot get approval for an additional secretary begins typing, filing and doing other activities more appropriate for subordinates.
Displacement 'Kick the dog who bites the cat.'	Redirecting pent-up emotions towards persons other than the primary source of the emotion.	You roughly reject a simple request from a subordinate after receiving a rebuff from the boss.
Compensation 'Tit for tat.'	Engaging in a substitute behaviour to make up for a feeling of inadequacy.	A manager who is not advancing professionally works very hard on volunteer activities.
Denial 'It ain't true.'	Refusing to absorb threatening information.	You are unwilling to accept that others see you as hostile when you are pressed for time.
Withdrawal 'If I'm not here, I don't have to deal with it.'	Physically or mentally leaving a situation that produces anxiety, conflict or frustration.	A person's idea is rejected by a committee, so he is either absent from future meetings or fails to participate.
Resignation 'If I got to do it, I got to do it, but not ' too well.	Withholding any sense of emotional or personal involvement in an unpleasant situation.	An employee who hasn't received praise no longer cares whether or not he does a good job.
Conversion 'It makes me hurt so bad.'	Transforming emotional conflicts into physical symptoms.	A salesman about to meet with a client who is anticipated to say no experiences a headache.
Counterdependence 'You can't make me.'	Suppressing feelings of dependence and expressing hostile independence.	A boss feeling confused and lost rudely rejects help from subordinates.
Aggression 'The best defence is a good offence.'	Instigating a hostile attack on another because you are frustrated or uncomfortable.	A manager makes a sarcastic remark to an employee who has just made a minor error.

Sources: adapted from Timothy W. Costello and Sheldon S. Zalkind (1963) *Psychology in Administration: A Research Orientation*, pp. 148–149. Reprinted by permission of Prentice Hall, Inc., Upper Saddle River, NJ; and D.I. Costley and R. Todd (1987) *Human Relations in Organizations*. St Paul, MN: West Publishing, pp. 232–235.

Your turn

What are your relationship needs?

Instructions Allocate between 0 and 9 points to indicate the degree to which each of the following six questions applies to you (where 0 = not at all and 9 = completely).

_____ 1 I like to invite people to join social activities.

_____ 2 I feel badly when other people do things without inviting me to join them.

_____ 3 I try to have other people do things the way I want them done.

_____ 4 Other people's preferences strongly influence my behaviour.

_____ 5 I try to develop close personal relationships with people.

_____ 6 I like people to act close and personal towards me.

_____ **Total points**

Scoring Add up the number of points for the six questions to determine your total interpersonal needs score. Your score will fall somewhere between 0 and 54. The point allocations to each of the six questions reveals the relative strengths of your interpersonal needs as follows: 1 – expressed inclusion; 2 – wanted inclusion; 3 – expressed control; 4 – wanted control; 5 – expressed affection; 6 – wanted affection. You can write these in the boxes in Exhibit 9-3 to visually depict the relative strengths of your interpersonal needs.

Interpretation There is no 'right' score. The value of this information is that it lets you know the relative strength of your own interpersonal needs. The average person, according to national studies, discussed by Whetton and Cameron (1995), has a total score of 29. Your highest scores on individual questions indicate which interpersonal needs are least satisfied and probably dominate your relationships with others.

Source: developed by Phillip L. Hunsaker for class discussion, University of San Diego, 1995.

EXHIBIT 9 – 3 Fundamental interpersonal relationship orientations

Behaviours	Interpersonal needs		
	Inclusion	Control	Affection
Expressed towards others	I want others to join me	I take charge and influence others	I get close to others
Wanted from others	I want others to include me	I want others to lead me	I want others to get close to me

resource graduates in business schools may have stronger interpersonal needs than accounting and systems analysis students. This indicates that students with higher interpersonal needs tend to select people-orientated careers, and vice versa. The findings do not necessarily predict success as a manager, however, because that depends to a large degree on the types of work and people you are supervising.

Research by DiMarco (1974) and Liddell and Slocum (1976) found that the degree of need compatibility between two or more people can make the difference between a happy and productive team and a dissatisfied and ineffective one. If one person has a high need to express dominance and control, and another has a high need to receive direction, they are likely to get along well. On the other hand, if they both have high needs to express dominance and low needs to receive it, conflict is probable. The key is whether the important needs of each person are complementary and to what degree they are satisfied in the relationship. Robbins and Hunsaker (1996) suggest that compatible individuals usually like each other more and work better together. Awareness of differences in interpersonal needs can help you adapt your own behaviours to let others satisfy their needs, which can enhance your relationships with them.

Feelings

People continually experience feelings about themselves and others, but many have not learned to accept and use feelings constructively. How you express feelings is a frequent source of difficulty in interpersonal relationships. Problems arise not because emotions are present, but because they are not used well. Rather than express them constructively, people often deny or ignore their own and others' feelings in an attempt to avoid rejection or struggle for control.

For example, you may have experienced immediate rapport or dislike towards someone you have only just met. What you are feeling has to do with things about the other person and yourself that you are only unconsciously aware of (O'Connell, 1994). Immediate liking for a person you have just met is often caused by seeing in them things you like in yourself, or traits you would like to have but don't, like charm or humour.

It is the negative reactions that can cause the most problems, however, especially if they are directed at a person you will be interacting with for a long time, like your boss or a co-worker. Therefore, it is important to try to understand what caused your reaction and why. It may be that the other person has characteristics that remind you of someone in the past who brought you pain. Alternatively, it might be that the person triggers awareness of your 'shadow self' – that is, parts of yourself that you are not aware of because you do not like them. Being egotistical, 'wimpy' or aggressive may be behaviours you repress in yourself, and seeing someone else who dares to act in these ways can cause negative reactions.

O'Connell (1994) suggests that maintaining a productive relationship requires that you first look at yourself to understand what it is about you that is causing the negative feelings. You may then see that it is not really the other person you do not like, but a particular characteristic that you also have yourself. Then you may be able to overlook the characteristic in the other, as you do in yourself. If self-analysis is not enough, it can be helpful to tactfully express personal feelings so that you and the other party can try to work out potential difficulties in a productive way.

Interaction setting

Often, what appear to be personality changes may just be two people's varying responses to different and incompatible job requirements. This frequently happens when people work in different parts of the organisation, under different organisational cultures, for different bosses, and in different jobs that make different demands.

Job requirements

Job requirements determine how psychologically close or distant two people need to be to perform their work. The depth of interpersonal relationships required by a job depends on how complex the task is, whether the people involved possess different kinds of expertise, the frequency of interaction in the job, and the degree of certainty with which job outcomes can be predicted (Cohen *et al.*, 1992).

Bennis *et al.* (1973) contend that work situations that are simple and familiar to both workers, may not require strong feelings, demand little interaction and have a high certainty of outcomes, call for minimal task relationships. Complex situations that require different knowledge from each person, high trust, much interaction, and have an uncertain outcome, may call for more intense interpersonal relationships and teamwork. An example of a minimal task relationship would be an operating room nurse and a surgeon, whose only required exchange is with regard to information about the patient's welfare and the surgeon's need for instruments. Teamwork requires that people collaborate in a complex task situation demanding trust and mutual support, as when two police detectives are attempting to arrest an armed criminal.

Organisational culture

As will be discussed in Chapter 16, the organisation's culture influences the general nature of employee relationships. People take cues from the culture they work in and usually respond to what they perceive as general expectations. Some cultures discourage intimacy and allow only distant, impersonal relationships. The more culture fosters competitiveness, aggressiveness and hostility, the greater the likelihood that people will be cautious and on guard with each other. Other cultures encourage family-like closeness. Steele and Jenks (1977) suggest that the more sociable and personal the culture, the more people are likely to share non-work information and feelings, while Golembiewski (1972) argues that different interaction patterns can be distinguished by the following four primary factors.

1 *Openness* is the degree to which participants share their thoughts and feelings with others.

2 *Trust* is the degree to which you believe someone else is honest and supportive.

3 *Owning* refers to taking responsibility for a problem to which you are a contributor versus blaming someone else.

4 *Risk to experiment* is the degree to which you are punished for trying something new, especially if it fails, versus doing things in safe, approved-of ways.

regenerative interaction patterns
Co-operative and caring relationships that promote openness, trust, rapport and intimacy.

In **regenerative interaction patterns**, people are open with each other, which develops trust and promotes rapport and intimacy. This is a 'win–win' relationship where people are 'for each other'; they want to help each other grow and consequently co-operate for their mutual benefit. Owning is high because people want to understand each other and learn from mistakes. The risk associated with trying new behaviours is low because trust and goodwill promote constant growth and improvement. If there are problems in a regenerative relationship, the parties try to understand and learn from past mistakes in order to develop an even more satisfying and productive relationship.

degenerative interaction patterns
Competitive and destructive relationships resulting in lack of openness, low trust, blaming and defensiveness.

In **degenerative interaction patterns**, on the other hand, any problems that develop result in blaming others, defensiveness, lack of trust and decreased openness. In such a 'win–lose' relationship, lack of trust leads to a reduction of openness, risking new behaviours that may fail, and owning up to past mistakes, because all of these can make you more vulnerable. Most people try to escape degenerative climates if they want to grow and relate productively with others. If they stay, it is usually because of a high need for power and dominance or very low self-esteem and high insecurity.

Trust levels

trust
The feeling of confidence that someone will act to benefit rather than harm you.

Trust is a key ingredient in any win–win relationship, whether personal or business. Trust exists whenever you choose to let yourself be dependent on another person whose future behaviour can affect your well-being. Johnson (1993) suggests that trust occurs to the degree that you are aware that another's behaviour can benefit or harm you, and you feel confident that the other person will act to benefit you. An example of trust occurs when a working mother leaves her baby at a daycare centre. She is aware that her choice could lead to harmful or beneficial consequences and feels relatively confident that the staff will behave to bring about the latter.

Relationships do not grow and develop until individuals trust each other. Trust is learned from past interactions with another. Goss and O'Hair (1988) contend that trust is earned as the parties self-disclose personal information and learn that they will not be hurt by making themselves vulnerable to each other. Increased trust leads to the sharing of more personal information between the parties, which enhances regenerative interaction patterns and contributes to improved problem-solving and productivity. Managing emotional intelligence not only helps with developing trust but also enhances the workplace (see the Eye on Ethics box).

Emotional intelligence: good call

Go through the keyhole at any call centre and you'll find roles that require conscientiousness, motivation and sensitivity.

It is almost impossible nowadays to avoid coming into contact with a call centre. From taking out a credit card to arranging a holiday, we are all accustomed to a phone conversation rather than a face-to-face interaction.

The challenge is to ensure that the right person is handling the right call in the right manner. While the industry does have an unfortunate image of being the sweatshop of the 1990s, a number of organisations are investing heavily in creating excellent working environments with clearly defined career opportunities.

With more than 65 per cent of the costs of a modern call centre being people costs, and with the industry as a whole suffering retention problems, it is essential that recruitment, training and development activities are tailored appropriately. Many senior industry figures have debated the links between behaviour profiles and performance in an effort to discover what type of employee best fits a customer service role.

Research with the Department of Works and Pensions, egg and Morgan Stanley, all of whom run large call centres, has tried to answer these questions.

Using the Higgs and Dulewicz Emotional Intelligence Questionnaire, 286 call centre employees were sampled to find the links between emotional intelligence (EI) elements and performance. The sample was chosen to ensure variations in age, tenure and appraisal performance rating. The results showed that the most important EI elements for call centre workers were conscientiousness, resilience, motivation and sensitivity. Interestingly, a negative relationship between intuitiveness and performance was discovered. This can be explained by the extensive use of scripts and standard operating procedures, which employees with high levels of intuitiveness find restrictive. It was found that the least significant EI element was influence.

eye on ethics

The research also discovered gender differences in EI elements, with women having on average a profile with higher levels of sensitivity and conscientiousness than their male colleagues. In addition, it was found that age was related to performance, with older workers demonstrating better customer service skills than younger workers, although tenure of role was not a significant factor.

The findings have a number of implications for the call centre industry. For instance, people with high EI intuitiveness could well be frustrated in a role that requires compliance with rules and regulations. They may even use this strength in a way that, while they are trying to be helpful to customers, can have unforeseen consequences for the company; for example, the employee may go 'off-message'. Recruitment of those with high EI intuitiveness should therefore be avoided in this environment. The researchers suggest that companies recruiting customer service staff should focus on those who demonstrate high levels of conscientiousness, motivation, resilience and sensitivity. Perhaps controversially, recruiters should target their processes towards attracting older women, although this does not mean that people under 40 should not be considered for these types of roles.

It is widely understood that some aspects of EI are capable of development, with certain elements being easier to achieve than others. This means that firms recruiting call centre staff should look particularly for conscientiousness and motivation in the selection process. But they should target development plans at improving elements such as self-awareness, influence and sensitivity.

As a result of the research, the organisations involved are already looking at using the findings to improve recruitment and selection.

Chris Stephenson, head of HR operations at egg, says egg had been looking at the whole call centre recruitment process and wanted to see what EI had to offer. 'I went into it slightly sceptically. EI is a buzzword and can be seen as a bit management faddish. However, it did identify some valid measures, especially around relationship building,' he says. 'Call centre work is viewed by the general population as a young person's game. The reality is that a major part of the work is about relationship building and the best people for that are those who have had life experience.

'We are looking at moving the age profile for recruitment to the more mature end of the employment market.'

The Department of Work and Pensions is looking at using the EI elements as part of its initial sift of applicants and combining this with the broader competence-based recruitment processes of its call centre.

Those involved in the exercise believe it has demonstrated ways in which the performance of call centre staff can be improved through effective selection and tailored development.

Time and emotion study

The Higgs and Dulewicz Emotional Intelligence Questionnaire uses seven elements of behaviour:

1 self-awareness – awareness of your own feelings and of how others respond to you
2 emotional resilience – ability to keep going in difficult situations
3 motivation – ability to pursue longer-term goals
4 interpersonal sensitivity – understanding others' feelings and having empathy

5 influence – ability to influence others through interaction

6 intuitiveness – ability to make decisions with limited or ambiguous information

7 conscientiousness – integrity and correlation between words and actions.

Source: Malcolm Higgs in *People Management*, 23 January 2003, p. 48.

Discussion questions

1 Do you think EI is more important than IQ?

2 How can you develop the elements of behaviour recommended above?

Whenever trust is broken the relationship suffers. The damage may be temporary or permanent, depending on the nature of the relationship. The Enron collapse and subsequent shredding of papers by Andersen Consulting is an example of what happens when people lose trust.

In his best-selling book, *The 7 Habits of Highly Effective People*, Stephen Covey (1989) uses the metaphor of an 'emotional bank account' to describe the amount of trust that has been built up in a relationship. To Covey, trust refers to the overall feeling of safeness that you have with another person. You make 'deposits' into an emotional bank account with another person through kindness, honesty and keeping commitments. These acts build up a reserve trust account that promotes confidence in you even if your communication is sometimes ambiguous or you make an occasional mistake. However, if you show disrespect, fail to honour commitments or take advantage of the other person, your trust account becomes depleted. The relationship then becomes degenerative, with hostility and defensiveness making it difficult to build up trust again.

Covey (1989) suggests six major deposits to build up emotional bank accounts.

1 *Understand and honour other people's needs and priorities*, which may be very different from our own.

2 *Attend to little things*, like showing kindness and being courteous, because they make big positive deposits in relationships.

3 *Keep commitments*. Breaking a promise can be a massive withdrawal that may prevent future deposits because people will not believe you.

4 *Clarify expectations* so that others do not feel cheated or violated if you do not behave in ways that they assumed you knew they desired, even though they never overtly told you.

5 *Show personal integrity* by keeping promises, being honest, fulfilling expectations and being loyal to all people equally, including those not present.

6 *Apologise sincerely when you make a withdrawal*, without rationalising or trying to shift some of the blame to the other.

As trust builds in our emotional bank account, it becomes the foundation of regenerative relationships with others. People learn to put all their cards on the table to deal with issues and solve problems without wasting energy focused on differences in personality or position. Without trust, you lack the credibility and safety for open communication, creativity, problem-solving or mutual learning.

Different styles of relating

When interacting with others, you sometimes get the reactions you want, but at other times you do not. Your **interpersonal effectiveness** is the degree to which the consequences of your behaviour match your intentions. According to Johnson (1993), you can improve interpersonal effectiveness by disclosing your intentions, receiving feedback on your behaviour, and modifying your behaviour until it has the consequences you intend it to have. Important aspects of your behaviour to be aware of include your self-presentation, orientation towards others, behavioural style, ethics, and reactions to people who differ in gender or ethnic background.

interpersonal effectiveness
The degree to which the consequences of your behaviour match your intentions.

Differences in self-disclosure

How well do other people know you? Are you easy to get to know? Do you feel free to tell others what you feel and think? In order to know you and be involved with you, I must know who you are and what you need. For that to happen, you must **self-disclose** how you perceive, think and feel about the present situation, along with any relevant information from your past. Without self-disclosure you cannot form a meaningful relationship with another person.

self-disclose
The process of revealing how you perceive and feel about the present.

Johari Window
A model of the different degrees of openness between two people based on their degree of self-disclosure and feedback solicitation.

The **Johari Window** proposed by Luft (1984), discussed in the previous chapter under communication, is a model of the different degrees of openness between two people. It is based on the degrees of self-disclosure and solicitation of feedback when sharing information with another person. The model presents four 'window-panes' of awareness of others and ourselves. (Refer back to Exhibit 8-5.)

In the *open area*, information is disclosed and known by both parties; mutually shared perceptions confirm both parties' frames of reference. In the *hidden area* lie things that you are aware of but do not share because you may be afraid that others will think less of you, use the information to their advantage or chastise you because they may hurt the other's feelings. The *blind area* encompasses certain things about you that are apparent to others but not to yourself, either because no one has ever told you or because you defensively block them out. Blind spots, however, make you less effective in interactions with others. A certain team member may be terrible at running meetings, for example, but may not know it because no one has given her any feedback. Finally, in the *unknown area* lie repressed fears and needs or potential that neither you nor the other are aware of.

Managing openness: guidelines for self-disclosure (Coffey et al., 1975)

Because openness is risky – having both potential costs and rewards – it can be difficult to decide how open to be and with whom. Sharing your feelings and needs with others can build strong relationships in which you feel understood and cared about, and have your needs satisfied. With the wrong parties, however, your openness could be used against you. With closed behaviour you may not risk rejection nor being taken advantage of, but you may incur the costs of possibly not satisfying your needs and goals. It is difficult to establish meaningful relationships if you do not let yourself be known to significant others. Either too much or too little openness can be dysfunctional in different types of interpersonal relationship.

Research focus: different styles of self-disclosure

Hanson (1973) argues that in important intimate and trusting relationships, above-board behaviour is called for and people self-disclose freely with each other. This is the *transparent style* of interacting illustrated by Luft in Exhibit 9-4, characterised by the large 'open' area. Transparent styles are appropriate for significant relationships in regenerative climates. They would not be appropriate with casual acquaintances, in competitive situations or where trust and goodwill have not been established.

A person with a relatively large 'hidden' area uses an *interviewer style* because this person asks a lot of questions when soliciting feedback but does not self-disclose to others. Consequently, others have a difficult time knowing how the person feels or what he or she wants. After a while, people can become irritated at continually being asked to open up and share things without any reciprocation from the interviewer. They may become suspicious about how the information will be used, and may begin to shut down on the quantity and quality of information they are willing to share.

People with large 'blind' areas give a lot of feedback but solicit very little from others. People with this *bull-in-the-china-shop style* frequently tell others what they think and feel and where they stand on issues, but they are insensitive to feedback from others. Since they do not 'hear' what others say to and about them, they do not know how they come across and what impact their behaviour has on others.

A person with a large 'unknown' area does not know much about him or herself – nor do others. He or she may be the silent observer type, who neither gives nor asks for feedback. This is the *turtle*, who carries an imaginary shell around himself that insulates him from others. People have a hard time knowing where he stands or where they stand with him.

EXHIBIT 9–4 Different self-disclosure styles

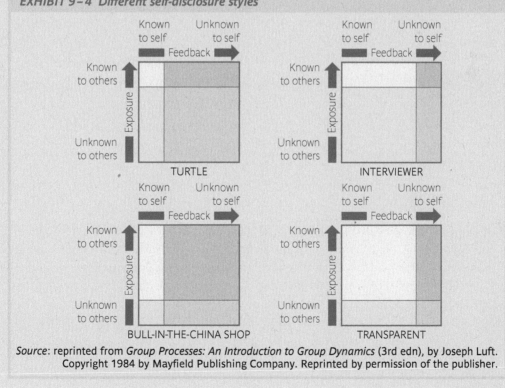

Source: reprinted from *Group Processes: An Introduction to Group Dynamics* (3rd edn), by Joseph Luft. Copyright 1984 by Mayfield Publishing Company. Reprinted by permission of the publisher.

Research focus: different behavioural styles

According to Hunsaker and Alessandra (1986), many times two people who cannot get along with one another (whether they are peers or boss and subordinate) have no difficulty interrelating with other people. Sometimes these differences can be accounted for by different frames of reference, needs, goals or self-presentation styles. Often they occur, however, because people have different preferred ways of being treated by others. If two people's preferred ways of interacting do not match, there is a high likelihood of conflict and tension.

behavioural style

A person's habitual way of interacting with other people.

A person's behavioural style is his or her habitual way of interacting with other people. It can be determined by examining two dimensions. *Responsiveness* is a person's degree of readiness to show emotions and develop relationships. *Assertiveness* refers to the amount of control a person tries to exercise over other people. Hunsaker and Alessandra summarise in Exhibit 9-5 the four primary behavioural styles determined by different levels of responsiveness and assertiveness.

People with different behavioural styles often irritate each other and have incompatible work methods. A major interpersonal skill is knowing how to adapt your own behavioural style to others' in order to avoid alienation. This is practising *behavioural flexibility*: treating others the way they want to be treated. Multinational corporations are realising the importance of being more considerate of others and are sending their managers to 'charm schools'. However, before you polish your charm you need to understand your own behavioural style and be able to determine that of others.

EXHIBIT 9–5 Characteristics of the four behavioural styles

High responsiveness

Amiable style

Slow at taking action and making decisions
Likes close, personal relationships
Dislikes interpersonal conflict
Supports and 'actively' listens to others
Weak at goal-setting and self-direction
Has excellent ability to gain support from others
Works slowly and cohesively with others
Seeks security and belongingness
Good counselling skills

Expressive style

Spontaneous actions and decisions
Likes involvement
Dislikes being alone
Exaggerates and generalises
Tends to dream and get others caught up in the dream
Jumps from one activity to another
Works quickly and excitingly with others
Seeks esteem and belongingness
Good persuasive skills

Low assertiveness ←——————————————→ **High assertiveness**

Analytical style

Cautious actions and decisions
Likes organisation and structure
Dislikes involvement with others
Asks many questions and wants specific details
Prefers objective, task-oriented, intellectual work environment
Wants to be right and therefore relies heavily on data collection
Works slowly and precisely alone
Seeks security and self-actualisation
Good problem-solving skills

Driver style

Firm actions and decisions
Likes control
Dislikes inaction
Prefers maximum freedom to manage self and others
Cool and independent; competitive with others
Low tolerance for feelings, attitudes and advice of others
Works quickly and impressively alone
Seeks esteem and self-actualisation
Good administrative skills

Low responsiveness

Source: P.L. Hunsaker and A.J. Alessandra (1986) *The Art of Managing People,* New York, NY: Simon & Schuster, p. 36. Copyright © 1980 by Phillip L. Hunsaker and Anthony J. Alessandra. Reprinted by permission of Simon & Schuster, Inc.

The expressive style

Expressives are animated, intuitive and lively, but they can also be manipulative, impetuous and excitable. They are fast-paced, make spontaneous decisions, and are not very concerned about facts and details. They thrive on involvement with others. They are verbal and good at influencing and persuading. They are the cheerleaders: 'I can, you can, we can make a difference.' They like to be recognised.

Expressives are very emotional and are relatively comfortable sharing their own feelings and hearing about the feelings of others. To maintain productive relationships with them it helps not to hurry a discussion and to be entertaining. When striving for an agreement with an expressive, make sure that you both fully understand all the details and summarise everything in writing so it will not be forgotten.

The driving style

Drivers are highly assertive but not very responsive. They are firm with others and make decisions rapidly. They are orientated towards productivity and concerned with bottom-line results, so drivers can be stubborn, impatient and tough-minded. Drivers strive to dominate and control people to achieve their tasks.

Drivers like expressing and reacting to tough emotions, but are uncomfortable either receiving or expressing tender feelings. You can maintain a productive relationship with a driver if you are precise, efficient and well organised. You should keep the relationship businesslike. To influence a driver in the direction you desire, provide options you are comfortable with, but let the driver make a decision.

The analytical style

Analyticals are not very assertive or responsive. They are persistent, systematic problem-solvers who sometimes appear aloof, meticulous and critical. They need to be right, which can lead them to rely too heavily on data. In their search for perfection, their actions and decisions tend to be extremely cautious. They do not shoot from the hip, they avoid being confrontational and think before they speak.

Analyticals suppress their feelings because they are uncomfortable with any type of emotion. To get along with an analytical, try to be systematic, organised and prepared. Analyticals require solid, tangible and factual evidence. Do not use gimmicks or push them for a fast decision. Take time to explain the alternatives, and the advantages and disadvantages of your recommendations.

The amiable style

Amiables are very responsive but unassertive, causing them to be supportive and reliable. Sometimes they appear to be complaining, soft-hearted and acquiescent. They are slow to act and want to know how other people feel about a decision before they commit themselves. Amiables dislike interpersonal conflict so much that they often tell others what they think they want to hear rather than what is really on their minds.

Amiables like expressing and receiving tender feelings of warmth and support, but abhor tough emotions like anger or hostility. They are good team players and have no trouble recognising the person in charge, unlike drivers who always act as if they are the boss. To get along with amiables, support their feelings and show personal interest in them. Move along in an informal manner and show the amiable that you are 'actively listening'.

Managing your openness means choosing when and how to be more open and authentic in your relationships with others. It means thinking before acting. In choosing how open to be in any situation, consider your own motives, the probable effects of your remarks on the other, and the recipient's readiness to hear your views. This includes an assessment of the degree of trust between you to determine if self-disclosure would be too risky (Goss and O'Hair, 1988). In mature relationships, for example, the bonds of trust between parties causes them to assume that the other will not use disclosed personal information in ways that risk negative consequences.

Male/female differences

No one denies that males and females are different. Because of these differences most people interact differently with same-sex than with different-sex communicators. Some of the most common sexual differences in interpersonal relationships concern communication styles, which were discussed in Chapter 8: relating strengths, interaction preferences and social-sexual behaviour.

Relating strengths

Different interacting psychological and social forces place women's early development in a context of *communion*, emphasising expressiveness, connection and relatedness, whereas men's early development occurs in a context of *agency*, emphasising independence, autonomy and instrumentality. Fletcher (1994) suggests that this early emphasis on relatedness and connection may cause women to develop, more highly than men, the qualities of vulnerability, empathy, and an ability to empower and enable others.

Men are socialised to deny feeling vulnerable and are encouraged to strive for self-reliance, strength and independence, while women are expected to attend to their own and others' feelings and connect emotionally with others. By being better able to comfortably recognise and respond to feelings of self-doubt, inadequacy and vulnerability, women are better able to non-judgementally address weaknesses in themselves and others, which are preconditions to personal growth, healthy interdependence and helping others.

Women learn to listen with empathy and to be responsive and sensitive to others' emotions. Men, on the other hand, are encouraged to be rational and strong and to deny feelings in order to maintain rationality and control. Women's stronger empathy is thought to be valuable in maintaining collaborative, growth-enhancing relationships.

Finally, women grow up expecting a two-directional pattern of relational growth, where contributing to the development of others will increase their feelings of effectiveness and competence and where others will be motivated to reciprocate. This is opposed to men's early training, which emphasises independence and competitiveness. Consequently, women may be more naturally adaptable to helping others at work in coaching or mentoring relationships (Kram, 1986).

Interaction preferences

Males and females differ in their reactions to authority figures and how they prefer to deal with conflict. These issues have grown in importance as more women have assumed positions of authority in organisations. In terms of supervisor preference, females tend to have more positive attitudes towards female managers than do males. They also perceive female managers as more competent than do males. Although female college students report that they would prefer a female boss upon graduating, more females with work experience prefer male supervisors (Wheeless and Berryman-Fink, 1985).

With respect to conflict, more female than male managers have been socialised to avoid confrontations altogether or to seek help in resolving them. More women than men settle for non-influential roles rather than become involved in power struggles and conflicts. In contrast, many men have been taught to over-emphasise power and strive for one-upmanship even when it is unnecessary or counterproductive.

Social-sexual behaviour

Social-sexual behaviour is any non-work-related behaviour having a sexual component; it includes things like sexual harassment, flirting and office romances. Analyses of office romances and sexual harassment have suggested that over half of all employees have received some kind of sexual overture from a co-worker of the other gender. Research by Gutek *et al.* (1990) found that about 10 per cent of all women have actually left a job because of sexual harassment. Lee (1992) also suggests that this includes leaving not only because of physical sexual advances but also due to unwelcome verbal abuse.

More than half of US women executives say they have suffered sexual harassment, a problem reported by 70 per cent of Japanese working women and 50 per cent of women working in European countries. In addition, 15 per cent of men in the United States say either female or male co-workers have harassed them. Harassment results in stress, absenteeism, productivity declines, turnover and legal action, which cost companies an average of about £200 per employee per year. According to Castro (1992), solutions include raising awareness, providing training, and consistent enforcement of clearly communicated rules and penalties.

The existence of genuine attraction between men and women in the workplace cannot be ignored. When men and women work closely and intensely together, they often become attracted to each other even if they did not intend it to happen. Sex goes to work with us every day, and we are naive if we assume that management can hand down an edict stating, 'We'll have no attraction here.' Since people choose whether or not to act on these feelings, it is better to give people guidelines and help in managing attraction productively. Effectively managing sexual attraction in relationships involves learning to communicate directly, setting personal boundaries and having a sense of ethics (Lee, 1992).

Lapland: A second look

We all agreed that experiencing the dramatic exposed our best and worst qualities in a way that astounded us and that it rapidly increased the speed of the bonding process. After all, you quite literally 'need each other' even to walk across flat ground where the snow is deep. You are also forced to recognise that other people's qualities, which you may have initially considered weaknesses, could in fact be valuable. I, for instance, hate being hurried at the cost of a good result, but realise a sense of urgency can be useful.

'Being so far away from home gives you the rare opportunity of taking off your baggage,' adds Kumud. 'In some cases, that's just inhibition or pressure and problems from work that you often bring with you to a training programme.'

Where else would you find yourself dancing to an Abba medley on the stage of a cheesy nightclub called Doris with people you had only just met and had every intention of trying to impress?

The activities for the latter half of the trip appeared, at first glance, to be 'just for fun'. We shed ourselves of our team badges and rode off on snowmobiles, husky dogs, rally cars, quad bikes and reindeer. A reward for all our hard work? Not so, says Mr Wallace. 'It's a way of improving self-motivation and self-confidence. There's bound to be some of those activities that scare you, and if you wind up going for it and getting over that fear, it gives you a sense of achievement and shows your potential. And because everyone notices that about everyone else, it builds up confidence between the team members.'

It also has the effect of ensuring that people do not feel their every move is under scrutiny. Mind you, we were undoubtedly more relaxed than during the more formal team exercises – something that co-ordinators were aware of, so they secretly checked out our responses and characteristics from time to time.

And it works a treat. Several times a few of us took one look at an activity and shrieked: 'No way!' But on at least half of those occasions, because of the unfamiliar surroundings as well as a lack of coercion, we found ourselves coming round to the idea and achieving the unthinkable.

Source: Kate Hilpern in *Independent*, 8 April 1999, p. 13.

Summary

- Executives emphasise the critical importance of interpersonal skills in achieving organisational objectives and managerial success.

- A good starting place for improving your competence in interpersonal relations is to understand the personality factors that influence them. These include things like self-concept, frame of reference, defences, feelings and need compatibility.

- Successful managers and executives also know the importance of emotional intelligence.

- Emotional intelligence encompasses many specific factors; however, the ability to develop positive interpersonal relationships ranks high in the skills desired by most firms.

- Additionally, it is important to recognise that emotional intelligence is not a fixed amount or number. Rather, emotional intelligence is something individuals can improve. Sometimes where interactions take place determines how effective they are.

- Job requirements determine the depth and range of possible interpersonal relationships. Some jobs require that people work closely together in tight quarters and with a high degree of interaction, while other jobs require only distant contact on relatively independent tasks.

- Another factor that determines how people interact emotionally is organisational culture. In some organisations, openness, trust, personal ownership and the ability to take risks are cultural values. The prevalent organisational culture will dictate how people interact on an emotional level, influencing the level of trust and intimacy.

- Other factors affecting how people relate are their degrees of openness in sharing information, their preferred behavioural styles, their comfort level in expressing emotions, and their tendencies to deceive one another.

- How much a person knows about herself and himself and how much they share with others, influences others' perceptions of these individuals. Some people know a lot about themselves but choose to disclose little, while others are just the opposite.

- People also exhibit different behavioural styles. Some people are very 'driving', while others are expressive, analytical or amiable in their style.

- Additionally, men and women have specific differences in relating strengths, interaction preferences, and reactions to social-sexual behaviour.

Areas for personal development

Since one of the biggest challenges managers face in the global work environment today is successfully managing interpersonal relations with different types of people in organisations, mastering interpersonal relations skills is of paramount importance. You can be more effective in developing and maintaining productive interpersonal relations if you remember to apply the following interpersonal skills.

1 **Focus on self-awareness.** Being aware of what you are feeling allows you to guide your own actions so that you can interact effectively with others. If you are able to recognise a mood or feeling, rather than suppressing or denying it, you can consider how it affects you. Then, instead of reacting spontaneously, you can choose how to act appropriately to maintain the relationship and get the results you want from others.

2 **Practise empathy.** Put yourself in the other person's shoes. What are his or her feelings, objectives and past experiences? Try to see the situation from the other person's frame of reference.

3 **Be aware of defensiveness.** Yours and others. Defensiveness occurs when you protect yourself by denying, excusing or rationalising your actions to protect your self-concept against the threat of being damaged by failure, guilt, shame or fear. The problem is that all defence mechanisms involve a degree of distortion of reality. So you need to be aware of your own and others' defence mechanisms. Then you can avoid doing things that promote defensiveness in others. You will also be better prepared to recognise and avoid defensive reactions in yourself.

4 **Determine interpersonal relationship needs and modify your behaviour appropriately.** The degree of compatibility between two or more people's needs for inclusion, control and affection can make the difference between a happy and productive team and a dissatisfied and ineffective one. First determine differences in interpersonal needs and then adapt your own behaviours to let others satisfy their needs. This consideration will enhance your relationships with them.

5 **Maintain regenerative interaction climates.** Always try to promote 'win–win' relationships where people are motivated to help each other grow and co-operate for their mutual benefit. Emphasise owning responsibility for problems so that people want to understand each other and learn from mistakes. Make sure that risks associated with trying new behaviours are low so that people are free to be creative and innovative.

6 **Develop high trust levels.** You earn trust by encouraging others to make themselves vulnerable to you by self-disclosing personal information and learning that they will not be hurt by you when they do. To build trust with others, understand and honour their needs and priorities. Second, show kindness and be courteous. Third, keep your commitments. Fourth, clarify your expectations. Fifth, show personal integrity by keeping promises, being honest, fulfilling expectations. Sixth, apologise sincerely when you violate others' trust without rationalising or trying to shift some of the blame.

7 **Self-disclose to others.** In order to know you and be involved with you, others need to know who you are and what you need. For that to happen, you have to share how you perceive, think and feel. Without self-disclosure you cannot form a meaningful relationship with another person.

8 **Solicit feedback from others.** To determine how you come across to others and learn about your interpersonal strengths and weaknesses, it is necessary to ask others to provide you with feedback. This will not happen automatically, especially from subordinates. Therefore, you need to request constructive feedback from significant others to improve your own effectiveness and your relationships with them.

9 **Practise behavioural flexibility.** Adapt your preferred style of interacting to meet the needs and preferences of others. By treating others the way they want to be treated you will avoid alienation and build positive relationships.

Questions for study and discussion

1 Why are interpersonal relationships in the workplace important? What are some relationships you have had that affected your productivity and satisfaction positively? Negatively?

2 What is emotional intelligence? Do you feel you have a strong emotional intelligence? What steps can you take to strengthen your emotional intelligence?

3 What is your present self-concept? Describe times when you had a diminished self-concept and what caused it. Have you experienced an inflated self-concept? Describe what happened.

4 Describe a negative relationship you have had with someone in terms of the A-B model. Do the same for a positive relationship. What are the key differences between the factors in each situation?

5 Describe a relationship with someone in whom you place great trust. What conditions create and maintain that trust? Describe a relationship with someone in whom you place little trust and the conditions that created it. What are the differences between the trusting and distrusting relationships?

6 What is your behavioural style? How does it influence your relationships with other people at work, at college and in your personal life? How can your knowledge of behavioural styles be applied to improve your relationships in these different settings?

7 What are the main relationship differences between females and males? Think of your most important relationship with a male and a female. How do the different relating preferences affect you specifically in these relationships?

8 Draw a Johari Window with the four quadrants reflecting your personal degrees of self-disclosure and solicitation of feedback. How does your Johari Window influence your relationships with others?

🔑 Key Concepts

emotional intelligence, *p. 406*

self-concept, *p. 412*

value system, *p. 412*

reciprocity, *p. 413*

personal frame of reference, *p. 414*

defence, *p. 414*

regenerative interaction patterns, *p. 420*

degenerative interaction patterns, *p. 420*

trust, *p. 421*

interpersonal effectiveness, *p. 424*

self-disclose, *p. 424*

Johari Window, *p. 424*

behavioural style, *p. 426*

Personal skills exercise
Comparing interpersonal needs

Preparation Complete the 'Your turn' exercise on page 418, then form discussion groups of three to six.

Time 30–60 minutes (depending on the size of the discussion groups)

Procedure Share your scores with others in your small group and discuss the implications for your interpersonal relationships according to the following questions (10 to 15 minutes for each student).

1 Examine your scores on each need category as they relate to each other. Your highest scores indicate which interpersonal needs probably dominate your relationships with others. How well do these scores describe your interpersonal behaviour in the various aspects of your life?

2 How do the other people in your group react to your scores in terms of how they experience you?

3 Examine how different you are relative to others on the six different interpersonal need scores. How are these differences perceived by others?

4 Your scores are also good indicators of how others are likely to react to you. Compare your scores to those of others in your group.

(a) Who are you compatible with – that is, one person wants what the other expresses?

(b) Who are you incompatible with – that is, one person expresses something another does not want, or both parties express the same thing (for example, if you have control, or neither wants something that is necessary, such as control)?

(c) What happens when two people emphasise the same need (for example, affection), as opposed to situations where they emphasise different needs (for example, control versus affection)?

5 Discuss the implications of your interpersonal needs for inclusion, control and affection for you as a manager.

6 Reflect back on the previous discussion with your group members. Do you behave in ways that you want to change? Share the changes you propose and see how others react.

Team exercise

Getting to know you: connecting by rubber bands

Preparation Requires a room with space to move about freely.

Time 35–40 minutes

Activity 1 All members of the class stand up and silently move around, greeting each other non-verbally. After you have greeted everyone (about 3 minutes) you non-verbally choose a partner for Activity 2.

Activity 2 Stand about 2 feet apart facing your partner. Put your hands out in front of you, almost touching the hands of your partner. Pretend that your hands are connected by rubber bands and that you are facing your partner in a mirror. Non-verbally move your hands around in a creative way (3 to 5 minutes).

Activity 3 Stay in your hand-mirroring position. Now pretend that your feet are also connected by rubber bands. Again, non-verbally move your hands and feet around. Be creative: see if you can move around the room, encounter other pairs, and so on (3 to 5 minutes).

Activity 4 With your partner, non-verbally choose another pair. Sit down together and share with the other pair what you learned about your partner from participating in Activities 1, 2 and 3. Rotate sharing until all are finished (10 minutes), then discuss the following questions in your group (15 minutes):

1 Who invited the other to be his or her partner? What did you learn about your and your partner's needs for including or being included?

2 What did you learn about your own and your partner's need for control from how your movements were initiated in the hand and feet mirroring?

3 Was there reciprocity with your partner, or did one person take charge?

4 What kind of behavioural style do you think your partner has from sharing this exercise with him or her?

5 What else did you learn about yourself and your partner?

Case study: **the Pete and Jenny fiasco**

Jenny Graham was a hot topic at Mastergram plc long before September 1980, when Peter Finch stood before more than 600 employees and denied that her rapid advancement had anything to do with 'a personal relationship that we have'. Graham joined the company in the previous June as a senior manager answerable to Peter Finch, after a three-hour interview in a top hotel. 'A meeting of kindred spirits,' she said. Exactly one year later, Finch gave her a bigger title – assistant director for public relations. Three months after that came the promotion to assistant director for strategic planning. Finch tried to confront the uproar that immediately followed by announcing to employees that his new assistant director and he were 'very, very good friends' but not romantically involved. The comment backfired, creating a national media furore so intense and so focused on Graham's youth, blonde hair and shapely figure that in the autumn of 1980 the Mastergram board of directors forced her resignation.

Inside Mastergram, gossip about the relationship between Graham and Finch began to reach a crescendo after her June promotion, and all sorts of things helped keep the noise level up. A TV camera focusing on a former cabinet minister at a conference happened to find Finch and Graham sitting next to him. Some Mastergram people suggested that Finch was less accessible than he had once been, and Graham's growing influence with him did not help to allay suspicions. She had called herself his 'alter ego' and 'most trusted confidante'; he said she was his 'best friend'. Then in August, Finch and his wife of 25 years divorced so quickly it surprised even top officials at Mastergram.

Top corporate executives had been accused of almost everything imaginable except having romances with one another. But, what was one to think? Here were two young, attractive, unattached people working together, travelling together, even staying in the same two-bedroom suite at luxury hotels. They had to be having an affair – and that would explain Graham's sprint up the ranks. Or was Graham, as one business journalist portrayed her in a four-part newspaper series, a brilliant, idealistic corporate missionary destroyed by jealous cynics? Another journalist interviewed Graham, and feminist leaders rallied to her defence asking whether this meant that young, talented, attractive, ambitious and personable female executives were permitted only slow climbs upward, lest they invite gossip?

Insisting that their relationship had been platonic until after she left Mastergram, Finch and Graham married in June 1982. The same year, after resurfacing as an assistant CEO at Marfon, Graham acted as Finch's unpaid adviser during Mastergram's attempted takeover of Marietta plc. But their ambitious plan collapsed when Mastergram was swallowed by Alliance plc in a merger that cost hundreds of Mastergram's employees their jobs. The fiasco was blamed, in part, on Finch's young wife, the strategic planner.

The couple escaped and started a small venture capital firm. In 1983, Jenny Finch founded a charity that helps single women with unplanned pregnancies. In 1988, Peter Finch was named CEO of Morksen plc.

In 1994 Morksen posted losses of £210 million and lurched towards bankruptcy. In February 1995, Finch was ousted as Morksen stock fell from £20 a share to £3.50; employees and pensioners alike watched their futures evaporate. In February, too, Jenny Finch resigned as executive director of the non-profit Morksen Foundation, a position critics say she used to benefit her own charity. Once more, the Finches were at the centre of a corporate ethics controversy – and this one seemed no less vitriolic than the last.

The Morksen community has not regretted the Finches' demise. It was not only the shareholders' losses and the hundreds of Morksen workers Peter Finch fired, but the fact that the Finches rubbed Morksen the wrong way – almost from the start. So much so that after being ignored at the town's private clubs and most prestigious boards, the couple and their two children abruptly relocated three years ago to a £2 million mansion a hundred miles away. Jenny Finch managed her charity and Peter

Finch ran Morksen by phone, fax and courier, and from a £12 million corporate Falcon jet that peeved Morkseners, dubbed 'Jenny's taxi'.

Now, with more than a dozen lawsuits filed by shareholders, charging that Peter Finch and the Morksen board wasted assets and managed the company recklessly, Jenny Finch's role is under legal as well as public scrutiny regarding the use of Morksen assets to benefit her charity. The lawyers are also eyeing the close relationship linking Morksen and its foundation with the charity's complex web of friendships, business interests and moral commitments. In 1992, half the Morksen board members had wives on Jenny Finch's charity board, while Peter Finch served on both boards. 'Once so many of the directors and their wives had joined with the Finches in ... a moral crusade, *Business Times* pointedly asked, 'how likely was it that they would challenge Mr Finch in the boardroom?'

Source: adapted from Berman (1995) and Bernstein (1980).

Questions for discussion

1 Was Jenny unfairly victimised by a society suspicious that attractive women advance on their wiles, not their wits?

2 Is any 29-year-old fresh from business school, no matter how smart, qualified to be the chief planning executive of a multibillion-pound company in the throes of a major restructuring?

3 Are the personal lives of Jenny and Peter – or any other corporate officials – anybody's business?

4 Once such an embarrassing controversy surfaces, how should an organisation deal with it?

5 What ramifications do romantic relationships at work have for other organisational members and for organisational effectiveness in general?

6 What are the probable reasons people reacted as they did to the actions of Peter and Jenny?

7 What mechanisms could organisations institute to avoid these kinds of problems?

8 What could Peter and Jenny have done differently to avoid the negative outcomes?

Applied questions

9 How can an organisation manage social-sexual behaviour in the workplace?

10 Exhibit 9-2 illustrates common defence mechanisms used in the workplace. Can you identify which could have been used by Jenny and Peter and say how successful they would have been?

WWW exercise

Manager's Internet tools

Web tips: emotional intelligence on the World Wide Web

The first part of this chapter examined the role and importance of emotional intelligence (EQ). Knowing the importance of EQ and an individual's understanding of his or her own EQ is not something to be taken lightly. As the business world increasingly becomes more competitive, the corporate search for the 'best people' becomes a tighter and tighter race. Companies are now defining the best people as individuals who possess trustworthiness, integrity, honesty, leadership, and other qualities that build teamwork and strong interpersonal relationships. Sheer technical skills or IQ alone will not define success. Rather, the ability to interact successfully with others and lead will define the best people.

General World Wide Web search exercise

EQ.org (http://www.eq.org/) is a website established to further the understanding of what EQ is and the importance of EQ for success. This website contains some of the latest research articles written on emotional intelligence, definitions of emotional literacy and suggestions for training to improve one's EQ. Check it out and find other sites using a search engine that deals with interpersonal relations.

From the EQ.org website, read some of the latest articles on EQ. What do these articles say or imply about the importance of EQ? How would you build these success factors into your work life?

Specific website exercise

Using a search engine type in 'emotional intelligence'. You will find that there are several agencies that offer support and advice on EQ. If you were a manager which company would you choose to deliver your programmes?

LEARNING CHECKLIST

Before you move on you may want to reflect on what you have learnt in this chapter. You should now be able to:

- ☑ appreciate the importance of good interpersonal relations at work
- ☑ understand the importance of emotional intelligence
- ☑ appreciate the impact of personality differences on relationships
- ☑ assess interaction climates
- ☑ recognise differences in self-disclosure
- ☑ deal effectively with male/female differences in work behaviours
- ☑ understand the importance of ethics in interpersonal relations
- ☑ develop strategies to deal with people who have different interpersonal styles.

Further reading

Bradberry, T. and Greaves, J. (2005) 'Heartless Bosses?', *Harvard Business Review* 83(12), December, p. 24.

Gabel, R.S., Dolan, S.L. and Cerdin, J.L. (2005) 'Emotional Intelligence as Predictor of Cultural Adjustment for Success in Global Assignments', *Career Development International* 10(5), pp. 375–397.

Liptak, J.J. (2005) 'Using Emotional Intelligence to Help College Students Succeed in the Workplace', *Journal of Employment Counseling* 42(4), December, pp. 171–179.

References

Bennis, W.G., Berlew, D.E., Schein, E.H. and Steele, F.I. (1973) *Interpersonal Dynamics* (3rd edn). Chicago, IL: Dorsey Press, pp. 495–518.

Berman, L. (1995) 'The Gospel According to Mary', *Working Woman*, August, pp. 47–49.

Bernstein, P.W. (1980) 'Things the B-school Never Taught', *Fortune*, 3 November, pp. 53–56.

Castro, J. (1992) 'Sexual Harassment: A Guide', *Time*, 20 January, p. 37.

Coffey, R.E., Athos, A.G. and Raynolds, P.A. (1975) *Behaviour in Organizations: A Multidimensional View* (2nd edn). Englewood Cliffs, NJ: Prentice Hall, pp. 150–151.

Cohen, A.R., Fink, S.L., Gadon, H., Willits, R.D. and Josefowitz, N. (1992) *Effective Behaviour in Organizations* (5th edn). Homewood, IL: Irwin, p. 256.

Costley, D.L. and Todd, R. (1987) *Human Relations in Organizations*. Los Angeles, CA: West Publishing Company, pp. 232–235.

Covey, S.R. (1989) *The 7 Habits of Highly Effective People*. New York, NY: Simon & Schuster, 1989, pp. 188–189.

Daft, R. (1999) *Leadership: Theory and Practice*. Fort Worth, TX: The Dryden Press, pp. 346–347.

DiMarco, N.J. (1974) 'Supervisor–Subordinate Life Style and Interpersonal Need Compatibilities as Determinants of Subordinate's Attitudes toward the Supervisor', *Academy of Management Journal* 17, pp. 575–578.

Edwards, A. (1991) 'The Enlightened Manager: How to Treat all your Employees Fairly', *Working Woman* 16(1), January, pp. 38–39.

Fisher, A. (1998) 'Success Secret: A High Emotional IQ', *Fortune*, 26 October, pp. 293–298.

Fletcher, J.K. (1994) 'Castrating the Female Advantage: Feminist Standpoint Research and Management Science', *Journal of Management Inquiry*, March, pp. 74–82.

Gallup (1991) *Challenge to Management Education: Avoiding Irrelevancy*. Morristown, NJ: Financial Executives Research Foundation, The Gallup Organisation, pp. 5–9.

Gibbs, N. (1995) 'The EQ Factor', *Time*, 2 October, p. 65.

Goleman, D. (1998) *Working with Emotional Intelligence*. New York, NY: Bantam Books.

Golembiewski, R.T. (1972) *Renewing Organizations: The Laboratory Approach to Planned Change*. Itasca, IL: F.E. Peacock Publishers, p. 31.

Goss, B. and O'Hair, D. (1988) *Communicating in Interpersonal Relationships*. New York, NY: Macmillan Publishing Company, pp. 47–48.

Gutek, B.A., Cohen, A.G. and Konrad, A.M. (1990) 'Predicting Social-sexual Behaviour at Work: A Contact Hypothesis', *Academy of Management Journal* 33(3), pp. 560–577.

Hanson, P.C. (1973) 'The Johari Window: A Model for Soliciting and Giving Feedback', *1973 Annual Handbook for Group Facilitators*. San Diego: University Associates, pp. 114–119.

Hill, R.E. (1974) 'Interpersonal Needs and Functional Areas of Management', *Journal of Vocational Behaviour* 4, pp. 15–24.

Hunsaker, P.L. and Alessandra, A.J. (1986) *The Art of Managing People.* New York, NY: Simon & Schuster, pp. 32–49.

Johnson, D.W. (1993) *Reaching Out: Interpersonal Effectiveness and Self-actualization.* Needham Heights, MA: Allyn and Bacon, pp. 32–47.

Kram, K. (1986) 'Mentors in the Workplace', in D.T. Hall (ed.) *Career Development in Organizations.* San Francisco, CA: Jossey-Bass, pp. 29–47.

Lee, C. (1992) 'Sexual Harassment: After the Headlines', *Training*, March, pp. 23–31.

Liddell, W.W. and Slocum Jr, J.W. (1976) 'The Effects of Individual-role Compatibility Upon Group Performance: An Extension of Schutz's FIRO Theory', *Academy of Management Journal* 19, pp. 413–426.

Luft, J. (1984) *Group Processes* (3rd edn). Palo Alto, CA: Mayfield Publishing Company, pp. 11–20.

Murray, B. (1998) 'Does Emotional Intelligence Matter in the Workplace?', *APA Monitor*, July, p. 21.

O'Connell, L. (1994) 'Gut Reactions Tell About Self', *San Diego Union-Tribune*, 26 September, p. E-3.

Robbins, S.P. and Hunsaker, P.L. (1996) *Training in Interpersonal Skills* (2nd edn). Englewood Cliffs, NJ: Prentice Hall.

Sanholz, K. (1987) *National Business Employment Weekly*, Fall.

Schutz, W.C. (1958) *FIRO: A Three Dimensional Theory of Interpersonal Behaviour.* New York, NY: Rinehart & Co.

Steele, F. and Jenks, S. (1977) *The Feel of the Work Place.* Reading, MA: Addison-Wesley Publishing, pp. 157–163.

Turner, A.N. and Lombard, G.F.F. (1969) *Interpersonal Behaviour and Administration.* New York, NY: The Free Press/Collier-Macmillan.

Weisinger, H. (1998) *Emotional Intelligence at Work.* San Francisco, CA: Jossey-Bass, pp. 214–215.

Wheeless, V. and Berryman-Fink, C. (1985) 'Perceptions of Women Managers and Their Communicator Competencies', *Communication Quarterly* 33, pp. 137–148.

Whetton, D.A. and Cameron, K.S. (1995) *Developing Managerial Skills* (3rd edn). New York, NY: HarperCollins, p. 81.

Chapter 10

Managing groups and teams

LEARNING OUTCOMES ☑

After studying this chapter you should be able to:

- ☑ **explain** the primary characteristics of groups
- ☑ **compare** the contributions of different types of groups
- ☑ **describe** the stages of group development
- ☑ **discuss** how group norms are developed and enforced
- ☑ **determine** sources of group cohesiveness
- ☑ **understand** threats to group performance
- ☑ **explain** how to develop a group into a team
- ☑ **discuss** the characteristics of high-performing teams
- ☑ **define** key team member roles
- ☑ **assess** and improve team performance.

Investment in teamwork can pay handsome dividends for a company, as can be seen in the example of Pocklington Coachworks in the opening vignette.

Pocklington Coachworks

Recognising needs, keeping promises, exceeding expectations...

If asked what the trademark of Pocklington Coachworks is, then the unanimous answer would be 'our commitment to total customer satisfaction. The way we achieve this is thanks to our attitude to innovation, our smart engineering and our quality manufacturing. We create vehicles that people want to look at, want to walk on board and want to own.'

▶

Every single vehicle is an original and begins life on the drawing board. Initial concept discussions start the ball rolling and, from these, we produce custom-built vehicles that are the result of immense skill, problem-solving and craftsmanship. Of course, the service does not stop with the production of the vehicle; we at Pocklington Coachworks offer ongoing support for the entire life of the unit – and beyond!

How do they do this? Pocklington Coachworks has recognised its need to invest in teamwork.

'People contribute to everything we are...'

Pocklington recognises that people really are the backbone of any business and by surrounding yourself with the right people you are assured of a certain degree of success. 'Certainly, everything we have achieved here at Pocklington Coachworks is down to the skill, hard work and loyalty of our team.'

Every single member of this team contributes to the business and shares an immense sense of pride in their contribution. People are, without doubt, the greatest asset, and through ongoing training and skills development, Pocklington maintains a team-based structure that guarantees ongoing success.

'This emphasis on investing in a 'team' rather than just a workforce, is recognised in our award-winning craftsmanship, our Investor In People accreditation and our great pride in what we consistently achieve.'

This was recognised when Pocklington Coachworks reached the finals of the *Evening Press* Business of the Year awards. In the previous year, it had reached the final in the Exporter of the Year category.

In 2001 it reached the finals of the Progress Through People award and its inspirational leader Fran Johnson is in the top line-up for Business Personality of the Year.

It has gone beyond its Investors In People status to create self-managed teams among its 68 staff, 47 of whom are on the shop floor and the balance support staff.

With the help of York-based training company Bergander and Business Link North Yorkshire, the innovative engineering company set up its 'winning teams' programme designed to highly train and develop team leaders to create a trickle-down of knowledge involving everyone in the business.

Mike Kitchen, a team leader of the Red Team, who has been with the company since 1995, recognises that through their investment in people he has been given many opportunities to progress to his current position.

There is also the firm's apprenticeship programme – now in its fourth year and part of an £80 000 investment in general staff training. This had impressed its clients, Subaru and Toyota Motorsport, who had written detailed testimonials in support of its nomination for the business award. This is backed up by Mark Walton, an apprentice with the company, who says 'I am in my second year as an apprentice and I have received first-class training. I see myself having a bright future here and it is great working for such a motivated company'.

The directors of Pocklington Coachworks believe that a major success ingredient for the continued growth of the business is to unlock the potential of everyone working within the company. Pocklington's aim is to achieve 'self-managed teams' throughout the business – brimful of business champions. To ensure the level of commitment of everyone, Pocklington has a business initiative called 'Winning Teams in Action'. This takes every team through a clearly understood and measured five-category process: taking the teams from the

'AWARENESS' stage, with everyone realising the journey to be undertaken, to 'CERTAINTY', where true self-managed teams are realised, controlling their own performance and working at optimum efficiency.

While the programme is challenging, enjoying the journey is essential and actively encouraged.

Source: www.pocklington.co.uk.

Discussion questions

1 How important are self-managed teams in increasing employee motivation?

2 Who should set the goals for the self-managed teams: the workers or management?

The case of Pocklington Coachworks shows that teamwork can not only improve performance but also motivation. Another example of a small business achieving dividends through group work is a small group of coal miners who bought out their coal mine when the government planned to close it and turned it into a profitable business. However, it is not just smaller companies that use self-managed teams, another example is Microsoft, where there are programming teams of about 12 developers who write and develop software. Team members each have their own specific responsibilities, but they are also expected to support and collaborate with each other, and they are rewarded for both (Rebello, 1996). However, according to Katzenback and Smith (1993a, 1993b) and Drucker (1992), for each of these success stories of outstanding team performance there are many times more about work groups that did not work at all. What makes the difference between high-performing teams and group failures is the subject of this chapter.

Most of you have had, or surely will have, the opportunity to experience teamwork with the popular business school learning tool 'the group project'. Faced with a group task, many students protest: 'Is there any way I can get out of doing this as a group project? I don't want to have to co-ordinate and depend on other people. I could do it better and faster by myself!' Actually this may be true if other students think: 'Great! I'll team up with some good students and then I won't have to do so much work!' Similar thoughts often go through the minds of managers and professionals when they are placed on committees, task forces, work teams, quality circles and other organisational groups.

Most of us enter team situations cautiously because ingrained individualism discourages us from putting our fates in the hands of others or accepting responsibility for others. According to Katzenback and Smith (1993a), this is with good reason. If members do not overcome their natural reluctance to trust their fate to others, the price of 'faking' a team approach is high. At best, members get diverted from their individual goals, costs outweigh benefits, and people resent the imposition on their time and priorities; at worst, serious animosities develop that undercut even the potential personal bests of individuals working alone.

Working with others is not easy. Nevertheless, groups constitute the basic building blocks of any organisation. In today's complicated and rapidly changing business environment, few individuals in an organisational setting can successfully go it alone. For many tasks, teams accomplish much more work in less time than the same number of individuals can working separately. Gates (1989) suggests that employees can also grow more quality conscious through group interaction as they learn about others' experiences, problems and solutions as work in progress flows through the organisation. When groups do not act like teams and are unproductive and dissatisfying, it is usually because their members lack the necessary attitudes, knowledge and skills to work together effectively. Alternatively, they have not been provided with clear objectives, structures and appropriate environments by management.

Although there is no guaranteed 'how to' recipe for building high team performance, there are a number of findings from studying successful teams that provide insights into the essential ingredients. One objective of this chapter is to enhance your awareness, appreciation and understanding of how groups function and contribute to organisations. Another is to provide you with the tools to participate as an effective group member. Finally, you will learn how to manage groups, develop them into high-energy teams when needed, and intervene when your team gets off track.

Groups and their functions

We all spend a great deal of time in group interactions long before we take jobs in organisations. Most of us are born into a family group, become part of one or more play groups, and soon enter the academic world of multiple-classroom groups. Later we may join clubs and teams and become members of social or religious groups, while for others a gang may become their dominant group. Some of these group memberships are mandatory, others are undertaken voluntarily. Yammarino and Dubinsky (1990) suggest that work groups are the manager's main vehicle for accomplishing organisational tasks. While Ashforth and Mael (1989) argue that groups also satisfy personal needs for friendship, self-esteem and identity.

group
Two or more people who perceive themselves as a distinct entity, regularly interact and influence one another over a period of time, share common values and strive for common objectives.

People riding in a lift, watching a movie or waiting in a doctor's office may constitute a physical gathering of individuals, but they lack the basic psychological characteristics of a group. A **group** can be defined as two or more people who meet regularly and influence one another over a period of time, perceive themselves as a distinct entity distinguishable from others, share common values and strive for common objectives (Shaw, 1981).

In most organisations, several different types of group exist, and most employees are likely to be members of more than one. Groups can be classified as formal or informal.

Formal groups

A **formal group** such as a committee, maintenance crew or task force is established by management and charged to perform specific tasks and accomplish organisational objectives. Some of the most common contributions that formal groups make to their two primary beneficiaries, the organisation and its individual members, are summarised in Exhibit 10-1.

formal group
A group intentionally established by a manager to accomplish specific organisational objectives.

standing task group
A permanent group formally specified in the organisational structure consisting of a supervisor and direct subordinates.

A **standing task group**, sometimes referred to as a command group, is permanently specified in the formal organisational structure and consists of a supervisor who exercises formal authority over direct subordinates. Specific departments such as accounting, quality control or shipping are examples of standing task groups. Standing task groups are the workhorses of organisations and they contribute the basic inputs to goal achievement. You see standing task groups at work in a university's admissions, finance and catering departments.

EXHIBIT 10 – 1 What formal groups contribute

Contributions to Organisations

1 Accomplish complex, interdependent tasks that are beyond the capabilities of individuals.
2 Create new ideas.
3 Co-ordinate interdepartmental efforts.
4 Solve complex problems requiring varied information and perspectives.
5 Implement action plans.
6 Socialise and train newcomers.

Contributions to individuals

1 Satisfy needs for affiliation.
2 Confirm identity and enhance self-esteem.
3 Test and share perceptions of social reality.
4 Reduce feelings of insecurity and powerlessness.
5 Provide a mechanism for solving personal and interpersonal problems.

Source: adapted from E.H. Schein, *Organizational Psychology* (3rd edn). Englewood Cliffs, NJ: Prentice Hall, pp. 149–151. Copyright 1980. Reprinted by permission of Prentice Hall, Inc., Upper Saddle River, NJ.

---

task group

A temporary formal group created to solve specific problems.

A **task group** is a temporary formal group that is created to solve specific problems. Examples include a product development team, a quality committee and a political candidate's campaign advisers. Task groups do not report to any particular department but are often made up of people from different standing task groups who possess complementary areas of expertise to solve the assigned problem. When the problem is solved, the task group usually disbands and members return to their standing task groups. Examples of task forces in action are given in the World Watch box.

Informal groups

An **informal group** emerges through the efforts of individuals trying to satisfy personal needs

informal group

A group that emerges through the efforts of individuals to satisfy personal needs not met by the formal organisation.

for support, friendship, growth and recreation. Membership in informal groups is based on common interests and mutual attraction versus being assigned, as it is in formal groups. Examples of work-related informal groups are the 'pub bunch', the darts team, the smokers who meet outside during the working day for a 'quick puff' and the car sharers. Meer (1985) and Ferris and Rowland (1983) argue that the subtle influence of informal groups over their members' behaviours often turns out to be more powerful than the vested authority of formal groups. This influence can be both positive and negative. For a pub bunch group, the informal group can lead to the generation of new and productive ideas and a positive rapport among the individuals. However, this group could become more of a 'clique', and individuals who are left out or uninvited can acquire negative feelings towards the members of the informal group.

An **interest group** is made up of individuals who affiliate to achieve an objective of mutual

interest group

An informal group consisting of individuals who affiliate to achieve an objective of mutual interest.

interest that may have nothing to do with their formal task group memberships. Working mothers who lobby together to get their organisation to ease childcare problems by providing daycare facilities on the premises, flexible working hours and shared job assignments, is an example.

Mitsubishi and Honda on competition and quality circles

The Japanese tend to do things in groups, place a high value on group membership and strive to be as cohesive as possible. This group orientation is exemplified by the now famous quality control (QC) circles instituted in Japanese industries right after the Second World War. Even in 1983 there were more than 100 000 such groups formally registered with the Japanese Quality Circle Association and more than a million others that were unregistered.

A typical QC group in Japan consists of from two to ten employees from a natural working group in which all members know one another's duties. The groups focus on any production or service problems or improvements that fall within the scope of their jobs.

However, in recent years, the Japanese have expanded the concept of the quality circle beyond just their own corporations. Honda, Toyota and Mitsubishi, traditionally known as fierce competitors in the auto industry, have combined forces in the form of a cross-company quality circle. The three companies made motor car history when they made a joint presentation at the 20th annual Association for Quality and Participation spring conference in 1998. Each company had used quality circles in its manufacturing processes for a long time, and the success of these companies can be attributed to the implementation of quality circles. Now, however, the goal was to take the quality circle concept one step further and create a quality circle with members from each company. The goal: learn from each other's successes. The companies feel that collaboration and competition are not mutually exclusive, and the use of a combined quality circle will make each company better.

Internally, each company uses quality circles in all aspects of its manufacturing processes. Furthermore, Mitsubishi and Honda even sponsor internal competitions among the various quality circles. The companies feel that the competition can be healthy and award a prize to the best quality circle. However, the prize is not for the presentation specifically, but rather the best process. While Toyota does not support the quality circle competition, all three of the car makers agree that the problem-solving process within the quality circle is the most important aspect.

Source: Sara Olberding (1998) 'Mitsubishi and Honda on Competition and Quality Circles', *Journal for Quality and Participation*, May/June, pp. 55–59. Reprinted with permission of the Association for Quality and Participation. Copyright 1998. All rights reserved.

Discussion questions

1 Do you think people from different companies can work successfully in groups? What is likely to hinder their success?

2 Does success in group work depend on a person's culture?

---

friendship group
An informal group based on common characteristics that are not necessarily work related.

reference group
A group with which an individual identifies to form opinions and make decisions regardless of whether he or she is an actual member.

A **friendship group** also develops based on common characteristics such as marital status, political views, college affiliations and sports. Friendship groups are important for their own sake because they satisfy the affiliation needs of their members. Enlightened managers maintain good relations with friendship groups because these groups have tremendous influence on their members that managers would prefer to have directed towards organisational goals (Hussein, 1989).

A **reference group** is any group with which an individual

identifies for forming opinions, making decisions or determining how to act. Reference groups are the bases for many friendship and interest groups, but they may also exist outside of the organisation and still influence a person's behaviour at work. Reference groups are based on things like race, gender, politics, religion, social class, education level and profession. According to Napier and Gershenfeld (1993), reference groups provide values for individuals on which to base personal decisions and norms that justify social behaviour, both of which may or may not be congruent with organisational preferences. Most of us have seen examples when individuals are more influenced by reference groups than organisations about how to dress or interact with others at work.

Although informal groups exist to satisfy individual needs, they also provide contributions to the formal organisation. Examples of some of the primary contributions of informal groups are given in Exhibit 10-2.

How groups develop

Groups have life cycles similar to people. They are born, grow, develop and often die. A group's effectiveness is influenced by its stage of development and how well its members have learned to work together. A newly formed task force reacts much differently to threatening changes than does an older, more stable formal standing task group (Hughes, 1991). To become stable, cohesive and effective, a group must resolve issues about goals, power and intimacy as it progresses through several stages of maturation (see 'Research focus').

EXHIBIT 10–2 What informal groups contribute

Without informal group memberships, individuals often feel lonely, insecure and alienated. They also have no way to verify their perceptions of events, expectations or contributions.

Contributions to individuals

1 Satisfaction of social and affiliation needs.
2 Satisfaction of needs for security and support.
3 Enhanced status for members if the group is perceived by others as prestigious.
4 Enhanced feelings of self-esteem if a member is valued by other group members.
5 Feeling more competent by sharing the power of the group to influence and achieve.

Contributions to organisations

1 Solidify common social values and expectations congruent with organisational culture.
2 Provide and enforce guidelines for appropriate behaviour.
3 Provide social satisfaction unlikely for anonymous individual workers to experience.
4 Provide a sense of identity that often includes a certain degree of status.
5 Enhance members' access to information.
6 Help integrate new employees into the informal expectations of the organisation.

Sources: summarised from P.K. Lunt (1991) 'The Perceived Causal Structure of Loneliness', *Journal of Personality and Social Psychology*, July pp. 26–34; and Keith Davis (1962), *Human Relations at Work* (2nd edn). New York, NY: McGraw-Hill, pp. 235–257.

Research focus: **the five-stage model of group development**

Several research-based theories suggest that most groups progress in sequence through the five stages of forming, storming, norming, performing and adjourning, as demonstrated by Tuckman and Jensen (1977) and later extended by Kormanski and Mozenter (1987). Different groups will remain at various stages of development for different lengths of time, and some may remain at a given stage permanently, either by design or because the group is stalled. By being aware of a group's progress, its leader can facilitate members' functioning at each stage and the transition to the next stage of development. This five-stage model of group development is illustrated in Exhibit 10-3.

Forming

In a newly formed group, many uncertainties exist about the group's purpose, structure and leadership. Members are concerned about exploring friendship and task potentials. They do not have a strategy for addressing the group's task. They do not yet know what behaviours are acceptable as they try to determine how to satisfy needs for acceptance and personal goal satisfaction. As awareness increases, this stage of group development is completed when members accept themselves as a group and commit to group goals.

EXHIBIT 10–3 Stages of group development

FORMING
Awareness:
Commitment
Acceptance

STORMING
Conflict:
Clarification
Belonging

NORMING
Co-operation:
Involvement
Support

PERFORMING
Productivity:
Achievement
Pride

ADJOURNING
Separation:
Recognition
Satisfaction

Storming

The next stage involves intragroup conflict about the clarification of roles and behavioural expectations. Disagreement is inevitable as members attempt to decide on task procedures, role assignments, ways of relating and power allocations. One objective at this stage is to resolve the conflicts about power and task structure. Another is to work through the accompanying hostility and replace it with a sense of acceptance and belonging that is necessary to progress to the next stage.

Norming

Co-operation is the theme of the norming stage, which involves the objectives of promoting open communication and increasing cohesion as members establish a common set of behavioural expectations. Members agree on a structure that divides work tasks, provides leadership and allocates other roles. Desired outcomes for this stage of group development are increased member involvement and mutual support as group harmony emerges. If groups become too contented, however, they can be stalled at this stage because they do not want to create conflict or challenge established ways of doing things.

Performing

In this stage of development, group members are no longer in conflict about acceptance and how to relate to each other. Now members work interdependently to solve problems and are committed to the group's mission. Productivity is at its peak. Desired outcomes are achievement and pride, and major concerns include preventing loss of enthusiasm and sustaining momentum. For permanent work groups it is hoped that this is the final and ongoing state of development.

Adjourning

The adjournment or separation phase occurs when temporary groups like task forces and committees disband after they have accomplished their goals. Feelings about disbanding range from sadness and depression at the loss of friendships, to happiness and fulfilment due to what has been achieved. The leader can facilitate positive closure at this stage by recognising and rewarding group performance. Ceremonial events bring closure to the desired emotional outcome of a sense of satisfaction and accomplishment.

Moderators to the five-stage sequence of group development

In task groups created to develop solutions to immediate problems within prescribed time periods, these developmental phases are less separate and distinct than the five-stage model of group development suggests. Two factors that affect the process are task deadlines and group composition.

- **Task deadlines.** Given a deadline for task completion, a group will develop its own distinctive approach to problem-solving until about halfway through the allotted time. At this midpoint, most groups change their approach to the task and apply a burst of concentrated energy, re-examining assumptions and ineffective behaviours and replacing them with new approaches that usually contribute to dramatic gains in progress. Gersick (1989, 1991) and Romanelli and Tushman (1994) suggested that these more productive behaviours are maintained until close to the deadline, when a final burst of activity to finish the job occurs.

▶

> ■ **Group composition.** Watson *et al.* (1993) suggest other developmental differences have been found between culturally diverse and homogeneous groups. Newly formed homogeneous groups are more effective than heterogeneous ones through the first part of the task (performing) stage. After settling into the performing stage, however, heterogeneous groups catch up and perform in a manner comparable to homogeneous ones. More diverse groups actually become slightly more proficient at identifying problems and generating solution alternatives if they continue to work together for long periods of time. Look at the case of Norwich Union in the Dynamics of Diversity box, and think about how a diverse workforce can be good for business.

Norwich Union gets feedback from older staff

In an effort to encourage older workers Norwich Union asked its workers why they had joined the firm, if their experience has matched their expectations, and how they find working with younger employees.

Norwich Union is surveying its older employees about their experiences to help it recruit more employees over the age of 45.

The insurance company has formed a number of focus groups made up of employees over 45 who have joined the company in the past year.

The workers will be asked why they joined the firm, if their experience has matched their expectations, and how they find working with younger employees, who in some cases are their managers.

Norwich Union plans to use the results to help it shape future recruitment strategy.

Currently, 78 per cent of Norwich Union employees are under 40, but the average age of its customers is 50. A large proportion of workers in its contact centres are aged between 18 and 24.

Sandy Wilson, head of HR policy and reward at Norwich Union, said there was a strong business case for increasing diversity.

'We are looking at improving our customer experience,' she said. 'Getting more older workers on the front line can only be a good thing. Our aim is to enrich our working environment by creating a workforce that is more flexible, creative and reflective of our customer base.'

A survey of 1000 people of working age conducted by Norwich Union found that more than a fifth (22 per cent) believed their employer culture did not support older workers.

The research also found that 17 per cent said a lack of part-time flexibility was preventing them from working longer.

'The role employers can play in encouraging employees to retire later is important,' said Wilson.

Source: originally published in *People Management*, 27 October 2005, Katie Hope, reprinted with permission.

Discussion questions

1 Why is it important to attract and keep older workers?

2 What advice would you give Norwich Union to help it implement a diversity policy?

Research focus: **Belbin's team roles**

In a study of business game teams at the Carnegie Institute of Technology in 1981 Belbin (1993) found that for a group to be effective there are eight necessary roles that, ideally, would be spread evenly among the team. These were known as the co-ordinator, the shaper, the plant, the monitor-evaluator, the resource investigator, the implementer, the team worker and the finisher. Belbin also identified a ninth person, the specialist, who would join the group when required; this person may be a legal expert, IT specialist or accountant, say.

Belbin noticed that when a group's task changes, individuals may move from one role to another and, in small groups, people may occupy more than one role.

Independent research by Fisher *et al.* (1998) confirms that groups that have a balance of member roles are the most effective, although there has been some argument as to whether as many as nine members are necessary in order for a group to be effective.

The research by Belbin and the subsequent self-perception inventory developed by Belbin and his colleagues, enables team members to be identified prior to a team's formation and can be useful when teams need to be assembled quickly. However, care needs to be taken when using this technique, to ensure the appropriate people are selected as people's roles are not necessarily static.

EXHIBIT 10–4 Belbin's (1993) team roles

Role	Characteristics	Strengths	Possible weaknesses	Contributions to work team
Co-ordinator	Calm Self-confident Disciplined Controlled	Optimist Self-disciplined Common sense Organisational skills	Average intellect or creative ability	Presides and co-ordinates, good at working through others
Shaper	Highly strung Dominant Extrovert	Challenges inertia Irritable Dynamic	Impatient Argumentative	Passionate about the task and is good at arousing others and spurring to action
Plant	Introvert Individualist Imaginative	Intellectual Creative thinker Unorthodox	Disregards practice or procedure Doesn't take account of reality	An innovative person full of imagination and ideas
Monitor-evaluator	Prudent Unemotional Unbiased	Discreet High intellect Rational Analytical	Uninspiring, 'a jobs-worth' Tactless	Analyses project and spots possible flaws, keeps the plant in check
Resource investigator	Popular Sociable Extrovert Relaxed	Good social skills Communicative	Not an originator of ideas Can easily lose interest	Good for networking and making contact outside the team
Implementer	Trustworthy Efficient Practical	Administrator Conscientious Systematic	Not a leader Inflexible	Transforms plans into action Often performs tasks others may consider boring

continued ▶

EXHIBIT 10–4 continued

Role	Characteristics	Strengths	Possible weaknesses	Contributions to work team
Team worker	Supportive Sensitive Diplomatic	Shows concern for others Team player	Indecisive in a crisis	Maintains team spirit and helps reduce conflict Often only noticed when absent
Finisher	Conscientious Thorough Anxious	Perfectionist Pays attention to detail	Worries over small details	Ensures the team concentrates on the necessary tasks to achieve deadlines Not always popular
Specialist	Independent Single-minded	Dedicated	Protective of expertise	Provides knowledge and skills when needed

Group structures

After a group has progressed through the stages of development described in the 'Research focus', certain stable patterns of relationships exist among its members. Communication networks have been established, bonds of intimacy and interpersonal attraction have emerged, powerful and influential members have been identified, agreement regarding appropriate behaviour has been reached, and the relative esteem for each team member has been established in a hierarchy. These patterns of relationships constitute the group's structure and directly impact each member's behaviours.

Functional group roles

A **role** is a set of recurring behaviours that is expected from a member by others in the group.

role
A set of recurring behaviours that are expected from a member by others in a group.

task roles
Roles that directly help accomplish group goals.

maintenance roles
Roles that help establish and maintain good relationships among group members.

personal roles
Roles that only meet individual needs and are usually detrimental to the group.

Kolb *et al.* (1991), Kayser (1990) and Benne and Sheats (1948) argue that some group roles are functional in that they help the group achieve its goals. Other roles, which are usually motivated by specific individual needs, are dysfunctional and interfere with group effectiveness. After a group has matured to the performing stage, personal behaviours detrimental to the group are mostly eliminated and members adopt behaviours beneficial to group performance.

Earlier research by Benne and Sheats (1948) had also found that it is necessary for two types of functional role to emerge for a group to continue to exist and accomplish its objectives in a satisfactory manner. They called these **task roles**, which directly help accomplish group goals. **Maintenance roles** help establish and maintain good relationships among group members. Examples of these roles are listed in Exhibit 10-5, along with some frequent **personal roles**, which are sets of behaviours that meet individual needs and are usually detrimental to the group's interaction. Personal roles need to be replaced with maintenance and task roles before a group can become an effective team.

EXHIBIT 10–5 Group roles

Task roles	Maintenance roles	Personal roles
Initiating	Encouraging	Blocking
Giving information	Harmonising	Seeking recognition
Seeking information	Setting group standards	Dominating
Summarising	Gatekeeping	Avoiding
Elaborating	Compromising	Seeking help
Consensus testing	Providing feedback	

Norms

Groups develop common expectations, called *norms*, to reinforce functional role behaviours

norms

Commonly held expectations about appropriate group member behaviour.

and prevent dysfunctional personal behaviours. **Norms** are expectations about appropriate individual and group behaviour commonly agreed on by members. They are established over time for behaviours that have a significant impact on a group, like facilitating its survival, increasing the predictability of member behaviours, ensuring member satisfaction, expressing values important to the group's identity, and preventing embarrassing interpersonal problems (Feldman, 1984).

Types of norm

Norms tell group members how to behave in certain situations. *Formal norms* exist as written rules and procedures for all employees to obey. Most norms, however, are *informal* in that they develop from group members' own experiences of what behaviours help and hinder their performance and satisfaction. Some informal norms are *functional* and others are *dysfunctional* in facilitating the achievement of organisational goals.

Goodman *et al.* (1987) contend that there are common classes of norm that appear in most work groups. Perhaps the most common are about *performance-related processes* that provide members with guidelines about things like how hard to work, how to do a job, how much to produce and how to communicate. There are usually norms about *appearance* that indicate appropriate dress standards, how to look busy and how to appear loyal to the company. *Informal social arrangements* are also dictated by norms regulating with whom members should joke around, eat lunch and become friendly. Finally, norms regulate the *allocation of resources* like who gets the corner office, assignment of onerous jobs and who gets new office equipment.

How norms develop

Norms usually develop gradually and informally as group members learn what behaviours are necessary to function effectively. They may also be established more rapidly in one or more of the following ways (Feldman, 1984). *Explicit statements by supervisors or influential co-workers* about actions that facilitate group success can define specific role expectations, determine acceptable personal behaviours (e.g. how colleagues address each other, lateness, personal phone calls) and define legitimate ways of accomplishing work. *Critical events* can establish important precedents that become accepted norms. For example, if a member tells people in other units about hiring plans, which results in the new position being lost, norms about secrecy might develop to protect the group in similar situations in the future.

Primacy refers to the first behaviour pattern that emerges in a group, which often sets group expectations. People usually continue to sit in the same seats they sat in at their first meeting even though original seats were not assigned and people could change where they sit at every meeting. On the other hand, some group norms emerge because members bring expectations with them from other work groups in previous organisations. Such *carry-over behaviours* from past situations increase the predictability of group members' behaviours in new settings. For example, students and professors bring with them relatively constant sets of expectations to each class. Consequently, students do not have to continually relearn their roles from class to class.

How norms are enforced

Groups want their members to conform to norms and can apply a wide variety of techniques to pressure individuals into changing their behaviours. If a member strongly desires to be accepted by the group, just being informed of group norms is often enough to cause compliance. Praising the member who exactly meets the group's production norms will reinforce commitment.

When a member is observed deviating from agreed-on behaviours, the group usually applies pressure to enforce conformance to its norms. The member is first reminded of the range of behaviours acceptable to the group and then perhaps teased. If norms are greatly exceeded, the deviant member may be ostracised.

A group is more likely to reject a person who violates its norms when he or she has not conformed or performed adequately in the past. On the other hand, a member can build 'idiosyncracy credits' by behaving consistently with group expectations and contributing effectively to group goals. These credits are spent when the person performs badly or violates norms. When credits are expended the person will most likely be punished for violating norms.

Status within groups

As a group proceeds in its work, some members will contribute more to the group's productivity and camaraderie, earning them greater respect or making them better liked than others. **Status** is a measure of relative worth and respect conferred on an individual by the group. Early in a group's life, status rankings are temporarily determined by each person's status outside the group, based on things like education, income, occupation or title. Over time a more permanent status pattern develops based on each member's role and contribution to group goals (Napier and Gershenfeld, 1993).

status
The measure of relative worth and respect conferred upon an individual by the group.

Higher status is more likely to be awarded to members who are willing to put in the necessary work to make the group successful. Members who intentionally violate group norms for personal benefit are usually ranked at the bottom of the social hierarchy because they pose a threat to the group's security and integrity.

Cohesiveness

Keyton and Springston (1990) argue that successful performance of both task and maintenance roles contributes directly to positive feelings about membership in a group. When members like one another and the group itself, the group is **cohesive** – that is, held together by the close interpersonal bonds of its members, who highly value their association and want to maintain it. The more cohesive a group, the more effective it will be in meeting member needs and the more conformity it can demand from its members.

cohesive
The degree of attractiveness of a group to its members and the closeness of the interpersonal bonds between group members.

Sources of cohesiveness

According to Summers *et al.* (1988), group cohesiveness springs from many sources. Eight of the factors that make membership attractive to group members are listed in Exhibit 10-6.

Cohesion is likely to be high if the *goals* of the group are clearly specified and compatible with member needs. Lack of agreement on goals or incompatibility of personal and group goals will disrupt cohesiveness. *Successful accomplishment* of goals generates positive feelings about the group and its members. Continued failure, on the other hand, can cause continued frustration or member withdrawal from the group. Losing sports teams, for example, frequently suffer from dissension and finger-pointing born of frustration from lack of wins.

Yetton and Bottger (1983) suggest that, as group *size* increases, both interactions and communications begin to break down and cohesiveness decreases. Groups of five to seven are large enough to provide diverse inputs and small enough to give members the opportunity to voice their opinions, make contribution, and be recognised. Groups of more than 15 members generate feelings of anonymity ('Who needs me?') in all but a few members.

If the group has a *charismatic leader* or consists of members who are personally *attracted* to one another, cohesiveness is likely to be high. Attraction may be based on common values, willingness to support one another, physical characteristics, common interests, or any number of other factors that members find desirable in one another.

Attacks from external entities that are perceived as threatening to the group's fundamental purpose create a shared resistance, increased commitment to the group, and tighter bonds among its members. Internal differences are minimised under these conditions, and cohesiveness increases as members dedicate themselves to common causes. Japanese business leaders are adept at creating cohesiveness based on an almost warlike vision of competing firms as 'enemies' to be defeated. Trades unions often use the same tactic against management.

Membership in a *high-status* group is valued more than membership in a group that others disdain. Group status may depend on past success, the importance of group activities, the group's level in the organisation, or the standards for admission. Think of the football teams people support. Those in the Premiership tend to have a much larger fan membership than those playing in lower leagues.

Competition within a group tends to decrease cohesiveness, while working together towards a common goal increases it. Tasks and reward systems that promote *co-operation* among members promote feelings of goodwill and discourage competitive win–lose situations and the resulting negative feelings.

Women are thought to be more co-operative and less competitive with people whom they see as friends or team-mates than are men. Studies such as that by Bettenhausen (1991), have consistently reported that all-female groups are more cohesive than all-male or mixed-sex groups.

Cohesive groups come in many styles and sizes. Consider the effectiveness of the different groups of public-sector workers and the type of support they need to give each other.

EXHIBIT 10 – 6 *Sources of group cohesiveness*

Common goals
Success experience
Small size
Interpersonal attraction
Challenge of a common enemy
High status
Co-operation among members
Female composition

Team loyalty: in good company

Corporate social responsibility (CSR) is a standard that can be applied to varying degrees. But what does it mean in real terms?

Some companies embrace CSR as an inherent part of their business strategy from day one. Others find it is something that evolves in tandem with the wider world as priorities change and responsibility climbs higher up the agenda.

Boots, a company that is more than 150 years old, has made great strides in CSR and has been nominated for a Business in the Community award this year. It was among the first to champion family-friendly policies for employees. And, in 2001, Boots became the first organisation to offer staff formal accreditation for their work in the community.

One of Boots' corporate statements says: 'A business will only thrive when it builds on the skills and retains the commitment of the people who work within it. It's a key part of our corporate responsibility to achieve this by the way we reward our employees, develop and train them, and earn their trust.'

Voluntary work plays a large part in its CSR programme. The company started a Skills for Life scheme that offered employees the chance to be involved in community activities during company time. In 2002, Boots employees spent 50 000 hours on voluntary activities, which equates to £500 000.

The company also began a My Health programme to support and develop initiatives and events delivering health promotion messages in the community. It has teamed up with primary care trusts, hospital NHS trusts and New College, Nottingham (NCN), to execute its many projects. One scheme is the creation of a dedicated 'Look Good ... Feel Better' beauty room at Nottingham City Hospital. This provides free workshops for women with cancer. Its 'Time for a Treat' programme expands on that concept, providing health and beauty treatments aimed particularly at elderly patients and the parents of neonatal babies, NHS staff and wider community groups, including those who are socially excluded, have mental health problems or self-harm. NCN trains volunteers from Boots to provide a basic therapeutic massage for these groups.

Each volunteering opportunity is matched to the skills required by a specific job role, including leadership, relationship-building and creativity. Employees work with their line managers to select the voluntary activities that will best complement any skills that need to be developed. This could take the form of managing someone on work experience, becoming a literacy volunteer, giving patients massages or mentoring – all activities that will help to improve someone's professional competency. 'Because the project is so strategically aligned to where the business is going, our people are inspired,' says Sandra Rose, personnel manager at Boots. 'We advertised for volunteers for the massage service and in 48 hours 30 people came forward, many of whom had not previously been involved in volunteer work in the community.' The company conducted a survey of its main site in Nottingham and found that 80 per cent of employees felt either 'very positive' or 'positive' about the company when told how much it gave back to the community.

Source: Joy Persaud in *People Management*, 10 July 2003, p. 36.

Discussion questions

1 How do you think the nature of the job can affect group cohesiveness?

2 Do you think these strategies prevent an 'us and them' situation?

Consequences of group cohesiveness

Members of cohesive groups have common goals and values, and satisfy their needs by being together. Members value their membership highly and want to maintain it. The result is a high degree of conformity to group norms and a high degree of group influence over individual members. High cohesiveness can, however, have either positive or negative consequences for group productivity, job satisfaction and growth.

Productivity

Highly cohesive groups have, according to Mullen and Copper (1994), the potential to be more productive than groups with low cohesiveness, but this potential is not always realised. Much depends on whether the group identifies with the organisation's goals and whether its norms support high productivity. Highly cohesive groups tend to have more uniform output among members than do less cohesive groups because cohesive group members adhere closely to production norms. Keller (1986) suggests that, as a consequence, productivity will be high if a group's norms support organisational goals, but productivity will be low if its norms oppose the organisation's goals. These relationships between cohesiveness, group norms and productivity are illustrated in Exhibit 10-7.

Satisfaction

Cohesive groups place a high value on themselves and their tasks, which raises the group's status in its members' eyes. The high degrees of acceptance and mutual attraction among group members result in less internal tension and more genuine camaraderie. Consequently, satisfaction of individuals' needs and feelings of well-being tend to run high in cohesive groups, regardless of whether this synergy is focused for or against organisational objectives.

Growth

If they are not cohesive, groups offer little support for sharing knowledge and teaching skills. In highly cohesive groups members share and learn from one another because members like one another and take pride in the group's performance. It is possible, however, that enforced compliance to group norms and standards may prevent members from achieving their task and interpersonal potential. If, for example, a highly cohesive group maintains low output norms and adheres to a rigid social structure, the development of a specific individual's technical skills and interpersonal satisfaction may be thwarted.

Group versus individual problem-solving

Although groups often take more time than individuals to make decisions, well-managed ones are usually more creative, produce better-quality decisions, generate more acceptance of

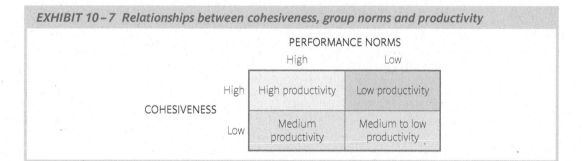

EXHIBIT 10-7 Relationships between cohesiveness, group norms and productivity

		PERFORMANCE NORMS	
		High	Low
COHESIVENESS	High	High productivity	Low productivity
	Low	Medium productivity	Medium to low productivity

decisions and have more commitment to effective implementation (Shaw, 1981). However, groups have characteristics that, if not managed properly, can impede their effectiveness. Some of the important advantages and disadvantages of group versus individual decision-making are summarised from work by Maier (1967) and Schwartz and Levin (1990) in Exhibit 10-8.

The threats to group effectiveness

The potential disadvantages of groups contribute to four well-studied threats to effectiveness. Inappropriate conformity and groupthink are directly related to members' needs for acceptance. Social loafing can be tied to ambiguous responsibilities. Individualism is a competing goals issue.

Inappropriate conformity

Asch (1951) suggests that when individual members go along with group decisions they believe are clearly wrong, they are conforming inappropriately. Most of us can think of at least a couple of times when we have gone along with the group against our better judgement. Plenty of examples exist of how business groups too often do the same thing in accounts of practices like sexual harassment, insider trading, 'cooking the books' and illegal hazardous waste disposal. The recent Enron scandal is a prime example of this.

EXHIBIT 10–8 Advantages and disadvantages of group problem-solving

Advantages groups have over individuals	Disadvantages groups have compared with individuals
■ *More knowledge and information.* A group of people meeting together to solve a problem has more breadth and, quite often, more depth of experience and knowledge than any one individual. This is especially true if members come from diverse backgrounds.	■ *Competing goals.* Group members often have prior commitments to other reference groups or have personal agendas that conflict. These differences can lead to disagreement about alternative solutions, and to destructive conflict.
■ *Diversity of viewpoints.* A number of people with different experiences can generate more options and creative alternatives. They also bring a greater number of approaches to solving the problem.	■ *Time consuming.* People have to plan and co-ordinate group meetings and then wait for everyone to arrive. The processes of being understood, resolving interpersonal conflicts and irrelevant side conversations also detract from group problem-solving efficiency.
■ *Increased understanding.* By participating in the problem-solving process, group members have a better understanding of the decision and why it was made.	■ *Social pressure to conform.* Especially in highly cohesive groups, members often conform to majority opinions that are not optimal in order to gain liking and acceptance.
■ *Increased acceptance.* Group members are more likely to accept a decision they understand. Also, a participative decision, in North American democratic-type societies, is often perceived as more legitimate than an autocratic decision by a single manager, which might be considered arbitrary.	■ *Domination by a few.* High status, power or just an assertive personality can cause certain members to dominate group discussions and influence decisions that they prefer. If the dominating people do not have the best ideas and those who do are kept silent, the quality of the group decision will suffer.
■ *Better implementation.* Participation in a decision creates a feeling of ownership of 'our decision' versus one by some authority figure. People want to show that they are right and consequently will work hard to implement it themselves as well as encouraging others to do the same.	■ *Ambiguous responsibility.* Since no one individual is held responsible for a group's decision, there is often uncertainty about who is accountable for implementing decisions and who gets the credit or blame for outcomes. Often this can lead to decisions that are more risky than is appropriate for the organisation, because no one in particular will be held accountable if the decision fails.

Research focus: the groupthink phenomenon

groupthink

A state in groups where the pressures for conformity are so great that they dominate members' abilities to realistically appraise alternative decision options.

According to Aldag and Fuller (1993), groupthink exists when pressures for conformity are so great they dominate group members' concerns for realistic appraisal of alternative courses of action. Groupthink occurs in highly cohesive groups that desire to agree. Classic governmental examples of groupthink occurred when Margaret Thatcher and her cabinet decided on the Poll Tax, or when the Conservative Government lost the 1997 general election after 18 years in power because it ignored warnings that 'sleaze' would make it unelectable.

Janis (1982) identified eight dominant symptoms of groupthink that can be gleaned from such disastrous situations. All these decision-making groups endeavoured to avoid disagreements, overlooked disturbing information, rejected valuable criticism and failed to voice dissenting opinions. Exhibit 10-9 highlights the symptoms of groupthink.

Studies by Janis (1982) of successful policy decisions reveal that effective groups do not exhibit these symptoms. It appears that groupthink can be avoided if a leader remains neutral, encourages criticism, asks for new ideas and brings in people from outside the group, like advisers or consultants, to raise alternative views.

EXHIBIT 10 – 9 Symptoms of groupthink

1 **Illusions of group invulnerability**. Members of the group feel they are invincible, resulting in risk taking (e.g. Pearl Harbor).

2 **Collective rationalisation**. Refusal to consider contradictory data or to consider unpleasant alternatives thoroughly (e.g. failure to consider engineers' warnings about the O-rings in the Challenger disaster).

3 **Illusion of group morality**. Members of the group feel it is 'right' and morally correct (e.g. in religious or ethnic wars like those between the Arabs and Jews, or Serbs, Croats and Muslims).

4 **Stereotypes of competitors**. Shared negative opinions of treating groups as weak, evil and stupid (e.g. communists versus capitalists, Muslims versus Christians).

5 **Pressure to conform**. Direct pressure to conform is applied to a member who suggests other alternatives or that the group may be wrong (e.g. L.A. police officer hitting Rodney King because the others expected him to even though he thought it was wrong).

6 **Self-censorship**. Members do not share personal concerns if contrary to overall group opinion (President Kennedy's cabinet members with doubts about the Bay of Pigs invasion remaining silent).

7 **Illusions of unanimity**. Erroneously believing that all are in agreement and accepting consensus prematurely (e.g. if one person would have opposed the Bay of Pigs invasion, Kennedy would have cancelled it, but no one did and consensus was assumed).

8 **Mind guarding**. Members of the group protect the group from hearing disturbing ideas or viewpoints from outsiders (e.g. keeping new conflicting test results suppressed just before a new drug is approved).

Source: Irving L. Janis (1982) *Groupthink: Psychological Studies of Policy Decision and Fiascoes* (2nd edn). Boston, MA: Houghton Mifflin Company. Copyright 1982 by Houghton Mifflin Company. Adapted with permission.

Social loafing

Common logic says that the productivity of a group should at least equal the sum of the productivity of each individual member, and the research on the advantages of groups over individuals suggests that they may be even more productive than the sum of individual member outputs in problem-solving situations. Research studies by Shepperd (1993) have determined, however, that individual efforts actually decline as group size increases. This tendency for individuals to exert less effort when working in a group than when working individually is called **social loafing**.

social loafing
The tendency of individuals to exert less effort when working in a group than when working individually.

One reason for social loafing, according to Jackson and Harkins (1985), is the possibility that if you perceive that other group members are not contributing their fair share, you might reduce your own input to re-establish a perceived equity of effort. Another possibility, suggested by Williams *et al.* (1981), is that if members think that individual inputs are not identifiable, this dispersion of responsibility will cause some to become 'free riders'. Finally, according to George (1992), if the group task is perceived as unimportant or is boring, and the previous two conditions exist, motivation may decrease even more. This research, according to Harkins and Szymanski (1989), has important implications for managers of groups, since social loafing does not seem to occur when group members expect their outputs to be measured.

Group composition

Social loafing has been found to be more prevalent in individualistic cultures like the United States or Great Britain, where people are competitive and motivated by personal gain, than in collectivist societies like Japan, China or Germany, which support group goals over self-interest (Earley, 1989). Consequently, groups in collectivist societies usually perform better than groups in individualistic societies.

Guzzo and Shea (1992) suggest that heterogeneous groups composed of dissimilar members are likely to have more *diversity* in experiences, information and viewpoints that can enhance their problem-solving effectiveness. Watson *et al.* (1993) found that this group advantage may be modified, however, if the group diversity is generated from differences in cultural background (racial, religious or national), which can promote lack of identification with the group and difficulties in communicating and solving conflicts. According to Adler (1991), these interpersonal problems can detract from task effectiveness and result in ambiguity, confusion and miscommunication, unless members learn how to be more open to different perspectives and manage their disagreements productively.

Smith-Lovin and Brody (1989) suggest that although men and women usually work well together in groups, *gender differences* can cause problems in group effectiveness. In mixed-gender groups, for example, men interrupt women significantly more than they do other men. Women, on the other hand, interrupt less often and less effectively, but do not discriminate between men or other women. This difference contributes to decreased power and influence for women.

Ott (1989) suggests that it can be even worse if women move into professions previously dominated by men. Men more often than women want to keep the other sex out and put up resistance that can manifest itself in discrimination and harassment. Group leaders need to be aware of sexual tensions in mixed-gender groups and be ready to prevent sexual harassment and discrimination.

Source: Working Women, October 1995.
© Signes Wilkinson, Cartoonists & Writers
Syndicate/cartoonweb.com.

Making groups more effective

Being aware of and compensating for the above threats to group effectiveness can go a long way towards improving group functioning. Effective leadership in facilitating the group process and running effective meetings can also help immensely. Finally, team-building activities that transform work groups into high-performance teams can boost group effectiveness where appropriate.

Leadership facilitation

According to Driskell and Salas (1991), whether a group will be effective or ineffective depends primarily on the skills of its members and its leader's ability to facilitate the process. For example, lower-status group members usually defer to those with higher status, even though they may be the ones with the best ideas. Group leaders need to ensure that all participants feel free to contribute. They should avoid trying to persuade others in the problem-solving group to adopt their own preference. Schwartz and Levin (1990) suggest that the leader's role is to establish a co-operative environment in which all opinions are heard and evaluated before a solution is reached. If the leader is not aware of the dynamics of the group process or is not effective in the role of facilitator, a cohesive group may succumb to threats like social loafing and groupthink.

Meeting guidelines

Despite numerous jokes and complaints about the time they waste, meetings are the group process used on a regular basis by most organisations to combine expertise and solve organisational problems. The attitudes, qualifications and behaviours of the people attending a meeting are important contributors to its effectiveness. All these factors can be influenced by the meeting leader who sets up formal procedures to control the process. Some established guidelines for facilitating meeting effectiveness are summarised in Exhibit 10-10.

> **EXHIBIT 10 – 10 Guidelines for conducting productive meetings**
>
> Although most meetings have well-deserved reputations for being both inefficient and ineffective, there are some well-established guidelines that can help improve the process. Running a meeting productively requires the following actions.
>
> 1 **Preparing and distributing an agenda well in advance of the meeting.** This allows participants to know who should attend, how to prepare and what the objectives are.
> 2 **Consulting with participants before the meeting.** This ensures that all participants have properly prepared and do not forget anything.
> 3 **Establishing specific time parameters.** To avoid wasting time and allow participants to plan other activities, meetings should begin and end on time.
> 4 **Maintaining focused discussion.** Disruptions, interruptions and irrelevant discussions should be discouraged so that the discussion can be directed to the issues at hand.
> 5 **Encouraging and supporting participation by all members.** The best ideas may be in the heads of silent members, who need to be encouraged to participate.
> 6 **Encouraging the clash of ideas.** Critical thinking, constructive disagreement and reality testing are necessary to avoid premature decisions.
> 7 **Discouraging the clash of personalities.** Personal attacks cause anger and hostility that detract from meeting effectiveness.
> 8 **Facilitating careful listening.** Model and encourage concentrated listening where the speaker is empathised with and receives responses from others to ensure understanding.
> 9 **Bringing proper closure.** Meetings should be ended by summarising accomplishments and allocating follow-up assignments.
>
> *Source*: adapted from S.R. Robbins and P.L. Hunsaker (1996) *Training in Interpersonal Skills* (2nd edn). Englewood Cliffs, NJ: Prentice Hall, 1996, pp. 171–184.

One way of increasing meeting efficiency is to allow participants to remain at their desks and interact through *electronic meeting systems (EMSs)*. EMSs consist of sophisticated computer software that keeps meetings on track and moves the group towards clear, well-thought-out decisions by allowing meeting participants to follow structured, non-personal procedures on personal computers to rapidly solve problems, generate new ideas, assess opinions, make decisions and resolve conflicts. EMSs allow for anonymous inputs so that participants can be completely honest without fear of reprisal, and they can cut meeting times in half because they eliminate digressions, allow several participants to talk at once, and structure the process. On the other hand, the lack of emotional elements and non-verbal inputs, and differences in keyboard skills can be drawbacks.

Motorola uses EMS tools for planning, ranking and rating employee performance, and plotting strategies for the future. At Westinghouse, EMSs are used for any kind of meeting where the need is to gather information and stimulate new ideas, rather than simply disseminate existing information. Westinghouse applies EMSs to develop strategic plans for international marketing, to collect and evaluate utility-customer opinions on proposed research and development funding options, to evaluate progress in customer satisfaction, and to plot areas for achieving competitive advantages (Finley, 1992).

Team building

team building
All activities aimed at improving the problem-solving ability of group members by resolving task and interpersonal issues that impede the team's functioning.

Team building includes all activities aimed at improving the problem-solving ability of group members by working through task and interpersonal issues that may impede the team's functioning. Team building can be applied when forming groups or as an intervention to improve existing groups.

Forming new groups

For both task and interpersonal effectiveness, it is usually easier to form a completely new group than to deal with the resistance that must be overcome when trying to change existing groups. New groups do not have to break down any barriers, bad habits, harmful attitudes, inappropriate working relations or procedures. According to Margerison and McCann (1990), addressing the following questions before the group begins to work can get a new group off to a productive start.

- **Where are we going?** Personal and team goals should be clarified so that members share a common vision, purpose and goals. Realistic priorities should be clarified for each person so he or she knows how participation on the team fits in with other commitments.

- **Who are we?** Members should share their expectations and concerns about working with the team. As group members share their strengths, weaknesses, work preferences, values and beliefs, diversity can be dealt with before it causes conflicts.

- **Where are we now?** Members can use the first two steps and determine their existing situation (Where are we now?) compared to their goals (Where are we going?) to determine the final step.

- **How will we get there?** This includes establishing operating guidelines about decision-making, work methods, participation, conflict resolution, work completion and team improvement.

Symptoms indicating that improvement of existing groups is required

Dyer (1987) suggests that a team-building programme is not usually initiated unless someone (the leader, a higher-level manager, a team member or consultant) recognises that the group is having problems working productively as a team. Dyer *et al.* (1990) also argue that there are a number of symptoms which indicate that groups are ineffective.

A common symptom of group problems occurs when members *communicate outside the group* instead of expressing disagreements and concerns during group meetings. Another symptom is *overdependency on the leader* when members should be moving ahead on their own when it is clear that action is needed. *Unrealised decisions* that are made but not carried out can indicate a lack of commitment to group goals. Decreased productivity and satisfaction can signal *hidden conflicts* that are causing group tension. *Fighting without resolution*, evident in continual open arguments and attempts to put down, deject or hurt others, calls for immediate intervention. Finally, the formation of *self-interest subgroups* that put themselves before the needs of the total unit indicates a lack of commitment to the superordinate goals of the team and organisation.

Determining how to improve group performance

Chapter 12 provides an in-depth discussion of the problem-solving process, tools and techniques. The same sequential problem-solving steps can be applied to solve group problems, improve their effectiveness, and build them into high-performance teams. After identifying problems through data gathering (interviews, questionnaires or observations) they are analysed, prioritised and assigned to task groups to solve. Driver *et al.* (1993) suggest that the resulting action plans are then implemented, results are evaluated, and follow-ups are continually applied to ensure that problems are solved effectively. According to Tjosvold (1991) and Katzenback and Smith (1993b), if this process reveals that traditional work groups are not appropriate to achieve objectives, high-performance teams may need to be developed because they often better utilise employee skills and are more adaptable to changing organisational demands. To determine how well a group of which you are a member performs as a team, complete the 'Your turn' rating form. Then discuss your ratings with other members of your group to build your team performance.

Your turn

How well do we work together as a team?

Instructions Think of a team you have recently been a member of (e.g. class project group, student body committee, volunteer group) and complete the following team self-evaluation by circling the number representing your evaluation for each question.

How well are we working together?

	Strongly disagree	Disagree	Neither agree nor disagree	Strongly agree	Agree
1 The team knows exactly what it has to get done.	1	2	3	4	5
2 Team members get a lot of encouragement for new ideas.	1	2	3	4	5
3 Team members freely express their real views.	1	2	3	4	5
4 Every team member has a clear idea of the team's goals.					
5 Everyone is involved in the decisions we have to make.	1	2	3	4	5
6 We tell each other how we are feeling.	1	2	3	4	5
7 All team members respect each other.	1	2	3	4	5
8 The feelings among team members tend to pull us together.	1	2	3	4	5
9 Everyone's opinion gets listened to.					
10 There is very little bickering among team members.	1	2	3	4	5

Scoring and interpretation

To find your total score, add the numbers you have circled. _____

To find your average score, divide the total score by 10. _____

If your average score is 4 or higher, teamwork is strong. If your average is between 3 and 4, teamwork is healthy, but there is room for improvement. If your average is 2 or lower, something is getting in the way of teamwork.

Whatever the score, discussing these issues together with an open mind is likely to improve teamwork.

If possible, meet with your other team members. Compare evaluations and identify which of the 10 items your team agreed were strengths of the team (ratings of 4 or 5) and those that you agreed were weaknesses (ratings of 1 or 2). Discuss what the team needs to do to work more effectively together.

Source: table from John H. Zenger *et al.* (1994) *Leading Teams: Mastering the New Role.* New York, NY: McGraw-Hill. Copyright 1994 The McGraw-Hill Companies. Reproduced with permission of The McGraw-Hill Companies.

How teams differ from groups

We defined a *group* as two or more people who regularly interact with and influence one another over a period of time, perceive themselves as a distinct entity distinguishable from others, share common values and strive for common objectives. Group members may share information, make decisions and help each other, but they produce individual outputs within individual areas of accountability. A work group's performance is the sum of what its members accomplish as individuals. Committees and task forces composed of individuals who work together are therefore not necessarily teams.

team

A relatively permanent work group whose members share common goals, are interdependent and are accountable as a functioning unit to the organisation as a whole.

As summarised in Exhibit 10-11, Katzenback and Smith (1993a) suggest that a **team** is a type of group that can be defined as a 'small number of people with complementary skills, who are committed to a common purpose, set of performance goals, and approach for which they hold themselves mutually accountable'. A team engages in collective work produced by co-ordinated joint efforts that result in more than the sum of the individual efforts, or *synergy*. Members are accountable for performance both as individuals and as a group.

All teams are not created equal, nor should they be

Drucker (1992) distinguishes among three kinds of teams that differ in structure – member behaviour requirements, strengths, vulnerabilities, limitations and requirements. To be effective, each should be matched to the appropriate types of task. If a certain type of team is assigned to the wrong type of task, the results are frustration and low performance, like playing baseball on a tennis court, or vice versa. Teams are tools designed for specific tasks.

The key to effectiveness is to match up team characteristics with situational demands. The first type of team is really like our definition of a group, where players are nominally *on* a team, but do not directly depend on or interact with each other to achieve objectives. Players have fixed positions and specialities that they perform alone. An example is an athletics team or bowling team, where group performance is the sum of individual accomplishments. In industry, it might be a traditional factory assembly line.

Advantages of athletics-style teams are that each member is accountable for specific goals and is evaluated individually. Because no one has to adapt to anyone else on the team, each position can be staffed by egotistical 'stars' that do their jobs in their own ways.

The second is like a *football team*, where players have fixed positions but also need to co-ordinate their efforts as a team. The design teams originated by Japanese car makers are football-type teams, where engineers, manufacturing staff and marketing people work in parallel. Other examples are a symphony orchestra or the casualty unit at hospital.

EXHIBIT 10 – 11 Differences between groups and teams

Groups	Criteria	Teams
Formal established	Leadership	Shared roles
Individual	Accountability	Shared and individual
Sum of individual outputs	Performance	Collective and synergistic
Diverse	Skills	Complementary

Third is the *tennis doubles team*, where a player has a primary rather than fixed position and is required to cover for his or her team-mate by adjusting to their partner's strengths and weaknesses and the constantly changing demands of the game.

Football and tennis doubles teams have flexibility and synergy, but they require more organisational factors than athletics teams. Football teams need a game plan, and everyone in the orchestra puts the Mozart symphony on his or her music stand; stars are only featured if a solo is called for, otherwise they subordinate themselves to the team. The 'flexible manufacturing' plant at General Motors, for example, developed small teams consisting of seven cross-trained members who were allowed flexibility with respect to individual work style as long as everyone contributed only to the one clear goal for the entire team.

Not all teams do the same things

According to Drucker (1992), in most organisations there are essentially three types of group that meet these descriptions of true teams. Katzenback and Smith (1993a, 1993b) suggest that these can be classified by their objectives: to recommend things; to do things; to run things.

Teams that recommend things

After studying and solving specific problems, some teams *recommend things*. They are usually temporary and disband after analysing problems, recommending solutions and formulating action plans for others to implement. Examples of these *problem-solving teams* are task forces, project groups and quality circles. As described in Chapter 3, quality circles are small groups (seven or eight people) from the same work area who voluntarily get together to identify, analyse and recommend solutions for problems relating to quality, productivity and cost reduction.

Teams that make or do things

Teams that *make or do things* are permanent work groups responsible for ongoing, value-added activities like manufacturing, marketing, sales or service. Sundstrom *et al.* (1990) give examples of such as *work teams* that produce things, interacting task groups, like airline flight crews, or autonomous, **self-managed work teams** that are given the authority for their own planning, scheduling, monitoring and staffing. One of the first experiments with autonomous work teams was in the 1970s when Saab built a new engine plant. The plant was designed with teams that were allowed to decide how to assemble engines, establish their work pace, and schedule their own breaks instead of the usual production line form of manufacturing. Results were that the previous annual 70 per cent turnover and 20 per cent absenteeism rates were practically eliminated and productivity increased to one engine per person every 30 minutes (Barker, 1993; Verespel, 1994).

self-managed work teams
Autonomous groups of workers who are given authority for planning, scheduling, monitoring and staffing themselves.

In 1990, 46 per cent of the most successful multinational companies had some employees in autonomous work groups. At the start of the new millennium, in the year 2000, close to half of workers were working on self-managed work teams. As illustrated by the Saab new plant design, it is easier to instal autonomous work teams when a new organisation is being created than to impose them on an existing structure because appropriate applicants and technology can be selected for the new system. According to Hughes (1991) and Manz *et al.* (1990), in well-established organisations, training and socialisation are required and reward systems need to be adapted to the new situation.

Companies such as General Motors, Hewlett-Packard, General Mills and Texas Instruments also report successful applications of self-managed work teams (Lublin, 1992; Hilkirk, 1993; Verespel, 1994). According to Zemke (1993), some organisations have been disappointed however. A review by Goodman *et al.* (1988) of 70 studies on autonomous work groups found that they generally had a positive impact on productivity and responsibility but no significant impact on satisfaction, commitment, absenteeism or turnover.

cross-functional team
A team composed of persons from several different functional units who work together to accomplish a task.

Another type of team that does things is the cross-functional team, which unites people from several different units at the same hierarchical level to accomplish a task. Boeing, the world's largest aeroplane manufacturer, uses cross-functional teams made up of marketing, engineering, manufacturing, finance and service representatives, so that each department knows what the other is doing. The result is better co-ordination of technical specialists, which increases the efficiency of product design and delivery (Yang and Oneal, 1990).

General Motors used cross-functional teams in the development of some of its cars to co-ordinate the entire project from the very beginning. Rubbermaid assembled a cross-functional team composed of engineers, designers and marketers. As a group it went to customers to determine the features preferred in a new portable 'auto office'. Contributions from several different functions ensured that all important design questions were answered, and first-year sales were running 50 per cent above projections (Dumaine, 1990). The Technology Transformation box describes how increased use of technology means that even more emphasis needs to be placed on teamwork.

Teams that run things

Teams that *run things* are made up of top managers of an organisation or its major subunits. These groups are responsible for determining the organisation's mission, goals, strategic plan and operating procedures, and then overseeing the activities of those reporting to them to ensure successful implementation and desired results. Teams run things at any level, from the total organisation down through divisions, departments and programmes, to ongoing functional activities.

How groups develop into teams

French and Bell (1990), Mascowitz (1985) and Dyer *et al.* (1990) have identified effective teamwork as a key characteristic of large companies. Nevertheless, it does not happen automatically. Smither (1991), however, suggests that without proper preparation, quality circles, autonomous work groups, cross-functional teams and other types of team, may not live up to expectations. According to Dyer *et al.* (1990), if members do not trust or support each other, meetings easily degenerate into fighting and arguing, and co-operation is nil.

Newly assembled groups, be they of football players or production workers, go through the same stages of group development described earlier until they reach the performing stage. Even at that stage they need to possess the following characteristics: the team mission is agreed by all; leadership is a shared activity; accountability is both individual and shared collectively; problem-solving is ongoing; effectiveness is measured by the group's collective accomplishments (Katzenback and Smith, 1993b).

Exhibit 10-12 provides some guidelines for managers desiring to build high team performance. Some related considerations are team values, organisational conditions, interpersonal skills and the match of team roles with member work preferences.

technology transformation

Teleworking: mind your manors

The rise of teleworking has brought with it concerns about employers' health and safety responsibilities for their staff who work from home.

In an age when people are increasingly encouraged to work from home or on the move, how far do their employers' health and safety responsibilities stretch? Ursula Huws, a writer and consultant specialising in teleworking, recounts a disturbing tale of an enthusiastic individual who took his laptop PC out on a London Underground train to do some work, dropped the machine on a fellow passenger's foot and promptly landed his employer, a major utility company, with a damages claim for a broken toe. The injured party had seen the company's logo on the machine and sued.

The story, Huws admits, is unusual, but the issue it raises is certainly a real one. 'It's increasingly being recognised that the employer's responsibility for workers' health and safety extends beyond the traditional workplace,' she says.

In recent years, a growing number of major British companies have been through the tentative telework pilot stage and moved on to a situation where working at home is a common practice, very often as part of a wider set of flexible working options. The latest data from the Office for National Statistics shows that the number of so-called 'homeworker teleworkers' has increased by 20 per cent in the past two years, while a looser category, that of people who typically work from home at least one day a week, has increased by 40 per cent in the same period. About 1.6 million people – almost 6 per cent of the UK workforce – are at least occasional teleworkers, it seems. Although teleworking can offer considerable benefits to both the employer and the individual, a successful teleworking policy must get the details right, and health and safety should be near the top of the agenda. The Nationwide Building Society, for example, first considered the issue when it was drawing up health and safety guidelines in the early 1990s. But it developed a far more comprehensive approach in 1998–99, when a cross-divisional working group came up with detailed policies and procedures.

Formal homeworking is prevalent mainly in the building society's technical division, where the number of people teleworking has grown from 20 to 60 in a year, although some employees in the retail recruiting teamwork from home too. The Nationwide also has teams of home-based mobile staff who visit customers who are in mortgage arrears.

Would-be homeworkers are asked to conduct a lengthy risk assessment of their home, which includes photographing the proposed work area. An application to telework requires approval from both the individual's line manager and the Nationwide's cross-divisional home-workers' user group. If the request is granted, a second-stage risk assessment is carried out as soon as the home office is equipped.

The Nationwide provides desks and chairs as well as computers and printers for its teleworkers. Pauline Henderson of the corporate personnel department, who led the homeworking policy team, describes a case where an employee was proposing to work from home using his existing portable PC.

'We said: "No." If homeworking is to be done formally, we can't condone using a laptop,' she says.

When homeworking is on the agenda, companies have to find out more about the homes of their staff than they would normally consider necessary – or indeed acceptable. This process generally incorporates the contractual right of the employer to visit the individual's home for health and safety purposes. The Co-operative Bank spelled out the implications of this right in a formal teleworking agreement, signed with the Bifu bank workers' union (now Unifi) in 1996, that is still used by other employers as a model. The agreement states that, before an employee can start teleworking, their home must be surveyed by a member of the property department. The bank also reserves the right to send in an electrician. Generally, the homeworker foots the bill if electrical work is deemed necessary for safety reasons, with the bank funding any modifications needed to install work-related equipment. After that, the bank claims the right to make ongoing home visits ('prearranged and at a mutually convenient time'). Union health and safety officers may also visit the home.

In the public sector, Kent County Council has been one of a handful of local authorities at the forefront of teleworking. The council's local agreement, devised in 1996 and revised two years later, also covers the sensitive issue of access rights. 'Reasonable notice' will usually be given to members of staff, but the council reserves the right to obtain urgent access to their homes if faulty equipment creates a serious health and safety problem or means that the employee cannot work; for urgent security and audit purposes; or, more generally, for occupational health and safety purposes.

The Nationwide also reserves the right to inspect the homes of its teleworkers, although Henderson says that in practice ways are found to minimise the need for this. 'It's a sensitive issue; managers feel they're intruding,' she points out, adding that the issue is even more delicate if the manager is male and the homeworker is female. The general duty to protect the health, safety and welfare of employees applies wherever they are working – albeit with the proviso 'as far as is reasonably practicable'. The obligation to undertake a risk assessment of work activities also applies where employees are working from home.

But there is insufficient case law to help employers gauge the extent to which they might be held liable for any mishap suffered by their homeworkers. After all, the health and safety legislation also imposes responsibilities on the employee. Kent County Council's agreement, for instance, reminds homeworkers that they are 'expected to co-operate with their line manager in ensuring a safe and healthy working space at home'.

In practice, employers will want to ensure that their liability insurance policies are broad enough to cover those working away from the office. Good employers will also advise employees to check their own household insurance, which can be invalidated if they start working from home.

It is relatively easy to assess the physical health and safety issues associated with a home office, but it is important for employers not to forget psychological issues such as stress. The International Labour Organisation's recent handbook on best practice in teleworking draws attention to the risk of workaholism, with homeworkers more likely than office-based employees to find work demands seeping through into their domestic lives.

Another concern for employers should be homeworkers' isolation. The TUC has suggested that teleworkers should hold regular meetings with managers and colleagues, and ideally spend at least one day every week in the office. This is the approach that the Nationwide adopts.

'I wouldn't advocate 100 per cent homeworking,' Henderson says. 'We still want our homeworkers to interact physically with the rest of their teams. Typically, they'll be homeworking three days out of five and hot-desking for the rest of the time.'

Source: Andrew Bibby in *People Management*, 9 August 2001.

Discussion questions

1 What is meant by teleworking?
2 How can groups be effective in such a fast-changing environment?

EXHIBIT 10–12 How managers can improve team performance

- Determine performance goals that can be immediately achieved to create early success.
- Make sure that members have the appropriate skills.
- Establish demanding performance standards and provide direction.
- Create a sense of urgency in the first meeting.
- Set clear rules of behaviour.
- The leader should model appropriate behaviours.
- Members spend lots of time together bonding as a team socially and while working.
- Continually give the team and individual members positive feedback and rewards.
- Regularly challenge the team with new projects or problems to solve.

Source: J.R. Katzenback and D.K. Smith (1993) 'The Discipline of Teams', *Harvard Business Review*, March–April, pp. 118–119. Reprinted by permission of *Harvard Business Review*. Copyright 1993 by the President and Fellows of Harvard College. All rights reserved.

Common values

Group members need to possess certain core values that reinforce collective accountability for co-operative outputs. Such key values encourage listening and responding constructively to others, giving the benefit of the doubt, providing support, recognising the interests of others and acknowledging their accomplishments (Katzenback and Smith, 1993a).

Supportive organisational conditions

Overall, teams work best if the following four conditions are met: management visibly supports teams; the teams, in turn, support organisational goals; team leaders are skilled at running team meetings; the organisation can afford to lose time and defer productivity while team members learn to work together (Smither, 1991).

Skilled team members

Successful teams are usually composed of members who possess a complementary mix of skills required to do the team's job. *Technical skills* are necessary to meet the team's functional requirements. *Problem-solving* and *decision-making skills* are needed to identify problems and opportunities, evaluate options, make necessary trade-offs, and decide how to proceed. Finally, according to Katzenback and Smith (1993a), *interpersonal skills*, like openness, active listening, feedback, support, trust, mutual influence and constructive confrontation, are required to establish common goals and collaborate to achieve them.

Matching team roles and preferences

If you were the coach of a football team, you would want to get your players into their best positions. You would find out quickly what skills they had and where they felt they could play best. Then you would assign them to specific defensive or offensive roles. During the game you would want your individual players to co-ordinate their specialised roles as defenders, attackers and shooters, rather than have each player try to do all the work alone. These basic principles are the same for managing a work team. Like a coach, a manager tries to accomplish a common goal by linking differentiated roles held by motivated team members (Davies, 1990).

When Lee Iacocca took over at Chrysler, he discovered that not only did it not have the right mix on its management team, but there was also very little co-ordination – that is, everyone worked independently. He was quick to realise that Chrysler's business and financial problems were, to a large extent, a result of its lack of teamwork: all Chrysler's problems really boiled down to the same thing – nobody knew who was on first. There was no team, only a collection of independent players, many of whom had not yet mastered their positions. It was this key organisational problem that Iacocca (1986) set out to resolve because it was the basis for the long-term improvement of the organisation.

How teams maintain and improve their effectiveness

To win games, a sports team must co-ordinate the efforts of individual players. A sports team practises hours each week for that one hour of critical playing time where its performance counts. Members review films of past games, identify mistakes, set goals and plan strategies for the next game. Then the team practises until weaknesses are eliminated and it is skilled at implementing its new action plans.

Work teams also need to co-ordinate the efforts of individual members in order to be effective. Most work teams, however, seldom take time to review their past actions to determine what worked and what did not. They do not spend time learning from past mistakes, nor do they consistently revise goals, plan new strategies, practise new ways of behaving, or get coaching on new methods of communicating and working together.

Even teams effective in the performing stage of development can lose their momentum and develop problems as they mature. Success and familiarity can lead to complacency, groupthink and decreased creativity (Kaeter, 1994). Let us address some actions that maintain and rejuvenate team effectiveness.

Maintaining balanced roles and preferences

Sometimes teams can correct imbalances by moving people around in the organisation or bringing new people in with new skills to fill in the gaps. It is also sometimes possible for team members to 'stretch' into areas not currently high on their list of preferences through appropriate skill training. In addition, people from other groups can be brought in to temporarily fill a certain role. Three more sophisticated techniques are sometimes used to clarify the role expectations and obligations of team members.

Role analysis technique

role analysis technique
Clarifies role expectations and obligations of team members through a structured process of mutually defining and delineating role requirements.

With the role analysis technique, each individual defines the rationale, significance and specific duties of his or her role with the inputs of other team members. According to French and Bell (1990), the final result is a mutually agreed-on set of written 'role profiles' summarising the activities, obligations to others and expected contributions from others for each role on the team.

Role negotiation technique

role negotiation technique
A controlled negotiation process between team members that results in written agreements to change specific behaviours by conflicting parties.

The role negotiation technique is a controlled negotiation process between team members who have problems based on power and authority. It requires team members to focus on work behaviours, not on personal feelings about each other, and to write down what they want others to do more of, do less of, stop doing, and maintain unchanged. The result, according to Harrison (1972), is a written agreement by conflicting parties to change specific behaviour.

Responsibility charting

responsibility charting
A technique for clarifying who is responsible for what on various decisions and actions within the team.

Responsibility charting clarifies who is responsible for which decisions and actions by having team members construct a grid with the types of team decisions and actions in a vertical column on the left side and the specific team members who are involved across the top. Then each team member is assigned one of the five following behavioural expectations for each of the actions: responsibility to initiate action; approval or veto rights; support for implementation; right to be informed (but with no influence); non-involvement in the decision (Beckhard and Harris, 1977).

Maintaining trust and openness

Team members cannot begin to improve their interpersonal relations unless they are made aware of the impact of their behaviours on others and how they can make these behaviours more productive. When individuals feel secure enough to ask others to explain how they perceive their behaviours and to provide suggestions for improvement, other team members can disclose their perceptions in constructive and supportive ways to help eliminate blind spots. By helping each other improve, team members start to trust each other more, become more open, feel better about others and form a cohesive team (Luft, 1984).

sensitivity training
Unstructured feedback meetings where members share observations and feelings about each other to help improve sensitivity of behaviour towards others and the team's ability to function.

structured feedback procedures
Meetings where members share feedback with each other by using a prepared format.

self-assessment inventories
Paper-and-pencil tests that reveal participant characteristics.

According to Pasmore and Fagans (1992), one way to do this is through **sensitivity training**. This is a series of unstructured meetings with no formal agenda, where participants share observations and feelings about team processes, relationships and unspoken consequences, to help each other understand and enhance team performance. There are also **structured feedback procedures** that facilitate the sharing of similar data when group members are more reticent and need more guidance. For example, team members can write what they perceive to be each other's role preferences, style strengths and weaknesses, and other data of interest. Then, each individual reads his or her list to the group and receives clarification (Otto, 1970).

Another approach is to administer **self-assessment inventories** that measure things like behavioural styles, values, tolerance of ambiguity and conflict management styles. These can be scored, interpreted and published for all group members to see. The team can then analyse the scores to better understand why others prefer certain ways of doing things and behave as they do. Incongruencies between personal styles and task assignments and relationship-style differences can be discussed and action plans generated to manage them more appropriately.

exercises and simulations
Activities participants engage in to generate behaviour for feedback that can be analysed and used to develop improvement plans.

Finally, **exercises and simulations** can be utilised to analyse behaviour in a non-threatening setting. How observed behaviours might help and hinder goal accomplishment and team development can then be discussed.

Pocklington Coachworks: a second look

Pocklington Coachworks recognises that, 'a massive part of our success is ongoing communications with the client and that is why we welcome visits to our site at any time so that the progress of your vehicle can be seen at first hand'.

They are quoted as saying 'We listen, we respond, we deliver.'

This has been recognised by Richard Cregan, general manager of Toyota Motorsport GmbH who has said:

> It has been a pleasure to work with everyone at Pocklington Coachworks over the duration of the building of our hospitality units. The level of professionalism and general friendliness afforded to Toyota makes us proud and totally justified in choosing Pocklington over stiff opposition from other companies to build these units.
>
> During the Hospitality Unit project I have come to know and appreciate how Pocklingtons run their company with their colleagues and staff, the teamwork, project management and the attention to detail shown by everyone at Pocklington, can be an example for success in all companies both large and small.

Pocklington's commitment to self-managed teams is one of the reasons it won three awards at the *Evening Press* Business Awards in 2001, winning Business of the Year, Progress through People, and Business Personality of the Year for their managing director Fran Johnson. This is an excellent result of which both the directors and employees of Pocklington can be immensely proud.

Pocklington also recognises that part of managing teams is dealing with change and, as such, has introduced a Champions of Change Award.

'At Pocklington, we do not just recognise team success but individual success too. Business Link and Bergander have been working alongside the directors of Pocklington Coachworks and have produced a system that recognises and rewards individuals, "Champions of Change". Champions are vital in all areas of the company.'

To be a Champion of Change, individuals must achieve the following criteria:

- have 'whatever it takes' attitude
- always positive
- kills negativity
- enthuses others
- passionate about Pocklington
- a proven winner.

All these strategies help to improve commitment and lead to a motivated workforce, which results in a successful company.

Source: www.pocklington.co.uk.

Summary

- The majority of an organisation's work is accomplished by people working on teams, such as quality circles, project groups and autonomous production teams.

- However, some groups work like a 'dream team', appearing to accomplish miracles, while others generate nightmares.

- What makes the difference? The answer lies in appropriate group membership, structures, processes and training. If group members with appropriate skills and attitudes are trained to understand their own and others' role requirements, they can develop themselves to collaborate without dysfunctional conflicts, to achieve common objectives.

- There are several paradoxes to be continually managed, however. One is that the cohesiveness of groups develops when members value their association with one another and their common goals can promote enhanced satisfaction and extra synergy, but it can also reinforce resistance to change and underachievement if members need to relinquish behaviours that are accepted as group norms.

- Another is that the very conformity that standardises behaviour and makes life comfortably predictable may also serve to stifle constructive conflict and creativity. In striving for group acceptance, many members show far less initiative and independent thought than they are capable of demonstrating as individuals.

- Deviators who intentionally violate group norms are often resented and forced back in line, but at times their behaviours can be breakthroughs for productive change.

- To transform groups into high-performing teams, group members need to develop high degrees of trust, open communication, participation and constructive confrontation skills.

- Also, individuals with appropriate skills and interests need to be matched to their preferred work function.

- High-performance teams need to apply team-building techniques aimed at improved working relationships.

- The process of improving team effectiveness includes continual data gathering and analysis to assess areas needing improvement; problem-solving to determine sources and solutions to problems; training and exercises to build the skills and processes necessary for continual high performance.

Areas for personal development

In a global economy, competition between corporations and firms is increasing at a breakneck speed. To compete, firms are required to introduce new products and services almost overnight. While superior technology will give some firms a competitive advantage, the best technology alone is not enough. The most competitive organisations will be the ones that have the 'best people' functioning as teams, using technology to achieve results. Speed will be dictated by how quickly people can respond to competition. Teamwork is therefore a powerful competitive advantage. The following skills will help you build productive teams.

1 **Recognise and facilitate stages of team development.** Knowing the five stages of team development will help you understand what management techniques and leadership styles need to be applied at specific times to maximise team effectiveness and progress. Learn to recognise when a team is forming, storming, norming, performing or adjourning, and respond to the team's needs appropriately.

2 **Understand and work with team norms.** Norms determine acceptable team member behaviours. What time people arrive at work, how late they stay at night, how hard people work, what they wear, and even how people interact with each other, are examples of such norms and behaviours. Inadvertently violating team norms can lead to considerable resistance, hostility and even retaliation. Reward and reinforce positive norms that are in the organisation's best interest, while providing incentives to drop or change negative norms.

3 **Promote team cohesiveness.** Assign people who are compatible with one another to teams so that they can commit to a common direction that is in alignment with overall corporate goals. Other factors that can promote cohesiveness are assigning a charismatic team leader, creating a feeling of competition with other teams, promoting the high status of the team, and including women on the team.

4 **Look out for barriers to group effectiveness.** Non-conformity, groupthink, social loafing and incompatible group member composition can destroy a team's effectiveness. It is important to recognise these negative threats and find ways of combating them in order for a group to be successful. One helpful technique is to bring in a person from outside the group who can provide an objective view of the situation.

5 **Look for symptoms indicating a need for team-building.** Things to look for include concerns being communicated outside the group, over-dependence on the leader, failure to implement decisions, decreased productivity and satisfaction, fighting without resolution, and formation of self-interest subgroups.

6 **Diagnose sources of team problems.** After identifying problems through data gathering (interviews, questionnaires or observations) the problems are analysed, prioritised and assigned to task groups to solve. The resulting action plans are then implemented, results are evaluated and follow-ups are continually applied.

7 **Recognise that teams differ from groups.** Not all groups need to function as teams. For example, machinists performing individual manufacturing functions may be located in a common group location but are not required to interact as a team with other employees working in the group area. Where interdependence and co-ordination are required, however, teams are necessary.

8 **Know how to build groups into teams.** Successful teams are built out of groups by several critical factors. Some examples are that team members have common goals, team goals are in alignment with organisational goals, team members possess the correct skills to perform the job required and individual team members' work preferences match their specific team roles.

9 **Know how to lead teams effectively.** Team leaders need to possess sufficient interpersonal and organisational skills to provide direction and keep the team on track. The leader also needs to possess the skills to conduct efficient and effective meetings.

10 **Maintain and improve team effectiveness.** A key process is to continually review past team actions to determine what worked and what did not. Another essential responsibility is maintaining balanced roles and preferences through the application of the role analysis technique, the role negotiation technique and responsibility charting. Finally, it is essential to maintain trust and openness.

❓ Questions for study and discussion

1 Think about the groups you belong to. What types of formal and informal groups are they? What are your primary reference groups? What effects do they have on your behaviour in actual groups?

2 Think about some groups of which you are or have been a member. Cite their specific norms. What group functions do these norms serve? How are these group norms enforced?

3 Think of a successful sports or project team you have been on. What key characteristics made it so effective?

4 Think of a team you have been on that was not effective. How did you feel being a part of this team? What were the main problems? What did you do about the situation? Why?

5 How would you go about forming a new team to complete a class project worth one-third of your mark? What questions would you want members to address? What work functions would you want to be certain to cover? What balance of member preferences would you desire? Would your decisions or processes change if the project was worth three-quarters of your mark? What about your entire mark?

6 How would you practise continual process improvement in your class project team? What interventions and techniques would you apply and why? How would you go about gaining their acceptance and implementation by other team members?

7 What factors would you consider in forming a new automobile joint venture team made up of American, Japanese and German managers? What processes would you recommend for building cohesion and avoiding conflicts?

🔒 Key Concepts

group, *p. 444*

formal group, *p. 444*

standing task group, *p. 444*

task group, *p. 445*

informal group, *p. 445*

interest group, *p. 445*

friendship group, *p. 446*

reference group, *p. 446*

role, *p. 452*

task roles, *p. 452*

maintenance roles, *p. 452*

personal roles, *p. 452*

norms, *p. 453*

status, *p. 454*

cohesive, *p. 454*

groupthink, *p. 459*

social loafing, *p. 460*

team building, *p. 462*

team, *p. 465*

self-managed work teams, *p. 466*

cross-functional team, *p. 467*

role analysis technique, *p. 471*

role negotiation technique, *p. 471*

responsibility charting, *p. 472*

sensitivity training, *p. 472*

structured feedback procedures, *p. 472*

self-assessment inventories, *p. 472*

exercises and simulations, *p. 472*

Personal skills exercise

Winter survival exercise (Johnson and Johnson, 1987)

Purpose This exercise is designed to demonstrate the potential advantages of participative group decision-making compared to individual decision-making.

Time 85 minutes for the complete exercise. If less time is available, leave out step 8 and shorten steps 6 and 7 by the time needed. For example, leaving out step 8 saves 20 minutes, and if 5 minutes are taken off of steps 6 and 7, the exercise can be completed in 55 minutes.

Materials A copy of the 'Winter Survival Situation' text (see below) for each member of the class.

Procedure

1 All the class reads the 'Winter Survival Situation' text (5 minutes).

2 *Individually rank* the 12 items shown in the Winter Survival Tally Chart according to their importance to your survival in the Winter Survival Situation. In the 'Individual ranking' column, indicate the most important item with a 1, going through to 12 for the least important. Keep in mind the reasons each item is or is not important (5 minutes).

3 Form groups of five or six members. Reach a *group consensus* on the best rank-order for the 12 items and record it in the second column of the Winter Survival Tally Chart. Remember that a consensus means that everyone agrees that this is the best ranking. It is not simply an average of the individual rankings (30 minutes).

4 Enter the *expert's ranking*, which will be provided by the instructor, in the third column.

5 Calculate the absolute difference (i.e. ignore minus signs) between the *individual ranking* and the expert's ranking for each item and record this information in the fourth column. Put the sum of the absolute differences for each item at the bottom of the fourth column.

6 Calculate the absolute difference for each item between the *team's ranking* and the expert's ranking. Add these absolute scores at the bottom of the fifth column (5 minutes for steps 4 to 6).

7 Compare the differences between your absolute difference score and your group's absolute difference score. Based on these results, discuss the merits of individual versus team decision-making (20 minutes).

8 Share your group's absolute difference scores and conclusions with the class. The class discusses common conclusions about the merits of individual versus team decision-making (20 minutes).

The Winter Survival Situation

You have just crash-landed somewhere in the woods of southern Germany or northern Austria. It is 11.32 a.m. in mid-January. The small plane in which you were travelling crashed into a small lake. The pilot and co-pilot were killed. Shortly after the crash the plane sank completely into the lake with the pilot's and co-pilot's bodies inside. Everyone else on the flight escaped to land without getting wet and without serious injury.

The crash came suddenly before the pilot had time to radio for help or inform anyone of your position. Since your pilot was trying to avoid a storm you know the plane was considerably off-course. The pilot announced shortly before the crash that you were 45 miles north-west of a small town that is the nearest known habitation.

You are in a wilderness area made up of thick woods broken by many lakes and rivers. The snow depth varies from above the ankles in windswept areas, to more than knee-deep where it has drifted. The last weather report indicated that the temperature would reach 5 degrees centigrade in the daytime and 15 degrees below zero at night. There is plenty of dead wood and twigs in the area around the lake. You and the other surviving passengers are dressed in winter clothing appropriate for city wear – suits, trouser suits, street shoes and overcoats. While escaping from the plane, your group salvaged the 12 items listed in the first column on the Winter Survival Tally Chart. You may assume that the number of persons in the group is the same as the number in your group, and that you have agreed to stay together.

Winter Survival Tally Chart

Items	Your individual ranking	Your group's consensus ranking	Survival expert's ranking	Difference between Column 1 and Column 3 values	Difference between Column 2 and Column 3 values
Ball of steel wool					
Newspapers (one per person)					
Compass					
Hand axe					
Cigarette lighter (without fluid)					
Loaded .45-calibre pistol					
Sectional air map made of plastic					
20 × 20-foot piece of heavy-duty canvas					
Extra shirt and trousers for each survivor					
Can of butter					
Bottle of 100-proof whisky					
Family-size chocolate bar (one per person)					
Totals					

Team exercise

Working together as a problem-solving team

Time 45 minutes

Procedure In groups of four, decide among yourselves which of you will play each character in the illustration to complete this exercise. If you have more than four people in your group, more than one person will have to play each character (or, if you would prefer, somebody can be the horse). If you have fewer than four people in your group, one of your group members will have to play the role of two of the characters.

Questions for discussion

1 As a group, create your own story about what happened to lead up to the events in the illustration, and decide how your character behaved in the time leading up to what you see occurring in this illustration. Be creative and have some fun in making up an interesting story about your team. Instead of referring to the characters as 'the guy holding the rope' or 'the one who's sweating', give each character a name. The names can be fictitious, or maybe you'd prefer to give them your names (15 minutes).

2 Each team presents its story to the class and fields questions (20 minutes).

3 The class as a whole compares stories and determines implications to real task team situations (10 minutes).

4 (Optional) Complete the team self-evaluation in the Your Turn exercise earlier in this chapter. Each member is to evaluate the team independently, using his or her own form (30 minutes).

Case study: **self-directed work teams at the City Zoo**

The City Zoo has been undergoing a metamorphosis from a traditional functional hierarchy where 50 departments, like animal keeping, horticulture and maintenance, worked in parallel without venturing out of their narrowly defined job responsibilities. In an effort to provide a healthier environment for plants and animals, better educate visitors about conservation issues and enhance visitor experience by immersion into natural habitats, the zoo developed bio-climatic zones that grouped together plants and animals in cageless enclosures that visitors walk through. Examples of these bio-climatic zones are Tiger River, Gorilla Tropics, Kopjhe Corner and Sun Bear Forest.

Zoo personnel quickly discovered that the separate departments did not work well for the co-ordinated operations required by the bio-climatic zones. The zoo's response was to develop separate self-managing teams of seven to ten members whose goal is to work together to successfully operate their particular bio-climatic zone. The teams are cross-trained and made up of specialists in horticulture, mammals, birds, fish, maintenance and construction, from the old departments. Because all now share responsibility for their zone, jobs blend together and team members all pitch in to do whatever kind of work is necessary regardless of their former department designation. Teams meet regularly to analyse the work required, set goals for themselves, manage their budgets and monitor their progress.

In the beginning, teams operated only in the bio-climatic zones, while the rest of the staff continued to operate in the traditional way. As the zoo completes additional renovations, the remaining zones will also be staffed by self-managed teams of employees from the original 50 functional departments.

The challenge for the zoo's department managers is to let go of their traditional managerial practices and learn new ones that better facilitate the new team-zone-based organisation. Managers now take on a coach/adviser role and use their technical expertise and big-picture perspective to support teams and act as liaisons for them.

So far the results have been exemplary. Zoo attendance is up 20 per cent and workmen's compensation claims within the self-managed teams have been significantly reduced.

Source: Stewart (1992); Allender (1993); Austin (1993); Cauldron (1993, 1992).

Questions for managerial action

1 How did the switch to bio-climatic zones challenge the specialists and managers of these separate departments?

2 What should the management of the City Zoo have considered before deciding to change to a self-managed team type of organisational structure (e.g. managers' loss of power, compensation and reward systems)?

3 What could have gone wrong with this type of change? Why?

4 Would being on one of these zone teams increase or decrease your job satisfaction versus being a part of a traditional functional department? Why?

Applied questions

5 How can managers improve team performance at City Zoo?

6 Using Exhibit 10-11, can you identify when groups of workers became a team? How has this improved performance?

WWW exercise

Manager's Internet tools

Web tips: teamwork on the web

This chapter has emphasised that by building a team, greater results can be achieved. While teamwork is not traditionally thought of as a 'discipline' area such as finance, accounting or information systems, it is a vital skill necessary for an organisation to function efficiently and effectively.

World Wide Web search

Log on to any of the job search databases on the web. Some sites are listed below, but there are several others you can find. Perform a search on these databases using the keywords 'team', 'teamwork' and 'cross-functional'. Once you retrieve some database hits, scan a few of the job descriptions. Some sites to look at are:

http://www.topjobs.co.uk
http://www.reed.co.uk
http://www.monster.co.uk

1 What types of jobs list 'teamwork' as a required skill?
2 If a job lists 'cross-functional' responsibilities, what are these cross-functional responsibilities?
3 How important does teamwork appear to be for career advancement?

Specific website – the Body Shop

The Body Shop prides itself on the way it does its business, as can be seen from the opening vignette in Chapter 3. It also prides itself as an employer. Look at the website at www.bodyshop.co.uk. What does it say about the company's culture? Look at the job listings, what does it ask for? Does it specifically mention teamwork, or is it implied by the nature of the job? Is the company successful because of its people or its culture? How are the two linked? What phrases are listed on the website that show they value teamwork?

LEARNING CHECKLIST

Before you move on you may want to reflect on what you have learnt in this chapter. You should now be able to:

☑ explain the primary characteristics of groups
☑ compare the contributions of different types of groups
☑ describe the stages of group development
☑ discuss how group norms are developed and enforced
☑ determine sources of group cohesiveness
☑ understand threats to group performance
☑ explain how to develop a group into a team
☑ discuss the characteristics of high-performing teams
☑ define key team member roles
☑ assess and improve team performance.

Further reading

Albanese, R. and Van Fleet, D.D. (1985) 'Rational Behaviour in Groups: The Free-rider Tendency', *Academy of Management Review* 10, April, pp. 244–255.

De Jong, A., De Ruyter, K. and Lemmink. J. (2005) 'Service Climate in Self-managing Teams: Mapping the Linkage of Team Member Perceptions and Service Performance Outcomes in a Business to Business Setting', *Journal of Management Studies* 42(8), December, p. 1593.

Dowling, W.F. (1973) 'Job Redesign on the Assembly Line: Farewell to Blue-collar Blues?', *Organisational Dynamics*, Autumn, pp. 51–67.

Haslam, N., Bastian, B., Bain, P. and Kashima, Y. (2006) 'Psychological Essentialism: Implicit Theories and Intergroup Relations', *Group Processes & Intergroup Relations* 9(1), 1 January, p. 63.

Maples, M.F. (1988) 'Group Development: Extending Tuckman's Theory', *Journal for Specialists in Group Work*, Fall, pp. 17–23.

Walther, J.B. and Bunz, U. (2005) 'The Rules of Virtual Groups: Trust, Liking and Performance in Computer-mediated Communication', *Journal of Communication* 55(4), 15 December, p. 828.

References

Adler, N.J. (1991) *International Dimensions of Organizational Behaviour* (2nd edn). Boston, MA: PWS-Kent, p. 99.

Aldag, R.J. and Fuller, S.R. (1993) 'Beyond Fiasco: A Reappraisal of the Groupthink Phenomenon and a New Model of Group Decision Processes', *Psychological Bulletin*, May, pp. 533–552.

Allender, H. (1993) 'Self-directed Work Teams: How Far is Too Far?', *Industrial Management*, September–October, pp. 13–15.

Asch, S.E. (1951) 'Effects of Group Pressure upon the Modification and Distortion of Judgments', in H. Guetzkow (ed.) *Groups, Leadership and Men*. Pittsburgh, PA: Carnegie Press, pp. 177–190.

Ashforth, B.E. and Mael, F. (1989) 'Social Identity Theory and the Organization', *Academy of Management Review*, January, pp. 20–39.

Austin, N.K. (1993) 'Making Teamwork Work', *Working Woman*, January, p. 28.

Barker, J.R. (1993) 'Tightening the Iron Cage: Concertive Control in Self-managing Teams' *Administrative Science Quarterly*, September, pp. 408–437.

Beckhard, R. and Harris, R.T. (1977) *Organizational Transitions: Managing Complex Change*. Reading, MA: Addison-Wesley, pp. 76–82.

Belbin, R.M. (1993) *Team Roles at Work*. Oxford: Butterworth Heinemann.

Benne, K.D. and Sheats, P. (1948) 'Functional Roles of Group Members', *Journal of Social Issues* 4(2), Spring, pp. 41–49.

Bettenhausen, K.L. (1991) 'Five Years of Groups Research: What We Have Learned and What Needs to be Addressed', *Journal of Management*, June, p. 362.

Cauldron, S. (1992) 'What a Zoo Can Teach You', *Fortune*, 18 May, pp. 55–57.

Cauldron, S. (1993) 'Are Self-directed Teams Right for Your Company?', *Personnel Journal*, December, pp. 76–94.

Davies, R.V. (1990) *The Team Management Systems Research Manual*. York, United Kingdom: Team Management Systems, pp. 1–2.

Driskell, J.E. and Salas, E. (1991) 'Group Decision Making Under Stress', *Journal of Applied Psychology*, June, pp. 473–478.

Driver, M.J., Brousseau, K.R. and Hunsaker, P.L. (1993) *The Dynamic Decisionmaker*. New York, NY: Jossey-Bass, pp. 216–231.

Drucker, P.F. (1992) 'There's More Than One Kind of Team', *Wall Street Journal*, 11 February, p. A16.

Dumaine, B. (1990) 'Who Needs a Boss?', *Fortune*, 7 May, pp. 52–60.

Dyer, W.G. (1987) *Team Building: Issues and Alternatives* (2nd edn). Menlo Park, CA: Addison-Wesley, pp. 97–108.

Dyer, W.G., Daines, R.H. and Giauque, W.C. (1990) *The Challenge of Management*. New York, NY: Harcourt Brace Jovanovich, pp. 346–350.

Earley, P.C. (1989) 'Social Loafing and Collectivism: A Comparison of the United States and the People's Republic of China', *Administrative Science Quarterly*, December, pp. 565–581.

Feldman, D.C. (1984) 'The Development and Enforcement of Group Norms', *Academy of Management Review*, January, pp. 47–53.

Ferris, G.R. and Rowland, K.M. (1983) 'Social Facilitation Effects on Behavioural and Perceptual Task Performance Measures: Implications for Work Behaviour', *Group & Organisation Studies*, December, pp. 421–438.

Finley, M. (1992) 'New Technology is Changing how Meetings are Conducted', *Office Systems*, May, pp. 44–47.

Fisher, S.G., Hunter, T.A. and Macrosson, W.D.K. (1998) 'The Structure of Belbin's Team Roles', *Journal of Occupational and Organisational Psychology* 71(3), pp. 283–288.

French, W.L. and Bell, C.H. Jr (1990) *Organization Development: Behavioural Science Interventions for Organization Improvement*. Englewood Cliffs, NJ: Prentice Hall, p. 127.

Gates, M. (1989) 'The Quality Challenge: Can Managers and Workers See Eye to Eye?' *Incentive* 163(8), August, pp. 20–22.

George, J.M. (1992) 'Extrinsic and Intrinsic Origins of Perceived Social Loafing in Organizations', *Academy of Management Journal*, March, pp. 191–202.

Gersick, C.J.G. (1989) 'Marking Time: Predictable Transitions in Task Groups', *Academy of Management Journal* 32, pp. 274–309.

Gersick, C.J.G. (1991) 'Revolutionary Change Theories: A Multilevel Exploration of the Punctuated Equilibrium Paradigm', *Academy of Management Review* 16, pp. 10–36.

Goodman, P.S., Devadas, R. and Griffith Hughson, T.L. (1988) 'Groups and Productivity: Analyzing the Effectiveness of Self-managing Teams', in J.P. Campbell, R.J. Campbell and associates (eds) *Productivity in Organizations*. San Francisco, CA: Jossey-Bass, pp. 295–327.

Goodman, P.S., Ravlin, E. and Schminike, M. (1987) 'Understanding Groups in Organizations', in L.L. Cummings and B.M. Staw (eds) *Research in Organizational Behaviour* 9. Greenwich, CT: JAI Press, p. 159.

Guzzo, R.A. and Shea, G.P. (1992) 'Group Performance and Intergroup Relations in Organizations', in M.D. Dunnette and L.M. Hough (eds) *Handbook of Industrial & Organizational Psychology* (2nd edn, vol. 3). Palo Alto, CA: Consulting Psychologists Press, pp. 288–290.

Harkins, S.G. and Szymanski, K. (1989) 'Social Loafing and Group Evaluation', *Journal of Personality and Social Psychology*, June, pp. 934–941.

Harrison, R. (1972) 'When Power Conflicts Trigger Team Spirit', *European Business*, Spring, pp. 27–65.

Hillkirk, J. (1993) 'Self-directed Work Teams Give TI Lift', *USA Today*, 20 December, p. 8B.

Hughes, B. (1991) '25 Stepping Stones for Self-directed Work Teams', *Training* 28(12), December, pp. 44–46.

Hussein, R.T. (1989) 'Informal Groups, Leadership, and Productivity', *Leadership and Organisation Development Journal* 10(1), pp. 9–16.

Iacocca, L. (1986) *Iacocca: An Autobiography*. New York, NY: Bantam Books.

Jackson, J.M. and Harkins, S.G. (1985) 'Equity in Effort: An Explanation of the Social Loafing Effect', *Journal of Personality and Social Psychology*, November, pp. 1199–1206.

Janis, I.L. (1982) *Groupthink: Psychological Studies of Policy Decisions and Fiascoes* (2nd edn). Boston, MA: Houghton Mifflin.

Johnson, D. and Johnson, F. (1987) *Joining Together* (3rd edn). Englewood Cliffs, NJ: Prentice Hall, pp. 107–113.

Kaeter, M. (1994) 'Repotting Mature Work Teams', *Training*, April (supplement), pp. 4–6.

Katzenback, J.R. and Smith, D.K. (1993a) 'The Discipline of Teams', *Harvard Business Review*, March–April, pp. 111–120.

Katzenback, J.R. and Smith, D.K. (1993b) *The Wisdom of Teams: Creating the High-performance Organization*. Boston, MA: Harvard Business School Press.

Kayser, T.A. (1990) *Mining Group Gold*. El Segundo, CA: Serif Publishing.

Keller, R.T. (1986) 'Predictors of the Performance of Project Groups in R&D Organizations', *Academy of Management Journal*, December, pp. 715–726.

Keyton, J. and Springston, J. (1990) 'Redefining Cohesiveness in Groups', *Small Group Research*, May, pp. 234–254.

Kolb, D.A., Rubin, I.M. and Osland, J.M. (1991) *Organizational Psychology: An Experiential Approach* (5th edn). Englewood Cliffs, NJ: Prentice Hall, pp. 213–214.

Kormanski, C. and Mozenter, A. (1987) 'A New Model of Team Building: A Technology for Today and Tomorrow', in J.W. Pfeiffer and J.E. Jones (eds) *The 1987 Annual: Developing Human Resources*. San Diego, CA: University Associates, pp. 255–268.

Lublin, J.S. (1992) 'Trying to Increase Worker Productivity: More Employers Alter Management Style', *Wall Street Journal*, 13 February, p. B1.

Luft, J. (1984) *Group Processes* (3rd edn). Palo Alto, CA: Mayfield Publishing Company.

Maier, N.R.F. (1967) 'Assets and Liabilities in Group Problem Solving', *Psychological Review* 74, July, pp. 239–249.

Manz, C.C., Keating, D.E. and Donnellon, A. (1990) 'Preparing for an Organisational Change to Employee Self-management', *Organisational Dynamics*, Autumn, pp. 15–26.

Margerison, C. and McCann, D. (1990) *Team Management Systems: The Team Development Manual*. Toowong, Queensland, Australia: Team Management Resources, pp. 19–36.

Mascowitz, M. (1985) 'Lessons from the Best Companies to Work For', *California Management Review*, Winter, pp. 42–47.

Meer, J. (1985) 'Loafing Through a Tough Job', *Psychology Today*, January, p. 72.

Mullen, B. and Copper, C. (1994) 'The Relation Between Group Cohesiveness and Performance: An Integration', *Psychological Bulletin*, March, pp. 210–227.

Napier, R.W. and Gershenfeld, M.K. (1993) *Groups: Theory and Experience* (5th edn). Dallas, TX: Houghton Mifflin, pp. 81–84.

Ott, E.M. (1989) 'Effects of the Male–Female Ratio at Work', *Psychology of Women Quarterly*, March, p. 53.

Otto, H.A. (1970) *Group Methods to Actualize Human Potential: A Handbook*. Beverly Hills, CA: The Holistic Press, pp. 50–59.

Pasmore, W.A. and Fagans, M.R. (1992) 'Participation, Individual Development, and Organisational Change: A Review and Synthesis', *Journal of Management*, June, pp. 375–397.

Rebello, K. (1996) 'Inside Microsoft', *Business Week*, 15 July, pp. 56–57.

Romanelli, E. and Tushman, M.L. (1994) 'Organizational Transformation as Punctuated Equilibrium: An Empirical Test', *Academy of Management Journal* 37, October, pp. 1141–1166.

Schwartz, A.E. and Levin, J. (1990) 'Better Group Decision Making', *Supervisory Management*, June.

Shaw, M.E. (1981) *Group Dynamics: The Psychology of Small Group Behaviour* (3rd edn). New York, NY: McGraw-Hill, pp. 11–12.

Shepperd, J.A. (1993) 'Productivity Loss in Performance Groups: A Motivation Analysis', *Psychological Bulletin*, January, pp. 67–81.

Smither, R.D. (1991) 'The Return of the Authoritarian Manager', *Training*, November, p. 40.

Smith-Lovin, L. and Brody, C. (1989) 'Interruptions in Group Discussions: The Effects of Gender and Group Composition', *American Sociological Review*, June, pp. 424–435.

Stewart, T. (1992) 'The Search for the Organization of Tomorrow', *Fortune*, 18 May, pp. 36–48.

Summers, I., Coffelt, T. and Horton, R.E. (1988) 'Work-group Cohesion', *Psychological Reports*, October, pp. 627–636.

Sundstrom, E., De Meuse, K.P. and Futrell, D. (1990) 'Work Teams', *American Psychologist*, February, pp. 120–133.

Tjosvold, D. (1991) *Team Organisation: An Enduring Competitive Advantage*. Chichester, England: Wiley.

Tuckman, B.W. and Jensen, M.A.C. (1977) 'Stages of Small Group Development Revisited', *Group and Organisational Studies* 2, pp. 419–427.

Verespel, M.A. (1994) 'Workers-managers', *Industry Week*, 16 May, p. 30.

Watson, W.E., Kuman, K. and Michaelson, L.K. (1993) 'Cultural Diversity's Impact on Interaction Process and Performance: Comparing Homogeneous and Diverse Task Groups', *Academy of Management Journal* 36, pp. 590–602.

Williams, K., Harkings, S. and Latane, B. (1981) 'Identifiability as a Deterrent to Social Loafing: Two Cheering Experiments', *Journal of Personality and Social Psychology*, February, pp. 303–311.

Yammarino, F.J. and Dubinksy, A.J. (1990) 'Salesperson Performance and Managerially Controllable Factors: An Investigation of Individual and Work Group Effects', *Journal of Management* 16, pp. 87–106.

Yang, D.J. and Oneal, M. (1990) 'How Boeing Does It', *Business Week*, 9 July, p. 49.

Yetton, P. and Bottger, P. (1983) 'The Relationships Among Group Size, Member Ability, Social Decision Schemes, and Performance', *Organisational Behaviour and Human Performance*, October, pp. 145–159.

Zemke, R. (1993) 'Rethinking the Rush to Team Up', *Training*, November, pp. 55–61.

Conflict management and negotiation

After studying this chapter you should be able to:

☑ **define** and describe the conflict process

☑ **recognise** symptoms of conflict

☑ **identify** sources of conflict

☑ **differentiate** between functional and dysfunctional conflict

☑ **utilise** conflict styles appropriately

☑ **apply** conflict management strategies

☑ **bargain** and negotiate.

The opening vignette looks at the issues involved when a trades union official becomes a manager, and the conflicts that can arise.

From shop floor to boardroom employment relations

Trades union officials are making the once unthinkable switch to management roles. And jumping moral hurdles, says Stephen Overell.

This summer, before the wildcat strikes at British Airways and the airline's outsourced caterer Gate Gourmet, Rory Murphy moved from union official to outsourcing consultant. He changed jobs with no qualms and for no extra money, thinking it might be 'challenging'. If any of his former colleagues at Amicus, a 1.2 m-strong manufacturing and financial services trades union, now feel him to be a traitor they have yet to say so to his face. He remains, he insists, 'instinctively pro-worker' and says his 'underlying philosophy' has not changed a bit.

▶

Like many former union officials who have changed sides, his move was a staging post on a journey that began many years earlier. Mr Murphy's doubts about the ability and willingness of unions to adapt to a fundamentally altered world of work date back to the early 1990s. Today, he suggests, unions may no longer be relevant to workers' needs.

'In the early 1970s, unions were strong because they were needed,' he says. 'But now unions have effectively won the battle. All the things they were fighting for – equality, lifelong learning, rights for part-timers – are well on their way to becoming a reality.

'If trades unions had a relevance, people would join them. But the world has moved on and unions have not. The workplace today is a significantly better place than it was in 1972.'

The continued retreat of union influence is not in doubt. According to the Workplace Employment Relations Survey, backed by the UK Government, in 1998 57 per cent of workplaces had no union members, while union members made up a majority of the workforce in 22 per cent of workplaces. By 2004, the figures had progressed to 64 per cent and 18 per cent respectively. However, the debate about why this decline has taken place remains lively.

Mr Murphy argues that justification for the unions' existence has been eroded by the expansion of employment protection legislation and employers' efforts to retain good staff.

Lack of appetite from employees, rather than shifts in the composition of the workforce, best explains their increasingly marginal role, he contends.

'The fundamental conflict identified by Marx between the interests of worker and employer may still be there,' he says. 'But the idea of "two sides" no longer makes much sense to people because there is so much common ground ... I just felt I could contribute more as a consultant.'

Former union officials who have moved into management – most frequently human resource management – are not as rare as they once were: union mergers have forced more ex-officials into the jobs market. Yet, by any standards, Mr Murphy's trajectory is a dramatic one: apostasy is one thing, outsourcing another.

Mr Murphy argues that outsourcing is 'a fact of life that is here to stay' and is 'not inherently anti-worker' provided it is done in the right way – which is also the policy of his former union.

He accepted the offer from Morgan Chambers, an outsourcing specialist, because the company stressed the need to improve the human side of outsourcing with early consultation and fair dealing for affected workers.

He says he views the controversial nature of the job as part of its appeal. Clients have been 'curious and interested in my skill-set,' he claims. However, some fellow consultants have been suspicious of his motivations. He says he does not know what erstwhile union colleagues think.

For Patrick Eraut, who joined the British Airports Authority as employee relations manager in 2002 after six years as a negotiator with Unify, the finance union that is now part of Amicus, the test of where his commitment lay came uncomfortably early.

Two months into the job, he had to advise on the dismissal of a union representative. While as a union official he had 'represented people who deserved to be dismissed', he nevertheless felt a conflict in helping to oust a trades unionist. 'I was clear that the grounds were solid, but I couldn't help thinking that if only there had been more dialogue years earlier, it wouldn't have been necessary.'

Today, he has no doubt that he is there to represent the interests of BAA; what is more, he no longer feels instinctive sympathy with workers when he reads about industrial disputes. 'There is so often fault on both sides,' he says.

Once more, there was no single event that sparked the move – rather a long-term accumulation of frustrations. Unions were slow to understand the more individualised outlook of workers, he believes, and failed to learn from other organisations, such as banks, about the use of 24-hour call centres in communicating with members. A lack of leadership was compounded by the slow nature of democratic decision-making in conferences and committees, he argues. His restlessness was further stirred by doing an MBA between 2000 and 2002, and being exposed to new insights on business.

Source: © Financial Times, 2005.

Discussion questions

1   What type of conflicts could arise if a union representative becomes part of management?

2   Is there no longer a need for a unionised workplace now that employees are protected by legislation?

Every relationship contains conflict, disagreement and opposed interests. Conflict has the potential to destroy relationships, put companies out of business and ruin careers, but these outcomes are not inevitable. Negative consequences usually arise from failure to handle conflict in constructive ways. As demonstrated by the opening vignette, however, constructive conflict management produces creative solutions to problems, higher-quality relationships and constructive change. Johnson (1993) suggests that unless relationships of any type are able to withstand the stress involved in inevitable conflicts, and manage them productively, they are not likely to endure. This chapter provides a game plan for understanding and managing conflict productively in both personal and organisational situations.

What is conflict?

conflict
A disagreement between two or more parties who perceive that they have incompatible concerns.

Conflict is a disagreement between two or more parties – for example, individuals, groups, departments, organisations, countries – who perceive that they have incompatible concerns. Conflicts exist whenever an action by one party is perceived as preventing or interfering with the goals, needs or actions of another party. Rahim (1992) proposes that conflicts can arise over a variety of organisational experiences, such as incompatible goals, differences in the interpretation of facts, negative feelings, differences of values and philosophies, or disputes over shared resources. As defined above, conflict sounds pretty negative. However, in some cases, it can actually stimulate creative problem-solving and improve the situation for all parties involved.

Functional versus dysfunctional conflict

The traditional view of conflict assumed that it was undesirable and led to negative outcomes like aggression, violence and hostility. This *dysfunctional view* of conflict implied that managers should determine the causes of conflict and eliminate them, and make sure that future conflicts

Research focus: philosophies of conflict

The unitarist perspective

This is the traditional view, which sees conflict as undesirable, destructive and to be avoided at all costs. In organisations it is assumed that everyone is on the same side, working towards the same goals; any differences are assumed to be the result of poor leadership, poor communication or some agitators looking for trouble. This simplistic view fails to see that differences of interest or opinion can be perfectly normal. Drucker (1984) identifies with this view in his writings about organisations, where he suggests that everyone should work together to fulfil a common goal. Morgan (1986) also acknowledges that it is popular with managers as it emphasises teamwork, and anyone who questions a manager can be discredited.

The pluralist perspective

An organisation is seen as a collection of different groups, all with their legitimate aims to pursue, and therefore a degree of conflict is normal. Pluralists propose the idea that conflict is natural and therefore procedures need to be in place to handle it so that it does not disrupt the organisation as a whole. This is the widely accepted view of conflict but, from a critic's viewpoint, it ignores the wider cultural issues of conflict.

The radical perspective

This is derived from the Marxist perspective and suggests that organisational conflict reflects the conflict in wider society between the capitalist owners and the workers. This perspective takes into account the wider social view but views conflict as vertical and considers that managers are the instruments of the owners, therefore it fails to acknowledge that managers may also have different views. It also fails to recognise that conflict can occur between people at the same level in an organisation.

The interactionist perspective

This view, proposed by McKenna (1994), sees conflict as neither good nor bad but simply inevitable. It is not too different from the pluralist perspective. It recognises that, when there is conflict, much of the organisation's energy will be challenged into its resolution, to the detriment of pursuing other goals. However, it also recognises that when there is no conflict, there is unlikely to be creativity and this will lead to complacency. This means there should be an optimum level of conflict that needs to be identified to enable the organisation to develop. The problem is finding the optimal level and learning how to manage the conflict effectively.

were prevented. One CEO of a car manufacturer was sacked for this reason. The CEO had created dysfunctional conflicts for influential people in the company. Although the CEO had rationalised his approach by saying, 'You don't change a company in bankruptcy without making a few waves', others viewed him as creating more work for people who were already working beyond capacity, playing people against each other, and intimidating managers, employees, and even outside suppliers and customers (DeGeorge, 1994; Smith, 1993).

However, if economic results improve, as was the case with the car manufacturer, conflict can be viewed as *functional* because of its potential to stimulate creative resolution of problems and corrective actions and to keep people and organisations from slipping into complacency.

Perhaps it should not matter if individuals dislike conflict. If it increases performance and is beneficial to the group or organisation as a whole, it is functional.

This outcome of the conflict is the criterion for determining whether it is functional or dysfunctional – that is, whether it has positive or negative outcomes for the decision-making group (e.g. department, organisation, stockholders). Perhaps the most appropriate attitude towards conflict is that it is inevitable and has the potential to be dysfunctional, but if managed constructively, conflict can be functional and enhance performance.

Exhibit 11-1 provides an overview of the conflict management process. The first thing a manager needs to do is determine what stage the conflict is in. Then the source of the conflict has to be established. Next, the manager can examine the consequences and performance outcomes of the conflict. Finally, the manager needs to decide which conflict style orientation and specific strategies can be applied most productively to manage the conflict. The following section of this chapter will focus on the first two parts of the conflict management process: the stages and sources of conflict.

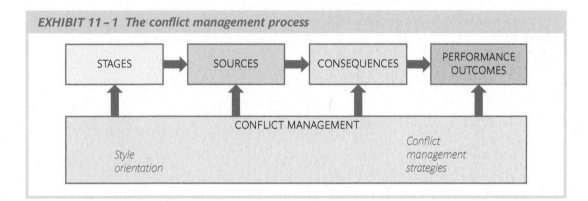

EXHIBIT 11–1 The conflict management process

Research focus: **the stages of conflict**

Thomas (1992) suggests that although a conflict does not exist until one party perceives that another party may negatively affect something that the first party cares about, the development of antecedent conditions (the sources of conflict) marks the start of the process. Afterwards, conflict usually proceeds through the five stages diagrammed by Pondy (1967) in Exhibit 11-2.

Stage 1: Latent conflict

When two or more parties need each other to achieve desired objectives, there is potential for conflict. Other antecedents of conflict, such as interdependence, different goals and ambiguity of responsibility, are described in the next section. They do not automatically create conflicts but, when they exist, they make it possible. Latent conflict often arises when a change occurs. Conflict might be caused by a budget cutback, a change in organisational direction, a change in a personal goal, the assignment of a new project to an already overloaded workforce, or an expected occurrence (such as a salary increase) that does not happen.

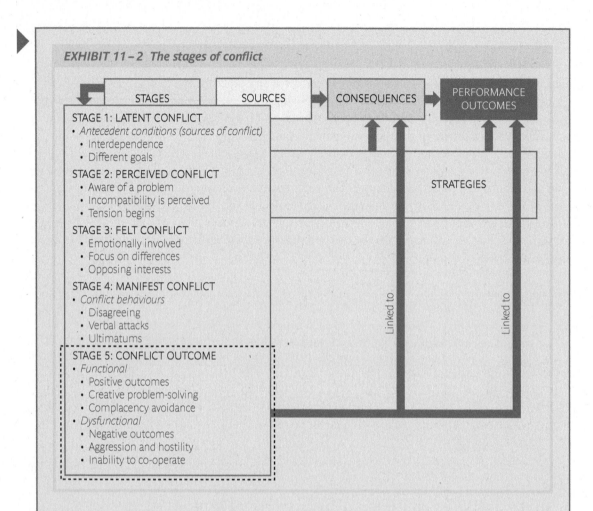

EXHIBIT 11–2 The stages of conflict

Stage 2: Perceived conflict

This is the point at which members become aware of a problem. Incompatibility of needs is perceived and tension begins as the parties begin to worry about what will happen. At this point, however, no one feels that anything that they care about is actually being overtly threatened.

Stage 3: Felt conflict

Now the parties become emotionally involved and begin to focus on differences of opinion and opposing interests, sharpening perceived conflict. Internal tensions and frustrations begin to crystallise around specific, defined issues, and people begin to build an emotional commitment to their particular position. Kuman (1989) argues that the type of emotion felt is important because negative ones produce low trust and negative perceptions of the other party's position, which can result in destructive win–lose tactics. Carnevale and Isen (1986) suggest more positive feelings, on the other hand, can contribute to a more balanced view of the situation and more collaborative endeavours. In either case, the result is a defining of what the conflict is actually about, which will determine the alternatives available for later resolution.

Stage 4: Manifest conflict

The obvious display of conflict occurs when the opposing parties plan and follow through with acts to achieve their own objectives and frustrate the other. Glasl (1982) suggests actions can range from minor disagreeing, questioning and challenging at one end of the conflict-intensity continuum, to verbal attacks, threats, ultimatums, physical attacks and even efforts to destroy the other party, at the other end.

Stage 5: Conflict outcome

The interactions of the conflicting parties in the manifest conflict stage result in outcomes that can be functional or dysfunctional for one or both parties. As conflict proceeds through the stages, functional resolution becomes more difficult. The parties become more locked into their positions and more convinced that the conflict is a win–lose situation. It is usually easier to achieve positive collaboration and win–win outcomes when the conflict is recognised early, before frustration and other negative sentiments set in.

Sources of conflict

In order for conflict to occur, certain conditions must exist. These conditions may be outwardly visible, or they may be latent and waiting to surface. Therefore, it is imperative to understand these underlying conditions that can cause conflict. Exhibit 11-3 presents the primary causes of conflict condensed into five general categories: goal incompatibility, structural design, role expectations, degenerative climate, and personal differences.

Goal incompatibility

An ideal situation exists when two parties perceive their goals as mutually enhancing and view each other's behaviours as contributing to the achievement of both sets of goals. In such a case, a high degree of co-operation is likely to result. Design research and marketing departments, for example, will probably enjoy a co-operative relationship because a new line developed by the former will provide the latter with the products it needs to meet its increased sales objectives. Several things can get in the way, however.

Mutually exclusive goals

When one side's goal achievement is perceived as threatening to another's, the resulting conflict is likely to engender win–lose competition. For example, both design research and marketing departments may interrelate poorly with a production department that has a goal of eliminating new and low-volume production runs. Another classic case of goal conflict often exists between sales departments who want increased volume and market share versus credit departments who want to limit sales to customers with the ability to pay.

Insufficient shared resources

Most organisations operate with a finite amount of money, personnel and equipment. As parties compete for their share of the organisational pie, conflict often results. If one party receives more power, higher status, better work assignments or more material resources, the remaining parties often get less. Kabanoff (1991) argues that dysfunctional conflict results from the win–lose competition that limited resources foster.

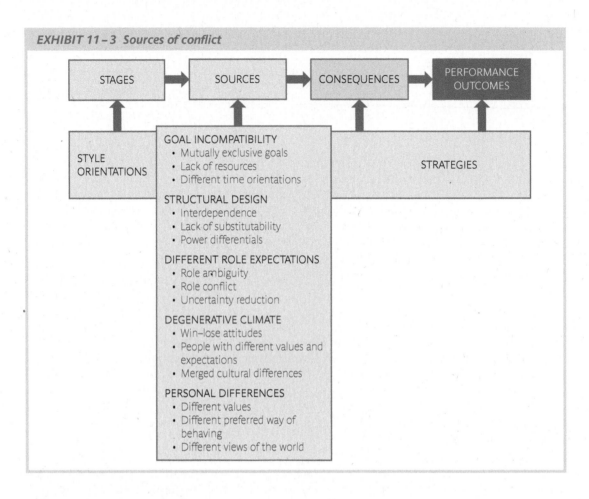

EXHIBIT 11–3 Sources of conflict

Different time orientations

Another potential source of conflict is the different time spans needed by parties to achieve their goals. Some parties have relatively short time orientations. Production crews, for example, may require hourly feedback about results. Marketing departments often focus on weekly sales volume, while research and finance departments may have to look several years ahead when developing new products or forecasting interest rates and other economic trends.

When parties suboptimise and focus only on accomplishing their own goals, their different time orientations can cause considerable conflict. The marketing department's goal of introducing new products immediately, for example, can conflict with the research department's need for at least six months to design and develop them and production's minimum two-month manufacturing period.

Structural design

interdependence

The degree to which interactions between parties must be co-ordinated in order for them to perform adequately.

Differences in goals, resource demands and time orientations are related to interdependence, or the degree to which interactions between parties must be co-ordinated in order for them to perform adequately. How relationships between parties are structured by the organisation determines how they interact to facilitate or hinder each other in accomplishing goals.

Interdependence

The relationships between parties can be visualised on a continuum, ranging from complete dependence to complete independence. When one party has the power to determine the performance outcomes and goal achievements of another, the second party is relatively dependent on the first. Two parties are independent only when their respective activities have no impact whatsoever on each other.

Most relationships fall somewhere between complete dependence and independence and are characterised by the need to co-ordinate certain activities for successful task performance. The more two parties share responsibilities and need to co-ordinate schedules and to co-operate in decision-making, the more interdependent they are. Exhibit 11-4, from Thompson (1967), illustrates three distinct types of interdependent task relationship: pooled, sequential and reciprocal.

Pooled interdependence exists when two parties are independent of each other for their own performance outcomes, but each makes a discrete contribution to the overall organisation that affects the well-being of all parties. An example would be a finance department and a marketing department. They rarely have cause to interact directly with each other, so no direct conflict is likely to occur. Both departments' performances, however, independently contribute to the overall profitability of the company, which affects profit sharing for employees in all departments.

pooled interdependence
Exists when two parties are independent of each other for their own performance outcomes, but each makes a contribution to the overall organisation that affects the well-being of both parties.

Sequential interdependence occurs when the output of one party provides necessary inputs for another to accomplish its goals. An example of this is when store room employees pull out of the warehouse the specified components needed for the manufacturing department to use in assembling products for customers. The receiving groups in these situations are dependent on the providing groups for the timing and quality of the goods or services needed to do their jobs. This one-way flow of activity can cause considerable anxiety for receiving parties because their goal attainment is dependent on inputs from the supplying party, which has no real need to see that their needs are met.

sequential interdependence
Occurs when the output of one party provides necessary inputs for another to accomplish its goals.

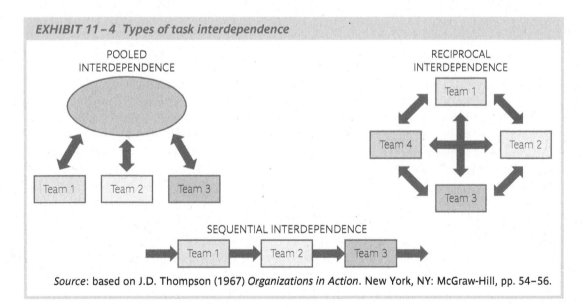

EXHIBIT 11-4 Types of task interdependence

Source: based on J.D. Thompson (1967) Organizations in Action. New York, NY: McGraw-Hill, pp. 54–56.

reciprocal interdependence
Exists if the outputs of two parties are inputs for each other.

Reciprocal interdependence exists if the outputs of two parties are inputs for each other. In such symbiotic relationships, each party supplies necessary inputs to the other. Salespeople, for example, relay information to the packaging department so that it can create packages of goods that meet customer requirements. If the packages do not satisfy customer demands, salespeople will have a more difficult time securing orders in the future. The potential for conflict between reciprocating groups is great because of the high need for co-ordination. Success requires effective communication and joint decision-making.

Awareness of the nature of interdependence is necessary to manage potential conflict and ensure optimal performance of interacting parties at any level: interpersonal, group, inter-group and multi-organisational. The complexity of relationships depends on the type of inter-dependence experienced by two groups. Pooled interdependence is the least complex relationship, while reciprocally interdependent interactions require the most co-ordination and collaboration.

When groups are dependent on one another for the completion of their tasks, the potential for conflict is high. This is especially true when effective task performance depends on reciprocal interaction. Imagine the potential for disaster if control tower personnel were to experience conflict with flight crew members on aircraft. The potential for conflict also exists among sequentially dependent subgroups. An assembly-line delay in the production of furniture, for example, can cost workers in the finishing department the opportunity to earn their incentive bonus.

Lack of substitutability

The more alternative sources of needed resources and services available to a party, the greater its degree of substitutability. Many organisations require that parties use the services of certain other parties within the organisation in order to ensure full utilisation of resources. This policy creates a sequential dependency relationship because the supplying party has power over the receiving party. The lack of available alternatives is often perceived as a conflict by the dependent party. This is because differences in goals and time orientations could be dysfunctional for them. Intergroup conflict could occur, for example, when a marketing department wants to introduce a wide variety of new products but is required to work only with the company's own small design research department, which is already stretched to capacity.

Power differentials

Each of the factors examined so far has the potential to create differences in influence and dependence between parties, which in turn contribute to differences in power. The firefighters strike of 2002/3 is an example of differences in power. The Fire Brigades Union (FBU) calls the brigade out on strike, the employers try to negotiate with pay linked to performance, then the government intervenes with the threat of outlawing the strike. It is then back to the beginning again as the FBU feels compromised.

If party A makes certain decisions that impact on party B's ability to accomplish its goals, party A has power over party B. The more dependent party C is on receiving vital inputs from party D, the more power supplier party D has over receiver party C. The more important party A's function in an interdependent situation, the more all other parties need it, and the more influence party A will command. Since most groups, like most individuals, do not like to be completely dependent on someone else, power differences can cause intergroup conflict, especially when areas critical to goal achievement or satisfaction are involved.

Different role expectations

role
A set of related tasks and behaviours that an individual or group is expected to perform.

role set
All the people who interact with a person or group in a specific role and have expectations about appropriate behaviour.

Khan *et al.* (1964) propose that a **role** is a set of related tasks and behaviours that an individual or group is expected to carry out. A **role set** is all the people who interact with a person or group in a specific role and have expectations about appropriate behaviour. A role set for a manager would include his or her supervisor and subordinates plus members of other groups who attempt to influence the manager's behaviour. Since all members of a role set depend on the incumbent's performance in some manner, they actively attempt to bring about behaviour consistent with their needs. Identifying a role set helps explain who influences a particular person or group to behave in certain ways.

Role ambiguity

role ambiguity
Exists when role sets do not make clear their expectations of role holders.

Role sets need to make clear what they expect from parties who fulfil specified roles. When members of a role set fail to transmit enough information about their expectations, incumbents experience **role ambiguity**. It is difficult to behave acceptably when it is not clear what others expect.

Role ambiguity has several causes. Sometimes those in the role set are not clear themselves about what should be required, so they do not say anything or the expectations that are communicated are vague. A role holder may, for example, receive feedback to be a 'better' group member but fail to glean any specifics as to what 'better' actually means. 'Better' may apply to standards of productivity, but it could just as easily apply to interpersonal relationships within the group. The resulting uncertainty can have paralysing effects. Another source of confusion is contradictions between communicated expectations and contrary reactions after a group member complies with the expectations. For example, a group member is told that teamwork is what counts but is later denied a salary increase because he or she did not exhibit 'outstanding individual achievements' relative to others.

Role conflict

role conflict
Exists when the behavioural expectations of the role holder and/or those of others in the role set do not agree.

When a party's own expectations and those of other role set members differ, **role conflict** occurs. Lubin (1991) suggests that Japanese managers who join western firms, for example, often face social ostracism from the close-knit community of Japanese expatriates when they adopt behaviours and customs expected in their western organisations that are contrary to Japanese customs. According to Khan *et al.* (1964), there are four types of role conflict.

1 **Intrasender conflict:** When prescriptions and proscriptions that come from a single member of the role set are inconsistent or conflicting, intrasender role conflict occurs. If, for example, a team leader is asked by the company's director to add the director's cousin to the staff, but at the same time to follow all equal opportunity guidelines, intrasender conflict may result. The team leader will be legitimately confused about the director's motives, the firm's commitment to equal opportunity, and how he or she should act.

2 **Intersender conflict:** When pressures from one member of a party's role set conflict with those from one or more others in the same role set, intersender conflict results. A classic

example occurs when a group member is promoted to a formal leadership position and finds it impossible to satisfy all the old peers' expectations as well as the new managerial mandates. A first-line supervisor supervising former peer-group members will surely receive pressures from 'old buddies' for favours that conflict with the goals of upper-level management.

3 **Interrole conflict:** When different roles held by the same party require mutually exclusive behaviours, interrole conflict exists. For example, to meet an impending deadline a project team's boss may request that everyone work late on a night when a team member has an important social engagement with his or her spouse (a conflict between work and personal roles).

4 **Person–role conflict:** When your role requires you to do something you do not want to do or feel you should not do, person-role conflict exists. Conflict between a person's needs and values and the demands of a role set is exemplified when an individual is asked by other group members to restrict production. If doing so is contrary to the group member's personal code of ethics, person–role conflict will result.

Role overload

Role overload occurs when role expectations exceed a party's ability to respond effectively. This often occurs when multiple role senders have legitimate expectations for a person's behaviour that are all impossible to fulfil within a given time limit. May and December, for example, is a time of role overload for many university students, especially those who have to work. They must prepare for examinations and typically write assignments for different courses simultaneously. It is also the start of the holiday season or summer sporting events, so those working in catering and retail or associated businesses must cope with their employers' demands to work longer hours. Others may feel the self-imposed pressure to work more hours to meet their own increased financial needs. In addition, relatives and friends expect that students will be available for socialising. Unfortunately, these conflicting expectations cause frustration and stress for students.

---

role overload

Occurs when role expectations exceed a party's ability to respond effectively.

Managing role problems

Anyone can experience any or all of these role conflicts. Different types of role problem are more likely to occur at different levels of an organisation, however. At lower levels of the organisation, role conflict is more prevalent. The first-line supervisor, for example, has to deal with conflicting expectations from subordinates, peers, union representatives and upper management. At higher levels, role ambiguity is more likely to be a problem. A new company chief executive, for instance, must somehow cope with the task of 'making the company more profitable' without really knowing what the relevant factors are or how to restructure them. Rizzo *et al.* (1970) argue that regardless of their specific source, role difficulties frequently cause dysfunctional conflict.

The pressures and negative consequences of role conflicts can be reduced in several ways. Both role ambiguity and conflict can be reduced by identifying who legitimate role-set members are, reducing interdependencies, and establishing more explicit role expectations. The role difficulties of a working single parent cannot be reduced appreciably, for example, but the roles of many organisation members can be streamlined by clarifying role expectations from above and delegating specific tasks downwards. A legal secretary who works for three lawyers, one senior and two junior associates, can ask for clear guidelines as to how to prioritise her tasks. There is a paradox to what we have just recommended, however: some role clarification can actually create dysfunctional conflicts. Uncertainty is the difference between what is actually known and what needs to be known in order to make correct decisions and perform adequately. Eliminating uncertainty requires establishing task clarity – that is, making sure that the responsibilities of parties are clearly stated and understood. It is fairly easy to eliminate task uncertainty for groups in routine jobs such as manufacturing by establishing policies, standard operating procedures and rules. Groups responsible for non-routine tasks, such as developing new products or marketing strategies, however, experience much higher levels of uncertainty and require customised responses.

Some groups are assigned the responsibility of reducing uncertainty for other groups by making decisions or creating rules and procedures that establish operating standards for them. A good example is when an accounting department provides regulations that control how sales representatives must handle expense accounts. Intergroup conflict often results from power differences created when the group assigned to reduce uncertainty imposes rules or procedures perceived to interfere with another group's goal accomplishment.

Degenerative climate

In Chapter 16 we will discuss in further detail how the organisation's culture influences the general nature of employee relationships. However, in Chapter 9, we demonstrated how some

degenerative interaction climate
An organisational climate that encourages dysfunctional conflict.

cultures encourage a degenerative interaction climate where 'win–lose' *attitudes* set the stage for dysfunctional conflict relationships to flourish. Degenerative climates are easy to establish and difficult to overcome. All it would take to destroy a co-operative overall organisational climate, for example, would be an accounting department that flaunts its power by reporting all expense-account errors to higher management and disclosing publicly the names of those 'caught' violating the established procedures.

Another way that climate can create dysfunctional conflict is in cases where people with different values and expectations established from experiences in previous organisational cultures must interact together. Many production workers, for example, have little formal education and are concerned with the pragmatic aspects of specific tasks in highly structured environments. Scientists in research and development groups, on the other hand, may have many years of formal education and spend most of their relatively unstructured work hours engaged in esoteric, future-orientated activities. These differences may make it virtually impossible for such groups to understand one another's values, expectations and priorities. Read the Eye on Ethics box to see how one set of values might not be understood by others.

Another example of culture clash occurred when General Electric acquired Kidder, Peabody & Company. There were big merged cultural differences between GE's organisation men, with their generous pension plans, and the entrepreneurial prima donnas of Kidder, who chafed at any management controls and made so much money they did not need a pension plan. The differences in previous cultures caused the Kidder and GE Capital groups to dislike each other intensely. The Kidder group referred to the GE people as 'credit clerks', and the GE Capital group thought the Kidder people were overpaid, arrogant and under-talented. Consequently, just about everything that could go wrong did, including destructive competition and loss of profitable business (Swartz, 1989).

Football players' strike: Taylor comes to the point of necessary return

Gordon Taylor, the chief executive of the Professional Footballers' Association (PFA), had constantly ducked one question. As the row over his organisation's slice of TV revenue had grown ever more bitter, culminating, while the parties were still in negotiation, in Taylor invoking strike action for televised Premiership and Nationwide League matches, the question remained unanswered. Did Taylor believe – or, more to the point, was he certain – that such extreme industrial action was legal? The first match affected was scheduled to be the noon kick-off between Chelsea and Manchester United. There had been much posturing by both sides, with hot air expended almost each and every day, and there would be more. For the most part Taylor had run a brilliant campaign, at least in terms of public relations, so much so that the players, as he was fond of reminding everybody, were 99 per cent behind him when the PFA balloted them over strike action. They were bound to be. Footballers are not renowned for thinking for themselves and, if the PFA boss tells them they need to go on strike, they will. After all, Taylor is a good bloke and he and his mates know what is what. But invoking the strike call made some wonder if Taylor may have blown it and if he could be forced to backtrack rather smartly. This was not because his case for more money had suddenly been weakened – even though the £50 million offered for the three years seemed an awful lot by anybody's standards – but because many lawyers working within the field of industrial relations seriously doubted whether this was a legitimate dispute. The arguments were that the PFA was not a genuine trades union and therefore that this was not a lawful conflict; that the PFA was seeking to induce the players into breaches of contract with the clubs who were, in effect, an innocent third party. And, on top of everything else, the legality of the wording of the strike ballot was now deemed by some lawyers to be suspect. On the other hand, should this whole sorry episode come to the high court, as it surely would unless the strike was lifted or a settlement reached, then the PFA may well have argued that the Premiership was no more than the instrument of the clubs, that they were one and the same, and that the PFA was therefore right in bringing the players into dispute. These were what lawyers, rubbing their hands in glee, were apt to call 'cracking good arguments', but they were ones that could leave the public perplexed and, perhaps, ultimately disillusioned. The Premier League and the Nationwide League had, without a doubt, conducted the affair with remarkable insensitivity, implicitly accusing the PFA of greed without ever fully explaining their own positions. 'It was hoped that wise counsel would prevail and the likely outcome would be a deal,' said Nick Smith of Queen Square Chambers, Bristol, a barrister specialising in employment and sports law. 'Everybody concerned will recognise the inherent risk in going to court, although it would represent a very interesting piece of litigation.' It was a huge risk. Nothing is certain in law and it would appear that the PFA was the one likely to incur the heavier costs. And what would it do should it lose? Sell the Lowry? Urge the players to dig deep into their pockets and bale it out? Or would the Premiership offer any more funding to an organisation which, as it sees it, was prepared to put the players' interests before the greater interests of the game. Taylor initially captured the high ground but had let it slip. A compromise had to be reached and reached quickly. The public, as the TV ratings demonstrated, were not over-enthused with the sport, while the lawyers sensed a protracted legal wrangle that would benefit only them. It was time for common sense to prevail and for the posturing to cease. In addition, it was time too, surely, for Taylor to justify his extremely large salary through further negotiation rather than a strike threat which, anyway, would ultimately prove to be empty.

Source: © Guardian Newspapers Ltd, 2001, Stephen Bierly.

Discussion questions

1 Why do so many negotiations involve the threat of strike action and how can strikes be avoided?

2 Is it ethical for football players who earn vast sums of money to strike?

Personal differences

As we discussed in Chapter 9 on interpersonal relations, there are some people you have an instant affinity with while others you immediately dislike. There is a high potential for conflict between people with different values, different preferred ways of behaving and different views of the world.

The next section describes in depth the consequences of conflict. As you will see, the consequences of conflict can be either functional or dysfunctional, with team or individual performance increasing or decreasing.

The consequences and outcomes of conflict

Conflict is inevitable in any organisation where individuals and groups must interact to produce complex outputs. Although conflict can often be destructive, Quinn (1988) suggests that at other times it may stimulate creativity, encourage flexibility and even be satisfying because it provides an interesting environment to work in. As illustrated in Exhibit 11-5, the key is to determine whether the conflict is functional or dysfunctional, and then to manage it appropriately.

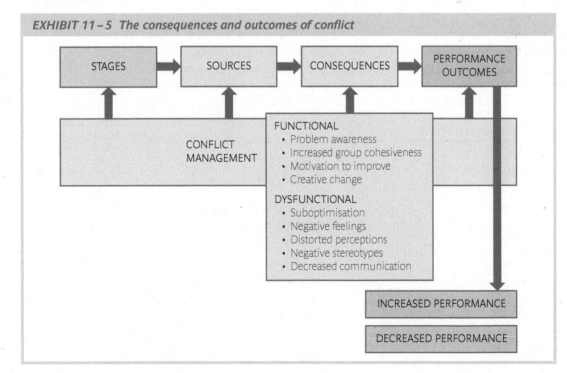

EXHIBIT 11–5 The consequences and outcomes of conflict

Functional conflict and performance

If you have grown up in the West, you may be well aware of the value of the kind of competition that stimulates individuals and groups to greater efforts that yield superior results. Spectators pay millions of pounds annually to share the excitement of skilled athletic competitive conflict. In the business world, competition inspires the creation of new products and establishes affordable pricing structures. International competition stimulates nations to advance their technology and develop their resource bases. These examples of functional conflict are between competing groups that are not part of the same formal organisational structure. These competing groups do not have to work together to solve common problems or achieve common goals. The reward system provides for one winner and one loser. However, in situations where the competing groups or individuals are part of the same organisational structure and must work together to achieve organisational goals, the objective is a win–win, as opposed to a win–lose, outcome.

functional conflict
Conflict between groups that stimulates innovations and production.

As we saw in Chapter 10, Cosier and Schwenk (1990) propose that conflict can improve the quality of decision-making in task forces by eliminating groupthink and allowing all points of view to be considered. Janis's (1982) analysis of major decisions made by four American presidents demonstrated that constructive conflict resulted in high-quality decisions, whereas decisions where all advisers easily conformed to majority opinion were often disastrous. Research scientists, according to Pelz and Andrews (1966), have also been found to be most productive when intellectual conflict exists.

Conflict is also positively related to productivity in well-established, permanent groups. One study by Hall and Williams (1966) found that high-conflict groups outperformed low-conflict groups by 73 per cent. As described in Chapter 10, culturally diverse groups that experience more conflict about different values, perspectives and approaches, are generally more creative and produce higher-quality decisions than do homogeneous groups (Kirchmeyer and Cohen, 1992).

Conflict is inevitable even between individuals or departments that are supposed to cooperate to accomplish organisational goals. To manage conflict so that motivation increases and the quality of work improves, managers need to make sure that interacting parties have cooperative goals and that procedures, attitudes and skills are in place to deal productively with conflict. According to Tjosvold (1986), a number of benefits can result in a conflict-positive organisation in which participants perceive conflict as an exciting opportunity for personal and organisational growth.

conflict-positive organisation
An organisation in which participants perceive conflict as an opportunity for personal and organisational growth.

- Discussing conflict openly can make organisational members more aware and better able to cope with problems.

- Attention is drawn to issues that may interfere with productivity, and organisational practices may be challenged and consequently improved.

- Successfully resolved conflict can strengthen relationships because organisational members understand each other better, release built-up tensions and learn that relationships are strong enough to work through problems productively.

- Personal development occurs as participants learn about their own conflict styles and increase their competencies in managing interpersonal and interdepartmental problems.

- As a break from standard operating procedures, conflict can be stimulating and fun as participants become involved in solving interesting interdependent problems.

Functional change within groups

One of the most important places to observe these positive results is within a group experiencing conflict with another group. Four changes typically occur in groups experiencing intergroup conflict: increased cohesion, increased loyalty, increased emphasis on task accomplishment, and acceptance of autocratic leadership (Schein, 1965).

Increased cohesiveness

When groups are threatened by other competing groups, members put aside their interpersonal differences and band together against the common enemy, and group membership becomes more attractive. This phenomenon is often seen when nations that traditionally compete economically and politically band together against a common aggressor in wartime. Examples are the Arab nations' co-operation against the common perceived Israeli threat and the European allies' coming together during the world wars.

Increased loyalty

Group goals take precedence over individual gain or satisfaction as members sacrifice for the common good. Members rigidly adhere to established rules and strictly enforce new ones to eliminate potential conflicts among members that might detract from task accomplishment.

Acceptance of autocratic leadership

In the face of a crisis, group members are more willing to accept the autocratic decisions of a central leader because they are more timely than democratic methods and other members are free to consolidate energy for winning the conflict.

Emphasis on task accomplishment

Personal goals and satisfaction are put aside so that all energy can be concentrated on meeting the challenge put forth by the competing groups. There is a sense of urgency, with no time for absenteeism or performing unrelated activities.

Functional changes between groups

Even dysfunctional intergroup conflict can produce positive consequences if participants learn from the experience and manage conflicts better in the future. Research by Tjosvold *et al.* (1992) has demonstrated that conflict can actually promote co-ordination between departments and contribute to task accomplishment, efficient use of resources and customer service, if the interacting departments have co-operative, but not competitive, goals. Miles (1980) confirms that potential positive consequences for relations between groups include:

- increased problem awareness
- decreased tensions after disagreements have been resolved
- more appropriate readjustments of tasks and resources
- establishment of mechanisms for obtaining feedback about intergroup problems
- clarification of priorities and tasks.

Dysfunctional conflict and performance

dysfunctional conflict
Conflict between groups in the same organisation that hinders the achievement of group and organisational goals.

Dysfunctional conflict occurs when the interaction between two or more parties hinders the achievement of individual, group or organisational goals. An example of a conflict with lose–lose outcomes was the coal miners dispute of the 1980s, which contributed to the industry's demise and had a catastrophic effect on local communities.

Dysfunctional changes between groups

Four common intergroup consequences of conflict are hostility, distorted perceptions, negative stereotyping and decreased communication. Sherif and Sherif (1953) suggest that these all serve to exacerbate negative outcomes in intergroup conflict.

Hostility

Hostility between groups (a 'we–they' attitude) often develops, causing each group to see itself as virtuous and the other groups as incompetent or unprincipled enemies. The intense dislike that develops makes reconciliation more difficult.

Distorted perceptions

Groups in conflict often develop distorted perceptions emphasising the negative and ignoring the positive traits of competing groups. At the same time, members often develop higher opinions of their own group.

Negative stereotypes

The resulting negative stereotypes of other groups contribute to decreased and distorted communication, suboptimisation and lack of co-ordination. Members perceive fewer differences within their own group and greater differences between their group and the 'enemy' than really exist, creating even greater conflict between groups and further strengthening cohesiveness within each group.

Decreased communication

These negative attitudes and stereotypes usually cause communication breakdowns between conflicting groups. Although groups often increase surveillance to detect the plans and weaknesses of competing groups, no real sharing of information takes place and this void is filled by the distorted perceptions and negative stereotypes already mentioned. Decreased communication is especially dysfunctional where sequential or reciprocal interdependence exists between groups.

Dysfunctional changes within groups

Many of the same problems that two individuals experiencing conflict must contend with manifest themselves within groups: lack of trust, decreased co-operation, decreased communication, and so on. Also, Jehn (1994) suggests that, in a group, as member satisfaction decreases so does cohesion and productivity, which can eventually threaten the very survival of a group.

The productive management of conflict

The first part of this chapter has shown how conflict can have negative and/or positive consequences for individuals, groups and organisations. The major variable that determines its outcome is how the conflict is managed. Exhibit 11-6 summarises conflict style orientations and conflict management methods.

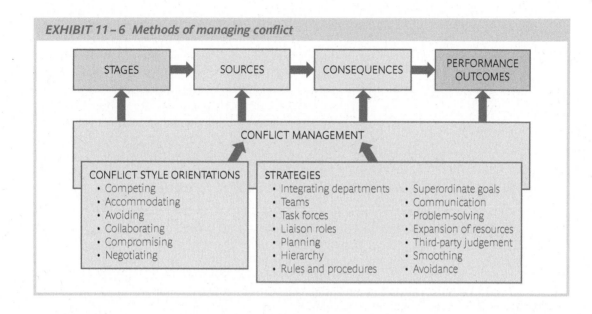

EXHIBIT 11–6 Methods of managing conflict

Conflict management style orientations

Parties engaged in a conflict usually have two main concerns: getting what they want for themselves and maintaining the kind of relationship they want with the other party. When people are primarily concerned for themselves, they are assertive in trying to satisfy their own needs. When they care about the other party and want to maintain a positive relationship, people are co-operative and concerned about making sure the other's needs are satisfied.

The most appropriate conflict management style orientation

None of these conflict management approaches is better or worse than any other per se. Their effectiveness depends on how appropriate they are for any particular situation. Most people, however, have a 'dominant' style that they most often use because it has been successful in the past and they are comfortable with the required behaviours. If their dominant style is not appropriate or does not work, people revert to 'back-up' styles in attempting to resolve conflicts. This involves stepping out of the comfort zone of your favourite style and adapting to the situation with a more appropriate style. To determine your dominant and back-up style hierarchy, complete the 'Your turn' self-assessment inventory.

If it is important to you to resolve a conflict in a way that enhances your relationship with the other party, collaboration or compromise is far more effective than avoidance or competition. As described by Alessandra and Hunsaker (1993) in the earlier chapters on communications and interpersonal relations, effective communications and constructive feedback are necessary to support more collaborative efforts and to work through confrontations that may develop. It is also necessary to be flexible and be able to negotiate and bargain with the other party.

Cultural and gender differences in conflict style orientations

Another factor that determines which conflict style orientation is most appropriate is the cultural backgrounds of the participants. If the two parties in a conflict are from similar cultures, a collaborative style orientation is more likely to be attempted. Participants usually share their

Research focus: conflict management style

conflict management style
The different combinations of assertiveness and co-operation that people emphasise when in a conflict situation.

Rahim and Magner (1995) suggest that the different degrees of emphasis that people place on these two basic concerns can be expanded into five specific **conflict management style** orientations: competing, accommodating, avoiding, collaborating and compromising. These are shown in Exhibit 11-7 (Thomas, 1992).

Competing

Competing is assertive and unco-operative behaviour, embodied in the parties' pursuit of their own concerns at others' expense. Competing behaviour is often used by power-orientated people who will use every technique available to win their point or defend their position.

Competing can be beneficial when quick, decisive action is vital, as in emergencies. It is also useful when unpopular actions, such as discipline or cost-cutting, must be implemented. Finally, competing is sometimes necessary to protect against people who take advantage of uncompetitive behaviour. If you are too competitive, however, you may find yourself surrounded by yes-men who have learned that it is unwise to disagree with you, which cuts you off from sources of important information.

Accommodating

Accommodating is the opposite of competing. It consists of unassertive and co-operative behaviour. Accommodating people frequently neglect their own concerns to satisfy the needs of others in order to maintain a positive relationship.

Accommodating is an appropriate strategy when the issue at stake is much more important to the other person. Satisfying another's needs as a goodwill gesture will help maintain a co-operative relationship, building up social credits for use in later conflicts. Accommodating is also appropriate when a manager wishes to develop subordinates by allowing them to experiment and learn from their own mistakes. Too much accommodation, however, can deprive others of your personal contributions and viewpoint.

EXHIBIT 11–7 Interpersonal conflict management styles

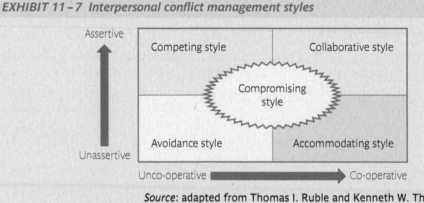

Source: adapted from Thomas I. Ruble and Kenneth W. Thomas (1976) 'Support for a Two-dimensional Model of Conflict Behavior', *Organizational Behavior and Human Performance* 16, p. 145.

Avoiding

Avoiding is unassertive and unco-operative behaviour. People with this conflict management style pursue neither their own concerns nor those of others. To avoid conflict altogether, a person might diplomatically sidestep an issue, postpone it or withdraw from the threatening situation.

Avoiding is appropriate when the issue involved is relatively unimportant to you. In addition, if you have little power or are in a situation that is very difficult to change, avoiding may be the best choice. Similarly, avoidance may be wise if the potential damage from confronting a conflict outweighs its benefits or you need to let people cool off a little in order to bring tensions back down to a reasonable level. On the other hand, you should not let important decisions be made by default or spend a lot of energy avoiding issues that must eventually be confronted.

Collaborating

Collaborating is the opposite of avoiding; it consists of both assertive and co-operative behaviour. It involves working with the other person to find a solution that fully satisfies both parties. This is a joint problem-solving mode involving communication and creativity on the part of each party to find a mutually beneficial solution.

Collaborating is a necessity when the concerns of both parties are too important to be compromised. Collaborating merges the insights of people with different perspectives. It allows you to test your assumptions and understand those of others, to gain commitment by incorporating others' concerns, and to work through hard feelings. Not all conflict situations, however, deserve this amount of time and energy. Trivial problems often do not require optimal solutions, and not all personal differences need to be worked through. It also does little good to behave in a collaborative manner if others will not.

Compromising

Compromising falls somewhere between assertive and co-operative behaviours. The objective is to find a mutually acceptable middle ground that partially satisfies both parties. This conflict management style splits the difference and makes concessions.

A compromise is appropriate when goals are moderately important but not worth the effort of collaboration or the possible disruption of competition. If a manager is dealing with an opponent of equal power who is strongly committed to a mutually exclusive goal, compromise may be the best hope for leaving both of them in relatively satisfactory positions. Compromise is also wise when a temporary settlement needs to be achieved quickly. It can be a useful safety valve for gracefully getting out of mutually destructive situations. On the other hand, too much compromising might cause you to lose sight of principles that are more important, values and long-term objectives. Too much compromise can also create a cynical climate of gamesmanship.

true concerns more openly, seek each other's opinions, and more fully reveal their bargaining strategy than if the parties were from different cultures.

Rahim and Blum (1995) suggest that participants from different cultures have different conflict style orientations consistent with their cultural value systems. Participants from different cultures perceive the same conflict situation differently and have different goals, values and priorities. Take, for example, the differences between people from collectivist cultures like Japan, where group goals are valued more than individual goals, and individualistic cultures like the United Kingdom, where personal achievement is the predominate value. Consistent with the

Your turn

Your conflict management style

Consider conflict situations in which your wishes differed from those of another person or group. Indicate how often you applied each of the following tactics.

	Rarely				Always
1 I argue to prove my position.	1	2	3	4	5
2 I negotiate for a compromise.	1	2	3	4	5
3 I try to meet others' expectations	1	2	3	4	5
4 I try to find a mutually acceptable solution.	1	2	3	4	5
5 I firmly pursue my position.	1	2	3	4	5
6 I keep conflicts to myself to avoid hassles.	1	2	3	4	5
7 I hold on to my solution no matter what.	1	2	3	4	5
8 I compromise through give-and-take tactics.	1	2	3	4	5
9 I share information to reach a joint decision.	1	2	3	4	5
10 I keep my differences to myself.	1	2	3	4	5
11 I accommodate the wishes of others.	1	2	3	4	5
12 I try for the best solution for everyone.	1	2	3	4	5
13 I propose middle-ground agreements.	1	2	3	4	5
14 I go along with the suggestions of others.	1	2	3	4	5
15 I avoid hard feelings by not sharing my disagreements.	1	2	3	4	5

Scoring To determine your primary conflict-handling style, transfer the number you assigned to each statement on the questionnaire to the scoring key below, and then add the columns. Your conflict handling style is the category with the highest total. See Exhibit 11-7 and the previous discussion for a complete description of these styles.

Competing	Accommodating	Avoiding	Collaborating	Compromising
1 _____	3 _____	6 _____	4 _____	2 _____
5 _____	11 _____	10 _____	9 _____	8 _____
7 _____	14 _____	15 _____	12 _____	13 _____

Total:

_____ _____ _____ _____ _____

Sources: M.A. Rahim (1983) 'A Measure of Styles of Handling Interpersonal Conflict', *Academy of Management Journal* June, pp. 368–376; and K.W. Thomas and R.H. Kilmann, *Thomas-Kilmann Conflict Mode Instrument*, Sterling Forest, NY: XICOM, Inc. 1977.

above model of conflict management style orientations, people from collectivist cultures prefer to collaborate or avoid conflict if both parties cannot be satisfied, in order to maintain cohesive relationships. People from individualistic cultures, on the other hand, tend to compete and fall back on compromise if they cannot get everything they want. It should be noted that collectivists collaborate only within their own group; Chen *et al.* (1998) contend that when they have a conflict with people outside their group, they can be just as competitive as individualists.

Karakowsky (1996) also suggests that although other factors may override its influence, gender is another factor that influences conflict style orientations. As discussed in Chapters 8 and 9, women seem to be more concerned than men about maintaining a positive, ongoing relationship between conflicting parties. This leads them to prefer a collaborative style orientation when entering a conflict, and to be more willing to compromise, or even accommodate, to preserve the relationship. Men, on the other hand, are usually more competitive and less concerned about the relationship.

Negotiating

Negotiating, or bargaining, is the practical application of the collaborating and compromising approaches to conflict management. According to Wall (1985), **negotiation** occurs whenever two or more conflicting parties enter into a discussion in an attempt to determine a mutually acceptable exchange rate for their respective goods or services. We know that lawyers and car salesmen spend a lot of time negotiating, but so, too, do managers. They have to negotiate salaries for incoming employees, make deals with superiors, bargain over budgets, work out differences with associates, and resolve conflicts with subordinates. Negotiating is actually something that just about everyone engages in almost every day, and most of the time without even realising it. Think back over your past several days. Did you have occasion to do things like clarify the time to meet for dinner, organise a day for a study group to meet, decide on a film to see with another person? Look at the Dynamics of Diversity box for an insight into the complexity of negotiations across cultures.

> **negotiation**
> A form of problem-solving where two groups with conflicting interests exchange things in order to reach a mutually agreeable resolution.

Bargaining strategies

The success of negotiations depends on the bargaining strategies that the respective parties choose to apply. There are two general approaches to negotiation: *distributive bargaining* and *integrative bargaining*.

Distributive bargaining

You see a used car advertised for sale in the newspaper. It appears to be just what you have been looking for. You go out to see the car. It's great and you want it. The owner tells you the asking price. You do not want to pay that much. The two of you then negotiate over the price. The negotiating process you are engaging in is called **distributive bargaining**. Its most identifying feature is that it operates under zero-sum conditions. That is, any gain I make is at your expense, and vice versa. Referring back to the used car example, every pound you can get the seller to cut from the car's price is a pound you save. Conversely, every pound more he or she can get from you comes at your expense. Thus the essence of distributive bargaining is negotiating over who gets what share of a fixed pie. Appropriate conflict style orientations for distributive bargaining start with compromise, followed by competition and accommodation, depending upon the relative importance to you of getting more of what you want versus maintaining a positive relationship with the other party.

> **distributive bargaining**
> The negotiating process whereby two parties negotiate over the price of an item.

Exhibit 11-8, suggested by Stagner and Rosen (1965), depicts the distributive bargaining strategy, which contains a bargaining zone of mutual acceptance. Let us assume that you and another party represent the two negotiators. Each of you has a *target point* that defines what you

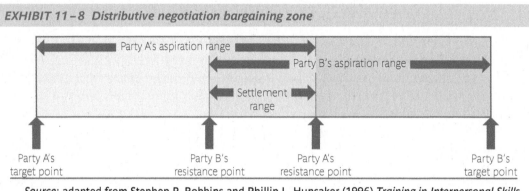

EXHIBIT 11–8 Distributive negotiation bargaining zone

Party A's aspiration range

Party B's aspiration range

Settlement range

Party A's target point

Party B's resistance point

Party A's resistance point

Party B's target point

Source: adapted from Stephen P. Robbins and Phillip L. Hunsaker (1996) *Training in Interpersonal Skills*. Upper Saddle River, NJ: Prentice Hall, p. 243.

dynamics of diversity

Four into one will go – at a push: KLM's alliance talks with the three EQA partners had progressed well, but the real repercussions of a deal were starting to emerge

It was all going so well. The rapid advance of alliance talks between KLM and the three European Quality Alliance (EQA) partners gave the impression that they were drifting towards the perfect marriage like graceful swans. But in reality there were feet paddling furiously beneath the surface to defuse the mounting barriers to such an agreement – even one that stopped short of a full merger.

The structure being considered by the presidents of KLM, SAS, Swissair and Austrian Airlines – a joint holding company that merged management functions while maintaining the notional independence of the four carriers – would have been a watershed for the European industry. Not only would it have propelled the partners into the British Airways/Air France/Lufthansa league, but it could also be a crucial moment for aeropolitical relations between the USA and Europe.

First the good news. Despite the obvious stumbling blocks – rationalising US alliance partners and competing hubs, and securing the agreements of governments and unions – the rationale behind the KLM–EQA link-up remained as strong as ever, even if Austrian Airlines' flirtation with Lufthansa had opened up the first gap in the united front presented by the four airlines.

The 16 working groups set up to evaluate the alliance had come out clearly in favour of a holding company called Euroair, jointly managed and split between KLM, SAS, Swissair (holding 30 per cent each) and Austrian (10 per cent), with a single balance sheet and offering a jointly branded product. Individual airline identities would be maintained, at least in the short term, with a full merger delayed until a more forgiving regulatory climate emerged.

The smooth progress of what were, perhaps, the most complex alliance talks ever attempted is attributed to the existing close relationships between senior management at the four airlines. 'It makes higher levels of discussion immediately possible,' says Paul Maximilian Mueller, head of external relations at Swissair. 'We are looking at doing something that has never been done before in Europe by considering a multi-cross-border joint venture.'

The EC Commission's competition and transport directorates faced a field day with this one, but also ran the risk that critics would have another opportunity to drive a wedge between their responses.

Talks between the airlines and the Commission were said to have progressed well, with the Commission obviously concerned about the impact on competition in the Community. In providing conditional approval for the deal, the Commission focused on the effect on competition between the partners' major hubs and on attempting to ensure that the dominant positions the four airlines already held in their respective domestic markets were not abused.

Although supportive the Commission wanted a favourable response to two key questions. First, how would the US partnerships be resolved, and what impact could this have on EC–US bilateral agreements? Second, would the new partnership be recognised as a Community carrier? The airlines insisted that the new company would be a Community carrier, but the Commission and third countries had to be convinced.

The issue was complicated by the fact that KLM and SAS were the only two Community airlines involved. Sweden and Norway were due to take on the third package – which includes the Community's common ownership legislation – in July. Austria should have been included in the second package by the end of the year, but this did not cover ownership, while Switzerland remained in limbo following its referendum vote against incorporating EC legislation, though a separate EC–Swiss agreement covering air transport could be negotiated.

Commission officials are reluctant to speculate about possible bloc negotiations, but they are a priority concern. In addition, that thinking was shared on the other side of the Atlantic. The deal called into question many assumptions upon which the bilateral negotiating system was based, including the importance of nationality to the airline business.

With managements bending over backwards to sell the merits of the proposal to governments and the financial community, there was predictable concern about its impact among the airlines' rank-and-file workforce. The unions (with the exception of those at Austrian) had not come out against the deal, despite the likely loss of jobs, and if anything were taking the realistic approach that the consolidating forces of the European airline industry could not be halted. But there was concern about the way in which employees were being treated.

Talks between airline managements had been paralleled by discussions between the unions representing staff at the four European carriers and their counterparts at the three US carriers involved. Despite the presence of union representatives on the boards of SAS, KLM and Austrian Airlines, the unions claimed there had been an unprecedented lack of consultation.

The first cracks had started to appear in the united KLM–EQA front amid concerns that the deal would marginalise Austrian Airlines. The carrier's senior management are reportedly split on the benefits of the alliance, its unions have come out against it and the Austrian Government is worried about any loss of sovereignty.

With so many countries and cultures involved moving forward was proving difficult.

Source: *Airline Business*, June 1993, p. 22(2), Reed Business Publishing Ltd (UK).

Discussion questions

1 With so many different organisations involved how could you build coalitions to smooth the process of negotiation?

2 What effect could the impact of culture have in negotiating deals?

would like to achieve. Each of you also has a *resistance point*, which marks the lowest outcome that is acceptable – the point below which you would break off negotiations rather than accept a less favourable settlement. The area between these resistance points is called the settlement range. As long as there is some overlap in the aspiration ranges, there exists a settlement area where each of your aspirations can be met.

settlement range
The area between resistance points where there exists an area where two parties can meet their aspirations.

When engaged in distributive bargaining, your tactics should focus on trying to get your opponent to agree to your specific target point or to get as close to it as possible. Examples of such tactics are persuading your opponent of the impossibility of getting to his or her target point and the advisability of accepting a settlement near yours; arguing that your target is fair, while your opponent's is not; and attempting to get your opponent to feel emotionally generous towards you and thus accept an outcome close to your target point.

Integrative bargaining

integrative bargaining
A collaborative approach where parties assume there is a win–win solution.

The collaborative conflict style orientation results in integrative bargaining, where the parties assume that it is possible to create a win–win solution. If successful, the result is satisfaction and positive long-term relationships. The following sales-credit negotiation provides an example of integrative bargaining in action.

Assume a sales representative for a women's sportswear manufacturer has just closed a £15 000 order from a small clothing retailer. The sales representative calls in the order to her firm's credit department. She is told that the firm cannot approve credit to this customer because of a past slow-pay record. The next day, the sales representative and the firm's credit supervisor meet to discuss the problem. The sales representative does not want to lose the business. Neither does the credit supervisor, but he also does not want to get stuck with an uncollectable debt. The two openly review their options. After considerable discussion they agree on a solution that meets both their needs: the credit supervisor will approve the sale, but the clothing store's owner will provide a bank guarantee that will assure payment if the bill is not paid within 60 days.

Many experts in negotiation have concluded that integrative bargaining is generally preferable to distributive bargaining. This is because the former builds positive long-term relationships and facilitates working together in the future. It bonds negotiators and allows each to leave the bargaining table feeling that he or she has achieved a victory. Distributive bargaining, on the other hand, leaves one party a loser. It tends to build animosities and deepen divisions between people who have to work together on an ongoing basis.

If this is the case, why is there not more integrative bargaining in organisations? The answer lies in the conditions necessary for this type of negotiation to succeed. According to Thomas (1992), these conditions include openness with information and frankness between parties, sensitivity on the part of each party to the other's needs, the ability to trust one another, and willingness by both parties to maintain flexibility. Unfortunately, many organisational cultures and interpersonal relationships are not characterised by these conditions. In these cases, too much openness and information sharing when trying to collaborate can make you vulnerable because the other party has more information and may use it against you. Fells (1998) suggests this can be very costly if the other party does not reciprocate, giving him or her more power to leverage a better deal. So, even if one party begins integrative bargaining by collaborating and attempting to establish trust, if the other party fails to reciprocate, the original collaborating party will usually shift to a distributive win–lose bargaining strategy for self-protection.

Guidelines for effective negotiating

During the actual negotiation process, the behaviours of the parties involved are very influential in determining the type and outcome of the negotiation. According to Robbins and Hunsaker (1996), the most essential behaviours for effective negotiation are summarised in the following guidelines.

Consider the other party's situation

Acquire as much information as you can about your opponent's interests and goals. What are his or her real needs versus wants? What constituencies must he or she appease? What is his or her strategy? This information will help you understand your opponent's behaviour, predict his or her responses to your offers, and frame solutions in terms of his or her interests. Additionally, when you can anticipate your opponent's position, you are better equipped to counter his or her arguments with the facts and figures that support your position.

Have a plan and concrete strategy

According to Lewicke *et al.* (1996), your chances of obtaining a favourable negotiation outcome increase if you plan and set goals before the action starts. Treat negotiation like a chess match. Expert chess players have a plan and a strategy. They know ahead of time how they will respond to any given situation. How strong is your situation and how important is the issue? Are you willing to split differences to achieve an early solution? If the issue is very important to you, is your position strong enough to let you play hardball and show little or no willingness to compromise? These are questions you should address before you begin bargaining.

Begin with a positive overture

Establish rapport and mutual interests before starting the negotiation. Then begin bargaining with a positive overture – perhaps a small concession. Concessions tend to be reciprocated and lead to agreements. A positive climate can be developed by reciprocating your opponent's concessions, also. But keep in mind that although concessions enable parties to move towards the area of agreement, establish good faith and provide information about the relative importance of various negotiation concerns, the meaning of making concessions does vary from culture to culture. For example, Russians typically view concessions as a sign of weakness while Chinese negotiators generally pull back when the other parties change from initial positions (Adler, 1991).

Address problems, not personalities

Concentrate on the negotiation issues, not on the personal characteristics of your opponent. When negotiations get tough, avoid the tendency to attack your opponent. If other people feel threatened, they concentrate on defending their self-esteem, as opposed to solving the problem. It is your opponent's ideas or position that you disagree with, not him or her personally. Separate the people from the problem, and do not personalise differences.

Maintain a rational, goal-orientated frame of mind

Use the previous guideline in reverse if your opponent attacks or gets emotional with you. Do not get hooked by emotional outbursts. Let the other person let off steam without taking it personally while you try to understand the problem or strategy behind the aggression.

Pay little attention to initial offers

Treat an initial offer as merely a point of departure. Everyone has to have an initial position. These initial offers tend to be extreme and idealistic. Treat them as such. Focus on the other person's interests and your own goals and principles while you generate other possibilities.

Emphasise win–win solutions

Bargainers often assume that their gain must come at the expense of the other party. As noted with integrative bargaining, that need not be the case. There are often win–win solutions. However, assuming a zero-sum game means missed opportunities for trade-offs that could benefit both sides. So, if conditions are supportive, look for an integrative solution. Create additional alternatives, especially low-cost concessions you can make that have high value to the other party. Frame options in terms of your opponent's interests and look for solutions that can allow your opponent, as well as you, to declare a victory.

Create a climate of trust

Of course, neither side is going to make themselves vulnerable by sharing information in pursuit of a collaborative agreement if they do not trust the other party. Consequently, you want to avoid words and phrases that may irritate the other party or cause mistrust. Skilled negotiators do not make exaggerated statements or absurd opening offers, or renege on commitments. They listen, ask questions and try to empathise with the other party, while being patient and avoiding defensiveness if the other party tests them in the beginning.

Insist on using objective criteria

Fisher *et al.* (1991) suggest that you should make your negotiated decisions based on principles and results, not emotions or pressure. Agree upon objective criteria that can aid both parties in assessing the reasonableness of the alternatives. Do not succumb to emotional pleas, assertiveness or stubbornness if the other party's underlying rationale does not meet these criteria.

Be open to accepting third-party assistance

When stalemates are reached, consider using a neutral third party. The two most common forms of third-party assistance are mediation and arbitration. *Mediators* can help parties come to an agreement, but they do not impose a settlement. Companies like Texaco have used ombudsmen to mediate conflicts in areas such as racial discrimination allegations in attempts to maintain a positive and trusting environment. *Arbitrators* hear both sides of the dispute and then impose a binding solution. They are often utilised in the final stage of union grievance negotiations.

Which approach is best depends upon the specific conflict situation. Mediation provides the greatest potential for employee satisfaction when dealing with minor conflicts because it allows the parties more responsibility in determining the outcome. Meyer *et al.* (1997) suggest that when the parties are at a definite stalemate, however, arbitration is usually most appropriate because its structured rules and processes provide the best sense of fairness.

Adapt to cultural differences

As with conflict style orientations, negotiation practices are heavily influenced by national culture. So, if you are negotiating with people from a different cultural background, take into consideration how cultural influences are likely to shape their goals and negotiating tactics. For example, do not expect a Chinese negotiator to quickly jump into bargaining with you if he or she does not know you. This is because the Chinese tend to place a strong emphasis on relationships so they prefer not to negotiate with people they do not know well or trust. After bargaining begins, Chinese negotiators' positions on an issue may become rigid if they feel their goals are being compromised. Nevertheless, according to Pye (1982), nothing should be considered final in negotiations with the Chinese until the terms have actually been realised.

It is also important to take into consideration how cultural influences are likely to shape your own goals and negotiating tactics, and how these come across to negotiators from different cultures. For example, generally the British play down status distinctions because they value equality and do not want to appear to be showing off. However, because of their task orientation, Britons also get frustrated with time delays when another negotiator has to wait for approval from superiors in his or her home country before obtaining closure to an agreement. They also prefer limited small talk and socialising, which is necessary in many countries to allow negotiators to get to know each other before bargaining begins. The British may also often become angry when their foreign counterparts adhere to different ethical standards, such as dishonesty or bribery, or backing out on an agreement (Graham and Herberger, 1983).

It is important to adapt to the cultural expectations of negotiators from different countries in order to maintain the rapport and credibility necessary for potential integrative outcomes. It is also important to keep in touch with your own cultural biases and styles so that they are not exploited by well-informed negotiators from other countries. Chinese negotiators, for example, have been known to consciously stall the bargaining process and inject long periods of silence when negotiating with westerners purposely to exploit the latter's propensity for impatience (Pye, 1982).

The advent and growth of the Internet is leading to many new and unforeseen challenges for international negotiators. The lack of face-to-face contact is disturbing for negotiators from countries where building rapport and relationships before establishing agreements is important, but is a welcome relief to task-orientated westerners. On the other hand, there are a host of additional problems that e-commerce has created for international negotiations. This situation is explored in the Technology Transformation box.

Conflict management strategies

Ancona (1990) suggests that it is a truism that parties, be they individuals, groups, organisations or countries, that co-operate with each other are usually more productive than those that do not. But there are many areas of potential conflict. Conflict erupted at Apple Computers in the early 1980s, although the groups involved were in independent divisions. The newly created Macintosh division was assigned the task of developing a creative breakthrough product as quickly as possible and was receiving a disproportionate share of the company's publicity and resources. At least this was how the Apple II division, which was bringing in most of the company's profits, saw it. This situation led to jealousy, resentment and name-calling between the two divisions.

Since dysfunctional conflict can have destructive consequences, it is important to detect, reduce and act to prevent its recurrence. On the other hand, according to Cosier and Schwenk (1990), even dysfunctional conflict is useful in that it signals needed changes. Also, functional conflict that serves to improve the quality of decision-making and stimulate creative breakthroughs should be judiciously managed to achieve the most beneficial results for the organisation. Consequently, the critical issue is not how to eliminate conflict but how to manage it productively to obtain positive change and avoid negative consequences.

technology transformation

Negotiating the e-commerce cyberspace

Technology enables e-commerce – the electronic distribution of goods and services. Business can be done from anywhere in the world, pushing globalisation to its limits. However, the rapid increase in the amount of e-commerce business leads to new international trade questions. Countries are being forced to converge on topics such as the following.

- What constitutes an electronic signature?
- What taxes apply in which countries?
- Is pornography legal?
- Can drug prescriptions be ordered over the Internet?
- How can Internet crimes be prevented?
- How will intellectual property rights be enforced?
- What should be done about Internet sites that give instructions on how to build weapons such as bombs, guns and hazardous chemicals?

These are just the tip of the iceberg when it comes to international trade negotiations about e-commerce. However, approaches to finding answers to these questions are as diverse as the countries involved. Different cultures place different values on just about every topic, making international negotiations very difficult. One country might try to prevent Internet pornography, while another country might concentrate on preventing the sale of imported items to 'protect the local culture'.

Where, traditionally, trade negotiators reported to one agency or government, regarding e-commerce, the roles and responsibilities of negotiators are shifting. Companies are leading the charge into new Internet goods and services; therefore, new pressures on trade issues are coming from companies and public interest groups, not governments. Negotiators find themselves caught in the middle. Furthermore, the skills necessary to negotiate multilateral agreements on technology are different to the skills required for negotiating agreements on manufacturing. Negotiators must be well versed in different high-technology areas while at the same time bridging cultural gaps. And, in the case of e-commerce, these gaps can be significantly wide.

Source: 'Horse Trading in Cyberspace: US Trade Policy in the Information Age', *Journal of International Affairs*, Spring 1998, pp. 473–496.

Discussion questions

1 Is it important to have convergence on the issues raised by e-commerce?
2 What conflicts are likely to arise if trading by e-commerce means that anything goes?

Attempts to manage intergroup conflict take the form of win–lose (competing and accommodating), lose–lose (avoiding), win–win (collaborating), or compromise (bargaining) outcomes. Win–lose outcomes are brought about by all-or-nothing competitive strategies that encourage one group to win at the expense of the other. Since organisations consist of ongoing relationships, zero-sum strategies create destructive political environments. Avoiding strategies do not solve problems, they leave the problems to fester and erupt later. At best, they allow some temporary productivity until the groups can address the conflict more effectively. Compromise strategies allow both groups to gain a little, but neither to obtain all that their respective members desire. Since win–win strategies allow both groups to obtain their goals through creative integration of their concerns, the best practice is to try a win–win strategy first. If this does not work, a compromise strategy can provide some benefits to both groups. Organisations with intergroup co-ordination strategies can often manage conflict productively without it becoming destructive.

Co-ordination strategies for avoiding intergroup conflict

Exhibit 11-9 identifies seven of the most frequently used methods for co-ordinating intergroup performance to avoid dysfunctional conflicts. The seven strategies are listed on a continuum of increasing cost in terms of resource and energy commitment. The strategies are not mutually exclusive. Galbraith (1973) suggests that in most organisations, the simpler strategies listed at the low end of the continuum are used in conjunction with the more complex strategies listed at the high end. For example, managers using task forces to co-ordinate intergroup performance are likely to be using rules and procedures in conjunction with the higher-level task force strategy.

Rules and procedures

One of the simplest and least costly ways of avoiding intergroup conflict is to spell out in advance the required activities and behaviours in the form of rules and procedures. Written standards tell interacting parties what to do in specific situations to ensure adequate performance and avoid having to work things through each time. If the typing pool is tied up with the finance department's quarterly report, for example, and if the personnel department knows ahead of time that under such conditions it is free to hire temporary help from an outside agency, no confrontational interaction between personnel and finance will be necessary.

The problem with rules and procedures is that they only help when activities are reoccurring and can be anticipated in advance. When uncertainty and change characterise the task environment, however, rules and procedures alone may not guarantee that no dysfunctional conflict will occur.

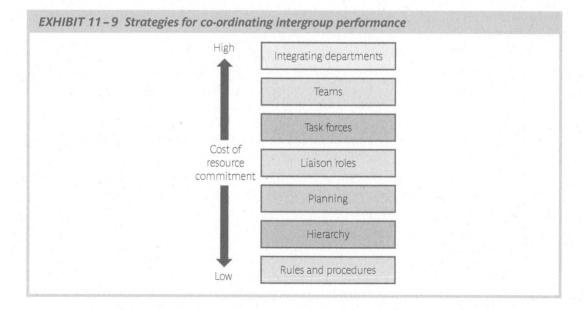

EXHIBIT 11–9 Strategies for co-ordinating intergroup performance

High

↑

Cost of resource commitment

↓

Low

- Integrating departments
- Teams
- Task forces
- Liaison roles
- Planning
- Hierarchy
- Rules and procedures

Hierarchy

When rules and procedures are not sufficient for coping with intergroup problems, conflict can be passed up the hierarchy to a common superior for resolution. If conflict arises between copywriters and graphic designers in an advertising department, for example, the advertising production manager may intervene as mediator. If the salesforce perceives itself to be in conflict with the entire advertising operation, the vice president in charge of marketing may have to resolve the issue.

Planning

In more complex situations, co-ordinating intergroup activities requires more than rules, procedures or hierarchies. Planning can be essential to task accomplishments when it is necessary to determine in advance the goals, roles and responsibilities of all the groups that need to co-operate.

A classic example of the need for planning is in building construction. Most interactions can be anticipated and the behaviours of various groups controlled in a programmed fashion. All groups – diggers, concrete pourers, bricklayers, carpenters, plasterers, painters – must know in advance what they are supposed to do and when. Activities are controlled by a master plan that co-ordinates the efforts of the interacting groups.

Liaison roles

When the number of interactions between several groups becomes more frequent or complex, organisations often establish co-ordinating personnel to handle these ongoing interaction requirements. A liaison expedites lateral communication much more effectively than could a cumbersome formal information system alone. Because liaisons are well acquainted with the nature of the work all parties perform, they can cut through the bureaucracy to provide quicker, more effective communication. An example would be an MBA graduate with an undergraduate degree in engineering who acts as a liaison between the engineering and production departments.

liaison
A party that expedites lateral communication between interacting groups by circumventing formal organisational boundaries.

Task forces

When several groups interact over time in a complex situation, another way of facilitating co-operation is to establish a temporary task force made up of one or more individuals from each of the interacting units. This group investigates problems, suggests solutions and facilitates communication among all groups involved. When the problem or task has been completed, the task group disbands and members return to their respective groups and resume their normal activities. A task force of a new product for a major customer, for example, might consist of individuals from production, research and marketing, along with the customer's representatives.

task force
A temporary group made up of individuals from interacting groups that resolves problems, facilitates co-operation and promotes integration of efforts.

Teams

When several groups must interact in a complex situation over a long period of time, more permanent teams can be formed to manage intergroup activities. Team members maintain their original roles in their functional department in addition to their new ones as co-ordinating team members. Task teams are established at universities to function as standing committees that periodically make decisions about such things as granting tenure to faculty members or allocating annual budgets. At an international paper company, the United Paper Workers Union and management agreed to create a team made up of the union president, a company director and three members of each group, whose goal was to enhance co-operation and avoid confrontation. This team has provided benefits such as an agreement that the company would steer clear of attempts to eliminate the union from certain plants in return for the union's willingness to grant cheaper pension formulas (Stevens, 1983).

Integrating departments

When the complexity of information flows between several interacting groups is beyond the capacity of plans, temporary task forces or permanent teams, an entire integrating department can be established. These are permanent departments with full-time individuals whose only responsibility is the effective co-ordination of intergroup activities. Since this is a very expensive method, it is usually used only if an organisation's business requires a lot of ongoing co-operation between groups with conflicting goals or if recurring, non-routine problems can significantly impact overall organisational success. Integrating departments is the most complex mechanism for managing intergroup co-ordination. If problems beyond the capabilities of such departments arise, a major organisational redesign is probably called for.

Strategies for reducing dysfunctional conflict

According to Ury *et al.* (1988), persistent dysfunctional conflict needs to be confronted. Schein (1989), Rahim (1989) and Likert and Likert (1976) suggest a variety of techniques that can reduce dysfunctional conflict and these are presented in this section. It should be kept in mind, however, that different cultures prefer different approaches to resolving conflicts. Some of these cultural differences are shown in Exhibit 11-10.

EXHIBIT 11–10 International conflict resolution approaches

	North Americans	**Arabs**	**Russians**
Primary negotiating style and process	Factual: appeals made to logic	Affective: appeals made to emotions	Axiomatic: appeals made to ideals
Opponent's arguments countered with . . .	Objective facts	Subjective feelings	Asserted ideals
Making concessions	Small concessions made early to establish a relationship	Concessions made throughout as a part of the bargaining process	Few, if any, small concessions made
Response to opponent's concessions	Usually reciprocate opponent's concessions	Almost always reciprocate opponent's concessions	Opponent's concessions viewed as weakness and almost never reciprocated
Relationship	Short term	Long term	No continuing relationship
Authority	Broad	Broad	Limited
Initial position	Moderate	Extreme	Extreme
Deadline	Very important	Casual	Ignored

Source: Nancy J. Adler and D.M. Hunt (1991) *International Dimensions of Organizational Behavior* (2nd edn). Boston, MA: PWS-Kent, pp. 179–217. Copyright 1991. Reprinted with permission of South-Western College Publishing, a division of Thomson Learning.

Superordinate goals

One of the most effective ways to reduce conflict is to determine an overriding goal that requires the co-operative effort of both conflicting parties. Such a goal must be unattainable by either party alone and of sufficient importance to supersede all their other goals. One fairly common superordinate goal is *survival* of the organisation. This usually requires the elimination of suboptimal strategies on the part of conflicting opponents. In the airline industry, for example, several unions have agreed to forgo pay increases and have even accepted temporary pay reductions when the survival of an airline was threatened.

This strategy *eliminates win–lose situations* as participants shift efforts towards co-operation so they all can pull together to maximise organisational effectiveness. Setting up an appraisal system that *rewards total organisational effectiveness* rather than individual or group accomplishments also supports these efforts. Marshall Industries, for example, did this to promote co-operation rather than competition between groups, resulting in the virtual elimination of conflicts and increased profits and share prices.

A derivative strategy to restore alliances and increase co-operation is focusing on a *common enemy*. At the international level, bickering nations unite against a common adversary in times of war or natural catastrophe. Players on football teams that normally compete in a particular league join together to produce a team to challenge another country. Nothing halts the internal squabbles of a political party faster than a reminder that the opposition party is gaining strength. Like all these factions, warring groups will suppress their conflicts and join together to help their organisation compete successfully against another. Sometimes, however, they must be reminded that the opposition is out there. See the World Watch box, which describes an international negotiation situation where it appears that a superordinate goal might have helped resolve the conflict.

Increased communication

In cases where conflicting parties are not competing for scarce resources or trying to achieve inherently opposed goals, devising means to increase communication can do much to correct misunderstandings, reduce negative stereotypes and develop more positive feelings among the parties. Requiring parties to meet together to solve common problems can reduce stereotypical images and faulty perceptions, and contribute to mutual understanding. NCR Corp. (formerly National Cash Register Company) began tearing down the walls between its engineering and manufacturing groups by putting people from design, purchasing, manufacturing and field support in adjacent cubicles to allow them to communicate with one another throughout the design and manufacturing process. This process reduced assembly time from 30 minutes to only 5 and permitted assembly without special tools. The free flow of information across groups enabled NCR to get better products to market much faster.

Problem-solving

Problem-solving is a more structured means of bringing together conflicting parties for a face-to-face confrontation. The purpose of a problem-solving meeting is to identify and solve conflicts through a mutual airing of differences, complaints and negative feelings. An effort is made to work through differences and bring about a greater understanding of the opposing party's attitudes, perceptions and position.

The problem-solving approach requires considerable time and commitment, but it can be effective when conflicts stem from misunderstandings or differences in perceptions. Specific problem-solving strategies and techniques can be found in Chapter 12.

International espionage or 'just doing my job!'

In the winter of 1997, Richard Bliss faced some cold realities. Before accepting a short overseas assignment, he probably never envisioned that he would end up in a Russian prison and an international espionage battle. Or did he?

Mr Bliss, a 29-year-old employee of the San Diego-based telecommunications firm Qualcomm, went to Rostov-on-Don, Russia, to assist Electrosviaz in the implementation of a £5.8 million wireless system. Carrying with him high-tech global positioning (GPS) and computer equipment, he was taken into custody by Russia's Federal Security Service (FSS) and accused of spying. Facing the death penalty or a 20-year prison sentence, the US Government moved quickly into negotiations with Russia to free Mr Bliss. Executive-level pressure from vice president Al Gore and the State Department permitted Mr Bliss's release, but not before he had spent 11 days in an isolation cell.

Since the end of the Cold War, Russia has maintained the image of a pro-western business environment. Under the leadership of Boris Yeltsin, Russia sought western help in the building of a telecommunications infrastructure. As Georgi Yurchenko, director of the local Russian mobile phone company Dontelekom, put it, 'We ask these westerners to come here to help us develop our communications, and then we arrest them for doing so. It's absurd.'

Why was Mr Bliss being held? Was he really spying, or were there other reasons for his imprisonment? Could a man that had no military background, no Russian language skills, no college degree, and who had never set foot outside the United States until this two-month assignment really be a spy? It is probably more plausible that he was being held for other reasons. Perhaps he or Qualcomm had not paid a local bribe to conduct business there. Or perhaps Qualcomm had not filed the appropriate documentation, In any case, the Russian Government appeared to realise that bigger things were at stake, and that putting US businessmen in prison would probably not attract future western investment. Mr Bliss was released in time to return to the United States for the Christmas holidays on the promise he would return to Russia to face the charges. To date, he has not returned nor has Russia pressed the issue.

Sources: 'Russia Says an American Accused of Espionage Can Return Home for the Holidays', *New York Times*, 24 December 1997, sec. A, p. 8; 'Russian Spy Case a Puzzler', *San Diego Union-Tribune*, 16 December 1997, p. C-1; 'Figure in "Spy" Case Settles Lawsuit; He Asked Qualcomm for £1 Million after Being Held in Russia', *San Diego Union-Tribune*, 31 August 1999, p. C-1.

Discussion questions

1 Conflicts always involve at least two opposing views, how can we remain impartial when resolving a dispute?

2 How could the conflict be resolved without either side losing face?

Expansion of resources

When the major cause of conflict is limited resources, the likely outcome is a win–lose situation in which one party succeeds at the expense of another. If at all possible, the organisation should eliminate this source of conflict by expanding its resource base. Additional investments may pay off handsomely in terms of increased productivity.

Third-party judgement

As described in the earlier section on negotiation skills, conflicting parties may appeal to a common boss or an outside judge to serve as a mediator in resolving their dispute. Often this is easier, less time consuming and less expensive than working through every issue with inter-group problem-solving techniques. At other times when more collaborative approaches have failed, arbitration may be the last resort.

Professional arbitrators are commonly brought in to resolve disputes between unions and management. The Arbitration and Conciliation Service (ACAS) is one such organisation used to resolve disputes between unions and management. Compare this to the other common option of expensive and time-consuming lawsuits (Bernstein and Schiller, 1991).

Within organisations, common superiors are often called in to recommend solutions to conflicts between individuals or departments. Managers acting as third-party arbitrators have significant clout because the warring parties agree beforehand to abide by the arbitrator's decision. Elangovan (1995) suggests that, depending on the criteria established for successful dispute resolution (e.g. fairness, performance effectiveness), managers may select a variety of intervention strategies ranging from investigation of facts to adversarial (e.g. trial-like) con-frontation meetings.

The advantages of arbitration can carry a hidden cost. An arbitrator usually hands down a win–lose decision that is unlikely to receive the loser's full commitment. Like a parental decision on who is 'right' when two children fight over a toy, an arbitrated outcome may solve the immediate problem but increase hostility between the conflicting factions. No one is left with an enhanced understanding of what caused the basic conflict or how future clashes can be prevented. When an arbitrator hands down a compromise solution that only partially fulfils the demands of both sides, neither group is totally satisfied with the outcome. Although this may be slightly preferable to a win–lose decision, the sources of conflict are likely to remain (Elangovan, 1995).

Changing organisational structure

According to Galbraith (1973), when the reasons for conflict are scarce resources, status differ-ences or power imbalances, changes in organisational structure may be the answer. Structural changes include things like rotating group members on a semi-permanent basis, creating liaison or co-ordinator positions and eliminating special-interest groups that exist within the organisa-tion. Some organisations, for example, rotate new employees through a variety of assignments in different groups to ease the competitive effects of single-group identification, enhance under-standing of interaction in the whole system and provide identification with the total organisa-tion. In other situations conflicting parties can be relocated, task responsibilities can be redefined and hierarchies can be decentralised. Sometimes two conflicting groups can be merged into one. If the conflict clearly centres on the personal animosities between two or more strong individuals, the key instigators can be removed.

Restructuring has produced increased quality, productivity and co-operation for companies such as Ford Motors and Hewlett-Packard, which are shifting their focus from how individual departments function to how different departments work together. Companies such as Conrail, Dun & Bradstreet Europe, Du Pont and Royal Bank of Canada have created network groups of department managers with appropriate business skills, personal motivations, resource control and positions, to shape and implement organisational strategy. According to Charan (1991), the free flow of information to all network group members who need it and the emphasis on hori-zontal collaboration and leadership have clarified joint business goals and helped meet deadlines.

Avoidance

Some groups may be able to ignore dysfunctional situations temporarily by looking the other way or disregarding the threatening actions of others in the hope that the situation will resolve itself. But most conflicts do not just fade away; usually, they worsen with time. Although avoidance is ineffective in the long run, certain controlled conditions can be established to lessen the short-term consequences of conflict. Sometimes conflicting parties can be physically separated, or the amount of interaction between them can be limited. Procrastination, disregard for the demands of others, and attempts at peaceful coexistence are all variations of the avoidance process.

From shop floor to boardroom employment relations: a second look

While the decision to change sides was a big one, Mr Eraut argues that he has not had far to travel: the distance between the pro-partnership wing of the trades union movement and the 'progressive' wing of employers is no longer vast, he believes. 'Both are about building constructive relationships and improving the experience of working. Work is a huge part of people's lives and dignity, and I remain absolutely committed to the goal that they should be treated fairly and with some generosity. In many organisations that goal still requires a third party to be involved, so there continues to be a need [for unions].'

For Aceneth Williams, the move from full-time Unison shop steward at Derbyshire Police, to human resources manager was in one sense not a move at all: she has been in the same office for more than 30 years. This longevity helped reduce animosity when she took the HR job in August 2004 – both from union colleagues and her family (she comes from a mining background), and from managers who were uncertain which hat she was wearing.

'I've been here a long time so I was able to command respect,' she says. 'But it certainly wasn't easy.' Like Mr Eraut, taking a course, this time in HR, contributed to the decision to move to management.

The day-to-day job is comparable to what she was doing before: listening, advising, smoothing out misunderstandings. Yet she advocates what has become an unfashionable view in HR circles: that part of her role is to 'represent' employees. She explains that observing working life from both sides had led her to doubt the concept of 'sides': 'It's all about doing the best for the individual and the best for the organisation. So often, conflict is down to management style, rather than anything more serious.'

But she admits the idea of shared interests between workers and managers is sorely tested from time to time: 'I have had to make people redundant when they are on long-term sick leave because their disability did not fit the legal definitions. The way I justified it is that it is the taxpayers that pay all our wages. You have to think about them.'

Source: Stephen Overell, 'From Shop floor to Boardroom EMPLOYMENT RELATIONS: Trade Union Officials are Making the Once Unthinkable Switch to Management Roles. And Jumping Moral Hurdles', *Financial Times*, 2005.

Summary

- Organisations are made up of interacting individuals and groups with varying needs, objectives, values and perspectives that naturally lead to the emergence of conflicts.
- When conflict occurs it can either stimulate new positive changes or result in negative consequences. Members of a group in conflict with another group, for example, often experience increased cohesion, loyalty, task concentration and autocratic leadership.
- Between themselves, however, the conflicting groups can experience dysfunctional hostility, distorted perceptions, negative stereotypes and decreased communication.
- Conflicts need to be managed appropriately to provide positive outcomes and avoid the negative possibilities.
- Interpersonal conflict management styles include competing, avoiding, accommodating, collaborating and compromising.
- Interacting groups can be co-ordinated through rules and procedures, hierarchy, planning, liaison roles, task forces, teams or integrating departments.
- Strategies for preventing and reducing dysfunctional intergroup conflict include emphasising the total organisation by focusing on superordinate goals or a common enemy, increasing communication, joint problem-solving, negotiating, expanding resources, obtaining a mediator, changing organisational structure, smoothing things over, and avoiding potential win–lose conflict situations.

Areas for personal development

It is difficult, if not impossible, to think of a relationship of any type that does not encounter disagreements at one time or another. Johnson (1993) suggests that unless relationships are able to withstand the stress involved in the inevitable conflicts, and manage them productively, they are not likely to endure. Because of inherent characteristics such as scarce resources, interdependence, different goals and the need for co-ordination, conflict is a natural phenomenon in organisational life. Consequently, it is not surprising that some organisation researchers (Tjosvold and Johnson, 1983) have concluded that 'no skill is more important for organisational effectiveness than the constructive management and resolution of conflict'. Listed below are the essential skills for managing conflict productively in both interpersonal and intergroup situations.

1 **Assess the nature of the conflict.** Conflict is natural to any relationship and it can never be completely eliminated, nor should it be. If not managed properly, conflict can be dysfunctional and lead to undesirable consequences like hostility, lack of co-operation, violence, destroyed relationships and even company failure. Nevertheless, when managed effectively, conflict can stimulate creativity, innovation and change, and build better relationships.

2 **Identify the sources of conflict.** Conflicts can arise for a large variety of reasons, such as incompatible goals, differences in the interpretation of facts, negative feelings, differences of values and philosophies, or disputes over shared resources. The five main sources in organisations to be on the lookout for are goal incompatibility, structural design, role expectations, degenerative climate and personal differences.

3 **Use the most appropriate style orientation for managing a specific conflict.** Each of us has a preferred style orientation for handling conflicts. Nevertheless it is important to be flexible and vary our conflict management style response according to each specific situation. Know when it is most appropriate to draw upon each of the five conflict style orientations of avoidance, accommodation, forcing, compromise and collaboration when attempting to resolve dysfunctional conflicts.

4 **Empathise with the other conflict parties.** Your chances of success in managing a conflict will be greatly enhanced if you can view the conflict situation through the eyes of the conflicting parties. Determine who is involved in the conflict, what interests each party represents, and each player's values, personality, feelings and resources.

5 **Have a plan and concrete strategy.** Lewicke *et al.* (1996) and Northcraft and Nealel (1994) both suggest that your chances of obtaining a favourable outcome increase if you plan and set goals before the action starts. Ask yourself questions such as how strong your position is, how important the issue is to both yourself and the other party, and if you are willing to negotiate and split differences.

6 **Address problems, not personalities.** Concentrate on the issues, not on the personal characteristics of your opponent. It is your opponent's ideas or position that you disagree with, not him or her personally. Separate the people from the problem, and do not personalise differences.

7 **Maintain a rational, goal-orientated frame of mind.** Do not get hooked by emotional outbursts. Let the other person let off steam without taking it personally while you try to understand the problem or strategy behind the aggression.

8 **Emphasise win–win solutions.** In conflict situations it initially appears that our gains must come at the expense of the other party. However, that need not be the case, and there are often win–win solutions. Nevertheless, assuming a zero-sum game means missed opportunities for trade-offs that could benefit both sides. So, if conditions are supportive, look for an integrative solution.

9 **Create a climate of trust.** Neither side is going to make itself vulnerable by sharing information in an attempt for a collaborative agreement if it does not trust the other party. Consequently, avoid words and phrases that may irritate the other party or cause mistrust. Listen, ask questions and try to empathise with the other party, while being patient and avoiding defensiveness if the other party is competitive in the beginning.

10 **Adapt to cultural differences.** Conflict style orientations and negotiation practices are heavily influenced by national culture. So, if you are negotiating with someone from a different cultural background, take into consideration how cultural influences are likely to shape the other person's goals and negotiating tactics.

❓ Questions for study and discussion

1 Review the major factors that cause intergroup conflicts. Now, think of a group to which you currently belong. How do these factors influence your behaviour and feelings towards other groups with which your group interacts?

2 Describe situations from your personal experience in which conflict was functional and situations where it was dysfunctional.

3 Discuss the mechanisms for resolving conflicts between students and faculty on your campus. Are they effective? Why or why not? What mechanisms do you suggest to better resolve such conflicts?

4 Explain this statement: 'An organisation can experience too little or too much conflict.'

5 Define pooled interdependence, sequential interdependence and reciprocal interdependence. In which situation is conflict most likely to occur? Why? Which type of interdependence exists between groups with which you are familiar?

6 Suggest the appropriate conflict reduction strategies for a collective bargaining stalemate in which both management and union groups have a record of hostility and non-co-operation. Could such potential conflict be prevented by the design chosen for a new industrial organisation? How?

7 What is the predominant intergroup conflict at your college or place of work? What is being done to resolve this conflict? What could be done?

8 What is your dominant conflict management style? How did you develop it? When does it work best for you? When doesn't it work?

🔑 Key Concepts

conflict, *p. 489*

interdependence. *p. 494*

pooled interdependence, *p. 495*

sequential interdependence, *p. 495*

reciprocal interdependence, *p. 496*

role, *p. 497*

role set, *p. 497*

role ambiguity, *p. 497*

role conflict, *p. 497*

role overload, *p. 498*

degenerative interaction climate, *p. 499*

functional conflict, *p. 502*

conflict-positive organisation, *p. 502*

dysfunctional conflict, *p. 504*

conflict management style, *p. 506*

negotiation, *p. 509*

distributive bargaining, *p. 509*

settlement range, *p. 512*

integrative bargaining, *p. 512*

liaison, *p. 518*

task force, *p. 518*

Personal skills exercise
Used car negotiation (Robbins and Hunsaker, 1996)

Purpose This is a role play designed to help you develop your compromise approach to conflict resolution through practising negotiation skills.

Procedure The class should first break into pairs. Then decide which person will play the role of the seller and which person will play the role of the buyer. You have 5 minutes to read the situation, your role and to prepare your targets. Do not read the other person's role. The negotiation should not take longer than 15 minutes. After that, the class will compare outcomes and discuss the various strategies utilised.

Situation You are about to negotiate the purchase/sale of a car. The buyer advertised the car in the local newspaper. Before advertising it, the buyer took the car to the local Volkswagen dealer, who has provided the following information:

- 1998 VW convertible
- white with red upholstery, tinted glass
- AM/FM, CD player
- 30 450 miles
- steel-belted radial tyres expected to last to 80 000 km
- 14 km per litre
- no rust; dent on passenger door barely noticeable
- mechanically perfect except exhaust system, which may or may not last another 10 000 miles (costs £150 to replace)
- *Glass's Guide* retail value, £5000; wholesale, £4400
- car has spent its entire life with one owner.

Buyer's role Your car was stolen and wrecked two weeks ago. You do a lot of travelling in your job, so you need a car that is economical and easy to drive. The convertible advertised looks like a good deal, and you would like to buy it right away if possible. The insurance company gave you £4000 for your old car. You have only £700 in savings that you had intended to spend on a trip with an extremely attractive companion – a chance you really don't want to pass up.

Your credit has been stretched for some time, so if you borrow money, it will have to be at an interest rate of 15 per cent. Furthermore, you need to buy a replacement car quickly, because you have been renting one for business purposes and it is costing you a great deal. The convertible is the best deal you have seen and the car is fun to drive. As an alternative, you can immediately buy a used 1999 Ford Escort for £3800 (the wholesale value), which does 28 miles per gallon and will depreciate much faster than the convertible.

The seller of the convertible is a complete stranger to you. Before beginning this negotiation, set the following targets for yourself:

1 the price you would like to pay for the car: _____
2 the price you will initially offer the seller: _____
3 the highest price you will pay for the car: _____

Seller's role You have bought a used Mercedes from a dealer. The deposit is £4700, with steep monthly payments. You are stretched on credit, so if you can't make the deposit, you will have to borrow at 15 per cent. You are going to pick up the Mercedes in two hours, so you want to sell your old car, the convertible, before you go.

You advertised the car (which is in particularly good condition) in the newspaper and have had several calls. Your only really good prospect at the moment is the person with whom you are about to bargain – a stranger. You don't *have* to sell it to this person, but if you don't sell the car right away, you will have to pay high interest charges until you do sell it.

The Mercedes dealer will only give you £4400 for the convertible, since he will have to resell it to a Volkswagen dealer. The local VW dealer is not anxious to buy the car from you since he has just received a shipment of new cars; in any case, he probably would not give you more than £4400 either.

Before beginning this negotiation, set the following targets for yourself:

1 The price you would like to receive for the car: _____

2 The price you will initially request: _____

3 The lowest price you will accept for the car: _____

👥 Team exercise

Win as much as you can (DeVito, 1982; Pfeiffer and Jones, 1974)

Purpose

1 To diagnose and manage a potential conflict situation within an organisation competing with another organisation.

2 To provide opportunities for practising negotiation skills.

3 To explore trust building and collaboration in a potential conflict situation.

Time The total exercise can last from 50–75 minutes depending on how much time is allocated for the following activities. Preparation takes from 10–15 minutes. The exercise takes 35 minutes for seven rounds. If you drop round 2, six rounds will take about 30 minutes. The debriefing time depends upon how much depth you go into, so it can vary from 10 to 25 minutes.

Procedure Divide the class into two or more organisations. Then divide each organisation into four one- to five-person departments. The four departments in each organisation should be far enough apart from each other so that members of each department can communicate without being overheard by other departments.

The exercise consists of seven rounds of decision-making in which each department selects either P (profit) or Q (quality) based on its prediction of what the other departments in its organisation will do and the pay-off schedule. Winnings or losses depend on what is negotiated and what the other departments decide to do.

Process

1 Each player invests £1.00 in his or her company (give the money to the instructor). If any student is uncomfortable risking a pound, or if it is a very large class, one option is to have each department assign an observer to help the instructor (a) collect and announce decisions; (b) observe internal and intergroup dynamics; (c) handle negotiations; (d) lead department debriefing; and (e) lead class debriefing.

2 Participants study the pay-off schedule, the scorecard and the profit distribution matrix (5 minutes).

3 There is to be no talking between departments, only within departments, except during negotiations.

4 There are opportunities to negotiate with other departments before the rounds with bonuses – that is, after rounds 2, 4 and 6. Departments must direct requests to negotiate to the instructor (or observer), and other departments can agree or refuse. If departments agree to negotiate, one representative from each department meets with one from another department in a private place. Negotiators are not allowed to show their scorecards to each other. Departments pick different members to negotiate with each of the other departments so that all get a chance to negotiate. Actual decisions for the next round can be made only through consensus of department members after they return from negotiations.

5 Departments have 10 minutes to get organised and determine their goals and strategy. Each decision round is 3 minutes. Each negotiation period is 5 minutes.

6 Scoring: departments keep their own cumulative scores on their scorecard. The instructor or observer duplicates a scorecard for each organisation on the board and keeps total organisation scores for each round (i.e. sum of scores for the four departments in each organisation).

7 Pay-off schedule directions: at the beginning of each of the seven successive rounds, choose either a P to maximise profit margin or a Q for highest quality. The pay-off for each round depends on the pattern of choices made by other departments in your organisation. The pay-off schedule, scorecard and profit distribution summary are included on the Decision Tally Sheet. Scores can be kept on this sheet in the book, but it should be duplicated and passed out to participants separately for easier use.

Profit distribution At the end of the seven rounds of play, add up the cumulative organisation and department scores. Write these on the board and distribute the total pot as follows.

- The organisation with the largest balance gets 40 per cent (distributed equally among the four departments).
- The department with the largest balance gets 30 per cent (can be either the winning or losing organisation).
- The department with the second-largest balance gets 20 per cent.
- The department with the third-largest balance gets 10 per cent.
- If there is no positive pay-off for either organisation, there will be no distribution, even if departments have positive balances. The instructor keeps all the money.

Questions for discussion

1 How would you describe the behaviour of the departments in your organisation?

2 How would you describe your own behaviour?

3 Is this real-life behaviour?

4 How do you feel about the way you played the game? How do you feel about how the other departments played the game?

5 What did you learn about yourself? About others?

Decision Tally Sheet

Directions At the beginning of each of the seven successive rounds choose either a P to maximise profit margin, or a Q for highest quality. The 'pay-off' for each round is dependent upon the pattern of choices made by other departments in your company.

Pay-off schedule

4 Ps: Lose £1.00 each

3 Ps: Win £1.00 each

1 Q: Lose £3.00

2 Ps: Win £2.00 each

2 Qs: Lose £2.00 each

1 P: Win £3.00

3 Qs: Lose £1.00 each

4 Qs: Win £1.00 each

Scorecard profit distribution

■ Company with largest balance gets 40 per cent (distributed equally).

■ Department with largest balance gets 30 per cent.

■ Department with second-largest balance gets 20 per cent.

■ Department with third-largest balance gets 10 per cent.

■ If no positive pay-off for any company, there will be no distribution.

Case study: **he said, she said . . . (Fritz *et al.*, 1999)**

Shirley and Abdul both work for a software development company. The manager of the new product division was originally the leader of a project team for which she interviewed and hired Abdul. Shirley, another project team member, also interviewed Abdul but strongly opposed hiring him for the project because she thought he was not competent to do the job.

Seven months after Abdul was hired, the manager left the project to start her own company and recommended that Abdul and Shirley serve as joint project leaders. Shirley agreed reluctantly – with the stipulation that it be made clear she was not working for Abdul. The general manager consented; Shirley and Abdul were to share the project leadership.

Within a month Shirley was angry because Abdul was representing himself to others as the leader of the entire project and giving the impression that Shirley was working for him. Now Shirley and Abdul are meeting with you to see if you can help them resolve the conflict between them.

Shirley says: 'Right after the joint leadership arrangement was reached with the general manager, Abdul called a meeting of the project team without even consulting me about the time or content. He just told me when it was being held and said I should be there. At the meeting, Abdul reviewed everyone's duties line by line, including mine, treating me as just another team member working for him. He sends out letters and signs himself as project director, which obviously implies to others that I am working for him.'

Abdul says: 'Shirley is all hung up with feelings of power and titles. Just because I sign myself as project director doesn't mean that she is working for me. I don't see anything to get excited about. What difference does it make? She is too sensitive about everything. I call a meeting and right away she thinks I'm trying to run everything. Shirley has other things to do – other projects to run – so she doesn't pay too much attention to this one. She mostly lets things slide. But when I take the initiative to set up a meeting, she starts jumping up and down about how I am trying to make her work for me.'

Discussion questions

A variety of strategies can be used to help resolve the conflict between Abdul and Shirley. Explore the concepts on conflict management presented in this chapter. Put yourself in the position of mediator between Abdul and Shirley and consider the following questions.

1 Abdul and Shirley seem to have several conflicts occurring simultaneously. Identify as many of these individual conflicts as possible.

2 Are there any general statements you can make about the overall nature of the conflict between Abdul and Shirley?

3 What are the possible ways to deal with the conflict between Abdul and Shirley (not just the ones that you would recommend, but all the options)?

4 Given the choices identified in item three, what is the best way for Abdul and Shirley to deal with the conflict between them?

5 Given all the benefits of hindsight, what could or should have been done to avoid this conflict in the first place?

Applied questions

6 What stage of conflict have Shirley and Abdul reached (refer to Exhibit 11-2)? How can they move forwards to reach a positive outcome?

7 How dependent are they on each other for the successful completion of tasks (refer to Exhibit 11-4)?

WWW exercise

Manager's Internet tools

Web tips: conflict management on the web

This chapter has focused on conflict and how conflict can be managed. The chapter gives several techniques and ideas on how to manage interpersonal and intergroup conflicts. Since conflict is a serious corporate issue, there are many additional resources for you to use when working with or managing conflict.

World Wide Web search

Using a search engine, perform a search on the phrase 'conflict management'. You should come up with several 'hits', including companies specialising in conflict management. You should also find pages that list tips for resolving conflict and successful negotiations. What are the similarities and differences between the information you find on the web and the concepts presented in the chapter?

Specific website

Take a look at the Arbitration and Conciliation Service's (ACAS) website at www.acas.org.uk. What does it tell you about negotiation and arbitration? How would you find the relevant information if you were an employee with a grievance, or an employer wishing to set up a code of practice for grievance procedures? What other advice does ACAS offer?

LEARNING CHECKLIST

Before you move on you may want to reflect on what you have learnt in this chapter. You should now be able to:

- ☑ identify the different philosophies of conflict
- ☑ define and describe the conflict process
- ☑ recognise symptoms of conflict
- ☑ identify sources of conflict
- ☑ differentiate between functional and dysfunctional conflict
- ☑ utilise conflict styles appropriately
- ☑ apply conflict management strategies
- ☑ bargain and negotiate effectively.

Further reading

Balachandra, L., Bordone, R.C., Menkel-Meadow, C., Ringstrom, P. and Sarath, E. (2005) 'Improvization and Negotiation: Expecting the Unexpected', *Negotiation Journal* 21(4), October, pp. 415–441.

De Dreu, C.K.W. (2006) 'When too Little or too Much Hurts: Evidence for a Curvilinear Relationship between Task Conflict and Innovation in Teams', *Journal of Management* 32(1), February, p. 83.

Huzzard, T. and Docherty, P. (2005) 'Between Global and Local: Eight European Works Councils in Retrospect and Prospect', *Economic and Industrial Democracy* 26(4), 1 November, p. 41.

Lobel, S.A. and McLeod, P.L. (1991) 'Effects of Ethnic Group Cultural Differences on Cooperative Behavior on a Group Task', *Academy of Management Journal*, December, pp. 827–847.

References

Adler, N.J. (1991) *International Dimensions of Organizational Behavior* (2nd edn). Boston, MA: PWS-Kent, pp. 179–217.

Alessandra, A.J. and Hunsaker, P.L. (1993) *Communicating at Work*. New York, NY: Simon & Schuster, Chapter 7.

Ancona, G. (1990) 'Outward Bound: Strategies for Team Survival in an Organization', *Academy of Management Journal*, June, pp. 334–356.

Bernstein, A. and Schiller, Z. (1991) 'Tell It to the Arbitrator', *Business Week*, 4 November, p. 109.

Carnevale, P.J.D. and Isen, A.M. (1986) 'The Influence of Positive Affect and Visual Access on the Discovery of Integrative Solutions in Bilateral Negotiations', *Organizational Behavior and Human Decision Processes*, February, pp. 1–13.

Charan, R. (1991) 'How Networks Reshape Organizations for Results', *Harvard Business Review* September–October, p. 179; and 'Theory P Stresses How Departments Interact', *Wall Street Journal*, 13 December 1991, p. B1.

Chen, C.C., Chen, X.P. and Meindl, J.R. (1998) 'How Can Cooperation Be Fostered? The Cultural Effects of Individualism-collectivism', *Academy of Management Review* 23, pp. 285–304.

Cosier, R.A. and Schwenk, C.R. (1990) 'Agreement and Thinking Alike: Ingredients for Poor Decisions', *Academy of Management Executive*, February, pp. 69–74.

DeGeorge, G. (1994) 'Why Sunbeam is Shining Brighter', *Business Week*, 29 August, pp. 74–75.

DeVito, J.A. (1982) *The Interpersonal Communication Book* (6th edn). New York, NY: Harper-Collins, pp. 360–361.

Drucker, P. (1984) *The Practice of Management*. London: Heinemann.

Elangovan, R. (1995) 'Managerial Third-party Dispute Intervention. A Prescriptive Model of Strategy Selection', *Academy of Management Review*, October, pp. 800–830.

Fells, R.E. (1998) 'Overcoming the Dilemmas in Walton and McKersie's Mixed Bargaining Strategy', *Industrial Relations* 53, Spring, pp. 300–325.

Fisher, R., Ury, W. and Patton, B. (1991) *Getting to Yes* (2nd edn). New York, NY: Houghton Mifflin.

Fritz, S., Brown, F.W., Lunde, J.P. and Banset, E.A. (1999) 'Case Study in Conflict Management: He Said, She Said...', *Interpersonal Skills for Leadership*. Upper Saddle River, NJ: Prentice Hall, pp. 208–209.

Galbraith, J.R. (1973) *Designing Complex Organizations*. Reading, MA: Addison-Wesley, pp. 103–117.

Glasl, F. (1982) 'The Process of Conflict Escalation and the Roles of Third Parties', in G.B.J. Bomers and R. Peterson (eds) *Conflict Management and Industrial Relations.* Boston, MA: Kluwer-Nijhoff, pp. 119–140.

Graham, J. and Herberger, R. (1983) 'Negotiating Abroad – Don't Shoot from the Hip', *Harvard Business Review*, July–August, pp. 160–169.

Hall, J. and Williams, M.S. (1966) 'A Comparison of Decision-making Performances in Established and Ad Hoc Groups', *Journal of Personality and Social Psychology*, February, p. 217.

Janis, I.J. (1982) *Groupthink: Psychological Studies of Policy Decisions and Fiascoes* (2nd edn). Boston, MA: Houghton Mifflin.

Jehn, K. (1994) 'Enhancing Effectiveness: An Investigation of Advantages and Disadvantages of Value Based Intragroup Conflict', *International Journal of Conflict Management*, July, pp. 223–238.

Johnson, D.W. (1993) *Reaching Out: Interpersonal Effectiveness and Self-actualization.* Boston, MA: Allyn and Bacon, pp. 205–207.

Kabanoff, B. (1991) 'Equity, Equality, Power, and Conflict', *Academy of Management Review*, April, pp. 416–441.

Karakowsky, L. (1996) 'Toward an Understanding of Women and Men at the Bargaining Table: Factors Affecting Negotiator Style and Influence in Multi-party Negotiations', Proceedings of the Annual ASAC Conference, Women in Management Division, pp. 21–30.

Khan, R.L., Wolfe, D., Quinn, R. and Snoek, J. (1964) *Organizational Stress: Studies in Role Conflict and Ambiguity.* New York, NY: Wiley.

Kirchmeyer, C. and Cohen, A. (1992) 'Multicultural Groups: Their Performance and Reactions with Constructive Conflict', *Group & Organizational Management*, June, pp. 153–170.

Kuman, R. (1989) 'Affect, Cognition and Decision Making in Negotiations: A Conceptual Integration', in M.A. Rahim (ed.) *Managing Conflict: An Integrative Approach.* New York, NY: Praeger, pp. 185–194.

Lewicke, R.L., Hiam, A. and Olander, K. (1996) *Think Before You Speak: The Complete Guide to Strategic Negotiation.* New York, NY: John Wiley.

Likert, R. and Likert, J. (1976) *New Ways of Managing Conflict.* New York, NY: McGraw-Hill.

Lubin, J.S. (1991) 'Japanese Are Doing More Job Hopping', *Wall Street Journal*, 18 November, p. B1.

McKenna, E. (1994) *Business Psychology and Organizational Behaviour.* Hove, UK: Erlbaum.

Meyer, J.P., Gemmell, J.M. and Irving, P.G. (1997) 'Evaluating the Management of Interpersonal Conflict in Organizations: A Factor-analytic Study of Outcome Criteria', *Canadian Journal of Administrative Sciences* 14, pp. 1–13.

Miles, R.H. (1980) *Macro Organizational Behavior.* Santa Monica, CA: Goodyear, p. 123.

Morgan, G. (1986) *Images of Organization.* Beverly Hills, CA: Sage.

Northcraft, G.B. and Nealel, M.A. (1994) 'Joint Effects of Assigned Goals and Training on Negotiator Performance', *Human Performance* 7, pp. 257–272.

Pelz, D.C. and Andrews, F. (1966) *Scientists in Organizations.* New York, NY: John Wiley.

Pfeiffer, J.W. and Jones, J.E. (eds) (1974) *A Handbook of Structured Experiences for Human Relations Training* (rev. edn) vol. III.

Pondy, L. (1967) 'Organizational Conflict: Concepts and Models', *Administrative Science Quarterly* 12, pp. 296–320.

Pye, L. (1982) *Chinese Commercial Negotiating Style.* Cambridge, MA: Oelgeschlager, Gunn & Hain Publishers.

Quinn, R.E. (1988) *Beyond Rational Management: Mastering the Paradoxes and Competing Demands of High Performance.* San Francisco, CA: Jossey-Bass, p. 2.

Rahim, M.A. (ed.) (1989) *Managing Conflict: An Interdisciplinary Approach.* New York, NY: Praeger.

Rahim, M.A. (1992) *Managing Conflict in Organizations* (2nd edn). Westport, CT: Praeger.

Rahim, M.A. and Blum, A.A. (eds) (1995) *Global Perspectives on Organizational Conflict.* Westport, CT: Praeger.

Rahim, M.A. and Magner, N.R. (1995) 'Confirmatory Factor Analysis of the Styles of Handling Interpersonal Conflict: First-order Factor Model and its Invariance Across Groups', *Journal of Applied Psychology* 80(1), pp. 122–132.

Rizzo, J.R., House, R.J. and Lirtzman, S.I. (1970) 'Role Conflict and Ambiguity in Complex Organizations', *Administrative Science Quarterly* 15, pp. 150–163.

Robbins, S.P. and Hunsaker, P.L. (1996) *Training in Interpersonal Skills: Tips for Managing People at Work* (2nd edn). Upper Saddle River, NJ: Prentice Hall, pp. 253–254.

Schein, D.H. (1965) *Organizational Psychology.* Englewood Cliffs, NJ: Prentice Hall, pp. 80–86.

Schein, D.H. (1989) *The Role of the CEO in the Management of Change: The Case of Information Technology.* Sloan School of Management, Massachusetts Institutes of Technology.

Sherif, M. and Sherif, C. (1953) *Groups in Harmony and Tension.* New York, NY: Harper, pp. 229–295.

Smith, G. (1993) 'How to Lose Friends and Influence No One', *Business Week*, 25 January, pp. 42–43.

Stagner, R. and Rosen, H. (1965) *Psychology of Union–Management Relations.* Belmont, CA: Wadsworth, pp. 95–96, 108–110.

Stevens, J.P. (1983) 'Paper Avoids a Replay', *Business Week*, June, pp. 33–34.

Swartz, S. (1989) 'Costly Lesson: GE Finds Running Kidder Peabody & Co Isn't All That Easy', *Wall Street Journal*, 27 January, p. B1.

Thomas, K.W. (1992) 'Conflict and Negotiation Processes in Organizations', in M.D. Dunnette and L.M. Hough (eds) *Handbook of Industrial and Organizational Psychology* (2nd edn) vol. 3. Palo Alto, CA: Consulting Psychologists Press, pp. 651–717.

Thompson, J.D. (1967) *Organizations in Action.* New York, NY: McGraw-Hill, pp. 54–55.

Tjosvold, D. (1986) *Working Together to Get Things Done.* Lexington, MA: D.C. Heath, pp. 111–112.

Tjosvold, D. and Johnson, D.W. (1983) *Productive Conflict Management: Perspectives for Organizations.* New York, NY: Irvington Publishers, p. 10.

Tjosvold, D., Dann, V. and Wong, C. (1992) 'Managing Conflict Between Departments to Serve Customers', *Human Relations* 45(10), pp. 1049–1050.

Ury, W.L., Brett, J.M. and Goldberg, S. (1988) *Getting Disputes Resolved: Designing Systems to Cut the Costs of Conflict.* San Francisco, CA Jossey-Bass.

Wall, J.A. Jr (1985) *Negotiation: Theory and Practice.* Glenview, IL: Scott, Foresman, p. 4.

Gate Gourmet

On a hot, balmy day in August 2005 passengers were preparing to depart Heathrow airport on their British Airways (BA) flight to far-flung destinations across the world. BA, which in the past had had industrial disputes and staffing problems, suddenly found itself embroiled in another industrial dispute as its ground staff walked out. However, this was not a dispute that involved BA, instead it involved the catering company Gate Gourmet, which provided the in-flight meals. The BA workers had come out in support of these workers, who they perceived to have been illegally sacked.

The walkout resulted in more than 100 000 passengers being stranded and cost the airline £40 million. It also left BA unable to provide normal in-flight meals once services resumed, with many passengers instead being given vouchers with which to buy their food from the airport.

After the BA staff had returned to work, the stand-off at Gate Gourmet rumbled on, with the sacked staff picketing outside the caterer's Heathrow factory.

The dispute was sparked off when Gate Gourmet sacked 670 workers in a dispute over working practices. According to the Transport and General Union (T&G) this was not the only problem. Fellow workers reporting for duty the next day were faced with the ultimatum of signing a new contract that would slash pay and conditions or face the sack. Catering assistants at the time were paid just £12 000 a year while drivers were paid less than £16 000 per year.

The T&G argued that: 'These are very low wages by any standards, but especially in London, one of the most expensive cities in the world. Yet Gate Gourmet is seeking to push them even lower, and the workers even closer to poverty.'

The T&G believed Gate Gourmet had engineered this situation and had made it clear that the flashpoint issue – the hiring of 130 seasonal workers – was a provocative move because never before had such extra staff been taken on while permanent staff were under threat of redundancy.

The T&G began a campaign to get the sacked workers their jobs back and it urged Gate Gourmet to re-employ the sacked workers and sit down with the T&G to resolve the dispute.

However, the T&G were accused by Tom Born, head of the catering company Gate Gourmet, of creating a fictional account of the summer's chaotic dispute in order to bring back secondary picketing.

Born decided to speak out after Tony Woodley, general secretary of the T&G, argued for a return to secondary picketing as a means of protecting 'weak and vulnerable' workers.

Born accused the T&G of a false portrayal of Gate Gourmet as an aggressive union-busting company, saying: 'It is disturbing for me to see how this dispute, which was an illegal action, is now being used to put forward a [conference] resolution that has nothing to do with what actually happened at Gate Gourmet. My view on secondary action is that the law is perfectly appropriate and any change would have a negative impact on the British economy.

'If we were such a bad employer, why would so many people want to come back? The T&G want everyone to come back. They call us a bad employer yet we pay above the market rate and have a final salary pension scheme. They can call us whatever they want for their political agenda but the facts are different.'

As the battle continued the following statements were put forward by the T&G as the facts about the dispute.

- Talks have been ongoing with Gate Gourmet for many months in order to improve the business. During this time the T&G has played an active role in meeting the business needs.

- In June this year a rescue package was put forward by the company. The T&G said that any restructuring proposals needed to be across the board and include management grades. The company then re-graded 147 shop-floor workers as managers, only to make them redundant. The original management team put themselves on higher starting salaries than before and made it clear they would not be part of the restructuring.

- Following this provocative and callous action, when the rescue package was put to the workforce it was rejected by nine to one.

- Since then T&G officers have been trying to find a way forward with the company and other parties to reach a solution.

- With the threat of redundancies hanging over the workers' heads, Gate Gourmet then announced that it wished to employ 120 additional temporary staff. Why were they seeking to make people redundant when they were planning to employ new staff? We would be happy for them to employ new workers if they removed the threat of redundancy from the original workforce.

- On 10 August 2005, the company brought in new workers without discussion. While the union sought clarity on the situation, staff assembled in the canteen in preparation for a meeting. Management then told staff that they had three minutes to get back to work or they would be sacked. They refused and remained in the building. Members starting the late shift also refused to come into work having heard the news. Those assembled in the car park were sacked by megaphone.

- It is becoming increasingly clear that Gate Gourmet had planned this action for some time. Private security guards were put on the gates. Extra workers were bussed in to replace those sacked. Dismissal letters were sent to all staff whether they are on leave or sick. The company had drivers in place six months ago to cover for this event. They also informed companies they trade with the day before that there would be a dispute.

- This dispute has been engineered by the company. This is a premeditated dispute designed to provoke action by workers so that they can be sacked without their due redundancy pay.

- This is a concerted attack on the airport workforce and their trades unions.

- This is irresponsible US-style union bashing, which has no place in UK industrial relations.

- Gate Gourmet's action is jeopardising workers' jobs, their communities, and the businesses and livelihoods of many of their colleagues. It must be resisted.

Gate Gourmet challenged what it called 'these T&G myths' with the following statement:

> The facts are that hundreds of former Gate Gourmet workers took the law into their own hands and on 10 August staged unauthorised, illegal industrial action. The TGWU was fully aware of this action and did nothing to stop it. A radical group of workers at the centre of this event has a history of similar illegal action, taking such measures seven times in the past three years.

Gate Gourmet also gave the following as its position in the dispute.

- Gate Gourmet London's number one priority is to ensure that the local company remains viable and that 1400 jobs at Heathrow are protected.

- Gate Gourmet will continue to negotiate in good faith with the union in the hope of reaching a fair and reasonable agreement.

- Gate Gourmet cannot even consider requests by dismissed workers for re-engagement unless all dismissed workers sign compromise agreements.

- Gate Gourmet will not, under any circumstances, re-engage the former employees who instigated the illegal job action on 10 August.

■ Gate Gourmet has offered ex-employees who are not re-engaged or employees who are leaving generous terms of compensation (if a compromise agreement is signed in the case of the ex-employees).

Gate Gourmet added that it was determined to do everything it could to find a solution through negotiation that would ensure the viability of the Heathrow business and protect the jobs and pensions of the 1400 loyal and hard-working employees. The company was committed to working with the union to find a fair and reasonable solution for the dismissed staff.

The arguments battled on. Born challenged what he called a series of T&G 'myths' about the dispute, while the T&G claims that Gate Gourmet plotted for a year to replace staff with agency workers on worse conditions.

Born responded that, 'This is utterly ridiculous. Why the hell would we spend a year trying to find a solution in negotiation with the union if this was our plan? And if it was a plot, why didn't we do it on 14 June when they all walked out then on illegal wildcat action?'

Born added that his managers held 30 meetings with the union earlier this year to work out a restructuring programme involving 675 redundancies, which was put to staff with union approval, only to be rejected in June.

To try to end the dispute, at the end of August Gate Gourmet had offered all staff – including those that had been sacked – redundancy packages. About 700 staff – 300 of those sacked and 400 from the existing Gate Gourmet employees – applied to accept the offer, according to the union.

However, one remaining disagreement was not resolved, which was Gate Gourmet's insistence that it would not re-employ 200 so-called 'troublemakers'.

Finally, after a series of negotiations conducted by the arbitration service ACAS, at the end of September a deal was struck.

Under the deal struck between the T&G and managers of Gate Gourmet, about 144 workers will be forced to take compulsory redundancy, while hundreds of others will take voluntary redundancy.

Woodley of the T&G made the following statement: 'I am pleased however that our shop stewards and members have accepted a settlement that will see the great majority of our members go back to work or take voluntary separation.'

If a resolution had not been reached, Gate Gourmet had said that its UK operation faced going into administration if it could not cut costs. It has since provisionally secured the improved BA contract it said its UK business needs to secure its financial survival, but the airline warned all along that this was dependent upon Gate Gourmet and the T&G coming to agreement. BA is Gate Gourmet's largest customer in the UK.

At the end of the dispute the T&G and Gate Gourmet made the following joint statement:

> Both the company and the union are pleased that a way forward has been found and, if the agreement is ratified, both sides have committed to working together to rebuild trust and confidence after all the difficulties of recent weeks.
> Source: www.bbc.co.uk; Charter (2005); www.tgwu.co.uk; www.gategourmet.co.uk.

Discussion questions

1 In your opinion why did the conflict escalate?

2 Is there a right or wrong party in the dispute?

3 How would you have conducted the negotiations if you were (a) the union leader, (b) the manager of Gate Gourmet?

4 Do you think the two parties have achieved a win–win solution? Explain your answer.

Applied questions

5 Using Exhibit 11-5, what are the functional and dysfunctional outcomes of the conflict?

6 Conflict moves from stages to sources to consequences to performance outcomes. How could management have better used conflict management strategies to end the dispute?

PART 4

The role of the manager: leadership practices

Part contents

Ethical problem-solving and decision-making

LEARNING OUTCOMES

After studying this chapter you should be able to:

- ☑ **explain** the nature of managerial problem-solving
- ☑ **identify** the five steps of the rational problem-solving process
- ☑ **appreciate** the value of ethics and morality in decision-making
- ☑ **describe** the strengths and weaknesses of different decision styles
- ☑ **utilise** quality management tools for problem-solving
- ☑ **apply** techniques to stimulate creativity and innovation.

The opening vignette explores how a change in management approach combined with an ability to solve problems can improve services in a failing London Council.

Planned escape from chaos: Josephine Kwhali, leading the overhaul of Hackney children's services

When she arrived at Hackney Council two years ago as head of the children's and families' service, Josephine Kwhali was shocked at what she found. 'Child protection files were stuffed in boxes and cupboards and nobody could tell me with any accuracy which children were on the protection register,' she says. 'About half those vulnerable children did not have an allocated social worker.'

Many staff were demoralised and management was generally poor or non-existent, says Kwhali. The service was fundamentally directionless.

The chaos surrounding child protection was just one example of the mess that Hackney's children's services had got itself into, resulting in a series of highly critical inspection reports, the placing of the east London authority on the government's 'special measures' list, and the imposition in 1999 of ministerial directions, forcing the borough to observe its statutory obligations.

The social services crisis was part of a wider collapse in Hackney, with its education standards under fire, the lowest council tax collection rate in London, political infighting among councillors, and a financial meltdown resulting in savage budget cuts.

Today, the borough still faces huge problems, but its children's services have staged a dramatic recovery. In her recent annual report, Denise Platt, chief inspector of the Social Services Inspectorate (SSI), praises the contribution of Kwhali and her colleagues in turning things round. Their work, she says, meant that Hackney was this year taken off the special measures regime, and the SSI team that visited the borough in the summer found 'real and positive improvement in children's services', more confident management and shared values among managers and staff.

'All [staff] were clear that the leadership of the head of children and families services had been a critical factor in the change,' says Platt. 'Staff were purposeful and talked about being able to do the job from the moment they arrived at work, not clearing yesterday's backlog.'

Kwhali, who had held senior posts at the London boroughs of Lambeth, Hammersmith and Fulham, and Greenwich before joining Hackney, is reluctant to take the credit and insists that other factors contributed to the improvement in social services. These, she says, included the re-forming of the department, which had been split into various free-standing units with no overall director during a much-criticised council restructuring in the late 1990s.

'Just before I joined, Hackney had appointed a new social services director, the political instability on the council was being tackled and there was a new managing director,' she says.

There was a recognition at the highest levels of the council that children's services needed to be turned around, although there have been complaints that this has been partly achieved by cuts to services for older people. Kwhali denies that these services were singled out, arguing that there was little left in children's services to cut and that the combined adult services had the largest share of the budget.

Of her role, she says: 'I was appointed with a clear agenda to sort out the mess and there was a lot of pressure because everyone knew we were in the "last chance saloon".' However, she knew by the end of her second week that dramatic improvements were feasible because she 'wasn't faced with a workforce resistant to change'. While there was low morale, 'there were also many staff who had kept faith with Hackney and were passionate about delivering a good public service and were prepared to be part of a change'.

The first priority was ensuring that Hackney delivered on its statutory responsibilities, notably in respect of children on the child protection register and those looked after in care. 'There's no point doing lots of innovative work if you're not doing the basics right,' Kwhali says. In this case, doing the basics meant a huge task of sorting through caseloads, reviewing cases and putting in place new systems and procedures, backed up with firm management monitoring.

By the time the SSI team reviewed Hackney's performance in the summer of 2002, there were rarely any unallocated cases of children looked after or on the protection register. 'All visits now take place in the statutory time frame, and in one year we doubled the number of looked-after children for whom adoption was secured,' says Kwhali.

Another improvement was the creation of specialist teams to address the needs of particular groups of children about whom there were serious concerns. But for Kwhali it was not enough to put in place proper management structures: it was also about winning 'hearts and minds'.

Source: © Guardian Newspapers Ltd, 2002, Patrick McCurry.

Discussion questions

1 Why do you think Josephine Kwhali was able to implement changes when her predecessors could not?

2 How did Josephine Kwhali implement her decisions?

Bass (1983) suggests that individual, managerial and organisational success all depend on making the right decisions at the right times. However, decision-making is just one component of the problem-solving process. Unless a problem has been defined and its root causes identified, managers are unlikely to be able to make an appropriate decision about how to solve it. Effective managers, like Hackney's Josephine Kwhali, know how to gather and evaluate information that clarifies a problem. They know the value of generating more than one action alternative and weighing all the implications of a plan before deciding to implement it. In addition, they acknowledge the importance of following through. This chapter explains decision-making and problem-solving and offers some guidelines for eliminating barriers to effective problem-solving.

The steps for rational problem-solving

problem-solving
The process of eliminating the discrepancy between actual and desired outcomes.

decision-making
Selecting the best solution from among feasible alternatives.

Problem-solving is the process of eliminating the discrepancy between actual and desired outcomes. Although, sometimes subconsciously, most people confront problems by first acknowledging that they exist. Next, the problem needs to be defined and analysed. Then alternative solutions need to be generated. **Decision-making** – selecting the best solution from among feasible alternatives – comes next. Finally, the solution needs to be implemented, which Europeans call 'taking' a decision. Archer (1980) suggests that, for optimal problem-solving, social scientists advocate the use of the rational problem-solving approach outlined in Exhibit 12-1.

A problem exists whenever the actual situation is not what is needed or desired. For example, when a work project needs to be done by a certain deadline and information needed to complete the assignment has not been supplied, a problem exists.

Problem awareness

A major responsibility for all managers is to maintain a constant lookout for actual or potential problems. Pounds (1969) argues that managers do this by keeping channels of communication open, monitoring employees' current performance, and examining deviations from present plans as well as from past experience. Four situations usually alert managers to possible problems: when there is a deviation from past experience; when there is a deviation from a set plan; when other people communicate problems to the manager; when competitors outperform the overall organisation. The Dynamics of Diversity box shows how Vitra tries to keep ahead of the competition.

Being aware that problems exist is not always easy, however. People may be genuinely unaware of a problem's source or reluctant to acknowledge that a negative situation actually exists. The problem may appear threatening to them, they may fear reprisal from a supervisor for their share of the responsibility, or they may not want to be considered inept.

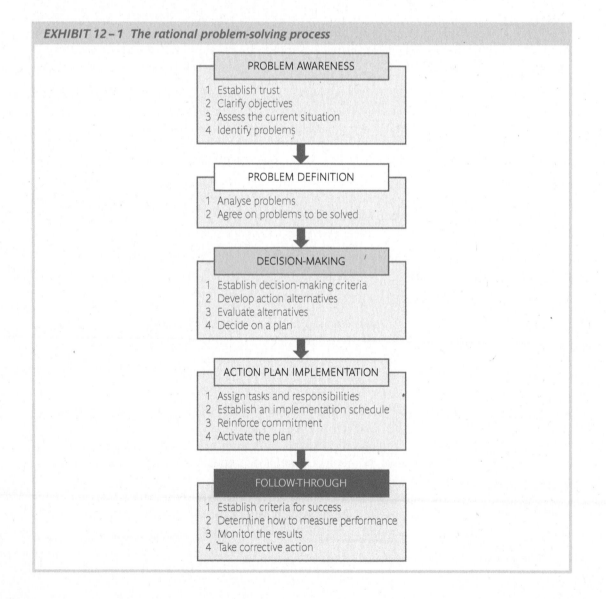

EXHIBIT 12–1 The rational problem-solving process

PROBLEM AWARENESS
1 Establish trust
2 Clarify objectives
3 Assess the current situation
4 Identify problems

PROBLEM DEFINITION
1 Analyse problems
2 Agree on problems to be solved

DECISION-MAKING
1 Establish decision-making criteria
2 Develop action alternatives
3 Evaluate alternatives
4 Decide on a plan

ACTION PLAN IMPLEMENTATION
1 Assign tasks and responsibilities
2 Establish an implementation schedule
3 Reinforce commitment
4 Activate the plan

FOLLOW-THROUGH
1 Establish criteria for success
2 Determine how to measure performance
3 Monitor the results
4 Take corrective action

Hot-desking: it's autumn, when thoughts turn to fashion, so just what will the modern office be wearing this season?

It was as if the dozen or so journalists had been invited to the Thunderbirds headquarters to meet Brains, only to find that he'd been cloned into an eerie, not-quite-matching pair. We had thought, quite reasonably, that we were in Basle, Switzerland, at the Frank Gehry-designed headquarters of Vitra, one of the world's most influential furniture manufacturers, for a press briefing. However, no. This was International Office Furniture Rescue. Moreover, it wasn't Brains at all. It was the Bouroullec brothers, the quizzical Bretons who are the hottest French design export since Philippe ('I can design a hotel in one day, zut-boff ker-ching!') Starck.

The Brains were here, after 18 months' wood-shedding, to reveal something called 'Joyn', an office furniture system featuring shower curtains, latticed plywood, fabric-covered desk dividers and dinky R2D2 filing cabinets on leads.

And there was a third Brain to consider: Mr Vitra, aka Rolf Fehlbaum – pared down, black-clad, smiling, preternaturally alert. As the trio sat in the conference room, patiently waiting for the audience to settle down, two unspoken questions hung in the air: can the Bouroullecs cut it; and has Fehlbaum, Europe's radical furniture savant, read the runes correctly?

It matters, big-time. Sales of designer office furniture are worth £830 million in Britain alone. In Vitra's case, we're talking serious kit, the kind of thing you find in venture capitalist boardrooms: office chairs designed by Charles and Ray Eames or Alberto Meda at well over £1000 a pop. And new product launches by the company are closely watched in the industry – not least by Vitra's rivals. The contract market – where specifiers regularly buy furniture pieces in the hundreds – is, after all, where the money is.

Talent is the first requirement. Fehlbaum has it. He took over the family business in 1977. In 1986 he acquired the rights to manufacture classic Eames designs in the lucrative markets of Europe and the Middle East. He's built on that success by 'breaking' hot new designers dozens of times since then: 'There are a lot of designers who produce a couple of interesting projects but there are very few who keep on producing projects with the depth and originality they do. There are too many designers praised for good, but not great work. I believe the Bouroullecs have the seeds of greatness in them. They interrogate typologies. They really think about how people want to use products.'

In addition, what have the Bouroullecs come up with so far? Why are they 'great'? Five years ago it was Les Vases Combinatoires, Ronan's riff on ceramic containers that could be put together in myriad ways; two years later, he struck again with a modular kitchen for Cappellini that was about as minimally detailed as you can get. Interlocking, moulded brick shelving, Hole Chairs, felt loudspeakers, the skinnily proportioned Glide Sofa and, the star of the Design Museum show, the Lit Clos sleeping cabin, a weirdly screened gerbil-hutch for two on needlethin legs.

The Joyn desk system, officially launched this Tuesday at the Orgatec exhibition in Cologne (the office furniture industry's equivalent of Cannes), sits on the same, strange cusp: these are products designed for mass-production, heavy marketing and profitability. And yet, these are also products that seek to break hierarchies, democratise decision-making processes and promote teamwork.

The system is based on 8 m-long tables with slide-in space dividers and a central spine that houses electrical and computer junctions and allows accessories such as trays, lights and file-stands to be slotted in. It's extremely simple to manipulate and reflects Fehlbaum's view that in the truly dynamic office 'personal organisation is more important than hierarchy. The new office has to deal with creativity. Everything that's an obstruction to natural work is an obstruction to success.' The idea is that work teams can be 'created rapidly and make communication and collective intelligence the normal thing'.

However, have they got it right, or will Joyn's almost domestic appearance (the white desks are so clean-looking you could eat off them) prove too avant-garde for office workers used to divisive cubicles and open-plan wastelands?

'We wanted to know what makes industry real,' says Erwan. 'We're trying to de-code things. This system allows you to break down cultural walls. We concentrated on ease of use to try to make people free. We don't promise that it's the twenty-first-century answer to everything – it's just that we tried to create the kind of buzz that will put some life into work.'

And Vitra into unknown territory. However, then, nobody said it was easy at International Office Furniture Rescue.

Source: © Jay Merrick, *Independent*, 19 October 2002.

Discussion questions

1 Can you identify how Vitra makes its decisions?
2 Who do you think controls the decision-making process?

Establish trust

When a problem involves others, they need to feel understood and accepted; they must have confidence that the problem can be resolved; they must trust management to see the problem as a learning experience and not as an excuse to punish someone. Hunsaker and Alessandra (1986) suggest that people need to feel secure enough to acknowledge that a problem exists and to acknowledge their own contributions to it.

Clarify objectives

> 'Cheshire Puss,' Alice began, 'would you tell me, please, which way I ought to walk
> from here?'
>
> 'That depends a good deal on where you want to get to,' said the Cat.
>
> 'I don't care where,' said Alice.
>
> 'Then it doesn't matter which way you walk,' said the Cat. (Carroll, 1975)

objective
Desired outcome that we want to achieve.

Unlike Alice in Wonderland, most of us have an **objective** or desired outcome that we want to achieve. If you do not know what your objectives are, it is difficult to know what your problems are, let alone what to do about them. Therefore, objectives must be set and clarified before a current situation can be assessed.

According to Morrisey (1977), setting objectives serves four main purposes. First, it provides a clear, documented statement of what you intend to accomplish. Written objectives are a form of acknowledgement and a reminder of commitment. Second, setting objectives establishes a basis for measuring performance. Third, knowing what is expected and desired provides positive motivation to achieve goals. And, fourth, knowing exactly where you are going is much more likely to get you there than trying many different solutions in a haphazard way.

It is a manager's responsibility to make sure that set objectives support overall organisational goals. To obtain commitment from employees, managers must define organisational objectives and point out how they support each employee's personal goals. Finally, the objectives for any particular person or group should mesh with the objectives of others who might be affected by them. One way to address these constraints is to conduct team goal-setting meetings so that all concerned parties can participate openly.

There is little motivational value in setting objectives that require nothing more than maintenance of present performance levels. On the other hand, very difficult objectives may appear unattainable and therefore be demoralising. While objectives should foster an improvement over present performance, they should also be clearly achievable.

Organisational decision-making

The decision-making process and what types of decision are made are largely determined by the structure of the organisation. Does the decision-making rest mainly with top-level management or can it be delegated to lower levels in the organisation? When we look at decision-making we need to look at the types of decision that are made, who makes them, and the organisational approaches to gathering information, evaluating alternative solutions and implementing the final decision.

Assess the current situation

When evaluating the current situation, participants must focus on both the 'what' and the 'how' of performance from two viewpoints: that of the organisation and that of the people involved. The immediate need is to determine if goals are met by the current situation. Do actual conditions match desired ones? If not, what are the differences? Mismatches usually show up clearly, but sometimes an inadequate current situation is taken for granted because it is how things have been for so long. If the matching process reveals discrepancies, the next step is to determine why.

Identify problems

Serious mistakes can be made if managers act before they accurately identify all the sources of a problem. To identify a problem accurately, it must be understood from all points of view.

The full determination of how a particular problem prevents people from accomplishing desired goals can be made only when all parties are free to participate in its identification without fear of being blamed or criticised. If problem-solving is perceived as a joint learning experience, people will be much more likely to contribute needed information than if they fear punishment for disclosing information that may indicate they have made mistakes.

Problem identification and solution are much easier in routine than non-routine situations. Routine problems are those that arise on a regular basis and can be solved through *programmed decisions* – standard responses based on procedures that have been effective in the past. One example of a programmed decision is a student's automatic probationary status when his or her grade point average sinks below a predetermined level. Another is the reordering of supplies as soon as stock on hand falls below a certain quantity. Most routine problems are anticipated, which allows managers to plan in advance how to deal with them and sometimes to delegate problem-solving to their subordinates.

Non-routine problems are ones not anticipated by managers. They are unique. No standard responses to them exist. These types of problem require *non-programmed decisions* – innovative solutions tailored to fit specific dilemmas. The fuel blockades of 2000 was a non-routine problem; if it had escalated it would have required new ways of distributing petrol and transporting goods and people. Catastrophes always pose non-routine problems. When Concorde crashed on take-off in Paris the remaining planes were grounded until their fuel tanks were reinforced. Stranded ticket holders, loss of custom, and idle pilots and flight crews were just some of the non-routine problems faced by decision-makers at many levels.

One way to be prepared for potential problems and to be able to quickly identify their cause is to thoroughly understand the process involved. A **flowchart**, or **process flow diagram**, is a pictorial representation of all the steps of a process. Flowcharts document a process and help demonstrate how the various steps relate to each other. See Exhibit 12-2 for a sample flowchart involving quality inspection of incoming parts.

flowchart (process flow diagram)
A pictorial representation of all the steps of a process.

The flowchart is widely used in problem identification. The people with the greatest amount of knowledge about the process meet to first draw a flowchart of what steps the process actually follows. Then they draw a flowchart of what steps the process should ideally follow. Brassard (1988) suggests that by comparing the two charts they find differences, because that is where the problems arise.

Problem definition

If the problem is not defined clearly, any attempt at solving it will be doomed to fail because the parties involved will not really know what they are working on (as the saying goes, 'rubbish in equals rubbish out'). All the remaining steps will be distorted because they will be based on insufficient or erroneous information. Lack of information often inhibits the generation of adequate alternatives and exploration of potentially negative consequences.

All necessary information should be gathered so that all relevant factors can be analysed to determine the exact problem that must be solved. The goal is to determine the root causes of the problem. If instruction forms are constantly misinterpreted, for example, are the forms incomplete or is the required information poorly supplied? Causes should not be assumed; instead, all plausible alternatives should be investigated before settling on the most probable cause(s).

Hasty assumptions can also result in symptoms being mistaken for sources of problems. When symptoms are eliminated, it is often mistakenly assumed that the problem has also been eliminated. This is like receiving medication from your doctor to control a skin rash, which is only a symptom that something is wrong. The medication clears the rash, but the actual cause of the problem is not identified until you and/or the doctor look for clues. When you discover that the onset of the rash coincided with the arrival of a new plant in your living room, you have identified the problem: an allergy to that plant.

Analyse problems

Checking to make sure that the problem is defined accurately and analysed completely provides a safeguard against incorrect assumptions, treatment of symptoms only, and incomplete understanding. The way a problem is actually defined has a major impact on what alternatives are considered, what decision is reached, and how the action plan is implemented. Failure to define an identified problem accurately can impede consideration and eventual application of the best solution.

EXHIBIT 12 – 2 Process flow diagram: receiving inspection

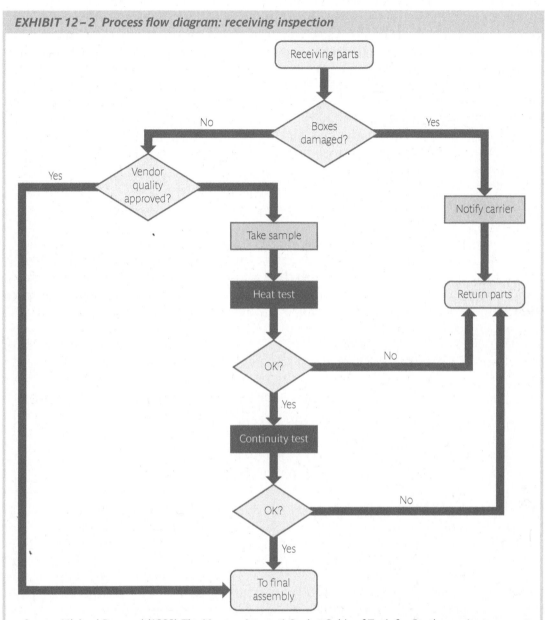

Source: Michael Brassard (1988) *The Memory Jogger: A Pocket Guide of Tools for Continuous Improvement*. Methuen, MA: GOAL/QPC, p. 10. Reprinted with permission from *The Memory Jogger™*. Copyright 1996 by GOAL/QPC.

Failure to thoroughly diagnose a problem can result from inadequate time and energy available to review all the possible causes and implications. Other times, underlying psychological reasons come into play, such as not wanting to know what the real problems are, fearing that we ourselves are to blame, being concerned that a close associate will be hurt, or anticipating that the problem will prove too big for us.

One technique for facilitating a thorough problem analysis, suggested by Brassard (1988), is the cause-and-effect diagram. A *cause-and-effect diagram*, or fishbone chart, is constructed to represent the relationship between some 'effect' and all possible 'causes' influencing it.

As illustrated in Exhibit 12-3, the effect or problem is stated on the right side of the chart and the major influences or causes are listed to the left. Although a problem may have various sources, the major causes can usually be summarised under the four 'M' categories of *manpower, methods, machines* and *material.* Data can then be gathered and shared to determine the relative frequencies and magnitudes of contribution of the different potential causes.

Agree on problems to be solved

If more than one problem has been identified and defined, the next step is to set priorities regarding which problem will be worked on first and which ones will be put aside temporarily or indefinitely. One criterion for rank ordering multiple problems is how much their solutions will contribute to desired objectives. The most important problems should be dealt with first, even if their solutions seem more difficult. One quality management tool that can help management do this is called 'Pareto' analysis.

Pareto chart

A vertical bar graph that indicates which problems, or causes of problems, should be solved first.

A **Pareto chart** is a vertical bar graph that indicates which problems, or causes of problems, should be solved first. To construct a Pareto chart, the problems to be compared and their rank order are determined by brainstorming and analysing existing

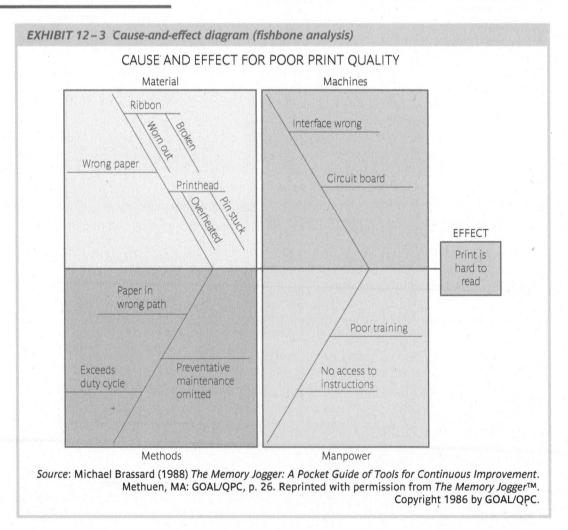

EXHIBIT 12-3 *Cause-and-effect diagram (fishbone analysis)*

CAUSE AND EFFECT FOR POOR PRINT QUALITY

Source: Michael Brassard (1988) *The Memory Jogger: A Pocket Guide of Tools for Continuous Improvement.* Methuen, MA: GOAL/QPC, p. 26. Reprinted with permission from *The Memory Jogger*™. Copyright 1986 by GOAL/QPC.

data. Then a standard for comparison, such as annual cost or frequency of occurrence, and the time period to be studied are selected. After necessary data for each category have been gathered, the frequency or cost of each category is compared to that for other categories. Brassard (1988) lists the categories from left to right on the horizontal axis in order of decreasing frequency or cost. A Pareto chart of field service customer complaints is illustrated in Exhibit 12-4.

Decision-making

After information has been gathered and goals have been clarified, situations assessed and problems identified, the next step is to develop a particular course of action that will either restore formerly acceptable conditions or improve the situation in a significant way. Since there is usually more than one way to solve a problem, it is critical to remain open to all possible solutions and arrive at several alternatives from which to choose.

Establish decision-making criteria

criteria
Statements of objectives that need to be met for a problem to be solved.

Decision-making criteria are statements of objectives that need to be met for a problem to be solved. Effective criteria should possess the following characteristics.

Specific, Measurable, and Achievable, Relevant, Timebound (SMART)

'I need to reduce scrap material waste by 10 per cent, avoid a reduction in product quality, and increase production by 5 per cent. This must be done in one month.' This is an example of a concise decision-making criteria statement. Decision-making criteria should be *specific*: 'I will increase productivity by 5 per cent', not just 'I want to increase productivity.' Second, they should be *measurable*: saying you want to increase employee morale is not as good a criterion statement as saying that you will increase employee morale as indicated by a 4 per cent reduction in absenteeism over the next three months. Third, to gain commitment to meeting criteria, there should be sufficient time, resources and expertise available to make them *achievable*. They must also be *relevant*: it is no good introducing a system of childcare to increase staff morale, if none of the employees has children. They must also be *timebound*, achieved within a time limit. This helps when measuring targets and also ensures that a problem does not linger on indefinitely.

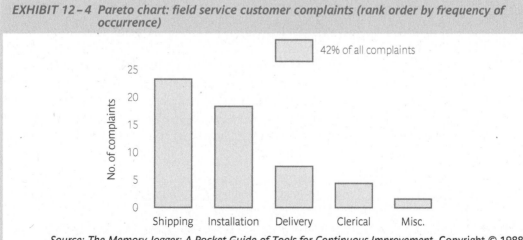

EXHIBIT 12–4 Pareto chart: field service customer complaints (rank order by frequency of occurrence)

Source: *The Memory Jogger: A Pocket Guide of Tools for Continuous Improvement.* Copyright © 1988 GOAL/QPC. Reprinted with permission from *The Memory Jogger*™. Copyright 1986 by GOAL/QPC.

Complementary

The criteria must also complement one another. The achievement of one should not reduce the likelihood of achieving another. For example, you would not improve the quality and detail of your written reports at the expense of spending the necessary time with those who must interact with you.

Ethical

Decision criteria should conform to what is considered morally right by society. Criteria should be legal, fair and observant of human rights. Organisations need to establish a commonly agreed upon set of ethical standards to guide decisions when individuals are confronted with conflicting obligations, cost–benefit trade-offs, and competing value choices. The following section on ethical decision-making expands on the many dilemmas of applying moral criteria.

Acceptable

Even the best technical decision will not be workable if it is unacceptable to the parties involved. You may be convinced, for example, that the best solution for meeting a production deadline without increasing costs is to have the department work weekends for the next month without additional compensation. However, this is not a viable action plan because it will not be acceptable to those on whom its implementation depends. Negative reactions to changes can create more problems than are solved. Sensitivity to emotional factors, personal values and individual objectives is vital in choosing a successful action plan.

Develop action alternatives

The value, acceptance and implementation of an action plan are enhanced by involving all affected parties in the generation and analysis of alternatives. Acceptance can be tested by soliciting feedback to determine if those involved understand the potential benefits and to assess their readiness to make the necessary commitment. As many solutions as possible should be generated to avoid picking a premature solution that does not meet all long-run criteria. Techniques to facilitate this step are provided in the following section on how problems can be solved more effectively.

Evaluate benefits and risks of alternatives

It is important to look at all the long-run consequences of the alternatives being considered. This is sometimes overlooked because of our tendency to avoid spending extra time and energy and our fear of discovering negative consequences in preferred solutions. Important criteria to consider in evaluating action alternatives are each alternative's *probability of success* and the associated *degree of risk* that negative consequences will occur. According to Natale *et al.* (1990) if the chance of failure is high and the related costs for an alternative are great, the benefits of an alternative may not justify its use. Risk can be personal as well as economic – just ask the person whose reputation is on the line or who is soon to undergo a performance review. The degree of risk can be separated into four categories: certainty, known risk, uncertainty and turbulence.

Certainty

Certainty exists if the exact results of implementing a problem solution are known in advance.

certainty
Exists if the exact results of implementing a particular solution are known in advance.

Certainty (of return) exists if you put your money in a savings account for one year, whereas it does not exist if you invest it in real estate or the stock market. Certainty is the exception rather than the rule in most managerial decision-making situations. Complete information and guaranteed outcomes are rare.

Known risk

known risk
Present when the probability that a given alternative will produce specific outcomes can be predicted.

Known risk is present when the probability that a given alternative will produce specific outcomes can be predicted. For example, an executive may know that by taking a commercial airline flight tonight, he or she has a 99.5 per cent probability of arriving on time for a business meeting in London tomorrow morning. If the executive lives in Glasgow, he or she will also know for certain that if the last flight is missed, the meeting tomorrow will also be missed. Probabilities based on historical records or statistical analyses are sometimes assigned to risky alternatives. At other times, probabilities are simply estimated through managerial intuition.

Uncertainty

uncertainty
Exists when decision-makers are unable to assign any probabilities to the consequences associated with an alternative.

Uncertainty exists when decision-makers are unable to assign any probabilities to the consequences associated with an alternative. Choices among uncertain alternatives are often based on intuition and hunches.

Turbulence

turbulence
Occurs when the environment is rapidly changing and decision-makers are not even clear about relevant variables, available solution options or potential consequences of decisions.

Turbulence occurs when the environment is rapidly changing and decision-makers are not even clear about relevant variables, available solution options, or potential consequences of decisions. In times of recession, economic reforms or military conflict, turbulence usually prevails.

Decide on a plan

As alternatives are evaluated according to these criteria, many will clearly be unsatisfactory and can be eliminated. Sometimes the evaluation will reveal that one alternative is decidedly superior to all others. At other times, none of the proposed action plans will be acceptable, signalling a need to develop additional alternatives. Most often, however, several alternatives will appear feasible, and the best one must be selected. Exhibit 12-5 illustrates a decision-making grid that summarises the above criteria for evaluating alternatives. Such a grid can help to visualise which alternative offers the maximum benefits with minimal risks and costs. The decision-making goal is to select the best solution alternative for solving the entire problem without creating any additional negative consequences for anyone else in the organisation.

EXHIBIT 12–5 Decision-making grid

ALTERNATIVES	CRITERIA					
	BENEFITS	PROBABILITY OF SUCCESS	COSTS	RISKS	ASSOCIATED CONSEQUENCES	TIMING
Alternative A						
Alternative B						
Alternative C						

Research focus: rational versus bounded rationality perspective

Perfect rationality

In a world of perfect rationality, all problems can be clearly defined, all information and alternatives are known, the consequences of implementing each alternative are certain, and the decision-maker is a completely rational being who is concerned only about economic gain. These conditions of *classical decision theory* allow for an optimal solution to every problem and provide the basics for ideal management decision-making.

The model of human behaviour known as the economic man model assumed the following.

- The decision-maker had access to perfect information concerning all aspects of the decision situation.
- The decision-maker could process all the relevant information when identifying and diagnosing problems.
- The decision-maker could identify all possible solutions to a problem and evaluate the outcomes of each alternative solution.
- Multiple goals of an organisation could be combined into a single, simple mathematical equation.
- A rational decision-maker would always select the alternative solution that would produce the maximum benefit to the organisation.
- All decision-makers process information in the same manner and make similar decisions.

The real world, however, is made up of real people with real problems, and it rarely conforms to these ideal conditions. Consequently, there are not many arguments in favour of the economic man approach, although most of the economic theories of human behaviour are based on these assumptions.

Bounded rationality

Behavioural decision theory has questioned the classical assumptions and recognised the real-world limitations to obtaining and processing all relevant information that might optimise decision-making. Simon argues that administrators exhibit bounded rationality when they reach satisfactory rather than 'perfect' decisions. According to Simon (1957), bounded rationality is necessary in the face of constraints on time, money and intellectual resources. While the goal of the decision model presented here is to optimise decision outcomes, satisficing – choosing the first satisfactory alternative that meets minimal requirements – probably describes the majority of daily managerial decision-making. Herbert Simon, a Nobel Prize winner, challenged early decision-making models of perfect rationality. The concept of bounded rationality implies that decisions are made under the following external and psychological constraints.

satisficing
Choosing the first satisfactory alternative that meets minimal requirements.

- Individuals do not have perfect information regarding the problem.
- Decision-makers are not aware of all feasible solutions.
- Even if all the information were available, they would probably not have the cognitive capacity to understand and remember it all.

The decision-maker's ability to analyse only a few things at a time is know as *cognitive limits of rationality*. This means that, contrary to the rational economic man approach, most decision-makers explore very few alternatives and make decisions on limited amounts of information.

A major implication of bounded rationality is 'satisficing' by decision-makers rather than 'maximising'. 'Satisficing' means that decision-makers are establishing a minimum level of acceptability for a solution and then finding alternatives until one reaching the minimum level is found. When the first suitable alternative is found, the search for other alternatives comes to an end. This means that decision-makers using the bounded rationality approach limit their information to the most convenient and least expensive solutions, unlike the rational approach, which implies decision-makers are 'maximisers' who will search for the solution that will be of maximum benefit in solving the problem. Another critical implication of the bounded rationality approach is that the search for alternative solutions and the process of evaluating them is influenced by the decision-maker's attitudes, values and cognitive processes. This means that personality and psychological implications have an impact in final decisions, as we will discuss later in this chapter.

Action plan implementation

A decision and action plan are of little value unless they are implemented effectively. How the action plan is to be accomplished connects the decision with reality. Implementation includes assigning tasks and responsibilities, and establishing an implementation schedule. Take a look at the Eye on Ethics box to see what happens when a government implements a decision in the foot-and-mouth crisis.

Faith and reason

True creativity is not the same as problem-solving. Now we have not one, but three inquiries into foot-and-mouth disease. But will any of them address the really awkward questions?

In the end, the government has decided upon not one inquiry into the outbreak of foot-and mouth, but three – one to look at its own handling of the epidemic, one to review the science, and one to consider the future of farming and food. There will be plenty of questions for the three inquiries to ask. But will they overlook the most important?

Foot-and-mouth disease has indeed been a tragedy; but ought we to see it as a problem? Dorothy L. Sayers would have said no. In her book about God, *The Mind of the Maker*, which is quite as excellent as her detective novels, she argues that we ought to stop treating life as a series of problems, and instead attempt to deal with it creatively. Creativity, as she knows well from experience, is a quite different thing from problem-solving.

Detective novels work precisely because the 'problem' is artificially designed. It must be neatly, completely and always soluble. Once the story is over, there must be no loose ends: we can put the book away satisfied. We discover the answer, though, just because the author was careful to set the question so that we could solve it according to the rules. Real life is not like that.

We are treating foot-and-mouth disease, as we treat most social issues, as a problem. That, indeed, is why the scourge has turned into a disaster. We decided in advance what question to ask: 'How can we eradicate it?' Politically, we have allowed ourselves to ask nothing else. We assumed, with no good reason, that there was a single and complete solution, and that when we

eye on ethics

found it we would be able to drop the 'problem' as casually as we can lay Sherlock Holmes aside when we get to the last page. We were wrong; yet we continue in the relentless pursuit of 'solutions' that only deepen the tragedy.

When someone sees a sick sheep they remember first that it is an animal, and ask, 'Can it be cured?' Mere problem-solvers assume that everything is there to be manipulated; the only constraint on action will be the limits of brute strength. They will ride roughshod over nature and law and custom alike. What does it matter if that flock belongs not to the state, but to this family, which has tended it for generations? If it must be commandeered and destroyed to 'solve the problem', then so be it.

For those who think in terms of problems, it is natural to reduce the complex richness of life to simplified abstractions, for these are easier to manipulate. In our society, that usually leads to questions of money. We know all about the effects of foot-and mouth: the millions lost to the tourist industry, the wealthy farmers sitting pretty with their vast payouts. It is much easier to ignore those awkward elements of genuine tragedy that do not fit easily with our predetermined view of the question. What of the families who have sacrificed themselves to months of lonely isolation and succeeded in keeping their flocks healthy, yet still had them destroyed? Or the experienced slaughtermen who have been reduced to despair by the brutal pointlessness of their commission? Why so little of them? If we attend to them, however, the 'problem' might become too complicated to solve.

Life does indeed throw up limited and solvable problems, and we must tackle them. But we should be worried when we catch ourselves thinking of the big issues simply as problems.

Source: © Martin Lindstom, *Independent*, 11 August 2001.

Discussion questions

1 Should it have been the government's responsibility to solve the problem, and how did it identify the solution for the mass slaughter of animals?

2 How does developing creativity differ from problem-solving?

Assign tasks and responsibilities

It is important to clarify both verbally and in writing what each person involved will do to make the new action plan work. To avoid misunderstandings it is essential to specify who is to do what, by when and how.

Establish an implementation schedule

To be implemented effectively, all necessary tasks need a specified time schedule for completion. One way to do this is to start at an end point (the date by which the objective should be completed) and work backwards. Action implementation steps can be listed in priority order and assigned a reasonable length of time for completion, starting with the last step before the objective is accomplished.

One of the earliest scheduling techniques was developed by Harry Gantt in the early 1900s. A **Gantt chart** is a graphic planning and control method that breaks down a project into separate tasks and estimates the time needed for their completion. The chart has a space for planned starting and completion dates, and actual dates filled in as implementation occurs. A sample Gantt chart is shown in Exhibit 12-6.

Gantt chart

A graphic planning and control method that breaks down a project into separate tasks and estimates the time needed for their completion.

EXHIBIT 12-6 Sample Gantt chart

Activity description (responsibility)	Dec 1992	Jan 1993	Feb 1993	Mar 1993	Apr 1993	May
	7 14 21 28	4 11 18 25	1 8 15 22	1 8 15 22 29	5 12 19 26	3 10
Process planning, routing and scheduling (Chuck Teplitz: Project Manager)	▬▬					
Material procurement (David Burt: Procurement)	▬▬▬▬▬▬▬▬					
Parts fabrication (Don Helmich: Manufacturing)						
Part No. 1			▬▬▬			
2			▬▬			
3			▬			
4			▬▬			
5			▬▬			
6			▬			
7			▬▬▬▬			
8				▬▬		
9				▬▬▬		
10				▬▬▬		
11			▬▬			
12			▬			
Subassemblies (Pam Schwerin: Assembly) A					▬▬▬	
B					▬▬	
C					▬	
D					▬	
E					▬	
Final assembly (Pam Schwerin: Assembly)					▬▬	

▢ Planned starting and completion dates
▨ Work completed

Source: L.W. Rue and L.L. Byars (1992) *Management Skills and Applications* (6th edn). Homewood, IL: Richard D. Irwin, p. 210. Adapted from Elwood S. Buffa (1993), *Modern Production Management* (4th edn). New York, NY: John Wiley & Sons, Inc., p. 576.

Gantt charts help to make certain that all implementation tasks are considered in relationship to each other and appropriate people are assigned to each task. They provide checkpoints for all tasks to ensure that they are finished on time. Gantt charts are developed by defining goals and setting completion dates, then bracketing time blocks based on the time required and completion date of each task.

Once an action plan is implemented managers often move on to another task. It is of major importance, however, to follow through to be sure that the solution is working effectively and that no additional problems have been created. Follow-through is the final stage of the problem-solving process.

Follow-through

Following through entails the development and maintenance of positive attitudes in everyone involved in the implementation process. There are several guidelines to help establish the positive climate necessary for the implementation steps that follow.

- Visualise yourself in the position of those doing the implementing so that you understand their feelings and perspectives.
- Establish sincere respect and concern.
- Make sure necessary resources are available.
- With this kind of positive climate set up, there are several sequential steps in the follow-through process. They include establishing the criteria for measuring success, monitoring the results obtained, and taking corrective action when necessary.

Establish criteria for measuring success

Unless the circumstances have changed, the criteria for measuring problem-solving success are the time, quality and quantity goals already developed in the action-planning stage. These criteria serve as *benchmarks* for measuring and comparing the actual results.

Monitor the results

The data on the results can be compared with the established criteria. If the new performance meets the criteria, no further action is necessary other than continued monitoring. If the new results do not measure up, the next step is to determine why. Each implementation step may alter the problem situation in unanticipated ways.

Take corrective action

The problem-solving process is a *closed-loop system*. If performance fails to match the success criteria, the problem needs to be identified by again applying the problem-solving process. For any new corrective action plan new measures and schedules need to be determined and new data need to be gathered and tested against the criteria.

Ethical decision-making

What is ethics?

Business ethics is concerned with moral issues in business. It is concerned with good and bad, right and wrong. It may also be concerned with fairness, justice and equity.

The study of ethics looks not only at what is good and bad but also examines moral duty and obligation. Ethics can be regarded as moral principles or values, and moral conduct relates to the principles of right or wrong behaviour. In business, ethical questions arise as to whether we should or should not perform certain actions.

Ethical theory, discussed above, creates a dilemma as to how should we act in business to ensure we are behaving ethically. According to Tsalikis and Fritzsche (1989), a large majority of managers agree that unethical practices occur in business, and a substantial portion (about 65 per cent) report that they have been pressured to compromise their own ethical standards when making organisational decisions. Ferrell and Gardiner (1991) suggest that some of the

Research focus: ethical theory

Ethics helps us to decide whether our actions are right or wrong. Ethics is a branch of philosophy and attempts to help us understand that which is right and distinguish it from that which is wrong. It can also be known as moral philosophy and can focus on the following themes:

- cognitivism and non-cognitivism
- religious morality
- consequentialism versus non-consequentialism
- utilitarianism – an ethic of welfare
- Kantianism – an ethic of duty
- natural law – an ethic of rights.

Cognitivism takes the position of what we can know. It is one of the first and most profound divisions of ethical theory and suggests that it is possible to know moral right from moral wrong. According to cognitivism there are objective moral truths that can be known and statements of moral belief that can be true or false. *Non-cognitivism* is concerned with what cannot be known. This suggests that an objective assessment of moral belief is not possible. In other words, there is no truth or falsity waiting to be discovered, there is only belief, attitude and emotional reaction. Advocates of non-cognitivism claim that:

- morality is a social invention
- morality is based upon cultural preferences
- the scope can vary, but they are without a supporting basis in reality
- nothing makes a preference any more true or false
- moral right or wrong is whatever the group says it is.

This means that the group 'norms' validate what is right and wrong and moral right and wrong is whatever the group says it is. For example, if the group 'norm' is to fiddle expense claims, then this could be seen as an appropriate way of behaving. This is referred to as moral relativism, which is the position that moral or ethical ideas do not reflect absolute or universal truths but are instead based on social, cultural, historical or personal 'norms'. This means that moral beliefs are not founded on the truth but are decided by the cultural group. Therefore no cultural group has superior or inferior moral beliefs. This means that in some countries bribes can be seen as acceptable as they are a cultural 'norm'.

Religious morality can be seen as an obvious source for defining views on morality. In other words, if God exists, who better that God to decide what is right and wrong, and if God is omniscient that surely he or she must be the infallible authority on matters of ethics. This theory, that actions are solely because God commands them, is known as Divine Command Theory. As a theory this is largely popular but radically incoherent. It raises certain questions and statements, such as:

- How does God decide what is right and wrong?
- Is God a dictator, by deciding right and wrong on a whim?
- If God commands humans not to harm each other, then it is human welfare that forms the basis of morality – the fact that God commands it is incidental.

Consequentialism forms part of the great divide in cognitivist thinking between theories that assess moral right and wrong in terms of consequences of actions and those that do not. The consequentialist theories look at the results of actions to determine the truth and falsity of moral judgements. This means that the test of whether an action is right or wrong is dependent on whether it causes benefit or harm. If it gives benefit it can be seen as a good action, if it causes harm then the action is bad. In other words it is the consequences of actions that matter. *Non-consequentialism*, however, takes the view that it is not useful to consider consequences in terms of benefit as good and harm as bad. Good and bad do not determine right or wrong as it is right or wrong that determine good and bad. Therefore the consequences of an action play no part in whether it is right or wrong. Some people when faced with ethical problems weigh up the costs and benefits of their action – these follow a consequentialist approach; others may consider whether an action is right or wrong and not the consequences – this is the non-consequentialist approach.

Utilitarianism refers to an ethic of welfare and is the best-known consequentialist theory. It is concerned with the usefulness of actions. Utility means usefulness, useful actions are seen as good because they provide benefit, while non-useful actions are bad as they create disutility. One of the earliest thinkers on this matter was Jeremy Bentham who suggests that utility is happiness: 'actions are right to the extent that they maximise happiness or at least minimise unhappiness, wrong to the extent that they maximise unhappiness or minimise happiness'. The result is a 'happiness theory' which says that we should choose the path that will provide maximum happiness for the majority even if a minority may suffer. This was, however, later modified as to disadvantage others was to create disutility, and intense suffering by a minority was seen to always outweigh any happiness of the majority, therefore a grossly exploited underclass should not be permitted.

Kantianism refers to an ethic of duty and can be attributed to Emanuel Kant in the eighteenth century. Kant suggests that an action is morally right only if the person performing it is motivated by goodwill and morally wrong if not. According to Kant an action is done from a sense of duty and nothing else. This is also known as deontological theory, from the Greek word for duty.

Natural law is the third tradition in ethical thinking and is traditionally about protecting people from unjust actions by governments. 'Natural law' sets limits to the power of rulers and proposes that unjust governments could be disobeyed. John Locke in the early eighteenth century was a key figure in the development of natural rights and many of the human rights laws have followed on from his thinking.

Many of the above ethical theories suggest that there is a clear distinction between right and wrong and good and bad. However, in the real world there tend to be lots of grey areas. Therefore, in the application of ethical theories the aim of serving the common good has to be tempered with the admission of right and duties. The problem is that rights and duties cannot be examined separately and neither can be considered without regard to collective welfare. When acting ethically it is important to consider the following questions: How will an action affect the common good? What is its likely degree of utility and disutility?

underlying causes for individuals and organisations making poor choices when considering ethical issues are:

- individuals and/or organisations are sometimes immature
- economic self-interest is overwhelming
- special circumstances outweigh ethical concerns
- lack of education in the areas of morality and ethics
- potential rewards outweigh possible punishments for unethical behaviour
- the culture or mindset is that 'all's fair in love, war and business'
- there is organisational pressure on individuals to commit unethical acts.

ethics
The discipline dealing with what is good and bad, and with moral duty and obligations.

ethical behaviour
Behaviour that conforms to accepted standards of conduct.

ethical reasoning
The process of sorting out the principles that help determine what is ethical when faced with an ethical dilemma.

ethical dilemma
A situation or problem facing an individual that involves complex and often conflicting principles of ethical behaviour.

As discussed in the 'Research focus', ethics is the discipline that deals with what is good and bad, and with moral duty and obligations. Ethical behaviour is that which conforms to accepted standards of conduct. Ethical reasoning involves sorting out the principles that help determine what is ethical when faced with an ethical dilemma. An ethical dilemma is a situation or problem facing an individual that involves complex and often conflicting principles of ethical behaviour. A classic example of an ethical dilemma would be the submarine commander who has to decide whether to stay afloat to save a downed pilot or to submerge immediately to avoid enemy aircraft. In business, ethical dilemmas often arise when managers face conflicting values. For example, a salesperson might face the dilemma of telling the truth about a product and thus losing a sale and his or her commission.

To prevent these ethical dilemmas, organisational decision-makers need to prioritise all competing values and standards of behaviour. Klein (1991) suggests that a commonly agreed upon set of ethical standards can then be developed to guide decisions when conflicting obligations, cost–benefit trade-offs and competing value choices are present. Baker (1992) recommends that, when thinking through particular dilemmas, the following questions can sharpen ethical sensitivity and moral awareness.

- Does this decision or action meet the highest societal standards about how people should interact with each other?
- Does this decision or action agree with my religious teachings and beliefs (or with my personal principles and sense of responsibility)?
- How will I feel about myself if I do this?
- Do we (or I) have a rule or policy for cases like this?
- Would I want everyone to make the same decision and take the same action if faced with these same circumstances?
- What are my true motives for considering this action?

Public justification criteria

One dilemma in determining ethical criteria concerns differences of opinion regarding what behaviours are appropriate. The rule of thumb in many business cultures is whether you would feel proud about your behaviour if every detail was published in the newspaper the next day. Baker (1992) suggests the following specific questions to ask yourself when contemplating an action using *public justification criteria*.

- How would I feel (or how will I feel) if (or when) this action becomes public knowledge?
- Will I be able to explain adequately to others why I have taken this action?
- Would others feel that my action or decision is ethical or moral?

This test does not eliminate ethical dilemmas between subcultures or different countries, however, because there are 'readers' with very different values. An international example concerning different expectations about bribery is given in the World Watch box.

Corruption in foreign aid

The United States hoped that, with the passage of the Foreign Corrupt Practices Act in 1977, other countries would follow suit. None has, however, which places American companies at a major disadvantage when operating in foreign countries with different views towards ethics. It takes only a casual vacation trip to Southeast Asia to see hundreds of copies of American products, some even with authentic-looking US company logos on them. In this part of the world it is commonplace for foreign companies to have to pay bribes to be able to conduct business, but even some westernised countries such as Germany permit legal tax deductions for bribes to win foreign business deals. How can American companies compete in such an environment?

However, the bribes and corrupt practices are not limited to private business alone; official US government aid to foreign countries for infrastructure development projects (road and water plant construction, communications projects, etc.) has been diverted for non-targeted uses. In a recent study, the World Bank received some shocking news – 40 per cent of overseas firms (including some US firms abroad) admitted to using bribery to win World Bank-sponsored projects.

A new Act is before Congress to combat the misuse of official funds from the United States – the Fair Competition in Foreign Commerce Act. The aim of this Act is twofold. First, it will block US Treasury funds from going to a country that does not have a third-party monitor in place. This action will require independent monitors to oversee the bidding on projects and disbursement of monies. Second, it will require recipient countries to establish their own anti-corruption programmes, including the use of third-party monitors.

While the aim of the Fair Competition in Foreign Commerce Act is twofold, so are the intended outcomes. This act will require countries to operate on a higher ethical level, eliminating bribery and the diverting of funds for non-specified uses (especially since these are US Government funds). Second, it should place US companies in a better position to compete with foreign firms when bidding on development contracts.

Source: adapted from James Srodes (2000) 'Curbs on Foreign Bribery – and Foreign Aid', *World Trade*, Irvine, February, p. 12.

Discussion questions

1 Should companies be able to use bribes to win business in countries where the practice is accepted?

2 If it is acceptable to use bribes overseas, would it be acceptable to use bribes in the home country?

Values as benchmarks

Since neither the home nor host country values are absolute, and nor do they hold for both countries, some type of transitional, or compromise, criteria need to be established that satisfy all parties concerned with the interactions. Nevertheless, there are some moral values that might be so important to a party that they should never be compromised. These are core values, or *absolute values*, like those established by the United Nations regarding basic human rights. *Compatible values* are statements of desirable ways of behaving that support absolute values. One example is a credo statement of a company that states how members should behave to live up to the company's absolute values. *Transitional values* are those that bend somewhat from absolute and compatible values to be more compatible with the different values of another culture. For example, the limits established for gift-giving in the United Kingdom might be less than those allowed for Japan, where the custom is to be more extravagant. These are values in tension, which may or may not endure depending on the consequences. Finally, there are *intolerable values*, which are so opposed to our core values that no interaction with the people holding them is possible. Donaldson (1996) suggests that countries allowing slave labour, or dangerous procedures with high death rates, would not be viable business partners for a company in a country where human rights are seen as important.

Source: *San Diego Union-Tribune*, 14 August 1999, p. C – 4. Copyright 1999 G.B. Trudeau.
Reprinted with permission of Universal Press Syndicate, Inc. All rights reserved.

Applying moral frameworks to ethical decisions

Competing ethical criteria can also create ethical dilemmas within the same culture. Take the dilemma faced by John Higgins in the following situation.

John Higgins is director of research for a large company in the electronics industry. He recently promoted Mary Jones to head the design team charged with developing a critical component for a new radar system. He evaluated Mary as having superior knowledge of the technical elements in the project. However, he had begun to hear that the members of the all-male team were complaining about a woman leading them. There was evidence that some team members were subtly sabotaging the project. John knew it was fair to give Mary this job based on her merits, but he also knew that the successful and quick completion of the project was essential both for the company's success and his own reputation. He wondered if he should remove Mary as team leader.

John Higgins' problem is typical of the complex decisions managers face much of the time. According to Boatright (1993), these problems can be viewed from different points of view, including economic, legal and moral frameworks. A strictly *economic* framing of this problem would consider what is most efficient and effective in terms of minimising costs and maximising efficiency and profits. From this point of view, Higgins would probably opt to remove Mary Jones as team leader. The *legal* view is concerned with whether or not a given act violates the law. Using a legal framework Higgins would ask such questions as: 'Would removing Mary be illegal because of gender discrimination?' and 'Does management have the legal right to assign duties?' From this viewpoint, Higgins may need legal advice in making his decision. Viewing this problem from a *moral* framework raises a different set of questions. Two basic ones are: 'Would such a move be right?' and 'Would it be fair and just?' A decision might be both economically wise and legal and still be immoral.

Some people believe that moral considerations apply to their personal lives but not to their business decisions. Those with this viewpoint believe that economic and legal considerations are the only relevant basis for making sound business decisions. What is most profitable overrides moral considerations, assuming legality. This does not mean such people believe business is an immoral activity. Rather they would see it as amoral, which means business runs according to its own rules. They assume that laws provide the necessary rules for conducting business, so the relevant questions are: Is the behaviour profitable, and is it legal? If John Higgins held this amoral view, he would probably replace Mary. However, he might believe that moral issues are relevant for work as well as for personal behaviour. Managers face difficult decisions when they must balance moral considerations and organisational goals.

Morality

morality
A set of principles defining right and wrong behaviours.

What, then, is a moral viewpoint? **Morality** is a set of principles defining right and wrong behaviours. Boatright (1993) suggests that a behaviour is considered moral if it conforms to a standard of right behaviour. The concept of ethics is closely related to morality, and the terms *moral* and *ethical* are frequently used synonymously.

Rest (1988), however, suggests that ethics cannot be taught. The reasoning, partially, is that people may be taught ethical behaviour, but that is no guarantee they will behave ethically. While this is true, the starting point is to teach people to recognise the ethical dimensions of a problem and to reason with ethical principles to decide on an ethical solution in a particular situation. A framework for applying moral principles to ethical dilemmas is presented below.

Moral principles

When individuals are confronted with ethical dilemmas – situations that involve conflicting or competing moral interests – it is helpful to have guiding principles for reasoning through the dilemma. Three major sets of moral principles are utilitarianism, rights and justice, as discussed in the 'Research focus' on ethical theory.

Utilitarianism

utilitarianism
Acting in such a way that the greatest good is achieved for the greatest number.

Fleming (1994) defines **Utilitarianism** as the means to act in such a way that the greatest good is achieved for the greatest number. To use utilitarianism for reasoning through an ethical dilemma, begin by identifying alternative courses of action. Then determine the benefits and harm resulting from each alternative for all relevant stakeholders that would be affected by the behaviour resulting from a decision being made. Next, select the alternative that encompasses the most benefits and least harm for the most stakeholders. This principle is similar to cost–benefit analysis, which is commonly used in business decision-making. Utilitarianism guides the decision-maker to choose the alternative that produces the greatest net social good when all the stakeholders are considered.

social good
Positive decision results such as happiness, benefit or least harm.

utility
The economic benefits realised in transactions.

In the context of a moral decision, **social good** is defined in general terms such as happiness, benefit or least harm. The broad nature of this definition sometimes makes application of the concept difficult, and people may differ in their assessments. It is easier to use the economics term, **utility**, but this has a narrower meaning, referring only to the economic benefits realised in transactions. It is much more difficult to measure happiness, benefit or good. The greater the number of stakeholders affected by a decision, the more difficult such measurement is.

Another weakness of utilitarianism is its focus on outcomes and not on the means for achieving the ends. If utilitarianism is the only principle applied, some courses of action may be suggested that conflict with other ethical principles such as rights and justice. The Higgins–Jones case exemplifies this point. Higgins might reason that he, the other employees and the company would be best served if the conflict surrounding Mary Jones was eliminated by removing her. However, such a decision would appear to violate Jones's rights, and many would question the fairness or justice of such a decision.

In spite of these limitations, the utilitarian principle can be useful. Its main value is that it helps guide decision-makers to act in ways that lead to the greatest social good. Appropriate application of utilitarianism requires considering the impact of decisions on all stakeholders and reaching decisions that benefit the largest number. Baker (1992) recommends the following questions be among those to ask when applying utilitarianism.

- What will be the short- and long-term consequences of this action?
- Who will benefit from this course of action?
- Who will be hurt?
- How will this action create good and prevent harm?

Rights

A second philosophic approach to reasoning about ethical dilemmas focuses on the rights of individuals. This approach is grounded in the work of Immanuel Kant, an eighteenth-century philosopher who believed that each individual has a right to be treated with dignity and respect and as a free and equal person. Fleming (1994) defines a right as a justified claim or entitlement that an individual can make to behave or to have others behave towards him or her in a certain way. The justification for such a claim is based on a standard accepted by a society. Sometimes

right
A justified claim or entitlement that an individual can make to behave or to have others behave towards him or her in a certain way.

these rights are explicitly stated. The Declaration of Independence identifies life, liberty and the pursuit of happiness as 'unalienable rights'. The UK's new Human Rights Act sets forth the rights of individuals. Interpretations of these specific rights are leading to many legal challenges and socially accepted moral rights.

Legal rights are codified in law, whereas *moral rights* are justified by society's generally accepted moral standards. An important basis for moral rights is Kant's principle that humanity must always be treated as an end, not merely as a means. This implies that treating another as a means is to use that person for one's own gain. Treating the individual as an end implies respect by allowing the person to choose for herself or himself in order to satisfy personal needs and goals.

Rights impose corresponding duties. These duties may either be to refrain from certain behaviour or to act out certain behaviour. For example, an individual's right to privacy imposes on others the duty to refrain from violating that privacy. Kant's notion that each individual should be treated with respect suggests that each individual has a corresponding duty to treat others with respect. If society accepts that each individual has a right to education or medical care, there are corresponding duties to provide them for those who cannot provide for themselves.

The rights approach suggests that actions that violate the rights of individuals are wrong. However, individual rights sometimes conflict. For example, the right to associate freely with whomever one chooses may conflict with the right not to be discriminated against. Fleming (1994) gives the following example: should a private club be able to determine that only men can be members? In such cases the decision-maker needs to determine which right is more important for sustaining human dignity. Is it free association or equality?

The rights approach to ethical dilemmas indicates that it is morally wrong to interfere with the moral rights of an individual. However, consideration of individual rights alone is insufficient for ethical decision-making because social costs must also be considered. Individual rights should not be achieved at an unreasonable cost to others in the society. The difficulty of defining, measuring and balancing these rights sometimes makes specific ethical decisions difficult. Both individual rights and the common good must be considered. Baker (1992) suggests the following questions be among those to ask when using the rights approach to solve ethical dilemmas.

- Would this action infringe or impinge on the moral rights or dignity of others?
- Would this action allow others freedom of choice in this matter?
- Would this action involve deceiving others in any way?

Justice

justice
Fairness in giving each person what he or she deserves.

Justice has been connected with ethics and morality more than any idea in western civilisation. **Justice** is fairness. It means giving each person what he or she deserves. Conflicts often develop when people disagree over how benefits and burdens should justly be distributed. The challenge is to determine morally what each person or group justly deserves.

One widely accepted principle that helps reason about such issues was stated by Aristotle over 2000 years ago. He postulated that equals should be treated equally and unequals unequally. Fleming (1994) suggests that, today, this principle is interpreted as meaning that 'individuals should be treated the same, unless they differ in ways that are relevant to the situation in which they are involved'. For example, two people of different gender or race who perform equally should be compensated equally. However, two people who perform and contribute differently should be paid differently, even if they are of the same gender or race. Differences based on such criteria as contribution, need and what one deserves, are sometimes used to justify unequal treatment. For example, it is widely accepted that it is just for the government to treat poor people differently than those who are wealthy. However, many would agree that it is not just, or fair, to treat Mary Jones differently than her male colleagues only because of gender.

distributive justice
The fair distribution of benefits and burdens across a group or society.

retributive justice
The fairness of blame or punishment for wrongdoers.

There are different types of justice. The kind we have been talking about so far is **distributive justice**, which refers to the fair distribution of benefits and burdens across a group or society. A second kind of justice is **retributive justice**, which is the fairness of blame or punishment for wrongdoers. For example, most would say that firing an employee for making a relatively small mistake the first time would not be fair. On the other hand, if that employee had been adequately trained and had made a similar mistake before, and if the mistake was relatively expensive, dismissal might be just.

compensatory justice
The fairness of compensation awarded to those who have been injured.

Compensatory justice is concerned with the fairness of compensation awarded to those who have been injured. For example, an employee who is sacked illegally is entitled to compensation for having been wronged. The extent of compensation that is just depends on such factors as how long the employee goes without getting work, how long the employee had been with the employer and how much hardship the illegal sacking caused the employee.

A key question to ask when making moral decisions is 'Am I treating all people equally and, if not, is such action justified?' In business and other organisations people are often treated differently in terms of their pay, job responsibilities and authority. If these differences are based on morally acceptable criteria, such as performance or experience, such unequal treatment is considered just. Differences of treatment based on such things as race, gender, religion or age are not considered just in the UK. Morally acceptable criteria, however, are different in different countries.

Baker (1992) suggests the following questions be among those to apply when deciding how to be just.

- Would I feel that this action was just (ethical or fair) if I were on the other side of the decision?
- How would I feel if this action were done to me or to someone close to me?
- Would this action or decision distribute benefits justly?
- Would it distribute hardships or burdens justly?

Cultural differences will make a difference in what is considered just, which can cause ethical dilemmas in international business transactions like those described in the World Watch box on corruption in foreign aid. The issue of bribery, for example, is one of the toughest to resolve in the international context. It regularly occurs in government as well as business even though it violates all the economic, legal and moral frameworks just discussed. The free market system is the best in the world for promoting efficient productivity, but it only works if transactions are based solely on price and quality considerations. No country in the world has laws that sanction bribery, so it is universally illegal. Furthermore, Donaldson (1996) argues that it violates the moral principles of justice (it is not fair), rights (those who produce the best quality with the lowest price are not necessarily rewarded) and utilitarianism (the greatest net social good for all stakeholders is not obtained).

As we have seen, however, not all issues can unequivocally be solved by applying previously agreed-upon standards of conduct, because such agreement is impossible. Baker (1992) suggests that, in such situations, the best that one can do is refer to personal intuition and insight. Some questions to ask yourself when dealing with these ambiguous ethical dilemmas are as follows.

- Have I searched for all alternatives? Are there other ways to look at this situation? Have I considered all points of view?
- Even if I can rationalise this decision or action, and even if I could defend it publicly, does my inner sense tell me this is right?
- What does my intuition tell me is the ethical thing to do in this situation? Have I listened to my inner voice?

Stakeholder theory

Stakeholder theory is about how a firm is managed to benefit the groups and individuals who have a stake in the organisation. This is more than just meeting the needs of its shareholders.

Attas (2004) suggests that stakeholder theory should have five conditions.

1 It must be an ethical theory in that decisions made by the organisation take into account the needs of all the stakeholders rather than the self-interest of the organisation.

2 It must clearly identify who the stakeholders are and what their stake is in the organisation.

3 The stakeholder must be identified on morally relevant grounds and not on the power they may have in the organisation.

4 The duties owed to stakeholders are specific to them because of the stake they have in the organisation and not because of their role as citizens.

5 The claims stakeholders can make are not held universally by everyone but are due to their special relationship with the organisation.

The above conditions suggest that there is a special relationship between the stakeholders and the organisation. Therefore, stakeholder theory is about considering the harm and benefits to the different groups involved in the organisation.

According to Evan and Freeman (1993) and Bowie (1998), this may mean following the Kantian theory about right treatment, or the principle of fairness as suggested by Phillips (1997). To some, stakeholder theory may be seen as another name for the ethical concerns that managers should consider as a normal part of their management of an organisation.

According to Phillips (2004), stakeholder theory 'maintains that normative or legitimate stakeholders are owed an obligation by the organisation and its leaders, while derivative stakeholders hold power over the organisation and may exert either beneficial or harmful influence on it'.

Different stakeholders want different things from organisations. Phillips (2004) argues that it is impossible to know exactly who wants what, but most often discussions revolve around who should have a stake in the wealth an organisation creates, rather than how the organisation has created its wealth.

The difficulty for managers is how to prioritise among an organisation's stakeholders; often it is the job of the human resource manager to find out what employees want, while the public relations manager may be tasked with the role of identifying the needs of the local community. However, the reality should be that all managers should take responsibility for stakeholder interaction and it should not reside in specialised departments.

Much of the debate around stakeholder theory is whether business ethics is different from everyday ethics. Carr (1968), in his comparison of the game of poker to business ethics, made this statement:

> Poker's own brand of ethics is different from the ethical ideals of civilised human relationships. The game calls for distrust of the other fellow. It ignores the claim of friendship. Cunning deception and concealment of one's strength and intentions, not kindness and openheartedness, are vital in poker. No one thinks any worse of poker on that account. And no one should think any worse of business because its standards of right and wrong differ from the prevailing traditions of morality in our society. (Carr, 1968)

This suggests that the ethics of business is of a lesser standard than the ethics of society, and some people have suggested that this should be the case. However, Phillips (2004) contends that the opposite should be true and that businesses should recognise that they need to act upon their obligations and responsibilities. He counteracts Carr's statement by saying:

> Running an organisation does not licence a manager to violate the norms and standards of society, but instead introduces a brand new set of moral considerations based on stakeholder obligations. In the respect of normatively legitimate stakeholders (e.g. financiers, employees, customers), the ethics of business implies more obligations rather than less. (Phillips, 2004)

Recognising an ethical organisation

Pastin (1986) provides the following four principles for highly ethical organisations.

1 They are at ease interacting with diverse internal and external stakeholder groups. The ground rules of these firms make the good of these stakeholder groups part of the organisation's own good.

2 They are obsessed with fairness. Their ground rules emphasise that the other person's interests count as much as their own.

3 Responsibility is individual rather than collective, with individuals assuming personal responsibility for the actions of the organisation. These organisations' ground rules mandate that individuals are responsible to themselves.

4 They see their activities in terms of purpose. This purpose is a way of operating that members of the organisation value highly. And purpose ties the organisation to its environment.

Another way is to identify if an organisation operates with integrity, this can be done by demonstrating if:

- there exists a clear vision and picture of integrity throughout the organisation
- the vision is owned and embodied by top management, over time
- the reward system is aligned with the vision of integrity
- policies and practices of the organisation are aligned with the vision; no mixed messages
- it is understood that every significant management decision has ethical value dimensions
- everyone is expected to work through conflicting-stakeholder value perspectives.

The following guidelines can help with the integration of ethics in an organisation.

Recognise that managing ethics is a process

Ethics is a matter of values and associated behaviours. Values are discerned through the process of ongoing reflection. Therefore, ethics programmes may seem more process-orientated than most management practices. Managers tend to be sceptical of process-orientated activities, and instead prefer processes focused on deliverables with measurements. However, experienced managers realise that the deliverables of standard management practices (planning, organising, motivating, controlling) are only tangible representations of very process-orientated practices. For example, the process of strategic planning is much more important than the plan produced by the process. The same is true for ethics management. Ethics programmes do produce deliverables (e.g. codes, policies and procedures, budget items, meeting minutes, authorisation forms, newsletters). However, the most important aspect from an ethics management programme is the process of reflection and dialogue that produces these deliverables.

The bottom line of an ethics programme is accomplishing preferred behaviours in the workplace

As with any management practice, the most important outcome is behaviours preferred by the organisation. The best of ethical values and intentions are relatively meaningless unless they generate fair and just behaviours in the workplace. That's why practices that generate lists of ethical values, or codes of ethics, must also generate policies, procedures and training that translate those values to appropriate behaviours.

The best way to handle ethical dilemmas is to avoid their occurrence in the first place

That's why practices such as developing codes of ethics and codes of conduct are so important. Their development sensitises employees to ethical considerations and minimises the chances of unethical behaviour occurring in the first place.

Make ethics decisions in groups, and make decisions public, as appropriate

This usually produces better-quality decisions by including diverse interests and perspectives, and increases the credibility of the decision process and outcome by reducing suspicion of unfair bias.

Integrate ethics management with other management practices

When developing the values statement during strategic planning, include ethical values preferred in the workplace. When developing personnel policies, reflect on what ethical values you'd like to be most prominent in the organisation's culture and then design policies to produce these behaviours.

Use cross-functional teams when developing and implementing the ethics management programme

It's vital that the organisation's employees feel a sense of participation and ownership in the programme if they are to adhere to its ethical values. Therefore, include employees in developing and operating the programme.

Value forgiveness

This may sound rather religious or preachy to some, but it's probably the most important component of any management practice. An ethics management programme may at first actually increase the number of ethical issues to be dealt with because people are more sensitive to their occurrence. Consequently, there may be more occasions to address people's unethical behaviour. The most important ingredient for remaining ethical is trying to be ethical. Therefore, help people recognise and address their mistakes and then support them to continue to try operate ethically.

Note that trying to operate ethically and making a few mistakes is better than not trying at all

Some organisations have become widely known for operating in a highly ethical manner (e.g. Ben & Jerry's, Johnson & Johnson, Aveda, Hewlett-Packard). Unfortunately, it seems that when an organisation achieves this strong public image, it's placed on a pedestal by some business ethics writers. All organisations are composed of people, and people are not perfect. However, when a mistake is made by any of these organisations, the organisation has a long way to fall. In our increasingly critical society, these organisations are accused of being hypocritical and they are soon pilloried by social critics. Consequently, some leaders may fear sticking their necks out publicly to announce an ethics management programme. This is extremely unfortunate. It's the *trying* that counts and brings peace of mind – not achieving heroic status in society.

Individual differences in decision styles

Driver *et al.* (1993) contend that individuals do not always follow ethical guidelines or the rational problem-solving process just described. Even when they do, there are variances due to individual information-processing habits. Some differences involve satisficing versus optimising preferences. Others are determined by the amount of information people prefer and the criteria they focus on when making decisions.

Decision styles refer to our learned habits for processing decision-making information. Whether one style is 'better' than another depends on the particular situation in which it is used. There are two primary ways that people differ in their decision-making habits: (1) in the amount of information they use; and (2) in the number of alternatives they develop to potentially solve a problem.

decision styles
Learned habits for processing decision-making information.

Amount and focus of information processing

Some people use a great deal of information in generating and evaluating alternatives, while others use very little. When faced with a problem, a *satisficer* uses just enough information to arrive at a feasible solution. The satisficer knows that more information about the problem might be available but decides that it is not worth the additional effort to obtain it.

A *maximiser*, on the other hand, continues to gather information until nothing new can be learned about the problem. A maximiser knows that a workable solution might be reached with less information but decides that important aspects of the problem might not be recognised unless all available information is considered.

Both methods are valuable in appropriate situations. For example, the satisficer has an advantage when time is important, whereas the maximiser has an advantage when problems are complicated and there is little time pressure.

Solution focus refers to the number of alternatives that a person develops for dealing with a problem. *Unifocus* people are committed to one dominate criterion and consequently favour a single solution to a problem. *Multifocus* people, on the other hand, apply several criteria and generate several solutions to a problem. The unifocus approach has an advantage when efficiency is important, when it is possible to adopt only one solution, or when rules and regulations narrowly limit the range of choices. The multifocus approach has an advantage when there is a need to find new ways of doing things or it is important to 'cover all the bases'.

The five dominant decision styles

From these differences in amount of information used and solution focus, five fundamentally different decision styles emerge. Exhibit 12-7 illustrates the relationships among the five decision styles.

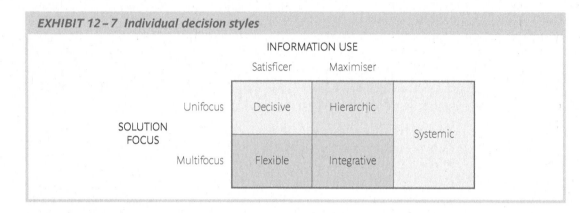

EXHIBIT 12–7 Individual decision styles

Decisive style

Decisive persons use just enough information to reach one workable solution. Decisives are fast-thinking, action-orientated people who place high importance on efficiency, promptness and reliability. They usually stick to one course of action for dealing with a particular problem.

Flexible style

People with this style also use a minimal amount of information, but they are multifocused and so produce several solutions to a problem. Like decisives, flexibles are action orientated, but they place greater importance on adaptability than on efficiency. They like to keep their options open.

Hierarchic style

People with the hierarchic style analyse a large amount of information thoroughly to develop a single, best solution to a problem. They place great emphasis on logic and quality. Hierarchical organisations tend to be slow to make decisions the first time they encounter a particular problem, but they speed up substantially after they develop a method for handling that type of problem.

Integrative style

People with this style utilise a very large amount of information to produce multiple solutions to problems. Integrative people value exploration, experimentation and creativity. They look at problems from many points of view and see numerous options for dealing with a single problem. Consequently, they sometimes have difficulty deciding on only one solution, which makes them appear indecisive. To counter this tendency, integrative people sometimes try to implement several courses of action simultaneously.

Systemic style

This two-stage decision style combines both integrative and hierarchic patterns. A person using the systemic style initially approaches a problem in the integrative way, viewing it from many points of view and exploring multiple solutions. After examining many options, however, the person becomes more hierarchic, subjecting various alternatives to a rigorous analysis that ends with a clearly prioritised set of solutions. The systemic person usually develops a very broad understanding of a problem. In many cases, systemic people examine multiple problems simultaneously to understand the broader implications of situations. Because of the thoroughness of their analyses, systemic people tend to be slow decision-makers.

Back-up styles

Although most people have a clear predisposition towards one dominant decision style, many shift to a different 'back-up' style occasionally. The shift between dominant and back-up styles is related to how much pressure a person experiences when making decisions.

Under the pressure of tight deadlines, high risk and significant consequences, people tend to shift to the less complex decisive or flexible styles, which are easier and faster to use. These styles are also frequently used under low pressure if there is not enough information to employ a more complex style. Under moderate pressure, people tend to use the more complex systemic, integrative or hierarchic styles because there is a lot of information available and sufficient time to analyse it in depth.

The importance of participation in decision-making

Who should be involved in the problem-solving process? Just the manager? A committee? A coalition of key individuals? The entire department? The Halewood case in Chapter 5 highlights the value of involving the workforce in decision-making.

Degrees of decision participation

Cotton *et al.* (1988) suggest that there is evidence that participation can enhance morale, satisfaction and productivity, but in emergencies or when others do not have sufficient information, an autocratic decision may be more appropriate. Vroom and Jago (1988) have developed a diagnostic framework for matching the amount of participation in decision-making with situational requirements. Their five possible decision-making processes, described in Exhibit 12-8, vary in the degrees of participation they allow.

Criteria for participation in decision-making

When deciding how much participation to use when making a decision, several factors need to be considered. Three of the most important criteria are the quality requirements, the degree that it is necessary for subordinates to accept the decision, and the time required to make the decision.

EXHIBIT 12–8 Types of participation in decisions

Key: A = Autocratic, C = Consultant, G = Group; I and II denote variations of a process

AI You solve the problem or make the decision yourself, using information available at the time.

AII You obtain the necessary information from your subordinate(s), then decide on the solution to the problem yourself. You may or may not tell your subordinates what the problem is in getting the information from them. The role played by your subordinates in making the decision is clearly one of providing the necessary information to you, rather than generating or evaluating alternative solutions.

CI You share the problem with relevant subordinates individually, getting their ideas and suggestions without bringing them together as a group. Then you make the decision that may or may not reflect your subordinates' influence.

CII You share the problem with your subordinates as a group, collectively obtaining their ideas and suggestions. Then you make the decision that may or may not reflect your subordinates' influence.

GII You share the problem with your subordinates as a group. Together you generate and evaluate alternatives and attempt to reach agreement (consensus) on a solution. Your role is much like that of chairman. You do not try to influence the group to adopt 'your' solution, and you are willing to accept and implement any solution that has the support of the entire group.

Source: reprinted from *Organizational Dynamics*, Spring 1973.
© 1973 with permission from Elsevier Science.

Quality requirements

Whether a decision is best made by an individual or a group depends on the nature and importance of the problem. Important decisions that have major impacts on organisational goal achievement need to be of the highest possible quality. In complex situations, it is unlikely that any one individual will have all the necessary information to make a top-quality decision. Therefore, the decision-maker should at least consult with others who are either closer to the problem or more 'expert' in dealing with it. One person with appropriate knowledge and experience, on the other hand, can decide what to do to solve simple routine problems.

Acceptance requirements

The effectiveness of the action plan decided upon is a combination of its quality and the effort put into implementing it. A top-quality decision, if not implemented appropriately, will not be effective. A lower-quality decision that receives enthusiastic support from all involved may be more effective than a higher-quality alternative that implementers do not 'buy into'.

Those affected by a decision are usually more highly motivated to implement the action plan if they have had an opportunity to influence it. Being involved usually increases participants' understanding and generates a feeling of commitment to make 'our' decision work, whereas an arbitrary, autocratic decision that is handed down often results in passive acceptance or even active resistance to implementation. This will be elaborated on in Chapter 17.

Time requirements

Allocating problem-solving and decision-making to a group requires a greater investment of time in meetings, which is then unavailable for usual tasks. Nevertheless, the level of acceptance and probability of efficient execution is greater for participative decisions than autocratic methods. In addition, a higher-quality decision may also result from the inclusion of a variety of perspectives and approaches. It is important to determine if this additional time investment produces significantly higher degrees of quality, acceptance and commitment.

Research focus: Vroom and Jago's decision tree – determining the appropriate degree of participation in decision-making

The specific needs for quality, acceptance and time provide the impetus for choosing from the five degrees of participation considering the optimum approach to a particular decision. Vroom and Jago (1988) have found that the answers to seven questions about decision quality and acceptance can indicate the most appropriate degree of participation in any given decision situation. Exhibit 12-9 illustrates the appropriate sequence of three questions regarding quality and four questions regarding acceptance, in a decision-tree format.

It is possible that more than one style will be appropriate for a particular problem situation. In that case, the optimal style indicated by this model is the more autocratic one because it will require the least amount of time to implement. Therefore, the decision tree is most useful in situations where time is a critical factor. It does not take into consideration such long-term factors as morale or employee development. In a situation where increased group cohesiveness and worker morale are important, it may be more appropriate to choose a more time-consuming decision style that emphasises team development. While the autocratic style takes far less time, it does not address the long-term developmental needs of the individuals involved.

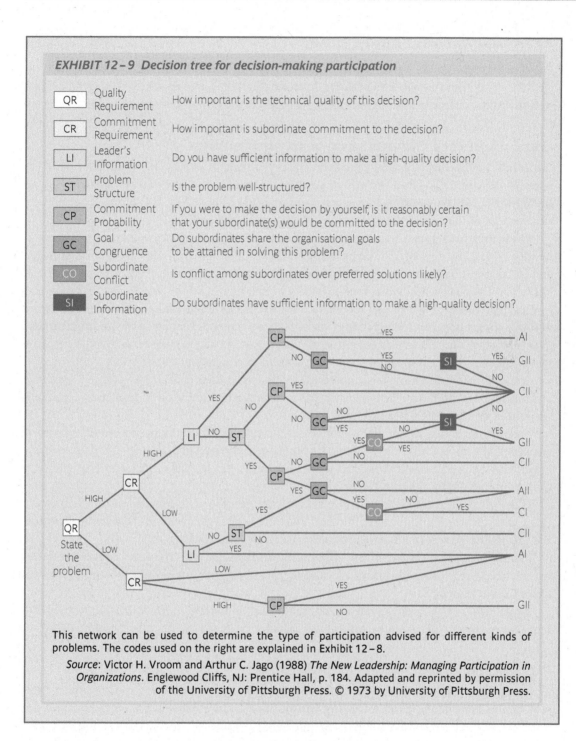

EXHIBIT 12–9 Decision tree for decision-making participation

QR	Quality Requirement	How important is the technical quality of this decision?
CR	Commitment Requirement	How important is subordinate commitment to the decision?
LI	Leader's Information	Do you have sufficient information to make a high-quality decision?
ST	Problem Structure	Is the problem well-structured?
CP	Commitment Probability	If you were to make the decision by yourself, is it reasonably certain that your subordinate(s) would be committed to the decision?
GC	Goal Congruence	Do subordinates share the organisational goals to be attained in solving this problem?
CO	Subordinate Conflict	Is conflict among subordinates over preferred solutions likely?
SI	Subordinate Information	Do subordinates have sufficient information to make a high-quality decision?

This network can be used to determine the type of participation advised for different kinds of problems. The codes used on the right are explained in Exhibit 12–8.

Source: Victor H. Vroom and Arthur C. Jago (1988) *The New Leadership: Managing Participation in Organizations.* Englewood Cliffs, NJ: Prentice Hall, p. 184. Adapted and reprinted by permission of the University of Pittsburgh Press. © 1973 by University of Pittsburgh Press.

Solving problems more effectively

Techniques for avoiding 'groupthink' and the liabilities of group decision-making discussed in Chapter 10 can enhance group problem-solving effectiveness. Other methods for solving problems better include encouraging creativity, structured processes for guiding interaction, and electronic information processing.

Encouraging creativity

For organisations to solve problems creatively, managers have to demonstrate that they value creativity and know how to deal with innovations when they are suggested. Research has identified how some characteristics of managers generate creativity in their organisations.

Characteristics of managers who generate creativity

Campbell (1978) suggests that managers who encourage creativity are willing to *absorb risks* taken by subordinates. They allow their people freedom, expect some errors, and are willing to learn from inevitable failures. Managers who are afraid of mistakes, on the other hand, restrict the freedom of their subordinates to experiment and be creative.

Productive managers of creativity can live with *half-developed ideas.* They do not insist that an idea be 100 per cent proven before supporting its development. They are willing to listen to and encourage subordinates to press on with 'half-baked' proposals that hold promise. They know that criticism can kill innovation.

Creative managers have a feel for the times when the company rulebook needs to be ignored and will *stretch normal policies* for the greater long-term good. Managers who permit no deviation from standard operating procedures will make predictable progress and avoid mistakes but will not obtain the giant breakthroughs that calculated risk-taking can promote.

Productive managers are *good listeners.* They listen to their staff, try to pull out good ideas, and build on suggestions. They do not try to impose new policies or procedures on people without listening to the other side first.

Creative managers *do not dwell on mistakes.* They are more future orientated than past orientated. They do not hold the mistakes of others against them indefinitely. They are willing to begin with the world as it is today and work for a better future. They learn from experience, but they do not wallow in the past.

When good ideas are presented, productive managers are willing to decide on the spot to try them without waiting for further studies. They are courageous enough to *trust their intuition* and commit resources to implementing promising innovations.

Finally, productive managers are *enthusiastic and invigorating.* They encourage and energise others. They enjoy using the resources and power of their position to push projects forward and make improvements.

To determine how creative you are, complete the 'Your turn' exercise. If your score is not as high as you would like, a number of ways to enhance creativity are described in the next section.

Promoting creative thinking in organisations

To encourage creativity, a manager needs to provide a bureaucracy-free environment that tolerates diverse behaviour. When a wealthy patron once asked Pablo Picasso what he could do to help him, Picasso looked at him and said succinctly, 'Stand out of my light' (Campbell, 1978). Cocks (1990) highlights several examples of how universities and businesses have promoted creativity by eliminating organisational barriers:

> In a course at one university, students are requested to build the tallest structure possible out of ice lolly sticks and then look for 'the insight in every failure'. Those who end up with the highest projects went through the most failures. Whoever followed a fixed idea from the outset never finished first.

Your turn

How creative are you?

Place a check mark by the 10 words in the following list that best characterise you.

energetic	persuasive	observant	fashionable	self-confident
persevering	original	cautious	habit-bound	resourceful
egotistical	independent	stern	predictable	formal
informal	dedicated	factual	open-minded	forward-looking
tactful	inhibited	enthusiastic	innovative	poised
acquisitive	practical	alert	curious	organised
unemotional	dynamic	polished	courageous	clear-thinking
helpful	efficient	perceptive	quick	self-demanding
good-natured	thorough	impulsive	determined	understanding
realistic	modest	involved	flexible	absent-minded
sociable	well-liked	restless	retiring	

Scoring key For each of the following adjectives that you checked, give yourself 2 points:

energetic	resourceful	original	enthusiastic	dynamic
flexible	observant	independent	perceptive	innovative
persevering	dedicated	courageous	curious	self-demanding
involved				

For each of the following adjectives that you checked, give yourself 1 point:

thorough	determined	restless	informal	self-confident
alert	open-minded	forward-looking		

The rest of the adjectives receive no points.

Add up your total number of points: _____

Interpretation

16–20	Very creative
11–15	Above average
6–10	Average
1–5	Below average
0	Non-creative

Source: adapted from Eugene Raudsepp (1981) *How Creative Are You?* New York, NY: Putnam, pp. 22–24.

Training students to learn from mistakes and try, try again may be good training for future careers in business. But 'You cannot just order up a good idea or spend money to find one', points out Jon Henderson, director of Hallmark Cards' Creative Resources Centre. 'You have to build a supportive climate and give people the freedom to create things.'

One famous example of how a creative climate can pay off is some advertising agencies, where employees are encouraged to devote some of their work time to non-job-related creative thinking. The advertising agency Saatchi & Saatchi has recreation rooms where designers can kick a ball around; staff may also be found watching *Teletubbies* on TV; they also have their own pub.

Despite the obvious benefits creative risk-taking has brought to companies, not all managers are comfortable with the adjustments necessary for creating a climate that nurtures creativity. Research by Alari (1991) has found that managers with negative feelings about creativity feel that it is uncontrollable, which is anathema to a manager whose job is to control. Consequently, many managers are fearful and unwilling to give up their power and control. For those managers who see the necessity for creativity but are still apprehensive, several structured alternatives to promoting problem-solving creativity exist that do not entail giving up control in the work environment. Among them are brainstorming, the nominal group technique and the Delphi technique.

Brainstorming

Brainstorming is a demonstrated approach for achieving high participation and increasing the number of action alternatives (Osborn, 1957). To engage in brainstorming sessions, people meet in small groups and feed off one another's ideas, which provide stimuli for more creative solutions. Rules for effective brainstorming promote the goal of quantity of ideas, no matter how far-fetched, allow no criticism or evaluation of ideas as they are generated, allow only one idea at a time from each person, and encourage people to build on each other's ideas.

brainstorming
A small-group approach for achieving high participation and increasing the number of action alternatives.

Brainstorming groups are encouraged to be freewheeling and radical. Through use of a non-evaluative environment that is intentionally fun, brainstorming ensures involvement, enthusiasm, and a large number of solution alternatives. The Garbage Can model shown in Exhibit 12-10 in the 'Research focus' box is one method that can be used in these situations.

Brainstorming generally works well in a participative, team-orientated climate where people are comfortable with each other and are committed to pulling together towards a common goal. In some situations it may not be effective, however. One example occurred in Paris, France, where the expatriate general manager from the United States attempted a brainstorming session with department managers and, instead of a number of excited ideas, was met with a room full of frowns and complete silence. When he enquired why there were no responses, he was told very seriously that he was the director general, and it was his job to tell them what to do. The staff's job was to follow orders and accept his suggestions, not to do his job for him.

At other times, a hostile or political climate might inhibit the free flow of ideas. In restrictive interpersonal climates, more structured techniques like the nominal group or Delphi group technique may be more effective. The recent development of electronic brainstorming, described in the Technology Transformation box, can also circumvent the need for face-to-face brainstorming meetings.

Nominal group technique

In the **nominal group technique**, Van de Ven and Delbecq (1974) suggest that participants meet together in a highly structured format that governs the decision-making process. First, participants independently write down their ideas about the problem. Second, each presents one idea to the group in a round-robin fashion without discussion. These ideas are summarised and written on a flip chart or whiteboard so all can see them. After a group discussion to clarify and evaluate the ideas, an independent ranking of the proposals takes place. These rankings are pooled to determine the proposal with the highest aggregate ranking, which is the group's decision.

nominal group technique
A highly structured group problem-solving format that governs the decision-making process.

Small business solutions: two laptops are better than one – using networked laptops in brainstorming sessions can yield more ideas

We have all been there. In a meeting, searching for ideas to create new business or solve an old problem, out comes the obligatory flip chart and a set of markers. Then the tired mantra 'all ideas are good ideas' is recited before all present attempt to come up with some groundbreaking creative thinking. However, do these traditional techniques actually work?

Ray Elmitt, founder of Crystal Interactive, which regularly runs brainstorming sessions for companies using wirelessly networked laptop computers, believes that traditional ways of generating ideas are largely unproductive.

'Ideas are batted up on to flip charts, and groups find it difficult to separate the generation of ideas from the evaluation stage. It slows down really fast as people start to criticise the ideas,' he says.

Elmitt estimates that in a traditional session with a group of about six people you are only going to get about 15–20 ideas. With the same group using wireless-enabled brainstorming technology, he often gets three times that number in about five minutes.

That probably explains why a range of companies from the BBC and ITV to major airlines are organising sessions on anything from strategy to product development using these new technology-based techniques.

In a typical Crystal Interactive brainstorming session, all participants are given their own laptop, which lets them input their ideas anonymously. Meanwhile, on their screen they can see all the other contributions that are being simultaneously submitted by other members in the session.

'Everyone has a PC so everybody can effectively speak at once instead of waiting their turn. You just key your ideas in. It's much faster because they are anonymous and people are not afraid to put forward ideas,' explains Elmitt.

He feels that in a traditional business environment ideas can be shot down, not on grounds of quality but simply because of the position of the person who suggested them.

The company works in advance with all of its clients to agree the subjects that are to be addressed by a team and then acts as a facilitator to assist the real-time collaborative process. 'We help the groups to generate loads of ideas, evaluate them and organise them into themes so they understand them. Then we home in on a few vital areas,' Elmitt explains.

He admits that the generation of a large volume of ideas is not in itself a guarantee of quality, but he points out that it does give more options to work with. Working anonymously, participants are invited to group results under headings and then they can vote in real time on issues of importance and the priority actions to be taken.

Dotcoms were famous for introducing flatter organisations to promote the faster sharing of information, and the Crystal Interactive approach carries forward this culture.

The tailored software that facilitates this new brainstorming process is a product called groupSystems; it was produced by Ventana Corporation, which is a commercial offshoot of the University of Arizona.

But what do the participants feel about this new way of exchanging ideas? Andrew Oldham, e-commerce standards manager for Intel, recently used the wireless laptops as part of an e-business workshop on investment issues and he felt the technology helped people overcome their normal inhibitions.

'You get good ideas, which traditionally you might not get because people might be unwilling to express them,' he says.

▶ Based in Kingston upon Thames, Crystal Interactive (www.crystal-interactive.co.uk) works with a permanent core staff of just three, but with extra help available on contract. A lot of the company's methods are used by organisations overseas and while the group decision-making technology is potentially available to anyone, it tends to be high-tech organisations and the financial services industry that use it the most at the moment.

Adrian Abbott, b2b finance manager for Sainsbury's, has been on a Crystal Interactive work-shop and he came away impressed with the efficiency of the process: 'The technology enables you to gather ideas from a wide variety of people very rapidly.'

Nevertheless, for small groups, he thinks face-to-face discussions are more effective and he feels the technology-based process does not allow enough scope for people to challenge and react to the instantly generated findings.

However, Peter Lewy, director of learning and development for Exel plc, a global supply chain management company, believes it is important for employees to feel their opinions are valued, and he likes the immediacy of technology-enabled brainstorming.

Exel has used Crystal Interactive in order to make its conferences more interactive. Rather than leaving staff to pay lip-service to someone addressing them from a stage, he explains they wanted to get employees more involved with the development of the organisation. 'Too much communica-tion is top down. This gives instant opportunities for sideways and upwards feedback.'

Copies of the output of the sessions are printed off quickly, but Lewy accepts that the use of the technology will not necessarily mean much unless the feedback is acted on. He also believes it will be a while before traditional managers make non-hierarchical group decision-making part of their day-to-day practices.

Source: © Guardian Newspapers Ltd, 2001, Justin Hunt.

Discussion questions

1 How does this method involve everyone in the decision-making process?

2 Using this process why is there likely to be a higher commitment to the chosen decision?

Research focus: **the Garbage Can model**

Garbage Can model
Views decision-making as a mix up of choice process, problems, solutions and participants.

The Garbage Can model deals with the pattern of flow of multiple decisions within an organisation, referred to by Cohen *et al.* (1971) as 'Organised Anarchy'.

It is used to explain the pattern of decision-making in organisations that experience extremely high uncer-tainty and does not rely on normal vertical hierarchies.

The Garbage Can model is based on three premises.

1 There are problematic preferences, where goals, problems, alternatives and solutions are ill-defined and ambiguity characterises each step.

2 There is unclear and poorly understood technology, which means the cause-and-effect rela-tionships are difficult to identify.

3 Turnover: employees change rapidly, or they are busy and offer only limited time to one decision.

stream of events
The choice of opportunities that flow in and out of an organisation.

According to the Garbage Can model (see Exhibit 12-10), the decision process is not seen as a sequence of steps but rather as a **stream of events**.

Stream of events

The stream of events consists of the following.

- **Problems:** the problems are the difference between the situation now and the desired situation. The problems are seen as independent from the alternatives and solutions.
- **Potential solutions:** the solutions are the constant flow of ideas through an organisation. In this model solutions are used to formulate problems rather than the other way around. This is the opposite to the classical model. It suggests that managers often do not know what they want until they have some idea of the potential solutions that are available.
- **Participants:** these are the members of the organisation who contribute to the decision-making process. They are not static and will bring different values, attitudes and experiences to the process.
- **Choice of opportunities:** these are the occasions when the organisation is expected to make a decision. Some of these decisions occur regularly, such as recruitment and selection of employees, others may result from a crisis, such as the fuel blockades of 2000.

Consequences of the Garbage Can model

- Solutions may be proposed even when problems do not exist.
- Choices are made without solving problems.
- Problems may persist without being solved.
- A few problems are solved but often this is only by chance.

The implications for management highlight an important feature of decision-making in organisations. Often the choosing and implementation of solutions is done by different people in the organisations and it is the job of managers to ensure that what was chosen is implemented. As we have said, many problems go unsolved as often there is no agreement between the match of problems to solutions. Often it is only when a problem and solution meet together by chance, and the decision-maker has recognised it as so, that a solution is implemented. Therefore, it is the focus of the manager to find the links between problems and solutions.

EXHIBIT 12 – 10 The Garbage Can model of organisational decision-making

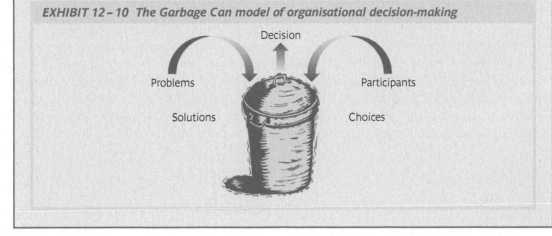

The nominal group technique offers the advantages of multiple idea generation, balanced participation and participant satisfaction. It is time consuming and does require participants to meet together at a common location. In any group decision-making situation, the advantages and disadvantages of a proposed technique should be weighed with respect to the nature of the participants and the specific decision being made.

Delphi technique

In the **Delphi technique**, Dalkey and Helmer (1963) recommend that participants do not meet together but interact through a series of written judgements and suggestions. After each participant has been presented with the problem, he or she writes down comments and possible solutions and sends them to a central location for recording and reproduction. Each participant then receives a copy of all other comments and solutions to use as a springboard for additional ideas or comments. These also are returned to the central location for compilation and reproduction, and an independent vote on solution priority is taken.

Delphi technique
A structured group problem-solving process where participants do not meet together but interact through a series of written judgements and suggestions.

The Delphi technique allows for the pooling of a variety of ideas, viewpoints, independent feedback and criticism at minimal expense, since participants do not have to congregate at a common meeting place. It does, however, take an extended period of time and there is really no control over the decision-making process. Depending on the nature of the decision group, participants' lack of face-to-face interaction can be either an asset or a liability.

Studies by Van de Ven and Delbecq (1974) have examined the effectiveness of both the nominal group technique and the Delphi technique and traditional interaction groups. These studies have revealed that significantly more ideas tend to be generated by the nominal group and Delphi techniques than the traditional group, and satisfaction tends to be higher using the nominal group technique than the Delphi or traditional groups (Van de Ven and Delbecq, 1974).

Group decision support systems

Group decision support systems are electronic and computer-supported data-processing tools that can facilitate group decision-making in certain situations. 'Same time-same place' interactions among team members can be facilitated by software tools such as mathematical models, spreadsheets, graphics packages and electronic brainstorming activities. 'Same place-different time' interactions are supported by such tools as retrieval systems for information sharing and display software. 'Same time-different place' group interactions can be accomplished through videoconferencing, which combines audio and video communications. 'Different time-different place' decision-making can be helped by such mechanisms as electronic mail and groupware. Alari (1991) suggests that group decision support system tools have been shown to increase the efficiency of group problem-solving, better document it and produce higher-quality decisions.

group decision support systems
Electronic and computer-supported data-processing tools that can facilitate group decision-making in certain situations.

Hackney: a second look

As a senior black social services manager, one of the reasons Josephine Kwali went to Hackney was its multicultural population and workforce. 'Probably 70 per cent of the staff are black, or from a visible minority, and it's a similar figure for the families we serve, so that gave me an extra spur,' she says. 'It meant there was a point of connection and shared experience with a large proportion of staff – and that helped in terms of bringing people with me in what we were trying to achieve.'

A white male, she thinks, may not have been as effective in leading the service at this time because of the disillusionment that many black staff felt with the previous regime. 'That's because leadership is not just about making the right decisions, but also inspiring and making a connection with staff.'

Two years ago, Hackney social services had such a poor image that it was rumoured that even agency staff refused to work there. Today, in common with other inner London boroughs, the council still has a recruitment problem, but it can build on a core of loyal and increasingly motivated staff.

'People tend to either love or hate Hackney,' says Kwhali. 'But for those staff that love it, the place gets in your blood.'

Source: © Guardian Newspapers Ltd, 2002, Patrick McCurry.

Summary

- The rational problem-solving process includes identifying the problem, clarifying objectives, analysing alternatives, deciding on a solution, implementing the solution and following through to ensure its effectiveness.

- To begin solving a problem, the current situation needs to be diagnosed to understand and define the problem as accurately as possible. Hasty assumptions often contribute to a failure to distinguish a problem's symptoms from its sources.

- The immediate and long-term effects of all alternative solutions on other people and situations should be considered.

- Effective action plans contain measurable criteria and time lines. Involving the people affected by the plan in the analysis of alternatives and in decision-making will build their commitment to its implementation.

- When evaluating action plan alternatives, benefits are weighed against possible negative consequences.

- Other considerations include probability of success; associated risk factors; potential money, time and energy costs; and the possible reactions of those affected.

- Effective implementation of an action plan depends on the parties' commitment to make it work.

- Commitment to the agreed-upon solution is usually gained when problems, needs and objectives are identified mutually, and solutions are reached through the participation and consensus of all involved.

- Specific tasks and responsibilities are assigned, schedules are established and personal commitment is reinforced as the plan is activated.

- The follow-through process involves the development of procedures to monitor and assist the implementation of the new action plan.

- A control process is applied to measure performance, monitor results and take corrective actions when needed.

Areas for personal development

1 **Apply all five steps in the problem-solving process,** as follows.

   - *Problem awareness.* Focus on correctly identifying problems versus symptoms of problems. Assess the importance of the problem relative to the overall goals of the team. Is it a 'mission critical' problem or a relatively minor situation?
   - *Problem definition.* As the saying goes, 'rubbish in equals rubbish out'. Make sure you correctly define the problem so you do not create new problems.

- *Decision-making.* Establish good criteria for a decision. Then come up with alternative solutions and assess the impacts (both positive and negative) of each alternative. Choose the best alternative.

- *Action plan implementation.* Assign specific work assignments to the most appropriate people and determine how long the individual tasks will take. Once actions are under way, reinforce team commitment to the actions.

- *Follow-through.* Identify success criteria and measure the results against it. If the results do not match the success criteria, determine why and how far off the results were. Identify new actions that need to be taken.

2 **Use problem-solving tools.** Use flowcharts to analyse processes, and cause-and-effect diagrams to uncover sources of problems. Use Pareto charts to identify graphically the major causes or priorities of problems. Use decision-making grids to establish criteria and alternatives for decisions. Use a Gantt chart to identify tasks and time lines for decision implementation.

3 **Identify the ethical concerns in each specific decision situation.** Ask yourself, if I made this decision and it was published in the *Financial Times* tomorrow, how would I feel? How would others feel?

4 **Use the most appropriate personal decision-making style.** Examine the strengths and weaknesses of your dominant decision style. In situations where other decision styles are more appropriate, use them yourself or enlist others more comfortable with other styles to aid you in the decision process.

5 **Determine when and how much group participation is optimal in each decision situation.** Some decisions and problems require an autocratic approach, while others need a consultative or group approach. Recognise the difference in problems and the level of participation needed to be successful.

6 **Encourage creativity.** Show others that you value creativity by absorbing risks, living with half-developed ideas, stretching normal policies, being a good listener, not dwelling on mistakes, and committing resources to the implementation of promising innovations.

7 **Use group decision-making to enhance problem-solving effectiveness.** Use group techniques like brainstorming, the nominal group technique and the Delphi technique to enhance creative group problem-solving. If available, take advantage of computer-supported group decision support systems.

Questions for study and discussion

1 Explain why it is so important to establish an atmosphere of trust in situations of group problem-solving. Can you cite situations where you have not trusted others with whom you were involved in solving a problem? Compare them with situations in which you have felt trust. Have you ever felt that others in a group distrusted you? Why?

2 What four purposes are served by clarifying objectives early in the problem-solving process? Whose objectives should be considered?

3 Explain this statement: 'No problem solution can be better than the quality of diagnosis on which it is built.'

4 With regard to selecting an action plan, indicate whether you agree or disagree with each of the following statements and why: (1) Experience is the best teacher; (2) Intuition is a helpful force; (3) Advice from others is always beneficial; (4) Experiment with several alternatives.

5 What difficulties might you anticipate when using the rational problem-solving process? Why? What additional difficulties might arise because of personal attributes? Which of these have you experienced? Explain. What were the consequences? How can these difficulties be avoided?

6 Which decision style would be most effective at each stage of the rational problem-solving process? Why? Explain which decision style would be best for making decisions under emergency circumstances. Which is best for solving a complex problem requiring considerable creativity?

7 Explain under what circumstances you would want to use participation to solve a problem. When would you rather solve the problem individually?

8 How can a manager encourage creative problem-solving by department members?

9 How would you, as a manager, motivate your employees to engage in ethical behaviour?

🔑 Key Concepts

problem-solving, *p. 545*

decision-making, *p. 545*

objective, *p. 548*

flowchart (process flow diagram), *p. 550*

Pareto chart, *p. 552*

criteria, p. 553

certainty, *p. 554*

known risk, *p. 555*

uncertainty, *p. 555*

turbulence, *p. 555*

satisficing, *p. 556*

Gantt chart, *p. 558*

ethics, *p. 563*

ethical behaviour, *p. 563*

ethical reasoning, *p. 563*

ethical dilemma, *p. 563*

morality, *p. 566*

utilitarianism, *p. 566*

social good, *p. 566*

utility, *p. 566*

right, *p. 567*

justice, *p. 568*

distributive justice, *p. 568*

retributive justice, *p. 568*

compensatory justice, *p. 569*

decision styles, *p. 573*

brainstorming, *p. 580*

nominal group technique, *p. 580*

Garbage Can model *p. 582*

stream of events *p. 583*

Delphi technique, *p. 584*

group decision support systems, *p. 584*

Personal skills exercise

Choosing a decision style

Purpose To learn how to apply the Vroom and Jago (1974) decision participation model.

Preparation Review the section entitled 'The importance of participation in decision-making?' on page 575 of this chapter. Make sure you understand the five decision participation styles (Exhibit 12-8) and the decision participation tree (Exhibit 12-9).

Stage 1: individual case analyses Individually read each of the hypothetical cases that follow. Decide which of the five decision participation styles from Exhibit 12-8 you would use in each situation. Record your decisions.

Case A You are a manufacturing manager in the north-eastern division of a large electronics plant. Upper management is always searching for ways to increase efficiency.

Recently management installed new machines and introduced a simplified work system, but to everyone's surprise (including your own) the expected increase in productivity has not been realised. In fact, production has begun to drop, quality has fallen, and the number of employee resignations has risen.

You do not believe there is anything wrong with the machines. You have requested reports from other companies that are using them, and their responses confirm this opinion.

You have also called in representatives from the firm that built the machines. These technicians have examined the machines thoroughly and report that they are operating at peak efficiency. You suspect that some elements of the new work system may be responsible for the decreased output and quality, but this view is not shared by your five immediate subordinates: the four first-line supervisors who head your four production sections and your supply manager. They have attributed the drop in production to various factors: poor operators, insufficient training, lack of adequate financial incentives, and poor worker morale. Clearly, this is an issue about which there is considerable depth of individual feeling. There exists a high potential for discord among your five key subordinates, and this may be just the tip of the iceberg.

This morning you received a phone call from your division manager, who had just reviewed your production figures for the last six months and was clearly concerned. The division manager has indicated that the problem is yours to solve in any way you think best but has requested that you report within a week what steps you plan to take.

Certainly you share your manager's concern and you know that, despite their differing views, your subordinates share it as well. Your problem is to decide what steps must be taken by whom in the effort to reverse the decline.

Case B You are the general team leader in charge of a large work team that is laying an oil pipeline. It is now necessary to estimate your expected rate of progress in order to schedule material deliveries to the next field site.

You know the nature of the terrain you will be travelling and have the historical data you need to calculate the mean and variance in the rate of speed over that type of terrain. Given these two variables, it is a simple matter to calculate the earliest and the latest times at which materials and support facilities will be needed at the next site. It is important that your estimate be reasonably accurate. Underestimates result in idle workers, and overestimates result in holding materials for a period of time before they are to be used.

Up to this point, progress has been good. Your five group team leaders and other members of the team stand to receive substantial bonuses if the project is completed ahead of schedule.

Case C You are supervising the work of 12 nurses. All 12 have similar levels of formal training and work experience, a condition that enables you to use them interchangeably on most wards. Yesterday your manager informed you that a request had come in from a hospital in the same Health Care Trust for four nurses to go on extended loan for a period of six to eight months. For a number of reasons, he argued (and you agreed) that this request should be met from your group.

All your nurses are capable of handling this assignment and, from the standpoint of present and future projects, there is no particular reason why any one should be retained over any other. The major problem is that the location of the other hospital is considered undesirable by most members of the organisation.

Stage 2: group discussion After individuals have recorded their opinions of the most appropriate decision participation style to be used in each of these cases, proceed with the following steps.

1 Divide the class into groups of three to five people. Designate one person from each group to keep a record of each group's discussion.

2 Each person shares with others in the group why he or she chose a particular decision style for each of the three cases.

3 Focus on determining all the reasons people chose different decision styles. One person should write down the styles chosen for each case and note briefly the associated reasons.

4 **Important:** the group should not try to reach a consensus; you merely want to discover how many different approaches were taken and why.

5 Using the decision-making tree in Exhibit 12-9, individually answer the questions at the top and work through the decision tree until you reach the recommended decision style for each of the three cases.

6 Repeat step 5 as a group. Now establish consensus as to the appropriate decision style prescribed by this model.

7 Check your answers with Vroom and Yetton's, which your instructor will provide. Discuss any variations and reread the chapter explanation if misunderstandings persist.

8 Discuss within the group how original decisions agreed with or varied from the Vroom and Yetton model. Speculate as to why. The recorder should note the outcome of this group discussion.

Stage 3: class discussion Reconvene as a class. Have the group recorders report group outcomes, including discrepancies between the original (individual) analyses and Vroom and Yetton's solutions. Note any sharp disparities among the groups' responses, and try to determine why they occurred. Participate in a class discussion based on the following questions.

1 To what extent do you agree with the model? What are its strengths and weaknesses in application?

2 Do you have a preferred decision style (AI, AII, CI, CII, GII)? Why or why not? Will knowledge of this model help you be more flexible in choosing a decision style?

3 How closely does your decision behaviour match that prescribed by the model? What evidence do you have that you are concerned more with time (efficiency) or with participation in choosing a decision style?

Team exercise

Ethical decision-making (Sammet, 1992)

Purpose To practise stretching and expanding your moral reasoning and ethical judgement and to sharpen your ethical sensitivity and moral awareness.

Time 55–110 minutes, depending on the number of cases assigned and the degree of class discussion

Procedure Participants assume that they are managers at Martin Marietta plc, which is undertaking an ethics training session. The exercise consists of deciding on ethical courses of action for ten mini-cases. (Time: 50 minutes (5 minutes per case). If time is limited fewer cases can be used.)

Instructions Form groups of four to six people and select a group leader who will lead the discussion of the first case. Your group will have 5 minutes to reach a decision for each case before moving on to the next one. Rotate leaders for the case discussions.

Note These cases reflect real-life situations. Consequently, you may sometimes feel that a case lacks clarity or that the precise choice you would have made is not available. Some cases have more than one satisfactory solution and others have no good solutions. In all cases, however, you must *decide on the one best solution* from those presented.

Debriefing After the decisions have been made for all the cases, the class should discuss each case in order. For each case, groups share their decisions and explain why they think their choice is the best. Then the tutor provides the point values and rationale assigned for each option by the Martin Marietta plc trainers. Each group keeps track of its score for each case. At the end of the discussion, groups add up their points for all 10 cases and the group with the highest score wins. (Time: 60 minutes. Less time is required if fewer cases are assigned or the total class discussion of group answers is omitted.)

Mini-case 1 A defence programme has not yet been formally approved nor have the funds been allocated. Nevertheless, because it all looks good and you need to get started in order to meet the schedule, you start negotiating with a supplier. What do you tell the supplier?

Potential answers
(a) 'This is a "hot" programme for both of us. Approval is imminent. Let's get all the preliminary work under way.'
(b) 'The programme is a certainty. I want you under contract as soon as possible.'
(c) 'Start work and we will cover your costs when we get the contract.'
(d) 'If you want to be part of the team on this important, great programme, you, like us, will have to shoulder some of the start-up costs.'

Mini-case 2 Two of your subordinates routinely provide their children with supplies from the office. How do you handle this situation?

Potential answers
(a) Lock up the office supplies and issue them only as needed and signed for.
(b) Tell these two subordinates that office supplies are for office use only.
(c) Report the theft of pens and paper to the head of security.
(d) Send a notice to all employees that office supplies are for office use only and that any disregard of the notice will result in disciplinary action.

Mini-case 3 Your operation is being relocated. The personnel regulations are complex and might influence your employees' decisions about staying on the 'team'. Relocating with no experienced staff would be very difficult for you. What do you tell your employees about their options?

Potential answers

(a) State that the relocation regulations are complex: you won't go into them right now. However, you tell them that everything probably will come out all right in the end.

(b) Suggest that they relocate with you, stating that a job in hand is worth an unknown in the bush.

(c) Present them with your simplified version of the regulations and encourage them to come along.

(d) Tell them only that you'd like them to relocate with you to preserve the team, which has worked so well together.

Mini-case 4 Your price is good on a project contract you are bidding for, but you think it will take you several months longer than your competitor to develop the system. Your client, the Ministry of Defence (MoD), wants to know the schedule. What do you say?

Potential answers

(a) Tell the MoD your schedule is essentially the same as you believe your competitor's will be.

(b) Show the MoD a schedule that you believe is the same as your competitor's (but believing you can do better than your engineers have told you).

(c) Explain to the MoD the distinct advantage of your system, irrelevant of schedule.

(d) Lay out your schedule even though you suspect it may cause you to lose points on the evaluation.

Mini-case 5 A friend of yours wants to transfer to your division, but he may not be the best qualified for the job. You do have an opening and one other person, whom you do not know, has applied. What do you do?

Potential answers

(a) Select the friend you know and in whom you have confidence.

(b) Select the other person who, you are told, is qualified.

(c) Request a qualifications comparison of the two from the human resources department.

(d) Request the human resources department to extend the search for additional candidates before making the selection.

Mini-case 6 Your new employee is the niece of the director of finance. Her performance is poor and she has caused trouble with her co-workers. What do you do?

Potential answers

(a) Call her in and talk to her about her inadequacies.

(b) Ask the human resources department to counsel her and put her on a performance improvement plan.

(c) Go and see her uncle.

(d) Maybe her problems are caused by the newness of the job; give her some time to come around.

Mini-case 7 You work in finance. Another employee is blamed for your error involving a large amount of money. The employee will be able to clear himself, but it will be impossible to trace the error back to you. What do you do?

Potential answers

(a) Do nothing. The blamed employee will be able to clear himself eventually.

(b) Assist the blamed employee in resolving the issue but don't mention your involvement.

(c) Own up to the error immediately, thus saving many hours of work.

(d) Wait and see if the matter is investigated and at that time disclose your knowledge of the case.

Mini-case 8 After three months you discover that a recently hired employee who appears to be very competent falsified her employment application in that she claimed she had a university degree when she did not. As her supervisor, what do you do?

Potential answers

(a) You are happy with the new employee, so you do nothing.

(b) Discuss the matter with the human resources department to determine company policy.

(c) Recommend that she be fired for lying.

(d) Consider her performance, length of service and potential benefit to the organisation before making any recommendation to anyone.

Mini-case 9 A close relative of yours plans to apply for a vacancy in the department that you head. Hearing of this, what would you say to that person?

Potential answers

(a) 'Glad to have you. Our organisation always needs good people.'

(b) 'I would be concerned about the appearance of favouritism.'

(c) 'It would be best if you did not work for me.'

(d) 'If you get the job, expect no special consideration from me.'

Mini-case 10 A current supplier contacts you with an opportunity to use your expertise as a paid consultant to them in matters not pertaining to your company's business. You would work only on weekends. What would you do?

Potential answers

(a) Accept the job if the legal department poses no objection.

(b) Accept the job.

(c) Report the pertinent details to your supervisor.

(d) Decline the position.

Case study: call for review over SATS test cheating

Teachers' leaders called on the education secretary, Charles Clarke, to urgently review national tests and league tables, after a *Guardian* newspaper investigation found widespread allegations of cheating in tests for 11 year olds.

Teachers' union heads said the government relied too much on external exams – including standard assessment tests (SATS) – and a rethink was long overdue.

Chris Woodhead, the former chief inspector of schools, said the government had ignored evidence that teachers were boosting children's results in primary school tests as much as five years ago. Methods included opening papers ahead of time, coaching children and helping them during tests.

'As chief inspector, I met heads who wanted to tell me that they knew cheating was a major problem. However, when I raised these concerns with the education department, they didn't want to know.'

He said the government's exam body, the Qualifications and Curriculum Authority (QCA), was also 'not keen' to look into the matter. 'I do feel the QCA has a vested interest in minimising the problem,' he said.

John Bangs, the assistant general secretary and head of education at the biggest classroom teaching union, the National Union of Teachers (NUT), said: 'The NUT is deeply concerned about "the terrible trio", testing, targets and tables, which drive the curriculum into a hole at the end of primary school and put enormous pressure on teachers. We cannot condone any teachers bending the rules, but this shows the climate the tests have created, whereby our children's futures are dominated by teachers "teaching to the test". We would urge Charles Clarke to launch a serious review into the entire testing system.'

David Hart, general secretary of the National Association of Head Teachers, said he felt cheating occurred only in a minority of schools: 'But the Qualifications and Curriculum Authority must monitor the situation and not pretend it is not going on. This evidence does show the enormous pressure teachers are under, and the impact of the government's target-setting and league table agenda, linked with the performance-related pay system.'

Damian Green, the shadow education secretary, said the government must launch an immediate investigation and reveal what evidence of cheating it already had. Phil Willis, Liberal Democrat education spokesman, called for a Royal Commission to investigate the entire exam system.

A spokesman for the Department for Education and Skills said: 'The government is absolutely committed to maintaining the integrity and security of the national curriculum key stage tests and takes any allegation of malpractice very seriously. The extremely small number of isolated incidents every year are investigated thoroughly, but it is clear there is absolutely no evidence of widespread cheating.'

The QCA released figures showing that 479 cases of cheating in exams were reported this year, more than double the complaints in 2001. However, only seven schools had their results annulled. The body appealed for teachers to report concerns.

Source: Angelique Chrisafis and Rebecca Smithers, *Guardian*, 29 October 2002, p. 3.

Questions for discussion

1 Why is there pressure to cheat and whose responsibility is it to control cheating?

2 How can the creative problem-solving process develop an action plan to prevent the problem of cheating in schools?

Applied questions

3 There are obviously some problems that need to be solved to achieve a foolproof system. As a manager can you identify the parts of the problem using a cause-and-effect diagram like that in Exhibit 12–3?

4 Using the different moral principles of utilitarianism, rights and justice, would your decisions be different depending on the approach used? Which is your preferred approach and why?

WWW exercise

Manager's Internet tools

Web tips: problem-solving skills on the web

This chapter provides a variety of tools for helping you solve problems and make decisions. They range from knowledge of the rational problem-solving process to group decision support systems consisting of electronic and computer-supported data-processing tools. Today there are many more databases and information-processing tools available on the Internet that can expand your problem-solving capabilities. Complete the exercises that follow to become more familiar with these alternatives.

World Wide Web search

There are many sites on the Internet, including many specific companies, devoted to improving problem-solving skills. Using a search engine, find some sites that are targeted to helping people develop their problem-solving skills. What do these sites and/or companies have to offer, and what are the similarities to the concepts presented in this chapter?

Specific website Creative Problem Solving Group – Buffalo

The Creative Problem Solving Group – Buffalo is a consulting group that, among other things, helps organisations solve problems creatively. On its website, the company has a pictorial representation of its problem-solving methodology. Go to the company's website, examine its mission, and then look at its problem-solving methodology (in the Services section).

Company: http://www.cpsb.com/
Problem-solving: http://www.cpsb.com/cps.html

Discussion questions

1 What are the key components to Buffalo's creative problem-solving approach? To what types of problem does the company think the model can be applied?
2 Is the model static, with defined beginning and end points, or is it a dynamic model? What difference does it make?

Specific website – the Future Problem Solving Program

The Future Problem Solving Program (FPSP) is an organisation established to expand students' thinking on problems.

The organisation hopes to inspire students to look at problems in different lights, and generate new and creative solutions to problems. The organisation developed a six-step process as a guideline for problem-solving. Go to the FPSP website and examine its six-step process on the Overview page. Then, look at the graphical representation on its FPSP History page.

Company: http://www.fpsp.org/
Problem-solving: http://www.fpsp.org/overview/history.html

Discussion questions

1 What are the key components of FPSP's approach to creative problem-solving? Are they different from Buffalo's components identified on the previous website?
2 What are the differences in the two models, and what might account for the differences? How significant are they?

LEARNING CHECKLIST ☑

Before you move on you may want to reflect on what you have learnt in this chapter. You should now be able to:

☑ explain the nature of managerial problem-solving

☑ identify the five steps of the rational problem-solving process

☑ appreciate the value of ethics and morality in decision-making

☑ describe the strengths and weaknesses of different decision styles

☑ utilise quality-management tools for problem-solving

☑ apply techniques to stimulate creativity and innovation.

Further reading

De Colle, S. (2005) 'A Stakeholder Management Model for Ethical Decision Making', *International Journal of Management & Decision Making* 6(3/4), p. 299.

McCabe, A.C., Ingram, R. and Conway Dato-on, M. (2006) 'The Business of Ethics and Gender', *Journal of Business Ethics* 64(2), p. 101.

Mellahi, K. and Wilkinson, A. (2004) 'Organisational Failure: A Critique of Recent Research and a Proposed Integrative Framework', *International Journal of Management Reviews* 5/6(1), p. 21.

References

Alari, M. (1991) 'Group Decision Support Systems: A Key to Business Team Productivity', *Journal of Information Systems Management* 8(3), Summer, pp. 36–41.

Archer, E.R. (1980) 'How to Make a Business Decision: An Analysis of Theory and Practice', *Management Review*, February, pp. 289–299.

Attas, D. (2004) 'A Moral Stakeholder Theory of the Firm', *Ethics and Economics* 2(2).

Baker, S. (1992) 'Ethical Judgment', *Executive Excellence*, March, pp. 7–8.

Bass, B.M. (1983) *Organizational Decision Making*. Homewood, IL: Richard D. Irwin.

Boatright, J.R. (1993) *Ethics and the Conduct of Business*. Englewood Cliffs, NJ: Prentice-Hall, Inc., p. 1.

Bowie, N.E. (1998) 'A Kantian Theory of Capitalism', *Business Ethics Quarterly* (special issue 1), pp. 37–60.

Brassard, M. (1988) *The Memory Jogger: A Pocket Guide of Tools for Continuous Improvement*. Methuen, MA: GOAL/QPC, pp. 9–13.

Campbell, D. (1978) 'Some Characteristics of Creative Managers', *Center for Creative Leadership Newsletter* 1, February, pp. 6–7.

Carr, A.Z. (1968) 'Is Business Bluffing Ethical?', *Harvard Business Review*.

Carroll, L. (1975) *Alice's Adventures in Wonderland*. New York, NY: Viking Press, p. 22.

Cocks, J. (1990) 'Let's Get Crazy', *Time*, 11 June, pp. 40–41.

Cohen, M.D., March, J.G. and Olsen, J.P. (1971) 'A Garbage Can Model of Organizational Choice', *Administrative Science Quarterly*, March, pp. 1–25.

Cotton, J.L., Vollrath, D.A. and Froggatt, K.L. (1988) 'Employee Participation: Diverse Forms and Different Outcomes', *Academy of Management Review*, January, pp. 8–22.

Dalkey, N.C. and Helmer, O. (1963) 'An Experimental Application of the Delphi Method to the Use of Experts', *Management Science* 9, pp. 458–467.

Donaldson, T. (1996) 'Values in Tension: Ethics Away from Home', Kenneth Robinson Fellowship Lecture, University of Hong Kong, 9 January.

Driver, M.J., Brousseau, K.R. and Hunsaker, P.L. (1993) *The Dynamic Decisionmaker*. New York, NY: Jossey-Bass, pp. 1–36.

Evan, W.M. and Freeman, R.E. (1993) 'A Stakeholder Theory of the Modern Corporation: Kantian Capitalism', in T.I. Beauchamp and N.E. Bowie (eds) *Ethical Theory and Business* (4th edn). Prentice Hall, Englewood Cliffs, NJ: Prentice Hall.

Ferrell, O.C. and Gardiner, G. (1991) *In Pursuit of Ethics: Tough Choices in the World of Work*. Springfield, IL: Smith Collins Company, pp. 9–13.

Fleming, J.E. (1994) 'Business Ethics: An Overview', University of Southern California, unpublished paper, p. 2.

Hunsaker, P.L. and Alessandra, A.J. (1986) *The Art of Managing People*. New York, NY: Simon & Schuster, pp. 224–226.

Klein, L.S. (1991) 'Ethical Decision Making in a Business Environment', *Review of Business* 13(3), Winter, pp. 27–29.

Morrisey, G.L (1977) *Management by Objectives and Results for Business and Industry* (2nd edn). Reading, MA: Addison-Wesley.

Natale, S.M., O'Donnell, C.F. and Osborne Jr, W.R.C. (1990) 'Decision Making: Managerial Perspectives', *Thought* 63(248), pp. 32–51.

Osborn, F. (1957) *Applied Imagination*. New York, NY: Scribners.

Pastin, M. (1986) *The Hard Problems of Management: Gaining the Ethics Edge*. San Francisco, CA: Jossey-Bass.

Phillips, R. (1997) 'Stakeholder Theory and a Principle of Fairness', *Business Ethics Quarterly* 7, pp. 51–66.

Phillips, R. (2004) 'Some Key Questions about Stakeholder Theory', *IVEY Business Journal*, IVEY Management Services, March/April.

Pounds, W.F. (1969) 'The Process of Problem Finding', *Industrial Management Review* II, Fall, pp. 1–19.

Rest, J.R. (1988) 'Can Ethics Be Taught in Professional Schools? The Psychology Research', *Easier Said Than Done*, Winter, pp. 22–26.

Sammet, G. (1992) *Gray Matters: The Ethics Game*. Orlando, FL: Martin Marietta Corporation.

Simon, H.A. (1957) *Administrative Behaviour* (2nd edn). New York, NY: Free Press.

Tsalikis, J. and Fritzsche, D.J. (1989) 'Business Ethics: A Literature Review with a Focus on Marketing Ethics', *Journal of Business Ethics* 8, pp. 695–743.

Van de Ven, H. and Delbecq, A. (1974) 'The Effectiveness of Nominal, Delphi, and Interacting Group Decision-making Processes', *Academy of Management Journal* 17, pp. 605–621.

Vroom, V.H. and Jago, A.G. (1974) 'Decision Making as a Social Process', *Decision Sciences* 5(4), October, pp. 734–769.

Vroom, V.H. and Jago, A.J. (1988) *The New Leadership: Managing Participation in Organizations*, Englewood Cliffs, NJ: Prentice Hall.

Power and politics

The opening vignette suggests that the fears that so many of us have about our working lives are in fact unfounded. We've never had a better chance to improve our working lives

No more dog eat dog

Sit in a busy sandwich bar in the centre of any British city at lunchtime and eavesdrop on the conversations around you. Rather than fevered discussion about the election, the subject is far more likely to be office politics. While the plots and characters vary, the dominant themes don't: the small injustices – the arbitrary, capricious exercise of boss power – and the wasting of time.

'She appointed him because she fancied him and put him above her departmental chief,' said a friend in a calm assessment of the war that is causing havoc in his office. 'He's a waste of space on a fat salary, but he makes sure to give stupid assignments and to pin the blame on his underlings, while claiming the credit for anything that works.'

The interplay of these conversations is deeply familiar: anxiety and a sense of grievance is met with sympathy and (perhaps) reassurance. And underlying it, accepted by both listener and speaker, is their complete powerlessness. The absurdity of some of these office dramas can only be likened to the court of an absolute monarch: a Louis XIV handing out goodies to his favourites, who run their fiefdoms with comparable patronage.

For most people in white-collar jobs for eight hours a day, the office is where they experience most directly other people's power over their lives. How work is organised – how power is distributed – is one of the most obvious forms of politics, and yet neither my friend nor any of the sandwich munchers expect work to feature in the election beyond a few references to full employment or flexible working time.

In the run-up to the election Alan Milburn may have talked a lot about people wanting more control over their lives, but no one ever imagined he was talking about the workplace. There is a bizarre disconnect between how, as consumers, our sense of control and individualism is inflated and flattered, while at work we are expected to park such notions and buckle down with self-sacrificial team spirit. Equally, the political realm may be full of rhetoric about democracy, human rights and active citizenship, but few outside the shrinking, marginalised trades union movement suggest that such principles have any relevance to the eight hours you spend at work.

Or look at the disconnect another way. The government is happy to tell us what to eat but not how to work. Yet we now know from meticulous international research that work has a huge impact on our health – most obviously life expectancy, but also conditions such as heart disease. Status, control over our work, the pace and intensity of that work and what support we have: these have a direct impact on our health, perhaps even more than diet. But while the government urges the country to eat its greens, there are no initiatives on stress, no investigating task forces, not even Jamie Oliver-style petitions to combat the stress epidemic.

The grumbles emanating over sandwiches are not just coming from a rump of whingers. On every indicator of job satisfaction in the British workforce, ratings have dropped sharply since 1990: hours, pensions, pace of job and workloads are the obvious ones; but, interestingly for a society that prides itself on being highly individualistic, there has been a marked decline in control over our work. A majority of the workforce don't trust their bosses to look after their interests. Most damning of all, an OECD study found that we bump along second only to South Korea in our sense of insecurity – not about keeping our jobs, but about our positions in the organisation.

Our workplaces are rife with cynicism, lack of trust and anxieties about status and position. Yet the only person who has managed to get working conditions on to the national agenda in recent years is comedian Ricky Gervais and his alter ego David Brent. The work-related political agenda is tightly circumscribed and amounts to Labour boasting of its employment record, the national minimum wage and its family-friendly policies. These three apart, work is a political no-go area.

The depoliticisation of work must be the most profound and enduring legacy of Thatcherism. She handed business the 'right to manage', unaccountable to all but its shareholders. The strategy was to pit everyone against everyone else: competition between companies but also within companies, within departments, within teams. The message was clear: unless you personally and your company are competitive, you are history. Competition was the spur to productivity.

▶   Parts of this legacy simply haven't worked. Our productivity is notoriously poor compared to that in Germany or Scandinavia, countries where (and it may be more than coincidence) the quality of working life has always been high on the political agenda, and governments – in alliance with employers and trades unions – have sponsored experimentation in work organisation and helped spread best practice. Other parts of the Thatcherite legacy were never more than myth and urgently need debunking, such as performance-related pay, which the research shows is based on a false premise – you can't measure an individual's output because it is always dependent on colleagues – and actually damages motivation.

Source: © Guardian Newspapers Ltd, 2005, Madeline Bunting.

Discussion questions

1 Are office politics an unavoidable part of working life?

2 How can organisations minimise the influence of politics in the workplace?

If power elicits social disapproval, politics cannot be too far behind. Power (and its companion, politics) is a force that people try to keep under wraps. People who have power generally feel obliged to deny that they have it or at least not to flaunt it. And those who want it often try to give the impression that they do not. (There are, of course, exceptions!) Such behaviours indicate that power is a very misunderstood phenomenon.

Power is neutral. It is neither inherently evil nor inherently good. The managers responsible for Reuters can use their power with the goal of increasing business. Powerful managers and leaders often have big egos, those at Reuters tried to use their power to protect themselves and in the end the organisation suffered.

Most of us realise that sometimes power is pivotal to a successful outcome. You have already read about using empowerment, organisational culture and job design to enrich the lives of employees and to improve the problem-solving capabilities of teams. These are examples of how increasing the power of people at work produces positive outcomes.

Power and how to gain it

Society expects parents to influence their children's social and moral development. Teachers and lecturers are expected to influence the intellectual and ethical development of students. Salespeople are rewarded when they influence customers' buying decisions.

In most social contexts, being influential is viewed as a positive quality, something that is expected if not admired. However, people often feel uneasy with power. We view it negatively if we feel manipulated, exploited or squelched, like a pawn in another person's game. According to Beeman and Sharkey (1987), power is a basic social force that alters the reality of those influenced by the power holder. Yet power can be a vital and positive change force within organisations.

MRS. GELLERMAN SEIZES AN OPPORTUN-
ITY TO SNAP A FEW PICTURES OF THE
BOSS NAPPING ON THE JOB WHICH SHE'LL
FILE FOR FUTURE JOB PROTECTION USE.

Source: reprinted by permission of Tribune Media Services.

Power goes beyond influence

Kanter (1977) defines **power** as the ability to alter circumstances so that another person does

---
power

The ability of A (the power holder) to alter circumstances impacting on B so that B does what A wants done.

---

what the power holder wants done. Leavitt (1978) gives the following example. If A has power over B, A can get B to do something that B might not otherwise do. A has power if he or she can overcome B's resistance to achieve A's objective. The outcome can be beneficial for both. A manager, for example, can place a subordinate who develops a proposal supportive of the manager's goals in an assignment that provides visibility and access to senior management – a career-enhancing move.

According to Schein (1985), power is the currency that buys changes in organisational outcomes: shapes goals, influences promotional decisions, resolves conflicts and brings about change in organisational structure. Cohen and Bradford (1991) suggest managers can be most influential if they can get colleagues to co-operate without resorting to formal authority or position of power. We will explain how to do this below.

Power can be abused and used selfishly, or it can be used constructively to revitalise the quality of life in organisations and subsequently the quality of products and services produced. The intentions of power determine its positive or negative effect. Sam Walton of Wal-Mart and Asda used power constructively to instil a philosophy that employees 'value the customer' and, in doing so, he created the largest retailing chain in the world: Wal-Mart. He empowered managers to be responsive to local customer and community needs.

Power arises from three non-mutually exclusive primary sources: position, personal behaviour, or situational forces. Yukl and Taber (1983), in Exhibit 13-1, summarise key power elements in these three power sources. A person's *formal position* may convey the power to exercise legitimate authority or control rewards. Alternatively, some people have *personal sources of power*, such as expertise, reference to others or networks of alliances – all essentially unrelated to organisational position. Finally, a person may seize a *situational opportunity* to exercise power, often drawing on associations with powerful persons, control of information

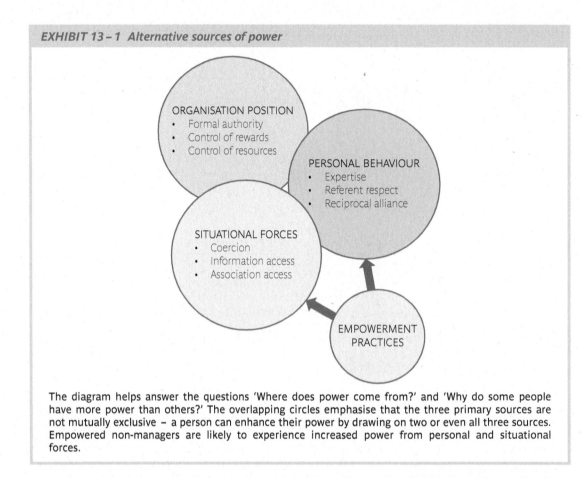

EXHIBIT 13–1 Alternative sources of power

ORGANISATION POSITION
• Formal authority
• Control of rewards
• Control of resources

PERSONAL BEHAVIOUR
• Expertise
• Referent respect
• Reciprocal alliance

SITUATIONAL FORCES
• Coercion
• Information access
• Association access

EMPOWERMENT PRACTICES

The diagram helps answer the questions 'Where does power come from?' and 'Why do some people have more power than others?' The overlapping circles emphasise that the three primary sources are not mutually exclusive – a person can enhance their power by drawing on two or even all three sources. Empowered non-managers are likely to experience increased power from personal and situational forces.

or even coercion. As suggested by the overlapping circles in the exhibit, a person often combines two or more power sources to gain greater leverage in altering the behaviour of others. Two of these power sources are potentially enhanced if an organisation empowers people at work.

Power often comes with organisational position

Emerson (1962) suggests that, although many sources of position power exist, one of the most common stems from B's dependence on A for something that B strongly desires. This dependence may stem from A's ability to provide advancement, recognition, security, information, acceptance, favourable positions or vital resources. **Position power** originates from the rights a person holds in the organisational hierarchy, such as legitimate authority, the ability to reward and the capacity to punish. According to French and Raven (1962), for managers, power usually goes with the job. Biggart (1984) suggests that managers need to realise, however, that position power is relative – commanding obedience is risky if the manager's performance depends on the creative action or expertise of subordinates.

position power
A form of power that originates from the rights a person holds by virtue of the organisational hierarchy – the legitimate authority to reward and punish.

Formal authority

formal authority
Legitimate power derived directly from a person's title and position in the organisational hierarchy.

The right to command is called **formal authority**. According to Bacharach and Lawler (1980), this type of power derives directly from a person's title and position in the organisational hierarchy. When people comply with orders issued from someone with formal authority, they do so because they have accepted the power associated with that person's job as legitimate to organisational governance. The effectiveness of authority ultimately depends on subordinates' acceptance of a manager's right to command.

Barnard (1938) suggests that if subordinates are willing to risk personal consequences and refuse to obey the directives of someone in a position of authority, then that person lacks legitimate power – their authority is questioned. Requests or directives believed to be within a legitimate 'zone of acceptance' will be obeyed, but orders falling outside the legitimate range of acceptable expectations will be questioned, if not rejected. A personal assistant, for example, may comply readily with requests to handle correspondence, schedule appointments, maintain documents and greet visitors, but may refuse to shop for gifts for the manager's family, pad the boss's expense account or work on Sundays.

If legitimate authority alone is used to influence behaviour, others will probably seek to gain counterbalancing power. Ng (1980) suggests that even the mere possession of formal authority isolates the manager from subordinates who inherently resist influence, fear possible punishment or are simply uncomfortable with authority figures. Nevertheless, formal authority is often necessary to resolve complex differences of opinion, as when a higher-level manager dictates a solution to how differences are to be resolved between two or more battling departments.

Research focus: French and Raven's 'Five Bases of Power'

As we have mentioned above, to understand how power is used in an organisation we need to understand why some individuals have more power than others. Several different ideas have been put forward and one of the best known is French and Raven's (1962) 'Five Bases of Power'.

Some of these bases, such as reward, coercive and legitimate power, are derived from the power holder's position in the organisation, while referent and expert power are more likely to be caused by personal characteristics.

Reward power

reward power
Demonstrated when a person offers to reward others for doing something he or she wants.

Managers are usually perceived as having the ability to supply desired rewards such as promotions, pay rises or sought-after job assignments. Reward power is demonstrated when a person actually or implicitly offers to provide others with rewards for doing something he or she wants. Its strength rests on the desirability and magnitude of the rewards and on the perception of others that the manager can (and will) provide the rewards if they comply with directives or requests.

Reward power influences motivation (a lesson introduced in Chapters 6 and 7). According to Duchon *et al.* (1986), problems develop if the actual rewards do not match expectations. Furthermore, some peers who do not receive equitable rewards may feel that the manager is 'playing favourites'.

Coercive power

coercive power
Based on the ability to withhold desired resources or make life unpleasant for those who do not comply with the power holder's requests.

A person can influence others by threatening to deprive them of things they value. Coercive power is the ability to withhold desired resources or make life unpleasant for people who do not comply with the power holder's requests. Coercive power is based on fear and is likely to arouse anger, resentment and even retaliation. One common reaction is 'malicious obedience', in which resentful associates soothe their hurt feelings by doing 'exactly' what the coercer told them to do – no less, but certainly no more. If the mission fails, it is the power wielder who ends up looking bad when the associate truthfully says, 'I did exactly what you told me to do!'

Kipnis (1976) suggests that coercion is one of the most commonly used forms of power. Yet some experts believe that it is useful only in limited situations. Cartwright (1965) proposes that a manager is most likely to be obeyed when both reward and coercive power are perceived as legitimate and used in combination. Coercion that is used like blackmail invites coercive reciprocity if given a chance.

Legitimate power

legitimate power
The authority to command the actions of others.

As we discussed earlier when we talked about formal authority, legitimate power arises from someone's formal position when they have the authority to make decisions or command the actions of others. Legitimate power is typically based on the formal organisational hierarchy. Legitimate power can be acquired through the organisational role, election or some other form of recognition. Subordinates play a major role in the exercising of legitimate power as their compliance is influenced by whether they perceive the use of power to be legitimate.

Expert power

expert power
Originates when a person is perceived to have superior knowledge, experience or judgement that others need and do not possess themselves.

A person has expert power when he or she is perceived to have knowledge, experience or judgement that other people need and do not possess themselves. Thomas (1984) contends that, given the increased complexity and technology throughout society, we have become dependent on experts. When advised by someone with expert knowledge of computers, taxation or the law, we usually accept their advice.

Your degree of expert power depends on your performance record over time, the importance of your area of expertise and the alternative sources of such knowledge available to others. Hollander (1979) suggests that if you exercise poor judgement or offer faulty advice, or if others find ways to solve problems without your help, your potential power over others diminishes. Expert power may also decrease if you make the receiver feel inferior or if you train others so well that they can carry on without you. A

mentor
A person with more expertise who helps those with less.

person who develops a reputation as a mentor – one to whom others turn for sustained personal coaching and guidance – enjoys expert power.

Referent power

referent power
Comes from being respected, likeable and worthy of emulation.

charisma
A quality of admiration when others identify with and are attracted to a leader they look up to.

Referent power is found in a person who is respected, likeable and worthy of emulation. Schweitzer (1984) suggests that when others identify with and are attracted to someone they look up to, that person is said to have charisma. People with charisma, such as Princess Diana, are admired and often serve as role models for others. Most people can develop referent power by demonstrating friendly, supportive and considerate behaviours towards others. You will learn in Chapter 14 that being considerate is one of the basic ways of enacting leadership style.

People are motivated to comply with requests from those who hold referent power because they want to please them and gain their approval. Some requests may be beyond the zone of acceptance however, and asking too much too often may cause a reduction of referent power. To retain referent power, its holders are under constant pressure to maintain their exemplary images and live up to others' expectations.

Control of resources

Managers are typically given budgets or authority to allocate resources in carrying out the work of their units. However, the positions they occupy often give them power beyond what is formally intended simply because they are in a position to control access to resources that others need. A purchasing technician (not even a manager), because of their position in the flow of processing purchase requisitions, can restrict or delay access to goods and services sought by people at higher levels within the organisation. Peer managers or even managers lower within the organisational hierarchy can use their control of special equipment or services to bargain for actions favourable to their goals.

Power gained by controlling access to resources others need or want often provokes ethical issues. Who is going to be better or worse off because of someone having resource control power? For example, Walt Disney's chief executive faced this dilemma about how to use his power to decide the entertainment and informational content of multimedia programming after Disney bought ABC Television (Scheinin, 1995).

Power originating from personal attributes

As French and Raven (1962) identified in their Five Bases of Power, respect does not arise merely because a person occupies a pivotal position in the hierarchy or can dole out certain rewards or sanctions. Mulder *et al.* (1986) suggest that the kind of respect that inspires high-quality performance is the respect people feel for those whom they admire and in whom they have confidence. Even a recent university graduate, new to an organisation, is likely to influence managers with state-of-the-art technical knowledge. Such personal power originates with expertise, personality and alliances.

Reciprocal alliances

Most power bases, especially those of personal origin, work best if part of an ongoing, reciprocal exchange. People who engage in mutually beneficial exchanges and build alliances or

reciprocity

The trading of power or favours for mutual gain: you help me, I'll help you.

networks will, over time, increase their power. **Reciprocity** is the trading of power or favours for mutual gain. Repayment need not occur at the time of a transaction, since payments can be banked for later exchange. According to Cohen and Bradford (1991), 'using reciprocity requires stating needs clearly without "crying wolf", being aware of the needs of an ally without being manipulative, and seeking mutual gain rather than playing "winner takes all"'.

Once people work together on successful projects, they have colleagues on whom they can call for future help. The scientist, accountant or marketer who heads a group for one project may the next time be in a supportive role. To promote reciprocal networks ('I'll help you if you'll help me'), Xerox CEO Paul Allaire valued the 'superordinate' or higher-level goal: 'You can't get people to focus on only the bottom line. You have to give them an objective like "satisfy the customer" that everyone can relate to. It's the only way to break down those barriers and get people from different functions working together' (Dumaine, 1991). Reciprocal alliances build on expanded social networks of give-and-take influence within the organisation.

Power originating from situational forces

Whereas power from organisational and personal sources seems to be rather specific as to why it originates, the situational category is less definitive. Situational forces typically involve more a blending of organisational and personal sources with opportunistic elements brought about by an event or circumstance. As Pfeffer (1992) reminds us, power often involves the fit between situational requirements and personal traits.

Information power

information power

Stems from the ability to control access to critical information and its distribution.

Information becomes power when we possess information others need but do not have. **Information power** stems from the ability to control access to critical information and its distribution. You need not be an expert to assimilate, overhear or read important information. People in accounting, information systems or purchasing often have access to information others seek. They can develop power through selective distribution of information and guarded communication.

Zand (1981) suggests that if you control information, the likelihood that your decisions will be challenged by others is reduced. Control over the distribution of critically needed information enables you to define reality for others in ways that serve your own objectives. According to Wexley and Yukl (1984), control over information also means that it can be selectively filtered and packaged to influence decisions made by persons dependent on this information. For example, a computer facility's manager could influence his firm's computer selection decision by providing information favouring one option and discrediting others. The risks of using information in this manner, however, include the decreased trust and loss of respect of those who find out they have been unfairly influenced. They will probably develop alternative sources of information.

Association power

association power

Arises when one person has influence with another who possesses power.

Some people manage to develop considerable power simply by being associated with a powerful person, even though they may have no personal or positional power of their own. **Association power** arises when one person has influence with another who possesses power. Family members, confidantes and close aides of

Research focus: **using power bases**

Yukl (1994) proposed guidelines to explain how managers should use the Five Bases of Power proposed by French and Raven (1962). These guidelines are shown in Exhibit 13-2.

The guidelines in the exhibit demonstrate that how a person responds to a person is largely determined by how the other person behaves. If person A tries to influence person B, person B may respond with commitment, compliance or resistance. Commitment will mean that B accepts the influence and is highly motivated to respond to the wishes of A. Compliance means that B is willing to respond to A providing the response will be adequately rewarded. Resistance means that B opposes A's wishes and will deliberately try to neglect or sabotage the request. Exhibit 13-2 explains how to obtain commitment rather than resistance. However, the guidelines assume that the goals of the employees are the same as those of the leader and the organisation. If the goals of the individual do not match those of the leader or organisation, compliance will depend on the personality of the persuader.

EXHIBIT 13 – 2 Using power bases

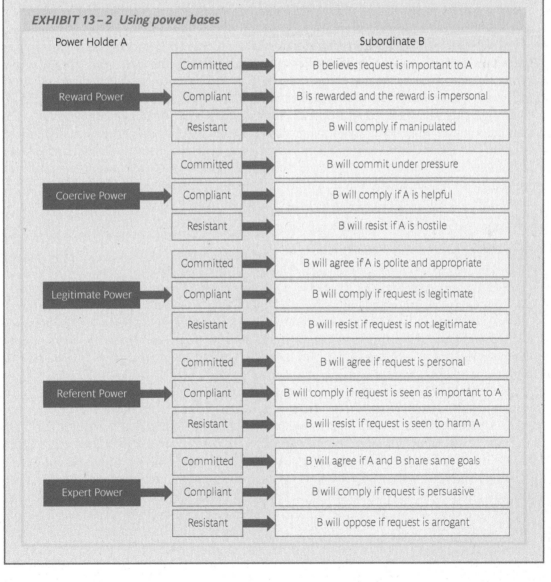

Power Holder A		Subordinate B
Reward Power	Committed	B believes request is important to A
	Compliant	B is rewarded and the reward is impersonal
	Resistant	B will comply if manipulated
Coercive Power	Committed	B will commit under pressure
	Compliant	B will comply if A is helpful
	Resistant	B will resist if A is hostile
Legitimate Power	Committed	B will agree if A is polite and appropriate
	Compliant	B will comply if request is legitimate
	Resistant	B will resist if request is not legitimate
Referent Power	Committed	B will agree if request is personal
	Compliant	B will comply if request is seen as important to A
	Resistant	B will resist if request is seen to harm A
Expert Power	Committed	B will agree if A and B share same goals
	Compliant	B will comply if request is persuasive
	Resistant	B will oppose if request is arrogant

public officials have association power. In some organisations, so do staff members who have developed close advisory relationships with the manager.

A personal assistant handles phone calls, correspondence and appointments. The loyal assistant also serves as a sounding board for the executive's ideas and frustrations, and knows who currently is in and out of favour with the boss. Association power has its place in organisations because it can help cut through the bureaucracy, as if an informal power structure exists in the shadow of the formal organisation.

Power enhanced by empowerment

Organisation position, personal attributes and situational forces are the three traditional sources of power in organisations. As described in Chapter 7, empowerment has recently emerged as a form of power for people unaccustomed to having power. Empowerment has become a popular topic of discussion and practice because of the widespread use of electronic information systems and the competitive pressure to flatten organisational structures. The result, according to Ford and Fottler (1995), has been that employees are increasingly asked 'to accept responsibility for the definition of the content of their jobs and the quality of their work'.

Employees have been granted authority to resolve problems encountered on the job as managers shift decision-making responsibility from themselves to the ones who directly engage problems. Empowerment is more than delegation. It involves sharing information and knowledge with employees and rewarding performance. Empowerment encompasses job enrichment by giving a person a whole job with decision responsibility, and providing him or her with sufficient information to know how that job fits into the organisation's overall purpose. One potential impact of empowered employees is to enhance their personal power and increase the likelihood they will experience situational power. Read the World Watch box to see how more women are being elected to powerful positions in Thailand, partly because of the efforts of pioneering female politicians to empower more women to follow in their footsteps.

world watch

Women rise to power in Thailand

As we enter the twenty-first century, examples of women gaining great respect and power are becoming increasingly more frequent. One such example is in politics in Thailand. Thailand is paving the way among the traditionally male-dominated Asian countries in electing women to politics. Unprecedented numbers of Thai women are being sent to public office, as the people of Thailand tire of the corruption and status quo that has permeated the Thai government for decades. Thai voters are putting their faith in women candidates to clean up and restructure the bureaucratic tangle of power in the government.

'It's four-wheel drive now,' says Smita Sorasuchart, one of a new and growing breed of Thai women who feel their place is in the corridors of power, not in the kitchen. The vivacious, western-educated wife of government spokesman Akapol Sorasuchart is already an active member of the ruling Democrat Party. She is also spokeswoman for the Science and Technology Ministry. And she plans to run in the general election to be held later this year.

Women from all walks of life are entering the political arena, not just the privileged like 40-year-old Smita. Born in Bangkok's sprawling portside slum area, Prateep Ungsongtham Hata, 47, is now a new senator, elected in the 4 March Senate polls, which saw a record 71 per cent voter turnout. And in June 2000, women will be vying for the office of Bangkok governor for the first time. 'Thai politics have certainly changed now,' says Smita.

'I deeply believe that most voters would like to elect women politicians at both national and local levels,' says Sudarat Keyuraphan, a member of the Thai Rak Thai (Thai Love Thai) Party and a Bangkok gubernatorial candidate. 'They have strong confidence that women politicians have better intentions and are less corrupt than male politicians.'

That more women are getting involved in Thai politics is not surprising considering the plethora of organisations that have been set up by pioneering female politicians in the past 10 years to help train and educate women for just that purpose. And given Thai society's relative openness and tolerance, women in Thailand face fewer barriers to entering the political arena than in other, more male-dominated Asian countries.

Indeed, Thailand is now following the lead of the Philippines, where women have long been active in politics. The Philippines is also the first – and so far, only – Southeast Asian country to have a female leader: Corazon Aquino, who became president in 1986. Thailand differs from many other Asian countries, though, in that, by and large, women politicians are not taking up the mantle of deceased husbands or fathers, such as Aquino or Indonesia's Megawati Sukarnoputri.

Prime minister's office minister Pavena Hongsakula, 50, predicts that the number of female representatives in the new 500-member lower house could easily double after the general election. That's because more women are planning to run, and political parties are supporting and promoting them more vigorously, she says. The Senate could have up to 20 female members after the March election results are confirmed – a slight increase from the old, appointed Senate.

In local government, nearly 1500 women, or 2.5 per cent of the total, were elected village heads in 1998, something that was unheard of before the 1990s. And this year (2000) the number of women elected to municipal and provincial councils in January and February more than doubled to 10 per cent from less than 5 per cent.

Some say the growing participation of women in the political process goes hand in hand with the political changes launched by the 1997 reformist constitution. Political observers will be watching closely to see how the three women candidates (Pavena, who has yet to formally declare her candidacy but has told friends she will run; Sudarat; and Kalaya Sophonpanich, sister-in-law of Bangkok Bank chairman Chatri Sophonpanich) fare in the race for Bangkok governor, against each other and their two male opponents.

If a woman becomes Bangkok governor, could a woman prime minister be next? 'There's nothing to say we can't be prime minister, but we have just started,' says Pavena. But they definitely are heading down the right path. Overall, women's organisations nationwide are giving Thai women the knowledge and encouragement they need to be more involved in politics, while the general mood of reform since 1997 is also a boon. As Pavena notes, 'The government should increasingly educate women that politics is now part of their daily life – everyone owns the country, not just men.'

Source: 'Ladies First', *Far Eastern Economic Review*, 13 April 2000, pp. 112–114.

Discussion questions

1 How does culture affect women's ability to gain power?

2 What type of political behaviour could women develop to gain power bases?

The effect of social networks on a manager's power

Managers and subordinates are linked in social networks infused with power expectations.

Grimes (1978) suggests that, over time, subordinates learn to expect that their behaviour will be altered by their manager. Realising this, they then tend to go with the flow rather than ignore, disobey or resist the manager's attempts to exercise power.

People expect social control

With social acceptance, power becomes normalised: according to Pfeffer (1981), social control of one's behaviour by others has become an accepted part of organisational life. Even though lower-level members might have the countervailing power to resist requests or directives from managers (by virtue of their expertise or control over access to needed information, materials, people), they seldom do so once the pattern of acceptance has been established.

Social control expectations are in part a product of cultural socialisation. However, different cultures create different expectations of social control and power sharing.

Power acceptance is a western belief

Industrial systems in Europe, North America and Australia/New Zealand have been built on the generally accepted belief that managers are the ones who make key decisions in organisations. This expectation of social control by managers has cost western society dearly – our organisations are not as internally co-operative and productive as they could be. Cole (1990) suggests that group problem-solving talent has often been under-utilised because traditional practices keep significant decision power in the hands of the managerial hierarchy. However, Ciampa (1992) argues that when power is expected to be a managerial prerogative rather than a force that also flows up from front-line employees, self-initiated problem-solving for continuous improvement does not occur. One alarming study (Yankelovich, 1983) of non-managerial employees demonstrated that the use of top-down position power is costly.

- Three-quarters said they could be significantly more effective than they are.
- Half said they put no more effort into their job than that necessary to hold it.
- Sixty per cent said they 'do not work as hard as they used to' Yankelovich.

Power diffusion is an eastern practice

Large businesses in Japan and some other Asian cultures are widely recognised as being built on a bottom-up decision model and group consensus. Power tends to be more diffused through widely shared information and involvement in contributing to a gradual course of action. According to Abegglen and Stalk (1985), inequalities in status and rewards between top managers and first-rung employees are much less pronounced in Japanese than in western firms, except between men and women, as you will learn in a moment. Except at the top, Japanese managers hold less formal authority and draw more on expertise than equal-level managers in the West. Consequently, according to Lincoln (1989), managers in Japanese firms usually seek the counsel of group members and build communication networks with a minimum of reliance on position power. However, Mroczkowski and Hanaoka (1989) argue that the recent necessity to increase the speed, flexibility and magnitude of decisions, has shifted more power to top executives in Japanese firms, a top-down shift that has unknown implications in the long run.

Western managers are slowly moving towards participatory and group-based models of decision-making in an effort to make the workplace more eastern in character. However, Levine (1990) suggests that quality circles, self-directed teams and gainsharing plans are still not widespread. Nevertheless, when managers move in the direction of power sharing, people feel empowered that they can make a difference, and quality usually improves.

Research focus: **Tannenbaum and Schmidt**

Thomas and Velthouse (1990) suggest that managers who share power generally increase their own power by strengthening the self-control of others. Exhibit 13-3 shows how power expands as a manager shares it. The classic Tannenbaum and Schmidt (1968) model portrayed power as largely a zero-sum game, bounded within the rectangle ABCD. As the manager shared decision power, presumably he or she gave up power to others. However, as power is shared (by shifting decision behaviours towards the right), subordinates perceive themselves as more in control of

EXHIBIT 13 – 3 *Decision power sharing increases subordinates' self-efficacy and managers' reputational power*

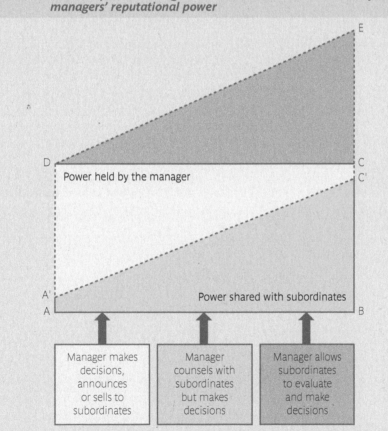

Power held by the manager

Power shared with subordinates

| Manager makes decisions, announces or sells to subordinates | Manager counsels with subordinates but makes decisions | Manager allows subordinates to evaluate and make decisions |

Sources: extended from Robert Tannenbaum and Warren Schmidt (1958) 'How to Choose a Leadership Pattern', *Harvard Business Review* 36, March–April, pp. 95–102; and Kenneth W. Thomas and Betty A. Velthouse (1990), 'Cognitive Elements of Empowerment: An "Interpretative" Model of Task Motivation', *Academy of Management Review* 15, October, pp. 666–681.

their environment, thanks to their manager. The manager thus does not lose power but potentially continues to hold power (the areas bounded by A'C'ED). It is even likely that, with strengthened relations between manager and subordinates, the manager's power will increase (the slope of DE will become steeper).

A method of measuring the influence of people in different levels of the organisation (Tannenbaum and Schmidt, 1968) resulted in individuals being asked the question: 'In general how much influence do you feel each of the following groups actually has in what they want in your plant?' The employees rate the amount of influence the individuals have at the different levels in the organisation, using a five-point scale, ranging from 1 for little or no influence to 5 for a great deal of influence. The responses from all the people at the different levels were then averaged to form a control graph, similar to the one shown in Exhibit 13-4.

The research by Tannenbaum and Schmidt (1968) provided the following conclusions:

- Even though the data were collected from a large variety of organisations, ranging from public to private and education to the military, the control graph was similar with members at the top level of the organisation exerting more control and influence than those lower down.

- The results from similar companies in different countries, such as the USA, Italy, former Yugoslavia, Israel's kibbutzim and Austria, produced the same pattern of hierarchical control despite having different political and ideological values.

- When those lower down the organisation were asked how much control and influence they would like, the majority indicated that they would prefer more. However, their ideal control is still less than the amount they would choose to delegate to senior managers.

- The total control in an organisation is not a fixed sum, nor does it remain constant. If power is increased at one level it is not necessarily decreased at another. Therefore, increasing the power at lower levels of the organisation will not mean that those higher up will have less power; instead, the total amount of power and influence the organisation has will increase.

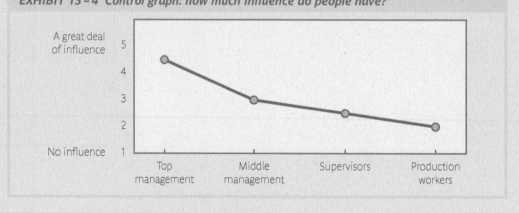

EXHIBIT 13–4 Control graph: how much influence do people have?

Central positions enhance power

The position a person occupies within a social network shapes that person's access to information and people. According to Brass (1984), people holding central positions in an informal network have the potential for greater power because of this access. Central positions, such as those occupied by middle and top managers, give people an opportunity to know who holds power and how powerful they are. They also provide more opportunities to cross-check information against multiple sources, making for more accurate perceptions of what goes on within the company. The more accurate a person's perception of the social network and of information, the more likely that person is to be influential.

Krackhardt (1990) suggests that people in central positions are sought after for advice, which becomes a source of power. People feed useful information to those who have reputations for being powerful. For example, a corporate controller may be seen by managers in other departments as centrally connected and accessible. People therefore seek out the controller for advice and special requests. These interactions are likely to provide the controller with even more information about people, events, resources and opportunities within the firm. As his or her information base and experience in getting things done increases, so will their reputational power.

Diversity is threatened by power relationships

Power involves interactions among people in a group or network, with one central person exerting dominant influence over time. According to Bacharach and Lawler (1980), sociologists refer to social exchange theory as the expectation that each individual caught in the dependency web of power relationships aims for positive outcomes. But Baldwin (1978) argues that exchanges are not equal, and for some not even positive. Social exchanges (the interplay of requests, ideas and commands) are always asymmetrical, meaning that there is an uneven distribution of power and unequal valuation of outcomes or benefits. Because of this, some players experience negative outcomes.

social exchange theory
Assumes that power and outcomes within a group are unevenly distributed, yet expects that each individual in a web of power relationships aims for positive outcomes.

One negative outcome occurs when ethnic minorities or women are confined to the low end of the power spectrum. Kanter (1977) and Fairhurst and Snavely (1983) suggest that, in part, such imbalances are caused by their fewer numbers and by token dynamics, in which the token minority or female complies with power strategies used by the majority. The abuses suffered range from sexual harassment to personal humiliation through choice of language. For example, the dominant male might refer to a woman as 'girl' or 'sweet young thing'. Or the boss might say, 'I want you boys to...' This off-hand remark may be taken as a racial put-down by the African-Caribbean in the group, who associates the term 'boy' with the historical oppression of his race. In doing business with Japanese men, western women are at a disadvantage unless they deliberately use power-equalising tactics.

In some cases, language is used as a power tactic to put down a minority or to be condescending. In others, offensive language is unintentional. Ironically, powerful managers who put down minorities and women may still accept their ideas and contributions. Unfortunately, those who are under-represented cannot go to the wall each time a slur occurs; to do so throws the relationship into a win–lose contest, and power often wins. One study, by Brass (1985), reports, however, that where women *are* able to break into the male-dominated coalition, they can end up being perceived as more central to the power network than their male counterparts. See the Dynamics of Diversity box for an example of the difficulties involved in managing politics at work.

dynamics of diversity

In a world where we are increasingly defined by our work, why do so many of us have such a poor understanding of office politics?

A decade ago, Rebecca was at the start of what she thought was a flourishing career. She had a good relationship with a difficult boss and, one year, while on a work trip to the Conservative Party conference, he told her that she would be promoted at the end of the month. That evening, one of Rebecca's contacts helped her gatecrash a party full of cabinet ministers. Going up the curving staircase, Rebecca met her boss, who was not on the guest list and who had been refused entry. 'Oh, don't worry, I'll get you in,' said Rebecca's contact, breezily. He did. 'And that's when it all went wrong,' Rebecca says.

The party was almost exclusively male and middle-aged; full of drunken Conservative politicians and newspaper editors. As a pretty woman under 30, Rebecca was immediately surrounded, but by her side, recognised by no one and of interest to nobody, stood her manager. With increasing desperation, Rebecca kept introducing him to the ministers who joined her circle, hoping that someone would treat him with the interest and deference he was accustomed to. No one did. 'The normal power relationship between us was being turned upside down,' says Rebecca, 'but the stupid thing was, I thought that at least he'd be pleased because he'd see I was trying to protect him.'

Back in the office the following day her manager first ignored her and then picked out her report for particular criticism. A week later several promotions were announced. Rebecca's name was not among them. Her relationship with her boss never recovered.

Rebecca had broken one of the unspoken rules of her hierarchical workplace: never witness the humiliation of your boss. Our workplaces are full of such hidden rules. Working within them is critical to our happiness and our success. But many of us take years to understand that they are there at all.

We go into workplaces with any number of preconceptions about other people's motivations and values, and we're often shockingly slow to adjust our assumptions in the face of reality. Work consumes a huge amount of our time, increasingly defines us to ourselves and other people, and largely determines our standard of living. The difference between getting it right and wrong is life-changing.

Rose worked, increasingly unhappily, for four different companies in 15 years before being frozen out of her senior job, and retreating to part-time and badly paid freelance work. She realises now that she never understood how to behave in her workplaces. Her education – modest home, grammar school, Oxford – gave her the illusion that the world was a meritocracy. In retrospect she can't believe her naivety. She says she never grasped that getting on with colleagues was more important than doing the job, and she didn't see the necessity of adapting to different office cultures. She was equally out of sympathy with the radical feminism of her first office, and the glamour-obsessed networking of her final one. 'It just didn't occur to me that all workplaces might be an arena for games-playing and manipulation. I thought office politics was something that only concerned people at the top of organisations, who were fighting for places on the board.'

Are things that different in more formal working organisations such as the civil service? John, a senior civil servant, says not. 'There's certainly a huge gulf between the explicit rules of the organisation and the real ones. Every year, we're appraised on a whole set of pretend criteria: creativity, project management, implementation. In practice there are only two criteria that really count, and they are: Are you a good chap? And have you caused any problems for your bosses by upsetting the politicians?

'You have to be very ambitious, but not show it – a team player on the surface, but really an individualist. You mustn't be seen to try too hard, or care too much. Urbanity is prized, and so is reserve. When I first arrived, young and green, I addressed my superiors as Mr so-and-so. I was told off for it, told that we don't have that kind of formality here; everyone uses Christian names. But that informality was completely deceptive. We were expected to show a high degree of deference, and to do exactly as we were told.'

The hidden rules of government service are even more complex for outsiders who suddenly find themselves having to work with career civil servants. Diane, a woman who worked at the top of government, learned quickly that power didn't go with a title. 'I came in as a policy adviser, and it was very destabilising, in a subtle way, when I arrived. Little things – you'd go into a meeting with civil servants, and they didn't look at you when they talked, or greet you when you came in.

'So I started kicking up a bit of a stink, but things only changed after some acid tests. It was never an easy relationship, though. I always felt excluded. You know that there are all these conversations and decisions being made by the men in the clubs and the bars, and as a female you're just never part of that.'

When I began to research this article, I didn't expect it to turn into a story about the continued problems of women in the office. But it rapidly became clear that women get the politics of the workplace wrong much more frequently than men do.

Last year Professor Carol Black, president of the Royal College of Surgeons, caused a furore by suggesting that the increasing domination of medicine by women would be disastrous for the profession, as all the evidence showed that any female-dominated sector lost power and influence as a result. She was much criticised by people who interpreted her remarks as being anti-women. I think she was making an important point.

On the whole, women are less attuned to power relationships, and less concerned by the exercise of power, than men are. The qualities for which they are so often praised – team-working, empathy, openness, conscientiousness – may be very good for the organisations where they work, but they are the opposite of the qualities required for individuals to succeed: single-mindedness, calculation and an acute consciousness of status.

Freya is a young academic who made a common mistake: she assumed that it was a mark of special favour when her managers asked her to take on extra work. She agreed to take on the financial management of her department when the full-time administrator left, believing it would demonstrate her commitment and competence. It had just the opposite effect. While her colleagues lunched with contacts, or wrote the papers that would get them their next job, she was staying late every evening to balance the books. 'I was such a fool. I never distinguished between prestigious tasks that would add to my marketability and the routine stuff that no one else wanted to do.'

Annie has worked as a senior account executive in four advertising agencies. She believes she now knows the hidden rules of her industry, but says it took her far too long to learn them. 'The first rule of advertising is: never admit to any mistakes. The clever thing to do is subtly blame someone inferior. You say something like: "I really thought it was right to give Juliet a chance here, but I'm afraid it's rather backfired. Turns out she's not quite ready, but don't worry, I'm on to it."

▶ 'The most critical rule is: find a mentor, preferably a much more senior management person who has either hired you, or whose empire you're in. Treat it like a new friendship – nurture it, ask their advice, admire them. That's how people do really, really well. A good mentor will accelerate you up the ladder.'

When I ask Adam, now a senior manager in a multinational company, whether he understood the rules of his workplace when he began, he is almost offended. 'Of course,' he says. 'I knew I had to be noticed. You work out who's powerful, and who's going up. Mark was very temperamental, hard to manage, but thought to be brilliant. I knew that the only way to stay attached to him was to make myself invaluable. So I identified his weaknesses – he wasn't good at writing reports, for instance, or at organisation – and I did all those for him. It made him look better, so he wanted to keep me on, and I learned a hell of a lot. I started doing all the things he did.

'I was a bit too cocky in the end, and he turned on me quite viciously. But by then I could do without him, because he'd already been so effusive about me to the head of department that my reputation was established.'

All workplaces have their own models of desirable behaviour, and their own criteria for defining who is in and who is out. Sidra, an Asian woman who works for a huge American finance company, says the route to acceptability in her workplace is a puritanical approach to your work and your body. 'This office is very head-down, no personal emails, no conversations at your desk, no personal calls, no unnecessary talking on the phone. They all seem very nice, but you never get a chance to talk. No one lunches.

'The one thing you're allowed to make time for in your working day is fitness. It's completely acceptable for someone to say, "Oh, I'm just off for my one o'clock run." It's what all the top people do, and it's how you get on. You meet really senior managers from other departments. People get offered jobs and decisions get made while running.'

Why do perfectly intelligent people end up working in environments that don't suit them? It's often because the explicit values of an organisation have nothing to do with the real values – they may even be the reverse. A black administrator I know had the unhappiest time of her life working for a left-wing council with admirable policies. The backstabbing, sexism, bullying and rudeness were intolerable. She moved to a right-wing council, quite out of tune with her political beliefs, and found it a comparative haven of politeness and harmony.

So many people are frustrated and unhappy because they are working in environments where the real values don't match their own. We would be far happier if we worked in places that respected the qualities we possessed at the time. Perhaps the best way to understand it is to consider that all organisations are meritocracies – it's just that the merits on which people are being judged may be rather hard to discern.

We are slow to recognise when we're in the wrong place. That's partly because we're averse to too much change, but also because we don't want to admit defeat. Stubbornly, blindly, we go on thinking that if we stay just a little longer or try a little harder, our true worth will be recognised. We couldn't be more wrong.

Source: © Jenni Russell, *Guardian* (2005).

Discussion questions

1　How can power in the workplace be managed effectively?

2　What can people do if they work in organisations that do not match their values?

Sexism sustains power imbalances/inequities

White males continue to dominate the power hierarchy in most western organisations, and even more so in Japan, China and several Asian cultures. Women are subjected to games and inequities that keep many discouraged, if not angry, about the imbalances of power. Evidence of sexism ranges from the subtleties of how women are treated in meetings to blatant harassment. Sexual harassment builds on the unequal distribution of power; for some men, harassment is a tactic that preserves the power separation. Power repercussions can haunt the woman who attempts to call attention to sexist practices, short of harassment, that keep women from advancing.

In meetings, women are more likely to be talked over and interrupted than men. They have to be more persistent to get a fair hearing of their ideas. Women are less often invited into the closed-door sessions that follow meetings, sessions where political alliances are bonded and offline decisions are struck to deal with sensitive issues. Women often feel they have to down-play their non-working role as mothers, whereas men can be boastful whenever they 'play mum', as if doing so is a real sacrifice, but one that wins them points for being human. Today as women have moved into management, the distinction between the 'mummy track' and the 'fast track' needs to be broken. According to Reardon (1993), even in organisations that do offer parental leave to either spouse there is an unspoken message that anyone who takes advantage of childcare and family programmes will not get ahead. Such institutional thinking retards equal gender access to power.

The effect of situational and personal factors on power

Power is situational dependent. Pfeffer (1981) suggests that a person may be able to influence people in some situations but not in others, which means power depends on the context or relationship. In fact, the balance of power can be reversed, depending on the circumstances. At the office, a manager may be recognised by subordinates as having power over the group. But if the boss joins other members of the department for a weekend of backpacking, it may well be that the subordinate who was once a forest ranger will end up telling every one what to do – even the manager! The context has changed.

Not everyone desires to be in a position of power. Even those who have strong needs for power differ in why they believe power is important and how they use it. To understand organisational power it is necessary to be sensitive to different situations and to individual power needs. Read through the Eye on Ethics box and think about how you would feel if your judgement of your tutors could influence their pay and promotion prospects.

Situational factors determine power relationships

Power in organisations stems from many situational factors. These include specialisation and task importance, perceptions of competence, the dependence of others, ambiguous roles, organisational uncertainty, organisational culture, and resource scarcity.

Specialisation and task importance

A fundamental characteristic of all organisations is the division of tasks to create specialisation of roles, functions and departments. According to Pfeffer (1981), in the process not all jobs or departments are created equally. Because of their contribution to performance, some demonstrate greater importance than others, and power is in part based on the importance of the role

The customer will not always be right if we link lecturers' pay to their popularity

Performance-related pay comes in many guises, but the latest suggestion is perhaps the most ridiculous. Among the ideas in the melting pot for the strategy document for higher education, due out in November (2002), the DfES is considering linking student feedback forms to individual·lecturers' pay as a means of enhancing teaching excellence – a disastrous prospect for students' education and lecturers everywhere.

The consequences of such policy madness are manifold. Who in their right mind will teach the least popular, but essential, courses? There would be a national shortage in statistics lecturers before the year was out, battles over the best lecture theatres and scraps over PowerPoint projectors.

The more cynical will find ways of working the system: giving out feedback forms before any coursework is marked and explaining the government term 'something for something' – a decent mark for good feedback. Photocopy budgets will rocket as handouts proliferate, ensuring that the spoon is placed firmly in every student's mouth. References to popular culture will abound as Channel 4's *Big Brother* discovers a new audience. And no lecturer will ever ask a question without answering it first.

There is a contradiction at the heart of this idea: the same people who are proposing beefing up the external examining system with the possibility of obligatory training for all who partake are assuming that students somehow know what a good course/lecturer is or does. What are they measuring? The subtle use of different theoretical perspectives to shed new light on a subject? The ability to convey complex ideas with clarity and enthusiasm? The extent to which they are challenged intellectually? I doubt it. More likely are the number of video clips and the amount of jokes included, oh and free beer often helps as well.

Research in this area shows that students judge lecturing styles and performances over and above content and academic rigour. They have also been known to judge on the basis of race, sexuality and gender.

But by far the worst consequence of putting our pay at the mercy of the student is the acceptance that the 'customer knows best'.

This is supermarket politics at its best. Students shop down the aisles of their universities, choosing which courses to add to their degree trolley. Some will base their choices on a whim – do as little work as possible; others will stick to a particular brand – the lecturers that are felt to mark highly. It is the logical end point of modularisation. But it misses a vital point: customers cannot exercise power of choice if they are unaware that certain foods or combinations of foods are not good for them. Few will opt for a healthy diet. Furthermore, choice is ever limited as the products are adapted and packaged in response to popular demand – junk education in bite-size chunks.

In higher education this means waving goodbye to degrees that attempt to equip the student with the critical skills and depth of knowledge to deal with a complex world, and to courses that are difficult and challenge students. To get to that upper second or first students will choose the path of least resistance. They already do this, of course, but at least we can still insist on core elements that we consider vital, though less popular.

In the land of performance-related pay through student assessment of courses and their lecturers, how long will this last? When the pay is so poor, the pressures so high, who can afford to take the moral high ground when all the fun of the fairground is what pays. The customer is always right.

Less popular courses will simply die and along with them the skill base for socio-economic stability. Just because languages, civil engineering, chemistry are all suffering in the popularity stakes does not mean that society needs fewer linguists, engineers and chemists. Far from it.

If individuals stand to lose pay over popularity, then who will decide to do PhDs in such subjects and take up the posts required when consumer fancy changes direction, as it always does?

If such an idea came to fruition it would not enhance teaching excellence, it would wreck it. There is nothing strategic about this idea, just sheer silliness.

Source: © Natalie Fenton, *Guardian*, 22 October 2002.

Discussion questions

1 What could be the consequences if student feedback impacted on lecturers' pay?

2 How does the government use politics to influence subjects offered at university?

Source: *San Jose Mercury News*, 19 and 20 June 1995.
Reprinted with special permission of King Features Syndicate.

within the organisation. In a brokerage house, the critical function might be credit analysis; in a bank, market development; in a software firm, programming; and for an aircraft manufacturer, engineering.

Perceptions of competence

People who perform well at organisationally critical tasks establish power for themselves. People who fail to perform to the expectations of others fall short of their power potential. Pfeffer (1981) suggests that power is also established by the people who convince others that their work is both necessary and valuable. When one manager replaces another in the same position, a shift in perceived power often follows. Depending on the perceived skills and competence of the new manager, he or she will be seen as more or less powerful than the former manager.

Dependence of others

A person's degree of power is also a function of other people's dependence on him or her to satisfy their needs. Emerson (1962) gives the following example. If Bob thinks he is dependent on Alice to attain his goal, Bob will be more apt to co-operate with Alice's wishes. The power of Alice over Bob has long been defined as 'equal to the dependence of B on A'. Consider a personal example. Suppose you need a specific course to attain the degree necessary for the job you want after graduation. Further suppose that Dr Kirk is the only one who teaches that course. Surely Dr Kirk now has more power over you than if several others taught the course or the course were not required. Dependence is often based on the number of alternatives available and the importance of the outcomes the power holder controls.

Ambiguous roles

Power plays are unlikely to affect workers in highly specific, routine jobs. But when job roles are ambiguous or professional in nature – when employees have discretion in decisions and actions – people are vulnerable to power overtures by others. The financial analyst who prepares an analysis of a proposed acquisition may skew the results to favour the position of the chief financial officer, who dangles the carrot: 'What you recommend could speed you onto a fast-track managerial career.' By contrast, the assembler who installs seat belts in cars as they pass his station is less likely to be the target of power plays by the team leader.

Organisational uncertainty

According to Pfeffer (1979), managers in organisations that are economically volatile or that are frequently buffeted by crisis rely more on power than do managers in stable organisations. In a stable organisation with a largely predictable future, employees expect their behaviour will be governed primarily by bureaucratic systems and standard operating procedures.

Organisations in turbulent environments are constantly changing – grasping for better product features and practices to increase reliability while cutting activities that add to costs. In this climate of uncertainty, managers and technical professionals resort to power plays to push for their favourite programmes. Power is more likely to be a factor influencing decisions in high-tech firms than in supermarkets, for example.

Organisational culture

Organisations differ in their predispositions to use power to influence behaviour. In some organisations, such as many public utilities, employees accept power-based decisions and political actions as a way of life. Because managers in high-power organisations act as power brokers to block or advance the careers of others, making the boss look good helps an employee's career progress. Kanter (1989) argues that by contrast, in highly task-focused organisations, position power has less influence on behaviour.

Resource scarcity

Shortages, cutbacks and general conditions of scarcity stimulate power tactics. Companies with abundant resources – a rarity these days – experience fewer power plays provided that members perceive the distribution of resources to be equitable. But, according to Pfeffer (1979), take away the resources, and power struggles intensify for whatever remains. This is especially apparent when a firm shifts from periods of growth to cyclical periods of austerity, as is common during economic recessions.

When once-successful computer and software firms shift to lay-offs and cutbacks in departmental and programme budgets during periods of declining gross margins, as happened with Apple Computers, survival instincts whet appetites for power and politics. This had been a factor contributing to the turmoil at Apple Computers. Managers and professionals used whatever influence they could muster to keep themselves and their groups insulated from lay-offs and downsizing.

In addition to the situational factors we have discussed, personal needs drive power practices. Not all people need power, and those who do have different motives.

People have different power needs

Who wants power? On the surface it seems that everyone might find it beneficial to have control over others. In actuality, individuals have different comfort levels concerning power over others. The power motive is the learned desire to have strong influence or control over others. McClelland (1975) found the power motive to be a reliable personality characteristic that varied from person to person. McClelland's research suggested that for managers to be successful leaders and to be able to influence others they should possess a high need for power. Think of your friends. Don't some like to take control and make decisions for the group more than others? What you see is differences in the need for power.

power motive
The socially acquired or learned desire to have strong influence or control over others.

Dual face of the power motive

People with a high need for power are more likely to seek out and remain in positions of authority because they enjoy influencing others to accomplish objectives. They will exercise personal power tactics to speed their promotion to positions that convey greater power. People with a low need for power, on the other hand, do not gain satisfaction from influencing others. They may lack the assertiveness and confidence necessary to direct others or to defend their group's interests in dealings with superiors and hostile outsiders. According to Winter (1973), the power motive has been found predictive of a manager's probability of rising through the hierarchy in bureaucratic organisations. However, Cornelius and Lane (1984) suggest it is less critical in technical or professional settings.

You may recall from Chapter 6 that a person's power needs can be personalised or socialised. People with personalised power needs exercise power to dominate others and keep them weak and dependent. They are often rude, sexually exploitive, aggressive, and concerned with acquiring symbols of power and status. A person with socialised power needs is more emotionally mature and exercises power for the benefit of others and of the organisation. McClelland and Burnham (1976) argue that the socialised power wielder minimises coercion, playing favourites and using power for personal gain.

Chusmir (1986) suggests that, while men and women have similar needs for power, women have a higher need for socialised power than do men. A person with a high need for socialised power is more likely to achieve visible managerial success than a person without a power need or with a personalised power need, although gender bias is a complicating factor. Strong personal power needs may improve short-run performance but bring about a later fall from power.

Power avoidance and powerlessness

Because of the responsibility it entails and the interpersonal conflicts associated with it, many people avoid power. To them it is easier and less anxiety provoking not to live up to the expectations that go along with being a powerful person. Using power inevitably embroils a person in conflict, where actions and motives are confronted and challenged. Many people would prefer to avoid emotionally charged confrontations at work.

Others publicly deny their desire for power – and sometimes even deny it to themselves – for several reasons. One is the widely held belief that power corrupts, which is supported by the way people with power have abused it in the past. Adolf Hitler is certainly a grim example. Kipnis (1976) argues that another reason for denial is that when people acquire power for its own sake, they may be covering up feelings of inferiority, compensating for deprivations, or substituting power for lack of affection. These are not images that readily fit most people's self-concepts.

Power avoidance notwithstanding, according to Kanter (1983), most people fear powerlessness, a key source of alienation. Salancik and Pfeffer (1977) argue that people realise power is one of the valid mechanisms for reality testing and getting things done in organisations. Powerlessness and organisational ambiguities contribute to a person's use of political behaviours. People who feel powerless invest their energy in dysfunctional behaviour like protecting their turf, avoiding difficult issues, covering up mistakes, avoiding risks and resorting to self-serving politics.

How people engage in organisational politics

Contrary to popular opinion, 'politics' originally referred to actions that served society. In the eighteenth century, being political meant engaging in public service. However, times and meanings have changed. Even the ideology underlying the formation of the Labour and Conservative political parties – that of serving large interest groups – has largely faded from political reality (Drucker, 1989).

Organisational politics has been defined, by Mayes and Allen (1977), as the deliberate 'management of influence to obtain ends not sanctioned by the organisation or to obtain sanctioned ends through non-sanctioned influence means'. Whereas, according to Allen *et al.* (1979), power can be a latent force (a capability), politics involves deliberate actions to develop and use power to counter the goals, ideas or plans advanced by competing interests.

organisational politics
The deliberate management of influence to achieve outcomes not approved by the organisation, or to obtain sanctioned outcomes through non-approved methods.

Because it functions outside the official system, the purpose of politics is to shift otherwise ambiguous outcomes to one's personal advantage. Thomas (1994) suggests that politics has been found to be an integral part of industrial life and critical to the management of change and innovation. Pfeffer (1992) even writes: 'Accomplishing innovation and change in organisations requires more than the ability to solve technical and analytic problems. Innovation almost invariably threatens the status quo, and consequently, innovation is an inherently political activity.'

While politics at times may be deceitful and even illegal, politically motivated employees often have the best interests of the organisation at heart. Political behaviour can still be service orientated, true to the original meaning of 'politics'. Politics invokes strategies intended to trip the balance of power and influence the outcome in one's favour. For example, imagine that a compensation manager believes he has a design for a better performance evaluation system. Knowing his ideas will appear radical, he meets several times with each individual who serves on the compensation policy committee to try to influence each to buy into the new scheme. His political actions are outside the required system, but his vision aims to benefit the organisation.

Organisational uncertainty increases conflict and politics

Conflict often results when performance criteria are ambiguous, goals inconsistent or dissimilar, rewards uncertain, work flows interdependent, communication lacking or organisational participants are highly competitive. Conflict among these variables is amplified when the stakes are high or power is diffused. According to Beeman and Sharkey (1987), political behaviours are likely to be intense under such conditions. By contrast, when performance standards are explicit and rewards rationally allocated, political activity usually declines.

Other conditions incite conflict and political behaviours. They emerge, for example, when resources are scarce or insufficient, so that people are motivated to manoeuvre outside the formal system to get their 'fair share'. Furthermore, it is difficult to avoid political behaviour when interacting with authoritarian personalities or people who externally attribute outcomes. Biberman (1985) suggests that since authoritarian personalities are less aware of their behaviour, they may take greater political risks, wanting to squash those who get in their way. Fandt and Ferris (1990), however, argue that politics is also likely when there is little trust among members and rewards are allocated on a zero-sum basis. But, according to Greiner and Schein (1988), perhaps most significantly political behaviour often occurs when peers work in lateral relationships in which no one has authority over the others.

As a means of dealing with inconsistent and uncertain conditions, organisational politics serves several positive functions. Political behaviour can help get the job done in spite of personnel inadequacies by working around the weak link. Politics can also be a force for change when qualified, politically active people tackle problems that resist formal solutions. A political network also serves as a grapevine for communicating with and influencing individuals throughout the organisation.

Important, decentralised decisions invite politics

As shown in Exhibit 13-5, people are more likely to become political when the decision outcome is important to them or to their group. However, according to Ferrell and Petersen (1982), because political behaviour often has costs, people tend to be selective. They do not waste their time becoming embroiled in issues where the potential outcome is insignificant.

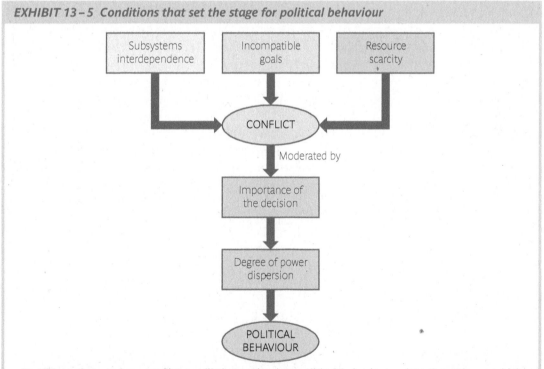

EXHIBIT 13–5 Conditions that set the stage for political behaviour

Conditions that produce conflict are likely to stimulate political behaviours when the stakes are high and power is widely diffused throughout the organisation. People then manoeuvre outside the formal system to 'get their fair share'.

Source: suggested by Jeffrey Pfeffer (1981) *Power in Organizations*. Marshfield, MA: Pitman Publishing, pp. 67–96.

The other factor moderating the use of politics is the extent to which power is dispersed or centralised. When power is concentrated towards the top of an organisation (or bureaucratic rules are widely accepted), there is less incentive to use political power to influence decisions. Politics comes into greater play when power is widely dispersed and decision-making processes are ad hoc. Coalitions then emerge, with each group supporting the position most favourable to its members.

Alternative forms of political behaviour

Political capacity is the ability and inclination to behave politically, to exercise power and influence. It has been stated by Beeman and Sharkey (1987) that 'the sum of someone's power and influence represents that person's capacity for political action. Although techniques for gaining power and influence vary, manipulating the behaviour of others is at the heart of political behaviour. Exhibit 13-6 shows that political manipulation can be positive or negative and based on power or influence. It identifies four forms of political manipulation: inducement, persuasion, obligation and coercion. Of the four, persuasion is the most gentle, coercion the most forceful.

Inducement is a stronger positive force that relies on the use of power. The manipulator offers some form of reward in exchange for compliance – perhaps more desirable assignments, greater autonomy, a larger budget or the promise of a more favourable performance review. To illustrate: 'If you back my plan with the general manager, I'll push for the capital investment you want for your lab.' However, since providing rewards may cost the manipulator, persuasion alone is often attempted first.

Obligation is a negative form of political manipulation that draws on feelings of owing the manipulator something. For example, Alex will remind Bess of the personal investment he has made in her welfare over the years. Alex may attempt to convince Bess that unless she does as he wants, she will be worse off. He might say, 'Remember how I saved your Taiwan joint venture? You've got to help me with this Singapore alliance or our entire Far East business goes down the drain.'

By contrast, in applying outright *coercion*, Alex will alter the situation so that Bess is actually worse off unless she complies. Alex might say, 'If you don't issue a purchase order for this industrial robot, I'll let management know you are contracting with a vendor who illegally disposes of toxic waste.' Coercion can backfire, so it must be used infrequently and exercised with caution. Experienced politicians often delegate coercive tactics to a committee or subordinate so they do not appear to be the 'heavy'.

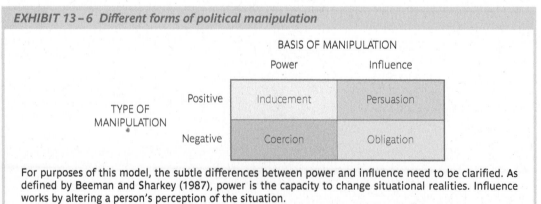

EXHIBIT 13 – 6 *Different forms of political manipulation*

		BASIS OF MANIPULATION	
		Power	Influence
TYPE OF MANIPULATION	Positive	Inducement	Persuasion
	Negative	Coercion	Obligation

For purposes of this model, the subtle differences between power and influence need to be clarified. As defined by Beeman and Sharkey (1987), power is the capacity to change situational realities. Influence works by altering a person's perception of the situation.

Source: reprinted with permission from *Business Horizons*, March–April 1987. Copyright 1987 by the Board of Trustees at Indiana University, Kelley School of Business.

Successful managers use a variety of other political tactics. One study asked people to describe incidents in which they succeeded in getting a superior, subordinate or co-worker to do what they wanted. It found that the variety of tactics used to influence another is fairly extensive. Examples of eight of these tactics appear in the 'Your turn' exercise. Take a moment to complete it now.

Your turn
A checklist of political tactics

Which of these behaviours have you used in your attempts to get others to do your bidding?

Which have others used on you? Why did they succeed or fail? Tick those used and make a note of the result.

	I have used on others	Others have used on me	Result and why
Assertiveness			
■ Point out that the rules require the person to do it.	☐	☐	_____
■ Repeatedly remind the person what is wanted.	☐	☐	_____
Ingratiation			
■ Act polite and humble while making the request.	☐	☐	_____
■ Sympathise about the hardships the request causes.	☐	☐	_____
Rational appeals			
■ Write a detailed plan justifying a request.	☐	☐	_____
■ Explain the reasons for your request.	☐	☐	_____
Sanctions			
■ Threaten to expel the person from the group.	☐	☐	_____
■ Threaten to complain to a higher authority.	☐	☐	_____
Exchanges			
■ Propose an exchange of favours.	☐	☐	_____
■ Remind the person of past favours you provided.	☐	☐	_____
Upward appeals			
■ Appeal to higher levels to support a request.	☐	☐	_____
■ Send the person to see a superior.	☐	☐	_____
Blocking			
■ Threaten to stop working with the person.	☐	☐	_____
■ Ignore the person and stop being friendly.	☐	☐	_____
Coalitions			
■ Obtain support of co-workers to back a request.	☐	☐	_____
■ Make request at meeting where others will back it.	☐	☐	_____

Source: David Kipnis, Stuart M. Schmidt and Ian Wilkson (1980) 'Intraorganisational Influence Tactics: Explorations in Getting One's Way', *Journal of Applied Psychology* 65, pp. 440–452.

Which specific influence tactic to use depends on the objective of the political attempt and the nature of the situation. Exchange and ingratiation tactics, for example, are likely to be used to obtain personal favours. Rational appeals and coalition tactics are likely to be used to gain acceptance of work-related changes. Assertiveness and sanctions are used to influence subordinates, while rational appeals are used to influence superiors.

Political tactics are learned skills

One of the more interesting realities of organisational politics is its reciprocal nature. 'I'll help you if you help me' provides the foundation for a political power base, so long as both are not direct adversaries. There will probably come a time in your career when achieving your goal hinges more on political activity than on your technical expertise. Kipnis (1983) suggests that, at the very least, you must be aware of how those around you use power in order to avoid being negatively manipulated. The tactics that follow, proposed by Greiner and Schein (1978), are common in many settings and can be learned. They may initially seem contrary to your behavioural preferences, but be forewarned – others will use them. Tactical skills include the following.

- **Maintain alliances with powerful people.** Forming coalitions and networking is basic to gaining power in any organisation. Coalitions are important not only in making committee decisions but also in day-to-day encounters. Maintain close alliances with those on whom you depend to accomplish your tasks. In addition to your boss and peers, establish working relationships with staff people who have expert or information power and with people in other departments whose work affects your own. An accommodating purchasing agent, shipper or accountant can make a big difference in how readily you get things done.

- **Avoid alienation.** In keeping with the tactic of maintaining alliances, do not injure someone who is or might soon be in a position to take revenge. The same principle applies to burning bridges that may be needed to cross future raging currents.

- **Use information as currency.** Politically astute organisational members understand the power implications of obtaining and carefully disseminating information. Sharing information with someone who needs it and has no other means of acquiring it enhances your power base. That person now owes you a favour and may perceive you as someone on whom he or she is dependent for future information.

- **Withdraw from petty disputes.** Some issues are so critical they are worth fighting for. But some conflicts are so petty that it makes more sense to concede and walk away. Be gracious in yielding on an issue that is important to another person but not to you. Doing so builds credibility and an indebtedness that might be reciprocated at a later date.

- **Avoid decisive engagement.** By advancing slowly towards a political end, it may be possible to progress undetected or at least remain sufficiently inconspicuous to avoid alarming and arming others. If an adversary's proposal appears to be gaining momentum and cannot be thwarted immediately, for example, it may be possible to refer it to a committee for further discussion. This gains a delay and a wider bargaining arena.

- **Avoid preliminary disclosure of preferences.** Appearing overly eager for a certain outcome may leave you in a vulnerable position. If the outcome of a situation is uncertain it may be advisable to support the aggressive efforts of someone else rather than take the lead yourself. This way you can get off the ship if it begins to sink. And if an impasse does occur, your timely 'fresh perspective' may be the approach that allows others to compromise.

- **Make a quick but successful showing.** Make a big, successful splash early in the game to get the right people's attention, especially if you are a newly appointed manager. Being visible, available and an apparent expert means you are likely to receive assignments and positions with more power and potential. Even once you are established in the organisation, sometimes it pays to 'shoot for the moon' on a project, so that you can later settle for less but in the process move people and programmes closer to your way of thinking.

- **Collect IOUs.** The 'Godfather' of book and film fame used IOUs to extend his realm of influence. He would do favours for 'family' members, but he made it clear that they owed him something in return. When these IOUs were called in, the debtor was expected to pay up – usually with interest. Extending favours or support to another is like depositing in a savings account, as long as you trust the person to reciprocate later.

- **Exploit possible negative outcomes.** Sometimes things must get worse before they get better. Bad news demands attention and may be the catalyst for desired change. A CEO could not convince the board to fund the acquisition of a supplier until the firm's sole source of supply was threatened by a vendor's cash-flow problems. By focusing on likely negative outcomes, those who would otherwise resist may switch to your side.

- **Divide and rule.** The assumption behind this principle is that those who are divided will not form coalitions themselves. One way to divide and rule is to approach individual members of your opponent's coalition and point out your common interests. Sociologists call this 'co-optation'. Another tactic is to identify your adversaries' weaknesses and publicise them, or reveal their behaviours that run contrary to organisational norms.

These tactics can be learned, and there are sound reasons for using them. As a rule political tactics are more successful if they are subtle and non-threatening – blatant power plays often lead to resistance, defensive reactions and retaliation. Because unobtrusive political tactics do not threaten other people's self-esteem or resource base, McCall (1978) suggests that they are less likely to cause negative reactions.

How power and politics can be moral

The use of power and politics within organisations invites a test of moral judgement. According to Cavanagh *et al.* (1981), a morally ethical manager or professional seeks to behave not just in compliance with the letter of the law or company policy, but within the spirit of it as well. Power and politically motivated behaviour need not be applied in an immoral or unethical fashion.

Morality and power are not mutually exclusive

When it comes to using power, a person's actions can be classified as moral, amoral or immoral (see Exhibit 13-7). You can evaluate your actions using this three-level classification scheme. It helps you to see whether you are applying or thinking of applying power too far beyond the boundaries of ethical propriety.

EXHIBIT 13–7 Three standards of managerial ethics

ETHICAL STANDARDS

Moral management — Treat others fairly and comply with spirit as well as letter of the law

Amoral management — Do not weigh ethical considerations in decisions, stay close to letter of the law

Immoral management — Actively oppose ethical principles; seek to get around the law

Source: reprinted with permission from *Business Horizons*, March–April 1987. Copyright 1987 by the Board of Trustees at Indiana University, Kelley School of Business.

Moral management

The **moral manager** strives to develop and adhere to ethical goals, motives, standards and general operating strategies. Power is exercised to pursue fair and just ends. The manager views laws as minimum standards of conduct. Moral management is essentially unselfish and not prone to self-serving politics. Moral management does not have to compromise performance; ethical behaviour promotes enduring self-interest.

moral manager
One who strives to develop and adhere to ethical goals, motives, standards and general operating strategies.

Moral management is consistent with innovation and continuous improvement. You can see this in the power-sharing, self-policing, continuous improvement redesigns that Japanese and German car manufacturers apply to their products to constantly upgrade quality, safety and operating performance. This has not always been the standard of conduct for other countries' car manufacturers, who at times have compromised safety to save a few pounds per vehicle in redesign costs. Moral managers support their people, recognise their accomplishments, are sensitive to their fears and needs, and communicate confidence in the organisation's purpose and products.

Immoral management

The **immoral manager**, according to Carroll (1987), is not only devoid of ethical principles, but also actively opposed to what is ethical. Selfishness is paramount for the immoral manager, whether focusing on using power for personal gain or maximising short-term gains for the firm. Senior managers of Beech-nut, the US baby food company, deliberately moved inventories of bottled sugar water (deceptively labelled as apple juice) from warehouse to warehouse in efforts to evade Food and Drug Administration investigators. According to Welles (1988), it was knowingly engaging in immoral (and illegal) behaviour. Cutting corners and concealing facts are common tactics for immoral managers obsessed with personal power. This seems to be the case in tobacco industry executives proclaiming that their product is non-addictive, and yet their proprietary research has revealed for decades the addictive capacity of tobacco.

immoral manager
One devoid of ethical principles and who is actively opposed to doing what is ethical.

Amoral management

Perhaps even more troubling than outright immoral management is the **amoral manager** who lacks any moral sensibility whatsoever. Managers who are amoral can be intentional or unintentional in approaching ethical issues. The intentionally amoral manager knowingly keeps ethics out of personal decisions within the organisation.

amoral manager
One who lacks any moral sensibility whatsoever; one who does not think about the moral implications of actions, or who chooses to keep ethics out of decisions

The unintentionally amoral manager does not think about ethics at all. He or she may lack ethical principles and thus not reflect on the broader consequences of how power is used. The amoral manager will operate within the letter of the law to the extent that it is known. However, one of the greatest dangers of amoral management is that decisions are made without anticipating negative consequences. Several well-known cases include Ford Motors. An advertising campaign in eastern Europe showing a group of Ford employees from Dagenham was altered to make all the employees white. It had even removed a turban from the head of one of the workers. Another example is Nestlé's decision to market concentrated baby formula in developing countries with impure water supplies (Carroll, 1987).

Technology poses a new ethical challenge. Bylinsky (1991) argues that technology now permits supervisors to eavesdrop on their staff's phone conversations and to secretly observe computer screens or even type in warnings when they see something they do not like. Whether the employee is a reservation agent or stockbroker, such use of power invades privacy with an aura of 'Big Brother is watching you'. Electronic eavesdropping is not only a questionable use of power, but it can accentuate negative feedback and lead to the overuse of punishment to boost performance.

How politics are pluralistic

Active political behaviour can be healthy because it forces the clash of ideas. Although the 'best' idea may not always prevail, at least people are encouraged to defend their views. Greiner and Schein (1988) refer to this as the 'pluralistic/political model', which they contend is the most realistic way to describe how organisational actors arrive at decisions. 'The pluralistic/political model sees organisations as composed of differing interest groups. Each party pursues its own goals, sometimes on selfish grounds but often for well-intended reasons based on its view of what is best for the organisation as a whole.'

Organisational politics requires dispersion of power throughout an organisation, which means people are free to disagree. When power is tightly centralised within a hierarchy, decisions are protected from politics. This applies to nations as well as to organisations. Pfeffer (1981) observes:

> There is more political activity in democratic countries with relatively equal political parties than there is in countries which are run by strong dictatorships. Ironically, when power is dispersed, decisions become worked out through the interplay of various actors with more equal power in a political process.

Only with knowledge of how political behaviour works can you analyse your own dependencies, assess the sources and strength of your power, and recognise when political tactics are being used to influence you. The degree to which you apply political skills depends on the nature of your situation and your personality. However, an awareness of their use and consequences will enhance your personal and organisational effectiveness. This is an awareness that government leaders need to be especially cognisant of, as illustrated in the Technology Transformation box.

technology transformation

'Wading upstream through treacle': modernisation – or the lack of it

The following case is an example of how, according to the view of a young policeman in southern England, politics can affect performance.

'I, along with my colleagues from other forces, am extremely frustrated with the organisation as a whole. Officers at command level are more interested in how their actions affect their careers than how they affect the community and their officers. I'll give you a recent example well known inside the south-coast grapevine.

'The latest weapon in the fight against crime is a US system called CompStat (computer comparison statistics). This is a system combining intelligence and computer software to give up-to-the-second tracking and mapping of where crime is happening. This tells a police force where it should patrol, and brings the hotspot to an early conclusion.

'A Sussex officer researched this system and introduced a home-made form of it in Hove. The crime rate fell by 30 per cent last year.

'This year, however, Hove and Brighton divisions were amalgamated. Under the revamped command team, the Hove system has lapsed, and crime hotspots have returned.

'When it comes to budgets and funding, a lot of things are beyond police forces' power to change. All I would say is that the management of police money is the most laughable thing since Lord Archer denied lying in court.

'Example. A search warrant is planned to be executed one Saturday at an address where two kilos of crack cocaine are believed to be stored, plus firearms. On the Thursday before, the targeted individual is unexpectedly arrested.

'The suspect is in police custody, away from any firearms – yet an immediate search is not authorised. The original plan is upheld, though it is much riskier and could end in lives being lost with use of guns. Why? Because it would incur no overtime.'

Geoff Hyams, 38, until recently a Met detective inspector running murder squads in southwest London; now head of the Internet portal Police Oracle:

'Britain has a world-renowned police organisation whose foundation is the officer on the street. But having moved into the private sector, I find it frustrating to see all the technology and expertise available here on the commercial side that would have helped me and my colleagues but about which we and most other operational police knew nothing. Such as: palmtop computers that can link with the police national computer and voter registers to make the use of stop-and-search powers more efficient; mobile fingerprint-recognition systems that could so easily help in the first few "golden hours" of a missing person or murder investigation; computerised property systems that lessen chances that the reliability of forensic evidence will be questioned in court, and that radically streamline police practices in holding and submitting exhibits.

'I have also seen private consortiums willing to put their knowledge into police organisations until they realise that the "not invented here" syndrome makes trying to get innovative public–private initiatives accepted about as easy as wading upstream through treacle.

'Products developed in-house can rapidly become obsolete, as police organisations do not have the commercial incentive to remain at the cutting edge. Private companies do. But police suspicion of the private sector and reluctance to add to its profits mean forces often don't modernise as quickly as they might if they let the private sector keep them at the forefront of technology.

'And management seem to accept with a shrug the often ridiculous waste of money stemming from lack of co-operation between forces. Research, consultancy and support costs are often multiplied by 40 or 50 times as each force goes it alone.'

These attitudes all need reassessing and the policing debate needs dragging wider to consider public–private partnerships in information technology, management support, crime prevention – and how best to get and keep staff at a time when lack of experience on the street is being exacerbated by an exodus of long-service staff.

Source: © Geoff Hymes, *Guardian*, 3 October 2002.

Discussion questions

1 Why does politics interfere with the performance of cracking crime?
2 How can political behaviour be reduced?

No more dog eat dog: a second look

This bleak Thatcherite 'dog eat dog' ideology of working life has sunk deep roots into the national psyche. If you talk about improving any aspect of working life – for example, the book I wrote on reducing working time last year – the most common response is fear about losing jobs to China and falling behind in the global rat race. In fact, as David Coats points out in his excellent *Agenda for Work* published last week, only 2–3 per cent of jobs are likely to be off-shored by 2020. Another myth to be debunked, which has been used by successive governments (Tory and Labour) to bully the British workforce, is 'no jobs for life'. In fact, job tenure has barely changed in the past 20 years, and is now even increasing.

The reality is that by dint of a combination of demographic trends and a strong economy resulting in near-full employment, the British workforce has probably never been in a stronger position to renegotiate and reimagine its conditions of labour – not just on pay, but on working time, trust, autonomy and empowerment. Why shouldn't our preoccupation with quality of life be applied as much to our working lives as our made-over homes and holidays? That's not a logic relished by New Labour, which has notably maintained much of the Thatcherite workplace legacy, and refuses even to drop the opt-out on the EU Working Time Directive for fear of antagonising business. The problem is that none of that incipient power will be realised unless workers see their interests as in common, not in competition, and develop the campaigning organisations – revived trades unions or something new? – to put those interests on the public agenda. The alternative is absolute monarchy.

Source: © Guardian Newspapers Ltd, 2005, Madeline Bunting.

Summary

- Power is the basic force managers use to change organisational realities by getting others to do what they want done. Anyone can have power, but managers and leaders have power advantages since their positions in social networks place them at the centre of information and decision exchanges; people thus expect them to act powerfully.

- Power can arise from a person's position (as do formal authority and reward power) or personal behaviour (as do expert and referent power). However, situational forces allow other power possibilities (such as coercion and access to information), which affect the degree to which a person can alter the realities of others and thus exercise power.

- Some people's socialised power needs energise them to act in keeping with organisational purposes. Others with high personal power needs have more self-serving aims. Some seek to avoid power altogether, not wanting the responsibility and potential conflict often associated with it.

- Organisational politics occur when people or groups seek to alter resources or outcomes in their favour. Political behaviours increase when conditions are uncertain, complex and competitive. Political manipulation can take the form of inducement, persuasion, obligation or coercion.

- Political tactics, such as maintaining coalitions with powerful people, using information as currency, avoiding premature disclosure of preferences and collecting IOUs, are learned skills.

- However, the practice of being political or exercising power does not need to be immoral or even amoral.

- Moral managers act fairly and legally to do that which is ethically right in the service of the organisation.

- Across nations as well as organisations, political activities abound when power is disbursed and multiple interest groups jockey for position. Tightly centralised power limits people's freedom to act politically.

Areas for personal development

Most people are wary of managers who hold power and exercise it freely. In an era focused more on collaboration and team effort, inappropriate use of power can result in organisational and career problems. However, there are times when a manager needs to use power to resolve problems within the organisation. You can be more effective in managing and applying power if you apply the following interpersonal skills.

1 **Do not rely on commanding obedience based on your formal authority.** Managers often have 'position power', which originates from the rights they hold in the organisational hierarchy, such as legitimate authority and the power to reward and punish. Managers can use that power to command obedience from their subordinates. However, requiring obedience at all costs may actually harm the organisation if the manager's performance depends on the creativity or expertise of the employees. Furthermore, if those receiving the orders refuse to comply, the manager's authority will be questioned. Managers can be more effective by working together with their employees to arrive at suitable solutions. However, in emergency situations or when problems involving complex differences of opinion arise, a manager should exercise his or her formal authority.

2 **Cultivate personal power.** Personal power may be more effective in dealing with employees, because it is unrelated to the manager's position within the organisation or other external factors. Subordinates are more inclined to follow a manager based on his or her qualifications, experience and behaviour than just on position in the company alone. You can enhance your personal power by increasing your expertise, developing strong interpersonal skills and building reciprocal alliances.

3 **Empower employees to increase their own personal power.** As subordinates' personal power increases, they will begin to feel more responsible for the quality of their work. A manager should share information and knowledge with his or her employees and reward good performance to empower employees to take responsibility for their contribution.

4 **Seek situations that enhance your power.** Situations that can enhance your power base include those where you are a specialist, your assigned task is important, others perceive you as being competent, others are dependent on you for information or services, you can resolve role ambiguity and organisational uncertainty, and you control scarce resources. Situations in which you are the only one with high power needs can also enhance your influence over others who do not have such desires.

5 **Manage language and actions to avoid bias.** Even in these times of growing acceptance and globalisation, preferences for some individuals or groups, or negative attitudes about minorities can still be found at all levels in organisations. Managers need to recognise that bias occurs and carefully structure their own behaviour to ensure that all subordinates are given equal treatment and that any negative behaviours or attitudes are dealt with immediately. Otherwise, your behaviour will come back to bite you in the form of retaliations and attempts to neutralise your power.

6 **Recognise and willingly engage in organisational politics where necessary.** Power may be a dirty word in the UK, but little can be accomplished without it. Although it is tempting to avoid power and politics because of the associated social disapproval, both are necessary to be a successful manager. Power is often pivotal to successful organisational change and to protect yourself from being manipulated, exploited or squelched, like a pawn in another person's game.

7 **Practise the different forms of political manipulation appropriately.** Use *persuasion* utilising emotion and logic to influence others to perceive the situation in a better light and feel better off. Use *inducement* by offering some form of reward in exchange for compliance. Use *obligation* by drawing on feelings of owing you something for past favours you have done. Finally, use *coercion* by threatening to alter the situation so that the other person is worse off unless he or she complies with your request. Coercion can backfire, however, so it must be used infrequently and with caution.

8 **Learn political tactics.** Be aware of and be skilled at utilising political tactics such as being assertive, ingratiating yourself with others, making rational appeals, threatening sanctions, suggesting exchanges, making upward appeals, blocking opponents' goals and forming coalitions. Even if you do not initiate these tactics yourself, you need to be able to recognise them in order to defend yourself against those who do.

❓ Questions for study and discussion

1 Power has been defined as the ability to alter another person's behaviour. In what ways can a manager use position power to alter someone's behaviour? How can a non-manager use personal power?

2 Why does position power seem to be more accepted in western societies such as the UK than in eastern societies such as Japan? Relate your answer to the concept of centrality within a social network.

3 Create a scenario that describes the ideal conditions under which a manager will have power over a group. Incorporate at least four situational factors into the picture you paint of power.

4 How do people's power needs differ? How do the different orientations towards power of people with high power needs influence their chances for personal and organisational success?

5 How do inducement, persuasion, obligation and coercion differ? If you were a manager, which form of political manipulation would you use most? Why?

6 Suppose your boss suggested that your contribution to the department would be stronger if you could draw on a more versatile portfolio of political behaviours. Identify four political tactics you would feel comfortable using and describe situations in which you might use each.

7 What is the difference between an immoral and an amoral manager? Comment on how you could use the political tactics you identified in Question 6 and still be a moral manager.

8 Why are political activities less likely to occur in a tightly centralised system? Do you foresee an increase or decrease in political behaviours in developing countries? Why?

🔑 Key Concepts

power, *p. 601*

position power, *p. 602*

formal authority, *p. 603*

reward power, *p. 603*

coercive power, *p. 604*

legitimate power, *p. 604*

expert power, *p. 604*

mentor, *p. 604*

referent power, *p. 605*

charisma, *p. 605*

reciprocity, *p. 606*

information power, *p. 606*

association power, *p. 606*

social exchange theory, *p. 613*

power motive, *p. 621*

organisational politics, *p. 622*

moral manager, *p. 628*

immoral manager, *p. 628*

amoral manager, *p. 629*

Personal skills exercise

Personal power strategies

Purpose To increase awareness of power bases and strategies actually used by members of the class and to provide feedback on how their political effectiveness can be enhanced.

Time This is a two-part exercise. For a class of less than 1 hour in duration, complete Part 1, which provides insights into personal applications of power bases. Part 2 can be completed in the next class session if desired. Part 2 also takes about an hour to complete and provides insights into positional versus personal power bases as well as individual influence tactics.

Preparation For both parts of the exercise, review the bases of power and influence strategies described in this chapter. Make sure you have as many index cards (or better yet, 'name tag' stickers) as you have participants. People in classes completing Part 2 need to bring £1.00 to class and be prepared to risk it. After the exercise is over, they may get their money back, lose it all or actually get more back. Members who do not want to 'buy into' Part 2 of this learning experience can opt to be observers.

Procedure Divide the class into groups of seven participants who remain together for both parts of the exercise. Within each group, complete the following tasks.

Part 1 (50 to 60 minutes)

Task 1 Discuss the seven bases of power: legitimate, reward, coercive, referent, expert, information and association. Through consensus, rank-order these bases from most important to least important in terms of their effectiveness in influencing classroom behaviour (15 to 20 minutes).

Task 2 Group members all stand up. Then they physically line up according to the degree of influence each person had in establishing the power base ranking in Task 1. Again use group consensus to determine a continuous order of influence from number 1, most influential, to number 7, least influential. Physically reposition and discuss the line-up until all are satisfied that it is the best possible representative ranking.

Each person is assigned the number corresponding to his or her place in the line-up. The most influential person becomes number 1, and so on. Each person writes his or her number on a card or sticker and displays it throughout the remainder of the task activity (5 to 10 minutes).

Task 3 Group members sit down and discuss why the rankings came out the way they did (15 minutes).

Task 4 The total class debriefs key learning from the exercise (15 minutes).

Part 2 (55 to 85 minutes) Part 1 must be completed before Part 2 can be experienced. There are four tasks for Part 2.

Task 1 Assign each person the number of votes that they now display (i.e. their place in the previous influence ranking). Collect £1.00 from each participant and place the coins in a pile in the centre of the group. Participants now decide how to divide up the total pot according to the following instructions (30 minutes).

- Your objective is to influence the group decision so as to win as much money for yourself as possible. You may use any personal influence strategies (e.g. coalition formation, holding out, charisma, rational development) not outlawed in these instructions.

- At least two people (one-third of the group) cannot receive any money back at all. The pot can be divided among the remaining group members in any proportion decided upon (e.g. one member can receive it all, it can be divided evenly among the remaining two-thirds, or it can be distributed in unequal proportions).

- The money allocation decision is to be determined by the casting of votes. Each group member may cast the number of votes on his or her place card or sticker (i.e. formal organisational power).

- The voting procedure is to be determined by the group. Possible procedures could include: (a) one voting round to place all your votes for the person(s) you want to receive all the money; (b) several rounds of voting for the people you want to receive equal shares of money until only two people are left out. For example, if five people are in the group, you would vote three times electing one recipient in the first vote, another is the second vote and the third in the final vote.

- Do not attempt a hasty vote. Wait until all group members have had their say and indicate a readiness to vote.

- It is *not legitimate* to: (1) use any chance procedures such as matching coins or drawing straws; (2) simply give your votes to someone else and not participate in the decision, (3) agree to return the original £1.00 contributions after the exercise; (4) agree to buy everyone drinks after class, etc. In other words, at least two people must never get their money back, and it is not possible to opt out of the political process.

Task 2 Individually write down the answers to the following questions (10 minutes).

1 What were your feelings as you participated in this exercise?

2 From what power bases did you draw?

3 What influence strategies did you utilise?

Task 3 Discuss your answers with others in your group (30 minutes).

- Give group members feedback regarding the effectiveness of their individual behaviour.
- Discuss why those winning the conflict were more successful.
- How might the outcome have been different in different circumstances?
- Finally, share what you learned about yourself regarding your feelings and your style of using power in conflict situations.

Task 4 The class debriefs the exercise by sharing key learning from the exercise (15 minutes).

Team exercise

The Power Game (Bowen *et al.*, 1997; Bolman and Deal, 1979)

Purpose To explore the dynamics of power at the individual, interpersonal, group and system levels. To create opportunities for students to examine their personal beliefs and attitudes about power, power strategies and reactions to power.

Step 1 Students each give the tutor a pound coin to be used in the exercise. How this money will be used will be explained later. This is your personal investment in the exercise. You may get more or less money back at the end of the exercise. Students not wanting to contribute a pound can serve as observers.

Step 2 Students are divided into three groups: the top group consisting of three to five members, the middle group consisting of six to ten members, the bottom group consisting of the remaining class members (at least twice as large as the middle group).

Step 3 The money is divided into thirds. Two-thirds of it is given to the top group to do with as it wishes. One-third is given to the middle group to do with as it wishes. No money at all is given to the bottom group.

Step 4 The groups are assigned to their workplaces. The top group gets the best place (e.g. office or lounge with comfortable chairs and door that can be shut). The middle group gets a suitable place like a seminar room, also with a door that can be shut. The bottom group gets the least desirable space (e.g. a hallway or a lecture hall with non-movable chairs).

Step 5 Groups go to their assigned workplaces and read the instructions provided below about their rules and tasks. Then the groups have exactly 60 minutes to complete their tasks.

Rules

1 Members of the top group are free to enter the space of either of the other groups and to communicate whatever they wish, whenever they wish. Members of the middle group may enter the space of the lower group when they wish but must request permission to enter

the top group's space (which the top group can refuse). Members of the lower group may not disturb the top group in any way unless specifically invited by the top group. The lower group does have the right to knock on the door of the middle group and request permission to communicate with it (which the middle group can refuse).

2   The members of the top group have the authority to make any change in the rules that they wish, at any time, with or without notice.

Tasks and responsibilities

1   **Top group:** to be responsible for the overall effectiveness and learning from the exercise, and to decide what to do with its money (two-thirds of the total coins collected).

2   **Middle group:** to assist the top group in maximising the overall effectiveness of the exercise, and to decide what to do with its money (one-third of the total coins collected).

3   **Bottom group:** to identify its resources to influence the other two groups and to decide how best to contribute to the learning and the overall effectiveness of the exercise.

Debriefing Each of the three groups discusses the following questions. They then choose two representatives to go to the front of the class and discuss their answers with representatives from the other groups.

1   Summarise what occurred within and among the three groups.

2   What are some of the differences between being in the top group versus being in the bottom group?

3   What can we learn about power from this experience?

4   Which groups and individuals were more influential or less influential? How was influence expressed in these groups (e.g. personal deals, negotiation strategies, coercive efforts)?

5   How close do you think this exercise is to the reality of making resource allocation decisions in large organisations?

Case study: time running out on outdated age discrimination legislation – an ageing population and reduced pensions mean that many people will be forced to delay their long-awaited retirement

British bosses will be comforting themselves today that the latest age discrimination case to hit the headlines has broken in America, the litigation capital of the world.

They will no doubt be reassured that, although 56-year-old Sharon Haugh is suing a UK company, the merchant bank Schroders, she is using US laws, which for many years have recognised the rights of an ageing workforce.

Schroders insists it is committed to equal opportunities and denies the claim. Yet, in Britain, to discriminate on the basis of age alone has never been illegal. But, by 2006, this will change and cases will become commonplace in British courts. In four years' time, ministers must meet their obligations to comply with European Union equality laws, which include tough rules on age discrimination.

British employment lawyers are already warning their City clients that when age discrimination becomes illegal, damages will start to mirror the kind of record payouts recently witnessed in sex and race discrimination cases.

This comes at a time when there is more incentive than ever for British employees to keep working. The ageing population, and the widespread abolition of final salary pension schemes, have forced many people to delay their plans for retirement.

While the appetite to keep working is often not reciprocated by many employers, some do value older staff keen to keep working.

Tesco, for example, embraces mature employees and is proud of the fact that one in six of the supermarket chain's 200 000 staff is over the age of 50.

Evidence that the benefits cut both ways was evident at Tesco's branch in Canary Wharf, East London, yesterday. Janakumar Vyas, 47, started his job three years ago after selling his Indian sweet-shop.

He said he had not encountered ageism at work and has not found age a hindrance to his tasks, which include restocking and shelf-stacking in the wine and spirits section.

'I feel I'm able to do my job properly, as well as anyone else at the store. I will keep on working until I feel otherwise,' Mr Vyas said.

James Davies, chairman of the Employment Lawyers Association working group on age discrimination, says that employers should immediately start drawing up workplace policies to 'avoid any inference of discrimination which can be based on age'. Although the government has until 2006 to comply with the directive it can act sooner if it wishes.

Under British law an older worker has very little protection from discrimination. Anyone dismissed will have to prove that he or she qualifies for compensation under the rules of unfair dismissal.

Mr Davies, an employment law expert with the London law firm Lewis Silkin, says that an employee who can show that the sacking was for reason of age alone will be able to win an unfair dismissal claim. But such claims are capped at a little over £50 000. Under the proposed change in the law, an older employee will not only be able to claim unlimited damages but will not have to wait to be sacked before starting a legal action.

Many charities and lawyers argue that there is a compelling case for Britain to be seen to want to eliminate age discrimination by acting now rather than being pushed into it by Brussels in 2006.

Debbie Smith, campaigns manager for Help the Aged, said yesterday: 'The case of Sharon Haugh demonstrates that age discrimination is rife in society today. This case, and many others like it, shows the need for action to be taken to outlaw age discrimination, in all its forms, now.

'Unless the government legislates against age discrimination now rather than the proposed 2006, the UK will continue to deny itself a huge wealth of talent, skills and experience from a large and growing section of the community.'

But all indications are that the government would much rather stall on this issue until it has solved the greater problem of how to support an increasingly ageing population against the uncertain future of the pensions market.

This month Patricia Hewitt, secretary of state for Trade and Industry, announced that ministers would be appealing against a tribunal ruling that gives thousands of workers aged over 65 the right to claim for unfair dismissal. The decision to make an appeal has mystified lawyers and age campaigners alike.

The tribunal decision, made in August, gives workers aged over 65 the right to claim for unfair dismissal and redundancy payments.

John Rutherford, 71, and Samuel Bentley, 74, won a claim for indirect sexual harassment when they were dismissed from their jobs in the clothing industry for being over 65. They argued that there were far more men than women working over the age of 65, and therefore the cut-off point at 65 years discriminated against men.

The Employers Forum on Age (EFA) is unhappy that the government is to appeal against the employment tribunal, whose landmark decision was widely seen as a step towards stopping age discrimination. 'Whether the government appeal is successful or not, when someone is unfairly dismissed they should be able to make a claim whatever their age, as a matter of principle,' said an EFA spokesman.

In a seemingly contradictory move, which highlights the government's growing uncertainty in this area, ministers are planning to change Inland Revenue rules to make it much simpler for employers to retain older workers.

Under reforms outlined this month by Andrew Smith, the Work and Pensions secretary, employees will be able to stay on at work after retirement age while drawing their company pension. Current Inland Revenue rules prevent anyone from taking a pension and salary from the same employer. This makes it virtually impossible for staff to wind down to part-time work or take a less senior position with the same company while supplementing their income with a company pension.

The government knows that time is running out on its plans to provide for the economic security of an ageing population. No worker wants to feel that the only way of supporting themselves into their retirement is by suing their boss over a case of age discrimination.

Source: Robert Veraik in the *Independent*, 9 October 2002, p. 15.

Questions for managerial action

1   What can companies do to protect themselves from legal action with regard to ageism?

2   What ramifications could this relationship have for other organisational members and for organisational effectiveness in general if people no longer have to retire?

3   Should the government legislate or should companies be left to decide their own workplace policies?

Applied questions

4   How can older people build political power in organisations to ensure that their views are represented?

5   Diversity can become threatened by power relationships. How can organisations ensure that power is dispersed throughout the workplace and that everyone has an equal value?

WWW exercise

Manager's Internet tools

Web tips: power for dealing with sexual harassment from the World Wide Web
Sexual harassment and gender discrimination cause businesses to lose millions of pounds each year in legal costs and lowered productivity. Yet, despite heightened awareness of such incidents in the workplace, many companies either deny their existence or do not implement enough measures to prevent their occurrence. This is partly due to fear and ignorance about how to proceed. The Internet provides a wealth of information to help both organisations and individuals understand and deal productively with sexual harassment.

World Wide Web search
Information about sexual harassment can be found by keying into a search engine. You may also want to look at online newspaper articles and review recent cases of sexual harassment and gender discrimination. Think about how companies could have avoided these cases. Do not forget there are also other forms of discrimination. How can these be avoided with explicit equal opportunities policies?

Specific website
Students are required to search for themselves.

Discussion questions
Choose a website for a company that you are interested in working for. Do they have policies on gender discrimination? How do these translate into action in the workplace?

1 From a sexual harassment website, read some of the latest cases about sexual harassment. What are some of the common power and political ramifications in these cases?

2 From a legal viewpoint, define and give examples of the two legally recognised types of sexual harassment.

3 If someone in the workplace uses profanity or other sexually explicit language that offends, does that create a hostile work environment?

4 How effective do you think your chosen company's policies and procedures are for preventing sexual harassment? Why?

5 What can an individual who is being sexually harassed do to deal with the harassment? Check the information on a sexual harassment website for some answers.

LEARNING CHECKLIST

Before you move on you may want to reflect on what you have learnt in this chapter. You should now be able to:

☑ understand why power is useful in organisations

☑ describe forms of power originating from position, personal characteristics, and situational forces

☑ explain how social networks create opportunities for managers to establish power

☑ identify situational factors that affect power and explain why power is context specific

☑ describe the differences among four forms of political manipulation – persuasion, inducement, obligation and coercion

☑ identify tactics for developing political power

☑ differentiate among moral, immoral and amoral modes of handling power

☑ explain why centralisation diminishes political behaviour.

Further reading

Abel, C.F. (2005) 'Beyond the Mainstream: Foucault, Power and Organization Theory', *International Journal of Organisation Theory and Behaviour* 8, Winter, pp. 495–520.

Miner, J.B. (1978) *The Management Process: Theory, Research, and Practice* (2nd edn). New York, NY: Macmillan, pp. 179–180.

Mintzberg, H. (1983) *Power In and Around Organizations*. Englewood Cliffs, NJ: Prentice Hall.

Rosen, C.C., Levy, P.E. and Hall, R.J. (2006) 'Placing Perceptions of Politics in the Context of the Feedback Environment, Employee Attitudes and Job Performance', *Journal of Applied Psychology* 91(1), January, p. 18.

Treadway, D.C., Adams, G.L. and Goodman, J.M. (2005) 'The Formation of Political Sub-climates: Predictions from Social Identity, Structuration and Symbolic Interaction', *Journal of Business and Psychology* 20(2), Winter, p. 201.

References

Abegglen, J.C. and Stalk Jr, G. (1985) *Kaisha: The Japanese Corporation*. New York, NY: Basic Books.

Allen, M.P., Panian, S.K. and Lotz, R.E. (1979) 'Managerial Succession and Organizational Performance: A Recalcitrant Problem Revisited', *Administrative Science Quarterly* 24, p. 177.

Bacharach, S.B. and Lawler, E.J. (1980) *Power and Politics in Organizations*. San Francisco, CA: Jossey-Bass, Chapter 3.

Baldwin, D.A. (1978) 'Power and Social Exchange', *The American Political Science Review* 72, pp. 1229–1242.

Barnard, C. (1938) *The Functions of the Executive*. Cambridge, MA: Harvard University Press, Chapter 12.

Beeman, D.R. and Sharkey, T.W. (1987) 'The Use and Abuse of Corporate Politics', *Business Horizons* 30, March–April, p. 27.

Biberman, G. (1985) 'Personality and Characteristic Work Attitudes of Persons with High, Moderate, and Low Political Tendencies', *Psychological Reports*, October, pp. 1303–1310.

Biggart, N.W. (1984) 'The Power of Obedience', *Administrative Science Quarterly* 29, pp. 540–549.

Bolman, L. and Deal, T.E. (1979) 'The Power Game', *Journal of Management Education* 4(3), pp. 38–42.

Bowen, D.D., Lewicki, R.J., Hall, F.T. and Hall, F.S. (1997) *Experiences in Management and Organizational Behavior* (4th edn). New York, NY: John Wiley & Sons, pp. 204–206.

Brass, D.J. (1984) 'Being in the Right Place: A Structural Analysis of Individual Influence in an Organization', *Administrative Science Quarterly* 29, pp. 518–539.

Brass, D.J. (1985) 'Men's and Women's Networks: A Study of Interaction Patterns and Influence in an Organization', *Academy of Management Journal* 28, June, pp. 327–343.

Bylinsky, G. (1991) 'How Companies Spy on Employees', *Fortune*, 4 November, pp. 131–140.

Carroll, A.B. (1987) 'In Search of the Moral Manager', *Business Horizons* 30, March–April, p. 9.

Cartwright, D. (1965) 'Leadership, Influence, and Control', in James G. March (ed.) *Handbook of Organizations*. Chicago, IL: Rand-McNally, pp. 1–47.

Cavanagh, G.F., Moberg, D.J. and Velasquez, M. (1981) 'The Ethics of Organizational Politics', *Academy of Management Review* 6, July, pp. 363–374.

Chusmir, L.H. (1986) 'Personalized vs Socialized Power Needs among Working Women and Men', *Human Relations* 39, February, pp. 149–159.

Ciampa, D. (1992) *Total Quality: A User's Guide for Implementation*. Reading, MA: Addison-Wesley, pp. 175–202.

Cohen, A.R. and Bradford, D.L. (1991) 'Influence without Authority: The Use of Alliances, Reciprocity, and Exchange to Accomplish Work', in B.M. Staw (ed.) *Psychological Dimensions of Organizational Behavior*. New York, NY: Macmillan, p. 384.

Cole, R.E. (1990) 'US Quality Improvement in the Auto Industry: Close but No Cigar', *California Management Review* 32, Summer, p. 77.

Cornelius, E.T. and Lane, F.B. (1984) 'The Power Motive and Managerial Success in a Professionally Oriented Service Industry Organization', *Journal of Applied Psychology* 69, pp. 32–39.

Drucker, P.F. (1989) *The New Realities*. New York, NY: Harper & Row, pp. 76–105.

Duchon, D., Green, S.G. and Taber, T.D. (1986) 'Vertical Dyad Linkage: A Longitudinal Assessment of Antecedents, Measures, and Consequences', *Journal of Applied Psychology*, February, pp. 55–60.

Dumaine, B. (1991) 'The Bureaucracy Busters', *Fortune*, p. 42.

Emerson, R.M. (1962) 'Power–Dependence Relations', *American Sociological Review* 27, pp. 31–40.

Fairhurst, G.T. and Snavely, B.K. (1983) 'Majority and Token Minority Group Relationships: Power Acquisition and Communication', *Academy of Management Review* 8, April, pp. 293–300.

Fandt, P.M. and Ferris, G.R. (1990) 'The Management of Information and Impressions: When Employees Behave Opportunistically', *Organizational Behavior and Human Decision Processes*, February, pp. 140–148.

Ferrell, D. and Petersen, J.C. (1982) 'Patterns of Political Behavior in Organizations', *Academy of Management Review* 7, July, pp. 403–412.

Ford, R.C. and Fottler, M.D. (1995) 'Empowerment: A Matter of Degree', *Academy of Management Executive* 9, August, pp. 21–29.

French Jr, J.R.P. and Raven, B. (1962) 'The Bases of Social Power', in Dorwin Cartwright (ed.) *Group Dynamics: Research and Theory*. Evanston, IL: Row, Peterson, pp. 607–623.

Greiner, L.E. and Schein, V.E. (1988) *Power and Organizational Development: Mobilizing Power to Implement Change*. Reading, MA: Addison-Wesley, pp. 18–23.

Grimes, A.J. (1978) 'Authority, Power, Influence, and Social Control: A Theoretical Synthesis', *Academy of Management Review* 3, October, pp. 724–735.

Hollander, E.P. (1979) 'Leadership and Social Exchange Process', in K.J. Gergen, M.S. Greenberg and R.H. Willis (eds) *Social Exchange: Advances in Theory and Research*. New York, NY: Winston-Wiley.

Kanter, R.M. (1977) *Men and Women of the Corporation*. New York, NY: Basic Books, Chapter 7.

Kanter, R.M. (1983) 'Power Failure in Management Circuits', in J. Allen and L. Porter (eds) *Organizational Influence Processes*. New York, NY: Scott, Foresman, pp. 87–104.

Kanter, R.M. (1989) *When Giants Learn to Dance*. New York, NY: Simon & Schuster, Chapter 6.

Kipnis, D. (1976) *The Powerholders*. Chicago, IL: University of Chicago Press, pp. 77–78.

Kipnis, D. (1983) 'The Use of Power', in J. Allen and L. Porter (eds) *Organizational Influence Processes*. New York, NY: Scott, Foresman, pp. 17–32.

Krackhardt, D. (1990) 'Assessing the Political Landscape: Structure, Cognition, and Power in Organizations', *Administrative Science Quarterly* 35, June, pp. 342–369.

Leavitt, H.J. (1978) *Managerial Psychology* (4th edn). Chicago, IL: University of Chicago Press, pp. 148–155.

Levine, D.I. (1990) 'Participation, Productivity, and the Firm's Environment', *California Management Review* 32, Summer, p. 86.

Lincoln, J.R. (1989) 'Employee Work Attitudes and Management Practice in the US and Japan: Evidence from a Large Comparative Survey', *California Management Review* 32, Fall, pp. 89–106.

Mayes, B.T. and Allen, R.W. (1977) 'Toward a Definition of Organizational Politics', *Academy of Management Review* 2, October, pp. 672–677.

McCall Jr, M.W. (1978) *Power, Influence, and Authority: The Hazards of Carrying a Sword*. Greensboro, NC: Center for Creative Leadership, Technical Report No. 10.

McClelland, D.C. (1975) *Power: The Inner Experience*. New York, NY: Irvington.

McClelland, D.C. and Burnham, D.H. (1976) 'Power is the Great Motivator', *Harvard Business Review* 54, March–April, pp. 100–110.

Mroczkowski, T. and Hanaoka, M. (1989) 'Continuity and Change in Japanese Management', *Human Resources*, Winter, p. 52.

Mulder, M., Koppelaar, L., de Jong, R. and Verhage, J. (1986) 'Power, Situation, and Leader's Effectiveness: An Organizational Field Study', *Journal of Applied Psychology* 71, pp. 566–570.

Ng, S.H. (1980) *The Social Psychology of Power*. London: Academic Press, Chapter 3.

Pfeffer, J. (1979) 'Power and Resource Allocation in Organizations', in R. Miles and W. Randolph (eds) *The Organizational Game*. Santa Monica, CA: Goodyear, pp. 232–246.

Pfeffer, J. (1981) *Power in Organizations*. Marshfield, MA: Pitman, p. 5.

Pfeffer, J. (1992) *Managing with Power: Politics and Influence in Organizations*. Boston, MA: Harvard Business School Press.

Reardon, K.K. (1993) 'Betty Friedan on "The Second Stage" in Business', *Journal of Management Inquiry* 2, March, pp. 8–11.

Salancik, G.R. and Pfeffer, J. (1977) 'Who Gets Power – and How They Hold on to it: A Strategic-contingency Model of Power', *Organizational Dynamics*, Winter.

Schein, V.E. (1985) 'Organizational Realities: The Politics of Change', *Training and Development Journal*, February, pp. 37–41.

Scheinin, R. (1995) 'Welcome to Disneyworld', *San Jose Mercury News*, 5 August, pp. 1E, 11E.

Schweitzer, S. (1984) *The Age of Charisma*. Chicago, IL: Nelson-Hall.

Tannenbaum, A.S. and Schmidt, W.H. (1968) *Control in Organizations*. New York, NY: McGraw-Hill.

Thomas, K.W. and Velthouse, B.A. (1990) 'Cognitive Elements of Empowerment: An "Interpretative" Model of Interpretative Task Motivation', *Academy of Management Review* 15, October, p. 673.

Thomas, R.J. (1984) 'Bases of Power in Organizational Buying Decisions', *Industrial Marketing Management* 13, October, pp. 209–217.

Thomas, R.J. (1994) *What Machines Can't Do: Politics and Technology in the Industrial Enterprise*. Berkeley, CA: University of California Press.

Welles, C. (1988) 'What Led Beech-nut Down the Road to Disgrace', *Business Week*, 22 February, pp. 103–106.

Wexley, K.N. and Yukl, G.A. (1984) *Organizational Behavior and Personnel Psychology* (rev. edn). Homewood, IL: Richard D. Irwin, pp. 228–229.

Winter, D.G. (1973) *The Power Motive*. New York, NY: Collier Macmillan.

Yankelovich, D. and associates (1983) *Work and Human Values*. New York, NY: Public Agenda Foundation, pp. 6–7.

Yukl, G. (1994) *Leadership in Organisations* (3rd edn). Englewood Cliffs, NJ: Prentice Hall.

Yukl, G. and Taber, T. (1983) 'The Effective Use of Managerial Power', *Personnel* 60, pp. 37–44.

Zand, D.E. (1981) *Information, Organization, and Power*. New York, NY: McGraw-Hill.

14

Leadership

After studying this chapter you should be able to:

☑ **distinguish** between the art of leadership and the practice of management

☑ **understand** the role of personality traits in leadership

☑ **contrast** group-centred leadership theories based on cognitive styles and observable behaviours

☑ **apply** emotional intelligence when choosing appropriate leader styles

☑ **explain** why most current theories of leadership are based on situational contingencies

☑ **diagnose** when transformational and transactional leadership are appropriate

☑ **show** why leadership is not necessary for all organisational circumstances.

The opening vignette illustrates how a charismatic leader can turn around a failing organisation, in this case a school.

Diane Maple: the charismatic head teacher who turned round Chantry Junior School in Luton with a combination of sheer determination and a great deal of charm

Diane Maple was looking out of the window of the infants' school where she was head teacher when she saw children from the neighbouring junior school set upon a teacher on the sports field. She rushed to help her colleague, who had made a routine umpiring decision in a Year 6 rounders match that had gone down badly – so badly that some of the 10 and 11 year olds were hitting her.

The teacher was shocked and intimidated so Maple frogmarched the offending children back into the junior school to deal with them. On the way they passed a Year 4 classroom where all the children were watching the drama unfold, leaning against the glass, hands banging against it, shouting at the top of their voices: 'We're on top, we're on top.' Inside were three teachers, all unable to keep the class in order.

This was Chantry Junior School in Luton four years ago, a school that Maple had just agreed to be head of after an Ofsted report had found it to be failing and had put it into special measures. Only 25 per cent of the children were reaching the standard expected of the average 11 year old in English, 23 per cent in maths and 27 per cent in science. Discipline was not too good either.

The school was under-subscribed. It was the kind of school to which anyone with any common sense would think at least twice before sending their children. It was the kind of school teachers fell over themselves to leave. One class had 17 different teachers in one year.

As Maple puts it: 'Everyone had been told they were rubbish, by Ofsted, by the local education authority. Self-esteem was at rock bottom. The teachers were disillusioned and they were putting their grief onto the children. Children were suffering because the teaching was so poor.'

Last year there was another Ofsted report. This one described the school, which by then had been combined with the infants' school, as very good, with an excellent head and a strong management team. Test scores had risen to 60 per cent in English, 47 per cent in maths and 73 per cent in science. Some year groups are now over-subscribed.

This autumn the whole school of more than 400 children was sufficiently well behaved to be able to walk to the nearby church with their teachers for a harvest festival. Four years ago swimming had to be cancelled, not just because the swimming teachers at the pool found the children too difficult to handle, but it was too dangerous to walk them there because of their behaviour in relation to road traffic.

Maple is some leader. She has turned round a school where staff were demoralised and children were, at the very least, underperforming and, in too many cases, out of control, in a very short space of time. In addition, this was in a school serving a housing estate in one of Luton's poorer areas that suffer high levels of unemployment and drug abuse. Some children in the school have parents who have died from drug addiction. One-third of the children have special needs. For some, the school is the only stable point in their lives.

So how has she done it? Well, largely just by being her. She is a woman who genuinely values others very highly and has an unerring talent for building self-esteem, whether it is in children or adults. She has natural authority supplemented by bucket-loads of charm, which she sprays liberally over children and adults alike. She is a lot of fun, too, and takes the gentle 'mickey' out of you in a way that makes you feel included, not criticised.

She is a practising Christian and this is a very important part of her life. Talk to her colleagues and you would think she could almost walk on water. One says: 'She's superhuman.' Another comments: 'When I think about her, it gives me goosebumps.'

Moreover, what does she think about them? 'I care about my staff deeply. They are fantastic. We are like an extended family.'

The staff, teachers and non-teaching, all talk about how much time she finds to discuss problems with them, whether they are work or personal ones, and how special she makes them feel individually. Many have worked in other schools and say they have never known an atmosphere like the one in this school.

They talk about how much they look forward to coming to school. As one says: 'I miss it in the holidays.' Not a comment you normally associate with teaching. They are working with some very challenging children, but they do not seem to find it a problem and they say it is because of Maple's leadership.

Parents are hardly less effusive. She has time for them and their problems, and makes them feel good about themselves and their children. She certainly exudes calm confidence and self-belief. She is the kind of person you instinctively feel would not be running round like a head-less chicken in a crisis. She is widely respected and consulted by other heads in Luton.

Nicky Steers, chair of governors with four children at the school, one with attention deficit hyperactivity disorder, says: 'I have left the area now but I still bring the children back. It is a family. Everyone is made to feel so welcome. My children would be distraught to leave.'

Maple knows all the children's names and she remembers the names of grandmas and aunties, too. One parent, who moved away after her first child went to the school, came back with the second, 11 years later, and the head still remembered her name.

However, Maple is no soft touch, either. If you step out of line, you know it. The boundaries of acceptable behaviour are thickly painted – whether you are a child, teacher or local authority official doing the wrong thing. Rules for behaviour in the school are firmly understood, enforced and largely obeyed. No one is excluded, in all senses of the word. In the early days while she was settling the school, 20 children would be on report for misbehaviour. Last year there were only two.

Source: © Wendy Berliner, the *Guardian*, 29 October 2002. Reprinted with permission.

Discussion questions

1 Do you think Diane Maple was born with leadership qualities or acquired them?

2 What qualities make Diane Maple a good leader?

Leaders such as Diane Maple are the people who create, grow and transform organisations. But as environmental events are anticipated and unfold, people like Maple are caught in a dilemma. On the one hand, they have to lead change processes and redirect people's energies together with other resources. They have to lead transformations of products, technologies and organisational practices that produce growth. Conversely, they must manage to preserve order and achieve productivity – in the opening vignette that meant improving test scores. They have to manage costs and timeta-bles, and co-ordinate tasks across departments so that quality and efficiency are achieved.

Maple is able to excel as a manager by developing innovative processes for getting work done more efficiently. She is also a visionary leader who provides a clear sense of direction for transforming ideas into successes, and she energises others by challenging them to help make possibilities come true. She is also good at communicating and making her staff and students feel valued. Diane Maple is both an accomplished manager and a superlative leader. However, are these terms synonymous? Alternatively, do 'leader' and 'manager' mean different things?

What distinguishes managers from leaders?

Managers are common at all levels of organisations, whether they are called supervisors, man-agers, directors, administrators or executives. Managers typically devote most of their day to managing resources, projects, deadlines, and so on. Leaders excite people about visions of opportunities and empower them to innovate and excel. Like managers, leaders can be found at all levels. Unlike managers, leaders do not necessarily need a title to exert leadership effectively – in fact, the leader may not be a manager at all. By contrast, managers are always given titles symbolic of the scope of their responsibilities.

Managers have authority to be in charge

managers
Persons granted authority to be in charge of an organisational unit and thus responsible for diagnosing and influencing systems and people to achieve appropriate goals.

authority
The right to make decisions and commit organisational resources based on position within the organisation.

accountability
Holding a person with authority answerable for setting appropriate goals, using resources efficiently and accomplishing task responsibilities.

leadership
The act of providing direction, energising others and obtaining their voluntary commitment to the leader's vision.

leader
A person who creates a vision and goals, then energises others to voluntarily commit to that vision.

As discussed in Chapter 2, a manager is a person granted formal authority to be in charge of an organisation or one of its sub-units. Managers diagnose and influence systems and are responsible for controlling activities to keep the flow of work running smoothly. They keep activities and programmes on track, maintain system predictability, and balance revenues against costs to achieve reasonable productivity and profitability. Authority is the right to make decisions and commit organisational resources based on one's position within the organisational hierarchy. Managers draw on their position authority to initiate problem-solving, decision-making and action. However, with authority come responsibility and accountability. Accountability means the manager is answerable for the setting of appropriate goals, the efficient allocation of resources and task accomplishment within the unit.

Leaders influence others to follow

According to Bennis and Nanus (1985), leadership is the process of providing direction, energising others and obtaining their voluntary commitment to the leader's vision. A leader creates a vision and goals, and influences others to share that vision and work towards the goals. As explained in Chapter 2, a vision is an articulated picture of the future that conveys purpose, direction and priorities. It illuminates the conditions, events, products and qualities that could be attained through focused human energy and selective use of resources. Leaders are thus concerned with bringing about change and motivating others to support that vision of change.

How do you recognise a leader? It is easy to think of a few public figures who have made the news: Richard Branson, the Queen, Margaret Thatcher, Anita Roddick or Winston Churchill. These we may recognise as *formal leaders* because they also hold position authority as a president, commander or other title. They exert influence over large numbers of people without having to interact with them on an interpersonal level. The CEO of a large company or the chief of a metropolitan police force can, through personal credibility and position power, influence members of the organisation to follow their lead without talking personally with most members. People at the top of an organisation who have formal authority have position power to change the values, strategies and culture of an organisation.

Not all leaders hold high positions of authority and leadership is not always trans-formational. Leaders can be found at all levels of the organisational hierarchy. In addition, not all immediately stand out from the crowd. When several non-managerial people are put together on a 'leaderless' task force or assigned to a self-managed team, one or two are likely to emerge as informal leaders. Such emergent leaders keep goals defined, agendas moving and ideas integrated so the project is completed on schedule. In ad hoc groups and in interactions with peers, leadership is observable even in the absence of formal managerial authority.

You may work with a visible professional who seems to be stirring up new ideas, championing new causes, and inspiring co-workers to pursue strategic visions. Such *informal leaders* do not have the advantage of formal authority; their spheres of influence are unrelated to organisational position. This commonly occurs when a mid-level manager of one department influences peers in other departments to support a favoured programme or a pilot project.

Think of leaders that you know, who inspire you and make you want to achieve. On a global level, the international statesman Nelson Mandela has cajoled and inspired political leaders to work towards reducing oppression and sharing political power. His goal has been to achieve racial equality in his historically segregated South Africa homeland. When he was president of South Africa he was definitely a leader. However, a manager? Probably not.

Managers do things right, leaders do the right things

Managers can be leaders, but leaders do not have to be managers. To understand the distinction between the two, compare their organisational impact. While one person might fill the roles of both manager and leader, those roles exhibit distinct systems of action.

Kotter (1990) observes that management involves coping with complexity, while leadership is about coping with change. Kotter states that 'each system of action involves deciding what needs to be done, creating networks of people and relationships that can accomplish an agenda, and then trying to ensure that those people actually do the job'. Exhibit 14-1 provides Kotter's basic distinction between how managers and leaders accomplish these three tasks.

In their book, *Leaders*, Warren Bennis and Burt Nanus (1985) provide a slightly different perspective on the difference between managers and leaders that none the less agrees with Kotter's basic theme. Although the distinction may sound trite, it suggests a difference in how efforts are focused:

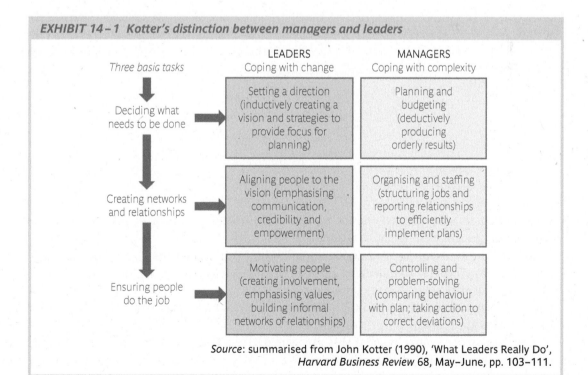

EXHIBIT 14–1 Kotter's distinction between managers and leaders

Three basic tasks	LEADERS Coping with change	MANAGERS Coping with complexity
Deciding what needs to be done	Setting a direction (inductively creating a vision and strategies to provide focus for planning)	Planning and budgeting (deductively producing orderly results)
Creating networks and relationships	Aligning people to the vision (emphasising communication, credibility and empowerment)	Organising and staffing (structuring jobs and reporting relationships to efficiently implement plans)
Ensuring people do the job	Motivating people (creating involvement, emphasising values, building informal networks of relationships)	Controlling and problem-solving (comparing behaviour with plan; taking action to correct deviations)

Source: summarised from John Kotter (1990), 'What Leaders Really Do', *Harvard Business Review* 68, May–June, pp. 103–111.

To manage means to bring about, to accomplish, to have responsibility for, to conduct. Leading is influencing, guiding in direction, course, action, and opinion. The distinction is crucial. Managers are people who do things right and leaders are people who do the right thing. The difference may be summarized as activities of vision and judgment – effectiveness [leading] – versus activities of mastering routines-efficiency [managing]. (Bennis and Nanus, 1985)

In attempting to manage complexities, managers emphasise systems, structures, controls and actions intended to achieve predictability and order. Leaders engage in extensive communication to elicit and act on ideas. Ultimately, leaders articulate thoughts in simplified visions that provide people with a sense of direction. Leaders promote change and are the trendsetters of organisational life. They empower others to work on causes, in part as a way of gaining commitment to the organisation. All organisations need both managers and leaders.

Are you more ready for managing or leading? Answer the questions in the 'Your turn' exercise to gain insights into your preferences.

Distinguishing leaders from followers

Packard (1962) provided an enduring perspective on leadership when he wrote, 'Leadership appears to be the art of getting others to want to do something that you are convinced should be done.' Leadership prompts followers to behave in ways they would not necessarily do without the leader's influence. To understand this art it helps to look at the leader's traits, cognitive style and behaviour with group members.

In ancient times, it was assumed great leaders were born into an upper-class heritage. Today, we recognise that leaders develop; they learn from and are formed by life's experiences. Zaleznik (1990) contends that many leaders have encountered adversity during their developmental years that cause them to look inward 'to reemerge with a created rather than an inherited sense of identity'. Andy Grove, CEO of Intel, for example, credits the paranoia he endured as a refugee in war-torn Europe during the Second World War as driving him to take risks to make bold, innovative moves, which keep his company number one in the world of microprocessors (Schlender, 1995).

Leader traits

According to Stogdill (1948, 1974) successful leaders do stand out from other people. However, traits such as drive and self-confidence by themselves are not sufficient to predict leadership success. Kirkpatrick and Locke (1991) suggest they are only preconditions or enablers from which leaders must initiate actions such as clarifying a vision, setting goals and role modelling. So, what is the right stuff that leaders are made of?

When followers look to leaders for direction and inspiration, they expect to find certain characteristics. Leaders, according to Kirkpatrick and Locke (1991), 'need to have the "right stuff" and this stuff is not equally present in all people'. Personal characteristics are important; however, they are merely a precondition for leadership. The leader's behaviour and cognitive skills are also important.

Read the World Watch box and try to picture Ricardo Semler interacting with people in his Brazilian organisation. Perhaps you can visualise how a leader's personality enables others to perceive in him effective leadership qualities in this situation.

Your turn

Your leadership potential

Questions 1 to 6 below are about you right now. Questions 7 to 22 are about how you would like to be if you were the head of a major department at a corporation. Answer yes or no to indicate whether the item describes you accurately, or whether you would strive to perform each activity.

Now

1 When I have a number of tasks or homework to do, I set priorities and organise the work to meet the deadlines.
2 When I am involved in a serious disagreement, I hang in there and talk it out until it is completely resolved.
3 I would rather sit in front of my computer than spend a lot of time with people.
4 I reach out to include other people in activities or when there are discussions.
5 I know my long-term vision for career, family and other activities.
6 When solving problems, I prefer analysing things myself to working through a group of people.

Head of major department

7 I would help subordinates clarify goals and how to reach them.
8 I would give people a sense of mission and higher purpose.
9 I would make sure jobs get out on time.
10 I would scout for new product or service opportunities.
11 I would use policies and procedures as guides for problem-solving.
12 I would promote unconventional beliefs and values.
13 I would give monetary rewards in exchange for high performance from subordinates.
14 I would inspire trust from everyone in the department.
15 I would work alone to accomplish important tasks.
16 I would suggest new and unique ways of doing things.
17 I would give credit to people who do their jobs well.
18 I would verbalise the higher values that both I and the organisation stand for.
19 I would establish procedures to help the department operate smoothly.
20 I would question the 'why' of things to motivate others.
21 I would set reasonable limits on new approaches.
22 I would demonstrate social non-conformity as a way to facilitate change.

Scoring Count the number of yes answers to even-numbered questions. Count the number of yes answers to odd-numbered questions. Compare the two scores.

Interpretation The even-numbered items represent behaviours and activities typical of leadership. Leaders are personally involved in shaping ideas, values, vision and change. They often use an intuitive approach to develop fresh ideas and seek new directions for the department or organisation. The odd-numbered items are considered more traditional management activities. Managers respond to organisational problems in an impersonal way, make rational decisions, and work for stability and efficiency.

If you answered yes to more even-numbered than odd-numbered items, you may have potential leadership qualities. If you answered yes to more odd-numbered items, you may have management qualities. Leadership qualities can be developed or improved with awareness and experience.

Source: Richard L. Daft (1999) *Leadership: Theory and Practice*. Fort Worth, TX: The Dryden Press, pp. 55–56.

Research focus: **trait theory**

Various studies into trait theory were based largely on the 'great man' theory that leaders were born and not made, which can be traced back as far as the Ancient Greeks. However, with the rise of the behaviourist schools of psychology the 'great man' theory became less acceptable.

Studies by Stogdill (1948, 1974), as can be seen in Exhibit 14-2, found that the majority of research into traits identified five traits related to leadership ability, such as energy, appearance and height; four intelligence and ability traits; sixteen personality traits, such as adaptability, aggressiveness, enthusiasm and self-confidence; six task-related characteristics, such as achievement, drive, persistence; and nine social characteristics, such as co-operativeness, interpersonal skills and administrative ability.

Research by Mann (1959) and Ghiselli (1971) noted correlations between leadership effectiveness and the traits of intelligence, supervisory ability, initiative, self-assurance and individuality in working methods. In fact, the relationship between self-confidence and leadership produced some of the highest correlations of any of the personality traits tested.

The outcome of the major reviews into trait theory concluded that effective leadership does not depend solely on a combination of personality traits. It is also necessary to take into account situational variables as they can often determine whether a particular personality trait will be effective. Therefore, leadership must be examined as an interaction between three variables: the characteristics of the leader, the characteristics of the subordinate and the nature of the task.

Updated research by Lord and Phillips (1982) analysed Mann's data and subsequent studies into trait theory, and concluded that there are leadership prototypes, which affect our perceptions of who is or is not an effective leader. Your leadership prototype is your mental idea of the traits and behaviours that you believe leaders possess. This has been confirmed by research on social-cognitive theory, which has found that people do use idealised personal traits to distinguish leaders from non-leaders. Schmidt and Posner (1982) suggest that, above all, followers look most for credibility in their leaders. Credibility, according to Kirkpatrick and Locke (1991), refers to being honest, competent, forward looking and inspiring. Six additional traits have been found to be used by followers to distinguish leaders from non-leaders: drive, leadership motivation, honesty and integrity, self-confidence, cognitive ability, and knowledge of the business. Exhibit 14-3 summarises these qualities.

leadership prototypes
The perception of traits and behaviours that a leader is seen to possess

social-cognitive theory
A line of research that finds people do use idealised personal traits or characteristics as a way to distinguish leaders from non-leaders.

credibility
One of the most characteristic traits of leaders, which refers to being honest, competent, forward-looking and inspiring.

EXHIBIT 14–2 Stogdill's personality factors most frequently associated with effective leadership

Capacity	Achievement	Responsibility	Participation	Status
Intelligence	Scholarship	Dependability	Activity	Socio-economic
Alertness	Knowledge	Initiative	Sociability	Popularity
Verbal facility	Athletic prowess	Persistence	Co-operation	
Originality	Personality adjustment	Aggressiveness	Adaptability	
Judgement		Self-confidence	Humour	
		Desire to excel		

> ### EXHIBIT 14–3 Traits that distinguish leaders from non-leaders
>
> As you read the following descriptions of the six traits, try to create an image of a leader at work. Does this describe you?
>
> 1 **Drive** – has the need for achievement through challenging assignments, the desire to get ahead, high energy to work long hours with enthusiasm, tenacity to overcome obstacles, and initiative to make choices and take action that leads to change.
>
> 2 **Leadership motivation** – exemplifies a strong desire to lead, the willingness to accept responsibility, the desire to influence others and a strong socialised desire for power (which means the desire to exercise power for the good of the organisation).
>
> 3 **Honesty and integrity** – demonstrates truthfulness or non-deceitfulness (honesty) and consistency between word and deed, is predictable, follows ethical principles, is discreet and makes competent decisions (integrity).
>
> 4 **Self-confidence** – gains the trust of others by being sure of own actions (and not being defensive about making mistakes), being assertive and decisive, maintaining emotional stability (not losing one's cool), and remaining calm and confident in times of crisis.
>
> 5 **Cognitive ability** – has a keen mind and thinks strategically, reasons analytically, and exercises good judgement in decisions and actions; has the ability to reason deductively and inductively.
>
> 6 **Knowledge of the business** – beyond formal education, develops technical expertise to understand the concerns of followers, comprehends the economics of the industry, and knows the organisation's culture and behaviour.
>
> *Source*: Shelley A. Kirkpatrick and Edwin A. Locke (1991) 'Leadership: Do Traits Matter?' *Academy of Management Executive* 5, May, pp. 48–60. Republished with permission of *Academy of Management Executive*. Permission conveyed through Copyright Clearance Center, Inc.

Brazilian firm 'hunts woolly mammoth'

By age 30, Ricardo Semler was president of Semco S/A, Brazil's largest marine equipment and food-processing machinery manufacturer. He had also authored a best-selling book, *Turning the Tables*. Semler is proud that his organisation functions more based on leadership than management. He took over a small family business, expanded it to serve global markets, and increased employment to over 800, making Semco one of Brazil's fastest-growing companies.

Unlike traditional Brazilian firms where paternalism creates a powerful, centralised family fiefdom, Semco is guided by three fundamental values: democracy, profit sharing and information. Semler states, 'One of my first moves when I took control of Semco was to abolish norms, manuals, rules and regulations' and replace them with common sense and reasonableness. As a highly participatory leader, Semler did a number of things that seem unconventional. He promoted 'civil disobedience' so people would challenge anything that was not working. Staff departments and specialised jobs were eliminated so that people either make or sell products – there is no one in between. He abolished all policies on things like travel expenses, allowing employees to charge whatever they thought reasonable. He has subordinates evaluate managers twice a year, and subordinates earn more than managers if they are more indispensable. Everyone gets an equal vote on key decisions such as where to locate a new plant.

Semler personifies a radical brand of leadership. He delights in portraying his organisation using the metaphor of a prehistoric woolly mammoth hunt. Hunting roles were filled by

world watch

▶ whoever was able to perform a task first or best in the hunt, giving the semblance of order without formal organisation. 'What I am saying is, put 10 people together, don't appoint a leader, and you can be sure that one will emerge. So will a sighter, a runner [for the hunt], and whatever else the group needs. We form the groups, but they find their own leaders. That's not a lack of structure, that's just a lack of structure imposed from above.'

Source: adapted from Ricardo Semler (1989) 'Managing without Managers', *Harvard Business Review* 67, September–October, quotes pp. 79, 82.

Discussion questions

1 What are the qualities of leadership that Semler possesses?

2 What does Semler mean when he says his organisation functions more on the basis of leadership than management?

Leader behaviours

Ultimately people evaluate leaders based on their behaviour and decide if they voluntarily want to follow their lead. Although using different terms, over 50 years of research reviewed by Likert (1961) and Stogdill and Coons (1957) has essentially differentiated between behaviours that focus on task production and behaviours that focus on building positive employee relationships.

Task and relationship behaviours

task-orientated behaviour
An approach to leadership that focuses on supervision of group members to obtain consistent work methods and job accomplishments.

initiating structure
Leader behaviour intended to establish well-defined patterns of organisation, channels of communication, and work procedures between leader and group.

employee-orientated behaviour
An approach to leadership that aims at satisfying the social and emotional needs of group members.

showing consideration
Leader behaviour to bring out friendship, mutual trust, respect and warmth in leader–member relationships.

Task-orientated behaviour focuses on careful supervision of group members to obtain consistent work methods and accomplishment of the job. It centres on initiating structure intended to establish 'well-defined patterns of organisation, channels of communication, and methods of procedure' between leader and group. Employee-orientated behaviour aims at satisfying the social and emotional needs of group members. Halpin (1959) suggests this focuses on showing consideration to develop 'friendship, mutual trust, respect, and warmth in the relationship between the leader and members of his staff'.

In extensive research by Korman (1966), neither behaviour ensured maximum performance effectiveness and work-group satisfaction. Although leaders high in *both* initiating structure and showing consideration tended to have better follower performance and satisfaction than leaders low in either or both, there were enough negative side effects (absenteeism and grievances) that the positive outcomes were not unconditional. Trying to predict group performance solely on the basis of a consistent leader behaviour turned out to be a futile endeavour.

Leader decision styles

A related line of research concentrates on studying leader behaviour in decision-making and its impact on productivity and satisfaction. Four principal *leader decision styles* were identified. The first is *autocratic*, characterised by unilaterally taking charge and giving assignments to others.

The *democratic* style is easy-going, using suggestions and encouragement to reach a group consensus. With the *laissez-faire* style the leader is passive and non-committal, which allows others to make their own decisions independently. The fourth decision style is *human relations*. It emphasises consulting with those who are involved to gather data and opinions before making a decision (Berkowitz, 1954). Exhibit 14-4 shows how these four descriptors of a leader's decision style can be distinguished when superimposed on the two broad behavioural dimensions of initiating structure and showing consideration (Lewin and Lippitt, 1938).

Leader states of mind

leadership states of mind
The thoughts held to be important to a leader (motives, attitudes, goals, sources of satisfaction) in guiding how the leader interacts with group members.

Beyond personality traits and observable behaviours, how the leader views him or herself when in a leadership role is also important. Leadership states of mind refer to the leader's cognitions (the motives, attitudes, goals and sources of satisfaction that exist in the mind) that guide interactions with group members. Some leaders think primarily about getting the job done; they are production focused and driven to achieve successful results. Other leaders are concerned primarily about gaining co-operation from their people and building relationships based on mutual respect – they believe high morale produces reasonable performance.

How leaders and managers adjust to situational contingencies

Several explanations of the thought processes and behaviours of leaders as they interact with immediate group followers over the course of changing circumstances have been proposed. These theories apply equally to chief executives, store managers or department managers, and their lessons serve as the starting point for developing managers. While it is probable that a leader will rely on one pattern of behaviour more than on others, an effective leader's behaviour is not as rigid as implied by the behavioural labels we have discussed so far. Let us look at a hypothetical leader, Michelle, as an example.

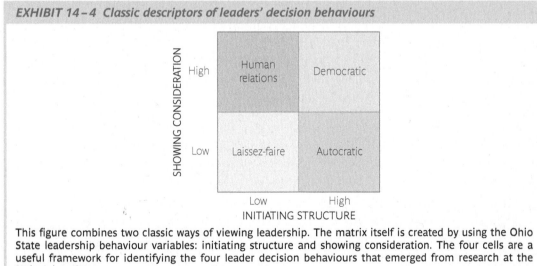

EXHIBIT 14–4 Classic descriptors of leaders' decision behaviours

This figure combines two classic ways of viewing leadership. The matrix itself is created by using the Ohio State leadership behaviour variables: initiating structure and showing consideration. The four cells are a useful framework for identifying the four leader decision behaviours that emerged from research at the University of Iowa.

Research focus: **Blake and Mouton's Leadership Grid®**

Leadership Grid®
A matrix used by Blake and Mouton to identify five leadership styles based on concerns for people and/or production.

One of the most popular explanations of cognitive style is the Leadership Grid developed by Blake and Mouton (1964). The Leadership Grid® is a matrix that identifies five leadership styles by interpreting leaders' concern for production and concern for people. A leader's style is diagnosed by a battery of questions that assigns point values ranging from 1 (low) to 9 (high) on the independent production and people attitudes. The five dominant styles are identified by points on the grid (see Exhibit 14-5).

For example, a leader who scores 9,1 subscribes to the *authority-compliance* style. Such task-focused leaders have great concern for output and presume that people obediently accept the influence of authority figures. By contrast, the 1,9 or *country club* style manifests a belief that if people's needs are thoughtfully attended to, they will feel comfortable and friendly with co-workers and as a result will co-operate. The *impoverishment* or 1,1 style seeks simply to get by with minimal effort (a condition more commonly associated with abdication, not leadership).

Blake and Mouton typically find that most respondents score towards the 5,5 *middle-of-the-road* style, one characterised by compromise and a desire to do things right by keeping divergent interests in balance. Organisations that employ the grid in leadership training do so with the goal of moving participants towards the 9,9, *team* style, purported to be the ideal. Empirical research by Beer and Kleisath (1967) does not necessarily support the abundant testimonials about the effectiveness of such 'ideal' styles. The power to predict leader effectiveness improves significantly when the leader's interaction with changing situations is considered in the contingency approach.

EXHIBIT 14–5 Blake and Mouton's Leadership Grid®

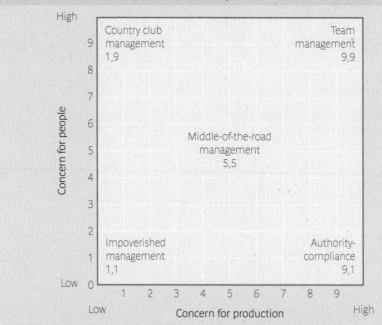

Source: The Leadership Grid® Figure from *Leadership Dilemmas – Grid Solutions*, by Robert R. Blake and Anne Adams McCanse (formerly the Managerial Grid Figure by Robert T. Blake and Jane S. Mouton), Houston, Gulf Publishing Company, p. 29. Copyright © 1991 by Gulf Publishing Company. Reproduced by permission.

The grid is popular with managers as a means of assessing their leadership style and is used extensively as a training and consultancy tool for diagnosing organisational problems. However, its usefulness has not been supported by research. Most of the research that supports the grid idea has been based largely on the interpretation of case studies. Empirical research has failed to show that a 9,9 leadership style is superior, as the situation, group members and task all impact on styles of leadership. Therefore, the 9,9 style is not always the most effective. Although useful for identifying and classifying managerial styles it does not tell us why a manager fails, for this we would need to look at the underlying causes, such as the personality of leader and followers, and the situation.

Nevertheless, this research does help identify the leadership roles performed within a group and it does imply that leadership consists of leader behaviours performed by any of the group members, regardless of whether they have been formally appointed as leaders.

Michelle is observed to interact infrequently with members of the graphic design group that she heads. When she does, it is usually to exchange a brief pleasantry or to inquire about or comment on a designer's project. Her dominant behaviour outwardly appears to be neither task nor relationship orientated, suggesting that she is a 'laissez-faire' or 'impoverished' type, to use grid terminology.

However, on occasion Michelle devotes considerable time to helping a group member through a stressful project or personal situation. She listens, questions, counsels, provides encouragement, and conveys empathy and understanding. This behaviour is high relationship, low task. Occasionally Michelle can also be seen working closely with some of her group on a project. She clarifies goals, defines priorities, provides guidelines for how a job is to be done, asks for progress reports and provides feedback about their performance. Such behaviour is high task, low relationship.

The general observation that Michelle most often uses what classical theorists call 'laissez-faire' leadership does not mean that Michelle is failing to do her job. In fact, Michelle may be a strong 'team-style' leader, with high concern for both people and tasks. However, she perceives that her group is capable and usually effective without her direct intervention. Michelle may be correctly adjusting her leadership behaviour to the contingencies of changing member needs and other circumstances by usually staying out of their way – she empowers them. Granting her group members autonomy also frees her to work more on influencing peers (over whom she has no direct authority) and external groups of customers and suppliers. Contingency theories propose the situational variables that influence leaders like Michelle, to change styles to match appropriately with the needs of different tasks and followers.

Contingency theory variables

Under what circumstances is a leader effective? This question has long piqued the curiosity of leaders as well as scholars. In *The Human Side of Enterprise*, McGregor (1966) observed, 'Managers who are successful in one function are sometimes, but by no means always, successful in another. The same is true of leadership at different organisational levels.'

contingency theory
The perspective that a leader's effectiveness is dependent on how he or she interacts with various situational factors – there is no one best universal approach.

Contingency theory emphasises that a leader's effectiveness is not independent from situational factors that influence the tasks to be undertaken. Leadership occurs within a task context that can vary in degree of specificity and complexity. Also involved in any leadership situation are people factors such as variations in the leader's style or behaviour in interaction with the capabilities and readiness of subordinates to perform a task.

Exhibit 14-6 illustrates four principal contingency factors associated with leadership effectiveness. As suggested by the arrows in the diagram, these four factors interact to shape the leader–follower relationship. They apply whether the perceived leader is appointed as a manager or emerges from the group. Two contingency factors identified in Exhibit 14-6 relate to the leader personally, his or her cognitive style and his or her actual observable behaviour. The two remaining contingency factors include work-related elements of the situation and the behaviour of followers.

The leader's cognitive style

Much of the research knowledge about leadership focuses on the leader's motives, concerns, knowledge and personality. People differ in how they want to be perceived as leaders and what they seek to get out of being a leader. As we have seen, some adopt a people-centred leadership style aimed at building trusting and caring relationships. Others assume a task-centred leadership style that embraces goal accomplishment and productive results. These approaches are learned from experience, are highly personal and tend to be consistent over time. The leader's mindset or cognitive style serves two purposes. According to Weiner *et al.* (1983), it affects the leader's perception of the situation, and it constrains the range of personal behaviours the leader chooses to use.

The leader's observable behaviour

While thoughts, personal motives and attitudes (that is, a leader's style) are not always transparent, a leader's behaviour is directly observable. Some leaders devote a great deal of time to structuring and directing task activities. Others concentrate on showing consideration, making people feel accepted and aware that their well-being is important. Some leaders handle power autocratically; others work to share power with their subordinates, empowering them to

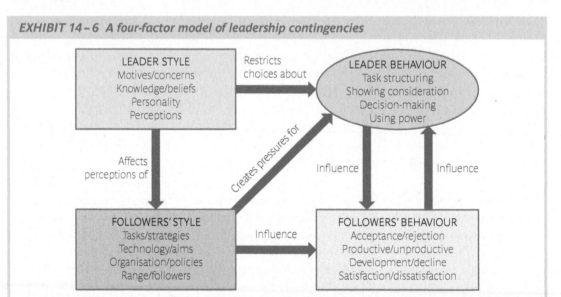

EXHIBIT 14-6 A four-factor model of leadership contingencies

Leadership research usually focuses on how the leader interacts with others – the leader's behaviour. But leader behaviour does not occur in a vacuum. The exhibit suggests that the cognitive structures or mindsets of leaders influence chosen behaviours. Similarly, effective leaders also consider the people with whom they are working, as well as other situational factors embodied in either the organisation or the task itself.

perform up to their potential. A leader's outward behaviour is the public face of leadership and is directly interpreted by those with whom the leader interacts.

Work-related situational variables

According to Tannenbaum and Schmidt (1958), the effective leader does not behave independently of situational realities. The nature of the job to be done (for example, whether it is routine and unchanging or complex and ambiguous), the technology and resources or time available, the organisation's culture, and the leader's power or managerial authority within the organisation – these and other issues set the stage for determining if leadership methods will be effective.

The behaviour of followers

People who are targets of influence become critical forces in determining how to lead. People differ in their competencies, motivation, attitudes and goals. A leader should consider these human idiosyncrasies, since they affect receptiveness to the leader's attempts to influence. They also affect the reciprocal influence others have over the leader. Especially when group members are from different ethnic, racial or cultural backgrounds, expectations about leadership and the willingness to accept authority can differ greatly.

Four influential contingency theories of leadership over the years have been: Fiedler's (1965) contingency theory about leader style and situational favourableness factors; Hersey and Blanchard's (1996) situational leadership theory focusing on the maturity of subordinates; House and Mitchell's (1974) path-goal theory; and Vroom and Yetton's (1973) group decision tree. A new approach to contingencies and leadership styles has been put forward by Goleman (2000), based on his concept of emotional intelligence.

Research focus: the Fiedler contingency model – matching leader style and situational favourableness factors

task-motivated style
Used by Fiedler to describe leaders whose satisfaction comes from pride of task accomplishment and group success in doing a job well.

relationship-motivated style
Fiedler's way of characterising leaders who are principally concerned with respect in interpersonal relations and in helping the group develop as a team.

This model, proposed by Cartwright and Zander (1960), maintains that leadership style remains stable across time and across various leadership experiences. Leaders who have a strong task-motivated style enjoy the feeling of pride in accomplishing a task or having their group do a job well. The relationship-motivated style leaders seek more to realise respect in interpersonal relationships and to experience satisfaction in helping a group to develop as a team.

The two different leadership styles are most effective in different situations. The job of the leader is to match his or her leader style to the most appropriate situation, which depends on the following three critical contingency factors (Fiedler and Chemers, 1974).

1 **Task structure:** the degree to which the job assignments are formalised and structured; ranging from high (specific) to low (ambiguous).
2 **Position power:** the degree of influence a leader has over activities such as hiring, firing, discipline, promotions and salary increases; ranging from high (formal authority) to low (informal authority).
3 **Leader–member relations:** the degree of confidence, trust and respect subordinates have for the leader; ranging from good (cohesive) to poor (hostile).

These three factors combine to produce situations that range from favourable to unfavourable for the leader. This can be seen in Exhibit 14-7.

Very favourable conditions for leader influence occur when all three factors are in the high, strong or good range. Conversely, the most unfavourable leadership situation exists when all three factors are low, weak or poor.

Fiedler's research about how style and circumstance relate to leadership effectiveness indicates that a task-motivated leadership style is likely to produce more effective group results when either very favourable or very unfavourable situations exist. For example, in the very unfavourable situation, the task-motivated leader is willing to take charge and structure the situation and members' tasks. A relationship-motivated style is more effective under mid-range or mixed circumstances – those that are moderately favourable. In these situations, achieving team co-ordination and realising group synergy are more productive than handing out detailed task assignments to individual group members.

Reviews of Fiedler's research have found that there is nothing automatic or good in either the task orientated or people satisfaction orientated style. Leadership depends on various elements in the group environment. Research by Yukl (1981) has also questioned the meaning of the 'least preferred co-worker' (LPC) score. Other research suggests that the model does not explain the causal effect of the LPC score on performance, neither have some of the findings of the research been statistically significant and situational measures may not be completely independent of the LPC score.

Nevertheless, it is important to recognise that effective leadership style is dependent on the situation. Fiedler's research drew attention to this and stimulated a great deal of research in this area.

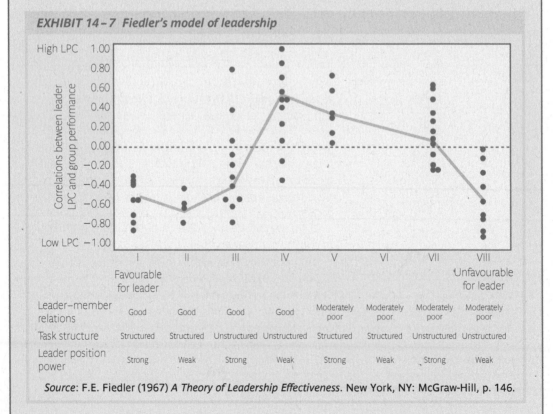

EXHIBIT 14–7 *Fiedler's model of leadership*

	I	II	III	IV	V	VI	VII	VIII
	Favourable for leader							Unfavourable for leader
Leader–member relations	Good	Good	Good	Good	Moderately poor	Moderately poor	Moderately poor	Moderately poor
Task structure	Structured	Structured	Unstructured	Unstructured	Structured	Structured	Unstructured	Unstructured
Leader position power	Strong	Weak	Strong	Weak	Strong	Weak	Strong	Weak

Source: F.E. Fiedler (1967) *A Theory of Leadership Effectiveness*. New York, NY: McGraw-Hill, p. 146.

Let us look at a hypothetical contrast between two leaders to see how Fiedler's contingency approach explains how different styles can be more effective in different situations. Jan is a task-motivated car sales manager who derives satisfaction principally from successful group performance, such as surpassing quotas, setting seasonal records, maintaining profit margins and outselling competitive agencies. James, a sales manager at a competitor across the street, is a leader with a relationship-orientated style. He finds satisfaction through good interpersonal relations: building camaraderie among his salesforce, following up on customer service, establishing a positive image for his firm in the community, and winning repeat customers.

Having a dominant leadership style does not mean, however, that a task-motivated leader like Jan will be unfriendly and autocratic towards her sales representatives or potential customers. It simply suggests that she will find greater personal satisfaction in achieving sales and profit (task) success than in caring for the needs of others. However, if Jan perceives that a group member is discouraged by three days without a sale, she may engage in friendly, sympathetic (relationship-building) conversation rather than re-emphasise sales techniques or demand improvement (task behaviours). Similarly, relationship-motivated James may reprimand a member of his salesforce and demonstrate how to close a sale if he feels that the salesperson's relaxed attitude is resulting in lost sales.

As mentioned in the 'Research focus', there is independent research by Peters *et al.* (1985) to support the validity of Fiedler's theory. Other research, by Kennedy *et al.* (1987), however, suggests that additional variables are needed as contingency factors and that more reliable measures of leader style are needed. In addition, since style is assumed to be a consistent personal motive, Fiedler (1965) recommends engineering job contingencies to fit the leader rather than trying to change the leader. But, administratively and politically, it is difficult to engineer such a precise fit. And what happens if the situation changes, possibly because of the leader's success? Many researchers and practitioners take exception to the premise that effective leaders cannot change their style to adapt to different situations.

Research focus: Hersey and Blanchard's (1996) situational leadership theory – matching leader behaviours to followers' needs

situational leadership theory (SLT)
The Hersey and Blanchard model of leadership effectiveness based on combinations of the leader's task and relationship behaviours as moderated by the job maturity of followers.

In Hersey and Blanchard's (1996) situational leadership theory (SLT) model, combinations of task and relationship behaviours are prescribed, based on the job maturity of followers. *Task behaviours* include things like organising and defining roles; explaining necessary activities that need to be done; and establishing an organisational structure, channels of communication and methods of getting jobs accomplished. *Relationship behaviours* include maintaining personal relationships with followers by opening channels of communication, providing socio-emotional support (psychological strokes), and facilitating behaviours.

Followers' maturity, or job readiness, consists of the degree of 'capacity to set high but attainable goals, willingness and ability to take responsibility, and education and/or experience of an individual or a group'. Maturity ranges along a continuum according to the degree to which followers are willing and able to complete tasks on their own. This, of course, varies with the task. For example, a saleswoman may be very responsible in securing new sales but very casual about completing the paperwork necessary to close on a sale. As a result, it is appropriate for her manager to leave her alone in terms of closing on sales, but to supervise her closely in terms of her paperwork until she can start to do well in that area too.

The pattern of effective leader behaviours in relation to follower maturity is presented in Exhibit 14-8. To determine the appropriate leadership style, select one of the four boxes indicating your estimate of a follower's readiness. Draw a line straight upwards and where it intersects the normal curve indicates the appropriate leader behaviour. Ideally, as a follower's job maturity changes, the leader's behaviour towards that person should change also. Leadership behaviours should be adjusted over time to develop subordinate competencies as well as to guide and control current performance.

SLT matches leader behaviours to follower readiness (job maturity). Looking at Exhibit 14-8, select one of the four boxes above the 'follower readiness' scale. Note where the dashed vertical line intersects the normal curve in the matrix. That point of intersection indicates the appropriate leader behaviour.

Consider a leader who has two subordinates low in job maturity – for example, inexperienced supermarket cashiers both of whom are in their first full-time job. The assistant store manager begins their socialisation by emphasising responsibilities and training them in how tasks should be performed (high concentration on task, or 'telling'). As the cashiers begin to demonstrate that they can handle basic jobs, the leader shifts to also providing reassurance and praise, and making each worker feel valued (high relationship, or 'selling' behaviours).

EXHIBIT 14–8 Hersey and Blanchard's situational leadership theory

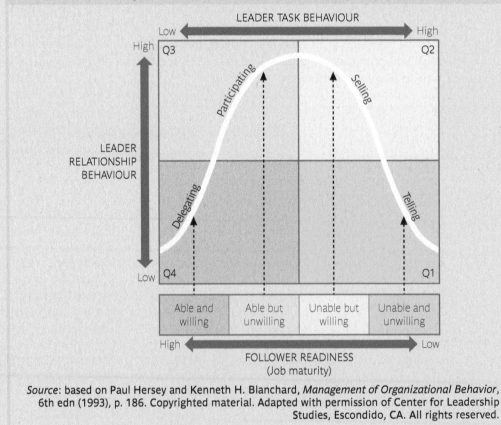

Source: based on Paul Hersey and Kenneth H. Blanchard, *Management of Organizational Behavior*, 6th edn (1993), p. 186. Copyrighted material. Adapted with permission of Center for Leadership Studies, Escondido, CA. All rights reserved.

Over time, the leader's task guidance diminishes as the two's performance becomes self-sustaining. Once the cashiers reach a high level of competence, the leader grants greater autonomy (for example, to cash cheques without approval by the manager). Interaction then occurs on an 'as needed', or 'participating' basis. Kram (1984) suggests that, in professional occupations, such a pattern often occurs between a mentor and protégé as the younger person gains professional skill, stature and reputation, ultimately becoming independent of the mentor.

However, if the job maturity of a person or group regresses, the leader needs to move backward along the bell-shaped curve in an effort to help followers regain their previous level of demonstrated maturity. One of the cashiers in our illustration may slip from a condition where 'participating' leadership is effective, back to where more 'selling' is needed when new computerised equipment is introduced.

The most significant conclusion from research on this situational leadership model is that leaders are unlikely to find a full range of job maturities among employees within a single job category or work group. Different levels of maturity are most directly associated with various classes of jobs, among the ranks of unskilled, semi-skilled, craft or professional. For example, according to Vecchio (1987), professionals are generally 'capable of and desirous of greater self-direction', whereas unskilled workers tend to 'expect and may prefer greater direction and less social-emotional attention on the part of supervisors'.

Research focus: Path-goal theory (House and Mitchell, 1974)

path-goal theory
The perspective that a leader should clarify goals, show acceptable paths for attaining goals, make the path easier to travel, and reward satisfactory performance.

The major concern of path-goal theory is how a leader can increase employees' motivation to attain organisational goals. As illustrated in Exhibit 14-9, by Cook (1980), a leader can increase follower motivation by clarifying performance goals, clarifying subordinates' pathways to obtaining organisational goals, and providing meaningful personal rewards. When clarifying paths to goals, leaders help subordinates identify and learn the behaviours that will enable them to successfully accomplish tasks. Second, leaders consult with subordinates to determine which rewards are important to them. According to Strebel (1994), the leader's job is then to increase personal pay-offs to subordinates for goal attainment and to make the paths to these pay-offs clear and easy to travel.

Like situational leadership, the path-goal approach indicates that leaders engage in instrumental (task) behaviours and supportive (relationship) behaviours that combine into four leadership styles (House and Mitchell, 1974). *Directive leadership* (highly task orientated) lets followers know what is expected of them, provides guidance as to what is to be done and how, clarifies performance standards and time schedules, and calls attention to work procedures and policies. *Achievement-orientated leadership* (highly task and relationship orientated) establishes challenging goals, seeks performance improvement and displays confidence that people will exert high levels of effort. *Participative leadership* (moderately task and highly relationship orientated) involves consulting with and soliciting the ideas of others in decision-making and action taking. *Supportive leadership* (highly relationship orientated) shows concern for the needs and goals of others and strives to make the work situation pleasant and equitable.

The path-goal approach suggests two important contingencies that determine which leadership style will be most effective for motivating subordinates in different situations. The first

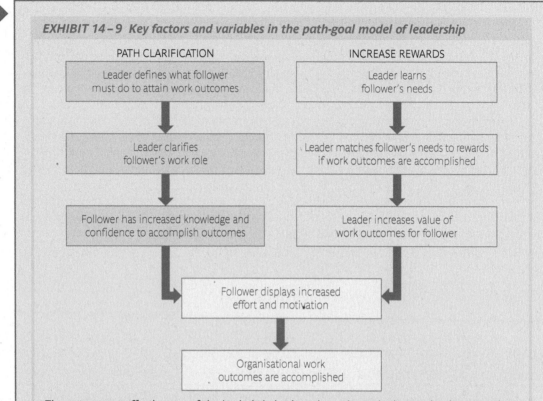

EXHIBIT 14–9 Key factors and variables in the path-goal model of leadership

PATH CLARIFICATION

INCREASE REWARDS

Leader defines what follower must do to attain work outcomes

Leader learns follower's needs

Leader clarifies follower's work role

Leader matches follower's needs to rewards if work outcomes are accomplished

Follower has increased knowledge and confidence to accomplish outcomes

Leader increases value of work outcomes for follower

Follower displays increased effort and motivation

Organisational work outcomes are accomplished

The outcome or effectiveness of the leader's behaviour depends on the interaction between situational variables (identified in the top of the diagram) and variations among followers (identified in the bottom). The leader's four basic behavioural options (the middle box on the left-hand side) depend on these six key situational and follower variables.

Source: based on Bernard M. Bass (1985) 'Leadership: Good, Better, Best', *Organizational Dynamics* 13, Winter, pp. 26–40.

one, like situational leadership, concerns the personal readiness level of subordinates: abilities, skills, needs and motivations. The second contingency factor concerns three environmental conditions similar to Fiedler's factors: (1) the degree of task structure – the extent to which tasks are well defined and have clear job descriptions; (2) the nature of the formal authority system – the degree of legitimate power the leader has and the extent of policies and rules that exist; (3) work group characteristics – the quality of interpersonal relationships among group members.

Researchers such as Schriesheim and Von Glinow (1977) have found the most useful application of path-goal leadership occurs when the follower's task is perceived to be ambiguous, ill-defined and lacking in routine or standardisation, as in jobs in product development or marketing research. Task-focused instrumental leader behaviour helps followers clarify ambiguous roles. Under conditions of low task structure (complex and/or ambiguous jobs), instrumental leaders have higher follower job satisfaction and goal attainment. However, in highly structured tasks – in purchasing or accounts payable jobs, for example – group members view instrumental leader behaviour as an attempt to exert added, unnecessary structure and control over their lives – too much management. In well-defined and routine situations, supportive relationship behaviour from the leader is more appropriate. Like other forms of relationship-building behaviour, supportive transactions aim to increase morale and co-operation by building on a base of consideration.

If the leader's path-goal behaviour is effective, it will produce greater employee effort by clarifying how subordinates can receive rewards, or changing rewards to fit their needs. According to Strebel (1994), the pay-off to leaders is that those who are being influenced are likely to accept the leader, expect that personal effort leads to better performance, expect that effective performance leads to relevant rewards, and are satisfied with their work and work situation.

The major contribution of the path-goal model is that it provides a method of viewing leadership in terms of rewards and punishments administered by the leader. It helps to explain why a particular style works best because of the rewards available in the environment and the leader's ability to administer such rewards or punishments.

Decision style influences group behaviour

How a leader makes decisions affects the likelihood that influence efforts will be positive. In earlier eras a boss's power tended to be absolute when workers were relatively unskilled and tasks were usually routine and simple. Then, a manager (more than a leader) could get results by being autocratic, by being the sole decision-maker. But, in many of today's work environments, tasks are complex and employees are highly educated and often more technically competent than the manager or leader. Participation by group members in decisions often produces better-quality decisions and increases commitment for effective implementation.

Tannenbaum and Schmidt's power-sharing model

One of the earliest contingency theories emphasised the extent to which the leader shared power with group members in making decisions. As previously demonstrated in Exhibit 13-3, the process of making decisions within a group can be described as a sliding ratio scale between 'leader-held power' and 'leader-shared power'. At one extreme are decisions in which all power is held by the leader (a 'make and announce' style). Power sharing increases if the leader 'sells' the decision, and increases further when they ask for feedback about possible alternatives before making the decision. Power sharing reaches its pinnacle when the leader delegates to the group the right to analyse problems and make decisions subject only to broad parameters.

A key lesson of this contingency theory by Tannenbaum and Schmidt (1958) is not that delegated decisions are necessarily better than unilaterally made ones. It is rather that effectiveness all depends on forces in the leader, forces in the followers and forces in the task situation. For example, if group members are not accustomed to making complex decisions and a life-threatening crisis faces the organisation needing a quick response, then a 'make and announce' decision by the leader is likely to be most effective. According to Thomas and Velthouse (1990), where members are highly talented and effectiveness is a function of group creativity and innovation, the effective leader probably helps crystallise a vision and involves group members in evaluating alternatives and collaboratively making a decision.

The Vroom and Yetton decision tree model

The concept that decision style shapes outcome effectiveness was extended by Vroom and Jago (1987). Their normative model is based on the premise that decisions affecting the group need to be timely, of high quality and accepted by group members. The Vroom and Yetton (1973) model presents three basic decision styles:

1 autocratic (where the leader unilaterally makes decisions)
2 consultative (where the leader solicits member inputs before deciding)
3 group (where the leader collaborates with members to arrive at a joint decision).

To guide leaders through the process of decision-making, the model uses a decision tree to structure the branching of decisions depending on considerations such as whether it affects an individual or the group, its complexity, and how quickly it must be made. A complete presentation of this model can be found in Chapter 12. Efforts to empirically validate the structured Vroom–Yetton (1973) model support the premise that working through a sequence of situational considerations leads to better decisions, both in the minds of leaders who evaluated past decisions and from independent raters.

Emotional intelligence and leadership styles

According to Goleman (2000), we know that the business world is constantly changing, and that effective leaders must respond accordingly. However, these changes take place daily, even hourly, so an important question is what contingency approach to apply when for best results. Recent research by the consulting firm Hay/McBer takes much of the confusion out of 'what style to use when' in order to be an effective leader. The research found six distinct leadership styles, each springing from different components of emotional intelligence, that have direct and unique impacts on team and organisational performance. Leaders with the best results did not rely on only one style, but used most of them every week depending on the situations they encountered.

So what were these six styles of leadership and when should they be applied for best results? *Coercive leaders* demand immediate compliance, which is necessary in a crisis or to deal with problem employees. When changes are required, or a clear direction is needed, *authoritative leaders* mobilise people towards a vision. *Affiliative leaders* are skilled at creating emotional bonds and harmony, which is a plus when teams are experiencing conflict or need to be motivated during stressful circumstances. *Democratic leaders* build consensus through participation, which is the best way to get input and acceptance from valuable employees. *Pacesetting leaders* set high standards for performance and expect self-direction when quick results from highly motivated and competent teams are required. *Coaching leaders* help employees improve performance and develop long-term strengths for the future through their empathy and self-awareness.

From what you have learned previously about leader traits, behaviours, mindsets and decision styles, these six leadership styles should sound very familiar. Moreover, the research finding that all styles are useful in certain situations confirms the validity of the contingency approach. The most effective leaders switched flexibly among the leadership styles as needed – not by mechanically matching their style to fit a checklist of situations, but by intuitively reading what is required in the first minutes of a conversation.

The key question is, how do they do it? According to Daniel Goleman, few leaders naturally possess all six styles in their repertoire, and even fewer know how or when to use them. So, how can you expand and effectively apply your leadership styles? One way to do this is to build a team with members who employ styles that the leader lacks. Another, which is recommended by Goleman, is for leaders to expand their own style repertoires by understanding which emotional intelligence competencies underlie the leadership styles they are lacking. Then, the areas of emotional intelligence the leader needs to build up to apply the style effectively need to be strengthened. Usually this requires changing old habits and acquiring new ones, which may take some time, practice and commitment. But, according to Goleman (2000), it is definitely worth the effort and will result in increased leadership effectiveness and team performance. Does this differ from male to female? The lack of women in upper management may suggest that women are less able at promoting themselves. Take a look at the Eye on Ethics box for a closer look at what diversity may mean for men.

Diversity boosted by men-only scheme

'The men felt that diversity meant everyone except white, male heterosexuals.'

Citigroup has piloted a men-only session where employees are encouraged to talk about how they view their female colleagues, as part of a programme to empower women.

Neil Cockroft, senior vice-president for diversity and talent management at Citigroup, said the workshop, Manpower Hour, allowed men to air their prejudices about gender diversity in a safe environment.

Speaking in the session, 'Shattering the Glass Ceiling', Cockroft said that men participating in Manpower Hour were honest about their feelings and the challenges they faced in working with women.

'The men felt that diversity meant everyone except white, male heterosexuals,' he said.

Cockroft said that one of the first steps in empowering women at Citigroup was educating men about the importance of gender diversity.

And, by encouraging men to openly discuss their prejudices, the organisation had the chance to change their mindsets.

'Unless their assumptions are on the table, you can't respond,' said Cockroft.

The diversity team had considered Manpower Hour high risk, but it has been so popular that one business unit has adopted it as a regular feature.

The bank is now looking at ways of building on the success of the workshop. It is one of a raft of measures to improve gender diversity at the firm, which include a maternity buddy scheme to optimise maternity exits and re-entry, mentoring and women's networks.

Speaking at the same session, Michelle Ryan, from the School of Psychology at the University of Exeter, explained why gender diversity was still needed in the workplace.

Ryan replicated research conducted in the 1970s that looked at masculine and feminine traits and how many of them overlapped with the characteristics of a good manager.

The results 20 years ago found 65 per cent of the male and management traits overlapped. Only 9 per cent of feminine traits overlapped.

Ryan conducted four studies with hundreds of participants to find out if the results would differ 20 years later. However she found that, although there was little variation in traits, women were definitely treated differently to men. The research suggests that women tend to be appointed to leadership positions under very different circumstances than men. More specifically, the research suggests that women are more likely to be appointed to leadership positions that are associated with an increased risk of criticism and failure. Women's leadership positions can thus be seen as more precarious than those of men.

Source: Julie Griffiths, originally published in *People Management*, 28 October 2005 and reproduced with permission.

Discussion questions

1 What could be the dangers of implementing such a scheme?

2 What are the masculine and feminine traits that could influence leadership style?

Transactional versus transformational leadership

So far, the discussion has centred on how transactional leaders get things done through people. They are implementing-type leaders who apply task and relationship behaviours to influence people to do what they want them to do in order to achieve organisational goals. However, it takes more than this to lead an entire organisation through major changes. For that task, transformational leaders are called for. They tend to be more visionary and concerned about charting a mission and direction. These pathfinders are entrepreneurs and charismatic leaders who are more concerned about where the organisation ought to try to go.

Organisations need both types of leader. Leavitt (1987) has summarised the distinctly different contributions made by pathfinders (transformational leaders) and problem-solvers and implementers (transactional leaders). *Implementing leaders* are skilled at getting things done through people. They work through social and emotional behaviours to energise people, whether building teams or cajoling, persuading, influencing or commanding. *Problem-solving leaders* engage in planning, organising and making decisions. They are rational, systematic and highly organised. They apply reason and logic to systematic equations to make order out of chaos. The *pathfinder* is an entrepreneur and charismatic leader who lives in a world of values and aesthetics, putting faith before evidence. According to Leavitt (1987), 'Pathfinding is about getting the right questions rather than the right answers. It is about making problems rather than solving them. It is not about figuring out the best way to get there from here, not even about making sure that we get there. It is rather about pointing to where we ought to try to go.'

Whereas transactional leaders promote stability, transformational leaders create significant change in both followers and organisations. Both types of leadership behaviour are necessary in organisations, and effective leaders exhibit both transactional and transformational leadership patterns, though in different proportions. Remember how Diane Maple, the head teacher in the opening vignette, demonstrates both transactional skills and transformational qualities as an organisational leader.

How leaders transform organisations

If you are inclined towards leadership, the early stages of your career will probably build on the concepts of leading groups already discussed. However, leadership beyond the face-to-face group level involves learning other qualities. When leaders seek to influence the entire organisation or one of its major units, they draw on transformational leadership. **Transformational leaders** energise others with visions and strategies of how to refocus and revitalise the larger organisation.

transformational leaders
Leaders who energise others with visions and strategies of how to refocus and revitalise the larger organisation so that change meets people's enduring needs.

The concept of the transformational leader is credited to Burns (1978), who emphasises that leadership involves changing organisations: 'The ultimate test of practical leadership is the realisation of intended, real change that meets people's enduring needs.' Leaders at the head of an organisation mobilise influence across the organisation so that others follow the path they envision without the necessity for interpersonal interaction.

Pathfinding

Pathfinding leaders are visionary types – dreamers concerned about charting a mission and direction. Pathfinding leaders who also have a capability for implementing provide the entrepreneurial stimulus to start new businesses and transform old ones. Pathfinders make the break-throughs, take the risks, and commit themselves to developing the newer and better. They are the divergent thinkers who, rather than converge on the 'one best answer', push people to consider creative possibilities from which choices can be made.

---

pathfinding leaders

Entrepreneurial and charismatic leaders who are visionary types – dreamers concerned with pointing to where an organisation ought to try to go.

Pathfinders are personified by General Electric's Jack Welch. Welch strategically refocused GE into 14 core businesses, departing from the unrelated conglomerate type of diversification that characterised GE in the 1970s. In undertaking this transformation, Welch practised the productivity improvements later confirmed by research as necessary for periodic organisational refocusing (Markides, 1992).

In transforming organisations, the pathfinding leader unsettles people with difficult questions such as: What do we really want to do with this company? What do we value? What kind of organisation would we love to build? Such strategic questions force soul searching and the possibility that people could do something uniquely different with their time and resources. Pathfinding leadership enables quality and continuous improvement to become the driver.

Behavioural strategies for transformational leaders

Kouzes and Posner (1995) and Bennis and Nanus (1985) suggest that leaders draw on at least three behavioural strategies in transforming organisations.

1 **They create a vision.** Depending on personal style (and through some combination of intuition, analysis, creativity, learning from others and deductive thinking), the leader articulates and champions a vision of a desired future state that is challenging, meaningful and credible. Visions give direction to organisational members in ways congruent with the leader's style and philosophy, and consistent with environmental pressures and organisational resources and constraints. The best visions, according to Collins and Porras (1995), are ones that take root within the organisation, and which build enduring capabilities that transcend changes in leaders and market conditions. Sam Walton of Asda Wal-Mart had a clear vision of bringing mass merchandising at low prices to rural communities when he created Wal-Mart, a vision that prospered even after his death. Anita Roddick is another example, her clear vision enabled the Body Shop to carry on when she stepped down as CEO.

2 **They mobilise commitment.** Acceptance by others is critical to making the new vision happen. Conger (1991) suggests that leaders demonstrate personal excitement and promote the vision to groups at every opportunity, replacing managing by dictate with articulating a message that is highly motivational. Look back at the Halewood case in Chapter 5, where inspirational leadership changed working practices and productivity at the Halewood car plant.

3 **They institutionalise change.** Rather than apply the quick fix or one-minute management solution, the transforming leader oversees system-wide shifts in problem-solving and decision-making processes. This involves seeing that new practices pervade the

organisation instead of being limited to a handful of elite managers. The transforming leader enables others to act on the vision and conveys the confidence to meet challenges. Michael Eisner did this when he took over as CEO of ailing Walt Disney Productions and shifted perceptions, standards and decision criteria to transform Disney into a powerful, diversified entertainment giant once again (Boje, 1995).

Transformation through dedication and continuous improvement

Given the fast and far-reaching rate of competitive, technical and geopolitical change, organisational strategies and practices that were effective five years ago have limited applicability in many industries today. This reality was driven home by Louis V. Gerstner Jr, two years into his transforming experience as CEO of IBM (a firm that in the first three years of the 1990s had net losses of £12 billion): 'One of the great things about this industry is that every decade or so, you get a chance to redefine the playing field. We're in that phase of redefinition right now, and winners or losers are going to emerge from it' (Sager, 1995). One winner is Jeff Bezos, CEO of Amazon.com, one of the first visionary leaders of the new economy. His experiences as a transformational leader in the emerging e-commerce industry are described in the Technology Transformation box.

Such turbulent conditions demand transformational change to lead strategies that develop new lines of business and deepen a commitment to quality and continuous improvement. Yet Bennis (1990) believes that many visions lack impact and staying power because they overlook two fundamental human needs that underpin change in today's organisations: quality and dedication. He writes:

> Modern industrial society has been oriented to quantity, providing more goods and services for everyone. Quantity is measured in money; we are a money-oriented society. Quality often is not measured at all but is appreciated intuitively. Our response to quality is a feeling. Feelings of quality are connected intimately with our experience of meaning, beauty, and value in our lives.
>
> Closely linked to the concept of quality is that of dedication to, even love of, our work. This dedication is evoked by quality and is the force that energises high-performing systems.

Bennis (1990) asserts that too many men and women in positions of high leadership fail to exercise needed transformational leadership. They get entrapped in managing daily routines and never lead the reform towards total quality through continuous improvement. Bennis, as well as other researchers such as Kouzes and Posner (1995), concludes that transformational leadership is a skill that can be learned. Transformational leadership skills can be developed by learning the best practices of others and from personal mistakes or setbacks. Five behavioural practices common to successful transformational leaders are summarised in Exhibit 14-10.

Marks & Spencer started as a small market stall at the beginning of the last century, and developed into a national institution. Changes in management have had their effect over the years and to keep its position it has had to diversify into food and finance. In the 1990s Marks & Spencer was finding it hard to maintain its position. Luc Vandevelde was brought in as CEO to revive the company, and by consolidating its European operation and diversifying into named labels, once again the business has managed to maintain its place in the retail market. Once Vandevelde had achieved his aim he was able to step down and allow others to carry on.

Paving the way to the future at Amazon.com

The success of the Internet has facilitated the emergence of the 'new economy' in just a couple of years. At first glance, leaders in the new economy can appear very different from the 'image' of business and political leaders that first comes to mind – distinguished, powerful and dressed in a three-piece suit. Quite the contrary, many of the leaders in the Internet sector are under 30, wear jeans to work, and dismiss many traditional business practices or boundaries. But they have the same core qualities that all leaders share – the ability to create a vision and motivate their followers to reach that goal, and to pursue that vision even in the face of opposition.

Just like the pioneers who shaped the industrial era, the new economy leaders take huge risks to follow their dreams. In the summer of 1994, one such visionary left his lucrative job at an investment firm, packed his car and, with his wife, moved to start what he thought would be a good business – selling books over the Internet. He was turned away time after time and investors thought he was crazy.

That man is Jeff Bezos, CEO of Amazon.com, one of the first visionary leaders of the new economy. He is widely credited with changing the way that business is conducted and for seeing into the e-commerce future of the Internet. He was named *Time*'s Person of the Year for 1999, and has a personal worth of approximately £7 billion. According to *Time* managing editor Walter Isaacson, 'Bezos is a person who not only changed the way we do things but helped pave the way for the future.'

Discussing some experiences, leadership and the focus of Amazon.com, Jeff Bezos speaks out: 'Being at the heart of the new economy is intense fun, really. It's a huge, good time to be near the centre of something that is going to change the world in some positive ways. Most people never have the opportunity, even in a small way, to make history, which Amazon.com is trying to do. It's work hard, have fun, make history. That's what we're trying to do.

'My day-to-day responsibilities have changed significantly over the last two years. We have built this extraordinary management team, which allows me to spend more time working on recruiting, which I devote a lot of time to. Mondays and Thursdays I try to keep clear of prescheduled meetings so I can wander around and talk with people; just basically be proactive on those days. So, yeah, there are some fundamental ways you can start to change your time when you have a very strong management team.

'My focus is now on the customer, customer, customer. I think everything falls out of that. It's especially true online, because the balance of power shifts away from the company and towards the customer. Customers have a bigger voice online. If we make a customer unhappy, they can tell thousands of people. Likewise, if you make a customer happy, they can also tell thousands of people. With that kind of a megaphone in the hands of every individual customer, you had better be a customer-centred company.'

Source: adapted from James Daly (1999) 'Paving the Way to the Future at Amazon.com', *Business 2.0*, 24 February, pp. 12–16. For the complete article visit www.thestandard.com.

Discussion questions
1 How is leadership changing with the advent of new technology?
2 Do you think visionary leaders make good managers?

EXHIBIT 14–10   How leaders get extraordinary things done

Researchers Kouzes and Posner (1995) focused on what leaders do whenever they are at their personal best and concluded that there are five behavioural practices common to successful leaders.

1 **They challenge the process.** They are willing to take risks to change the status quo. They make mistakes to push innovation.

2 **They inspire a shared vision.** They have a dream – a purpose, mission, goal or agenda. They live their lives backwards by starting with a picture in their mind, then enlisting others to share passionately in that vision and make it happen.

3 **They enable others to act.** They focus on 'we' to build coalitions and encourage collaboration. They build teams and empower others. (This is the most significant of the five practices.)

4 **They model the way.** They are clear about their business beliefs and behave consistently with those beliefs. They show others their values by behaving as they expect others to act.

5 **They encourage the heart.** They use celebrations to offer dramatic encouragement and rewards. They show team members they can win and winning is exciting. They love their customers, their products, their people and their work.

Source: James M. Kouzes and Barry Z. Posner (1995) *The Leadership Challenge: How to Get Extraordinary Things Done in Organizations*. San Francisco, CA: Jossey-Bass. Copyright 1995 Jossey-Bass Publishers. Reprinted by permission of Jossey-Bass, Inc., a subsidiary of John Wiley & Sons, Inc.

Is leadership always necessary?

Some researchers, such as Kerr and Jermier (1978), take issue with theories that assume leadership will always be useful. One of their studies found that leadership theories fail to systematically account for much of the change in group performance. While group members need guidance and psychological strokes or emotional support, they may not necessarily be dependent on the manager or leader for them. Quite simply, there are substitutes for leadership; three are described in Exhibit 14-11.

The first two substitutes (personal expertise and intrinsic task satisfaction) reflect professionalism or a high degree of job maturity, to use the Hersey and Blanchard terminology. The third condition (rules and procedures) may occur when job technology acts as a control even when job maturity is not advanced. These and other conditions that substitute for leadership further support the contingency philosophy. They confirm that the extent of the need for leadership and leader behaviour are situationally dependent.

EXHIBIT 14–11   Three substitutes for leadership

Leadership interventions are needed less, if at all, when the following conditions are found within a group.

1 **Individual job expertise.** The highly mature individual in a profession, a craft or a technical job knows when and how to perform the task. Years of experience and training and working with a number of supervisors enable the individual to work without dependence on a leader except when receiving assignments or new goals.

2 **Intrinsic task satisfaction.** People who obtain high personal satisfaction from working on a particular task do not need a supervisor's influence to keep them productive. When satisfaction comes from the task itself rather than from extrinsic rewards administered by a manager, the best leadership role is largely supportive, not interfering.

3 **Formalised rules and procedures.** Tightly structured tasks with specific understood procedures reduce worker dependency on supervisors. Leadership may be superfluous when the employee does not have to exert judgement in order to perform the task successfully.

Source: Steven Kerr and John M. Jermier (1978) 'Substitutes for Leadership: Their Meaning and Measurement', *Organizational Behavior and Human Performance* 22, December, pp. 375–403. Used by permission of Steven Kerr, visiting professor, University of Michigan.

The originators of the path-goal theory of leadership also note that when a group's goals as well as the paths to goals are clear, leadership is not really necessary. According to House and Mitchell (1974), under these conditions – when employees know what to do, how to do it and when to do it – 'attempts by the leader to clarify paths and goals will be both redundant and seen by subordinates as imposing unnecessary, close control'. Leaders should be aware of a group's situational needs, for there are times when influence need not be exerted.

Diversity issues in leadership

Within western organisations, white males have had a decided advantage for rising to prominent leadership positions. Few women and people of differing ethnic origin have been able to break the barriers for entry into the ranks of senior management and its opportunities to exert broad, transforming leadership. When Dee Bodine, a 52-year-old black woman, director of marketing, was interviewed and asked if people of ethnic minorities face barriers or special problems in advancing into top management, she replied:

> Yes, absolutely, there are barriers to moving into senior management. It starts at the one-on-one level. People see us as weaker, less qualified, and a bigger risk. Therefore, we don't get picked for key assignments that would give us visibility and credibility. The few of us who do get chosen live in a very non-supportive, lonely, pressure cooker kind of environment. The personal perceptions translate into both formal and informal practices that exclude us. (Morrison, 1992)

This same study by Ann Morrison (1992) found that the most critical barriers to advancement by women and people of ethnic minorities are:

1 Prejudice, of treating stereotyped differences as weaknesses.
2 Poor career planning, where minorities are blocked from high-profile, challenging jobs.
3 A lonely, hostile, unsupportive working environment for non-traditional (minority) managers.
4 A lack of organisational savvy of knowing 'how to play the game' of politics.
5 Career comfort by executives in dealing with their own kind (the inside group).
6 Difficulty in balancing family and career, especially for women.

On this last point, one story was told where a woman on the verge of being promoted opted instead to be demoted because her husband was critical of the amount of travel she was doing. She also reported that no man within the company had accepted a demotion rather than be promoted within at least the last five years. Another meta-study, by Blum *et al.* (1994), concluded that 'management jobs are still dominated by men and that, given the option, many organisations still prefer to hire or promote men into administrative and management positions'. Several writers on organisations have started to relate sports coaching to leadership; for more examples of this look at the Dynamics of Diversity box.

Yet, surprisingly, an increasing number of women who make it into responsible management positions, even senior management, are reassessing their lives and opting to leave their posts rather than be bored or unfulfilled. A survey by Morris (1995) of 300 career women (94 per cent managers and executives) between the ages of 35 and 49 found that 87 per cent had made or were seriously considering making a significant change in their lives. In contrast to common perceptions, it was not motherhood or glass ceilings that pulled these women

dynamics of diversity

A question of sport

Sports coaching may be a good way to motivate your top team, but to score in the long term you need to leave the playing field behind and address your business goals.

When it comes to improving the performance of a business's top team, dragging them up a mountain and across a river, or sitting them in front of a highly motivational sports coach, may produce some very short-term benefits, but it won't necessarily deliver long-term improvement.

For the record, I don't hate sports and coaches. In fact, from the late 1980s to the mid-1990s I worked in the Sport Psychology Department at the US Olympic Training Centre and as a sports psychologist with professional sports teams and athletes across the USA. Since then I've worked with senior teams in some of the world's largest and most successful businesses, so I can offer some impartiality.

If one takes a step back and thinks about the differences between senior business teams and sports teams, my opening remark should be obvious.

A typical top-level sportsperson is young, physically gifted and extremely committed to both their own results and the success of their team. They will often share identical objectives with their team-mates and be focused on a specific goal, whether this is an individual match or a longer-term competition.

Their progress is highly visible, and both the individual and the team usually receive immediate feedback on their performance – even if, for some, this might be at the hands of the tabloid press.

For the coach or manager, there are daily opportunities to discuss performance and explore actions to improve it. Also, the motivational strategies implemented by coaches read like a formula for how to find oneself in front of an industrial tribunal. If you're looking for a micro-managing bully, you could do a lot worse than start with many successful sports coaches.

By comparison, the leader of a senior business team is faced with a very different set of challenges. These may lie in the divergent personal perspectives and goals of their team members, most of whom will be older than the typical elite sportsperson.

Succeeding in business also requires highly developed analytical skills and the ability to cope with many ambiguous, unpredictable tasks simultaneously.

In sport, the parameters are fewer and more predictable. Although, just as in business, sports teams can employ better skilled team members, they can't suddenly decide to double the number of players on the field in a way your business competitor could suddenly decide to spend its entire annual advertising and promotions budget in one month.

Even defining winning and losing is more complex in business – is it about net profit, net margin, market share, return on capital employed, share price or shareholder added value?

There may be value in using sports coaches or outdoor activities for motivational purposes. But for the serious business of securing long-term performance improvement from a senior team, training should be focused on three core issues: alignment of commercial goals and priorities, and developing understanding of these within teams; clarity of team purpose and necessary procedures; and addressing team dynamics – although only if they're interfering with the agreement or achievement of business priorities.

And you don't even have to get your feet wet.

Source: Michael Greenspan (2005) 'A Question of Sport', *People Management*, 13 October, p. 7. Michael Greenspan is a partner at organisation and management consultancy Kiddy & Partners.

Discussion questions

1 What are the differences between the performance of a top athlete and a business leader?
2 Why do leaders need to understand the importance of group dynamics?

away from corporate leadership. Many were striking out on their own to become entrepreneurs, consultants or involved in philanthropic pursuits – quests to become more fulfilled and satisfied.

Typical of many, Claire Irving left her career in corporate mergers and acquisitions to start her own detective agency. She gave this reason for her change: 'It wasn't burnout, it was boredom.' Satisfied with her switch, she remarked, 'I am doing it for me.' Ironically, at the very time society begins to expect more women in positions of corporate leadership, it seems that significant numbers of those who achieve business success redirect their lives so that life is more manageable and personally meaningful. Perhaps the lesson is that from the viewpoint of leader satisfaction, there can be as much (or more) joy in leading five as in leading 500 or 5000.

Diane Maple: a second look

Certainly, the atmosphere in the school is outstanding. Everyone smiles at you, not just the teachers and children but the receptionists, the secretarial staff, the dinner ladies and the parents – it's quite infectious.

You could call it Happy Valley primary school and it wouldn't be going too far. Yet Happy Valley it isn't. This is a deprived area and, while the inside of the school may be an oasis of calm, the outside isn't. The lead was stolen off part of the school building this autumn. It's not the first time but people living near the school dare not report it while it's happening for fear of getting their cars torched.

Every child in the school planted a tree against one of the boundary fences and every one was stolen. One notable day staff and children were trapped in the school by a police shoot-out with drug dealers in a building across the road. As Maple says: 'We don't give up. If you did, you would give up totally.'

She is shocked by winning the award because, to her, she is not doing anything that is special. 'I just do my job to the best of my abilities. I have had the privilege to lead a school out of special measures and the joy of seeing the children blossom again. There are so many people out there who do what I do every day. This is an award for all head teachers.'

Source: © Wendy Berliner, the *Guardian*, 29 October 2002. Reprinted with permission.

Summary

- Managers carry out a broader set of functions than do leaders. Managers focus on using their authority to cope with complexity, see that things are done right, and ensure resources are used efficiently.

- Leaders emphasise change and continuous improvement, and they seek to visualise the right thing to do by questioning practices and possibilities.

- Leaders seek to influence followers so they will want to work towards the leader's goals. Leaders also appear to have certain traits in common that help others to have confidence in their credibility, a phenomenon explained by social-cognitive theory.

- Several streams of research have focused on the leader's style or behaviour as he or she interacts directly with the group to be influenced. Although many labels have been employed to describe this behaviour, in essence they distinguish between the leader's task-orientated and relationship-orientated behaviours or between the leader's underlying cognitive styles (motives and concerns).

- Because predictions of effectiveness based solely on the leader's behaviour or style have generated inconsistent results, most contemporary models incorporate one or more situational variables. These are called contingency theories.

- Fiedler equates effectiveness to task versus relationship styles in combination with three contingency variables.

- Hersey and Blanchard pay attention to how the leader's task and/or relationship behaviours are adapted to followers' job maturity competencies.

- House and Mitchell view the leader's behaviour as clarifying goals and showing the path to them.

- Vroom and Yetton consider leadership effectiveness options by working through a decision tree of group and situational factors.

- A different form of leadership is necessary at the level of the larger organisation, where the leader acts as a visionary pathfinder and a transformer of organisational strategies and practices. At this level, leaders must learn the skills of creating a vision, mobilising commitment and institutionalising change. They get extraordinary things done by being dedicated to continuous improvement and enabling others to act.

- Some research suggests that there are times when leadership is not necessary or may even get in the way. There are even conditions that may be substitutes for leadership.

- Women and ethnic minorities face the dilemma that while they have more obstacles to overcome to break into responsible leadership positions, many who do succeed find the experience less than fulfilling. They choose to downsize the complexities in their lives by breaking away from big organisations to follow other more personal pursuits.

Areas for personal development

Although the extent and type of leadership may be dependent on the characteristics of a specific situation, there is no doubt that effective leadership is a crucial variable in organisational success. You can be a more effective leader if you apply the following interpersonal skills.

1 **Act as a leader or manager as appropriate.** Both leadership and management are needed in organisations. Leadership is required to focus on the big picture, to form a vision for followers, and to empower them to innovate and excel. Management, on the other hand, is needed to focus on daily operations and managing people, tasks and resources. While many managers can be leaders, not all leaders are managers. Leaders are present at all levels in an organisation.

2 **Use leader task behaviours** when it is necessary to obtain consistent work methods and accomplish a job by specific deadlines.

3 **Use leader relationship behaviours** to satisfy social and emotional needs when team morale is low, when there is conflict among employees, or when certain team members feel alienated from the rest.

4 **Adapt your leadership style to situational contingencies.** The most appropriate leadership style to use depends on the situation. Check situational variables like task structure, follower maturity, relationships with subordinates and other relevant factors to determine what leader behaviours are required. Set aside your own preferences and use the style that is most appropriate to best solve the problem or get the desired results.

5 **Expand your style repertoire by understanding which emotional intelligence competencies underlie the leadership styles you are lacking.** Build up the areas of emotional intelligence you need to apply all leadership styles effectively. Usually this requires changing old habits and acquiring new ones, which may take some time, practice and commitment. Nevertheless, it is definitely worth the effort and will result in increased leadership effectiveness and team performance.

6 **Clarify paths to goals for followers.** A leader can increase follower motivation by clarifying performance goals and subordinates' pathways to obtaining organisational goals, and by providing meaningful personal rewards. When clarifying paths to goals, help subordinates identify and learn the behaviours that will enable them successfully to accomplish tasks. Second, consult with subordinates to determine which rewards are important to them. Then increase personal pay-offs to subordinates for goal attainment and to make the paths to these pay-offs clear and easy to travel.

7 **Create a vision.** Articulate and champion a vision of a desired future state that is challenging, meaningful and credible. Visions give direction to organisational members in ways congruent with the leader's style and philosophy and consistent with environmental pressures and organisational resources and constraints.

8 **Encourage commitment.** Acceptance by others is critical to making the new vision happen. Leaders demonstrate personal excitement and promote the vision to groups at every opportunity, replacing managing by dictate with articulating a message that is highly motivational.

9 **Institutionalise change.** Enable others to act on the vision and convey the confidence that they can meet the challenges. Be sure that new practices pervade the organisation instead of being limited to a handful of elite managers.

10 **Outline contingent plans to keep moving towards the vision.** Most of the time things do not go according to plan en route to achieving a vision. A leader should formulate other plans of action for when inevitable problems or changes derail the current path of progress.

11 **Anticipate and accept change.** Not everyone is totally comfortable with change, but an effective leader has to understand that change happens and be prepared to deal with it. Learn from observing the best practices of others and from personal mistakes and setbacks. Then make appropriate changes.

Questions for study and discussion

1 Both leadership researchers and corporate executives contend that too many organisations are over-managed and under-led. In your own words, what are the differences between managers and leaders? Why do organisations need both?

2 The idea of identifying leaders based on personality traits was once popular, became discarded, and now has rising popularity again. What are some of the reasons personal characteristics are useful in thinking about leaders and how they are perceived? What are some of the traits or characteristics that seem to distinguish leaders from the rest of the crowd, in the minds of followers?

3 Many of the popular theories of leadership generated over the past four decades incorporate a task and a relationship dimension to describe the leader (although several labels have been used). Although they use similar terms, what is the difference between the behaviour-based theories and those that apply a cognitive style interpretation? Why have efforts to predict group effectiveness using only the leader's behaviour or style produced inconclusive results?

4 Draw a four-cell matrix using 'initiating structure' (task) and 'showing consideration' (relationship) as your two behaviour axes. Add 'high' and 'low' labels on each axis. In each of the cells, write examples of how a leader would behave. Then describe the circumstances that would allow each set of behaviours to be effective.

5 Compare and contrast the leadership style model of Fiedler with the situational theory of Hersey and Blanchard. Both are contingency theories, but how does their use of the concepts 'task' and 'relationship' differ? Which one seems most useful? Why?

6 What were your scores on emotional intelligence when you took the 'Your turn' self-assessment inventory in Chapter 9? Take a couple of minutes now to look back at this and review emotional intelligence – the ability to manage ourselves and our relationships effectively. Based on your scores and understanding of the components of emotional intelligence, which of the six leader styles are most natural for you and which areas of emotional intelligence do you need to improve in order to enhance your leadership effectiveness?

7 How does a transformational leader bring about change? What personal behaviours help the transformation process?

8 What are the circumstances when leadership may not really be necessary? Comment on the observation that the relationship between leaders and followers is not always an equitable one.

Key Concepts

Personal skills exercise
Don't topple the tower (Cook, 1978)

Purpose This action exercise helps to examine leader–member relationships that affect team performance on a tangible production project. In teams of three or four people, the objective is to see how many folded index cards can be stacked two cards per tier, with each tier at a 90-degree angle to the tier below, to form a multi-tiered tower of up to 20 cards. You say it sounds easy? Wait until you are a worker and try to do it blindfold!

Primary attention is on the thoughts and interaction behaviours of the leader. During each production debriefing, other situational factors are examined: skill differences among workers; worker needs, expectations and perceptions; physical factors, and so on.

Time 35–65 minutes

Materials Large index cards (12 × 18 cm size recommended), 20 per team. Strips of cloth suitable for blindfolds, two per team.

Procedure

1 Assign participants to three- or four-person teams. If the available time is limited to about 45 minutes, use three-person teams to allow sufficient time for each member to serve in a leadership role during one 5-minute building period. If time is not so limited, four-person teams provide more comparison data.

2 The production exercise will be repeated (in 5-minute intervals, timed by the instructor) as many times as there are persons per team. Roles are to be rotated following each action cycle. The roles are:

   ■ leader or supervisor (one person)

   ■ subordinates, builders (two people)

   ■ process observer (one person, but only if using four-person teams).

3 Once teams are assembled, each team receives its 20 index cards and two blindfolds. Fold cards lengthwise in the middle to form 'tents'. If 12 × 18 cards are used, each tent will be 53–55 cm high × 18 cm long, flared about 2 cm at the bottom.

4 After teams and materials are assembled, develop whatever procedures you believe will be necessary to ensure good performance, so long as they are consistent with the instructions. During the planning and preparation time, it will be the *leader's responsibility* to *establish a team output goal* (expressed as the number of cards stacked without toppling the tower). Blindfold the two initial builders, and designate them as worker A and worker B. If you have time, practise until the instructor is ready to start all teams on the first 5-minute production period.

Production instructions

1 Using the non-dominant hand for stacking cards, blindfolded worker A will place the first card tent in the middle of a desk or table. Blindfolded worker B places the second card, parallel to the first, as close or far apart as directed by the leader. This forms the base tier. Worker A then places the third card at right angles to the base; worker B places the fourth card parallel to the third. Work continues in this manner, with workers alternating the stacking of each card, with two parallel cards per tier.

2 Since workers are blindfolded, the leader/supervisor must guide the work verbally through instructions to the work team. The supervisor cannot touch either the workers or the cards at any time during the 5-minute timed production period.

3 The round is terminated for a work team when (a) the goal is achieved, i.e. the tower is 10 tiers high; (b) a card that was previously stacked on the tower is knocked off; (c) the entire tower topples; (d) the instructor calls time at the end of five minutes. If a worker is placing a card and it slips off without knocking off another card, the leader may direct the worker to retrieve the card and resume building.

4 After each round, the instructor records on the board each team's goal and actual results. This can be done in matrix form with numbers inserted as each round is completed.

5 At the end of each round, each team privately debriefs the factors that contributed to productivity or problems, satisfaction and developmental learning. The observer (if one is used) should lead this discussion using notes of observed behaviours. Questions can be

asked of workers and the leader about their experiences. Did they feel anxiety, tension or frustration? What were their thoughts, motives and suggestions for improving performance? Following a few minutes for team debriefing and planning, the instructor may debrief the class with one or more focusing questions. If time is scarce, the debriefing can be held until after the final round. The objective of the debriefing phase is to move beyond having fun and help focus learning from this direct experience.

Team exercise
Dividing up leadership (a role play)

Purpose This role-playing exercise initially involves all class members and gives everyone an opportunity to exert leadership influence in one of six groups. Through the two-phase dynamics of the exercise, students form impressions about their own leadership tendencies and learn through social observation what leadership behaviours do and do not work in the present situation. The first phase focuses on emergent leadership within self-selected groups; in the second phase, representatives from each group vie to influence others as to the merits of their group's recommendation and their share of a £500 000 budget.

Time about 45 minutes

Materials Copies of the background notes for the six groups from the *Instructor's Manual*. Each note represents one of the six major activity centres for the Multi-Phase Products Company: research, manufacturing, marketing, administration, scientific instruments division, and medical instruments division.

Pre-group preparation: a background note on Multi-Phase Products Co. The entire class should read the following background material before beginning phase 1.

Multi-Phase Products, is a midsize firm in the medical and scientific instruments industry that has begun to experience difficulties. The firm is organised along functional lines, and it has two business divisions that produce and sell products. Now 12 years old, the firm currently employs about 700 people. Last year it generated revenues of £120 million with profits before tax of £3 million. Now three months into the financial year, managers within the firm are troubled by declining profit margins. Three years ago, net profit margins before tax peaked at 10 per cent of gross revenues; this quarter a loss is projected. Gross margins have also declined (from 55 per cent three years ago to 40 per cent this quarter). In part, this is because of the higher costs involved in introducing a new technology within the medical instruments division. There has also been an erosion of price points in the maturing scientific instruments division, which is facing intensified competition in both domestic and foreign markets. In several specific product market areas, customers have the perception that the quality of Multi-Phase products has slipped relative to that of competitors.

Procedure for Group Phase 1: selection and recommendations After everyone has read the background note, progress through the following three steps.

1 The instructor asks for six volunteers whose job is simply to act as resource persons and pass along information to group members once groups form. Each volunteer is handed one of the six group background information notes (obtained from the *Instructor's Manual*) and a sign indicating the group's organisational unit. The six volunteers then stand around the perimeter of the room (at the four corners and midpoints of the two longest sides) and hold up their organisational unit sign.

2 All others in the class then stand and move to one of the six locations. Use any criteria you wish in selecting a group, such as its function, the people who seem to be attracted to it, or the number of people in the group. Groups need not be equal in numbers, but the largest must have no more than twice as many members as the smallest.

3 Now the work begins. The resource volunteer shares verbally (by paraphrasing, not reading) information contained in the 'group note' with his or her group. Members discuss ideas for improving the firm, restoring quality and selecting an approach that seems reasonable. They also decide what share of a £500 000 'quality improvement budget' they believe their recommendation merits. They then select one member to represent their interests as a leader at the 'task force' meeting. (Instructor will allocate time – about 10 minutes.)

Procedure for Phase 2: task force budget meeting The six task force leaders now assemble in front of the room (seated, if movable chairs are available). Each presents his or her group's recommendations and discusses them with the other five. This is a leaderless group, in the sense that no one is appointed to officiate as chairperson.

The six-person group will then decide on the merits of the six proposals by allocating the £500 000 quality improvement pool of funds the CEO has budgeted for this purpose. The allocation that is finally accepted by the task force group should be proportionate to the perceived value of the six proposals for improving Multi-Phase products. (The instructor may call an end to negotiations if the group seems to be at an impasse – about 15 minutes.)

Debriefing The instructor guides a discussion of questions such as the following.

1 Why did you choose to volunteer (or not to volunteer) as a resource person? To what extent did resource persons become group leaders at the multigroup negotiations?

2 What behaviours were influential in deciding on the group's recommendations? Were the behaviours of influential persons examples of leaders showing consideration, or were they instrumental in nature? Did some people actively seize the opportunity to influence the group? For people who were influential, what were you seeking to accomplish by both the content and manner of expressing your ideas?

3 Why were some of the leaders apparently more able to convey a vision of their plan in the budget negotiations? Did the most visionary exert greater influence on the task force?

4 What was the basis for leadership at the Group Phase 1 level? To what extent was the outcome of the budget allocation process in Phase 2 a reasonable reflection of the pathfinding leadership qualities of the group leaders?

Case study: going independent – freelance executives for hire; 'overstretched businesses can benefit from the skills and experience of independent directors'

Need a chairman in a hurry? Has your finance director left you in the lurch? Perhaps you are gearing up for a float on the stock market and need to add a bit of weight to the boardroom. Or perhaps the squalls in the economy have blown you over, and you are looking for someone with the skills to steer you back to an even keel.

Britain's biggest venture capital company 3i has pioneered a service that provides companies with temporary executives to help them out with specific tasks or periods of development. Patrick Dunne helped set up 3i's Independent Directors Programme (IDP) in the late 1980s and as a director of the company has led its expansion into markets here and overseas.

'We now have about 600 members on 1200 boards, and about a third of those are outside the UK. Taking one of our independent directors onto your board is a great way to get to know 3i,' says Dunne.

The idea is simple. The skills that make for a good entrepreneur who can launch and build a new business are quite different from those needed to run a medium-sized, maturing operation. They are certainly not the skills needed if the business gets into difficulties, as can easily happen with fast-growing companies. This is where the IDP comes in. It recruits people who usually have a history of being entrepreneurs themselves, who have spent their career in management, and are now free to go into 3i's client companies and help out for a limited period. It is a hybrid form of management consultancy.

The service is free to companies that 3i has already invested in. It could also be of interest to others, either potential clients of 3i, or companies that are prepared to pay a fee for the IDP's services.

Often these 'parachuted in' managers are entrepreneurs themselves who have built up their own business and sold it. They have money but are still young enough to want to do more. But they don't want to go through the start-up process themselves again, says Dunne. Spending a limited period with a business appeals to them. 'Many of these IDP people will have experience of turning around troubled companies – an occupational hazard when you're dealing with fast-growing companies. If you've been involved in a high-growth phase, turnaround work comes naturally,' Dunne says.

These independent directors focus on four key roles: chairman, chief executive, finance director and independent director. Globally 3i makes 200 appointments of independent directors a year. 'We introduce five or six candidates to the managing director of the company that has requested the help. We agree a specification with the company. The client picks the person, so they feel they are in control of the process, they have ownership of it: with our existing pool of independent directors we can introduce rescue chairmen at short notice to a troubled business, for example. Then they can recruit a chief executive, and so on. We provide independent directors to a lot of distressed businesses, either existing clients or ones that we think have a good recovery potential.'

Dunne is also an author, and he uses one of his books, *Directors' Dilemmas*, to illustrate common management problems at the IDP's quarterly regional events. 'We do a lot of training and development for people on the IDP. For instance, there is a "Twenty Questions" game, "What makes a good finance director?" This is very useful for meetings between a non-executive director and a potential finance director.'

Dunne says the starting point for sorting out the problems of an under-managed medium-sized business is getting clarity. 'In family owned and run businesses, there is often a lack of clarity about who is responsible for what on the board. Very often the first thing the independent director has to do is to help the existing management to "keep out of jail", as it were. For instance, avoiding bankruptcy. Finance directors are usually the most valuable in this role, sorting out cash-flow problems. Then the independent director can turn to more long-term issues.'

Most important of these is usually the prosaic subject of how the company is run. 'Good governance doesn't get entrepreneurs' attention,' laments Dunne. Entrepreneurs typically don't like talking about 'core board processes'. These include framing strategy, something most entrepreneurs make up as they go along. Second, key appointments to strengthen the board. Third, running board meetings properly, not something that headstrong owner-managers take naturally to. A board should represent the views of key stakeholders, not just the entrepreneur and his chums. There is also setting the agenda. All these things Dunne describes as 'the plumbing' of the board. 'You will get leaky plumbing if you don't get it right,' he says.

The IDP is active abroad, particularly in France, Germany, the Netherlands and Finland. 'We also offer access to Independent Directors to clients in Japan,' says Dunne. 'We can offer UK clients a

Japanese board member, for instance. This kind of thing can be very important when British companies are trying to operate in different cultures. Expanding into Japan and the USA is where a lot of British SMEs come to grief.'

As a director of Britain's biggest venture capital company, Dunne is sensitive to oft-quoted suggestions that this country suffers from a 'funding gap' for small, growing companies. The charge is that there is a gap between funding from an ordinary bank overdraft secured on your house, say, and investment from a venture capitalist who will want to put in a big enough sum to make an adequate return. Between these two extremes, many small companies fail to find the right kind of funding, or so the argument goes.

Is this a true picture? 'Absolutely not,' declares Dunne. 'In fact in the UK there is an excess of capital raised. In addition, it is not just for technology start-ups either. For any company with a good plan, getting capital is not much of an issue in the UK,' he says emphatically. 'Good venture capitalists make money by making investments, after all. There's a lot of money around.'

Dunne admits the scene varies at the smaller end of the scale. The type of investment start-ups can attract depends on their growth plans, he says. Companies such as 3i are most interested in those with plans for serious growth, preferably including expansion into foreign markets. It is difficult for manufacturers to sustain rapid growth relying on the UK market alone, he says, although this isn't such a problem for service companies.

For instance, 3i has one client called Pixology, which has developed a system to remove the 'red eye' effect from photographs. 'It has great international potential,' says Dunne. 'We provide risk capital, therefore we require a reward when things go well. We invest into private companies by underpinning their capital. In most of them we take a minority position. The buyouts we do are much larger. With these we usually help management to buy out a subsidiary and then we sell it to the stock market.'

Source: John Willcock, *Independent*, 15 July 2002, p. 7.

Questions for discussion

1 Do you think that bringing in managers from the outside when needed is useful? Why, or why not?

2 What kind of leadership qualities will these board directors need?

3 What is the idea behind 3i's vision?

4 How would you feel if the company you worked for kept changing directors?

Applied questions

5 Kotter distinguishes between leaders and managers. Using Kotter's diagram in Exhibit 14-1, how could a temporary manager fulfil a leadership role?

6 Leaders and managers need to adjust to situational contingencies. Using Blake and Mouton's Leadership Grid®, which style would suit a temporary manager? What contingencies would need to be taken into account?

WWW exercise

Manager's Internet tools

Web tips: providing leadership through the Internet

As the Internet economy generates tremendous wealth in the developed parts of the world, the gap between rich and the poor widens, and constantly changing political landscapes threaten the stability and peace in many countries. The World Economic Forum (WEF) is one of the most influential global partnerships of business, political, intellectual and other leaders of society committed to improving the state of the world. Its members, constituents and collaborators together engage in processing, developing and sharing ideas, opinions and knowledge of the key issues on the global agenda. The Forum is independent, impartial to political influences, non-profit, and based on the belief that entrepreneurship brings about positive change in the global public interest to further economic growth and social progress. According to Warren Bennis:

> The World Economic Forum/Booz Allen & Hamilton study team is doing something profoundly important and original by focusing on organisational attributes rather than on individual leaders. By creating diagnostic tools that measure institutional alignment and adaptability, and then linking those to strategic interventions and enabling systems, they have made a significant breakthrough in both theory and practice, with the real promise of enhanced organisational performance.

World Wide Web search

The WEF is committed to integrating all members of the global society into its activities, and has created a website to increase its reach and exposure worldwide. According to the CEO, Klaus Schwab, the organisation is focused on 'building the network society ... this means that elites will more and more disappear [and] the new network society will be open and access should be guaranteed to everybody'. Learn about the world and how you can help. Visit WEF at www.weforum.org and check out how the WEF promotes world leadership through its many projects, including Transition to Peace, Global Leadership for Tomorrow and the Digital Infrastructure Initiative.

Specific website: Global Leaders for Tomorrow Website

With the launch of the joint Strategic Leadership Project, with Booz Allen & Hamilton, the organisation presents a novel approach to the study of leadership in organisations, proposing that leadership is an outcome fostered by environments that encourage it. The initiative is based on the premise that CEOs, managing directors and other senior executives generate such environments by empowering employees, and employing systems and processes that encourage leadership behaviours which, in turn, drive organisational performance. Visit this site (http://www.weforum.org./glt/) to learn about WEF's Global Leadership for Tomorrow programme, which has established a worldwide network of young leaders from diverse backgrounds to analyse and provide solutions to world problems.

1 How does the WEF approach have significant application in helping developing countries establish organisational cultures conducive to creating leaders?

2 What is the mission of the Global Leadership for Tomorrow programme?

3 How do members of the Global Leadership for Tomorrow programme prepare for tomorrow's world problems?

4 Look at some of WEF's projects, conference reports and future events. How significant a role do you think this organisation plays in providing vision and strategy for world leadership? How could it be even more powerful?

LEARNING CHECKLIST ☑

Before you move on you may want to reflect on what you have learnt in this chapter. You should now be able to:

☑ distinguish between the art of leadership and the practice of management

☑ understand the role of personality traits in leadership

☑ contrast group-centred leadership theories based on cognitive styles and observable behaviours

☑ apply emotional intelligence when choosing appropriate leader styles

☑ explain why most current theories of leadership are based on situational contingencies

☑ diagnose when transformational and transactional leadership are appropriate

☑ show why leadership is not necessary for all organisational circumstances.

Further reading

Bennis, W. (1993) *An Invented Life: Reflections on Leadership and Change.* Reading, MA: Addison-Wesley, 1993, pp. 19–22.

Blake, R.R. and Mouton, J.S. (1975) 'An Overview of the Grid', *Training and Development Journal* 5, May, pp. 29–36.

Blake, R.R. and Mouton, J.S. (1985) *The Managerial Grid III.* Houston, TX: Gulf Publishing.

Field, R.H. (1990) 'A Test of the Vroom–Yetton Normative Model of Leadership', *Journal of Applied Psychology* 67, pp. 523–532.

Kotter, J.P. (1990) *A Force for Change: How Leadership Differs from Management.* New York, NY: Free Press.

Kramer, R.M. (2006) 'The Great Intimidators', *Harvard Business Review* 84(2), February, p. 88.

McGregor, D. (1960) *The Human Side of Enterprise.* New York, NY: McGraw-Hill.

Prakash Prabhakar, G. (2005) 'An Empirical Study Reflecting the Importance of Transformational Leadership on Project Success Across Twenty Eight Nations', *Project Management Journal* 36(4), December, pp. 53–61.

Somech, A. (2006) 'The Effects of Leadership Style and Team Process on Performance and Innovation in Functionally Heterogeneous Teams', *Journal of Management* 32(1), 1 February, p. 132.

References

Beer, M. and Kleisath, S. (1967) 'The Effects of the Managerial Grid on Organizational and Leadership Dimension', in S.S. Zalkind (ed.) *Research on the Impact of Using Different Laboratory Methods for Interpersonal and Organizational Change*. Washington, DC: Symposium of the American Psychological Association, September.

Bennis, W. (1990) *Why Leaders Can't Lead*. San Francisco, CA: Jossey-Bass, pp. 23–24.

Bennis, W. and Nanus, B. (1985) *Leaders: The Strategies for Taking Charge*. New York, NY: Harper & Row, p. 20.

Berkowitz, L. (1954) 'Group Standards, Cohesiveness, and Productivity', *Human Relations* 7, pp. 509–514.

Blake, R.R. and Mouton, J.S. (1964) *The Managerial Grid*. Houston, TX: Gulf Publishing.

Blum, T.C., Fields, D.L. and Goodman, J.S. (1994) 'Organization-level Determinants of Women in Management', *Academy of Management Journal* 37, April, p. 241.

Boje, D.M. (1995) 'Stories of the Storytelling Organization: A Postmodern Analysis of Disney as "*Tamara*-Land"', *Academy of Management Journal* 38, August, pp. 997–1035.

Burns, J.M. (1978) *Leadership*. New York, NY: Harper & Row, p. 461.

Cartwright, D. and Zander, A. (1960) *Group Dynamics: Research and Theory*. New York, NY: Harper & Row.

Collins, J.C. and Porras, J.I. (1995) 'Building a Visionary Company', *California Management Review* 37, Winter, pp. 80–100.

Conger, J.A. (1991) 'Inspiring Others: The Language of Leadership', *Academy of Management Executive* 5, February, pp. 31–45.

Cook, C.W. (1978) 'Debriefing with Serialized Theory Development for Task-team Development', *Exploring Experiential Learning: Simulations and Experiential Exercises*. Tempe: Bureau of Business and Economic Research, Arizona State University, pp. 7–8.

Cook, C.W. (1980) 'Guidelines for Managing Motivation', *Business Horizons* 23, April, p. 63.

Fiedler, F.E. (1965) 'Engineering the Job to Fit the Manager', *Harvard Business Review* 43, September–October, pp. 115–122.

Fiedler, F.E. and Chemers, M.M. (1974) *Leadership and Effective Management*. Glenview, IL: Scott, Foresman, p. 70.

Ghiselli, E.E. (1971) *Explorations in Managerial Talent*. Pacific Palisades, CA: Goodyear Publishing Company.

Goleman, D. (2000) 'Leadership That Gets Results', *Harvard Business Review*, March–April, pp. 78–90.

Halpin, A.W. (1959) *The Leadership Behavior of School Superintendents*. Chicago, IL: Midwest Administration Center, University of Chicago, p. 4.

Hersey, P. and Blanchard, K.H. (1996) *Management of Organizational Behavior: Utilizing Human Resources* (7th edn). Upper Saddle River, NJ: Prentice Hall, Chapter 8.

House, R.J. and Mitchell, T.R. (1974) 'Path-goal Theory of Leadership', *Journal of Contemporary Business* 3, Autumn, pp. 81–97.

Kennedy, J.K., Houston, J.M., Korgaard, M.A. and Gallo, D.D. (1987) 'Construct Space of the Least Preferred Co-worker (LPC) Scale', *Educational and Psychological Measurement*, Fall, pp. 807–814. (LPC refers to a semantic differential instrument that asks leaders to describe their 'Least Preferred Co-worker' using pairs of bipolar adjectives, such as pleasant/unpleasant.)

Kerr, S. and Jermier, J.M. (1978) 'Substitutes for Leadership: Their Meaning and Measurement', *Organizational Behavior and Human Performance* 22, December, pp. 375–403.

Kirkpatrick, S.A. and Locke, E.A. (1991) 'Leadership: Do Traits Matter?', *Academy of Management Executive* 5, May, pp. 48–60.

Korman, A.K. (1966) 'Consideration, Initiating Structure, and Organizational Criteria – A Review', *Personnel Psychology*, Winter, pp. 349–361.

Kotter, J.P. (1990) 'What Leaders Really Do', *Harvard Business Review* 68, May–June, pp. 103–111.

Kouzes, J.M. and Posner, B.Z. (1995) *The Leadership Challenge: How to Get Extraordinary Things Done in Organizations.* San Francisco, CA: Jossey-Bass.

Kram, K.E. (1984) *Mentoring at Work.* Glenview, IL: Scott, Foresman.

Leavitt, H.J. (1987) *Corporate Pathfinders.* New York, NY: Penguin, p. 3.

Lewin, K. and Lippitt, R. (1938) 'An Experimental Approach to the Study of Autocracy and Democracy: A Preliminary Note', *Sociometry* 1, pp. 292–300.

Likert, R. (1961) *New Patterns of Management.* New York, NY: McGraw-Hill, p. 36.

Lord, R.G. and Phillips, J.S. (1982) 'Schematic Information Processing and Perceptions of Leadership in Problem-solving Groups', *Journal of Applied Psychology*, August, pp. 486–492.

Mann, R.D. (1959) 'A Review of the Relationships between Personality and Performance in Small Groups', *Psychological Bulletin* 56, pp. 241–270.

Markides, C.C. (1992) 'Consequences of Corporate Refocusing: Ex Ante Evidence', *Academy of Management Journal* 35, June, pp. 298–412.

McGregor, D. (1966) *Leadership and Motivation.* Cambridge, MA: The MIT Press.

Morris, B. (1995) 'Executive Women Confront Midlife Crisis', *Fortune* 132, 18 September, pp. 60–86.

Morrison, A.M. (1992) *The New Leaders: Guidelines on Leadership Diversity in America.* San Francisco, CA: Jossey-Bass, p. 29.

Packard, V. (1962) *The Pyramid Climbers.* New York, NY: McGraw-Hill, p. 170.

Peters, L.H., Hartke, D.D. and Pohlmann, J.T. (1985) 'Fiedler's Contingency Theory of Leadership: An Application of the Meta-analysis Procedures of Schmidt and Hunter', *Psychological Bulletin*, March, pp. 274–285.

Sager, I. (1995) 'The View from IBM', *Business Week*, 31 October, p. 142.

Schlender, B. (1995) 'Andy Grove Can't Stop', *Fortune* 131, 10 July, pp. 88–98.

Schmidt, W.H. and Posner, B.Z. (1982) *Managerial Values and Expectations: The Silent Power of Personal and Organizational Life.* New York, NY: American Management Association.

Schriesheim, C. and Von Glinow, M.A. (1977) 'The Path-goal Theory of Leadership: A Theoretical and Empirical Analysis', *Academy of Management Journal* 20, September, pp. 398–405.

Seashore, S.E. (1954) *Group Cohesiveness in the Industrial Work Group.* Ann Arbor, MI: University of Michigan Survey Research Center.

Stogdill, R.M. (1948) 'Personal Factors Associated with Leadership: A Survey of the Literature', *Journal of Psychology* 25, pp. 35–71.

Stogdill, R.M. (1974) *Handbook of Leadership: A Survey of Theory and Research.* New York, NY: Free Press, pp. 49–63.

Stogdill, R.M. and Coons, A.E. (1957) *Leader Behavior: Its Description and Measurement.* Columbus, OH: Ohio State University, Bureau of Business Research, p. 75.

Strebel, P. (1994) 'Choosing the Right Change Path', *California Management Review* 36, Winter, pp. 29–51.

Tannenbaum, R. and Schmidt, W. (1958) 'How to Choose a Leadership Pattern', *Harvard Business Review* 38, March–April, pp. 95–102.

Thomas, K.W. and Velthouse, B.A. (1990) 'Cognitive Elements of Empowerment: An Interpretative Model of Task Motivation', *Academy of Management Review* 15, October, pp. 666–681.

Vecchio, R.P. (1987) 'Situational Leadership Theory: An Examination of a Prescriptive Theory', *Journal of Applied Psychology* 72, August, pp. 444–451 (quote on p. 450).

Vroom, V.H. and Jago, A.G (1987) *The New Leadership: Cases and Manual for Use in Leadership Training.* New Haven, CT: Yale University.

Vroom, V.H. and Yetton, P.W. (1973) *Leadership and Decision Making.* Pittsburgh, PA: University of Pittsburgh Press.

Weiner, B., Graham, S., Taylor, S.E. and Meyer, W.U. (1983) 'Social Cognition in the Classroom', *Educational Psychologist* 18, Summer, pp. 109–124.

Yukl, G.A. (1981) *Leadership in Organizations.* Englewood Cliffs, NJ: Prentice Hall.

Zaleznik, A. (1990) 'The Leadership Gap', *Academy of Management Executive* 4(1), pp. 7–21.

Part 4: Integrated case study

eBay

Pierre Omidyar was just 28 when he sat down over a long holiday weekend to write the original computer code for what eventually became an Internet superbrand – the auction site eBay. However, it wasn't actually called that at the time of its launch on Labor Day, Monday 4 September 1995. It first appeared under the more prosaic title of Auction Web. That opening day was not exactly a roaring success. In fact, the site attracted no visitors at all in its first 24 hours. But, within weeks, a few dozen items were already being offered for sale, including a warehouse in Idaho and a 1937 Rolls-Royce.

By the end of 1995, several thousand auctions, attracting more than 10 000 bids, had taken place. Now eBay has 157 million users in 34 countries, with annual profits expected to reach $1bn this year.

'It's certainly a poster-child of the dotcom boom,' says Charles Abrams, research director for technology analysts Gartner.

eBay holds the philosophy that:

> We believe people are basically good
> We believe everyone has something to contribute
> We believe that an honest, open environment can bring out the best in people
> We recognise and respect everyone as a unique individual
> We encourage you to treat others the way that you want to be treated

Legends and myths have grown up about the early days of Auction Web, which changed its name to the more familiar eBay in 1997. According to one myth, the site came into being because Mr Omidyar's fiancee, Pam Wesley, wanted to contact other people who shared her hobby of trading Pez sweet dispensers.

That story was a product of public relations – but it is true that the first item sold was Mr Omidyar's own broken laser pointer, which went for $14 despite being essentially worthless. After that modest start, the milestones came thick and fast.

- Auction Web starts charging users a percentage of the sale fee in February 1996, becoming a real business for the first time.

- Monthly revenues reached $10 000 in June 1996, prompting Mr Omidyar to leave his job and run the site full-time. In 1997, the newly renamed eBay marks its 1 000 000th sale – a Big Bird toy, based on the *Sesame Street* TV character.

- Meg Whitman joins as chief executive in 1998. Later that year, the company goes public – more than one million people are registered users and 8 per cent of the items on sale are Beanie Babies.

- In 1999 eBay sets up local sites in the UK and Germany, and overcomes a serious crash that closes the site for 22 hours. Surviving the dotcom bust, it overtakes Amazon as most visited e-commerce site in 2001 and buys the PayPal online payment service in 2002. However, it suffers a setback in Japan, withdrawing from the market after losing out to Yahoo!

This original star of Silicon Valley's dotcom boom is still growing at over 40 per cent, and now earns half a billion pounds a year.

With its extraordinary range of goods for sale, from the original 'collectors items' – like Elvis and *Star Wars* memorabilia – to cars and even property, eBay has expanded its reach to over 100 million registered users, with its own branded sites in more than 30 countries.

Today in the UK, according to eBay, 10 000 people earn all or some of their income from trading on the site. They are people like Paul and Elaine Harrison from Berkhamsted, who make a living selling movie props. They recently got £500 for the actual diary used in the first *Bridget Jones* film, after Paul had built a special presentation case for it – complete with lights, pictures and even a microphone to make the lights react to music.

Or there's George Crudgington from Derby, whose garage is full of £100 000 of porcelain, ready to sell on eBay. Having built a successful business with that, now he's moving into French antiques, taking advantage of prices in a country where eBay hasn't yet taken hold as it has here.

Every eBay trade makes money for the company through a basic listing fee – which can be as low as 15p – together with a small percentage of the final sale price. With millions of users worldwide, it all adds up. Yet eBay's very success makes it vulnerable. While past enthusiasm for eBay shares has pushed their value up, now the financial markets are alert to the slightest stumble in the company's performance.

eBay's shares have slid suddenly, by about a third since the New Year. The fall was triggered by a company announcement of a minuscule shortfall in earnings compared with analysts' predictions.

As one commentator put it: 'It's not often a company's quarterly sales and profits shoot up by 44 per cent only to have its stock plummet by 19 per cent the next day.'

But future jitters are likely to be caused not by eBay's own performance, but by factors outside its control.

London investment manager Nick Train describes eBay as 'part of the black economy' and warns that it will be government intervention, rather than the market, that will clip its wings. He adds that, 'If the company continues to grow at current rates, sooner or later it is going to impinge upon the consciousness of tax collectors and excise agents around the world.'

eBay's business represents a massive growth in 'person-to-person' trading, which governments have, until now, found hard to regulate.

But with the total value of trades on eBay now amounting to $34bn a year, it's an area that the tax authorities are going to be increasingly keen to regulate.

Nick Train points out that if eBay's trading were the total economic activity of a nation state, it would represent the 59th largest economy in the world, just behind Kuwait. And, of course, most national governments would be delighted with a growth rate one-tenth of eBay's.

Last year the Inland Revenue visited eBay's UK headquarters in Richmond-upon-Thames, and eBay says it will be putting up a link to the Revenue's website to encourage traders to declare taxable earnings. But, to date, that link has not appeared, and if you search eBay's Help section for advice, you'll get the message 'Sorry, no topics were found for "income tax".' However, Doug McCallum, eBay UK's managing director, insists that eBay traders 'are paying their taxes', and that 'Gordon Brown and the Treasury should be absolutely delighted that eBay has unleashed an astonishing army of entrepreneurs in this country'.

However, according to the Inland Revenue, 'For a person disposing of an unwanted personal possession, whether through the newspaper small ads or on the Internet, his or her activities would not amount to trading.'

For its part, the Inland Revenue has refused to admit that there is a grey area for eBay traders, between those who are buying and selling privately, and those who are doing it 'professionally' or to supplement their income. A spokesman for the Inland Revenue commented that, 'There is usually no dispute that the activities carried on by a particular taxpayer do amount to a trade: the butcher, the baker and the candlestick maker all know, without getting into semantics, that they are carrying on a "trade".'

'On the other hand, for a person disposing of an unwanted personal possession, whether through the newspaper small ads or on the Internet, his or her activities would not amount to trading.'

Some observers believe that the Inland Revenue will have to take further action over eBay and its traders.

Hellen Omwando, market analyst at Forrester Research, says: 'Of course they're going to look at some way of taxing eBay, and eBay will carry that down to consumers.'

If that happens, eBay will have to increase its fees to traders, which could trigger another bout of share price jitters.

Until then, eBay traders in Britain will continue to do well.

George Crudgington, having traded porcelain from his home in Derby for seven years, has just bought a house in the French countryside using the profits of seven years of eBay trading.

That's not bad, considering he only started because he was out of work and short of money. eBay has changed all that.

Of course, eBay's rise to global prominence has not met with universal acclaim.

Some users object to its reliance on the feedback mechanism to root out dishonest traders and want the company to take more decisive anti-fraud action.

US jeweller Tiffany's has even tried to make eBay liable for the sale of counterfeit goods in its auctions, by suing for damages of up to $1m for every counterfeit Tiffany's item sold.

For its part, eBay says the listing of such items in its auctions is prohibited and reserves the right to remove them from the site.

But in the words of Charles Abrams, eBay's achievement lies in 'empowering the end-user – enabling consumers, and later businesses, to compete in a universal market in ways that they could not before'.

He told the BBC News website: 'If I wanted to sell a collector's plate 15 years ago, I would have to go to my local antique store and hope they would give me a fraction of the price. I would not have had a mass market open to me.'

However, Mr Abrams believes the old view of eBay as mainly the preserve of individuals selling collectable items is increasingly out of date, even if the company still prides itself on its community spirit.

'Sixty percent of eBay postings today are being done programmatically – that is, by machines,' he said. That means that small businesses, using the latest web services technology to automate listings, are playing a growing role in e-commerce.

eBay continues to develop as more commercial sellers are using the site. The service Prostores gives sellers their own web address but processes their sales through eBay's own systems. More and more people are using eBay as a shopfront for fixed-price sales, and the company is keen to encourage them to stay with its services.

It also wants to rebuild relationships with sellers some six months after threatening a sharp price rise.

In the decade since it was founded, eBay has become one of online commerce's biggest success stories, outlasting all its competitors. It made a profit of $256m in the three months to March, up 28 per cent on the same period of 2004, on sales of more than $1bn.

But its core business – auctions – seems to be topping out, meaning the firm needs to focus more on keeping happy the thousands of people who use the site as a shop window for fixed-price goods.

More than 100 000 regular sellers have no site of their own, eBay general merchandise manager Michael Dearing says, and Prostores was intended to make it easier for them to build one: 'The marketplace will continue to be a foundation for a long time, but we know that sellers are interested in finding buyers all over the place and this can help them do that.'

The service – initially available only to people in the USA – will start at $6.95 a month and will charge a fee of 0.5–1.5 per cent per transaction, to be processed through eBay's payment subsidiary PayPal.

Users will not have to be existing eBay sellers, although those already paying for an 'eBay store' will get a cheaper rate. The next step, he argues, is for eBay to become a business-to-business platform as well, offering a channel for large-scale supply and procurement.

eBay spokesman Richard Ambrose confirms that the company intends to make the site more user-friendly for businesses trading in bulk.

'If you want to sell, say, 50 000 Jiffy bags or 25 000 bricks, you can do it, but it's not a great experience,' he told the BBC News website. 'In the next few years, we will be making it easier to whole-sale items on the site.'

Mr Ambrose says that, despite eBay's dominant market position in many countries, the company is not complacent about the future. 'We're in a strong, but not impregnable position,' he says. 'We're under severe pressure from Yahoo! in Asia – we're in a fierce battle with them in China.'

eBay stirred up controversy among users by increasing some of its fees earlier this year. Mr Ambrose says this was to ensure that certain popular ways of making sellers' listings stand out were not devalued through overuse.

'From the outside, it's easy for it to seem that we're trying to flex our muscles. But in the long term, we want people to grow on eBay and maximise their profits. When they grow, so do we.'

In 2005, eBay saw profits for the three months to June had risen to a record $291.6m from $190.4m a year earlier. Revenues had jumped 40 per cent to $1.09bn, exceeding forecasts of $1.04bn, while all other key measures, such as active users, had also surged.

'eBay achieved remarkable results . . . excellent momentum in the USA and Germany, as well as at PayPal, all helped deliver an impressive jump in revenues and profit,' president and chief executive Meg Whitman said.

However, the rise in trade is not without controversy and the company has come under fire for raising charges for its sellers and failing to clamp down on so-called 'mischief makers'.

In July, the UK press was up in arms after eBay refused to act against vendors who put tickets for Live8 up for sale. It later banned the re-sale of tickets for the charity concerts.

Sources: *The Money Programme*, 'eBay: Money for Old Rope?', broadcast on BBC2, Friday 25 February 2005, at 1900 GMT; www.bbc.co.uk; www.ebay.co.uk.

Discussion questions

1 What are the ethical responsibilities of an organisation such as eBay?

2 Who are the stakeholders and what is their stake?

3 How can eBay build power across cultures?

4 How does eBay make decisions in an organisation that crosses so many countries?

Applied questions

5 Using Exhibit 14-1, can you differentiate between good leadership and good management?

6 Using Fiedler's contingency model, does the leadership style match the structure of eBay?

Developing the organisation

Part contents

Organisational structure and design

The opening vignette illustrates the impact of changing work patterns on the design and structure of organisations

Working from home or skiving? The teleworking phenomenon

Problems with public transport, traffic jams and time wasted on travelling are beginning to persuade employers to allow their staff to work from home.

Research from the UK Labour Force Survey shows that 1.7 million people – about 6 per cent of the British workforce – now work from home in their main job at least one day a week, using

▶

a computer and a telephone. The figure falls to 1.1 million, or 4.2 per cent, if you exclude those who do it only occasionally.

Datamonitor, an industry analyst, estimates that the number of people working from home across Europe could jump by more than 50 per cent between now and 2005.

The driving force is the desire among employees for a better balance between work and home life and, among employers, a wish to hang on to the best people.

British Telecommunications has been examining the issues of home working longer than most. It started in 1992 with the aim of saving £180 million in property costs by the end of the millennium, by encouraging staff to work more flexibly. Now 7500 of its 130 000 employees are formally based at home. Another 40 000 or so have remote access to the company's computer systems.

Having saved money on its office costs, BT formed something called its 'Workstyle Consultancy Group' to pass on its experience to paying clients.

Peter Jones, a business development manager with the consultancy urges companies to be clear about their aims and objectives when drawing up a policy of home working, or teleworking as it is often called.

'Companies need to understand what it costs to have somebody in an office building and what they could save if he or she weren't. They have to ask: if I made my people work more flexibly, what would it do to their approach to the business?'

All the evidence suggests not only that employees invariably feel happier working at home but also that they are more productive. Research shows that productivity improves by between 20 and 40 per cent.

'Home working should not be a way to get people to work harder, because we know that they will. It is important that companies show that they trust their employees,' says Jones.

The need to trust workers based at home changes not just the way they are managed but also the way a company views its workforce.

Source: adapted from *Financial Times*, 31 January 2002.

Discussion questions

1 How does the change in working patterns impact on the design and structure of the organisation?

2 How can management maintain control when it can no longer physically see employees at work?

To put teleworking into practice by organisational design, organisations will need to think about the type of business they have. A people-orientated industry where customers expect face-to-face dealings with staff would find teleworking impractical, although it may be possible for the administrative aspects of the business. How are the staff to be managed? Many bosses may feel they lose control if they cannot physically see their employees at a workstation, therefore work needs to become task orientated with goal-setting, rather than time orientated, which depends on hours worked. Teleworking not only changes the design of an organisation but also the culture. To work effectively many people need social contact and managers need to think about how to manage this. Will they have weekly meetings? If so, where will they be held if a physical building no longer exists? Managers will also need to think about the functions of how to plan, lead, organise, co-ordinate and control when they no longer see their employees. This again needs to be built into the organisational design.

Organisation is the architectural alignment of people and processes around which enterprises are designed. As in any architectural design, there are trade-offs and compromises. But unlike the design of a vehicle or building, organisational structures and networks are expected to change substantially and fairly frequently to accommodate growth and keep the organisation viable. This realisation that organisational design must be a fluid, ever-evolving process is exemplified by the British Telecommunications vignette. BT's executives realised in the early 1990s that the organisation needed to be more flexible, especially with increasing property costs. It used emerging technology as a tool not only to save money but also to boost staff productivity, as it was found that staff working from home were more productive. It then used its expertise to give itself a competitive advantage by setting up a consultancy. So what started as a cost-cutting measure has resulted in a money-making business.

To respond to the changing world order, BT took the bold step of reconfiguring both its organisational structure and the mindset of people. The goal of BT's reorganisation was to save money. The result has been a contented workforce with more flexibility in where it works and staff no longer have the stress of battling with failing transport systems – leaving more time to be spent working on tasks.

The focus of this chapter is on organisational designs as they impact people's work behaviours. The design of organisations is intended to support and help people carry out the strategies of an enterprise. To appreciate variations in organisational design, however, it is helpful to understand the ways in which technology is changing the way work is performed. With increased use of information technologies and flatter structures, teams of a largely self-managed nature play a greater role in performing task responsibilities.

Organisational design should no longer be thought of simply as the static, mechanical arrangement of boxes and lines of reporting relationships that generations of employees have known as the 'organisation chart', and that symbolises an organisation's 'structure'. Organisational design also involves the alignment of the systems and processes managers put in place to guide behaviour or, in the case of BT, the methods with which people approach their work.

Organisational designs change over time

One lesson of Chapter 2 is that, for a strategy to be carried out, management needs to realign organisational structure and processes to support its objectives. Strategies require the orchestrated capabilities of people, resources and systems to make them work in ways that produce a competitive advantage. For this to happen, managers engage and draw on five principal options that typically are the *targets for internal change* within the organisation when changing or adapting its strategy. These internal options are people, tasks, technology, organisation and culture. The arrows in Exhibit 15-1 show that, potentially, there can be complete interactions among these five variables that we call the 'organisation star'. A change in one might affect one or more of the other variables.

Although a major focus of this book is on the people variable, a person's behaviour at work is not entirely based on free will. Surrounding situational factors present changing stimuli that either constrain or liberate what a person does in carrying out work responsibilities. The design of organisational structures and the design of work teams are two of those situational

EXHIBIT 15–1 *The organisational star offers organisational targets for change*

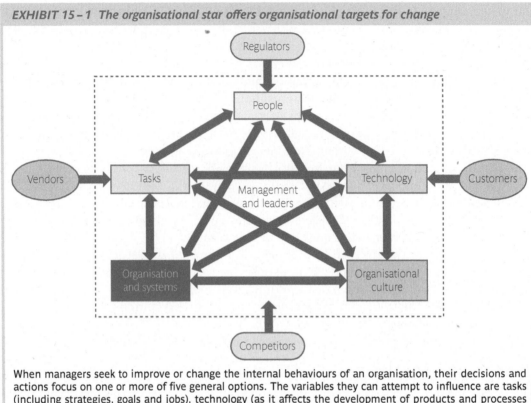

When managers seek to improve or change the internal behaviours of an organisation, their decisions and actions focus on one or more of five general options. The variables they can attempt to influence are tasks (including strategies, goals and jobs), technology (as it affects the development of products and processes for getting work done), organisation and internal systems, organisational culture (values and beliefs), and people (their numbers, attitudes, capabilities and behaviours). Surrounding the organisation (within the dashed border) are four forces comprising the transacting environment of the enterprise: vendors, customers, regulators and competitors.

factors we examine in this chapter (others are in later chapters). We also introduce the contributing role of technology, which has become a major catalyst to organisational change. Because rapid advances in technology – especially information technology – are having a tremendous impact on management practices and organisational design, let us begin with it as a driving force of change.

A digital revolution, manifest by the combination of information technology and wireless telecommunications symbolic of the new economy, is transforming work and organisations. People are united independently of time and geography through tools such as interactive databases, teleconferencing, email, the Internet and groupware. Schneider and Perry (2000) suggest that **electronic business** (e-business or e-commerce) makes corporate boundaries transparent by enabling employees, vendors and customers to be connected through a network of electronic transactions that enables instant and simultaneous access to the same data. The result is a faster, cheaper and more informed flow of action to move information, money and goods around the globe.

electronic business
An information network called e-business or e-commerce that makes corporate boundaries transparent by enabling employees, vendors and customers to be simultaneously connected to the same data and information, resulting in faster and cheaper transactions to move information, money and goods around the globe.

A study of more than 75 networked companies concluded: 'Where work is carried out through (information) networks, an organisation's structure changes whether you want it to or

Research focus: **the Joan Woodward study**

Technology drives changes in the structuring of work

You may think the impact of technology is a new phenomenon, yet as long ago as 1965 Joan Woodward, a British industrial psychologist, conducted a study that looked at the relationship between organisational design and technology.

Woodward's (1965) research began as a field study of management principles. Her study was designed when the universal principles of management were considered as one of the best ways of managing an organisation and when it was considered that for every manager there should be a span of control of six subordinates.

To test the universal principles, Woodward, through the use of questionnaires, interviews and observations, surveyed 100 manufacturing companies to identify how they were organised. Woodward (1965) gathered information on a wide range of structural characteristics, such as:

- the span of control
- levels of management
- ratios of management to administrators
- management style
- measures of performance regarding economic success.

In the first analysis of the data, it was found that firms varied widely in their span of control, number of hierarchical levels, administrative levels and amount of verbal communication. It seemed that the size of an organisation did not account for differences in structure, neither were the structural variables related to economic success. Therefore, they could not find support for the universal principles of management.

The researchers then looked at structural differences to determine whether these were affected by market share, profitability, capital expenditure and factors such as reputation and employee behaviour. Again, no link was found and a relationship could not be established between effectiveness and organisational structure.

Woodward and her team then began to look at the technology in organisations. They found that technology influenced the appropriate organisational structure. From this Woodward developed a scale of technical complexity that represented the extent of mechanisation and predictability of the manufacturing process. High technical complexity meant that most of the work was performed by machines, while low technical complexity meant that workers had a larger impact on the production process. Woodward originally identified 10 categories of technical complexity, but these were later reduced to three basic technology groups:

1 small batch and unit production – small orders to meet specific customer needs; it is not highly mechanised

2 large batch and mass production – long production runs of standardised products; uses mass production technology

3 continuous process production – the entire process is mechanised and there is an ongoing flow of materials.

Woodward discovered that using this classification of technology produced significant relationships between technology and structure and technology and performance. The more complex the technology used the greater the number of management levels, but there was an increase in the number of administrators required to support the machinery. Woodward also found that the span of control, formalised procedures and centralisation were high for mass production, but as the jobs tended to be standardised there was little communication, even though the employees were less skilled. The other two technologies required more skilled workers and increased communication to adapt to the changing conditions. The relationship between technical complexity and structural characteristics can be seen in Exhibit 15-2.

Woodward's examination of the relationship between performance and technology discovered that successful firms tended to have a structure that fitted their technology. Woodward's conclusion was that each of the three technologies required a specific organisational structure and the most successful organisations were those whose ratios and numbers on each of the structured variables were close to the median, as illustrated in Exhibit 15-2. Less successful firms tended to have numbers either lesser or greater than the median. It was also found that smaller batch and continuous process organisations were more likely to have organic structures, while mass production organisations tended to have mechanistic structures.

Woodward's study was an important step in the development of organisational theories and her findings moved research away from the universal principles of management onto the search for situational variables.

Later studies, by Zwerman (1970) in the USA and Marsh and Mannari (1981), supported Woodward's findings in that the type of technology was closely related to organisational structure.

Perrow (1966) extended the work by Woodward and drew attention to two major dimensions of technology:

1 the extent to which the task is predictable or variable

2 the extent to which the technology can be analysed.

EXHIBIT 15 – 2 *Relationship between technological complexity and structural characteristics*

Structural characteristics	Technology		
	Unit production	Mass production	Continuous process
Number of mgt levels	3	4	6
Supervisor span control	23	48	15
Direct/indirect labour ratio	9:1	4:1	1:1
Management/total personnel ratio	Low	Medium	High
No. skilled workers	High	Low	High
Formalised procedures	Low	High	Low
Centralisation	Low	High	Low
Amount of verbal communication	High	Low	High
Amount of written communication	Low	High	Low
Overall structure	Organic	Mechanistic	Organic

Source: Joan Woodward (1967) *Industrial Organisation: Theory and Practice*. London: Oxford University Press.

This combination provides a continuum of technology from routine to non-routine, with non-routine technology requiring more complex problem-solving. Perrow argues that, by classifying organisations according to their technology and routineness of task, we would be better able to predict the most effective form of organisational structure.

Another study, by Collins and Hull (1986), in the USA, questioned the relationship between the span of control as a by-product of technology. They identified the effects of size, task complexity and mechanisation as an impact on the span of control, and suggested that other considerations need to be taken into account in the size-versus-technology debate. As technology moves on, many other variables need to be taken into account; the digital revolution makes the management of organisations less predictable.

not. I can't find a single case where it doesn't happen' (Stewart, 1994). Increasingly data connect people to people directly, without the need of managers in a hierarchy to filter and pass along information and hand down decisions. Not only does information technology pressure an organisation to flatten its hierarchy, it also pressures changes in jobs – including management. The traditional concept of the boss who knows more than his subordinates quickly fades when talented people have access to information – and, through information, access to stakeholders such as customers and vendors. Perhaps nowhere is this universal connectivity to information and empowerment of the frontline employee more apparent than in the technology practices of Federal Express, as noted in the Technology Transformation box.

Technology encompasses the scientific knowledge, processes, systems and equipment used to create products and services and help people carry out their tasks. Technology is typically the motivating force behind continuous improvements in what an organisation produces and the means by which human productivity is increased. Some examples of specific technological processes that are transforming work methods include enterprise resource planning (ERP) software, electronic data interchange (EDI), statistical process control (SPC), manufacturing resource planning (MRP II), just-in-time (JIT) inventory, management information systems (MIS), and computer-integrated manufacturing (CIM). For the individual worker, an upgrade in technology might be as basic as replacing a stand-alone computer with networked computing or a hand tool with an electrically powered one.

technology
The scientific knowledge, processes, systems and equipment used to create products and services and to help people carry out their tasks.

Jobs shift to new knowledge-based technologies

In a perceptive view of our past and future, Toffler (1996) used the metaphor of colliding waves to visualise three distinct, work-related changes transforming civilisation. The waves shift from agriculture to industrial manufacturing to the current information and knowledge-based third wave, a new way of organisational life based on information technologies and new work patterns. Electronics alone now employs considerably more people in the UK, USA and Canada than steel, autos and aerospace combined (Grove, 1992).

We all know that the technological push towards electronic miniaturisation and doing more with less has enabled more power and speed to be packed into smaller microprocessor packages that control such products as computers, vehicle climate systems, watches and video cameras. Even something as basic as long-distance telephone services requires fewer resources and yet provides an improved quality of service because of a shift in transmission from copper wires to

technology transformation

Information moves Federal Express around the globe

Fred Smith received a grade of C+ on his Yale University term paper that conceived a business of delivering express material on an overnight basis. Not deterred, Smith opened Federal Express in April 1973 and shipped a total of 14 packages on day one. Today FedEx is the world's largest express company with time-definite delivery, employing 130 000 people serving 325 airports across 212 countries. Its key to success is not its 600 or so aircraft and nearly 40 000 trucks, but the way it employs technology to organise business processes around information.

The FedEx information network processes about 60 million electronic transactions per day, scanning each shipment 13+ times from pick up to delivery. The company plans to go entirely paperless to some 350 million online customer transactions per day in a 100 per cent electronic format. To handle that volume of electronic transactions used to track, bill and collect payments, FedEx is organised by what the company calls a six-corner network model. The model includes four data centres in the United States, plus Brussels serving Europe and Singapore serving the Asian region. There is built-in redundancy among the centres so if one has disruptions (as occurred once in Memphis due to a major ice storm), the system is not interrupted.

To place information at the fingertips of couriers and customers alike, FedEx has developed a number of systems and processes with an information-age ring:

- COSMOS – the tracking system that scans and displays the status of a shipment
- Supertracker – a computer network that processes all scanned information for worldwide access
- Powership – a custom PC-type device given to customers to enable them to print labels, invoices, and so on
- Customer service workstations – special computer screens to enable agents to quickly process customer calls.

Most companies the size of FedEx would break their organisation into various business units that are autonomous profit centres. But because a shipment FedEx picks up in London or Anchorage could go anywhere in the world, the business is organised as one operating unit. FedEx has six data centres and thousands of satellite operations, and 'the only thing that can pull that together is technology'.

Source: adapted from Cynthia H. Spangler (vice president of Corporate Headquarters Systems at Federal Express) (1998) 'Global Manufacturing, Logistics, Organisational Issues', in Fariborz Ghadar (ed.) *New Information Technology and its Impact on Global Business Management.* University Park, PA: The Center for Global Business Studies, pp. 119–130.

Discussion questions

1 How would FedEx operate if the technology failed? What is holding the structure together?

2 What would be the implications for the organisation if it were to operate as autonomous business units?

hair-thin fibre-optic cable. But cellular technology enables wireless telecommunications to be available anywhere, and the portable mobile phone has become ubiquitous in most regions of the world, especially in developing nations where the waiting time for installation of a wired phone is often measured in years.

The contemporary challenge is to continually increase productivity in the sectors employing most of the population, the knowledge and service sectors. In the knowledge sector, career opportunities are increasingly limited to people with advanced education. Because most people lack academic degrees, a challenge for managers of such employees is to teach them how to use technology tools to improve productivity and job satisfaction in less-skilled service jobs. Exhibit 15-3 offers several skill-building ideas from Drucker (1991) to meet this challenge.

Illustrative of one application, the jobs of supermarket workers were transformed in the late twentieth century by electronic checkouts that combined optical scanning, barcodes, and database technology. In the modern alternative, a customer can go online through the Internet and, with the aid of screen prompts, key in necessary information for the purchase of books, airline tickets, and other goods and services without human interaction. According to Kaufman (1995), information technology 'allows near-instantaneous electronic transmission of sales and inventory information, enabling even the largest retailers (or smallest dotcom) to keep abreast of what customers want without communicating with them personally'.

Retail supermarkets such as Tesco and Sainsbury's have an electronic record of each item sold for use in stock control, merchandising, analysing the profit contributions of each product and comparing performance among stores. Because administrators represent the largest occupational group in developed nations, such applications of technology are having major impacts on transforming jobs and organisational designs throughout retailing and the service sector.

Technology creates global competition for jobs and skills

National boundaries still exist for political and ethnic reasons, but economically the factory worker or administrator in Birmingham is competing as much with employees in Frankfurt, Seoul, New York or Tokyo as with workers in London or Edinburgh. Increasingly, products and services blend together, and often it is the service component that affords competitive

---

EXHIBIT 15 – 3 Drucker defines five skills for improving the person–job match

To improve the productivity of knowledge and service employees, Peter Drucker advises managers to develop five types of skills.

1 First, ask, 'What is the task? What are we trying to accomplish? Why do it at all?' In manufacturing and transportation jobs, the task is more observable; in knowledge and service jobs, tasks need to be evaluated frequently and changed. In any industry, the most profound route for improving performance and the person–job match is often to eliminate tasks altogether – to stop doing that which really does not need to be done.

2 Second, take a hard look at the ways in which jobs add value. Where does real value occur? Many activities only add costs rather than value. Cost generators such as unnecessary meetings or reports written to impress higher managers should be candidates for elimination.

3 Third, define performance in terms of what works. Quality only comes by analysing the steps in the process that produce value-added performance. Managers then need to wipe out unnecessary steps and build in those that are necessary but lacking.

4 Fourth, managers need to develop a partnership with people who hold potentially productive jobs and get them to improve the process. This means relying on job-holders to identify obstacles to improved performance and to build in corrective action. Drucker says quite simply, 'To find out how to improve productivity, quality, and performance, ask the people who do the work.'

5 Finally, to sustain continuous learning, people at all levels need to teach. Drucker says, 'The greatest benefit of training comes not from learning something new but from doing better what we already do well. Equally important . . . knowledge workers and service workers learn most when they teach.'

Source: Peter F. Drucker (1991), 'The New Productivity Challenge', *Harvard Business Review* 69, November–December, pp. 69–79. Reprinted by permission of *Harvard Business Review*.

advantage because it is not easily replicated. The competitive objective for world-class firms is to create products that are specialised and add value due to their high service component. The Co-operative Bank demonstrates how it reaches customers in out-of-the-way locations and brings them a service that they may otherwise not receive (see the Dynamics of Diversity box).

Service workers empowered by technology are often called 'knowledge workers'. According to Reich (1991), three *universal work skills* drive the success of the knowledge worker because each skill provides high value to the customer.

1 Problem-solving skills, or the ability to put things together in unique ways, be they movie scripts, software, mortgages or semiconductor chips.

2 The skills to help customers understand their needs and how those needs can best be met by taking advantage of the customised product offered.

3 The skills to link problem-solvers with problem identifiers, or the management and brokerage of ideas.

Such skills reflect the changing organisational requirements that people must meet if they are to be effective in a global labour market.

The Co-operative Bank

The Co-operative Bank, established in 1872, has long been known for asking customers what it should do with their money while it is in the bank and for the last 10 years it has also been asking its customers to vote on ethical issues. It is also known for its management of diversity.

While the main big banks are finding it uneconomical to maintain branches in rural locations, the Co-operative Bank is using satellite technology to enable it to provide free LINK automatic teller machines (ATMs) at 750 Co-op convenience stores throughout the country. They are available to all banks and building societies and the Co-operative Bank will not charge for using them. This means that by harnessing the latest technology, the Co-operative Bank has been able to bring free cash to the most remote parts of the country. The Bank has installed a cash machine in a Co-op convenience store on the tiny island of South Uist in the Outer Hebrides. The islanders previously had no access to cash through the LINK cash machine network. Other rural locations to benefit include Blaenau Ffestiniog in North Wales and Broadford on the Isle of Skye.

Spokesperson for the Bank, Simon Williams, director of corporate affairs, said: 'The way the cash machine network in the UK has developed means that machines tend to be clustered in the centres of towns and cities, while many other areas have been left as cash machine deserts.... We have proved that, by installing cash machines in Co-op convenience stores, we can provide a service to the community and at the same time encourage customers to visit the stores.'

The Co-operative Bank and the retail Co-op Societies share the costs and the benefits of these new cash machines. They can do this because they are all part of the same Co-operative family.

This is not the only way the Co-operative Bank meets the needs of its diverse customer base. In 2001 the Bank sponsored and initiated a report called 'Access to Credit for Families on Low Incomes'. The report looked at the credit options available to Britain's financially excluded, who could not gain loans from banks and other mainstream providers and who were often left at the mercy of 'loan sharks', whose high interest rates ensured that borrowers' debts increased rather than diminished.

The report, by Paul Jones of Liverpool John Moores University, showed how families on low incomes gain extra money to finance basic needs, like furniture or children's clothing, from a flourishing alternative lending market. This included buying on credit from mail-order catalogues, home credit and, as a last resort, unlicensed money lenders. The research highlighted the fact that it was the affordability of the weekly payments rather than the high interest rates that concerned borrowers who, although aware that they were charged high rates of interest, their priority was obtaining a loan to meet an immediate need.

As a result of this research the Co-operative Bank became a major supporter of Credit Unions throughout the UK. Credit Unions exist to encourage savings and lend money to the poorer communities, who do not always have access to the major banks. They are usually based on large inner-city housing estates and, to qualify for a loan, the potential borrower must save a small amount for a period of time.

The Co-operative Bank's approach to managing diversity, whether by providing free access to banking in rural communities or its approach to the financially disadvantaged, has enabled the Bank to hold its head up high when many of its competitors are receiving bad publicity for alleged consumer rip-offs.

Source: www.co-operativebank.co.uk.

Discussion questions

1 How has technology changed the organisational structure?
2 How is the Co-operative Bank's structure organised?

The environment and organisational design and structure

Another influence on organisational design and structure is the degree of stability or instability in the environment. Research has found that different organisational structures are needed to cope with environmental uncertainty. Two classic studies, one by Burns and Stalker (1966) into divergent systems of management practice and another by Lawrence and Lorsch (1969) into the effects of environmental uncertainty, have looked at the changing nature of the external environment and its management structure.

The basic organisational design structures

One of the managerial requirements of any enterprise employing more than a few dozen people is to assign tasks and responsibilities to individuals and groups (be they teams, departments or other work units). Task responsibilities, whether designed for individuals or groups, then have to be arranged in a structure and governance process that promotes integration of work flows towards strategies that support the enterprise mission. Organisation design is the name given to this process of assigning responsibilities and structuring work to support enterprise goals, objectives and strategies. It is one of the key functions of management.

Research focus: the Burns and Stalker (1966) study

Research by Burns and Stalker studied the differences in the technological and market elements of the environment that affected the organisation structure and management processes.

The study looked at 20 manufacturing firms from several different industries in the UK and classified their environments between stable and predictable and unstable and unpredictable. The study found that organisations could be grouped into two main categories where the management practices and structures were considered to be in response to the environment. These were known as the mechanistic organisation and the organic organisation.

The mechanistic organisation

Such organisations are seen as a rigid structure, usually found in a stable environment. The characteristics are:

- organisational tasks are divided into specialised and functional duties, whereas individual tasks are likely to be more abstract
- roles have a detailed definition of rights and responsibilities and are related to functional position
- a hierarchic structure of control and authority is reinforced by vertical structures; knowledge is held by those at the top of the hierarchy
- loyalty and obedience are insisted on by superiors.

The organic organisation

- Knowledge and experience is valued for its contribution to the common task. Individual tasks are seen as relating to the organisation as a whole.
- Individual tasks are continually redefined through interaction with others.
- Responsibility is shared, with control, authority and communication having a lateral rather than vertical direction.
- Knowledge may be located anywhere in the organisation, with power based around knowledge.
- Communications are seen as giving information and advice rather than instructions.
- Importance and prestige are attached to those with expertise rather than position.

The mechanistic and organic types of organisation are seen as opposite ends of a continuum. Most organisations would expect to have a mix of both types. However, organisations that tend to be mechanistic will have vertical structures, standardised rules and procedures, high levels of specialism and centralised control. In contrast, organic organisations are likely to be flatter and people are likely to be more goal orientated.

The Burns and Stalker study found a clear link between the environment and structures. They also found that values and attitudes were important in the different organisational structures. Therefore, organisational structures need to be matched by the appropriate organisational cultures. We will look at this in more detail in the next chapter.

Research focus: the Lawrence and Lorsch (1969) study

Lawrence and Lorsch examined organisations in three different industries: plastics, packaged food products, and paper containers. They chose these industries because they faced a high degree of uncertainty either due to technology or rapid changes in customer demand.

In analysing how the firms interacted with the environment, two key concepts were identified.

1 Differentiation – the degree of specialisation and departmentalisation. This included employee behaviour in highly specialised departments.

2 Integration – refers to the co-ordinating processes of achieving unity of effort among the various subsystems to achieve the organisation's goals.

Lawrence and Lorsch found significant relationships between the degree of uncertainty in the three industries and the amount of differentiation and integration. Organisations with a fairly certain environment, which were also fairly undifferentiated, tended to adopt a mechanistic structure. They were organised along functional lines with a highly centralised authority structure. Co-ordination was achieved through direct supervision and formal written procedures. A bureaucratic organisational structure was seen as consistent with the degree of certainty in the industry.

Organisations facing an uncertain environment adopted an organic environment. They had a highly differentiated structure with highly specialised internal departments to deal with the high degree of uncertainty. Co-ordination was achieved through cross-departmental teams and co-ordinators who liaised between departments. The most successful of this type of organisation needed high levels of differentiation plus high levels of integration to co-ordinate them.

The research by Lawrence and Lorsch helps our understanding of organisational design by highlighting the effects of environmental uncertainty on organisational structure. It found:

■ environmental uncertainty – means frequent changes in information processing to achieve co-ordination

■ highly uncertain environments and highly differentiated structure – may need a manager assigned to manage the integration across departments through the use of committees or liaison teams

■ simple and stable environments – may not need anyone with an integration role.

The analysis by Lawrence and Lorsch can be developed from the organisational to the departmental level within an organisation. Large organisations may have different departments operating in different environments. Therefore one department, such as production, could be mechanistic while another, such as marketing, may be organic.

In some respects the Lawrence and Lorsch studies can be seen as an extension of Burns and Stalker's ideas. Although, where Burns and Stalker see organisations as undifferentiated, Lawrence and Lorsch see differentiation and integration at the very centre of organisational design.

The critics of the theory argue that organisations are treated as passive recipients of environmental influence with the one-way flow from environmental factors to appropriate structure to economic performance. This shows the environment as the independent variable, structure as the factor that needs to be adjusted, which results in performance as the dependent variable. This ignores the idea that most organisations will try to influence their environments rather than change their organisational structures. Let us now venture into the basic structures of organisation design.

For start-up businesses and small enterprises, decisions about organisational design are simple and easy to implement. Organisations of up to 100 or so people typically have a few basic departments structured around functions performed. Each has a supervisor or manager who is responsible directly to the chief executive. The owner or executive personally acts as leader, decision-maker and controller over the single line of business. However, as a firm grows in size to employ tens of thousands, organisational designs become complex – sometimes maze-like and, for others, more like a loosely coupled network – changing periodically to accommodate growth or realignment needs.

Purposes served by organisational design

For over 2000 years, organisations have been 'structured' as a means of getting large numbers of people to work towards a common goal, be it building a pyramid or fighting a war.

organisational structure

The networked arrangement of positions and departments through which the essential tasks of an enterprise are subdivided and grouped to create the systems, decision centres and behavioural linkages that carry out business strategies.

organisational chart

The symbolic structure of boxed titles and lines that represent positions and reporting relationships.

Organisational structure provides the systems architecture through which the essential tasks of an enterprise are subdivided and grouped to create the processes, decision centres and behavioural network that carry out enterprise strategies.

For centuries, an organisational structure has been represented by the boxes and lines on an organisational chart – the tangible symbols of the positions and reporting relationships throughout an enterprise. Such approaches to organisation have been essentially hierarchical in structure, which thus affects human behaviour because structure can make it easy or difficult for people in separate work units to talk and work with one another. Structure affects the way people size up situations, the way they interact with others, what they value and believe to be important, time horizons and even management styles – a phenomenon called 'differentiation', which has been described previously in the Lawrence and Lorsch (1969) 'Research focus' and which we will meet again later in the chapter.

Largely during your lifetime, organisational designs have shifted to be less hierarchical, less structured, yet grouped and linked in ways that promote creativity and continuous improvement behaviours rather than conformity. Organisational design

organisational design

The process managers go through to create meaningful structures, decision and information networks, and governance systems.

is the process managers go through to create meaningful structures, decision and information networks, and governance systems. According to Mohrman and Cummings (1989), Hanna (1988) and Lawler (1988), organisational design provides for (1) the dividing and grouping of tasks; (2) networks to convey information; (3) a structure for locating decision centres or authority; (4) processes for co-ordination, control and conflict resolution; and (5) the means to link key work units with appropriate external stakeholders such as customers and suppliers. Designing an organisation involves deciding how the enterprise should be managed and led as much as it does creating structures to subdivide and allocate tasks.

Four basic structures set the stage for organisational design

Throughout the last half century, four basic structures have served as common approaches for grouping people and subunits within social systems, whether they be business firms, police departments or the postal service. These four basic designs group by function, geography, product and customer, respectively. Traditionally, the chosen structural arrangement is summarised as an organisational chart and, traditionally, organisations have been built around a dominant structural form, and then other forms are blended in for special purposes. This hybrid approach is logical because each basic structure has weaknesses as well as strengths. Lawler (1992) emphasises this contingency aspect of organising in his remark: 'Depending upon the choices about strategy that organisations make, different organisational designs and structures are appropriate, for one simple reason: different designs produce different behaviours and different outcomes.'

To illustrate the rationale and pros and cons for these four structures, we describe the organisational designs of the Whitbread company, as it grows in complexity over time. Whitbread was founded in 1742 when Samuel Whitbread started his brewing business at the Goat Brewhouse, Whitecross Street, London. This was the first purpose-built mass production brewery in Britain and it started small, with just a few employees and Samuel Whitbread managing the business functions, from selling to accounting. The quality and consistency of its beer and its ability to deliver using drays pulled by shire horses, made Whitbread a name synonymous with the brewing industry; that was over 250 years ago. Two centuries later, what was a small family business has expanded and with it has come increased task complexity and an increased span of control. The next few pages of text and organisational charts describe how this firm used each of the four basic designs to cope with different strategies and task-grouping needs over time.

Organisational design by function

organisational design by function
Grouping people into departments or subunits based on similar skills, expertise and functions performed – such as product design, production and marketing.

Over time Whitbread's brewery grew. As business expanded, essential activities were grouped into three key functional areas. An organisational design by function groups people into departments or subunits based on similar skills, expertise and functions performed – such as production, sales and accounts. As a still small firm, Whitbread's key functions included production, sales and office management. Exhibit 15-4 shows this simple structure, consisting of three supervisors, each responsible to the owner for specialised

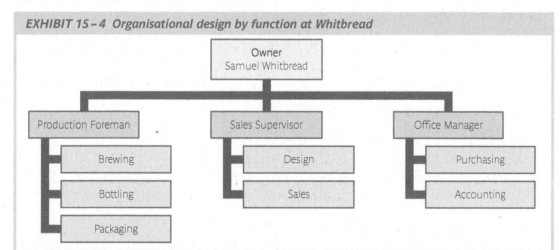

EXHIBIT 15–4 Organisational design by function at Whitbread

Functional design structures the organisation on the basis of the key functions (tasks or activities) to be performed. Each major group or subunit is responsible for performing a particular type of activity, such as production, sales or the office administrative functions. The major functional managers in the Whitbread organisational chart are also responsible for supervising the subfunctions reporting to them.

activities common to the function under which they are grouped. The supervisors would report to the owner and lines of communication would be vertical.

Advantages and disadvantages of design by function

Thompson and Strickland (1995) suggest that organisations dominated by a functional architecture work best when a company has a single line of business and/or is relatively small. A functional structure is ideally suited to encourage specialisation and prompt people to keep up with the latest technical developments in their specialist field. If departmental tasks are relatively independent, a high level of functional efficiency is possible. Because of departmental specialisation, the functional form relies on pushing decisions to a higher level of management for control and co-ordination. This makes the job of the general manager important and visible to all, but it may not be an efficient use of managerial time.

Extreme specialisation, however, creates tunnel vision. People tend to perceive multifunctional problems from the vantage point of their narrow area of expertise. This leads to conflict and turf protecting, which can strain the process of communication and co-ordination in the absence of a decisive leader. Decisions that are complex or span two or more functions tend to get pushed to the top for resolution, slowing decision responsiveness, as the organisation becomes larger and more layered. Maintaining quality becomes difficult, since few people genuinely feel responsible for customer satisfaction or the acceptance of decisions. A functional design also complicates the process of developing broad-based general managerial skills, because functional managers have a limited range of specialised experiences.

Organisational design by geography

Typically, as an organisation grows, it spreads its coverage to new regions or territories, and relies in part on an **organisational design by geography**. In the case of Whitbread, it started to buy pubs in which to sell its beer and began to branch out away from London. For larger firms or those that compete on a global stage, geographic expansion might logically be into other countries.

organisational design by geography
With organisational growth, this design creates units focused on serving the needs of a region or territory, which could include organising by country or hemisphere.

For Whitbread, the route to growth meant buying public houses and tying them to the brewery, so that they could sell only Whitbread products; these were known as 'tied houses'. To make this manageable, divisions were formed and managers were put in charge of specific areas, although the central operations were still directed from the brewery. Exhibit 15-5 illustrates this.

Advantages and disadvantages of design by geography

Organising by location emphasises local adaptation to market and/or supplier conditions. It is especially well suited to retail chains, the postal service, public accounting partnerships, police departments and fast-food restaurants. For organisations engaged in customer service, a regional structure allows local personnel and managers to be responsive to pressures and opportunities in their region. It promotes competitiveness and quality. Geographic design also makes it possible to create many profit centres where local general managers are responsible for both revenues and expenses.

On the downside, maintaining consistency of image and service can be compromised by a geographic design. The dilemma faced by headquarters managers is how much freedom to allow local managers versus how much control to exercise centrally. This decision typically depends on the size and complexity of the territory to be managed locally. A multinational firm,

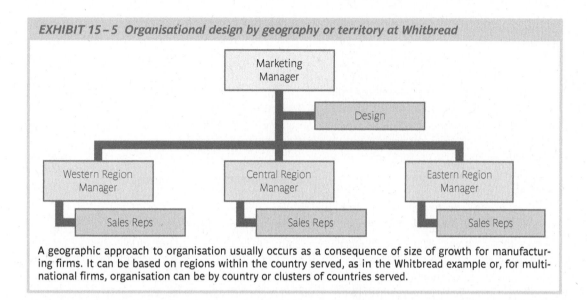

EXHIBIT 15 – 5 Organisational design by geography or territory at Whitbread

A geographic approach to organisation usually occurs as a consequence of size of growth for manufacturing firms. It can be based on regions within the country served, as in the Whitbread example or, for multinational firms, organisation can be by country or clusters of countries served.

such as pharmaceutical giant Pfizer International (with diverse operations in more than 100 countries), will grant greater autonomy to its business unit managers in foreign countries than Safeway will grant to its supermarket store managers within a single metropolitan region. Pfizer managers face more complex and diverse issues due to unique country cultures and different lines of business than those encountered by Safeway store managers in their local communities.

Organisational design by product line

With guaranteed sales through its tied pubs, the volume of Whitbread's business increased. It also moved into the restaurant business and became one of Britain's leading chain restaurant groups with its Beefeater brand and later with Brewer's Fayre. The combination of increased volume and the different drinking preferences in the regions meant more products were developed. This put considerable pressure on the production function. **Organisational design by product line** groups activity centres based on the unique product or service each provides. Whitbread continued to produce beer but it now also engaged in centralised production for its restaurant outlets to ensure standardisation of products across the chains.

organisational design by product line
A structural grouping on the basis of the unique product or service each activity centre provides.

However, a product-based design rarely exists as a pure organisational form. Of necessity, some functions will be duplicated, causing some redundancy of functional responsibilities. A centralised production kitchen can produce products for two different styles of restaurant, and reduce duplication of functions, although because of the nature of the industry functions will be duplicated at the point of service, in the actual restaurants.

Yet at the highest level of production, the two unique operations were separated into independent divisions, each organised, staffed and equipped appropriately for the two distinct product lines, custom and stock products. Factories were set up to mass produce beer and centralise production for its food outlets, which later included Pizza Hut, Cafe Rouge, Bella Pasta, Mama Amalfi and TGI Friday's. Exhibit 15-6 shows the organisation now divided into the three types of business: restaurants, breweries and public houses. Below these manager levels, tasks are still organised by function.

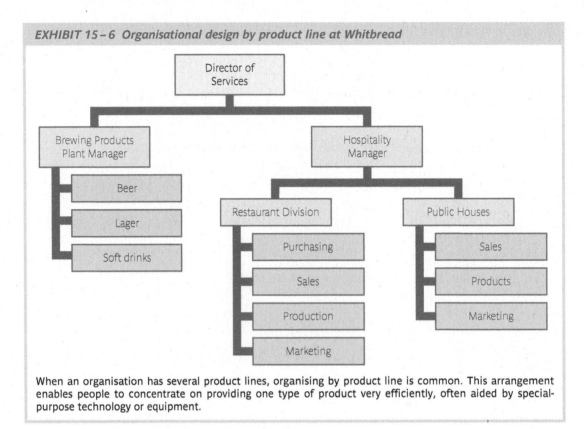

EXHIBIT 15 – 6 Organisational design by product line at Whitbread

When an organisation has several product lines, organising by product line is common. This arrangement enables people to concentrate on providing one type of product very efficiently, often aided by special-purpose technology or equipment.

Advantages and disadvantages of design by product line

For large, multibusiness firms such as Whitbread, decentralising based on products or lines of business promotes entrepreneurial behaviour. Even a car manufacturer such as Ford, with its relatively basic cluster of products all derived from a core motor car technology, has historically organised around product divisions: Transit, Ka, Galaxy, and so on. Product-line executives typically have profit centre responsibility to reinforce accountability.

The potential weakness of decentralised, product-based entities is the difficulty of co-ordinating related activities across business units. Rivalry is likely to exist – rivalry not only for customers but also for corporate resources, such as investment money or additional staff positions. If several business units draw separately on similar core technologies for the research and design of products, they probably forgo economy-of-scale savings and may be slow to share with other units the technological breakthroughs discovered in one unit. Moreover, as noted, some duplication of function specialisation is almost inevitable.

Organisational design by customer/market channel

After the acquisition of restaurants came the acquisition of hotels, the formation of the Whitbread Hotel Company and the purchase of the UK rights to the Marriott brand. The booming market in fitness saw Whitbread move into the leisure area with the purchase of David Lloyd Leisure. Whitbread realised that its customer requirements and market channels were becoming more diverse. The process of selling beer was no longer its only business, indeed the year 2000 saw the sale of its brewery followed by the sale of its pubs in 2001, due partly to political changes. Whitbread now had several distinct companies trading under different names and

organisational design by customer

Clustering human talent and resources so that each organisational unit focuses on the unique sales/service requirements for each type of customer or channel of distribution – such as the home market, commercial accounts or resellers.

viewed very differently by its customers. In fact many customers may not have realised they were visiting a Whitbread-owned hotel or restaurant.

Therefore, the managerial structure was focused on divisions and regions. This **organisational design by customer** enables the staff to focus on the unique sales/service requirements for each type of customer or channel of distribution. Exhibit 15-7 illustrates organisation by customer, with groupings into distinct divisions with a director for each and further divisions into the specific brand.

Advantages and disadvantages of design by customer/market

Customer or market channel-based structures are usually used in combination with one or more other designs. They serve well the needs of the business when product lines can be marketed to very distinct customer segments. Their advantage is that special customer needs can focus quality service throughout each organisational unit. For example, by relying on market feedback from a customer segment, such as hotel bedrooms needing coffee-making facilities, employees serving that segment can make changes in everything from the design of special product features to pricing and methods of providing sales and service.

To create high employee involvement, Lawler (1992) believes the customer-based design is optimum. He writes, 'A company should usually organise profit centres around customers, for one simple reason: this structure makes it easiest for the organisation to align its employees with an external customer who can give feedback and who makes purchasing decisions.' Focusing on the customer enables the competitive market – not hierarchical controls or supervisor whims – to affirm or modify employee behaviour. The challenge for companies offering several lines of products to the same customer is to balance product expertise (a benefit of

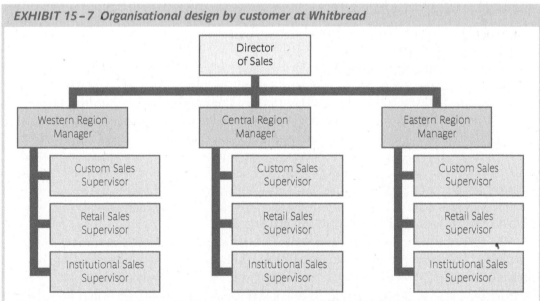

EXHIBIT 15 – 7 Organisational design by customer at Whitbread

When key business activities (such as sales and service) are differentiated on the basis of customers or market segments, a customer-based organisational design makes sense. This allows specialisation according to the unique needs of particular customer groups.

product-focused designs) with the simplicity of having one voice speak to the customer. Market-focused designs also tend to require duplication of sales and marketing staff, with two or more groups selling the same product line.

Combining designs over the organisational life cycle

Few businesses enjoy predictable, sustained growth and Whitbread has demonstrated this throughout the last century. More typically, organisations grow during their early years and then experience contractions as the core business begins to mature and/or as economic cycles disrupt performance. As they *age* and grow in *size*, firms pass through an organisational life cycle in which they move from simple to progressively more complex structures and systems. Mintzberg (1983) suggests that, with the possible exception of high-tech firms, what starts as a simple structure typically becomes either a professional bureaucracy or machine-type bureaucracy with complex layers and structures of departments. As size expands, where possible the organisation divides quasi-independent activity centres into separate business unit divisions. The ultimate design for a firm diversified into several lines of business is to take on the characteristics of a *network*, loosely coupled by central resource allocations.

organisational life cycle
Organisational structures progress from simple to complex designs and systems as they age and grow in size.

During both the expansion and contraction phases of the life cycle, reorganisations are commonplace. The focus of most reorganisations is to better align organisational design with business strategies and competitive forces, although at times 'reorganisation' is simply a euphemism for reducing headcount by lay-offs. Whitbread's restructurings are typical of a firm that periodically needs to realign how people, activities and resources are grouped into work units. We described and provided a separate organisational chart for each of the four basic structures. In practice, however, these different designs are combined into a more complex organisational structure. A more complete picture of Whitbread's organisation at this point in its life cycle is presented in Exhibit 15-8.

A hybrid combination – the matrix organisation

Some managers and organisational scholars include the matrix organisation as one of the fundamental forms of organisational design. A matrix organisation incorporates dual responsibilities and reporting relationships connecting selected functions with specific products or projects. Mohrman *et al.* (1995) suggest that, although the matrix structure originated in aerospace, it can be used in an industry where people with functional expertise need to be temporarily assigned to a project, but where it is expected people will be reassigned to another project once a designated milestone (timetable and accomplishment) is reached. Exhibit 15-9 presents an illustration of a matrix structure.

matrix organisation
A structure that incorporates dual responsibilities and reporting relationships connecting selected functions with specific products or projects.

The project manager is typically given overall responsibility for bringing the project in on time, on budget, and meeting the product requirements. This manager has budget authority to make the investments and expenditures necessary to assure project success. However, the project manager is dependent on pulling talent temporarily from specialised functions and paying the salaries of those functional team members. The functional manager is responsible for assuring the assigned personnel are keeping up with their professional development, such as state-of-the-art technical knowledge and skills. Individual specialists (be they production, designers, accountants or marketers)

EXHIBIT 15–8 Integrated organisational design at Whitbread

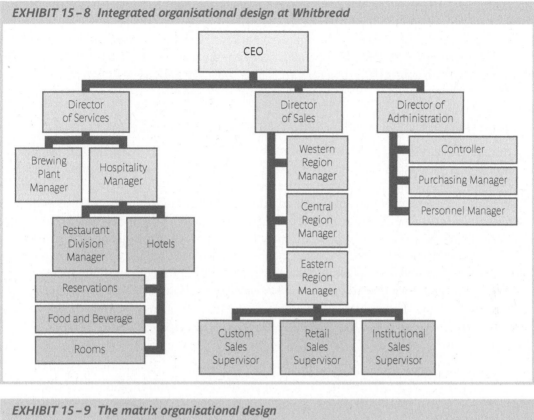

EXHIBIT 15–9 The matrix organisational design

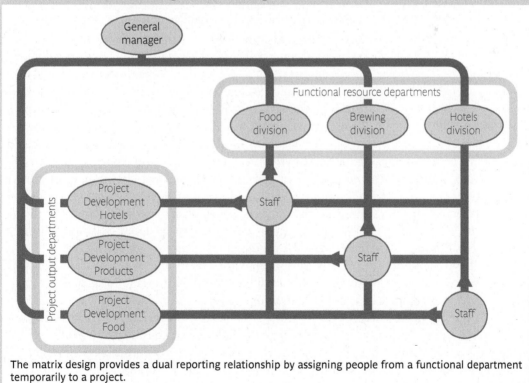

The matrix design provides a dual reporting relationship by assigning people from a functional department temporarily to a project.

thus have to contribute to the needs of the project, and yet continue to interface with their functional manager. Managers in the matrix organisation need to become skilled at managing conflict, for at times there will be differences in perspective and priority. Galbraith (1995) argues that the conflicting pressures within the matrix design underscore the managerial lesson that structuring an appropriate organisational design involves balancing a series of trade-offs.

The trade-offs in balancing organisational design

The advantages and disadvantages associated with each of the four basic designs suggest the managerial task of organising is one of making compromises. Except in very small enterprises, organisational design involves striking a balance among opposing forces, needs and goals. In addition, once designed, an organisation's structure seldom stays in place very long in today's volatile and competitive environment. According to Chandler (1962), a long-standing principle is to have structure follow and support strategy rather than allow an out-of-date structure to constrain strategic options. Among the key trade-offs that make organisational design challenging is the need to strike an accord between centralisation and decentralisation. Managers also seek a working balance among autonomy, control and integration.

Balancing centralisation and decentralisation

Historically, basic organisational trade-offs come into play when managers consider where in the organisation certain decisions should be made. The central trade-off pits pressures for centralisation against the need for decentralisation. **Centralisation** is the concentration of authority and decision-making towards the top of an organisation. **Decentralisation** is the dispersion of authority and decision-making to operating units throughout an organisation. Most medium-to-large organisations have a degree of both centralisation and decentralisation in their structures.

centralisation
An organisational structure that concentrates authority and decision-making towards the top.

decentralisation
An organisational structure that disperses authority and decision-making to operating units throughout the organisation.

According to Connor (1992), larger enterprises with highly competent and skilled employees tend to diffuse decision-making, allowing greater participation and less centralisation. However, Maynard *et al.* (1992) suggest that large firms that perpetuate centralised management tend to be slower in recognising how their hierarchical structure restrains organisational effectiveness over time. Central structures work reasonably well in slow-changing industries but are less adaptable in complex, fast-changing environments. Microsoft, Intel, Johnson & Johnson, or Cisco could not lead their markets if governed by a highly centralised hierarchy. Even the venerable Coca-Cola took the drastic action of cutting its workforce by 6000 – its first lay-off in 81 years – as a step towards decentralisation following a health scare in Europe. Take a look at the Eye on Ethics box for more on Coca-Cola.

According to Alexander (1991), as environmental uncertainty and complexity increase, senior managers move incrementally towards decentralised control to promote local adaptability and decision-making. In particular, implementation of strategies and operating policies are decision areas normally delegated to local or lower-level managers. However, major resource allocation decisions such as acquisitions or investments in new plants are typically retained by the top management team. As another example, the board of directors of a bank authorises personal bankers to approve unsecured personal loans up to £15 000, and home mortgage loans up to £200 000. Commercial loans and those above the branch limits are reserved for central office approval.

Coca-Cola reorganises in light of bad press

One of the world's best recognised and most successful brands closed the book on the twentieth century amid controversy, disappointment and the sudden resignation of its CEO, Douglas Ivester. Financially, profits had fallen for two successive years, with 1999 earnings down by 31 per cent. Contributing to the decline was controversy surrounding a health scare in several European countries during that summer, when more than 250 people reported becoming ill after drinking Coke.

In his two years as Coke's CEO, Douglas Ivester briefly endured several defining moments – most of them negative. Described as an accounting-trained superrational CEO, Ivester assumed people around the globe viewed the world with the same rationality as he: a place where everything would add up. As a seven-days-a-week workaholic, he believed he could control every aspect of Coke's business and found it difficult to delegate.

At the close of three weeks of work in Paris, trying to salvage a troubled acquisition, Ivester heard that some Belgian school children had become sick after drinking Coke. Technical experts at Coke determined it came from a batch with a bad mix of carbon dioxide. Ivester flew home to Atlanta the next day as planned.

An unrelated batch of Coke was shipped from the firm's plant in Dunkirk, France, with fungicide on the bottom of cans, which gave the product an off smell. 'There is no health issue,' Ivester told his managers and French officials. However, health officials banned further sale of the product in Belgium, and after a week of unrelenting bad press, he flew back to Brussels. The next day, Belgian newspapers carried a full-page ad with a letter from Ivester that began, 'My apologies to the consumers of Belgium. I should have spoken with you earlier.' Although the government ban was lifted later that week, this was but one in a series of errors in judgement that led to Ivester's resignation on 6 December 1999.

The company was criticised for its slow response to reports that Coke consumption was making people sick. Speed of response to acknowledge the possible side effects of a bad batch of product and issuance of a fast and complete recall have become the hallmarks of ethical handling of such events. (Other bad press flowed from a racial discrimination suit filed by black employees and former employees.)

Successor executive Douglas Daft took decisive action as Coke entered the twenty-first century by slashing 6000 jobs from its workforce, part of a massive downsizing and corporate restructuring. The European scare was not the only contributing factor to the reorganisation, but it dramatised the cumbersome nature of too much centralised decision-making in the Atlanta international headquarters, especially in quickly responding to issues bridging quality and ethics. Atlanta's bureaucracy endured 2500 of the job cuts, brought about to delegate decision authority and increase local control in the offices where Coke operates in 200 countries.

Within his first two months at the helm, Douglas Daft remarked that the restructuring 'announcement is the culmination of a careful review during the past six months of each of our business functions. The world in which we operate has changed dramatically, and we must change to succeed.' For a company not in the habit of making changes, such a dramatic move to streamline the organisation (which eliminated 20 per cent of its workforce) symbolised an effort to shake off complacency and simplify an unwieldy corporate structure. With fewer decision-makers and greater local autonomy, Coke needs also to educate its managers to make the right decisions, uncompromising in anything that might appear to be unethical or trying to bottle up controversy.

Sources: Richard L. Jones 'Coca-Cola Layoffs Hit Atlanta Hard', Knight Ridder News Service, 27 January 2000 in *San Diego Union Tribune*, p. C-2; Patricia Sellers, 'Crunch Time for Coke', *Fortune*, 19 July 1999, pp. 72–78; and 'Debunking Coke', *The Economist*, 12 February 2000, p. 70.

Discussion questions

1 How did Ivester's management style impact on the Coca-Cola organisation?

2 Using Lawson and Lorsch's model, how would you describe the Coca-Cola organisation?

Balancing autonomy and control

As a variant on the centralisation–decentralisation issue, managers struggle with the dilemma of how to strike a balance between maintaining control and granting autonomy to others. An emphasis on **control** limits the authority given managers to shape decisions and resource allocations by specifying parameters and providing for higher-level reviews, often with approvals before proceeding. Organisations that emphasise control are concerned with *consistency* of action. Policies define the expected processes for conducting recurrent activities, and elaborate measures provide a check against budgets and plans.

In contrast, **autonomy** means granting power and responsibility to followers to initiate innovative action that improves processes and performance with results assessed against general goals. An organisation that emphasises autonomy is more concerned with promoting creativity and freedom of action in the belief that people will do what is right. Autonomy pushes decision prerogatives to those who are closest to the action and who have the relevant information, with the expectation that people will accept responsibility for producing favourable results.

The control–autonomy conflict is often framed in terms of maintaining consistency and predictability versus promoting innovation and flexibility. It is not unusual to find within the same organisation considerable differences in how these management principles are handled, depending on the type of function performed and the degree of environmental stability or turbulence encountered. Managers of sales and research and development (R&D) departments generally grant considerable autonomy because results require individual initiative and creativity.

Manufacturing and service operations departments tend to be governed by greater control because of the need for efficiency, quality assurance and conformity with design specifications. Harry (1994) suggests that functions involving routine processes are prime candidates for the six sigma approach to quality, with the goal of measuring performance to reduce variance and improve consistency. General Electric's Jack Welch committed his organisation to six sigma and, within two years and after investing more than a billion dollars in the effort, realised savings of three-quarters of a billion dollars beyond that investment (Goett, 1999).

Johnson & Johnson (J&J), a large diversified pharmaceutical firm with hundreds of product lines, is structured into 160 or so largely independent business units (Weber, 1992). The

control
Bounds the authority given managers to shape decisions and resource allocations by specifying parameters and providing for higher-level reviews and often approvals.

autonomy
Grants power and responsibility to followers to initiate innovative actions that improve processes and performance, and then assesses results against general goals.

presidents of the business units are given reasonable autonomy to run their own units consistent with a code of ethics. The objective of these small, self-governing units is to make each manageable and ethically responsive to market forces. One divisional president remarked, 'I don't ask permission. I'm almost never distracted by J&J management.' 'Distracted' is an interesting word choice, for in many large firms senior management creates a lot of distractions for line managers. However, at J&J, each business unit (with its unique product line and market) prepares its own budgets and marketing plans, and often manages its own research and development. The intent is to use a decentralised, autonomous structure to provide operating executives a sense of ownership of a business and an entrepreneurial motivation to be aggressive in the pharmaceutical marketplace.

Balancing differentiation and integration

A long-standing concern of managers is the question of what do people identify with as their source of organisational allegiance and goals? Do people identify more with their department, function or discipline, or with the larger enterprise? Are their goals heavily localised to the immediate work unit level, or linked to more holistic organisational outcomes?

differentiation
The psychological identification and attachment to a subpart of an organisation, to a particular department, discipline or function.

integration
A psychological orientation that identifies with the 'big picture' perspective of the larger organisation or a major division within it, combined with the realisation that co-ordination and combining of actions across subunits is of greater importance than individual departments or functions.

Differentiation, as we mentioned earlier, distinguishes the cognitive-emotional orientations people hold towards a subpart of an organisation – to one's work unit, be it a particular department, discipline or function. **Integration** reflects the quality and form of collaboration between work units to shift expectations to a 'big picture' perspective of the larger organisation. Lawrence and Lorsch (1969) suggest that integrative forces bring with them the realisation that, ultimately, it is the co-ordination and combining of actions across subunits that is of greater importance.

Differentiation promotes specialisation and functional expertise, whereas integration promotes synergy and co-ordination. With strong differentiation, the prevailing mindsets of managers differ in goals, time horizons and interpersonal styles across departments, which reinforce departmental differences in the formality of structure. For example, the manufacturing managers of a firm might have goals focused on productive efficiency, emphasise short time horizons and exhibit task-driven interpersonal styles, whereas the marketing managers focus on customer satisfaction and moderate time horizons, with a more social style of interacting. Conflict across work units is more likely since the implicit goal is to have one's department win in struggles over resources or product or programme developments. We see this a lot in colleges and universities when faculty identify more with their discipline, such as finance or marketing, than they do with the school. This complicates curriculum development or reform as each discipline tries to 'win' by getting more of its content into the programme. By contrast, where faculty have more of an integration identity with the school or college, they tend to work through curricular issues faster and more smoothly, with the objective of designing what is best for students and meeting the needs of employers.

Traditionally, organisations that have allowed people to become highly differentiated in their mindset have tended to mesh or co-ordinate work-flow issues through structural means – decisions are pushed up and actions thrust down the hierarchy. An extreme case of differentiation was seen in the Ford Motor Co. situation during the 1980s and early 1990s, where 'fiefdoms' (to use the word chosen by CEO Nasser, the CEO at that time) became all prevalent to the detriment of an integrating corporate identity. Not only were the fiefdoms focused on a regional mindset – the CEO remarked that Ford Europe executives would not listen to corporate-level suggestions – but they were strongly polarised by function and management versus union within a region's operations.

With increased globalisation and use of information technology, integration has become a stronger need where the whole, not just the sum of the parts, is important for success in fulfilling expectations of customers, shareholders and other stakeholders. As you will learn shortly, the expanded use of teamwork, and especially cross-functional teams, has become one means to promote collaborative processes to accept responsibility and integrate decisions and actions for the greater good. According to Dean and Susman (1989), cross-functional teamwork becomes more pronounced, even necessary, with increased technological complexity, the speed-up of product introductions, and the need for flexibility in producing customised products and services for customers. Lawler (1992) suggests that, under these conditions, 'work teams simply allow more decisions and more co-ordination activities to be pushed lower in the organisation – particularly if the production or service process is complicated and involves a number of steps'.

According to Keidel (1990), the need for integration and collaboration can be thought of as a linking-pin to help balance autonomy and control trade-offs when quality and speed of decision-making are critical. Exhibit 15-10 graphically portrays a three-way relationship between control, autonomy and integration by identifying the principal trade-offs involved in deciding how to balance the three. The use of integration (collaboration) promotes flexibility and synergy among activities. Conversely, when control (centralisation) is the pivotal organising strategy, consistency and a more global perspective prevail. Autonomy (decentralisation) emphasises accountability with an overlay of responsiveness to local or unique market conditions.

EXHIBIT 15 – 10   Trade-offs among control, autonomy and co-ordination

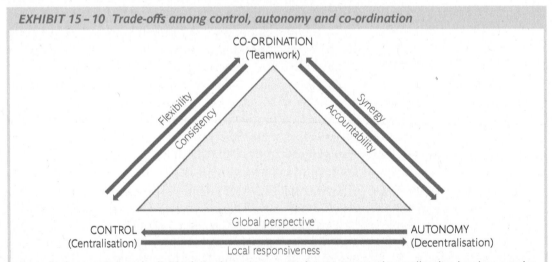

Organisations can't have it all. The interplay among control, autonomy and co-ordination involves a series of trade-offs, or compromises. The pairs of arrows show the opposing forces between each set of factors involved in the trade-off. For example, on the left side of the triangle, as an organisation becomes more control-orientated, it increases consistency at the cost of reducing flexibility.

Source: adapted from Robert W. Keidel (1990) 'Triangular Design: A New Organisational Geometry', *Academy of Management Executive* 4, November, pp. 24, 26.

Bureaucracy versus organic, postmodern structures

Issues of control – autonomy – integration spill over into the 'look and feel' of organisational designs. As enterprises move into the twenty-first century, Pasmore *et al.* (1982) suggest they accelerate movement away from tightly structured, mechanistic approaches to organisation towards structures and processes that are looser, organic, adaptive networks. As we have already discussed in the Lawrence and Lorsch 'Research focus', a mechanistic organisation is highly structured and formalised, leading to conforming behaviours to handle routine functions within an essentially stable environment. According to Hackman (1989), an organic organisation relies on the adaptive capacities of individuals, facilitated by empowerment and a collaborative network, to cope with dynamic internal and external forces. Bergquist (1993) and Heckscher and Donnellen (1994) suggest that the qualities of a mechanistic organisation are classically associated with bureaucracy, whereas organic organisational qualities have been described using many labels: postmodern, open systems, post-bureaucratic, virtual organisation, high-involvement organisation, the networked organisation, and others.

mechanistic organisation
An organisation with a traditional 'look and feel' that is highly structured and formalised, desiring conformance behaviours to handle routine functions appropriate to stable environments.

organic organisation
An organisation with a looser 'look and feel' that relies on the adaptive capacities of individuals to cope with dynamic internal and external forces, facilitated by empowerment and a collaborative network.

Bureaucracy as a model

For decades managers embodied a philosophy in which people were cast into well-defined job roles. The same or similar roles were grouped into work units headed by a supervisor or manager, with groups of work units linked by a hierarchy of reporting relationships. Conceptually, this perspective was first advocated and described by the German scholar Max Weber (see Chapter 1 for historic detail). As conceived by Weber in Vesey (1991), bureaucracy is an efficiency-orientated system of organisation that emphasises the formalisation of roles and rules to promote control. The classic bureaucracy is shaped like a pyramid and structured on a rational–legal system of authority.

bureaucracy
A classic pyramid-shaped structure created as a rational–legal system of authority emphasising formal roles and rules with the intent of being efficiency-orientated.

As a system of organisation, bureaucracy came into being in part to emphasise technical requirements and to rationalise policies without regard to the political patronage and favouritism that had characterised German organisations in the early half of the twentieth century. By specifying rules and procedures, managers are freed from making routine decisions – such matters can be delegated to subordinates. However, because of its formalism and codified protocol, bureaucracy (like power) has become a dirty word to those who do not understand its intent. People often speak with disdain of the 'bureaucratic red tape' associated with vast hierarchies. They are critical of the routine paper shuffling that stifles creative responses to novel situations, and employees who seem uncaring. Conventional wisdom holds that, in bureaucracies, the head appears not to know where the feet are going.

Yet, according to Sager (1999), bureaucracies can be very efficient. IBM's was for years. However, the early 1990s slowed its adaptiveness to a crawl, so CEO Louis V. Gerstner Jr began dismantling the bureaucracy and transforming the organisation to function more like an entrepreneurial network. As IBM discovered, a bureaucratic approach to organisation can flourish when routine operations are fitted to rather stable, predictable environments. Bureaucracies enhance predictability and conformance to standards, and can be highly efficient when handling large volumes of largely repetitive work. With today's computerised information systems, the bureaucratic organisation makes sense for handling much of the work performed in service firms such as banks, insurance firms and telephone companies. However, this is not the case for fast-changing organisations facing global competition, such as IBM.

The organic, flexible alternative

The limitations of the bureaucratic, mechanistic model when confronted with turbulent environments have spawned a number of experiments with alternative structures. These go by many names, as suggested by Bennis (1993), and include characteristics such as 'networks, clusters, cross-functional teams, temporary systems, ad hoc task forces, lattices, modules, matrices'.

Organic organisations empower individuals and teams to pursue continuous improvement through flexible adaptation. Task roles are expected to change continually or are ambiguously defined, and organisational design is fluid and features frequent structural reorganisations. Goals are diverse, complex, less measurable and more likely to change than in the mechanistic organisation. Planning flows up, down and across organisational units rather than being passed up and down. Structurally, the organisation is flatter.

Organic organisations are designed to promote effectiveness in complex, fast-changing environments, especially when technology is a driving force for change. Lawler (1992) suggests that the organic organisation promotes high involvement, which helps people provide high-quality products and services at competitive costs, and to respond quickly to opportunities or threats. Donald Petersen began the transformation of a sluggish Ford Motor Co. during the 1980s, a change that accelerated as Jacques Nasser became CEO in the late 1990s. Petersen was convinced that, to revitalise the way people work, it is necessary to change from the traditional top-down organisational design and management practices. In his book, *A Better Idea*, Petersen begins by presenting his ideology:

> I'm writing this book to express my belief that business can and should be conducted in a better way than it has been in the past. We need to foster an attitude of trust, cooperation, and respect throughout our organisations ... [to] help the company or organisation transform itself from a place where everybody hates to come to work to a place where people trust one another and enjoy working together. (Vesey, 1991)

Now that you have had an exposure to many of the differing characteristics involved in organisational design, it is time to take stock of what you may be looking for in the employer organisation(s) you join. Take a minute to complete the 'Your turn' exercise.

How organisations become leaner, flatter, more integrated

The purpose of organisation is to encourage behaviours appropriate to goal and task needs. Given the trend for mental tasks to replace menial ones, a corresponding organising trend is to flatten the organisational hierarchy, either by breaking businesses into autonomous units or by improving horizontal work-process flows and decreasing the intensity of supervision. Lawler (1992) contends that, where such structural changes are made, higher involvement results from pushing decisions closer to people with first-hand information – those in the firing line.

Your turn

What type of organisation do you prefer?

Describe the characteristics you prefer to experience in an organisation. Use your personal beliefs and values as a guide to score each of the 12 characteristics on a 5-point scale, where 5 means 'strongly agree' with the statement and 1 means 'strongly disagree'. Circle your preference.

	Agree				Disagree
1 People should know where they fit in a well-defined hierarchy of explicit authority–status relationships.	5	4	3	2	1
2 Supervision, decisions and controls should be exercised through a chain of command with clearly understood roles.	5	4	3	2	1
3 Codified systems of formal rules, policies and procedures should simplify the handling of routine activities.	5	4	3	2	1
4 Division of labour should be refined through job specialisation.	5	4	3	2	1
5 Technical competence and seniority should be the basis for job staffing.	5	4	3	2	1
6 Promotions and pay should be based on individual performance merit.	5	4	3	2	1
7 Roles should be fluid, changing with new goals and needs.	5	4	3	2	1
8 Planning should take place throughout the organisation; plans should not simply be handed down from the top.	5	4	3	2	1
9 Personal involvement in challenging, complex tasks should be a greater source of motivation than management style or formal rewards.	5	4	3	2	1
10 Teams rather than individuals should be the primary source of output.	5	4	3	2	1
11 Primary work tasks should occur more in a horizontal work flow than within specialised functional departments with vertical responsibilities.	5	4	3	2	1
12 Performance should be measured more by external results (customer satisfaction) than by internal statistics (costs per hour).	5	4	3	2	1

Scoring and interpretation

Enter the sum of your scores to questions 1 to 6 here: _____ M

Enter the sum of your scores to questions 7 to 12 here: _____ O

Subtract the smaller score from the larger. If M is larger, on balance you prefer more mechanistic or bureaucratic organisations. If O is larger, your preference is for organic or flexible organisations. If the difference between your M and O scores is 17 or greater, your preference is quite strong. If the difference between the scores is 9 to 16, a moderate preference is indicated; if 1 to 8, your preference is slight. Obviously, a difference of zero is neutral. As you read on in the chapter, you will understand the differences between these two organisational prototypes.

During the mid-1980s through to the mid-1990s, it was popular for managers to streamline organisations by use of the three Rs: restructuring, re-engineering and rightsizing. Unfortunately, these three tended, for the most part, to be euphemisms for lay-offs, for reducing the number of people employed. According to O'Neill (1994), the goal of all three was to improve financial performance (re-engineering also aims to improve customer service), but the human consequences of such programmes were often traumatic. Anytime an organisation reduces its workforce by 10 000 to 50 000, there are going to be unemployed casualties who do not recover. Nevertheless, organisations will continue to draw on several tactics to flatten structures.

Mandel (2000) argues that the new millennium ushered in a continual effort to flatten organisations and make them more organic as a source of competitive advantage. Much has been said and written about the 'new economy' with its rapid globalisation through an exponential rise in the applications of information technology. Unemployment in the United Kingdom, as one characteristic of the new economy, has dropped to an all time low, and inflation is a minor issue at about 2–3 per cent. Organisations are undertaking significant risky investments in technology and are restructuring financial markets. In addition, at the heart of this are new perspectives on organisational design.

Widen the span of control

span of control

In describing organisational structures, denotes the number of people supervised by one manager, or the ratio of managers to persons managed.

One way to flatten organisations is to widen the span of control. **Span of control**, as we discussed earlier, denotes the number of people supervised by one manager, or the ratio of managers to persons managed. While organisations that seek high involvement may no longer emphasise 'control', the span-of-control concept is still useful. Exhibit 15-11 shows the interplay between span of control, hierarchical levels and organisational size. The only way a large organisation – say one with 100 000 or more people – can maintain flexibility without becoming overly hierarchical is to increase the average span of control and reduce the number of management levels (and thus the number of managers). Executives today generally aim to have seven or fewer levels, in stark contrast to the 14 to 19 levels common to bureaucracies such as General Motors.

According to Lawler (1992), in organisations that hold to the old principle of narrow span of control, people are under-motivated and under-utilised. A manager with five people in his/her department (a narrow span), is likely to interact with them more often – and be more

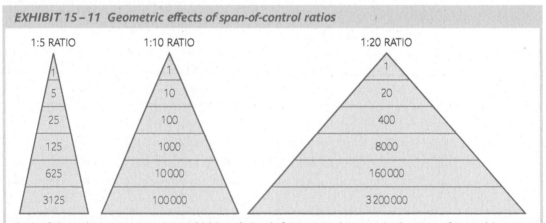

EXHIBIT 15–11 Geometric effects of span-of-control ratios

1:5 RATIO	1:10 RATIO	1:20 RATIO
1	1	1
5	10	20
25	100	400
125	1000	8000
625	10 000	160 000
3125	100 000	3 200 000

Each of these three structures (pyramids) has six levels from top to bottom. As the span of control (average number of people reporting to a manager) increases, the organisation becomes 'flatter', because proportionately fewer managers are required to manage a greater number of people. Simply by doubling the span from 5 to 10, a six-level organisation can increase its employee base about 32-fold, from 3125 to 100 000. Another doubling of span (from 10 to 20) increases total employees another 32 times (from 100 000 to 3 200 000).

controlling – than with a wide span of 15 to 30. AT&T used to believe six was the optimum span of control for most managers – a number that allowed the manager to issue directives and expect subordinates to follow them. Nevertheless, as the number of people in a manager's unit increases, the opportunity for the manager to directly control their behaviour decreases while the empowerment potential increases.

Lawler (1992) concludes, in reflecting on structures in organisations, 'Most organisations, even very large ones, should be able to operate effectively with no more than six or seven levels of management. Usually spans of management should never be less than fifteen and, in most cases, should be larger.' According to Hill and Hoskisson (1987), ultimately, a manager's span of control is constrained by his or her information-processing capabilities. Such a contemporary guideline, of wide spans and shallow levels, contrasts greatly with the narrow and deep beliefs held by generations of managers beginning in the early twentieth century.

Flatten levels of management

Pyramidal hierarchies shape an environment in which power is not shared. Power firmly held at the top transmits the message that people lower in the organisation are not to be trusted to think and act independently. By structuring to eliminate layers of management, an organisation pushes power to lower levels and encourages employee involvement. When the board of directors of General Motors pressed chairman and CEO Robert Stempel to resign, and then appointed John F. Smith Jr as CEO in the 1990s, critics stated, 'Smith must force a fundamental change in GM's culture by holding managers accountable for their performance while encouraging them to take risks. That means pushing power to make decisions down into the ranks' (Kerwin and Peterson, 1962).

All these flattening efforts are not undertaken without difficulty. In the 1980s, General Electric reduced positions and managerial levels but found that most work tasks remained, overtaxing the managers. It then focused on eliminating unnecessary hierarchy-related work, such as reports, meetings and multiple levels of approval for decisions. In the 1990s, GE acknowledged that the firm has been 'pulling the dandelions of bureaucracy for a decade, but they don't come up easily and they'll be back next week if you don't keep after them'.

Information technology provides a tremendous boost to the concept of pushing decisions to lower levels. By providing open access to commonly shared information, management has less of a role to play in synthesising information and thus making decisions. Decisions are made faster, transactions are simplified, costs decline and organisational structures are streamlined through innovative and repetitive use of Internet applications. IBM cut about £1 billion out of costs by improving employee access to information (Sager, 1999).

line positions
Job assignments that directly contribute to creating customer value by either designing products, producing them, financing needed resources, marketing to create demand, and/or selling and servicing the product.

staff positions
Jobs that support the line positions through carrying out advisory and internal 'overhead' support activities such as accounting, purchasing and human resource functions.

Shift control from staff to line

Organisations historically have two types of members and positions: line and staff. **Line positions** more or less directly contribute to creating value added for the customer by designing products, producing them, financing the needed resources, and marketing and selling them. **Staff positions** are supposed to support the line, providing technical advice such as legal counselling or carrying out 'overhead' activities such as accounting and human resource functions to relieve managers of specialised administrative burdens.

When staff groups grow in numbers, staff managers often try to expand the scope of their 'services' by developing guidelines and rules intended to co-ordinate (standardise) daily activities ranging from employee evaluations to purchases of supplies. Expanding the scope of staff control carries two costs: the cost of employing staff and the added cost (especially in time requirements) to line people who have to comply with staff procedures.

Goold (1991) suggests that, with the push towards leaner, customer-responsive, global enterprises, many organisations have cut back on staff and limited their tasks to providing information and advice, not making decisions or requiring reports. Streamlining staff functions with the aim of empowering line people is common at John Lewis department stores and SAS (the international airline). Both firms eliminated their detailed procedure manuals (produced by staff) and simply instruct employees to 'satisfy the customer'.

The elimination of non-revenue-producing staff has been aggressively pursued by the Europe-based firm, Asea Brown Boveri (ABB) (Wolff, 1999). When it acquires businesses, ABB typically reduces their corporate staff by up to 90 per cent. To emphasise that it can be done, its corporate home office numbers only about 150 (out of some 250 000 employed across 1300 frontline companies in 140 countries). Even IBM concentrated on cutting staff and headquarters employees when it downsized, by displacing nearly 100 000 through the early 1990s. IBM's personnel staff shrank 90 per cent (from 400 to 40), and the European headquarters was trimmed from 2000 to less than 200 (Kirkpatrick, 1992). See the case of Shell in the World Watch box.

Re-engineer from vertical flows to horizontal work processes

One of the more widely used approaches to creating a lean organisation has been the shift from emphasising vertical relationships to focusing on horizontal work flows. This shift feeds on changes in high-involvement work teams, the electronic distribution of information, and managing business processes rather than functional departments. For example, in GE's Bayamon, Puerto Rico, plant, about 170 hourly employees work in teams of 10 or so without supervisors, and there are only 15 salaried 'advisers' plus one general manager (Stewart, 1992). Each team's representative works with both upstream (distributors, customers) and downstream operations (such as receiving, assembly and shipping) to ensure that value is added in each link of the horizontal chain of processes. By rotating jobs every six months, employees learn new skills and see how one team's work affects others in the work-flow stream.

Emphasise cross-functional co-ordination

Re-engineering reconfigures work processes to serve customers better. To use the definition popularised by Hammer and Champy (1993), **re-engineering** entails the 'radical redesign of business processes to achieve dramatic improvements in critical, contemporary measures of performance, such as cost, quality, service, and speed'. Champy (1995) and Keidel (1994) conclude that re-engineering seeks to make two major changes. At the personal level, it aims to shift the mindsets of people caused by working within the 'silos', 'chimneys' or 'smokestacks' of vertical, functionally aligned organisations (as in the Ford of yesteryear). At the competitive level, work flows are redesigned to make sense from a customer's perspective. The 're-engineering' emphasis is on rearranging business processes so they cut across functions in a horizontal flow. Each set of operational processes should have a definable beginning and end, such as the flow from new product development to customer acquisition, concluding with order fulfilment. The objective is to achieve integration among task interdependencies.

re-engineering
The radical redesign of business processes to achieve dramatic improvements in measures such as cost, quality, service and speed.

Shell innovates with cyber teams

Think the commercial aspects of the World Wide Web are just for cutting costs and speeding up transactions? At Shell Group, the worldwide petroleum company, the web is used to stimulate and manage innovation. Six teams of six employees each meet weekly in Rijswijk, Netherlands, and in Houston, Texas, to sort through, evaluate and selectively act on ideas sent to them via email. The teams, known as GameChangers, are rounding up over 300 useful ideas per year with billions in pay-offs.

Of Shell's recent five top business initiatives, four were processed through GameChanger teams. One example is a new 'Light Touch' method for discovering oil by using laser technology to sense hydrocarbon emissions released naturally into the air from underground reserves. The technology helped locate some 30 billion barrels of oil reserves in Gabon.

Such 'knowledge markets' put bright ideas in the hands of teams who can quickly convert the best into products or projects. By harnessing the web throughout Shell's far-flung organisation, these small entrepreneurial teams drive innovation faster than the firm has ever experienced. In effect these cyber teams function like start-up enterprises fuelled with corporate money as venture capital. Says Harvard professor Clayton Christensen, 'The trend now is to decentralise operations, to build idea factories, or idea markets. This is a way to bring the start-up mentality inside [the existing organisation].'

They do this by soliciting ideas across the seas and continents, pick the most promising, and then either pass the project off to an established business unit or, alternatively, create and fund a new start-up. In the latter case, they can create a virtual organisation by using web communications to collaborate with experts wherever they may be. Pay-offs for those involved range from cash bonuses to stock options.

The pay-off to Shell is a revitalisation of a mature bureaucracy, by pushing decision-making deep within the organisation. Innovative entrepreneurial GameChanger teams serve as models, and many operating units have replicated the process and structure to create their own local team. As autonomous groups, the teams are in charge of their own resources, write their own policies, hire employees, create their own 'idea-reward systems', and often report to the most senior executive in the region. Math Kohnen, director of GameChanger Initiatives, states a simple objective: 'What it says is, innovation is everybody's responsibility.'

Source: Marcia Stepanek (1999) 'Using the Net for Brainstorming', *Business Week*, 13 December, pp. EB-55–57.

Discussion questions

1 How would you describe the structure of the Shell organisation?
2 How is the World Wide Web affecting the design of organisations?

Hammer and Champy (1993) argue that re-engineering applies to real work processes, not to single departments. One of Ford Motor's early ventures into redesign began as an initiative to cut costs within the accounts payable department, the unit that paid supplier bills. Ford's breakthrough in thinking occurred when it shifted from accounts payable to examine the entire business process of procurement. Procurement was more encompassing, involving purchasing and receiving as well as accounts payable. Much of accounts payable's work involved matching up documents: the originating purchase order, the receiving document and the invoice. Most of the time the documents did not match – the quantity delivered differed from that ordered, or unit costs were different.

Actually, Pareto's law of maldistribution was at work. Often known as the 80/20 rule, Pareto's law states that 80 per cent of an outcome or observed phenomenon is caused by only 20 per cent of the input or contributing events. For example, it is not uncommon for 80 per cent of an activity's costs to be contributed by 20 per cent of the steps involved, or for 80 per cent of a firm's accidents to be caused by only 20 per cent of the employees.

Pareto's law

Known as the 80/20 rule, this principle states that 80 per cent of an observed result is caused by 20 per cent of the activities, or efforts, or people involved.

Ford's new process is largely automated through the use of an electronic database accessible by people in all three functions. Instead of paying on receipt and verification of an invoice, payment authorisation is now automatically issued when the receiving clerk confirms that an incoming delivery of parts corresponds to the purchase order displayed on the computer screen.

Caution: probabilities of disappointment and anxiety run high

As firms re-engineer and otherwise work to design more flexibility into their organisations, the boundaries that once compartmentalised groups of people and effectively insulated most employees from outside forces begin to break up. Good working relationships do not happen automatically when people are thrust into teams or given more freedom. The struggle to learn new skills begins when senior managers give up some of their authority, encouraging participation and teamwork. According to Hirschhorn and Gilmore (1992), re-engineering should help people look at their work from different perspectives: 'the task is to allow sufficient boundaries to give individuals and work groups an identity, but to keep them focused outward, not inward. . . . The issue is to organise around issues as well as tasks.'

Redesigning organisations does not come easy, and the outcomes are not always positive. One piece of research, by Cameron (1993), of the consequences of 150 corporate restructurings (involving downsizing) found that 75 per cent ended up in worse shape. (However, there was no control for the severity of crisis that precipitated the redesign – they could have ended up in even worse shape without reconfiguring.) Even re-engineering, which reorganises the way work is done (not just realigning boxes on an organisational chart), is not without problems. Hammer (1993), who helped popularise the intervention, estimates that between 50 and 70 per cent of re-engineering initiatives fail to achieve their objectives. Another researcher emphasises the need to reconceptualise or rethink individually and collectively more than just organisational and process designs:

> Organisational rethinking ... means conceptualizing design in a manner that incorporates organizational identity, or character – who we are, and what we stand for; organizational purpose, or constituencies – for whose benefit we exist; and organizational methods, or capabilities – how we satisfy customers/consumers. (Keidel, 1990)

Thus, before launching a top-down redesign using one or more of the three Rs (restructuring, re-engineering and rightsizing), executives might do well to rethink their pending actions by pulling the three Cs noted above to the forefront: character, constituencies and capabilities. These design lessons apply to organisational structures that focus on teams to support human and strategic efforts.

Designing work around self-managing teams

To bring about continuous improvement and innovation, routine tasks of production and in-person service jobs are increasingly bundled into teams to work in harmony with technology.

Firms are moving to abandon what have been narrowly defined job classifications. For example, 'craft' boundaries in union shops have historically prevented a firm's carpenters from moving an electrical outlet or pipe when relocating a wall in a production facility. Such skill rigidities are dysfunctional to employees and to the enterprise.

Involvement and innovation

Many organisations give team members broad responsibilities and greater discretion to define their jobs so they can respond to whatever challenge the group encounters. Teams now carry out many of the planning and problem-solving functions previously reserved for managers. Ford Motor Co. can produce as many cars today as it did in the late 1970s with half as many employees. The most important factor, according to Templin (1992), in this improvement is increased co-operation of the workforce to help find ways to reduce costs. Ford worked with union participation to eliminate work rules with narrow job classifications in the company's formerly least productive stamping plant, a change that saved £20 million per year. (Look back at the example of the Halewood plant in Chapter 5.)

The movement to give a work group or team more responsibility for performing tasks in the workplace is gaining momentum. Lawler (1992) writes: 'Despite the fact that individual enrichment has important advantages and should be used in certain situations ... the preferred work design for most high-involvement situations is the team approach.' Propelling this trend has been the growth of quality management and continuous improvement practices.

Traditional organisational practices place responsibility for improvement on the manager. There is evidence from Schonberger (1994), however, that managers often make erroneous assumptions about what is wrong – for example, with manufacturing quality. Although managers may assume that quality problems stem from a poor workforce, poor work quality, and poor maintenance of production facilities and equipment, in reality the problems may be due to poor quality of incoming parts or poor design – factors that people doing the work contend with every day. Mitroff (1988) observes that, 'You can't get quality through blame or through fixing the wrong part of the whole system.' Participative teams are often more resourceful in bringing about continuous quality improvement.

Options for participative team management

Although managerial authority still prevails in most organisations, the shift towards non-managers participating in decisions is increasing. Managers are learning that, to be competitive, they 'should count on the ideas and judgement of production workers, as well as their physical effort' (Hossein Safizadeh, 1991). Until recently, UK and US managers have been slower than their Japanese and Swedish counterparts to accept and learn from work teams. According to Cole (1989), one source of resistance has been fear of potential power loss, but that fear often causes managers to neglect the value of potential improvements that are easily seen by those working in non-managerial jobs.

Managers who wish to allow non-managers to participate in making decisions face two questions: In what types of decisions should employees participate? How much latitude should they be granted to implement their recommendations? Exhibit 15-12 uses these two issues to identify a matrix of different participation possibilities. The three team-based participation models through which performers can influence work practices and policies are quality circles, self-managed work teams and cross-functional teams. Self-managed teams and cross-functional teams enjoy greater authority to act on their own recommendations than do quality circles. Quality circles essentially provide an analysis and advisory function, and offer a starting point for teamwork in many organisations.

EXHIBIT 15–12 Participation in decision-making

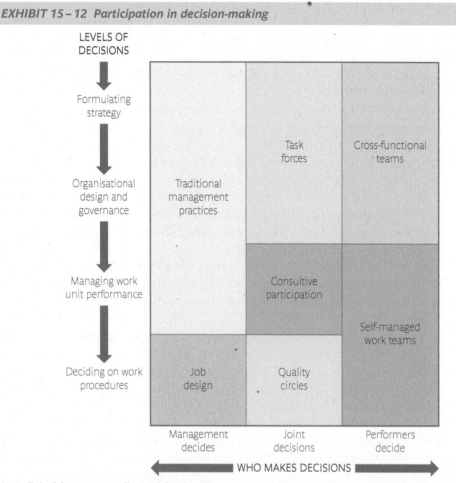

Not all decisions are equally participative. Once management moves beyond traditional management practices, in which decisions reside with managers, the intermediate step is usually joint decisions, where performers can make recommendations (as usually practised by quality circles, consultative participation and task forces). Only when decisions are completely delegated to the performers (as with self-managed teams and cross-functional teams) is participation at its highest level.

Source: adapted from Edward E. Lawler III and Susan A. Mohrman (1987) 'Quality Circles: After the Honeymoon', *Organizational Dynamics*, Spring.

Quality circles

Ciampa (1992) and Dewar (1980) highlighted a movement to promote decentralisation and capture the creative power of workers using quality circles which began in Japan in the 1960s. Although the concept originated in the United States, it was not practised there until introduced by Lockheed in the 1970s. According to Shea (1991), a **quality circle (QC)** is a group process that operates parallel to the traditional managerial structure by involving volunteers in applying technology tools to produce problem-solving recommendations. Quality circle members study ways to improve quality incrementally, although normally they do not have authority to implement changes. Instead, they sell the merits of group analysis and recommendations to management, in what is at best a form of joint decision-making.

quality circle (QC)

A group process that operates apart from but parallel to the traditional managerial structure by involving volunteers in analysing problems and recommending solutions.

Quality circles provide a means for people in technical or operational capacities to become responsible for solving problems and improving practices. They learn that their ideas do make a difference. A nine-person team of physicians, technicians and managers at a Norfolk general hospital made a difference when they eliminated 14 steps to cut X-ray processing time from an average 72.5 hours to 13.8 hours (Anderson, 1992). Because it trains participants and managers alike to share responsibility, the QC experience provides a positive skill-building prelude to true self-managed work teams.

Self-managed teams

Although work teams have existed for centuries, only recently have self-managed teams become a key approach to organising work within large organisations. A self-managed team is a work unit whose members are granted responsibility and authority to make the decisions necessary to produce a product or service. Teams are given the right to be largely self-governing, to make decisions about scheduling and assigning tasks, to decide on work methods and who gets hired, and even in some cases to adjust rates of pay. Because they are part of the regular organisational system, teams are intended to create high rates of member involvement and commitment.

self-managed team
A work unit whose members are granted responsibility and authority to take the decisions and actions necessary to produce a product or service.

Much of the pioneering work on teams originated from the Tavistock Institute in the UK. Daft and Steers (1986) conducted early experiments with work teams under the label of 'socio-technical systems design'. Ironically, what the Tavistock researchers observed in their pioneering study was how technology and work reorganisation broke up naturally functioning self-managing teams of coal miners. These researchers reasoned that work organisation needed to consider both the *technical* requirements (for equipment, tools and work processes) *and* the *social-system* aspects of work if teams are to be motivated.

socio-technical systems design
A systems approach to enhance motivation and productivity by structuring work groups to achieve a balance between technical and human subsystems.

The goal of socio-technical systems design is to achieve a balanced fit between the technical system and the human system as a group. Whereas traditional job design focuses on ways of assigning responsibilities and achieving greater motivation for individual employees, socio-technical systems design seeks these benefits for entire work groups. Pasmore *et al.* (1982) reported on over 130 examples of change towards socio-technical systems design involving organisations as varied as a railway maintenance depot, car manufacturing, textile mills and pet food production. According to Mohrman *et al.* (1995) these approaches have used a variety of other nomenclatures to describe their team concept, including self-managing teams, autonomous work teams, self-directing teams and self-regulating teams.

Cross-functional teams

Bringing new or improved products to market is traditionally organised as a series of sequential processes to transform ideas into products. Three to five separate functional groups are typically involved, each doing their own work and then handing it off to the next upstream group. Vesey (1991) suggests that, to attack the cost of product introduction delays, some firms have moved to cross-functional teams as integrators. Cross-functional teams pull together people from different functions or disciplines to co-ordinate separate but

cross-functional teams
A way of organising that pulls people together from several different functions or disciplines to emphasise co-ordination of separate but interrelated tasks in achieving product and service quality.

interrelated tasks that affect overall product or service quality. They often take the form of development teams who band together only long enough to complete a particular project and then disband.

Ford Motor Co. created the original Team Taurus when management decided to design and build the Taurus and Sable automobiles in the 1980s. The cross-functional team assembled designers, production specialists, engineers, customers, accountants and others to generate a simultaneous flow of ideas about designs, cost estimates, organisational processes and other aspects, to speed development and production of the vehicles. 'Before the first clay model was built, they knew how the car would be assembled. Under the previous system, manufacturing managers didn't see the cars they were going to build until eight or nine months before production started' (Vesey, 1991). Taurus became the best-selling car in America by the early 1990s. However, to make it attractive to younger buyers, a second Team Taurus assembled in the basement of Ford's Design Centre, nicknamed 'The Dungeon'. Starting with 150 members the team expanded to 700 engineers handling chassis, engine and manufacturing chores, working alongside designers, marketers, bean counters, suppliers and factory-floor workers to design and test the vehicle together. Says team leader Landgraff, 'How we managed this programme is as important to Ford as the vehicle we engineered' (Kerwin, 1995).

Teleworking: a second look

Steve Treadwell started a computer company producing software for database marketing in the early 1990s. He began with no office, so employees worked at home; and apart from a small administration centre he never got an office.

'Everybody said it would work with five people but not with 10. When we got to 10 full-time employees, they said the limit would be 20, and so on. In the end we had nearly 200 people, all of them working from home,' says Treadwell.

Having sold the company, he has recently started Virtesse, a consultancy that advises on the benefits and pitfalls of teleworking.

'One of the biggest changes is that work becomes task orientated, not hours orientated. We would say to our people so long as the job is done by Friday or whenever it was needed, then we don't mind when you do it,' he says.

But employees still need contact with each other, whether they are working from an office or from home.

'The whole company would get together every six weeks or so. We would spend a day together – half the time on purely business things, the rest on just getting to know each other.'

Of course some jobs are better suited to teleworking than others. The UK Labour Force Survey shows that the bulk of teleworkers are in managerial, professional or administrative jobs.

They are twice as likely to be graduates than the national average and most are employees. Men also outnumber women by two to one, making up 67 per cent of the UK's teleworkers.

How quickly teleworking grows will depend on the demand for staff. A looser market for skilled professionals, thanks to a slowing economy, will make it easier for companies to hire those they need, on standard terms and conditions, and so slow the growth in home working.

However, the trend towards flexible working of all kinds, particularly for senior managers and those in professions, is well established.

As Ursula Huws, director of the Emergence Project, a study funded by the European Commission into the effect of information technology on employment, and an associate fellow of the UK's Institute for Employment Studies, says: 'These days almost everybody whose job is based on knowledge or intellectual content is using telecommunications as a generic tool. Your place of work is almost immaterial. People are now expected to be flexible and to have all the functionality of teleworkers.'

For that reason, she says, the future is likely to be a hot desk – whether it is at home or in the office.

Source: adapted from *Financial Times*, 31 January 2002.

Summary

- Organisational structures and systems are designed to support strategies by providing the architecture for assigning responsibilities, making decisions and integrating work flows.

- However, strategies are changed (as you learned in Chapter 2) with the objective of improving the match between organisational capabilities and shifting environmental conditions.

- One environmental factor that by itself is causing changes in organisational design is technology. Information technology in particular is altering the nature of jobs by speeding the tempo of decisions, thus compressing layers of management and producing flatter, more organic organisational structures.

- Organisational design is the structural arrangement for grouping essential tasks (jobs) and providing a behavioural network for making decisions and co-ordinating work flow. Managers design the structure of organisations by using variations on four basic forms: function, geography, product and customer (and to a lesser degree, the matrix design).

- Organisational design supports the strategies of an enterprise and helps focus employee behaviour. Managers intend that design will help strike a balance among the needs to control behaviours, allow reasonable autonomy and integrate actions across work units.

- Because of accelerated shifts in global competition and technology, there is a tendency for organisations to become less mechanistic (or machinelike) and more organic (flexible). Bureaucracy, which for decades promoted efficiency and predictability through rules and control, is softening to practices that create greater employee involvement and adaptation. With organic involvement come flatter structures and a wider span of control for managers.

- Re-engineering has also promoted the creation of leaner, more cost-efficient organisations by emphasising the interconnection of process work flows across functional areas. Creating lean structures helps an organisation both to cope with increasing size and to respond to environmental conditions.

- With the increasing complexity of operations, organisations are building in greater participation opportunities for non-managers.

- Groups ranging from quality circles to self-managing and cross-functional teams are involved in continuous-improvement projects and running their own operations. With high involvement, people are challenged to rethink systems and processes – to eliminate tasks that no longer add value.

Areas for personal development

The design of organisational structures is a strategy supporting the creative process usually reserved for top managers. Nevertheless, there are some skill-building activities that even non-managerial students can begin practising. Because much of your working life will probably be devoted to organisations, the better you understand the impact of organisational design on your performance individually and collectively, and on your sense of satisfaction and fulfilment, the more you will feel in control of your environment.

1 **Anticipate the impact of technology on the tasks you perform.** Develop an appreciation of how technological change alters the methods by which one works over a lifetime. Unless you are 40 or more years of age, develop this 'historic' perspective by talking to two or three people who have worked for 20 or more years. Ask questions about what tools and technology they had available when they started their careers. What do they have now? How has newer technology affected how they do their jobs? Are their reporting relationships any different because of, say, changes in information practices? How have their organisations changed their structures because of technological advances?

2 **Learn what it is like to work in different organisational structures.** Although you cannot actually experiment with working in, say, a functional, geographic, customer, product or matrix-type structure, again you can interview others to learn vicariously through their experiences. Ask about the pros and cons of different approaches to structural emphasis from the perspective of someone who has worked in two or more. Ask also about the realities of mixed hybrid structures, for rarely is only one approach used.

3 **Sketch organisational charts for two or more organisations.** Few medium-sized to large organisations rely on only one or two approaches to designing their structures. Select two organisations based on your ease of access (either in person or through others or published sources). Start with non-managers in several types of position, and begin to sketch a diagram of who reports to whom. You will find there are seldom easy answers.

4 **Think about your preferences for trade-offs among autonomy, being controlled and collaboration.** Turn back to Exhibit 15-10, which was presented as a model for how managers emphasise their needs or uses of each of the three factors. Change the frame of reference to what you might prefer to experience if this represented three elements in your working environment. First, if you had to choose one condition, which would it be: to be controlled by others, to be autonomous, or to collaborate to integrate actions with others? Now, if you could select a point along one of the sides of the triangles that represented a preferred balance, place an X at that point and answer why you chose that point. Finally, if you could function in the space within the triangle, place a Y at the point that reflects how close or far away from each extreme you would like to be. Why that point? How could you change your employment situation to become perfectly positioned over time?

5 **Determine an effective span of control.** Think about span of control from two perspectives. First, as a follower, what span would you like your leader to experience? Obviously his or her span of control depends on many factors, such as the complexity and certainty of the task and the size of the overall organisation. But, generally, how

much supervision and interaction with your boss do you believe you need? Want? Do you see this changing as you gain experience? Next, think about how many people you would feel comfortable supervising when you find yourself in a management position. How do your personal needs affect your preference for closeness or distance?

6 **Play different roles in self-managed teams.** Here you do have an opportunity to gain experience while you experiment with unique learning assignments. On team projects, do not just fall into the rut of taking one role – such as doing the spreadsheets, or the graphics, or the writing, or the data collection. Volunteer for different assignments as a way of learning how to function in a team environment, so that you view team tasks from multiple points of view.

Questions for study and discussion

1 The character of work and the structuring of organisations are changing due to dramatic changes in technologies, products and services. What do you believe to be two significant technology-induced challenges facing managers responsible for shaping the work tasks people perform? Explain.

2 Describe and sketch the distinguishing characteristics of the four basic structural forms of organisation: design by function, product, geography and customer. Give at least two reasons why each would be used (advantages) and two limitations.

3 Describe an organisation that would have the characteristics of both centralisation and decentralisation.

4 Under what circumstances would managers want to emphasise autonomy with integration more than control and differentiation?

5 What were the original purposes of a bureaucratic approach to organisation? Why does bureaucracy receive a 'bad press'? What makes an organisation organic? Which gets better results, a bureaucracy or an organic organisation? Why?

6 Develop an argument that a span of control of 15 is more effective than a span of 5.

7 What are the behavioural differences involved? Base your argument on an organisation built on five levels of management.

8 What do quality circles, self-managed teams and cross-functional teams all have in common? How do they differ?

🔑 Key Concepts

electronic business, *p. 700*

technology, *p. 703*

organisational structure, *p. 710*

organisational chart, *p. 710*

organisational design, *p. 710*

organisational design by function, *p. 711*

organisational design by geography, *p. 712*

organisational design by product line, *p. 713*

organisational design by customer, *p. 715*

organisational life cycle, *p. 716*

matrix organisation, *p. 716*

centralisation, *p. 718*

decentralisation, *p. 718*

control, *p. 720*

autonomy, *p. 720*

differentiation, *p. 721*

integration, *p. 721*

mechanistic organisation, *p. 723*

organic organisation, *p. 723*

bureaucracy, *p. 723*

span of control, *p. 726*

line positions, *p. 727*

staff positions, *p. 727*

re-engineering, *p. 728*

Pareto's law, *p. 730*

quality circle (QC), *p. 732*

self-managed team, *p. 733*

socio-technical systems design, *p. 733*

cross-functional teams, *p. 733*

Personal skills exercise
Visualising the ideal workweek

Purpose To enable students to visualise the work and organisational qualities that most appeal to them (and ideally, time permitting, to compare and contrast those ideals with those of peers). The process should draw out considerations of person–job fit and differences in expectations among students for organisational design qualities.

Time and procedure Requires about 10 minutes if working alone (Phases 1 and 2) or about 30 to 40 minutes if using group sharing and feedback (Phases 3 to 5 – less if using two-person groups).

Phase 1: list individual work attributes (5 minutes) Working alone, list qualities or attributes you would ideally like to experience at work in the first year following your graduation. Think comprehensively, using the following questions as prompts.
(a) What is the nature of the job; what tasks will you perform?
(b) How will you use technology?
(c) How frequently and in what ways do you expect to interact with others?
(d) What skills are likely to be required or useful?
(e) Do you prefer to be held personally accountable for results (or your team, or others)?
(f) What form of performance measures should indicate results?
(g) What personal outcomes or benefits do you expect to achieve?
(h) What do you expect of the organisational environment (stability, chaos, etc.)?

Phase 2: individual story preparation (3 minutes) Now project ahead to fantasise a perfect week at work one year after graduation. Think of what you will be doing, with whom, under what organisational conditions and with what result. Prepare a framework for a story about the highlights of that week.

Phase 3: group formation and story telling (7–10 minutes) Team up with two or three other students. Take turns telling your story. Embellish with as much detail as possible. Keep the storyline plausible, even though it is an ideal situation.

Phase 4: group introspection and comparisons (7–10 minutes) Once the stories have been told, discuss the similarities and differences. Probe to understand why people tell the stories they do; look for underlying motives. You might use the following questions to facilitate your discussion.
(a) What job attributes seem to be important to you? To others?
(b) What do the people in your group want out of work?
(c) What do they want out of the organisational environment or design?
(d) How do another person's desires compare to your own?
(e) Who within your group seems to be the team player? The individual contributor? Why?
(f) What will probably be required for the ideal to come true?

Phase 5: class debriefing (7–10 minutes) Discuss as a total class the personal meanings of the exercise. Think along the following lines.
(a) Did you (or others) find it difficult to envision your ideal work tasks? Why? How much do you think about future work?
(b) Into what broad job categories did preferences fall? Did anyone desire a routine production job? Managerial work? A career directly providing personal service to others? A career analysing information?

(c) Which was the most popular job choice? Why?

(d) Was there much interest in self-managed teams? Why, if yes or no?

(e) To what extent do any of the tasks in your stories build on skills learned in school?

(f) Now, think ahead 10 years. Would your stories change substantially? Why? How does experience affect expectations?

Team exercise
Nominal group technique (NGT) focuses person–organisation fit

Purpose This exercise helps students relate the behavioural implications of different approaches towards organising, to a match between personal values and expectations. A second bonus is to learn how to employ the nominal group technique (NGT). This technique is a structured, group problem-focusing technique developed by Delbecq *et al.* (1975) that works best when trying to understand a complex question that has many possible answers. Thus, students not only gain insights into organisational design, but also develop a working understanding of NGT as a problem-focusing, problem-solving technique, useful when equal participation is desired (Cook, 1993).

Materials One or two sheets of newsprint for each group of six to seven persons and one felt-tip marker for each. One roll of masking tape for posting results. Each student will bring a sheet of note paper and a pen or pencil to the group.

Time It will require about 30–45 minutes to complete all six phases of the exercise, longer if debriefing is emphasised.

Procedure

1 **Form teams and select question theme (3–5 minutes).** Divide the class into groups of six to seven persons. Each group then selects (on a first request, first served basis) an organisation theme that it will explore during the exercise. Several theme possibilities are suggested below; others can be chosen, subject to the constraint that a theme must invite a large variety of possible responses. Your team may select a theme from the list below or originate your own to insert into the following focusing question.

   The focusing question What values, skills and behaviours do people need in order to be personally successful and valued organisational contributors in an enterprise characterised by this approach to organisation: [insert theme]?

   Suggested themes
   (a) Organisational design emphasising functions
   (b) Organisational design emphasising product line
   (c) Organisational design emphasising customers or market segments
   (d) A mechanistic bureaucracy
   (e) An organic/adaptive (postmodern) organisation
   (f) A highly centralised organisation
   (g) A highly decentralised organisation
   (h) An organisation emphasising self-managed and/or cross-functional teams.
   Once a theme has been selected, take a couple of minutes to make sure everyone understands the question and theme/concept.

2 **Work through the processes of the NGT (20 minutes)** Your instructor will provide detailed action steps (from the *Instructor's Manual*). The basic sequence is as follows:
   (a) individual brainstorming (3–4 minutes)
   (b) round-robin sharing/listing (about 10 minutes)
   (c) clarifying ideas (about 5 minutes)
   (d) individual balloting (3–4 minutes)
   (e) pooling of rankings (3–4 minutes).

3 **Interpretive discussion and debriefing (5–10 minutes)** As a final wrap-up, discuss the implications of the exercise.

   The findings Why did your team select the theme that it did? What did you discover about this organisational model/characteristic that surprised you or caused you to rethink your attraction to it? To what degree does its personal success factors fit your own expectations?

The NGT process Was NGT as satisfying as a general free-for-all discussion? How likely was it that it produced more detailed results? Under what circumstances might you expect the NGT to be of value as an organisational process tool at work?

Case study: **the Salisbury Hotel**

The Salisbury Hotel prides itself on the high standards of personal service it gives its customers. As a four-star hotel with 80 bedrooms, a function suite and a 60-seat restaurant, it certainly has a lot of potential. Set in an old Tudor-style mansion, in a picturesque village near Stratford-upon-Avon, it can tap into the local tourist trade and appeal to overseas tourists who want to capture something of old England.

However, despite its appeal, the Salisbury Hotel has had a severe downturn in business, partly due to the drop in tourism from an outbreak of foot-and-mouth disease on local farms, but also more recently due to the terrorist attacks on 11 September 2001.

The hotel is privately owned and is run by a manager, Tom Banks, who was appointed two months ago. Recently he has been instructed by the owners to cut costs. As the hotel has a reputation for its high levels of personal service, cutting the number of employees does not look like an option, although some streamlining of employee roles may be possible. Tom decides that a more appropriate way to proceed would be to call a staff meeting of department managers and discuss how to cut costs.

The Salisbury Hotel is organised by function, with a front office manager who also has responsibility for sales, an executive head chef, a restaurant manager, a bars manager, a head housekeeper and an events manager. Each manager is responsible for several employees; the restaurant has the largest number of staff with eight full-time employees and a bank of 30 casual staff members, who can be called on for functions, such as weddings and conferences.

Tom calls the managers to a meeting and explains the situation. He asks each manager to identify where there is wastage and how it can be eliminated.

The front office manager, Irene Morgan, complains that it is not so much the wastage but the poor procedures. She says, 'Yesterday, a customer phoned the restaurant for room service and gave an order for smoked salmon sandwiches and a bottle of champagne, yet the restaurant had not passed the receipt on to reception. Therefore the customer checked out without being billed for it, and this is not the first time.'

'That's not true,' replies Aldo Mariniera, the restaurant manager, 'We leave the receipts at reception, but your receptionists are too busy chatting to take any notice.'

'Anyway, if any department needs to cut costs it is the kitchen. They are forever cooking themselves steaks and the amount of brandy they requisition for cooking is unbelievable, it certainly doesn't end up in the food.'

'How dare you say that,' shouts Jean-Claude Le Maire, the head chef. 'Your waiters are forever picking at food in my kitchen, and they encourage the staff to make bigger portions, so that they can get more tips. We never benefit from that.'

'You may not get tips, but everyone's seen you doing deals with suppliers. Anyway, your staff are paid more than mine,' retorted Aldo.

'That's true,' replies Will Yates, the bars manager. 'His staff are paid much more than the rest.'

'That's because mine are artists, they take years to train and if the restaurant gets a Michelin star, it's down to my team, yet you'll all take the benefit.'

At this point Tom decides to end the meeting. 'Look,' he says, 'If we want to keep our jobs we need to work together as a team. I suggest you go away and look at what you are doing then report back to me.'

'Typical of management,' mumbles Jean-Claude, as they leave the meeting. 'All they ever think about is costs and profit, where's the art in that?'

Tom realises he has a problem with his management team. How is he going to get them to work together when not only are they barely talking to each other, but some of them are openly antagonistic?

He decides to think about what managerial action is necessary before he next meets with the team.

Questions for managerial action

1 What organisational concepts are involved in the Salisbury Hotel? What clues lead you to these conclusions?

2 What are the behavioural implications of the organisation of the hotel? What is going well? What is not?

3 What are the obstacles to improved performance?

4 What must Tom do to try and meet the owner's objectives? Think of all the alternatives.

Applied questions

5 Using the organisational star in Exhibit 15-1, can you identify the targets for change?

6 Burns and Stalker (1966) identified the mechanistic and organic organisation. Can their findings be applied to a service industry, and what conclusions can be drawn?

WWW exercise

Manager's Internet tools

Web tips: getting a feel for an organisation on the web

This chapter's opening vignette and 'second look' examined the challenges of teleworking for the organisational structure and mindset within a rapidly changing business environment. CEOs of such companies know that the structure and mindset needs to change to allow their company to compete effectively in a global marketplace. In order to do this, a shift in culture is needed at executive, managerial and employee levels.

World Wide Web search

Pick a company you are interested in possibly working with. Browse its website for information on careers and jobs at the company. See if the website contains information about how the company is organised and what the company expects of its employees. Is the company looking for individuals to work in a functional manner, or does it expect employees to move around within the company, even possibly working on longer-term assignments overseas? What does this imply about the structure of the organisation?

Specific website: www.ford.co.uk

Look at the Ford Motor Company's website, paying particular attention to the section on 'Careers and Career Programmes'. The website will list areas of the company by function, such as human resources, Ford Land, finance, and marketing sales and service. Examine a couple of these areas and note some of the 'expectations' for employees. Also, pay attention to the Graduate Recruitment Programmes and the comments under Career Expectations.

1 Even if you are interested in one particular area – say, finance – does the website lead you to believe that you will be performing finance activities in only one area? What do you think your career in finance might be like at Ford?

2 How is Ford reinforcing its CEO's commitment to deliver and compete in a global environment through its hiring, training and rotation programmes?

LEARNING CHECKLIST

Before you move on you may want to reflect on what you have learnt in this chapter. You should now be able to:

☑ explain why significant changes in the nature of jobs and organisational design are occurring as a result of information technology

☑ draw the four most basic organisational designs and cite two advantages and disadvantages of each

☑ explain how the issues of autonomy, control and integration affect decisions about centralised versus decentralised authority in the design of organisations

☑ contrast the characteristics, strengths and weaknesses of bureaucracy with those of organic, postmodern organisations

☑ state how differences in span of control, hierarchical levels and size produce flatter and more lateral networked organisations

☑ compare the similarities and contrast the differences among quality circles, self-managed teams and cross-functional teams.

Further reading

Furrer, O., Krug, J.A., Sudharshan, D. and Thomas, H. (2004) 'Resource Based Theory and its Link to the Global Strategy, Structure and Performance Relationship: An Integrative Framework', *International Journal of Management & Decision Making* 5(2, 3), p. 99.

Gantman, E.R. (2005) 'The Future of Work: How the New Order of Business will Shape Your Organisation, Your Management Style and Your Life', *Organization Studies* 26(8), p. 1258.

Tan-Solano, M. and Kleiner, B.H. (2001) 'Effects of Telecommuting on Organizational Behaviour', *Management Research News* 24(3/4), pp. 123–126.

Taylor, W. (1991) 'The Logic of Global Business: An Interview with ABB's Percy Barnevik', *Harvard Business Review* 69, March–April, p. 92.

Von Glinow, M.A. and Mohrman, S.A. (eds) (1990) *Managing Complexity in High Technology Organisations.* New York, NY: Oxford University Press.

References

Alexander, J.A. (1991) 'Adaptive Change in Corporate Control Practices', *Academy of Management Journal* 34, March, pp. 162–193.

Anderson, K. (1992) 'Dramatic Turnaround', *USA Today*, 10 April, p. 5B.

Bennis, W. (1993) *An Invented Life: Reflections on Leadership and Change.* Reading, MA: Addison-Wesley, p. 105.

Bergquist, W. (1993) *The Postmodern Organization.* San Francisco, CA: Jossey-Bass.

Burns, T. and Stalker, G.M (1966) *The Management of Innovation.* Tavistock Publications.

Cameron, K.S. (1993) cited in Richard A. Melcher, 'How Goliaths Can Act Like David', *Business Week/Enterprise*, p. 193.

Champy, J. (1995) *Reengineering Management.* New York, NY: Harper Business.

Chandler, A.D. (1962) *Strategy and Structure: Chapters in the History of the Industrial Enterprise.* Garden City, NY: Anchor.

Ciampa, D. (1992) *Total Quality: A User's Guide for Implementation.* Reading, MA: Addison-Wesley; and Donald L. Dewar, *The Quality Circle Handbook.* Red Bluff, CA: The Quality Circle Institute, pp. F1–F7.

Cole, R.E. (1989) *Strategies for Learning: Small-group Activities in American, Japanese, and Swedish Industry.* Berkeley, CA: University of California Press.

Collins, P.D. and Hull, F. (1986) 'Technology and Span of Control: Woodward Revisited', *Journal of Management Studies* 23(2), March, pp. 143–164.

Connor, P.E. (1992) 'Decision-making Participation Patterns: The Role of Organizational Context', *Academy of Management Journal* 35, March, pp. 218–231.

Cook, C.W. (1993) 'Nominal Group Methods Enrich Classroom Learning', in Charles M. Vance (ed.) *Mastering Management Education: Innovations in Teaching Effectiveness.* Newbury Park, CA: Sage, pp. 179–186.

Daft, R.L. and Steers, R.M. (1986) *Organizations: A Micro/Macro Approach.* Glenview, IL: Scott, Foresman and Company, pp. 273–274.

Dean Jr, J.W. and Susman, G.I. (1989) 'Organizing for Manufacturable Design', *Harvard Business Review* 67, January–February, pp. 28–36.

Delbecq, A.L., Van de Ven, A.H. and Gustafson, D.H. (1975) *Group Techniques for Program Planning.* Glenview, IL: Scott, Foresman.

Dewar, D.L. (1980) *The Quality Circle Handbook.* Red Bluff, CA: The Quality Circle Institute.

Drucker, P.F. (1991) 'The New Productivity Challenge', *Harvard Business Review* 69, November–December, pp. 69–79.

Galbraith, J.R. (1995) *Designing Organizations*. San Francisco, CA: Jossey-Bass, pp. 77–79.

Goett, P. (1999) 'Jack Welch: He Brings Good Things to GE', *Journal of Business Strategy*, September–October, pp. 39–40.

Goold, M. (1991) 'Strategic Control in the Decentralized Firm', *Sloan Management Review*, Winter.

Grove, A.S. (1992) 'Technology Industries Outlook', Outlook Conference, San Francisco, CA: The Bay Area Council, 11 March.

Hackman, J.R. (ed.) (1989) *Groups That Work (And Those That Don't): Creating Conditions for Effective Teamwork*. San Francisco, CA: Jossey-Bass.

Hammer, M. (1993) quoted in Thomas A. Stewart, 'Reengineering: The Hot New Managing Tool', *Fortune*, 23 August, p. 42.

Hammer, M. and Champy, J. (1993) *Reengineering the Corporation: A Manifesto for Business Revolution*. New York, NY: Harper Business.

Hanna, D.P. (1988) *Designing Organizations for High Performance*. Reading, MA: Addison-Wesley.

Harry, M.J. (1994) *The Vision of Six Sigma: A Roadmap for Breakthrough*. Phoenix, AZ: Sigma.

Heckscher, C. and Donnellon, A. (eds) (1994) *The Post-bureaucratic Organization*. Thousand Oaks, CA: Sage.

Hill, C.W.L. and Hoskisson, R.E. (1987) 'Strategy and Structure in the Multiproduct Firm', *Academy of Management Review* 12, April, pp. 331–341.

Hirschhorn, L. and Gilmore, T. (1992) 'The New Boundaries of the "Boundaryless" Company', *Harvard Business Review* 70, May–June, pp. 104–115.

Hossein Safizadeh, M.H. (1991) 'The Case of Workgroups in Manufacturing Operations', *California Management Review* 33, Summer, p. 62.

Kaufman, S. (1995) 'Superstores' Low Prices Leave Retailing's Independents Dazed', *San Jose Mercury News*, 10 July, p. 5D.

Keidel, R.W. (1990) 'Triangular Design: A New Organizational Geometry', *Academy of Management Executive* 4, November, pp. 21–37.

Keidel, R.W. (1994) 'Rethinking Organizational Design', *Academy of Management Executive* 8, November, pp. 12–27.

Kerwin, K. (1995) 'The Shape of a New Machine', *Business Week*, 24 July, p. 63.

Kerwin, K. and Peterson, T. (1962) 'Fixing GM: Pages from a Radical Repair Manual', *Business Week*, 16 November, p. 46.

Kirkpatrick, D. (1992) 'Breaking up IBM', *Fortune* 126, 27 July, p. 53.

Lawler III, E.E. (1992) *The Ultimate Advantage: Creating the High-involvement Organization*. San Francisco, CA: Jossey-Bass.

Lawler III, E.E. (1988) *High-involvement Management*. San Francisco, CA: Jossey-Bass.

Lawrence, P.R. and Lorsch, J.W. (1969) *Organization and Environment*. Homewood, IL: Irwin, pp. 23–39.

Mandel, M.J. (2000) 'The New Economy: It Works in America. Will It Go Global?' *Business Week*, 31 January, pp. 73–77.

Marsh, R.M. and Mannari, H. (1981) 'Technology and Size as Determinants of Organisational Structure of Japanese Factories', *Administrative Science Quarterly* 26, pp. 35–56.

Maynard, M., Healey, J.R. and Clements, M. (1992) 'Board Gives Tough Task to Fresh Talent', *USA Today*, 3 November, pp. B1–B2.

Mintzberg, H. (1983) *Structure in Fives: Designing Effective Organizations*. Englewood Cliffs, NJ: Prentice Hall.

Mitroff, I.I. (1988) *Break-away Thinking: How to Challenge Your Business Assumptions.* New York, NY: John Wiley & Sons, p. 21.

Mohrman, S.A. and Cummings, T.G. (1989) *Self-designing Organizations: Learning How to Create High Performance.* Reading, MA: Addison-Wesley.

Mohrman, S.A., Cohen, S.G. and Mohrman Jr, A.M. (1995) *Designing Team-based Organizations: New Forms for Knowledge Work.* San Francisco, CA: Jossey-Bass, pp. 19–21.

O'Neill, H.M. (1994) 'Restructuring, Re-engineering, and Rightsizing: Do the Metaphors Make Sense?' An introduction to the special issue of the *Academy of Management Executive* 8, November, pp. 9–11.

Pasmore, W., Francis, C.E. and Haldeman, J. (1982) 'Sociotechnical Systems: A North American Reflection on Empirical Studies of the 70s', *Human Relations* 35, pp. 1179–1204.

Perrow, C. (1966) *Organisational Analysis: A Sociological View.* Tavistock Publications.

Reich, R.B. (1991) *The Work of Nations.* New York, NY: Alfred A. Knopf, pp. 84–85.

Sager, I. (1999) 'Inside IBM: Internet Business Machines', *Business Week,* 13 December, pp. EB20–EB38.

Schneider, G.P. and Perry, J.T. (2000) *Electronic Commerce.* Cambridge, MA: Course Technology.

Schonberger, R.J. (1994) 'Human Resource Management Lessons from a Decade of Total Quality Management and Reengineering', *California Management Review* 36, Summer, pp. 109–123.

Shea, G.P. (1991) 'Quality Circles: The Danger of Bottled Change', in J. Henry and D. Walker (eds) *Managing Innovation.* London: Sage, pp. 117–126.

Stewart, T.A. (1992) 'The Search for the Organization of Tomorrow', *Fortune,* 18 May, pp. 92–98.

Stewart, T.A. (1994) 'Managing in a Wired Company', *Fortune,* 11 July, p. 44.

Templin, N. (1992) 'Team Spirit: Response to Crisis Made Ford Factories in US More Efficient', *Wall Street Journal Europe,* 17 December, pp. 1, 7.

Thompson Jr, A.A. and Strickland III, A.J. (1995) *Strategic Management: Concepts and Cases* (8th edn). Chicago, IL: Irwin, Chapter 9.

Toffler, A. (1996) *The Third Wave.* New York, NY: Bantam; and 'Riding the Waves', *Worth,* June, pp. 94–100.

Vesey, J.T. (1991) 'The New Competitors: They Think in Terms of "Speed-to-market"', *Academy of Management Executive* 5, May, pp. 23–33.

Weber, J. (1992) 'A Big Company that Works', *Business Week,* 4 May, pp. 124–132.

Wolff, M.F. (1999) 'In the Organisation of the Future, Competitive Advantage Will Lie with Inspired Employees', *Research Technology Management,* July–August, pp. 2–4

Woodward, J. (1965) *Industrial Organisation: Theory and Practice.* London: Oxford University Press.

Zwerman, W.L. (1970) *New Perspectives on Organization Theory.* Westport, CT: Greenwood Press.

Chapter 16

The impact of organisational culture at work

LEARNING OUTCOMES ☑

After studying this chapter you should be able to:

☑ **explain** why organisational assumptions are important and identify three types of assumption that give meaning to culture

☑ **identify** four steps of organisational cultures based on the origin and content of the underlying cultural value systems

☑ **illustrate** how an organisation's core ideology, if truly visionary, provides sustaining consistency of behaviour regardless of changes in strategies and practices

☑ **articulate** how organisational culture guides behaviour

☑ **read** an organisation's culture by observing its physical settings and rituals, and by asking questions about its underlying assumptions and values

☑ **explain** how a founder establishes culture in a new organisation and how subsequent leaders adapt cultural elements to promote adaptive change

☑ **distinguish** four factors useful in comparing and contrasting national cultures.

The opening vignette illustrates how culture can permeate through an organisation and influence its function, yet is difficult to observe and understand.

Hewlett-Packard Company: visionary ideology and organisational culture

Hewlett-Packard (H-P) has the reputation of being an ethical, quality-focused organisation that is driven to innovate. Its success has been guided by a set of core ideology and principles put in place decades ago by founders William Hewlett and David Packard. In a moment of introspective reflection, Bill Hewlett wrote in 1990: 'As I look back on my life's work, I'm probably most proud of having helped to create a company that by virtue of its values, practices, and success has had a tremendous impact on the way companies are managed around the world. In addition, I am particularly proud that I'm leaving behind an ongoing organisation that can live on as a role model long after I'm gone.'

What sets H-P apart from most not so visionary companies is the collective focus on building an organisation first and foremost that would sustain innovation and an environment conducive to the creation of great products. Products and profits are a function of the commitment to make technical contributions to the fields in which the company participates, to build in respect and opportunity for H-P employees, and to contribute to the communities in which the company operates. These are some of the ideological values that are fundamental to H-P's way of doing business. They are articulated and lived in an organisational culture code of conduct long known as the 'H-P Way', which Dave Packard summarised in a post-retirement retrospective as follows.

1 **Put profits into perspective.** Maintain balance between short-term profits and the need to invest for long-term strength and growth.

2 **Act only when you can make a contribution.** Expand and diversify only when you can build on strengths and have the capacity to make a contribution.

3 **Put customers first.** Every person should think continually about how their activities relate to servicing our customers.

4 **Commit the business to quality.** From the start we had more reason than most to emphasise quality, as customers relied on the accuracy of our measurement instruments.

5 **Have trust in people.** Pick the most capable people for each assignment, then keep them enthusiastic about what they are doing.

6 **Keep the organisation flexible.** Even widely decentralised companies should be alert to signs of cumbersome bureaucracy, the same liability that drags down centralised organisations.

7 **Keep the doors open.** People using the open door must never be subjected to reprisals or other consequences.

8 **Manage by objectives.** Overall goals are clearly stated and agreed to, and people are given the flexibility to work towards those goals in ways they determine are best.

For decades these cultural ideals have served the H-P organisation well as it has transitioned from a scientific instruments business to a computer systems and computer printer business to unknown future possibilities. Hewlett-Packard has not been without its moments of crisis and disappointments from product failures, but its core ideology has provided a constancy of purpose and the general ways for getting there. The leaders, strategies and products change, but the ideological values endure and drive the company to 'develop an environment in which individuals can be creative'.

The core values lead to an inner drive to continuously improve and innovate. As conveyed by a marketing manager, people within H-P cannot rest on past laurels: 'We're proud of our successes, and we celebrate them. But the real excitement comes in figuring out how we can do even better in the future. It's a never-ending process of seeing how far we can go. There's no ultimate finish line where we can say "we've arrived". I never want us to be satisfied with our success, for that's when we'll begin to decline.'

Sources: adapted from David Packard (1995) *The HP Way: How Bill Hewlett and I Built Our Company*. New York, NY: Harper Business; James C. Collins and Jerry I. Porras (1994) *Built to Last: Successful Habits of Visionary Companies*. New York, NY: Harper Business; and Eric Nee (2000) 'Hewlett-Packard's New E-vangelist', *Fortune*, 10 January, pp. 166–167.

Discussion questions

1 How would you describe the culture at Hewlett-Packard?
2 How can only one person influence the culture of an organisation?

Organisational culture is not always easy to observe and understand, for it tends to subtly permeate most aspects of organisational life. Although culture is one of the newer organisational concepts, it has quickly been recognised as a key predictor of employee satisfaction an competitive performance. The rapid acceptance of its importance in understanding and influencing organisational behaviour moved from obscurity to world-class prominence during the last quarter of the twentieth century. Although misunderstood by some as fuzzy and soft, organisational cultures, like organisational structures, can play a powerful role in supporting missions and strategies. Jacob (1995) observes, 'Corporate cultures that tend to put their three constituencies – shareholders, customers, and employees – on the same plane, as opposed to putting shareholders first, are perversely the ones that do best for shareholders.' Hewlett-Packard excels at balancing concern for these constituencies.

How assumptions give meaning to organisational culture

The concept of culture is about as old as civilisation itself. Linton (1945) provides a timeless definition of **culture** as 'the configuration of learned behaviour and results of behaviour whose

culture
The pattern of learned behaviours shared and transmitted among the members of a society.

component elements are shared and transmitted to the members of a particular society'. So defined, China has a culture – a commonality of beliefs, experiences, values and expectations – that sets it apart from Egypt, India, Poland and Mexico.

For centuries people have expected national or ethnic cultures to cause the people of one region to behave differently from those of neighbouring countries. For example, Australia's 'She'll be right' mentality causes inhabitants to concentrate primarily on enjoying life, believing the natural resources of their country provide the means to do so. This is substantially different from the more competitive and achievement-orientated behaviour found in the ancestral homes of most New Zealanders. The American's ability at self-promotion is often seen as boasting by the more modest English. Similarly, today's managers know the culture of British Airways differs from that of easyJet or Go. In addition, within each major division of such large organisations, employees will experience somewhat unique localised subcultures. By virtue of organisational membership and its prevailing culture, employees thus behave in predictably different ways.

Organisational assumptions guide behaviour

As a relatively new concept, organisational culture is open to many interpretations. Pascale (1984) suggests that some managers think of organisational culture as simply 'the way we do things around here', while others believe it is a more complex 'set of shared values, beliefs and assumptions that get everyone headed in the same direction'. Still others might say that culture inculcates members in the ways of an organisation and gives it meaning. Whatever the interpretation, most managers agree that when members are aware of the organisational culture, formal controls are less necessary.

organisational culture
The fundamental assumptions people share about an organisation's values, beliefs, norms, symbols, language, rituals and myths – all the expressive elements that give meaning to organisational membership and are accepted as guides to behaviour.

According to Pettigrew (1979), **organisational culture** describes the fundamental assumptions people share about an organisation's values, beliefs, norms, symbols, language, rituals and myths that give meaning to organisational membership and are collectively accepted by a group as guides to expected behaviours. The critical element is for these collections of fundamental assumptions to be *shared and accepted* by organisational members. When these assumptions are accepted as inviolate keys to organisational success, behaviours will tend to be more consistent with these guides to action.

Schein (1985) suggests that patterns of assumptions emerge as a group learns from founders and through discovery or invention to cope with its problems of external adaptation and internal integration. More of Edgar Schein's definitions of culture can be seen in the 'Research focus' box. Management philosopher Peter Drucker has even built a theory of business around three key assumptions people make about their organisation, assumptions that emerge through experience over time. Drucker (1994) writes:

> The assumptions about *environment* define what an organisation is paid for. The assumptions about *mission* define what an organisation considers to be meaningful results ... Finally, the assumptions about *core competencies* define where an organisation must excel in order to maintain leadership.

As organisational members become aware of core assumptions, they learn the limits of acceptable behaviours. Some behaviours are prescribed and encouraged, such as IBM's tenet of working with customers to help solve problems and extend product applications. Other behaviours are proscribed and are to be avoided, such as the Inland Revenue's norm that an inspector should never accept a free lunch from a client or organisation, to avoid a potential conflict of interest.

Schein (1983) suggests that most organisations develop patterns of cultural assumptions that answer such fundamental questions as: How does our organisation relate to its environment? How do we learn and communicate? What do we expect of people and relationships? What constitutes successful results? At what do we excel? As answers emerge through actions and behaviours that seem to work, they become incorporated into patterned sets of

strong culture
Achieved when most members
accept the interrelated assumptions
that form an internally consistent
cultural system.

fundamental assumptions that create an enduring cultural system. Exhibit 16-1 shows two contrasting examples of basic elements woven into internally coherent cultural patterns. According to Schein (1984), we say an organisation has a **strong culture** when most members accept a set of interrelated assumptions that forms an internally consistent cultural system that endures over time.

Assumptions define relationships to the environment

Some environmental assumptions refer to the natural environment: will the organisation exploit or seek harmony with nature? This is an issue for home developers, oil companies, forest products firms and public utilities. One study, by Henriques and Sadorsky (1999), classified 400 firms into four environmental profiles – reactive, defensive, accommodative and proactive – and found that proactive firms take the time to manage environmental issues with all stakeholders (except the media).

More often this set of assumptions refers to the industry environment created by organisational decisions. According to Weick (1969), each organisation shapes or *enacts* its own unique environment as managers make decisions and selectively respond more to some external elements than to others. Environmentally related assumptions concerning customers, markets and competitors frame the reason for the organisation's existence and make it unique.

EXHIBIT 16–1   GEM and MAX: two contrasting cultural systems

GEM Corporation
The cultural system
1   People are responsible and motivated to govern themselves.
2   Individuals are the ultimate source of ideas.
3   Truth is pragmatically discovered by using groups to test ideas and competitively try out alternatives.
4   Opposing ideas are healthy because members view themselves as an organisational family that will take care of each other.

The observable behaviours
People work in an open office landscape with few doors on offices; there is much wandering around; conversations are intense and at times argumentative; informality prevails.

MAX Corporation
The cultural system
1   People are disciplined and loyal in carrying out directives.
2   Organisational relationships respect hierarchy; they are linear and vertical.
3   Truth comes from better-educated, older, higher-status members.
4   Each person has a niche or turf that cannot be invaded.
5   The organisation will take care of its members within each department unit.

The observable behaviours
People work inside their offices with doors closed; there is little conversation except by prearranged appointments; meetings are conducted with strict agendas; deference to authority is respected; formality prevails.

Sources: 'Culture in Organizations: A Case Study', by William G. Dyer Jr, Working Paper #1279–82. Copyright 1983 by the Sloan School of Management. All rights reserved. The MAX example is reprinted from 'Coming to a New Awareness of Organizational Culture', by Edgar H. Schein, *Sloan Management Review*, Winter 1984, excerpts from p. 5, by permission of publisher. Copyright by Sloan Management Review Association. All rights reserved.

Research focus: **Edgar Schein**

One of the most accepted definitions of culture is the one given by Schein (1984). He argues that:

> [Culture is] . . . a pattern of basic assumptions – invented, discovered or developed by a given group as it learns to cope with its problems of external adaptation and internal integration – that has worked well enough to be considered valuable and, therefore, to be taught to new members as the correct way to perceive, think and feel in relation to those problems.

Schein suggests that culture has three interwoven levels, some of which may be seen while others are invisible. These three levels are:

1 basic assumptions – how and who makes decisions, the belief in the firm's ability to compete, the type of desirable behaviour in the workplace or how individuals earn respect

2 values and beliefs – the type of rewards, the values placed on honesty, trust, effort

3 artefacts and creations – norms, rites, myths, stories, language.

Schein suggests that these basic assumptions form the innermost core of a culture – they are the fundamental beliefs that are buried in people's consciousness and are often taken for granted.

As organisations evolve, the history and traditions, often put there by the founder, can have a huge impact on its culture and although the goals of an organisation may change, there is often a tenuous link back to the early days. Culture does not remain static, but as it changes there is always a link with the previous phase. Schein calls this 'hybridisation of culture'. It is a slow process and Schein has identified two generic problems that occur at every stage. These are:

- ensuring external adaptation and survival – such as developing consensus with regard to mission and goals

- ensuring internal integration – such as working groups, division of power, rewards and incentives.

Once the culture is established new members need to be socialised into the appropriate ways of behaving. This is seen as cultural replication and maintenance. Schein explains this as happening during the selection process. The selection of new members is based on the perception that they will fit in. Although new members are unlikely to be a perfect match, peer pressure helps them to conform; if they are later found to deviate then they are removed.

Edgar Schein's contribution is useful in that it has a sound theoretical base and can help us explain organisational culture; but care needs to be taken with the view that culture can be taught, as it is more usual for it to be learnt through observation, imitating role models and the desire to fit in.

Asda's owner, Wal-Mart, is either loved or hated because of its strategy of expanding rapidly to dominate general merchandise retailing in its chosen locations. But more important than its choice of store location is its fundamental commitment: 'We exist to provide value to our customers – to make their lives better via lower prices and greater selection in clean modern stores; all else is secondary' (Collins and Porras, 1994). Culturally, managers work to bond associates (non-management employees) to the firm's ideal of putting customers first by working in partnership with associates to create passion and commitment through spontaneously leading cheers, giving out awards and promoting contests.

By contrast, Waitrose, part of the John Lewis Partnership, tends to have its stores in more affluent areas. The stores are smaller and the focus is on quality rather than being cost competitive. The products are concentrated in the food area; it does not sell electrical goods. The staffing policies are different: although Asda calls its staff colleagues, Waitrose calls them partners, which, because of its profit-sharing scheme, enables staff to benefit from the company's profits. Although these two retailers often share the same markets, their widely divergent patterns of relating to their environments (from stakeholders to physical space) have created entirely different organisational cultures.

Assumptions promote learning and communicating

Learning involves seeking to understand reality and discover the basis for truth. Senge (1990) suggests that organisations are capable of learning just as are individuals, and thus differ in how employees are expected to define reality. Some organisations seek to learn empirically through experimenting and gathering feedback. Others believe truth is revealed intuitively or comes only from higher management. At a practical level, these issues frame assumptions about management's planning time frame (short or long term), concepts of space and equity (open cubicles or private offices), and beliefs about how to achieve innovation (whether driven by management or teams throughout the organisation).

Language and communication norms also help define organisational reality. In some bureaucracies managers are conditioned that unless they 'put it in writing', nothing gets done. In faster-changing, more informal environments, managers expect that once they leave a meeting, their agreed-upon actions will be performed without their having to exchange minutes or memos – a spoken tradition prevails. Depending on what has and has not worked in the past, members of an organisation develop an acceptable and somewhat unique basis for learning and communicating.

Assumptions tell about people and relationships

Organisations tend to develop common assumptions about human nature and how people are to be treated. Nahapiet and Ghosal (1998) suggest that practices within some politically active organisations presume people are self-centred, personally competitive and willing to sacrifice others for personal gain. In other organisations, people are believed to be team players willing to make self-sacrifices for the common good, developing 'social capital' through a network of relationships. According to Bianco (2000), Charles B. Wang assembled Computer Associates International into the second largest software firm (after Microsoft) in part by insisting on unquestioned employee loyalty and ruthless candour in relationships.

The culture also reflects assumptions about who is to have power and how power is to be used, which affects relationships among people. In founding Ford Motor Co., Henry Ford built the firm on core values about 'reasonable profits', 'good wages' for workers, and 'spiritual principles' that for a while seemed to be forgotten when Henry Ford II managed the firm. Under his long reign, the company was notoriously centralised and capricious, which encouraged political competition among managers. In contrast, while he was CEO of Chrysler, Lee Iacocca (equally flamboyant) initiated practices that delegated more and created a team atmosphere. Chrysler's team climate brought out the best in its people as a way of helping to manage costs, reduce break-even volume levels, and redesign quality cars to meet customer wants (Flint, 1990; Petre and Schlender, 1999; Wetlaufer, 1999).

One disturbing research study by Blum et al. (1994) found that dimensions of organisational culture were good predictors of the degree to which women would be accepted into management positions. The process of cumulative efforts by the organisation to adapt to environmental forces shaped attitudes and behaviours towards women in management. Even though the percentage of management positions filled by women has approximately doubled in the past 25 years (to about 40 per cent), the culture in many organisations, especially in manufacturing, perpetuates the stereotype that management is for men. Some firms actively monitor and put systems into place to redress the balance.

Assumptions link competencies to mission

As emphasised in earlier chapters, the organisational mission has meaning when stakeholders buy into it, when it is assumed to provide focus for success. The companion for enabling the *mission* to be reality based is for managers and employees to also hold common assumptions about the *competencies* that give them advantage in the market *environment*. In making this observation, Drucker (1999) subsequently reflected on the competence and productivity of one type of employee – knowledge workers – where continuous learning and teaching have to be built into the job. Making productive use of technically competent knowledge workers is necessary for organisational survival and viability: 'The ability to attract and hold the best of the knowledge workers is the first and most fundamental precondition.'

Assumptions about what constitutes technological competencies and how to enable knowledge workers to create innovation differ across organisational cultures. One study of 440 firms in 34 technical fields, by Granstrand *et al.* (1997), found that the most robust set of assumptions and practices focused more on 'distributed' rather than 'core' competencies. Organisations that expect their technical talent to focus on core competencies limit inquisitiveness and exploration to a narrow range of technologies that feed into established, more certain product lines. Organisations that encourage 'distributed' competencies realise a more diversified base of technological involvement, across an increasing number of technical fields, in different parts of the organisation and among different strategic objectives. The distributed emphasis stimulates creative discovery and competence enhancement that leads to combining technological competencies into a more diverse stream of emerging, uncertain products and services. Furthermore, Dyer and Singh (1998) suggest that organisations that develop technology-sharing relationships or networks in collaboration with other organisations are more likely to produce a sustained comparative advantage.

Why organisational value systems differ

The assumptions most critical to organisational behaviour are those shared values that lie at the heart of human character and societal behaviour. Rokeach (1973) defines values as the enduring beliefs and expectations held to be important guides to behaviour by a person or group of people. An individual's personal values learned from formative early experiences guide his or her other behaviour throughout life. Thumin *et al.* (1995) found if a certain set of values is held to be very important, it enables the person to behave consistently across different situations. When asked to rank 15 organisational value statements, a sample of professionals in organisations generated high agreement that the top five organisational values are:

values
The enduring beliefs and expectations that a person or group holds to be important guides to behaviour.

1 provide excellent service to customers

2 operate in a highly ethical manner at all times

  3 provide products and/or services of excellent quality

  4 consistently make a fair and reasonable profit (not maximise profits)

  5 staff the organisation with high-calibre employees from top to bottom.

Just as occurs in business education and training, religious and fraternal or service organisations have long sought to pass along their values to new members or to people generally. People who participated in scouting in their youth may remember the scout oath, that 'a scout is trustworthy, loyal, helpful, friendly, courteous, kind', and so on. Or, for many religions, the Ten Commandments serve as reminders that 'Thou shall not...'. The laws of a nation are usually based on shared values as to how people ought to behave and what the consequences should be if a person violates those codified values. Before reading on, consider your own values as expressed in elements of organisational culture by completing the 'Your turn' exercise.

Your turn

What do you value in organisational culture?

For each question, circle the most valued option.

  1 Which would you prefer as an organisational motto?
  (a) The customer is king.
  (b) We're number one.

  2 In discussions with colleagues, which would you value?
  (a) A focus on goals, processes and organisational systems.
  (b) Stories of success and superiority over competition.

  3 What would you prefer to find in offices and work areas?
  (a) An emphasis on function over form and getting work done.
  (b) Elegance, attention to symbols of success, clean desks.

  4 With which organisation would you rather identify?
  (a) One with a reputation for conservative stability.
  (b) One noted for the bold moves of its leader.

  5 How would you like to be socialised in organisational lore?
  (a) Hear stories about average people doing good things.
  (b) Hear stories about the exploits of founders.

  6 On which would you rather base your organisational identity?
  (a) A history of providing good service and fair treatment.
  (b) Your association with a dynamic industry leader.

Scoring In each of the four fields identified below, give yourself 1 point for each of the responses you circled:

Functional: 1A 2A 3A = _____   Elitist: 1B 2B 3B = _____
Traditional: 4A 5A 6A = _____   Charismatic: 4B 5B 6B = _____

From your scores in each of the rows above, circle the word that had the highest score in the pair, either functional or elitist, and either traditional or charismatic. Now, turn to Exhibit 16-2 and circle on the model the combination you seem to value the most. The text explains your organisational culture preference.

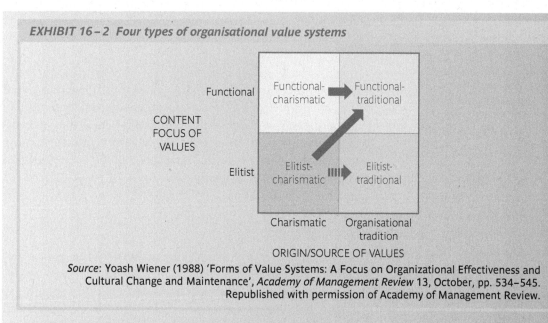

EXHIBIT 16–2 Four types of organisational value systems

Source: Yoash Wiener (1988) 'Forms of Value Systems: A Focus on Organizational Effectiveness and Cultural Change and Maintenance', *Academy of Management Review* 13, October, pp. 534–545. Republished with permission of Academy of Management Review.

When organisational values are strong, one of these four systems typically emerges as the dominant pattern. Since charismatic types are inherently more unstable, the arrows show possible movements towards greater organisational effectiveness (with solid arrows stronger than dashed). Values embedded in tradition with a functional focus are thus more effective in bringing about behaviours necessary for long-term success.

Factors defining organisational value systems

Every organisation is capable of generating and passing along a set of values that is more or less unique to it. An organisation's values convey what behaviours and beliefs are important to its success. According to England (1967), a set of values becomes an **organisational value system** when those core values are shared by the majority of organisational members. Values take on meaning within an organisation through what is espoused (what people say) and by inference (what people do). To understand the impact of organisational values on behaviour, you need to look both at the origin of those values and at their content or meaning.

organisational value system

A core set of values shared by the majority of organisational members, typically differentiated by the origin and content of those enduring values.

Origins of organisational values

charismatic-based values

Values originating from a strong leader, usually the founder, which tend to be internalised by members as long as they look to the leader for guidance and inspiration.

Research by Wiener (1988) suggests that organisational values originate from either charismatic leadership or organisational traditions. **Charismatic-based values** originate from a strong leader, usually the founder, and tend to be internalised by members only as long as they identify with the leader, to whom they look for guidance and inspiration. As the pioneer of IBM, Tom Watson is credited with making explicit and inculcating many of the values that help give IBM meaning and guidance today. For better or worse, the same was true of Margaret Thatcher's long reign and influence on shaping the 'me' culture of the 1980s. Certainly Anita Roddick created an enduring organisational value system for the Body Shop. For most small firms, the values of the founder-owner directly shape the organisational culture.

tradition-based values
Values deeply rooted in historical practices, which provide stability as they are passed from generation to generation.

Alternatively, values can emerge out of organisational traditions that are more anonymous in origin. Tradition-based values are deeply rooted in historical practices and lend stability to the organisation because they are readily passed from generation to generation of organisational members. British Airways and the Royal Marines each has a culture that has been passed on largely by tradition. People working for each organisation are well aware of what it stands for and how individual members can expect to be treated.

Content of organisational values

functional values
Express a normative mode of conduct that tells members what they should pay attention to (e.g. customer service, innovation, quality).

elitist values
Focus on the perceived superiority of the organisation in comparison to others.

The content or interpreted meaning of values is based on either functional or elitist ideals. Functional values express a normative mode of conduct that tells members what they should pay attention to, such as customer service, innovation, speed and quality. Elitist values focus more on the perceived superiority of the organisation in comparison to other organisations. Functional values offer more constructive guidance for members' behaviours. For example, if a firm values quality, everyone should be empowered to make continuous improvements and eliminate dysfunctional practices. Elitist values, on the other hand, attempt to instil pride in membership, creating a 'we're number one' mentality. Elitist values can create an aloofness that weakens members' abilities to confront changing realities.

Four alternative value systems define organisational cultures

Exhibit 16-2 presents what researchers call a '2 by 2 model' identifying four types of organisational value system. Of the four, the elitist-charismatic value system is weakest and least stable; the functional-traditional is strongest and most enduring.

Functional-traditional values

Wiener (1988) contends that the functional-traditional values are 'most likely to contribute to the development of environmentally viable values and, consequently, to organisational effectiveness', functional values that emerge from traditional practices are most supportive of managers' needs to set consistent goals, policies and strategies. Hayes (1985) suggests that, rather than being pushed from the top down, they evolve slowly through feedback from incremental changes, which both gives these values permanence and makes them difficult for competitors to copy. The values of co-operation, a sense of shared obligations, quality, loyalty and focused effort, which characterise Japanese firms, are typical examples. They are also infused in such successful British firms as the Virgin Group, TXU Energy and the John Lewis Partnership.

Elitist-charismatic values

At the opposite end of the long-term effectiveness spectrum are elitist-charismatic values. These values usually come from the flamboyant, eccentric personality of a founder who creates a product or service that meets early market success. Members often revere the charismatic leader's 'cause' and what he or she has been able to achieve. Anita Roddick imparts such values at the Body Shop. Apple Computer began as a culture based on charismatic leadership (from Steve Jobs and Steve Wozniak) and elitist attitudes ('we're out to change the world'). With changes in leadership (from Jobs to John Sculley to Gil Amelio then back to Jobs), Apple struggled in the early and mid-1990s to refocus organisational values and strategy, and is probably in the functional-charismatic domain today.

Functional-charismatic values

This culture has the potential for longer-term effectiveness and probably represents a transitional phase along the path towards functional-traditional values. Any value system of charismatic origin tends to be temporary, linked to the personal ideals of the founder. But dedication to functional values such as quality and risk-taking puts the focus on doing what is right rather than on elitist pride. Asda's owner, Wal-Mart, made this transition in the 1990s whereas Hewlett-Packard and McDonald's completed the shift long ago.

Elitist-traditional values

Finally, some organisations use tradition as a way of intentionally sustaining long-term elitism. Usually these are smaller, niche marketers who appeal to clients attracted by snob appeal or the long tradition of being perceived as superior or exclusive. Some universities, law firms and brokerage houses convey elitist traditions and successfully control client access to uphold the elitist posture. The bank Coutts & Co. is an example of this; it is known as the Queen's Bank and has offices in some of the best locations, such as London's Mayfair.

The critical question is how well the culture with its system of values serves the organisation during periods of change, especially when environmental forces are shifting. When a new strategy is required, strong cultures that once served an organisation well are now likely to inhibit its adaptation. Following increased competition in the 1990s, Marks & Spencer struggled for years to accept the decline of its once dominant household name in the marketplace. Its long-standing elitist-traditional values, which assumed it had superiority over its competitors with its 'buy British' policy, fell apart when its competitors were offering the same quality at a cheaper price by purchasing from overseas. Alternatively, as will be seen at the end of the chapter (in the 'second look' section) when Carly Fiorina took over as Hewlett-Packard's new CEO, she sought to sharpen the focus of long-standing values within the prevailing 'H-P Way' culture. She is reinforcing H-P's core ideology.

A core ideology connects purpose and values

In their landmark longitudinal study of 18 'visionary companies' in paired comparisons with 18 not-so-visionary companies, Collins and Porras (1994) found that all the companies that others sought to emulate built their organisations on a foundation core ideology. An organisation's core ideology combines essential and enduring core values as a small set of guiding principles with a purpose that uniquely defines the fundamental reasons for its existence beyond making money. Ideology provides for stability over generations of management; it is a set of precepts around which the organisation functions irrespective of its leaders, its strategies, its lines of business and its practices as they change over time.

core ideology
Combines essential and enduring core values as a set of guiding principles with a purpose that uniquely defines the fundamental reasons for the organisation's existence (beyond making money).

Purpose more than profits

Collins and Porras drew two interesting conclusions about the power of core ideology that run contrary to conventional wisdom. These visionary companies discarded the 'profit maximisation myth'. In 17 out of 18 paired cases, they built the organisation around ideology that had more than economic purpose relative to their comparison firms. The ideology defines: 'This is who we are; this is what we stand for; this is what we are all about.' With a clear ideology, an organisation builds a driving motivation around a purpose that serves society and as a derivative generates a stream of earnings to sustain the enterprise.

David Packard defined H-P's purpose as 'first and foremost to make a contribution to society' and that 'our main task is to design, develop, and manufacture the finest electronic [equipment] for the advancement of science and the welfare of humanity'. This purpose combined with values in the H-P Way (described in the vignette at the beginning of the chapter) to shape the enduring, visionary ideology. Packard also made it clear that anyone who could not accept profit as one of the company's objectives 'has no place either now or in the future on the management team of this company' (Packard, 1957).

Ideologies vary across organisations

A second key finding was that there was not a consistency of the themes or values embedded in the core ideologies of sustainable visionary companies. Collins and Porras report that 'although certain themes show up in a number of the visionary companies (such as contribution, integrity, respect for the individual employee, service to the customer, being on the creative or leading edge, or responsibility to the community), *no single item shows up consistently across all the visionary companies*'.

Some firms, such as Johnson & Johnson and Wal-Mart, make *customers* central to their ideology; others, such as Waitrose and Marriott, focus on *concern for employees*; some, such as Ford and Disney, place *products or services* as central to their core; firms such as Sony and Boeing made audacious *risk-taking* a central element; while some, such as 3M and Motorola, target *innovation* as the key to ideology.

What was central to all, however, was the *authenticity* of the ideology. Behaviour and actions that are consistently aligned with the stated ideology are more critical than the content of the ideology per se. This general principle was emphasised by IBM's Thomas J. Watson Jr in his booklet, *A Business and its Beliefs*: 'If an organisation is to meet the challenges of a changing world, it must be prepared to change everything about itself except [its basic] beliefs as it moves through corporate life ... The only sacred cow in an organisation should be its basic philosophy of doing business.'

The functions of organisational cultures

Small firms draw on organisational culture to help establish competitive advantages in niche markets. This is very true of easyJet and British Airways, one with no-frills cheap air transportation, the other now aiming at the business market and clients who wants comfort over price. Large firms, such as Unilever, IBM and Sony, create global markets and worldwide competition through deliberate strategies and cultures of disciplined managerial practices. Similar actions and behaviours are used by the various branches of the military, drawing on the one hand on sets of rational managerial tools (strategy, technology, organisational structure, information systems, policies) and on the other on organisational cultural elements (ritual, tradition, symbols) to carry out co-ordinated missions. Although less overt than the traditional managerial tools, organisational culture contributes as a guide to consistent behaviour by reinforcing capabilities and strengthening sources of competitive advantage.

Culture complements rational managerial tools

Organisations use many tools and processes to channel, guide and change behaviour. Unlike the rational tools in the manager's portfolio, organisational culture cannot provide a quick fix or abruptly change organisational behaviour. Culture epitomises the expressive character of organisations; it is communicated less through objective realism and more through symbolism, feelings and the meaning behind language, behaviours and physical settings. Exhibit 16-3 contrasts the elements of organisational culture with the rational tools of management.

Hewlett-Packard has used management tools to change its organisational structure as it periodically branched into new lines of business. Company policies (more management tools) are extensive and detailed in writing, intended to provide consistency in the performance of routine tasks. But H-P also seeks to influence employee behaviour in less direct ways by promoting the H-P Way, cultural beliefs supported by management that emphasise a disciplined, team approach to innovation. When John Young, the first non-founder CEO of H-P announced his retirement, he noted that the H-P Way withstands changing times and is transportable worldwide: 'The thing that fascinates me as much as anything is to go to Britain or China or Hungary or Czechoslovakia, and already they have the same team spirit and the value system in place.'

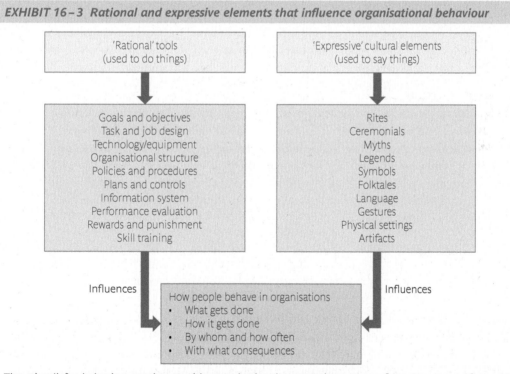

EXHIBIT 16–3 Rational and expressive elements that influence organisational behaviour

'Rational' tools
(used to do things)

'Expressive' cultural elements
(used to say things)

Rational tools	Expressive cultural elements
Goals and objectives	Rites
Task and job design	Ceremonials
Technology/equipment	Myths
Organisational structure	Legends
Policies and procedures	Symbols
Plans and controls	Folktales
Information system	Language
Performance evaluation	Gestures
Rewards and punishment	Physical settings
Skill training	Artifacts

Influences   Influences

How people behave in organisations
- What gets done
- How it gets done
- By whom and how often
- With what consequences

The stimuli for behaving consistent with organisational expectations comes from two types of sources. Each can be equally effective in getting things done in organisations. Cultural elements are defined throughout the chapter.

Source: the rational tools are common to organisation practice; the expressive cultural forms were suggested by Janice M. Meyer and Jarrison M. Trice (1994) 'Studying Organizational Cultures through Rites and Ceremonials', *Academy of Management Review* 9, October, pp. 653–669.

Rational tools such as technology and structure are designed to do things. The *expressive practice of culture* reflects more a way of communicating the way we do things. One of these elements aims to initiate deliberate rational actions, the other to influence the ways in which human behaviours carry out the actions. Managers, engineers and other trained professionals who just want to get on with the jobs to be done, may not perceive the expressive qualities conveyed in organisational rites, rituals, legends and other cultural elements. But, according to Beyer and Trice (1987), 'to overlook these expressive consequences is to miss much of the significance of what is really happening in organisations'.

Culture supports (or resists) strategic changes

For better or worse, the intended strategy of a firm is affected by the behaviours of the people expected to carry it out. Culture serves as a rudder to keep the firm's strategy on course. Reimann and Wiener (1988) suggest that, increasingly, managers and consultants are recognising that 'while corporate strategy may control a firm's successes or failure, corporate culture can make or break that strategy'. Changes in technology are having a major impact on how organisations behave, as can be seen from the Technology Transformation box.

Strategy is a rational management process that leads to actions intended to match a firm's product and service offering to a specific market or type of customer. Culture is the expressive back-up that influences how well the strategy is implemented. Managers are often blindsided when they try to introduce radical strategic changes that run contrary to cultural expectations. For example, in the mid-1970s, the petroleum industry appeared to face diminished growth and mounting geopolitical pressures from oil-exporting nations. Two CEOs of major oil companies were determined to diversify their businesses to reduce their dependence on oil (a major strategy change). But after five years of failing with various acquisition attempts, both firms remained firmly committed to oil – and both CEOs were ousted. *Business Week* concluded:

> Each of the CEOs has been unable to implement his strategy, not because it was theoretically wrong or bad but because neither had understood that his company's culture was so entrenched in the traditions and values of doing business as oilmen that employees resisted – and sabotaged – the radical changes that the CEOs tried to impose ... If implementing [strategies] violates employees' basic beliefs about their roles in the company, or the traditions that underlie the corporation's culture, they are doomed to fail.

In strong culture organisations, such as H-P, the Body Shop or John Lewis, core ideologies are widely shared among employees, and certain behaviours are honoured, even celebrated. What do you suspect happens when two strong culture firms join together through a merger?

Culture helps socialise new members

According to Wanous (1980), many firms try to hire people they believe will be compatible with the culture – that is, who will 'fit in and be one of us'. Experienced members then work to socialise newcomers in the ways of the culture, which involves changing attitudes and beliefs to achieve an internalised commitment to the organisation. Socialisation is the process by which new members are indoctrinated in the expectations of the organisation and its cultural norms, or unwritten codes of behaviour. One organisa-

socialisation

A process by which new members are indoctrinated into the expectations and rituals of the organisation – its cultural norms or unwritten codes of behaviour.

Boeing's cutting-edge digital system will make its debut in the new *Star Wars* film

With the latest release of the *Star Wars* movie, a high-tech revolution is taking place a few miles down the road in Brixton, south-east London.

Star Wars: Episode II – Attack of the Clones is the world's first blockbuster movie to have been shot entirely on digital camera and premiered using digital technology. The industry believes it is only a matter of time before projector reels and wheels, even 35 mm film, are obsolete.

Films of the future will be transmitted exclusively using the superior digital format. When the Odeon premiered *Star Wars* it used digital technology. But the Ritzy Cinema in Brixton will go one further, making use of cutting-edge satellite systems when it starts screening the film.

The two cinemas are among the few in the UK to boast digital technology.

For both the film industry and cinemas, the switch to digital makes financial sense. Hollywood spends £800 million a year copying and distributing films to cinemas, the move to digital will cut costs by £100 million.

The major pioneer in the world of digital cinema has been the aircraft manufacturing giant Boeing. Its technology, which uses satellite, fibre-optics and physical media technologies, has been installed in 23 US cinemas.

The advantage of the satellite method is that a file can be transmitted to many destinations simultaneously; this will save 75 per cent of distribution costs.

Digital should also help eliminate piracy and even has environment benefits, as celluloid, costly and messy to dispose of, has to be destroyed after only three weeks of use.

So what's the catch?

As with new technology, the costs of buying and installing the digital equipment are high. This means it may be affordable only to the largest players, that smaller film-makers may find themselves priced out of the market and audiences will be forced into the multiplexes, where they are likely to have to pay more.

Source: *Financial Times*, 12/13 May 2002.

Discussion questions

1 What impact does new technology have on culture?

2 Does new technology mean culture is becoming global?

technology transformation

---

tional researcher emphasises that it is the perceived attractiveness of an organisation's culture that enables it to recruit and retain the technical talent necessary to build competitive capabilities:

> The assets of Intel and Motorola are actually the knowledge and energy of the engineers who create the designs. The ability of Intel and Motorola to compete in the new economy depends on their ability to attract, retain, motivate, and co-ordinate talented engineers. (Galbraith, 1995)

Organisations with strong ideologies and cultures devote considerable time to indoctrinating and training new members in the ways of the organisation. Bureaucratic organisations typically devote attention to detailed explanations of rules and procedures. Those who emphasise rules sprinkle their explanations with folklore and myths about the errant soul who tried to introduce personal reforms or who took exception to the rules, only to be castigated for not operating within expected bounds. For such organisations, myths about heroes retell the virtues of paying your dues and being a loyal member over the long term. This can have an adverse affect when health and safety issues are involved, as can be seen from the Eye on Ethics box.

By contrast, socialisation into younger, more entrepreneurial organisations is less formal; it may even appear non-existent except for introductions all around and perhaps an explanation of benefits. Established members informally tell tales of heroes described either as mavericks (non-conforming risk-takers who singlehandedly solve difficult problems) or charismatic team leaders with compelling visions. The message is to model the behaviour of the hero. However, managers of firms based in the UK generally devote less time to socialising newcomers than do managers in other countries, especially in Asia. Consequently, according to Beyer and Trice (1987), 'UK workers often form stronger alliances to their occupations [professional disciplines] than to their work organisations – an outcome that may be neither desirable nor inevitable.'

Culture promotes expected behaviours

Although the expressive character of organisational culture gives it the appearance of being a weak factor in managing organisations, cultures work best when strong. An organisation has a strong culture when members accept and buy into a common set of beliefs, values and assumptions, as if their behaviours were guided by an invisible hand. A strong culture has such widely accepted modes of conduct that certain behaviours are expected, and others would never occur.

Culture works best when people forget why they are doing certain things, but keep on doing them. For example, how often are you conscious of why you shake hands when meeting someone? We forget that the origin of shaking hands was to prove that your hand was free of a weapon and therefore extended in peace. But the strong culture that promotes consistent behaviour also makes it difficult to adapt when old ways no longer fit new realities. IBM knows well how a strong, once elitist culture constrained the shift to new, more flexible and customer-responsive behaviours.

Boje (1995) suggests that where culture is strong, powerful forces spread to all aspects of organisational life. For example, Walt Disney Productions encountered serious cultural rigidities following Walt's death in 1966. For almost two decades, his successor managers attempted to follow exactly in Walt's footsteps. 'What would Walt have done?' was the usual question raised in contemplation of a decision. By trying to second-guess their brilliant founder, they were not only forever mired in the past, but they lacked Walt's creativity and sense of marketing. Not until Michael Eisner was brought in as CEO in 1984 did Disney begin to revitalise both its culture and its strategy. Eisner believed that Disney's cultural strength was dedication to entertainment experimentation and innovation – not rigid adherence to traditional 'family entertainment' (Fulmer and Fulmer, 1988).

Subcultures facilitate organisational diversity

According to Duncan (1989), few organisations other than small to mid-size enterprises in a single line of business have a uniform, monolithic culture. While central tendencies towards shared assumptions promote a dominant culture throughout a large organisation, subcultures coexist as adaptive responses to diverse needs.

Industry putting profits before workers

Despite increasing pressure from the Health and Safety Commission to cut workplace accidents and deaths, industry leaders are still putting profits, customer satisfaction and staff training above the health and safety of their workers.

The revelation follows a British Safety Council/MORI poll of presidents, managing directors and chairs of companies in the FTSE 500. The leading industrialists were asked to list the three main corporate objectives for their business.

Top of the list was generating profits for shareholders (84 per cent), with increasing customer satisfaction coming second at 80 per cent. Next came the desire for new products or services, greater productivity and better training for staff.

Only one company in six, or 16 per cent, singled out improving health and safety as important enough to find a place in their top three priorities. This is at a time when workplace fatalities are at their highest for 10 years, with 295 deaths last year – a third up on figures for 2000. Commenting on the survey, David Ballard, director general of the British Safety Council, said: 'The results show the top executives are still failing to take their responsibilities seriously at a time when the government is determined to drive up safety standards. This is sheer complacency.'

Under new legislation proposed for the next parliament, three new charges of corporate killing, reckless killing and killing by gross carelessness, are expected by campaigners. Two of the charges carry maximum life sentences, while a company director found guilty of killing by gross carelessness faces a maximum sentence of 10 years.

When questioned over whether they were making provisions for the anticipated change in health and safety law, just over half said they were demonstrating a commitment to health and safety as a result.

Over a third claimed that they would be appointing a health and safety director while under a third said they were providing additional health and safety resources. Most of those who took part in the survey listed higher insurance costs, loss of reputation and loss of profits as the most likely results of a corporate killing prosecution.

In a bid to find out the likely impact of the new legislation on the construction industry – the most dangerous sector, with deaths averaging two a week – the BSC conducted a further telephone poll, which revealed that the introduction of the new offences is likely to make company directors resign their posts.

Two-thirds of companies questioned felt that health and safety provisions were adequate, with only 10 per cent saying they would be providing extra resources or appointing additional health and safety staff. 'Our view is that the new laws will force managers and directors to create healthier and safer workplaces,' said Ballard. 'But this can never be achieved by legal penalties alone, but by developing a safety culture.'

Source: *Environmental Health News* 17(8), CIEH.

Discussion questions

1 How can organisational culture be changed to improve safety?

2 If profits come before people what does this say about the culture of the organisation?

Subcultures
Localised subsystems of values and assumptions that give meaning to the common interests of small clusters of people.

Subcultures are localised subsystems of values and assumptions that give meaning to the common interests of smaller clusters of people within the overall organisation. A subculture may identify the members of a specific department, activity centre or division. Or it may emerge when a fairly broad cross-section of organisational members share a particular experience or perspective. Gregory (1983) suggests that perhaps the perspective is the result of having served under a particular leader, or having attended a common university, or sharing a common background such as all being engineers or English, Scottish or Welsh.

Subcultures have three possible impacts on the organisation: they can (1) serve to enhance the dominant culture; (2) promote an independence from it, as commonly occurs among divisions of diversified firms; or (3) function as countercultures when they are at odds with it.

Anita Roddick's method of adapting to different subcultures is to franchise Body Shop stores in different countries. This enables the managers of the stores, who are local people, to operate successfully but still share the core values of the Body Shop and use its logo. Knowing the nuances of various national cultures in which the enterprise operates is necessary if a company is not to become unstuck. Body Shop found this out to its cost when it took some unauthorised photos of tribespeople in Brazil and had to pay them compensation. When working across cultures not only do you have to know the mindset, the culture and the language but also the wants and needs of the people. Each of these functions within a subculture depending on whether a person works in sales, accounts or personnel. Each has expectations and assumptions and to be successful they need to be addressed.

countercultures
Subcultures that reject the values and assumptions of the host organisation and develop opposing beliefs, frequently based on elitist notions of a charismatic leader.

According to Cooke and Rousseau (1988), countercultures reject the values and assumptions of the host organisation and develop opposing beliefs, often based on elitist notions that may be promulgated by a charismatic leader. Such groups within an organisation function more as adversaries than as partners. When Steve Jobs and his maverick band of programmers and designers developed the original Macintosh computer, there was such rivalry between his elitist group and the rest of Apple Computer that a showdown with John Sculley, then CEO, led to the ousting of Jobs, one of Apple's co-founders. (Sculley was subsequently ousted, and Steve Jobs is back as CEO after a brief tenure by Gil Amelio – evidence of a strong power dynamic within the Apple culture.) Countercultures such as the Macintosh group can be strong, but they often focus on thwarting the efforts of the larger organisation.

The foregoing experiences and examples demonstrate why cultures are important to organisational performance, as part of the genetic code that maps patterns of behaviour. They also demonstrate why effective managers have to learn to interpret and guide their organisations' cultures.

Valuing diversity creates flexibility

Valuing diversity is important as it can help an organisation respond to the needs of its customers, but it is also important to remember that different people have different needs and therefore organisations also need to be flexible.

Diversity is important as it adds value to an organisation. People of different backgrounds are likely to bring different ideas to the organisation and that has to be good for business. Not only that, valuing diversity shows that an organisation values its employees, which should mean increased involvement and an improvement in productivity.

According to Spencer (2005) diversity matters for the following reasons.

- Improved access to markets or clients, other stakeholders and the wider community. If an organisation does not understand the culture and values of its market group then it will have trouble reaching them.

- Attractiveness to employees, as an organisation that values employee diversity will be an attractive place to work.

- Avoiding the cost of discrimination. Organisations that discriminate may pay the price, not only in the shape of legal action but also in terms of low morale and disaffected customers.

Diversity is about valuing differences; our differences are unique to us and are what makes us special. Spencer (2005) suggests that the starting point for organisations is to recognise the value of, and then actively seek to benefit from, the diversity of their staff team. Diversity is about inclusion and, according to Spencer (2005):

> organisations who want to maximise the quality, productivity and sustainability of their goods and services need to strive to fully engage the commitment, abilities, energy and diversity of experience, perceptions and approaches of all their people, all of the time. To achieve this, organisations need to understand the critical importance of managing inclusion, and seek to develop the skills of their people to be competent managers of inclusion.

This means that organisations need a coherent strategy on how people will be included in an organisation; this strategy needs to be implemented and it needs to work.

How members read their organisation's culture

Cultural clues suggest how a company chooses to succeed. They reveal insights into how problems have been solved and what is held to be important in the conduct of business. Pettigrew (1979) argues that managers need to learn how to read cultural clues, for often there are inconsistencies between what is said and what is done, or between subcultures and the overall culture. They can begin by observing objects – physical settings and artefacts. Then they might probe into the behavioural side by observing clues revealed through rites, rituals and people's public actions. Finally, skill in reading culture evolves by asking people questions and listening to how they respond as much as to what they say. Greetz (1973) suggests the search is less for precise answers than for a general understanding. Analysis of culture is 'not an experimental science in search of law, but an interpretative one in search of meaning'.

Observe physical settings and artefacts

Any newcomer to an organisation – whether just considering employment, reporting the first day on the job or attending his or her first staff meeting – can pick up clues by observing physical settings and artefacts. Here are a few non-behavioural clues to watch for.

Facilities

According to Wolf (1964), Coffey *et al.* (1985) and Deal and Kennedy (1982), physical facilities tell a tale of what is important, and not so important, to an organisation (see Exhibit 16-4). They reflect values and performance expectations. You might find that although the reception and office areas are reasonably well maintained and tidy, the production facility is cluttered with scrap, chemical stains blotch the floor, heat and noise are excessive, lighting is dim, and

---

EXHIBIT 16 – 4 How physical surroundings reveal cultural clues

Bricks and mortar
- What is the physical appearance of the facility? Is it well maintained, with an aesthetically pleasing sense of decor, or unkempt, dingy and run-down?
- Do work areas show individual flair (with artwork or awards and other artefacts on display), or does everything appear to be stock issues and monotonously uniform?

Use of space
- Do space allocations seem equitable and well used, or do some departments seem to have more than they need while others are shoehorned into a corner?
- In office settings, does an open layout invite spontaneous conversations, or are people protected by private offices (behind closed doors)?
- Does the allocation of space clearly reinforce status differences among people in different positions, or does it appear that most people have about the same amount of space?

Equipment, symbols and artefacts
- How ostentatious or spartan are the furnishings and decor? Are the walls painted? Wallpapered? Panelled with inexpensive veneer or solid hardwood?
- What adorns the walls in the reception area: gallery-quality paintings or mass-produced prints? Award plaques and trophies?
- Are the computers, fax machines and other technological equipment state of the art?

---

paint is peeling from walls and machines. Obviously the physical facilities needed for a manufacturing operation differ from those needed for a sales office. However, does one appear the neglected stepchild, as if management has failed to reinvest in its future?

Organisations that function around elitist values tend to convey status differentials in the location and sizes of offices. Status is denoted by being higher up in a building, having a corner office, being located around the perimeter of a floor and having an office rather than a cubicle. People have been known to fight to get a window office in organisations where status symbols are important.

Dress

Maney (1992) suggests that what people wear can say as much about the organisation as about them as individuals. Such clues offer an insight into the degree of formality expected of people. The once universal white shirts and conservative pinstriped suits of IBM's sales and service force are legendary, in contrast to the informality of T-shirts and jeans within many high-tech firms. Dress also makes a statement about the expected flexibility and individuality encouraged (or discouraged) by the culture. Dress-down Fridays or business casual represent attempts by formal organisations to slightly loosen up, to appear more humanistic. As you make inferences from physical symbols, you will begin to see a cultural paradigm emerge.

Find meaning in organisational rites

According to Beyer and Trice (1987), rites provide convenient forums for reading an organisation's culture based on what is said and done in public. Values, beliefs and other assumptions typically surface and are reaffirmed at the rites that bring people together for public occasions. A **rite** is a planned public performance where other forms of cultural expression, such as recounting company legends, are woven into a single event. Because rites have a clear beginning and end, they are a good opportunity to observe expressions of cultural assumptions that lie slightly beneath the surface.

rite
A planned public performance or occasion where diverse forms of cultural expression are woven into a single event.

An 'Avon lady' on the podium at a recent conference stated: 'Do you think I was born with BMW car keys in my hand? Time is no excuse. Direction will create time. Motivation will create energy. Keep working girls: you'll soon have a sleek, silver machine like mine.' Avon is an industry based on selling cosmetics through direct selling. It uses high-energy conferences to create a culture of success, and inspires its salespeople through incentives.

Legends

Stories and legends are often told at rites. Every IBM employee has heard the story about former CEO Tom Watson Jr's being denied access to a secure area by a young security guard. Even though she recognised Watson, he wore the wrong colour badge for that area. To his credit, Watson waited patiently while an aide retrieved the proper badge – he made no attempt to pull rank. For IBM members, the message is that all rules and policies apply equally to everyone. Watson also made it clear that he did not want to surround himself with 'yes men' and proudly proclaimed, 'I never hesitated to promote someone I didn't like. The comfortable assistant – the nice guy you like to go fishing with – is a great pitfall. I look for those sharp, scratchy, harsh, almost unpleasant guys who see and tell you about things as they really are' (Stewart *et al.*, 1999). This is the stuff legends are made of.

Meetings and away days

As the most frequently practised rite in organisations, meetings make statements about culture. Some organisations stand on ceremony by meeting at the same time, same place each week, with detailed agendas circulated before the meeting, followed by minutes of who said what. The entire event is a ritual to keep people informed and conforming to predictable behaviours. For other organisations, meetings are impromptu. People get together when someone encounters a problem or perceives an opportunity that needs the ideas of others, and creativity and problem-solving are preferred over conformity.

Organisations with turbulent, fast-changing environments frequently engage in 'offsite' meetings. The 'away day' is a day-long or multi-day forum designed to bring critical players together to question basic assumptions, raise critical issues, and resolve or plan responses to challenges. Some away days are held at regular intervals and involve people across the organisation, such as a quarterly sales planning session. Others are sessions for issue-focusing and problem-solving within a single department. Overtly used for rational purposes, both are rich in expressive behaviours that also help socialise newcomers and reinforce beliefs and values.

Ask questions and observe responses

When used in isolation, observation often seems an inefficient means of seeking cultural clues. Asking questions is more efficient and direct, even though responses cannot always be taken at face value. Managers rely on questioning as a means of interpreting meaning and testing their assumptions about culture on others. The few questions that appear in Exhibit 16-5 are easy to remember and go a long way to prepare you to extract cultural assumptions from organisational members.

Questioning and listening also have the practical advantage of providing a database on which personal advancement can be built. Many people have heard stories of a tea-boy who became chairman of a multinational company (Stewart *et al.*, 1999). So, ask questions, then listen and act on what others say and learn more about culture in the process.

By now you should understand the kinds of assumptions that underlie organisational culture, know how cultures vary, and know how to pick up clues that provide insights into cultures. Now consider what leaders do to build adaptiveness into the culture.

EXHIBIT 16 – 5 *How questions uncover cultural assumptions*

To surface underlying cultural assumptions, ask the following types of question. Look both for consistencies and variations in what people tell you. The greater the consistency, the stronger the culture.

1 What is the relevant history of this company? How did it come into being? (Founders always imprint their beliefs on an organisation to convey perspectives they want to perpetuate.)

2 What accounts for the success of this company? If growth has been irregular, how has this organisation been able to recover from downturns? (Responses suggest beliefs about what accounts for performance and where the firm is going to place its bets.)

3 What kind of people work here? What do you have to do to get ahead? (People usually find it easy to talk about people. Watch for what is said about revered heroes, as their behaviour indicates what the organisation values.)

4 What do you think about this as a place to work? What happens here during a typical day? How do decisions really get made? (While part of the responses will be evaluative, they'll also reveal glimpses into accepted behaviour. In addition, they will reveal something about the rites that are important to stakeholders.)

Source: Terrence E. Deal and Allan A. Kennedy (1982) *Corporate Cultures: The Rites and Rituals of Corporate Life*, pp. 132–133, © 1982 by Addison-Wesley Publishing Company, Inc. Reprinted by permission of Perseus Books.

How leaders build flexible, responsive cultures

An organisation's founder or founders begin to shape a culture when choosing the first people they hire. Culture really begins to take on meaning as those early hires encounter problems, solve them, and receive feedback from the founder(s) and the environment. Out of responses to crises comes growth, and depending on the lessons learned, certain values and core assumptions take on meaning while others are rejected or become irrelevant. Once established, an organisation's culture takes on a life of its own, resisting pressures to change – even if feedback confirms that the firm's relationship to its environment has deteriorated. Yet, over time, cultural modifications often become necessary.

First-generation managers develop a culture

During the formative period when the enterprise is still under the control of the founder(s), culture emerges from two sources: the founder's behaviours and from direct experience. First, founders bring to the start-up firm beliefs about how to succeed in business. Usually assumptions about products/services, markets and technology that underlie the business's mission are confirmed or denied rather quickly in the marketplace. Either the business takes hold or it fails. Other assumptions, about styles of decision-making and how to compete, take longer to test. Employees who are committed to the founder's concept of doing business seem to tolerate organisational or managerial imperfections as the cost of getting the business established. Schein (1983), who we discussed earlier, suggests that founders manifest three important behaviours:

1 the behaviours they deliberately use to role model, teach and coach

2 what they pay attention to in the organisation or its environment – what they measure and control

3 how they react to critical events and organisational crises, or their demonstrated methods of coping.

Second, another early source of culture is active experimentation (trial and error), where group members learn what really works and what fails. Whether passed along by the founder or learned through experimentation, only attempted solutions that seem to work are repeated and taught to newcomers. These lessons range from how to treat people, to how to develop creative ideas, to how to secure a foothold in a market environment. As members learn patterns of problem-solving, assumptions become confirmed. In the early days employees at Virgin learned that unconventional practices and a willingness to find new ways of doing things quickly enabled their firm to become an industry leader and a well-known brand name.

The second generation adapts a culture

Culture typically comes under threat once the founder begins to hire into key positions people who are not part of the first generation. While welcomed for their technical or managerial skills, newcomers are viewed by old-timers as less loyal and thus not fully trustworthy. The first generation of employees tends to operate more on the basis of personal relationships than the formal systems more characteristic of the second generation. 'The real test of the effectiveness of a corporate culture comes when the organisation's environment changes. Sometimes a strong culture can be like a millstone around the neck of a firm that is trying to respond to environmental changes' (Reimann and Wiener, 1988).

Unless the culture emphasises continuous innovation and product–market adaptation, a strong culture and ideology makes the introduction of change more difficult. Even IBM, a once elitist firm that employees assumed was invincible, encountered this 'millstone around the neck' as it struggled to slough off its mainframe mentality when the market for computers shifted to PCs and then to networks between the mid-1980s and mid-1990s.

Hewlett-Packard has found that its H-P Way permits reasonably fluid adaptations to business conditions over the decades as leaders come and go. As re-emphasised by John Young, the first CEO to lead the firm following the co-founders' retirements.

> Our basic principles have endured intact since our founders conceived them. We distinguish between core values and practices; the core values don't change, but the practices might. We've also remained clear that profit as important as it is – is not *why* the Hewlett-Packard Company exists; it exists for more fundamental reasons.

The alternative to a strong culture such as that found in the H-P Way is to have no consistency of beliefs and values – in effect, a weak culture. In a weak culture, people are not sure what is expected of them, much less how the organisation believes it will succeed. According to Trice and Beyer (1984), purposeful change may be even more difficult in weak-culture organisations, but for different reasons: 'Without the security and sense of purpose provided by a relatively strong culture, organisational members may feel impotent and unable to act decisively. These are not qualities that foster change.'

weak culture
The absence of common assumptions and norms, which means people are unsure of what is expected of them or how the organisation believes it will succeed.

A research study of 207 firms in 22 industries by Kotter and Heskett (1992) found that strong-culture organisations performed significantly better than weak-culture companies on measures such as increased revenues (682 per cent versus 166 per cent), improved net income (756 per cent versus 1 per cent) and expanded workforce (282 per cent versus 36 per cent). Such differences contribute to the reasons second and subsequent generations of managers often feel compelled to redefine values, clarify the purpose and promote a shift in culture towards an enduring ideology.

Growth prompts revolutionary shifts in culture

Greiner (1972) suggests that almost every period of evolutionary growth in an organisation's history is followed by a revolutionary upheaval as systems, people and structure shift towards a mode that allows another period of growth. Out-of-date cultural assumptions are usually at fault whenever members' behaviours seem overly unethical, unconcerned about quality, intentionally untruthful and manipulative of each other for personal gain. Several other situations that prompt a shift in culture are identified in Exhibit 16-6.

New leadership, new teaching practices

According to Rubenson and Gupta (1992), rather than expect the executives who have led an organisation for several years to change their culture incrementally, cultural change is typically more revolutionary and the result of a change in leadership. With a new management team, new assumptions and practices are introduced. The old ways and beliefs are challenged, especially if the organisation's progress has hit a plateau or declined. As new initiatives are introduced, employees question the cultural underpinnings of their organisation. Often there is a period of scepticism, resistance and complaining about 'losing our values' – the conditions that enabled a previous period of growth.

Champy (1995) writes in his book on re-engineering management that the power of managers to make significant changes in their organisations

> is limited not by the precepts of re-engineering but by the very nature of a culture. A company's culture cannot be proclaimed or easily manipulated. At best they [managers] can lead the way – that is, they can 'model' the behaviour, enable it, and educate it, drawing out what is already there, or what they hope is there.

Cultural change thus needs to be led, guided and nurtured because, like a large ship at sea, it takes time to turn.

teachable point of view
A process where the leader defines his or her values and beliefs about what it takes to succeed in the organisation's chosen businesses and in business generally, and then projects those ideas as a teacher throughout the organisation.

One of the methods some leaders use to help refocus a culture and 'turn the ship' is to apply the teachable point of view. To have a **teachable point of view**, the leader defines his or her values and beliefs about what it takes to succeed in the organisation's chosen businesses and in business generally, and then projects those ideas as a teacher throughout the organisation to motivate people towards a common goal. As described by Tichy

---

EXHIBIT 16 – 6 Situations prompting a shift in culture

Cultural changes may be necessary whenever organisations need to:

- break away from a rigid bureaucratic culture and become more responsive to change
- diminish the belief that power or policies get things done, and shift more towards satisfying customers and the marketplace
- create an identity and set of values for a mediocre, culturally weak organisation
- integrate an acquisition (with its own culture) into the ways of a new parent
- blend two cultures into one following a merger
- establish a unique, autonomous culture after a division is spun off or divested
- permit a division or major task unit to develop a subculture supportive of its task
- infuse stronger cultural elements into a weak-culture firm through rites and symbols.

(1999), it begins with a written personal statement (of about two pages), and then it is shared live with the next level of followers in interactive discussion as a teacher to students, who in turn become teachers. Tichy believes the teachable point of view makes better leaders, has a multiplier effect as it cascades down the organisation, and expedites developing people who behave congruently with the newly focused cultural norms. It has been successfully used by Jack Welch at GE, Jacques Nasser at Ford Motor and Andy Grove of Intel, among others.

Ethnic diversity sensitises organisational cultures

Many enterprises, even smaller businesses, are rapidly becoming multi-ethnic and multicultural because of the imported backgrounds employees bring with them. This is especially true in countries such as Germany, Spain and the UK where there is a big influx of immigrants from all over the world.

What you are learning about managing people's organisational behaviour gives you a British and American view of the world. The managerial approaches that work for us (and a few other Anglo societies) do not necessarily stand up well in other countries. Unfortunately for managers outside North America and the British Commonwealth, the vast majority of what has been researched and written about management during this century originated in English-speaking countries. As an export, North American-based management research and recommendations do not always work well unless adapted to fit the local culture. This has also been the case when American companies have tried to impose their culture on British companies. Nevertheless, innovative management practices often originate in North America, and are then exported all over the world (especially through university graduates who return to their home countries). In the Dynamics of Diversity box look at what happened when the Americans tried to import their culture into France at EuroDisney.

With our diverse workforce many organisations have taken on a multicultural complexion. Subcultures of various ethnic groups circulate within organisations. The emphasis is more on diversity than the melting pot of assimilation that prevailed in earlier generations of immigrants. While most rural areas outside the large cities remain predominantly Caucasian, many inner cities are culturally diverse.

Working with people from different ethnic and cultural backgrounds is a challenge and a source of opportunity for managers and organisational cultures. Although far from perfect, the British culture today is more accepting of ethnic and racial diversity than are most cultures of the world. Japan tends to be a very closed ethnic culture, the eastern European republics tend not to be tolerant of some minorities, and stories of the plight of blacks within South Africa, before the collapse of apartheid are legion. Such characteristics suggest that, as enterprises become global, managers need to understand how national cultures constrain the degree to which an organisational culture can fit within the values and practices of other nations.

How national cultures impact on global business

Most successful firms need at times to rework cultural elements to become more adaptive. One test of organisational culture occurs when a firm moves into a foreign country or when many of its new employee recruits are foreign born. While business people may share some commonality of values across national cultures (such as 'providing excellent service to customers'), a country's culture and business environment can cause value elements to differ significantly across national borders. In one study, by Johnson *et al.* (1995), of how accountants from four

dynamics of diversity

French weave fresh magic at Disney

The opening of a long-awaited second theme park at Disneyland Paris was in stark contrast to the launch of the first, 10 years ago. At that time, the French press savaged Disney, accusing it of a US cultural invasion. Wandering around the park at that launch, one could not help but think that if it wasn't for the grey drizzle, one could have been in Florida. Everything was done the American way, from the ban on alcohol inside the gates to the use of American English on the voiceovers and menus.

As the financial results got worse and worse, Disney realised its market research was not all it was cracked up to be. It started replacing some of the expensive sit-down restaurants with more family-orientated burger bars. It introduced beer on the menu and even changed the image-tarnished name EuroDisney to Disneyland Paris in a bid to get the turnstiles moving. After a long slog, it now makes an operating profit and the new park is expected to make visitors stick around for longer than the current average of two days.

On visiting the new Walt Disney Studios Park, it was painful to see how hard Disney bosses had gone the other way to be accepted in France. CEO Michael Eisner said: 'When we first came in there were questions that we were too American. People recognise that we are not actually American, we are Disney European.' He pointed out that Disney is behind *Amélie*, the biggest-grossing French film ever to hit America. Others emphasised the great connection between Disney and Europe saying that *Cinderella*, *Pinocchio* and *The Hunchback of Notre Dame* have their roots here. Every opportunity to highlight the European connection is milked. The stunt show scenery is based on the French Riviera and the studio Tram Tour shows London being scorched by dragons.

Many shows are in French verse then, if you are lucky, English. Songs are mainly in French, and children will need to have a pretty high reading age to understand the English subtitles in studios where they explain how animated films and special effects are created. Disney tunes are crooned in French, and at attractions such as the Disney Animation Gallery the songs switch in and out of French, English, Italian and German.

You get the feeling that people with a real sense of humour and fun put the studio together rather than the slick corporate machine Disney is famous for. By accepting that it is in Europe and that Europe has different wants and needs from America, Disney's new understanding of diversity may well be reflected in increased profits.

Source: Jeanette Hyde, *Observer*, 17 March 2002.

Discussion questions

1 What could Disney have done to ensure it had more of an understanding of European culture?

2 How can a lack of cultural awareness affect business success?

countries ranked 15 value statements, the most significant variability was found among two business values involving job satisfaction and profit maximisation (where low number rankings mean the item is more valued):

	United States	Holland	China	India
Employee motivation and job satisfaction	8	4/5	11	6
Consistently strive to maximise profits	12	14	2	10

Chinese accountants place much less importance on motivation and job satisfaction than do the Dutch, but Indians value it more than Americans. By contrast, the Chinese highly value profit maximisation (presumably as a means of economic development), but accountants in the other countries place it rather far down in their rankings of organisationally important values.

Culture has international and ethnic implications

You are undoubtedly aware of the cultural differences among countries, whether you have travelled outside your home country or simply read and watched TV and movies. Arab cultures differ from Asian, Mediterranean and western European cultures. One apparent difference among countries is the symbolism of language. But values, beliefs and behaviours also have patterned differences, and students of management should be aware of these.

While the productivity differences among countries are largely due to education, national or ethnic values also give people different predispositions towards work and business practices. Cultural differences also influence management styles. For example, researchers Ouchi and Jaeger (1978) found that, compared to American managers, Japanese managers tend to be more focused on the long term, more involved in group decision-making, less likely to delegate responsibilities to an individual, more willing to accept a go-slow approach to career promotions, less focused on a clear career path, more comfortable with informal controls, and more concerned about the welfare of the entire organisation. Ouchi's research identifies how a culture can be adapted and he identifies a Theory Z environment, as can be seen from the 'Research focus' below.

Beyond this comparison, what are some of these systematic differences in national cultures? Other studies, by Hofstede (1980, 1994) and Trompenaars and Hampden-Turner (1999), have attempted to identify differences in national cultures, as can be seen from the following, 'Research focus' boxes.

Research focus: Ouchi's Theory Z culture

Theory Z refers to an American adaptation of the Japanese style of management that became popular in the 1980s. At that time comparisons between the two countries' industries suggested that management styles in Japan were far superior to those in America. As a result companies such as IBM, Hewlett-Packard and Marks & Spencer attempted to adopt Theory Z characteristics.

The main feature of a Theory Z organisation is the sense of collaboration between managers and employees. Firms that successfully implement a Theory Z culture find that employees have a sense of belonging and involvement. Views are shared across the organisation and, from this, shared norms and values begin to emerge, which in turn help the organisation to improve and move forward.

A comparison of the main distinguishing features of a Theory A (typical American organisation) with those of a Theory Z organisation can be seen in Exhibit 16-7.

The Theory Z organisation is not one culture transplanted into another. It has been adapted to make it work. The ideal Theory Z organisation combines a basic cultural commitment to individual values common in western culture with a highly collective pattern of interaction common in Japanese culture. It also offers a holistic orientation towards life and tries to find a work–life balance. To implement a Theory Z organisation the organisation needs to be flexible and responsive to change.

EXHIBIT 16 – 7 Comparison of three organisational cultures

Theory A (American)	Theory J (Japanese)	Theory Z (modified American)
Short-term employment	Lifetime employment	Long-term employment
Individual decision-making	Consensual decision-making	Consensual decision-making
Individual responsibility	Collective responsibility	Individual responsibility
Rapid evaluation and promotion	Slow evaluation and promotion	Slow evaluation and promotion
Explicit formalised control	Implicit informal control	Implicit, informal control with explicit, formalised measures
Specialised career path	Non-specialised career path	Moderately specialised career path
Segmented concern	Holistic concern	Holistic concern including family

Source: G. Ouchi and A.M. Jaeger (1978) 'Type Z Organisation: Stability in the Midst of Mobility', *Academy of Management Review* 3(2), April, pp. 308, 311.

Research focus: the Hofstede framework

The landmark research of Geert Hofstede (1983) provides an insightful look at the similarities and differences in cultural values among 50 countries. His pathfinding research was drawn from over 100 000 IBM employees in countries throughout the world (excluding the former Soviet republics). The essence of country culture is national mental preprogramming, which is that part of our collective learning 'that we share with other members of our nation, region, or group but not with members of other nations, regions, or groups'. Hofstede provides several examples of national mental preprogramming at work:

national mental preprogramming
Geert Hofstede's concept for that part of a country's collective learning that is shared with other members of that nation, region or group, but not with members of other nations, regions or groups.

> In Europe, British people will form a neat queue whenever they have to wait; not so, the French. Dutch people will as a rule greet strangers when they enter a small, closed space like a railway compartment, doctor's waiting room, or lift; not so, the Belgians. Austrians will wait at a red pedestrian traffic light even when there is no traffic; not so, the Dutch. Swiss [people] tend to become very angry when somebody – say, a foreigner – makes a mistake in traffic; not so the Swedes. All these are part of an invisible set of mental programmes which belongs to these countries' national cultures.

As Hofstede (1983) interpreted survey results, he noticed that responses to questions about values were rather stable within nationality groups, but attitudes were not. Values, as defined earlier, are rather permanent desires or beliefs people hold to be important

attitudes
Temporal beliefs based on evaluative interpretations of current conditions.

independent of situations. Attitudes are temporal beliefs based on evaluative interpretations of current conditions. When IBM members responded to attitude questions such as 'How do you like your job?' the responses showed no national pattern; they depended on the current situation for each individual. In contrast, responses to value questions such as 'How would you describe an ideal job?' were similar within, but different across, nationalities.

Four largely independent dimensions, based on patterns of enduring values, provide the framework for describing national cultures: (1) individualism versus collectivism; (2) centralised versus diffused power; (3) strong versus weak uncertainty avoidance; and (4) masculinity versus femininity.

Individualism versus collectivism

All societies deal with the relationship between the individual and other people. In highly *individualistic societies*, the individual is expected to look out for his or her own self-interest, and maybe that of the immediate family. At the other extreme, *collectivist societies* assume that close ties exist among people and the interests of the individual are subordinated to the group, be it extended family, tribe, village and/or employer. Individualistic nations are loosely integrated (do your own thing), collectivist tightly integrated (honour thy group heritage). Interestingly, per capita economic wealth correlates with individualistic behaviour – collectivist nations are poorer.

As you might expect, the United States, Great Britain, Australia and the Netherlands are very individualistic. Some highly collectivist nations are Colombia, Pakistan, Panama, Taiwan, Venezuela and South Korea. Among those in the middle are Japan, Spain, Israel, Austria, Argentina and India. However, Chen *et al.* (1998) argue that within any nation can be found individuals tending towards each perspective, or the emergence of co-operation mechanisms to reduce extreme behaviours. Generally, individuals orientated towards a collectivist ideology are more co-operative when working within groups, whereas individualists tend to ignore group needs. Nevertheless, according to Wagner (1995), even among individualists, their willingness to co-operate increases if the group size is small, if individual behaviour can be identified and evaluated, and if individuals feel that their behaviours are indispensable to the success of the group endeavour. These are the mediating conditions under which strong individualists, as often found in North America, can be team players.

Centralised versus diffused power

How to deal with inequalities among people is another fundamental value issue for nations. *Centralised power societies* permit unequal intellectual or physical capabilities to grow into blatant inequalities in the distribution of power and wealth. *Diffused power societies* play down individual differences by sharing or decentralising power. Societies that deliberately promote greater power differences among people tend to centralise authority. They permit and even promote autocratic leadership as part of their mental conditioning of people.

Nations with distinct power hierarchies are poorer and collectivist. Their people accept unequal distributions of power as almost inevitable, given their psychological dependence on others. Prime examples are the Philippines, India, Venezuela, Guatemala, Pakistan, Panama and Arab countries. At the opposite extreme, Anglo-Saxon nations promote low stratification of power and embrace democratic ideals, just as they believe strongly in individualism. This culture cluster includes the United States, Australia, Great Britain, New Zealand, Canada and the Netherlands. Japan, Argentina and Spain score in the middle of the power distance scale.

Strong versus weak uncertainty avoidance

Culture conditions people to cope in different ways with future uncertainty. Societies accepting of uncertainty use organised creativity to reduce the risk of uncertainty: technology to control nature; laws to discourage deviant behaviour; and religion in the broadest sense of the word to promote desired behaviour. Nations with a strong need for *uncertainty avoidance* usually claim that absolute truth originates from a dominant religion. To them the future is a challenge to be overcome and is associated with high levels of anxiety, emotionality and aggressiveness. Strong uncertainty avoidance nations include the Latin European and Latin American countries; Mediterranean countries such as the former Yugoslavia, Greece and Turkey; and Japan and South Korea.

People in weak uncertainty avoidance countries accept the unknown future and are not troubled by it. They take risks rather easily and are tolerant of different behaviours and opinions since they are relatively secure. Such nations include Denmark, Sweden, Singapore, Hong Kong and Jamaica. More middle of the road on uncertainty avoidance are Britain, the United States and Canada, Finland, Norway, East Africa (Kenya, Ethiopia, Zambia) and West Africa (Nigeria, Ghana, Sierra Leone).

Masculinity versus femininity

This dimension resolves the division of social roles between the sexes. Some nations make sharp distinctions between roles based on sex, wherein men take on the more dominant and assertive roles while women assume the more care-taking, service roles. Nations with such clear sex-role divisions are called 'masculine' by Hofstede. *Masculine values* permeate societies where the hero is the successful achiever, where showing off and displaying wealth are accepted. Other societies are more tolerant of a wider distribution of roles almost independent of sex and are called 'feminine'. *Feminine values* include respecting the underdog, putting relationships before wealth, and tending to quality of life and the environment.

Among nations, the most masculine country is Japan, followed by German-speaking nations and some Latin American countries, such as Mexico and Venezuela. The most feminine are the Scandinavian countries. More nations are clustered towards the middle than on any other dimension, with Britain and the United States in this group but leaning towards the masculine side. Only recently have women in Britain begun to break into jobs that were once the exclusive domain of men (such as firefighting and prominent roles in the armed services).

Comparing cultural central tendencies

Index scores of Hofstede's four dimensions are shown for several countries in Exhibit 16-8. However, they should be interpreted cautiously. According to Oritz (1987), cultural dimensions exist along a continuum, whether applied to an organisation or a nation. The index scores from Hofstede's research represent central tendencies or averages based on a large number of respondents. If you have done a statistics course, you will know there is always variance about the statistical mean. For example, not all British men are 1.75 m in height, even if this might be the national mean.

Similarly, when describing how nations score on any particular cultural variable, it is easy to stereotype, jumping to the conclusion that a particular behaviour or belief describes all the people of a country. In fact, some individuals display very few or even none of the dominant cultural characteristics. One extensive research study of the Hofstede theory examined the extent

EXHIBIT 16–8 *Four independent cultural dimensions: how select countries/regions score*

Country/region	Approximate dimension index score (0–100)[a]			
	Individualism	Power distance	Uncertainty avoidance	Masculinity
Arab countries[b]	40	80	65	50
East Africa[c]	30	60	50	40
Brazil	40	70	75	50
Mexico	30	85	80	70
Panama	10	95	85	45
India	50	80	40	60
Indonesia	15	80	45	45
Korea	20	60	85	40
Japan	45	55	90	95
France	70	65	80	45
Great Britain	90	35	35	65
Germany	65	35	65	65
Sweden	70	30	30	5
United States	90	40	45	65
Canada	80	40	40	55

Notes

a Hofstede used a series of index scores to plot variables on two-dimensional graphs, with the higher number having higher value for the dimension identified. Numbers in this exhibit represent approximate index scores as interpreted from the graphs, rounded to the closest five points; thus, all values are relative, not absolute.

b Arab countries include Egypt, Lebanon, Libya, Kuwait, Iraq, Saudi Arabia, UAE.

c East African countries include Kenya, Ethiopia, Zambia.

Source: interpreted from Geert Hofstede (1983) 'The Cultural Relativity of Organizational Practices and Theories', *Journal of International Business Studies* 14, Fall, pp. 75–89.

to which national cultures or organisational cultures created role stress for individuals, whether they were confused by role ambiguity or upset by role conflict. The results of a 21-nation study were clear:

> Role stress varies substantially more by country than by demographic and organisational factors ... The power distance and individualism concepts are the ones most closely linked to the role stresses. Petersen (1995) suggests that, overall, managers from high-power-distance countries report greater role overload than managers from low-power-distance countries.

Evaluation of Hofstede's work

There has been much criticism of Hofstede's work. His methodology has been questioned as his sample was drawn from only one company and the company itself had a very strong corporate culture. However, Hofstede argued that this was not important, as the samples were matched and the differences were in the external social environment, which genuinely reflected the

▶ different cultures. Other critics argue that Hofstede treats national boundaries as being the same as national cultures: he does not take into account regional variations, which can be quite extreme in some countries. The work is also criticised as a scheme that *describes* cultures rather than explaining how cultures arise and are maintained, although Hofstede argues that he never set out to explain cultures, but to document differences in attitudes and work-related values caused by culture.

Nevertheless, Hofstede's work has been used as a base for many researchers, who use it to examine cross-cultural effects in the workplace.

Research focus: **Fons Trompenaars' framework**

A framework developed by Trompenaars and Hampden-Turner (1999) draws on the work of Hofstede and also that of Kluckhohn *et al.* (1952), and is a useful tool for understanding and dealing with cultural differences. Trompenaars questioned respondents from 47 national cultures and suggests that cultures vary in how their members solve problems. He identified three major types.

1 The relationships with people – five major cultural differences were identified, as can be seen below.

2 Attitudes towards time – suggests that societies view time differently and how the past, present and future interrelate.

3 Attitudes towards the environment – relates to whether individuals are either a part of nature or separate from it; how much individuals are a master of their fate.

Trompenaars identified five major cultural differences in how relationships with other people are handled, and these are as follows.

1 **Universal versus Particular** – Universal: the emphasis is on rules and regulations. Particular: the emphasis is on relationships and flexibility.

2 **Individual versus Collective** – Individual: the emphasis is on freedom and responsibility. Collective: relates to group emphasis and consensus.

3 **Neutral versus Affective** – Neutral: the emphasis is on objectivity and detachment. Affective: emphasis is on displays of emotion.

4 **Specific versus Diffuse** – Specific: the emphasis is focused and narrow, and focused to the task. Diffuse: the emphasis is on the building of relationships.

5 **Achievement versus Prescription** – Achievement: the emphasis is on performance. Prescription: the emphasis is on the idea that status comes from age, education, gender.

Trompenaars' work is useful in linking the dimensions of culture to other aspects of organisational behaviour. The work has since been developed with Charles Hampden-Turner and they have extended their field of analysis. Neutral–Affective has been replaced with Equality–Hierarchy, and this now corresponds more closely with Hofstede's findings.

The work of analysing culture has resulted in a common thread emerging, in that organisations operating in a global environment need to be aware of cultural differences in order to avoid potential problems. It also suggests that there is no formula for reconciling cultural differences, that each culture should be viewed on its own merit and that one culture is not superior to another.

National cultures: pressures to adapt to promote global business activity

According to Earley and Singh (1995), the key to effective management practices or quality organisational research is to understand the cultural contexts 'in which firms and individuals function and operate'. Jung and Avolio (1999) and Gibson (1999) suggest that adaptations to those contexts can range from shifting leadership styles and degree of task uncertainty when working with small groups to modifying more extensive practices within a nationwide organisation. Organisations that choose to operate on a transnational basis, especially businesses, must obviously build in some capacity of adaptiveness to function harmoniously within host national cultures. In a recent 'Organisation of the Future' conference, the European domiciled Asea Brown Boveri (ABB) was selected as the model of a transnational corporation for its culture of promoting entrepreneurial behaviour within the 140 countries where it does business, yet maintaining consistency with common core principles. (See the World Watch box for how ABB achieved this world adaptiveness.)

However, just as business organisations must adapt to national cultures as they become global, country cultures are not beyond the reach of global change realities. As information technologies and financial interdependencies literally link the world, national cultural values are also under pressure to adapt on a much more subtle scale.

Japanese capitalism

Research by Johnson (1993) indicates that the Japanese practise a very different form of capitalism than the Anglo-American model. Capitalism to the Japanese emphasises managerial autonomy from the interests of shareholders and employees, economic priorities that emphasise producers over consumers, industrial policy in which government acts as the guiding hand, and a strong state ethic made legitimate more by economic accomplishments than by public consent. However, according to Faw (1999), these practices, fuelled by national cultural values, are now clashing with serious economic tensions. The organisational model that was the darling of the 1970s and 1980s did not hold up in the 1990s as the world globalised through information technology with service-orientated business practices as the drivers for creating world-class value. As Japan entered the new economic century mired in recession, citizens as consumers were not spending because of persistent fears of lay-offs and declining wages. Bremner (2000) suggests that what had become a cultural belief in lifetime employment and benevolent monolithic employers now clashes with major corporate restructurings, mergers and bankruptcies as Japanese executives focus 'on raising returns, not job stability'.

Capitalistic socialism

Travelling a few thousand kilometres to the west, it will be interesting to see how effective will be the former Soviet republics (now the Commonwealth of Independent States), including giant Russia, in their struggle to become democratic, market-based economies with widespread private ownership of property. To change an economic system without changing cultural values is risky; sustaining that change will be nothing short of revolutionary. Burlingham (1992) argues that so far among communist-socialist nations, only the Chinese have attracted free-enterprise investment funds on a large enough scale to be on the verge of emerging as a global economic force.

To support these business changes, national cultures will also have to change. People have to experience success with a different system if they are to change their fundamental assumptions and beliefs. So far the old communist system of direct rationing and price setting is believed to

Asea Brown Boveri (ABB): success based on a multidomestic culture

The cohesiveness of national cultures constrains the efforts of a business firm from another country to import the values of its corporate culture into the foreign national culture. An exception is when the firm functions as a transnational operation, actively promoting a multidomestic blend of cultures, as personified by Asea Brown Boveri (ABB). Created as a result of a 1987 merger between two century-old firms, one Swedish, one Swiss, founding CEO Percy Barnevik planned ABB to be a global business resting on three internal contradictions. Says Barnevik, 'We want to be global and local, big and small, decentralised with centralised reporting.'

Each of ABB's 50 or so lines of business is effectively a national business enterprise with its own president and financial statements in targeted countries. It is the job of the 1300 or so national presidents to create an organisation and culture that enable the business to best serve and penetrate the domestic market in their host country – to focus ABB's local presence regardless of where the product is manufactured. This approach 'allows us to optimise our businesses globally and maximise performance in every country in which we operate,' says Barnevik. 'We get a truly multidomestic organisation.'

At a conference jointly sponsored by the Conference Board and the Peter F. Drucker Foundation for Nonprofit Management, ABB was described as a success model. It became a transnational firm reconfigured from a 'grab-bag of second tier companies' into 'an organisation that enshrines idea generation, individual initiative, autonomy and co-operation across boundaries, while at the same time making performance more transparent and measurements more meaningful, with management expected to deliver against quantifiable economic targets'. ABB became the most competitive company in its industry by successfully creating an integrated network model of a transnational corporation 'with a culture based on empowerment and responsibility'.

Sources: adapted from Michael F. Wolff (1999) 'In the Organisation of the Future, Competitive Advantage Will Lie with Inspired Employees', *Research Technology Management* 42, July–August, pp. 2–4; William Taylor (1991) 'The Logic of Global Business: An Interview with ABB's Percy Barnevik', *Harvard Business Review* 69, March–April, pp. 91–105; and William E. Halal (1994) 'From Hierarchy to Enterprise: Internal Markets Are the New Foundation of Management', *Academy of Management Executive* 8, November, pp. 69–83.

Discussion questions

1 What is meant by the expression 'an organisation with a culture based on empowerment and responsibility'?

2 Why is it important for a global organisation to understand local culture?

produce shortages for the masses and allow the privileged to lead a good life. But the economic infrastructure (factories, roads, etc.) of the former Soviet republics is so run-down that there is insufficient capacity to allow a freer price mechanism to allocate resources.

European economic integration

Even the more gradual shift towards an economically integrated European community (five decades in the making) has not been problem-free. The introduction of the euro monetary system and plan to reduce tariffs notwithstanding, each European nation has its favourite industries to protect, people to keep employed, beliefs about the role of government in manag-ing business, preferences about distribution systems, and so on. The BMW/Rover merger was a good example of this.

But where European firms encounter even greater obstacles is in seeking to establish a multinational presence within the United States. The strong national cultural value of independence and autonomy complicates the integration of US acquisitions into a European multinational corporation – the Daimler/Chrysler merger purports to preserve both a German and an American organisational culture. In part this difficulty of cultural assimilation occurs because most Americans have little or no international experience nor have they sought it until recently because of the large size of the US market. Says one French multinational executive with substantial activities in the United States:

> It is difficult for Americans to develop a world perspective. It's hard for them to see
> that what may optimise the worldwide position may not optimise the US activities.
> We have to remind them continually of the need to think globally and encourage
> exchanges of people. None of this is surprising, because most US firms have not
> had much international experience. (Rosenzweig, 1994)

Thus, there is an adaptive interplay between organisational cultures and national cultures. While national cultures may take decades to produce a noticeable modification in values and norms, we expect organisations to adapt much more quickly to the national context in which they choose to operate. Occasionally we even see an organisation such as ABB that actively incorporates elements of the host country national culture into a business unit's corporate culture framework. The result is a blend of values that promotes local adaptability without sac-rificing key assumptions that have made the enterprise a global force.

Hewlett-Packard: a second look

Carly Fiorina had made a name for herself as a leader within Lucent (the telecommunications company) when she was selected as Hewlett-Packard's CEO in 1999, the first 'outsider' to lead H-P. She quickly initiated changes on two fronts: one focused on operating practices by cutting costs, reorganising divisions and changing the sales compensation plan; the other initiated entrepreneurial efforts to find new businesses, new services and new ways of doing business. Her actions, although intended to move the firm into new fields of business, were consistent with the eight principles of the H-P Way and the core ideology that had developed within the company over 60 years.

Within her first six months, she revived an old H-P tradition – that of 'corporate maverick'. She did so by tasking former marketing manager Nick Earle with the job of starting as many new Internet businesses as he could. Earle now runs a network called the 'e-services.solutions group' and has up to $150 million to invest in Internet start-up ideas that surface throughout H-P. He is also to work in innovative ways with other companies to build a network of firms that bring web services to business-to-business customers. As H-P's CEO at the turn of the century, Carly Fiorina has moved boldly to imprint her leadership initiatives on the organisa-tion, but seems to be doing so by using the strengths of a well-established visionary ideology and very visible corporate culture.

Source: Eric Nee (2000) 'Hewlett-Packard's New E-Vangelist', *Fortune*, 10 January, pp. 166–167.

Summary

- Culture conveys expected behaviour. An organisation's culture is a powerful collective force of values, beliefs, assumptions and norms that are communicated through rites, legends and other forms of employee socialisation and ritual.

- Organisations develop value systems that can be described as originating either from charismatic leaders or from tradition, and in content either as functional or elitist. Of the four possible combinations, traditional functional values build the strongest culture, charismatic-elitist the least enduring and adaptable.

- The combination of enduring values and a sense of purpose grounded in serving and adding value to society (rather than simple profit maximisation) produces a core ideology about which everything else in the organisation can change.

- Culture is important to organisations not only as the foundation for strategy implementation, but also because it promotes consistent behaviour and helps socialise newcomers in the ways of the organisation.

- Future managers need to be skilled observers of organisational culture and able to make their culture more responsive to change. You can learn to read corporate cultures by developing the skills of observing and by questioning the expressive meanings of organisational rites and rituals.

- Managers should be aware that the expressive look and feel of organisational culture can be a useful way of influencing behaviour and reducing reliance on rational managerial tools such as policies and budgets.

- When an organisation has a strong culture (that is, when most members agree on a set of underlying assumptions), people tend to resist adapting to new environmental pressures unless change and experimentation are embedded in cultural values.

- Conflict and resistance to change originate within subcultures and countercultures, and especially in mergers between two cultures.

- Given the increasing globalisation of business and governmental relations, managers should be sensitive to the impact of country cultures or ethnic differences on human behaviour.

- One paradigm, by Hofstede, is useful in comparing national cultures by examining whether they are individualistic or collectivist, hold centralised or diffused power, have strong or weak uncertainty avoidance, and are masculine or feminine.

- Companies that expand globally find that such dimensions constrain the direct transfer of the organisational culture. Even within domestic organisations, managers need to be sensitive to the ethnic or cultural predispositions of members and customers, especially to those whose backgrounds are other than Anglo-Saxon.

Areas for personal development

As an expressive quality of an organisation's assumptions, beliefs and values, culture per se is not a skill to be learned. Nevertheless, individuals can learn how to interpret an organisation's culture and what to look out for as organisational members who have yet to enter the ranks of senior management. Build your skills by having in mind an organisation you know well (from your experience at work, college, etc.) as you work through the following tasks.

1 **Build a portfolio of organisational assumptions.** Assumptions are all-encompassing – from values, to beliefs, to lessons learned from the 'way we do things' in this organisation. List and categorise what you believe to be the organisation's key assumptions. Use any categories that make sense to you, possibly including its purpose, relationship to its environment, relationship to people and stakeholders.

2 **Define the organisational value system.** Use the sources of origin (charismatic leaders or tradition) and content (functional or elitist) to identify its current alignment. Now, if it is something other than traditional-functional, what actions should be initiated to provide some movement in that direction?

3 **Scrutinise its core ideology.** Some researchers and executives argue that an organisation's core ideology is most fundamental to its existence and long-term viability. Think of ideology as the interplay between enduring values and its externally orientated purpose. Does your organisation have a core ideology? What is it? Does it provide the platform for continual or periodic changes in strategies and practices? Does it hold up across transitions in leadership? If you see weakness in ideology, what could your organisation do to build a more solid foundation?

4 **Evaluate your socialisation.** As a new member, what, if anything, was done to bond you into the organisation? If anything was done, were you talked to (by a member of management or human resources or by another authority figure)? Were you given something to read? Did you attend a class or formal newcomer's induction? Did a peer take you on and become a sort of mentor? Were you part of an interactive learning experience? What was the content of what you were told? Was the emphasis on stories about people succeeding, about organisational history, or about the future directions and policies? What would you like to have experienced? What will you do when you have an opportunity to socialise newcomers into your organisation?

5 **Wander around and read its cultural clues.** What do you observe in the design and layout of buildings, offices and work spaces? Artwork or objects placed on walls in public places? Member dress? Behavioural interactions between members? Ways in which conflict or disagreements are handled? Formality or informality of conversations and formal gatherings (meetings, classes)? How do these observable clues match up with the organisation's professed values, its ideology? If you notice a mismatch, what would it take to achieve stronger congruence between what is observed and what is professed?

6 **Know your subcultures and countercultures.** Not all organisations have them, but if it is of a fair size, chances are an organisation will have multiple subcultures. Probe by asking questions and making observations as to what purpose the subcultures play and the extent to which they are anchored with the overall core ideology. Experience also, vicariously if necessary, what life is like within a subculture. Since culture is the expressive side of the organisation, how do you (and subculture members) feel in terms of empowerment,

self-efficacy and commitment to overall organisational purposes? If you find a counterculture, why is it allowed to exist and does it serve a functional purpose? Develop the detective skill to be on the lookout for countercultures, and anticipate the personal costs (and benefits?) of becoming seduced into joining the cause.

7 **Find ways of letting a foreign culture 'happen to you'.** Undoubtedly there are some students from other countries within your college. Strike up a purposeful conversation with two or three from diverse national cultures. Ask them questions about life in their native culture using Hofstede's four dimensions as a guide for framing your questions and organising answers. Anticipate how you would function if working in that national culture by playing out 'What if?' scenarios across several hypothetical situations with your international colleagues. In what ways would you behave as 'normal' in your native culture? In what ways might you adapt?

❓ Questions for study and discussion

1 What does it mean to say organisational culture is 'a pattern of basic assumptions that a given group has invented, discovered or developed'? Identify three basic assumptions that underlie the organisational culture of your college.

2 What are the four types of organisational value systems formed by the interaction of charismatic/tradition and function/elite dimensions? Which is most responsive to change? Least responsive? Why?

3 What are the building blocks of an organisation's 'core ideology' and in what ways does their stability, if well defined, foster change and innovation over successive generations of leaders?

4 Why is organisational culture considered an 'expressive' way of influencing behaviour rather than a 'rational' managerial tool?

5 What organisational characteristics provide clues to reading an organisation's culture? Which two do you believe to be the most revealing? Why?

6 Why is a strong-culture organisation at risk of being unresponsive to change? Why is a change in top management often desirable when an organisation's culture is no longer adaptive? Give an example of how leadership can promote cultural change.

7 What are Hofstede's four fundamental factors that shape national mental conditioning? Using his framework, what country (or countries) do you believe to be most unlike the United Kingdom? Most like the United Kingdom?

8 What can organisations that conduct business on a global stage do to promote adaptability to local national cultures while still preserving the core values and norms of the larger organisation?

🔑 Key Concepts

culture, *p. 750*

organisational culture, *p. 751*

strong culture, *p. 752*

values, *p. 755*

organisational value system, *p. 757*

charismatic-based values, *p. 757*

tradition-based values, *p. 758*

functional values, *p. 758*

elitist values, *p. 758*

core ideology, *p. 759*

socialisation, *p. 762*

subcultures, *p. 766*

countercultures, *p. 766*

rite, *p. 768*

weak culture, *p. 771*

teachable point of view, *p. 772*

national mental preprogramming, *p. 776*

attitudes, *p. 777*

Personal skills exercise*

Draw a culture

Purpose Much of what we communicate about organisations depends on language. But other, non-verbal, means of expression can transcend the constraints of language. This exercise gives you the opportunity to visualise and communicate an abstract idea using the tools of the artist.

Time The exercise can be completed in 5 minutes if done individually (15–20 minutes are needed if extended to class or group sharing).

Materials Each student uses his or her own pen or pencil and one sheet of paper. The instructor brings one roll of masking tape (if class sharing).

---

* Can be enhanced with group sharing.

Procedure Think of an organisation you know quite well. It could be your current or past employer. Or you might select a student organisation with which you have been actively involved, your church or your college. Choose a specific organisation with which you have had enough experience to form definite impressions about its values, beliefs, rites and generally accepted assumptions.

Once you have an organisation clearly in mind, *draw a picture* of your organisation *as a vehicle of transportation.* You do not have to literally draw a specific kind of vehicle such as an aeroplane, automobile, bicycle, tank or ship. Be creative. Imagine some kind of hybrid vehicle that conveys the characteristics of the organisation and will make a statement about its culture. Draw as many features as you can, adding people, symbols and other images. When you have finished your drawing, on the back of the paper connect the symbols in your picture with words. Write brief interpretations of what the different features of your picture mean. How did some quality of the culture lead to the representation in your picture?

Public showing (optional) When you have finished, your tutor may ask you either to share your drawings in ad hoc small groups or, time and class size permitting, to tape all pictures to the wall to share them with the entire class. Observe the drawings of your classmates. Your tutor may ask a few students to explain what they have drawn and why. Experience suggests that powerful insights into organisational culture are often revealed once you are freed from the confines of language.

😯 Team exercise

Where is the organisational culture?

Purpose This exercise puts students' powers of perception to the test in reading the culture of your educational institution. If time permits, a walk around campus can add focus to what students look for in reading their organisational culture.

Time This activity takes about 15–20 minutes without a campus walk, 45 minutes or so with one.

Materials In class, it helps to have one blank flip-chart sheet and a marker for each group (of four to six students), and masking tape to affix charts to a wall.

Procedure Organise into groups of four to six members each.

Group work Your group's task is to develop a list of cultural attributes of your school (university, school or college) based solely on what you have observed. Time permitting, your instructor may give each group some time (15–20 minutes) to walk around the building and write down a list of everything that suggests a cultural characteristic based on what can be seen. Without the walk, simply exchange ideas within your group about what you have noticed that seems to provide a cultural clue. Use the following questions to prompt your analysis.

1 What do the buildings suggest? Tradition (ivy-covered brick) or functional?

2 What about equipment, furnishings and decor? Pristine, elegant elitism, or neglect and impoverishment? State-of-the-art technology, or make do hand-me-downs? Size of classrooms? Are classrooms named?

3 What are people wearing? Students? Faculty? Staff?

4 What are people doing outside of class? Are people interacting or isolated? Are the doors of tutors' offices open? Are they in their offices (when not in class)?

5 What story do the bulletin boards tell? Are trophy cases or other symbols of achievement and winning visible?

Class presentation After the allotted time, each group displays its flip chart and briefly provides its interpretation of what observable features tell about organisational culture. Then as a class discuss questions such as the following.

1 To what extent are there elements of commonality among the group's conclusions?
2 Are there differences of interpretation of what the same observable features mean?
3 Do these pictures of your campus confirm your assumptions about its culture?

Case study: **is it stop or Go for Stelios and Cassani?**

Conflict and mergers, but what about the culture?

Before easyJet and Go merged, reports of conflicts and clashes of culture were emerging. This is how their talks were perceived by those outside the organisation before the merger took place.

Cracks have started to appear in the relationship between easyJet founder Stelios Haji-Ioannou and Go chief executive Barbara Cassani.

The relationship between Haji-Ioannou and Cassani is icy. Cassani, Go's American boss – and recently named Business Woman of the Year – has reacted unfavourably to the idea that her beloved airline might be swallowed up by easyJet, even though the deal would create the largest no-frills airline in Europe and make her an extremely wealthy woman.

The first sign of acrimony came with the leaking of a message Cassani had recorded for her staff, saying she had tried to persuade 3i, the venture capital fund that owns most of Go, not to pursue the deal. Stelios and Cassani then communicated with each other only through the press. Cassani insisted she had never been offered a role at easyJet and did not want to have any part in the combined business. Haji-Ioannou countered by saying that he had offered the number two job in a merged airline.

Clearly with this acrimony these two will not be working together in the new airline, but with such animosity what effect is this going to have on the merged company culture at lower levels in the organisation?

Although both Go and easyJet are no-frills airlines, they have a different philosophy of what this means. easyJet has a policy of not allocating seats, while Go allocates; cheaper flights on Go involve a Saturday-night stop-over, not so with easyJet. Then there is the coffee: Cassani prides herself on being the no-frills airline that sells fresh coffee in cafetieres, while easyJet has instant in plastic cups. Cassani's philosophy is 'cheap does not mean poor quality'. The other issue is that Go was once owned by British Airways and was set up in direct competition with easyJet. British Airways, although privatised in 1987, still sees itself as Britain's airline and a British institution. Does Go also have this mentality?

So, what are the plans? Plan A for easyJet was to roll out the easyJet model across Europe and compete with mainline carriers. If Go is now to come under the easyJet umbrella these plans will have to be revised dramatically. But it needs to be seen where the synergy with Go will be.

The final result was a takeover of Go by easyJet. Go is no more and easyJet now flies to all the destinations previously served by Go, which is now a distant memory.

Source: adapted from *Financial Times*, 12/13 May 2002.

Discussion questions

1 How would you describe the concept of organisational ideology in relation to easyJet and Go?
2 What inferences do you draw about the merger of easyJet and Go for organisational cultures?

3 What would your proposals be for a management structure following a merger? Under what conditions might the dual executive arrangement work?

4 Does the disagreement appear to be more the victim of organisational culture or power politics?

Applied questions

5 Using Schein's definitions of culture, what are the basic assumptions, values and beliefs, artefacts and creations of easyJet?

6 How have the rational and the expressive elements that influence organisational behaviour created one dynamic organisation?

WWW exercise

Manager's Internet tools

Web tips: discerning corporate culture on the web

The Internet is an excellent vehicle for corporate communication. Beyond just company products, services and financial information, the web can also be used to communicate a message about the company's culture. This can be a daunting task, however, since to know the true culture requires that one be inside the company. Yet, a company can still use the Internet to reveal some of the basic core values or beliefs that guide the company.

One might think that three of the largest computer manufacturers would be the same. However, there are some dramatic differences among the cultures of Dell, Compaq and Gateway. Each organisation is different in size, organisation and culture. Pretend you are interested in a career with one of these computer manufacturers. Ignoring such things as the physical location of the company, salary and specific job responsibility, try to determine which company you would be more interested in working for by assessing its culture as depicted on its website.

Look at such things as the management team and the corporate mission statement, and pay particular attention to areas that list 'values'. Search for statements about people, culture or any message that the company is trying to convey about what life would be like at that company.

http://www.compaq.co.uk
http://www.dell.co.uk
http://www.gateway.co.uk

1 What is your perception of the cultures of the three computer manufacturers? Do you view the cultures to be similar or different? What might account for the differences?

2 From a culture perspective, which company would you be more interested in working for? Why?

3 Do you think that culture, or some aspects of culture, can be communicated on the Internet? Why, or why not?

LEARNING CHECKLIST ☑

Before you move on you may want to reflect on what you have learnt in this chapter. You should now be able to:

☑ explain why organisational assumptions are important and identify three types of assumption that give meaning to culture

☑ identify four steps of organisational cultures based on the origin and content of the underlying cultural value systems

☑ illustrate how an organisation's core ideology, if truly visionary, provides sustaining consistency of behaviour regardless of changes in strategies and practices

☑ articulate how organisational culture guides behaviour

☑ read an organisation's culture by observing its physical settings and rituals, and by asking questions about its underlying assumptions and values

☑ explain how a founder establishes culture in a new organisation and how subsequent leaders adapt cultural elements to promote adaptive change

☑ distinguish four factors useful in comparing and contrasting national cultures.

Further reading

Dervitsiotis, K.N. (2005) 'Creating Conditions to Nourish Sustainable Organisational Excellence', *Total Quality Management & Business Excellence* 16(8, 9), October/November, p. 925.

Flynn, F.J. (2005) 'Identity Orientations and Forms of Social Exchange in Organisations', *Academy of Management Review* 30(4), October, p. 737.

Lok, P., Westwood, R. and Crawford, J. (2005) 'Perceptions of Organisational Subculture and their Significance for Organisational Commitment', *Applied Psychology* 54(4), October, p. 490.

Wolff, M.F. (1999) 'In the Organisation of the Future, Competitive Advantage Will Lie with Inspired Employees', *Research Technology Management* 42, July–August, pp. 2–4.

References

Beyer, J.M. and Trice, H.M. (1987) 'How an Organisation's Rites Reveal its Culture', *Organisational Dynamics* 15, Spring, p. 7.

Bianco, A. (2000) 'Software's Tough Guy', *Business Week*, 6 March, pp. 132–144.

Blum, T.C., Fields, D.L. and Goodman, J.S. (1994) 'Organization-level Determinants of Women in Management', *Academy of Management Journal* 37, April, pp. 241–268.

Boje, D.M. (1995) 'Stories of the Storytelling Organization: A Postmodern Analysis of Disney as "*Tamara*-Land"', *Academy of Management Journal* 38, August, pp. 997–1035.

Bremner, B. (2000) 'Doctor, I Just Can't Make Myself Spend', *Business Week*, 27 March, p. 57.

Burlingham, B. (1992) 'China, Inc.', *Inc.*, December, pp. 110–121.

Champy, J. (1995) *Reengineering Management: The Mandate for New Leadership.* New York, NY: Harper Business, p. 35.

Chen, C.C., Chen, X.P. and Meindl, J.R. (1998) 'How Can Cooperation Be Fostered? The Cultural Effects of Individualism-collectivism', *Academy of Management Review* 23, April, pp. 285–304.

Coffey, R.E., Athos, A.G. and Raynolds, P.A. (1985) *Behaviour in Organizations: A Multidimensional View* (2nd edn). Englewood Cliffs, NJ: Prentice Hall, pp. 38–52.

Collins, J.C. and Porras, J.I. (1994) *Built to Last: Successful Habits of Visionary Companies.* New York, NY: Harper Business.

Cooke, R.A. and Rousseau, D.M. (1988) 'Behavioural Norms and Expectations: A Quantitative Approach to the Assessment of Organisational Culture', *Group and Organisational Studies* 13, pp. 245–273.

Deal, T.E. and Kennedy, A.A. (1982) *Corporate Cultures: The Rites and Rituals of Corporate Life.* Reading, MA: Addison-Wesley, pp. 129–139.

Drucker, P.F. (1994) 'The Theory of the Business', *Harvard Business Review* 72, September–October, p. 100.

Drucker, P.F. (1999) 'Knowledge-worker Productivity: The Biggest Challenge', *California Management Review* 41, Winter, pp. 79–94.

Duncan, W.J. (1989) 'Organizational Culture: "Getting a Fix" on an Elusive Concept', *Academy of Management Executive* 3, August, pp. 229–236.

Dyer, J.H. and Singh, H. (1998) 'The Relational View: Cooperative Strategy and Sources of Interorganizational Competitive Advantage', *Academy of Management Review* 23, October, pp. 660–679.

Earley, P.C. and Singh, H. (1995) 'International and Intercultural Management Research: What's Next?', *Academy of Management Journal* 38, April, p. 338.

England, G. (1967) 'Organizational Goals and Expected Behaviour of American Managers', *Academy of Management Journal* 10, June, pp. 107–117.

Faw, R. (1999) *World's Best Value: Global Competition in the Information Age.* Safety Harbor, FL: Worldsbestvalue.com.

Flint, J. (1990) 'The New Team's Plans for Moving Iron', *Forbes*, 1 October, p. 78.

Fulmer, W.E. and Fulmer, R.M. (1988) 'Walt Disney Productions', in A.J. Strickland III and A.A. Thompson Jr (eds) *Cases in Strategic Management* (3rd edn). Homewood, IL: Richard D. Irwin, pp. 71–94.

Galbraith, J.R. (1995) *Designing Organizations.* San Francisco, CA: Jossey-Bass, pp. 2–3.

Gibson, C.B. (1999) 'Do They Do What They Believe They Can? Group Efficacy and Group Effectiveness Across Tasks and Cultures', *Academy of Management Journal* 42, April, pp. 138–152.

Granstrand, O., Patel, P. and Pavitt, K. (1997) 'Multi-technology Corporations: Why They Have "Distributed" Rather than "Distinctive Core" Competencies', *California Management Review* 39, Summer, pp. 8–26.

Greetz, C. (1973) *The Interpretation of Cultures.* New York, NY: Basic Books, p. 5.

Gregory, K.L. (1983) 'Native-view Paradigms: Multiple Cultures and Culture Conflicts in Organisations', *Administrative Science Quarterly*, September, pp. 359–376.

Greiner, L.E. (1972) 'Evolution and Revolution as Organizations Grow', *Harvard Business Review* 50, July–August, pp. 37–46.

Hayes, R.H. (1985) 'Strategic Planning-forward in Reverse?', *Harvard Business Review* 63, November–December, pp. 111–119.

Henriques, I. and Sadorsky, P. (1999) 'The Relationship between Environmental Commitment and Managerial Perceptions of Stakeholder Importance', *Academy of Management Journal* 42, February, pp. 87–99.

Hofstede, G. (1980) *Culture's Consequences: International Differences in Work-related Values.* Beverly Hills, CA: Sage Publications.

Hofstede, G. (1983) 'The Cultural Relativity of Organizational Practices and Theories', *Journal of International Business Studies* 14, Fall, p. 76.

Hofstede, G. (1994) 'Management Scientists Are Human', *Management Science* 40(1), pp. 4–13.

Jacob, R. (1995) 'Corporate Reputations', *Fortune*, 6 March, p. 54.

Johnson, C. (1993) 'Comparative Capitalism: The Japanese Difference', *California Management Review* 35, Summer, pp. 51–67.

Johnson, J.H. Jr, Thumin, F.J., Kuehl, C. and Jiang, W.Y. (1995) 'Toward Harmonization: A Cross-cultural Empirical Study Examining Managerial Values of Accountants from Four Countries', *Journal of Global Business*, September, pp. 35–37.

Jung, D.I. and Avolio, B.J. (1999) 'Effects of Leadership Style and Followers' Cultural Orientation on Performance in Group and Individual Task Conditions', *Academy of Management Journal* 42, April, pp. 208–218.

Kluckhohn, C., Rapoport, R., Roberts, J. and Vogt, E. (1952) 'Culture: A Critical Review of Concepts and Definitions', *Peabody Museum of Archaeology and Ethnology* 47(1). Cambridge, MA: Harvard University Press.

Kotter, J.P. and Heskett, K.L. (1992) *Corporate Culture and Performance.* New York, NY: The Free Press.

Linton, R. (1945) *The Cultural Background of Personality.* New York, NY: Appleton-Century Crofts, p. 32.

Maney, K. (1992) 'Workplace Dresses Down in '90s', *USA Today*, 24 July, p. B-1.

Nahapiet, J. and Ghoshal, S. (1998) 'Social Capital, Intellectual Capital, and the Organizational Advantage', *Academy of Management Review* 23, April, pp. 242–266.

Oritz, A.A. (1987) 'The Influence of Locus of Control and Culture on Learning Styles of Language Minority Students', in J.J. Johnson .and B.A. Ramierez (eds) *American Indian Exceptional Children and Youth.* Reston, VA: ERIC Clearinghouse on Handicapped and Gifted Children, Council for Exceptional Children, pp. 9–16.

Ouchi, W.G. and Jaeger, A.M. (1978) 'Type Z Organization: Stability in the Midst of Mobility', *Academy of Management Review* 3, April, pp. 305–314.

Packard, D. (1957) 'Objectives of the Hewlett-Packard Company', January, HP archives.

Pascale, R. (1984) 'Fitting New Employees into the Company Culture', *Fortune*, 28 May, p. 28.

Peterson, M.F. (1995) 'Role Conflict, Ambiguity and Overload: A 21-nation Study', *Academy of Management Journal* 38, April, p. 446.

Pettigrew, A.M. (1979) 'On Studying Organisational Cultures', *Administrative Science Quarterly* 24, December, p. 574.

Reimann, B.C. and Wiener, Y. (1988) 'Corporate Culture: Avoiding the Elitist Trap', *Business Horizons* 31, March–April, p. 36.

Rokeach, M. (1973) *The Nature of Human Values.* New York, NY: The Free Press, p. 5.

Rosenzweig, P.M. (1994) 'The New American Challenge: Foreign Multinationals in the United States', *California Management Review* 36, Spring, p. 117.

Rubenson, G.C. and Gupta, A.K. (1992) 'Replacing the Founder: Exploding the Myth of the Entrepreneur's Disease', *Business Horizons* 35, November–December, pp. 53–57.

Schein, E.H. (1983) 'The Role of the Founder in Creating Organisational Culture', *Organisational Dynamics*, Summer, pp. 13–28.

Schein, E.H. (1984) 'Coming to a New Awareness of Organizational Culture', *Sloan Management Review*, Winter, p. 4.

Schein, E.H. (1985) *Organizational Culture and Leadership.* San Francisco, CA: Jossey-Bass.

Senge, P. (1990) *The Fifth Discipline: The Art and the Practice of the Learning Organization.* New York, NY: Doubleday.

Spencer, L. (2005) 'Diversity and Equal Opportunities: Why Do They Matter?', *Training Journal,* June, pp. 54–58.

Stewart, T.A., Taylor III, A., Petre, P. and Schlender, B. (1999) 'Henry Ford, Alfred P. Sloan, Tom Watson Jr, Bill Gates: The Businessmen of the Century', *Fortune,* 22 November, pp. 108–128.

Thumin, F.J., Johnson, J.H. Jr, Kuehl, C. and Jiang, W.Y. (1995) 'Corporate Values as Related to Occupation, Gender, Age, and Company Size', *The Journal of Psychology* 129, pp. 389–400.

Tichy, N. (1999) 'The Teachable Point of View: A Primer', *Harvard Business Review* 77, March–April, pp. 82–83;.

Trice, H.M. and Beyer, J.M. (1984) 'Studying Cultures through Rites and Ceremonials', *Academy of Management Review* 9, October, p. 666.

Trompenaars, F. and Hampden-Turner, C. (1999) *Riding the Waves of Culture* (2nd edn). London: Nicholas Brealey.

Wagner III, J.A. (1995) 'Studies of Individualism-collectivism: Effects on Cooperation in Groups', *Academy of Management Journal* 38, February, pp. 152–172.

Wanous, J.P. (1980) *Organizational Entry: Recruitment, Selection, and Socialization of Newcomers.* Reading, MA: Addison-Wesley, p. 171.

Weick, K. (1969) *The Social Psychology of Organizations.* Reading, MA: Addison-Wesley.

Wetlaufer, S. (1999) 'Driving Change: An Interview with Ford Motor Company's Jacques Nasser', *Harvard Business Review,* March–April, pp. 76–88.

Wiener, Y. (1988) 'Forms of Value Systems: A Focus on Organizational Effectiveness and Cultural Change and Maintenance', *Academy of Management Review* 13, October, pp. 534–545.

Wolf, W.B. (1964) 'The Nature of Organizations', in W.B. Wolf (ed.) *Management: Readings toward a General Theory.* Belmont, CA: Wadsworth, pp. 18–23.

The role of human resource management in the organisation

LEARNING OUTCOMES

After studying this chapter you should be able to:

- ☑ **identify** the historical developments and their impact on HRM

- ☑ **outline** the development and functions of HRM

- ☑ **understand** the differences between HRM and personnel management

- ☑ **evaluate** 'hard' and 'soft' approaches to HRM

- ☑ **understand** how diversity is an issue in HR practice

- ☑ **consider** the HRM as an international issue.

The opening vignette illustrates why human resource management (HRM) is important in helping to achieve competitive advantage in the competitive mobile phone industry.

O2: batteries recharged

If all goes well in the summer of 2005, there will be sighs of relief around the boardroom table at O2. Not because the mobile phone company will have fought off a take-over; nor because one of its major competitors will be in trouble. Simply surviving the month without the firm losing its most valuable employees will be enough – a sign that the executive committee members spotted a potential disaster in time to be able to take steps to avoid it.

Among those on the committee, the one with most reason to be satisfied will be group HR director Andrew Harley. Originally recruited into BT's IT department, Harley transferred to HR in 1997 and slowly worked his way up the ladder.

In conversation at O2's headquarters, he concedes that he might have been verging on the melodramatic when he warned his colleagues of the 'perfect storm' the company was heading for this summer. But he says that he knew unless something was done urgently, the outlook for O2 was bleak.

'There were a few reasons for my pessimism,' he says. 'By July, a lot of our executive share options would be maturing – when that happens people always look elsewhere. And, for good or bad, O2 is seen by many headhunters as a good company to get people from.'

Harley was also worried that the company had worked people too hard without investing sufficiently in their development. 'There comes a time when people have been running up and down escalators so much that they start to think it's about time they tried something different,' he says.

The firm came into existence in November 2001 when BT Wireless demerged from its parent as Cellnet (it became O2 in February 2002). By then Harley was its HR director.

'I'd spent 14 years in IT and initially went into HR for only six months. But I really enjoyed it. I did a variety of roles, although mostly in computing to start with. The aspect I liked most was executive development within the global business. It was fascinating. You had to work out how to connect all these people, whether they were French, German, English, or working in Asia or America.'

Then, in 2001, after a series of ever more senior roles for Harley, came Cellnet. 'I was asked to be HR director. I jumped at the chance.'

Back then, the thought of the company even surviving as far as 2005 was far-fetched. 'We were in survival mode,' says Harley. 'Everyone was focused on minute-by-minute, hour-by-hour delivery.

'It was only later on that I realised we weren't OK. I'd never run HR in a plc before, or worked at executive committee level. There was a very rapid growing-up in terms of identifying the things that I didn't know about – all those 'I wish I'd known then what I know now' aspects.

'It's funny looking back now, because no one gave us a prayer – everyone was telling us we'd be around for three months, then be eaten up by a Telefonica or a Telecom Italia. And, in HR terms, we didn't give much thought to the long term because we'd done the compensation and the share plans – all we were focused on was managing a performance culture and driving things month by month.'

Adding to the stress of the demerger was the fact that Cellnet had only a small HR team of around 40. This wasn't really enough, given that it was also having to take on such work as corporate social responsibility, for which BT had a good reputation. 'It wasn't something we could just drop. Mobiles are contentious, whether it's the potential health hazards of masts, recycling or children's use. So we took it very seriously.'

The analogy Harley uses is that it was like a first move away from home. 'You suddenly realise what your parents do for you – the washing, the shopping, the tidying. It sounds like we were a bit naive, but we just didn't see it all coming.'

Yet another stress factor was an approach from telecoms firm KPN to buy the company. This meant more HR activity in terms of settling employees and supporting the teams that were responding to the approach.

However, as O2 emerged intact from that last year, the focus gradually turned to the longer term. 'The big thing that has changed over the past 18 months has been a realisation that we can survive,' says Harley. 'Our revenue grew by £1 billion last year. A lot of FTSE 100 companies don't even have that as a revenue.'

When he was able to raise his head above the parapet for the first time, Harley picked up on the fact that O2 needed to start investing in its people. 'You need three things to keep people – they have to have interesting work, they need be told how well they're doing, and they need someone who is interested in their development. We definitely have interesting work, and we have a tough performance-management system so people know how they're doing, but had we invested in them? I didn't think we had. We hadn't spent much on development because we were in survival mode.'

This realisation, along with the approaching maturity of the executive stock options, led to a two-pronged strategy: to revisit reward and to create an executive development plan (EDP). The strategy does seem to have averted the perfect storm – although it wasn't as simple as it sounds.

'Our work has had a really big impact, but it hasn't been cheap. It's probably the most expensive intervention we've done in terms of investing in people,' says Harley.

'We've had to focus on total reward and say to people, "Yes, you have got money coming up", but we also show them what they are due to receive in 2007, 2008 and 2009. There's a ramp – if they stay, they will continue to earn good money. We also remind them about the more intangible benefits, whether it's pensions or healthcare. We've done that for 90 people so far.'

Harley explains that selling the concept to the board wasn't straightforward. 'If you say to the executive committee – a lot of whom have come from different companies – that you want an EDP, they'll say, "Oh, we had them in our old companies, they're just a glorified pat on the back."'

So Harley outlined his plans for an EDP that would improve the bottom line and made sure the committee was aware just how real the perfect-storm scenario was. Fortunately, they listened.

O2's EDP is run with Templeton College, Oxford – by coincidence, it was set up by the HR team's Mark Templeton. Much to his relief, Harley has been assured by participants that it is effective.

'We've made people stop and think about what they do. That's a really impressive thing because everyone is so busy that it's relatively easy for them to say: "No, I'm going to stick to the tried-and-trusted ways of doing things." One of my favourite sayings is that, for every problem, there's a simple solution that's unfortunately wrong. If they stopped and thought about it, they'd come up with something better.'

And the stakes are high. In the UK alone, O2 has 10 000 employees and is a £3 billion company. It also has eight operators competing with it. 'We need people who can set strategy and be inspirational in front of 1000 or 2000 employees,' says Harley. 'You can't afford for someone to come up against a problem and do something that's suboptimal. They've got one chance, and it has to be right.'

It is hoped that the EDP will take care of that problem, so the next challenge for Harley is to improve the O2 customer experience. With the market close to saturation, there is a growing need to keep the customers O2 already has, as well as attract new ones.

To do this has meant reducing some teams in marketing, technology, finance and HR, while increasing front-line people such as retail sales and customer-contact agents. Up to 500 managers will leave in the next six months, and over the next 12–24 months the company will hire up to 2000 retail and customer-contact people.

It seems the work of an HR director is never done, but there is little time for complacency. As if to remind him of this, CVs land on Harley's desk daily, many of them from one of O2's main rivals. 'I see CVs from all our competitors, but this company's share scheme has paid out and it's had – or is still in – a bit of a perfect storm,' says Harley.

'That's not to say it won't come out of it, because it's got good marketing people and very strong customer orientation. We are just hoping we won't be in the same position when it comes to July and August and our own people get their cheques.'

He is confident O2 won't be. 'We've explained to employees where the future lies and we've shown them that we're investing in them.'

He then adds that he's just had a meeting with his UK executive team. 'It was very reassuring,' he says. 'They told me – completely unsolicited – that they'd seen a real change in the HR team. They thought we'd really moved on.'

If he sighed with relief, you couldn't really blame him.

Source: © Steve Smethurst, *People Management* magazine, 5 May 2005.
Reproduced with permission.

Discussion questions

1 How can the role of HR influence the success of an organisation?
2 Why is it important for managers to retain staff?

The opening vignette demonstrates the importance of human resource management as part of the management function. This chapter introduces you to the role of human resource management and its importance for organisational behaviour.

Whether you work as a supervisor in a supermarket with responsibility for the checkout operators, the general manager of the local branch of a multinational bank, the union representative for a major airline or the director of HRM in a technology organisation, you will be responsible for managing people. You may have decided to choose people management because you have a love of people, but empathy for people is not necessarily what makes human resource practitioners effective. According to Hunt (1999), what is important for HR managers is an understanding of the structures and climate in which people's potential can be released, developed and rewarded. Andrew Fastow of Enron, although misguided, discovered this in his famous quote: 'Eat what they hunt – only then will they hunt well'. However, he failed to understand the necessity of developing the whole organisation and the results are history. The Enron view of people management is not the view taken by all organisations. The John Lewis Partnership, for instance, also believes in giving its employees, or 'partners' as they are referred to by the company, a stake in the organisation. It achieves this by encouraging workers to co-operate to fulfil the company's aims. In turn, employees are rewarded with a share of the profits.

This chapter introduces you to the role of the people manager and human resource specialist. At the moment, HR is in a constant state of change with Hunt (1999) suggesting that one of the following could happen.

■ HR goes into decline – outsourcing and downsizing has removed the HR specialist from organisations and placed the HR role with the overworked line manager.

vision
The view of how the organisation sees itself developing and achieving its objectives.

■ Human resource management is an important function, which will begin to play an important role in top management. The HR function will be closely integrated into the **vision** and strategy of the organisation.

■ HR will continue as it has done in the past, due to the limitations of labour markets, unions, legislation, etc. This implies that it stands still and does not develop.

Whatever the view of HR and how it develops in the future, it is important to understand where it has come from and what has influenced it. To set the scene of where we are today, we will now take an overview of the historical developments of the profession.

History of HRM
The late nineteenth century

Wherever people have needed to be employed there has been some form of people management, although it has only been in recent years that a consistent view has emerged on how to develop people.

At the end of the nineteenth century many workers were employed in the manufacturing sectors, where they had to put in long hours and conditions were often harsh. The welfare state did not exist and no work could mean destitution. However, even in such unenlightened

paternalist
An employer viewed as a father figure in the organisation.

times some employers did value their workers and took on a **paternalist** role for their employees. Such famous names as Cadbury, Rowntree and Bournville, all chocolate manufacturers, and Lever, a soap manufacturer, all took their employees' welfare

very seriously and established the provision of health and education as part of their role as a responsible employer. These enlightened employers tended to be Quakers and were some of the first employers to employ welfare officers. The welfare officers were often women and were concerned not only with visiting sick employees but also with supervising moral welfare. Pressures were also coming from an emerging labour movement and trades unions were gaining influence with a campaign for 'industrial betterment' (Cannell, 2004).

The 1900s also saw the development of personnel management as a professional body, with the formation of the Welfare Workers' Association, a forerunner to the CIPD.

Scientific management

Human resource management as we know it today also developed from a range of theories from sociologists, psychologists, and management and organisational behaviourists. One of the

scientific management
An early 1900s movement, which held that the scientific observation of people would reveal the one best way to do any task.

earliest can be traced back to the United States in the early 1900s with the development of 'time and motion' studies, which would find the 'one best way' of performing a task. The father of what became known as **scientific management** was Frederick Taylor. Taylor replaced haphazard rules of thumb with precise measure principles. He was one of the first to emphasise the prediction of

behaviour and encouraged the use of training and other management techniques to influence work outcomes. Taylor identified the skills needed for a particular job and would hire and train workers to perform to the required standards. Employees were rewarded with a 'differential piece rate' pay system that rewarded work output. Many managers took on the ideas of Taylor often without the pay incentives. Although Taylor, publicised his ideas as a success, the reality was threats of industrial action, redundancies and disgruntled management (Rose, 1975).

Fordism

The USA was also leading the way in developing large-scale industrialisation with car manufacturers such as Henry Ford. Ford continued with the scientific management approach and developed an assembly line where the workers were allowed a minimum amount of time to complete a task before the car moved to the next stage in the production process. Employees unable to keep up were fired; this led to a high level of absenteeism as well as high employment turnover. To counteract the high staff turnover Ford introduced 'the five dollar day' bonus, which would double workers' wages. However, the bonus was payable only to employees whose moral and work ethic was seen as appropriate both at home and at work. Management control was also increased, through the use job evaluation and a pay system that was matched to the difficulty or status of the job. Workers had to be with the company six months to qualify for the scheme, and young people under 21 and women were not eligible (Benyon, 1973). With mass production, the role of managing people became a science and managers were expected to have not only technical expertise but also managerial ability. In the UK, however, reliability and the ability to impose discipline were seen as far more important than technical knowledge.

The human relations movement

The **human relations** movement began to grow in the 1920s with Elton Mayo and the famous Hawthorne experiments. This shifted the view of people management away from the mechanistic principles of scientific management and towards a behavioural approach of satisfying the social needs of workers. The results of the Hawthorne approach taught managers that concern for people did not mean lower production, but the reverse. This was seen as an anti-Taylor perspective as it argued against Taylor's 'one best way', although it agreed with Taylor's idea of sufficient rest breaks for workers.

human relations
The movement which proposed the view that the social side of work was important for improving performance.

Research in the UK was also emerging from the National Institute of Industrial Psychology (NIIP). It investigated methods of work and its relation to fatigue, and concluded that fatigue was not only psychological but also physiological. The resulting research, by what became known as the human relations school and other work psychologists, identified the importance of the human factor of work. They discovered that people were more effective if they were allowed a say in how to perform tasks and that social relations were often more important than money in maintaining morale.

The First World War

The war years of 1914–18 saw major developments in personnel management. The Munitions of War Act 1915 passed to ensure a sufficient supply of labour to munitions factories made the provision of welfare services compulsory. This led to a large increase in the number of welfare officers, many of whom were men as it was considered more appropriate for them to oversee the welfare of boys.

However, women were also being recruited in large numbers to replace the men sent to the trenches. This led to some bitter disputes with trades unions, which saw craftsmen's jobs being filled by unskilled women. It led to the government having to enter into discussion and consultation with the unions (Cannell, 2004).

Another development was the role of 'labour officers', needed to assist in the recruitment, selection, discipline and industrial relations on the shop floor of unionised workers. Labour officers also had to interpret the many government directives concerning the employment of civilians in wartime and aspects concerning discipline and dismissal. Many labour officers were male and came from an engineering and works management background (Evans, 2003).

Between the wars

The engineering industries developed the role of the personnel manager, and job titles such as 'labour manager' or 'employment manager' became more common. Their role was to handle recruitment, dismissal, absence and pay. Pay negotiations were becoming more common and officials appointed by employers' federations negotiated national pay rates with the unions.

The inter-war years also saw the emergence of the title 'personnel manager', in companies such as Marks & Spencer. The personnel manager dealt with many of the functions of the human resource that we know today. However, senior management more often dealt with any industrial relations problems (Cannell, 2004).

Personnel was not the only name to change: the Worker's Welfare Association, after evolving through several name changes, finally became the Institute of Labour Management in 1931, and eventually the Institute of Personnel Management (IPM) in 1945.

The Second World War

The 1939–45 war saw more government regulations introduced to regulate employment and increase morale in a bid to boost the war effort. The role of the welfare and personnel manager was seen by government as a vital part of the drive to greater efficiency. Strikes were also made illegal and productivity improvements became part of a joint consultation and negotiation between unions and the government. By the end of the war the personnel profession had expanded and had approximately 5300 practitioners; many of the HRM practices in use today can trace their origins back to the war years.

The post-war years

With the post-war years came a time of economic boom, with manufacturing at its peak. Unemployment was low and personnel practices such as planning, recruitment and selection became important aspects of the personnel manager's role. During the war much of the personnel role had been to implement government rules, and the emerging personnel profession tended to be very bureaucratic and based on function (Cannell, 2004).

Industrial relations also took on a new role. During the war years negotiations were centralised and often government led. With large companies now developing their own employment policies, negotiations became more and more decentralised with local shop stewards and local bargaining. Official and unofficial strikes became damaging to the economy and the UK became notorious for its poor industrial relations. Eventually, a report by Lord Donovan in 1968 criticised employers, managers and unions for their failure to negotiate and failure to plan for industrial relations strategies. Much of the criticism of the failure of industrial relations was directed at the failure of employers to give personnel management a high priority. The higher profile of personnel today can partly be seen as a response to the criticism made by Donovan (Cannell, 2004).

The 1960s also saw the introduction of new legislation, such as contracts of employment, training and redundancy payments. The 1970s saw the introduction of equal opportunities legislation and employment protection, but there were also attempts to control trades union activity. The economy was also in decline and personnel departments were not only expected to implement the new legislation, but also directives on pay regulations to curb the spiralling inflation. New techniques needed to be developed to improve performance and much of the work done by social scientists, management and organisational behaviour theorists in the USA, such as Herzberg's theory of motivation, found their way into the personnel departments.

The main features of personnel management as it is today were in place by the end of the 1970s and are summed up by Cannell (2004) as follows:

- **The collective bargaining role** – centred around dealing with trades unions and the development of industrial relations strategies.

- **The implementer of legislation role** – implying understanding and implementing a growing amount of legislation.

- **The bureaucratic role** – implementing a series of rules about behaviour at work, dealing with recruitment, managing absence, and so on.

- **The social conscience of business role**, or 'value champion' – a residue from the welfare worker function.

- **A growing performance improvement role** (in some organisations and sectors) – about integrating the personnel function with business needs and taking a more strategic view.

The rise of HRM

The election of a Conservative Government under Margaret Thatcher in 1979 marked a change in shift from collectivism to individualism. Legislation was introduced to control the perceived abuse of union power by banning sympathy strikes and removing the concept of the 'closed shop', where union membership was compulsory. High unemployment of over three million, and the decline of the manufacturing industries, also led to decline in the strength of the unions.

The 1980s also saw the term 'human resource manager' (HRM) introduced to the UK from America. The meaning of the term HRM has led to many debates and academic discussions, as can be seen below. To some, it was seen as a way of minimising trade union influence and the name change from 'personnel' symbolised this. Others saw HRM as a more strategic role in the achievement of organisational objectives, with an HR director at board level. Before moving on to the personnel management versus human resource management debate, developments through the 1980s and 1990s, such as the rise of the training specialist, as well as the reward, resourcing and diversity specialists that exist in many large organisations are now seen as an important part of the personnel function.

As can be seen throughout the last century, the role of the HR professional continues to evolve, develop and have a significant impact on the effectiveness of organisations. The debate between personnel and HRM continued into the 1990s and is discussed in the following section.

Personnel management versus HRM

Personnel management is often considered an old-fashioned name for human resource management, and in some organisations, there may well be little difference between the old personnel department and today's HR department. But HRM can also mean a particular philosophy of the role of HRM in organisations, and how people are developed and nurtured to achieve organisational goals.

The foundations of HR activity

The traditional view of HRM can be explained by the four objectives that form the foundation of the human resource activity. These can be identified as staffing, performance, change management and administration objectives, and are illustrated in Exhibit 17-1.

These are the underlying objectives that support the HR function and enable managers not only to ensure compliance with legislation but also to enable a move towards strategic development, which will be discussed in the next chapter. An explanation of why they are important is given below.

Staffing objectives

Staffing ensures that the right staff are available at the right time in the right place. This involves identifying the nature of the job and implementing a recruitment and selection process to ensure a correct match. Staffing objectives also need to ensure that once the people are recruited they can be retained, either through a reward package and/or development process. There is nothing new about this, as can be seen from the overview of the history of HRM: even Henry Ford had to offer an incentive of the 'five dollar day' in an attempt to reduce staff turnover, and today many workers in the financial sector eagerly await their end-of-year bonuses.

Performance objectives

These are a continuation of the staffing objectives. Once the staff are in place they need to be motivated to perform. This can take place through the development processes. Performance targets may be introduced through an appraisal system where employers invite members of staff to discuss their performance and future ambitions and develop strategies to enable them to be

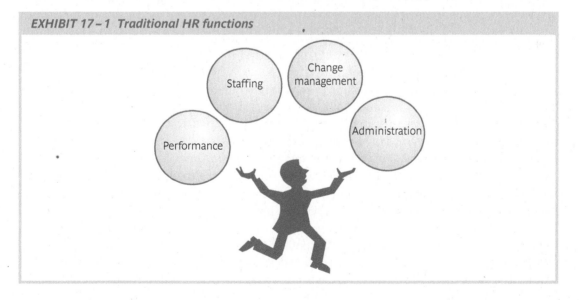

EXHIBIT 17–1 Traditional HR functions

met. House of Fraser stores use the appraisal system not only to identify future managers but also to enable sales staff to receive training, either in work-related issues such as customer care, or personal development areas such as improving IT skills. Training and development are often used to close the gap between current performance and expected future performance. But, as House of Fraser identified, they can also be used for maintaining commitment and empowerment, which in turn will improve performance. Performance objectives can also identify the disengaged worker, who for whatever reason no longer feels committed to the organisation. Again strategies can be put in place to return these workers to fuller participation in the workplace.

Change-management objectives

These are required if organisations are to be effective in developing an innovative and fast-moving organisation that can keep up with the fast pace of development in a modern society. Organisations need to be adaptable and flexible, which means that policies and objectives need to be in place to manage change. Many of the IT industries need to be adaptable and fast changing to keep up with changes in modern technology. For example, Apple Computers' market share was in decline due to the monopoly of the Microsoft Windows operating system, but it has reinvented itself with the iPod, and is now leading the way in music technology. Without change management objectives Apple would have found it much harder to respond to rapid changes. For this reason the recruitment, selection and development strategies all need to feed into the change-management objectives.

Administration objectives

These need to be complied with in order for the organisation to operate smoothly. Employees need to be paid regularly, tax needs to be collected to comply with legislation, and data need to be accurate and relevant to the organisation's goals. Employment legislation needs to be adhered to and records maintained, where appropriate, to demonstrate this is happening. When companies expand rapidly, they need to ensure that their administration systems are adequate for their needs. One such market research company, based in St Albans, expanded from a team of two people to an organisation employing 20 people. There were no systems in place to deal with the increase, and this resulted in poor allocation of tasks, not knowing who was on duty and at what time, as well as staff not being paid on time. The result: demotivated staff and a high staff turnover, which eventually affected business performance.

Distinguishing between HRM and PM

All the above objectives need to be taken into account, whether personnel management or HRM. However, personnel management is viewed as **workforce centred** and more operational in focus. Personnel managers recruit, select and carry out administrative procedures in accordance with management's requirements. They act as a bridge between the employer and the employee. As a result, personnel managers were seen as functional specialists rather than strategic managers and often had little power or status in the organisation. The personnel manager needed to understand the needs of the manager and the employee, and articulate those needs to both sides.

workforce centred
Refers to personnel managers who concentrate on protecting the workers from managers.

Some organisations, however, see HRM as a particular approach in the management of people. HRM can be seen as a radical new approach linked to strategy and viewing people as assets who need to be actively managed as part of the long-term interests of the organisation. HRM can be viewed as a radical integrated approach to the management of people in an organisation and, as such, can be seen as a general management function. Where personnel managers can be viewed as specialists, HRM can be seen as the responsibility of *all* managers, particularly senior managers, and as such is proactive rather than reactive.

Guest (1987) identifies the differences in his model illustrating the differences between personnel and human resource management (see Exhibit 17-2).

Guest (1987) shows a model of HRM that is commitment based, which is distinct from compliance-based personnel management. According to Guest, HRM is:

- linked to the strategic management of an organisation
- seeks commitment to organisational goals
- focuses on individual needs rather than the collective workforce
- enables organisations to devolve power and become more flexible
- emphasises people as an asset to be positively utilised by the organisation.

Guest (1987) sees HRM as a distinct approach to managing the workforce and argues that, although personnel management will also select and train staff, it is the distinct approach in the selection and training that matters. HRM's approach should be linked to high performance and commitment rather than compliance. Guest (1997) recognises that, although empirical evidence is only just beginning to show the link between HRM and performance, evidence is already suggesting that HRM works. The view from industry is also suggesting that HRM is taking on a strategic role in industry. The CIPD (2003) HR survey identified HR issues as now being regularly discussed at executive boards and HR managers seeing their role as that of a strategic business partner, with the HR function now focused on achieving key business goals and developing employee capabilities.

Storey defines the elements that differentiate HRM as follows.

- Human capability and commitment: Storey argues that this is what differentiates organisations.
- Strategic importance of HRM: it needs to be implemented into the organisational strategy and considered at the highest management level.

EXHIBIT 17–2 The differences between personnel and HRM

	Personnel	HRM
Time and planning	Short term, reactive ad hoc marginal	Long term, proactive, strategic, integrated
Psychological contract	Compliance	Commitment
Control systems	External	Self-control
Employee relations	Pluralist, collective, low trust	Unitarist, individual, high trust
Structures and systems	Bureaucratic/mechanistic, centralised, formal	Organic, devolved, flexible
Roles	Specialist/professional	Largely integrated into line management
Evaluation criteria	Cost minimisation	Maximum utilisation (human asset accounting)

Source: Guest (1987).

- The long-term importance of HRM: it needs to be integrated into the management functions and seen to have important consequences for the ability of the organisation to achieve its goals.
- The key functions of HRM: seen to encourage commitment rather than compliance.

Storey (1992) identifies a model with 27 points that differentiate HRM from personnel and industrial relations (IR) practices. Storey's model is based on an ideal type of organisation and is a tool used to present what Storey sees as the essential features of personnel and HRM in an exaggerated way.

Storey identifies four categories in which the 27 points fit. These are: beliefs and assumptions, strategic concepts, line management, and key levers, which include the functions of HR such as selection, pay, and so on.

Storey's model can be viewed as an 'ideal type' of HRM and has been used as a tool for research and analysis of organisations. In practice, HRM would use some elements of his 27 points but would be extremely unlikely to include all of them. As such the model is useful as a research tool but does not reflect what happens in practice (see Exhibit 17-3).

Storey's (1992) 27 points of difference identify personnel management as being bureaucratic, based on rules and procedures and seen as a separate function from general management. On the other hand, HRM is seen as related to the business need, and central to the corporate plan and the responsibility of all managers.

Storey (1992) proposes another model as a means of comparative analysis, for identifying the shift organisations may take from personnel management to HRM. This is illustrated in Exhibit 17-4.

Storey (1992) suggests in the model depicted in Exhibit 17-4 that, for an organisation to gain competitive advantage, a strategic response needs to be given to the beliefs and assumptions of the organisations and that line managers should take on part of this role. Line managers would have a responsibility for the change in key levers, which would move the organisation away from being locked into bureaucratic procedures towards becoming a flexible organisation that would encourage commitment through performance-related goals.

Your turn

Where would you prefer to work?

Consider the main differences between personnel and human resource management. Would you prefer to work in a company that follows personnel management practices or HRM practices?

Defining HRM: soft versus hard HRM

hard HRM
Views people as a resource used as a means of achieving organisational goals.

soft HRM
Encourages employers to develop strategies to gain employee commitment.

Within the HRM view, two approaches have been identified. Storey (1989) labelled these two approaches hard HRM and soft HRM. The 'hard' approach, rooted in manpower planning, is concerned with aligning human resource strategy with business strategy, while the 'soft' approach is rooted in the human relations school, has concern for workers' outcomes and encourages commitment to the organisation by focusing on workers' concerns.

EXHIBIT 17-3 *Storey's 27 points of difference between personnel and IR practices and HRM practices*

Dimension	Personnel/IR	HRM
Beliefs and assumptions		
1 Contract	Careful delineation of written contracts	Aim to go 'beyond contract'
2 Rules	Importance of devising clear rules/mutuality	'Can-do' outlook; impatience with 'rule'
3 Guide to management action	Procedures	'Business need'
4 Behaviour referent	Norms/custom and practice	Values/mission
5 Managerial task vis-à-vis labour	Monitoring	Nurturing
6 Nature of relations	Pluralist	Unitarist
7 Conflict	Institutionalised	De-emphasised
Strategic aspects		
8 Key relations	Labour management	Customer
9 Initiatives	Piecemeal	Integrated
10 Corporate plan	Marginal to	Central to
11 Speed of decision	Slow	Fast
Line management		
12 Management role	Transactional	Transformational leadership
13 Key managers	Personnel/IR specialists	General/business/line managers
14 Communication	Indirect	Direct
15 Standardisation	High (for example, 'parity' an issue)	Low (for example, 'parity' not an issue)
16 Prized management skills	Negotiation	Facilitation
Key Levers		
17 Selection	Separate, marginal task	Integrated, key task
18 Pay	Job evaluation (fixed grades)	Performance related
19 Conditions	Separately negotiated	Harmonisation
20 Labour management	Collective bargaining contracts	Towards individual contracts
21 Thrust of relations with stewards	Regularised through facilities and training	Marginalised (with exception of some bargaining for change models)
22 Job categories and grades	Many	Few
23 Communication	Restricted flow	Increased flow
24 Job design	Division of labour	Teamwork
25 Conflict handling	Reach temporary truces	Manage climate and culture
26 Training and development	Controlled access to courses	Learning companies
27 Foci of attention for interventions	Personnel procedures	Wide-ranging cultural, structural and personnel strategies

Source: Storey (1992, p. 38). Reproduced with permission of Blackwell Publishers.

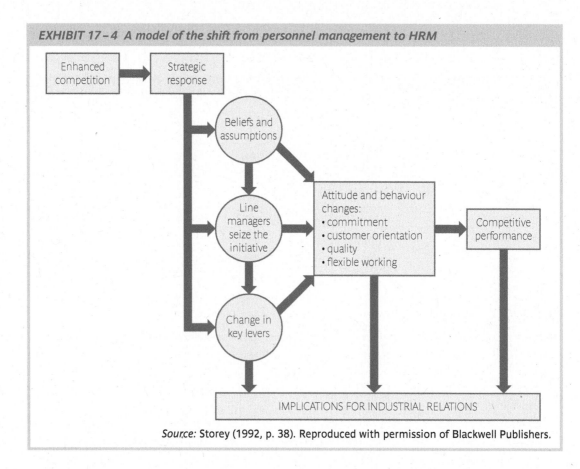

EXHIBIT 17–4 A model of the shift from personnel management to HRM

Source: Storey (1992, p. 38). Reproduced with permission of Blackwell Publishers.

Soft HRM

The soft view of HRM, developed by Storey (2001), popularised a distinctive approach to managing the human resource. Beer *et al.* (1984) proposed the Harvard model as a means of improving managers' methods of managing people. Walton (1985) argued that the role of HRM was to develop strategies to gain employees' commitment, not to be a means of controlling them.

Beer *et al.* (1984) suggest that managers need to be more responsible for HRM. The Harvard model opened the debate in the 1980s and proposes four human resource categories, as is demonstrated in Exhibit 17-5.

The issues proposed by Beer *et al.* (1984) argue that managers need to take responsibility for employee influence, human resource flow, reward systems and work systems, regardless of the size of the organisation. They recognise that different stakeholders have different interests and, for an organisation to be effective, managers need to take these interests into account.

Employee influence

This refers to how managers disperse their power and authority throughout the organisation while ensuring that the organisational goals are met.

The human resource flow

This refers to issues of recruitment, selection, development and ending the contract for the people in the organisation. The model argues that managers must work together to ensure that the right people are in the right place at the right time.

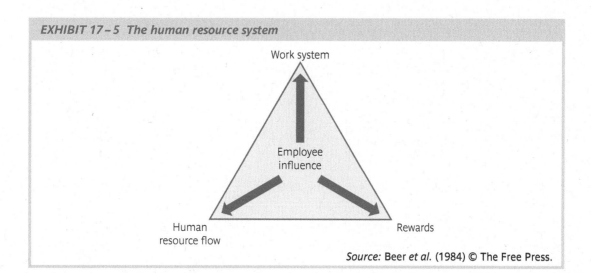

EXHIBIT 17–5 The human resource system

Source: Beer *et al.* (1984) © The Free Press.

Rewards systems

These are concerned with how employees are rewarded for their work. They include monetary reward such as pay, bonuses and profit sharing, and non-monetary rewards such as holidays and health insurance. They are also concerned with intrinsic rewards such as job fulfilment and empowerment, which help to maintain a motivated and productive workforce. The **Harvard model** recommends that employees are involved in the design of the reward system, while managers must ensure it is consistent with the organisation's goals.

Harvard model
A soft model of HRM to encourage employee commitment through employee influence, HR flow, reward and work systems.

Work systems

This refers to the organisation of work to ensure that it is efficient and productive and, again, can meet the organisation's goals. Work systems need to ensure that the communication channels work and the correct technology is in place at the various levels of the organisation.

As can be seen from Exhibit 17-6, the human resource system forms one part of the Harvard model and cannot be considered without taking into account stakeholder interests, situational factors, HR outcomes and the long-term consequences of decisions.

Stakeholder interests

This refers to shareholders who have a financial interest in the business. These range from the management, who need to ensure that organisational goals are met, to employee groups, either formal or informal. Externally, the government also has an interest in how organisations operate: this includes legislation to ensure that people are protected and to monitor how the organisation contributes to the economy. Often in communities where one type of organisation is a major employer, the community may also have a stake in the organisation. This was the case in the 1980s when, with the demise of the coal mines and manufacturing industries, many communities were destroyed as people moved away to find work. Unions may also have an interest in the organisation and, although many unions lost their power after the 1980s, workers still have the right to belong to a union and employers have a duty to recognise this.

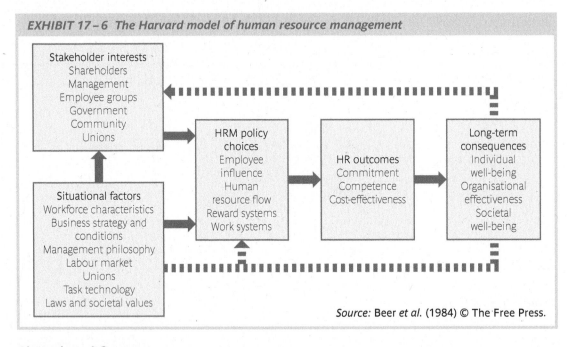

EXHIBIT 17–6 The Harvard model of human resource management

Source: Beer et al. (1984) © The Free Press.

Situational factors

These include the characteristics of the workforce, which in turn include labour markets, union representation, laws and societal values. Questions need to be asked such as: Who are they? Where do they come from? What is the culture? The business environment also needs to be considered, such as the economic conditions, strategic issues as to the direction of the organisation, and the management philosophy that drives the organisation. The technology and work systems also need to be taken into account to ensure that the workers can be effective.

These lead to the HRM policy choices of employee influence, human resource flow, reward systems and work systems, which were illustrated in Exhibit 17-5.

HR outcomes

These follow on from the HRM policy choices and are concerned with commitment, competence, congruence and cost-effectiveness. Managers need to ask: 'How can we gain commitment from our workers to enable the achievement of organisational goals? How can we ensure we have a trained and competent workforce who are able to perform productively? How can we sustain congruence; in other words, ensure that our workers are compatible with the management style and will fit in with other employees?' Finally, how can managers ensure they are cost-effective while maintaining employee satisfaction?

Long-term consequences

These follow on from HRM policy and outcomes and refer to individual well-being. Will the outcomes ensure that individuals are looked after and their needs considered? Will the organisation still be able to be effective and compete or provide a service in the external market? How will the HR outcome satisfy the wider needs of society and the community as a whole.'

Managing diversity is another important issue for managers today, which is why HR managers need to be aware, not only of legislation, but also how it can affect the morale of employees. Managing for diversity ensures that all employees can feel valued as part of the organisation. An example of this is illustrated in the Dynamics of Diversity box.

Post haste: Royal Mail wants to recruit and retain women at all levels

The male remains dominant in mail. With a workforce comprising 85 per cent men, Royal Mail is a company that still has to bridge the gender gap. As one of the largest employers in the UK, it wants to know not only how it can attract more women, but how it can ensure they are represented at all levels of the business.

'Like many organisations, the further up the hierarchy you look, the fewer women there are,' explains Satya Kartara, director of diversity and inclusion at Royal Mail.

The motivation to change this situation came in 2002, when current chairman Allan Leighton arrived. It was a time when Royal Mail was losing over £1m each day, morale among its employees was at rock bottom and the group's reputation in terms of service delivery was plummeting. One of the four key objectives introduced by Leighton to reverse the slump in fortunes was to implement a policy of diversity and inclusion.

'One of the things Mr Leighton is very keen to do is make Royal Mail a great place to work, and we believe that having a much more representative workforce will help achieve this goal,' explains Kartara.

So far, the organisation has focused on two areas: flexible working and making its advertising more female friendly. 'In our ads, we are clearly stating that we want more women to join us,' she says. 'Meanwhile, our current flexible-working initiatives include job sharing.'

Royal Mail is also looking at other solutions, such as changing the way its offices prepare for deliveries. 'A lot of the very early morning work is spent sorting the mail. We are exploring the idea of structuring the shifts so that a separate set of people can do the sorting to those doing the delivering. This would mean that women who want to come into work a bit later could do so, but they'd still be able to finish work relatively early and spend time with their families,' says Kartara.

Royal Mail is also demonstrating its commitment at the top of the organisation. 'We have a diversity champions group made up of very senior managers, and they are the ones who ensure our ideas actually happen on the ground. Vanessa Leeson, our gender champion, is committed to ensuring there are no blockages to our strategies.'

On the downside, the Equal Opportunities Commission recently investigated allegations of widespread sexual harassment of Royal Mail's female postal workers. However, the probe has been suspended following an agreement based on a wide-ranging action plan to stamp out harassment.

Despite such measures, Royal Mail is keen to do much more to attract, retain and promote women. 'It's early days,' admits Kartara. 'We've only been looking at this issue in a really serious way for the past nine months, and we're open to ideas about what else we can do. Ideally, we want to change things as quickly as possible.'

Dianah Worman, adviser, diversity, the Chartered Institute of Personnel and Development (CIPD), says: 'It is clear that the challenges we face in managing diversity are not open to quick-fix solutions. Fundamental change is needed, and that includes tackling flexible working and extending such opportunities to employees at all levels.

'Flexible working is vital in helping people to manage their work/life balance, and is often a factor taken into account by successful women in considering top-level roles. Work/life provisions won't be a positive differentiator in the market for talent in the longer term, but a negative one if options are not available.

'Royal Mail is not alone in the domination of top positions by men, and CIPD research makes it clear that cultural change in the boardroom is the next thing employers will have to tackle to attract and retain more highly qualified women.'

Andrew McNeilis, European commercial director, Hudson (recruitment consultancy), suggests 'Royal Mail is probably the only UK business that can count every member of the public as a customer, and it should capitalise on that. Your customers are your potential future workforce – they need to hear about the steps you are taking to encourage diversity, and see opportunities for themselves.

'Use women in all your advertising, not just recruitment, and target women's publications to show the advantages of working at Royal Mail. Companies that ensure their workforce mirrors their customer base win on both sides.

'A cultural shift like this takes time – it's a marathon, not a sprint. But promote the commercial and social benefits that a diverse workforce has brought to the business so far. Success breeds success, and the more positive examples of diversity in practice that can be showcased to current employees, the better.

'Finally, talk to, and learn from, other organisations that have tackled diversity in their recruitment and are now reaping the rewards.'

Tony Burnett, director, Performance Through Inclusion (consultancy), says: 'It's tempting to start with recruitment, but if you recruit women into a hostile environment, they'll leave very quickly. The key is culture, so it's essential that Royal Mail continues to create an environment in which women are treated with dignity and respect. That means having effective policies and practices that give women career and life choices.

'At the same time, the organisation should consider a thorough review of all recruitment processes to assess whether any bias exists. Further, it could help external recruitment partners to develop inclusive practices that would attract more women and create an equal platform for them to succeed.

'Finally, women will add a new dimension to the business, and Royal Mail should use that as a core part of it message.

'It is not about women for the sake of representation, it's about women because it makes business sense.'

Source: adapted from Kate Hilpern © the *Independent*, 2005.

Discussion questions

1 What is the role of the HR manager in managing diversity?
2 How can an organisation change to reflect a more diverse workforce

The soft view of HRM proposed by the Harvard model recognises the importance of people and that stakeholder interests are more likely to be met if HR policy choices and outcomes ensure the long-term consequences of individual well-being, which impact on societal well-being and increase organisational effectiveness. The Harvard model suggests that organisations that encourage employee influence in decision-making are likely to be more effective provided they are consistent with organisational goals.

Development of the soft HRM model

Guest (1987) extended the Harvard model's four HR policy choices of employee influence, human resource flow, reward systems and work systems to a total of seven. These seven policy areas included: organisational job design; policy formulation and implementation and management of change; recruitment, selection and socialisation; appraisal training and development; manpower flows; reward systems and communication systems. The correct policy choices will lead to HR outcomes of commitment, competence and cost-effectiveness, and result in the long-term consequences of individual well-being, organisational effectiveness and societal well-being.

Organisational and job design

This is similar to the Harvard model's *work systems* and includes how the design of a job fits into the organisational design. It takes into account the suitability of the tasks and technology used to achieve organisational goals. The design of organisations should reflect a high commitment model to HR and demonstrate how work design can be related to organisation strategy. For example, workers would be empowered to take control of their work as a means of increasing commitment to the organisation. The organisational structures would be designed to enable this to happen, power is more likely to be dispersed and management would be less authoritarian.

Policy formulation and management of change

This means using HR policy to identify and manage change in a business environment. This extends from the Harvard model, which has not identified change as a separate policy. It is especially important in a fast-changing business environment to manage change effectively to ensure competitiveness. Apple Computers managed to develop the iPod and gain competitive advantage by having policies for managing innovation and change.

Recruitment, selection and socialisation

human resource flow
The movement of people through the organisation, from recruitment and selection to termination of employment.

This is covered in the Harvard model's **human resource flow**. As the name suggests, it covers aspects of how and where employees are recruited, selected and inducted into the organisation, to ensure that they will be suitable in achieving organisational outcomes. However, this is more than just having the right people in the right place at the right time: it also needs to ensure that the workforce will be involved in the achieving of organisational goals.

Appraisal, training and development

This is not covered in the Harvard model as a separate policy. Guest (1987) argues that policies are necessary to ensure that employee performance is evaluated, which in turn ensures that the appropriate training and development take place. The aim is for a motivated, skilled, involved and contented workforce. Competing commitments, such as union involvement and work/life balance, would be identified and strategies would be developed to ensure that workers are able to be fully committed.

Manpower flows

These ensure that systems are in place to monitor employees throughout their life in the organisation. They can provide information on how staff are promoted or why they may leave the organisation. The Harvard model covers this in its *workflow* policies. It is important, as high staff turnover can indicate a problem with morale. Poor morale leads to poor productivity and low commitment to the organisation.

Reward systems

As with the Harvard approach, these cover the type of monetary and non-monetary rewards the organisation uses to maintain employee commitment. It needs to ensure that appropriate rewards are available, desirable and achievable. For example, if performance-related pay is part of the reward system then the criteria for achieving qualifying targets need to be transparent and achievable. If targets are imposed that are perceived to be out of reach, employees are less likely to feel committed to achieving them.

Communication systems

This refers to the processes the organisation has in place to ensure that efficient communication takes place and that information can be shared between employees and managers. Communication is seen as a vital part of ensuring employee participation and commitment. In a high-commitment organisation communication would be open and effective. Employees need to feel they are listened to and their opinions and concerns taken into account. Employers cannot be expected to meet the goals of the organisation if these have not been communicated to them, which is important for a high-commitment organisation. Poor communication also often leads to a disgruntled and dissatisfied workforce and poor employee relations.

Guest (1987) continued with the theme of a soft HRM model, but argued that policies and practices should be designed to achieve the organisational outcomes of strategic integration, employee commitment, workforce flexibility and quality. This is demonstrated in Exhibit 17-7.

The distinguishing feature of Guest's model is that HR policies should be designed to achieve the following outcomes.

strategy
The process of envisioning and planning to create a match between organisational competencies and goals.

Strategic integration

This ensures that the HR policies and business policies are integrated. It argues that HR strategies and planning form part of a manager's role and that the HR **strategy** should form part of the business strategy and not be treated as a separate entity.

EXHIBIT 17-7 Guest's model of HRM

Policies	Human resource outcomes	Organisational outcomes
Organisational job design	Strategic planning/implementation	High job performance
Policy formulation and implementation/management of change	Commitment	High problem-solving
Recruitment, selection and socialisation	Flexibility/adaptability	Successful change
Appraisal, training and development	Quality	Low turnover
Manpower flows – through, up and out of the organisation		Low absence
Rewards systems		Low grievance level
Communications systems		High cost-effectiveness

Source: Guest, D. (1997) 'Human Resource Management and Industrial Relations', *Journal of Management Studies* 24(5), September, pp. 503–521.

This means that managers take responsibility for the human resource and need to ensure that they have the right people in the right places to ensure that the business strategy can be achieved.

Employee commitment

This encourages employees to have 'buy in' to the organisation, which in turn encourages high levels of productivity. Commitment is gained through 'winning their hearts and minds', rather than imposing management sanctions. This means that the employment relationship should be more than an economic exchange where employees receive a financial reward for their services. It should also include a psychological relationship of shared goals and values and a sense of belonging. The Eye on Ethics box demonstrates how managing absence can improve employee commitment.

Mental arithmetic

Stress-related sickness absence costs society £3.7 bn per year, with up to five million people in the UK feeling very or extremely stressed by their work. Mental health problems associated with work include depression and anxiety, which can lead to alcohol misuse and sickness absence.

A joint review by the Ministerial Task Force for Health and Productivity and the Cabinet Office concluded that: 'the public sector has higher recorded long-term absence (particularly stress related) than the private sector ... and both the incidence and duration of stress-related absence is increasing'.

Nottingham City Council, a large local government organisation with more than 14 000 staff, became concerned about levels of sickness absence due to mental health problems. It decided to recruit an experienced mental health nurse (MHN) with a community nursing background as a mental health adviser in a bid to tackle the problem. It was agreed that the project, which was funded by the Neighbourhood Renewal Fund, should run for a year before evaluating the findings.

The adviser's role was to advise managers and the human resources department on a broad range of issues relating to employee mental health, and to see employees with mental health issues. It was decided that the employee's line manager would initiate this process by completing a referral form in collaboration with HR and the employee.

The referral form allows the manager to ask specific questions and provide background information. A one-off assessment is then carried out. The broad aim of this process is to assess the current mental health state of the employee, identify possible causative factors, advise on potential supportive measures and, if appropriate, provide the basis of a return-to work plan. Issues around redeployment, ill-health retirement and the Disability Discrimination Act can also be explored if required.

The adviser does not act as a staff counsellor, and strict boundaries are adhered to in order for any subsequent advice to remain objective. However, if appropriate, the adviser provides the employee with impartial advice and support during the assessment and can provide information on relevant services.

The employee is shown the information contained in the referral, and is offered a copy of the resulting report. This is done to ensure that the process is valuable for all concerned and there is openness and trust between the relevant parties. Managers are also encouraged, if applicable, to involve the employee in the referral process.

▶ Multidisciplinary working is an important part of the MHN role, as it is sometimes appropriate for the MHN to request further information from an employee's general practitioner, or other professionals involved in their care. However, this is only done with the employee's written consent. Liaising with other professionals, such as local mental health teams, in order to support staff may also be necessary.

Another aspect of the role is to provide managers, team leaders and human resources staff with training in mental health awareness and the management of mental health issues in the workplace. Training takes the form of two half-day sessions. The first is designed to increase knowledge and awareness of mental health and mental ill-health. Issues around stress, stigma and factors that influence views are discussed. In terms of mental illness, the course primarily concentrates on depression and anxiety. This is because these are the most common mental health problems in our society, and also the most relevant to managers dealing with stress-related employee sickness.

The second part of the course explores the relevance of mental health issues in today's workplace, and what is currently considered best practice in managing employees who are experiencing mental health difficulties.

Other aspects of the adviser's role include: working with teams with significant levels of sickness absence due to mental illness; being a member of a working party responsible for developing a mental health strategy for the organisation; and raising the profile of mental health issues within the organisation.

The study found that the most prevalent mental illness was depression, closely followed by anxiety. In the vast majority of cases the symptoms were stress-related. In some cases, the origin of the stress, such as work or home life, was clear, while in others there appeared to be a combination of external factors and poor coping skills. Staff with a previous diagnosis of bi-polar affective disorder (manic depression) or a psychotic illness were also assessed, but the incidence of these conditions within the workplace was low.

Introducing a mental health adviser into the Occupational Health (OH) department appears to have had a positive impact. During the first 12 months of this project there have been both qualitative and quantitative gains. There has been an overwhelmingly positive response from line managers and HR staff regarding the benefits of this service. Both groups reported feeling more confident in dealing with cases that at times can be very complex and have also felt better able to support their employees through difficult periods.

An important aspect of the success of this project appears to have been the ability of the OH department to provide specialist advice, reflected in the results for the usefulness and relevancy of this advice. The OH department has been able to provide advice that reflects its knowledge of a wide variety of different roles and working environments within the organisation. This is essential when advising on reasonable adjustments to duties and additional support from within the departments.

Accessibility has also been an important part of this role. Those involved in managing sickness absence have been encouraged to contact the adviser for informal advice if appropriate. This could be to discuss the appropriateness of a potential referral or to seek advice regarding an employee, without going down the route of a formal referral. One of the most common queries is for information on what other services or support may be available for an employee. Although the focus of this role is primarily on advising line managers and HR staff, employees involved in the casework also reported finding the informal advice beneficial.

The findings for type of illness and work role reflect national statistics for these areas. The most prevalent mental illness in the UK is depression, which affects one in six people. A recent, highly publicised study by business psychologists Robertson Cooper found that teachers and social workers were in the top three most stressful occupations in the UK, along with those in public-sector security (i.e. police, prison officers and the armed forces). There are also local reasons for certain departments making more referrals. For example, a factor in the high prevalence of social services referrals is that this department employs the largest number of staff in the organisation.

In response to these findings, training sessions specifically for head teachers and social work managers have been planned. The possibility of providing interventions for a specific team was also explored. A team from the social services department was identified as having the highest sickness levels, attributable to mental health problems. Discussions were held with the team manager to explore whether an intervention would be appropriate. A training need was subsequently identified, and the adviser is now developing an educational session specifically for this team.

The reduction in sick days attributable to mental health difficulties by 21 per cent is significant, and part of this reduction may be linked to the introduction of a specialist adviser. However, it is acknowledged that other factors may also have impacted on this figure.

Training sessions for managers throughout the organisation will continue to be provided. Demand is high, and a number of managers have requested sessions for their teams. The first half of the mental health awareness course is felt to be appropriate for the majority of staff, as it is only the second part of the course that focuses on management. Mental health awareness sessions have now been run with several teams, and this is likely to develop further.

Following the initial 12-month period, it was agreed that the role was valued and that the outcomes had been very positive. Further funding was secured and the role of mental health and well-being adviser is now a permanent post within the Occupational Health department. The project has also resulted in a neighbouring local authority employing a nurse to perform an equivalent role.

The mental health adviser role is expected to develop further, with an emphasis on supporting specific departments and teams.

Source: adapted from Chilton, S. (2005) 'Mental Arithmetic', *Occupational Health* 57(11), November, pp. 26–28.

Discussion questions

1 Why is it important for managers to be concerned with the health and well-being of their employees?

2 Why is it important for managers to manage absence?

Workforce flexibility

This ensures that the workforce is adaptable and flexible; this in turn will mean that the organisation can respond to changes. Training to enable increased flexibility will be integral to the HR strategy and will be designed to encourage a motivated, skilled and involved workforce.

Quality

A high-quality workforce will ensure that the products and services provided are of the highest standards. The drive for quality will be encouraged through a high-commitment model, which also encourages effective commitment to the organisation.

Guest (1987) argues that the HR outcomes will result in organisational outcomes of high job performance, high problem-solving ability, a greater ability to adapt to change and improved cost-effectiveness. The HR outcomes will also reduce employee turnover, absence and grievances. However, Guest proposes that this will happen only if a strategic approach is taken to integrate HRM policies into business policies and they have the support of all the managers in the organisation.

Keenoy (1990) criticises Guest's model as being too simplistic and unrealistic in that it would be hard to implement in a realistic working environment. In response, Guest (1997) argues that progress in the UK in integrating HR policies has been slow and, for soft HRM to work, managers need to take into account social market attitudes and develop long-term thinking through consultation within the workforce. Many managers do not take a long-term view for their organisations and, as a consequence, many HRM policies are also short term and follow fashion rather than ensuring long-term commitment to the organisation through its people.

Both the Harvard model and Guest's model represent the soft approach to HR. The ideas they propose should create highly committed workforce managers who have concern for workers' outcomes and are able to link these to the organisation's outcomes. In conclusion, the soft approach to HR ensures that employees are competent to perform, are committed and that this is congruent with organisational goals, which in turn should result in cost-effective HRM and lead to the organisation achieving competitive advantage.

Hard HRM

Storey (2001) identifies the 'hard' model of HRM as that proposed by Fombrun *et al.* (1984), also referred to as the **Michigan model**.

Michigan model
The model that develops hard HRM as a means of using people as an organisational resource to achieve organisational goals.

The 'hard' model of HRM emphasises that employees should be treated as a means of achieving the organisation's goals. This means that employees are a business resource and successful organisations are those that best deploy their human resources.

'Hard' HRM assumes that increasing performance will be the manager's main reason for improving HRM. Fombrun *et al.* (1984) argue that the external environment of increased competition and market instability will necessitate HRM strategies be designed to achieve the goals of the organisation.

Fombrun *et al.* (1984) also argue that organisations exist to accomplish a mission or achieve objectives, and strategic management takes into account three interconnected issues of mission and strategy, organisation's structure and human resource systems. See Exhibit 17-8 to find out how these fit together.

Mission and strategy

mission
The fundamental purpose of an organisation that defines the nature of its business and provides strategic direction unifying human and other resources.

This refers to the organisation's reason for being. The **mission** articulates the organisation's fundamental purpose and defines the nature of the business. It is there to unify human and other resources. Organisations exist to achieve a mission and managers need to think strategically about how people are managed and deployed to this end.

EXHIBIT 17–8 Strategic management and environmental pressures

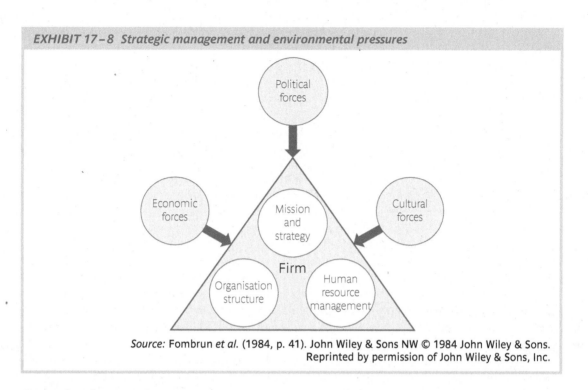

Source: Fombrun et al. (1984, p. 41). John Wiley & Sons NW © 1984 John Wiley & Sons. Reprinted by permission of John Wiley & Sons, Inc.

Organisation structure

This refers to the requirements and tasks needed to achieve the organisation's goals. These include accounting systems and communication networks, as well as the personnel required at the different levels and the tasks to be accomplished.

Human resource management systems

These establish the need for people to be recruited and developed, which in turn will enable them to achieve the organisational goals and maintain performance.

The Michigan model shown in Exhibit 17-8 recognises the external and internal forces of HRM as a triangle. Management decides the mission and strategy, it designs the organisational structure to meet the strategy and mission, and integrates and organises HRM to fit in with the structure and to fulfil the mission and strategy. The mission, strategy, organisational structure and human resource management cannot operate in isolation. They also need to respond to the external forces of politics, economics and culture. Once these have been taken into account, managers can begin to design the human resource system.

Devanna *et al.* (1984) describe the four functions of the cycle as follows:

> Performance is a function of all of the human resource components: selecting people who are best able to perform the jobs defined by the structure, appraising their performance to facilitate the equitable distribution of rewards, motivating employees by linking rewards to high levels of performance, and developing employees to enhance their current performance at work as well as to prepare them to perform in positions they may hold in the future.

The Michigan model's human resource cycle is illustrated in Exhibit 17-9. Fombrun *et al.*'s concept of HRM was influenced by much of the well-known literature on management style, such as Mayo (1933), Chandler (1962) and Galbraith and Nathanson (1978).

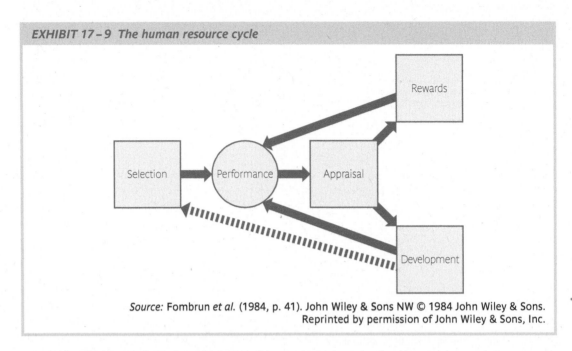

EXHIBIT 17–9 The human resource cycle

Source: Fombrun *et al.* (1984, p. 41). John Wiley & Sons NW © 1984 John Wiley & Sons. Reprinted by permission of John Wiley & Sons, Inc.

The Michigan model is based on strategic control, organisational structure and systems put in place for managing people. It identifies the need for human assets to be managed to achieve strategic goals. Motivation and rewards are important but only as a means of achieving the organisational mission and goals.

An organisation operating 'hard' HRM would aim to have a rational fit between the organisation's strategy, structure and HRM systems. The management style would see employees as a means of achieving business goals, and employees would be valued only if their worth had a positive effect on business strategy. The hard model of HRM is much closer in its philosophy to free market thinking with the use of hiring, firing and cost-cutting to ensure that the human resource is fully utilised.

Empirical research by Truss *et al.* (1997) into large organisations such as BT, Lloyds TSB and Hewlett-Packard has not produced evidence of organisations' systematic and consistent practice of HRM. However, it did find that employees were strategically controlled in order for them to achieve organisational goals, which is consistent with the hard approach.

The context of human resource management

Human resource management cannot take place in isolation from the internal organisation or the external environment where the political, economic, societal, technological and international context can have an impact on how the organisation operates and how HRM is managed within that context. The **context** within which HR takes place will impact on organisational policies and have implications for the functions of HR. This has been highlighted earlier in the example of the Beardmore Conference Hotel, whose flexible benefits reflected the local society and culture as well as the economic environment, where managers recognised the need to attract and retain staff at that time.

context
The external and internal environment within which HR operates.

Context has many layers, which build up to impact on how the organisation does business. Exhibit 17-10 demonstrates how organisations operate within a given context.

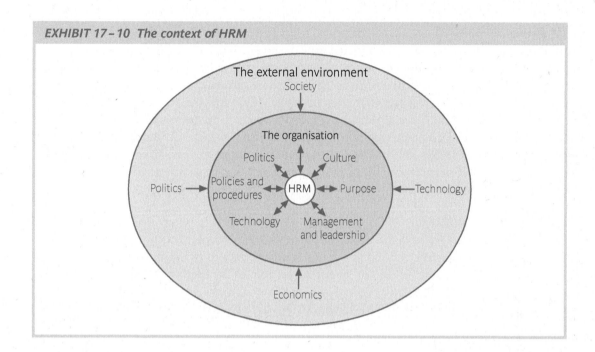

EXHIBIT 17–10 The context of HRM

The organisational context

To operate successfully the organisation needs to ask itself the following questions. What business are we in? How can we carry out our business to be as effective as possible and to meet out

stakeholders
Identifiable clusters of people who have an economic and/or social interest in the performance of an organisation.

stakeholders' needs? The organisational context is also influenced by the external context; it interacts with its environment and this in turn impacts on HR. For this reason, HR practices need to be designed to reflect the organisational context. However, in a fast-changing working environment this is often difficult to achieve: new technologies are developed, governments and attitudes change. Policy will, in turn, inform practice but needs to be flexible enough to respond to the influences of the external environment. For example, changes in working hours have meant changes in policies, which in turn have led to changes in practice, which in theory has meant a reduction in working hours for some workers.

The external context

The external environment influences the external context of the organisation. An organisation would not be effective if it ignored the external context of politics, economics, society and technology. In London and the south-east of England, there is a shortage of key workers, such as nurses and teachers, and many workers have been employed from abroad to fill the vacancies. For organisations, this means a review of policies to ensure that new workers' needs are considered. On a practical side, new aspects of training may have to be delivered to meet lan-

open system
System influenced by the external environment and inputs, making it complex and difficult to control.

guage needs. To do this an organisation needs to operate as an **open system**, which can change to meet the needs of its external environment. Katz and Kahn (1966) identify open systems as those that interact with the environment; this makes them complex and difficult to control.

The political context

The political context not only refers to the type of government in power at the time, but also whether the country is democratic or not. In the UK the political context changes depending on which political party is in power. In the past, the Conservative Government has tended to favour the employer over the employee; an example of this was the removal of the minimum wage. Traditional Labour Governments have focused on the employee and have had close links with the unions. With New Labour the lines have become somewhat blurred: although they have reintroduced the minimum wage, they have also formed close links with industry by encouraging public/private partnerships. With every change of government the HR practitioner needs to identify the impact on the organisation and the HR department.

The economic context

The economic context refers to the health of the nation. If business is booming and unemployment is low, it may be harder to find and retain staff. In times of economic decline, unemployment increases and a greater choice of labour is available to the employer. However, economic decline may also mean that your organisation has to 'downsize' and the HR department will then face the dilemma of dealing with redundancies. An organisation may also need to answer to shareholders, who expect to see a healthy return on their investment. For the HR professional this could mean developing operations overseas where labour is cheaper, such as Prudential moving its call centres to India. It may also mean outsourcing some or all of the functions of HR, as the organisation pursues its competitive advantage. An example of outsourcing is discussed in the Technology Transformation box.

The social context

The social context refers to the culture, politics, leadership and management style that influence the organisation. An HR manager must be able to identify the culture within which the organisation operates. This means she or he needs to recognise and understand the values the organisation is trying to promote. However, they also need to understand the **culture** and society from which their employees are recruited. Schein (1985) offers the following as a definition of culture as:

culture
The pattern of learned behaviours shared and transmitted among the members of society.

> a pattern of basic assumptions – invented, discovered or developed by a given group as it learns to cope with its problems of external adaption and internal integration – that has worked well enough to be considered valuable and therefore, to be taught to new members as the correct way to perceive, think and feel in relation to those problems.

Many industries in the past have grown up in particular regions. For example, coal mining in the north-east of England, steelworks in Wales, pottery in the Midlands, financial services in London. Even though many of these industries have now gone, society often clings to past tradition. As new industries move in, the HR manager needs to adapt and change the culture to match the new organisation.

An HR manager should not underestimate the importance of the societal context of business as, in many instances, businesses have foundered due to a lack of understanding of the culture. Examples are EuroDisney Paris, whose lack of understanding of European culture and its failure to embrace all things American, had a serious impact on business. Or, Wal-Mart in Argentina, which failed to understand how the Argentines liked to shop, and could not understand why business was not booming in its bright and shiny new supermarkets.

A sunrise industry

The term 'outsourcing' has created lots of debates among economists, politicians and sociologists. But this way of doing business goes back to the barter age. The magnitude of outsourcing has increased considerably resulting in a widening of the scope of services in all spheres of activity. The world is witness to an era of globalisation: to business beyond borders in a world without frontiers, thanks to the explosion of the Information Superhighway.

'Why outsourcing?' is a good question. Burgeoning businesses, pressure of competition, shrinking time spans, easier communication, the concept of a global village with seamless synergies, abundant hard-working and skilled personnel at low costs, and the ability to work 24/7 due to time zone differences, are some of the reasons for the surge in outsourcing. Using third-party service providers has become the rule rather than an exception. The benefit that the USA derived by outsourcing to the rest of the world is reported to have been more than $60 billion in 2004.

It is in the field of financial outsourcing that GKM has been using both offshore and domestic capabilities for data transformation for the past three years. Such dual capabilities enable it to sustain quality, adhere to delivery schedules and contain costs. Technology and telecommunications have improved considerably in recent years. The costs of high-bandwidth telecom links to India have fallen, while imaging software has improved. This helps companies to scan documents and send them electronically to India to provide all types of accounting and financial services.

The scope of services that was thought of originally was to provide preparation of tax returns but has now enlarged to write-ups, payroll processing, auditing, project costing, AP vouchering and compliance verifications, as well as providing manpower during peak tax seasons – so much so that GKM actually maintains the appointment diaries for some CPAs and sends birthday greetings to clients on behalf of some. With substantial increases in the level of trust, its scope of services is widening day by day. Originally, outsourcing was considered to be economical but now the CPAs realise that it has other benefits, such as consistency, ability to adopt best practices, reduced training cost of employees and avoidance of peak tax season workload.

Overcoming challenges

What makes outsourcing work even better is the perfect synergy between American business acumen and inherent Indian mathematical ability.

The challenge in this industry lies in managing human resources. The training of employees and their retention makes all the difference to the quality of deliverables. GKM's culture of training and learning not only inspires current employees but also attracts new talent from the job market. GKM's attrition rate is one of the lowest in the industry. It has realised the need for training since inception and maintains constant focus on the same. Right from classroom training to videoconferencing with US CPAs, GKM enables employees to keep abreast of the latest developments in taxation and related matters.

In addition to being an ISO-certified company, the policies and procedures are reviewed on a constant basis to align it to the needs of its CPA clients. Motivational exercises include family get-togethers, educational tours and participation in special seminars to keep employees rejuvenated at all times.

Tasks involving value addition require a high degree of expertise, training and judgement based on complex skill sets. Errors made by workers result in highly magnified goodwill breaches for the client. Some may be attributed to the origin where the outsourcer is not clear in specifications or provides insufficient or faulty raw data. Yet some may happen due to poor quality in transition. But most errors are due to lack of training and documentation at the back office. An experienced back office has an edge over a new one in this regard.

These companies of standing are past their teething troubles and understand the front-end requirements better. One way to cope with the situation is to document processes clearly and coherently as well as familiarise the employees with the maintenance and use of these processes through constant and consistent training programmes. Those who skimp on training pay the high price of losing the customer.

Staying secure

One of the major concerns of the CPA is information security and confidentiality of data. GKM has located its server in San Francisco, which has state-of-the-art monitoring systems with the highest possible level of security. Workplace security is on a par with the best in the industry and includes biometric scanners, predefined access and output devices GKM uses 128-bit secured socket layer encryption for any data transfers. Employees are apprised at frequent intervals of the importance of security and the need to follow procedures scrupulously and diligently.

It makes no difference if the processor is headquartered right down the street or in India. The requirement is due diligence to ensure that a company's needs would be met by a reliable, fiscally healthy partner. 'Outsourcing is a must, not a choice,' says Viji Sudhakar, president of GKM. She maintains that outsourcing to a different country does not challenge the integrity of the company itself since these companies scrupulously abide by US laws and regulations. 'The first step is to train offshore workers and continuously monitor and audit the transition at all stages. Compliance as laid down by clients is verified at every stage to ensure that accuracy is not compromised.'

In answer to the criticism that the quality of service suffers because of opting for outsourcing, one must note that even Gucci doesn't make its authentic Italian footwear in Italy any more. Companies may keep all their logistics, marketing and financial departments at the strategic level within their country, so that the heart and soul is native while the brain is foreign. Even this is an exaggeration since in most cases outsourcing only involves execution of given tasks in a certain predefined manner.

GKM enables CPA firms to focus on value-added services while routine functions are carried out at the back office. Some of its CPA clients have remarked that, by outsourcing, they can focus on the latest opportunities such as those presented by Sarbanes-Oxley compliance assignments.

To answer all detractors, outsourcing is a sunrise industry – one where world business trends indicate the sun might never set. The challenges ahead lie not only in maintaining the current velocity but also in developing established synergies further, in exploring frontiers never reached before, in achieving higher and higher levels of customer satisfaction, and truly making outsourcing a win–win proposition for client and service provider alike.

Source: adapted from Keyan, K. (2005) 'A sun rise industry', *Accounting Technology*, Boston, November, pp. 14–15.

Discussion questions

1 How is technology transforming human resource management?

2 What can be the problems of outsourcing routine functions?

The technological context

The technological context refers to the technology available for the organisation to use. In today's world, technology has a major impact in ensuring an organisation can maintain competitive advantage. For the HR manager it means keeping up to date with the technology available and the implications for using that technology. Thirty years ago the HR manager would have kept paper records, probably with the minimum of information. Today, the HR manager is expected to collect tax and national insurance, administer pensions and keep the information secure to comply with legislation such as the Data Protection Act. The HR manager also needs to ensure that staff are trained and developed to allow the company to embrace a fast-changing technological environment. Then there are the implications of technology replacing people or using technology to relocate sectors of the organisation such as customer services. There are also the new ways of working made possible through the use of email, videoconferencing and the Internet, where organisations can exist virtually. The HR manager needs to understand how to manage in the context of technology.

The global context

Today, many organisations operate in a global context. Globalisation is directing HR managers to develop an international strategy, which can impact on the activities of the HR department. Managers need to work across cultures and direct activities either externally from the home country or internally in the host country. This means the HR manager needs to have an understanding of international issues; each chapter of this book opens with a vignette that has an international perspective, to give readers an insight into global issues.

The **world watch** box gives an insight into the changing nature of HR in an international context.

China's labour shortage worries factories

Dongguan, China – In a country with 1.3 billion people, it's hard to imagine a labour shortage, but that's what the furniture and other industries are facing in southern China and elsewhere in the country as they compete for skilled and unskilled workers.

It's a concern for furniture retailers relying on quick and consistent delivery from China. Furniture plants that lose workers to other industries must constantly recruit and train new employees, and that can slow production.

In late August, Lacquer Craft, one of China's largest furniture makers, with 7000 workers, was running at 80 per cent capacity. President Mohamad Amini attributed that in part to difficulty in finding workers: 'It's been a little challenging to have the right people in place to run [our factories] at 100 per cent,' he said. 'It is taking longer to train and recruit.'

The *International Herald Tribune* reported last March that the government in Guangdong Province estimated 1 million workers were needed to fill jobs.

The squeeze has arisen largely because of the number of industries competing for workers in the Pearl River Delta in southern China. With new plants opening throughout the region, furniture companies often lose workers to plants willing to offer more pay or benefits.

Some blame the problem on the difficulty of drawing workers from rural areas for a mere $100 a month – a typical salary for a furniture production worker. For some, that just isn't enough to justify leaving family and friends in those areas.

world watch

The government is reportedly making it more attractive for farmers to remain in rural areas by offering them increased subsidies. Word also has spread about dirty working conditions and unfair labour practices in some plants, including furniture plants.

In early November, some 3000 workers went on strike at a DeCoro leather upholstery plant in Shenzhen. The strike was in response to pay cuts and the alleged beating of three workers by foreign supervisors.

While perhaps extreme, the incident highlights the growing tensions between management and furniture production workers seeking better working conditions, pay and benefits.

'Improved working conditions and living conditions, these are the key things involved in recruiting or keeping employees,' said Lacquer Craft's Amini. Lacquer Craft is dealing with the labour shortage by offering workers better pay and other incentives such as overtime for longer shift work. The longer hours not only help meet production deadlines, they also help increase plant efficiency.

Amini declined to reveal specifics about wages. But he estimated that in the past couple of years, the monthly wage in the industry has risen about 10 per cent. In the past five years, he said it has risen 20 per cent.

Samuel Liu, senior vice president of case goods manufacturer Omexey Enterprise, said it was a lot easier to get workers four years ago. His company has hired an agent to recruit workers from central and western China.

'We try to get people from the same villages and towns so they have family and friends and will not quit their job that easily,' said Liu, who estimated his factory's turnover rate for production workers at about 10 per cent. The administrative side is more stable, he said.

Richie Chen, general manager of case goods manufacturer Passwell Wood Mfg Corp., remembers how not too long ago people waited at his factory gate to fill out an application. 'Now it's not so many,' he said, citing competition from other industries and the increased government farm subsidies.

Like Omexey, Passwell sends recruiters to rural areas, and tries to retain workers by improving working and living conditions, including better food.

Gary Gone, an assistant to Amini who works at the Shanghai-area Lacquer Craft plant, said that, before this past May, there were about 100 people on any given day waiting outside the gate to fill out job applications.

Between May and August, the factory lost about 1000 workers, who returned to farms to take advantage of the higher subsidies. Today, the company offers workers bonuses if they help recruit a friend or family member.

Lacquer Craft also recruits students attending area vocational schools. New workers are typically trained in about four to six weeks, often starting out in delivery or courier roles before moving on to more technical production positions.

Younger, less experienced workers tend to leave sooner, while older, more experienced workers tend to stay longer.

Labour shortages and turnover are especially significant to producers such as Winny Overseas Ltd, which makes product for higher-end importers such as Sherrill, Hooker, Harden, The Platt Collections and Sansegal Home Designs. It can take months training workers to produce these higher-end goods.

But here, too, most of the turnover occurs at the entry level and not among more experienced workers, said Winny President Steven Lee.

Chen, of Passwell, said it takes about two months to get a worker ready to run machines in the plant, and about a year for them to get really proficient. He said the company tries to keep these workers on board by offering better living and working conditions.

Omexey tries to lower turnover through a training programme called Omexey College, a three-month course that gives workers a chance to land supervisory jobs if they agree to stay with the company for at least three years.

Still, the company faces competition from area shoe factories, said Liu. Although the pay may be similar, workers leave because shoe factories are seen by some workers as better and cleaner places to work.

How long the situation will persist is anyone's guess. Some don't see an end in sight because of demographic and other trends. Others are more optimistic, believing furniture makers can continue to compete for good workers.

'We don't see this problem as a long-term, serious problem,' said Lacquer Craft's Amini. 'Nevertheless, it is an issue everybody needs to pay attention to.'

Source: adapted from Russell, J. (2005) 'China Labour Shortage Worries Factories', *Furniture Today* 30(10), 14 November, pp. 1–2.

Discussion questions

1 How can HR ensure that the right people with the right skills are in the right place at the right time?

2 What can managers do to retain workers?

The role of the HR manager

The opening vignette talked about the functions of HR and how they need to be organised to achieve a sufficiently integrated approach to management. The role of the manager is to enable individuals to achieve **organisational goals** and objectives. Managers get things done through people. To do this successfully, they need to know who these people are, where they are from, how they can be developed not only for personal fulfilment but also to help achieve the organisational goals, and the impact of external constraints such as legislation, competition, employee relations, and education and training. The HR manager needs to know how these come together to form the function of HRM (see Exhibit 17-11).

organisational goals
The desired outcomes of an organisation that enable managers to assess and measure performance.

The different functions of HR

Exhibit 17-11 demonstrates how the HR manager has to juggle the different functions of HR in the internal environment of the organisation while keeping an eye on what is happening in the external environment. Below is a brief overview of each of these functions.

Planning, resourcing and retention

Managers need to know how many staff they will need in order to achieve the organisational goals. They need to identify where the staff will be needed, how many and at what times. This is especially important in organisations where business fluctuates, such as the retail and hospitality sectors. Managers also need to be able to identify the level of skills required. The general

EXHIBIT 17–11 The human resource functions

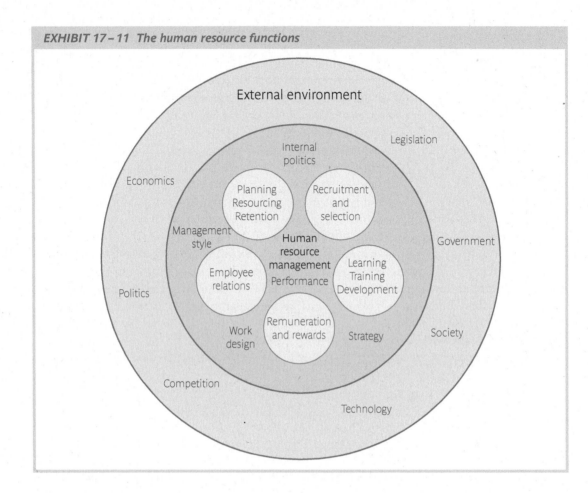

manager of your local Tesco knows that Friday and Saturday are likely to be the busiest days. S/he can look back at the past sales history and identify peak times. The store manager will ensure that s/he has trained checkout operators available, extra customer service staff and shelf packers to replace items. This is part of the **planning** and **resourcing** process. The retention of staff is also important, as recruiting staff is an expensive and time-consuming process. A manager needs to ensure that staff are happy in their work as not only will they be more productive, they will also be more likely to remain with the organisation.

planning
The method used to achieve organisational goals.

resourcing .
The pool of resources available for the manager to use to fulfil the plan and achieve objectives.

Recruitment and selection

When the need for people has been ascertained, the next task is to find them, and ensure that the right people are selected and recruited for the organisation. If the wrong people are recruited then there could be difficulties in achieving organisational goals and business could suffer. Employees may be over-qualified for jobs and leave, or under-qualified and not be able to perform adequately. This could have serious implications for the organisation. Think of the last time you took a flight in an aircraft, whether on a low-cost carrier such as easyJet or Ryanair, or on one of the larger airlines such as British Airways: the company representatives you came in contact with all

recruitment
The procedure used to attract staff to an organisation.

selection
The methods used to identify suitable staff who will match the requirements of the organisation.

projected a company image. The recruitment and selection process would ensure that only those candidates compatible with company goals would be recruited. The methods used could be IQ tests or psychometric tests, or as is often the case with airlines, guidelines for acceptable weight and height. If the wrong people had been recruited there could be serious implications for passenger safety and ultimately company reputation.

Training and development

training
The methods used to bridge the gap between where the employee is now to where the employer wants them to be.

In order to get the best from employees they need to be trained. Training is done to fill gap between the skills and knowledge they have at present and the skills and knowledge the organisation wants them to have in order to fulfil set goals. It ensures that employees are able to perform to the required standard. Whenever someone new is employed they need to be trained; this may take the form of an induction programme to make the new employee feel welcome and orientate them to the culture and working methods of the organisation, or it may be to enable the employee to develop a new skill and become more effective. Even working at McDonald's requires some form of training from the company induction programme, where new recruits are introduced to the philosophy and culture of the McDonald's organisation, through to learn-

development
Continuous learning to enable employees to fulfil themselves in their careers, which in turn increases commitment and motivation.

ing about hygiene, health and safety, and the methods used for preparing and serving products. Development ensures that employees can fulfil their potential. Development goes beyond the skills required for the job and takes into account individual aspirations. A developed workforce is able to accept change and is more fulfilled and motivated. An engineering firm may have a policy of promoting from within the company. The company needs to recognise which employees aspire to be the managers of the future, but it also needs to recognise that if the engineers are not developed they are likely to have problems, as the skills required for engineering are different from the skills required to manage an organisation effectively.

Remuneration and reward

pay
The monetary reward for providing a service.

reward
A monetary or non-monetary reward used as an inducement to increase performance or gain commitment.

Employees need to be paid so that they are able to live. Pay needs to be adequate and equitable. Money is not the only reward and may not motivate employees to be more productive; other benefits also need to be looked at. These can range from benefits such as pensions, healthcare and other financial incentives, to non-financial rewards such as those that come from empowerment and job satisfaction. Employers are now realising that employees have different needs and a fixed reward system is unlikely to suit everyone. Flexible benefits are becoming more common. The Beardmore Conference Hotel near Glasgow, is one example of an organisation that offers flexible benefits. Employees can choose from a range of benefits, such as flexible hours, childcare vouchers, pensions or driving lessons. With flexible benefits, an employee who needs childcare could choose childcare vouchers as part of their reward package, while older workers may prefer a company pension. The ability for employees to be able to choose their rewards means that they feel valued as individuals, which in turn means that they are more likely to stay with the organisation.

Employee relations

Healthy relations need to be maintained with employees to ensure a productive workforce. In the event of disputes and conflict arising, managers need to be able to manage successfully in order to ensure win–win outcomes. They need to be able to communicate and negotiate with unions and other employee representatives to ensure that a stable working environment is maintained. In 2003 British Airways check-in staff at Heathrow staged a walkout over new working practices. The result was hundreds of flights cancelled, summer holidays ruined and chaos at Heathrow, one of the world's busiest airports. Representatives from the union and BA then conducted angry exchanges in front of the media. Could it have been avoided?

The functions of human resource management cannot be carried out in isolation from the wider context of the organisation, or the society in which the organisation operates. The external environment can impact on how the functions are designed and implemented. This is why an HR manager needs to understand developments and changes in economics, politics, government, legislation, technology, external competition and society, and be able to manage change to respond to them effectively. An effective HR manager needs to able to respond to current issues and new developments. The internal environment also needs to respond to external influences. To do this it may develop a more strategic approach to HRM. Strategy can filter through the organisation, through the managing and development of performance, and by increasing employee participation and empowerment.

An HR manager also needs to consider issues of work and job design in response to the demands of society and the legal implications of health and safety, stress and employee welfare. Society also demands fair treatment, which means the HR manager not only has to be familiar with equal opportunities to comply with the law but also must know how s/he can value diversity to ensure employees are valued.

Human resource managers have a complex role in the organisation and, while people management is the role of all managers, it is the role of the HR specialist to develop a holistic and systematic approach to the management of people to enable the organisation to achieve its goals.

O2's executive development plan: a second look

So, has the executive development plan (EDP) worked? 'Well, we haven't lost anybody,' says O2 group HR director Andrew Harley, 'and when we talk to people they say they appreciate the company investing in them.'

But surely such casual feedback isn't the hardest of measures? 'No,' concedes Harley, 'but when someone who's very hard-bitten, who's working very long hours, looks you in the eye and says, "I really appreciate you doing this for us", it means something.'

He stresses that O2's EDP is not one of those wishy-washy, 'you're great and we're going to give you a certificate to prove it' courses. 'It's more: "You're going to work very hard, do a project for an executive committee member – and do your day job at the same time,"' he says.

The course is made up of three residential modules, each lasting two and a half days, at Templeton College, Oxford. There is also a project that has a life outside the course. The three modules are titled 'The informed leader', 'The bold leader' and 'The inspirational leader'.

Karan Martin, head of online customer service at O2 UK, explains the modules. '"Informed leader" looks at the environment we operate in and some potential options for us as a business.

"Bold leader" looks at the context of the industry and tries to develop strategic thinking. "Inspirational leader" looks at you as both a person and a leader, and aims to make the most of the leadership style that you have.'

Martin's project was to look at customer service team leaders to see exactly how much time they spent actually inspiring and coaching their teams in order to deliver an 'excellent customer experience'.

She recalls: 'We did a lot of analysis work, then ran a pilot where we stripped away anything that didn't support the purpose of their role, such as logging the times of people's arrival at work, logging holiday time on various systems, and a lot of general administrative work. As a result, we introduced an administrative role to give the team leaders support. They can now spend more time on side-by-side coaching of their people.'

Another satisfied customer is Anthony Soothill, head of billing at O2 UK: 'The EDP has been extremely important because it invested in what is effectively the second tier of management,' he says.

'If you look at recent announcements that we are investing more money in customer-facing roles and taking people out of back-office administrative functions, the whole of the senior management structure was behind this before it was announced. There was a collective understanding of why we were going to do it.'

Wise in hindsight

Several lessons have emerged that O2's group HR director Andrew Harley wishes he'd known in the first few months after the demerger:

- surround yourself with good people
- if you think it's wrong, it probably is
- always look back and see exactly how far you've come
- encourage yourself more – it's too easy to be your own harshest critic
- you will be out of your comfort zone, but relax; when we're stressed we perform below par and miss important cues and clues.

Source: Steve Smethurst in *People Management* magazine, 5 May 2005, p. 24.

Summary

- An HR manager needs to recognise that human resource management is in a constant state of change and that they need to recognise the importance of their role as a management professional.

- HR management has progressed from an ad hoc role to the professional body of the CIPD. It can trace its routes from the paternalistic principles of the nineteenth century, through to the era of scientific management and human relations, to its current state.

- The terms personnel management and HRM are part of the debate that informs the role of the HR manager. HRM is viewed as a means of moving people along to achieve organisational goals through staffing, performance, change management and administrative objectives. Personnel management has often been seen as a bridge between employer and employee.

- 'Hard' HRM, characterised by the Michigan model, is seen as viewing people as a resource needed to achieve organisational goals.

- 'Soft' HRM, characterised by the Harvard model, is seen as a method of developing strategies to encourage employee commitment through employee influence, human resource flow, reward and work systems.

- The functions of HR include: planning and resourcing; recruitment and selection; training and development; pay and reward; employee relations. These enable the HR manager to achieve organisational goals.

- Understanding the HR context in relation to the organisational and external context is important for an effective HR manager. The organisational context refers to the structures, processes, culture and systems in the organisation, while the external environment refers to the external politics, economics, technology and society that influence the organisation and, in turn, impact on the HR professional.

Areas for personal development

1 **Understand how HR is divided into different functions.** If you work for an organisation, look at its functions. When you applied for the job did you fill in an application form, how were you interviewed? Did you know what the selection criteria were? How are you motivated? Is it through pay or are there other rewards on offer? What type of training have you been offered? Could you develop a career with this organisation? This should give you an idea of how the functions of HR are carried out.

2 **Identify how history has contributed to the current state of HR.** A knowledge of historical developments can help us to understand the present. Do you know any organisations or

managers that view people as machines required to perform to their maximum capacity? Can you see problems in the operation of this type of organisation?

3 **Recognise the implications of the HR vs personnel debate.** Identify a company with which you are familiar, either somewhere you work or have contact with. Does it have an HR department or a personnel department? Can you identify how the departments view themselves. Look for clues such as policies, practices, control and rewards. Do they give an indication of the importance of people management?

4 **Determine the impact of the 'hard' and 'soft' approaches to HR.** Which model would you use as a manager? Which would be more effective for organisational performance and competitive advantage? Can you identify any organisations that follow either the 'hard' or 'soft' approach of HR? Is it effective?

5 **Recognise the importance of the context of HR.** Identify and describe the external environment that surrounds your organisation. How does this affect the internal organisation? What is the role of HR in both the internal and external context. Are there specific recruitment policies? Are there diversity issues that need to be addressed? Is there high labour turnover? Is the HR department effective in managing in context?

❓ Questions for study and discussion

1 What are the functions of human resource management?

2 Explain what the term 'personnel management' means.

3 Why are staffing, performance, change management and administration objectives important to HRM?

4 How does Storey define the elements that differentiate HRM from personnel management?

5 What does the term 'hard' HRM mean?

6 Guest (1987) argues that 'policies and practices should be designed to achieve organisational integration, employee commitment and workforce flexibility'. How can the HR manager implement policies and practices to achieve the above aims?

7 Critically analyse the Harvard model of HR. What implications does it have for the HR manager?

8 The Michigan model of HRM identifies the need for human assets to be managed to achieve strategic goals. What are the implications for an HR manager?

9 Why is it important for an HR manager to understand the context in which she or he operates?

10 What is the impact of technology on the practices of an HR manager in an organisation?

🔑 Key Concepts

vision, *p. 799*

paternalist, *p. 799*

scientific management, *p. 799*

human relations, *p. 800*

workforce centred, *p. 804*

hard HRM, *p. 806*

soft HRM, *p. 806*

Harvard model, *p. 809*

human resource flow, *p. 813*

strategy, *p. 814*

Michigan model, *p. 818*

mission, *p. 818*

context, *p. 820*

stakeholders, *p. 821*

open system, *p. 821*

culture, *p. 822*

organisational goals, *p. 827*

planning, *p. 828*

resourcing, *p. 828*

recruitment, *p. 829*

selection, *p. 829*

training, *p. 829*

development, *p. 829*

pay, *p. 829*

reward, *p. 829*

Personal skills exercise

Purpose To develop an approach to strategic thinking.

Time 40 minutes

Procedure Many employers require HR professionals to think strategically. Study the job advertisement below for an assistant HR manager. Draft an application in which you persuade the employer of your strategic capabilities. You may also want to include your CV.

Alternatively, if you are just starting out in the HR field, identify the skills you would need to develop to be in a position to apply for such a job and write down the strategies needed in order to develop the identified skills.

Walco Supermarkets plc
Assistant Human Resource Manager
Salary £25K + benefits

As a member of Walco's management group, you will assist the HR manager in identifying strategic business issues and will ensure that implementation of appropriate HR solutions results in enhanced operational capability and an increase in customer focus. The role requires an individual who is capable of assisting in the pioneering of leading-edge approaches to people development and driving significant culture change.

The successful applicant will have a good honours degree in Human Resource Management or a related field and be a member of the CIPD with a view to attaining graduate status and will have one year's experience in a strategic HR/OD role. You will be resilient and flexible in handling competing priorities and will have some experience of managing change.

To apply, visit 'job vacancies' at our website: www.walco.co.uk

Walco is an equal opportunities employer

Team exercise

Purpose To gain an understanding of how HR professionals develop strategic thinking.

Time 40 minutes

Procedure You are part of an HR team for Walco plc, a large chain of supermarkets. Your director of HR has just come back from an MBA management weekend and has decided that the HR team needs to be more strategic. The team has decided to get together and link the functions of HR to strategy. The problem is that the organisational strategy is unclear. You looked at the mission statement on the company's website and it says 'Walco – leading on price, leading on quality.' But it says very little about how it proposes to do this. Although, it does mention that Walco's people are a valuable asset.

Each one of the team members is responsible for a different function, such as planning, resourcing, recruitment, selection, training, development, pay, reward and employee relations.

- Decide who will be responsible for which areas.
- Choose a group member to chair the meeting.
- Outline the strategies that could be developed for each of the functions.

Case study: police – marching to a modern beat; massive investment and a clear framework will increase the performance of all police forces

'The police service is going through a period of radical change,' says Jane Stichbury, chair of the Association of Chief Police Officers for the Personnel Management Business Area. 'Reform is improving and enhancing the professionalism of the service and there are now better opportunities for staff than ever before.'

Indeed, the first National Policing Plan for England and Wales was published by the Home Secretary last year. This three-year plan sets out a clear framework for raising the performance of all forces, delivering improved police operation and greater public reassurance.

Coupled with an investment increase of £1.8 bn over the last three years into the service, conditions for employees have greatly improved. The pay system is being modernised to improve rewards for the most difficult and demanding front-line posts, as well as increasing basic pay to boost recruitment and retention. Following extensive training, a new recruit can now expect a starting salary of £26 000 in London. A recent allocation of £20 m has also been provided specifically to improve police stations, modernise officers' working surroundings and update technology.

'We're also delivering an environment now that is far more supportive, where there is strong leadership and a range of new policies that offer people flexibility,' says Stichbury. Indeed, mentoring programmes, part-time working and job sharing are increasingly common options in many forces. Support networks and welfare provisions, such as counselling, have also been extended.

In a climate where public confidence in pensions is low, police staff can also be assured of a secure retirement. 'You can pull your police pension after 30 years, regardless of how old you were when you joined,' says Bob Carr, head of recruitment for the Metropolitan Police Service, who will be eligible for retirement at just 49. 'The vast majority of people go on to serve their full term. So you have security of tenure when you're in the job and when you've finished.'

Police officers frequently cite the satisfaction and challenge of the varied workload as the most rewarding aspects of their jobs. Indeed, police in Britain deal with about six million 999 emergency calls a year and have cut overall crime by 22 per cent in the last five years. They are, however, faced with more and more complicated crimes, often high profile and in the public eye.

'When a police officer comes to work they have no idea what they are going to be faced with over the next eight hours,' says Jan Berry, chair of the Police Federation of England and Wales and a serving police officer with 28 years' experience. 'It can be tough as you are dealing with life and death situations, but this is part of the attraction, the challenge of being able to turn your hand and deal with a small child who is lost one second to a raging fire or shootout the next.'

There are now a record number of police officers employed by the 43 forces across England and Wales, with 5400 more officers than two years ago. However, the good news is that recruitment is still highly active. Indeed, numbers are set to increase, with a government target of 132 500 police officers by 2004. In addition, a further 4000 Community Support Officers are being recruited by forces who have limited powers to deal with low-level crime and disorder. Measures are also being introduced to increase the numbers and effectiveness of Special Constables.

When joining the police service, whether as a school leaver, a graduate or later in life as a second career, the same basic training programme will apply, lasting for 15 weeks at a National Police Training Centre or 18 weeks within the Metropolitan Police Service. This is followed by a two-year probationary period as a patrolling Police Constable in a borough, dealing with local events such as road accidents, public order and crime incidents. Once the two years is up, promotion and specialism into one of the many areas, such as Firearms, Drugs Squad, Criminal Investigation Department (CID), Traffic Patrol or Underwater Search Teams, is a popular route.

For those with the potential to rise quickly to Inspector level or higher, there is the choice of applying for the new High Potential Development Scheme (HPD), which if successful will offer a fast-track route into some of the most challenging managerial jobs. The scheme, although tough, gives a thorough grounding in police work, with an emphasis on substantial responsibility early on. There is no age limit, and some recent successful candidates have been in their late thirties.

Competition for joining the police service is fierce, with more than 35 000 people in England and Wales applying every year. Of these, only about 5000 are successful.

Unlike many jobs, no formal qualifications are required, although an educational standard is required to pass the initial recruitment tests. Recruiters will be looking for candidates who show self-confidence, good levels of fitness and the ability to think on their feet. 'Personal qualities are more important than qualifications,' says Bob Carr. 'You need to be resourceful, determined and flexible. It's not a nine-to-five job, so someone who is willing to go out of their way to make a difference is likely to be successful.'

Source: Jacqueline Freeman in the *Independent*, 30 January 2003, p. 1.

Discussion questions

1 If you were responsible for HR in a local police force, how would you organise the HR function?

2 What role would the HR manager have in managing change in the police force?

3 How important do you think job satisfaction is in maintaining morale?

4 How would you devise a policy to attract new recruits to a police force?

Applied questions

5 Using Guest's model, illustrated in Exhibit 17-2, do you think the police are using HRM or personnel management?

6 Beer *et al.* (1984) suggest that managers need to take responsibility for employee influence, human resource flow, reward systems and work systems. Has this happened in the above case?

WWW exercise

Choose a company that you would be interested in working for in the future. Go to the recruitment section of its website.

1 What information is available?

2 Are you able to make an informed choice about your future career prospects?

3 Does the website give an indication of how the company views the HR function?

4 Why are you interested in working for this company?

Specific web exercise

The Chartered Institute of Personnel and Development (CIPD) is the professional body that represents HR professionals in the UK. Visit its website at: www.cipd.co.uk.

1 How does the CIPD support the HR professional?

2 How can you use the CIPD to gain a better understanding of the HR profession?

LEARNING CHECKLIST ☑

Before you move on you may want to reflect on what you have learnt in this chapter. You should now be able to:

- ☑ outline the development of HRM
- ☑ understand the differences between HRM and personnel management
- ☑ evaluate 'hard' and 'soft' approaches to HRM
- ☑ understand the role of strategic HRM
- ☑ understand how diversity underpins HR practice
- ☑ understand the international forces that drive HRM.

Further reading

Boselie, P. and Paauwe, J. (2005) 'Human Resource Function Competencies in European Companies', *Personnel Review* 34(5), pp. 550–568.

Hendry, C. (1994) 'The Single European Market and the HRM response', in P.S. Kirkbride (ed.) *Human Resource Management: Perspectives for the 1990s.* London: Routledge.

Hendry, C. and Pettigrew, A. (1990) 'Human Resource Management: An Agenda for the 1990s', *International Journal of Human Resource Management* 1(1), pp. 17–43.

Legge, K. (1995), *HRM: Rhetorics and Realities.* Basingstoke: Macmillan Business.

Rothwell, W.J., Prescott, R.K. and Taylor, M.W. (1998) *The Strategic Human Resource Leader: How to Prepare Your Organisation for the Six Key Trends Shaping the Future.* Palo Alto, CA: Davies-Black Publications, p. 5.

Treven, S. (2006) 'Human Resources Management in a Global Environment', *Journal of American Academy of Business* 8(1), March, pp. 120–125.

References

Beer, M., Spector, B., Lawrence, P.R., Quinn Mills, D. and Walton, R.E. (1984) *Managing Human Assets.* New York, NY: The Free Press.

Benyon, H. (1973) *Working for Ford.* Harmondsworth: Penguin.

Cannell, M. (2004) *Personnel Management: A Short History.* London: CIPD.

Chandler, A.D. (1962) *Strategy and Structure: Chapters in the History of American Industrial Enterprise.* Cambridge, MA: MIT Press.

Devanna, M.A., Fombrun, C.J. and Tichy, N.M. (1984) 'A Framework for Strategic Human Resource Management', in C.J. Fombrun, M.A. Tichy and M.A. Devanna (eds) *Strategic Human Resource Management.* New York, NY: John Wiley & Sons.

Evans, A. (2003) *The History of the CIPD.* London: CIPD.

Fombrun, C.J., Tichy, N.M. and Devanna, M.A. (1984) *Strategic Human Resource Management.* John Wiley & Sons.

Galbraith, J.R. and Nathanson, D. (1978) *Strategy Formulation: Analytical Concepts*. St Paul, MN: Publishing Company.

Guest, D.E. (1987) 'Human Resource Management and Industrial Relations', *Journal of Management Studies* 24(5), pp. 503–521.

Guest, D.E. (1997) 'Human Resource Management and Performance: A Review and Research Agenda', *International Journal of Human Resource Management* 8(3), June, pp. 263–276.

Hunt, J. (1999) 'The Shifting Focus of the Personnel Function', *Personnel Management* 16(2), February, pp. 14–19.

Katz, D. and Kahn, R.L. (1966) *The Social Psychology of Organizations*. New York, NY: Wiley.

Keenoy, T. (1990) 'HRM: Rhetoric, Reality and Contradiction', *International Journal of Human Resource Management* 1(3), pp. 363–384.

Mayo, E. (1933) *The Human Problems of an Industrial Civilization*. New York, NY: Macmillan.

Rose, M. (1975) *Industrial Behaviour: Theoretical Development Since Taylor*. Harmondsworth: Penguin.

Schein, E. (1985) *Organization Culture and Leadership*. San Francisco, CA: Jossey-Bass.

Storey, J. (1989) *New Perspectives on Human Resource Management*. London: Routledge.

Storey, J. (1992) *Developments in the Management of Human Resources: An Analytical Review*. Cambridge, MA: Blackwell.

Storey, J. (2001) *Human Resource Management: A Critical Text* (2nd edn). London: Thomson Learning.

Truss, C., Gratton, L., Hope-Hailey, V. and McGovern, P. (1997) 'Soft and Hard Models of Human Resource Management: A Reappraisal', *Journal of Management Studies* 34(1), p. 53.

Walton, R.E. (1985) *Human Resource Management: Trends and Challenges*. Harvard Business School Press.

Chapter 18

Organisational change, development and innovation

• The opening vignette looks at GCHQ and the strategies it used to change its working practices.

Out in the open

Decades of ingrained culture don't change easily. But when Government Communication Headquarters (GCHQ) had the chance to design its own future HQ, the door was open for a radical reappraisal of the way the agency worked.

What images spring to mind when you try to visualise GCHQ? Tweed-jacketed, code-cracking geniuses straight out of the film *Enigma*, perhaps? Echoing corridors and paranoiac levels of security, almost certainly. The reality couldn't be more different (although, admittedly, you will bump into the odd genius). GCHQ today is housed in a state-of-the-art building that, on the inside at least, looks more like the headquarters of a high-tech business, complete with open-plan layout, desk sharing and a central garden. The whole building has 'campus' written all over it, not 'spooks'. It's all been designed with the aim of creating a new culture. And HR has been at the heart of it.

Rewind to the late 1990s and the picture would have looked completely different. GCHQ started life at Bletchley Park in Buckinghamshire and moved to Cheltenham shortly after the Second World War. By the end of the last decade it occupied around 50 buildings and, according to Alan Green, the man who planned the move out of those buildings, every one of them was occupied by a unique 'tribe'. 'The one thing they had in common was a belief that GCHQ would be a great organisation if the other 49 started doing things they way they did,' he says.

But the pressures for change were gradually building. For one thing, GCHQ's mission was being redefined. 'We'd built a highly efficient factory for fighting the Cold War,' says Green, 'and then the Cold War went away.' In place of a static enemy with relatively limited communications to monitor, almost overnight GCHQ was having to focus on terrorism as the main threat, while the Internet was rewriting the rules of the game. Inflexible working systems were wholly inappropriate for this new reality.

By 1997 change was also being demanded by the incoming Labour Government, which put a new stress on delivery, and a new director, David Omand – the first ever to be appointed from outside GCHQ. Omand set in train a modernisation programme that has proved to be remarkably resilient, surviving three changes at the head of the organisation. This included a leadership development programme, Lead 21, which Green says has resulted in some 'radical changes in people's self-perception and behaviour – including at very senior levels'.

The really dramatic catalyst for change came in 1998 when the Treasury demanded that GCHQ think about using Private Finance Initiative (PFI) funding for its next round of building renewal. At first this suggestion was met with incomprehension, according to Green; how could a super-sensitive organisation such as GCHQ rent its headquarters from a private landlord? But gradually the realisation dawned that this was an exciting opportunity to make a fresh start on one site – and so a brief was drawn up for the 'new accommodation project', which, over the 50-year lifetime of the PFI contract, will be worth around £1 billion.

This is where Alan Green came in. A GCHQ 'lifer', he started out as an engineer, then moved into general management, becoming head of HR in 1994, a role he held until 1998 when he returned to engineering as head of the department. In 2001 Green, who was part of the team that wrote the original brief for the move, was appointed business change manager for relocation, effectively responsible for all the people management issues involved in relocating a workforce of nearly 5000 in summer 2004.

'This was an exciting challenge for me,' he says. 'In my previous role I'd led an HR reform programme, changing our processes and services, driving forward the leadership development programme and introducing a competency framework. When I moved into HR I met lots of people who had good ideas, but no clue of how to make them happen. That's what I was good at.'

The first thing that Green and his team decided was that the walls had to come down – in the existing buildings, two-thirds of all staff worked in cellular offices, and silo working was rife.

The new building was therefore designed to be open plan from the very beginning, with only a few exceptions; ironically, that included parts of HR itself.

Initially there was a fair amount of resistance to this idea, particularly from managers, who feared the loss of their status symbols of offices and big desks, but most have been won round. 'We thought we would lose lots of people because of the shift to open plan,' says Green, 'but in the end fewer than 10 people left as a result. It was nowhere near as dire as people had feared.'

The new building, known as 'the doughnut', is a huge circular structure built around a central courtyard, or 'secret garden'. On the ground floor, a central walkway, 'the street', runs right around the structure, with restaurants, a gym and meeting rooms on either side. Like the famous street at BA's headquarters, it's deliberately designed to encourage chance meetings and spontaneous interaction.

'Seemingly, every corporate HQ has an internal street today,' says a British Construction Industry award citation for the building. 'GCHQ's is refreshingly different.' Above this central corridor is a huge atrium stretching up to the glass ceiling, bisected by bridges that connect the open-plan working areas on the first and second floors; these bridges are equipped with chairs and coffee tables, to act as impromptu meeting spaces. White noise and carefully designed acoustics prevent anyone from being overheard, although employees have had to get used to speaking at a lower volume than they might be used to – even in the 'pods' set aside for conversations people will be overheard if they start shouting.

Not everyone proved to be compatible with pure open-plan working. Many of the agency's mathematicians are introverts by nature and work best in seclusion, with no distractions apart from the occasional frenzied brainstorming session. Although they are based on the open floor with everyone else, Green's team had to modify these people's workstations to give them greater privacy.

The second radical departure for the new building was a 'work anywhere' principle. All data is stored on central computers, and the IT infrastructure is designed so that staff can log on at any workstation and their information and phone calls will automatically be routed to their location. This was a massive undertaking: the IT investment alone cost £300 million (£380 million were spent on the buildings), but it was long overdue.

'It took Y2K to teach us how little we understood about our IT,' says Green. 'We have the most sophisticated networks this side of the Atlantic, and the computers in this building use more power than the rest of Cheltenham put together, but we were running seven different email systems and we didn't have a common infrastructure. Now we do.'

One of the most obvious benefits of the new building – not to mention the significant energy savings – is that teams can be configured and reconfigured at a moment's notice. On 11 September 2001, it took GCHQ 24 hours to work out how to structure a team to respond to the new terrorist threat, and three months for the new team to be fully installed. Within 24 hours of the London bombings in July 2005, the GCHQ response team was fully functional.

There is another benefit, though: desk sharing. In part this is driven by necessity. Between the writing of the brief and the actual relocation to the new building, GCHQ's workforce grew by an unanticipated 25 per cent, and there simply wasn't enough room to accommodate everyone in the new headquarters. This isn't unique to GCHQ, Green says. 'Everyone we've spoken to about this says the same thing: no one ever builds enough space when they relocate.'

However, on any given day 15 per cent of the workforce is out of the office, so desk sharing was an obvious solution. Everyone has their own pedestal for storing paperwork and other items, but not everyone has their own desk – including, crucially, board members.

The target for desk sharing was initially set at 5 per cent – 19 desks for 20 people – but that's now been pushed up to an average of 10 per cent and some areas are operating at around 30 per cent. That still means a substantial number of staff have to be located off-site, at one of the old GCHQ buildings, which is one of the biggest disappointments for Green and his colleagues.

You get the sense, though, that GCHQ would still be desk sharing even if there were more space. This is an organisation that's passionate about modernisation and about creating a new, empowered culture, but still has a strong *esprit de corps*.

Source: Steve Crabb. Originally published in *People Management*, 2005, and reproduced with permission.

Discussion questions

1 Why did GCHQ feel the need to change?

2 How did the organisation implement its change strategies?

Argyris, Putnam and Smith (1985) suggest that change is one reality with which individuals, groups and organisations must constantly cope in order to survive. Change is the coping process of moving from the present state to a desired state that individuals, groups and organisations undertake in response to dynamic internal and external factors that alter current realities. GCHQ began its transforming change process with a modest vision to improve productivity and quality of communication. However, the changes have had a much better impact than could have been envisaged at the start.

change
The process of moving from one condition to another.

Giants such as Virgin and British Airways know that to survive they must adapt to accelerating and increasingly complex environmental dynamics. Virgin was more successful than BA at managing change post-11 September 2001. However, recently BA has increased its profits through downsizing and repositioning its market.

Why is change important to managers and organisations? Simply stated, organisations that do not bring about change in timely ways are unlikely to survive. One reason that the rate of change is accelerating is that knowledge and technology feed on themselves, constantly creating new innovations at exponential rates. Few leaders would have envisioned in the mid-1990s the revolutionary impact the Internet and World Wide Web would have on business practices in the early twenty-first century.

The factors that cause change

Changes in organisations are stimulated by multiple external and internal forces, often interacting to reinforce one another. Managers' responses to these factors, in turn, often have a significant impact on individuals within the organisation. Some of the dominant forces that stimulate change in organisations are summarised in Exhibit 18-1.

To survive and prosper, organisations must respond and adapt to these multiple forces. They must innovate and continuously improve their products and services to meet changing

EXHIBIT 18 – 1 Forces and examples of change

Technology
Internet and World Wide Web
Information technology (enterprise resource management – ERP)
Genetic engineering
Computers and robots
Statistical quality management techniques
Process re-engineering

Economic conditions
Recession or expansion
Interest rate fluctuations
International labour rates
Regulatory changes

Global competition
Southeast Asia's economic success
Unification of the European Union (and East/West)
Mergers and consolidations

World politics
Unstable conversion of former Soviet communist republics
Unpredictable role of China in world trade: uneasy relations with Taiwan
World sanctions applied to countries violating human rights
Civil wars and religious/ethnic conflicts in dozens of regions

Social and demographic changes
Increasing environmental concerns
Increasing cultural diversity
Increased education levels of the workforce
Increasing gap between haves and have-nots

Internal challenges
Behavioural problems: high turnover, absenteeism, strikes, sabotage
Process problems: communications and decision-making breakdowns or innovations
Struggles between work ethic and social ethic in many countries
Destructive organisational politics and conflict

customer demands and competition. Technologies must be updated, and new and better ways to organise and manage must be found. As the airline industry has found out, complacency and the status quo are dangerous.

Although external factors can mandate adaptation, the internal changes that occur in organisations sometimes severely and negatively affect the individuals who work in them. For example:

- an aerospace engineer employed for 20 years by a large defence contractor may be suddenly confronted with a lay-off because his company's business is declining
- a semi-skilled factory worker who lacks technical skills and knowledge to operate new, high-technology machinery finds their employment terminated
- the 50-year-old manager employed for 25 years is no longer needed because the company eliminated two managerial levels from its structure
- fear is instilled in those who are still working after 4000 people have been laid off because of a major merger, as they wonder if they will be next.

Changing workforce demographics also influence companies. Increasing numbers of women and minorities in managerial and professional positions enhance the human resources available to companies but raise ethical issues about advancement opportunities and pay.

Beer and Nohria (2000) concluded that, 'The brutal fact is that about 70 per cent of all change initiatives fail.' In attempting to 'crack the code of change', these researchers conclude that there are two primary theories of change: one is based on 'hard' economic value (e.g. financial return to shareholders); the other is based on 'soft' organisational capabilities. The economic strategy involves use of economic incentives, downsizing, drastic lay-offs, and restructuring. The organisational approach develops corporate culture, human capabilities, feedback, and measurements and reflections on evolutionary progress (as Hewlett-Packard has often exhibited over the decades). A few firms are able to move between both economic and organisational strategies, as masterfully demonstrated by General Electric under Jack Welch's leadership.

The norm of pervasive change brings problems, challenges and opportunities. According to Faw (1999), those individuals, managers and organisations that recognise the inevitability of change and learn to innovate or to adapt to and manage it while focused on creating world-class best value will be most successful. Both people and organisations frequently resist change, even if it is in their best interests, especially in large, established organisations. In the next section, we will identify some of the reasons for this resistance.

Why change is often resisted

It is not difficult to recognise resistance to change when explicitly manifest through things like strikes, slowdowns and complaints. It is more difficult to detect and cope with implicit resistance, like decreased motivation or loyalty, errors, absenteeism and foot-dragging when changes are introduced. Once resistance is detected, however, this does not mean that it should immediately be eliminated. Resistance to change is sometimes beneficial because it promotes functional conflict and debates that can promote more thorough analyses of alternatives and their consequences – if a timely response is not crucial to success. On the other hand, excessive or irrational resistance can hinder progress and even survival, particularly if competitors are faster acting. Many times, however, change is resisted even when its benefits outweigh its costs. Why does this happen? There are several overlapping reasons why people and organisations resist change.

Why individuals resist change

Likert (1967) suggests that individuals at all organisational levels are prone to resisting change. The leaders of many of the companies that have not sustained their organisation's performance failed to recognise the need to change and adapt in order to survive.

Earlier chapters concerning personality, perception, learning and motivation provide the basic characteristics of individuals that make them inclined to resist change. The following discussion summarises five of the main reasons individuals resist change. You can assess your own comfort level with change by completing the 'Your turn' exercise.

Your turn

Are you ready for change?

People vary in their comfort with change. By answering the following questions you can get an insight into one aspect of your readiness for change.

Instructions Circle the number after each question that represents your response. Key: 7 = strongly agree (SA); 6 = moderately agree; 5 = agree; 4 = neither agree nor disagree; 3 = slightly disagree; 2 = moderately disagree; 1 = strongly disagree (SD).

		SA						SD
1	An expert who doesn't come up with a definite answer probably doesn't know much.	7	6	5	4	3	2	1
2	I would like to live and work in a foreign country for a while.	7	6	5	4	3	2	1
3	There is really no such thing as a problem that can't be solved.	7	6	5	4	3	2	1
4	People who fit their lives to a schedule probably miss most of the job of living.	7	6	5	4	3	2	1
5	A good job is one where what is to be done and how it is to be done are always clear.	7	6	5	4	3	2	1
6	It is more fun to tackle a complicated problem than to solve a simple one.	7	6	5	4	3	2	1
7	In the long run it is possible to get more done by tackling small, simple problems rather than large and complicated ones.	7	6	5	4	3	2	1
8	Often the most interesting and stimulating people are those who don't mind being different and original.	7	6	5	4	3	2	1
9	What we are used to is always preferable to what is unfamiliar.	7	6	5	4	3	2	1
10	People who insist on a yes or no answer just don't know how complicated things really are.	7	6	5	4	3	2	1
11	A person who leads an even, regular life in which few surprises or unexpected happenings arise really has a lot to be grateful for.	7	6	5	4	3	2	1
12	Many of our most important decisions are based on insufficient information.	7	6	5	4	3	2	1
13	I like parties where I know most of the people more than ones where all or most of the people are complete strangers.	7	6	5	4	3	2	1
14	Teachers or supervisors who hand out vague assignments give one a chance to show initiative and originality.	7	6	5	4	3	2	1
15	The sooner we all acquire similar values and ideals the better.	7	6	5	4	3	2	1
16	A good teacher is one who makes you wonder about your way of looking at things.	7	6	5	4	3	2	1

Interpretation The instrument you have just completed assesses your *tolerance of ambiguity*, which is the ability to cope with uncertain, conflicting or complex situations. People who feel comfortable with sudden change, novelty and uncertainty have a high tolerance for ambiguity, and those who feel uncomfortable have a low tolerance for ambiguity. The above questions measure three dimensions:

1 One is your tolerance for *novelty* – new and unexpected situations

2 The second is your tolerance for *complexity* – lots of information that may not all be relevant and organised, and that may be conflicting or incomplete

3 The third dimension is your tolerance of *insoluble problem-solving* situations in which answers are not easily discovered.

People with a high tolerance of ambiguity are better able to cope with unstructured and dynamic situations characterised by uncertainty and ambiguity. It is not surprising that effective managers usually have a high tolerance for ambiguity. The level of an individual's tolerance for ambiguity is a fairly fixed personality trait, but it can be modified and changed with conscious effort by those who want to make such a change. Becoming more accepting of ambiguity as a natural condition in the world today facilitates coping with the change and uncertainty that inevitably faces each of us.

Scoring instructions for tolerance and ambiguity:

1 Reverse the scores for even-numbered items. This means, for the even-numbered items only, $7 = 1, 6 = 2, 5 = 3, 4 = 4, 3 = 5, 2 = 6$ and $1 = 7$.
2 Add the scores for all 16 items (using the reverse scores from step 1) to get your total score.
3 Compute your subscores using the following:
   (N) novelty score (2, 9, 11, 13)
   (C) complexity score (4, 5, 6, 7, 8, 10, 14, 15)
   (I) insolubility score (1, 3, 12).

Total score The average range is 44 to 48. Scores below 44 indicate high tolerance for ambiguity. Scores above 48 indicate high intolerance for ambiguity.

Source: from Stanley Budner (1962) 'Tolerance for Ambiguity Scale', *Journal of Personality* 30, pp. 29–50. Reprinted with permission of Blackwell Publishers.

Selective perception

In Chapter 4, we observed that people sometimes perceive the same thing differently. When changes are initiated, individuals tend to focus on how they personally will be affected rather than seeing the big picture for the entire organisation. For example, assume a manager announces that members of his group will henceforth be paid on a piecework rather than an hourly basis. Irma, who is fast and highly skilled, may eagerly embrace the change as an opportunity to increase her pay. Angela, a new employee, may object for fear she will fall behind the others. At other times, individuals may perceive that change is incompatible with personal beliefs and values.

Lack of information

People will resist change if they lack knowledge as to what is expected or why the change is important. Many people take the attitude that 'if it's not broken, don't fix it'. If the reasons for change are not clearly presented, they tend to fill in the missing pieces with speculation, which often assumes the worst in terms of initiator intentions and personal impact. In addition, if people do not have enough information about how to change, they may fear making mistakes, so they will not try.

Fear of the unknown

Individuals resist change when they are uncertain about how it will affect their well-being. According to Argyris (1957), they ask themselves, for example, 'How will downsizing or new web-based b2b marketing affect my job security?' Other fears include uncertainties about not knowing how to change or of not being able to perform as well as before the change, losing position, income, status or power. There is also the possibility that work will be less convenient or more difficult, and the potential of losing desirable social interactions.

Habit .

Many people prefer familiar actions and events, even if they are not optimal. Have you ever tried to break a bad habit like smoking, drinking too much coffee or not exercising? Breaking a habit is difficult because it takes hard work and involves giving up perceived benefits from the habit, even if the new behaviour has more desirable consequences.

Resentment towards the initiator

If a change seems arbitrary or unreasonable, or its timing and manner of implementation lack concern for the people expected to carry it out, resentment and anger are often directed towards those initiating the change. People also resent being controlled and losing autonomy over their work lives when their thoughts and feelings are not considered by change initiators. Finally, without trust in the initiators' intentions, people may resist the change out of resentment or fear of possible unknown consequences.

Why organisations resist change

Hall (1987) suggests that organisations resist change for many of the same reasons individuals do. In addition, many organisational practices minimise risk taking; if a process is working satisfactorily, they quite often will not change it until they are forced to. According to Kanter (1989), there are also many forces inside an organisation that create resistance to changes initiated by environmental conditions. Some of the main ones are summarised below.

Power maintenance

Changes in decision-making authority and control of resource allocations threaten the balance of power in organisations. Units benefiting from the change will endorse it, but those losing power will resist it, which can often slow or prevent the change process. Managers, for example, often resist the establishment of self-managed work teams. Or, manufacturing departments often resist letting purchasing departments control input quality. There are even occasions when a CEO will resist change, denying that it is his responsibility to promote socially responsible behaviour throughout a global network, as demonstrated by the Nike saga in the latter half of the 1990s (see the World Watch box).

Structural stability

Recall from Chapter 15 that organisations create hierarchies, subgroups, rules and procedures to promote order and guide behaviours. People who 'fit' these desired behavioural criteria are hired and shaped to conform further through the socialisation process and organisational conditioning. These organisational structures, rules and conditioning are designed to develop consistent, predictable behaviours. Such behaviours resist change. Furthermore, as we described in Chapter 2, an organisation is a system of interrelated structures or subsystems. A change in any one area will have effects on others, which may not be acceptable.

Functional suboptimisation

Differences in functional orientation, goals and resource dependencies can cause changes that are seen as beneficial to one functional unit but that can be perceived as threatening to another. Functional units usually think of themselves first when evaluating potential changes. They support those that enhance their own welfare, but resist the ones that reduce it or seem inequitable.

What has Nike learned about change management on a global scale?

Nike and the Nike 'swoosh' are among the most globally recognised symbols of branding success. Even in remote locations, people can be witnessed wearing Nike products – a pair of Nike shoes or a Nike athletic shirt, perhaps featuring David Beckham. However, the Nike name was tarnished when the company suffered a barrage of negative publicity beginning in 1995. The media published accusations that Nike was using child labour, paying wages below defined minimum levels and allowing worker abuses in the Indonesian manufacturing plants that made Nike products.

Philip H. Knight, the founder, CEO and chairman of the Nike Corporation, responded to the allegations of unethical or abusive factory conditions and poor wages by highlighting the fact that factories in Indonesia and Southeast Asia were subcontractors and not part of the Nike Corporation. Nike 'steadfastly maintained that because it did not own its overseas contractors, workplace standards inside their factories were not its responsibility'. Therefore, Nike claimed, the working conditions were beyond company control. 'There's some things we can control and some things we can't control,' said Knight, who emphasised that through its subcontracting arrangements, the Nike Corporation created over 500 000 jobs throughout Southeast Asia.

Amid all the negative publicity, Nike launched its own public relations campaign, a campaign that focused on how the company was creating and bringing jobs to impoverished lands. Nike also contracted for independent studies on its factory workers. Researchers at Dartmouth College reported that workers in Nike subcontracted factories 'make above the minimum wage for both [Indonesia and Vietnam] with money left over for savings'.

Nevertheless, the negative publicity was just too much. In an unprecedented move, Phil Knight on 22 September 1997, suddenly severed business ties with three Indonesian subcontractors. He cited poor conditions for local employees, excessive hours and neglect in observing the local minimum wages. 'Good shoes come from good factories, and good factories have good labour relations,' Knight said. His new view emphasised that Nike's relationship to subcontractors was 'more than just a subcontractor relationship . . . a partnership – not in the legal sense – but in the moral sense'. It took a cumulative external effect of human rights activists, negative publicity and protests for Knight to take seriously the subcontractors' treatment of local employees.

The Nike experience raises a fundamental question: To what degree does a western-world enterprise have a moral and business obligation to demand that its contract vendors in developing nations adopt business practices that do not exploit workers? Nike's resistance to promote and enforce change in Indonesian employment practices teaches the lesson that inaction or an attitude of 'it's not my problem' can have dangerous effects on a company's reputation and revenues.

Sources: condensed from Christopher W. Cook, 'It's a Jungle Out There', paper for USD, GBA 508 (May 2000), which drew on: 'Mastering Global Business', *Financial Times*, London, 27 March 1998; Elizabeth Malkin, 'Pangs of Conscience', *Business Week*, 29 July 1996; Timothy Burn, 'Nike Says Overseas Workers Well-paid', *Washington Times*, 17 October 1997; 'How Should Multinational Set Global Workplace Standards?', *Financial Times*, London, 27 March 1998; and Jim Lehrer, 'The Nike Story', *The News Hour*, PBS Video, 1997.

Discussion questions

1 How can a poor ethical image affect business?

2 How could Nike have changed the employment practices in Indonesia instead of withdrawing its contract from the factories?

Organisational culture

Chapter 16 discussed how organisational culture – that is, established values, norms and expectations – acts to promote predictable ways of thinking and behaving. Organisational members will resist changes that force them to abandon established assumptions and approved ways of doing things.

Group norms

As discussed in Chapter 10, groups develop their own norms to promote desirable behaviours. Most members conform to these norms, especially in cohesive groups. Consequently, any change that disrupts group norms, tasks or role relationships will probably be resisted. Groups also sub-optimise to ensure their own self-interests, often at the expense of the larger organisation. This means that groups will often resist changes that do not directly benefit them individually.

Managers sometimes mistakenly assume that subordinates will perceive the desired changes in the same way they do and so have difficulty understanding the resistance. As we have just discussed, there are more reasons to assume that people will perceive the desired change differently. A key task is to determine and understand the reasons behind people's resistance when it occurs. Then the challenge is to find ways to reduce or overcome that resistance.

Research focus: Kotter and Schlesinger – overcoming resistance to change

Research by Kotter and Schlesinger (1979) has identified six general strategies for overcoming resistance to change. Exhibit 18-2 illustrates the kinds of situation in which these approaches might be used, along with the advantages and disadvantages of each. The following paragraphs describe each strategy. It is the manager's job to match the demands of a change situation with the best approach to overcoming resistance with minimum disruption.

Education and communication

Help people learn beforehand the reasons for the change, what form it will take, and what the likely consequences will be. Keffeler (1991) suggests that even if the consequences of a change are generally perceived as positive, extensive communication is required to reduce anxiety and ensure that people understand what is happening, what will be expected of them and how they will be supported in adapting to change.

Participation and involvement

Encourage those involved to help design and implement the changes in order to draw out their ideas and to foster commitment. Participation increases understanding, enhances feelings of control, reduces uncertainty and promotes a feeling of ownership when change directly affects people. It is difficult for people to resist changes that they themselves have helped bring about.

Facilitation and support

Provide encouragement, support, training, counselling and resources to help those affected by the change to adapt to new requirements. By accepting people's anxiety as legitimate and helping them cope with change, managers have a better chance of gaining respect and the commitment to make it work.

EXHIBIT 18 – 2 Methods for dealing with resistance to change

Approach	Commonly used	Advantages	Drawbacks
Education and communication	Where there is a lack of information or inaccurate information and analysis	Once persuaded, people will often help with the implementation of the change	Can be very time consuming if lots of people are involved
Participation and involvement	Where the initiators do not have all the information they need to design the change, and where others have considerable power to resist	People who participate will be committed to implementing change, and any relevant information they have will be integrated into the change plan	Can be very time consuming if participants design an inappropriate change
Facilitation and support	Where people are resisting because of adjustment problems	No other approach works as well with adjustment problems	Can be time consuming, expensive, and still fail
Negotiation and agreement	Where someone or some group will clearly lose out in a change, and where that group has considerable power to resist	Sometimes it is a relatively easy way to avoid major resistance	Can be too expensive in many cases if it alerts others to negotiate for compliance
Manipulation and co-optation	Where other tactics will not work, or are too expensive	Can be a relatively quick and inexpensive solution to resistance problems	Can lead to future problems if people feel manipulated
Explicit and implicit coercion	Where speed is essential, and the change initiators possess considerable power	It is speedy, and can overcome any kind of resistance	Can be risky if it leaves people mad at the initiators

Source: reprinted with permission of the *Harvard Business Review*. Excerpt from 'Choosing Strategies for Change' by John P. Kotter and Leonard A. Schlesinger, vol. 57, March–April 1979, p. 111. Copyright © 1979 by the President and Fellows of Harvard College. All rights reserved.

Negotiation and agreement

Bargain to offer incentives in return for agreement to change. This tactic is often necessary when dealing with powerful resisters, like bargaining units. Sometimes specific things can be exchanged in return for help in bringing about a change. At other times, general perks can be widely distributed to help make the change easier to undertake.

Manipulation and co-optation

Manipulation is framing and selectively using information and implied incentives to maximise the likelihood of acceptance. An example would be if management tells employees that accepting a pay cut is necessary to avoid a plant shutdown, when plant closure would not really have to occur. *Co-optation* is influencing resistant parties to endorse the change effort by providing them with benefits they desire and non-influential roles in the process.

> ### Explicit and implicit coercion
>
> Some managers use authority and the threat of negative incentives to force acceptance of the proposed change. Management might decide that if employees do not accept proposed changes, then it has to shut the plant down, decrease salaries, or lay people off.

How managers prepare for planned change

Change can be planned or unplanned. Unplanned change just happens in the natural course of events or is imposed on an organisation by external forces. Organisations and individuals then react to these unplanned changes to minimise disruption, or to maintain or improve their situation. On the other hand, **planned change** is the result of consciously preparing for and taking actions to reach a desired goal or organisational state. It involves proactively making things different rather than reacting to changes imposed from outside the organisation. The key questions to be answered when planning change are as follows.

planned change
The process of preparing and taking actions to move from one condition to a more desired one.

1 *What* do we want to achieve? What are our goals?
2 *Why?* What are our performance gaps?
3 *Who* will be the change agents responsible for making the change?
4 *How* do we plan to make it happen? What targets do we want to change and what process will we apply to change them?
5 What organisational *consequences* do we anticipate from the change?

Goals of planned change

Planned changes attempt to accomplish two general types of outcome. The first type is aimed at improving the organisation's ability to cope with unplanned changes that are thrust on it. Changes in this area include increasing the effectiveness of information-gathering and forecasting systems, and the organisation's flexibility so that it can adapt in appropriate and timely ways. Advanced knowledge of competitors' new products, changes in governmental regulations or supply limitations, can prepare organisations for what they need to do to adapt.

A second type of planned change is targeted at changing employees' behaviours to make them more effective contributors to the organisation's goals. Changes in this category include instilling new attitudes, values and ways of visualising the organisation and employee roles in it, as well as training to improve productivity, interpersonal relationships and creative contributions.

Performance gaps between present and desired futures

To sharpen the focus in determining the reasons for change, various processes can be used to dramatise the difference between the status quo and the desired new standard of performance or desired organisational state. The six-panel photo essay in Chapter 3 (see page 110) showed the steps some managers use to engage those involved in the change in creating a visual gap analysis.

Source: *San Jose Mercury News*, 31 October 1999.
Dilbert reprinted by permission of United Feature Syndicate, Inc.

Change agents

Individuals or groups who assume responsibility for changing behaviour and systems are called **change agents**. Ford's former CEO Donald Petersen was the chief change agent responsible for significantly transforming the way people performed at Ford Motor Company in the 1980s. But often it is the managers or staff at lower levels in organisations who serve as change agents. Their role is to recognise the need for innovation or altering the status quo, and to plan and manage the implementation of the desired changes. According to DeAngelis (1994) psychologists and consultants are frequently called into organisations as quasi-independent change agents to help members devise new ways to cope and even thrive with dramatic changes.

change agents
Individuals or groups responsible for changing behaviour and systems.

Targets and process of change

Change agents identify the level at which their efforts will be directed. Levels can be targeted to change individuals, groups and/or entire organisations. Each represents a different level, or unit, of change. Change efforts may even be directed towards the *trans-organisational level*, which means the relationships between one company and others. For example, Ford Motor Company worked to change its relationships with several of its suppliers during the 1980s to develop just in-time (JIT) delivery schedules. But the General Motors experience of 1996 demonstrated that taking less than a system-wide approach at changing to an efficient JIT inventory flow can leave the organisation vulnerable. Strikes in two GM brake plants quickly caused closures of 23 of GM's 29 assembly plants and lay-offs of over 100 000 employees because of parts shortages (Vlasic, 1996).

Change agents also must focus on specific targets to alter in attempting to close performance gaps and reach desired objectives. Organisational targets for change include people, technology, jobs and work flows, organisational structure, processes, culture and management. Exhibit 18-3 shows examples of how each of these targets can be changed. After the level and target have been decided on, the change agent needs to determine what will actually be changed –

EXHIBIT 18 – 3 Targets for organisational change

Targets	Examples
Individual	■ Discharge a person and replace him or her with someone new ■ Change knowledge, skill, attitude or behaviour
Technology	■ Replace existing technology with a more modern machine, system or way of doing work
Structure	■ Change from a functional structure to a product division structure ■ Add a new department or division, or consolidate two existing ones
Processes	■ Change procurement from person-to-person negotiations to web-based transactions from a selective list of approved vendors
Culture	■ Implement a programme to encourage valuing quality and service
Management	■ Encourage participation in the diagnosis and solution of problems by empowering people at lower levels to minimise a top-down approach

the *content* – and what *process* will bring it about. For example, assume a manager is concerned about decreasing productivity among the clerical staff and thinks the cause might be excessive talking among staff members. In order to discourage talking among the clerical staff, the manager may decide to move their desks farther apart or place partitions between them. This is a content change.

How this manager introduces and implements the change is the process. For example, the manager may decide to announce the change by memo or in a staff meeting, or even have the desks moved during the night so that the staff find out about the change when they come to work the next day. Each of these three approaches to process might lead to different results, some quite unintended – including more serious morale problems within the organisation.

More change efforts fail, or achieve less-than-expected results, because of inadequate process than because of poor content. Successful change often requires as much thought, or even more, given to process as to content. Top-level managers and staff people sometimes neglect process because they are removed from the day-to-day happenings in a particular work unit. They focus on the logic and quality of the content and forget or underestimate the importance of how people will perceive and react to any change they decide to initiate. Managers sometimes assume that others will perceive the logic and value of the change just as they do. Often they are badly mistaken.

When planning change and evaluating alternatives, managers must pay attention both to the quality of the proposed content and to the probability of its acceptance. For instance, in the desk-arranging example, the manager should assess whether the benefits of the change in desk arrangement will outweigh potential costs. The manager should also predict the probability of acceptance of the change by employees. If that probability is too low and the benefits of the idea are marginal, a different approach to improve productivity must be found.

Anticipating organisational consequences: the systems approach

Because these various elements are all part of an interdependent system, a change in any single target often leads to changes in the others. For example, when companies introduced networked computers to improve productivity, a series of changes followed. First, people had to learn new skills because of the new technology. Often, a new data-processing department was introduced into the structure. People throughout the organisation had to learn a new vocabulary, and the way information was processed began to change. Over time, jobs were altered. For example, the need for middle managers decreased in many companies as computers linked to databases (such as enterprise resource planning (ERP) systems) and eventually web-based processes facilitated the organisation and flow of information and made decision-making possible at lower levels.

Not all change is as pervasive as the introduction of information technology, but it is common for changes to ripple throughout an entire organisation. Managers sometimes make a 'simple' change without considering the systems implications. This often leads to unintended consequences.

For example, assume that manager Jean Brown wants to improve her assistant's attendance record. Brown offers to let her have one day off for every two months of perfect attendance. Indeed, her effort is successful in that her assistant seldom misses a day of work. However, she also tells the other assistants in the department, who complain to their bosses that they do not have a similar incentive. Their bosses in turn complain to Brown's supervisor, who reprimands her. This result might have been avoided if Brown had discussed her approach with her peers and supervisor before unilaterally making the change.

Managing the planned change process

Most effective plans for managing change recognise that achieving organisational change is not a one-step process; rather, there are a series of processes through which those affected by the change must travel.

On the other hand, sometimes the need for change is less obvious. If all appears to be going well, there is little or no incentive to change. This applies to both individuals and companies. For example, assume that John is performing satisfactorily in his accounting job but has neglected to update his ERP system skills. Without warning, John's manager announces a change in the programs being used that requires skills John lacks. Frances, on the other hand, has completed a specialised computer skills course and knows the new program. The manager decides that Frances will take over John's position, and John is moved to a lower-level job. John mistakenly assumed that his ability to handle his current job translated into future security. He failed to anticipate the changing demands created by changes in technology. Frances anticipated the change and was better prepared to adapt when it came.

Companies also miss signals in changing markets and, because they are performing successfully, assume all is well. Significant changes can occur suddenly, causing serious trouble. IBM, for example, epitomised success in the computer industry in the 1980s. Unfortunately, its leaders initially failed to recognise the speed and scope of changes occurring both in its customer base and among competitors. Constant changes in microchip technology led to progressively more powerful personal computers that could do the work done previously by larger mainframe computers for many types of tasks, and then lead to Internet applications. IBM executives failed to appreciate the impact the more powerful personal computers would have on IBM's mainframe business. It took a new CEO, Louis Gerstner, to recognise the future of the Internet and to begin rebuilding IBM in the 1990s into what is now called the 'biggest dotcom of them all' (Sager, 1999).

Both individuals and managers need to monitor their environments to anticipate and recognise changes that might affect them. These changes can occur in knowledge, skills and technology. Companies also face changes in customers, regulators, competitors and suppliers. One of the key roles of top managers is to monitor environments and to adapt strategies to achieve success.

Research focus: three phases of planned change

One of the earliest and most utilised ways of identifying the phases of planned change was developed by Lewin (1951), a noted social psychologist. His model, illustrated in Exhibit 18-4, contains three phases: unfreezing, changing and refreezing.

unfreezing

Raising awareness that current conditions are not satisfactory and reducing resistance to desired change.

Unfreezing involves helping people to see that a change is needed because the existing situation is not adequate. Existing attitudes and behaviours need to be altered during this phase so that resistance to change is minimised. The manager in the previous desk-arranging example must give some thought to how employees should be prepared for the change. This might be done by explaining how the change can help increase productivity, but there will also probably be the need to convince the staff that their social satisfaction will not be lowered or that this cost will be worth some other gain they care about. The manager's goal is to help the staff see the need for change and to increase their willingness to make the change a success.

moving

Letting go of old ways of doing things and adopting new behaviours.

The second phase involves **moving**, or making the change, which involves letting go of old ways of doing things and initiating relationships for new ones. This is difficult because of the anxiety involved in letting go of the comfortable and familiar to learn new ways of behaving, with new people, doing different tasks with perhaps more complex technology. In the desk example, that means moving the desks and reinforcing the desired attitudes and behaviours of the clerks. In more complex changes, several targets of change may need to be changed simultaneously.

refreezing

Reinforcing the changes made to stabilise new ways of behaving.

The third phase, **refreezing**, involves reinforcing the changes made so that the new ways of behaving become stabilised. Cummings and Worley (1993) suggest that if people perceive the change to be working in their favour, positive results will serve as reinforcement. If they perceive the change as not working in their favour, it may be necessary for the manager to use external reinforcers, which can be positive or negative. For example, the manager might encourage the employees to keep working at the change by predicting that desired positive results will come. Or a small reward might be promised, such as a lunch or an afternoon off,

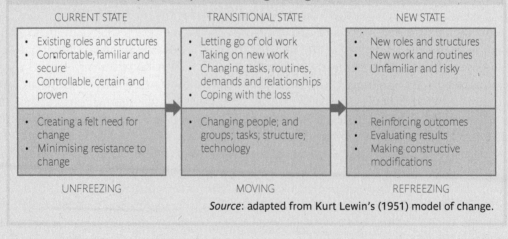

EXHIBIT 18 – 4 Three phases of planned change in organisations

CURRENT STATE	TRANSITIONAL STATE	NEW STATE
• Existing roles and structures • Comfortable, familiar and secure • Controllable, certain and proven	• Letting go of old work • Taking on new work • Changing tasks, routines, demands and relationships • Coping with the loss	• New roles and structures • New work and routines • Unfamiliar and risky
• Creating a felt need for change • Minimising resistance to change	• Changing people; and groups; tasks; structure; technology	• Reinforcing outcomes • Evaluating results • Making constructive modifications
UNFREEZING	MOVING	REFREEZING

Source: adapted from Kurt Lewin's (1951) model of change.

when the change has been completed successfully. Sometimes a more coercive approach to reinforcement is either necessary or appropriate. The goal of this phase of the change process is to cause the desired attitudes and behaviours to become a natural, self-reinforcing pattern.

Recognising the need for change

Building on Lewin's three phases of planned change, Exhibit 18-5 shows the steps required in planning and implementing change. In real situations, these steps are not always followed in sequence, but effective change normally includes each of them. The need for change is sometimes obvious, as when results are not in line with expectations, things are clearly not working well or dissatisfaction is apparent. As the 'pain' in such situations increases, so does the incentive to change.

Managers create planned change by altering the restraining and driving forces. A careful analysis is needed to determine how the restraining forces can be reduced or how the driving forces can be strengthened.

Lewin's force-field analysis has been a useful model for analysing change programmes and predicting the effects of future change. From this theory three explanations have been proposed by Bennis *et al.* (1976) to explain the underlying motives for behaviour as to why change occurs. These are as follows.

1 *Education* change assumptions are based on the idea that new information creates change. This has been called a rational-empirical change strategy since it is assumed that once people are educated about the change they will act rationally and agree to it.

2 *Reinforcement* – this method has been called the power-coercive strategy. It involves the application of power to force people to change. The power may be applied through the use of rewards or punishments.

3 *Peer group influence* recognises the influence of social norms and group dynamics in forcing change and is known as a normative-re-educative change strategy.

EXHIBIT 18–5 The planned change process

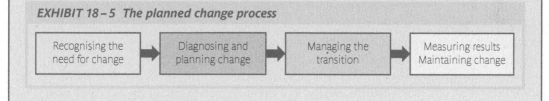

Diagnosing and planning change

Once the need for change has been recognised and a decision made to make a change, several questions need to be answered.

- What are our specific goals?
- Who are the stakeholders involved?
- What are the forces driving and restraining change?
- What contingencies should be considered?
- What process strategies will we use?
- What interventions will we use?
- How will we measure success?

Goals

The general planned change goals of preparing an organisation to cope with external changes and enhancing its employees' competencies were discussed in the section above on planning change. The first thing a change agent needs to do is determine what specific things need to be changed to achieve the desired situation. In doing so, it is important to distinguish between immediate and longer-term objectives, and between means and objectives.

For example, assume that a production manager needs to achieve greater output. He may assume that the way to accomplish this is to add machines to increase capacity. If he mistakenly defines his goal to be adding more machines without evaluating other options, he decreases the chances of making the best decision. He could consider another option to add people and operate a second shift. Another would be to re-engineer existing processes to achieve greater efficiency with existing machines and people. Both of the latter options offer more flexibility in case the need for increased output is temporary. It helps a manager choose the appropriate alternative if both short-term and long-term goals are clearly defined.

Stakeholders

When planning a change, all groups of people who might be affected by it should be considered. They are the stakeholders discussed in Chapter 2. Such groups might include employees, managers, owners/stockholders, suppliers, customers and even regulators. For example, management might decide to increase employees' pay to encourage motivation, but in doing so might irritate stockholders, who view the increase as an unnecessary expense that cuts into earnings. Alternatively, a manager might eliminate a step in his department's procedures to increase his group's efficiency, but thereby cause the work of another department to increase.

Driving and restraining forces

Lewin (1951) envisioned any potential change situation as an interplay of multiple opposing forces. Social systems tend towards a state of equilibrium, or balanced stability. For change to occur, it is necessary to tip the balance of forces so that the system (be it an individual, group or organisation) can move towards a new level of balance. Lewin developed the model of a force field to promote comprehensive and systematic analysis of potential factors that should be considered when evaluating alternative ways to promote positive changes.

force-field analysis
The process analysing the forces that drive change and those that restrain it.

Force-field analysis is the process of analysing the forces that drive change and the forces that restrain it, and then altering the balance. *Driving forces* push towards courses of action that are new or different from the status quo. *Restraining forces* exert pressure to continue past behaviours or to resist new actions. If these opposing forces are approximately equal, there will be no movement away from the status quo. For change to occur, the driving forces must be increased (in number or intensity) and/or the restraining forces must be reduced. An example of force-field analysis is diagrammed in Exhibit 18-6.

Force-field analysis is a useful diagnostic tool for the change agent. First, it assumes multiple forces, thus preventing oversimplified cause-and-effect thinking. Second, it recognises that change can be brought about by different strategies, including increasing driving forces, reducing restraining forces or combining the two strategies. It can be especially useful if the manager as change agent analyses forces from two different perspectives – first, relative to his or her own goals, and then from the point of view of those who are expected to implement change. This exercise typically reveals overlooked forces. See the Dynamics of Diversity box for a discussion of how some organisations attempt to develop through innovative work practices.

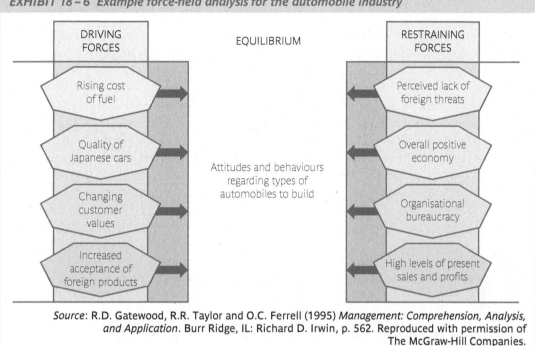

EXHIBIT 18 – 6 Example force-field analysis for the automobile industry

| DRIVING FORCES | EQUILIBRIUM | RESTRAINING FORCES |

Driving Forces:
- Rising cost of fuel
- Quality of Japanese cars
- Changing customer values
- Increased acceptance of foreign products

Equilibrium: Attitudes and behaviours regarding types of automobiles to build

Restraining Forces:
- Perceived lack of foreign threats
- Overall positive economy
- Organisational bureaucracy
- High levels of present sales and profits

Source: R.D. Gatewood, R.R. Taylor and O.C. Ferrell (1995) *Management: Comprehension, Analysis, and Application*. Burr Ridge, IL: Richard D. Irwin, p. 562. Reproduced with permission of The McGraw-Hill Companies.

Considering contingencies

The best way to change a given situation depends on various contingency factors – the critical factors in the situation that make one strategy more appropriate than another. According to Kotter and Schlesinger (1979), key contingent factors to consider include time, importance, anticipated resistance, power positions, ability, knowledge and resources required, and source of relevant data.

For example, if a change needs to be made quickly, is not critically important and resistance is not anticipated, using direct authority may be appropriate. However, if the change is important, resistance is anticipated and the power position of the 'changees' is relatively high, a participative approach might be more suitable. The key point is that change agents should consider the situation in terms of its contingent factors and then select the most appropriate strategy for intervention.

intervention
A planned process that introduces change.

Social, structural and technical change techniques that are guided by a change agent are referred to as *interventions*. An **intervention** is a planned process of introducing change involving an individual, group or organisation, usually with its help. It must be decided who will do what, when, where and how. We will discuss a sample of interventions in the following section on organisational development interventions.

Measuring results

The last step in the diagnostic and planning process includes deciding the criteria for success, how results will be measured, and what will determine when the change effort can cease – or should revert to a contingency plan.

dynamics of diversity

Ghana's sweet taste of global success

No matter how hot it gets in Ghana's capital, Accra, Golden Tree chocolate never seems to melt. It is an incredible advantage for chocolate vendors, who jostle with those selling football shirts, water and coconuts to push their wares through car windows in the many traffic jams that clog up the city.

The Cocoa Processing Company (CPC) has been making chocolate since 1965 and says it has mastered the art of making chocolate able to withstand the African sun.

Ghana is the world's-second biggest cocoa producer after neighbouring Ivory Coast, and CPC is a rare example of an African company adding value to its core product.

Much of the world's cocoa may come from West Africa, but as is the situation in many African commodity exporters, most of the value is added in Europe and America when it is turned into cocoa butter, cake and liquor – the ingredients for chocolate and confectionery. Currently, only about 20 per cent of Ghana's cocoa beans are processed locally, by companies such as CPC, West African Mills and international cocoa giant Barry Callebaut. The Ghanaian Government wants to see this percentage double and cocoa regulator Cocobod says it has several applications to set up processing facilities in Ghana, with investors attracted by the high quality of Ghanaian beans and incentives such as access to cheaper beans.

Cocoa firm Barry Callebaut is among those looking to process more beans in Ghana.

It is to double its processing capacity to 60 000 tonnes by the beginning of next year, managing director Gotzon de Aguirre says.

Similarly, CPC is also to double its processing capacity to 65 000 tonnes by the end of next year, CPC managing director Richard Amarh Tetteh says.

CPC makes chocolate for export to America and other countries and regions, but it has to jump through several hoops to do so, a fact that makes the African market more attractive. 'We can sell in America, by going through these guys who have gone through the processes and established the brand,' says Amarh Tetteh.

Some international firms say that processing cocoa beans in Ghana means they have access only to local beans, which is no good when they want a choice of flavours from around the world. Erratic power supply is also a disadvantage.

The irony is that, even as Ghana tries to make more money from processing its beans into semi-finished or finished products, in the automated world of international confectionery where the real value lies with the brand and not with the bar of chocolate, it seems unlikely this will lead to more jobs.

The Barry Callebaut factory employs 70 people and while CPC currently employs 600 people, it says that the high level of automation means the doubling of its capacity is unlikely to lead to more jobs. For CPC's Richard Amarh Tetteh, however, the logic to adding value is clear.

'We can't forever be suppliers of raw beans or semi-finished products, which have very little margin.'

Source: Orla Ryan, 'Ghana's Sweet Taste of Global Success', www.bbc.co.uk/business.

Discussion questions

1 How can the chocolate manufacturers use innovative work practices to develop new markets?

2 How can governments help and hinder innovation?

Managing the transition

Groves (1992) suggests that introducing and implementing a change seldom leads immediately to the desired results because people often require time to learn how to behave differently. Individual performance often declines during the learning period, which sometimes induces fear and anxiety among employees. During this period, there may be a strong desire to return to more familiar and proven behaviours. This doubt and fear may be reinforced if individuals share their concerns and complaints with one another.

Change agents can help people get through the transition period by anticipating underperformance and attitude problems, and being ready with increased support, education, encouragement and resources to help employees adapt. As people learn how to perform under the changed conditions and as they begin to perceive positive results, the external supports given by the change agent can be reduced. People begin to internalise their newly learned behaviours.

During the transition, the change agents need to set up managing structures to monitor results and keep actions on track. Usually special project managers, committees and interest groups are set up to assess and manage the change transition.

Measuring results and maintaining change

According to Cummings and Worley (1993), the change agent needs to determine if the change is progressing as planned and accomplishing desired results. Information needs to be gathered through feedback mechanisms such as surveys, sensing groups or interviews, and then compared to desired outcomes. If, as is often discovered, initial enthusiasm has faded as changes encounter operating problems, change agents need to intervene to sustain the momentum by providing assistance, training and resources. It also helps to develop support groups, set up special meetings and off-site retreats, and provide the means for steady reinforcement (e.g. praise, bonuses, celebratory award events) of those changing.

The practice of organisational development (OD)

A special subset of planned change is organisational development. It started out as an eclectic set of behavioural science tools and practices but has now become a professional field of social action and scientific inquiry. According to Cummings and Worley (1993) and Porras and Robertson (1992), **organisational development (OD)** is a system-wide application of behavioural science knowledge to the planned development and reinforcement of organisational strategies, structures and processes for improving an organisation's effectiveness.

organisational development (OD)
The system-wide application of behavioural science knowledge to the planned change process to improve organisation effectiveness.

The nature of organisational development

OD encompasses a wide variety of planned-change interventions, built on participative values, that seek to improve organisational effectiveness and employee well-being. Organisational effectiveness includes productivity (efficiency and effectiveness), people's satisfaction with the quality of their work life, and the ability of the organisation to revitalise and transform itself over time. OD can be differentiated from manager-led change in the following ways.

- Generally, OD focuses on changing an *entire system* in contrast to only one or a few components. (A system might include a group, department, division, organisation or even a group of organisations.)

- OD involves the application of *behavioural science* knowledge and techniques in contrast to operations research, industrial engineering or other deterministic disciplines.

- OD focuses on helping people and organisations *learn* how to diagnose and solve their own problems in contrast to relying on others for solutions.

- OD is often more adaptive and *less rigid* than structural-mechanistic change approaches. Although it does include a formal planning component, OD is a flexible, ongoing process of diagnosing and solving people-related problems, which can change with new discoveries and developments.

OD values and practitioners

Case *et al.* (1990) suggest that OD is a value-driven process. Brown and Covey (1987) argue that it emphasises human and organisational growth, collaborative and participative processes and a spirit of inquiry. According to Pasmore and Fagans (1992), the underlying OD meta-values include the following.

- **Respect for people.** People should be treated with dignity and respect because they are perceived as responsible, conscientious and caring.

- **Trust and support.** Effective organisations have regenerative interaction climates (see Chapter 9). They are characterised by trust, authenticity, credibility, openness and support.

- **Power equalisation.** To achieve the best collaboration, organisations should emphasise egalitarian participation (with power sharing) and not emphasise authority and control hierarchies.

- **Confrontation.** Problems should be shared and confronted so that they can be dealt with openly by all concerned.

- **Participation.** Those who will be living with the change should be involved in planning and implementing it. If they understand it, and participate in planning it, they will be more committed to implementing it.

Hunsaker (1983) suggests that OD is usually carried out by a professional change agent who is either a consultant from outside the organisation or from an internal staff department within it that is separate from the unit being assisted. External consultants offer their services to many organisations, while internal consultants provide their services to units within a single organisation. Both kinds of OD consultant help individuals and groups diagnose their own problems, develop solutions, and take action to improve processes and outputs.

In addition, Beer and Walton (1987) suggest that to bypass either source of full-time professionals, some managers and staff people have developed sufficient knowledge and skill to be able to apply OD approaches to their own work areas. A growing number of companies, including General Motors, Hewlett-Packard, Polaroid and General Electric, have programmes to train managers in how to develop and change their own work units (Kanter, 1983). Other managers develop competence in specialised areas such as reward systems, stress management, executive coaching, or career planning and development. This has enabled some organisations to manage change both faster and more effectively. Other companies, like Procter & Gamble, have programmes that develop managers' OD skills by rotating them into full-time OD roles (Cummings and Worley, 1993).

OD processes

According to Cummings and Worley (1993), OD processes have emerged from four primary sources originating in both the United States and Europe. These have been combined to form an eclectic approach that is centred around the action research model described below.

Sources

The first source was the development of *sensitivity training groups* by the National Training Laboratories as a way of giving individuals feedback about themselves in unstructured situations. Over time, more structured approaches developed into what we know today as team-building, which was discussed in Chapter 10.

A second source was the development of *survey research* and feedback. The thrust of this approach is to survey people at various levels in organisations to ascertain their attitudes towards work, supervision, working conditions, pay and benefits, and other related job factors. In many cases, the survey data are shared with supervisors and workers, who use them to decide how to work more effectively.

The emergence of OD can also be traced to the focus on productivity and quality of work life. One important contributor to this new emphasis was London's Tavistock Institute of Human Relations. Eric Trist and others developed what was to become known as a *socio-technical systems* approach to organisational development, discussed in Chapter 15.

Fagenson and Burke (1982) suggest that this approach combines the existing interest in human satisfaction at work with the technical aspects that increase efficiency and productivity – for example, reward systems, work flows, the physical work environment and management styles.

A fourth source of OD is *action research*. Action research engages the client organisation in generating and sharing research findings with action applications to help organisational members change and become more effective. According to Lawler (1985), action research emphasises the collaboration of social scientists and organisational members in designing, changing and measuring efforts to improve organisational effectiveness.

The action research model

action research
Data collection, analysis and problem diagnosis, the results of which are provided to the client system to help decide on plans for improvement.

Because it is such a generic change strategy, action research serves as a common model for planned change. Usually, a client system is at least symptomatically aware of a problem or need to change. Thus, their involvement in the research collection, analysis and action process is often desired over more structural or top-down approaches. The change agent and participants collaboratively engage in multiple processes to bring about change. The model is diagrammed in Exhibit 18-7. In practice the multiple steps overlap, and they provide only a general guide to what must be done. OD is not an exact science, and part of the art is developing steps to be taken as the process moves along. Rigid, standardised approaches are seldom successful, and the best practitioners are adept at innovating and adapting to the unfolding situation.

This adaptive approach is illustrated in the insurance company example described in the Eye on Ethics box. In this example, an outside consultant faced the ethical dilemma of providing the training that a group of managers originally wanted, or doing what he believed appropriate given his preliminary diagnosis of the situation.

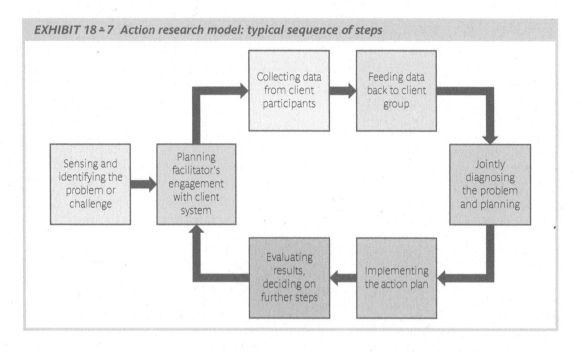

EXHIBIT 18·7 *Action research model: typical sequence of steps*

General Insurance Company: the ethics of escalating OD interventions

Sometimes a consultant feels ethically compelled to not give a client what they ask for. Elsie White, a line manager at General Insurance Company, telephoned Rob Henry, who had worked with the company for several years on a variety of problems. Elsie asked if Rob would conduct a two-hour team-building session for the administrative staff. When pressed to identify what she and a committee of four other line managers wanted to achieve with such a seminar, she explained that morale was low, absenteeism was high and co-operation was lacking. Rob quickly began to believe that a brief team-building session would not help. 'Could I meet with you and the other managers before making a hasty judgement as to what is needed?' asked Rob.

The meeting brought out a lot of issues within the 12 claims units, where each unit had one grade 4 secretary and one grade 3 mail and file administrator. The managers concluded the problems ran deeper than staff just not getting along, and agreed Rob could talk with a sample of administrative staff to get an idea of staff members' perceptions. Rob found administrative perceptions varied widely. Of the results, which Rob fed back to the managers, most were not surprising (such as grade 3 administrators feeling inferior and lacking advancement opportunities). But the managers had overlooked some obvious clues. The most co-operative pair were a secretary and administrator who were the same age and had their desks near each other. The least co-operative pair were a secretary and administrator who were 15 years apart in age and had their desks where they could not even see or hear one another, which made phone duties difficult. In addition, all secretaries and clerks agreed that there was not enough work for two.

As Rob fed back the data, the superintendents concluded that the problems were a combination of structural and interpersonal. They decided that a one-time two-hour team-building seminar would not bring about the desired outcome. With Rob facilitating the problem-solving and alternative-generating discussion, the group decided on several actions. They presented to senior management a convincing case to promote the administrators to grade 4 as soon as they were qualified. Senior management also agreed each unit could have two grade 4 employees. The line managers also agreed to redesign the work and organisation so fewer people would be needed. The reduction would occur through attrition, so that no one was punished for offering ideas to improve efficiency. These changes were explained to all those involved, and an announcement was made that Rob as an outsider whom most knew, would conduct a half-day team-building seminar without any managers present.

The secretaries and administrators had fun at the morning seminar, and made several useful suggestions for improving work processes. This morning session was immediately followed by a celebratory lunch at a nearby restaurant where the line managers expressed their appreciation for the administrative staff's involvement in team problem-solving.

Six months later, Rob conducted a review with the line managers, after first talking with the secretaries and administrators. Since the seminar, five grade 3 administrators had been promoted to grade 4 secretaries, one grade 4 secretary was promoted and not replaced, and another left and was not replaced. Several offices had been rearranged to enable a closer working relationship, the motivation and morale of the other grade 3 administrators were up significantly, absenteeism was down significantly, and complaints about lack of co-operation were greatly reduced. Rob reiterated to the line managers that his interventions were more extensive than they had originally wanted (a two-hour seminar), but that with a minimum of fact finding he could not in good conscience intervene without opening their thinking to options that would be more likely to solve most of the problems. The group felt good about the progress, expressed their appreciation to Rob, and agreed that he no longer needed to be involved.

Source: provided by Robert E. Coffey, co-author of this text in the two earlier editions.

Discussion questions

1 Why was change necessary and how did Rob know what that change should be?

2 How was the change implemented without being resisted?

OD interventions

The Eye on Ethics example demonstrates how managers and OD practitioners make interventions, often in a series of adaptive actions, to improve organisational processes and outputs that result in better performance and satisfaction. These interventions also helped people and the organisation become more effective in diagnosing and solving their own problems.

According to Cummings and Worley (1993), OD interventions have three major characteristics.

1 They are based on an understanding of how the organisation or unit actually functions, not just on how it is supposed to function according to charts, manuals or ISO 9000 documentation. We saw previously that data collection and diagnosis made up an important early step in the OD process.

2 The interventions must reflect the organisational members' free and informed choices. OD practitioners do not order people to intervene in a certain way. Instead, they strive to help organisation members participate in both the diagnosis of problems and the decisions about what interventions to make.

3 To be successful, the interventions must gain the internal commitment of those affected, not just their outward compliance. Internal commitment usually results from people having been involved in diagnosing the problem and determining interventions. This participation leads to their feeling some ownership of and responsibility for actions taken and results achieved.

OD interventions can be classified in different ways. Cummings and Worley (1993) suggest that one is by what organisational *issues* they intend to resolve. Another is by the organisational *level* (individual, group, organisation) at which the intervention is made. Exhibit 18-8 shows types of

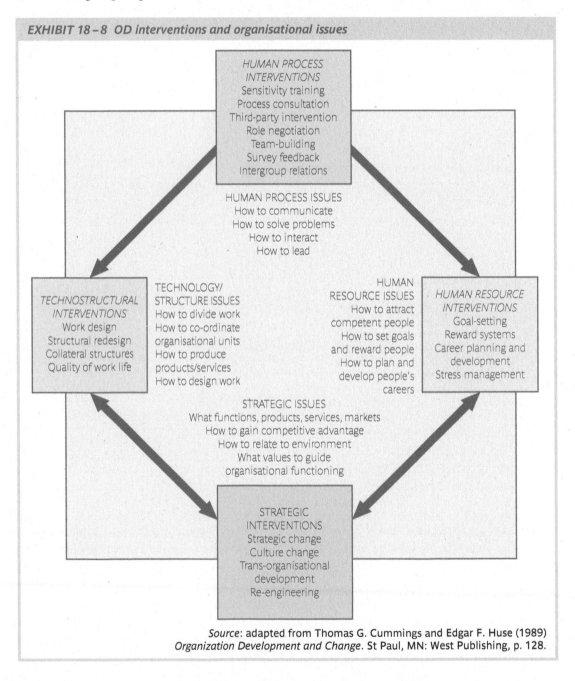

EXHIBIT 18–8 OD interventions and organisational issues

Source: adapted from Thomas G. Cummings and Edgar F. Huse (1989) *Organization Development and Change*. St Paul, MN: West Publishing, p. 128.

OD intervention and some of the issues they help resolve. Although 18 specific interventions are identified in the model, to give a sampling of such methods we simply describe three in which students often participate in the early years of their careers.

Role negotiation

When there is evidence of friction or misunderstanding among group members about who should do what, this intervention can be helpful. Role negotiation clarifies individual or group responsibilities and what each person is to give to and receive from others so that all may perform effectively.

Survey feedback

The purpose of this intervention is to collect data and feed it back to managers and employees with the intention of helping them identify problems and solutions. Information is usually collected by questionnaire. The OD practitioner helps facilitate the process, but the emphasis is on having those involved design ways to improve their performance and satisfaction.

Re-engineering

re-engineering
The redesign of a work process to achieve more quality, efficiency and effectiveness.

A relatively new concept, re-engineering describes the total rebuilding of important organisational processes. It involves fundamental rather than gradual change. The goal is to analyse critical work processes (e.g. purchasing, accounting, product design, sales) in detail so they can be redesigned to achieve more quality, efficiency and cost-effectiveness. Re-engineering usually leads to significantly changed processes that look little like the originals. Effective re-engineering includes consideration of important human resource systems such as rewards, appraisal and participation.

Ethical concerns in organisational development

This process of influencing change sometimes leads to ethical dilemmas. A few years ago an informal group of leaders from the various associations developed a set of ethical guidelines for OD practitioners. According to Cummings and Worley (1993), some of the key areas of ethical concern are those described below.

- **Interventions.** We have already seen that OD practitioners are value orientated, and many develop specialised skills. It is not considered ethical for the OD practitioner to choose an intervention he or she is not fully qualified to administer. It is also not ethical to use a favourite intervention familiar to the OD practitioner when it is neither appropriate for nor desired by the client.
- **Information.** Some of the information gathered during an intervention is personally and organisationally sensitive. OD practitioners must scrupulously avoid the misuse of such information. Misuses include revealing confidential information to the wrong parties and misusing confidential information to manipulate the client system for personal advantage.
- **Dependency.** The very nature of a helping relationship often leads to dependency. It is considered unethical for OD practitioners to prolong that dependency relationship. The role of the OD person is to help the client become independent by developing her or his own ability to manage the change and other processes involved.

■ **Informed choice.** At times clients do not understand the processes being proposed. The OD practitioner is obligated as much as possible to inform clients of interventions that might be suitable and to help them understand what they entail. Then the client should have the freedom to choose whether a particular intervention is used.

A natural goal of organisational development is to transform the organisation into a self-sufficient, problem-solving and learning organisation. A successful 'learning organisation' continues the change process internally on an independent, ongoing basis.

How 'learning organisations' promote change

To undertake purposeful change requires a collective capacity for learning. Organisations that focus energy and resources on learning from mistakes and opportunity-seeking are likely to 'learn faster than the competition, change before they're forced to, and always try to marry personal and financial performance', according to Peter Senge *et al.* (1995). Senge has popularised the concept of the learning organisation. A **learning organisation** develops tools and methods to analyse, change and re-evaluate its organisational systems so that employees respond more effectively and quicker to the same work-related stimulus than they did in the past, and to novel stimuli almost as quickly. Learning should be seen as a two-way process, with people and practices influencing each other, which will lead to change following naturally.

learning organisation

A deliberate effort by organisational members to develop models, tools and techniques for their organisation to change and grow faster than competitors.

According to Pedler *et al.* (1991), a learning organisation is one that facilitates the learning of all its members and continuously transforms itself as a whole. The result should be an organisation that is continually expanding and shaping its future with disciplines of personal mastery, mental models, building a shared vision, team learning and systems thinking.

According to Pedler *et al.* (1997), it is characterised by three stages:

1 implementing the things it does well

2 improving to do things better

3 integrating to do better things.

This means actions are required such as retaining staff, encouraging and rewarding them for using their abilities, and recognising that sanctions will be applied if they do not.

The learning organisation establishes a culture in which learning and questioning are fundamental to the organisation's development. The people in the organisation are continually reinterpreting their work and are constantly challenging accepted practices of doing business.

One successful learning organisation, Royal Dutch Shell, became committed to systematising learning when its research into older companies found that learning was their key to survival. Christensen and Overdorf (2000) suggest that the alternative is to be plagued with 'learning disabilities', which retard adaptiveness to change and can be fatal, causing organisations to prematurely shorten their life span. Like individuals, organisations that do not know how to learn to maximise the effectiveness of appropriate capabilities may survive but never live up to their potential. Marci (1996) argues that those firms that become effective learners are the ones most likely to succeed in increasingly turbulent, competitive global markets.

According to Garvin (1993), a learning organisation is skilled at creating, acquiring and transferring knowledge, and at modifying its behaviour to reflect new knowledge and insight.

Here are some examples that show how two managers view the power of learning within their organisations.

1 Ron Hutchinson, vice president of customer service for Harley-Davidson Motor Company Inc., says: 'To be effective long term, we must have an organisation in place that understands what caused prior mistakes and failures – and most importantly what caused successes. Then, we need to know how we can inculcate the successes and inculcate the preventive measures to avoid additional failures' (Solomon, 1994).

2 Human resources manager Laura Gilbert says her Educational Computing Company has become 'a place that has a proactive, creative approach to the unknown, encouraging individuals to express their feelings, and using intelligence and imagination instead of just skills and authority to find new ways to be competitive and manage work' (Solomon, 1994).

The characteristics of learning organisations

Five characteristics required for a learning organisation are summarised in Exhibit 18-9. They are personal mastery, mental process models, shared vision, team learning and systems thinking. Systems thinking is the most important because all the others are a part of it. In a learning organisation, people are willing to let go of old defences and ways of behaving in order to learn with others how their organisation really works. Senge (1990) suggests they can form a common vision of where they want to go, develop mental models of how organisational processes work, design a plan to get there, and implement it as a committed team.

Armed with these characteristics, learning organisations are better equipped to cope with the traditional organisational constraints of fragmentation, competition and reactiveness. Instead of separating different organisational functions into competing fragments, learning organisations emphasise the total system and how each function contributes to the whole process. Instead of competing for resources and trying to prove who is right or wrong, learning organisations promote co-operation and sharing of knowledge for the benefit of all. Finally, Kofman and Senge (1993) argue that instead of reacting to problems like a firefighter, learning organisations encourage innovativeness and continual improvement so that problems do not occur in the first place, or will not recur in the future.

EXHIBIT 18-9 Characteristics of a learning organisation

- **Systems thinking.** Members perceive their organisation as a system of interrelated processes, activities, functions and interactions. Any action taken will have repercussions on other variables in the system. It is important to see the entire picture in the short and long run.

- **Shared vision.** Belief and commitment towards a goal deeply desired by all. Sublimation of competing departmental and personal interests for the achievement of the shared vision.

- **Personal mastery.** Continual learning and personal growth by all organisational members. Individuals are willing to give up old ways of thinking and behaving to try out possible better ones for themselves and the organisation.

- **Mental process models.** Shared internal images of how individuals, the organisation and the world work. Willingness to reflect on the reasoning underlying our actions and to change these assumptions when necessary to create a more appropriate process for doing things.

- **Team learning.** Organisation members openly communicate across departmental and hierarchical boundaries to help all members solve problems and learn from each other. Decreasing the need for personal wins in order to increase the search for the truth for the good of the entire team.

Types of organisational learning

As we discussed in Chapter 5, individuals prefer different learning styles. So do organisations. Research by Rheem (1995) has identified four basic types of organisational learning: competence acquisition, experimentation, continuous improvement and boundary spanning.

Competence acquisition

Christensen and Overdorf (2000) suggest that organisations that learn by competence acquisition cultivate new capabilities in their teams and individuals – capabilities including resources, processes and values. They demonstrate public commitment to learning by continuously seeking new ways to work and by promoting learning as a fundamental part of their business strategies.

Experimentation

Organisations that learn by experimentation try out new ideas. They are innovators who attempt to be the first to market with new processes or products. (We elaborate on the process of innovation in the closing section of this chapter.)

Continuous improvement

Organisations that learn by continuous improvement strive to master each step in the process before moving on to the next. Their goal is to become the recognised technical leader for a particular product or process.

Boundary spanning

Organisations that learn by boundary spanning continuously scan other companies' efforts, benchmarking their processes against those of competitors. Like many organisations that learn from others, Porsche sent engineering teams to Japanese car factories to compare assembly times and discover how to improve its own processes.

Research by Rheem (1995) has found that, in general, companies that learn by experimentation are better able to compete and change than those that rely on the other learning methods. This does not mean that experimentation is best for all companies. To maximise competitiveness, an organisation's dominant type of learning should match its culture. For instance, a bureaucratic organisation proud of tradition would have a difficult time trying to learn by experimentation.

Creating learning organisations

How can a traditional reactive organisation be changed into a continual learner? Richards (1994) suggests that instituting any process that enlarges the organisation's knowledge base and improves the way knowledge is interpreted and put to use will help. Four specific actions are to establish a learning strategy, redesign organisational structure, infuse enterprise resource management systems, and modify the organisation's culture.

Establish a learning strategy

Management needs to develop and make explicit a strategic intent to learn. Slocum *et al.* (1994) argue that this includes a commitment to experimentation, a willingness to learn from experiences and a willingness to implement necessary changes in the spirit of continuous improvement. One strategy worthy of elaboration in the closing part of this section is the stimulation of double-loop learning rather than conventional single-loop learning.

Redesign the organisational structure

Traditional hierarchical organisational structures that emphasise authority, separate departments into competing domains and enforce formal communication networks impede organisational learning. Richards (1994) suggests that to enhance organisational learning, communication can be increased by encouraging informal face-to-face interaction and electronic distribution to all concerned. Competition can be replaced with co-operation through the establishment of common performance measures and rewards. Authority levels are reduced by instituting cross-functional teams and eliminating departmental boundaries.

Infuse enterprise resource management systems

Enterprise resource planning (ERP) systems are software packages (such as SAP-R3 or Peoplesoft) that integrate all facets of a business, including manufacturing, accounting, procurement, human resources and sales (Schneider and Perry, 2000). ERP and other forms of integrative software are increasingly web-based and designed to permit anyone who has a need to know to call up real-time information. Such instant access to data sources of information promotes learning by enabling people throughout the organisation to analyse situations and to make timely, more informed decisions. Peters (2000) refers to enterprise software as 'white-collar robots' that will transform organisational productivity in the early twenty-first century much like robots and mechanised automation transformed blue-collar efficiency in the latter half of the twentieth century.

Modify the organisation's culture

Learning happens best in the context of organisational cultures that value growth, openness, trust and risk-taking. Known as the regenerative climate (described in Chapter 9), emphasis is on high openness, trust and owning of responsibility. Managers promote experimentation, trying new things, constructive criticism, learning from past mistakes and bringing functional disagreements into the open. Management establishes regenerative climates by publicising what is desired, acting accordingly themselves and rewarding desired behaviours. According to Porras and Robertson (1992), the organisational development process is concerned with developing learning organisations to improve individual and organisational effectiveness.

To be effective, Garvin (2000) suggests that six common characteristics are necessary:

1 a culture that is willing to stimulate, to test and to adopt new ideas
2 a learning culture that encourages and rewards skill development
3 a diversity of attitudes and perspectives are accepted and tolerated
4 feedback from customers and suppliers is provided regularly
5 the culture encourages appropriate risk-taking
6 knowledge is shared not just in the organisation but also with stakeholders.

It should be remembered that a learning organisation is not just a collection of individuals who are learning. Learning can take place at individual, departmental and organisational levels, and demonstrates that there is an organisational capacity for change.

Research focus: Chris Argyris – managers can shift from single-loop to double-loop learning

From research involving 6000 people across a wide variety of countries, ages, ethnic identities, educational levels, power levels, experience, and from both sexes, Chris Argyris, a renowned academic, concluded that many modern techniques that promote communication between managers and employees are dysfunctional. Techniques such as total quality management, management by walking around, focus groups and organisational surveys inhibit learning *if* used in a one-dimensional way.

Single-loop learning displaces employees' responsibility

single-loop learning
Occurs when a manager shifts responsibility from employees to himself or herself by asking simple unidimensional questions that produce simple impersonal responses.

According to Argyris (1994), when learning is of a single-loop character, the responsibility for learning and action shifts from subordinate to manager. Argyris emphasises: 'single-loop learning asks a one-dimensional question to elicit a one-dimensional answer' wherein outcome responsibility resides with the manager doing the asking.

For example, the manager who asks others to identify the major obstacles to faster product innovation actually shifts accountability for innovation from employee to the manager. Although on the surface it may appear as if employees are being empowered because their opinions are being asked for, the implication is that the manager takes responsibility for acting on the advice.

Double-loop learning keeps accountability on followers

To enter into double-loop learning, the leader would have to shift accountability back to employees. This might be done by asking tough questions, such as: How long have you known

double-loop learning
Shifts accountability for actions and learning to employees by having a manager ask complex questions about the employee's motivation for solving a problem.

about these problems? What goes on in this company that prevented you from questioning these practices and getting them corrected or eliminated? Double-loop learning turns questions back on people in the form of follow-ups – to ask not only for facts, but also for the motives and action implications behind the facts, with the implication that changing the situation is their responsibility.

Managers often contribute to the problem if they have been trained to emphasise positive regard of others, being considerate and employee morale. Such motives and attitudes 'deprive employees and themselves of the opportunity to take responsibility for their own behaviour by learning to understand it. Because double-loop learning depends on questioning one's own assumptions and behaviour, this apparently benevolent strategy [of single-loop learning] is actually *anti*-learning', according to Argyris (1994). An illustration of how technology, along with staff empowerment through learning and improved communications, promotes business agility is presented in the Technology Transformation box.

Consistent positive regard probably diminishes learning

All too often, managers use socially 'upbeat' feedback and behaviour to unconsciously inhibit learning, when honesty and candour would produce more responsible behaviour. Organisational members learn a set of rules to deal with difficult situations in ways that do not embarrass or threaten psychological well-being. Managers end up sending mixed messages when they reply along the lines of 'your recommendation is a good one, but I have to overrule it because...'. By saving face with subordinates while nevertheless thinking the idea is not a good one, managers are telling employees that their job is to make suggestions, and the manager's job is to make decisions and act. Rather than confront others with candour and forthrightness, managers who absolve others are talking the talk but not walking the walk. Rather than promoting empowerment of others, they are creating dependence. Argyris writes:

> Once employees base their motivation on extrinsic factors – [such as] the CEO's promises – they are much less likely to take chances, question established policies and practices, or explore the territory that lies beyond the company vision as defined by management. They are much less likely to learn. A generation ago, business wanted employees to do exactly what they were told, and company leadership bought their acquiescence with a system of purely extrinsic rewards ... Today ... managers need employees who think constantly and creatively about the needs of the organisation. Argyris (1994) suggests that they need employees with as much intrinsic motivation and as deep a sense of organisational stewardship as any company executive.

How an organisation learns to innovate

Innovation is a special case of planned change and learning that either transforms current

innovation
Planned change and learning that transforms products, services and markets, or dramatically creates an entirely new market and line of business.

products, services and markets, or, in a more dramatic leap forward, creates an entirely new market by introducing a radically new product or service. An organisation is considered an innovator if it stirs up the marketplace and simultaneously creates competitive pressures (threatens to displace currently available products/services) and thus new opportunities for organisations that quickly adapt. It has long been recognised that innovation success in an established organisation requires a balancing of contradictions between stabilising the efficiency of the current market offerings and building in capabilities to create and develop offerings for future, unknown markets. Peter Drucker (1998) has described this tug-of-war thus:

> The search for innovation needs to be organisationally separate and outside of the ongoing managerial business. Innovative organisations realise that one cannot simultaneously create the new and take care of what one already has. They realise that maintenance of the present business is far too big a task for the people in it to have much time for creating the new, the different business for tomorrow. They also realise that taking care of tomorrow is far too big and difficult a task to be diluted with concern for today. Both tasks have to be done. However, according to Drucker (1974), they are different. Innovative organisations, therefore, put the new into separate organisational components concerned with the creation of the new.

Cycles of innovation through 'new ventures' capabilities

In reality, achieving these dual capabilities within the same organisation is difficult if managers seek to promote significant innovation beyond continuous improvement. Empirical evidence

technology transformation

What makes a business more agile?

In order to remain productive and competitive, businesses need to be agile. Staff empowerment, cost efficiency and improved communications are some of the key elements that define business agility.

Over the last few years a huge wave of technological innovation has been unleashed that is rapidly changing society, the nature of work and the ways in which companies are interacting with their customers.

The introduction of text messaging, always-on Internet connectivity and the possibilities of mobile working are prompting companies to fundamentally review their internal processes and the way they operate in order that they can keep up and survive in a more dynamic and demanding society.

Martin Heath, head of communications consultancy for KPMG in the UK, says the biggest test for companies in today's rapidly moving marketplace is learning how to manage the implementation of new technologies that will enable them to respond faster to change. 'Technology is a means to an end. Simply putting in a new broadband link does not create any value in itself. It's only when you change your strategies and automate your processes that technology can bring business benefits. Technology is an enabler and you need to make sure you change your structures to account for that technology.'

Despite the difficulties associated with implementing new technologies, he believes that companies need to embrace new concepts, such as mobile working, in order for them to remain agile and productive in the marketplace. 'As soon as any of us are away from our desks, our productivity goes down. We no longer have access to our email. We no longer have access to knowledge management systems.'

Heath sees the traditional office eventually extending outwards through networks that staff can tap into. 'The office will be on your laptop, PDA and phone. All the technology you get in the office will be on a mobile device.'

As the world becomes increasingly interconnected through a plethora of fast and pervasive communications platforms and as customers demand service every day of the week, companies are having to introduce flexible working arrangements. The traditional nine-to-five model is no longer adequate in a 24/7 environment and employers also know if they want to retain skilled staff, especially those with children and other family obligations, they are going to have to be open to part-time working and job-sharing arrangements, otherwise they could severely restrict the resources they can recruit from.

'Organisations can become more agile by deploying infrastructures that support them becoming agile. Your IT structure and networks have to permit flexible job patterns, instant messaging and videoconferencing,' explains Danny McLaughlin, managing director of BT Major Business, a division of BT Retail. He argues that businesses need to take full account of the fact that electronic communications are fundamentally changing the nature of work. 'Work is what you do and not where you go. We use web-based meetings so we can bring together the right specialists who may be based in different parts of the country. But there has to be the right infrastructure in place before you can have an e-enabled workforce.'

McLaughlin adds that the company has plans to provide all of its 5200 home workers with access to ADSL. He argues that if companies can allow individuals to work more on their own terms then they will feel empowered and motivated, which is likely to lead to a rise in productivity levels. 'If you create a satisfied employee base then it is going to impact upon customer satisfaction. If you equip people with the right kind of infrastructure and tools, they are more empowered to do their job and they can make decisions quicker.'

In order to make itself more agile, Virgin Atlantic recently launched a collaborative website for its 18 marketing offices around the world. The site stores product photographs, approved copy, videos of ads, poster campaigns and radio commercials in audio formats. The idea behind this online collaborative tool is that the airline's international marketing teams can upload their work, access material and share ideas in real time with others around the world. There are also contact numbers for external agencies who have carried out specific types of work so that they can be re-hired for future campaigns.

'It's improving internal processes simply because it channels everyone to one specific area. It means we can be more responsive globally, whereas before it might have taken a bit of time for campaigns to kick in,' explains Bill Gosbee, Virgin Atlantic's UK design manager. He adds that new collaborative web-based tools have a unifying effect and he feels they are most relevant for companies with a fragmented workforce.

Christoph Michel, chief executive of Hyperactive, which develops collaborative knowledge management systems, has helped advertising agencies to set up sites similar to the one deployed by Virgin Atlantic. He believes it is in the self-interest of companies to disseminate and share information more quickly online. 'Essentially they are after efficiencies for themselves and the business. The advertising gets done a lot quicker and they can have meetings online.' He adds that easily searchable information can make it less expensive for businesses to expand; local offices can easily tap into existing corporate knowledge and call up previous examples of work to help them pitch to new clients without having to pay to fly in executives from other countries to assist them.

Jonas Hjerpe, marketing director for Parity Technology, whose clients include Royal Mail, believes that a flexible IT architecture is crucial to the ability of a company to remain agile: 'Companies that tend to be successful have more strategic views of their information techno-logy.' He points out that it is not just the private sector that is harnessing technology in order to become more agile; local councils across the UK are piloting web-based technologies so they can, for example, purchase goods and services online in paperless environments. Leeds City Council has set up a web-based tendering service so suppliers can log on and see what is being tendered, and then download and upload tender information.

'It's giving people who want to apply for the council's contracts more time to do it. Instead of waiting for material to be published in the newspaper and then contacting us, they can go straight in and download it,' explains the Council's information manager Teddi Coutts.

And councils in Cornwall have clubbed together to pilot advanced multi-functional smart cards, which can be used by a variety of organisations to make services more accessible to people in rural areas. In the initial rollout, cards are being made available through schools for registration and meal payments. The cards are being used in libraries (as replacements for stan-dard cards) and for paying for tickets in local car parks and on buses.

'The world outside a company's four walls is quite different to the world about four years ago. Enterprises have to have very fluid structures and must quickly align their skills and knowledge to deliver what a market opportunity wants,' explains Andy Mulholland, chief technology officer for Cap Gemini Ernst & Young. He says the speed at which a company responds has to be dictated by the market and not by the traditional internal structures of the organisation.

He explains how companies such as Dell are now enjoying competitive advantages because they are using web-based channels to make new computers to order, while car companies such as Audi are enabling customers to configure the car models of their choice online. Tasks that were traditionally performed by a sales team are being supported by web-based tools that help customers design and swiftly order new products.

The agility of a business depends largely on the ability of management teams to rethink how their companies operate. In addition, many business consultants believe that UK directors are still a long way off from fully understanding how they can best integrate new technologies into their operations. Take mobile communications, for example. This sounds promising in theory, in terms of being able to send marketing information to consumers on the move, but few businesses appear to be fully geared up to deliver tailored individual marketing messages to consumers on mobile devices. Many are still mass media-orientated.

Mobile working sets executives free from their desks but it has its disadvantages as well, as KPMG points out. Not least is the fact that many companies are extremely worried about the security of data as they travel out of the physical office and through the air to someone's mobile device, which could be lost or stolen. 'There are big concerns over security,' admits Heath. 'I think the security issues are manageable. But the real debate is around the changing work practice issues.'

Finding smart ways to apply technology is not easy. Technology can facilitate home working, for example, and create significant savings as space is not required in traditional office premises. Such practices are open to abuse and require a significant amount of trust. It is by no means clear to companies how you manage home workers effectively and keep them motivated. Nor is home working suited to everyone. Many prefer the social interaction of working with other people.

While there are clearly many new possibilities, there is still some way to go before the concept of business agility is successfully mastered by UK directors. 'I don't think the process has been cracked yet,' says Heath. 'We're just at the stage where we are beginning to learn how to deal with this huge wave of technology innovation.'

Source: Justin Hunt, *Guardian*, 9 May 2002.

Discussion questions

1 How does technology influence innovation?

2 What are the negative factors associated with technological change?

suggests there is a cyclical pattern of building up internal corporate new venture programmes (to provide both capital and incentives for starting new businesses), and then diminishing them after a few years. These waves, or cycles, of innovation through corporate venturing are similar to the periods of revolutionary growth followed by slower, evolutionary stabilisation described in a classic article by Greiner (1998).

During the 1960s and early 1970s, a quarter of *Fortune* 500 (the American equivalent of the FTSE 100) firms built up such internal venturing capabilities. The firms that did so disbanded most of these venturing capabilities in the late 1970s, only to find renewed interest in the early 1980s, but then with the market downturn in 1987, the venturing capabilities were again discontinued. However, Chesbrough (2000) claims that, with the extended bull market in the late 1990s, they have now been reintroduced.

As an example of this last wave, Lucent created its New Ventures Group (NVG) in 1997, to commercialise emerging technologies being created in its Bell Laboratories that did not fit with Lucent's established businesses. Within its first two years of operation, the NVG had invested in 19 new ventures, mainly in the areas of Internet, networking, software, and wireless and digital broadcast. Technology firms are the typical players in this last wave of corporate venturing, with Adobe, Intel, Sun Microsystems, Xerox and Texas Instruments representative of firms using this strategy to drive innovation.

Distinguishing sustaining and disruptive innovations

sustaining innovations
Incremental innovations typically introduced by industry leaders to provide greater customer choice within established markets.

disruptive innovations
Revolutionary industry changes usually introduced by smaller, more entrepreneurial organisations to provide customers with new ways of doing things.

Few innovations are truly revolutionary; most are evolutionary. Sustaining innovations are evolutionary with continual or periodic improvements in products and services, and an occasional new product that provides greater choice within established markets. Sustaining innovations are almost inevitably developed and introduced by leaders within an industry, as they move incrementally from generation to generation of product.

Revolutionary changes are most often introduced by start-ups or smaller, more flexible entrepreneurial organisations. According to Christensen (1997), these disruptive innovations create an entirely new market by providing a product or service that offers customers new ways of doing things, although at first it may seem that the quality is ragged or even less than that of conventional alternatives.

Intel's movement across a family of Pentium microprocessors, each with greater speed, is an example of a sustaining innovation, as was Merrill Lynch's original introduction of its Cash Management Account. At the disruptive innovation end of the scale, Charles Schwab's initial entry as a low-cost discount broker or Yahoo!'s free Internet search engine are representative of the market-transforming effects of such innovation.

Innovative capabilities

Christensen and Overdorf have identified three overarching capabilities that enable innovation: resources, processes and values. *Resources* include both tangible assets such as people, equipment, cash and technologies; and the intangibles such as brands, relationships with suppliers and customers, and information. *Processes*, such as patterns of interaction, communication and decision-making (applied to product development, manufacturing, distribution and budgeting), are used to transform resources into products or services of value. For most organisations, processes are a catch-22 as they are used to promote consistency, not to introduce change. Finally, *values* in the innovation context are the standards by which employees set priorities and decide issues such as whether an idea for a new product is worthwhile or not, or whether a customer is more or less important.

Values reflect the business model of the organisation – its cost structure and its expected gross margins. Leaders of large established firms believe they must continually grow to sustain increasing economic shareholder value as part of their values. This means that disruptive innovations are often difficult to justify, as their expected gross margins often fall below the conventional threshold, or the initial revenue yield is too small to add significant impact to growth targets. Thus, to sustain growth and market capitalisation, big firms often turn to acquiring other firms. The expectation with acquisitions is that they produce access both to new capabilities (including technology or innovation) and to substantial revenue streams.

Strategies to strengthen innovation capabilities

Capabilities migrate as an organisation grows. In the start-up stages, what gets done is largely attributable to the organisation's resources, specifically people. Over time, the emphasis shifts to process and value capabilities. Notwithstanding attention given to re-engineering processes, the process capabilities of most organisations are less adaptable to change than are resources and values. For established organisations to be innovative, they need to develop flexibility across a range of capabilities. Christensen and Overdorf (2000) suggest that, to achieve this, they can choose from among three primary strategies.

1   Create new capabilities by originating new structures charged with innovating new ventures and businesses within the existing organisational boundary. These may be product development teams, new business start-ups, or an incubator that provides venture capital and key services to spawn dozens of new businesses. The 'new ventures' organisational units noted earlier personify this organisational strategy.

2   Create capabilities by spinning-off new ventures that do not fit the company's business model (which may be because it is more of a disruptive innovation), yet retain an equity investment position both for technology and earnings infusion back to the parent. Hewlett-Packard management did this when they realised ink-jet technology was a low-margin business that competed with its high-margin laser technology. Responsibility was transferred to a new division in Vancouver, British Columbia, to develop aggressively the future of H-P's ink-jet business.

3   Create capabilities through acquiring companies that have the capabilities the company wants. However, to prevent the larger parent organisation's values and processes from driving down entrepreneurial risk-taking enthusiasm and focus on a singular business activity, it is better to allow the fledgling enterprise to stand alone, insulated from managerial tendencies to integrate it into the mainstream processes and values. Cisco Systems has become a master at deciding which high-potential acquisitions to leave alone, and which acquisitions to integrate because they offer resources more than new business models (Gillmor, 2000).

Sources of innovation

It was none other than Drucker (1998) who wrote:

> There are, of course, innovations that spring from a flash of genius. Most innovations, however, especially the successful ones, result from a conscious, purposeful search for innovation opportunities, which are found in only a few situations. Four such areas of opportunity exist within a company or industry:
>
> ■ Unexpected occurrences
> ■ Incongruities
> ■ Process needs
> ■ Industry and market changes
>
> Three additional sources of opportunity exist outside a company:
> ■ Demographic changes
> ■ Changes in perception
> ■ New knowledge

One unusual approach to innovation and organisational change that builds on most of these sources of opportunity is reflected in the actions of Vulcan Ventures, the private holding company of Paul Allen, co-founder of Microsoft. Allen now concentrates on significant investments in some 140 companies, all synergistically related to his vision of creating a 'wired world'. Allen says, 'Today you have to take ideas and turn them into products or websites very quickly. That's just reality. When we created Interval Research (a product development think tank) we wanted to have substantial impact, spinning off start-ups and potentially changing the industry' (Kirkpatrick, 2000). Everyone's dream, Allen's reality.

GCHQ: a second look

Outside the cosy 'secret garden' and the friendly street, there's one way in for visitors and that leads through a museum devoted to GCHQ's glorious past: Enigma and other German, British and American cipher machines sit in cases beside decoded telegrams and press cuttings from the 1920s. Beyond that, the whole 'doughnut' is encased in a protective wall that GCHQ's own corporate literature likens to a 'medieval fortress', and that's surrounded by razor wire and high-security surveillance systems.

So, is there a conflict between the empowered, boundary-free culture being built inside GCHQ and the forbidding face it shows to the outside world? Not according to Alan Green: 'I don't have a problem with that at all,' he counters. 'Our core values are to be modern and professional. Our security systems show we take that seriously.'

Online bank egg has also used the built environment to achieve a cultural turnaround, but this was done without relocating. When the company moved into its premises in Derby's Pride Park area in 1998, the new building was designed to foster collaboration, high-energy working and a culture that supported the brand. However, thanks to egg's growth, by 2003 the building was accommodating half as many people again as it was initially designed to take.

The solution was a change programme aimed at resetting the 'being' of the building itself. 'By "being" we mean the essence of the structure, which builds and drives patterns of behaviour, and therefore forms a layer within the individual and communal "beings",' says egg's chief people officer, Neil Rodgers.

'We used traditional success factors of cost, time and risk quality as the core of our cost analysis. But we also designed the building to reinforce egg's purpose and strategy and make them live, in terms of how the building is experienced by the people that work there.'

The resulting refit saw the introduction of new areas aimed at stimulating conversations between staff, study zones for e-learning, quiet reflection and research, a multi-purpose studio, equipped to host events, and plasma screens to broadcast information on the changing nature of the business.

The past decade has seen a profound switch from an industrial to a post-industrial economy, according to If Price, professor of facilities management at Sheffield Hallam University – but the way we design and use our buildings simply hasn't caught up.

Price, whose research work has included collaborations with GCHQ and Internet bank egg, says: 'Stan Aronoff and Audrey Kaplan, the authors of *Total Workplace Performance: Rethinking the Office Environment*, make the point that when electric power became widely available in factories, it took another 20 years before people stopped designing manufacturing lines as if there was only one power socket. The same thing's happening to the way we design offices today.'

▶ 'The physical workspace is the most important and the least appreciated tool of contemporary knowledge management. Conversations are the production process of the knowledge economy, and conversations are heavily influenced by the spaces in which they occur.'

Research by Price's team has found that employees value the ability to interact with colleagues above all other aspects of workplace design, but such issues are often given low priority when a move is being planned.

The enthusiasts for new ways of working can often be their own worst enemies, says Price. 'There's no point introducing open plan for its own sake and expecting it to work. Actively managing this, including involving people in the designing of their own workspaces, is important.'

The vocabulary used is also crucial. 'Some people are frightened by terms such as "hot-desking", whereas the reality may be far less painful,' he says

Source: Steve Crabb, 'Out in the Open', *People Management* magazine, 13 October 2005, p. 24.

Summary

- Pervasive change has become the norm as organisations and individuals adapt to rapid and often unexpected change to survive and prosper. External change forces include technology, economic conditions, global competition, world politics, and social and demographic factors.

- People seek change that is favourable and resist change perceived as harmful or ambiguous. They make cost–benefit assessments of potential changes, which influence their degree of acceptance or resistance. To be skilled at managing change, managers and other change agents begin by identifying performance gaps and the targets of their change efforts. They must understand both the content and process of change and how their efforts affect their organisational system.

- Three phases of change are unfreezing, changing and refreezing. Planned change involves: (1) recognising the need for change; (2) diagnosing and planning; (3) considering contingencies; (4) taking action and measuring results; and (5) managing the transition.

- Organisational development (OD) is a system-wide application of behavioural science knowledge designed to improve organisational effectiveness and people's satisfaction and quality of work life. OD is concerned with both the technical and social aspects of work and system design and improvement.

- Increasingly, OD practitioners work on strategy, culture development and technology integration. Typical steps include: (1) sensing the problem and engaging an OD practitioner; (2) entering and contracting; (3) collecting data and diagnosing; (4) planning and implementing interventions; and (5) evaluating results and deciding on further steps. While a variety of specific interventions are available, the process of influencing change is potentially open to ethical dilemmas, and OD practitioners have developed guidelines to deal with them.

- In the long run, planned change interventions seek to create learning organisations that are skilled at creating, acquiring and transferring knowledge, and at modifying behaviour to reflect new knowledge and insights. Five characteristics required for a learning organisation are personal mastery, mental process models, shared vision, team learning, and systems thinking.

- Innovation is a special form of change that can be either sustaining (more evolutionary changes in products and processes) or disruptive (revolutionary change that creates new markets). Three key capabilities to promote innovation are resources, processes and values, with different mixes of each depending in part on the size and extent to which leadership is entrepreneurial or working within a bureaucracy.

- For large organisations to have a chance at disruptive innovation, their major strategic options are to organise new structures (such as a venture creation group), spin off new ventures to provide them freedom from well-defined process constraints, or acquire hot emerging businesses.

Areas for personal development

Because change is ubiquitous throughout a lifetime, it helps to master skills early in your career that provide you with the flexibility and responsiveness so that change works to your advantage.

1 **Develop a tolerance for ambiguity.** If your score on the 'Your turn' exercise (page 846) was high (49 or above), you need to work on becoming more accepting of ambiguity. Break away from everyday structured routines; engage once a day or a few times a week in a novel activity and learn to appreciate the unexpected. Take in information from multiple sources to feel more comfortable with complexity; access the web more often if you normally shy away from it, and work to search out more sources when writing a paper (do not minimise the number of references).

2 **Be on guard for change resisters.** They are everywhere and can pull down group performance. If you can avoid them (so they do not directly impact your work), then do so. However, when resisters impact you (say, even on a class team project), learn to educate them, communicating accurately the goals and reasons why attaining them are important; draw out their participation by providing involvement that is not overwhelming or threatening to them; and negotiate or bargain with them when necessary.

3 **Practise force-field analysis.** Learn to assess change-orientated issues or dilemmas by working through a listing and weighting of driving forces and restraining forces causing the status quo. Become adept at identifying forces you can alter to tip the scales in favour of moving in the direction you believe you (and/or others) need to go.

4 **Use the three phases of planned change.** Get used to envisioning change as a three-step process of unfreezing, changing and refreezing. Unfreezing can begin with a force-field analysis to lower resistance or enhance the felt need for change. Then work through taking on new tasks or building new relationships. Relinquish old routines; perhaps have a ceremony to cope with throwing out the old. Evaluate results and reinforce new outcomes so that the change is refrozen into your behaviour set.

5 **Adopt the values and methods of the OD practitioner.** While you may never consider yourself an OD change agent, in almost any career it helps to become a facilitator of the group process. As to values, respect people's diversity, be open and authentic, share power and be confronting to pull issues out into open discussion. Engage others in collecting and sharing data and diagnosing the problem or issue, which should lead to joint action planning. Evaluate results together and debrief the process.

6 **Be your own learning organisation.** Actively engage in competence acquisition by taking on novel tasks, experiment with new ideas and new ways of doing things, seek continuous improvement in all that you do (benchmark against your past personal best), and seize opportunities to span the boundaries of organisations as a way of building your network of people on whom you can call for information and feasibility testing of ideas or proposed courses of action.

7 **Be on the lookout for innovation opportunities.** There really are few boundaries on the opportunities to innovate. While not all innovations are disruptive (in the sense that they create new markets), even continuous improvements strengthen the likelihood of adaptiveness and viability. You do not have to be the source of creative ideas. Scan your environment by listening and reading; you will find clues to practices you currently engage in that could be done differently – innovation to you.

❓ Questions for study and discussion

1 Think of an organisation you know and identify what you think is the most significant change it has made in the last five years. What factors influenced the change? Was the change resisted? If so, by whom and why? Apply a force-field analysis to your example.

2 The manager of the business office for a 250-bed hospital wants to improve the handling of patient record-keeping. She shows you a proposed reorganisation of the department in which several currently specialised functions (admitting, funding, and the like) are combined into 'patient representative' positions. The 30 restructured roles will handle patient files almost from entry to exit. The manager plans to announce the change at the next staff meeting. What would you communicate to her to minimise resistance to the proposed change?

3 Think of an organisation or group to which you belong. Identify a change you think would improve the organisation. How would you go about planning and implementing the change? Include Lewin's three phases of unfreezing, changing, refreezing in your answer. Also, distinguish between content and process in developing your plan.

4 OD practitioners use two basic strategies to achieve their objectives: the human process and the techno-structural approaches. Distinguish between these two and give an example of each.

5 What are one or two examples of ethical dilemmas that change agents or OD practitioners might encounter? How would you suggest they think about those dilemmas?

6 Give examples of learning organisations that you have been a part of or heard about. How would these types of organisation benefit or harm individual members compared to traditional organisations?

7 How might two firms in the same industry, one large and one small, differ in their approaches to promote innovation?

ⓘ Key Concepts

change, *p. 843*

planned change, *p. 852*

change agents, *p. 853*

unfreezing, *p. 856*

moving, *p. 856*

refreezing, *p. 856*

force-field analysis, *p. 858*

intervention, *p. 859*

organisational development (OD), *p. 861*

action research, *p. 863*

re-engineering, *p. 867*

learning organisation, *p. 868*

single-loop learning, *p. 872*

double-loop learning, *p. 872*

innovation, *p. 873*

sustaining innovations, *p. 877*

disruptive innovations, *p. 877*

Personal skills exercise

Force-field analysis to improve a personal problem

Purpose Problems can be defined as the difference between a current situation and a desired situation.

Discussing problems is beneficial when it:

1 helps to reduce our anxiety
2 leads to a reduction of the problem or discomfort caused by it through a redefinition of the problem, or
3 leads to constructive action that alleviates the problem.

This exercise is designed to accomplish all three purposes. Force-field analysis is based on the concept that there are opposing forces in equilibrium that keep us stuck in our current situations when we want to move to a more desirable situation.

Time For the personal force field, about 25 minutes. Another 30 minutes is necessary if pairs are formed to provide feedback.

Procedure

Part 1: Individually complete the force-field problem-solving module below for a current problem you are experiencing personally. The problem could be a habit you are trying to break (e.g. drinking coffee, smoking, procrastination), or something you want to improve in but have trouble working on (e.g. public speaking, learning a foreign language, mastering a new computer program) or any other type of problem you are putting off solving for some reason (e.g. looking for a new job, breaking off a dysfunctional relationship, starting a diet or exercise programme to get in shape) (20–30 minutes).

1　**Describe the current situation that you want to change.** Often, part of the problem is that no one knows exactly what the problem is. To start the process, describe a current situation as accurately and briefly as possible.

2　**Describe the desired situation.** This is not necessarily the ideal situation, which can often be an impractical solution. Indicate the direction and realistic change you desire.

3　**List the opposing or restraining (negative) forces** that resist improvement in the situation using the following force-field analysis diagram.

4　**List the driving or pushing (positive) forces** that are motivating you to change in the following force-field analysis diagram.

5　**Review the driving and restraining forces** and number them according to their impact on the situation (1 is most important, 2 is second in impact, 3 is third, etc.).

Force-field analysis

Current situation　　　　→　Desired situation

_____　　_____

_____　　_____

_____　　_____

Driving forces　　　　　→　Restraining forces

_____　↔　_____

_____　↔　_____

_____　↔　_____

_____　↔　_____

6　**Action options.** These are your *action steps* aimed at directly changing the forces that maintain the current problem situation. Change procedures modify the strength of the forces, to alter the dynamics of the current situation. You may either (1) increase the strength of or add driving forces, or (2) decrease the strength of or take away restraining forces. Concentrate on the most important forces (identified in step 5) and brainstorm as many *action steps* as possible.

(a) Add driving forces. _____

(b) Increase the strength of driving forces. _____

(c) Eliminate restraining forces. _____

(d) Reduce the strength of restraining forces. _____

7　**Priorities.** Arrange actions listed in (a) to (d), above, in order of priority. Use ease of implementation and strength of possible effect as two criteria.

8 **Organisation of resources.** For the five top priority action steps (step 7), list the materials, people and other resources available.

Action step   Resources

_____   _____

_____   _____

_____   _____

9 **Agenda.** Action implementation steps for each strategy:

- What is going to be done? _____
- Who is going to do it? _____
- When is it going to be done? _____
- Evaluation: how will you determine when the step is completed and accomplished?

_____

10 **Commitment.** Make a personal statement about your intentions and desired consequences.

_____

Part 2 (optional) When you complete all the steps in your force-field analysis, pick a partner who has also finished and share your work. Your partner's job is to ask for clarification, provide you with feedback about additional information you may want to add, and reality-test your plans so that you can make sure you have the best possible chance of success for implementation (15 minutes).

Part 3 (optional) Reverse the procedure in Part 2. Now the second partner shares his or her force-field analysis and gets feedback (15 minutes).

Team exercise

Changing the grading system

Purpose

- To practise stakeholder analysis.
- To practise making a force-field analysis.
- To plan briefly what needs to be done to bring about change.

Time 30–54 minutes

Background Assume that several students have petitioned your instructor to grade your current course in managing organisational behaviour on a pass-fail basis. Your instructor has reservations about this, but was willing to ask the Dean if there was a possibility of changing the grading in this course from an A through F basis to pass-fail. The Dean expressed willingness to consider the question but asked for a more detailed proposal, including the pros and cons and how such a plan might be implemented. Your instructor, in turn, has asked your group to develop a preliminary analysis of how such a change might be made.

Procedure

Step 1 Join a group of four to six students to do the following.

1 Develop a stakeholder analysis. Identify all stakeholders and their interests and concerns (5–7 minutes).

2 Prepare a force-field analysis. Identify the pushing and restraining forces and estimate the intensity and importance of each (10–12 minutes).

3 Prepare a preliminary plan for introducing and implementing the change. Identify who will do what and when. Be specific about the order and priority of actions (5–10 minutes).

4 Prepare a brief recommendation indicating whether or not your group thinks your instructor should proceed (5 minutes).

Note This is a simulated exercise and is not intended to influence your instructor to change the grading system!

Step 2 Entire class reconvenes. As time permits, do the following.

1 Each group reports its recommendation.

2 Class discussion: class discusses learning from this experience and how this process would be similar to and different from analysing and planning a change at work.

3 Compare the analyses (10–20 minutes for all of Step 2).

Case study: Walford Golf sell off

After many years of decline in the quality of its golf courses, Walford town outsourced the management and operation of East Park GC, City Park GC and West Park GC. Up to this time, the golf courses had been managed by Walford Parks & Recreation Department (PRD) under a contract to a private company (concessionaire).

Under the terms of that contract, the concessionaire operated the pro shops, took in the green fees and remitted to PRD a fixed percentage of all revenues. Golf course maintenance was the responsibility of PRD's maintenance employees, all of whom belonged to UNISON. For many years, PRD was unable to collect sufficient revenue to undertake needed course improvements and the concessionaire lacked any contractual incentive to do anything other than point customers to the first tee.

For the decade leading up to the outsourcing, the golf facilities lost substantial monies and there was an accumulation of £20 million in deferred maintenance projects. The end result was a sustained worsening of the condition of the golf courses (including associated facilities such as clubhouses, restaurants and a driving range) and widespread public disaffection.

Walford Golf – a private non-profit organisation – was formed to manage the golf courses. Its mission was to restore the facilities to a level equivalent to other public golf courses in the Greater Walford area, to improve course maintenance procedures and to build capital reserves to begin to address deferred maintenance projects. Under the terms of its outsourcing agreement, Walford Golf contracted with the city to manage the golf facilities for 12 years with renewable five-year options.

Walford Golf would have responsibility for the operation of the town's entire golf facilities. It would remunerate the city when the organisation made a profit, and then only after Walford Golf had accumulated capital reserves for improvements as specified in the contract. Without the benefit of working capital, Walford Golf commenced operations utilising a bank line of credit.

The town of Walford and PRD did not favour the outsourcing of the golf facilities that resulted from public hearings on the matter. However, public dissatisfaction with PRD's management of the facilities, coupled with its failure to make any significant improvements, made it impossible for the city to resist this alternative.

The town council was willing to go only so far in the call for privatisation. It required that Walford Golf retain the golf course maintenance crews as town employees under union contract. This meant that the maintenance crews would continue to report to PRD rather than to Walford Golf. To supervise the maintenance crews, PRD appointed its former manager of golf as its liaison to Walford Golf.

Walford Golf hired a CEO who reported to the president of Walford Golf's volunteer board of directors, all of whom had been picked by a selection committee created by PRD. As he set about the task of creating a going concern, the CEO requested operating budget data from the liaison in order to prepare the organisation's first annual budget. It is worth noting that the PRD liaison officer had unsuccessfully applied for the job of CEO for Walford Golf.

PRD's liaison officer did not respond to the CEO's request and complied only after the maintenance budget was negotiated internally with UNISON and was approved by the town council. In succeeding months, the following occurred.

■ During a summer heatwave, PRD refused to alter the work schedules of maintenance crews so that areas of need could be watered in the afternoon. The union threatened to file a grievance against Walford Golf if it had its own employees do the watering.

■ PRD 'loaned' turf care equipment owned by Walford Golf to other town departments without consultation or approval.

■ PRD's liaison officer made an ongoing series of derogatory written and verbal statements about Walford Golf, its board members and the CEO, all of which suggested that the golf facilities were being mismanaged. These statements were published in the major local newspaper.

■ Confidential matters discussed at board level regarding personnel, pricing and capital improvements were regularly leaked to the press, causing continuous public relations problems for Walford Golf.

■ A number of board members exerted pressure on the CEO to grant contracts to specific vendors, to hire personal friends, to provide discounted pricing for golf merchandise, and to relax enforcement of contract provisions on one particular vendor.

From a business standpoint, Walford Golf thrived during its first two and a half years of operation. Strict cash control and stock procedures were put in place, the golf courses were data-linked using networked point-of-sale systems, retail sales in the pro shops surged, capital reserves of more than £500000 were accumulated, and an equivalent amount was invested in new equipment and facility enhancements.

Source: based on *Seattle Golf Change Constraints within a Public–Private Partnership*, by Christopher M. Redo, University of San Diego.

Questions for managerial action

1 What steps would you take next if you were the CEO? Be specific.

2 What leverage does the CEO have regarding PRD and the liaison? What are the limits of his authority to change the situation?

3 What should be the role of Walford Golf's board of directors? What should be the limits of their involvement in management of the golf courses?

4 Evaluate the proposition of a public–private partnership for public facilities?

5 Assuming the CEO sought greater degrees of freedom in changing policies and procedures to improve club operations, what are the driving and restraining forces that now prevent further change? What could be done to begin unfreezing the situation?

Applied questions

6 Using Lewin's phases of planned change, illustrated in Exhibit 18-4, How could management encourage employees to accept the outsourcing of work?

7 Learning organisations are more responsive to change; how can managers shift from single-loop to double-loop learning to ensure organisational flexibility?

WWW exercise

Manager's Internet tools

Web tips: continuous improvement

Using a search engine, look on the web for a change management consultant. What do they say about the management of change? How do they see their role in guiding organisations through the change process?

Specific web exercise

Choose a company that you are interested in working for. Look at its website and try to answer the following questions. You may have to search in the corporate information section of the website for the answers.

1 What are some of the events in past performance that have helped to instil a culture of change and continuous improvement?

2 How has the organisation committed itself to quality? Does it list some of the internal initiatives it has undertaken to ensure a quality product both internally and with external customers?

3 How linked are the concepts of quality and continuous improvement? Can you find specific examples?

4 What are the core business principles? How do you think the company reinforces these core principles in day-to-day activities?

5 What steps has the company taken to inculcate continuous improvement in people and teams?

6 How does the company measure and define success?

LEARNING CHECKLIST

Before you move on you may want to reflect on what you have learnt in this chapter. You should now be able to:

☑ identify what factors cause change

☑ understand why people and organisations resist change

☑ discuss the phases of change

☑ describe how change can be planned and implemented

☑ explain the processes of organisational development

☑ explain the characteristics of learning organisations

☑ articulate three strategies by which mature organisations stimulate innovation.

Further reading

Brunetto, Y. (2001) 'Mediating Change for Public Sector Professionals', *International Journal of Public Sector Management* 14(6/7), pp. 465–481.

Marcic, D. (1996) 'Summary of The Fifth Discipline by Peter Senge', in J.L. Pierce and J.W. Newstrom (eds) *The Manager's Bookshelf: A Mosaic of Contemporary Views* (4th edn). New York, NY: HarperCollins, pp. 105–112.

McCann, L., Hassard, J. and Morris, J. (2005) 'A Tale of Three Cities: Organisational Change and Middle Managers in British, North American and Japanese Urban Administrations', *Management Research News* 28(9), pp. 65–67.

Smith, K.D. and Taylor, W.G.K. (2000) 'The Learning Organisation Ideal in Civil Service Organisations: Deriving a Measure', *The Learning Organisation* 7(4), p. 194.

References

Argyris, C. (1957) *Personality and Organization.* New York, NY: Harper & Row.

Argyris, C. (1994) 'Good Communication that Blocks Learning', *Harvard Business Review* 72, July–August, pp. 77–85.

Argyris, C., Putman, R. and Smith, D.M. (1985) *Action Science.* San Francisco, CA: Jossey-Bass.

Beer, M. and Nohria, N. (2000) 'Cracking the Code of Change', *Harvard Business Review*, May–June, pp. 133–141.

Beer, M. and Walton, E. (1987) 'Organization Change and Development', *Annual Review of Psychology* 38, pp. 229–272.

Bennis, W.G., Benne, K.D. Chin, R. and Corey, K.E. (1976) *The Planning of Change.* New York, NY: Holt, Rinehart and Winston, pp. 22–45

Brown, L.D. and Covey, J.G. (1987) 'Development Organizations and Organization Development: Toward an Expanded Paradigm for Organization Development', in R.W. Woodman and W.A. Pasmore (eds) *Research in Organizational Change and Development, vol. 1.* Greenwich, CT: Jai Press, p. 63.

Case, T.L., Vandenberg, R.J. and Meredith, P.H. (1990) 'Internal and External Change Agents', *Leadership and Organizational Development Journal* 11(1); and Bennis, W. (1969) *Organization Development: Its Nature, Origins, and Prospects.* Reading, MA: Addison-Wesley.

Chesbrough, H. (2000) 'Designing Corporate Ventures in the Shadow of Private Venture Capital', *California Management Review*, Spring, pp. 31–49.

Christensen, C. (1997) *The Innovator's Dilemma: When New Technologies Cause Great Firms to Fail.* Boston, MA: Harvard Business School Press.

Christensen, C.M. and Overdorf, M. (2000) 'Meeting the Challenge of Disruptive Change', *Harvard Business Review*, March–April, pp. 66–76.

Cummings, T.G. and Worley, C.G. (1993) *Organization Development and Change* (5th edn). St Paul, MN: West Publishing Company, p. 63.

DeAngelis, T. (1994) 'Psychologists Balance Company Needs', *Monitor*, November, pp. 34–35.

Drucker, P. (1974) *Management: Tasks, Responsibilities, Practices.* New York, NY: Harper & Row, p. 799.

Drucker, P.F. (1998) 'The Discipline of Innovation', *Harvard Business Review*, November–December, pp. 149–157.

Fagenson, E.A. and Burke, W.W. (1982) 'Organization Development Practitioners' Activities and Interventions in Organizations During the 1980s', *Journal of Applied Behavior Science* 26(3), pp. 285–297.

Faw, R. (1999) *World's Best Value: Global Competition in the Information Age*. Safety Harbor, FL: Worldsbestvalue.com.

Garvin, D.A. (1993) 'Building a Learning Organization', *Harvard Business Review* 71(4), pp. 78–91.

Garvin, D.A. (2000) *Learning in Action: A Guide to Putting the Learning Organization to Work*. Harvard Business School Press.

Gillmor, D. (2000) 'Chambers: "A Leader's Got to Walk the Talk"', *San Jose Mercury News*, 21 May, pp. 1f, 2f, 6f.

Greiner, L.E. (1998) 'Evolution and Revolution as Organizations Grow', *Harvard Business Review*, May–June, pp. 55–68.

Groves, J.M. (1992) 'Leaders of Corporate Change', *Fortune*, 14 December, pp. 104–114.

Hall, R.H. (1987) *Organizations: Structures, Processes, and Outcomes* (4th edn). Englewood Cliffs, NJ: Prentice Hall, p. 29.

Hunsaker, P.L. (1983) 'Role of the Inside Change Agent: Strategies for Changing Organizations', in D.D. Warrick (ed.) *Contemporary Organizational Development*. Glenview, IL: Scott, Foresman, & Company, pp. 123–137.

Kanter, R.M. (1983) *The Change Masters*. New York, NY: Simon & Schuster.

Kanter, R.M. (1989) *When Giants Learn to Dance: Mastering the Challenges of Strategy*. New York, NY: Simon & Schuster.

Keffeler, J.B. (1991) 'Managing Changing Organizations: Don't Stop Communicating', *Vital Speeches*, 15 November, pp. 92–96.

Kirkpatrick, D. (2000) 'Why We're Betting Billions on TV', an interview with Paul Allen, *Fortune*, 15 May, pp. 249–261.

Kofman, F. and Senge, P.M. (1993) 'Communities of Commitment: The Heart of Learning Organizations', *Organizational Dynamics*, Autumn, pp. 5–23.

Kotter, J.P. and Schlesinger, L.A. (1979) 'Choosing Strategies for Change', *Harvard Business Review* 57, March–April, pp. 106–114.

Lawler III, E.E. (1985) *Doing Research that is Useful for Theory and Practice*. San Francisco, CA: Jossey-Bass.

Lewin, K. (1951) *Field Theory in Social Science*. New York, NY: Harper & Row.

Likert, R. (1967) *The Human Organization*. New York, NY: McGraw-Hill.

Pasmore, W.A. and Fagans, M.R. (1992) 'Participation, Individual Development, and Organizational Change: A Review and Synthesis', *Journal of Management*, June, pp. 375–397.

Pedler, M. (1997) *Action Learning in Practice* (3rd edn). Aldershot: Gower.

Pedler, M., Burgoyne, J. and Boydell, T. (1991) *The Learning Company: A Strategy for Sustainable Growth*. Maidenhead: McGraw-Hill.

Peters, T. (2000) 'Visions 21: What Will We Do for Work?', *Time*, 22 May, pp. 68–71.

Porras, J.I. and Robertson, P.J. (1992) 'Organizational Development: Theory, Practice, and Research', in M.D. Dunnette and L.M. Hough (eds) *Handbook of Industrial & Organizational Psychology* (2nd edn), vol. 3. Palo Alto, CA: Consulting Psychologists Press, p. 734.

Rheem, H. (1995) 'The Learning Organization: Building Learning Capability', *Harvard Business Review*, March–April, pp. 3–12.

Richards, G. (1994) 'Organizational Learning in the Public Sector: From Theory to Practice', *Optimum* 25(3), 22 December, p. 3.

Sager, I. (1999) 'Inside IBM: Internet Business Machines', *Business Week*, 13 December, pp. EB20–EB38.

Schneider, G.P. and Perry, J.T. (2000) *Electronic Commerce.* Cambridge, MA: Course Technology, pp. 307–308.

Senge, P. (1990) *The Fifth Discipline: The Art and Practice of the Learning Organization.* New York, NY: Doubleday.

Senge, P., Roberts, C., Ross, R.B., Smith, B.J. and Kleiner, A. (1995) *The Fifth Discipline Fieldbook: Strategies and Tools for Building a Learning Organization.* New York, NY: Currency Doubleday.

Slocum, J.W. Jr, Mcgill, M. and Lei, D.T. (1994) 'The New Learning Strategy: Anytime, Anything, Anywhere', *Organizational Dynamics* 23(2), 22 September, p. 33.

Solomon, C.M. (1994) 'HR Facilitates the Learning Organization Concept', *Personnel Journal* 73(11), November.

Vlasic, B. (1996) 'Bracing for the Big One', *Business Week*, 25 March, pp. 34–35.

The culture of change in the NHS

King's Lynn and Wisbech Hospitals NHS Trust in Norfolk, one of the first trusts to achieve the new NHS gold standard in people management, has boosted communications and involved employees in decision-making. But, like its peers up and down the country, it is facing testing times, with, among other things, the implementation of Agenda for Change and ongoing financial difficulties. Then there's MRSA. The trust says it is doing plenty to tackle the issue, but it does seem to have a particular problem – earlier this year the local paper, the *Lynn News*, revealed it was the fourth-worst performer in the country in what the paper described as the Health Protection Agency's 'league of shame'.

Against this backdrop, the trust, based at the Queen Elizabeth Hospital in King's Lynn, has done particularly well to emerge as one of the first in the UK to achieve 'Practice Plus' accreditation in the Department of Health's Improving Working Lives (IWL) standard, a year and a half ahead of the final deadline.

The national programme, launched a few years ago, awards trusts kitemarks against their commitment to improving employees' working lives. There are three stages – bronze, silver and gold – with Practice Plus being the gold standard, demonstrating that a trust is implementing IWL across the whole organisation in all staff groups. By next April, all NHS organisations are expected to achieve Practice Plus by demonstrating best practice in a variety of areas, including human resources strategy and management, equality and diversity, communications and staff involvement, flexible working, and training and development.

HR director Amanda Lyes, who joined the trust in August 2003 from Ipswich Hospital NHS Trust where she was deputy HR director, is proud of its achievements and the work that went into gaining the standard in October last year. 'We could have chosen to take our eye off the ball,' she says. 'But we're proud of what we do, we've got excellent staff-side [union] relationships and we've got nothing to hide.'

Among the many improvements that have been implemented as part of IWL are the appointment of a communications manager and a scheme to improve attendance at work, which is currently being piloted. A work–life balance co-ordinator has also been appointed to work across both the hospital and the local primary care trust, with specific responsibility for helping with childcare.

Other initiatives include changing the role of a member of staff to training and education co-ordinator after he helped another employee learn to read and write; plans to develop a support group as part of the induction programme for medical staff and their families who join the hospital from overseas; and reviewing the trust's harassment and bullying policy to change its emphasis to 'managing mutual respect'.

From the start, the trust set out to involve employees in the IWL programme. A main steering board was set up to drive the initiative and around 30 staff were recruited as 'IWL advisers' to sit on focus groups and 'share the word'. 'They were our champions, if you like,' says Lyes.

A 'take a breather' day was also organised to promote IWL to staff. The day, which it is hoped will be repeated this year to mark the Queen Elizabeth Hospital's 25th anniversary, included activities such as a themed buffet, stress-relieving massages and a special staff lottery draw.

Lorna Benefer, a corporate nursing secretary who is on secondment to the Agenda for Change project team, became one of the IWL advisers. She believes the initiative is changing working lives, although she admits it can sometimes take 'a little while to make culture changes'.

'IWL has made a difference and I think it will continue to do so,' she says. 'There are many advantages to working here that people take for granted, either because of the culture or because they have worked in the NHS for the whole of their working lives.'

The unions have also been actively involved in IWL – sitting on the steering board and acting as advisers – and this, says Lyes, played a significant role in helping the trust to achieve Practice Plus. 'We have an informal, relaxed environment and our staff-side representatives know they can talk to any member of staff, whether they are management or otherwise. We are very open as an organisation, and staff know that they can influence decisions,' she says. 'The staff opinion survey reflects this. For the past few years we have seen year-on-year improvements in how staff perceive communication.'

David Coe, an electrician, shop steward for Amicus and chairman of the Hospitals Joint Staff Consultative Committee, says it would be wrong to say that everything is rosy at the trust – for instance, a lot of the wards have not been painted for years and publicity surrounding MRSA has dented staff morale – but he believes communication has greatly improved.

'I used to go on about how communication in the trust was terrible, but now it is both up and down,' he says. 'Years ago we felt we were just getting lip-service but times have changed. We are never going to agree on everything but we get there in the end.'

And he adds that, although the unions may have their differences with HR, the relationship is very amicable. 'The thing about HR here is that there is a real open-door policy.'

This openness is reflected in the trust's decision to involve staff in tackling its financial problems – the deficit at the end of the past financial year was still to be confirmed as PM went to press, but is expected to be around £8 million.

'We should all take ownership. That is how we can move forward as an organisation,' says Lyes. 'The message of the trust's board is that we need to be working together on trust issues.'

Employees were asked for ideas and suggestions to reduce expenditure and improve efficiency, and many of these were incorporated into the financial recovery plan, which was published at the end of last year.

A database of suggestions, such as using email where possible instead of paper, and second-class post instead of first class, is available on the intranet, and the financial position is communicated monthly to the workforce.

'The financial recovery group is now looking at turning the ideas into action. Quite a few of the suggestions have already been put into action, resulting in several hundreds of thousands of pounds being saved,' says Lyes.

Among the major cost-cutting schemes in the plan are reducing sickness absence through the attendance reward scheme, tackling overtime and introducing 'e-recruit'. The trust had been spending more than £200 000 in advertising for new staff, but now expects to eliminate virtually all of this through online recruitment. By the end of this financial year (March 2006), it is anticipated that the trust will have transferred entirely to e-recruitment through the hospital website and the NHS jobs website.

It is also hoped that the trust can provide payroll services for other trusts on a shared-service basis because it was one of only three organisations to pilot the national electronic staff record system, which is being rolled out across the NHS. But the move – which would generate additional income of £100 000 – is 'very much an ambition' at the moment.

All this means the HR department is very busy, but Lyes seems happy to rise to the challenge. 'I love my job,' she says. 'It's exciting and fast-paced. The nicest thing about HR is that you can make a difference to people's working lives.

'HR is crucial to the NHS in terms of developing our workforce not only for now but also for tomorrow. If you haven't got the right people with the right skills, then that is going to have an impact on patient care.'

Managing sickness

Sickness absence is one area where the King's Lynn and Wisbech Hospitals NHS Trust hopes to make significant savings, and it is piloting a scheme to reward attendance.

Last year, absence increased to just over 6 per cent of the workforce – or an average of 10 days a year per employee – although this was affected by a virus that hit the trust in October and led to staff taking several days off at a time. By the end of March this year, absence had reduced, with just under 5 per cent of the 2800-strong workforce off sick at any one time.

'In the current financial climate that is not good,' says Lyes, 'but we do believe that, working with our staff, managers and occupational health, we can reduce sickness further.'

Sickness absence – which, says Lyes, is about average for the NHS – costs the £100 million-turnover trust around £4.5 million a year, including the cost of bank and agency staff.

With this in mind, part of the IWL initiative focused on devising a scheme to reward attendance at work.

'We recently revised the sickness absence policy with our staff, but we felt we needed to do more,' says Lyes. 'Another reason for piloting such a scheme is that we have a managing sickness absence target of 4 per cent.'

Staff in Sterile Services and a department in the medical directorate are currently taking part in the three-month pilot scheme, which started in April and will be rolled out to the rest of the trust if it proves to be successful. For every quarter of full attendance, staff get a half day off, which means that over the course of a year they can get up to two days' extra leave if they don't take time off sick. 'It may not seem like a lot, but it's a good incentive and it really accumulates,' says Lyes.

The trust has shown that it is not just management but also leadership that is important. According to Herminia Ibarra, professor of organisational behaviour at Insead, management is about efficiency while leadership is about creating change. 'Learning to lead is partly about what you do, but it is also about who you are,' she says. 'It is not enough to be good with people; you must be able to move a group.'

Aspiring leaders can struggle with selling ideas, working through networks, communicating clear messages and improving leadership style, says Ibarra. And learning 'to be' happens in a different part of the brain to learning 'how'. 'They are different types of learning. Learning to lead needs motivation, practice and feedback.'

The trust has implemented its change strategy by involving people from across all sectors of the organisation. As can be seen, the collective imagination and energy in organisations is immense. Yet many managers feel that to implement change is to tell people what they need to do rather than letting it come from within.

The following strategies can help the focus on change to develop from within the organisation.

Trust people

'No one turns up for work actually wanting to do a bad job.' Managers need to learn to trust their colleagues to come up with the best way of making a project work. The more leeway and space people have to interpret any information they've been given, the greater their contribution will be.

Show them the money

It's important to help people understand why they should contribute. One manager stated 'I've told them about the importance of brand until I'm blue in the face, but they just don't get it.' One argument against this would be that it was not the wilful ignorance of her colleagues that was the problem, but the 'telling'. It is possible to lead without telling people exactly what they should be doing. If you need people to innovate, to solve problems and to make the right judgements for themselves, they need a good reason to make that effort. Being told what to do is not reason enough.

Give them the time and space to understand the context for their efforts and why they are important. Go out of your way to help them understand the impact their efforts will have, and to come to their own conclusions. Be obsessive in planning communications that will feed back evidence of what impact they actually did have. This means hard evidence such as numbers.

Get people to act

The important thing in internal communications is not what you do, but what the people you are communicating with do. If you get people doing stuff, then you have communicated; if not, you haven't. This is why so many well-meaning newsletter and e-zine campaigns don't have much of an impact.

Say thank you

Thank people or, at the very least, make sure that when they have put something of themselves into your project, you acknowledge it. If you don't, you might have one successful internal communications effort, but you won't have another. Your communications need to be the start of a dialogue, not the end of it. If you want people to make your project better, you need to show that you are listening to their input and doing something as a result.

Get and give feedback

Internal communication is often seen as the end point of a process. But if communication is focused on supporting a project, strategy or initiative, will it be more or less effective if it allows the people you're communicating with to contribute, critique and feed back? If you aren't willing to develop the subjects of the communications, it's not communicating, it's simply telling.

Source: adapted from Barber, A., *People Management* magazine, 19 May 2005, p. 44; Ibarra, H., 'To Be or Not to Be, That is the Question', *People Management* magazine, 21 April 2005, p. 15; Warren, C., *People Management* magazine, 30 June 2005, p. 32.

Discussion questions

1 How has the NHS trust been successful in encouraging employees to accept the culture of change?

2 Five strategies have been identified for the successful implementation of change. Can you identify where they have been used in the NHS trust?

3 Why do so many internal communications efforts concentrate on telling people exactly what to do, hedging them in and directing their efforts when there's a much better way of using internal communication to bring about change?

4 Why is communication so important to managers?

Applied questions

5 Kotter and Schlesinger have identified six general strategies for overcoming resistance to change. Which strategies were used in the NHS trust?

6 Organisational development (OD) encompasses a wide variety of planned change interventions. How can OD be differentiated from manager-led change? Does the above case provide any examples?

Index